THE BOOK OF TOFU

THE BOOK OF
TOFU

Protein Source of the Future... Now!
VOLUME I

WILLIAM SHURTLEFF & AKIKO AOYAGI

Illustrated by Akiko Aoyagi

Ten Speed Press
A Soyfoods Center Book

BY THE SAME AUTHORS

Tofu & Soymilk Production (Soyfoods Center)
Miso Production (Soyfoods Center)
The Book of Tempeh (Ten Speed Press)
Tempeh Production (Soyfoods Center)
History of Soybeans and Soyfoods (Soyfoods Center)
Soyfoods Industry and Market: Directory & Databook (Soyfoods Center)
50 Bibliographies on Soyfoods and Soybeans (Soyfoods Center)
SoyaScan Database—62,000 records from 1100 B.C. to present (Soyfoods Center)

Cover Illustration: Akiko Aoyagi

Special edition *Book of Tofu and Miso,* copyright © 2001 by William Shurtleff and Akiko Aoyagi

Ten Speed Press
P.O. Box 7123
Berkeley, CA 94707
www.tenspeed.com

Book Design and Typography by Beverly Stiskin
Cover Design by Akiko Aoyagi

ISBN: 1-58008-358-7

Printed in Canada

For Suzuki Shunryu roshi (1906-1971)
Zen master and friend

Winter's plum tree blossoming

gaté gaté pāragaté parasamgaté bodhi svāhā

Contents

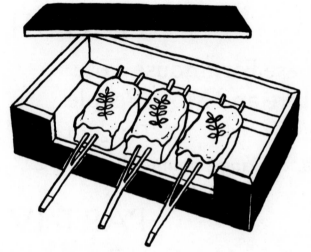

PART III

Japanese Farmhouse Tofu: Making Tofu for More and More People

PART IV

The Practice of Making Tofu: The Traditional Tofu Shop

Preface

After returning to America from my first visit to Japan, a summer in 1967 practicing Zen meditation, I had the good fortune to meet Shunryu Suzuki *roshi,* head abbot of the Tassajara Zen Mountain Center. Moved by his example, in June 1968 I joined the Tassajara community, nestled in the wild beauty of the Santa Lucia Mountains near Big Sur, California. Working as a cook in the Center's fine kitchens, I grew to appreciate the value of our natural food, vegetarian diet. We served tofu on special occasions, and miso soup and cooked whole soybeans several times a week. In late 1969 I wrote an informal book containing 167 recipes served at Tassajara: four of these used tofu. Then 25 copies of the typewritten, homemade book were sent to friends as Christmas presents.

Tassajara—uninsolated life in a place of breathtaking beauty. I soon came to feel that the utterly simple way of life and practice that Suzuki *roshi* brought to the West was the most wonderful gift I had ever received.

After two and a half years at Tassajara, I spoke to Suzuki *roshi* about returning to Japan to continue practicing meditation, study the culture and language from which his teaching emerged, and learn more of the art of Buddhist vegetarian cookery. He encouraged me in my desire to help bring more of the East to the West, and in January 1971 I found myself a penniless student in Kyoto, enrolled in a Japanese language school and living with a Japanese family. The local tofu shop was a few minutes walk away. It was thus out of necessity that I first made tofu—also known in the West as soybean curd—a part of my daily diet, grateful that it was both nutritious and inexpensive.

Nahum and Beverly Stiskin arrived in Japan in June 1969 after studying in Boston for about two years with Michio and Aveline Kushi, Japanese teachers of macrobiotics. The Kushis encouraged the Stiskins to go to Japan to teach Japanese about macrobiotics and brown rice, and to study and record traditional Japanese culture before it was lost to modernization and the "economic miracle." The Stiskins settled in Kyoto and in September 1969, just after the birth of their first child, enrolled in the Japanese language school. In 1971 they started a small publishing company named Autumn Press, and that same year published their first book, *The Looking-Glass God,* written by Nahum, about Shinto, Japan's oldest religion.

For nearly a year the Stiskins and I attended the same language school (*Nihongo Gakko*) in Kyoto, yet we barely met. I was aware of their new publishing company, and one evening I attended a talk at their home by Helen and Scott Nearing.

After almost a year in Kyoto, in December 1971, I moved to Tokyo and enrolled in a university to continue my study of Japanese language and culture. Akiko and I met later that month and quickly found that we shared an interest in the traditional lifestyles and arts of East Asia. She was working as a clothing designer and illustrator; she was also a good cook. Knowing that I was intrigued by tofu, she prepared me many of her favorite recipes using each of Japan's seven different types of tofu.

In Tokyo, I lived in a small upstairs apartment near the University with my good friend from Tassajara, Jeffrey Broadbent, and his new wife, Gretchen. Jeffrey and I were taking the same intensive course in written and spoken Japanese. We bought tofu almost daily from the local tofu maker who delivered it on his bicycle and blew a little horn to announce his arrival. Soon Gretchen became so interested in tofu that she began visiting the local tofu shop and studying the process. She shared her discoveries and enthusiasm with me. At the end of the school year, for Akiko's sister's wedding, Gretchen baked an unforgettable many-layered all-natural non-dairy wedding cake—with tofu frosting!

On October 22, 1972, Akiko and I visited our neighborhood tofu shop in Tokyo, and for the first time we watched the traditional tofu making process first hand. Deeply impressed, we decided to write a booklet on tofu. But who would publish it? Two months later, on December 22, Jeffrey and Gretchen Broadbent called. They had just spent the evening with Nahum and Beverly Stiskin, who were now living in Hayama, south of Tokyo. Nahum was increasingly involved with his publishing. Something clicked. I asked for their phone number, then immediately called Nahum—who I hadn't seen for more than a year, since Kyoto days—and asked if Autumn Press might be interested in publishing a booklet on tofu. To my astonishment he replied: "I think that's a great idea!" He invited us to Hayama on January 13 to discuss the matter. I took a handwritten table of contents and one short chapter. It quickly became clear that all four of us shared a vision of tofu as a key protein source of the future; this was exciting. We believed that the West was ready for a book on tofu. Akiko and I left our meeting, unexpectedly, with a signed agreement in hand. Our idea for a booklet had just turned into a book—and we four had become a team.

One evening, about two months later, a mutual Japanese friend and Zen student, Mr. Nishimura, who considered himself a tofu connoisseur, introduced us to the world of tofu haute cuisine at *Sasa-no-yuki*; founded in 1703, it is probably Japan's oldest and most renowned tofu restaurant. The dinner was composed of twelve small dishes, each artistically presented and each featuring tofu in one of its many forms. Here, indeed, was tofu like we had never tasted it before. We were invited to return to the kitchen to learn how each recipe was made; many appear in this book.

We soon began to explore the realm of tofu cookery in earnest. Each morning we walked to our neighborhood tofu shop—one of the 38,000 scattered throughout Japan—and bought out supply for the day, always freshly prepared. I had never imagined that tofu could be coaxed into such a range of forms and textures, nor that it could combine harmoniously with so many different foods and flavors. Our low-calorie meals grew richer in protein and more deliciously varied, while our food bill remained as low as ever.

At first our repertoire was largely Japanese. We began to visit tofu restaurants throughout Japan, enjoying what seemed like an endless variety of tofu dishes served in elegant but simple settings: next to a garden in autumn colors, by a pond with its symphony of cicadas, or in a quiet temple over looking a garden of white sand raked into wavelike eddies. Whenever possible, we met with the head cook at these restaurants and stood at his elbow watching, taking notes, trying to absorb the subtleties of

his art as he prepared each of his specialties. Later, we tried each of these recipes at home—sometimes over and over again—until we were satisfied with the results. We then grew bolder and began experimenting with tofu in traditional Western-style dishes. Akiko's creative touch yielded delicious tofu dips and puréed dressings, egg dishes and casseroles, salads and soups, barbecued tofu, and deep-fried tofu burgers.

As our interest in tofu deepened, we asked the master of our local tofu shop, Mr. Toshio Arai, if we could return to study the tofu-making process in greater depth at *Sangen-ya*. We were deeply impressed with the feeling of alertness and care in his work. His movements were precise and graceful, joined in an effortless rhythm that, at times, flowed like a dance. A true master, he held in highest esteem the traditional, natural way and the spirit of fine craftsmanship. Working in an attractive, compact shop attached to his home, he used only natural ingredients to prepare the tofu he sold from his shop window and throughout the neighborhood. Like the traditional sword-maker or potter, his daily life was a practice, a spiritual path or, as the Japanese say, a Way. It was obvious that his work was its own fulfillment and reward.

I returned again and again to watch this master at work. Finally I asked to become his disciple and apprentice. Over a period of more than a year, he gradually taught me the techniques of making tofu in the traditional way.

This man urged us to record the methodology and, if possible, the spirit of his art both for Westerners seeking meaningful work and for future generations of Japanese who might someday wish to rediscover the rewards of fine craftsmanship presently obscured by modern industrial values and westernization. Throughout my apprenticeship, Akiko and I were encouraged to scour Japan to seek out every traditional tofu master we could find. To do so, we spent the warm months traveling up and down the islands, carrying backpacks and the tools necessary for our study. Often spending the night in temples, we met many Zen masters and practiced meditation with their students. And on many mornings, under a sky full of stars, Akiko and I wound our way to the one lighted shop on the sleeping streets of Japan's towns or cities to join a tofu master at his work.

Traditional tofu makers had often spoken to us with nostalgia and praise of the fine tofu once made in farmhouses throughout the country. To locate this legendary tofu and learn the secrets of its preparation, we backpacked early one spring into the remotest parts of Japan. We learned the traditional art from grandmothers in the mountainous back country while, to our surprise, the members of Banyan Ashram—a farming and meditation community on tiny Suwanose Island—taught us a remarkably simple way of making tofu, unknown to even the more professional craftsmen with whom we studied.

As we continued our work, several simple facts came together to broaden our perspective. The writings of nutritionists, ecologists, and experts studying world food and population problems convinced us that a meat-centered diet makes very inefficient use of the earth's ability to provide human beings with protein. It soon seemed to us imperative that the West learn to use soybeans directly as a source of inexpensive, high-quality protein, as people in East Asia have been doing for thousands of years. Here, where density of population has long posed serious problems, tofu is the most important and most popular way of transforming soybeans into a delicious food. Yet how unfortunate it seemed that there were fewer tofu shops in the combined countries and continents of India, Africa, South America, Russia, Canada, Europe, and America, than within the space of one-half square mile in Tokyo, Taipei, Seoul, or Peking.

We also came to feel that the tofu shop, requiring a minimum of energy resources, technology, and capital, could serve as a model for decentralized home or cottage industries throughout many parts of the developing and developed worlds. With this thought in mind, we took to studying shops in Japan and Taiwan which, we felt, combined the best of both traditional and modern techniques, making possible the large-scale production of good-quality tofu at relatively low cost. We also visited Japan's largest and most modern tofu factories to study their production-line methods in detail.

Traditional tofu masters have a saying that there are two things they will not show another person: how to make babies and how to make tofu. But to our continual surprise, these men invited us in—sometimes hesitatingly at first—to observe them at work and ultimately opened their hearts and homes to us in a way that was an ongoing source of inspiration to our research. We returned again and again to our favorite shops, each time with new questions, each time able to understand things we had not noticed or grasped before. Perceiving the sincerity of our intention to transmit the fundamentals of their craft to the West, they ended up sharing secrets with us that they would never have dreamed of revealing to their compatriots. We only hope that our efforts here do justice to their kindness, and to the care and patience they showed us in making sure that we *really* understood.

A rhythm emerged between our research in the field, writing, artwork, and daily meditation, which nurtured our growing book. Over a period of almost three years, we prepared and enjoyed more than 2,500 tofu dishes. This book contains only the 500 recipes which seemed to us best suited to Western tastes. Each recipe uses only natural foods and none requires the inclusion of meat.

As our work neared its completion, both Akiko and I realized that perhaps our finest teacher had been tofu itself. Like water that flows through the worlds, serving as it moves along, tofu joyfully surrenders itself to the endless play of transformation. Pierced with a skewer, it sizzles and broils above a bed of live coals; placed in a bubbling, earthenware pot over an open fire, it settles down next to the mushrooms and makes friends; deep-fried in crackling oil, it emerges crisp and handsome in robes of golden brown; frozen all night in the snow under vast mountain skies, it emerges glistening with frost and utterly changed. All as if it knew there was no death to die, no fixed or separate self to cling to, no other home than here.

A true democrat in spirit, tofu presents the same face to rich and poor alike. Placed before nobility in East Asia's finest haute cuisine, it is humble and unpretentious. Served up as peasant fare in rustic farmhouses, it is equally at home. Though unassertive, it is indispensable in the diet of more than 900 million people. Holding to simplicity, it remains in harmony with all things, and people never tire of its presence. Through understatement and nuance, it reveals its finest qualities.

Since earliest times, the people of East Asia have honored tofu in poem and proverb. Known as "meat of the fields" and "meat without a bone," tofu has provided them with abundant sustenance. In yielding and offering itself up, it seems to find its perfect balance in the greater dance. In the coming decades and centuries, tofu could nurture people around the world. To this end, we wish to send it on its way in the four directions.

Tokyo, Japan
March 1975
(Revised, March 1999)

Acknowledgments

WE WOULD like to thank the following people for their help in making this book: Mr. Toshio Arai, who gave us hundreds of hours of his time, taught us the traditional art and practice of making tofu, and prepared the tofu we ate and enjoyed each day; Mr. Shinji Morii, master of Morika, one of Japan's oldest and most famous tofu shops; Mr. Koryu Abe, Japan's foremost tofu historian; Mr. Hiroyoshi Masuda and his father, masters of one of Kamakura's finest traditional tofu shops; Ms. Kisa Asano and Mr. Mankichi Nagai, head craftspeople at two of Kyoto's oldest and finest yuba shops; Mr. Kiyoichi Oya, vice president of the Japanese National Tofu Union and president of the Tokyo Tofu Union; Mr. Tokuji Watanabe, director of the National Food Research Institute in Tokyo and one of the world's foremost authorities on tofu; Mr. Takichi Okumura, owner of Tokyo's renowned Sasa-no-yuki restaurant, and his head chefs, Mr. Sugita and Mr. Fushimi; Mr. Shigemitsu Tsuji, master and chief chef at Kyoto's Nakamura-ro restaurant, famous throughout Japan as a lecturer and writer on Japanese cuisine and tofu, and author of a recent book on tofu cookery; Mr. Toshio Yanaihara, author of many works on tofu and head of a large Japanese cooking school; Messrs. Scott Sawyers, Lloyd Reid, and Jack Yamashita of the American Soybean Association in Japan; Dr. Harry W. Miller, the West's foremost authority on soymilk and pioneer in the field of using soybeans as foods; Mr. Teisuke Yabuki, president of the Luppy Soymilk Company; Mmes. Ito Kidoguchi, Kazuko Ozawa, and Minoru Watanabe, all in their seventies, who first taught us how to make farmhouse tofu; the members of Banyan Ashram who taught us how to make tofu solidified with sea water and introduced us to the riches of their simple way of life; Mr. Kyo Ko, owner of Fukyo-dofu, Tokyo's largest manufacturer of Chinese-style tofu; Mr. Tadashi Honma, director of research for Japan's largest manufacturer of dried-frozen tofu; Messrs. Itaro Hayashi, Ei Tamura, Daisaburo Noma and Kinjiro Sugai, each masters of fine traditional tofu shops at which we studied; Messrs. Shotaro Yoshikawa and Minoru Narahara, two leaders of Japan's movement to return to the use of natural nigari solidifier; Mr. Kiyoshi Takato, manager of one of Japan's largest and most modern tofu factories; and tofu makers throughout Taiwan, Korea, and America who gave generously of their time and experience.

Finally, we would like to give special thanks to our parents for their aid and encouragement, to Mr. Tyler Smith for his editorial suggestions, and to our publisher, Nahum Stiskin, whose faith and support were with us from the first conception of this book until its completion.

PART I

Tofu:
Food for Mankind

Protein East and West

FOR OVER TWO millenia in China and 1,000 years in Japan, soybeans have served as one of the most important sources of protein. In countries such as these, where people have long had to live with the problem of overpopulation, soybeans have been prized for their remarkable ability to produce over 33 percent more protein from an acre of land than any other known crop and *twenty* times as much usable protein as could be raised on an acre given over to grazing beef cattle or growing their fodder (fig. 1). It is thus easy to understand why meat protein is a great deal more expensive than soy protein and why, as population pressure on the land increases, it seems inevitable that more and more farmers all over the world will be planting soybeans. Their "protein efficiency" is the first and, perhaps, primary reason why soybean foods have played such a key role in the daily diet of the people of East Asia.

Not only is the protein yield of soybeans high in terms of quantity—soybeans contain about 35 percent protein, more than any other unprocessed plant or animal food—it is also excellent in terms of quality. Soy protein includes all of the eight essential amino acids in a configuration readily usable by the human body. It is now becoming common knowledge that there is no essential difference between plant and animal proteins. From the body's point of view, the amount of usable protein contained in ½ cup of soybeans is no different from that contained in 5 ounces of steak. And inexpensive soybean foods contain no cholesterol, almost none of the relatively indigestible saturated fats found in most animal foods, and an extremely low ratio of calories to protein. These basic facts, now scientifically well documented, have been understood intuitively throughout East Asia since earliest times.

But just as Westerners prefer to transform whole kernels of wheat into breads, pasta, and other foods made from flour, so have the people of East Asia preferred to transform whole soybeans into other forms. Since long before the Christian era, men and women throughout Asia have participated in a

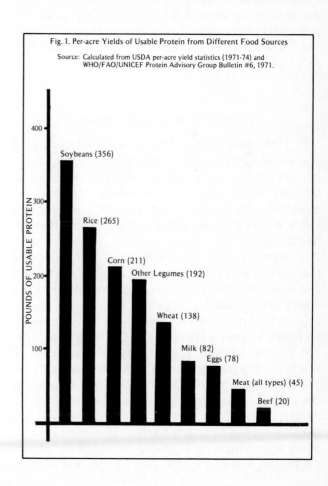

Fig. 1. Per-acre Yields of Usable Protein from Different Food Sources

Source: Calculated from USDA per-acre yield statistics (1971-74) and WHO/FAO/UNICEF Protein Advisory Group Bulletin #6, 1971.

POUNDS OF USABLE PROTEIN

- Soybeans (356)
- Rice (265)
- Corn (211)
- Other Legumes (192)
- Wheat (138)
- Milk (82)
- Eggs (78)
- Meat (all types) (45)
- Beef (20)

vast experiment to find simple yet effective ways of creating soybean foods that are versatile, easily digestible, and, above all, delicious. Centuries of creative endeavor have yielded three great products which now serve as the cornerstones of East Asian nutrition and cuisine: *tofu*, *miso* (fermented soybean paste), and *shoyu* (soy sauce). Whereas miso and shoyu are essentially high-protein seasonings, tofu is a food that can serve as the backbone of a diet in much the same way that meat and dairy products are now used in the dietary pattern of the West. The development of traditional technologies and methods for transforming soybeans directly into these foods may someday be regarded as one of East Asia's greatest contributions to mankind, and a major step in the direct utilization by man of the earth's bounty of protein.

Today, throughout much of Asia, tofu is by far the most important way of using soybeans as a daily food. Indeed tofu is as much a part of Oriental culture, language, and cookery as is bread in the West. In America, a country with twice the population of Japan, there are 19,000 bakeries and the average annual consumption of bread is 73 loaves per person. The tofu made in Japan's 38,000 tofu shops provides the average Japanese with about seventy 12-ounce cakes each year. And it is estimated that in Taiwan and China, the per capita consumption is considerably higher than it is in Japan.

America's Soy Protein Tragedy

Now imagine how strange it would seem if, in the world's largest wheat producing country, most of the people had never tasted bread. Yet no less unusual is the present situation in America, the world's largest producer of soybeans, where the majority of people have not yet tasted, seen, or even heard of tofu.

America now produces about two-thirds of the world's soybeans. They are presently our largest and most important farm crop, leading second-place wheat in both total acreage and dollar value. The 47 million tons of soybeans harvested in 1973 is enough to provide every person in the United States with 165 pounds of pure, high-quality protein. If all of this protein were used directly as food—in the form of tofu, for example—it would be sufficient to fulfill the average adult protein requirement of every American for about 3 years! And if the protein obtainable from one year's harvest of America's soybeans were distributed equally among all people on the planet, it would fulfill about 25 percent of their yearly protein requirements, according to even the most conservative Western standards.

But the tragedy of our present situation is that less than 15 percent of America's non-exported soy protein ever reaches human beings: 1½ percent directly in soybean foods and about 13 percent indirectly in the form of meat and dairy products.

What happens to all the rest? To understand the answer to this question we must first recognize that, while in East Asia soybeans have traditionally been used to make tofu and other soybean foods, in the West they have been viewed primarily as an oilseed. Almost all of America's non-exported soybeans are shipped to huge modern factories where their oil is extracted in a continuous, automated process. The largest and most important piece of machinery employed is a counter-current hexane solvent extractor, capable of handling over 4 million pounds of soybeans per day. Soy oil, which contains no protein, is degummed, refined, bleached, deodorized, and winterized by industro-chemical processes and then sold as cooking or salad oil. Some of the oil is hydrogenated to produce margarine and vegetable shortenings. The defatted soybean meal, a byproduct of the oil extraction process, contains about 2½ times as much protein by weight as steak.

Now, *where* does this protein go? In America, about 95 percent of all non-exported soy protein ends up as feed for livestock, and of this, 77 to 95 percent is irretrievably lost in the process of animal metabolism. In addition, we feed livestock 78 percent of all our grain, most of which could be used directly as food. American farmers use more of their soybeans and grain as fodder than farmers in any other country. These losses, creating the appearance of scarcity in the midst of actual plenty, are a direct result of our failure to understand and make use of the soybean's great potential as a food. For if the total protein available from these crops were utilized directly by human beings, it could make up an estimated 90 percent of the world's protein deficiency.

The process described above, inherent in the Western meat-centered diet, is the cause of our immense protein waste. In *Diet for a Small Planet*, Frances Moore Lappé shows how we use the cow as a protein factory in reverse: we feed it from 14 to 21 pounds of protein from sources that could be used directly as food, and we obtain only 1 pound of protein from the meat. In this highly inefficient process, only 5 to 7 percent of the total protein consumed by a feedlot steer or cow is returned for human consumption as meat. Likewise only 12 percent is returned by a hog as pork, 15 percent by a chicken as meat and 22 percent as eggs, and 23 percent by a cow as milk. In her appeal for a more rational use of the earth's bounty, Ms. Lappé urges Westerners to get off the "top" of the food chain and begin to utilize sources of high-quality, non-meat protein.

Although Americans make up only 6 percent of the world's population, they account for 30 percent of its total meat consumption. The per capita American consumption of beef, pork, and poultry presently runs about 254 pounds per year, or 316 grams per day. This is about 5 times the world average and 15 times the average intake for people in East Asia. In order to produce this much meat, American farmers plant an astounding 50 percent of their total acreage in feed crops, and U.S. livestock are fed 120 million tons of feed-grains each year. Consequently, the average American now consumes the equivalent of 2,000 pounds of grain and soybeans annually, roughly 90 percent of which is in the form of meat, poultry, and eggs. But in developing countries—where most grains and soybeans are used directly as food—the average person consumes only about 400 pounds of grain per year. Hence the birth of one meat-eating American has the same effect on world food resources as the birth of *five* children in India, Africa, or South America. On the other hand, a reduction in American meat consumption of only 10 percent could free 12 million tons of soybeans, corn, wheat, and other grains, enough to meet the annual grain requirements of 60 million people in less developed countries.

Worldwide Protein Crisis

It is now generally conceded that the world is facing a serious food crisis. More precisely, it is a protein crisis, and not one that is likely to go away or even become less critical during the coming decades. We have watched regional famines spread and become more frequent, and experts are no longer as optimistic as they once were about the "green revolution," with its climatically sensitive "miracle" seeds, its petroleum-based chemical fertilizers and toxic pesticides which steadily deplete the soil, and its heavy dependence on expensive and complex Western technology.

It is now estimated that more than one-fourth of the world's four billion people (including 450 million children equalling more than twice the population of the United States!) confront hunger or famine during at least some part of each year. In developing countries, according to United Nations statistics, 25 percent to 30 percent of all children never see their fourth birthday, largely due to malnutrition.

And many who do survive are permanently damaged physically and mentally because of the lack of sufficient protein in their diet. These facts so boggle the mind that most of us are simply unable or unwilling to face them. But this crucial problem of our age *must* be faced and understood *now,* for each of us can begin *today* to contribute directly to its solution.

The food crisis is continually aggravated by two basic trends that all experts agree must be reversed as rapidly as possible. The first trend, understood since the time of Malthus, is that linear increases in food production fall farther and farther behind exponential increases in population. In the less developed countries, the amount of food available to each person is steadily decreasing. With the world's population doubling every 35 years and expanding onto what is now farmland, and with most of the earth's good-quality land already under intensive cultivation, the cost of farming previously unused land on mountain sides or in deserts and jungles grows increasingly expensive. And hungry people are the least able to pay these costs.

The second trend, which is just now beginning to be recognized, concerns the relationship between affluence and the consumption of basic foods. As people develop a higher standard of living, they generally desire a larger proportion of meat and other animal protein in their diet (fig. 2). During the past 12 years, cattle herds have increased 30 percent in the United States and 28 percent throughout the rest of the world. During the same period per-capita livestock meat consumption has increased 22 percent in the United States, 26 percent in France and Canada, 30 percent in Russia, 33 percent in West Germany, 94 percent in Italy, and an astonishing 364 percent in Japan. (Japan, however, still has the lowest annual per capita meat consumption of any of the above countries; its 51 pounds per year is only 20 percent of top-ranking America's 254 pounds.) Since more than 14 pounds of fodder protein are needed to produce 1 pound of protein from beef, a small increase in demand for meat leads to enormous increases in the indirect consumption of soy and grain proteins. This results in a sharp decrease in the amounts of these foods available for human consumption, especially in poorer countries. In addition, rising demand for soybean and grain fodders pushes up their prices, creating a vicious cycle that further aggravates the shortages in poorer countries.

To reverse the first trend, every effort must be made to reduce population growth and raise agricultural productivity by increasing per-acre yields, bringing more land under cultivation, and using this

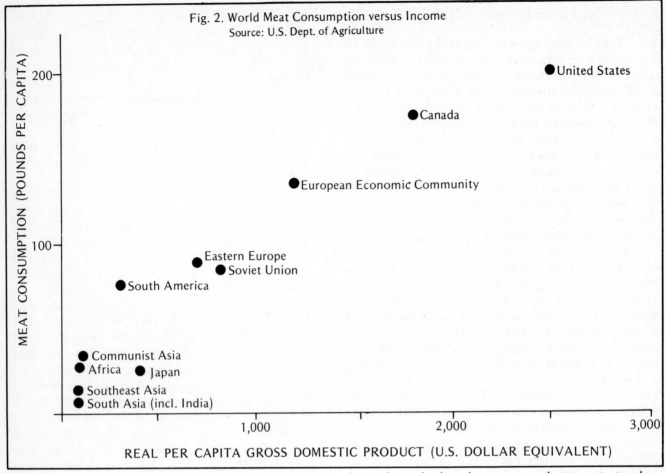

Fig. 2. World Meat Consumption versus Income
Source: U.S. Dept. of Agriculture

MEAT CONSUMPTION (POUNDS PER CAPITA)

200 — United States

Canada

European Economic Community

100 —

Eastern Europe
Soviet Union
South America

Communist Asia
Africa   Japan
Southeast Asia
South Asia (incl. India)

1,000   2,000   3,000

REAL PER CAPITA GROSS DOMESTIC PRODUCT (U.S. DOLLAR EQUIVALENT)

land for essential high-protein food crops (rather than cash crops such as coffee, tobacco, cocoa, and tea, which have little or no nutritional value). One hope for the coming decades is that developing countries with suitable topography and climate will follow the lead of Brazil in realizing the tremendous economic and nutritional potential of soybeans. From a mere 650,000 tons in 1968, Brazil's soybean production soared to 10.5 million tons in 1974, a *sixteenfold* increase in only 6 years. Having recently surpassed China to become the world's second largest soybean producer, Brazil is now working to boost production to 15 million tons by 1980 and hopes eventually to overtake first-place America. With exports totaling almost 1 billion dollars annually, soybeans have now surpassed coffee as Brazil's chief export crop, and the government is actively encouraging farmers to turn their coffee plantations into soybean farms.

(At the same time, however, industrialized nations are now becoming increasingly aware of the limits and dangers of conventional agricultural methods to create an ever-expanding food supply. Intensive use of pesticides and chemical fertilizers, the two main factors responsible for the great postwar jump in agricultural output, and attempts to clear more and more land for agricultural use are beginning to place such heavy stresses on the planet's basic ecosystems that they could easily create environmental problems of a greater magnitude than the food problems they are now intended to solve.)

While most Westerners—and particularly those not involved in agriculture—can participate directly in the reversal of the first trend only through family planning, every Westerner can participate in a very vital and immediate way to reverse the second trend, and thereby actively help to relieve the suffering that afflicts millions of our fellow human beings around the world. We can and must make more efficient use of the food presently available on the planet. And we must understand clearly the fact, often overlooked in discussing world food shortages, that there is presently more than enough food and protein for all the people in the world. The extremely complex problem of distributing this food in a just and compassionate way, avoiding large-scale misuse of its great nutritional potential, demands our fullest attention. Not the earth's natural limitations but the wisdom with which we use the earth's bounty will determine whether or not there is sufficient food for all human beings during the coming decades.

Most experts agree that to make fullest use of the protein we now have, the citizens of the world's affluent, industrialized nations will have to make basic changes in their eating habits. Most important, they will have to start eating less meat—especially beef. All of man's food comes initially from plant sources and, in fact, 70 percent of the world's protein is still consumed directly from plants. By rediscovering the wisdom inherent in traditional dietary patterns that make use of non-meat protein sources, we can free millions of tons of high-quality soy and grain protein to be used directly as food. (Since, according to various government estimates, the average American now receives from 12 to 45 percent more protein than his body can even use, Americans can perhaps most easily reduce their consumption of expensive protein foods.) In a world where the affluent nations appear to many as islands of plenty in a sea of hunger, each of us must make a personal effort to rectify this dangerous imbalance. We can begin by working to make best use of our ample protein supplies.

Hopefully, more and more people, recognizing that a meat-centered diet squanders the earth's food resources, will turn to nutritionally and ecologically viable alternatives—such as tofu. Many have already found that a meatless diet, low in saturated fats and cholesterol, makes sense in terms of good health, mental alertness, and a general feeling of physical well being. For many more people, the determining forces may well be primarily economic: skyrocketing meat prices. The basic inefficiencies of land use inherent in meat production have led food experts and economists to predict that in the coming decades, the prices of most meats could rise to the point where only the very rich could afford them. Yet whether we are moved by economic, ecological, religious or health considerations, or by a feeling of identification with the millions of hungry people around the world, each of us can help solve the world food problem by starting now to change the way we eat.

The Growing Importance of Soy Protein

One thing is virtually certain: Over the coming years, we can expect soy protein to play an increasingly important role in our daily lives. Although scientists continue to explore futuristic protein sources (such as cottonseeds, algae, petroleum, microbes, tree leaves, and synthetics), most experts now consider soybeans to be the most realistic and promising source of low-cost, high-quality protein available in large enough quantities to meet human needs on a worldwide scale. Hence, throughout the world, there is great interest in finding ways of using soybeans directly as a source of protein. In the United States, where 70 percent of all food protein presently comes from animal sources and only 30 percent from plants, major food research firms estimate that within 10 to 20 years these figures will be reversed. And the most rapid increase is, of course, seen in the use of soy protein. Whereas an estimated 150,000 tons of the latter were used in U.S. foods in 1972, it is predicted that more than *twelve* times this amount will be used by 1980.

Although these figures sound promising, an examination of their actual relevance to the world food crisis seems to suggest several problems. We must remember that the total amount of soy protein now used directly as food in the U.S. is still extremely small—only about 1½ percent of the total available from the domestic crop. Most of this protein is used in the form of plain or defatted soy flour (containing 40 to 52 percent protein), which is purchased primarily by the food industry and used in small amounts as a conditioner, extender, emulsifier, or moisture retainer in canned foods, baked goods, and processed meats. The presence of this soy additive is usually acknowledged only in small print on the label, and the word "soy" is often carefully omitted. Some soy flour is sent to developing countries in food supplements as part of America's worldwide nutritional aid program. Yet it is not expected that these ways of using soy protein will be of major importance during the coming decades.

Rather, experts in the food industry foresee the use of advanced Western technology to create a wide range of new, synthetic soybean foods. Many of these are already available: protein concentrates, isolates, spun proteins and, most important, textured vegetable proteins. The latter, extruded from defatted soybean meal (or whole soy flour) in highly sophisticated factories, are generally added as extenders to ground or processed meat products in order to lower their cost (and levels of saturated fats) while raising their protein content and improving their cooking qualities. Spun proteins, composed of tiny fibers or monofilaments of almost pure protein, are used to make imitation livestock products and meat analogs. By compressing the protein fibers to simulate the fibrous texture of meat, and adding the appropriate flavorings and colorings, food technologists are able to create imitation bacon, ham, sausages, beef, chicken, and a wide variety of new high-protein snacks. Many of these fabricated products are now available in Western supermakets. For relatively affluent Westerners, such foods can provide protein which is somewhat less expensive than that found in meat, while also helping to make more efficient use of domestic soy protein. Yet it is now clearly understood that the technology for producing these foods is far too complex and costly to be of use in developing countries where hunger is most acute. And to the growing number of Westerners interested in natural foods, these highly refined products are bound to be of limited appeal.

As a clear and practical alternative, we must turn our attention to traditional East Asian methods for transforming soybeans into foods; methods that recognize food to be man's most direct link with the nurturing earth and which bind season and soil, man and food into a holistic, organic cycle. Each of the seven basic types of tofu can be made in any Western kitchen, or in small, decentralized enterprises using technology on a human scale and employing a minimum of energy. The tofu shop can be adopted as easily in Bangladesh, Brazil, and Nigeria as in the industrialized or "post industrial" societies of the West.

In tofu shops now located throughout America, craftsmen have already begun making tofu available at reasonable prices. We believe these shops are situated at an historic crossroads, and that they can and will make an invaluable contribution to the betterment of life on our planet during the years ahead.

2

Tofu as a Food

NUTRITIONALLY, the various types of tofu—there are seven in Japan and even more in China—have much the same importance for the people of East Asia that dairy products, eggs, and meat have for us in the West.(In figures 3 and 4, tofu products are listed and illustrated in the approximate order of their availability in the U.S.) When looking for alternate sources of protein and when considering the benefits of a meatless way of eating, many people ask: "What will we use to replace meat?" Some experiment with eggs and dairy products, or with soybeans and grains. The traditional answer throughout East Asia has been tofu.

Before replacing all or part of the meat in our diet with less expensive protein from another source, most nutrition-conscious people will want to have enough sound, factual information to make this important decision with complete confidence. We feel that the following facts show tofu to be a truly remarkable food. And tofu's excellent nutritional record, extending over a period of thousands of years in China and Japan, gives practical substantiation to the findings of modern research.

Rich in High Quality Protein

The value of any food as a protein source depends on two factors: the *quantity* of protein in the food and the *quality* of that protein. Quantity is usually expressed as a simple percentage of total weight. By comparing the following figures, it can be seen that the highest percentages of protein are found in plant rather than animal foods:

Food	Percent Protein by Weight
Dried-frozen tofu	53
Yuba, dried	52
Soy flour (defatted)	51
Soy flour (natural)	40
Soybeans (whole, dry)	35
Cheeses	30
Fish	22
Chicken	21
Beef (steak)	20
Cottage cheese	20
Agé (Tofu Pouches)	19
Ganmo (Tofu Burgers)	15
Whole-wheat flour	13
Hamburger	13
Eggs	13
Doufu (Chinese-style Tofu)	11
Thick agé (Tofu Cutlets)	10
Tofu	8
Brown rice (uncooked)	6
Milk (whole)	3

(Source: *Standard Tables of Food Composition* [Japan] and *Diet For a Small Planet*)

Furthermore, we notice that dried-frozen tofu and *yuba* (a close relative of tofu) contain the highest percentages of protein found in any natural foods in existence. Moreover, the top five protein sources are all derived from soybeans. The data presented in figure 5 shows the percentages of protein and other nutrients in the various types of tofu now available

Fig. 3. Tofu Products Available in the West

Name Used in This Book	Other Names	Description	Where Sold*	How Sold
Tofu	Soybean Curd	Regular, Medium-firm Japanese-style tofu	N,J,C,S,T	12- to 21-ounce cakes water-packed in plastic tubs or cartons; also canned
Chinese-style Tofu	Doufu, Dow-foo, Bean Cake	Chinese-style firm tofu	N,J,C,S,T	Two or more 6-ounce cakes water-packed in plastic tubs
Silken Tofu	Kinugoshi, Soft, or Custard Tofu, Shui Dow-foo, Sui-doufu	Soft Japanese-style tofu	N,J,C,S,T	12- to 20-ounce cakes water-packed in plastic tubs or cartons
Deep-fried Tofu Cutlets	Thick Agé, Nama-agé, Atsu-agé, Raw-fried Tofu	Deep-fried tofu cakes	N,J,C,S,T	Cakes or slices of 5 ounces or less, dry-packed in plastic cartons or tubs; also sold in small triangles and cubes
Deep-fried Tofu Pouches or Puffs	Aburagé, Agé or Agé Puffs	A hollow pouch or puff of deep-fried tofu	N,J,C,S,T	Three ½- to 1-ounce pieces dry-packed in a cellophane bag
Hollow Deep-fried Tofu Cubes	Hollow Agé Puffs, Dow-foo Bok, Yudoufu	Chinese-style, hollow 1½-inch cubes of deep-fried tofu	N,J,C,S,T	15 cubes, each ⅓ ounce, dry-packed in a cellophane bag
Soymilk	Dou-jiang, Tonyu, Soyalac	Regular or flavored with honey or carob	N,J,C,S,T	1-pint glass, paper, or plastic containers
Tofu Pudding	Fresh Soybean Pudding, Soft Tofu Curds	Soft curds of soymilk	N,J,C,S,T	1-pound portions in plastic tubs
Wine-fermented Tofu	Doufu-ru, Fuyu, Chinese Cheese, Bean Curd Cheese	Chinese-style soft cubes of fermented tofu in brining liquor	C	White varieties in 1-pint bottles; red varieties in small cans
Deep-fried Tofu Burgers	Ganmo, Ganmodoki	Deep-fried tofu patties or balls containing minced vegetables	J	3½-ounce patties or 2-ounce balls dry-packed in plastic bags; or canned
Grilled Tofu	Yaki-dofu	A cake of firm regular tofu which has been grilled or broiled	J	10-ounce cakes water-packed in plastic tubs; or canned
Dried-Frozen Tofu	Koya-dofu, Kori-dofu	Very lightweight cakes of tofu which have been frozen and then dried	J,S	Five to ten 1-ounce cakes in an airtight carton
Instant Powdered Tofu	Dehydrated Instant Tofu	Do-it-yourself, instant home-made tofu	J,S	A foil-wrapped package of powdered soymilk accompanied by a small package of solidifier
Okara	Soy Pulp, Tofu Lees, Unohana	Insoluble portions of the soybean remaining after filtering off soymilk	J,T	8- to 16-ounce portions in plastic bags, balls, or mounds
Dried Yuba	Bean Curd Sheets	A high-protein film made from soymilk	J,C	4- to 8-ounce portions in paper or cellophane bags
Soymilk Curds	Oboro	Unpressed soft curds of coagulated soymilk	T	Available directly from tofu shops by special order
Pressed Tofu	Doufu-kan, Dow-foo Gar	Chinese-style small cakes of very firmly pressed tofu	C	Three 4-ounce cakes sealed in a plastic pouch
Savory Pressed Tofu	Wu-hsiang Kan, Flavored Soybean Cake	Pressed tofu seasoned with soy sauce and spices	C	Three 4-ounce cakes sealed in a plastic pouch

*N Natural and health food stores   J Japanese food markets   C Chinese food markets
 S Supermarkets, especially co-op markets   T Available at most tofu shops by special request

Fig. 5. *Tofu products available in the West*

Tofu

Chinese-style Tofu
(Doufu)

Silken Tofu
(Kinugoshi)

Deep-fried Tofu Cutlets
(Thick Agé)

triangles

cubes

cakes

Deep-fried Tofu Pouches &Puffs
(Agé)

Hollow Deep-fried Tofu Cubes

Soymilk

Tofu Pudding

Wine-fermented Tofu
(Doufu-ru; white and red)

Deep-fried Tofu Burgers
(Ganmo; patties, balls,
and treasure balls)

Grilled Tofu

Dried-frozen Tofu

Instant Powdered Tofu

Okara

Dried Yuba

Soymilk Curds

Pressed Tofu

Savory Pressed Tofu

Fig. 5. Composition of Nutrients in 100 grams of Tofu

Sources: *Standard Tables of Food Composition* (Japan), *FAO Food Composition Tables, and USDA Composition of Foods* (Wash., D.C.)

Type of Tofu	Food Energy Calories	Moisture Percent	Protein Percent	Fat Percent	Sugars Percent	Fiber Percent	Ash Percent	Calcium Mg	Sodium Mg	Phosphorus Mg	Iron Mg	Vit. B₁ (Thiamine) Mg	Vit. B₂ (Riboflavin) Mg	Vit. B₃ (Niacin) Mg
Tofu	72	84.9	7.8	4.3	2.3	0	0.7	146	6	105	1.7	0.02	0.02	0.5
Chinese-Style Tofu (Doufu)	87	79.3	10.6	5.3	2.9	0	0.9	159	7	109	2.5	0.02	0.02	0.6
Silken Tofu (Kinugoshi)	53	88.4	5.5	3.2	1.7	0	1.2	94	23	71	1.2	0.02	0.02	0.3
Deep-fried Tofu Cutlets (Thick Agé)	105	79.0	10.1	7.0	2.8	0	1.1	240	15	150	2.6	0.02	0.02	0.5
Deep-fried Tofu Pouches (Agé)	346	44.0	18.6	31.4	4.5	0.1	1.4	300	20	230	4.2	0.02	0.02	0.5
Soymilk	42	90.8	3.6	2.0	2.9	0.02	0.5	15	2	49	1.2	0.03	0.02	0.5
Wine-fermented Tofu (Doufu-ru)	175	52.0	13.5	8.4	13.6	1.2	11.6	165	458	182	5.7	0.04	0.18	0.6
Deep-fried Tofu Burgers (Ganmo)	192	64.0	15.4	14.0	5.1	0.1	1.4	270	17	200	3.6	0.01	0.03	1.0
Grilled Tofu	82	83.0	8.8	5.1	2.1	0	1.0	180	15	120	1.9	0.02	0.02	0.4
Dried-Frozen Tofu	436	10.4	53.4	26.4	7.0	0.2	2.6	590	18	710	9.4	0.05	0.04	0.6
Okara	65	84.5	3.5	1.9	6.9	2.3	0.9	76	4	43	1.4	0.05	0.02	0.3
Dried Yuba	432	8.7	52.3	24.1	11.9	0	3.0	270	80	590	11.0	0.20	0.08	2.0
Pressed Tofu and Savory Pressed Tofu	182	61.6	22.0	11.0	6.0	0.1	1.9	377	16	270	4.4	0.05	0.05	0.6
Dry Soybeans	392	12.0	34.3	17.5	26.7	4.5	5.0	190	3	470	7.0	0.50	0.20	2.0
Defatted Soybean Meal	322	8.0	49.0	0.4	33.6	3.0	6.0	220	4	550	8.4	0.45	0.15	2.0
Kinako & Roasted Soybeans	426	5.0	38.4	19.2	29.5	2.9	5.0	190	4	500	9.0	0.40	0.15	2.0

Note: Regular Japanese tofu varies in protein content from 6 to 8.4, and in water content form 87.9 to 83.9 percent; the mineral data above refer to tofu (and kinugoshi) solidified with calcium sulfate. Kinugoshi and the rich soymilk prepared at tofu shops vary in protein from 4.9 to 6.3, and in water content for 89.7 to 87.4 percent. Commercially-distributed soymilk varies in protein from 3.6 to 5.8, and in water content from 90.8 to 88.2 percent. Thick agé prepared with nigari often contains up to 17.7 percent protein and only 58.7 percent water. Differences in composition depend primarily on the method of preparation, the type of solidifier, and the grade and protein content of the soybeans used.

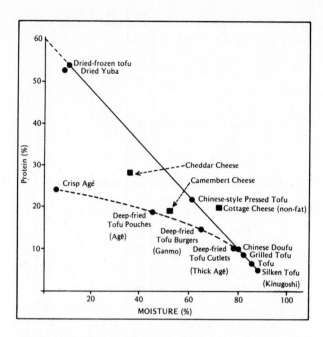

Fig. 6. Tofu Protein versus Moisture Content
  *For Non-deep-fried Tofu:
    Protein (%) = 59.6 — .61 × Moisture (%)

Wheat germ	67
Beef and hamburger	67
Oatmeal	66
Tofu	65
Chicken	65
Soybeans and soy flour	61
Peanuts	43
Lentils	30

(Source: *Diet for a Small Planet*)

From the body's point of view, the protein in tofu is identical to the protein in chicken. Note that tofu has the fourth highest NPU of any plant food. It also has the highest NPU rating of all soybean products and all members of the protein-rich legume family. The soybean is the only legume which is a "complete protein," that is, one containing all of the eight essential amino acids. And the amino acid analysis of tofu is remarkably similar to that of most animal protein (including casein milk protein).

By combining the two sets of figures given above we can compare the true value of various protein sources. Regular tofu, for example, contains 7.8 percent protein, 65 percent of which is actually usable by the body. Thus, a typical 8-ounce (227 gram) serving of tofu can supply us with 227 x .65 x .078 or 11.5 grams of *usable* protein. This is a full 27 percent of the daily adult male protein requirement of 43.1 grams. The same amount of usable protein could be supplied by 3¼ ounces of steak (at a much higher cost) or 5½ ounces of hamburger.

in the West; figure 6 illustrates the relationship between protein and moisture content in the different types of tofu.

Protein quality refers to the percentage of protein in a food that can be utilized by the body; it is usually expressed in terms of NPU (Net Protein Utilization), "biological value," or "protein score." The NPU of a food depends largely on the food's digestibility and on the degree to which the configuration of the eight essential amino acids making up the protein matches the pattern required by the body.

It is a common misconception that the protein found in animal foods is somehow basically different from (and superior to) plant protein. In fact, there is no basic difference. It is simply a question of degree. The higher the NPU of any food, the more completely the body is able to utilize that food's protein. The following figures show that, although animal foods tend to have the highest NPU ratings, a number of plant foods—including tofu—rank quite high on the scale:

Food	NPU (Percent)
Eggs	94
Fish	80
Cottage cheese	75
Brown rice	70
Cheeses	70

High Protein Complementarity

Tofu is an excellent food to use in combining proteins since it contains an abundance of lysine, an essential amino acid that is deficient in many grain products. Most grains, on the other hand, are well endowed with the sulfur-containing amino acids methionine and cystine, the limiting amino acids in soybeans (fig. 7). Thus soy and grain proteins, having exactly the opposite strengths and weaknesses, complement each other. By serving foods such as tofu and whole-grain bread or rice at the same meal and combining them in the correct ratios, we are able, in effect, to "create" new protein at no extra cost. The NPU of the resultant combination is considerably higher than that of either of the individual foods and, therefore, the total usable protein is much greater than if the foods were served at separate meals. Applying this principle of protein complementarity in planning our daily meals allows us

Amino Acids	MDR (gm)	Tofu (gm)	MDR (%)
(Methionine-Cystine)	1.10	0.20	17
Tryptophan	0.25	0.12	47
Methionine	0.20	0.10	52
Leucine	1.10	0.59	52
Valine	0.80	0.43	53
Isoleucine	0.70	0.41	59
(Phenylalanine-tyrosine)	1.10	0.75	67
Lysine	0.80	0.57	71
Threonine	0.50	0.37	72
Phenylalanine	0.30	0.48	160
Protein, usable (gm)	43.10	5.06	12

Note: Amino acids in shortest supply are listed first. Those in parentheses are important combinations of essential and non-essential amino acids with common properties. Thus 100 grams of regular Japanese tofu (7.8% protein) contains 0.20 grams of the sulfur-containing amino acids (methionine-cystine), or 17 percent of the minimum adult daily requirement of 1.10 grams.

to make fullest use of the earth's abundant protein supplies. For example, by serving only 3½ ounces of tofu together with 1¼ cups brown rice, we obtain 32 percent more protein than if we served these foods separately. Thus, tofu's unique amino-acid composition makes it not only a basic protein *source*, but also a truly remarkable protein *booster*. As the figures below show, the use of even small amounts of tofu combined with grains and other basic foods (in the ratios indicated) can produce large increases in usable protein. Herein lies the key to tofu's value as an essential daily accompaniment to the grain-centered diet, the way of eating characteristic of virtually all traditional societies since earliest times. Furthermore, the use of whole grains together with soy products creates a "protein-sparing effect": the body uses the grain carbohydrates as its source of fuel or energy and allows the protein to fulfill its basic function of tissue growth and repair.

Each of the following combinations provides exactly 50 percent of the daily adult male requirement of usable protein, or the equivalent of that found in 4½ ounces of (uncooked) steak. (All quantities of grains refer to the raw, uncooked product.)

Combination	Percent Increase
1 cup whole-wheat flour, 1½ tablespoons sesame butter, 3 ounces tofu	42
1 cup whole-wheat flour, 4½ ounces tofu	32
1¼ cups brown rice, 3½ ounces tofu	32
3 tablespoons each peanut and sesame butter, 4 ounces tofu	25
3/8 cup each whole-wheat flour and brown rice, 1¼ tablespoons peanut butter, 6¾ ounces tofu	24
¾ cup cornmeal, 1 cup milk, 5 ounces tofu	13

(Adapted from: *Diet for a Small Planet*)

The protein-rich combinations of tofu with whole-wheat flour suggest a variety of tofu (and nut butter) sandwiches or deep-fried tofu burgers, noodle or bulgur wheat dishes, and even *chapati*, *taco*, or pizza preparations. The traditional East Asian combination has, of course, been with rice.

Easy to Digest

While many high-protein foods, such as meats, dairy products, and beans, are quite difficult for some people to digest, tofu, prepared by a process that carefully removes the crude fiber and water-soluble carbohydrates from soybeans, is soft and highly digestible. Indeed, with a digestion rate of 95 percent, it is by far the most digestible of all natural soybean foods, and is much more digestible than cooked whole soybeans (68%). Thus, tofu can be an excellent food for babies, elderly adults, and people with digestive problems. The Chinese say that sages, yogis, and monks, who rely for sustenance on nothing but the mists of heaven and the fresh morning dew, are particularly fond of tofu as their third choice.

An Ideal Diet Food

Tofu is also the ideal diet food. A typical 8-ounce serving contains only 147 calories. An equal weight of eggs contains about 3 times as many calories, and an equal weight of beef about 4 to 5 times as many. Perhaps more important, next to mung- and soybean sprouts, tofu has the lowest ratio of calories to protein found in any known plant food. One gram of total protein costs you only 9 calories, and 1 gram of usable protein only 12 calories. The only animal foods which have a lower ratio are some types of fish and seafoods. Because of its low carbohydrate content, tofu is widely recommended for starch-restricted diets by doctors throughout East Asia. While providing 27 percent of your daily protein requirements, an 8-ounce serving of tofu costs you only 5 grams of carbohydrate and less than 7½ percent of the recommended daily adult requirement of 2,200 calories.

Low in Saturated Fats and Cholesterol

Tofu is unique among high protein foods in being low in calories and saturated fats and entirely free of cholesterol. And in this fact may be its greatest potential importance as a key to good health and long life. There is now a near consensus among doctors on the contributive role of animal fats and cholesterol to heart disease, the number-one health problem in the United States. It is well known that most doctors recommend a reduction in the consumption of animal foods as the first step in the treatment of heart disease, high blood pressure, arteriosclerosis, and atherosclerosis. Yet the standard American diet contains one of the world's highest proportions of saturated fats and cholesterol, since Americans presently obtain about 70 percent of all their protein from animal foods. And many low-carbohydrate reducing diets, because they depend on a large intake of meat, eggs, dairy products, and fish, result in an even larger intake of saturated fats and cholesterol. (The latter, present in all animal foods, is never found in tofu or other plant foods.) Moreover, the problem is becoming increasingly more serious as the proportion of saturated fats in the diet continues to rise: during the past 20 years, per capita American consumption of beef has more than doubled, while poultry consumption has increased by 150 percent. It is largely for these reasons that the American Heart Association now recommends that Americans cut their per capita meat consumption by one third while further reducing their intake of beef and pork in favor of poultry, which is lower in saturated fats.

Cross-cultural studies seem to indicate a clear relationship between low intake of animal fats and freedom from the heart and circulatory diseases mentioned above. The Japanese, for example, blessed with one of the world's lowest rates of these diseases, obtain only 39 percent of their protein from animal sources—primarily fish which are relatively low in saturated fats—and have about one-eighth the intake of saturated fats of most Americans. In China, where only 10 percent of the protein comes from animal sources, the cholesterol level is less than half that of most Americans. And observers have reported that the healthy, long-lived Hunzas rely on animal foods for only 1½ percent of their protein intake.

There is also a clear correlation between problems of overweight and the intake of animal foods high in saturated fats. Large-scale studies among Americans show that people practicing a meatless way of eating are 20 pounds below the national average weight, and that people following a standard meat-centered diet are 12 to 15 pounds above their ideal weight. Tests taken throughout the world likewise show that in societies with relatively low meat consumption (such as Japan), the people more closely approach their ideal weight.

Using tofu in place of livestock products as a basic protein source is an easy way to greatly reduce total intake of saturated fats and cholesterol. Regular tofu contains only 4.3 percent vegetable-quality fats. These are very low in saturated fats (15%), high in unsaturated fats (80%), and remarkably high in linoleic acid, one of the most important polyunsaturated fatty acids. By comparison, beef fat is high in saturated fats (48%), low in unsaturated fats (47%), and contains only 9 percent linoleic acid. An essential fatty acid, linoleic cannot be synthesized by the body and must therefore be obtained directly from sources such as soy products. Like natural lecithin, which is also found in abundance in tofu's unrefined oils, linoleic acid performs the vital functions of metabolizing, dispersing, and eliminating deposits of cholesterol and other fatty acids which have accumulated in the vital organs and blood stream. Soybeans, the best known source of lecithin and linoleic acid, are used for the extraction of these products now so popular in tablet form at Western health food stores.

Rich in Minerals and Vitamins

Tofu is an excellent source of calcium, an essential mineral for building and maintaining sound teeth and bones, and one which is often deficient in the diets of people who cannot afford dairy products. When solidified with calcium chloride nigari or calcium sulfate—as is most of the tofu presently made in America—regular tofu contains 23 percent, and *kinugoshi* 50 percent, more calcium by weight than dairy milk. A standard 8-ounce serving of tofu, therefore, provides 38 percent of the average daily calcium requirement. As shown in figure 5, tofu is also a good source of other minerals such as iron, phosphororus, potassium, and sodium, of essential B vitamins, and of choline and fat-soluble vitamin E.

A Health-giving Natural Food

Tofu is a traditional, natural food, prepared in essentially the same way today that it was more than one thousand years ago. Unlike so many high-protein foods, it has an alkaline composition which promotes long life and good health. In America, as in Japan, tofu is now a popular item in many natural- and health food stores, and Japanese doctors regularly prescribe it (and soymilk) in curative diets for diabetes, heart disease, hardening of the arteries, and a variety of other circulatory problems. Except for the loss of crude soybean fiber, tofu is a whole food made from simple, natural ingredients. Whereas cow's milk is curdled or solidified with an acid (rennet) to make cheese or curds, soymilk is generally solidified with either *nigari* or calcium sulfate to make tofu. Nigari—also called bittern—is the mineral-rich mother liquor that remains after natural sea salt is extracted from sea water. Calcium sulfate, now generally used in its refined form, was traditionally prepared from ground, lightly roasted gypsum, which is found in abundance in the mountains of East Asia.

Backbone of the Meatless Diet

For the rapidly increasing number of Westerners who find that a meatless or vegetarian diet makes good sense, tofu can serve as a key source of protein just as it has since ancient times for the millions of people throught East Asia practicing similar ways of eating.

Free of Chemical Toxins

Tofu—like other soybean products—is unique among high-protein, high-calcium foods in being relatively free of chemical toxins. It is well known that heavy metals, herbicides, and pesticides tend to concentrate in the fatty tissues of animals at the tops of food chains. Meat, fish, and poultry contain about 20 times more pesticide residues than legumes. Dairy foods, the next most contaminated group, contain 4½ times more. Since soybeans are an important legume feed crop at the base of the beef and dairy food chains, their spraying is carefully monitored by the Food and Drug Administration to keep the level of contamination at an absolute minimum.

Low in Cost

In addition to tofu's many fine qualities as a source of protein and basic nutrients, another endearing feature is its low cost. At the time of this writing, a typical 8-ounce serving of American-made tofu costs only 19½ cents. If the tofu is purchased directly from a tofu shop, the cost may be as low as 14 cents, and if the tofu is prepared at home, only 6½ cents! Storebought tofu costs only 56 percent of the price of an equivalent weight of hamburger, 34 percent of chicken, and 15 percent of lamb rib chop. Furthermore, unlike most meats, a pound of tofu is a pound of tofu: no fat or bones. As the following figures show, the cost of one day's supply of usable protein (43.1 grams for an adult male) derived from or purchased in the form of tofu is relatively low compared with other common protein sources:

Food	Cost
Whole dry soybeans ($0.35/lb)	$0.16
Tofu, homemade (.13/lb)	.24
Whole eggs, medium (.66/doz)	.35
Tofu, Packaged Lactone Kinugoshi (in Japan; 5.5% protein [.15/lb])	.38
Tofu, dried-frozen (in Japan) (1.72/lb)	.47
Tofu, regular (in Japan) (.26/lb)	.49
Tofu, regular, at U.S. tofu shops (.28/lb)	.52
Hamburger, regular grind (.69/lb)	.56
Whole milk, nonfat (.35/qt)	.59
Cottage cheese, from skim milk (.60/lb)	.60
Tuna, canned in oil (1.30/lb)	.65
Tofu, regular, at U.S. supermarkets (.39/lb)	.74
Spaghetti (.51/lb)	.75
Swiss cheese, domestic (1.64/lb)	.83
Peanuts (1.02/lb)	.84
Cheddar cheese (1.70/lb)	.93
Whole-wheat bread (.59/lb)	1.02
Chicken, breast with bone (1.16/lb)	1.04
Pork loin chop, med. (1.29/lb)	1.36
Yogurt (.43/lb)	1.75
Porterhouse steak, choice grade w. bone (1.99/lb)	2.10
Lamb rib chop (2.59/lb)	3.14

(Source: Prices sampled at California and Tokyo supermarkets and tofu shops, Feb. 1975. Figures calculated from data in *Diet for a Small Planet*.)

Note that in Tokyo, where the cost of living is now higher than in the United States, the retail price of tofu is relatively low. As tofu becomes more popular in the West and the number of shops making it increases, we can expect similar price reductions due to greater competition, elimination of middlemen, and the economies of large-scale production and distribution.

Because tofu is inexpensive, it is a truly democratic food that can be enjoyed by people throughout the world, especially those whose nutritional needs are the greatest. In Taiwan, for example, a pound of tofu presently retails for about one-fourth the cost of tofu in America.

Easily Made at Home

Each of the different varieties of tofu can be prepared at home using utensils found in most kitchens and ingredients which are readily available. Homemade tofu will be ready in an hour, and the cost drops to about one-third the retail price. Like fresh bread warm from the oven, fresh tofu prepared at home has a richness and delicacy of flavor that is rarely matched by storebought varieties.

Quick & Easy to Use

Like yogurt, cottage cheese, or cheese, each of the different types of tofu are ready to eat and re-quire no further cooking. We find that most of our favorite ways of serving tofu are the simplest, sometimes taking less than a minute to prepare. For people who are often in a hurry and like their food ready instantly, this ease of use will, no doubt, add to tofu's appeal.

Versatile

Finally, tofu is so versatile that it can serve as an ingredient in almost the entire range of your favorite dishes and be used in the national cuisine of countries around the world. Perhaps no other food has such a wide range of interesting forms, textures, and flavors; each variety invites experimentation, ingenuity, and inventiveness. We have found again and again that tofu can transform even the simplest dishes into something completely new. Among the most adaptive of foods, it may be used in both virtuoso and supporting roles. Like the taste of water from a mountain stream or a breath of crisp autumn air, simple flavors are often the most satisfying. And because its simplicity is inexhaustible, tofu, in its many forms, can be enjoyed day after day, adding body and richness of flavor—as well as protein—to your daily meals.

3
Getting Started

THERE ARE presently more than 180 tofu shops in the United States (see Appendix B). Since these are often small Japanese or Chinese family-run operations, tofu products and their names vary slightly from shop to shop. Each shop prepares a number of varieties of fresh tofu each day and retails them through a rapidly growing number of food stores in its area. Larger shops often distribute their tofu up to 200 miles away. In many cases, tofu is available at reductions of 25 percent if purchased directly from the tofu shop or if ordered unpackaged in bulk.

Look for fresh tofu in the refrigerated foods section of most markets. If your local market does not carry tofu, you may wish to give its management the name of the nearest tofu shop from which tofu can be ordered. In cities near tofu shops, good tofu cuisine is often served at Japanese, Chinese, and natural food restaurants.

Buying and Storing Tofu

What are the most important things to look for when buying tofu? First, try to buy tofu as soon as possible after it has been made; fresh tofu has by far the best flavor. In Japan, almost all tofu is served within one day after it is prepared. In the West, most fresh, packaged tofu now comes with a date stamped on the container indicating the date before which the tofu should be served. For regular tofu this date is 7 days, and for deep-fried tofu 10 days, after the tofu was made. Since many American tofu shops start work at 2 o'clock in the morning, their fresh

tofu is often available in local food stores early the same day.

Next, look for the name of the tofu solidifier, which will be printed in small letters on the package. Traditional-style tofu will be made with a nigari-type solidifier (natural nigari, calcium chloride nigari, or magnesium chloride nigari). Similarly, try to find tofu advertized as being cooked in an iron cauldron over a (wood) fire, rather than with steam. If the tofu is prepared with organically grown (Japanese-variety) soybeans and/or well water, so much the better. Almost all tofu made in America is free of preservatives and other chemical additives, but check the label to make sure.

When storing tofu (including doufu, kinugoshi, and grilled tofu), keep in mind the following points:

* Keep tofu under constant refrigeration but do not allow it to freeze. See that it is not allowed to stand in a warm place before being refrigerated.

* If tofu was purchased water-packed and is not to be used right away, slit the top of the container along one edge and drain off the water. If you plan to serve the tofu within 24 hours, seal and refrigerate (without adding more water). If you are unable to serve the tofu until a later date, re-cover with cold water and refrigerate. Drain the tofu and add fresh water *daily*. It can be kept up to ten days in this way without spoiling, although naturally there will be some loss of flavor and texture. Since tofu keeps better when covered with plenty of water, you may wish to transfer the tofu from its small container to a pan or bowl containing several quarts of cold water; cover or seal the container before refrigerating.

* Always drain water-packed tofu briefly before use. For slightly firmer tofu, drain for several hours or overnight. Effective draining procedures are described on page 96.

* Tofu that is several days old can be refreshed by parboiling (p. 96).

* Regular or deep-fried tofu can be stored indefinitely as homemade frozen tofu (p. 230).

When storing deep-fried tofu, simply refrigerate in an airtight container. Do not store under water.

Basic Ingredients

We recommend the use of whole, natural foods. Since cans and bottles tend to contribute to environmental clutter, the recipes in this book call for ingredients which can be purchased free of non-biodegradable packaging. The rarer ingredients used in Japanese-style recipes are defined in the glossary at the the end of this book. Many basic Oriental foods are now widely available at natural food stores and supermarkets, as well as at Japanese and Chinese markets. Or contact the Japan Food Corporation with offices in San Francisco, Los Angeles, New York, Chicago, Houston, Columbia (Md.), and Sacramento (Calif.). The following ingredients, listed alphabetically, are those we consider basic to tofu cookery:

Flour: Since all-purpose white flour contains only about 75 percent of the protein, 36 percent of the minerals, and 25 percent of the vitamins found in natural whole-wheat flour, we generally prefer to use the latter for baked goods, sauces, and the like. However, in tempura batters and pie crusts where lightness is essential, we recommend the use of unbleached white flour or a mixture of equal parts whole-wheat and white flours.

Miso: Also known as fermented soybean paste, miso is one of the basic staples and seasonings in every Japanese and Chinese kitchen. Its range of flavors and colors, textures and aromas is at least as rich and varied as that of the world's fine cheeses or wines. Miso has a consistency slightly softer than peanut butter and comes in both smooth and chunky textures. It contains an average of 14 percent high-quality soy protein and is very low in calories. Traditionally sold out of handsome cedar kegs, it is now also widely available in the West in polyethylene bags (fig. 8). Miso can be substituted for salt or shoyu (soy sauce) in almost all recipes in this book; for ¼ teaspoon salt or 1 teaspoon shoyu, use 1½ teaspoons salty miso or 1 tablespoon sweet miso. Although most miso may be stored indefinitely at room temperature, sweet varieties should be refriger-

Fig. 8. Miso

ated. (For additional information, see *The Book of Miso,* by the authors of the present work, listed in the bibliography.) The basic types of miso are:

Rice miso: Made from rice, soybeans, and salt. Basic varieties include red, light-yellow, semi-sweet beige, sweet red, and sweet white miso.

Barley miso: Made from barley, soybeans, and salt. Basic varieties are (regular) barley miso and sweet barley miso.

Soybean miso: Made from soybeans and salt. Basic varieties include Hatcho miso and one-year soybean miso.

Special Japanese miso: Finger Lickin' Miso has a relatively sweet flavor and chunky texture and is fermented together with chopped vegetables. The most popular varieties are *Kinzanji* miso, *moromi* miso, *hishio,* and *namémiso.* Sweet Simmered Miso (p. 41) and *akadashi* miso (p. 45) are other varieties used as tofu toppings.

Chinese chiang: The Chinese equivalent of miso, its main varieties are sweet wheat-flour chiang (*tien-m'ien chiang*), chunky chiang (*tou-pan chiang*), and red-pepper chiang (*la-chiao chiang*).

Oil: For best flavor, use cold-pressed, natural vegetable oils. For sautéing and salad dressings, we prefer soy, corn, or "salad" oil—often mixed with small amounts of sesame oil; for deep-frying, rapeseed or soy oil. Olive oil works well in Western-style dressings. Sesame oil, especially popular in Chinese dishes, is now widely available in the West. No recipes require the use of hydrogenated oils or animal fats.

Rice: Polished or white rice contains an average of only 84 percent of the protein, 53 percent of the minerals, and 38 percent of the vitamins found in natural brown rice. We prefer the flavor, texture, and nutritional superiority of the natural food.

Salt: Natural, unrefined sea salt contains an abundance of essential minerals which are lost during the refining process. Its flavor is richer and more concentrated than that of pure-white, refined table salt.

Shoyu: The skillful use of authentic shoyu (and miso) is the key to most tofu cookery. An all-purpose seasoning as important to Oriental cuisine as salt is to Western cookery, shoyu is called for in a majority of the recipes in this book. Containing 6.9 percent protein and 18 percent salt, natural shoyu has been a mainstay of Japanese cooking for more than 500 years. We use the Japanese name to distinguish this fine product from the modern, synthetic soy sauces now widely used in the West. In most recipes in this book, 1 teaspoon of shoyu may be substituted for ¼ teaspoon of salt. Sold traditionally in re-usable cedar kegs and returnable bottles, shoyu is now also widely sold in cans (fig. 9). The four basic types of shoyu and soy sauce available in the United States are:

Natural Shoyu: This traditional product is always brewed using a natural (rather than temperature-controlled) fermentation process, generally for 12 to 18 months. The finest varieties are prepared from whole soybeans, natural salt, and well water fermented together in huge cedar vats. All types also contain *koji* spores and roasted cracked wheat. All natural shoyu presently available in the West—some of which is sold as *Tamari* shoyu—is imported from Japan. Actually, Japanese *tamari*, the progenitor of shoyu, is a different product prepared without the use of wheat; it has a distinctive, slightly stronger flavor and aroma.

Shoyu: At present, this is the standard shoyu sold in Japan. A high quality product now produced on a large scale in the U.S., its flavor, aroma, and color are quite similar to those of the finest natural shoyu, and its price is considerably lower. Using techniques based on the traditional method but first developed during the 1950s, it is generally prepared from defatted soybean meal and brewed in large tanks for about 4 to 6 months under conditions of strictly controlled temperature and humidity.

Chinese Soy Sauce: This traditional Chinese product, which has a stronger and saltier flavor than shoyu, is also made by natural or temperature-controlled fermentation. Although some varieties are excellent, they are not widely available in the West. Our Chinese recipes call for this product. If unavailable, substitute shoyu.

Synthetic or Chemical Soy Sauce: This domestic product, sold under various Chinese brand names, is what most Westerners mean when they speak of soy sauce. It is not brewed or fermented but is prepared from hydrolyzed vegetable protein (HVP) by the reaction of defatted soybeans with hydrochloric acid. Its flavor and coloring come from additives such as corn syrup and caramel. Since it takes only a few days to prepare, the production costs are quite low. Some varieties may contain sodium benzoate or alcohol preservatives.

Sugar: Most recipes in this book call for natural or brown sugar, generally used together and balanced with shoyu or miso in the minimum amounts we consider necessary to create the desired flavor. In most recipes, 1¼ teaspoons of honey can be used to impart the same sweetening as 1 teaspoon of natural sugar. (We feel it is important that decreases of meat in the diet be accompanied by proportional decreases of sugar usage.)

Fig. 9. Shoyu

Vinegar: Use either Western-style cider or white wine vinegar, or the milder, subtly-sweet Japanese rice vinegar (*su*). The latter is especially tasty in salad dressings, sweet-sour sauces, and sushi rice. For 1 teaspoon rice vinegar, substitute ¾ teaspoon cider or mild white vinegar.

NOTE: Monosodium glutamate—also known as MSG or *ajinomoto*—is a crystalline, pure-white powder widely used as a chemical flavor-enhancing agent in contemporary Japanese and Chinese cooking. Because of the growing awareness that excessive use of this product may cause burning sensations, headaches, a feeling of pressure in the chest, and other discomforting symptoms, and because it is a highly refined substance prepared by the hydrolosis of petroleum, cane molasses, or starch with hydrochloric acid, it does not appear in any recipes in this book.

Japanese Kitchen Tools

The Japanese chef (like most Japanese craftsmen) uses only a small number of relatively simple tools in his work. While the recipes in this book can be prepared using only the utensils found in most Western kitchens, the following tools may make cooking with tofu somewhat easier and more enjoyable. Most of these tools are inexpensive and are available at many Japanese and Chinese hardware stores, as well as at some large Japanese markets.

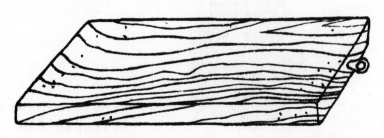

Cutting board: A board about 19 by 9 by 1 to 2 inches thick, the *manaita* is designed to be set across the kitchen sink and hung on the wall when not in use. Excellent for pressing tofu.

Japanese vegetable knife: One of the finest knives ever designed for cutting vegetables, the *hocho* makes the art of cutting and slicing a true joy. Most varieties are quite inexpensive. The finest of these knives are handmade and bear the stamp of the craftsman on the blade near the knife's wooden handle.

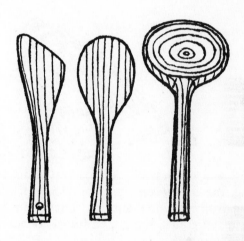

Wooden spatulas, rice paddles, and spoons: These utensils make the work of sautéing, stirring, and serving easier and more enjoyable.

Bamboo colander: Usually round and slightly concave, a typical *zaru*, made of thin strips of woven bamboo, is about 12 inches in diameter. It is used for draining and straining foods, for separating curds from whey when preparing homemade tofu, and as a serving tray for such foods as tempura and parboiled green soybeans.

Suribachi: An earthenware grinding bowl or mortar with a serrated interior surface, the usual *suribachi* is 10 inches in diameter and 3½ inches deep, and is accompanied by a wooden pestle (*suri-kogi*).

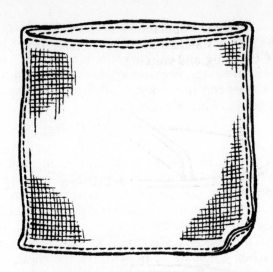

Pressing sack: A simple cloth sack about 15 inches wide and 15 inches deep made of coarsely woven cloth is very helpful in squeezing, crumbling, or reshaping tofu, as well as in preparing all varieties of homemade tofu and soymilk.

Japanese grater: A metal tray about 9 inches long, the *oroshi-gane* has many sharp teeth protruding from its upper surface. Since there are no holes in the grater, the grated foods collect in the trough at one end.

Serrated tofu-slicing knife: A small, all-metal knife with a vertically serrated blade, this is used in fine tofu restaurants and shops to create a fluted surface when cutting kinugoshi tofu.

Sudare: A bamboo mat about 10 inches square used for rolling sushi and other foods. A small bamboo table mat makes a good substitute. One special variety, called the devil's sudare (*oni-sudare*), is made of triangular bamboo slats designed to leave a distinct corrugated impression in the rolled foods.

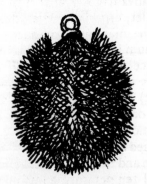

Tawashi scrub brush: Made of natural palm fiber, the *tawashi* is the perfect utensil for scrubbing root vegetables or washing pots. It is inexpensive and outlasts most synthetic brushes.

Wok set: Popular now in the West, the wok is the Orient's standard utensil for deep-frying, stir-frying, steaming, and sautéing.

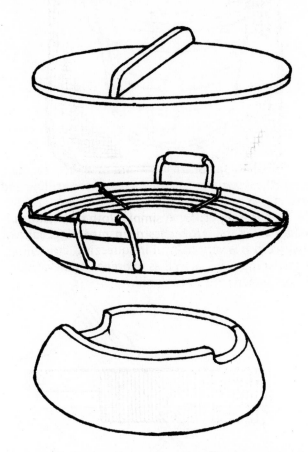

1. *The wok:* The wok itself is a metal pan about 13 inches in diameter and 3½ inches deep. Always used over a gas or charcoal burner, it is not suitable for use with electric ranges. Surprisingly low in cost and now widely available in the West, its design has numerous advantages over that of a regular flat-bottomed skillet, especially when deep-frying: a) It provides the maximum oil surface and depth with the minimum necessary oil volume (3 to 5 cups); b) Each piece of food can be slid gently down the wok's sides rather than dropped with a splash into the oil; c) Freshly-fried foods can be drained into the pan on an inobtrusive rack which saves oil and allows more thorough draining when the foods are later placed on absorbent paper; d) The wok's rounded bottom and thin metal sides allow for quick heating and oil temperature adjustment; e) During stir-frying and sautéing, the wok's large surface area allows each piece of food to have maximum contact with the bottom of the pan, yielding crisp-textured foods in minimum cooking time; f) Cooked foods can be scooped out easily and thoroughly and, when all is done, the wok is easier to clean or wipe free of oil than angular, flat-bottomed pots. After sautéing or stir-frying, wash the hot wok immediately with water and a scrub brush. Do not use soap.

Wooden lid: Used when simmering foods, the lid fits inside the wok's rim.

Draining rack: A semi-circular rack, the *hangetsu* is attached to the wok during deep-frying so that excess oil from the draining foods drips back into the wok.

Wok support: Used in most Chinese kitchens to give the wok stability and focus the strong fire at its base.

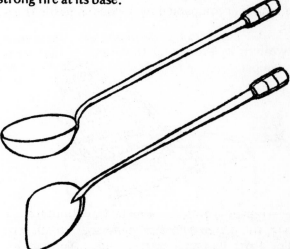

Stir-frying ladle and spatula: In Chinese kitchens, these large, sturdy tools are used during stir-frying. The ladle is employed to measure (by eye) and add all liquids and seasonings to foods cooking in the wok.

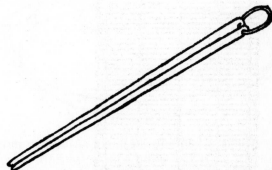

Long cooking-chopsticks: Shaped like regular Japanese wooden chopsticks but about 10 to 14 inches long and often joined with a string at one end, these *saibashi* are used mostly during deep-frying for turning foods in the hot oil or transferring cooked foods to the draining rack. Substitute a pair of long cooking tongs.

Mesh skimmer: Used for skimming debris from the surface of the hot oil during deep-frying and for removing very small deep-fried foods.

Deep-frying thermometer: Use a regular Western-style deep-fat thermometer that measures temperatures up to 380°.

Charcoal brazier: Made of baked earthenware, the *konro* or *shichirin* is used for grilling and broiling, as well as for heating *nabe* dishes (p. 143) or the family teapot. When preparing *nabe*, you may substitute a tabletop gas burner, heating coil, or chafing-dish warmer.

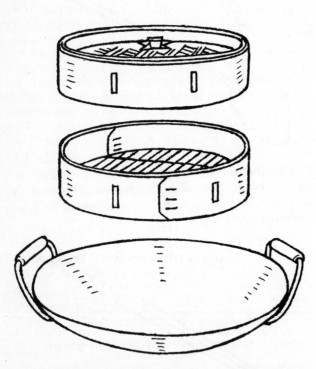

Chinese bamboo steamer: Although most varieties of *seiro* are round and are set into a *wok* during steaming, some types are rectangular. They are made of slatted or woven bamboo with ¼-inch gaps between the bottom slats. This design allows steam to rise through the steamer's lid and prevents it from collecting and dripping on the steaming foods. Two to four steaming compartments may be stacked in layers during steaming.

Broiling screen: This double-layer, 8-inch-square screen rests atop a stove burner and is used for broiling. Both layers are made of thin metal sheets, the bottom one perforated with 1/8-inch, and the top with 3/8-inch holes. The top layer slides out for easy cleaning. Broils foods faster and with less fuel than a Western oven broiler.

Basic Preparatory Techniques

The following preparatory techniques will be referred to in many of the recipes in this book. We list them all here for easy reference.

Salt-rubbing

This process softens and seasons vegetables (and *konnyaku*) without cooking.

Place thinly sliced vegetables into a bowl and sprinkle with salt. Rub the salt into the vegetables with your fingertips until the vegetables are fairly soft, then let stand for 15 to 20 minutes. Fill the bowl with water and rinse away the salt. Empty vegetables into a strainer or colander and drain briefly. Wrap vegetables in a clean cloth and squeeze gently to expel excess moisture.

Rinsing and Pressing Leeks or Onions

This is a quick and easy method for neutralizing the harsh and evoking the mild, sweet flavors of these vegetables.

Slice leeks or onions into thin rounds or slivers. Combine with several cups water in a small bowl and soak for 2 or 3 minutes. Pour into a cloth-lined strainer, gather the cloth's corners to form a sack, and press vegetables gently between your palms. Use immediately or refrigerate in a covered container.

Soaking Burdock Root

Burdock root has a slightly harsh, alkaline flavor that is easily removed by proper cutting and soaking. If unsoaked, burdock will lose its white color and turn a dark reddish brown soon after it is cut and exposed to the air.

Holding the root under running cold water, scrape off its dark peel with a knife or scrub it off with a scrub brush (*tawashi*). Cut the root into 2-inch lengths and submerge the lengths in cold water. Cut one section at a time into matchsticks and return these immediately to the water. Soak for about 10 minutes, then change the water and soak for 20 to 40 minutes more. Soaking time can be decreased by using warm or hot water, but some of the burdock's flavor will be lost. Drain quickly before sautéing.

Reconstituting Dried Sea Vegetables, Wheat Gluten, and Kampyo

Dried Hijiki: Immerse in several cups (warm) water and allow to soak for 20 to 30 minutes. Stir gently, then lift *hijiki* carefully out of water so that any grit stays at bottom of bowl. Place *hijiki* in a colander or strainer and press lightly to rid it of excess moisture. Note: ¼ cup (27 gm) dry *hijiki* yields 1 cup (200 gm) reconstituted.

Dried Wakame: Rinse *wakame* once, then soak for 15 to 30 minutes. Strain, reserving the nutritious liquid for use in stocks. Remove the midrib of each leaf only if it is unusually large. Squeeze *wakame* firmly, place in a compact mound on a cutting board, and cut at ½-inch intervals. (Place fresh *wakame* in several quarts of water, rinsing and squeezing 2 or 3 times to rid it of excess surface salt.) Note: 25 gm dried *wakame* yields 1 cup (125 gm) reconstituted.

Agar *(Kanten)*: Tear agar stick crosswise into halves and soak in 1 quart water for several minutes. Lift out agar and squeeze firmly. Change water and resoak briefly. Squeeze again, then tear into small (1-inch) pieces.

Dried Wheat Gluten: Soak for several minutes in water. Press lightly with fingertips to expel excess moisture before use.

Kampyo: Soak for 15 minutes in water to cover seasoned with a pinch of salt. Drain briefly, then rub lightly with salt.

Parboiling

To parboil vegetables, drop them into more than enough boiling water to cover, and cook until just tender. When parboiling green vegetables, add about ¼ teaspoon salt for each 2 cups water to help the vegetables retain their color. Vegetables that are easily overcooked may be plunged into cold water as soon as they are done. Length of cooking depends both on how finely the ingredients have been cut and on whether they will be cooked again. Shredded or slivered vegetables, or leaves that will be simmered again in a seasoned liquid, may be parboiled for 30 to 60 seconds; boil for 30 to 60 seconds more if they will not be recooked. Small rectangles of *konnyaku* and root vegetables should be parboiled for 1 to 2 minutes. Larger pieces may be boiled for as much as 3 to 4 minutes.

Cutting Tofu and Vegetables

Most of the cutting techniques used in the recipes presented in this book are familiar to any Western cook. A few, however, deserve special mention. The Japanese pay great attention to the way in which each ingredient is cut, because careful cutting not only lends beauty to the preparation when it is served but also assures that each uniform piece will be cooked to precisely the desired degree of tenderness.

Cutting tofu into small rectangles: Cut the cake of tofu lengthwise into halves, then cut crosswise into slices about ½ inch thick.

Cutting vegetables into small rectangles: Cut thick vegetables (carrots, *daikon*, etc.) into 1½-inch lengths, then cut each section vertically into thirds. Now place each piece on its largest surface and cut lengthwise into small rectangles about 1/8 inch thick.

Cutting into matchsticks: This technique is used with long, thin root vegetables. Cut crosswise into 2-inch lengths; then stand each piece on end and cut vertically into 1/8-inch-thick pieces. Stack these on top of one another and cut lengthwise into 1/8-inch-wide strips the size of wooden matchsticks. Slivering or cutting *julienne* are variations on this basic technique.

Cutting into half moons: Use with long, thick roots or tubers. Cut lengthwise into halves, then cut each half crosswise into pieces about ¼ to ½ inch thick.

Cutting into ginkgo leaves: Cut lengthwise into quarters, then cut crosswise into thin pieces.

Using Sesame Seeds

When roasted and ground, sesame seeds have a wonderful nutty flavor and aroma, and almost every Japanese kitchen is equipped with a *suribachi* and *surikogi* (a serrated earthenware bowl and wooden pestle, p. 34). used for grinding them. Small quantities of seeds can also be ground in a pepper grinder, a spice or coffee mill, or a special grinder that fits over the mouth of a jar of sesame seeds and is sold at Japanese hardware stores. If you are using ½ cup or more of seeds, you can grind them in a hand mill or meat grinder, or, in some cases, purée them in a blender with a dash of oil or shoyu. You may wish to make enough to last for several days or to use in Sesame Salt (p. 51). Grind the seeds with a firm but light touch until they are well crushed but not oily.

Two parts of ground roasted seeds impart about the same flavoring as 1 part pre-packaged sesame butter or *tahini*.

(Proper care of the *suribachi* is very important. Before use, scrub the *suribachi* with hot water and douse with boiling water. Dry with a dishcloth, then turn the bowl upside down and dry thoroughly with one edge raised to allow air to circulate. After use, fill the *suribachi* with hot water and soak for 1 hour; then scrub and dry as above.)

Heat a heavy skillet until a drop of water flicked across its surface evaporates instantly. Add seeds and reduce heat to low. Shaking the pan and stirring seeds constantly, roast for about 3 minutes or until seeds are fragrant and light brown and just begin to pop. (A seed pressed between the thumb and little finger should crush easily.) Transfer about ½ cup seeds at a time to the *suribachi* and grind with the pestle until no more than 10 to 15 percent of the seeds remain whole. For best flavor and aroma, use seeds immediately. To store, allow leftover seeds to cool, then seal in an airtight container in a cool, dry place. Prepare just enough for a week.

Toasting Nori

Wave a sheet of *nori* over medium heat for about 30 seconds or until crisp and slightly green.

Preparing a Steamer

Chinese Bamboo Steamer: Set the steamer over a wok filled with water to a depth of about 1½-inches. Bring water to a boil over high heat, then reduce heat to medium. Place the food in the steamer, cover with the bamboo lid, and steam for the required length of time. The woven bamboo lid prevents dripping by allowing steam to pass out. With this tool, several layers of food can be steamed at one time.

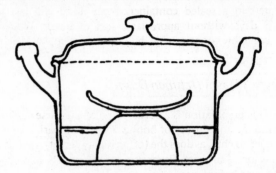

Covered Pot Steamer: Fill a 10- to 12-inch-diameter pot with water to a depth of about 1 inch. Bring to a boil over high heat, then reduce heat to low. Into the pot place a collapsible French steamer, a colander, or a plate set on top of an inverted bowl (above). Now put in the food to be steamed. (In many cases, tofu will be wrapped in a *sudare* bamboo mat before insertion.) Place a single layer of absorbent toweling or paper over the mouth of the pot to prevent moisture from dripping onto the food, then cover the pot. Steam as directed.

Chawan-mushi Steamer: Prepare as for a covered pot steamer, but place the cups directly in the water (above). If the cups do not have individual lids, cover with a sheet of absorbent paper topped with a plate to hold the paper in place. (Omit the toweling over the mouth of the pot.) Cover pot and steam for the required length of time. Good for custards and the like.

Basic Recipes

The following stocks, sauces, toppings, dressings, rice and noodle dishes, and other basic preparations are often served with tofu. They play important supporting roles in tofu cookery, so we have grouped them all together here. They will be called for frequently in later recipes.

SOUP STOCKS AND BROTHS

The different varieties of fresh *dashi* (Japanese soup stock) serve as the basis for a wide variety of tofu preparations and are easily made from natural ingredients. An instant dried dashi (dashi-no-moto) is now available in the West. Refrigerated in a sealed container, fresh dashi will last for 2 to 3 days without appreciable loss of flavor. Western-style vegetable or vegetable bullion stocks make satisfactory substitutes.

Number 1 Dashi *(Ichiban Dashi)*   MAKES 3 CUPS

This preparation is a cornerstone of Japanese cooking. The amount and variety of bonita flakes used varies slightly from chef to chef, as does the (often highly secret) method of preparation. For best flavor use flakes which have been shaved just before use.

3 cups water, Kombu Dashi, or Niboshi Dashi
¼ to 1 cup bonita flakes (15 to 30 grams)

Heat the water until quite hot in a small saucepan. Add bonita flakes and bring to a boil. Turn off heat and allow to stand for 3 minutes, or until flakes settle; skim off foam. Filter the dashi through a (clothlined) strainer placed over a saucepan. Press flakes with the back of a spoon to extract remaining dashi, then reserve flakes. (Some cooks add fine-textured flakes to simmered broths, *nabe* dishes, and miso soups together with the dashi, or simply omit straining.)

For a richer flavor, use a relatively large amount of flakes, simmer flakes for 2 or 3 minutes, and allow the dashi to stand (covered) for 15 to 30 minutes before straining.

Number 2 Dashi *(Niban Dashi)*   MAKES 2½ CUPS

The basic dashi ingredients are generally reused at least once to make a milder-flavored "Number 2" dashi. Thereafter the kombu may be slivered and simmered in shoyu and *mirin* to make *tsukudani* (a garnish for rice), pressure cooked with brown rice (p. 50), or cut into strips, each of which are tied into a simple loop and simmered in Oden (p. 175) or Nishime (p. 178); whole pieces are sometimes used to prepare vinegar- or *nukamiso* pickles (p. 326).

Whereas Number 1 Dashi is featured primarily in Clear Soups, this stock is generally used when simmering vegetables, with miso soups, or in noodle broths.

2½ cups water
Bonita flakes and *kombu* reserved from Number 1 Dashi

Combine all ingredients in a small saucepan and bring just to a boil. Remove *kombu* immediately, then simmer for 1 more minute. Strain and allow to cool.

Two tablespoons of fresh bonita flakes may be added to the boiling water after removing the *kombu;* reduce heat to lowest point and simmer for 5 minutes before straining. Leftovers may be reboiled in 1¼ cups water to make Number 3 Dashi.

Kombu Dashi *(Kombu Stock)*   MAKES 3 CUPS

Used in many homes as the basis for Number 1 Dashi (see above), this stock is featured in its own right in Zen Temple Cookery. *Kombu's* flavoring components (such as glutamic acid) reside mostly on its surface; be careful not to remove them by washing. Since they and the *kombu's* nutrients pass quickly into the stock, lengthy cooking is unnecessary, and actually leads to a decline in flavor.

1 strip of *kombu*, about 3 by 7 inches, wiped lightly with a damp cloth
3 cups water

Combine *kombu* and water in a saucepan and bring just to a boil. Turn off heat, remove *kombu*, and reserve for use in other cooking. Use dashi as required or, if preparing Number 1 (or *Niboshi*) Dashi proceed to add bonita flakes (or *niboshi*) immediately.

For a more pronounced flavor but somewhat more viscous consistency, score *kombu* surface across grain at ½-inch intervals; simmer for 3 to 5 minutes before removing; double the amount of *kombu* if desired.

VARIATIONS
*Cold Water Method: Combine water and *kombu* and allow to stand for at least to six hours, preferably overnight. Romove *kombu* and use dashi as required. (Some cooks bring the stock just to a boil before removing the *kombu*.) The lengthy soaking is often said to make best use of the *kombu's* nutrients and give the finest flavor.
*Shiitake & Kombu Dashi: Select 2 or 3 *shiitake* mushrooms, preferably ones having thick, partially opened caps and whitish (rather than darkish or yellowish) gills. (Or use ¼ cup dried stems or broken pieces.) Rinse briefly under running water, then soak either in cold water with the *kombu* or for 30 minutes in hot, freshly prepared Kombu Dashi. Strain dashi before use; do not squeeze *shiitake* to extract absorbed dashi lest stock turn a dark brown.

Soybean Stock   MAKES 1 QUART

Prepare Pressure Cooked or Boiled Soybeans (p. 59) doubling the amount of water used. (At the end of cooking, about 1 quart cooking liquid should remain for each cup soybeans.) Strain stock before serving beans.

Shiitake Dashi *(Mushroom Stock)*

The preparation of Shiitake Dashi as an integral part of the process for making miso soup is described on page 219. In Chinese Buddhist vegetarian restaurants and temples, a soybean & *shiitake* stock is prepared by adding 1 to 2 cups washed and drained *shiitake* stems or pieces to the ingredients for Soybean Stock (see above). The *shiitake* are usually removed before serving the beans.

Niboshi Dashi (Sardine Dashi)

MAKES 3 CUPS

3 cups water or Kombu Dashi (p. 39).
¼ to ½ cup tiny (2-inch-long) dried sardines

Combine ingredients and bring to a boil over medium heat. Reduce heat to low and simmer for 3 to 5 minutes, skimming off any foam that rises to the surface. Strain through a (cloth-lined) sieve, reserving fish for use in other cookery. Use dashi as required or, if preparing Number 1 Dashi, proceed to add bonita flakes immediately.

Clear Broth (Sumashi)

MAKES 1½ CUPS

1½ cups Number 1 Dashi (p. 39) or Kombu Dashi (p. 39)
1 teaspoon shoyu
½ teaspoon salt
½ teaspoon sake or *mirin* (optional)

Bring the dashi just to a boil over moderate heat. Reduce heat to low and stir in the shoyu, salt, and, if used, the sake or *mirin*. Proceed immediately to add the ingredients called for in the particular recipe in which the broth is used.

Noodle Broth
(Mentsuyu or Sobatsuyu)

MAKES 2½ CUPS

2 cups dashi (p. 39), stock, or water
4 tablespoons shoyu
1 tablespoon natural sugar
2 tablespoons sake or *mirin* (optional)
¼ teaspoon salt

Combine all ingredients in a saucepan and bring to a boil. Serve hot or cold over cooked noodles.

Sweetened Shoyu Broth

MAKES ½ TO ¾ CUP

In Japan, this preparation is widely used to season thinly sliced vegetables before using them in other recipes. If a large quantity of vegetables is being prepared, double or triple the recipe.

¼ to ½ cup dashi (p. 39), stock, or water
2 tablespoons shoyu
2 tablespoons natural sugar
1 tablespoon sake or *mirin* (optional)

Bring all ingredients to a boil in a small saucepan. Add thinly sliced vegetables and return to the boil. Reduce heat to low, cover, and simmer, stirring until all liquid is absorbed or evaporated. If crispier vegetable pieces are desired, simmer for only 2 to 3 minutes. Drain off broth, reserving it for later use.

BASIC SHOYU DIPPING SAUCES
(TSUKE-JIRU)

The following preparations are widely used with Chilled Tofu (p. 105), Crisp Deep-fried Tofu (p. 156), and Simmering Tofu (p. 142). Mirin-Shoyu is also used with Agédashi-dofu (p. 133), while *Nihaizu* and *Sambaizu* are favorite dressings for the many Vinegared Salads (*Sunomono*) which feature tofu.

Shoyu Dipping Sauces

SERVES 1

Pour 1½ teaspoons shoyu into a small (3-inch-diameter) dish. Stir in any of the following:

½ teaspoon grated gingerroot or juice pressed from grated gingerroot
¼ teaspoon grated *wasabi* or *wasabi* paste
¼ teaspoon crushed or minced garlic
½ teaspoon slivered *yuzu*, lemon, or orange peel
¼ teaspoon hot mustard
½ teaspoon sesame butter, *tahini*, or ground roasted sesame seeds (p. 38)
½ teaspoon nut butter (peanut, almond, cashew, etc.)
½ to 1 teaspoon orange, lemon, lime, or *yuzu* juice
1 to 3 tablespoons grated *daikon*

Vinegar-Shoyu
(Nihaizu or Sujoyu)

MAKES 2½ TABLESPOONS

2 teaspoons shoyu
2 tablespoons (rice) vinegar

Combine ingredients, mixing well.

Lemon-Shoyu (Ponzu-Joyu)

MAKES ¼ CUP

2 tablespoons shoyu
2 tablespoons lemon, lime, or *yuzu* juice

Combine ingredients, mixing well. Vary their proportions to taste. Tangy.

Mirin-Shoyu (Wari-shita)

MAKES 2/3 CUP

5 tablespoons dashi (p. 39) or soup stock
3 tablespoons shoyu
2 tablespoons *mirin*
2 teaspoons grated gingerroot

Combine ingredients in a small saucepan and bring just to a boil. Serve hot or cold, garnished with grated gingerroot.

Grated Daikon & Shoyu Dipping Sauce   SERVES 1

½ cup grated *daikon* (from top of fat daikon for best sweetness)
2 teaspoons shoyu
3 green beefsteak leaves, slivered; or ½ teaspoon grated gingerroot or carrot (optional)

Combine all ingredients in a small bowl; mix well. Serve with deep-fried tofu or tempura.

Sweetened Vinegar-Shoyu   MAKES ¼ CUP
(Sambaizu)

2½ tablespoons vinegar
2 teaspoons shoyu
4 teaspoons sugar
½ teaspoon sake or white wine (optional)
Dash of salt

Combine ingredients in a small saucepan and bring just to a boil. Remove from heat and allow to cool to room temperature. To use as a dressing, add 6 tablespoons dashi, stock, or water.

Tangy Shoyu Dipping Sauce   MAKES 1 CUP
(Chirizu)

¼ cup shoyu
¼ cup lemon, *yuzu*, or lime juice
2 tablespoons *mirin* or sake
1/3 cup grated *daikon*
½ leek or 2 scallions, sliced into thin rounds (1/3 cup)
Dash of 7-spice red pepper

Combine all ingredients, mixing well. Serve cold.

Chinese-style Soy Dipping Sauce   MAKES ¼ CUP

3 tablespoons soy sauce
½ teaspoon hot mustard
1 teaspoon sesame oil
2 teaspoons vinegar

Combine ingredients; mix well.

Korean-style Soy Dipping Sauce   SERVES 1

1 tablespoon soy sauce
¼ teaspoon sesame oil
Pinch of minced red peppers, or dash of tabasco or 7-spice red pepper
¼ teaspoon crushed or minced garlic

Combine ingredients on a small dish; mix lightly.

Tosa-joyu   MAKES 1 CUP
(Shoyu Dipping Sauce for Simmering Tofu)

¾ cup shoyu
3 tablespoons *mirin*

Combine ingredients in a small saucepan and bring just to a boil.

For variety, add ¼ to ½ cup bonita flakes to the ingredients and proceed as above. Strain before serving. Increase the proportion of *mirin* (up to 5 tablespoons), or substitute sake or pale dry sherry.

MISO TOPPINGS

Five basic types of miso toppings are widely used in tofu cookery: Sweet Simmered Miso, Miso Sauté, Special Miso Toppings, Finger Lickin' Miso, and regular miso. All varieties make excellent toppings for Crisp Deep-fried Tofu, Chilled Tofu, and many grain and vegetable dishes.

Sweet Simmered Miso
(Nerimiso)

Nerimiso derives its name from the verb *neru* which means "to simmer, stirring constantly, until smooth and thick." These tasty toppings are prepared by combining miso with sugar, water or dashi, seasonings and, in some cases, nuts, vegetables, or seafoods. Some varieties of Sweet Simmered Miso—such as peanut, walnut, *tekka* and *yuzu* miso— are sold commercially in Japan. Most varieties are made at home and in traditional or Zen-temple restaurants, where this type of preparation is said to have originated. Nerimiso is generally prepared as a preserved food meant to be served over a period of several weeks. One or 2 cups are usually prepared at a time and are kept in a small attractive container, often an earthenware crock. Nerimiso is served as a convenient topping or seasoning for cooked grains and fresh or cooked vegetables and salads, as well as for tofu. The sweeter varieties also make delicious spreads for toast or sandwiches, waffles, crêpes and pancakes, potatoes, sweet potatoes, and steamed vegetables (such as cauliflower or broccoli). Unused portions will keep their peak of flavor for 2 to 4 weeks if refrigerated in a sealed container.

Vary the amount of sugar to taste. If *mirin* is unavailable, use a mixture of honey and sake (or white wine) as described on page 322.

Red Nerimiso

MAKES ½ CUP

This is the simplest and most basic form of Sweet Simmered Miso; all other recipes may be thought of as variations or elaborations on this fundamental theme. By adding different ingredients and seasonings (sesame, gingerroot, grated lemon rind, etc.) to those listed below, you can create a wide array of delicious toppings.

5 tablespoons red or barley miso
2 to 4 tablespoons natural sugar
1 tablespoon water
1½ teaspoons sake, white wine, or *mirin* (optional)

Combine all ingredients in a small saucepan or skillet. Simmer for 2 to 3 minutes over low heat, stirring constantly with a wooden spoon or spatula, until mixture has a slightly firmer consistency than that of regular miso. Remove from heat and allow to cool to room temperature before serving. Cover and refrigerate unused portions.

VARIATIONS
*Rich Red Nerimiso:

   6 tablespoons red or barley miso
   3½ to 4 tablespoons natural sugar
   ¼ cup *mirin*
   2 tablespoons sake
Prepare as above. A favorite for use in Miso Oden.

Hatcho Nerimiso: Use Hatcho miso and reduce the amount of sugar used above by about one-third. This preparation has a deep, chocolate-brown color and savory aroma.
Crunchy Granola Miso: Prepare ½ cup Red Nerimiso (using a relatively small amount of sugar) and allow to cool to room temperature. Combine with ½ to 2/3 cup crunchy granola, mixing well.
*For use in Tofu Dengaku (p. 139), divide prepared Red Nerimiso into two equal portions. To one portion add ½ to 1 teaspoon hot mustard or ½ teaspoon *sansho* pepper.

White Nerimiso

MAKES 1¼ CUPS

1 cup sweet white miso
3 tablespoons *mirin*
1½ tablespoons sake
1 egg yolk
3 tablespoons ground roasted sesame seeds (p. 38), or 1½ tablespoons sesame butter or *tahini*

Prepare as for Red Nerimiso (see above).
      For use in Tofu Dengaku (p. 139), divide the prepared miso into two equal portions. To one add any of the following: ½ to 1 teaspoon grated gingerroot; 2 to 3 tablespoons thinly sliced leeks or green onions; 3 to 4 tablespoons ground

roasted sesame seeds (p. 38) or sesame butter; 1 to 2 tablespoons bonita flakes and 1½ teaspoons water.

Sesame Miso

MAKES ¾ CUP

¼ cup sesame butter, *tahini*, or ground roasted sesame seeds (p. 38)
1/3 cup red, barley, or Hatcho miso
2 to 3 tablespoons natural sugar
1 tablespoon sake or white wine
1 tablespoon water
1 to 2 teaspoons grated orange or lemon rind (optional)

Prepare as for Red Nerimiso (see above).
      For the sweet, chocolate-like flavor of Chinese Tien M'ien Chiang, use akadashi miso (p. 45) instead of red miso.

Peanut Miso

MAKES ½ CUP

½ cup whole (roasted) peanuts or ¼ cup peanut butter
¼ cup red, barley, or Hatcho miso
2 to 3 tablespoons natural sugar, honey, or *mizuame*
2 tablespoons water; or 1 tablespoon each water and sake, white wine, or *mirin*

Prepare as for Red Nerimiso (see above).

VARIATIONS

Peanut & Raisin Miso: Use ¼ cup each peanuts and raisins, and 1½ to 2 tablespoons sugar. Add 1 to 2 tablespoons whole or ground roasted sesame seeds if desired.
*Substitute whole cashews, almonds, or sunflower seeds for the peanuts.
*Use akadashi miso and reduce the sugar to 1½ tablespoons.

Walnut Miso

MAKES ¾ CUP

1½ tablespoons oil
½ to 1 cup walnut meats, whole or sliced
1/3 cup red, barley, Hatcho, or akadashi miso
3 to 4 tablespoons natural sugar
1½ teaspoons water
1 tablespoon sake (optional)

Heat a skillet or wok and coat with the oil. Add **walnut** meats and sauté for about 1 minute. Stir in remaining ingredients and proceed as for Red Nerimiso (above).
      For variety, pre-roast walnuts until fragrant in a dry pan and/or add ¼ cup sesame butter to the ingredients listed above.

Yuzu Miso

MAKES 1 CUP

½ teaspoon grated *yuzu* peel, or substitute 1 to 2 teaspoons grated lime, lemon, or orange peel.
½ cup red, barley, or Hatcho miso
5 to 6½ tablespoons natural sugar
6 tablespoons water

Prepare as for Red Nerimiso (above).

Lemon Miso

MAKES ¼ CUP

¼ cup red, barley, or Hatcho miso
1 to 2 tablespoons natural sugar
1 tablespoon water
1 teaspoon lemon juice
1 teaspoon grated lemon rind

Combine the first three ingredients in a skillet and proceed as for Red Nerimiso (p. 42). After removing from heat, stir in lemon juice and rind; allow to cool to room temperature.

Garlic Miso

MAKES ¼ CUP

3 cloves of garlic, thinly sliced or crushed
¼ cup red, barley, or Hatcho miso
1½ to 2½ tablespoons natural sugar
2 teaspoons sake, white wine, or water (optional)

Prepare as for Red Nerimiso (p. 42), but simmer over very low heat for 8 to 10 minutes, or until quite firm.

Gingerroot Miso

MAKES ½ CUP

2 to 3 teaspoons grated gingerroot
5 tablespoons red, barley, or Hatcho miso
2 to 3 tablespoons natural sugar
2 teaspoons sake, white wine, or water

Prepare as for Red Nerimiso (p. 42).

Kinome Miso
(Miso with Fresh Sansho Leaves)

MAKES ½ CUP

60 *kinome* leaves (not sprigs) (about ¼ cup)
5 tablespoons sweet white miso
1 tablespoon natural sugar
2½ tablespoons water
1 teaspoon shoyu (optional)
1½ teaspoons *mirin* or sake (optional)
Dash of *sansho* pepper (optional)

Place leaves in a strainer, douse with boiling water, and drain well. Grind leaves thoroughly in a *suribachi* (or mortar), or mince with a knife. Combine the next five ingredients in a small saucepan and prepare as for Red Nerimiso (p. 42). Add contents of saucepan and pepper, if desired, to ground *kinome* in *suribachi*; mix well.

VARIATIONS

*Jade-Green Miso: Collect 4 ounces of the tender tips of *(horenso)* spinach and/or *daikon* leaves. Mince thoroughly, then grind almost to a paste in a *suribachi* or mortar. Pour in 1 cup water and, using your fingertips, free the ground leaves from the grooves in the bowl. Now pour the contents of the *suribachi* into a fine sieve set over a small saucepan and rub the leaves through the sieve with the back of a large spoon. Heat contents of saucepan over high heat until puréed leaves float to the surface, then reduce heat to low and simmer for 1 minute. Pour contents of pan into a cloth-lined strainer; drain well. Using a small spoon, carefully remove green purée (called *aoyose*) from cloth. Add 1 teaspoon *aoyose* to Kinome Miso, stirring well, until the miso has turned a delicate green.

Egg Yolk Miso

MAKES 1 CUP

6 tablespoons sweet white miso
2 egg yolks
2 tablespoons natural sugar
6 tablespoons dashi (p. 39), stock, or water
Dash of *sansho* pepper (optional)

Prepare as for Red Nerimiso (p. 42).
    For use in Tofu Dengaku (p. 139), divide the prepared miso into 2 equal portions. To one add 1 teaspoon *aoyose* (see preceeding recipe) and 60 *kinome* leaves prepared as for Kinome Miso. Stir in these ingredients just after removing miso from the heat.

Miso Sauté
(Abura Miso)

    Each of these distinctly different toppings is prepared following the same basic pattern. Experiment with other vegetables and nuts, or even with fruits. Serve with chilled or deep-fried tofu, brown rice, rice porridge, or fresh vegetable slices. Refrigerated, unused portions will keep for up to 1 week.

Plain Miso Sauté

MAKES ¼ CUP

1½ tablespoons (sesame) oil
4½ tablespoons red, barley, or Hatcho miso

Heat a skillet and coat with the oil. Add miso and sauté over low heat for about 1 minute, or until miso just begins to stick to skillet. Allow to cool before serving.

Mushroom Miso Sauté

MAKES ½ CUP

2 tablespoons oil
10 mushrooms, thinly sliced
1 tablespoon, red, barley, or Hatcho miso
1½ to 2 teaspoons natural sugar

Heat a skillet or wok and coat with the oil. Add mushrooms and sauté over medium heat for about 1 minute or until tender. Reduce heat to low, add miso and sugar, and cook, stirring constantly, for about 1 minute more, or until mushrooms are evenly coated with miso. Allow to cool to room temperature before serving.
    Or, substitute butter for one-half of the oil, and sauté over low heat, adding ¼ cup chopped walnut meats.

Each of the following recipes is prepared in basically the same way as Mushroom Miso Sauté. Use 1½ to 2 tablespoons oil, 1 to 1½ tablespoons miso, and 1½ to 3 teaspoons natural sugar.

*Lotus root: Sauté 1½ cups ginkgo leaves of lotus root over low heat for about 5 minutes, or until tender but still crisp. Proceed as above.

*Kabocha: Use ¼ onion cut into thin wedges and 1½ cups thinly sliced pieces of *kabocha*, squash, or pumpkin. Sauté over medium-high heat for 4 to 5 minutes, or until softened. Add 1 tablespoon sesame butter, *tahini*, or ground roasted sesame seeds (p. 38) together with the miso and sugar.

*Eggplant: Use 1 diced onion and 1½ cups 2-inch matchsticks of eggplant. Sauté just until all oil is absorbed, then add miso and sugar.

*Sweet potato: Use 1¼ cups of sweet potato, yam, or Irish potato cubes. Sauté over high heat for 3 to 5 minutes until softened. If desired, sauté ½ diced onion and ½ thinly sliced carrot for 3 to 4 minutes before adding potatoes.

*Burdock root: Use 1½ to 2 cups matchsticks of burdock root, soaked (p. 37), and 1 carrot cut into matchsticks or grated. Sauté burdock root over high heat for 8 to 10 minutes, or until softened. Add carrot and sauté for 5 minutes more, or until both vegetables are tender. If desired, add 1 to 2 tablespoons roasted sesame seeds together with the miso and sugar.

*Onion: Use 2 onions, cut into thin wedges, and 1 carrot, thinly sliced, slivered, or grated. Sauté both vegetables together over medium heat for 5 to 6 minutes, or until carrot is tender. Proceed as for Mushroom Miso Sauté.

Lemon-Walnut-Mushroom Miso Sauté

MAKES ¾ CUP

1½ teaspoons oil or butter
4 (*shiitake*) mushrooms, thinly sliced (about 1/3 cup)
1 tablespoon minced lemon, lime, or *yuzu* rind
¼ to ½ cup chopped walnut meats
1/3 cup red, barley, or Hatcho miso
2½ to 4 tablespoons natural sugar
¼ cup water

Prepare as for Mushroom Miso Sauté (p. 43) but sauté mushrooms for 2 minutes, then add lemon rind and walnuts, and sauté for 1 minute more.

Crumbly Tekka Miso

MAKES ¾ CUP

The word *tekka* is composed of the Chinese characters "metal" and "fire," since this all-purpose condiment was traditionally simmered for a long time on a metal griddle or in a heavy iron pot. It is a favorite topping for brown rice as well as all types of tofu.

2 tablespoons sesame oil
¼ cup minced burdock root
3 tablespoons minced carrot
2 tablespoons minced lotus root
½ teaspoon grated gingerroot
½ cup Hatcho, barley, or red miso
2 to 4 tablespoons roasted soybeans (optional)
Dash of 7-spice or minced red pepper (optional)

Heat a wok or skillet and coat with the oil. Add the burdock and sauté over high heat for about 1 minute. Reduce heat to medium, add carrots and lotus root, and sauté for 2 or 3 minutes. Mix in gingerroot, miso, and, if used, soybeans and red pepper; sauté for 2 minutes more. Reduce heat to low and cook, stirring constantly with a wooden spatula, for 20 to 30 minutes, or until miso is crumbly and fairly dry. Allow to cool. Store unused portions in an airtight container.

Sweetened Tekka Miso

MAKES 1¼ CUPS

1 tablespoon oil
2/3 cup thin rounds of burdock root, soaked (p. 37)
½ carrot, cut into matchsticks
½ cup diced lotus root (optional)
1/3 cup Hatcho, red, or akadashi miso
¼ cup natural sugar
1 tablespoon sake or white wine
2 tablespoons ground roasted sesame seeds (p. 38), sesame butter, or *tahini*.
¼ cup roasted soybeans (p. 63) or soynuts

Heat a wok or skillet and coat with the oil. Add burdock and carrot and sauté over medium-high heat for 3 or 4 minutes. Reduce heat to low, then stir in next four ingredients and sauté for 3 or 4 minutes more. Stir in soybeans and remove from heat. Transfer to a bowl and allow to cool. Use as an all-purpose condiment.

Carrot & Red Pepper Miso Sauté

MAKES ¾ CUP

Many delicious varieties of Miso Sauté may be prepared without the use of sugar using the basic techniques given in the following two recipes.

3 tablespoons sesame oil
¼ teaspoon minced red peppers, Chinese red-pepper *chiang*, or tabasco sauce
1 carrot, grated fine
1 tablespoon grated gingerroot
¼ cup red, barley, or Hatcho miso

Heat a wok or skillet and coat with the oil. Add the red pepper and sauté for 15 seconds. Add grated carrot and gingerroot and sauté for 1 minute more. Stir in miso and sauté for 6 more minutes. Remove from heat and allow to cool before serving.

Onion-Sesame Miso Sauté

MAKES ½ CUP

1 tablespoon sesame oil
½ cup minced wild onions, scallions, leeks, or onions
3 to 4 tablespoons sweet red miso
Dash of 7-spice red pepper, tabasco sauce, or paprika

Heat the oil over high heat in a wok or skillet. Add onions and sauté for about 1 minute. Stir in the miso and red pepper, reduce heat to low, and sauté for 2 or 3 minutes more.

Garlic & Green Pepper Miso Sauté

MAKES ½ CUP

1 tablespoon oil
½ clove garlic, crushed or minced
1 or 2 green peppers, thinly sliced
2 tablespoons barley, red, or Hatcho miso
1 tablespoon natural sugar
3 tablespoons water

Heat a wok or skillet and coat with the oil. Add garlic and sauté over high heat for about 15 seconds. Add green peppers and sauté for 1 minute more. Reduce heat to medium, stir in remaining ingredients and cook, stirring constantly, for 2 more minutes. Allow to cool before serving.

Spicy Korean Miso Sauté

MAKES ¾ CUP

2 tablespoons sesame oil
1 clove of garlic, crushed
1 tablespoon grated gingerroot
2 green peppers, minced
½ small onion, diced
Dash of minced red pepper, tabasco sauce, or 7-spice red pepper
3 tablespoons red, barley, or Hatcho miso
2 teaspoons soy sauce
1 tablespoon sake or white wine

Heat a wok or skillet and coat with the oil. Add the next five ingredients and sauté for 2 minutes. Stir in the miso, soy sauce, and sake, return just to the boil, and remove from heat. Allow to cool before serving.

Vinegar Miso Sauté (Abura-su Miso)

MAKES ½ CUP

The addition of vinegar to many varieties of Miso Sauté gives a tangy flavor which is particularly well suited to deep-fried tofu.

1 tablespoon oil
1 small onion or leek, thinly sliced
1 clove of garlic, crushed or minced
1½ tablespoons red, barley, or Hatcho miso
1½ to 3 teaspoons natural sugar
1 tablespoon vinegar

Heat a wok or skillet and coat with the oil. Add onion and garlic and sauté over high heat for 2 minutes. Reduce heat to low, mix in miso and sugar, and simmer for 1 minute more. Remove from heat, mix in vinegar, and allow to cool.

For variety, substitute for the onions an equal volume of thinly sliced green peppers, mushrooms, or bamboo shoots.

Special Miso Toppings and Dipping Sauces

These preparations are delicious with chilled or deep-fried tofu. Or they may be used in many of the same ways as Shoyu Dipping Sauces.

Mixed Miso Toppings

MAKES ABOUT ¼ CUP

¼ cup red, barley, or Hatcho miso
Seasonings: Choose one of the following:
  2 cloves of garlic, grated
  4 teaspoons minced *umeboshi* (about 10) and, if desired, 2 tablespoons bonita flakes.
  1 teaspoon freshly grated *wasabi* or *wasabi* paste and, if desired, 2½ teaspoons natural sugar
  ¼ cup bonita flakes
  1 tablespoon each sesame butter and bonita flakes (or grated cheese) and ¼ teaspoon grated lemon rind. Serve in a hollowed half-lemon rind.
  ½ to 1 teaspoon hot mustard and 2 tablespoons *mirin*, sake, or white wine.

Combine miso and seasoning(s); mix well.

Peking Duck Dipping Sauce
(Homemade Tien M'ien Chiang)

MAKES ½ CUP

¼ cup Hatcho miso
1½ teaspoons sesame oil
½ teaspoon vegetable oil
¾ teaspoon sake or white wine
1 teaspoon shoyu
2¾ tablespoons natural sugar
¼ cup water

Combine the first five ingredients, mixing well. Dissolve sugar in water, then stir into the miso mixture until smooth. Refrigerate unused portions in a sealed container.

Akadashi Miso

MAKES ¼ CUP

2 tablespoons Hatcho miso
2 tablespoons red or light-yellow miso
2 tablespoons natural sugar
½ to 1 teaspoon shoyu

Combine all ingredients, mixing well.

Broiled Miso *(Yakimiso)*

Spread 1 to 2 teaspoons, red, barley, or Sweet Simmered Miso in a thin layer on the underside of a lid to an earthenware bowl, on a thin cedar plank the size of a large matchbox, in a clam or scallop shell, or on the concave surface of a large spoon. Holding the miso just above an open fire, move it slowly back and forth and broil for about 15 seconds, or until fragrant. (If broiling the miso on a lid, place the lid immediately on an empty bowl to minimize loss of aroma.) Serve miso as soon as possible (in container in which it was broiled) as an accompaniment for Crisp Deep-fried Tofu (p. 156) or Chilled Tofu (p. 105).

Gingerroot-Miso Barbeque or Dipping Sauce

MAKES ½ CUP

1½ teaspoons oil
½ teaspoon minced gingerroot
3½ tablespoons red, barley, or Hatcho miso
¼ cup water, stock, or dashi (p. 39)
1½ tablespoons natural sugar
1½ tablespoons *mirin*, dry sherry, or white wine
Dash of 7-spice red pepper or *sansho* pepper (optional)

Heat a wok or skillet and coat with the oil. Add gingerroot and sauté for 1 minute, or until just fragrant. Add the next four ingredients and cook, stirring constantly, for 3 minutes, or until mixture has the consistency of a thick sauce. Stir in the red or *sansho* pepper and remove from heat. Allow to cool before serving. Delicious with deep-fried tofu, barbequed foods, tempura, or fresh vegetable slices.

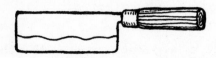

Vinegar Miso Dressings
(Sumiso)

These tangy preparations are widely used in Japanese-style tofu salads *(Aemono)* or as toppings for deep-fried tofu. Try adding small amounts of your favorite herbs and use with Western-style salads containing regular or deep-fried tofu and fresh vegetables.

Vinegar Miso Dressing

MAKES ¼ CUP

2 tablespoons red, barley, or Hatcho miso
1 tablespoon vinegar or 5 teaspoons lemon juice
4 teaspoons natural sugar
½ teaspoon *mirin*

Combine all ingredients, mixing well.

Mustard-Vinegar Miso Dressing *(Karashi Sumiso)*

MAKES ½ CUP

3 tablespoons sweet white miso
3 tablespoons vinegar
1 tablespoon natural sugar
1 teaspoon *mirin* (optional)
¼ teaspoon hot mustard

Combine all ingredients, mixing well.

Sesame-Vinegar Miso Dressing

MAKES ¼ CUP

1 tablespoon red, barley, or Hatcho miso
1 tablespoon vinegar
1 tablespoon ground roasted sesame seeds (p. 38), sesame butter, or *tahini*
1 to 1½ tablespoons natural sugar

Combine all ingredients; mix well.

MISO SALAD DRESSINGS

When used with salads containing regular or deep-fried tofu, these Western-style dressings serve as delicious seasonings able to evoke tofu's subtle, delicate flavors.

Floating-Cloud Miso Dressing

MAKES ½ CUP

6 tablespoons oil
2 tablespoons (rice) vinegar or lemon juice
2 tablespoons red, barley, or Hatcho miso
¼ teaspoon sesame oil
½ clove garlic, crushed
Dash of powdered ginger
Dash of dry mustard

Combine all ingredients; whisk or shake well.

Miso-Sour Cream Dressing

MAKES ¾ CUP

3 tablespoons sour cream
1 tablespoon red, barley, or Hatcho miso
1½ tablespoons cream cheese or Roquefort cheese, softened
4 tablespoons oil
2 tablespoons lemon juice
1 tablespoon minced onions or chives

Combine all ingredients, mixing well.

Miso-Cream Cheese-Mayonnaise Dressing

MAKES ½ CUP

4 tablespoons mayonnaise
2 tablespoons lemon juice
1 tablespoon red, barley, or Hatcho miso
1½ tablespoons cream cheese, softened
1 tablespoon sesame or peanut butter
1½ teaspoons grated onion and juice

Combine all ingredients, mixing well.

NUT AND SEED BUTTER TOPPINGS, SPREADS, AND DRESSINGS

These uncooked Western-style preparations, seasoned with a little salt, miso, or shoyu, can be used in much the same way as miso toppings and dressings. Delicious with deep-fried tofu or Dengaku (p. 139) as well as on sandwiches and toast.

Miso-Walnut Butter

1 cup walnut meats, lightly roasted and ground to a paste
¼ cup red, barley, or Hatcho miso
3 to 4 tablespoons water or stock

Combine all ingredients, mixing well.

Cinnamon-Sesame Butter

MAKES ¼ CUP

2 tablespoons sesame butter or *tahini*
1 tablespoon honey or natural sugar
1 tablespoon water
Dash of cinnamon
Dash of salt or ½ teaspoon red miso

Combine all ingredients, mixing well.

Lemon-Sesame Butter

MAKES ¾ CUP

5 tablespoons sesame butter or *tahini*
½ teaspoon grated lemon, lime, or *yuzu* rind (or 2 teaspoons of their juice)
2 tablespoons red, barley, or Hatcho miso; or 4 teaspoons shoyu
1½ tablespoons water or stock
1 tablespoon honey or natural sugar (optional)

Combine all ingredients, mixing well.
To make a sauce or dressing, use 1 tablespoon miso and 3 to 4 tablespoons water.

Spicy Sesame Butter

MAKES ¼ CUP

3½ tablespoons sesame butter
2 teaspoons shoyu
1 tablespoon natural sugar or honey
2 tablespoons water
Dash of 7-spice red pepper or tabasco sauce

Combine all ingredients; mix well.

Vinegar-Peanut Butter

MAKES ¼ CUP

2 tablespoons peanut butter
2 tablespoons oil
4 teaspoons vinegar
1 tablespoon natural sugar
½ teaspoon salt or 1 tablespoon red miso

Combine all ingredients, mixing well.

Miso-Peanut Butter

MAKES ¼ CUP

3 tablespoons peanut butter
1 tablespoon red, barley, or Hatcho miso
1 tablespoon honey
2 tablespoons water

Combine all ingredients, mixing well.
For variety, use 1 tablespoon each sweet white miso and peanut butter, 2 teaspoons each honey and vinegar, and a dash of shoyu.

White Sesame-Vinegar Miso Dressing

MAKES ¼ CUP

3 tablespoons sweet white miso
1½ tablespoons vinegar
1 tablespoon sesame butter or *tahini*, or 1½ tablespoons ground roasted sesame seeds (p. 38)
½ teaspoon natural sugar

Combine all ingredients; mix well.

Peanut-Vinegar Miso Dressing

MAKES ¼ CUP

1 tablespoon sweet white miso
2 teaspoons vinegar or lemon juice
20 peanuts, minced
2 teaspoons honey
½ teaspoon shoyu

Combine all ingredients, mixing well.

BASIC SAUCES

Each of these sauces may be served with a wide variety of different tofu preparations. They will all be called for in recipes throughout this book.

Onion Sauce
MAKES 3½ CUPS

This naturally sweet, rich brown sauce is prepared slowly like the basis for a French onion soup. Its basic form and many variations go well with a number of different types of tofu. For best results, make a large quantity at one time since the flavor improves after several days and re-warmings. It may be served hot or cold to equal advantage.

2 tablespoons oil
6 onions, thinly sliced
2 tablespoons shoyu; or 3 tablespoons red miso creamed in ¼ cup water
1 tablespoon butter

Heat a large casserole or heavy pot and coat with the oil. Add onions, cover, and simmer over low heat for about 2 to 3 hours, stirring thoroughly once every 10 minutes. When onions are a rich brown and very soft, mix in the butter and shoyu and simmer for 10 to 15 more minutes. (If using miso, return just to the boil, then remove from heat.) Serve hot or, for best flavor, allow to cool overnight and serve reheated or chilled the next day.

VARIATIONS:

*To ½ cup chilled Onion Sauce add 1 to 2 tablespoons shoyu or miso. Serve as a topping for chilled or deep-fried tofu. For variety garnish with diced or grated cheese or thinly sliced onions.

*Seasoned Onion Sauce with Nut Butters: Thin your favorite nut butter with a small amount of water or stock and, if desired, some lemon or orange juice, and add to 2 parts Onion Sauce. Season with herbs, 7-spice red pepper, shoyu, or miso. Garnish with thinly sliced green onions or parsley. For variety add large chunks of nuts, diced cheese, or sprouts. Serve with Chilled Tofu or as a topping for any variety of deep-fried tofu.

Mushroom Sauce
FOR 2 TO 3 SERVINGS

1½ tablespoons butter
½ teaspoon minced garlic
1 tablespoon minced onion
½ teaspoon grated gingerroot
4 to 5 small mushrooms, thinly sliced
1/3 cup ketchup
1 tablespoon red miso (optional)
Dash of pepper

Melt butter in a skillet. Add garlic, onion, and gingerroot and sauté for about 1 minute. Add mushrooms and sauté for 2 more minutes. Add ketchup, miso, and pepper and sauté for 1 minute more. Serve with Tofu Burgers (p. 127), Okara Chapati (p. 83), Crisp Tortillas (p. 170), or as a topping for Chilled Tofu (p. 105).

White Sauce
MAKES 1 CUP

Also known as Cream- or Béchamel Sauce, this traditional Western favorite acquires a distinctive flavor and creaminess when seasoned with miso. Season lightly for use with vegetables (such as cauliflower or potatoes) and more prominently for use with tofu dishes. Numerous variations prepared with soymilk and containing tofu are given on page 207.

2 tablespoons butter or oil
2 tablespoons (whole-wheat) flour
1 cup milk (soy or dairy); or stock
3 to 4 teaspoons red miso; 2 to 2½ teaspoons shoyu; or ½ to 2/3 teaspoon salt
Dash of pepper, paprika, or cayenne
1 tablespoon minced parsley (optional)

Melt the butter (or heat the oil) in a skillet. Add flour and, stirring constantly, cook over low heat for 1 to 2 minutes, or until flour is well blended and its raw taste has vanished. Add ½ cup milk (or stock) a little at a time, continuing to stir, then mix in the miso and slowly add the remainder of the milk. Increase heat to medium and cook, whisking or stirring, for 3 to 4 minutes more, or until sauce develops a smooth, nicely thickened consistency. Stir in pepper and parsley and remove from heat.

Note: Many cooks prefer to heat the milk to just scalding before it is added. In this case, after sautéing flour, remove skillet from heat until flour stops bubbling. Then pour in the near-boiling milk. When it stops steaming, stir briskly until smooth and proceed as above.

Brown Sauce

Prepare as for a white sauce except cook the flour until it is lightly browned and fragrant.

Teriyaki Sauce
MAKES 2/3 CUP

Generally used in Japan to baste broiled fish, this savory sauce is now used by many Westerners with shish kebab and other barbequed preparations. Also good as a dip for fresh vegetables or a topping for deep-fried tofu.

¼ cup shoyu or 6 tablespoons red miso
3 tablespoons sake or white wine
3 tablespoons brown sugar
1 teaspoon grated gingerroot or 1½ teaspoons powdered ginger
2 cloves of garlic, crushed
1 tablespoon sesame or vegetable oil
¼ teaspoon dry mustard

Combine all ingredients, mixing well. Marinate foods (deep-fried tofu, green peppers, onions, tomatoes, etc.) for at least 1 hour before skewering and broiling. Use remaining sauce to baste.

Gingerroot Sauce

MAKES 1¾ CUPS

1 cup dashi (p. 39), stock, or water
¼ cup shoyu
2 to 2½ tablespoons natural sugar
1 tablespoon cornstarch or arrowroot, dissolved in 4 table-
    spoons water
1 tablespoon grated gingerroot
Dash of 7-spice red pepper

Combine the dashi, shoyu, and sugar in a small saucepan and bring to a boil. Stir in the dissolved cornstarch to thicken. Mix in the grated gingerroot and season with the pepper. Delicious with deep-fried tofu dishes.

Ankake Sauce

MAKES 1¼ CUPS

1 cup dashi (p. 39), stock, or water
5 teaspoons shoyu
1 tablespoon natural sugar
2 teaspoons cornstarch, arrowroot, or *kuzu*, dissolved in 1½
    tablespoons water
½ teaspoon grated lemon rind or gingerroot (optional)

Combine dashi, shoyu, and sugar in a small saucepan and bring to a boil. Stir in dissolved cornstarch and, if used, the lemon rind, and cook for about 1 minute more until thick.

For a Mild Ankake Sauce use 3½ teaspoons shoyu, 1 teaspoon sugar, and 1½ teaspoons cornstarch. Omit lemon rind.

Rich Gingerroot-Ankake Sauce

MAKES 1 CUP

2/3 cup dashi (p. 39), stock, or water
3 tablespoons shoyu
2 tablespoons natural sugar
2 teaspoons arrowroot or cornstarch, dissolved in 2 table-
    spoons water
2 teaspoons freshly grated gingerroot or gingerroot juice

Prepare as for Ankake Sauce, above.

Korean Barbeque Sauce

MAKES ¼ CUP

2 tablespoons shoyu
2 teaspoons natural sugar
2 teaspoons sesame oil
1 tablespoon ground roasted sesame seeds (p. 38) or 1 tea-
    spoon sesame butter or *tahini*
1 tablespoon diced leeks or onions
1 clove garlic, crushed
¼ teaspoon 7-spice red pepper or tabasco sauce
Dash of pepper

Combine all ingredients, mixing well. Serve with Grilled Thick Agé (p. 174), Grilled Tofu (p. 223), or any variety of deep-fried tofu.

Sweet & Sour Sauce

MAKES 1¼ CUPS

1 tablespoon oil
½ onion, thinly sliced
½ small carrot, cut into irregular pieces
1 green pepper, cut into irregular pieces
¾ cup water or stock
2 tablespoons shoyu
2½ tablespoons natural sugar
2 teaspoons rice vinegar
1½ teaspoons cornstarch dissolved in 1½ tablespoons water

Heat a skillet or wok and coat with the oil. Add onion, carrot, and green pepper, and sauté for 3 to 4 minutes, or until onion is transparent. Add the next four ingredients, bring to a boil, and simmer for 3 minutes. Stir in dissolved cornstarch and cook for 30 more seconds or until thick.

For variety, omit the oil and vegetables, and add 1 teaspoon grated gingerroot and 1 tablespoon sake or white wine to the remaining ingredients.

Tomato & Cheese Sauce

MAKES 1¼ CUPS

2 tablespoons butter
1¼ cups chopped tomatoes
½ onion, minced
¾ cup grated cheese
½ teaspoon salt, 1 tablespoon shoyu, or 1½ tablespoons red
    miso
¼ teaspoon paprika
¼ teaspoon oregano or basil
Dash of pepper

Melt butter in a skillet. Add tomatoes and onions and sauté for 2 minutes. Cover, reduce heat to low, and simmer for 3 minutes. Uncover and continue simmering, stirring occasionally, for 15 minutes more, or until sauce is thick. Stir in remaining ingredients and remove from heat. Delicious served over deep-fried tofu.

Ketchup-Worcestershire Sauce

MAKES 6 TABLESPOONS

¼ cup ketchup
2 tablespoons Worcestershire sauce

Combine ingredients, mixing well. Serve with deep-fried tofu.

Tangy Ketchup & Lemon Sauce

MAKES ¾ CUP

1/3 cup ketchup
5 teaspoons lemon juice
1 teaspoon shoyu
1 teaspoon minced onions

Combine all ingredients, mixing well.

For variety add ¼ to ½ teaspoon hot mustard, 1 teaspoon horseradish, ½ teaspoon crushed anise or ground roasted sesame seeds, or 1 tablespoon minced parsley.

RICE, NOODLES, AND
OTHER BASIC PREPARATIONS

Brown Rice
MAKES 4 CUPS

The Japanese say that when cooked, both regular and *sushi* rice are at their peak of flavor when the rice at the bottom of the pot is golden brown and slightly crisp. And even moderns prize the aroma of rice cooked in a heavy iron pot over a wood fire.

2 cups brown rice, rinsed and soaked overnight in 2 2/3 cups water

In a heavy covered pot, bring water and rice to a boil over high heat. Reduce heat to low and simmer for 45 to 50 minutes or until all water is absorbed or evaporated. Uncover pot, remove from heat, and stir rice thoroughly with a wooden spoon. (If a slightly drier consistency is desired, transfer rice to a wooden bowl before stirring). Allow to cool for several minutes, then cover pot (or bowl) with a double layer of cloth until you are ready to serve.

To pressure cook: Rinse and drain 1 cup rice. Without soaking, combine in a pressure cooker with 1 cup water. Bring to pressure (15 pounds), reduce heat to low, and simmer for 25 minutes. Allow pressure to come down naturally for 10 to 15 minutes. Open pot and mix rice well. Allow to stand uncovered for 3 to 5 minutes, then cover with a cloth as above.

Brown Rice Porridge
SERVES 2 OR 3

Called *Congee* in China and *Okayu* in Japan, this is a popular main course at breakfast in many homes and temples. Easy to digest, rice porridge is considered the ideal food for sick people, and nursing mothers sometimes skim the creamy liquid from the porridge's surface to feed their babies as a breast milk supplement. In China, rice porridge is often served garnished or seasoned with doufu-ru (p. 264), as are the hundreds of varieties of rice gruel. The latter, a close relative of Japan's *Zosui* (p. 138), is prepared by cooking vegetables (often leftovers) with rice porridge and seasoning the mixture with miso or soy sauce.

½ cup brown rice, soaked overnight in 4½ cups water

Prepare as for brown rice, setting lid slightly ajar and simmering for about 90 minutes, or until rice develops a porridge-like consistency. Serve immediately, seasoned with Sesame Salt (p. 00) or salt- or miso-pickled vegetables. If desired, add crumbled *nori* and minced leeks.

Or combine 1¼ cups (leftover) cooked rice with 3½ cups water and, without soaking, proceed as above.

To pressure cook: Rinse and drain ½ cup rice. Without soaking, combine in a pressure cooker with 2½ cups water. Bring to pressure (15 pounds), reduce heat to low, and simmer for 45 minutes. Allow pressure to come down naturally for 10 to 15 minutes. Open pot and mix porridge well. Allow to stand uncovered for 3 to 5 minutes before serving.

Sushi Rice
(Rice in Vinegar Dressing)
MAKES 2½ CUPS

1 cup short (brown) rice, soaked in 11/3 cups water overnight in a heavy 2- to 4- quart pot
Vinegar Dressing:
    2 1/3 tablespoons (rice) vinegar
    1 tablespoon natural sugar
    2 teaspoons mirin (optional)
    1/2 teaspoon salt

Bring soaked rice to a boil in a covered pot. Reduce heat to low and simmer for 40 to 50 minutes or until all water has been absorbed and rice is quite light and dry. (If using white rice, simmer for only 15 to 20 minutes). Remove rice from heat and allow to stand for 5 minutes. Transfer hot rice to a large wooden bowl, platter, or other non-metallic container and immediately sprinkle on the dressing. With a wooden spoon, chopsticks, or a wide fork in one hand, and a fan or flat pot lid in the other, mix the rice vigorously while fanning to cool it as quickly as possible. Fan and stir for about 3 minutes, then allow rice to cool to room temperature.

For variety, prepare Unsweetened Sushi Rice by omitting the sugar and *mirin* in the dressing, and by increasing the vinegar to 4 tablespoons and the salt to 1½ teaspoons.

Noodles
SERVES 2 OR 3

4½ to 5 ounces dry buckwheat or whole-wheat noodles (*soba* or *udon*)

Bring 2 to 3 quarts of water to a rolling boil over high heat. Scatter noodles slowly over surface of water and return to the boil. Lower heat until water is boiling actively but does not overflow. Cook uncovered for about 5 minutes, or until noodles are tender but not soft. Pour noodles into a colander placed in the sink and drain briefly, then transfer to a large container filled with circulating cold water. Stir noodles with chopsticks for several minutes until they cool to temperature of water, then transfer noodles back into colander; drain well and serve.

To serve hot: Bring about 1 quart of fresh water to a boil in a saucepan. Place 1 individual portion of noodles into a small strainer, dip noodle-filled strainer into boiling water for about 5 seconds, then shake strainer above saucepan to rid noodles of excess moisture. Transfer noodles to individual serving bowls, pour on Noodle Broth (p. 40), and top with garnishes. Serve immediately.

In many fine Japanese soba restaurants, a portion of the nutritious hot water in which the noodles were initially cooked is poured into a small teapot and served after the meal. Each guest seasons his portion to taste with leftover Noodle Broth.

Sesame Salt *(Gomashio)*   MAKES ABOUT ½ CUP

A delicious all-purpose seasoning for grains, salads, beans, eggs, cereals, and sautéed vegetables, Sesame Salt is generally made with about 7 parts whole sesame seeds to 1 part salt. Please begin by studying instructions for preparing ground roasted sesame seeds (p. 38).

2 teaspoons sea salt
5 tablespoons white or black sesame seeds

Heat a heavy skillet. Pour in the salt and roast, stirring constantly, for about 1 minute. Add the sesame seeds and roast until done. Grind the salt-sesame mixture in a *suribachi* or hand mill as for Ground Roasted Sesame Seeds (p. 38). Store in an airtight container.

Sweet Vinegared Gingerroot *(Gari)*

3 tablespoons vinegar
2 tablespoons natural sugar
Dash of salt
1 piece of gingerroot, sliced into paper-thin rounds (¼ cup), parboiled, drained, and patted dry with a towel

Combine the first three ingredients in a small saucepan and heat, stirring constantly, until the sugar just dissolves. Now combine with the sliced gingerroot in a small bowl so that the gingerroot is fully immersed in the liquid. Cover and refrigerate overnight or for at least several hours. Serve with Inarizushi, Sushi Rice, or other rice dishes.

Paper-thin Omelets   MAKES ABOUT 8

These omelets may be made into an envelope or purse (*chakin*) used to contain Sushi Rice or Sushi Okara, or they may be cut into thin strips called "threads of gold" and scattered over the top of Sushi Rice.

4 eggs
¼ teaspoon salt
1 teaspoon ground roasted sesame seeds (p. 38) (optional)
1 to 2 teaspoons oil

In a small bowl, combine eggs, ¼ teaspoon salt and sesame; mix well. Heat a small skillet and coat lightly with oil, pouring off any excess. Pour about one-eighth of the egg mixture into the skillet, swishing it around quickly so that it just covers the bottom of the pan. Cook over high heat for about 20 to 30 seconds on one side only to form a thin omelet. Transfer omelet to a plate and allow to cool. Prepare 8 omelets, oiling the pan lightly after every 3 or 4. Sliver to use as a garnish.

Among the more than 500 dishes in this book, there are certain ones we enjoy again and again, and like to serve to guests as an introduction to tofu cookery. Most take very little time to prepare and use readily available Western ingredients. We have starred those we suggest you make your very first dishes. In later chapters we list our favorites first.

PART II

Cooking with Tofu:
Recipes from East and West

4

Soybeans

WHOLE DRY soybeans are the essential ingredient in the tofu maker's art. Each evening, he concludes his daily cycle of work by measuring out 15 to 20 gallons of beans in a special wooden box made with precisely mitered corners and a brand of the gods of good fortune burned into one of its sides (fig. 10). One of the gods is *Ebisu*, the deity of craftsmen, tradesmen, and fishermen; he symbolizes the hard worker who earns his living by honest toil. The other is *Daikoku*, the happy god whose wealth is so vast that he does not mind the rats nibbling at his bales of grain. The tofu maker washes the measured beans in a large cedar barrel bound together with hoops of brightly-polished brass, then sets them aside to soak overnight. He and the beans sleep under the same roof.

The story of tofu must begin with the story of soybeans. Officially known as *Glycine max* and botanically a member of the family *Leguminosae* (legumes), the soybean plant stands about 2 feet tall, has a slightly woody stem, and sprouts its leaves in groups of three. The leaves, stems, and pods are covered with soft brownish-green hairs, and the plant's seeds—soybeans—are borne in the pods which grow near the stalk in clusters of three to five (fig. 11). Each pod usually contains two to three seeds. Fresh soybeans are similar in color and size to green peas. The mature, dried beans are usually tan, beige, or yellow, but some varieties are also black, brown, green, or bi-colored. American beans are slightly smaller and yellower than most Japanese varieties. They grow from Louisiana in the south to Minnesota in the north, and from Texas in the west to the Carolinas in the east. Planted from May to June in rows about 40 inches apart, the fresh green beans are ready to eat by mid-July; the mature beans are harvested in September or October, after the leaves have fallen and the seeds have dried on the vine.

Soybeans are pulses, a term which refers to the seeds of leguminous plants such as peas, lentils, and beans. These plants have a symbiotic relationship with bacteria called *rhizobia*, which form nodules in the plants' roots. *Rhizobia* capture nitrogen (the essential element in all protein) from the air and fix it in the soil, thereby greatly enhancing the soil's fertility. Hence, many of the first soybean plants grown in the United States were used simply as cover crops or "green manure"; even today, all farmers, after harvesting the beans, plow under the remainder of the plant to create nitrogen-rich humus soil. Easy to grow in small vegetable gardens or window boxes, the soybean plant is a favorite with organic and bio-dynamic gardeners, too, for much the same reason.

Where did the word "soybean" come from? The present-day Chinese call soybeans *ta-tou*, or "great beans." The Japanese pronounce the same written characters as *daizu*. It is obvious that neither of these words resembles the word "soy." But in a Chinese dictionary dating from about the beginning of the Christian era, soybeans are called *sou*. In addition, the Japanese pronounce the word for soy sauce (*chiang-yu*) as *shoyu*. The etymology of the English word may therefore be traced either to the Japanese word for soy sauce or to the ancient Chinese word for soybean.

The origins of the soybean plant are obscured by legend and the Oriental urge to endow all things worthy of respect with ancient ancestry. It is said

Fig. 10. A soybean measuring box

that long ago, sages and wise rulers bestowed the bounty of soybeans upon the generations of mankind. The numerous myths, legends, and historical accounts of its ancestry all reflect a common wish to honor the soybean for the service it has given to humanity.

From evidence based on distribution, it seems likely that soybeans originated in Eastern Asia, probably either in northern China or Mongolia. Legend has it that soybeans are one of the oldest crops grown by man, extensively cultivated and highly valued as a food for centuries before written records were kept.

In an eighteenth-century Chinese encyclopedia, the discovery of the soybean was attributed to two legendary characters, *Yu-hsiung* and *Kung-kung shih,* who were said to have lived more than five thousand years ago. But it is not clear whether they discovered beans in general or soybeans in particular. A more widely known theory states that in 2838 B.C., a Chinese emperor named *Sheng-nung* wrote a *Materia Medica* which describes the plants of China and includes a description of the soybean together with a long discourse on its medical properties. And in writings reported to be published as early as 2207 B.C., Chinese agricultural experts give detailed tech-

nical advice concerning soybean planting and soil preferences.

It is known from reliable historical sources that soybeans were cultivated in China before the Han Dynasty (206 B.C.-220 A.D.) and that they were used in processed form as food by the second century B.C., when the ruler Liu An of Huai-nan is said to have discovered the process for making tofu. According to the ten-volume *Chi'min Yaushu,* mankind's oldest encyclopedia of agriculture, compiled in the sixth century, soybeans were initially brought to China by the great Chinese explorer *Choken,* who was the first to make contact with Greece, Rome, and India, and to open the Silk Road.

The transmission of soybeans from northern China or Manchuria to Japan, probably via Korea, may have taken place sometime between the sixth and eighth centuries, concurrent with the spread of Buddhism. (The discovery of charred soybeans together with husked rice in neolithic dwellings in Japan suggests that soybeans may actually have arrived in Japan long before the existence of written records.) Mention is made of soybeans in Japan's earliest existing documents, the famous *Kojiki* of 712 A.D. and the *Nihonshoki* of 720 A.D.. Records from the Nara period (710-794) show that soybean foods (such as miso and the progenitor of shoyu) were taxed by the government, and thus were an important part of the Japanese way of life even then.

Along with rice, wheat, barley, and millet, soybeans were included among China's venerated *muku*, or Five Sacred Grains, as early as the beginning of the Christian era. Since soybeans are not technically a grain, some scholars believe that it was beans in general rather than the soybean that were given this lofty title. Nevertheless, living close to the earth, the people of East Asia grasped the dependence of human life upon these basic crops. Their sense of the sacred grew out of a feeling of interrelationship—and gratitude—and determined their way of relating to soybeans and other essential foods.

The sense of the sacredness of soybean foods is still alive in Japan today; here the words tofu, miso, and shoyu are commonly preceeded in everyday speech by the honorific prefix *o*. Rather than saying *tofu*, most people say *o-tofu*, meaning "honorable tofu." And on the last day of winter, as determined by Japan's traditional lunar calendar, roasted soybeans play a key role in one of the country's most ancient and widely observed celebrations of ritual purification. In homes and temples throughout Japan, these *fuku-mame* or "beans of good fortune" are scattered by the handful in each room, then tossed through an open window into the cold night air with everyone chanting "Out with all evils; in with good fortune."

Today, the soybean has become the king of the Japanese kitchen. Indeed, the arrival of tofu, miso, and shoyu in Japan initiated a revolution in the national cuisine. Now when Japanese connoisseurs speak of these foods, they use many of the same terms we employ when evaluating cheeses or wines; traditional tofu masters often say that the consummation of their art is but to evoke the fine flavors latent in the soybean. Again and again we have heard them declare that "only *nigari* can unfold the delicate nuances of sweetness and the fine, subtle bouquet in the best domestic beans." And when the new crop of soybeans arrives at tofu shops late each fall, ardent devotees sample the first tofu with the discrimination and relish of French vintners.

Many Japanese grow soybeans in their vegetable gardens and they are cultivated extensively along the paths which separate one rice paddy from another. Varieties considered to have the finest flavors have been known for centuries by such names as "child of the white cranes" or "waving sleeves."

Except for Manchuria, the countries of East Asia have not traditionally pressed or crushed soybeans on a large scale to extract their oil. Nor have they generally baked, boiled, or ground the beans into flour. Using simple tools and processes, countless generations have discovered other ways of trans-

Fig. 11. The soybean plant

forming soybeans into delicious foods. After almost 1,000 years of use in China, the soybean was transmitted to Japan. Over the period of another millenium, the Japanese modified each of the basic Chinese soybean foods and created a number of new ones. Finally, at the beginning of the present century, the Japanese made the first major commercial shipment of soybeans to the Western world. In its contact with the West's unique patterns of cooking, farming, and food-processing, the soybean entered a new phase in its long history.

A German botanist, Englebert Kaempfer, spent 3 years in Japan from 1690 to 1693 and was the first Westerner to study and write about Japanese soybean foods. The first small samples of seed soybeans arrived in the West as early as 1790 and were planted in England's Botanical Gardens. The fact that their arrival corresponded with the beginning of the industrial revolution was to have a profound effect on the way in which soybeans came to be used. In 1804 the soybean was first mentioned in American literature in *Willic's Domestic Encyclopedia*, and in 1854, the Perry Expedition brought two soybean varieties back from Japan. In 1908, when the first commercial shipment of soybeans from Asia to the West was received in England, they were processed for oil to be used in the manufacture of soap, while the meal was fed to dairy cattle. This pattern of use, so different from that in Asia, has remained basically unchanged up to the present time.

In America, the first soybeans were used as a forage crop and for green manure rather than as a food for people. The first small-scale processing of soybeans to obtain oil was begun in 1911. In 1920 the American Soybean Association was organized and by 1922 Decatur, Illinois, had become the center of soybean processing in the U.S. In 1923, Charles Piper and William Morse wrote *The Soybean*, the first comprehensive book in English on this subject. Showing great interest in all of the basic Oriental soybean foods, they studied their methods of preparation in detail and included a large number of recipes using them in Western-style cookery. With remarkable insight, they wrote in the preface to their classical study:

> The importance of the soybean lies largely in the fact that the seeds can be produced more cheaply than those of any other leguminous crop. This is due to both its high yielding capacity and to the ease of harvesting. These facts alone insure the increasing importance of the crop in the future when the land shall be called upon to yield its maximum crop of food. There can be little doubt that the soybean is destined to become one of the major American crops. (p. v).

When Piper and Morse wrote these words, soybeans were still a relatively unknown commodity. It was not until 1935 that the acreage of beans used for oil extraction equalled that used for forage. Blessed with expanses of territory well suited by climate and soil quality for soybean production, and equipped with a technology that has made it possible to produce a bushel of beans with less than 8 minutes labor, the U.S. farmer was able by the 1950s to grow soybeans competetive price- and quality-wise with those originating in the Orient. By 1973, the U.S. soybean crop had reached the phenomenal figure of 1½ billion bushels (47 million tons), a *twentyfold* increase in size since 1940 and a 24 percent increase over the previous year. Over the same period, the yield per acre increased 68 percent to a high of 27 bushels. Recent tests plots have yielded as much as

60 to 100 bushels per acre, and experts feel that in the near future a nationwide average of 40 bushels may be possible. It is not likely that such large increases in production and yield will ever again be duplicated by soybeans or any other crop.

In the short space of two generations, America has become the world's largest producer of soybeans, supplying over 65 percent of the planet's total output. The number-two producer, Brazil, supplys about 18 percent, and China about 13 percent. Canada, Australia, Russia, and Indonesia also produce fairly large crops. Soybeans are now the number one U.S. farm export, and foreign demand is ever on the rise. Worth an astounding 5 *billion* dollars in 1974 and accounting for more than 8 percent of our total exports, soybean sales abroad generate a large proportion of the foreign currency used to import oil and other basic raw materials.

Thus, a nutritional cornerstone of East Asian cuisine has emerged as the most important American cash crop. Called "meat of the fields" in Asia, soybeans are now known among American farmers as "gold from the soil." Nevertheless, as late as September 1973, the then president of the United States could make a statement—that made headlines throughout Japan—to the effect that he had never seen a soybean. A majority of adult Americans are reported to have first heard the word "soybean" less than ten years ago and many have never seen a soybean plant, nor tasted fresh (green) or whole dry soybeans, or soybean sprouts. Yet, having become so well established in our agriculture and economy, soybeans are now gradually becoming part of our language and culture. At least one relatively large-scale American farming enterprise, a Tennessee-based new-age community called *The Farm*, has taken the historic step of cultivating them for use primarily as a food staple in the vegetarian diet of its members. *The Farm* is bound to be only the first of many as, over the coming years, the soybean becomes an ever-more integral part of our national cuisine.

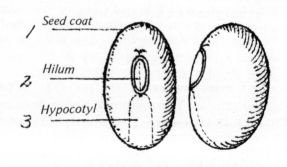

COOKING WITH WHOLE DRY SOYBEANS

In Japan, soybeans are only occasionally cooked at home. To save time and the cost of lengthy cooking, most people purchase ready-made soybean dishes, usually at the local delicatessen. Many of these store-bought preparations contain large amounts of shoyu and/or sugar to serve as natural preservatives. Whole (tan) soybeans are also available commercially deep-fried in a sweetened batter and sold as Soy Brittle (p. 62), while black soybeans are often used in confectionery treats.

But when most of us in the West set out to use soybeans, we usually start with those available in their whole, dry form at natural food stores and supermarkets. Presently the least expensive known source of usable protein, whole soybeans are also rich in iron, and vitamins B_1 and B_2. A truly remarkable food, they contain 1½ times as much protein as any other legume (34% to 38%), and are low in carbohydrates. Many recent cookbooks, especially those emphasizing natural foods, have begun to include a wide variety of recipes using boiled or baked soybeans in Western-style salads, soups, casseroles, and spreads.

Fresh, new-crop soybeans—the tastiest type—are generally available from the beginning of November. When storing large quantities, always use cloth rather than plastic sacks. When soybeans are kept over long periods, a small harmless moth and its eggs may appear among the beans. These can be easily removed by sifting and then exposing the beans to direct sunlight for one day.

Once you decide to make soybeans, tofu, and soymilk a basic part of your diet, buy a 60- to 100-pound sack of food- or seed grade beans at greatly reduced prices from a wholesaler or farmer's supply store; avoid the little packages retailed at inflated prices.

To ensure best flavor, digestibility, and deactivation of trypsin inhibitor (see p. 70), soybeans must be cooked—preferably pressure cooked—until they are very soft; a single bean should be easily crushed between the thumb and ring finger or between the tongue and roof of the mouth. The beans should also be throughly soaked in plenty of water (see graph, p. 289), the water discarded, and new water used for cooking; this helps remove the oligosaccharides believed to cause flatulence. When pressure cooking, some cooks add 1½ teaspoons oil for each cup of beans in order to prevent the seed coats from clogging the steam escape valve; some also prefer to add salt and seasonings before pressure cooking. If cooking the beans at only 10 pounds pressure, double the cooking times given in the following recipes.

Pressure Cooked Soybeans Plus
MAKES 2¼ CUPS

1 cup dry soybeans, rinsed and soaked for 2 or 3 hours in 2 quarts water
2 cups water
A thin wedge of lemon or lime (optional)

Drain and rinse soaked beans; combine with 2 cups water in a pressure cooker. Bring to full pressure (15 pounds) over high heat, then reduce heat to low and simmer for 45 minutes. (If soaked overnight, simmer beans for only 20 minutes.) Remove from heat and allow to stand for 10 to 15 minutes as pressure returns to normal. Cool lid under running cold water and open.

Return cooker to stove, stir in any of the ingredients listed below, and simmer uncovered over low heat for 10 to 15 minutes, or until flavors are nicely married. If necessary, add ¼ cup water during simmering. Stir from time to time. Serve hot or cold.

*2 tablespoons red, barley, or Hatcho miso (creamed with a little of the cooking liquid), or 4 teaspoons shoyu, or 1 teaspoon salt. If desired, add 1 teaspoon lemon juice or 1 tablespoon butter. For a deliciously rich flavor, add 1 (sautéed) minced onion together with the miso and stir in ½ cup grated or ¼ cup Parmesan cheese just before removing from heat.

*2 to 4 tablespoons molasses (honey or natural sugar) and 1 to 1½ tablespoons miso or shoyu.

*¼ cup sesame butter, *tahini*, ground roasted sesame seeds, or peanut butter, and 1 tablespoon miso or shoyu.

*3 to 4 tablespoons dry *hijiki* or slivered *kombu* (reconstituted, p. 37), 1 tablespoon shoyu or 1½ tablespoons red miso, 3 tablespoons sesame butter, and 1 onion or ¾ cup grated carrot (pre-sautéed in 1 tablespoon oil, if desired). For extra sweetness, add 1½ teaspoons honey or sugar.

*½ to 1 cup diced tomatoes, onions, carrots, celery, mushrooms, lotus root, burdock root, sprouts, fresh or dried *daikon*, or *kombu*. Add vegetables alone or in combination. Season with ½ teaspoon salt or 2 tablespoons shoyu (or miso). Add ½ teaspoon curry powder and 1 clove of crushed garlic with the onions or carrots.

*In any of the above recipes, after the beans and seasonings have finished cooking, try sautéing the mixture for a few minutes in a little (sesame) oil.

Boiled Soybeans
MAKES 2¼ CUPS

This recipe is for those who don't own a pressure cooker. You may wish to prepare 2 or 3 times the amounts given and refrigerate the unused portions.

1 cup dry soybeans, rinsed and soaked overnight in 2 quarts water
6½ to 7 cups water
½ to 1 teaspoon lemon juice (optional)

Drain soaked beans and combine with 4 cups water in a heavy pot. Bring to a boil over high heat, then reduce heat to low. Cover pot, leaving lid slightly ajar, and simmer for 2 hours. Add 1 cup water and simmer for 1 hour more. Again add 1 cup water and simmer for 1 hour. Add ½ to 1 cup water and simmer for 1 to 1½ more hours, or until beans are soft enough to be easily crushed between the thumb and ring finger. Add seasonings and/or vegetables and proceed as in the previous recipe.

Combine cooked soybeans and rice, mixing well. Serve hot or chilled, topping each portion with a large dollop of the mayonnaise and, if desired, a sprinkling of parsley.

Soybeans in Tortillas   SERVES 4

2 tablespoons oil
3 onions, minced
1 cup soybeans, pressure cooked (p. 59), drained, and mashed
¼ cup soybean cooking liquid
2 tablespoons shoyu or 3 tablespoons red miso
Dash of tabasco sauce or ½ teaspoon cumin (optional)
12 tortillas, warmed and buttered
1½ cups grated cheese
1 tomato, chopped
1 cup shredded lettuce or ½ cup thinly-sliced leeks

Heat a skillet and coat with the oil. Add onions and sauté for 6 minutes, then remove from heat and mix with the next four ingredients. Spoon into a bowl and serve together with the tortillas and remaining condiments, each in separate bowls. Invite guests to spoon soybean-onion mixture in a line across the center of a tortilla and top with a little of the cheese, tomato, and lettuce. Roll up tortilla and eat like a taco.

Soybean Spreads and Dips   MAKES ABOUT 2 CUPS

1 cup cooked soybeans (p. 59), mashed or puréed
¼ to ½ cup diced onions, raw or sautéed; or 1 clove garlic, crushed
¼ to ½ cup nut butters, sesame butter, sunflower seeds, cheese, yogurt, diced apple, or raisins
1 to 2 tablespoons lemon juice, shoyu, or honey
Dash of pepper, cardamon, coriander, chili powder, or grated orange peel

Combine all ingredients in a bowl and mix together to make a thick spread.

Tangy Sesame-Soybean Spread   MAKES 2½ CUPS

1 cup cooked soybeans (p. 59), mashed or puréed
1/3 cup sesame butter
2 tablespoons lemon juice
1/3 cup diced raw onion
1 clove of garlic, crushed or minced
1 tablespoon honey
1 tablespoon shoyu or 1½ tablespoons red miso
Dash of pepper

Combine all ingredients and mash together until smooth.

Soybeans Pressure Cooked with Brown Rice   SERVES 4 TO 6

This simple preparation is our favorite for using whole soybeans and is also popular in many Zen temples. The combination of rice and beans increases the total available protein by over 30 percent.

2 cups brown rice
½ cup soybeans
2½ cups water

Combine rice and beans in a pressure cooker, rinse well, and drain. Add the 2½ cups water, cover, and bring to full pressure (15 pounds) over high heat. Reduce heat to low and simmer for 25 minutes. Set aside and allow to stand for 10 minutes as pressure returns to normal. Cool pot under running cold water and open. Mix gently with a wooden spoon to distribute soybeans evenly. Cover cooker with a dish towel until ready to serve. Delicious with Sesame Salt (p. 51), Tekka Miso (p. 44), Finger Lickin' Miso (p. 31), or Sweet Simmered Miso (p. 41).

VARIATION

*Soybeans with Brown Rice Porridge: To the ingredients for Brown Rice Porridge (p. 50) add ¼ cup water and ¼ cup dry soybeans soaked for at least 3 hours in water to cover and drained. Proceed as for porridge. If desired, stir in any or all of the following just before serving: 1 tablespoon shoyu, 1½ tablespoons red miso, 1 tablespoon butter, 1 tablespoon minced parsley.

Soybeans & Brown Rice Stroganoff   SERVES 4 TO 6

2¼ cups Pressure Cooked Soybeans Plus (p. 59; season with miso or shoyu)
1 cup brown rice, cooked (p. 50)
2 cups Tofu Mayonnaise (with garlic; p. 107)
2 to 3 tablespoons minced parsley (optional)

Soybean Salads

SERVES 6

Cooked, chilled soybeans make a nice addition to a wide variety of salads. Experiment with your favorites or try the following:

1 cup soybeans, pressure cooked (p. 59)
1 small apple, diced
6 tablespoons raisins
1 carrot, grated
1/3 onion, minced, rinsed, and pressed (p. 37)
¾ cucumber, cut into thin rounds
1 green pepper diced
5 tablespoons (tofu) mayonnaise (p. 107)
¼ teaspoon salt
Dash of pepper

Combine all ingredients in a salad bowl; mix lightly.

Soybean Soups

Cook 1 part soybeans with 3½ to 4 parts water as for Pressure Cooked Soybeans (p. 59). Add diced, sautéed vegetables and salt, shoyu, or miso. Simmer uncovered for 30 to 40 minutes. Season with a favorite spice.

For a tasty summertime dish, add cheese or yogurt to the cooked soup. Purée the mixture in a blender and serve chilled, topped with dollops of yogurt.

Soybean Casserole with Corn and Tomatoes

SERVES 4

1 cup cooked soybeans
1 cup cooked corn
1 cup cubed tomatoes
¼ teaspoon paprika
¾ teaspoon salt
½ teaspoon natural sugar
1 teaspoon minced onion
2 ounces grated cheese
¼ cup chopped peanuts

Preheat oven to 350°. Place the first seven ingredients in a lightly oiled casserole. Top with the cheese and peanuts, and bake for 45 minutes.

Soybeans and Sautéed Vegetables with Noodles

SERVES 4

2¼ cups Pressure Cooked Soybeans (p. 59; unseasoned), drained
3½ tablespoons shoyu
2 tablespoons oil
1 clove of garlic, minced or crushed
1½ cups shredded cabbage
1 cup thinly sliced leeks or onions
½ cup grated carrot
6½ ounces (buckwheat or Chinese) noodles, cooked (p. 50)
Dash of pepper

Combine cooked soybeans and 2 tablespoons shoyu. Mix well, mash one-half of the beans, and set aside. Heat a wok or large skillet and coat with the oil. Add garlic and sauté for 30 seconds. Add cabbage, onions, and carrot, sauté for 4 minutes more, and turn off heat. Add soybeans, mixing until evenly distributed. Stir in noodles, sprinkle with the remaining 1½ tablespoons of shoyu, and season with pepper; mix lightly. Delicious hot or chilled.

Soyburgers

MAKES 8

Now increasingly available at natural food stores, soyburgers are also easily prepared at home; we like to make a large batch and freeze the leftovers. The addition of brown rice boosts the protein content. We find that deep-frying gives the finest flavor and texture, although slow broiling or pan-frying also give good results.

2¼ cups Pressure Cooked Soybeans (p. 59; unseasoned), drained and mashed
1¼ cups cooked Brown Rice (p. 50)
½ onion, diced
½ cup grated carrot
2 cups bread crumbs or bread crumb flakes; or substitute up to ½ cup (toasted) wheat germ or pre-cooked rolled oats
1 egg, lightly beaten
1 clove of garlic, minced or crushed
2 tablespoons minced parsley
2½ tablespoons shoyu or 3½ tablespoons red miso
¾ teaspoon curry powder or ¼ teaspoon ground dill seeds
Dash of pepper
Oil for deep-frying

Combine all ingredients, mixing well until mixture has the consistency of hamburger; shape into patties. Heat the oil to 350° in a wok, skillet, or deep-fryer. Drop in patties and deep-fry until golden brown (p. 130); drain well. Serve hot or cold as for Ganmo Burgers (p. 188). Also delicious topped with Tofu Mayonnaise (p. 107), fried with eggs and grated cheese, crumbled and used as a *taco* filling, or added to casseroles.

VARIATION:

*Soy "Meatballs": Shape mixture into 1-inch balls and deep-fry. Use in place of tofu in Stir-fried Noodles (p. 138) or Tofu Italian Meatballs (p. 123).

Deep-fried Soybeans

MAKES 4 CUPS

2 cups soybeans, soaked overnight in water and drained
Oil for deep-frying
Salt, onion salt, or garlic salt

Spread the beans out on a baking sheet and place in a 200° oven for 5 to 10 minutes until beans are dry. Heat oil to 350° in a wok, skillet, or deep-fryer. Deep-fry beans ½ cup at a time for 6 to 8 minutes, or until crisp and golden brown (p. 130). Drain beans on absorbent paper, season with salt, and serve immediately. Stored in an airtight jar, deep-fried soybeans keep quite well.

Curried Soy Fritters

SERVES 6

1 cup soybeans, cooked (p. 59) and drained
¾ cup soybean cooking liquid
1 clove of garlic, crushed or minced
1 onion, minced
1 cup (whole-wheat) flour
1½ teaspoons salt or 3 tablespoons red miso
1½ teaspoons curry powder
2 eggs, lightly beaten; or 2 teaspoons baking powder
Dash of pepper
Oil for deep-frying
Tofu Mayonnaise (with onion or curry; p. 107), Tofu Tartare
    Sauce (p. 109), Pineapple Sweet & Sour Sauce (p. 166), or
    Ketchup-Worcestershire Sauce (p. 49)

Mash three-fourths of the soybeans, leaving the remainder whole. Combine with the next eight ingredients, mixing well, to form a very thick batter. Heat oil to 350° in a wok, skillet, or deep-fryer. Drop in batter by large spoonfuls and deep-fry until golden brown (p. 130). Drain well on absorbent paper; serve immediately, accompanied by the mayonnaise or sauce.

Deep-fried Soy Brittle

SERVES 3 OR 4

¼ cup dry soybeans, soaked in water to cover for 1 hour,
    drained in a colander and allowed to stand overnight
Batter: Prepare as for Tempura Batter (p. 134)
    2 tablespoons (whole-wheat) flour
    4 teaspoons arrowroot, cornstarch, or kuzu
    2 teaspoons natural sugar
    3 tablespoons water
    1/8 teaspoon salt
    Dash of cinnamon (optional)
Oil for deep-frying

Combine drained beans and batter in a large bowl; mix lightly. Heat oil to 350° in a wok, skillet, or deep-fryer. Spoon several tablespoons of the bean-batter mixture onto a (wooden) spatula, then smooth to form a thin layer. Using chopsticks or a second spatula, slide the beans-and-batter mixture into the hot oil so that it forms a thin patty in the oil. Deep-fry for about 8 minutes until golden brown (p. 130). Drain well. Serve as hors d'oeuvre.

Soybean & Miso Garnish

MAKES 1 CUP

2 tablespoons sesame oil
1 cup cooked soybeans (p. 59), well drained
2 tablespoons red, barley, or Hatcho miso
½ teaspoon grated gingerroot
Dash of 7-spice red pepper (optional)

Heat a skillet or wok and coat with the oil. Add soybeans and sauté for 2 or 3 minutes. Reduce heat to low, add remaining ingredients, and sauté for 2 minutes more. Allow to cool to room temperature. Serve as a garnish or seasoning for Brown Rice or Rice Porridge.

Deep-fried Soybean Croquettes

Prepare Pressure Cooked Soybeans Plus (p. 59). Mash together with sautéed onion and carrot (diced), and shape the mixture into patties. Dust patties with flour, dip into beaten egg, and roll in bread crumbs. Deep-fry until golden brown.

Budomame (Sweet Soybeans)

12 SERVINGS

This and the following preparations are often sold in Japanese delicatessens and served in very small portions as desserts or hors d'oeuvre. Budomame means literally "grape soybeans," perhaps because of the rich, sweet flavor.

1 cup soybeans, rinsed and drained
7 cups water
4 to 6 tablespoons natural sugar
2 teaspoons shoyu or ½ teaspoon salt

Combine soybeans, 5 cups water, and two-thirds of the sugar; soak overnight. Bring to a boil, reduce heat to low, and simmer covered for 2 hours. Add 1½ cups water and simmer for 1 hour more. Add ½ cup water, the remaining sugar and the shoyu, and simmer for 50 minutes more, or until most of the liquid has been absorbed or evaporated. Cool before serving as a dessert or side dish.

OTHER SOYBEAN DELICATESSEN PREPARATIONS

*Kombu Mame: Add 2 tablespoons dried kombu (cut into strips 2½ inches long and ¼ inch wide) together with the shoyu.
*Kuro Mame: Soak black soybeans overnight in lightly salted water. Simmer (without draining) as above. Add one-half of sugar and simmer for 10 minutes. Add remaining sugar (omitting shoyu), season with salt and finish cooking as above. A favorite New Year's preparation.
*Gomoku Mame: Simmer soybeans in water seasoned with equal parts shoyu and sugar until beans are tender. Add small amounts of diced carrots, burdock root, lotus root, kombu, and konnyaku, and simmer for 30 minutes more.

ROASTED SOYBEANS
(Iri-mame)

Many delicious varieties of roasted soybeans or soy nuts are now available in the West in natural food and health food stores. Dry-roasted varieties contain a remarkable 47 percent protein. (By comparison peanuts contain only 27 percent protein and almonds and cashews only 19 percent.) They are usually lightly salted and have a nut-like flavor and crunchy crisp texture. Oil-roasted varieties are available salted or unsalted with plain, garlic, or barbeque flavors, and contain 37 percent protein.

Roasted soybeans can be eaten like peanuts as a snack, or used to add a crunchy texture and nutlike flavor to a wide variety of salads, sauces, casseroles, and miso preparations. In the West roasted soybeans are also used in health food "candy" such as soy honey- or nut bars. In their ground form, they are used in commercial soy spreads.

In Japan, these are the "beans of good fortune" enjoyed on the first day of the lunar spring. Roasted beans covered with multiple coatings of sugar, starch, and *nori* are sold commercially as *Mishima Mame* and served as a sweet snack. Green soybeans, roasted with salt until they have a crunchy texture and greenish-beige color, are sold as *Irori Mame*.

Homemade Roasted Soybeans   MAKES 3 CUPS

3 cups whole dry soybeans, rinsed and soaked for 5 to 6 hours

Drain beans well, then spread between layers of dry towelling for 1 hour. Transfer to large unoiled cookie tins or baking pans and spread 1 layer thick over the surface of pans. Place in an unheated oven and roast at 200° to 250° for 2 to 2½ hours, or until beans are light brown. Shake pans once every 15 minutes for the first hour, then every 30 minutes thereafter. Do not allow beans—which are inside tan hulls—to turn dark brown. While beans are still slightly soft, remove from oven, salt lightly, and set aside to cool until crunchy. Serve as is, like nuts, or use to make Roasted Soy Grits (see below).

For a salty variety, soak the beans in a mixture of 4 cups water and 2 tablespoons salt before roasting.

In Japan, roasted soybeans are prepared on a community scale in a large screen basket held over a strong flame and shaken like popcorn for about 40 minutes. The flame is then reduced to low and the beans cooked without shaking for 5 to 7 minutes until golden brown.

Roasted Soy Grits

Prepare either Roasted or Deep-fried Soybeans. Place in a blender and chop at low speed for about 30 seconds until chunky. (Do not grind to a meal or powder.) Use like nuts in casseroles, salads, soups, granola, cooked vegetables, or grain dishes.

FRESH GREEN SOYBEANS
(Edamame)

Many Westerners who have lived or traveled in East Asia find it remarkable that fresh green soybeans have not yet become a favorite summertime vegetable in the West—as they are in Japan. The green beans, simmered in the pod until tender, lightly salted, and then cooled are served as a delicious hors d'oeuvre—often with sake or beer—or as part of a meal. From mid-June until October, the beans' brilliant emerald color graces the dining tables of restaurants and private homes throughout Japan.

Immediately after soybean plants are uprooted, the dirt is shaken from the roots, most of the leaves are removed, and about 15 pod-bearing plants, each approximately 2½ feet long, are tied into bundles. About 10 to 12 soybean pods are clustered along the stalk of each plant, and a single 3-inch pod usually contains 3 green soybeans. The plants are taken to markets where they are sold by the bunch. After boiling the beans in the pods, the housewife may use the stems as fuel.

Highly digestible and containing over 12 percent protein, a typical 3½ ounce serving of green soybeans supplies more than 40 percent of an adult's daily protein requirement. They also contain as much vitamin C as oranges, and are rich in vitamin B_1. Although best served fresh and in season, green soybeans may also be frozen or canned like green peas; in the West they are generally available in the latter form. In Japan, cooked green soybeans (*hitashi mame*) are now available packaged in a sausage-shaped plastic container together with a little of the cooking liquid.

Green Soybean Hors D'oeuvre

SERVES 2

Like potato chips, these little devils are positively addicting.

2 cups green soybeans (in pods)
4 cups water
½ teaspoon salt

Combine soybeans and 4 cups water in a large pot and bring to a boil over high heat. Reduce heat to low and simmer for 15 to 20 minutes, or until pods just begin to open. Drain, sprinkle beans with salt, and allow to cool. Serve in the pods.

Or, after draining, combine beans in a small saucepan with ¼ cup water and 2 tablespoons each shoyu and natural sugar. Simmer for about 20 minutes, stirring occasionally. Drain and allow to cool. If desired, serve Japanese-style in a small (bamboo) basket or colander accompanied by cold drinks or hot tea.

Hot Buttered Soybeans

SERVES 3 TO 4

1 pound fresh green soybeans (in pods)
½ teaspoon salt
Butter

To shell beans, cover with boiling water and allow to stand for 5 minutes. Drain and cool briefly. Break pods crosswise and squeeze out beans (yielding about 1½ cups).

Bring 1 cup water to a boil in a small saucepan. Add beans and salt and return to the boil, then cover and simmer for 15 to 20 minutes. Drain well and serve hot (like lima beans or green peas) topped with butter. Salt lightly if desired.

Prepared this way, green soybeans also make an excellent addition to salads.

Green Soybeans with Brown Rice

Substitute 1 to 1½ cups fresh, shelled green soybeans for the dry soybeans in Soybeans Pressure Cooked with Brown Rice (p. 60). Serve as in the basic recipe or use as a filling for Agé Pouches (p. 192) or Inari-zushi Pouches (p. 194).

To prepare *Aomame Meshi*, combine in a heavy pot the above shelled green soybeans and rice plus 3½ cups water, a 4-inch square of *kombu*, and ½ teaspoon salt. Allow to stand overnight, then bring water to a boil and remove *kombu*. Cook as for Brown Rice (p. 50). For best flavor, allow to stand for several hours before serving.

Green Soybean Tempura

Shell, then parboil the beans until just tender. Stir into tempura batter (p. 134); deep-fry and serve as for Kaki-agé (p. 136).

Sweet Emerald Bean Paste *(Jinda)*

Shell and parboil green soybeans, then grind in a *suribachi* or purée in a blender. Combine 2 parts beans with 1 part sugar or honey. Use like *an*—a sweetened paste usually made with adzuki beans—as a filling for various *mochi* treats or cupcakes.

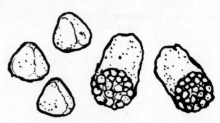

KINAKO
(Roasted Full-Fat Soy Flour)

Kinako is a tan or beige flour made by grinding whole roasted soybeans. It has a nutty flavor and fragrance and contains over 38 percent protein. Many of Japan's most popular confections are dusted with a light coating of sweetened kinako. These confections usually consist of a grain such as *mochi* (pounded glutinous rice), or steamed, pounded millet filled with *an* (sweetened adzuki bean paste). In the Kyoto area alone more than twelve popular confections are prepared with a covering of sweetened kinako. In a number of Japanese health-food treats (such as *kinako amé, gokabo, kokusen,* and *kankanbo*) kinako serves at the main ingredient; it is mixed with *mizuame* to give a chewy taffy-like texture and rich sweetness. We feel that kinako itself and a number of the following preparations—especially Kinako Butter, Kinako Candy, and Kinako Coffee—could be produced in cottage industries and sold commercially with excellent results.

A delicious and inexpensive source of high-quality protein, kinako is generally sold in ¼-pound bags and used in small quantities.

Homemade Kinako

MAKES ½ CUP

¾ cup whole dry soybeans

Place the beans in a large heavy skillet and roast over low heat, stirring constantly, for about 20 minutes, or until beans are light brown and slightly fragrant. Grind to a fine powder using a blender or hand mill. Sift through a fine mesh strainer to remove particles of the soybean hulls. The resulting kinako should be light yellowish beige and have a subtly sweet, fragrant aroma.

For commercial kinako, 5 to 10 gallons of unsoaked, whole soybeans are turned in a large (4-foot-long, 18-inch-diameter) rotating screen drum over an open fire for 30 to 40 minutes. When browned, and while still warm, they are ground to a flour or powder between slowly-turning stone wheels.

Kinako Butter

MAKES ½ CUP

This preparation tastes like a cross between sesame and peanut butter but is less expensive and higher in protein than both.

2½ tablespoons oil or butter
½ cup kinako
1 teaspoon red miso or shoyu; or ¼ teaspoon salt
2 to 3 teaspoons honey
1½ to 2 tablespoons water

Heat the oil in a skillet, then turn off heat. Add remaining ingredients, mixing until smooth. Delicious on crackers, canapés, or fresh vegetable slices. Covered and refrigerated, unused portions will last indefinitely.

Creamy Kinako Butter

MAKES ½ CUP

This tasty, high-protein preparation is now sold in natural food stores in Japan.

½ cup kinako
¼ cup butter or soybean margarine
1 to 2 teaspoons honey
Dash of cinnamon

Combine all ingredients, mixing well. Serve as a spread on toast or sandwiches.

Kinako-Peanut-Sesame Spread

MAKES 1 CUP

¼ cup kinako
2½ tablespoons peanut butter
¼ cup sesame butter
¼ cup water
1 tablespoon oil
1 tablespoon red miso or ½ teaspoon salt
½ clove garlic, crushed (optional)
1 tablespoon minced onion

Combine all ingredients in a small bowl; mix well. For best flavor, cover and refrigerate overnight. Use like any nut butter. Try it as a sandwich spread with tomatoes, cucumbers, and thinly sliced tofu (regular or deep-fried).

Apple-Cucumber Salad with Kinako Dressing

SERVES 2

½ apple, cut into thin wedges
½ cucumber, sliced into thin rounds
Dressing:
    1 tablespoon Kinako Butter (above)
    1½ tablespoons lemon juice
    2½ teaspoons honey

Combine all ingredients in a bowl and mix gently.

Kinako in Brown Sauces and Roux

Add 1 to 2 tablespoons (lightly roasted) kinako for every 2 tablespoons (whole-wheat) flour. While contributing a nut-like toasted flavor and complementary soy protein, kinako does not further thicken sauces since it contains almost no gluten.

Kinako in Breads and Muffins

Use kinako like soy flour, adding 10 to 15 percent to your favorite baked goods in order to boost the protein content by up to 32 percent, and to give a richness of flavor. Kinako Butter (above) works well as a filling for rolled loaves and pastries.

Sweetened Kinako

MAKES ¼ CUP

This preparation is used as a coating for many Japanese treats.

3 tablespoons kinako
1½ to 2 tablespoons natural sugar
Dash of salt

Combine all ingredients, mixing thoroughly. Place in a shallow bowl in which the treats may be rolled or dusted.

Abekawa Mochi

SERVES 3

This preparation is the most popular way of serving kinako in Japan.

6 cakes of *mochi* (each about 3 by 2 by ½ inch thick)
¼ cup Sweetened Kinako (see above)

Broil or bake *mochi* in a medium oven (or on a grill over a fire) until each cake swells to twice its original size and is crisp and nicely browned. Dip cakes immediately into very hot water, then roll in the kinako. Serve hot or cold as a dessert.

For a richer flavor, reduce the amount of sugar in the kinako mixture and omit the salt. Dip hot *mochi* into shoyu rather than water before rolling in kinako.

Chinese-style Kinako & Peanut Butter Balls

MAKES 12

These sweet, almost crumbly delicacies are a favorite in China where they are sold commercially.

½ cup kinako
2 tablespoons peanut butter
2 to 3 teaspoons natural sugar
1 teaspoon honey
Dash of salt

Combine all ingredients and shape into small balls.

Kinako Candy
(Kinako Amé or Genkotsu Amé)

MAKES 16

This rich, chewy treat is a favorite throughout Japan. Watch out!

1 cup kinako, approximately
2 tablespoons water
3 tablespoons *mizuame* (millet or barley malt), or substitute honey and reduce the amount of water above by ½ tablespoon
1 tablespoon natural sugar

Place ¾ cup kinako in a heatproof bowl. Combine remaining ingredients in a small saucepan and simmer over low heat, stirring constantly, for about 7 minutes, or until thick. Pour contents of pan into kinako, mix well and knead until firm, adding more kinako if necessary. Roll out onto a breadboard dusted with 2 tablespoons of kinako and continue kneading until dough is very stiff. Roll out into a long cylinder ¾ inch in diameter, and cut into ¾-inch lengths. For best flavor and a chewier texture, chill overnight.

For variety, try adding 2 tablespoons ground roasted sesame seeds (or carob) and a pinch of salt to the dough just before kneading.

VARIATIONS

Kokusen and Kankanbo: Prepare as above, but use slightly less water and more sugar, and add ground sesame seeds for *kokusen:* Roll out and cut to form small cylinders the size of cigarettes. Dry or bake in a slow oven until brittle.

Gokabo: Prepare dough as for Kinako Candy using *mizuame* but add 1 tablespoon water. Allow to cool, then roll out on a bread board (well-floured with kinako) to form a thin 6- by 8-inch rectangular sheet. Combine 2/3 cup puffed rice, rice crispies, or minced popcorn with 2 tablespoons softened *mizuame* or honey, mix well, then sprinkle in an even layer over kinako sheet. Roll up sheet from one side to form a compact cylinder, then gently roll back and forth under palms of hands on bread board until cylinder doubles in length and is reduced to 1 inch diameter. Cut crosswise into 1½-inch lengths, dust pieces liberally with kinako, and chill briefly before serving.

Kinako Coffee

SERVES 4

Caffeine-free, easy to prepare, and rich in protein, this hearty brew, with its roasted nutlike aroma, will surprise and delight even the staunchest coffee lover.

½ cup kinako, or substitute full-fat soy flour
3 cups (hot) water

Roast kinako over low heat in a heavy, dry skillet, stirring constantly for 3 to 4 minutes, or until dark brown and fragrant. Mix in water, bring to a boil, and simmer for 2 minutes. Filter through a fine-mesh strainer, cloth, or coffee filter. Serve hot or chilled, adding rich soymilk (or cream) and sugar (or a pinch of salt) to taste. Also delicious with malt or carob.

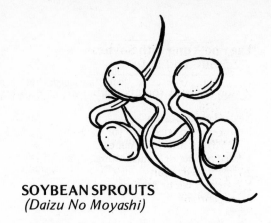

SOYBEAN SPROUTS
(Daizu No Moyashi)

One of the world's finest diet foods, soybean sprouts contain less calories per gram of protein than any other known vegetable food. Although mung bean sprouts are the most popular both in the West and in East Asia, soybean sprouts are inexpensive, tasty, and easy to prepare at home. Most contain both the bright yellow soybean and the sprout root which will grow to a length of 3 to 5 inches in 5 to 7 days. Soybean sprouts may be served as a green vegetable throughout the year either parboiled in fresh salads (where they serve as a good source of vitamin C) or in soups, sautéed, or baked dishes.

Homemade Soybean Sprouts

MAKES 3 TO 6 CUPS

1 to 1½ cups dry soybeans

Prepare a sprouter by making small holes in the bottom of a 10- to 12-inch-deep plastic container, milk carton, or coffee can. Pour in soybeans to a depth of at least 2 inches, then place sprouter in a slightly larger pot and fill with water to more than cover beans. Cover pot and allow beans to soak for 4 hours (no longer). Lift out sprouter and drain beans being careful not to mix or agitate them. Cover sprouter and place in a dark place at 72°F. Rinse beans 3 to 4 times daily by sprinkling with water, again taking care not to mix them. Repeat for 5 days or until sprouts are about 4 inches long. Transfer sprouts to a large pot and rinse with plenty of water; pour off loose hulls and remove unsprouted beans. Refrigerate unused sprouts in a sealed container.

Soybean Sprout Salad with Tofu

SERVES 3

2 cups soybeans sprouts, parboiled for 6 to 8 minutes and well drained
½ cup grated carrot
1 cucumber, thinly sliced
5 ounces deep-fried tofu (or 12 ounces regular tofu, pressed; p. 96), cut into bite-sized cubes
Dressing:
  2 tablespoons vinegar
  2 tablespoons sesame oil
  1½ tablespoons shoyu
  Dash of 7-spice red pepper or tabasco sauce

Combine the first four ingredients in a salad bowl. Add dressing and toss lightly. Also tasty with French dressing.

Egg Foo Yung with Soybean Sprouts and Tofu

SERVES 4

2 cups soybean sprouts, parboiled for 4 to 6 minutes and drained
6 eggs, lightly beaten
5 ounces deep-fried tofu (or 12 ounces regular tofu, pressed; p. 96) cut into small cubes
1 green pepper or 2 mushrooms, thinly sliced
½ cup minced onion
½ teaspoon salt or 2 teaspoons soy sauce
8 teaspoons oil
Pepper

Combine the first six ingredients, mixing well. Heat 2 teaspoons oil in a heavy skillet or wok. Pour in one-fourth of the egg-tofu mixture to form a thin omelet. Cook for about 2½ minutes on each side until nicely browned. Repeat until all ingredients have been used. Serve hot, topped with a sprinkling of soy sauce and pepper. Or top with Ankake or Gingerroot Sauce (p. 49). A delicious accompaniment for brown rice.

For variety, substitute ½ cup firmly packed okara for the tofu.

Chop Suey or Chow Mein with Soybean Sprouts and Tofu

SERVES 2 OR 3

8 teaspoons butter
12 ounces tofu, diced
1 cup thinly sliced celery pieces
1 small onion, thinly sliced
2/3 cup water or stock
2/3 teaspoon cornstarch, dissolved in 2 teaspoons water
1 cup soybean sprouts
2 tablespoons soy sauce

Melt 4 teaspoons butter in a skillet. Add tofu and fry, stirring occasionally, for 5 minutes, or until tofu is nicely browned, then transfer tofu to a separate container.

Melt remaining 4 teaspoons butter in the skillet. Add celery and onion and sauté for 2 to 3 minutes. Add cooked tofu and water, bring to a boil, and simmer for 5 minutes. Stir in the dissolved cornstarch, sprouts, and soy sauce. Return to the boil and simmer for 2 to 3 minutes. Serve hot as is, or over steamed rice. For *Chow Mein*, serve over fried Chinese noodles.

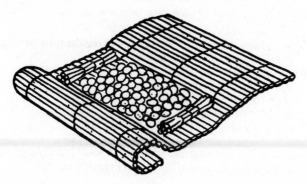

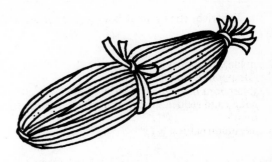

Fig. 12. Natto wrapped in rice straw

NATTO
(Sticky Fermented Whole Soybeans)

Natto are prepared (commercially or at home) by steaming soaked soybeans until they are soft, innoculating the warm (104°) beans with the bacteria *Bacillus natto*, and then allowing them to ferment for 15 to 24 hours in a humid environment at about 104°. The dark-brown beans have a fairly strong and unusual aroma and flavor, and a sticky, slightly slippery surface texture. When lifted from the bowl with chopsticks (fig. 13), like some varieties of melted cheese, they form gossamer-like threads. Although most whole soybeans are somewhat difficult to digest, natto are highly digestible because the beans' complex protein molecules have been broken down by the bacteria during fermentation. A whole, natural food, natto contain 16.5 percent protein and are rich in vitamins B_2, B_{12}, and iron. In Japan and in Japanese grocery stores in the West, natto are sold in small (3 to 4 ounce) packages wrapped in straw, from which they traditionally received bacteria for fermentation. Generally served as a topping for rice, natto are also used in miso soups and *Aemono*-dressings or sautéed with vegetables. In the provinces, they are mixed with a little sugar and served as an hors d'oeuvre. About 50,000 tons of soybeans are made into natto each year in Japan, about one-fourth the amount used to make either miso or shoyu.

Natto Topping For Brown Rice

SERVES 2

½ cup natto (1 package)
1½ tablespoons thinly-sliced leeks; or minced onions or *daikon* leaves
1½ tablespoons bonita flakes
¼ to ½ teaspoon hot mustard
1½ tablespoons powdered green *nori*, or crumbled toasted *nori* (optional)
1½ tablespoons shoyu or 7 teaspoons red miso

Combine the first five ingredients, mixing with chopsticks for about 1 minute until cohesiveness develops. Stir in shoyu and serve as a topping for hot rice, rice gruel, or crackers.

Natto are often mixed with only shoyu or with sugar and powdered green *nori* when served over rice.

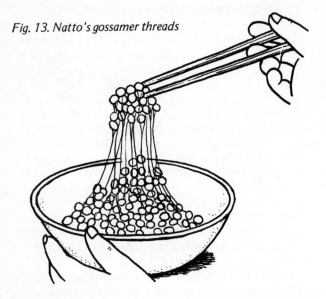

Fig. 13. Natto's gossamer threads

Natto Miso Soup

SERVES 2 OR 3

1¼ cups dashi (p. 39), stock, or water
2 (Chinese) cabbage leaves, cut lengthwise into halves, then crosswise into 1½-inch-wide strips
1 tablespoon red, barley, or Hatcho miso
2 tablespoons sweet white miso
½ cup natto
¼ cup thin rounds of leek or scallion
Dash of 7-spice red pepper

Bring dashi to a boil in a saucepan. Add Chinese cabbage, cover, and simmer for 2 to 3 minutes. Add miso creamed in a little of the hot broth. Add natto and return just to the boil. Sprinkle on leeks and remove from heat. Serve seasoned with a sprinkling of the red pepper.

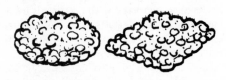

TEMPEH
(Fermented Soybean Cakes)

These cakes of cooked soybeans, bound together by a fragrant, white mycelium of *Rhizopus* mold, have a delectable flavor: fried or deep-fried, they taste remarkably like fried chicken or veal cutlets. Rich in protein (18.3% fresh or 48.7% dried), tempeh is also highly digestible, and *Rhizopus* serves as an effective deactivator of trypsin inhibitor (p. 70). Like other fermented soy products (miso, shoyu, natto) and sea vegetables, tempeh is one of only a few non-meat sources of vitamin B_{12}.

For centuries prepared daily on a cottage scale throughout Indonesia (where it is a basic food for millions of people and makes use of more than 50 percent of the country's soybean crop), tempeh is also an important staple in New Guinea and Surinam, and is eaten on a small scale in Malaysia and Holland. Its adaptability to household industries and its low cost should make it, like tofu, a food of worldwide commercial interest during the coming decades.

Before you begin, you will need to obtain tempeh starter, which is available from Farm Foods, 156 Drakes Lane, Summertown, TN 38483 or from USDA/NRRC, 1815 North University Street, Peoria, II 61604.

For a more detailed, illustrated description of making tempeh at home and hundreds of delicious recipes, see *The Book of Tempeh*, available from The Soyfoods Center.

Homemade Soy Tempeh
MAKES 30 OUNCES

2½ cups whole dry soybeans, washed and drained
18 to 20 cups water
1½ tablespoons (distilled white) vinegar
1 teaspoon tempeh starter

1. **Precook Soybeans:** Combine soybeans and 7½ cups water in a large cooking pot, cover, and bring just to a boil. Remove from heat and allow to stand, covered, at room temperature, for 8 to 16 hours. (Or simmer for 20 minutes and allow to stand for 1 hour.)

2. **Dehull Soybeans:** Carefully pour off water from pot and discard. Now rub or squeeze beans vigorously with hands for 3 to 4 minutes to remove hulls. Fill pot with water, stir gently in a circle to cause hulls to rise, then pour off water and hulls. Repeat until hulls are removed.

3. **Cook Soybeans:** Add 10 cups (hot) water and the vinegar to the drained beans in the cooking pot. Bring to a boil and cook, uncovered, at an active boil for 45 minutes.

4. **Dry and Inoculate Cooked Soybeans:** Drain beans in a colander or strainer for several minutes, then shake well to expel moisture. Line beans over toweling in an even layer, and allow to cool for 20 to 30 minutes, to body temperature. Transfer beans to a clean, large mixing bowl, sprinkle on tempeh starter, and mix well, for 2 minutes.

5. **Put Soybeans in Incubation Container:** Perforate two 7-by-8-inch plastic Ziploc bags with an ice pick over their entire surface at ½-inch intervals. Spoon half the inoculated soybeans into each bag, seal mouth, place on a flat surface, and press upper surface of bag with palm of hand to distribute beans in a uniform layer about ¾ inch thick.

6. **Incubate:** Place tempeh containers on a rack in a warm place (such as an oven with the door ajar or over a hot water heater) at about 86 to 88° F for 22 to 26 hours. Check temperature occasionally, especially toward the end of the fermentation, when it may rise rapidly. Tempeh is done when the beans are bound into a firm, compact cake by a dense, uniform, white mycelium, which has a pleasant, clean, mushroomy aroma. Gray or black spots, indicating sporulation, are not harmful if the smell is fresh and clean.

The tempeh is now ready to cook.

*Deep-fried or Fried: Deep-fry cakes (or pan-fry on both sides) until crisp and golden brown. Serve topped with shoyu, ketchup, Worcestershire, or any of the following Basic Sauces (pp. 48 to 49): Onion, Mushroom, Sweet & Sour, Ketchup-Worcestershire, or Tomato & Cheese. Also delicious in sandwiches and soups.

*Tempeh Goreng (*Savory Cutlets*): Score both surfaces of 3 fresh tempeh cakes to a depth of 1/8 inch. Combine 3 tablespoons water, ½ teaspoon salt, ½ clove of crushed garlic, and ¼ teaspoon coriander. Add tempeh, marinate for 5 minutes, and drain well. Deep-fry in (coconut) oil (p. 130). Serve as an accompaniment for rice dishes, topped with red-pepper sauce (*sambal*) if desired.

*Tempeh Kemul (*Crisp Chips*): Cut 3 tempeh cakes horizontally into paper-thin slices; sun-dry for 5 minutes if desired. Combine 6 tablespoons (rice) flour, 1 clove of crushed garlic, ¾ teaspoon salt, and ¼ teaspoon coriander. Mix in enough (coconut) milk to form a fairly thin batter, then add tempeh slices and allow to stand briefly. Deep-fry until crisp, and serve like potato chips. For variety use a well-salted tempura batter.

*Tempeh Bacham (*Rich Fillets*): Combine in a skillet ¼ grated onion, ¾ teaspoon salt, 3 to 4 tablespoons brown sugar, and 1¼ cups water. Add 3 tempeh cakes (cut crosswise into fourths), bring to a boil, and simmer until all liquid has evaporated. Deep-fry cakes and serve as for Tempeh Goreng.

*In Soups: Add diced fresh tempeh to soups and simmer for 30 minutes. Season with salt, miso, or shoyu.

*Baked or Roasted: Bake at 350° for about 20 minutes, or until nicely browned and fragrant. If desired, use as the basis for a pizza-type preparation, or serve topped with any of the sauces mentioned above.

HAMANATTO AND DAITOKUJINATTO
(Raisin-like Natto)

Hamanatto is a unique variety of natto soybeans which looks like raisins except that its surface has a grayish black tinge and is smooth and soft. Hamanatto beans have a pleasant, somewhat salty flavor resembling that of mellow Hatcho miso. Sprinkled over rice or rice gruel, served as an hors d'oeuvre with green tea, or cooked with vegetables as a seasoning, they add zest to bland dishes. A similar type of natto, called *Daitokuji natto*, is prepared in Daitokuji temple in Kyoto. Hamanatto are also widely enjoyed in China where they are known as *toushih*.

MODERN WESTERN SOYBEAN FOODS

This section would be incomplete without a brief description of the following foods. Of particular importance is soy flour which now appears in a large number of recipes for baked goods in Western-style cookbooks. The contrast between the character of most of these highly refined foods and the traditional East Asian products described above serves to emphasize the strikingly different roles that soybean foods play in the East as compared with the West.

Natural Soy Flour: This full-fat product, containing 35 to 40 percent protein and 20 percent natural oils, makes an excellent addition to breads, pasta, and pastries. It is used in amounts of about 10 to 15 percent of the total flour content.

Soy Granules: Containing 50 percent protein, this newly developed product is available at most health food stores. Easy to use, granules can be added to soups, stews, casseroles, or even puréed beverages.

Defatted Soy Flour and Grits: Containing about 50 to 52 percent protein, these foods are left over after the oil is extracted from whole crushed soybeans using hexane solvent. The least expensive source of soy protein in the West, they are now widely used in bakery products, processed and simulated meats, breakfast cereals, dietary and infant foods, and confections.

Soy Protein Concentrates: Containing 70 percent protein (on a moisture-free basis), these refined products cost only about 10 percent more than flour and grits and are used in processed meats, breakfast cereals, and infant foods.

Soy Protein Isolates: Containing 90 to 98 percent protein (on a moisture free basis), these products are prepared like concentrates from defatted flakes and flours. Resembling a white powder with a bland flavor, they cost about twice as much as flour or grits. First widely used in meat analogs, sausages, and canned meats as binding agents, they are now also employed to make simulated dairy products such as coffee creams, whipped toppings, and frozen desserts (imitation ice cream). Now sold as Natural Soy Protein in 1-pound bags at many health food stores.

Spun Protein Fibers: These are made by dissolving or suspending protein isolates in alkalai, then extruding them through spinnerettes into an acid-salt bath to form tiny monofilaments. Combined with ingredients such as wheat gluten, egg albumen, fats, flavoring, and coloring agents, they are formed into simulated meat items.

Textured Vegetable Protein: TVP is made from low-cost soy flour continually extruded under heat and pressure to form small chunks. When hydrated, these have a chewy texture and are capable of carrying a variety of colors and flavors. Considerably less expensive than both isolates and spun protein fibers, TVP is now becoming widely used as an extender in ground or simulated meats, and in infant foods.

Soy Oil Products: Although it contains no protein, refined soy oil is rich in polyunsaturates and linoleic acid, and low in cost. In the U.S. over 2½ billion pounds are produced yearly and used as cooking or salad oils, or in salad dressings. Another 4 billion pounds are hydrogenated to make margarine and vegetable shortenings.

5

Gô (Fresh Soy Puree)

Gô is a thick white purée of well-soaked un-cooked soybeans. It is more full-bodied in texture than whipped cream, but not as thick as cream cheese. It is interesting to note that the Japanese character for gô is also used to represent the verb *kureru* meaning "to give." This is appropriate, since gô is the source of each of the various tofu products (fig. 14); it is the first transformation of whole soybeans in the alchemy of tofu-making. As in an archetypal image from the Chinese *Book of Changes,* the soft beans, heaped high, pass downward between heavy granite millstones. Turning slowly, the whispering stones merge the many bright-yellow soybeans into cream-white, smooth gô, which flows over the sides of the lower, stationary stone and is caught in a large cedar tub (as shown on the cover illustration of this book). Nearby, in a massive black cauldron, boiling water awaits with the benediction of fire.

Gô is the only stage in the tofu making process where the entire soybean is still together; in the next step, the gô will be separated into *okara* and soymilk. Thus by using gô in cooking, we can enjoy the full range of the soybean's nutrients in their natural balance and completeness.

By soaking and grinding the soybean into gô, we greatly reduce the amount of time and fuel required for its thorough cooking, just as it is quicker and more economical to cook rolled- rather than whole-grain oats. Moreover, unlike most other grains and pulses, soybeans contain a substance called "trypsin inhibitor" (TI), which obstructs the func-

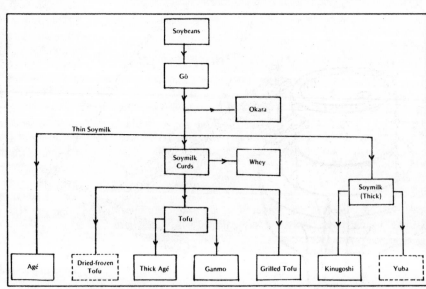

Fig. 14.
Gô as the Source of all Tofu Products

70

Fig. 15. *Hand-turned grinding stones*

Fig. 16. *Push-pull grinding stones*

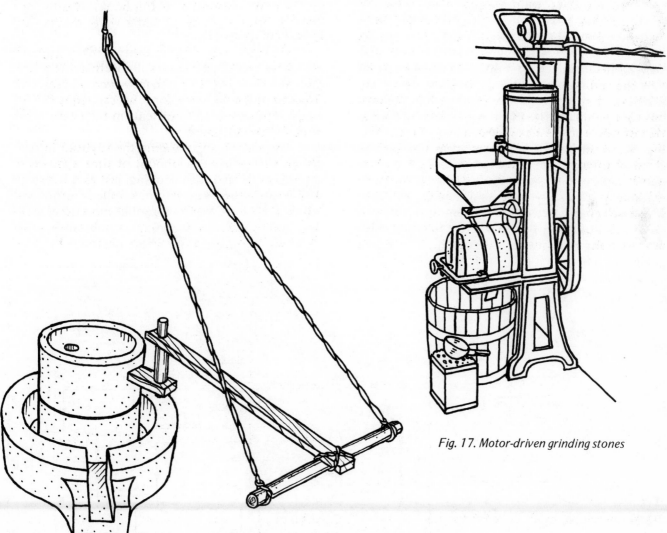

Fig. 17. *Motor-driven grinding stones*

tioning of the pancreas-secreted trypsin enzyme essential for the digestion of protein and the maintenance of proper growth. TI can—and must—be inactivated by cooking. Laboratory tests show that 70 to 80 percent of all TI present in the soybean must be destroyed if the body is to make use of the full array of nutrients in the bean. They also show that soaking and grinding whole soybeans greatly reduces the cooking time to attain this level of inactivation. Nutritionists recommend that well-soaked whole soybeans be simmered for four to six hours or pressure cooked (at 15 pounds) for 20 to 30 minutes. Gô, however, need be simmered for only 15 minutes or pressure-cooked for 10 if it is to be used directly as a food (or be further processed into soymilk); it requires as few as 10 to 15 minutes of simmering if it is to be made into tofu, since TI is contained in the soluble carbohydrates that dissolve in the whey during the curding process.

To prepare gô with the best flavor and nutritional value, soak your soybeans for the correct length of time (see graph, p. 289). Purée or grind them to a fine, smooth-textured consistency using an electric blender, a Corona- or Quaker City-type hand mill, a meat grinder with a fine attachment, an electric grain mill, a coffee mill, a mortar and pestle, a *suribachi*, or a juicer. Most important, cook the fresh gô without delay, and do not overcook, lest some of the protein value be lost.

The word "gô" is used by Japanese tofu makers in three different ways. First, it refers to the white purée mentioned above. Second, it is used to refer to a property of dry soybeans, similar to the gluten in wheat, which is a measure of the quantity and quality of the protein in the beans. The presence of this property depends on the soybeans' variety and grade, the region, climate, and soil in which they were grown, and their particular year of "vintage."

It is important in determining the amount of tofu that can be made from a given quantity of beans, and it determines the cohesiveness and delicate resilience of both the purée and the tofu made from it.

Finally, "gô" may refer to an elusive essence of the purée which determines the amount of tofu it will yield. Improper treatment of the purée can cause a decrease in this vital essence; tofu makers assert that this gô can "fall" or "drop out." Combining the three usages into a single sentence, a tofu maker might say: "To make fine tofu, use soybeans containing good gô, grind them between slowly-turning stones to make smooth, fine-textured gô, and cook immediately, to prevent any of the essential gô from escaping"!

Since ancient times and until really quite recently, most Japanese kitchens were equipped with a pair of 10-inch-diameter, hand-turned grinding stones (fig. 15). These were used to grind soybeans into gô during the preparation of farmhouse tofu or Gôjiru soup (p. 74). On special occasions, they were used to grind whole grains into flour, roasted soybeans into *kinako*, or tender tea leaves into *matcha* used in the tea ceremony. In farmhouses where tofu was made regularly or in large quantities, and in traditional tofu shops throughout Japan and China, an interesting design was developed whereby large, heavy stones were turned using a push-pull system (fig. 16). While one person worked the push-pull handle that revolved the upper stone, another ladled soaked soybeans into the stone's upper surface. Working in this way, it often took 1 or 2 hours for tofu makers to grind enough beans for a single

Fig. 18. Water-powered millstones

cauldronful of tofu yielding 120 cakes. Work usually started as early as 2 o'clock in the morning and, during the summer, the beans were often ground and cooked in two separate batches each day to ensure freshness. In several of Kyoto's elegant old tofu and yuba shops where granite stones are still used, the stone floor near the base of the grinding platform is distinctly indented and worn smooth in the spots where many generations of fathers and sons pivoted their feet as they turned the great stones by hand.

While all of the gô made in Japanese tofu shops is still ground between stone wheels, the great majority of the shops presently use relatively small, lightweight wheels that revolve more rapidly than the traditional, heavy stones. Some shops, however, have carefully preserved their beautiful heirloom millstones, mounting them vertically and driving them with a fanbelt and electric motor (fig. 17). The tofu master must chisel the cutting grooves of both stones every three months to keep them sharp. Like the finest Western stone-burr mills used for making stone-ground flours, these heavy stones yield gó, and hence tofu, of the finest quality.

It is interesting to note that although grinding stones have been used for more than 2,000 years in East Asia, the power to revolve them was traditionally provided entirely by man. It apparently never occurred to these craftsmen that natural forces—such as wind and water—could be used as energy sources. Less than a century ago, most of the flour prepared in the West was freshly ground each morning in stone mills powered by either water wheels (fig. 18) or windmills (fig. 19). The large stones were 3 to 4 feet in diameter and 12 inches thick, whereas in Japan and China, we have never seen a stone larger than 17 inches in diameter and 5 inches thick.

The same basic principles used in making high-quality whole-grain flours are also applied in preparing gô. Each morning the tofu maker drains and rinses his well-soaked soybeans, then places them in a hopper above the grinder. He runs a slow trickle of water—often drawn from the shop's deep well—over the beans, down through the hopper and in between the stones to give his gô the desired thickness. The stone wheels revolve slowly and at medium pressure to ensure that the germ, skin, and body of the beans are smoothly blended, and to avoid overheating, which would cause the essential gô to escape. This way of grinding yields gô with a very fine grain; the latter, in turn, increases the tofu yield. It also helps to develop the natural cohesiveness or glutinous quality found in soybeans in much the same way that kneading develops gluten in bread.

Lest the essential gô escape, the purée should be used as soon as possible after it has been ground. Thus, in tofu shops it is scooped immediately into a cauldron of boiling water. Gô loses its potency the longer it sits unused and the tofu yield consequently declines.

In modern Japan, most of the gô made in tofu shops is used directly in the tofu-making process. Only occasionally do the more tradition-minded order it from the tofu shop for use in home cooking. Since most homes are now equipped with a blender, cooks can make their own.

Gô can be added to soups or breads, or it can be sautéed with vegetables, mixed with diced foods and deep-fried, or used as a protein-rich base for casseroles and other baked dishes. Try using it in place of pre-packaged soy flour, meal, or grits in your favorite recipes; in most cases, cooking time will be reduced by 50 percent or more. This creamy-white, smooth purée invites imaginitive experimentation to find new uses for a food that is rarely, if ever, mentioned in Western cookbooks.

Fig. 19. Wind-powered millstones

Homemade Gô Purée

MAKES 2 CUPS

Gô purée has the consistency of a thick milkshake. Ground gô (below) is a thick paste. The two types may be used interchangeably in most recipes. To make 2 cups of gô purée from ground gô, simply mix the latter thoroughly with 7/8 cup water. (Note: 1 cup dry soybeans expands to about 2½ cups when soaked overnight.)

½ cup dry soybeans, soaked for 8 to 10 hours in 1 quart water
7/8 cup water

Rinse, then drain the beans in a colander. Combine beans and water in a blender and purée at high speed for about 3 minutes, or until smooth. Or, if a crunchier texture is desired, purée for only 1 minute. Use as an ingredient in other recipes.

Homemade Ground Gô

MAKES 1¼ CUPS

This variety of gô is slightly thicker than that made in most tofu shops, but resembles that made traditionally in Japanese farmhouses using either hand-turned grinding stones or a *suribachi*.

½ cup dry soybeans, soaked for 8 to 10 hours in 1 quart water

Rinse, then drain the beans in a colander. Using a hand mill or meat grinder with a fine-blade attachment, grind beans to a smooth paste.

Gô Cracker Dip or Spread

MAKES 1½ CUPS

1 tablespoon butter
½ cup minced onion
1 clove of garlic, crushed
1 cup Gôjiru (below)
¼ cup (tofu) mayonnaise (p. 107)
¼ teaspoon salt
Dash of pepper

Melt the butter in a skillet. Add onion and garlic and sauté until onion is nicely browned. Combine in a blender with remaining ingredients and purée until smooth. Serve as a dip for potato chips, crackers, or fresh vegetable sticks, or use as a sandwich spread.

Gôjiru
(Thick Miso Soup with Gô)

The most popular way of using gô in Japanese cookery, this famous wintertime soup is said to have originated in Japan's snowy northeast provinces. It can be prepared using a wide range of vegetables, seasonings, or garnishes. Experiment with whatever is available, in season, or simply appealing. Some cooks like to make Gôjiru as thick as porridge; others prefer to use more water and fewer vegetables and beans to create a texture resembling that of typical miso soup.

2 tablespoons oil
1 onion, thinly sliced; or 1 leek cut into 2-inch lengths
½ carrot, cut into thin half moons
2 ounces agé, cut into thin strips
3 mushrooms, thinly sliced
2 inches *daikon*, cut into half moons; or ½ cup chopped celery
1 potato, sweet potato, yam, or taro, diced
2 cups Homemade Gô Purée
3½ to 4 cups water, stock, or dashi (p. 39)
5 to 6 tablespoons red miso or 3½ tablespoons shoyu

Heat a heavy pot and coat with the oil. Add the next six ingredients and sauté over medium heat for 5 to 10 minutes, or until potatoes are softened. Add gô and water, bring to a boil, and simmer uncovered for 10 to 15 minutes, stirring occasionally. Add miso thinned in a few tablespoons of the hot broth and simmer for 1 minute more. Serve immediately or, for a richer, sweeter flavor, allow to cool for about 6 hours. Use leftovers in Gô Cracker Dip (see above) or in a casserole *au gratin* as described as a variation under Thick Onion Soup with Gô (see above).

VARIATIONS

*Any of the following garnishes or seasonings may be added to the soup with the miso or sprinkled on top of individual servings: 7-spice red pepper, powdered green *nori*, *sansho* pepper; minced trefoil, sake lees, slivered *yuzu* or lemon rind; pepper, crushed garlic, croutons, sage, or thyme.
*Experiment using other vegetables such as green beans, celery (including leaves), snow peas, *kombu*, or shelled green soybeans. Substitute an equal quantity of green soybeans for the dry soybeans when preparing the Homemade Gô Purée. When preparing a thin soup, add several lightly beaten eggs together with the miso.
*Seasoned Gôjiru with Deep-fried Potatoes: Sauté the vegetables and agé given in the recipe above, omitting the potatoes. Add 3 tablespoons each shoyu and natural sugar, cover pan, and simmer for 5 minutes. Cut 2 potatoes into thin rounds, deep-fry until golden brown, and add to the soup with the gô.
*Suritate and Hikitate: These are two country-style variations on the Gôjiru theme. In *Suritate*, which contains no vegetables, the gô is seasoned only with shoyu and simmered in water or dashi. *Hikitate* is made by parboiling, then thoroughly grinding soybeans and adding them to regular miso soup just before adding the miso.

Thick Onion Soup with Gô

SERVES 6

Use gô in place of *roux* or cream sauces to give body, flavor, and a rich infusion of protein to your favorite soups. The following two recipes work well as patterns for experimentation.

2 tablespoons oil
4 onions, thinly sliced
2 cups Homemade Gô Purée (p. 74)
3¼ cups water
3½ tablespoons shoyu or 5 tablespoons red miso
2/3 cup grated cheese
2 tablespoons butter
Dash of pepper
1 cup croutons (sautéed lightly in butter, if desired)
¼ cup minced parsley (optional)

Heat a heavy pot or large casserole and coat with the oil. Add onions and sauté for 5 minutes. Mix in purée and water and bring to a boil. Reduce heat to low and simmer for 10 minutes, stirring occasionally. Stir in the shoyu, cheese, butter, and pepper, and return to the boil. For best flavor, allow to stand for at least 6 hours. Serve as is or reheated, garnished with croutons and parsley.

VARIATIONS

*Add 5 to 10 ounces diced thick agé or ganmo together with the purée. Increase shoyu to 4 (or miso to) 6 tablespoons.
*Use leftovers to make a delicious casserole as follows: To each cup of leftover soup add 1 lightly beaten egg and, if desired, ¼ to ½ cup leftover vegetables or grains. Mix well, place into a baking pan or casserole and sprinkle lightly with cheese. Bake at 350° for 20 minutes, or until nicely browned.

Scrambled Eggs with Gô

SERVES 3 OR 4

2 tablespoons butter
¼ cup diced onion
¼ cup diced mushrooms
1 cup Homemade Gô Purée (p. 74)
2 eggs, lightly beaten
½ teaspoon salt
Dash of pepper
¼ cup grated cheese (optional)

Melt the butter in a skillet. Add onion and mushroom and sauté until onion is just transparent. Add gô and, stirring constantly, cook for 5 to 7 minutes, or until purée has a subtly sweet fragrance. Mix in remaining ingredients and cook for a few more minutes until eggs have set.

Go in Oven Cookery

When used in place of, or together with, eggs as a basis for casseroles, baked grain or egg dishes, or even for cheesecake-like desserts, gô lends body and flavor to each dish while providing the tasty richness and high protein usually supplied by dairy milk.

Whole-wheat Bread with Gô

MAKES 6 LOAVES

This high protein bread has a delightfully moist texture and rich flavor. By properly combining soy and wheat proteins, we increase the total amount of usable protein by about 30 percent.

2 cups soybeans, soaked overnight in water, drained and rinsed
4 cups lukewarm water
2 tablespoons dried yeast
½ cup honey or natural sugar
22 cups whole-wheat flour, approximately
¼ cup oil
2½ tablespoons salt

Combine half the beans and 2 cups water in a blender; purée for about 3 minutes, or until smooth. Pour the purée into a large mixing bowl. Purée the remaining beans in the same way and add to the bowl together with honey, yeast, and 4 cups flour. Using a large wooden spoon, mix for about 5 minutes to form a smooth sponge. Cover bowl with a moist towel, and allow to stand for about 40 minutes in a warm place until sponge doubles in volume.

Add the oil and salt. Fold in about 2 cups flour at a time to form a smooth, firm dough. Turn dough out onto a well-floured bread board and incorporate the remaining flour while kneading. When dough has been kneaded 200 to 300 times and is fairly light and smooth-textured, place in a large, lightly oiled bowl, cover, and allow to double in volume. Punch down and allow to rise once again.

Preheat oven to 350°. Turn dough out onto a lightly floured bread board and divide into 6 equal portions. Knead each portion about 20 times, shape into a loaf, and place into a lightly oiled bread pan. When the last loaf is in its pan, allow all loaves to rise for 5 to 10 minutes more. Bake for 40 to 50 minutes, or until nicely browned. Serve warm with butter.

Corn Bread with Gô

MAKES 1 LOAF

½ cup soybeans, soaked overnight in water and drained
2 tablespoons oil
1 tablespoon honey or natural sugar
2 tablespoons sesame butter, *tahini*, or ground roasted sesame seeds (p. 38)
1½ teaspoons salt
2 cups water
1½ cups cornmeal
Oil

Preheat oven to 375°. Combine the first five ingredients in a blender, adding 1½ cups water; purée for 3 minutes or until smooth. Pour into a mixing bowl and add remaining ½ cup water and cornmeal; mix well. Bake in a lightly oiled square pan for about 45 minutes. Serve with butter, molasses, or sesame butter—or try cottage cheese.

Gô Casserole

SERVES 2 OR 3

2 cups Homemade Gô Purée (p. 74)
½ cup milk (soy or dairy)
2 tablespoons melted butter
2 tablespoons ground roasted sesame seeds (p. 38), sesame butter, or *tahini*
½ teaspoon salt
Dash of pepper
2 tablespoons bread crumbs

Preheat oven to 350°. Combine the first six ingredients in a bowl; mix well. Pour into a lightly oiled casserole or bread pan and top with a sprinkling of bread crumbs. Bake for 30 to 40 minutes, or until nicely browned.

Egg Casserole with Cheese and Gô

SERVES 2 OR 3

2 cups Homemade Gô Purée (p. 74)
5 eggs, lightly beaten
¾ teaspoon salt, 1 tablespoon shoyu, or 1½ tablespoons red miso
Dash of pepper
1½ tablespoons butter
2 ounces sliced or grated cheese
Ketchup or Ketchup-Worcestershire Sauce (p. 49)

Preheat oven to 350°. Combine the first five ingredients in a large bowl; mix well. Pour the mixture into a lightly oiled bread pan or casserole, dot with butter and top with cheese. Bake for 40 to 50 minutes, or until nicely browned. Serve hot or cold with ketchup or the sauce.

Deep-fried Gô Patties *(Bakudan Agé)*

SERVES 3 OR 4

2 cups Homemade Gô Purée (p. 74)
2 cups bread crumbs or bread crumb flakes
½ carrot, diced or slivered
1 small onion, diced
½ teaspoon salt
1 tablespoon ground roasted sesame seeds (p. 38), sesame butter, or *tahini* (optional)
Oil for deep-frying

Combine the first six ingredients in a large bowl, mixing well. Shape the mixture into 2½-inch patties or 1¼-inch balls. Heat oil to 350° in a wok, skillet, or deep-fryer. Slide in patties or balls and deep-fry for about 2 minutes, or until golden brown (p. 130). Serve topped with ketchup, Ketchup-Worcestershire Sauce (p. 49) or Tofu Tartare Sauce (p. 49).

VARIATION
*Gô Croquettes: Into 1 cup Homemade Ground Gô (p. 74) mix ¼ cup minced and steamed sweet potatoes or yams and ¼ cup minced onions. Add just enough bread crumbs to hold the mixture together, season lightly with salt, and shape into 2-inch patties. Dust each pattie with flour, dip in lightly beaten egg, and roll in bread crumbs. Deep-fry and serve as above.

Or, substitute grated lemon or *yuzu* rind for the potatoes. Use grated glutinous yam as a binding agent, adding flour only if necessary.

Rice Pudding with Gô and Apple

SERVES 4 TO 6

¾ cup gô (made from ¼ cup dry soybeans soaked overnight, drained, and blended with 6 tablespoons water)
2 cups cooked Brown Rice (p. 50)
1½ tablespoons dark brown sugar
½ cup raisins
2 cups milk (soy or dairy)
1 apple, diced
1 tablespoon butter
¼ teaspoon salt
¼ teaspoon cinnamon

Combine the first six ingredients and, stirring constantly, bring just to a boil. Reduce heat to low and, continuing to stir, simmer for 10 minutes. Mix in remaining ingredients and remove from heat. Allow to cool uncovered for about 2 hours before serving.

Or, combine all ingredients and bake for 1 hour at 350°.

Rich and Spongy Loaf with Gô

SERVES 2 OR 3

2 cups Homemade Gô Purée (p. 74)
½ cup milk
¼ cup raisins
1 tablespoon butter
1 tablespoon honey
2 tablespoons natural sugar
1 egg, lightly beaten
Butter
¼ cup thinly sliced or grated cheese

Preheat oven to 350°. Combine the first seven ingredients in a bowl; mix well. Pour the mixture into a bread pan coated lightly with butter, and top with the cheese. Bake for about 30 minutes, or until nicely browned. Serve hot or cold.

6

Okara or Unohana

UNOHANA *(Deutzia scabra)* is a tiny white flower that grows in thick clusters on briar bushes and blossoms in the spring (fig. 20). In 1869, the *haiku* poet Basho, on his last long trek to the back country of northern Japan, wrote of unohana in his journal:

> *Mounting towards the Shirakawa barrier*
> *"Autumnal winds" hummed in my ears,*
> *"The maple" stood imagined,*
> *But leaf-green branches haunting too.*
> *Against unohana white white briars,*
> *As if pushing through snow.*
> > *(CID CORMAN translation)*

The word "unohana" is also used in connection with tofu. After gô is ladled into a cauldron of boiling water and simmered, it is transferred to a heavy cloth sack set on a rack on top of a wooden curding barrel. The sack's mouth is twisted closed and the sack is pressed. In farmhouses a grinding stone is set atop the sack; in tofu shops the sack is pressed either with a traditional lever (fig. 21) or with more modern equipment. In each case liquid soymilk filters through the sack into the curding barrel. The soybean pulp—called *okara* or unohana—remains in the sack. The soymilk is eventually made into tofu; the okara has its own special uses.

Okara is beige in color and has a crumbly, fine-grained texture. Some Westerners have remarked—only half in jest—that its appearance reminds them of moist sawdust. But the Japanese, in line with their ancient tradition of honoring even the simplest and most humble of foods, place the honorific prefix

Fig. 20. Unohana

o before the word *kara*, which means "shell, hull, or husk." Thus o-*kara* means "honorable shell." In Chinese it is called "child of tofu lees" (*doufu chatsu*), "soy lees" (*doucha*), or "tofu's head" (*douto*) in contrast with the soft curds which are called the "tofu's brain." Trying to translate any of these words into descriptive English is almost impossible; terms such as "soybean lees, grounds, mash, pulp, fines, residue, dregs," or the like hardly do justice to this fine food.

When Japanese refer to okara as an ingredient in cooking, they call it *unohana*, in honor of Basho's tiny white blossoms. And, indeed, it deserves this high evaluation for, when properly prepared, it is a tasty and nutritious food which serves as an important ingredient in traditional Japanese cuisine. Okara dishes are available in most delicatessens and at many fine restaurants. Light and almost fluffy, okara absorbs flavors well and gives body to sautéed vegetable dishes, soups, casseroles, breads, and salads.

The most important constitutent of okara is what nutritionists and doctors call "dietary plant fiber" and now consider to be an essential part of every well-balanced diet. Fiber, by definition, is indigestible. Composed of carbohydrates found in the outer bran layers of whole grains and the cell walls of natural vegetables and pulses, it passes unchanged through the human digestive tract performing two key functions: it provides the "bulk" or "roughage" necessary for regular bowel movements and the prevention of constipation; and it absorbs toxins (including environmental pollutants) and speeds their passage out of the body.

The recent re-evaluation of the importance of fiber-rich foods such as okara has resulted from the recognition of three dangerous trends in the dietary patterns of most industrialized nations: 1) our intake of dietary fiber is now only 20 percent of what it was one hundred years ago due both to the rapid rise in the consumption of sugar, meat, fats, and dairy products (all of which contain *no* fiber) and the decrease in the use of grains and vegetables; 2) a large proportion of the grains we do consume are in their refined, processed forms (such as white bread, rice, or pasta) which have been stripped of their fiber-rich (and nutritious) outer layers; 3) the average person has a steadily increasing intake of toxic substances from both food additives and the environment. Serving okara, therefore, allows us to make use of natural soybeans in the most holistic and health-giving way.

Containing about 17 percent of the protein in the original soybeans, okara itself consists of 3.5 percent protein by weight, or about the same proportion found in whole milk or cooked brown rice. While it is perhaps unfortunate that all of this protein is not transferred to tofu, its presence in okara is just that much more reason for utilizing this byproduct of the tofu-making process.

The tastiest and most nutritious okara is that removed in the process of making kinugoshi tofu, a variety made from very thick soymilk. Since this okara is pressed only once, it retains a great deal of the soymilk's flavor and nutrients, and has an obviously moist, cohesive texture. In the process of making regular tofu in tofu shops, soymilk is filtered through first a coarsely woven and then a finely woven sack. The small quantity of very fine-grained okara that collects in the second sack is usually pressed by hand (rather than with a press) so that it, too, retains a large portion of the soymilk taste and food value. During the winter months when the cold air ensures their freshness, both varieties are shaped into 4½-inch-diameter balls or sealed in small plastic bags to be sold for a few pennies per pound. Some tofu makers present okara to their customers free of charge as a token of appreciation for their patronage.

Before World War II, most tofu-shop okara was sold for use in cooking. Young apprentices at the shop were often allowed to cook the day's okara any way they wished and then sell their creations from door to door. At New Year's, okara croquettes and other tasty dishes, made and sold in this way, earned an impoverished apprentice a little pocket money.

In some parts of China, okara is pressed into cakes about 6 inches in diameter and 1 inch thick, and allowed to ferment for 10 to 15 days until each is covered with a mycelium of white mold. The cakes are dried for a few hours in the sun, then deep-fried or cooked with vegetables and sold as a nutritious flavoring agent called *meitauza*. In Indonesia, a similar product called *ontjom* is said to be well liked for its tasty almond-like flavor.

In Japan, a typical tofu shop produces about 15 gallons of okara daily, or roughly 1 gallon for each gallon of dry soybeans used. But at most, only one gallon or so of this is retailed. The remainder is picked up daily at the shop by local dairymen who feed it to their cows to stimulate milk production and enrich the milk's nutrient content. In China, many tofu makers run small hog farms and use okara as their principal source of fodder. Okara also works well as an organic mulch and fertilizer, or as a free, high-protein pet food. (In Japan it is now used commercially in dried dog- and cat foods.)

Nursing mothers have used okara for centuries to enrich their milk and stimulate its flow. It also serves as a traditional cure for diarrhea. Wrapped in a cloth and used to rub down the household woodwork, okara's natural oils coat and darken the wood, thus serving as a wax and polish.

At present in the United States, okara is available at some Japanese and Chinese groceries and, of course, at all tofu shops. But the easiest way to obtain okara is to prepare Homemade Tofu (p. 99) or Soymilk (p. 204). If you prepare enough tofu for two people, you will have as a byproduct about 1 cup of okara, or enough for two to four servings.

Fig. 21. A traditional lever press

Roasting or Parching Okara

The dry-roasting or parching called for in some recipes is meant to reduce okara's water content and give it a light, almost fluffy texture. When added to breads, muffins, cookies, or croquettes, roasted okara not only saves on flour but also gives much lighter results.

To roast using a skillet or wok, heat but do not oil the pan. Put in the okara and roast over low heat, stirring constantly with a wooden spoon or spatula, for about 3 minutes or until okara is light and dry but not browned.

When parching okara in an oven, spread the okara out on a large baking tin. Place in an unheated oven set at 350° and heat for 5 to 10 minutes.

Homemade Okara

The 1 cup of okara which results as a byproduct left over from the preparation of homemade tofu, soymilk, or kinugoshi is superior in taste, texture, and nutritional elements to that which is available from commercial tofu shops. It is also free. Since the soybeans are ground in a blender rather than between heavy stones, the okara has a slightly crunchy texture like that of finely chopped nuts. And since okara is pressed by hand rather than mechanically, it retains the flavor and nutrition of the unpressed soymilk. The okara that remains after making soymilk or kinugoshi is the tastiest and most nutritious, since some of the thick soymilk always remains in it. Since the okara from homemade tofu is generally separated from the soymilk before the milk is thoroughly cooked however, it is important that the okara be cooked slightly longer than commercial okara, hence the cooking times in the recipes that follow.

To prepare homemade okara, refer to the recipes for Homemade Tofu (p. 99), Soymilk (p. 204), or Kinugoshi (p. 215).

OKARA IN SALADS

Okara Salad with Noodles and Greens   SERVES 4

3 tablespoons oil
7 chrysanthemum, Chinese cabbage, chard, cabbage, or spinach leaves, cut into 1-inch-wide strips
2/3 cup okara, firmly packed
2/3 cup cooked noodles (rice flour or buckwheat)
1 tablespoon ground roasted sesame seeds (p. 38)
1 teaspoon grated gingerroot
½ teaspoon salt
Dash of pepper

Heat a skillet or wok and coat with the oil. Add the green leaves and sauté briskly over high heat. Reduce heat to medium, add okara and cooked noodles, and sauté for 5 to 10 minutes more, or until okara is light and fluffy. Stir in gingerroot, add salt and pepper, and remove from heat. Allow to cool to room temperature before serving.

For variety, mix in 1 diced apple and 1 teaspoon lemon juice after the salad has cooled. Serve topped with Tofu Mayonnaise (p. 107) and a sprinkling of roasted sesame seeds.

OKARA IN SOUPS

Okara may be added to most vegetable and miso soups. To prepare a thick soup, use about 4½ parts liquid to 1 part firmly packed okara. For a thin soup, use a ratio of 8 or 9 to 1. In Japanese okara soups, the vegetables are either sautéed in the pot until tender and then simmered briefly in the stock, or uncooked vegetables are added to the stock and simmered slowly until tender. The okara is generally added after the vegetables have been sautéed or partially simmered. In miso soups, use 6 tablespoons (3½ ounces) of okara to serve 4.

Chilled Okara Soup *(Unohana-jiru)*   SERVES 4

2 tablespoons oil
2 onions, diced
8 small mushrooms, thinly sliced through crown and stem
2/3 cup okara, firmly packed
3 cups water or stock
1 teaspoon salt
Dash of pepper
2 tablespoons butter
6 or 7 tablespoons red or barley miso; or 4 tablespoons shoyu
2 tablespoons sake or white wine (optional)
Minced parsley or chives

Heat a skillet or wok and coat with the oil. Add the onions and mushrooms and sauté over medium heat for 2 or 3 minutes. Add okara and water and bring to a boil; reduce heat to low. Add salt, pepper, butter, miso, and, if used, the sake, and simmer for 10 to 15 minutes more. Allow to cool, then chill overnight or for at least several hours. Serve garnished with parsley or chives.

OKARA IN SAUCES

Use small amounts (about 10% by volume) of okara (roasted or unroasted) as a thickener in mushroom, onion, curry, or spaghetti sauces.

OKARA WITH EGGS

Okara Scrambled Eggs SERVES 3 OR 4

3 eggs
½ cup milk
¼ teaspoon salt
Dash of pepper
½ cup okara, firmly packed
1½ tablespoons butter

Combine the first four ingredients in a mixing bowl; whisk or mix with a fork. Now stir in the okara. Melt the butter in a skillet, add the egg-and-okara mixture, and scramble over high heat for about 3 minutes or until firm but not dry. Serve hot or cold.

Okara & Egg Patties with Raisins SERVES 4

2 cups okara, firmly packed
2 eggs, lightly beaten
¼ cup raisins
1 tablespoon natural sugar
¼ teaspoon salt
1 teaspoon baking powder
1 to 2 teaspoons oil
2 tablespoons butter

Combine the first six ingredients in a large bowl; mix well. Heat a skillet and coat lightly with part of the oil. Shape the okara mixture into 2½-inch patties. Pan-fry patties on both sides until golden brown. Serve hot, each pattie topped with a dab of butter.

Or, bake the patties on a lightly oiled cookie sheet in a medium oven for about 20 minutes until nicely browned.

Okara Eggs with Sweet Potatoes and Raisins SERVES 2 OR 3

1½ tablespoons butter
½ cup okara, firmly packed
1 sweet potato or yam (5 inches long), steamed and diced
¼ cup raisins
½ cup water or stock
1 egg, lightly beaten
¼ teaspoon salt
Dash of pepper

Melt butter in a skillet. Add the next four ingredients. Stirring constantly, simmer until water is absorbed. Mix in the egg, season with salt and pepper, and cook, stirring constantly, for about 2 minutes until egg is firm and slightly fluffy. Allow to cool before serving.

OKARA BAKED

Okara may be used in your favorite recipes for stuffed, baked vegetables. Okara & Vegetable Sauté (below) can serve as a delicious filling for green peppers, mushrooms, potatoes, or eggplants. Use small amounts (about 10%) of okara in casseroles or breads, adding the okara to your ingredients either as is, lightly roasted (p. 79), or simmered in Sweetened Shoyu Broth (p. 40). Okara is also delicious in baked desserts (p. 84).

Scalloped Okara & Mushrooms SERVES 4 TO 6

3 tablespoons butter
3 tablespoons whole-wheat flour
1½ cups milk (soy or dairy)
Dash of pepper
1½ tablespoons oil
12 mushrooms, thinly sliced
1½ onions, thinly sliced
1½ cups okara, lightly packed
2½ tablespoons shoyu
½ cup grated cheese
2 tablespoons bread crumbs
2 tablespoons Parmesan cheese

Preheat oven to 350°. Use the first four ingredients to prepare a White Sauce (p. 48). Heat a skillet and coat with the oil. Add mushrooms and onions, sauté for 4 to 5 minutes, and remove from heat. Combine with the sauce, okara, shoyu, and cheese; mix well, then spoon into a lightly oiled loaf pan or casserole. Top with a sprinkling of bread crumbs and Parmesan; bake for 30 minutes.

Okara-Onion-Cheese Soufflé SERVES 2

Use ingredients for Okara Dessert Soufflé (p. 84) except omit the honey and vanilla. Add to the okara: ½ onion, minced and sautéed until transparent, ¼ cup grated cheese, 2 tablespoons grated carrot, salt and pepper to taste. Proceed as for the dessert.

OKARA STIR-FRIED, SAUTÉED, AND DEEP-FRIED

Okara Burgers

MAKES 4 TO 5

1 cup okara
½ cup whole-wheat flour
1 egg, lightly beaten
¼ cup minced onion
¼ cup grated carrot
1 clove of garlic, minced or crushed
1 tablespoon shoyu
¼ teaspoon curry powder
Dash of pepper
Oil for deep-frying

Combine the first nine ingredients, mixing well, and shape into patties. Heat the oil to 350° in a wok, skillet, or deep-fryer. Drop in patties and deep-fry until crisp and golden brown (p. 130). Serve as for Ganmo Burgers (p. 188).

If deep-frying is inconvenient, patties may be fried or broiled.

VARIATIONS

*Okara Fritters: Add 6 tablespoons (soy) milk and 1 egg to the above ingredients. Drop by spoonfuls into the hot oil to deep-fry. Mix skimmings from oil back into batter after each batch has been deep-fried. Delicious topped with Tofu Mayonnaise (p. 107). Makes 12 to 14.

Okara Tempeh

SERVES 3 TO 4

This delicious preparation, developed at *The Farm* in Tennessee (p. 316), is a variation on the traditional Indonesian *tempeh* recipe (p. 68). It is important to use okara which has been well cooked during the preparation of the soymilk. Coarse-textured okara seems to allow the best air circulation during fermentation; it must be pressed as firmly as possible to expel soymilk, thereby giving a light, high-quality product. For best results, prepare a shallow incubation tray having a bottom made of rustproof aluminum screen.

2½ cups well-pressed okara, cooled to room temperature
2 teaspoons vinegar
½ teaspoon tempeh starter or ¼ to ½ cup minced tempeh from a previous fermentation

Combine all ingredients, mixing well. Spread to a depth of ½ to ¾ inch in a shallow tray or pan and cover with a sheet of perforated plastic wrap as for Homemade Tempeh (p. 68). Proceed to incubate, cook and serve as directed in the basic recipe.

Okara-Potato Pancakes

MAKES 5 TO 6

1 cup coarsely-grated mature potatoes
2/3 cup okara
3 eggs, lightly beaten
1 teaspoon salt
1½ tablespoons minced onion
1½ tablespoons whole-wheat flour
Oil for frying
Applesauce or butter

Place potato gratings in a cloth towel and wring towel to extract as much moisture from potatoes as possible. Combine in a bowl with the next five ingredients; mix well. Shape into ¼-inch-thick patties and fry in a well-oiled skillet on both sides until golden brown. Serve hot, topped with either applesauce or butter.

Okara Croquettes

MAKES 10

1 cup White Sauce (p. 48; use 1 teaspoon salt for seasoning)
2 teaspoons oil
½ onion, minced
2 tablespoons grated carrot
1 cup okara
¼ cup whole-wheat flour
1 egg, lightly beaten
2/3 cup bread crumbs or bread crumb flakes
Oil for deep-frying

Prepare White Sauce and set aside to cool. Heat a skillet and coat with the oil. Add onion and carrots, and sauté for 4 to 5 minutes, then add to the sauce together with the okara; mix well. Shape into (soft) cylinders 1 inch in diameter and 2½ inches long. Dust with flour, gently dip into egg, and roll in bread crumbs; set aside briefly to dry.

Heat oil to 350° in a wok, skillet, or deep-fryer. Drop in croquettes and deep-fry until golden brown (p. 130). Serve hot or cold, as is or topped with Tofu Tartare Sauce (p. 109) or Tofu Mayonnaise (p. 107; with onion).

Okara & Vegetable Sauté
(Unohana no iri-ni)

SERVES 3 OR 4

This dish, sold ready-made in Japanese markets and delicatessens and prepared at fine restaurants, is the most popular way of serving okara in Japan. Most recipes call for carrots, *konnyaku*, *shiitake* mushrooms, leeks, and agé as the basic ingredients, but almost any other vegetables may be added or substituted. The flavor of this dish is substantially improved by allowing it to cool to room temperature. It is served as a side dish.

2 tablespoons oil (up to half of which may be sesame)
½ carrot, cut into matchsticks
2 onions or leeks, thinly sliced
1 cup okara, firmly packed
1½ cups water, stock, or dashi (p. 39)
2 to 3 tablespoons natural sugar or honey
3 tablespoons shoyu
1 tablespoon sake or white wine

Heat a skillet or wok and coat with the oil. Add carrot slivers and sauté for about 2 minutes, then add onion slices and sauté until transparent. Mix in remaining ingredients and bring just to a boil. Reduce heat to low and simmer, stirring occasionally, for 10 to 15 minutes, or until most of the liquid has evaporated. Remove from heat and allow to cool to room temperature. Do not reheat to serve. For best flavor, refrigerate overnight or for at least 5 hours.

*To the ingredients listed above, add 2 thinly sliced mushrooms (fresh, or dry *shiitake*), ¼ cake of *konnyaku* cut into small rectangles, and 2 ounces of agé cut into thin strips; sauté together with the onions. (Some cooks prefer to parboil carrot slivers, mushroom slices, and *konnyaku* chunks before sautéing them, and add them to the leeks about 30 seconds before the okara has finished cooking.) Other vegetables commonly sautéed with the okara include lotus root, bamboo shoots, burdock root, *udo*, snow or green peas, green beans, sweet potatoes, yams, or cabbage. Serve garnished with slivers of gingerroot.

*Use Okara & Vegetable Sauté as a filling for stuffed peppers, eggplants, or tomatoes, or in Agé or Inari-zushi Pouches (p. 192 and 194).

***Deep-fried Okara Balls in Thickened Sauce:** Prepare Okara & Vegetable Sauté and allow to cool. Combine in a small bowl with 1 egg and mix well. Sauté mixture in a lightly oiled pan until egg is firm, then allow to cool for 5 to 10 minutes. Shape into 1¼-inch balls, roll in cornstarch, and deep-fry until golden brown. Cut some of the balls into halves and top with Ankake Sauce, Gingerroot Sauce, or Sweet & Sour Sauce (p. 49). Allow to cool before serving.

Unsweetened Fried Okara SERVES 4 TO 6
(Unohana-iri)

2 tablespoons oil (up to ¼ of which may be sesame)
1 small onion, diced
4 mushrooms, thinly sliced
½ carrot, cut into matchsticks
½ cup diced lotus root
2 or 3 ounces agé, ganmo, or thick agé, diced (optional)
1 cup okara, firmly packed
1 cup water or stock
1 tablespoon shoyu
½ teaspoon salt

Heat a wok or skillet and coat with the oil. Add onion and sauté over high heat for 30 seconds. Reduce heat to medium, add mushroom, carrot, lotus root, and, if used, deep-fried tofu, and sauté for 2 to 3 minutes. Add remaining ingredients and bring just to a boil, then simmer for 3 minutes more. Allow to cool to room temperature (at least 3 to 4 hours) or refrigerate before serving.

If desired, use with any of the variations listed in the previous recipe.

Fried Okara Patties SERVES 2 OR 3
(Unohana Dango)

½ cup okara
¾ to 1 cup arrowroot or cornstarch
½ teaspoon salt
Water or milk
Oil
Worcestershire sauce or shoyu

Combine okara, arrowroot, and salt, mixing well. Add just enough water or milk to form a stiff dough and knead briefly. Shape dough into 1-inch balls, then press into 2-inch patties. Oil a skillet very lightly and fry patties on both sides until golden brown. Serve hot (like *mochi*) topped with a sprinkling of the sauce or shoyu.

Deep-fried Okara Balls in Sweet & Sour Sauce SERVES 4

1 cup okara, firmly packed
1 clove of garlic, crushed or minced
1 leek or onion, minced
1 teaspoon grated gingerroot
¼ cup ground roasted sesame seeds (p. 38)
2 tablespoons red or barley miso
¼ cup cornstarch or arrowroot
Oil for deep-frying
2½ cups Sweet & Sour Sauce (p. 49) or Pineapple Sweet & Sour Sauce (p. 166).

Combine the first six ingredients in a large bowl, mixing well. Form the mixture into 16 balls and roll the balls in the cornstarch. Heat the oil to 350° in a wok, skillet, or deep-fryer. Slide in the balls and deep-fry until golden brown (p. 130). Prepare the sauce. Just after it thickens, add the okara balls and simmer, stirring constantly, for 1 minute. Cut 8 of the balls into halves and allow all to cool to room temperature before serving.

Ankake or Gingerroot Sauce (p. 49) may be substituted for the Sweet & Sour Sauce. If desired, lightly roast the okara (p. 79) and add lightly beaten egg to aid in binding the mixture.

OKARA WITH GRAINS AND SUSHI

Okara has been used for centuries in Japan as a substitute for rice in sushi preparations. And in times when rice was scarce (due to war or famine), okara was cooked with or even served in place of rice as a staple food. By combining soy protein with that of grains, the okara boosted the total protein content by as much as 32 percent.

Okara also may be used in waffles, cornmeal muffins, spoonbread, and all yeasted breads. Use 2 parts flour to 1 part packed okara.

Okara Chapaties

MAKES 8

1¼ cups whole-wheat flour
½ cup okara, firmly packed
½ teaspoon salt
2 tablespoons water
1 tablespoon oil (optional)

Preheat oven to 350°. Combine 1 cup flour with remaining ingredients in a large bowl, mixing well. Knead for about 5 minutes to form a smooth dough. Divide dough into 8 parts and roll out each one on a floured board into a very thin 6-inch round. Place rounds on large baking trays and bake for 5 to 10 minutes, or until nicely browned. Allow to cool for at least 5 minutes, or until crisp. Serve topped with Mushroom Sauce (p. 48), butter, or a tofu spread (p. 109), or mounded with a salad or grain preparation.

The make *puri*, roll *chapati* dough into 4-inch rounds and deep-fry in 350° oil. Turn after about 30 seconds and continue deep-frying until *puri* have puffed up and are golden brown.

Okara Whole-wheat Pancakes

MAKES 10

1¼ cups whole-wheat flour
1 tablespoon baking powder
1 teaspoon salt
1 1/3 cups milk
¼ cup oil
2 tablespoons honey
½ teaspoon vanilla extract
3 eggs, separated into yolks and whites
¾ cup okara, lightly packed

Combine and sift the first three ingredients. In a separate container, combine the milk, oil, honey, vanilla, and egg yolks; mix well, then stir in okara. Beat egg whites until stiff. Lightly mix dry ingredients into wet ingredients, then fold in egg whites; avoid overmixing. Spoon batter in 6-inch rounds into a lightly oiled skillet and fry on both sides until golden brown. Serve with butter and either honey or maple syrup.

Wonderful Okara & Barley Flour Muffins

MAKES 12

1¼ cups barley flour
2 teaspoons baking powder
¼ teaspoon salt
1¼ cups milk
¼ cup honey or natural sugar
¼ cup oil
¼ teaspoon vanilla extract
¾ cup okara, lightly packed

Preheat oven to 400°. Roast barley flour in a heavy skillet, stirring constantly, until well browned and fragrant. Cool briefly, then combine with baking powder and salt, mixing well. Combine the next four ingredients in a separate bowl, mix thoroughly, then stir in okara. Fold dry ingredients lightly into wet. Spoon batter to a depth of about ¾ inch into a lightly oiled muffin tin and bake for about 35 minutes or until well browned. Invert on a rack and cool thoroughly before serving.

For variety, omit roasting; use Japanese-style pre-roasted barley flour *(mugi-kogashi)* or the regular Western variety.

Okara Rice

SERVES 4

1½ tablespoons oil
¼ cup diced carrot
2 onions or leeks, thinly sliced or diced
½ cup diced lotus root (optional)
2/3 cup okara, lightly roasted (p. 79)
2 cups cooked Brown Rice (p. 50)
2 tablespoons shoyu
2/3 teaspoon salt
Minced parsley and/or crumbled toasted *nori*

Heat a skillet or wok and coat with the oil. Add the carrot and onions and sauté for 3 or 4 minutes, or until onions are transparent. Add lotus root and sauté for 1 minute more. Add okara, rice, shoyu, and salt, mixing thoroughly. Cook for 2 or 3 minutes more, stirring constantly, until rice is well heated. Serve hot or cold, garnished with the parsley and/or *nori*.

For variety, cool the mixture, then shape into small patties. Dip patties in lightly beaten egg and roll in bread crumbs. Deep-fry until golden brown (p. 130) or pan-fry in butter. Serve with ketchup.

Sushi Okara *(Vinegared Okara)*

MAKES ¾ CUP

½ cup okara, firmly packed
1½ to 2 tablespoons rice vinegar
1 tablespoon natural sugar
1½ teaspoons sake or white wine (optional)
¼ teaspoon salt or 1½ teaspoons Sesame Salt (p. 51)

Roast okara for about 3 minutes until light and dry (p. 79). Transfer to a large bowl and allow to cool for 1 minute. Meanwhile, combine the remaining ingredients in a small bowl, mixing well. Stir mixture into okara as when preparing Sushi Rice (p. 50). Serve in any of the following ways:

*Garnished with slivered gingerroot as a topping for rice. (This may also be prepared as follows: In a skillet or wok, combine all the ingredients in the above recipe except the vinegar. Add 1 lightly beaten egg, 1 tablespoon hemp- or sesame seeds, and 2 tablespoons water or dashi. Simmer together until okara is light and dry, then remove from heat and stir in the vinegar.)

*Prepare 4 Inari-zushi pouches (p. 194) or plain Agé Pouches (p. 192) and serve filled with Sushi Okara. (Or, to make this filling, combine 1 part Sushi Okara with 1 part

Sushi Rice (p. 50) or plain Brown Rice (p. 50). If desired, add to the mixture any of the following diced or slivered vegetables simmered until tender in Sweetened Shoyu Broth (p. 40): carrots, lotus root, mushrooms, *kampyo*, or snow peas. The addition of whole or ground roasted sesame seeds (p. 38) or slivered Paper-thin Omelet (p. 51) to the mixture further enhances its flavor.)

*Substitute Sushi Okara for Sushi Rice in Nori-wrapped Sushi (p. 170).

Okara-Omelet Pouches
(Sushi Okara Chakin)

MAKES 8

These little pouches filled with vinegared okara are close relatives of Inari-zushi. Here, thin omelets take the place of agé pouches and Sushi Okara replaces Sushi Rice.

½ carrot, diced
1 tablespoon shoyu
1 tablespoon natural sugar
1 ounce agé, ganmo, or thick agé, diced (optional)
¾ cup Sushi Okara (p. 83)
8 Paper-thin Omelets (p. 51)

Bring 1½ cups water to a boil in a small saucepan. Drop in the carrot and simmer for 2 minutes; drain, reserving ¼ cup of the cooking water. In the same saucepan, now combine reserved water, cooked carrots, shoyu, sugar, and, if used, the agé. Simmer uncovered for 4 to 5 minutes until liquid is absorbed or evaporated, then set aside to cool.

In a large bowl, combine the carrot-agé mixture with the Sushi Okara, mixing lightly. Spoon equal portions of this filling onto the center of each of the omelets, then fold over each omelet to form an envelope (fig. 22). Serve as hors d'oeuvre or as part of a meal.

VARIATIONS

*Okara Chirashi-zushi: Prepare 2 Paper-thin Omelets (p. 51). Arrange the Sushi Okara—and—carrot mixture in a large (wooden) bowl and top with the slivered omelets.
*Five-Color Okara Sushi (Okara Gomoku-zushi): Double the amount of shoyu, sugar, and cooking water used in the seasoned broth. Simmer together with the carrot at least three of the following vegetables: snow peas, lotus root half-moons, green beans, *kombu* slivers, *(shiitake)* mushroom slivers, *kampyo* strips, or leek pieces. Mix the cooked vegetables with Sushi Okara and serve on a large platter garnished with a sprinkling of crumbled toasted *nori*.

OKARA DESSERTS

Okara Granola

MAKES 1½ CUPS

This is our favorite okara recipe. Golden brown, crumbly, and slightly sweet, it has much the same nutty aroma as toasted wheat germ, for which it makes an excellent substitute. You may wish to prepare a large quantity and store it in sealed jars.

2 cups okara
4 to 5 tablespoons natural sugar or honey
2 tablespoons oil
1 tablespoon vanilla
1/8 teaspoon salt

Preheat oven to 350°. Combine all ingredients, mixing well. Spread in a large, shallow pan and roast, stirring occasionally, for 50 to 60 minutes, or until nicely browned, crumbly, and fragrant. Serve with milk (try using the soymilk from which the okara was extracted) and top with raisins or fresh fruit. Also delicious as a topping for (soymilk) yogurt, a lightweight mix to take on hiking trips, or a substitute for bread crumbs in casserole toppings. Serve small portions; it expands!

For a crunchier texture and richer flavor, add ¼ cup any or all of the following: raisins, shredded coconut, toasted sunflower seeds or pine nuts, chopped almonds or walnuts, minced dates or apricots, toasted sesame seeds or wheat germ. Mix in these ingredients 5 minutes before the end of toasting. Use in any of the recipes in this book calling for crunchy granola.

Okara Dessert Soufflé

SERVES 4

3 eggs, separated into yolks and whites
½ cup okara
2 tablespoons honey
¼ teaspoon vanilla
1 tablespoon oil
Dash of salt
2 tablespoons raisins (optional)

Preheat oven to 400°. Beat egg yolks, then combine with the next five (or six) ingredients; mix well. Beat egg whites until stiff, then fold into okara-egg yolk mixture. Spoon into a lightly oiled loaf pan and bake for about 30 minutes, or until nicely browned.

Fig. 22. Okara Omelet Pouches

Okara Sponge Cake

SERVES 4

Use ingredients for Okara Dessert Soufflé, but double amounts of honey and vanilla; omit salt, oil, and raisins. Sift together ½ cup whole-wheat flour, 1 teaspoon baking powder, and ¼ teaspoon salt; stir into okara-egg yolk mixture before folding in egg whites. Proceed as for soufflé. Delicious topped with Tofu Icing (p. 149).

Baked Okara-Apple Dessert

SERVES 4

1 cup okara, firmly packed
2 small apples, cut into thin wedges
¼ cup raisins
2 eggs, lightly beaten (optional)
3 tablespoons natural sugar
¾ cup milk
Dash of salt
2 tablespoons bread crumbs
2 tablespoons butter
¼ teaspoon cinnamon
2 ounces grated cheese (optional)

Preheat oven to 350°. Combine the first seven ingredients in a bowl, mixing well. Spoon mixture into a lightly oiled casserole. Top with bread crumbs, dot with butter, and sprinkle with cinnamon and, if used, grated cheese. Bake for about 30 minutes, or until nicely browned.

Okara Doughnuts

MAKES ABOUT 10

2/3 cup okara, firmly packed
2/3 cup flour
1 egg, lightly beaten
1½ teaspoons baking powder
½ teaspoon salt
¼ cup raisins
3 to 6 tablespoons natural sugar
½ teaspoon cinnamon
Oil for deep-frying

Combine the first eight ingredients in a bowl; mix well to form a dough. Roll out on a floured board and cut as for doughnuts. Heat the oil to 370° in a wok, skillet, or deep-fryer. Slide in the doughnuts and deep-fry until golden brown (p. 130).

To make lighter doughnuts, roast the okara lightly (p. 79) before combining with ½ cup flour and 1 or 2 eggs.

Okara Peanut Butter Cookies

MAKES 20

¼ cup butter
¼ cup sifted natural sugar
1 egg, lightly beaten
½ cup peanut butter
¼ teaspoon salt
¼ teaspoon baking soda
¾ cup okara, lightly roasted (p. 79) if desired
¼ teaspoon vanilla

Preheat oven to 375°. Beat butter until soft. Blend in sugar, then mix in the remaining ingredients. Form this mixture into small patties and place on a lightly oiled baking tin. Bake for about 15 minutes or until nicely browned.

VARIATIONS

*Substitute ½ cup Kinako Butter (p. 65) for the peanut butter and add ½ cup grated coconut to the ingredients listed above.
*Omit the salt and vanilla. Substitute 1 cup sweet white miso for the peanut butter and add 6 tablespoons raisins to the ingredients listed above.

7
Curds and Whey

THE ART OF preparing homemade butter and cheese, and the vocabulary that went with it, are slowly disappearing from Western culture. But it was once commonly understood that when a solution of rennet—an enzyme extracted from the membrane of the fourth stomach of unweaned calves, lambs, or kids—was added to cow's milk, or when the milk was left uncovered for several days in a warm place, it curdled, separating into a thin, watery liquid (whey) and soft white semi-solids (curds). The curds, primarily coagulated milk protein called "casein," could then be fermented and aged to make cheese, or churned to make butter.

Although many Westerners today have never seen or tasted curds, they were widely enjoyed by our forefathers and are still a common delicacy in countries such as India where they are served in curries and puddings with sliced bananas and oranges. When Yogananda, one of the first great Yoga masters to teach in the West, was considering a life of blissful meditation in solitude rather than one of working for the spiritual benefit of others, he was asked critically by his master: "Do you want the whole divine *channa* (curds) for yourself alone?" And the Indian saint, Ramakrishna, indicating how people tend to chit-chat aimlessly until something vital appears in their lives, once said: "When the curds, the last course, appear, one only hears the sound 'soop-soop' as the guests eat the curds with their fingers."

The process of making tofu curds from soymilk resembles that for making dairy curds from cow's or goat's milk. Soymilk can be curdled or solidified with either a "salt" (such as nigari or magnesium chloride) or an acid (such as lemon juice or vinegar). When solidifier is stirred into hot soymilk and the soymilk is allowed to stand undisturbed for several minutes, the milk separates into delicate, white curds and pale yellow whey.

Soymilk Curds

After stirring nigari into the soymilk in his large, cedar curding barrel, the tofu craftsman covers the barrel with a wooden lid and allows the nigari to begin its work. Slowly it solidifies the soybean protein, which forms into curds and separates from the whey. After 15 or 20 minutes, the tofu maker rinses off a large, handsome bamboo colander and wraps its underside with cloth (fig. 23). He sets this on the surface of the mixture in the barrel and it slowly fills with whey. (The cloth keeps out the finer particles of curd.) The whey in the colander is ladled off and reserved for later use, and the colander is then weighted with a brick and replaced until it is again full (fig. 24). This whey, too, is ladled off into a large wooden bucket where it forms a billowy head of

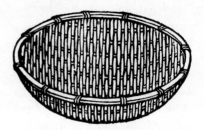

Fig. 23. A bamboo colander

86

Fig. 24. Weighting the colander

Fig. 25. Ladling whey from curds

foam (fig. 25). When all the whey has been removed, only white curds remain in the barrel.

The Japanese refer to curds as *oboro,* meaning "clouded over, hazy, or misty." The same word is used in the translation of the Biblical passage "through a glass darkly," and for describing a moon half hidden in clouds. The term "oboro" is particularly appropriate when used in reference to the tofu-making process, for a container of curding soymilk looks like a translucent, amber sky filled with soft white clouds. Curds made with nigari generally resemble cirrus clouds—long, thin, and wispy. If stirred or handled too roughly, they vanish. Curds made with calcium sulfate are more substantial and billowing, like cumulonimbus.

Like the clouds it resembles in so many other ways, *oboro* is transient; in a few moments it will be gone, only to reappear as tofu. But before it vanishes or changes form, it may be tasted. As soft as the most delicate custard, warm fresh curds have the richness of cream and a wonderful subtle sweetness.

When inviting guests to sample his *oboro,* the tofu maker scoops up a small dipperful of curds,

which he empties carefully onto a bamboo pressing mat, allowing the curds to drain briefly. He then slides the curds gently into a lacquerware bowl, seasons them with a few drops of shoyu, and asks his guests to partake of them while they are still warm. Many traditional masters have treated us to fresh curds in this way as we watched them making tofu.

When curds are ladled into cloth-lined settling boxes and pressed to make tofu, their fragile, almost insubstantial nature is given body and firmness. In most shops the finished curds are then soaked in water for several hours to firm and cool them, and thereby ensure maximum freshness. During the soaking, however, some of the rich and subtly sweet flavor of the curds is inevitably lost. Hence there are two simple ways to make their full goodness available commercially: one can either sell curds before they are pressed, or one can refrain from soaking finished tofu in water. In Taiwan and China, the warm curds themselves, called "flowers of tofu," are sold from pushcarts by street venders (fig. 104, p. 253). And many Chinese take a small pot or bowl to the neighborhood tofu shop each morning to

Fig. 26. Percentage of Original Soybean Protein Contained in Byproducts of the Tofu-making Process

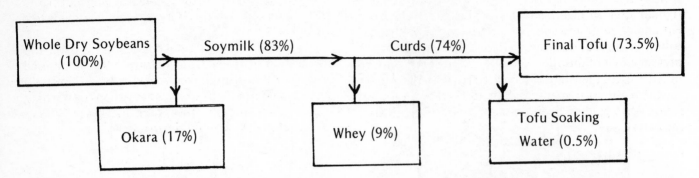

purchase these "flowers" for the family breakfast.

Almost all Japanese farmhouse tofu, and most commercial tofu in China and Taiwan, is allowed to cool either in the settling box or on a wooden pallet. Since these varieties of tofu are never soaked in water, their flavor remains closest to that of fresh curds. Homemade tofu can also be easily prepared in this way to keep it at its peak of flavor.

In Japan during the New Year's season, some tofu makers deliver warm curds from door to door. These are generally added to miso soups or seasoned with a little shoyu and any of the garnishes used for Chilled Tofu(p. 105). Curds are much more widely used in daily cookery in China than in Japan, being added there to noodle dishes, soups, and even sautéed vegetable dishes.

Many people may wonder why soymilk curds have never been fermented and aged in order to make Western-style cheeses. Research begun in the 1960s in California and Japan indicates that, in fact, tasty mild-flavored cheeses can be prepared inexpensively using bacteria from a dairy cheese starter and allowing well-pressed soymilk curds to ripen naturally for 3 to 9 weeks. These will soon be available commercially in flavors such as Cheddar.

In some parts of the United States, soymilk curds are now sold as Fresh Tofu Pudding, available in sealed polyethylene containers.

Whey

In the process of making tofu, whether at home or in a tofu shop, there are two inevitable byproducts: okara and whey. Containing valuable nutrients, both can be used in cooking. Whey is composed of 1 percent solids, 59 percent of which are proteins that were not solidified during the curding process. As shown in figure 26, whey contains 9 percent of the protein originally found in the dry soybeans,

plus much of the B vitamins and some of the natural sugars. It is produced in abundance whenever tofu is prepared; the curding process reduces 10 volumes of soymilk to about 1 part firmly-pressed curds and 9 parts whey.

At tofu shops, where more than 15 to 20 gallons are produced each day, whey is used as a gentle biodegradable soap. Hot whey is especially effective in cutting oils and quickly forms a head of suds when poured or stirred. The tofu maker carefully reserves the whey produced in his shop and uses it at the end of work each day to wash his tools. Both the deep-frying utensils and the barrels and dippers used for handling soymilk—which latter contains the natural oils found in soybeans—quickly become sparkling clean. On cold winter mornings, hot whey is also used to wash and warm the hands.

Some women use whey as a facial wash to remove oils and treat the complexion; others use it as a shampoo. It is also excellent for washing dishes, work clothes, or even fine silks. In Taiwan we noticed that many people come to tofu shops with a large pail to take home enough free "soap" to last for the day. In many homes it is used for washing and polishing wooden floors or woodwork, and for helping to give new woodwork a natural, seasoned look. Whey can also be used at home as a plant nutrient.

Like okara, warm whey is used to fatten livestock. Cows and horses are said to be able to gulp down a 3-gallon bucketful without taking a single breath. A tofu master in Kyoto told us how he offered a dray horse a pailful of whey one morning outside his shop (fig. 27). It seems that for years afterwards, whenever the horse passed, he stopped and refused to move until he was given his morning refresher.

Whey is collected in two different ways at tofu shops. First, as described above, it is ladled out of the curding barrel and reserved in a separate barrel or bucket. In addition, as it is pressed out of the tofu it is collected in the large wooden whey catch-box positioned underneath the settling boxes (see figure, p. 304).If soymilk has been solidified with just the right amount of nigari, its whey will have a transparent amber color and subtly sweet flavor. If too little solidifier is used, the whey will be cloudy due to the presence in it of unsolidified soymilk proteins. If too much is used, the whey will be bitter. To preview the flavor of the tofu, many craftsmen therefore take a sip of whey as they begin to ladle it out of the curding barrel.

About 70 percent of the solidifier added to soymilk dissolves in and is separated off with the whey. Sometimes, therefore, when a little uncurdled soymilk remains in the bottom of the curding barrel, the tofu maker will solidify it by stirring in some warm whey.

The 6 or 7 cups of whey resulting from the preparation of Homemade Tofu (p. 99) can be used place of water or milk when making bread, in cooking as a broth or soup stock, or as a soap for washing your tofu-making (or other) utensils. At last, a soap so mild and delicious you can drink it!

Fig. 27. A morning refresher

For each dumpling, moisten a 4- to 6-inch square of cheese-cloth (or a thin cotton cloth) and place it over the mouth of a cup. Push the cloth about 1/3 of the way into the cup to form a concave surface, and slip a rubber band around the rim of the cup to hold the cloth in place. Place 1 ladleful of warm curds onto the cloth (fig. 28), heaping the curds above the rim of the cup to give an evenly rounded upper surface. Allow curds to stand for 10 minutes, then immerse cloth and attached dumpling in cold water. After several minutes, carefully peel away the cloth; slip a small dish under each dumpling, lift out, and drain.

Karashi-dofu
(Curd Dumplings with Mustard)

MAKES 4

Prepared in many traditional tofu shops, these dumplings are sometimes filled with ginkgo nuts or some of the other ingredients used in ganmo.

Mix 1 teaspoon powdered hot mustard with just enough water to form a very thick paste. Cut a sheet of *nori* into 4 rectangles, each 1 by ½ inch. Form the mustard paste into 4 small cylinders about ½ inch long, then roll up each cylinder in one of the *nori* rectangles.

Prepare 4 cups, each 2½ inches in diameter, with cheesecloth squares set over their mouths as for Awayuki (see recipe above). Indent the cheesecloth to a depth of about 1½ inches below the rim of each cup and slip a rubber band around the rim of the cup to hold the cloth in place. Sprinkle the concave surface of each cloth with ¼ teaspoon powdered green *nori*, then using a small dipper or ladle (fig. 28), place a single scoop of curds in the cloth, filling it just to the rim. Place 1 *nori*-mustard roll in the center of the curds in each cup, then top with an additional half scoop of curds so that the upper surface of the curds in each cup is slightly rounded. Fill each of the cups in this way, then place the 4 cups close together, cover the curds with a moistened cloth and top with a cutting board. Place a 2-pound weight on the board and press the tofu for 20 to 30 minutes. Carefully remove the cloths from the curds and serve in any of the following ways:
  *Deep-fry the dumplings (without batter) in moderately-hot oil until golden brown; drain. Dip dumplings briefly into boiling water to remove excess surface oil, then simmer for 20 minutes in a mixture of 1 cup water or dashi, 3 tablespoons sugar, and 1½ tablespoons shoyu. Serve with a little of the cooking broth and garnish with thinly sliced leek or scallion rounds.
  *Serve in iced water as for Chilled Tofu (p. 105). Accompany individual servings with a small dish of shoyu, a garnish of grated gingerroot, and a topping of thinly sliced leek or scallion rounds.
  *Serve dumplings (chilled, warm, or deep-fried) topped with Ankake Sauce (p. 49) or Gingerroot Sauce (p. 49).

Warm Soymilk Curds *(Oboro-dofu)*

Proceed as for Homemade Tofu (p. 99). Just after ladling the whey out of the cooking pot (i.e. before ladling the curds into the settling container), scoop curds by the ladleful from the firm upper layer in the pot. Carefully place each ladleful of curds into a soup bowl and allow to stand for 1 minute. Holding the curds with your fingertips, pour off any excess whey that may have accumulated in the bowl. Serve immediately as is or:
  *Top warm curds with a few drops of shoyu, some whole or ground roasted sesame seeds, and/or a dash of *sansho* pepper. Or serve with any of the dipping sauces, garnishes, or miso toppings used with Chilled Tofu (p. 105).
  *Serve ¼ to ½ cup fresh curds in each cup of your favorite miso soup (p. 118).
  *Add curds to individual servings of tomato, onion, split pea or your favorite Western-style soups, then try seasoning lightly with shoyu or miso.
  *Place individual servings of curds in deep bowls and top with Ankake Sauce (p. 49). Season each portion lightly with a dab of grated gingerroot or a few drops of lemon juice, or serve with Gingerroot Sauce (p. 49) or the sauce for Takigawa-dofu (p. 210).
  *Mix curds with lightly beaten eggs and stir into Chinese egg-flower soups.
  *Gently stir curds into curry sauces or noodle dishes just before serving.
  *Serve curds Chinese-style seasoned with soy sauce, minced garlic, red pepper, and sesame oil, or topped with Spicy Korean Miso Sauté (p. 45).

Awayuki *(Homemade Curd Dumplings)*

Awayuki, meaning "light snow," is an excellent description of the texture and color of these soft and delicate dumplings. Traditional tofu shops prepare and sell them for use in various soup and *nabe* dishes.

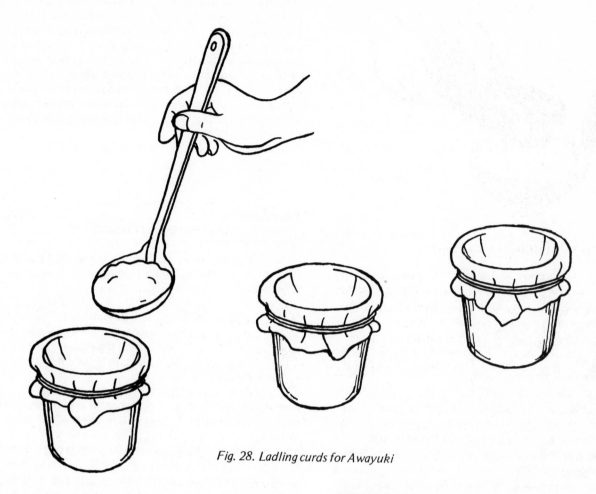

Fig. 28. Ladling curds for Awayuki

Kinugoshi Curds

SERVES 4

Prepare Homemade Kinugoshi (p. 215) or Soft Tofu (p. 216). After stirring in solidifier, allow tofu to stand for only 8 to 10 minutes, or until it is firm but still warm. Fill serving bowls with ¾ cup curds and serve topped with a few drops of shoyu or with the following sauce, popular in Taiwan and China.

> **Sweet Peanut Sauce**
> ¾ cup water
> 3 to 4 tablespoons unsalted peanuts
> 1½ tablespoons natural sugar or honey
> ½ teaspoon shoyu

Combine all ingredients in a small saucepan and bring to a boil. Reduce heat to low, cover pan, and simmer for 5 to 10 minutes. Serve hot. For a thicker preparation: after sauce has finished cooking, stir in ¼ teaspoon cornstarch dissolved in 1 tablespoon water and simmer for 30 seconds more.

Chilled Curds

When chilled, soymilk curds lose a bit of their subtle sweetness and fragile texture but make a refreshing summer-time treat or dessert. Any type of tofu curds can be used. Place several scoops of the chilled curds into small bowls and serve topped with fruit cocktail, orange sections, honey, maple syrup, or fruit syrup. Or serve in iced water as for Chilled Tofu (p. 105). (In the western United States, Tofu Pudding or Fresh Soybean Pudding, made from chilled soft tofu, is now available commercially.)

Homemade Whey

Reserve the 6 to 7 cups of whey which separate from the curds in the process of preparing Homemade Tofu (p. 99) for use as stock with soups or stews, in breads, or in simmered vegetable dishes. Or serve hot, like tea, as is. The most delicious whey comes from tofu that has been solidified with natural (clean) seawater which evokes the whey's subtly sweet flavors.

8
Tofu

J UST AS the word "bread" is used in reference to a wide variety of baked goods, the word "tofu" in its broad sense refers to a number of different soybean foods. Each of the seven basic types of Japanese tofu will be discussed in the following chapters; the many varieties of Chinese tofu will be treated in Chapter 15.

The word "tofu" is also used in a more limited sense to refer to "regular tofu," the simplest, least expensive variety and the one most widely known in the West (fig. 29). This tofu has no exact equivalent in Western cuisine and does not quite fit the English terms "soybean curd" and "soybean cheese" often used to describe it. Tofu is made *from* soybean curds just as cheese is made *from* dairy curds: after ladling off whey from the soymilk curds in his curding barrel, the tofu maker scoops the curds into two cloth-lined wooden settling boxes and tops them with a pressing lid and heavy weight for about thirty minutes (fig. 30). During this time the curds are firmed and made *into* tofu. Similarly, although the finished tofu, stored under water in deep sinks, has the color and shape of a light cheese, it is not fermented, aged, or ripened; hence the name "soybean cheese" is also inappropriate. (For a more detailed description of the tofu-making process, see Part IV.)

Of East Asia's three great soybean foods—tofu, miso, and shoyu—only tofu has a theory associated with its historical origin. According to ancient Chinese and Japanese references, as well as to popular tradition, the method for preparing both soymilk and tofu was discovered by Lord Liu An of Huai-nan in about 164 B.C. A famous scholar and philosopher, ruler and politician, Liu An is said to have been inter-

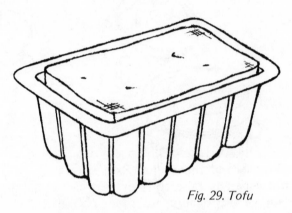

Fig. 29. Tofu

ested in alchemy and Taoist meditation. A close friend of many Taoist students, he may have undertaken his experiments with tofu as a way of introducing nutritious variety into their simple meatless diet. Historians believe that Liu An's tofu was probably solidified with either nigari or seawater and had a firm texture similar to most of the tofu made in China today.

There are two basic theories which try to account for the discovery of tofu. Lord Liu An or earlier Chinese may have discovered the method for curding soymilk quite by accident. Since soybeans were considered one of the Five Sacred Grains, they were probably dried like other grains before being cooked. If later boiled, they would either be added to water whole, or first ground or mashed into a purée. If used in purée form, the result would be a thick "soup" that would have to be seasoned. If the cook added natural salt—which contains bittern (nigari)—curds would soon form: the salt, intended as a seasoning, would have worked as a solidifying agent. The cook may later have decided to remove the fibrous okara from the purée to give the resulting

Fig. 30. Pressing tofu in settling boxes

curds a finer, more delicate texture. The next step, pressing, would have helped the food stay fresh longer and would have given it a texture firm enough to keep its form after being cut. The final result would then have been very similar to present-day tofu.

The second theory proposes that, since they did not generally raise cows or goats for milk, the Chinese were probably not familiar initially with the curding process; they may have learned it from the Indians in the south or the Mongols in the north, both of whom made curds and cheese. Advocates of the "importation theory" also note that the three other mild-flavored foods most favored by the Chinese—shark fins, swallow's nest, and trepang (sea slugs)—were also imported.

Tofu next appears in Chinese history about 800 years later. It is said that Bodhidharma, who lived in China from about 520 to 528 and founded the Chinese *Ch'an* (Zen) school, engaged tofu in "Dharma combat" to probe tofu's understanding of the Buddha's way. Bodhidharma later praised tofu for its simplicity, its honest, straightforward nature, and its "lovely white robes."

The earliest existing document containing mention of tofu is the *Seiiroku*, written during the Sung Dynasty (960-1127), more than 1,000 years after the food's discovery. Numerous other books of this period refer to a work written about 60 to 100 B.C. (but no longer in existence) which contained the story of Lord Liu An and the earliest tofu. In a work of the late Sung Dynasty, there is a description of the

menu served by a king to a prince, and tofu is included.

Tofu reached Japan during the eighth century and was probably brought from China by the numerous Buddhist monks and priests who were going back and forth between the two countries. Tofu is thought to have entered Japanese society through the upper classes, those who were connected with Chinese cultural and economic interchange, the court nobility, and the priesthood. Buddhist monks probably used tofu as a daily food in Japanese temples at a very early date. Emphasizing the value of a meatless diet, they were certainly a major factor in the early spread of tofu as a popular food. Some scholars believe that all of Japan's (and China's) earliest tofu shops were located within large temples or monasteries and were run by Buddhist priests and temple cooks.

During the Kamakura period (1185–1333), there was a large-scale movement to make Japanese Buddhism available to the common people. The five major Kamakura Zen temples each opened Buddhist vegetarian restaurants within their temple compounds, and existing records show that tofu was included on the menus. Laymen, having tasted tofu there for the first time, apparently learned from the monks how to prepare it, then opened their own shops in the capital cities of Kamakura and Kyoto. It was only later that tofu-making spread from the cities to the countryside.

During the Kamakura period, the new *samurai*

Transferring tofu-filled settling box to sink

Cutting tofu into cakes under water

ruling class practiced a simple, frugal, and down-to-earth way of life. These warriors greatly simplified the national cuisine by their example. It is said that tofu and miso replaced fresh river fish as the ruling shogun's prized delicacies, and that the samurai came to cherish agé and tofu, particularly as ingredients in their breakfast miso soup. It was also at this time that farmers started growing soybeans on a large scale in Japan's cold, dry provinces.

During the Muromachi period (1336-1568) tofu spread throughout Japan and became a popular daily food at all levels of society. Many of the great tea masters of the period used tofu extensively in their Tea Ceremony Cookery, which helped to bring tofu into the world of Japanese haute cuisine and to introduce it to famous chefs and restauranteurs. Since most Japanese followed the Buddhist practice of refraining from eating the meat of "four legged animals," tofu was welcomed as a source of inexpensive and tasty protein. The Japanese went on to invent several new forms of the food, including dried-frozen tofu, agé, ganmo, grilled tofu, and nigari kinugoshi.

As tofu became widely used in Japan, its basic character was gradually changed. In the hands of native craftsmen, tofu became softer, whiter, and more delicate in flavor. Farmhouse tofu alone retained some of the firmness and rich flavor of its Chinese predecessor.

When the Chinese Zen master, Ingen, came to Japan in 1661 he was surprised to find tofu unlike any he had known in China. In praise of this new food he composed an intricate yet simple proverb which is well known to this day. It described both the character of Japanese tofu and that of a man who wishes to pass freely and peacefully through this fleeting, illusory world. The proverb went:

> *Mame de*
> *Shikaku de*
> *Yawaraka de*

Each line had a double meaning, allowing the poem to be read either:

Made of soybeans, *or*	Practicing diligence,
Square, cleanly cut,	Being proper and honest
And soft.	And having a kind heart.

The word "tofu" first appears in a Japanese written document (the diary of Nakatomino Sukeshige) in 1183, where it is mentioned that tofu was used as a food offering at an altar. Mention is again made of it in a letter of thanks from the famous Buddhist priest Nichiren Shonin, written in 1239. The word "tofu" written with the present characters did not appear in Japan until the 1500s. The first Japanese "Book of Tofu" (*Tofu Hyaku Chin*) was written in 1782 and contained 100 tofu recipes culled from throughout Japan. A famous book in its day, it is still widely quoted.

Throughout its long history in Japan, tofu has appeared in numerous forms, some of which no longer exist. For example, when the Zen master Ingen, mentioned above, established the well-known

Mampuku-ji temple south of Kyoto, he taught the monks and local tofu masters how to prepare Chinese-style Pressed Tofu (see p. 251). Although this very firm variety became popular during the next century, it is now prepared by only one shop in Japan and is featured in Zen Temple Cuisine only in restaurants near Mampuku-ji. A closely related type of firm tofu called *rokujo-dofu* was prepared by tying 5 pieces of pressed tofu together with rice straw (fig. 90, p. 228), then drying them in direct sunlight until they were dark brown and quite hard. Finely shaved, rokujo-dofu was used like bonita flakes; it is presently prepared only in Fukushima prefecture. A third variety of virtually extinct tofu was walnut tofu, prepared by mixing chunks of walnuts into soybean curds just before they were pressed. Chinese fermented tofu (called *nyufu* in Japan and *doufu-ru* in China) was transmitted to Japan in early times and became popular among the aristocracy, in temples, and in a few rural areas. Its strong flavor, however, led to its gradual decline; today it is rarely if ever seen.

As tofu became a part of the language and culture in both Japan and China, it came to be used in proverbs and sayings. In China, finding fault with a person is compared to "finding a bone in your tofu." When a Japanese wants to tell a person to "get lost," he may say "Go bump your head against the corner of a cake of tofu and drop dead." Or when speaking of something as being hopeless he might say "It's as futile as trying to clamp two pieces of tofu together."

Tofu became a part of the culture in other ways too. For example, in the Women's Mass for Needles, started 1600 years ago by the Emperor Nintoku and still practiced in Japan, a cake of tofu is placed on the household altar and all the needles that have been bent or broken during the year are thrust into it. Each needle is thought of as a living being whose body has been sacrificed in service, and the woman of the house, as an expression of her gratitude, gives it this soft resting place as a reward for its hard work.

Up until the start of World War II, virtually all Japanese tofu was prepared in small household shops from gô cooked over a wood fire in an iron cauldron and soymilk solidified with natural nigari. Only after World War II did new solidifiers (such as calcium sulfate) and ways of cooking (such as with pressurized steam) come into vogue. In recent years, large shops and factories have begun to mass-produce tofu; each 10½ ounce cake is water-packed in a polyethylene container, thermally sealed with a sheet of transparent film, and pasteurized by immersion for one hour in hot water to give a shelf life of up to 1 week. Distributed over an area of several hundred miles in refrigerated trucks, this tofu is sold in supermarkets and neighborhood grocery stores at a price slightly below that of the tofu sold in most neighborhood shops.

About 900 years passed from the time of the discovery of tofu in China until its arrival in Japan. Another 1200 years passed before it made the leap westward across the Pacific Ocean to America where there are now more than 50 tofu shops, the oldest of which has been making tofu since the turn of the century. The history of tofu in the West, therefore, has only just begun.

PREPARATORY TECHNIQUES

The following procedures are used regularly in cooking with tofu. Try to master them from the outset, since each gives the tofu a unique consistency and texture. The eight techniques listed below are in order of the amount of water each allows to remain in the tofu. Thus parboiling, the first technique, expels very little water, while crumbling rids the tofu of more than 65 percent of its moisture, leaving it very firm and containing more than 20 percent protein. Figure 31 shows the effect of each technique on the weight, protein, and moisture content of a 12 ounce cake of tofu originally containing 7.8 percent protein and 84.9 percent water. For a graphic description of the relationship between protein and moisture content in different types of tofu, see figure 6 on page 25.

When fresh tofu is mashed or blended, 9 ounces yield 1 cup, and 12 ounces yield approximately 1½ cups.

Fig. 31. Effects of Preparatory Techniques on 1 Cake of Tofu

Preparatory Technique	Final Weight of 12 oz of Tofu (oz)	Percent Protein in Final Tofu (%)	Percent Reduction in Weight from Loss of Water (%)
Parboiling	11.5	8.0	3.5
Draining	10.0	8.5	17.0
Pressing	8.5	10.0	30.0
Squeezing	6.5	13.0	47.0
Scrambling	6.3	13.5	48.0
Reshaping	4.5	19.0	63.0
Crumbling	4.0	20.5	66.0
Grinding	4.0	21.0	67.0

Parboiling

This technique is used with both regular and kinugoshi tofu for at least four different purposes: 1) To warm the tofu before serving it topped with hot sauces; 2) To freshen stored tofu that shows signs of spoiling; 3) To make the tofu slightly firmer so that when simmered in seasoned broths it absorbs flavors without diluting the cooking medium; 4) To impart to the tofu a slight cohesiveness desired when preparing *aemono* (Japanese-style tofu salads).

The addition of a small amount of salt to the water seasons the tofu slightly, imparts to it a somewhat firmer texture, and makes possible longer parboiling without the tofu developing an undesirably porous structure. (It is for these reasons that *kombu* or salt are generally added to the broth of Simmering Tofu [p. 142] and other *nabe* preparations.)

Because parboiling causes a slight loss in some of the tofu's delicate flavors, it should be used only when necessary.

*Regular Parboiling: Bring 1 quart water to a boil in a saucepan. Reduce heat to low and drop in tofu. Cover and heat for 2 to 3 minutes, or until tofu is well warmed. (For a firmer texture, cut tofu into 4 equal pieces before parboiling.) Lift out finished pieces with a slotted spoon.

*Salted Water Method: Bring 2 cups water to a boil in a saucepan. Add ½ teaspoon salt, drop in (uncut) 12-ounce cake of tofu, and return to the boil. Remove pan from heat and allow to stand for 2 to 3 minutes. Remove tofu, discarding water.

Draining

Draining or storing tofu out of water (for no more than 12 hours) gives it a fairly firm texture and also helps preserve its flavor, since its subtle natural sweetness is lost quite easily in water. A 12-ounce cake of tofu drained for 8 hours will lose moisture equal to about 17 percent of its weight. The protein content of the final 10-ounce cake thereby increases from 7.8 to about 8.5 percent.

Place the tofu in a 1- or 2-quart flat-bottomed container. Cover well and refrigerate for 1 to 2 hours or, for a firmer texture, overnight.

If set on a small colander or folded towel placed into the container beforehand, the tofu will drain even more thoroughly.

If two cakes are stacked one on top of the other, the one on the bottom will be almost as firm as if it were pressed (see below).

If the tofu was purchased in a sealed plastic tub, prick a tiny hole in bottom of tub, drain out any water, and place tofu and tub in container as described above.

Pressing

When pressing tofu, it is important to preserve the form and structure of the cake so that it may later be cut into thin slices. Tofu is fully pressed when it can be picked up and held vertically in the air without crumbling. Pressing time may be varied to suit the dish being prepared: light pressing preserves the tofu's softness for use in tossed salads, while lengthy pressing gives firmer, stronger tofu for use in deep-frying.

Because of its delicate texture and unique structure (which holds water in millions of tiny "cells"), kinugoshi is almost never pressed. Doufu (Chinese-style firm tofu) has a cohesive structure and low water content and may be used without further pressing in any recipe calling for pressed tofu. Pat its surface dry with a cloth before use.

*Towel and Fridge Method: Wrap the tofu firmly in a small terry-cloth or cotton towel folded into fourths (facing), and set on a plate in a refrigerator for 1½ to 2 hours or overnight. To decrease the pressing time, drain the tofu beforehand, place a 2- or 3-pound weight on top of the tofu, and replace the damp towel with a dry one after about 30 minutes. Or cut the cake horizontally into halves before pressing and place in the towel as illustrated.

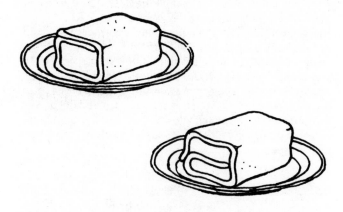

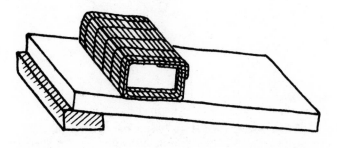

*Slanting Press Method: Wrap the tofu in a towel or bamboo mat *(sudare)* (or sandwich the tofu between bamboo mats) and place on a cutting board, tray, or large plate next to the sink; raise the far end of the board several inches. Set a 2- to 4-pound weight on the tofu and let stand for 30 to 60 minutes (below).

*Sliced Tofu Method: Cut the tofu crosswise into ½- to ¾-inch-thick slices and arrange on two towels placed on a raised cutting board (below). Cover the slices with a double layer of towels and pat lightly to ensure even contact. Allow to stand for 30 to 60 minutes. This method is commonly used when preparing tofu for deep-frying. For faster results, top with a cutting board and 5-pound weight and change the towels after 10 minute intervals.

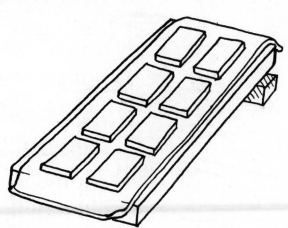

Squeezing

This process results in a mashed tofu that is slightly cohesive and has a texture resembling that of cottage cheese.

Place drained, parboiled, or pressed tofu (or doufu) at the center of a large dry dishtowel and gather its corners to form a sack. (Or use a tofu pressing sack [p. 34] if available.) Twist sack closed, then squeeze tofu firmly, kneading it for 2 or 3 minutes to expel as much water as possible (below). Squeeze lightly enough so that no tofu penetrates the sack. Empty the squeezed tofu into a mixing bowl.

Scrambling

This technique causes a further separation of tofu curds and liquid whey resulting in a texture similar to that produced by squeezing, but one which is slightly firmer and more crumbly.

Place tofu in an unheated skillet. Using a (wooden) spatula, break tofu into small pieces. Now cook over medium heat for 4 to 5 minutes, stirring constantly and breaking tofu into smaller and smaller pieces until whey separates from curds. Pour contents of skillet into a fine-mesh strainer; allow curds to drain for about 15 seconds if a soft consistency is desired, or for about 3 minutes for a firmer consistency. Spread curds on a large plate and allow to cool to room temperature.

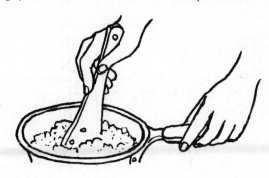

Reshaping

This process yields a tofu cake having a very firm and cohesive consistency similar to that of natural cheese, Chinese doufu-kan (p. 251), or processed ham. Called *oshi-dofu*, or "Pressed Tofu," in Japan, it is used in recipes calling for pieces the size of French-fried potatoes which hold their shape during cooking or tossing.

The first method given below takes about twice as long as the second, but yields a tofu that retains more of its natural flavor and texture. The addition of salt that it calls for prevents the tofu from developing a somewhat elastic, web-like structure while also seasoning it. The second method yields a firmer structure that holds together better during sautéing. The tofu undergoes a slight loss in flavor that is not very noticeable if served with a well-seasoned sauce in the typical Chinese style.

*Firm Seasoned Tofu: Combine 24 ounces tofu and 1 teaspoon salt in a saucepan; mix well. Stirring constantly, cook over medium heat for about 4 minutes or until tofu begins to boil vigorously. Pour the tofu into a cloth-lined colander in the sink and allow to drain for several minutes. Transfer the cloth onto a cutting board and carefully fold the edges of the cloth over the tofu; shape the tofu into a cake about 5 inches square and 1 inch thick. Place a pan filled with 3 or 4 quarts of water on top of the cloth (below) and press for 1 to 2 hours in a cool place. Unwrap and cut as directed; or re-wrap in a dry towel and refrigerate for later use.

*Very Firm Tofu: Boil the tofu in unsalted water as when crumbling (see below). Drain tofu, then proceed as above, pressing the tofu for 30 to 60 minutes.

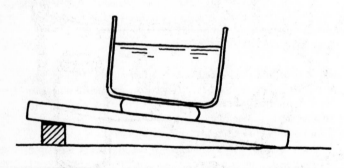

Crumbling

By reducing its water content to a minimum, we can obtain tofu with much the same texture as lightly sautéed, crumbly hamburger. Yet the tofu is slightly firmer, lighter, and fluffier, which makes it ideal for use in tossed salads, egg and grain dishes, spaghetti or curry sauces, and casseroles. (Kinugoshi, too, can be crumbled, either by the method described below or by scrambling [p. 97] and then pressing as follows.)

Combine 12 ounces tofu and 1 cup water in a saucepan. With a wooden spoon or spatula, break the tofu into very small pieces while bringing the water to a boil. Reduce heat and simmer for 1 to 2 minutes. Place a colander in the sink and line with a large cloth (or a tofu pressing sack). Pour the contents of the pan onto the cloth, gather its corners to form a sack, then twist closed. Using the bottom of a jar or a potato masher, press the tofu firmly against the bottom of the colander to expel as much water as possible. Empty the pressed tofu into a large bowl and allow to cool for several minutes. Now break the tofu into very small pieces, using your fingertips or a spoon.

Grinding

This process yields tofu having much the same light, dry consistency as crumbled tofu, but with a texture that is finer and more uniform.

Using either regular tofu or kinugoshi, prepare reshaped or crumbled tofu (p. 98). Refrigerate tofu in a covered container until well chilled. Then, cutting into chunks if necessary, run through a meat grinder with a medium-fine attachment.

HOMEMADE TOFU

If you find that fresh tofu is not available at a nearby store, try preparing your own at home using either whole soybeans or powdered soymilk. It's as enjoyable as baking bread— and considerably faster.

Homemade Tofu

MAKES 33 TO 39 OUNCES

We have found the following recipe, based on the traditional Japanese farmhouse method, to be easy to follow and virtually foolproof. The tofu will be ready 50 to 60 minutes after you start. One pound of soybeans yields about 3½ to 4 pounds of tofu at a cost about one-third to one-fourth that of commercial tofu and less than one-half the cost (on a usable protein basis) of hamburger. Solidified with nigari, made from soymilk simmered over an open fire (rather than steamed), and served at its peak of freshness, homemade tofu contains a fullness of flavor and subtle sweetness seldom found in even the finest storebought varieties.

Utensils

To make fine homemade tofu, you will need the following common kitchen tools (fig. 32):

An electric blender, food- or grain mill, or meat grinder
A "cooking pot" with a capacity of 2½ to 3 gallons
A "pressing pot" with a capacity of 1½ to 2 gallons, or a basin of comparable size
A 2-quart saucepan
A wooden spatula, rice paddle, or wooden spoon with a long handle
A shallow ladle or dipper about 1 inch deep and 3 or 4 inches in diameter, or a large spoon
A rubber spatula
A sturdy 1-quart jar or a potato masher
A 1-cup measuring cup
A set of measuring spoons
A large, round-bottomed colander (that will fit into the "pressing pot")
A flat-bottomed colander ("settling container") preferably square or rectangular
A shallow fine-mesh strainer or bamboo colander (*zaru*)
A coarsely-woven cotton dishcloth, 2 feet square, or a "pressing sack"
A 2-foot square of cheesecloth, or a light cotton dishtowel of comparable dimensions.

Fig. 32. Utensils for making tofu

Two special pieces of equipment, both easy to assemble, will make the work even easier:

*Make a "pressing sack" of the coarsely-woven cotton dishtowel mentioned above, or use a piece of sturdy linen cloth with about the same coarseness of weave as cheesecloth.. Fold the towel or cloth end to end and sew up the sides to form a sack about 15 inches wide and 15 inches deep. Or use a small flour sack with a fairly coarse weave.

*The flat-bottomed colander listed above is for use as a "settling container" which gives its shape to the finished tofu. If a 1-quart strainer or small, round-bottomed colander is used in its place, the tofu will naturally be rounded.

The three settling containers in figure 33 can easily be made at home. Container (a) is prepared from a 1½-quart wooden, tupperware, or plastic box with an open top and non-removable bottom. In containers (b) and (c) the bottom is removable, allowing for easy removal of the tofu without immersing the container in water. Good dimensions for the container are 4½ inches square by 4½ inches deep, or 6½ by 3½ by 4½ inches deep. Use a drill or heated icepick to bore ³/₈-inch-diameter holes about 1½ inches apart in the bottom and sides of the container. Fashion a flat wooden or plastic pressing lid (with or without holes) to fit down inside the rim of the box. Good woods to use are Philippine mahogany, vertical-grain Douglas fir, pine, maple, cedar, or cherry. An easy-to-use, high-quality TOFU KIT containing everything you need (including Philippine mahogany box, nigari solidifier, muslin pressing sack, and cloths, but **not** soybeans) is now made in America. For a free list of suppliers, send a self-addressed, stamped envelope to Soyfoods Center.

Ingredients

You will need only the following readily available ingredients:

Soybeans

The soybeans now sold at almost all natural- and health food stores, most co-op stores, and many supermarkets will make good tofu. However, to obtain the highest yield, try buying soybeans directly from a tofu shop in your area (see Appendix B), for they have been carefully chosen by the tofu maker.

Solidifier

The solidifiers most readily available in the West are Epsom salts, lemon or lime juice, and vinegar. All make delicious tofu, although they are not used in Japanese tofu shops. Japanese-style solidifiers are available from many natural food stores, local tofu shops, Japanese food markets, chemical supply houses (check your phone directory), or your local school chemistry lab. Usable seawater can be retrieved from clean stretches of ocean. Natural nigari comes in the TOFU KIT described on this page and is sold at some natural food stores, or it can be prepared at home using natural salt (p. 283). We recommend the use of refined nigari unless the natural nigari is certified to have come from a clean source of sea water. While we believe the nigari-type solidifiers are the easiest to use and result in the best tasting tofu, Epsom salts and calcium sulfate seem to give somewhat higher bulk yields and a softer end product by incorporating more water into the tofu. The yield of tofu solids or nutrients is about the same regardless of the type of solidifier used, except that lemon juice and vinegar give rather small yields. (Note: Calcium sulfate, a fine white powder, is sometimes mislabeled in the West and sold as nigari. The latter usually has a coarse, granular or crystaline texture; natural nigari is beige and refined nigari is white.)

The recipe below calls only for "solidifier." Your choice of solidifier depends upon the type of tofu you want.

For subtly sweet, nigari tofu use: 2 teaspoons magnesium chloride or calcium chloride (refined nigari); or 1½ to 2¼ teaspoons granular or powdered natural nigari; or 1½ to 2½ teaspoons homemade liquid nigari; or 2 to 4½ teaspoons commercially prepared liquid nigari; or 1½ cups seawater (freshly collected; p. 282).

For mild, soft tofu use: 2 teaspoons Epsom salts (magnesium sulfate) or calcium sulfate; or 1½ tablespoons each calcium lactate and lemon juice (the latter being stirred into the soymilk just after the last of the calcium lactate has been added).

For subtly tart or sour tofu use: 4 tablespoons lemon or lime juice (freshly squeezed); or 3 tablespoons (apple cider) vinegar.

Fig. 33. Three designs for a homemade settling container

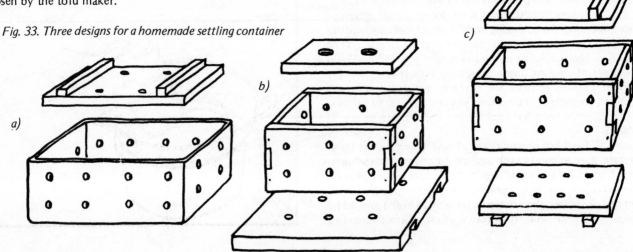

a)

b)

c)

Method

1½ cups soybeans, washed, soaked in 6 cups water for 10 hours (see graph, p. 289), rinsed and drained
16 cups water, approximately
Solidifer

Prepare in advance:

Place pressing pot in sink and set colander into pot. Moisten pressing sack lightly and line colander with sack, fitting mouth of sack around rim of colander. Or line colander with a moistened 2-foot-square dish towel (fig. 34a).

Moisten cheesecloth or thin cotton dishtowel and use to line bottom and sides of settling container. Place container on rim of large bowl or pan placed in sink.

After making the above preparations, proceed as follows:

Fig. 34. Preparing homemade tofu

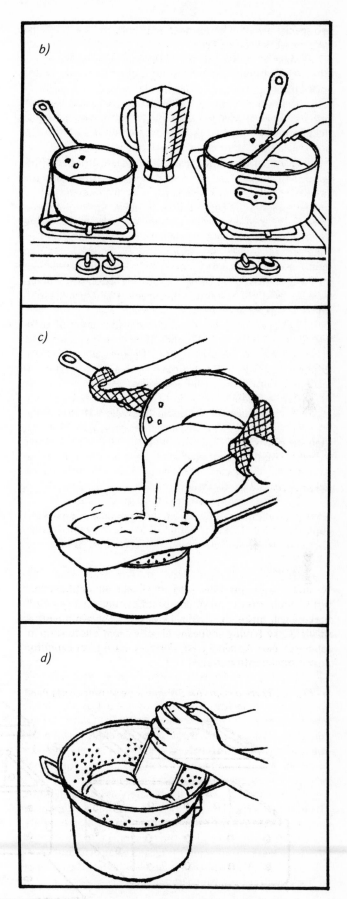

1) Heat 7½ cups water over high heat in cooking pot. While water is heating, divide beans into two equal portions. Combine one portion with 2 cups water in a blender and purée at high speed for about 3 minutes, or until very smooth. Add purée (gô) to water heating (or boiling) in cooking pot, then purée the remaining soybeans with 2 cups water in the same way and add to the pot. (If using a food mill or meat grinder, grind beans without adding water and add 4 cups more water to cooking pot.) Rinse out blender with a little water to retrieve any purée that may cling to blender's walls.

2) Taking care that pot does not boil over, continue heating on high heat, stirring bottom of pot frequently with a wooden spatula or spoon to prevent sticking (fig. b). When foam suddenly rises in pot, quickly turn off heat and pour contents of cooking pot into pressing sack (fig. c). Using a rubber spatula, retrieve any soybean purée that may still cling to the sides of the cooking pot and transfer to pressing sack. Quickly rinse out cooking pot and replace on top of stove.

3) Twist hot pressing sack closed. Using a glass jar or potato masher, press sack against colander, expressing as much soymilk as possible (fig. d). Open sack, shake okara it contains into one of its corners, close and press again. Now empty okara into the saucepan (or a large bowl) and add 3 cups water; stir well, then return moist okara to pressing

sack set in the colander. Close sack and press well as before; squeeze by hand to express the last of the soymilk (fig. e). Empty okara into the 2-quart saucepan and set aside.

4) Measure solidifier into dry 1-cup measuring cup and set aside.

5) Pour soymilk into cooking pot and bring to a boil over high heat, stirring frequently to prevent sticking. Reduce heat to medium and cook for 5 to 7 minutes; turn off heat and remove pot from burner.

6) Add 1 cup water to solidifier in measuring cup (unless using seawater) and stir until dissolved. With a to-and-fro movement, stir soymilk vigorously 5 or 6 times and, while stirring, pour in 1/3 cup solidifier solution. Stir 5 or 6 times more, making sure to reach bottom and sides of pot. Bring spoon to a halt upright in soymilk and wait until all turbulence ceases; lift out spoon (fig. f). Sprinkle 1/3 cup solidifier over surface of soymilk, cover pot, and wait 3 minutes while curds form. Using a measuring spoon, stir remaining 1/3 cup solidifier solution, uncover pot, and sprinkle solution over surface of soymilk.

7) Very slowly stir upper ½-inch-thick layer of curdling soymilk for 15 to 20 seconds, then cover pot and wait 3 minutes. (Wait 6 minutes if using Epsom salts or calcium sulfate). Uncover and stir surface layer again for 20 to 30 seconds, or until all milky liquid curdles.

(White "clouds" of delicate curds should now be floating in a clear, pale-yellow liquid, the whey. If any milky, uncurdled liquid remains suspended in whey, wait 1 minute, then stir gently until curdled. If milky liquid persists, dissolve a small amount of additional solidifier [about ¼ of the original amount] in 1/3 cup water and pour directly into uncurdled portions; stir gently until curdled.)

8) Place cooking pot next to settling container in sink. Gently press fine-mesh strainer into pot and allow several cups whey to collect in it. Ladle all of this whey into settling container to re-moisten lining cloths (fig. g). Set strainer aside.

9) Now ladle curds—and any remaining whey—into settling container one layer at a time. Ladle gently so as not to break curds' fragile structure (fig. h). Fold edges of cloth neatly over curds (fig. i), place a lid on top of cloth (a small board or flat plate will do), and set a ½- to 1½-pound weight on top of lid for 10 to 15 minutes, or until whey no longer drips from settling container (fig. j).

10) Fill pressing pot, a large basin, or sink with cold water. Remove weight and lid from atop tofu, then place container holding tofu into basin of water (fig. k). Slowly invert container, leaving cloth-wrapped tofu in water; lift out container. While it is still under water, carefully unwrap and cut tofu crosswise into halves. Allow tofu to remain under water for 3 to 5 minutes, until firm. To lift out, slip a small plate under each piece of tofu; drain briefly (fig. l).

For best flavor, serve immediately as Chilled Tofu (p. 105) or Simmering Tofu (p. 142). Store tofu in a cool place until ready to serve. (If not to be served for 8 or 10 hours, store under cold water.) Use the remaining 6 to 7 ounces (1 firmly packed cup) okara in the recipes given in Chapter 6, or refrigerate in an airtight container. Use the 6 to 7 cups whey in stocks and/or for washing your utensils.

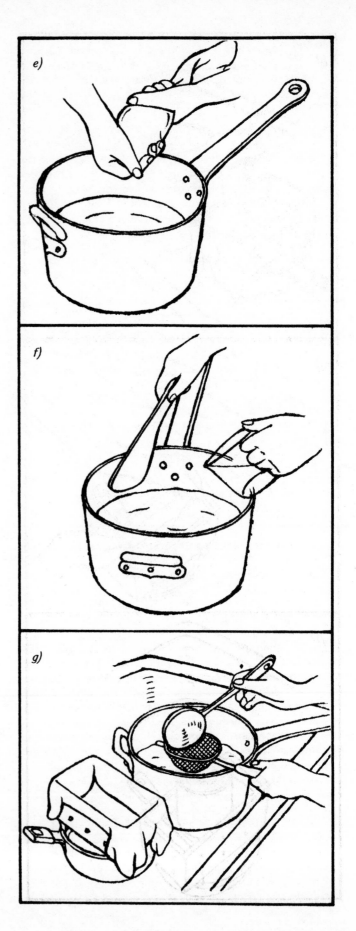

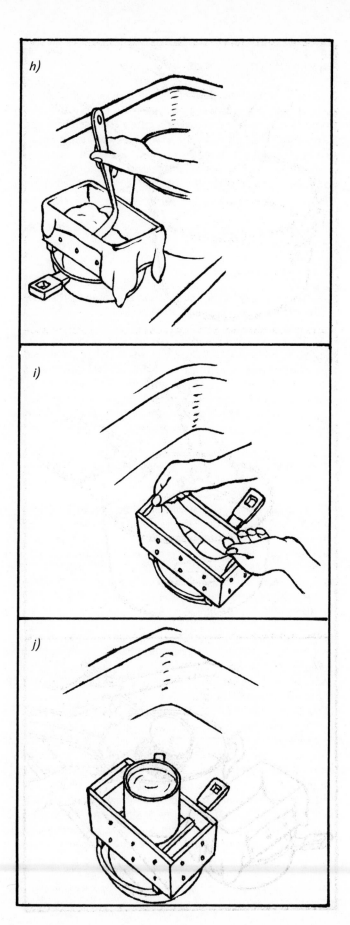

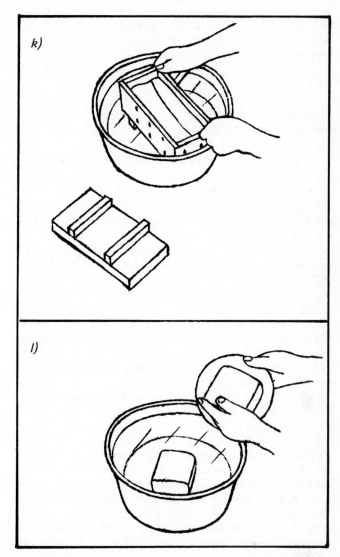

VARIATIONS

*Firm Farmhouse- or Chinese-style Tofu: We find this tofu to have the finest flavor, texture, and aroma. The apparent drop in bulk yield is due only to a loss of water, not of protein or other nutrients.

Cook the puréed soybeans in a heavy iron pot over an open wood fire. Use a nigari-type solidifier and, if possible, new-crop, organically grown (Japanese) soybeans. Ladle the curds quickly and not too carefully into the settling container, and press for 30 to 40 minutes with a 2-pound weight. Then invert the container leaving the tofu resting on the lid. (Or lift off the sides of a farmhouse-style container [fig. 35].) Remove the cloths and serve the tofu without immersing it in water.

*Omit Rinsing and Re-pressing Okara: This simplifies the basic method but gives a slightly lower yield. Begin by heating 7 rather than 5 cups water in cooking pot. After first pressing okara, open pressing sack in colander and allow okara to cool for 3 to 5 minutes. While okara is cooling, reheat soymilk. Holding pressing sack over cooking pot, squeeze by hand to expel any soymilk remaining in okara.

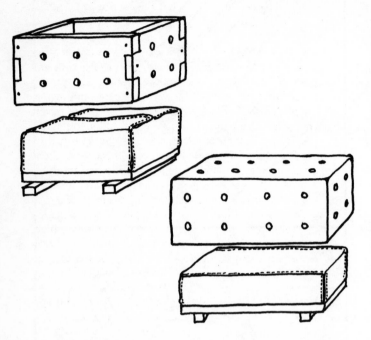

Fig. 35. Removing tofu from a farmhouse-style settling container

Homemade Tofu   MAKES 20 TO 23 OUNCES
(from Powdered Soymilk)

Tofu made from powdered soymilk is not quite as delicious as, and is somewhat more expensive than, tofu made from whole soybeans. However the process takes only about 35 minutes—as compared with 50 minutes when using whole soybeans—and is considerably easier since it is not necessary to grind the beans or remove and press the okara. One cup of powdered soymilk gives about the same yield as one cup of whole soybeans. Note that when using powdered soymilk, the whey which separates from the curds will be somewhat milkier than the whey from whole soybeans, even after the curds are well formed.

1 cup powdered soymilk
9 cups water
Solidifier: Use any of the solidifiers in the amounts listed in the recipe for Homemade Tofu (p. 99)

Combine powdered soymilk and water in a 1- to 1½-gallon pot. Whisk milk until well dissolved, then bring to a boil over high heat, stirring from time to time. Measure solidifier into a dry, 1-cup measuring cup and set aside. Reduce heat and simmer soymilk for 3 minutes. Add 1 cup water to solidifier and stir until dissolved. Proceed from step 6 as for Homemade Tofu.

Homemade Tofu   MAKES 18 TO 22 OUNCES
(Fermentation Method)

In this method, closely related to that for making Soymilk Yogurt (p. 205), bacteria present in the kitchen air enter the warm soymilk and produce lactic acid. The latter serves as solidifier, curdling the soymilk protein to form curds.

1½ cups soybeans, washed, soaked overnight in 1 quart water, rinsed and drained
10 cups water, approximately

Prepare soymilk as in steps in 1 through 5 of Homemade Tofu (p.99), but heat only 2¼ (rather than 7½) cups water in cooking pot. Remove pot from heat and allow soymilk to cool slightly, then pour soymilk into wide-mouthed jars and allow to stand uncovered for 8 to 10 hours. Cover jars and allow to stand at room temperature (at least 70°) for 18 to 36 hours, or until curds have solidified and just begun to separate from whey.

Gently pour curds into a strainer or colander lined with a tofu pressing sack or coarse-weave cloth; allow to drain for 20 minutes, then tie closed mouth of sack. Combine 4 cups water and 1 teaspoon salt in a pot and bring to a boil. Drop in sack, return to the boil, and allow to simmer for 20 minutes. Remove sack and proceed from Step 8 as for Homemade Tofu (p. 99) or press tofu in sack as for Reshaped Tofu (p. 98).

Since this tofu generally has a slightly sour flavor and crumbly texture (like cottage cheese), it is best used in dips, spreads, or dressings.

*Cook Soymilk Completely Before Pressing Okara: This method is similar to that used in most tofu shops, however here water rather than oil and limestone is used as bubble extinguisher (see p. 287). Unless a heavy-bottomed pot is used, the soymilk will overflow. Using a 2½- to 3-gallon pot, cook soybean purée in 9 cups water. When foam begins to rise, reduce heat to low and immediately sprinkle ¼ cup water over surface of foam while stirring with a wooden spoon. Stirring constantly, allow foam to rise 3 more times, adding water and stirring down each time. (Total simmering time should be about 15 minutes.) Empty contents of pot into pressing sack as in basic method and press okara thoroughly. (Omit rinsing and re-pressing of okara.) When all soymilk has been squeezed from okara, dissolve solidifier in 1 cup warm water and add to soymilk in pressing pot. Amount of solidifier used may have to be increased slightly due to lower temperature of soymilk.

*Soft High-yielding Tofu: Allow soymilk to cool to 170° before stirring in magnesium sulfate or calcium solidifier. Wait for 15 minutes before ladling curds very gently into settling container. Press curds with a 3-ounce weight for 15 minutes, then immerse tofu in cold water and allow to stand for 10 minutes before unwrapping cloths. For a milder flavor, allow to soak for 1 hour more.

*Lightly Seasoned Tofu: Combine 2 cups water and 1 to 1½ teaspoons salt in a bowl or large-mouth jar; mix well. Cut cooled tofu into 1½-inch cubes, place into brine, and cover jar. Refrigerate for at least 8 hours. For a more subtle seasoning, bring brine just to a boil before removing and serving tofu.

Five-Color Tofu (Gomoku-dofu)   MAKES 21 OUNCES

Although no longer widely available in Japan, this delicious tofu used to be prepared in traditional tofu shops on festive occasions or on special order. It was then usually deep-fried like thick agé (p. 180). The deep-fried variety is still available in the food section of several of Japan's finer department stores.

Ingredients for Homemade Tofu (p. 99)
¼ cup grated carrot
¼ cup grated burdock root or minced lotus root
¼ cup minced mushrooms or cloud-ear mushrooms
¼ cup green beans, fresh corn, or ginkgo nuts, parboiled in lightly salted water

Prepare soymilk as in steps 1 through 5 of Homemade Tofu. After cooking soymilk for 5 minutes, stir in vegetables. Now proceed as for homemade tofu, steps 6 through 10. Serve as Chilled Tofu (p. 105) or, for best flavor, deep-fry and serve as Homemade Thick Agé (p. 182).
VARIATIONS: (Use 2 to 4 tablespoons of each finely cut ingredient.)
*Seashore Gomoku: *Hijiki*, powdered green *nori*, bamboo shoots, sesame seeds, burdock root, and leeks.
*Wild Mountain Vegetable Gomoku: Osmund fern, cloud-ear mushroom, butterbur, and bamboo shoots.
*Gohoji-dofu: Use ¾ cup parboiled green soybeans.

Fig. 36. Chilled Tofu

TOFU QUICK AND EASY

In Japan, the quickest and easiest ways of serving tofu are also generally considered the most delicious. Here, in the preparation of food as in all the arts, simplicity is honored as the foundation of fine taste and beauty. The following dishes can be served at any meal and require no cooking at all.

Chilled Tofu (Hiya-yakko)   SERVES 1

Many connoisseurs maintain that this is the only recipe you need to know when using tofu. They are quick to add, however, that a creative cook can serve Chilled Tofu in a different way each day of the year if full use is made of seasonal garnishes, subtly flavored dipping sauces, and richly seasoned toppings.

Chilled Tofu is at its best, though, on hot summer afternoons and balmy summer evenings. Both regular tofu and kinugoshi (p. 211) may be used in preparing it: kinugoshi is preferred for its smooth, custard-like texture, and regular tofu for what many consider to be its more full-bodied flavor. Most important is the quality and freshness of the tofu itself.

It is said that this simple way of enjoying tofu first appealed to Japan's *yakko*, or lowest ranking samurai, about 300 years ago. A combination feudal retainer-servant-valet-and-footman, the yakko was not allowed to carry a sword, but was well known to the common folk because he marched at the very front of the procession whenever his lord made a public appearance. His prescribed uniform was a navy blue, waist-length coat with large square sleeves resembling heraldic banners. A distinctive 6- to 8-inch white square, the yakko's "crest" or "coat of arms," was dyed on the center of each sleeve. Since the color and shape of this square resembled the cubes of chilled tofu the yakko loved to eat, the new dish came to be known as "chilled yakko." And to this day, Japanese recipes call for cutting a 12-ounce cake of tofu into *yakko*, meaning 6 cubes. Chilled tofu is best cut and eaten with chopsticks since the cut surface is then better able to hold or absorb dipping sauces and garnishes.

6 to 8 ounces tofu (regular or kinugoshi), chilled
1½ to 2 teaspoons shoyu, Shoyu Dipping Sauces (p. 40), Sweet Simmered Miso (p. 41), Finger Lickin' Miso (p. 31), or regular miso (p. 31)
Garnishes and Condiments (see below)

Place the tofu on a small plate or in a shallow bowl. If desired, cut tofu into 1-inch cubes.

If using shoyu or a shoyu dipping sauce, sprinkle it over the tofu and top with your choice of garnishes and/or condiments. Or serve the shoyu separately in a small dish and arrange the garnishes on a platter nearby (fig. 36). Invite each person to add garnishes to the shoyu to taste.

If using miso or a miso topping, place a dab of the miso on top of the tofu and serve without garnishes.

Garnishes and Condiments (in order of popularity):
   Thinly sliced leeks or onions, rinsed and pressed (p. 37)
   Grated or slivered gingerroot
   Crushed or minced garlic
   Bonita flakes
   Thin strips of *nori*
   7-spice red pepper
   Slivered *yuzu* peel
   Grated fresh *wasabi* or *wasabi* paste
   Wasabi pickled in sake lees

Grated *daikon*
Diced green beefsteak leaves
Slivered or diced *myoga*
Minced red pickled gingerroot
Hot mustard
Diced *asatsuki*, chives, or wild onions
Ground roasted sesame seeds
A mixture of equal parts grated *daikon* and carrot
Beefsteak plant blossoms or buds
Tiny dried *oboro* shrimp
Benitade or *akame*
Kinome sprigs
Powdered green *nori*
Grated cucumber, or a mixture of equal parts grated
   carrot and grated cucumber
Slivered *kombu tsukudani*
Nori tsukudani
Chopped hard-boiled eggs
Diced cheese
Sesame butter

Popular Combinations:
   Gingerroot and leeks
   Bonita flakes, gingerroot, and leeks
   Nori and bonita flakes
   Hot mustard and bonita flakes
   Gingerroot, leeks, 7-spice red pepper, and bonita
      flakes
Other Sauces and Toppings:
   Mirin-shoyu (p. 40)
   Chinese oyster sauce
   All basic sauces (p. 48)
   Worcestershire or Worcestershire-Ketchup Sauce (p.
      49)
   Special Miso Toppings (p. 45)
   All varieties of Miso Sauté (p. 43)
   Nut and Seed Butter Toppings (p.47)

VARIATIONS

*Menoha-dofu: Serve chilled tofu uncut, set in a glass bowl on several pieces of *wakame*. Top with thinly sliced green peppers and cucumbers, and diced *myoga* and green beefsteak leaves. Surround with chunks of ice and serve with a dipping sauce made of equal parts shoyu and vinegar (or lemon juice).

*Nameko-dofu: Mix *nameko* mushrooms with grated *daikon*. Season with shoyu, vinegar, and sugar, then whip with chopsticks until bubbles form. Serve over Chilled Tofu and top with grated *wasabi* and thin strips of toasted *nori*.

Iceberg Chilled Tofu   SERVES 1

6 to 8 ounces tofu, cut into 1-inch cubes
Shoyu or Shoyu Dipping Sauces (p. 40)
Garnishes and Condiments for Chilled Tofu (p. 105)

Place the tofu cubes in a small serving bowl. Arrange 4 to 6 ice cubes around tofu, then add enough cold water to just cover tofu. Serve the shoyu or dipping sauce in a separate small dish accompanied by a variety of garnishes. Serve immediately to prevent tofu's subtle sweetness from being lost to the water.

SERVING HINTS

*When serving a group, float the cubed tofu in a large salad bowl at the center of the table. Provide guests with slotted spoons, or let each person remove the tofu with chopsticks. Float thin slices of radish, cucumber or lemon, or parsley sprigs in the iced water as both decoration and garnish.

*Place tofu cubes in attractive natural wooden boxes—about 6 by 8 by 2 inches deep—each box coated with red or black lacquerware, or in large sections of bamboo cut lengthwise into halves. Surround tofu with several large chunks of ice, but do not add water. Place a thinly sliced crescent of watermelon next to the tofu.

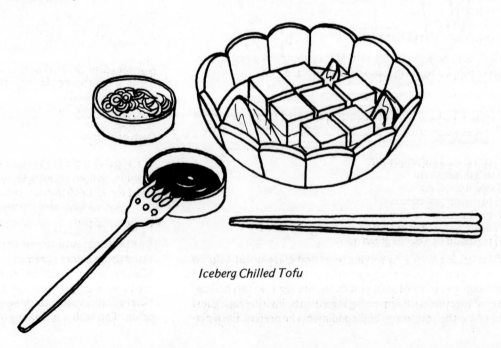

Iceberg Chilled Tofu

Chinese-style Chilled Tofu
(Ryanban-doufu)

SERVES 1

6 to 8 ounces doufu or tofu, chilled
1½ teaspoons minced leeks or onions
1½ teaspoons minced *cha-tsai* or *takuan* pickle
1 teaspoon tiny dried shrimp or bonita flakes
Dash of red-pepper *chiang* (p. 31), tabasco sauce, or minced pepper
½ teaspoon sesame oil
1½ teaspoons soy sauce

Place the doufu in a shallow bowl. Arrange the next four ingredients on top of the doufu, then sprinkle with the sesame oil and soy sauce.

Or, omit the pickles and red-pepper *chiang* and use 1 tablespoon each minced leeks and soy sauce, 1½ teaspoons sesame oil, and ¼ cup dried shrimp or bonita flakes.

Sweet-and-Crunchy Chilled Tofu

SERVES 1

6 to 8 ounces tofu, chilled
1 to 1½ teaspoons honey
1½ tablespoons (toasted) slivered almonds or walnut meats
½ banana, sliced into thin rounds
1½ tablespoons raisins
Dash of nutmeg

Place the tofu in a bowl and top with the remaining ingredients.

Chilled Tofu with Applesauce & Granola

SERVES 2

6 ounces tofu, drained (p. 94) and chilled
¼ teaspoon salt
1 cup applesauce, chilled
½ cup raisins
Dash of cinnamon
¼ cup crunchy granola or nuts

Mash tofu together with salt. Mix in applesauce and raisins. Serve topped with cinnamon and granola.

Chilled Tofu with Glutinous Yam and Egg
(Imokake-dofu)

SERVES 1

½ cup grated glutinous yam
6 to 8 ounces tofu
1 egg, uncooked
½ teaspoon grated *wasabi*
1 to 2 teaspoons shoyu
¼ sheet *nori*, cut into thin strips
½ teaspoon powdered green *nori*

Place grated yam in a serving bowl and place uncut tofu on top of yam. Hollow out 1 spoonful of tofu from the center of the upper surface of tofu and break the egg into this hollow. Serve together with remaining ingredients, inviting each guest to chose the seasonings and condiments he prefers. Each person cuts the tofu into bite-sized pieces and mixes the ingredients together in the serving bowl.

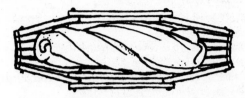

TOFU DRESSINGS, SPREADS, DIPS, AND HORS D'OEUVRE

Using an electric blender, you can make a wide variety of Western-style tofu preparations in less than a minute. When blended or mashed, a 12-ounce cake of tofu makes about 1½ cups. Fresh or dried herbs make excellent additions to many of these recipes.

A word to dieters: although most salads are excellent slenderizers, many conventional dressings definitely are not. Use tofu to create rich-and-creamy dressings which work together with your favorite salads to save you calories and reduce saturated fats.

Most of the following dressings plus Tofu Sour Cream can also be used with excellent results as sauces: spoon them over cooked vegetables just before serving. To prevent separation, do not reheat.

Tofu Mayonnaise Dressing

MAKES ABOUT 1 CUP

These delicious mayonnaise dressings, dips, and spreads take only 30 seconds to prepare. Whereas commercial mayonnaise must, by law, consist of at least 65 percent fat (most homemade varieties contain even more), the following tofu-based preparations contain no eggs and very little oil, making them ideal for use in low-calorie, low-fat diets. Refrigerated in a covered container, they will stay fresh for 1 or 2 days. A similar mayonnaise can be prepared by substituting soymilk for the tofu (p. 206).

6 ounces tofu, drained or pressed (p. 96) if desired
1½ to 2 tablespoons lemon juice or vinegar
2 tablespoons oil
½ teaspoon salt, or 2 teaspoons shoyu, or 1 tablespoon red miso
Dash of pepper

Combine all ingredients in a blender and purée for about 30 seconds, or until smooth. Or mash all ingredients and allow to stand for 15 to 30 minutes before serving.

For variety, add 1 tablespoon finely chopped parsley, or use equal parts lemon juice and vinegar.

VARIATIONS: Add any of the following ingredients to those listed above before puréing:
*Onion: ¼ cup diced onion. Excellent on all types of deep-fried tofu and with many vegetable dishes.
*Curry: ½ teaspoon curry powder and 2 tablespoons minced onion. Top with a sprinkling of 1 tablespoon minced parsley.

*Cheese & Garlic: ¼ cup Parmesan or grated cheese and ½ clove of garlic or ¼ onion, minced. Serve topped with a sprinkling of minced parsley.

*Gingerroot: 1 teaspoon grated or 1½ teaspoons powdered gingerroot and a dash of (7-spice) red pepper or tabasco sauce. Try over a tomato & cucumber salad. Top with 1 tablespoon minced parsley.

*Dill & Garlic: ¼ teaspoon dill and 1 clove minced garlic. Omit the pepper.

*Pickle: 2 small Western-style cucumber pickles, minced. Try over tomato wedges.

*Celery & Onion: 3 tablespoons each diced celery and onion. Serve with Tofu Cutlets (p. 134) or with squash dishes.

*Sweetened: 2 tablespoons each natural sugar and minced parsley. Use only a dash of salt and omit the pepper. Serve with Apple-Raisin Salad (p. 113) or melon balls.

*Sesame: 2 tablespoons sesame butter or tahini and 3 tablespoons minced celery.

*Walnut: ¼ cup each walnut meats and ketchup. Try over a salad of hard-boiled eggs, asparagus, and tomato wedges.

*Spicy Onion: 2 tablespoons diced onion, ¼ teaspoon paprika, and a dash of 7-spice red pepper, tabasco sauce, or cayenne.

*Ketchup: 5 tablespoons ketchup. Top with 2 tablespoons minced parsley.

*Sweetened Miso: 1 tablespoon red, barley or Hatcho miso and 1 or 2 tablespoons natural sugar. Omit the salt. Try over tomato wedges.

*Sweet White Miso: 2 tablespoons sweet white miso and ¼ cup chopped leeks, scallions, or onions.

*Miso & Peanut: 1 tablespoon red or akadashi miso, and 2 tablespoons each peanuts and minced parsley. Omit the salt.

*Egg Yolk: 1 egg yolk (or press the tofu and use 1 whole egg). If desired, add 1 teaspoon sugar, ½ teaspoon hot mustard, and a dash of red pepper.

*Mustard: 1 teaspoon hot mustard. Delicious with fresh tomatoes, steamed broccoli, or deep-fried tofu.

*Garlic: 1 to 1½ teaspoons minced or pressed garlic. Serve over tomato salads. If desired, add 3 tablespoons minced onion and top with chopped parsley.

*Raisin: 2/3 cup raisins. Use only ¼ teaspoon salt. Serve as a dessert topping over apples or on Waldorf salads.

*Green Beefsteak: 2 green beefsteak leaves.

*Umeboshi: 1/3 onion (minced), 1 tablespoon ground roasted sesame seeds or sesame butter, and 4 pitted umeboshi. Omit the salt.

*Herb: ½ teaspoon fresh or dried herbs (oregano, marjoram, sorrel, caraway).

*Substitute for part of the lemon juice or vinegar: sake or white wine, 1 teaspoon beet juice, or 1½ tablespoons orange juice.

Creamy Tofu Dressings and Dips   MAKES 1¼ CUPS

These preparations resemble tofu mayonnaise but contain no oil and are often slightly sweet. If a blender is not available, simply mash the ingredients together with a fork.

6 ounces tofu
1 tablespoon grated gingerroot
2½ teaspoons shoyu
1 tablespoon ground roasted sesame seeds (p. 38), sesame butter, or tahini
1 tablespoon natural sugar

Combine all ingredients in a blender and purée until smooth. Delicious with Green Bean Salad (p. 115), parboiled beansprouts, or over cucumbers mixed with thin slices of deep-fried tofu.

VARIATIONS: Proceeding as above, use the following ingredients:

*Tofu-Peanut Butter Dressing
    6 ounces tofu
    3 tablespoons peanut butter
    1 tablespoon vinegar or lemon juice
    1 to 2 tablespoons natural sugar

    Try with cucumber salads

*Tofu-Sesame-Miso Dressing
    6 ounces tofu
    1½ tablespoons sweet white miso
    1 tablespoon ground roasted sesame seeds (p. 38), sesame butter, or tahini
    2 teaspoons natural sugar
    ½ teaspoon mirin

Serve over fresh vegetables, or a combination of carrots, konnyaku, and (shiitake) mushrooms simmered in Sweetened Shoyu Broth (p. 40).

*Tofu-Garlic-Shoyu Dressing
    6 ounces tofu
    1 clove garlic, minced
    1½ tablespoons shoyu
    Juice of ½ lemon
    ¼ teaspoon oregano
    ¼ teaspoon marjoram

*Tofu-Sour Cream Dip
    6 ounces tofu
    2½ to 3 tablespoons sour cream
    2½ teaspoons red, barley, or Hatcho miso
    ½ teaspoon lemon juice or vinegar
    1½ teaspoon minced parsley
    Dash of pepper

Chinese-style Tofu-Sesame-Shoyu Dressing   MAKES 1½ CUPS

12 ounces tofu
2 tablespoons shoyu
2 teaspoons sesame oil
¾ teaspoon natural sugar
1 to 2 tablespoons minced leek, scallion, onion, or parsley (optional)

Combine all ingredients, mashing well. Serve over tomato and cucumber slices.

Tofu Tartare Sauce

MAKES 2½ CUPS

1 cup minced Western-style cucumber pickles
8 ounces tofu
4 tablespoons oil
5 tablespoons lemon juice
1 teaspoon salt
½ teaspoon hot mustard
2 hard-boiled eggs
2 tablespoons diced onions
2 tablespoons minced parsley
2 tablespoons chopped green olives (optional)

Combine ¼ cup minced pickles with the next five ingredients and purée in a blender until smooth. Combine with the remaining pickles and other ingredients and mix well. Serve with deep-fried tofu and tofu croquettes. If desired, top with a sprinkling of parsley.

Tofu Cream Cheese

MAKES 1 CUP

Easily prepared at home, tofu cream cheese contains no animal fats and costs about one-fourth as much as its dairy counterpart. Use as you would dairy cream cheese but do not reheat.

12 ounces tofu, squeezed (p. 97)
2 tablespoons oil
3/8 teaspoon salt
Dash of white pepper
1 teaspoon lemon juice (optional)

Combine all ingredients in a blender and purée until smooth and thick.

Tofu Sour Cream

MAKES 1½ CUPS

12 ounces tofu, parboiled (salted water method, p. 96) and squeezed (p. 97)
2 tablespoons lemon juice
¼ teaspoon salt

Combine all ingredients in a blender and purée until smooth.

Tofu Cottage Cheese

MAKES 1 CUP

12 ounces tofu, pressed (p. 96) if desired
½ teaspoon salt
Dash of pepper

Combine all ingredients and mash together; stir well to develop texture. Serve as cottage cheese.

VARIATION

*Sweetened Tofu Cottage Cheese: Use the ingredients for Tofu Whipped Cream (p. 148) and prepare as above. Try adding a few drops of vanilla. Serve with fresh fruit salads topped with raisins, slivered almonds, or sunflower seeds.

Tangy Tofu Cottage Cheese

SERVES 2

12 ounces tofu, drained (p. 96) if desired
2 tablespoons oil or ¼ cup mayonnaise
3 tablespoons lemon juice or vinegar
1 teaspoon salt or 4 teaspoons shoyu
1 clove minced garlic
Dash of pepper

Mash together all ingredients. Allow to stand for 30 minutes. Serve as a dressing for fresh vegetable salads.

For a deliciously rich flavor, omit the garlic and salt; add 3 tablespoons red miso and 2 tablespoons each natural sugar and minced parsley. If desired, top with a sprinkling of ground roasted sesame seeds.

Or try using any of the variations listed at Tofu Mayonnaise (p. 107).

VARIATIONS: Proceed as above:

*Deviled Tofu

12 ounces tofu
¼ cup mayonnaise
½ teaspoon dill
1 clove garlic, minced
1 tablespoon shoyu or 1½ tablespoons red miso
2 tablespoons oil
2 tablespoons vinegar or lemon juice
Dash of pepper

Tofu-Egg Spread

MAKES 1½ CUPS

12 ounces tofu, squeezed (p. 97)
2 hard-boiled eggs, diced
2 tablespoons oil
1 to 2 tablespoons lemon juice
½ teaspoon salt or 1 tablespoon red miso
2 tablespoons minced onion (optional)
1 tablespoon minced parsley

Combine the first six ingredients in a blender and purée for 30 seconds. Garnish with the parsley and serve as a sandwich spread.

Tofu-Nut Butter Spread or Topping

MAKES 2 CUPS

Serve as is on whole-grain bread or crackers, together with sprouts and fresh vegetables in sandwiches, or as a topping for fresh or cooked vegetables and vegetable salads.

12 ounces tofu, drained (p. 96)
6 tablespoons peanut or sesame butter
1 tablespoon honey
2 teaspoons lemon juice
2 tablespoons red or barley miso; or ½ teaspoon salt

Combine ingredients and mash together with a fork.

For a crunchier texture, add ¼ cup each raisins and peanuts (or sunflower seeds).

Tofu Guacamole

MAKES 2 CUPS

12 ounces tofu, squeezed (p. 97)
1 avacado, peeled and seeded
2 tablespoons red miso, or 4 teaspoons shoyu, or 1 teaspoon
   salt
2 tablespoons sesame butter or *tahini*
2 tablespoons minced onion
¼ tomato, diced
2 or 3 teaspoons lemon juice
1 clove garlic, crushed
Dash of paprika and/or pepper
2 tablespoons minced parsley or ¼ cup alfalfa sprouts

Combine the first nine ingredients and mash together with a fork until smooth. Serve as a dip, spread, or dressing, garnished with the parsley.

Tofu Pickled in Miso
(Tofu no Misozuke)

MAKES 6 OUNCES

This preparation, salty and richly fragrant, has a soft, cheeselike consistency resembling that of Chinese fermented tofu (doufu-ru). The many commercial varieties of Chinese firm tofu pickled in miso—called *chiang-doufu* or *chiang-doufu chin*—are generally served cut into small cubes as a seasoning for rice or rice porridge. Kept in a cool place, the tofu gradually grows saltier and will last indefinitely.

12 ounces tofu, well pressed (p. 96)
Miso Bed:
   ½ cup red, barley, or Hatcho miso
   ½ teaspoon grated gingerroot
   ½ teaspoon sesame oil
   1 teaspoon sake or white wine
   Dash of 7-spice red pepper or tabasco sauce

Cut pressed tofu crosswise into ½-inch-thick slices and parboil for 3 minutes (p. 96); drain and allow to cool to room temperature. Combine all ingredients to make miso bed, mixing well. Place one-half the mixture into a shallow 1-quart container and smooth to form an even layer. On this arrange the tofu slices, cover with remaining miso mixture, and then with a layer of plastic wrap spread over miso surface to keep out air; allow to stand for 12 to 15 hours. Remove tofu carefully from container and wipe off miso on tofu surface with a damp cloth. Cut into ½-inch cubes and serve with rice or, for best flavor and aroma, broil on both sides until well browned before serving. Also delicious as hors d'oeuvre.

VARIATIONS

*Dry very well-pressed tofu in a slow oven for about 1 hour. Cut each cake crosswise into thirds and embed in miso for one year. Sold commercially in Japan, the flavor, texture, and appearance of this product resemble those of a very firm cheese. Some varieties are wrapped with *kombu* and beefsteak leaves before pickling in semi-sweet barley miso.

*Embed miso for 24 hours or more in plain red miso. Mash and serve as a cracker spread topped with a slice of tomato or cucumber, or combine with equal parts Tofu Cream Cheese (p. 109), a little diced onions, and your choice of herbs to use as a dip.
*Combine 3 tablespoons mashed miso-pickled tofu with 2 tablespoons sesame or peanut butter, 1 tablespoon honey, and ½ teaspoon lemon juice; mix well. Serve as a sandwich spread or cracker dip.
*Sprinkle parboiled tofu slices with ¼ teaspoon salt and embed for 2 days in a mixture of 1½ cups sweet white miso and 2 teaspoons sake (or white wine). Broil and serve as above.
*Tofu Pickled in Shoyu: Press and cut tofu as above, then soak overnight in shoyu rather than miso.

Four-Color Tofu Hors D'oeuvre

MAKES 30 TO 40

1 cucumber, cut diagonally into thin ovals
1 carrot, cut into ovals
3 ounces cheese, cut into thin slices each 1½ inches square
1 sweet potato or yam, steamed and cut into thin rounds
¼ cup red miso, Sesame Miso (p. 42), or Sweet Simmered
   Miso (p. 41)
16 ounces tofu, pressed (p. 96) and cut into small rectangles

Arrange the first four ingredients on serving platters. Spread the surface of each vegetable piece and cheese slice with a thin coating of miso, then top with a slice of tofu. If desired, pierce with foodpicks. If miso is unavailable, dip each slice of tofu in shoyu.

Tofu Canapés

MAKES 16

16 slices of buttered bread or toast, each 1 by 3 inches
1½ tablespoons red miso or Walnut Miso (p. 42)
3 tablespoons sweet white, red, or Sweet Simmered Miso (p. 41)
12 ounces tofu, pressed (p. 96) and cut crosswise into 16 slices
Canapé Toppings: Your choice of the following, thinly sliced:
   Hard-boiled eggs
   Cucumbers
   Tomatoes
   Green peppers
   Cheese
   Snow peas or green beans, parboiled
   Potatoes or sweet potatoes, steamed
   Carrots

Spread half of the bread pieces with red miso and half with white miso. Cover each piece with a slice of tofu, and top with one slice of any of the canapé toppings. Pierce with foodpicks if desired.

If miso is unavailable, sprinkle the tofu and topping with a few drops of shoyu. Substitute crackers for the bread.

TOFU IN SALADS

Tofu is a wonderful addition to almost any salad. Its soft texture complements the crisp crunchiness of fresh vegetables. And because tofu has so few calories per gram of protein, tofu salads can be enjoyed by weight-watchers.

Tofu can take at least 6 different forms when served in salads. Mashed or squeezed and lightly seasoned, it resembles cottage or ricota cheese. Lightly drained and cubed, it can be used with or in place of croutons. Well-pressed and diced, it has the texture of soft cheese and goes well in marinated salads. Parboiled and crumbled, it may be used to keep a salad light. Reshaped and cut into thin strips, it has the consistency of firm cheese or ham. Finally, blended and seasoned, tofu can be turned into a variety of rich and creamy salad dressings.

Western-style Salads

We have divided the following tofu salads into Western and Japanese varieties depending on the type of dressing used and the method of preparation. Thus, a number of the Western salads—characterized by the use of a dressing containing oil and/or dairy products generally served over fresh, crisp greens and vegetable slices—also may contain typically Japanese ingredients.

Cauliflower Salad with Mashed Tofu   SERVES 4

1 small cauliflower
12 ounces tofu, mashed
2 ounces cheese, diced (optional)
¼ cup sunflower seeds (optional)
Caesar or Miso-Cream Cheese Dressing (p. 47)

Steam cauliflower for 10 minutes or until tender. Allow to cool, then separate into flowerets. Combine in a large bowl with remaining ingredients; toss lightly.

Or, marinate flowerets overnight in a well-seasoned oil and vinegar dressing.

Carrot, Raisin & Walnut Salad with Tofu   SERVES 4

6 ounces tofu, pressed (p. 96) and mashed
1 cup grated carrots, or diced apple or celery
½ cup raisins
½ cup (roasted) walnut meats, diced
1½ tablespoons red, barley, or Hatcho miso
2 teaspoons natural sugar
1 teaspoon sake or white wine
2 tablespoons sesame butter
4 lettuce leaves (optional)

Combine all ingredients, mixing well. If desired, serve mounded on lettuce leaves. Also delicious in sandwiches and on toast.

Curried Rice Salad with Tofu   SERVES 6

18 ounces tofu, pressed (p. 96) and broken into very small pieces
2½ cups cooked Brown Rice (p. 50), chilled
3 tablespoons minced green onion or leek
2 tablespoons minced parsley
2 green peppers; one slivered and one cut into rings
Dressing:
    6 tablespoons oil
    1/3 cup (rice) vinegar
    1 tablespoon lemon juice
    1 teaspoon curry powder
    ¼ teaspoon (7-spice) red pepper
    1 clove of garlic, crushed
    ¾ teaspoon salt
    Dash of pepper
4 lettuce leaves
1 tomato, cut into wedges

Combine the first four ingredients with the slivered green pepper. Add dressing, mix lightly and, for best flavor, allow to stand for several hours. Serve mounded on lettuce leaves in a large bowl; garnish with tomato wedges and green pepper rings.

Tofu Cottage Cheese Salad with Tomatoes and Walnut-Miso   SERVES 3

1½ tablespoons Lemon-Walnut Miso Sauté (p. 44) or Sesame Miso (p. 42)
3 tablespoons mayonnaise
12 ounces tofu, scrambled (p. 97)
3 tablespoons minced parsley
1 tomato, cut into thin wedges
¼ cup chopped walnut meats (optional)
Dash of pepper

Combine miso and mayonnaise, mixing well. Place tofu in a serving bowl and lightly mix in the miso-mayonnaise, parsley, tomato and, if used, the chopped nutmeats. Season with a sprinkling of pepper. Chill before serving.

Sweet Potato & Cucumber Salad with Mashed Tofu
SERVES 2

1 cucumber, cut into matchsticks
1 sweet potato, steamed and cut into ¼-inch-thick half moons
3 Chinese cabbage or lettuce leaves, cut into thin strips
6 ounces tofu, mashed
½ cup Caesar or Miso Sour Cream Dressing (p. 46)

Combine all ingredients; toss lightly.

Lettuce and Tomato Salad with Mashed Tofu
SERVES 4

12 ounces tofu, mashed
Caesar, bleu cheese, or Floating Cloud Miso Dressing (p. 46)
4 lettuce leaves
3 tomatoes, cut into wedges
2 cucumbers, cut into ovals
¼ cup sunflower seeds (optional)

Combine tofu and dressing in a bowl; mix well. Divide lettuce leaves among 4 serving dishes. Place tomato wedges and cucumber slices on top of lettuce, then top with tofu-dressing mixture and a sprinkling of sunflower seeds.

Western-style Vinegared Shira-ae (Shirozu-ae)
SERVES 2

6 ounces tofu, pressed (p. 96) and mashed
1 tablespoon sesame butter or *tahini*
1 tablespoon lemon juice
1½ tablespoons vinegar
½ teaspoon salt or 1 tablespoon red miso
1 teaspoon sake or white wine
1 cucumber or small carrot, sliced into thin rounds
2 hard-boiled eggs, chopped
¼ cup walnut meats
¼ cup raisins
2 tablespoons minced cucumber pickles (optional)

Combine the first six ingredients, mixing until smooth. Gently stir in the remaining ingredients and serve immediately.

Western-style Shira-ae
SERVES 2 OR 3

1 cucumber, cut into thin ovals
3 celery stalks, diced
6 ounces tofu, pressed (p. 96) and mashed
4 teaspoons sugar
½ teaspoon salt
4 teaspoons peanut butter or sesame butter
4 teaspoons rice vinegar

Combine the first five ingredients in a large mixing bowl. Cream the peanut butter and vinegar in a separate cup and pour over the tofu mixture. Mix all ingredients together lightly. For best flavor, chill before serving.

Tossed Green Salad with Soft Tofu Cubes
SERVES 4

6 to 8 lettuce or Chinese cabbage leaves
1 tomato, cut into thin wedges
2 fresh mushrooms, thinly sliced
1 large cucumber, cut into thin ovals
1 green pepper, thinly sliced
1 hard-boiled egg, diced
¼ cup French or Floating Cloud Miso Dressing (p. 46)
6 ounces tofu, drained (p. 96) and cut into ½-inch cubes
½ teaspoon salt
¼ cup sunflower seeds (optional)

Tear lettuce into salad-sized pieces and combine with the next five ingredients. Add the dressing and toss lightly. Now add the tofu cubes and season with salt; toss again. Serve topped with a sprinkling of sunflower seeds.

Marinated Salad with Diced Tofu
SERVES 4

12 ounces tofu, pressed very firm (p. 96) and cut into ½-inch cubes
1 cucumber, diced
1 small carrot, diced
1 tomato, chopped fine
10 green beans, parboiled (p. 37) and chopped fine
Dressing:
    2 tablespoons shoyu
    3 tablespoons (sesame) oil
    1 tablespoon (rice) vinegar
    ½ teaspoon natural sugar

Combine tofu and vegetables in a large bowl. Add dressing, cover bowl, and marinate for 8 to 10 hours in a cool place. Drain vegetables lightly before serving.

If desired, season the dressing with oregano or 7-spice red pepper. Or drain the salad well and use as a filling for Agé Pouches (p. 192).

Mushroom Tomato Salad with Crumbled Tofu
SERVES 4

4 lettuce leaves
4 small tomatoes, thinly sliced
4 large fresh mushrooms, thinly sliced
12 ounces tofu, crumbled (p. 98)
1 tablespoon minced parsley
Dressing:
    1 tablespoon shoyu
    ½ cup salad oil
    ¼ cup lemon juice
    ½ clove of garlic, crushed or minced
    Dash of pepper

Arrange lettuce leaves on serving dishes and distribute tomato slices around edges of leaves. Combine mushrooms and tofu and divide among the 4 lettuce leaves. Top with a sprinkling of parsley, then the dressing.

Hard-Boiled Egg Salad with Soft Tofu Cubes

SERVES 4

3 hard-boiled eggs, diced
5 Chinese cabbage or lettuce leaves, cut into thin strips
1 green pepper, thinly sliced
12 ounces tofu, drained (p. 96) and cut into ½-inch cubes
3 mushrooms, thinly sliced
Garlic dressing or Tofu Mayonnaise Dressing (p. 107)

Combine the first five ingredients in a salad bowl and top with the dressing; toss lightly.

Tofu Potato Salad

SERVES 5 OR 6

8 ounces tofu, cut into 1-inch cubes
2 cups cubed boiled potatoes
1 large cucumber, thinly sliced
½ cup celery, thinly sliced
Dressing:
    6 tablespoons (tofu) mayonnaise (p. 107)
    2 teaspoons shoyu
    Dash of pepper
6 lettuce leaves
Radish roses (optional)

Combine the first four ingredients with the dressing and toss lightly. Serve on the lettuce leaves, garnished with radish roses.

Tossed Green Salad with Reshaped Tofu

SERVES 3 OR 4

24 ounces tofu, reshaped (p. 98) and cut into matchsticks
    or pieces 3 inches long and ½-inch square
4 Chinese cabbage or lettuce leaves, torn into small pieces
3 small mushrooms, thinly sliced
1 tomato, cut into wedges
1 small cucumber, cut into thin ovals.
½ cup garlic dressing or Tofu Mayonnaise Dressing (p. 107)
¼ cup roasted peanuts or sunflower seeds

Combine tofu and vegetables in a salad bowl; dress and toss lightly. Serve topped with a sprinkling of peanuts.

Squash or Pumpkin Salad with Tofu Mayonnaise Dressing

SERVES 3 OR 4

2 cups 1-inch cubes of boiled or steamed *kabocha*, squash,
    or pumpkin
1 tomato, diced
¼ onion, diced
½ cucumber, slivered
2 tablespoons minced parsley
2 to 4 ounces deep-fried tofu, cut into thin strips (optional)
¾ cup Tofu Mayonnaise Dressing (p. 000)

Combine all ingredients in a large bowl; toss.

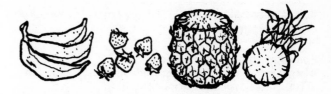

Fresh Fruit Salads with Tofu Dressings

*Tofu Whipped Cream (p. 148): Serve over any or all of the following: strawberries, thinly sliced apples, bananas, pears, peaches, or melon balls.
*Tofu Cottage Cheese (p. 109): Especially tasty as a filling for pear halves.
*Sweetened Tofu Cottage Cheese (p. 109): Serve in the same way as for Tofu Whipped Cream. Add a few drops of vanilla if desired. If using apples as the basis of the salad, top with raisins, slivered almonds or walnuts, sunflower seeds, and a sprinkling of toasted wheat germ and cinnamon. If using bananas, try the same toppings but substitute nutmeg for cinnamon.

Tofu-Banana Salad

SERVES 4

6 ounces tofu, mashed
3 bananas, cut into thin rounds
1 tablespoon honey
4 large lettuce leaves
¾ cup Tofu Whipped Cream (p. 148)
3 tablespoons toasted wheat germ

Combine tofu, bananas, and honey in a large bowl; mix gently. Spoon the mixture onto lettuce leaves, top with whipped cream, and sprinkle with wheat germ. Serve chilled.

Apple-Raisin Salad with Tofu Dressing

SERVES 4

2 apples, diced
½ cup raisins
½ cup peanuts or walnut meats
1 celery stalk, diced (optional)
½ teaspoon salt
1 cup Tofu-Peanut Butter Dressing (p. 108)

Combine all ingredients in a large bowl; mix well.

Tofu Fruit Salad

SERVES 2 OR 3

6 ounces tofu, cut into 1-inch cubes
1 cup orange sections or ½ cup pineapple chunks
2 tablespoons peanuts
¼ cup walnut meats
French dressing
1 cup alfalfa or bean sprouts

Combine the first four ingredients, add the dressing, and toss lightly. Serve mounded on the sprouts.

Mushroom Salad with Tofu Mayonnaise

SERVES 2 OR 3

8 white mushrooms, thinly sliced
4 large Chinese cabbage leaves, thinly sliced
½ cup Tofu Mayonnaise Dressing (p. 107)

Combine all ingredients in a salad bowl; toss lightly.

Tofu & Tomato Aspic or Molded Salad

SERVES 3 TO 4

½ stick of agar (4 gm), reconstituted and torn into small
    pieces (p. 37)
1 cup tomato juice
1 tomato, chopped
6 ounces tofu, rubbed through a sieve, puréed in a blender, or
    diced
4 teaspoons vinegar
2 tablespoons ketchup
1 tablespoon shoyu or ¾ teaspoon salt
1 teaspoon natural sugar
¼ teaspoon basil or oregano
Dash of black pepper
¼ cup chopped green pepper
½ cup chopped celery
Lemon wedges or Tofu Mayonnaise Dressing (p. 107)

Combine agar and tomato juice in a saucepan and bring to a
boil. Simmer, stirring constantly, for 2 to 3 minutes, or until
agar dissolves. Stir in the next eight ingredients, remove from
heat, and allow to cool until partially thickened. Mix in green
pepper and celery, pour into a mold, and refrigerate until set.
Serve chilled, topped with freshly-squeezed lemon juice or
dollops of the mayonnaise dressing.

Jelled Tofu (Kanten-dofu)

MAKES 2½ CUPS

Diced cubes of jelled tofu make an excellent addition
to tossed green salads and fruit cocktail mixtures. Or try
serving them accompanied by a dipping sauce of Vinegar-
Shoyu (p. 40), or the sauce used with their close relative
Takigawa-dofu (p. 210).

1 stick of agar (8 gm), reconstituted and torn into small
    pieces (p. 37)
1¼ cups water
12 ounces tofu, rubbed through a sieve or puréed in a blender
¼ teaspoon salt

Combine agar and water in a saucepan and bring to a boil.
Simmer, stirring constantly, for 2 to 3 minutes, or until agar
dissolves, then pour through a (warmed) strainer into a second pan. Add tofu and salt, mixing well, then pour tofu-agar
mixture into a (moistened) mold and allow to cool to room
temperature. Cover and refrigerate for several hours, or until
set. Cut into cubes, drain briefly if necessary, and serve as
for Tofu & Tomato Aspic.

Japanese-style Salads

In Japan, mixed foods served with a seasoned dressing
are called *aemono*. Unlike most Western salads, which are
made with vegetables in their raw state, these *aemono* salads
are generally prepared with lightly cooked vegetables and
served in tiny portions as an accompaniment to a main dish,
which they are meant to complement in color, texture, and
taste. Most *aemono* contain little or no oil, mayonnaise, or
dairy products. The dressing, generally prepared with vinegar
(or lemon juice) and shoyu or miso, is often quite sweet.
Aemono are generally named after the dominant seasonings
in the dressing: Sesame Miso-ae, Mustard-Vinegar Miso-ae,
Walnut Miso-ae, etc.

Shira-ae with Miso and Kinome

SERVES 4

Shira-ae, or "white salad," is one of Japan's most popular—and, in our opinion, most delicious—tofu dishes. All
varieties are at their best when chilled for 4 to 6 hours before
serving. They are delicious used as fillings for agé pouches or
as spreads for buttered toast or sandwiches. Any of the following recipes may be prepared without sugar, or with less
than half the amount ordinarily used. To make tangy *Shirozu-ae* (p. 112), add several tablespoons of vinegar or lemon
juice to your favorite variety of Shira-ae, and reduce the
amount of sugar slightly.

1 cake of *konnyaku,* cut into small rectangles (p. 37) and
    parboiled (p. 37)
1 carrot, cut into small rectangles
½ cup dashi (p. 39), stock, or water
½ teaspoon shoyu
½ teaspoon salt
3 tablespoons natural sugar
4 tablespoons ground roasted sesame seeds (p. 38); or 2½
    tablespoons sesame butter, or *tahini*
4 ounces tofu, parboiled and pressed (p. 97).
2 tablespoons sweet white miso or 1 tablespoon red miso
4 sprigs *kinome,* or substitute minced mint leaves

Combine the first five ingredients with 1 tablespoon sugar in a small saucepan. Simmer until all liquid is absorbed or evaporated, then allow vegetables to cool to room temperature. To the sesame seeds in the *suribachi* add tofu, miso, and 2 tablespoons sugar; grind together with a wooden pestle, then mix in the vegetables. Serve individual portions garnished with a sprig of *kinome*.

Shira-ae with Mushrooms and Sweet White Miso   SERVES 4 OR 5

4 ounces *daikon*, cut into small rectangles (p. 37)
¼ carrot, cut into matchsticks
½ cake of *konnyaku*, cut into small rectangles
1¼ teaspoons salt
3 mushrooms (fresh or dried), thinly sliced
2 teaspoons shoyu
4 teaspoons *mirin*
1 tablespoon ground roasted sesame seeds (p. 38), sesame butter, or *tahini*
8 ounces tofu, pressed (p. 96)
3 tablespoons sweet white miso or 1½ tablespoons red miso
1 teaspoon natural sugar

Combine the first three ingredients in a small bowl; rub vegetables with 1 teaspoon salt, then rinse and press (p. 37). Heat a dry skillet or wok. Add *konnyaku* and fry for several minutes, stirring constantly, until *konnyaku* is dry and begins to shrink; transfer to a bowl and allow to cool.

    Combine mushrooms, shoyu, and 1 teaspoon *mirin* in a small saucepan. Simmer until most of the liquid is absorbed or evaporated, then drain and allow mushrooms to cool.

    To the sesame seeds in the *suribachi* add ¼ teaspoon salt, the tofu, miso, sugar, and remaining 1 tablespoon *mirin*; grind together thoroughly. Mix in the *daikon*, carrot, konnyaku, and mushrooms. Serve chilled.

Shira-ae with Sweet Potatoes and Konnyaku   SERVES 4 TO 6

½ small carrot, cut into matchsticks and parboiled (p. 37)
1 cake of *konnyaku*, cut into matchsticks and parboiled
3 tablespoons dried (cloud-ear) mushroom, reconstituted (p. 37), drained, and cut into thin strips
3 tablespoons sugar
2 tablespoons shoyu
6 tablespoons ground roasted sesame seeds (p. 38); or 3 tablespoons sesame butter, or *tahini*
¼ teaspoon salt
12 ounces tofu, well pressed (p. 96)
1 small sweet potato, steamed and cut into ½-inch cubes

Combine the first four ingredients with 2 tablespoons sugar in a small saucepan. Simmer until most of the liquid has been absorbed or evaporated. Cool to room temperature, then drain. To the ground sesame seeds in the *suribachi* add salt, tofu, and 1 tablespoon sugar. Grind or mash together well. Mix in the potatoes and vegetables.

Or, omit the sesame and garnish with thin strips of toasted *nori* (p. 38).

Lotus Root Salad with Tofu Dressing   SERVES 2 OR 3

6 lettuce leaves
1 tomato, cut into thin wedges
Tofu-Garlic Dressing:
    6 ounces tofu, mashed
    ½ clove garlic, crushed
    1½ tablespoons lemon juice
    3 tablespoons oil
    ¼ teaspoon salt
    Dash of pepper
½ cup thin half-moons of lotus root, parboiled (p. 37)

Spread lettuce leaves in individual salad bowls and arrange tomato wedges around the leaves. Combine dressing ingredients in a small bowl and mix with a whisk or chopsticks until smooth. Stir in the lotus root and mound the mixture on the lettuce leaves.

Burdock and Green Beans with Tofu Sauce   SERVES 4

2 cups matchsticks of burdock root, soaked (p. 37) and parboiled (p. 37)
½ cup dashi (p. 39), stock, or water
1 tablespoon sugar
½ teaspoon salt
16 to 20 green beans, parboiled
¾ cup Quick Tofu-Sesame Sauce (p. 121)

Combine the first four ingredients in a small saucepan and simmer until most of the liquid has been absorbed or evaporated. Allow to cool to room temperature, then drain. Serve garnished with green beans and topped with the sauce.

Hailstones Salad   SERVES 3 or 4
(Arare-dofu no Aemono)

24 ounces tofu, reshaped (p. 98) and cut into ½-inch cubes or 2-inch matchsticks
1¾ ounces *narazuke* pickles, or substitute 2 small carrots, cut into matchsticks
1 tablespoon diced leeks or onions
1 tablespoon diced pickled red gingerroot *(beni shoga)*, or substitute Western-style cucumber pickles
Dressing:
    1 tablespoon Sesame Miso (p. 42) or red miso
    2 tablespoons water (or tea)
    ½ teaspoon salt
    1 teaspoon shoyu
    ¼ teaspoon vinegar

Combine the first four ingredients in a bowl; dress and toss lightly.

Shira-ae Stuffed Vegetables

SERVES 2

4 large mushrooms, with stems removed
2 green peppers, with seeds removed
1 cup Shira-ae (any variety; pp. 114 to 115)
2 tablespoons whole roasted sesame seeds
6 sprigs of *kinome* (optional)

Broil the mushrooms and peppers until lightly browned and fragrant. Use half the Shira-ae to stuff the peppers, and mound the remainder on the mushrooms. Sprinkle with sesame seeds and top with *kinome*.

TOFU WITH SANDWICHES AND TOAST

Tofu sandwiches may be used as the main course for a high-protein, low-calorie lunch. Thin slices of pressed tofu contribute to sandwiches much the same texture as a soft, mild cheese. The firm crunchiness of whole-grain toast and the softness of tofu make a particularly nice combination. The use of miso or shoyu is the key to seasoning. Due to protein complementary (p. 25), serving tofu and whole-wheat bread together can yield up to 42 percent more protein.

Tofu-Grilled Cheese Sandwich

SERVES 4

4 slices of whole-wheat bread, buttered
2 teaspoons mustard
¼ cup (tofu) mayonnaise (p. 107)
4 thin slices of tomato
12 ounces tofu, pressed (p. 96) and cut crosswise into eighths

Shoyu or 2 teaspoons red miso
4 slices of cheese

Spread each piece of bread with mustard and mayonnaise, and top with a slice of tomato and 2 slices of tofu. Season tofu with a few drops of shoyu or a thin layer of miso, then cover with the cheese. Broil until cheese melts.

Or place tofu on top of cheese and broil until tofu is lightly browned.

Open-faced Vegetable Sandwiches with Sliced Tofu

SERVES 4

If the sandwich is to be served immediately after it is prepared, little or no pressing of the tofu is required. However, if the sandwiches are to be used in a box lunch, press thoroughly to rid the tofu of excess moisture.

4 slices of whole-grain bread or toast, buttered
4 teaspoons red miso, Miso Toppings (p. 41), or Finger Lickin' Miso (p. 31); or 4 tablespoons Nut Butter Spreads (p. 47) or Kinako Butter (p. 65)
12 ounces tofu, well drained or pressed (p. 96) and cut crosswise into eighths
Your choice of the following, thinly sliced or minced:
    Lettuce
    Cucumber
    Tomatoes
    Onions or grated gingerroot
    Cheese, grated or sliced
    Hard-boiled eggs
    Parsley or alfalfa sprouts
Shoyu and/or Sesame Salt (p. 51)
Pepper (optional)

Spread each piece of bread or toast with the miso and top with 2 slices of tofu. (If desired, mash tofu with a fork to give a cottage cheese-like texture.) Cover with several varieties of vegetables and season to taste with a few drops of shoyu and a dash of pepper.

Sliced Tofu on Toast with Onion Sauce

SERVES 4

4 slices of whole-grain toast, buttered
1 cup Onion Sauce (p. 48), cooled
1¾ teaspoons shoyu
2 ounces cheese, grated
12 ounces tofu, pressed (p. 96) and cut crosswise into eighths

Shoyu

Arrange the toast on individual serving plates. Combine onion sauce and shoyu in a bowl; mix well. Spoon the mixture over the toast, sprinkle on cheese, and top with 2 slices of tofu. Season with a few drops of shoyu.

Additional Suggestions for Serving Tofu with Sandwiches

*Use Tofu-Nut Butter Spreads (p. 47), Tangy Tofu Cottage Cheese (p. 109), or Tofu Cream Cheese (p. 109). Serve on buttered bread or toast, as is, or with fresh vegetable slices.
*The many varieties of Tofu Mayonnaise (p. 107) may be combined in sandwiches with ingredients ranging from diced hard-boiled eggs to lettuce, tomatoes, and cucumbers.
*Western-type salads made with mashed tofu (p. 112) and Japanese cooked salads such as Shira-ae (p. 114) go deliciously on buttered toast.

TOFU IN SOUPS

Fresh tofu adds flavor, protein, and a delightful texture to almost any soup. Cut into small cubes, crumbled, thinly sliced, or made into dumplings, it should be added to the soup 1 or 2 minutes before you have finished cooking. (If cooked over high heat or for too long, tofu loses some of its softness and delicate texture.) Use about 2½ to 3 ounces of tofu per serving. In each of the following recipes, kinugoshi, deep-fried tofu, grilled tofu, frozen tofu, or yuba may be substituted for the regular tofu.

Western-style Soups

Some of the Western-style soups we believe go best with tofu include onion, tomato, mushroom, cabbage, squash or pumpkin, bean, split pea, and lentil. The addition of a small amount of miso or shoyu, and perhaps an egg or some grated cheese, to a soup containing tofu often enhances its overall taste and texture.

Cream of Tomato Soup with Tofu — SERVES 3 OR 4

1 tablespoon oil
1 onion, diced
1 tomato, diced
1 cup milk (soy or dairy)
3 tablespoons red miso or 2 tablespoons shoyu
Dash of pepper and/or tabasco sauce
¼ teaspoon oregano or marjoram
12 ounces tofu or 6 ounces deep-fried tofu, diced
2 tablespoons minced parsley

Heat a pot and coat with the oil. Add onion and sauté over medium heat until transparent. Add tomato and sauté for 2 or 3 more minutes. Add the next five ingredients and cook, stirring constantly, for 1 minute. Remove from heat and allow to cool briefly, then transfer to a blender and purée until smooth. Return to heat and bring just to a boil. Add tofu, return to the boil, and remove from heat. Chill for 4 to 5 hours. Serve garnished with parsley.

Creamy Tomato-Rice Soup with Tofu — SERVES 5 OR 6

1 cup cooked Brown Rice (p. 50)
1¼ cups milk (soy or dairy)
¾ cup water
½ onion, diced
2 large tomatoes, diced
4 teaspoons shoyu or 1 teaspoon salt
Dash of pepper
1 teaspoon natural sugar (optional)
Dash of basil or oregano
¾ cup grated cheese
12 ounces tofu or 6 ounces deep-fried tofu, diced

Combine the first nine ingredients in a blender and purée until smooth. Transfer to a heavy-bottomed pot and bring just to a boil. Cover and simmer for 15 minutes, stirring occasionally. Mix in the cheese and tofu, return just to the boil, and remove from heat. Serve hot or, for a richer, sweeter flavor, chill for 4 to 6 hours.

Gazpacho Guadalahara with Diced Tofu — SERVES 8

This Latin American favorite is at its best chilled on hot summer afternoons. Many varieties of *gazpacho* are also prepared without cooking.

6 cups tomato juice
1 teaspoon Worcestershire sauce
2 teaspoons lemon juice
½ teaspoon (seasoned) salt or 2 teaspoons shoyu
1 small clove of garlic, crushed; or 2 tablespoons minced mint leaves
1 small bay leaf
4 green onions, sliced into thin rounds
2 tablespoons finely chopped parsley
1 avocado, cut into bite-sized pieces
4 to 6 ounces tofu, cut into small cubes
1 small cucumber, thinly sliced
½ cup thinly sliced celery
¼ cup chopped green pepper

Combine the first six ingredients in a pot and simmer for 15 minutes. Cool to room temperature and add remaining ingredients. Chill for several hours and remove bay leaf before serving.

Thick Pumpkin or Squash Soup with Tofu — SERVES 4 OR 5

1½ tablespoons oil
1 pound seeded (*kabocha*) pumpkin or squash, cut into ½-inch squares
2 onions, thinly sliced
2 cups water or stock
¼ teaspoon nutmeg or cinnamon
1 clove garlic, minced
4 tablespoons red, barley, or Hatcho miso; or 3 tablespoons shoyu
12 ounces tofu, cut into ½-inch cubes
3 tablespoons parsley, minced
½ cup croutons or dry bread pieces
2 tablespoons ground roasted sesame seeds (p. 38) (optional)

Heat the oil in a casserole or large pot. Add pumpkin, onion, and water, cover, and bring to a boil. Reduce heat to low and simmer for 25 minutes. Stir in nutmeg, garlic, and miso thinned in a little of the hot soup. Add tofu, return just to the boil and remove from heat. For best flavor, allow to cool to room temperature. Serve cold or reheated, topped with parsley, croutons and, if used, the sesame seeds.

Tofu-Onion Soup

One of the most delicious of all Western-style soups with tofu. Simply substitute 12 ounces tofu for the deep-fried tofu in the recipe on page 162.

Japanese-style Soups

Savory miso soups and delicately flavored clear soups almost always feature tofu and are among the most popular of all home and restaurant preparations.

About Miso Soup

In Japan, more tofu is used in miso soup than in any other type of cookery. Of the three most popular ways of serving tofu—chilled, simmering, and in miso soup—only the latter is enjoyed throughout the year and at any of the day's three meals. And since miso soup is an indispensable part of the traditional Japanese breakfast—together with rice and *tsukemono* (salt-pickled vegetables)—tofu makers generally start work long before sunrise to be sure that fresh tofu is ready for early morning shoppers.

In Japan, entire cookbooks are devoted to the preparation of miso soup. By using fresh seasonal vegetables, sprigs and even flowers, the sensitive cook is able to reflect in a dark lacquerware soup bowl the great rhythms of the four seasons. And by combining various types of miso with the proper choice of seasonings and seasonal garnishes, it is quite easy to prepare a unique type of miso soup each day of the year. In fact some Japanese cookbooks contain detailed and elaborate charts suggesting different ways of preparing miso soup each day of the week at both breakfast and dinner throughout the year.

Yet of all the many ingredients used in miso soups, tofu is the most essential and widely used. The most popular forms are small cubes of regular tofu and thin slices of agé, although each of the other types of tofu and yuba are also used on occasion.

For the Japanese, miso soup is much more than just a food; it is a cherished and traditional cultural possession which can inspire poetry and touch the heartstrings while warming the body and soul. For some, miso soup is one of the keystones of good health and family harmony, the hallmark of a good wife who expresses her love and judgment through cooking. A well-known Japanese proverb even goes so far as to say that only when a young woman has mastered the art of making fine miso soup is she ready to become a bride!

Miso Soup with Tofu and Onions   SERVES 2

2 cups dashi (p. 39), stock, or water
1 small onion, thinly sliced
2½ to 3 tablespoons red, barley, or Hatcho miso
4 to 6 ounces tofu, cut into 3/8-inch cubes
Dash of 7-spice red pepper

Combine dashi and onion in a small covered saucepan and bring to a boil. Reduce heat to medium and cook for 4 to 5 minutes. Place miso in a small cup, cream with about ½ cup cooking broth, and add to the soup. (Or, place miso in a small strainer or sieve, partially immerse strainer into broth in saucepan, and rub miso through strainer with the back of a wooden spoon. If desired, add to soup any kernels of grain or soybeans left in strainer.) Stir soup lightly, add tofu cubes and return just to the boil; remove from heat. Season with red pepper and serve immediately, Japanese-style if you wish, in covered lacquerware bowls.

Or use 1 piece of broiled agé cut into thin strips or 6 tofu dumplings (p. 127) instead of the diced tofu.

VARIATION
*Picnic Miso Soup: Combine 3 tablespoons miso with 2 table-spoons bonita flakes in a small bowl. Mix well, then shape into 2 balls. Skewer and roast each ball over a burner until its surface is well browned. Place miso balls, sliced onion, tofu, and seasoning into a picnic container. To serve, divide ingredients among 2 soup bowls, cream the miso in the bowls with a little hot water, then stir in remaining hot water.

Creamy Miso Soup   SERVES 4

1 tablespoon oil
1 onion, thinly sliced
1½ to 2 cups half-moons of eggplant or cauliflowerets
2 tablespoons butter
2 tablespoons (whole-wheat) flour
1 cup milk (soy or dairy)
½ cup water
2 ounces cheese, grated or minced
12 ounces tofu or 5 ounces deep-fried tofu, cut into small
    rectangles
2 tablespoons light-yellow or red miso
Dash of pepper

Heat the oil in a casserole. Add onions and sauté for 3 minutes, or until lightly browned. Add eggplants and sauté briefly or until all oil is absorbed; turn off heat.

Using the butter, flour, and milk, prepare a white sauce (p. 48). Add the sauce and ½ cup water to the casserole, cover, and simmer over low heat for 5 minutes. Add cheese and tofu, increase heat to medium, and cook for 3 minutes. Stir in miso thinned in a little of the cooking broth, and season with pepper. Stirring constantly, simmer for 1 minute more. Serve hot or cold.

Miso Soup with Tofu, Leeks, and Wakame

SERVES 2

2 cups dashi (p. 39), stock, or water
¼ large leek, or ½ onion, cut into thin rounds
3 to 4 ounces tofu, cut into 3/8-inch cubes
¼ to 1/3 cup fresh or refreshed *wakame* (p. 37), cut into 1-inch lengths
2 tablespoons red or light-yellow miso
Dash of 7-spice red pepper or 1 tablespoon thinly-sliced leeks

Bring dashi to a boil in a saucepan. Add leek or onion and return to the boil. Add tofu and *wakame*, and simmer for 1 minute. Stir in miso creamed with a little of the hot broth and return just to the boil. Serve immediately, garnished with the red pepper or leek slivers.

Serving Tofu in Miso Soups Throughout the Year

Many Japanese cookbooks contain charts suggesting different ways of serving tofu in miso soups with seasonal vegetables and garnishes. The following suggestions are examplary:

*Spring, Sunday dinner: egg tofu, *junsai* (water shield), red miso, *sansho* pepper

*Fall, Tuesday breakfast: tofu, *nameko* mushrooms, Hatcho miso, hot mustard

*Fall, Wednesday dinner: *shimeji* mushrooms, tofu, chrysanthemum leaves, white and red miso, *yuzu* peel

*Winter, Monday morning: tofu, milk, chives or *asatsuki*, light-yellow miso, pepper

*Winter, Friday morning: tofu, bean sprouts, red miso, thinly sliced leeks

*Winter, Friday evening: tofu, salmon roe, sweet white miso, grated Mandarin orange peel

*Winter, Saturday dinner: tofu, oysters, leeks, red miso, *sansho* pepper

*Summer, Tuesday dinner: tofu, onion, egg, barley miso, parsley

OTHER SUGGESTIONS FOR SERVING MISO SOUPS

*Garnishes and Seasonings: In addition to those mentioned above, the following are also used to add the crowning touch: grated gingerroot or its juice; all wild, springtime sprouts, sprigs, and buds; *kinome, myoga,* slivered cucumber, ground roasted sesame seeds, minced parsley, *shiso* leaves, buds and seeds, *daikon* leaf tips, *wasabi,* trefoil, powdered green *nori,* crumbled toasted *nori,* butter, and sake.
*Other Common Basic Ingredients: *Daikon,* turnips, pota-

toes, sweet potatoes and taro, burdock root, wild vegetables, cooked soybeans, *konnyaku,* carrots, lotus root, dried or fresh wheat gluten, *mochi, (kabocha)* pumpkin and squash, noodles, ginkgo nuts, cottage cheese, and fresh peas and beans.
*For a description of the large-scale preparation of miso soup, combining the preparation of Number 1 and Number 2 Dashi, see page 219.
*Substitute 12 ounces of tofu for 5 ounces of deep-fried tofu or 2 ounces of dried-frozen tofu in miso soup recipes in those sections.

About Clear Soup
(Suimono)

The dewlike freshness and utter simplicity of Japanese clear soups are a subtle delight to the senses. Within the dark hollow of a lacquerware bowl, the chef creates a miniature floating world in which textures, colors, and shapes are as mindfully balanced as flavors. For as the Japanese say, "A man eats with his eyes as well as his mouth." A tiny crescent of *yuzu* or lemon peel, a brilliant green sprig of *kinome,* or as few as two slender white mushrooms and a small cube of tofu can form a still life in the fragrant, steaming broth.

When used in clear soups, tofu may be cut into a variety of attractive shapes: chrysanthemum leaves, circles, half moons, cherry blossoms, triangles, tiny cubes called "hail-stones" and larger cubes called "yakko," cylinders (which are then sometimes broiled), maple or ginkgo leaves, or little loops and bows. Some of these shapes are also used in miso soups.

Clear soups are usually served at the beginning of the meal. The ingredients are generally limited to about three, and each must be fresh and attractive. They are used either fresh or parboiled, then carefully arranged in the bottom of a lacquerware bowl. To avoid disturbing the decorative arrangement, the broth is then poured very gently down the sides of the bowl.

Clear Soup with Citrus Fragrance

SERVES 2

1½ cups Clear Broth (p. 40)
6 ounces tofu, drained (p. 96) and cut into 1½-inch cubes
½ leek or 2 scallions, cut into thin rounds
4 slivers of lemon or *yuzu* peel

Bring broth to a boil in a small saucepan. Add tofu and simmer for 2 minutes, until heated through. Remove tofu carefully with a slotted spoon and divide among two soup bowls. Garnish with sliced leeks and lemon peel, then carefully pour in the simmering broth. Serve immediately.

VARIATION

*Clear Soup with Tofu Bow (Musubi-dofu): Prepare reshaped firm tofu (p. 98). Cut into long strips the shape of thin French-fried potatoes. Carefully tie each of 4 strips into a simple overhand loop. Add to the broth in place of the tofu cubes.

Egg Flower Soup with Onions and Tofu

SERVES 2

1½ cups Clear Broth (p. 40)
¼ small onion, thinly sliced
1 egg, lightly beaten
3 ounces tofu, cut into 3/8-inch cubes

Bring broth to a boil in a small saucepan. Add onion and simmer for 3 minutes. Now bring broth to a rolling boil and pour in beaten egg while stirring briskly in a circle. Reduce heat to medium, add tofu, and cook for 1 minute more. Serve hot in covered bowls.

Clear Soup with Chrysanthemum Tofu
(Kikka-dofu)

SERVES 2

6 ounces tofu, cut into 2 equal pieces
Dash of salt
A 4-inch square of kombu (optional)
1½ cups Clear Broth (p. 40)
24 *nameko* mushrooms or 4 to 6 white mushrooms
2 cakes of dried wheat gluten
4 slivers of *yuzu* or lemon peel

Hold one of the pieces of tofu in the palm of one hand immersed in a bowl of water. Using a sharp knife, cut the large surface of the tofu into ¼-inch squares, cutting half way down through the piece of tofu (fig. 37). Set the cut piece of tofu under water on the bottom of the bowl and repeat with the second piece.

Bring 3 cups water to a boil. Add salt, *kombu,* and water, then carefully add the tofu. Return to the boil and simmer for 30 seconds. Using a slotted spoon or mesh skimmer, transfer tofu to empty soup bowls.

Bring clear soup broth to a boil in a small saucepan, add mushrooms and return just to the boil. Pour broth and mushrooms into bowls containing tofu. Garnish each serving with wheat gluten and *yuzu* peel.

Kenchin-jiru

SERVES 5

This popular dish derives its name from an unusual anecdote. It is said that several centuries ago in the Kamakura Zen temple Kenchin-ji, a young monk carelessly dropped a cake of fresh tofu on the kitchen floor. Since the floor was always kept immaculately clean, the head cook unhesitatingly gathered up the scattered curds and used them in the evening soup. In honor of this spirit of using each thing fully, the tofu was thereafter crushed or broken into small pieces before being added to the soup.

According to another tradition, this soup, with its distinctive sesame flavor, has its origins in Chinese-style *shippoku* cookery. The word *kenchin* derives from the Chinese *kenchen* and means "rolled slivers of food" or "rolled parched food." In one famous version of this dish, the sautéed tofu and vegetables are served rolled in yuba and deep-fried rather than as part of a soup.

1½ tablespoons sesame oil
18 ounces tofu, pressed (p. 96) and broken into small pieces
½ cup shaved burdock root
1 cup half-moons of *daikon*
5 *shiitake* or cloud-ear mushrooms, thinly sliced
1 to 1¼ cups large irregular chunks of sweet potato, yam, or taro
½ cup gingko-leaf pieces of carrot (p. 37)
½ cake of *konnyaku,* broken into small pieces and lightly salted
2¼ cups dashi (p. 39), stock, or water
3½ tablespoons shoyu or 5 tablespoons red miso
¼ teaspoon salt
2 teaspoons sake or *mirin*
Garnishes: 7-spice red pepper, slivered leeks, crumbled *nori,* and/or grated lemon or *yuzu* rind

Heat the oil in a heavy-bottomed saucepan. Add consecutively: tofu, burdock root, *daikon,* mushrooms, sweet potato, carrot, and *konnyaku,* sautéing each over medium heat for about 1 minute. Reduce heat to low, and add broth, shoyu, salt, and sake. Cover pan and simmer for 30 to 40 minutes, or until *daikon* is transparent. For best flavor, allow to stand for 6 to 8 hours, then serve individual portions topped with a sprinkling of the garnishes.

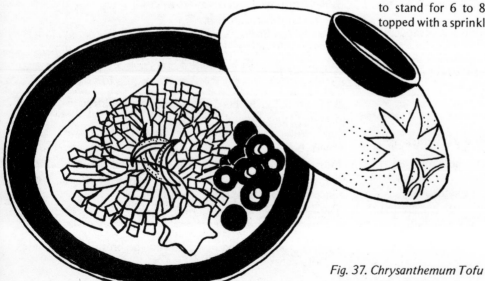

Fig. 37. Chrysanthemum Tofu

TOFU IN SAUCES

Friends or extra guests arriving just before mealtime? The spaghetti or curry sauce will only feed 6 but there will be 12 for dinner? Mash 2 or 3 cakes of fresh tofu, season with shoyu or miso, and stir into the sauce, thereby adding body, flavor, and plenty of protein. Seasoned this way, tofu also makes an excellent and inexpensive replacement for meat in many sauces. Most sauces become even more delicious if reheated or served cold after the flavors are given time to marry. Tofu may also be used with good results in most Basic Sauces (p. 48), Soymilk Sauces (p. 207), and Deep-fried Tofu Sauces (p. 165). The various types of Tofu Mayonnaise, Tofu Tartare Sauce, Creamy Tofu Dressings, and Tofu Sour Cream (pp. 107 to 109) also work well as sauces when served over cooked vegetables.

Quick Tofu-Sesame Sauce   MAKES 1¾ CUPS

12 ounces tofu
¼ cup sesame butter, *tahini,* or ground roasted sesame seeds (p. 38)
1 tablespoon shoyu
½ teaspoon salt
2 tablespoons natural sugar or honey

Combine all ingredients in a blender and purée until smooth. (Or mash ingredients together with a fork.) Serve over cooked vegetables or deep-fried tofu. If desired, substitute nut butters for the sesame.

Tofu Spaghetti Sauce   SERVES 4 TO 6

Regular or deep-fried tofu makes an excellent addition to any spaghetti sauce and may be used to replace meat. Use it in your favorite recipes or try the following:

2 tablespoons oil
1 clove garlic, crushed
2 onions, diced
2 large tomatoes, diced
2 green peppers, diced
3 mushrooms, thinly sliced
½ carrot, grated or diced; or 2 leaves of Chinese cabbage, thinly sliced
6 green beans, thinly sliced (optional)
2 cups water
1 bay leaf
24 ounces tofu, crumbled (p. 98); or 10 ounces thick agé, diced
7 cakes of dried wheat gluten (optional)
½ cup ketchup
3 tablespoons butter
¾ teaspoon salt or 2½ tablespoons shoyu
Dash of pepper
1/3 cup grated or Parmesan cheese

Heat a large heavy pot and coat with the oil. Add garlic and onions and sauté for 3 to 4 minutes. Add the next five ingredients and sauté for 3 to 4 minutes more. Add water, drop in bay leaf, and bring to a boil; cover pot and simmer for 15 minutes. Add the next six ingredients and re-cover; simmer, stirring occasionally, for about 1 hour. Remove from heat and cool to room temperature. Remove bay leaf and serve, either reheated or cold, over spaghetti or buckwheat noodles. Top with cheese.

For variety, season with grated gingerroot, green beefsteak leaves, oregano, or basil.

Tofu-Apple-Onion Curry Sauce   SERVES 3 OR 4

Substitute 18 ounces tofu (pressed; p. 96) for the deep-fried tofu in the recipe on page 166. Sauté the tofu in a little oil until tofu is firm and crumbly; add apples, potato, and water, and proceed as directed. For best flavor, allow sauce to stand for 6 to 8 hours before serving.

TOFU IN BREAKFAST EGG DISHES

One of the easiest and most delicious ways to incorporate tofu into your breakfast menu is by serving it in traditional Western-style egg preparations. Tofu goes well with cheese and all those vegetables which lend variety and zest to egg dishes. The Japanese often season their tofu-egg preparations with shoyu or Sesame Salt (p. 51) and a little sugar.

Butter-fried Tofu with Fried Eggs   SERVES 2

6 ounces tofu, pressed (p. 96)
1 tablespoon butter
2 eggs
Salt and pepper, or shoyu

Cut tofu lengthwise into halves, then crosswise into ¾-inch-thick pieces. Place pieces between cloth towels for several minutes until pieces are firm.

Melt the butter in a large skillet. Add tofu and sauté over medium heat for about 1 minute until golden brown. Turn tofu pieces with a spatula and cook second side. Use spatula to clear a small space at center of pan between the tofu pieces. Break the eggs into this space, cover skillet, and cook until eggs are firm. Season with salt and pepper, or shoyu. Try in place of bacon-and-eggs.

VARIATIONS

*Break the tofu into small pieces and sauté together with your choice of vegetables. Top the eggs with cheese and minced parsley just before covering the skillet.
*Poached Egg on Toast with Butter-fried Tofu: Cut the tofu as above and fry in butter. Cover several pieces of buttered whole-grain toast with the tofu slices, sprinkle lightly with shoyu, and top with poached eggs.

Tofu Sautéed in Butter with Scrambled Eggs

SERVES 2

1 tablespoon butter
6 ounces tofu
2 eggs, lightly beaten
Salt and pepper

Melt the butter in a skillet. Add tofu and mash, then sauté over medium heat until lightly browned. Add eggs and scramble until firm. Season with salt and pepper.

If desired, sauté any of the following together with the tofu: chives, bean or alfalfa sprouts, crushed garlic, mushrooms, scallions or onions, green peppers or lotus root (each diced or thinly sliced). Season with ½ to 1 teaspoon shoyu.

Scrambled Eggs with Tofu and Gingerroot

SERVES 2

3 eggs, lightly beaten
3 tablespoons shoyu
1½ to 2 tablespoons natural sugar
1 tablespoon grated gingerroot
12 ounces tofu

Combine eggs, shoyu, sugar, and gingerroot in a bowl; mix well. Place tofu in a skillet over medium heat and, using a spatula, cut tofu into small pieces. Stirring constantly, cook tofu for about 2 minutes until it is no longer moist. Pour in egg-shoyu mixture and scramble until firm. Serve hot or cold.

Scrambled Eggs with Tofu and Mushrooms

SERVES 4

12 ounces tofu, pressed (p. 96) and mashed
3 eggs, lightly beaten
2 tablespoons butter
1 cup diced fresh mushrooms
¼ teaspoon salt
Dash of pepper

Combine tofu and eggs in a bowl; mix well. Melt the butter in a skillet. Add mushrooms and sauté for several minutes until fragrant and tender. Pour in tofu-egg mixture and scramble until firm. Season with salt and pepper. Serve hot or cold.

Japanese-style Tofu, Eggs & Onions (Tamago-toji)

SERVES 2

1 tablespoon oil
1 small onion, thinly sliced
1 egg, lightly beaten
6 ounces tofu, thinly sliced
2 teaspoons shoyu
2 teaspoons natural sugar

Heat the oil in a skillet. Add onion and sauté for 3 to 4 minutes, or until transparent. Stir in remaining ingredients, cover, and cook for 2 or 3 minutes until egg is firm.

If desired, serve seasoned with *sansho* pepper or topped with grated cheese. Or serve as a topping for buckwheat noodles and garnish with crumbled, toasted *nori* (p. 38).

Tofu Poached Egg

SERVES 1

6 to 8 ounces tofu, pressed (p. 96) or well-drained

½ teaspoon shoyu or 1 teaspoon red miso
½ teaspoon lemon juice
1 egg

Scoop a deep hollow out of the upper surface of the tofu. Pour shoyu and lemon juice, then break the egg into this hollow.

Bring 1 inch of water to a boil over high heat in a saucepan. Carefully slide in tofu and return to the boil (fig. 38). Reduce heat to low, cover, and simmer for 3 minutes, or until egg is just firm. Scoop out tofu with a large slotted spoon and serve hot.

To distribute shoyu-lemon seasoning more evenly, mix tofu and egg together just before serving.

Fig. 38. Tofu Poached Egg

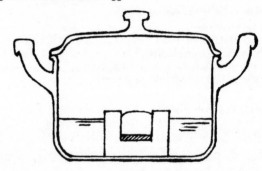

Tofu-Egg Omelet with Mushrooms

SERVES 2 OR 3

6 ounces tofu, pressed (p. 96) and diced
3 eggs, lightly beaten
1 tablespoon shoyu
½ teaspoon natural sugar
2 tablespoons ground roasted sesame seeds (p. 38), sesame butter, or *tahini*
1 tablespoon butter or oil
3 large fresh mushrooms, cut into thin strips
2 leeks or onions, cut into thin rounds

Combine the first five ingredients in a large bowl; mix well. Melt the butter in a skillet. Add leeks and mushrooms, and sauté for 2 or 3 minutes until fragrant and tender. Pour in tofu-egg mixture and cook over low heat. When omelet has an even consistency, fold and serve.

If desired, fill with grated cheese, cream cheese, or tomato wedges and minced parsley. Japanese chefs often cover omelets with several sheets of *nori* before rolling, then season the omelets with *sansho* pepper, powdered green *nori*, or Worcestershire sauce.

Tofu-Eggs a là Caracas

SERVES 3

2 tablespoons butter
8 ounces tofu, diced
2 tomatoes, minced or puréed
½ teaspoon salt or 1½ teaspoons shoyu
1 tablespoon minced onion
3 eggs, lightly beaten
¼ cup grated cheese
Dash of cinnamon

Melt the butter in a skillet. Add the next four ingredients, cover, and simmer over low heat for 20 to 30 minutes, or until tomatoes form a thick sauce. Add eggs, cheese, and cinnamon and cook, stirring constantly, for 2 or 3 minutes until eggs develop a creamy consistency. Serve hot or cold.

Chinese-style Egg Tofu

SERVES 2 OR 3

(Nanjen-dofu or Iritsuke-dofu)

1 tablespoon oil
12 ounces tofu, drained (p. 96) and cut crosswise into ¾-inch-thick pieces
2 eggs, lightly beaten
Sauce:
    ½ cup water
    1 tablespoon soy sauce
    ¼ teaspoon salt
    ¼ teaspoon sesame oil
    Dash of (7-spice) red pepper
    1 teaspoon cornstarch or arrowroot
¼ cup slivered leeks, scallions, or onions

Heat the oil in a wok or skillet. Add tofu and stir-fry for 2 or 3 minutes, being careful not to break individual pieces. Add eggs and stir-fry for 30 to 60 seconds more. Add the sauce and cook, stirring constantly, until thickened. Remove from heat and stir in leeks. Serve hot.

Okonomi-yaki *(Tofu-Egg Pancakes)*

SERVES 4

In Japan's many tiny restaurants specializing in *O-konomi-yaki*, each guest cooks his own pancakes on a small tabletop grill, then chooses seasonings and garnishes from the wide assortment available.

2/3 cup whole-wheat flour
2/3 cup milk (soy or dairy) or water
3 eggs
¼ teaspoon salt or 1 teaspoon shoyu
12 ounces tofu, pressed (p. 96)
½ carrot, grated
¼ onion, diced
3 mushrooms, thinly sliced
2 tablespoons corn kernels, parboiled (p. 37)
2 tablespoons green peas, parboiled
1 cup shredded cabbage
4 teaspoons oil
Worcestershire sauce, shoyu, or any Miso Topping (p. 41)
Powdered green *nori* or grated cheese

Combine the first four ingredients and mix well to make a batter. Stir in the tofu and vegetables. Heat 1 teaspoon oil in a large skillet. Spoon in one-fourth of the batter to form several pancakes and cook over low heat on both sides until golden brown. Repeat with remaining batter. Serve piping hot topped with a sprinkling of Worcestershire sauce and *nori*.

TOFU BAKED

Tofu may be used with excellent results in the baked dishes of countries throughout the world. It goes particularly well with all dairy products and with grains. The Japanese often sauté and season their vegetables with a little shoyu or miso (and sugar) before adding them to tofu baked dishes in order to give a richer and more distinctive flavor. Always use pressed tofu or doufu in casseroles where a firm or slightly dry consistency is desired. Experiment freely using tofu in your favorite recipes for oven cookery. Since baking—which uses a relatively large amount of fuel or energy—has never been a traditional Japanese way of cooking foods, most of the following recipes are typically Western. For baked desserts, see page 150.

Tofu Italian Meatballs

SERVES 2 OR 3

A remarkably good facsimile of its namesake, this preparation is one of the many creative and delicious tofu recipes served as part of the vegetarian cuisine at Tokyo's Seventh-day Adventist Hospital.

12 ounces tofu, well pressed (p. 96) or squeezed
¼ cup chopped walnut meats
½ onion, minced
¼ to 1/3 cup bread crumbs
1 egg, lightly beaten
3 tablespoons minced parsley
Dash of pepper
4 teaspoons red miso or ½ teaspoon salt
Oil for deep-frying
¼ cup tomato juice or tomato soup
¼ cup ketchup
Dash of oregano
3 tablespoons Parmesan or grated cheese

Combine the first seven ingredients and 1 tablespoon miso. Mix well and shape into 1½-inch balls. Heat oil to 350° in a wok, skillet, or deep-fryer. Drop in balls and deep-fry until cooked through and well browned (p. 130). Drain balls, then arrange in a loaf pan. Preheat oven to 350°. Combine remaining 1 teaspoon miso with tomato juice and ketchup, mixing to form a sauce, and pour over tofu balls. Top with a sprinkling of cheese and bake for 15 minutes, or until nicely browned. For best flavor, allow to stand for 6 to 8 hours. Serve hot or cold, as is or as a topping for spaghetti. Also delicious in Tofu Spaghetti Sauce (p. 121).

For variety, bake topped with Mushroom Sauce (p. 48) or Soymilk Cheese Sauce (p. 207).

Tofu & Brown Rice Casserole

SERVES 4

4½ teaspoons oil
1½ tablespoons butter
1½ onions, thinly sliced
1 cup cooked Brown Rice (p. 50)
12 ounces tofu, pressed (p. 96); or 9 ounces doufu
1 teaspoon salt
Dash of pepper
1 cup milk (soy or dairy)
¼ to ½ cup bread crumbs
2 ounces cheese, grated

Preheat oven to 350°. Heat a large skillet or wok and coat with 2 teaspoons oil and the butter. Add onion and sauté until lightly browned. Add brown rice, then tofu, sautéing each for 2 minutes. Season with salt and pepper. Place tofu-onion mixture in a casserole or bread pan coated with remaining oil. Pour in the milk, then sprinkle with bread crumbs and cheese. Bake for about 15 to 20 minutes, or until cheese is nicely browned.

Mushroom & Onion Casserole with Tofu

SERVES 3

2 onions, diced
8 mushrooms, thinly sliced
1 tomato, cut into thin wedges
1 teaspoon oil
1 pint yogurt
2 ounces dried onion soup or mushroom soup
24 ounces tofu, cut into ½-inch cubes
2 tablespoons roasted sesame seeds

Preheat oven to 350°. Combine the first three ingredients in a bowl; mix lightly. Layer one-half of mixture at the bottom of a lightly oiled casserole. Combine yogurt and dried onion soup in a bowl, mixing well. Pour one-fourth of yogurt-soup mixture over vegetables in casserole, and top with a layer of one-half of the tofu and 1 tablespoon sesame seeds. Then pour another one-fourth of the yogurt mixture over the tofu. Use the remaining ingredients to form an identical series of layers. Bake for 30 minutes.

Tofu-Cheese Soufflé

SERVES 4

3 slices of whole-wheat bread
2 tablespoons butter
6 ounces tofu, cut into ½-inch-thick slices
6 ounces (sharp cheddar) cheese, grated
1 tablespoon chopped onion or ¼ teaspoon onion powder
1¼ cups milk (soy or dairy)
2 eggs, lightly beaten
½ teaspoon salt or 2 tablespoons red miso
Dash of pepper

Butter the bread and tear each slice into 4 or 5 pieces. Coat a casserole lightly with butter, then layer bread, tofu, cheese, and onion, repeating the layers until all ingredients are used. Combine milk, eggs, salt or miso, and pepper, and pour into the casserole; allow to stand for 1 to 2 hours. Bake casserole in a pan of water for 45 minutes in a preheated 350° oven.

Mushroom & Tofu Soufflé

SERVES 6

2 ounces butter
1 pound fresh mushrooms
¼ cup diced onions
½ teaspoon salt and dash of pepper
½ cup (tofu) mayonnaise (p. 107)
6 slices of (whole wheat) bread, buttered and broken into
　　½-inch squares
8 ounces tofu, cut into ½-inch cubes
2 eggs, lightly beaten
1½ cups milk (soy or dairy)
2 cups white sauce (p. 48)

Melt butter in a skillet. Add mushrooms and sauté until tender. Add onions and sauté for 1 minute more, then remove from heat. Add salt, pepper, and mayonnaise; mix well.

In a lightly buttered casserole, layer the bread, tofu, and mushrooms, repeating until all ingredients are used. Combine eggs and milk and pour into the casserole. Allow to stand for at least 2 hours, preferably overnight. Pour white sauce evenly over casserole, then bake for 1 hour in a preheated 325° oven.

Tofu Loaf with Onions and Cheese

SERVES 4

4 tablespoons butter
2 tablespoons whole-wheat flour
1 cup milk (soy or dairy)
¾ teaspoon salt
1 onion, minced
4 ounces cheese, diced
12 ounces tofu, pressed (p. 96) and mashed
¼ cup bread or cracker crumbs

Melt 2 tablespoons butter in a skillet. Add flour and sauté until fragrant and lightly browned. Gradually add 1½ cups milk, stirring constantly, to form a smooth brown sauce. Season with the salt, then simmer until sauce is thick. Stir in onion, cheese, and tofu and remove from heat.

Coat a pie tin with 1 tablespoon butter and fill with tofu-sauce mixture. Sprinkle on bread crumbs and dot with remaining 1 tablespoon butter. Bake in a 350° oven for about 15 minutes, or until set.

Delectable Tofu & Onion Gratin

SERVES 4 OR 5

18 ounces tofu, diced
3½ cups Onion Sauce (p. 48)
2 cups dry bread pieces or croutons
2 teaspoon shoyu or 1 tablespoon red miso, dissolved in ½
　　cup water
¼ cup Parmesan or grated cheese

Combine the first four ingredients, mixing well, and pour into an oiled or buttered casserole or large bread pan; allow to stand for 1 to 2 hours. Preheat oven to 350°. Sprinkle casserole with cheese and bake for 20 to 30 minutes, or until nicely browned. Serve hot or cold.

For variety, press 4 to 6 hard-boiled egg halves into the tofu-onion mixture. Top with cheese and bread crumbs, and dot with butter before baking.

Tofu-Cheese Patties

MAKES 6

2 tablespoons oil
½ onion, minced
1 green pepper, diced
12 ounces tofu, pressed (p. 96)
1/3 cup mashed baked potatoes
½ cup bread crumbs
2 ounces cheese, grated or diced
½ teaspoon salt
Dash of pepper

Preheat oven to 350°. Heat a small skillet or wok and coat with 1 tablespoon oil. Add onions and peppers and sauté until onions are lightly browned. Combine tofu, potatoes, bread crumbs, cheese, and onion-green pepper mixture in a mixing bowl. Season with salt and pepper, mash together with a fork, and shape into 6 patties. Arrange patties on a baking tin lightly oiled with remaining oil, and bake for 40 minutes or until nicely browned. Serve topped with ketchup, Ketchup-Worcestershire Sauce (p. 49), or Onion Sauce (p. 48).

Savory Tofu-Pumpkin Delight

SERVES 4

2 tablespoons oil
½ onion, thinly sliced
3 cups boiled and mashed *kabocha* or pumpkin
12 ounces tofu, pressed (p. 96) and diced
1 egg, lightly beaten
3 tablespoons shoyu
3 tablespoons natural sugar
Dash of salt
Dash of cinnamon or *sansho* pepper (optional)

Preheat oven to 350°. Heat a large skillet or wok and coat with 1 tablespoon oil. Sauté onion until lightly browned, then turn off heat. Add pumpkin, tofu, egg, shoyu, sugar, and salt, mixing well. Coat a pie tin with 1 tablespoon oil and spoon in the tofu mixture; sprinkle with cinnamon or *sansho*. Bake for about 15 minutes, or until set.

Tofu & Pumpkin Patties

MAKES 8

2 cups boiled and mashed *kabocha* or pumpkin
24 ounces tofu, pressed (p. 96) and mashed
1 tablespoon salt
Dash of pepper
1 teaspoon oil
1/3 cup raisins
2 ounces cheese, grated or diced
2 tablespoons butter

Preheat oven to 350°. Combine pumpkin and tofu in a large bowl, mixing well, and season with salt and pepper. Shape the mixture into 4-inch patties and place on a baking pan coated with the oil. Dot the top of each pattie with raisins, cheese and butter. Bake for 20 to 30 minutes, or until lightly browned. Or bake in a pie shell as for pumpkin pie.

Buckwheat Noodle Gratin with Tofu

SERVES 5

3 tablespoons oil
1 onion, cut into thin wedges
½ carrot, cut into thin half moons
6 ounces tofu, pressed (p. 96) and mashed
1¼ teaspoons salt
2 tablespoons whole-wheat flour
½ cup milk (soy or dairy) or water
10 ounces *(soba)* buckwheat noodles, cooked (p. 50)
¼ cup minced parsley
5 slivers of *yuzu* or lemon peel

Preheat oven to 350°. Heat a skillet and coat with 1 tablespoon oil. Add the onion and sauté until transparent. Add the carrot and tofu and sauté for 4 to 5 minutes more. Transfer to a large bowl and season with ½ teaspoon salt.

Reheat skillet and coat with 1 tablespoon oil. Add flour and sauté until fragrant and lightly browned. Gradually add the milk, stirring constantly, to form a smooth brown sauce. Simmer until sauce is thick, then season with ¾ teaspoon salt.

Place noodles in a lightly oiled gratin dish. Add sautéed vegetable-tofu mixture, then pour on the sauce. Sprinkle with 1½ teaspoons oil and bake for about 20 minutes, or until slightly crisp and nicely browned. Serve hot or cold, topped with parsley and garnished with slivered *yuzu*.

Or, sauté ¼ cup yuba with the vegetables, and add 1 tablespoon sesame butter to the sauce just after stirring in the milk. Substitute rice flour noodles for buckwheat, and top with grated or Parmesan cheese before baking.

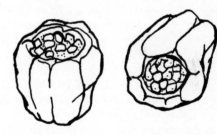

Tofu-Stuffed Green Peppers

SERVES 4

2 tablespoons oil
1 onion, minced
½ cup cooked Brown Rice (p. 50) or mashed potatoes
12 ounces tofu, pressed (p. 96); or 9 ounces doufu
2 tablespoons ketchup
½ teaspoon salt
4 large green peppers, cut vertically into halves and seeded

Preheat oven to 350°. Heat the oil in a skillet or wok and sauté onion until nicely browned. Add rice and sauté for 1 minute more. Add tofu, mash it in the pan, and sauté for about 2 more minutes; season with ketchup and salt. Use the mixture as a stuffing for the green peppers. Coat the outside of each pepper lightly with oil, arrange stuffed peppers on a lightly oiled pan, and bake for 20 minutes.

Baked Potatoes with Tofu Stuffing   SERVES 6 TO 8

4 potatoes, baked and cut lengthwise into halves
12 ounces tofu, pressed (p. 96); or 9 ounces doufu
2 ounces cheese, grated or diced
½ teaspoon salt
Dash of pepper
1½ tablespoons butter
1 onion, minced
1 tablespoon oil

Preheat oven to 350°. Scoop potato out of shells, then spoon 1 cup of potato into a mixing bowl and reserve the remainder. Mash tofu and cheese with potato in bowl; season with salt and pepper. Melt butter in a skillet and sauté onions until nicely browned. Mix onions into potato-tofu mixture, then divide the mixture among the potato shells. Coat a cookie tin with the oil and bake stuffed potatoes on tin for about 30 minutes, or until nicely browned. Delicious served topped with butter (or sour cream) and minced chives (or parsley).

Additional Suggestions for Serving Tofu in Baked Dishes

*Tofu makes a very nutritious addition to vegetable pies and quiches, tamale casseroles, and ravioli dishes. Use thin strips of pressed tofu as one of the ingredients in pizza toppings. In *enchiladas, tostadas, tacos,* or *quesarillas,* well-pressed, diced tofu may be used with or in place of beans, mixed with shredded lettuce, tomatoes, cheese, or other fillings.
*Kenchin-yaki: Sauté ¼ cup each slivered mushrooms, carrot, onion, and 3 tablespoons green peas. Combine with 12 ounces pressed tofu, 1 egg, 1½ tablespoons shoyu, and 2 teaspoons each sake and sugar. Mix well and bake in a loaf pan for 15 to 20 minutes.

TOFU SAUTÉED, STIR-FRIED, OR TOPPED WITH SAUCES

There are many ways of using tofu with cooked vegetables. Mastery of the Chinese technique for stir-frying will add a new dimension to your cooking repertoire. Sautéing with oil previously used for deep-frying (p. 130) will add flavor and savory aroma to even the simplest preparations.

Butter-fried Tofu Teriyaki   SERVES 2

1/3 cup Teriyaki Sauce (p. 48)
12 ounces tofu, pressed (p. 96) and cut into 12 small rectangles about ½ inch thick
1½ tablespoons butter

Place sauce and tofu in a shallow pan. Marinate for 1 hour, turning tofu rectangles over after 30 minutes. Melt the butter in a skillet. Add tofu and fry for 2 to 3 minutes on each side until golden brown. Serve any remaining marinade as a dipping sauce.

Tofu with Onion Sauce and Cheese   SERVES 4

3 tablespoons oil
6 onions, thinly sliced
5 tablespoons shoyu
24 ounces tofu, pressed (p. 96) and cut into 1-inch cubes
2½ teaspoons natural sugar (optional)
1 tablespoon sake or white wine
1 egg, lightly beaten
2 ounces cheese, thinly sliced
4 slices of whole-wheat toast (optional)

Using the oil, onions, and 3 tablespoons shoyu, prepare an Onion Sauce (p. 48). Add tofu cubes, sugar, sake, and the remaining 2 tablespoons shoyu, and simmer over low heat for 10 to 15 minutes. Turn off heat, then pour egg over surface of sauce; top with a layer of cheese. Cover and allow to stand until cheese melts. Serve as is or over toast.

Fried Tofu Patties with Eggs and Vegetables   MAKES 8

24 ounces tofu, squeezed (p. 97)
Thin tips and leaves of 1 celery stalk, minced
1 small onion, minced
¼ cup green peas or thinly sliced green peppers or leeks (optional)
4 eggs, lightly beaten
2 tablespoons ground roasted sesame seeds (p. 38), sesame butter or *tahini*
½ teaspoon salt
1 tablespoon shoyu
4 teaspoons oil
½ cup ketchup or Ketchup-Worcestershire (p. 49); or 4 teaspoons shoyu

In a large mixing bowl, combine the first eight ingredients; mix well to form a batter. Heat a skillet and coat with ½ teaspoon oil. Spoon about one-eighth of the batter into the pan and press lightly with a spatula to form a patty about 3/8 inch thick. Fry until nicely browned, then flip with the spatula and press again until patty is about ¼ inch thick. Fry until second side is golden brown. Repeat with remaining oil and batter until all are used. Serve patties hot or cold, topped with ketchup.

VARIATIONS

*Egg Patties with Oatmeal: Use 20 ounces tofu, ¾ cup quick-cooking oatmeal, ½ cup minced green onion, 2 eggs, ½ cup shredded carrot, and ½ cup diced green pepper. Use the batter to make ½-inch-thick patties and fry in butter for about 2 minutes on each side. Top with a sprinkling of shoyu, or pass sour cream or yogurt to spoon on top.
*Tofu-Yam Patties with Sweet Simmered Miso: Mix 12 ounces well-pressed tofu (p. 96) with ¼ cup grated glutinous yam and ¼ teaspoon salt. Shape into thin patties and fry in oil until golden brown. Serve topped with Sweet Simmered Miso (p. 41) and seasoned with *sansho* papper. Or serve topped with melted butter.

Tofu Burgers with Mushroom Sauce   SERVES 3

3 tablespoons oil
1 small onion, minced
24 ounces tofu, crumbled (p. 98) and allowed to cool
3 eggs, lightly beaten
½ cup bread crumbs or bread crumb flakes
¾ teaspoon salt
Dash of pepper
Mushroom Sauce (p. 48) or ketchup

Heat a skillet and coat with 1 tablespoon oil. Add onion and sauté for 3 minutes, then allow to cool. Combine onion with tofu, eggs, bread crumbs, salt, and pepper in a large bowl, and use the mixture to make 8 patties. Heat the skillet and re-coat with 1 tablespoon oil. Add 4 patties, cover, and cook over low heat for about 5 minutes on each side. Repeat with remaining 4 patties. Serve hot or cold, topped with the sauce.

Tofu Dumplings with Mushroom Sauce   SERVES 3 OR 4

24 ounces tofu, squeezed (p. 97)
1 egg, lightly beaten
1 tablespoon cornstarch or arrowroot
½ teaspoon salt or 3 tablespoons red, barley, or Hatcho miso
1 clove garlic, crushed
3 tablespoons parboiled minced vegetables (green peas, mushrooms, etc.)
¼ cup ground roasted sesame seeds (p. 38) (optional)
Mushroom (p. 48), Spaghetti (p. 121), or Sweet & Sour Sauce (p. 49)

Combine the first six ingredients, mixing well, and shape into 1-inch balls. Bring 1 quart water to a boil over high heat in a large pot. Drop in the balls and return to the boil. Reduce heat to medium and cook until dumplings float to surface. Scoop out dumplings with a slotted spoon, drain, and allow to cool briefly.
   Prepare the sauce of your choice, adding balls about 10 minutes before sauce has finished cooking. For best flavor, allow to cool for 4 to 6 hours, then reheat or serve cold.
   This dish also makes an excellent topping for spaghetti, noodles, or brown rice. Try using the dumplings in your favorite soups or in place of tofu in any of the soup recipes in this book. Or use in Oden (p. 175) or *nabe* dishes.

Butter-fried Tofu   SERVES 4

24 ounces tofu, pressed (p. 96)
3 to 4 tablespoons butter
½ onion, sliced very thin, rinsed and pressed (p. 37)
1 tablespoon minced parsley
2 ounces cheese (grated or Parmesan)
1 tablespoon slivered lemon peel
Dash of salt

Cut tofu lengthwise into halves, then crosswise into ½-inch-thick pieces. Melt the butter in a skillet. Add the tofu and fry on both sides until golden brown. Arrange pressed onions, parsley, cheese, and lemon peel in separate condiment dishes. Serve tofu hot, sprinkled with your choice of condiments and a little salt.
   For variety, serve with any of the shoyu dipping sauces and garnishes used with Chilled Tofu (p. 105), or top with Sesame Miso (p. 42).

Chinese-style Bean Sauce with Tofu   SERVES 3

   Although this popular type of preparation is called a "sauce," it is generally served as an entrèe in its own right.

2 tablespoons oil
1 teaspoon grated gingerroot
1 teaspoon crushed or minced garlic
2 small *(togarashi)* red peppers, minced
5 mushrooms, thinly sliced
3 green onions, whites thinly sliced and greens cut into 2-inch lengths
16 ounces tofu, pressed (p. 96) and cut into ½-inch cubes; or 12 ounces doufu
2 tablespoons red miso creamed with ½ cup water
1 tablespoon soy sauce
1 tablespoon honey
1 tablespoon cashew or sesame butter
½ teaspoon vinegar
1 teaspoon arrowroot or cornstarch, dissolved in 2 tablespoons water

Heat the oil in a wok or skillet. Add gingerroot, garlic, and red peppers, and sauté for 2 or 3 minutes. Add mushrooms and onion whites, and sauté for 2 or 3 minutes more. Add onion greens and tofu cubes and sauté for 1 minute. Combine miso, soy sauce, honey, cashew butter, and vinegar; mix well. Stir into tofu-mushroom mixture and simmer for 1 minute. Stir in dissolved arrowroot and simmer for about 30 seconds more, or until thick.

Tofu Sautéed with Bean Sprouts (Okinawa-style)   SERVES 4 TO 6

1¼ tablespoons oil
24 ounces tofu, well pressed (p. 96) and broken into ¾-inch pieces
8 to 10 ounces bean sprouts
3 to 4 scallions, cut into 2-inch lengths
1 tablespoon sake or white wine
1¼ teaspoons salt
1 teaspoon shoyu

Heat a wok or skillet and coat with the oil. Add tofu and stir-fry over high heat until golden brown. Add bean sprouts and scallions and stir-fry for about 2 minutes more, or until scallions are tender. Mix in sake, salt, and shoyu, and cook for 30 seconds more. Serve steaming hot.
   If desired, add slivered *daikon*, Chinese cabbage, leeks, onions, or *hijiki* to the ingredients listed above.

Sautéed Tofu with Lotus Root & Carrot

SERVES 4

1½ tablespoons oil
1 small lotus root, diced
1 small carrot, diced
12 ounces tofu, pressed (p. 96) and diced
2 tablespoons shoyu
1½ tablespoons natural sugar

Heat a skillet or wok and coat with the oil. Sauté the lotus root and carrot over low heat for 2 or 3 minutes. Add enough water to cover the vegetables, cover pan, and simmer for 10 to 15 minutes, or until soft. Add tofu, shoyu, and sugar, mixing well. Re-cover pan and simmer for 5 minutes more.

Chinese-style Tofu Sauté

SERVES 2 OR 3

2 tablespoons oil (up to one-half of which may be sesame oil)
½ carrot, cut into half moons
3 small green peppers, thinly sliced
1 small onion, cut into very thin wedges
12 ounces tofu, pressed (p. 96); or 9 ounces doufu
2 tablespoons soy sauce
3 tablespoons natural sugar
1 tablespoon vinegar
1½ tablespoons arrowroot or cornstarch, dissolved in ¼ cup water

Heat the oil in a wok or skillet. Add consecutively: carrot, green peppers, onion, and tofu, sautéing each for about 2 minutes, or until just tender. Add soy sauce, sugar, and vinegar, and simmer for 3 minutes more. Stir in dissolved arrowroot and cook for 30 seconds more, or until thick.

Iridofu (Crumbly Scrambled Tofu)

SERVES 3 OR 4

One of Japan's most popular tofu dishes, *Iridofu* has a light, dry texture and is remarkably similar to Western-style scrambled eggs in both flavor and appearance. This dish may be prepared with or without eggs, sweetened or unsweetened, and with or without the addition of any of the diced or slivered vegetables that are generally used in scrambled eggs.

1 tablespoon oil
1 small onion, diced
1 small carrot, diced
24 ounces tofu, crumbled into very small pieces (p. 98)
2 tablespoons ground roasted sesame seeds (p. 38) (optional)
½ teaspoon salt
2 teaspoons shoyu
Dash of pepper

Heat a skillet or wok and coat with the oil. Add onion and carrot and sauté for 3 to 4 minutes until onion is lightly browned. Add crumbled tofu and the remaining ingredients. Stirring constantly, sauté over medium-low heat for about 5 minutes, or until tofu is light, dry, and almost fluffy. Serve hot or cold.

VARIATIONS

*Add ¼ cup of any of the following with the tofu: parboiled green peas, diced (*shiitake* or cloud-ear) mushrooms, diced bamboo shoots, dried yuba flakes. Or add 1 to 2 pieces of diced agé or 1 teaspoon grated gingerroot. Try sautéing the vegetables in sesame oil.
*Add 1 or 2 eggs, 2 to 3 tablespoons natural sugar, and 1 tablespoon sake. Use only 2 tablespoons shoyu and a dash of salt, adding these together with the tofu. Add the lightly beaten egg after tofu has been sautéed for about 2 minutes.

Mabo-dofu
(Chinese-style Tofu with Red Pepper Sauce)

SERVES 2

The most popular Chinese-style tofu dish in Japan, *Mabo-dofu* usually contains a small amount of ground beef. It is representative of the many Chinese tofu dishes sautéed with pork, shrimp, chicken, or beef.

1 tablespoon corn or soy oil
1½ teaspoons sesame oil
1 clove garlic, crushed
¼ cup minced leeks, scallions, or onions
½ teaspoon minced red peppers
4 mushrooms, diced
½ cup water, stock, or dashi (p. 39)
1½ teaspoons sake
2½ teaspoons soy sauce
½ teaspoon salt
Dash of *sansho* or 7-spice red pepper
1½ teaspoons ketchup
24 ounces tofu or kinugoshi, cut into pieces 1¼ inches square by ½ inch thick
2 teaspoons cornstarch, dissolved in 2 tablespoons water
1 tablespoon minced leek or scallion greens

Heat a wok or skillet and coat with both types of oil. Add the garlic, leeks, and red peppers, and stir-fry over high heat for 15 seconds. Reduce heat to medium, add mushrooms, and sauté for 1 minute. Add water and next five ingredients, bring to a boil, and cook for 30 seconds. Add tofu and return to the boil. Stir in dissolved cornstarch and simmer until thick. Serve hot, garnished with the greens.

Chinese-style Oyster Sauce & Tofu
(Hao-yu Doufu)
SERVES 1 OR 2

3½ tablespoons oil
3 tablespoons leeks, cut into ½-inch lengths
2 tablespoons gingerroot, cut into ½- by ½- by 1/8-inch pieces
½ cup mushrooms, thinly sliced through the caps
¼ cup water
12 counces tofu or 9 ounces doufu, cut into 1½- by ½-inch pieces
¼ cup green peas
3 tablespoons sake
3 tablespoons oyster sauce (available at Chinese food markets)
2 tablespoons soy sauce
½ teaspoon salt
2 tablespoons cornstarch, dissolved in 3 tablespoons water

Heat the oil in a wok over high heat. Add the leeks and gingerroot and stir-fry for 30 seconds. Add the mushrooms and stir-fry for 30 seconds more. Add the next four ingredients and cook for 1 minute, stirring occasionally. Add the oyster sauce and cook for 1 minute. Add the soy sauce and salt and cook for 1 minute more. Mix in the dissolved cornstarch and cook for about 2 more minutes, lifting the wok occasionally and swishing its contents around the hot sides to aid evaporation of the cooking liquids. Serve hot on a large oval plate or platter.

Chinese-style Sautéed Firm Tofu
SERVES 4

24 ounces tofu, reshaped (p. 98)
2 tablespoons oil
½ teaspoon salt
1 small onion, thinly sliced
6 mushrooms or 1 large cooked bamboo shoot, thinly sliced
1 small carrot, cut into matchsticks
2 green peppers, cut into thin strips
1 tablespoon sake or white wine
1½ tablespoons soy sauce
1 teaspoon grated gingerroot
1 tablespoon natural sugar
1 tablespoon water
1 teaspoon cornstarch, dissolved in 3 tablespoons water

Cut tofu crosswise into pieces the shape of French-fried potatoes. Heat a wok or skillet, coat with the oil and sprinkle on the salt. Add onion, then the mushrooms, stir-frying each over high heat for about 30 seconds. Reduce heat to medium-low and add carrot, green pepper, and tofu, in that order, sautéing each for about 1 minute. Reduce heat to low and add sake, soy sauce, gingerroot, sugar, and water; simmer for 3 to 4 minutes. Stir in dissolved cornstarch and simmer for 30 seconds more.

For extra tang, add 2 teaspoons vinegar together with the sake.

Fanchie-dofu
(Chinese-style Tofu & Tomatoes)
SERVES 4

24 ounces tofu
5 tablespoons oil
1 teaspoon salt
2 tomatoes, each cut into 8 wedges
1 clove of garlic, crushed or minced
1 teaspoon sake or rice wine
3 tablespoons stock or water
½ leek or onion, diced
1 tablespoon cornstarch or arrowroot, dissolved in 3 tablespoons water
1 cup green soybeans or green peas, parboiled (p. 37)

Cut tofu lengthwise into halves, then crosswise into ½-inch-thick pieces. In a small saucepan bring 3 cups water to a boil. Drop in the tofu and return to the boil, then quickly empty tofu into a colander to drain.

Heat a wok or skillet and coat with 4 tablespoons oil and the salt. Add tomatoes and sauté until soft. Add tofu, garlic, and sake and sauté for 2 or 3 minutes. Add stock (or water) and leek, reduce heat and simmer for 4 to 5 minutes. Stir in dissolved cornstarch and remaining 1 tablespoon oil and simmer for 1 minute more until thick. Add green soybeans just before serving.

Braised Tofu
SERVES 4

¼ cup flour
2 eggs, lightly beaten
1½ teaspoons salt
9 tablespoons oil
24 ounces tofu, pressed (p. 96) and cut crosswise into 8 pieces; or 18 ounces doufu
2 tablespoons minced leeks
1½ cups dashi (p. 39), stock, or water
2 teaspoons shoyu
1½ tablespoons sake, *mirin*, or white wine
1½ teaspoons cornstarch, dissolved in 3 tablespoons water

Combine flour, eggs, and salt in a bowl, mixing lightly to form a batter. Heat 6 tablespoons oil in a skillet. Use the batter to coat each piece of tofu, then fry on both sides until golden brown. Drain and set aside, reserving excess oil.

Heat remaining 3 tablespoons oil in a skillet. Add leeks and brown lightly. Add fried tofu pieces, dashi, shoyu, and sake, mixing gently. Stir in dissolved cornstarch and simmer for about 30 seconds more, or until thick. Serve immediately.

Crispy Fried Tofu

12 ounces tofu, well-pressed (p. 96); or 9 ounces doufu
1 teaspoon salt
5 tablespoons (whole-wheat) flour
5 tablespoons oil
2 tablespoons shoyu

Cut tofu lengthwise into halves, then crosswise into thirds. Pat each piece lightly with a cloth towel to remove surface moisture, then sprinkle with salt and roll in flour. Heat the oil in a skillet until it is quite hot but does not smoke. Add tofu and fry on both sides until golden brown and fairly crisp. Drain on absorbent paper and serve immediately to be seasoned with shoyu to taste.

For variety, sprinkle powdered green *nori* on the fried tofu and top with grated *daikon* or gingerroot before sprinkling with shoyu. Or omit salt and roll tofu in cornstarch or arrowroot instead of flour.

Additional Suggestions for Serving Tofu Sautéed or Stir-fried

*Tofu in Fried Mexican Dishes:** Try tofu (pressed, then mashed or crumbled) in any of the following: *tostadas, enchiladas* with cheese, *chili rellenos,* or refried beans. Fry tofu in oil and season with shoyu and red peppers.
*Tofu with Fried Potatoes:** Combine well-pressed, mashed tofu with potatoes when preparing hashed browns, potato pancakes, or thinly-sliced browned potatoes.
*Fried Tofu Topped with Sauces:** Fry thin slices of well-pressed tofu in butter or oil until golden brown. Serve topped with any of the following sauces: Mushroom (p. 48), Sweet & Sour (p. 49), Tomato & Cheese (p. 49), or Lemon-Miso White Sauce (p. 207).

Fig. 39. Filling a wok with oil

TOFU DEEP-FRIED

Although three varieties of deep-fried tofu are available at most tofu shops (p. 154), tofu can also be deep-fried at home. One of the culinary arts raised to great heights by the Japanese, the technique of deep-frying comprises a world of its own, yielding light, crisp textures and delicate, delicious flavors. Learning to prepare fine, deep-fried foods is quite easy once you master the basic principles. This section contains recipes using nine different closely related methods for deep-frying tofu, listed here in order of ease of preparation: 1) without coating or batter; 2) rolled in *kuzu*, arrowroot, or cornstarch; 3) rolled in bread crumbs, bread crumb flakes, flour, or cornmeal; 4) dipped in lightly-beaten eggs and rolled in bread crumbs, *kuzu*, cornstarch, or flour; 5) rolled in flour or *kuzu* and dipped in eggs; 6) dipped into a thick batter of *kuzu* (or cornstarch) and egg whites; 7) dipped into a moderately thick batter of *kuzu* (or cornstarch) and water; 8) dusted with flour, dipped in lightly-beaten eggs, and rolled in bread crumbs to form a bound breading; and 9) coated with tempura batter.

About Deep-frying

Although deep-fat frying has long been a part of Western cookery, it has never attained the degree of popularity or artistry that it enjoys throughout the Orient, and particularly in Japan. Deep-frying is as common in the typical Japanese kitchen as baking is in the West, while it is faster and uses much less fuel. In only a few minutes, it transforms the simplest fresh vegetables, pieces of tofu, and even leftovers into prize creations. The art of deep-frying is a joy to practice and, fortunately, one of the easiest ways to begin learning is by making your own deep-fried tofu.

In Japanese, the verb *ageru* means "to deep-fry," and *agé-mono* or "deep-fried things" are the many foods that make up this vast world. The simplest form of deep-frying is called *kara-agé* or "deep-frying without a coating or batter." The three basic types of deep-fried tofu—thick agé, ganmo, and agé—are each prepared in this way. After mastering this technique, you should find no difficulty in perparing fine, crisp tempura.

If you wish to make deep-frying a permanent part of your repertoire of cooking techniques, it is best to start with the proper tools. Most important is the deep-frying pot. While many Westerners use a heavy 3- to 4-quart kettle, or an electric deep-fryer, most Japanese use either a wok (see p 35) or a heavy-bottomed skillet 2½ to 3 inches deep and 10 to 12 inches in diameter.

For best results use a simple vegetable oil. Japanese tofu masters prefer rapeseed oil, but many Western tofu shops also use soybean or cottonseed oil. Some chefs specializing in vegetable tempura prefer a combination of oils. If 10 to 30 percent sesame oil is added to any of the above basic oils, it will give the foods a delicious, nutty flavor. Other popular combinations are: peanut or corn (70%) and sesame (30%); peanut (75%), sesame (20%), and olive (5%); cottonseed (85%), olive (10%), and sesame (5%). For a light, crisp texture, avoid the use of animal fats in deep-frying.

Used deep-frying oil should be kept in a sealed jar and stored in a cool, dark place. When sautéing vegetables or frying eggs, you may use some of this oil to impart added flavor to the foods and help use up the oil. When deep-frying, try to use about one part fresh oil and one part used. Dark or thick used oil has a low smoking point and imparts a poor flavor. Foods deep-fried in used oil only are not as light and crisp as they could be. Pour oil from the storage jar into the deep-fryer carefully so that any sediment remains at the bottom of the jar. Then add fresh oil to fill the wok or skillet to a depth of 1½ to 2 inches (fig. 39).

Maintaining the oil at the proper temperature (about 350°) is the most important part of deep-frying. At first it may be easiest to measure the temperature with a deep-frying thermometer. More experienced chefs or tofu makers judge the oil's temperature by its appearance, aroma, and subtle crackling sound. If the oil begins to smoke, it is too hot. Overheating shortens the life of the oil Japanese say it "tires" the oil— and imparts a bad flavor to the foods cooked in it. Tempura chefs drop a little batter into hot oil to test its temperature. If the batter submerges slightly, then rises quickly to the surface where it browns within about 45 seconds, the temperature is just right (fig. 40). If the batter sinks to the bottom and rises only slowly to the surface, the oil is not hot enough; if it remains on the surface and dances furiously, the oil is too hot. Oil which is too hot will smoke—and burn the batter—whereas that which is too cold will not give the desired crispness.

Keeping the oil clean is another secret of successful deep-frying. This is especially important when using the batter or bound-breading methods. Use a mesh skimmer, or a perforated metal spatula or spoon, to remove all particles of food and batter from the oil's surface. Most cooks skim after every two or three batches of ingredients have been cooked. Place the small particles of deep-fried batter skimmed from the oil into a large colander or bowl lined with absorbent

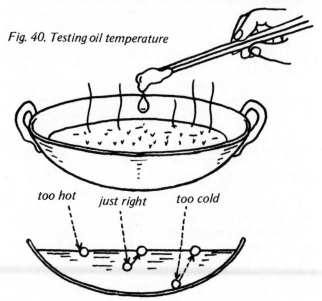

Fig. 40. Testing oil temperature

too hot   just right   too cold

paper, and allow to drain thoroughly. These may be used later as tasty additions to soups, salads, sautéed vegetables, noodles-in-broth, or other grain dishes.

To ensure that tofu and other deep-fried foods are served at their peak of texture and flavor, do your deep-frying just before you are ready to serve the meal, preferably after your guests have been seated at the table. If you have a large quantity of ingredients to deep-fry and wish to serve them simultaneously, keep freshly cooked pieces warm in a 250° oven.

After all foods have been deep-fried, allow the oil to cool in the wok or skillet, then pour it through a mesh skimmer or fine-weave strainer held over a funnel into your used-oil container. Seal the jar and discard any residue in the skimmer. Wipe all utensils with absorbent paper (washing is unnecessary) and store in a sealed plastic bag.

Crisp Agé Slices *(Tofu no Kara-agé)* — SERVES 2

The following technique is the basis of all types of deep-frying; 12 ounces of tofu yield 5 ounces of Crisp Agé Slices. Please begin by studying illustrations of the closely-related tempura process given on page 134.

Oil for deep-frying
12 ounces tofu, pressed (p. 97; sliced tofu method)

Use the oil to fill a wok, heavy skillet, pot, or deep-fryer to a depth of 1½ to 2 inches. Heat over high heat until temperature registers 350° on a deep-frying thermometer. Reduce heat to medium and slide half the tofu pieces down the side of the wok into the oil. Deep-fry for 1½ to 2 minutes, or until tofu is light golden-brown and floating near surface of oil. Turn each piece with long chopsticks or tongs and continue deep-frying for 1 to 3 minutes more until each piece is golden brown. Using chopsticks, transfer freshly cooked pieces onto the draining rack and allow to drain for several minutes. Skim surface of oil, check oil temperature, and slide in remaining tofu. Transfer well-drained tofu onto pieces of absorbent paper placed on a large tray or platter and allow to drain for several minutes more. Arrange tofu on plates, or serve Japanese style in a basket, bamboo colander, or serving bowl lined with neatly folded white paper. Serve immediately as for Crisp Deep-Fried Tofu (p. 156), or use in any of the recipes in Chapter 9. For variety, marinate for 1 hour in Teriyaki Sauce (p. 48) before serving.

Tofu French Fries — SERVES 2

12 ounces tofu, pressed (p. 97; sliced tofu method); or 9 ounces doufu
Oil for deep-frying
½ teaspoon salt

Cut tofu crosswise into pieces about the size of French-fried potatoes. Heat oil in a wok, skillet, or deep-fryer. Drop in tofu and deep-fry until golden brown (p. 130). Drain, then sprinkle with salt. Serve hot and crisp. Delicious with Ganmo Burgers (p. 188) and Tofu-Banana Milkshake (p. 149).

Tofu Mock Eels (Unagi-dofu)

MAKES 16

12 ounces tofu, pressed (p. 96) and mashed
¼ cup whole-wheat flour
1½ to 2 tablespoons red, barley, or Hatcho miso
2 teaspoons natural sugar
1 tablespoon sesame butter
½ teaspoon grated gingerroot
2 sheets of *nori*, each cut into 8 equal squares
Oil for deep-frying

Combine the first six ingredients, mixing for 2 to 3 minutes, then spread in a thin layer on the upper surface of each *nori* square. Heat the oil to 350° in a wok, skillet, or deep-fryer. Drop in the squares and deep-fry until golden brown. Drain well on absorbent paper and serve as a topping for brown rice or as an hors d'oeuvre.

Crispy Deep-fried Tofu

SERVES 2

The key to obtaining a crisp, delicately crunchy crust lies in using powdered *kuzu* (Japanese arrowroot), although other coatings also work well.

12 ounces tofu, well pressed (p. 96); or 9 ounces doufu
3 to 5 tablespoons *kuzu*, cornstarch, arrowroot, or whole-wheat (pastry) flour
Oil for deep-frying
Shoyu

Cut tofu into 6 rectangular pieces and roll each piece in the *kuzu*. Heat oil to 350° in a wok, skillet, or deep-fryer. Drop in tofu and deep-fry until golden brown (p. 130); allow to drain. Invite each person to season his or her tofu to taste with shoyu and garnishes such as grated gingerroot, *daikon*, *wasabi*, or thinly sliced leeks. Also delicious served with lemon wedges and a little salt, or with Tempura Dipping Sauce (p. 134).

VARIATIONS

Iso Agé (Deep-fried Nori-wrapped Tofu): Cut well pressed tofu crosswise into sixths, then wrap a 1- by 5-inch piece of *nori* around the center of each piece, moistening end of *nori* in water to seal. Roll *nori*-wrapped tofu in *kuzu* and deep-fry as above. Accompany each portion with a small bowl containing a mixture of 1/3 cup grated *daikon*, 1½ teaspoons shoyu and, if desired, a sprinkling of minced parsley. Or serve with Tempura Dipping Sauce.

Shinano Agé (Tofu Deep-fried in Buckwheat Flour): Roll tofu slices in buckwheat flour and deep-fry as above. For the dipping sauce, mix 1/3 cup dashi (p. 39), 1 tablespoon shoyu, and 2 tablespoons minced leeks. Or serve as for Thunderbolt Tofu, below.

Thunderbolt Tofu (Kaminari Agé)

SERVES 2

This popular recipe derives its name from the crackling sound made when the soft tofu is dropped into the hot oil.

12 ounces tofu, cut crosswise into halves and drained (p. 96)
¼ cup *kuzu*, cornstarch, or arrowroot
Oil for deep-frying
¾ cup dashi (p. 39), stock, or water
3 tablespoons shoyu
3 tablespoons *mirin* or sake
2 tablespoons grated *daikon*
2 tablespoons thinly sliced leeks or scallions
1 sheet of *nori*, cut into 1/8-inch-wide strips

Pat the tofu pieces with a dry cloth to remove surface moisture and roll them in *kuzu* powder. Heat oil to 350° in a wok, skillet, or deep-fryer. Drop in tofu and deep-fry until golden brown (p. 130); allow to drain, then place into deep serving bowls. Combine dashi, shoyu, and *mirin* in a small saucepan and bring almost to the boil. Pour this sauce over the tofu and top each portion with grated *daikon*, leek slices, and *nori*.

Tofu-Brown Rice Croquettes

MAKES 10

Oil for deep-frying
½ onion, diced
12 ounces tofu, pressed (p. 96); or 9 ounces doufu, cut crosswise into 1-inch-thick slices
1 cup cooked Brown Rice (p. 50)
1 tablespoon shoyu
2 teaspoons Sesame Salt (p. 51)
½ cup bread crumbs or bread crumb flakes
¾ cup Tofu Tartare Sauce (p. 109) or ketchup

Heat a skillet and coat with 1 tablespoon deep-frying oil. Add onion and sauté for 3 or 4 minutes until transparent. Add tofu and sauté until onion is lightly browned. Now add brown rice, season with shoyu and Sesame Salt, and cook for several minutes until rice is well heated. Transfer mixture to a separate bowl and shape into ten 2-inch patties; roll in bread crumbs.

Heat the oil to 350° in a wok, skillet, or deep-fryer. Drop in the patties and deep-fry until golden brown (p. 130). Drain, then serve topped with Tofu Tartare Sauce.

Tofu-Sweet Potato Croquettes

SERVES 4

24 ounces tofu, squeezed (p. 97)
2 cups cooked sweet or Irish potatoes, mashed
¼ cup chopped onions, scallions, or leeks
½ teaspoon salt
½ teaspoon curry powder (optional)
Dash of pepper
1 cup bread crumbs or bread crumb flakes
Oil for deep-frying
Tofu Mayonnaise (with onion; p. 107), Tofu Tartare Sauce (p. 109), or ketchup

Combine the first six ingredients in a large bowl; mix well. Shape into 2½-inch patties, roll in bread crumbs, and tap lightly to remove excess crumbs. Set aside to dry for 5 to 10 minutes.

Heat the oil to 350° in a wok, skillet, or deep-fryer. Slide in the croquettes and deep-fry until golden brown (p. 130); drain briefly. Serve with the Mayonnaise or Tartare Sauce.

For variety, substitute 1 cup parboiled corn kernels for 1 cup sweet potato. Dust patties with flour and dip in lightly-beaten egg before rolling in bread crumbs.

VARIATION

*Tofu Croquettes with Leftovers: Mash drained tofu together with leftover grains, diced fresh or cooked vegetables, thick soups, beans, or bread pieces. Season lightly with miso or curry powder. If necessary, add bread crumbs or bread crumb flakes to create a croquette consistency. Shape into patties, dip in beaten egg, and roll in bread crumbs or bread crumb flakes. Deep-fry as above. Serve topped with ketchup, Ketchup-Worcestershire (p. 49), or your favorite sauce. Extra croquettes may be refrigerated or frozen for later use. To reheat, fry lightly in butter.

Agédashi-dofu
(Deep-Fried Tofu in Dipping Sauce)
SERVES 4

Agédashi is one of Japan's favorite deep-fried tofu dishes. Its name is composed of two Chinese characters meaning "to deep-fry" and "to serve." What could be quicker or easier? The key to the texture lies in the use of *kuzu* and in serving the tofu immediately after it is deep-fried. The key to the flavor lies in the use of sesame oil and in cutting the tofu with chopsticks (rather than with a knife) after placing it in the dipping sauce. The roughly cut surface helps the sauce's flavor permeate the tofu. Agédashi is prepared with or without batter and is served in any number of different dipping sauces.

2 cakes of tofu (each 12 ounces), pressed (p. 96); or 18 ounces doufu
Oil for deep-frying (3 parts vegetable and 1 part sesame, if available)
1 egg, lightly beaten
¼ to ½ cup *kuzu*, arrowroot, or cornstarch
Mirin-Shoyu, Lemon-Shoyu, or Vinegar-Shoyu (p. 40)
2 teaspoons grated gingerroot or a mixture of 1 teaspoon each grated *daikon* and grated carrot.
2 tablespoons minced leeks

Cut each cake of tofu lengthwise into halves, then crosswise into thirds. Pat each piece with a dry cloth. Heat oil to 350° in a wok, skillet, or deep-fryer. Dip tofu into egg, then roll in *kuzu*. Deep-fry until golden brown. Serve accompanied by a dipping sauce and garnishes.

VARIATION

*Agédashi-dofu (without coating): Cut tofu as above but deep-fry without using eggs or *kuzu* coating. Serve with Mirin-Shoyu, garnished with either grated *daikon* or a mixture of 6 parts grated *daikon*, 2 parts grated gingerroot, and 1 part bonita flakes.

Deep-fried Tofu with Rice and Broth
(Tendon)
SERVES 2

¾ teaspoon sesame oil
5 teaspoons shoyu
1½ teaspoons natural sugar
½ teaspoon salt
1 tablespoon sake or white wine
1 teaspoon grated or minced gingerroot
2 teaspoons minced leeks, scallions, or onions
12 ounces tofu, drained (p. 96) and cut into 16 small rectangles (p. 37)
3 to 4 tablespoons (whole-wheat) flour
1 egg, lightly beaten
Oil for deep-frying
2/3 cup water
2 mushrooms, minced
2 cups cooked Brown Rice (p. 50)
¼ cup minced leek or scallion greens
Dash of 7-spice red pepper

In a flat-bottomed container, combine ¼ teaspoon sesame oil, 1 tablespoon shoyu, 1 teaspoon sugar, and the salt, sake, gingerroot, and leeks; mix well. Add tofu and marinate for 10 minutes on each side. Remove tofu, reserving the marinade, dust each piece with flour, and dip in the egg. Heat the oil to 350° in a wok, skillet, or deep-fryer. Slide in the tofu and deep-fry until golden brown (p. 130).

In a saucepan, combine the water and mushrooms with the remaining marinade, ½ teaspoon sesame oil, 2 teaspoons shoyu, and ½ teaspoon sugar. Bring to a boil over high heat, then add the deep-fried tofu. Return to the boil, reduce heat to medium, and cook uncovered for about 3 minutes.

Divide the rice among 2 large serving bowls. Top with the tofu and a sprinkling of scallions and red pepper. Now pour on the broth and serve steaming hot.

VARIATION

*Chinese-style Seasoned Deep-fried Tofu (Goda-dofu): Prepare the marinade using ¼ teaspoon each sesame oil and salt, ½ teaspoon each sugar and minced gingerroot, 1 teaspoon minced leeks, and 1½ teaspoons each soy sauce and sake. Marinate, then deep-fry the tofu as above. In a saucepan combine 1/3 cup soup stock or water, 1 diced mushroom, ¼ teaspoon sesame oil, and the remaining marinade. Bring to a boil, add the tofu, and simmer uncovered until all liquid is absorbed or evaporated. Sprinkle with 2 tablespoons diced leek greens and serve immediately, as is, or over rice as for Tendon.

Sizzling Tofu with Gingerroot-Ankake Sauce

SERVES 4

Deep-frying with a *kuzu* & egg white batter gives each piece of tofu a crisp and billowy coating, light and delicate as spindrift.

¼ cup *kuzu*, arrowroot, or cornstarch
2 egg whites
24 ounces tofu, pressed (p. 96); or 18 ounces doufu
Oil for deep-frying
1 cup Rich Gingerroot-Ankake Sauce (p. 49)

Combine *kuzu* and egg whites in a small bowl; mix until smooth. Cut tofu into 12 equal cubes (or thin rectangles; p. 37), dip into the batter, and deep-fry as for Crisp Agé Slices (p. 131). Serve immediately, topped with the hot sauce.

For variety, substitute 2/3 cup water for the egg whites. Or use the cornstarch & egg white batter described at Crispy Thick Agé (p. 168).

Breaded Tofu Cutlets *(Tofu Furai)*

SERVES 2

12 ounces tofu, pressed (p. 96); or 9 ounces doufu
1/3 cup flour or cornstarch
1 egg, lightly beaten (with 2 or 3 teaspoons of water or milk, if desired)
¾ cup sifted bread crumbs or bread crumb flakes
Oil for deep-frying
Salt
Tofu Mayonnaise (with onion; p. 107) or Tofu Tartare Sauce (p. 109)

Cut tofu lengthwise into halves then crosswise into ½-inch-thick pieces. Place between absorbent towels and allow to dry for several minutes. Gently dust tofu, one piece at a time, with the flour, then dip in the egg and roll in the bread crumbs. Place on a rack and allow to dry for 10 to 15 minutes; tap off any excess crumbs.

Heat the oil to 350° in a wok, skillet, or deep-fryer. Drop in the tofu and deep-fry until golden brown (p. 130). Add a piece of tofu to the oil about once every 15 seconds. No more than 6 pieces should be in the oil at one time. Drain briefly, then serve, inviting each guest to season the tofu with salt to taste, and top with the Mayonnaise or Tartare Sauce.

VARIATION

*After rolling each piece of tofu in flour, dip it in lightly beaten egg whites and roll in a dish of ¼- to ½-inch-long strips of transparent noodles. Deep-fry, then serve with salt and lemon juice, Tempura Dipping Sauce (p. 134), or thickened Gingerroot Sauce (p. 49). Or substitute *(somen)* thin noodles, cracker crumbs, cereal flakes, or minced carrots for the transparent noodles.

About Tofu Tempura

Tempura stands as one of Japan's great contributions to the art of fine cooking. Described by various foreign writers as "the pride of Japanese cuisine," "delicately flavored, light as air and wonderfully crisp," and "light and dry as spindrift," tempura's fine flavors and textures epitomize the beauty and subtlety of Japanese cuisine.

Nevertheless, tempura was originally "imported" from the West. It was probably brought to Japan by Portuguese sailors or Spanish missionaries during the 16th century, and is said to have been Japan's first contact with the art of deep-frying with batter. Good Catholics, the Portugese did not eat meat on Ember days, which occur four times each year. Instead, they asked for deep-fried shrimp. The word *tempura* is a corruption of the ancient Latin term *Quator Tempora*, meaning "four times." The Japanese now write the word using Chinese characters, the first of which, pronounced *ten*, means "heaven," perhaps in honor of the flavor.

Restaurants specializing in tempura are among Japan's most popular. The chef does his deep-frying behind a clean, natural-wood counter right in front of his customers. At its peak of crispness and flavor, each delicacy is quickly and artfully placed on a carefully-folded piece of white paper set on a bamboo tray that is then whisked across the counter to the waiting patron.

Tempura Batter

FOR 4 TO 6 SERVINGS

1 cup ice-cold water
1 egg yolk or whole egg
1¼ to 1½ cups (coarsely ground) unbleached white flour
½ teaspoon salt (optional)

In a mixing bowl, combine the water and egg yolk and beat well with a wire whisk or chopsticks. Sprinkle the flour and, if used, the salt evenly over the mixture. With a few quick strokes of the whisk (or a wooden spoon) lightly stir in the flour until all flour is moistened and large lumps disappear. (The presence of small lumps is alright.) Do not stir batter again after the initial mixing. Use as soon as possible and do not place too near the heat.

For variety, use your favorite fritter batter. Or omit the egg in the recipe above and add sesame seeds; decrease the amount of white flour used and compensate for the difference with several teaspoons of arrowroot or cornstarch.

Tempura Dipping Sauce *(Ten-tsuyu)*

FOR 4 TO 6 SERVINGS

1 cup dashi (p. 39), stock, or water
3 to 4 tablespoons *mirin*, sake, or pale dry sherry
¼ cup shoyu
4 to 6 tablespoons grated *daikon*
4 to 6 teaspoons grated gingerroot

Combine the dashi, *mirin*, and shoyu in a small pan. Bring just to a boil over high heat, then set aside to cool. Divide the dipping sauce, grated *daikon*, and grated gingerroot among 4 to 6 small serving bowls and serve with the tempura (fig. 42).

Each guest holds the container of dipping sauce in one hand, then transfers a piece of tempura from his place into the sauce, and cuts the food with chopsticks. The roughly cut surface helps the sauce's flavor to penetrate the tofu thereby giving the finest flavor.

The use of *daikon*, which is rich in the enzyme diastase, aids in the digestion of oils in the tempura. Each of the following accompaniments is also widely used in place of the dipping sauce and garnishes described above:

*Shoyu with Grated Daikon: A small dispenser of shoyu and some *daikon* are placed on the table. Each guest combines about 1½ teaspoons shoyu with 2½ tablespoons *daikon* in a small dish. In some cases 1 part grated gingerroot is mixed with 3 parts grated *daikon*. Or a few drops of lemon juice may be added to the shoyu-*daikon* mixture.

*Lemon Juice and Salt: Serve each portion of tempura garnished with several lemon wedges. Each guest squeezes a little lemon juice over the tempura, then sprinkles each piece with salt or dip it in salt served in a separate tiny dish.

*Salt or Shoyu: Tofu tempura is delicious sprinkled with either of these.

Fig. 41. Deep-frying tofu tempura

Tofu and Vegetable Tempura   SERVES 4 TO 6

12 ounces todu, well pressed (p. 96); or 9 ounces doufu
Vegetables:
      6 mushrooms
      24 green beans
      ½ sweet potato or yam
      1 onion
      2 green peppers
      2 inches of lotus root
Oil for deep-frying
Tempura Batter (see above)
Tempura Dipping Sauce and garnishes (see above)

Cut tofu crosswise into sixths and press for several minutes more using the sliced tofu method (p. 97). Cut sweet potatoes, onion, and lotus root into ½-inch-thick rounds, and cut pepper lengthwise into quarters. To rid vegetables of excess moisture, pat the cut surfaces lightly with a dry cloth.

Pour the oil into a wok, skillet, or deep-fryer and heat over low heat. Meanwhile quickly prepare tempura batter. When the oil temperature reaches 350° (test with a few drops of batter), dip tofu pieces into batter and slide them into oil. Deep-fry on both side until golden brown, drain briefly on a wire rack, then transfer onto absorbent paper. Dip vegetable slices into the batter and deep fry 6 to 8 at a time until golden brown. Arrange tofu and vegetable tempura in individual portions (atop fresh sheets of white paper) on serving plates or small bamboo colanders *(zaru)*. Serve accompanied by the dipping sauce and garnishes (fig. 42).

If any batter is left over, add this in spoonfuls to the oil and deep-fry. Combine these deep-fried batter balls with the pieces skimmed from the oil during deep-frying and use in (miso) soups or salad dressings, or with sautéed vegetables or Japanese-style noodle dishes.

VARIATIONS

*Other ingredients which make excellent tempura are tender eggplants, carrots (and green tops), *(kabocha)* pumpkin, all squashes, snow peas, cauliflower, apple, pear, banana, bamboo shoots, chrysanthemum leaves, green beefsteak leaves, *nori*, burdock root, ginkgo nuts, and yuba.

*Flower Tofu (Hana-dofu): Cut the pressed tofu horizontally into two ½-inch-thick slices. Use milk instead of water to make a slightly thick batter. Serve the tofu tempura topped with mild Red Nerimiso (p. 42). Garnish with leek slivers which have been soaked in water for 15 minutes and then drained.

*After dipping tofu or vegetables in tempura batter, roll in bread crumbs, bread crumb flakes, cereal flakes, finely diced carrots, ¼- to ½-inch long pieces of transparent noodles, or thin noodles *(somen)*. During deep-frying, the noodles puff up and become light and crisp.

Fig. 42. Serving Tofu and Vegetable Tempura

Fig. 43. Making Kaki-age

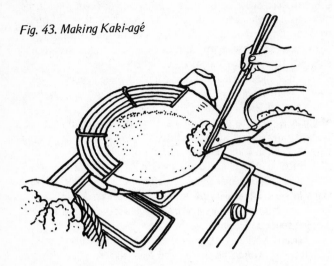

*Kaki-agé: Cut the pressed tofu and other vegetables into 3/8-inch cubes or matchsticks. Mix these in a bowl with batter that has been thickened slightly with flour. Place about 2 tablespoons of the batter-and-vegetable mixture on a (wooden) spatula. Using chopsticks, flatten the mixture to form a 2½-inch round, then carefully slide round into hot oil (fig. 43) and deep-fry as above.

*Skewered Tabletop Tempura: Heat the oil over a tabletop burner. Have each guest skewer three or four ingredients on a 12-inch bamboo or metal skewer. The skewer is dipped into batter and immersed in hot oil while being held at one end. Ginkgo nuts and green beans skewered on foodpicks are often prepared in this way: they are placed into the oil using chopsticks.

*Floured Tempura Retouched with Batter: This technique gives a very light, whispy coating to the tempura. Roll each ingredient lightly in flour before dipping it into batter. Deep-fry at 340°. When the ingredients float to the surface, dip both chopsticks (or two fingers) into the batter, then touch the batter quickly to the top of each piece of tempura bobbing in the oil. Repeat several times with each piece of food. Turn each piece with chopsticks and retouch the second side. Turn again and cook until crisp and golden brown.

Deep-fried Onions with Tofu Mayonnaise

SERVES 4

Oil for Deep Frying
2/3 cup flour
2 eggs, lightly beaten
1½ cups bread crumbs
4 onions, cut into ¼-inch-thick rounds; or ½ kabocha cut into thin wedges
¾ cup Tofu Mayonnaise (p. 107) or Tofu Tartare Sauce (p. 109)

Heat the oil to 350° in a wok, skillet, or deep-fryer. Quickly dust a slice of onion with flour, dip in egg, then roll in bread crumbs. Deep-fry until crisp and golden brown (p. 130); drain briefly. Serve with Tofu Mayonnaise for dipping.

Additional Suggestions for Serving Tofu Deep-fried

*Deep-fried Walnut Tofu: Mix 3 parts well-pressed tofu with 2 parts coarsely chopped walnuts. Season with salt and, if desired, add a small amount of egg white as a binder. Shape into patties (or roll out into a 1-inch-diameter cylinder, wrap in a sheet of nori and dip into tempura batter). Deep-fry and serve with a Shoyu Dipping Sauce (p. 40).

*Deep-fried Tofu-Miso Patties: Mix 2 to 4 tablespoons Hatcho, red, or barley miso, or Sweet Simmered Miso (p. 41) with 12 ounces tofu (well pressed). Shape into patties, roll in kuzu, flour, or cornstarch, and deep-fry. Serve with shoyu or a Shoyu Dipping Sauce (p. 40).

*Stuffed Deep-fried Tofu: Cut a 12-ounce cake of tofu diagonally into halves and deep-fry. Slit each half open along its long side, scoop out soft tofu and fill with fried rice and vegetables seasoned with a little shoyu.

*Deep-fried Tofu with Umeboshi (Bainiku): Mash well-pressed tofu, season lightly with salt, and shape into patties. Place a seeded umeboshi in the center of each pattie. Dip in tempura batter, press a green beefsteak leaf against one side of pattie, and deep-fry. Serve with salt and lemon juice.

*Deep-fried Rolled Tofu (Isobe-maki): Mash well-pressed tofu and mix with slivered carrots, green peas, and mushrooms. Season with salt and mix in sesame seeds. Any of the other ingredients used in Homemade Ganmo (p. 186) may also be added. Place a sheet of nori, yuba, or agé on a bamboo rolling mat. Spread the tofu mixture on the nori and roll the nori to form a 1½-inch-diameter cylinder. Dip into tempura batter and deep-fry. Cut into 1½-inch lengths and serve with shoyu or a Shoyu Dipping Sauce (p. 40).

*Tofu Bourguignon: This dish, originally made with beef, is now often served at fondue restaurants using bread instead of tofu. Fill a small metal pot half full of peanut oil and heat to 350° over a tabletop burner. Cut pressed tofu into 1-inch cubes and skewer on long (fondue) forks. Invite each guest to deep-fry the tofu in the oil until golden brown. Dip in shoyu or a Shoyu Dipping Sauce (p. 40). Or top with Sweet Simmered Miso (p. 41) or Tofu Tartare Sauce (p. 109).

*Deep-fried Bananas with Tofu Toppings: Deep-fry thin banana ovals covered with tempura batter (p. 134) or egg-and-bread crumbs. Serve immediately, topped with Banana-Lemon Whip (p. 148) or Tofu Whipped Cream (p. 148) seasoned with a little nutmeg and a few drops of lemon juice.

*Deep-fried Tofu Dumplings Filled with Mustard: Prepare Karashi-dofu (p. 90), dust each piece lightly with wheat-or rice flour, and deep-fry at 350° until golden brown. Serve in deep bowls topped with Simmering Tofu Dipping Sauce (p. 142) and garnished with thinly sliced leeks or beefsteak leaves.

*Deep-fried Chinese-style Tofu: This dish is a specialty of the Hakuun-an restaurant near Mampukuji temple. Simmer a 3-inch square of reshaped tofu (p. 98), or well-pressed regular tofu, for 2 hours in shoyu to cover. Allow to dry, dust with kuzu or arrowroot, and deep-fry. Serve with a dip of shoyu mixed with grated gingerroot or wasabi.

TOFU WITH GRAINS

Serving tofu with grains can increase the availability of their combined protein content by as much as 30 to 40 percent. A number of the best combinations and proportions are given on page 26. Tofu may be used in grain salads; fried, stir-fried or baked grain and noodle dishes; or sauce toppings. Use tofu with leftover grains in gruel (p. 170).

Tofu-filled Enchiladas

SERVES 2 OR 3

4 teaspoons oil
1 clove of garlic, minced or crushed
1 onion, minced
1 tablespoon whole-wheat flour
1½ tablespoons red miso or 1 tablespoon shoyu
1 cup water
Dash of 7-spice red pepper or tabasco sauce
Dash of white or black pepper
¼ teaspoon oregano
2 tablespoons tomato ketchup
6 tablespoons Parmesan cheese
8 ounces tofu
1 green pepper, minced
5 tortillas, each 5 inches in diameter

Heat a skillet and coat with 1 tablespoon oil. Add garlic and sauté for 30 seconds. Add one half the onion and sauté for 3 to 4 minutes. Mix in flour and sauté for 30 seconds, then add 1 tablespoon miso and sauté for 15 seconds more. Add water a little at a time, stirring constantly until smooth. Mix in the next four ingredients and 2 tablespoons Parmesan, cover, and simmer for 15 minutes. Remove sauce from heat and allow to cool, then mix in 2 tablespoons minced raw onion.

While sauce is cooling, heat a wok or skillet and coat with 1 teaspoon oil. Add green pepper and the remaining onion, and sauté for 3 minutes. Stir in the remaining 1½ teaspoons miso, season with white pepper, and remove from heat. Combine with tofu and 2 tablespoons Parmesan; mash well.

Preheat oven to 350°. Pour one half the sauce into a loaf pan or casserole. Dip one surface of a tortilla into remaining sauce, then holding this side upward, spread with one fifth of the tofu mixture. Roll tortilla loosely and place into loaf pan. Repeat with remaining tortillas and tofu until all are used. Pour remaining sauce over tortillas in pan and top with a sprinkling of 2 tablespoons Parmesan. Bake for 15 to 20 minutes, or until nicely browned. Serve hot or cold.

Brown Rice Porridge with Tofu and Vegetables

SERVES 3

½ cup brown rice
1 tablespoon (sesame) oil
½ small carrot, slivered or diced
2 onions, thinly sliced
½ cup diced celery, cabbage, or vegetable leftovers
12 ounces tofu
2½ tablespoons shoyu or 3½ tablespoons red miso
Dash of pepper

Use the rice to prepare Brown Rice Porridge (p. 50). About 15 minutes before porridge is ready, heat a wok or skillet and coat with the oil. Add carrot and sauté for 3 minutes. Mix in onion and celery and sauté for 5 minutes more. Add tofu, mash well, and sauté for 3 minutes. Stir in shoyu and pepper and remove from heat. Add sautéed tofu-vegetable mixture to the finished porridge, mix well, and allow to stand for 5 to 10 minutes before serving.

If desired, substitute 5 to 10 ounces diced deep-fried tofu for the regular tofu. Top with crumbled *nori* and diced leeks.

Bulgur Pilaf with Tofu

SERVES 4

3 tablespoons butter or oil
1 cup bulgur wheat
1 small onion, minced
2 cups water or stock
¼ teaspoon oregano
Dash of (freshly ground) pepper
9 ounces tofu
2 teaspoons shoyu or 1 tablespoon red miso
Sesame Salt (p. 51) or salt

Melt butter in a heavy skillet. Add bulgur and onion and sauté for 4 to 5 minutes. Add stock, oregano, and pepper, cover pan, and bring to a boil. Reduce heat and simmer for 15 minutes, or until all liquid is absorbed. Combine tofu and shoyu in a small bowl and mash together, then stir into the cooked grain. Serve hot seasoned with sesame salt.

For variety stir in 2 tablespoons minced parsley or 1/3 cup grated cheese just before serving.

Tofu & Eggs Domburi

SERVES 4

1 tablespoon oil
1 cup minced leek, scallion, or onion
1 cup grated carrot
2 ounces agé or ganmo (or 4 mushrooms), diced
12 ounces tofu, pressed (p. 96) and mashed; or 5 ounces thick agé, minced
¼ cup cooked, chopped spinach (optional)
2 tablespoons shoyu
1½ tablespoons natural sugar
¼ teaspoon salt
2 eggs, lightly beaten
1½ cups brown rice, cooked (p. 50)

Heat a skillet or wok and coat with the oil. Add the next four ingredients and sauté for 4 minutes. Add tofu and sauté for 2 minutes more. Mix in spinach, shoyu, sugar, and salt; cook for 1 minute. Stir in eggs, cover, and remove from heat.

Spoon hot rice into 3 large *(domburi)* bowls and top with tofu-and-eggs; serve immediately or allow to cool to room temperature. In Japan, the latter version is widely used in box lunches.

VARIATION

*Use Crumbly Agé Soboro (p. 169) or Iridofu (p. 128) as the topping.

Tofu with Fried Grains and Vegetables

SERVES 4

2 tablespoons oil
1 clove garlic, crushed
2 onions, thinly sliced
1 cup diced mushrooms, lotus root, celery, or eggplant
1 small carrot, grated or slivered
2 cups cooked (buckwheat) Noodles (p. 50) or Brown Rice (p. 50)
24 ounces tofu, crumbled (p. 98); or 12 ounces tofu, pressed (p. 96) and diced
1 to 1½ tablespoons shoyu
4 to 5 tablespoons ketchup
2 tablespoons Sesame Salt (p. 51) or ½ teaspoon salt
½ cup crumbled *nori* (optional)

Heat a skillet or wok and coat with the oil. Add consecutively: garlic, onions, mushrooms, carrot, and noodles (or rice), sautéing each for about 1 to 2 minutes. Add the next four ingredients and cook. stirring constantly, for about 3 minutes more. For best flavor, allow to cool for 4 to 6 hours. Serve topped with *nori*.

Italian-style Spaghetti with Tofu Meatballs

SERVES 4 OR 6

4½ to 5 ounces (whole-wheat) spaghetti or *(soba)* buckwheat noodles, cooked (p. 50)
Tofu Italian Meatballs (p. 123)
Tofu Spaghetti Sauce (p. 121)
Parmesan cheese and/or tabasco sauce

Divide the hot spaghetti among individual bowls and top with the meatballs and spaghetti sauce. Pass the cheese and tabasco.

Zosui or Ojiya *(Rice Gruel)*

SERVES 1 OR 2

Zosui (known colloquially as *Ojiya*) is a popular way of using rice or rice porridge and either miso- or clear soup, foods served daily in most Japanese homes. During the winter, thick Zosui served piping hot is prized for its ability to warm body and soul. The amounts of rice and soup can be varied considerably depending on the amounts of leftovers available.

1½ cups Tofu-Miso soup (p. 118) or Clear Soup with Tofu (p. 119)
1 cup cooked Brown Rice (p. 50) or Rice Porridge (p. 50)
4 to 6 ounces tofu, diced (optional)
1 to 2 eggs, lightly beaten (optional)
7-spice red pepper or grated gingerroot (optional)
Crumbled toasted *nori*, powdered green *nori*, slivered leeks or citrus rind, or minced parsley

Bring miso soup just to a boil in a saucepan. Mix in rice and return to the boil. Cover and simmer for 15 to 30 minutes, or until rice is soft. Just before removing from heat, stir in tofu and eggs. Season with the red pepper, garnish with *nori*, and serve immediately.

Tofu-Oatmeal

SERVES 2

1½ cups water
½ cup rolled oats or oatmeal
¼ teaspoon salt
1 tablespoon Sesame Salt (p. 50)
2 tablespoons butter
1/3 cup raisins
½ cup milk
1 tablespoon honey
12 ounces tofu, diced or mashed

Bring the water to a boil in a saucepan. Gradually stir in the rolled oats, add salt, and cook for 15 minutes or until softened. Stir in the remaining ingredients and cook, stirring constantly, for several minutes more. Serve hot or cold.

Tofu With Tacos

MAKES 6

12 ounces tofu
2/3 cup brown rice or bulgur wheat, cooked (p. 50)
¼ cup peanuts
½ green pepper, diced
2 cloves of garlic, crushed
¼ teaspoon chili powder
¼ cup ketchup
½ teaspoon salt or 1 tablespoon red miso
2 to 3 tablespoons oil
6 *tortillas*
Garnishes:
    Chopped tomato
    Minced onion
    Shredded lettuce
    Grated cheese
Tabasco or taco sauce

Combine the first eight ingredients in a large bowl; mash thoroughly. Heat the oil in a skillet and fry the *tortillas*. Top each *tortilla* with your choice of garnishes, spoon on the tofu mixture, and season with tabasco sauce.

Additional Suggestions for Serving Tofu with Grains:

*Grains with Tofu Sauces: Serve cooked brown rice or (buckwheat) noodles topped with any of the basic Tofu Sauces (p. 121), or with Japanese-Style Tofu, Eggs & Onions (p. 122).
*Gomoku-dofu: Substitute crumbled tofu (p. 98) for the okara or rice in Sushi Okara (p. 83) or Okara-Omelet Pouches (p. 84).
*Tofu in Chop Suey or Chow Mein: See p. 67.

TOFU BROILED

Since grilled tofu is one of the basic types of tofu prepared at tofu shops, regular tofu is not ordinarily grilled, broiled, or barbequed in the home. With one important exception: *Tofu Dengaku*. There are also many broiled dishes made from tofu that has already been deep-fried, since these acquire a particularly delicious flavor from direct contact with fire and lend themselves to basting and marinating.

Tofu Dengaku

SERVES 4

In *dengaku*, one of Japan's most popular treatments of tofu, firm pieces the size of small match boxes are pierced with bamboo skewers and lightly broiled. A topping of Sweet Simmered Miso is then spread on one of the tofu's surfaces, and the tofu is rebroiled until lightly speckled.

The two Chinese characters which form the word *dengaku* mean "rice paddy" and "music." It is said that the name originated about 600 years ago, when an ancient form of folk drama consisting of music and dance was popular in Japan's rural villages. In one famous play using a rice paddy as its stage setting, a Buddhist priest mounted a single stilt (resembling a pogo stick) called a "heron's leg." Precariously balanced, this character was called Dengaku Hoshi (fig. 44), and he did a dance known as the *dengaku*, or "music in the rice paddy." The newly conceived broiled tofu dish, with its distinctive, individual bamboo skewers, apparently reminded many people of the dengaku dancer, and the tasty preparation soon became known as Dengaku.

About 400 years ago, Nakamura-ro (p. 307) in the Gion geisha section of Kyoto became the first restaurant to serve dengaku. Attractively dressed women kneeling at small tables in front of the restaurant near the famous Yasaka shrine cut the tofu in a swift staccato rhythm to the accompaniment of shamisen music, and the new dish soon became known locally as Gion-dofu. Today the dengaku at Nakamura-ro is famous throughout Japan, especially its springtime variety which is topped with fresh bright-green sprigs of *kinome* and served with thick sweet sake *(amazake)*. It is prepared over a bed of live coals and served in lacquerware boxes (fig. 45).

From the early 1600s until the late 1900s many tofu shops prepared and delivered dengaku to order, and by about 1775 it had become very fashionable for Tokyo tea shops, way stations, and inns to serve this delicacy.

According to ancient chronicles, some of Japan's earliest types of dengaku were prepared in country farmhouses, especially during the winter. We have enjoyed sizzling-hot dengaku prepared from homemade tofu and homemade miso in several mountain villages. The well-pressed tofu is cut into pieces about 4 by 3 by 1 inch, or into ¾-inch-thick rounds. Each piece is pierced with a flat skewer 12 inches long made of green bamboo which has been soaked overnight in lightly salted water to prevent it from burning. The butt end of each skewer is poked into the sand or ashes around an open-hearth fireplace so that the tofu leans a few inches above and over a bed of live coals (p. 221). The savory broiled tofu is spread

*Fig. 44. Dengaku Hoshi
(from the "Tofu Hyaku Chin")*

田楽法師高足曲

with plain miso on both sides, quickly rebroiled until the miso is fragrant, and served as a light wintertime snack with tea. This traditional method of broiling, which imparts a savory fragrance of woodsmoke to the tofu, is practiced at the Dengaku restaurant in Kamakura (p. 309). Gifu Prefecture is especially famous for the dengaku served as a special treat during nighttime displays of fireworks. And in some villages, a special offering of dengaku—said to be the favorite food of the local gods—is made each year on November 14 at all *Ichi-fusha* shrines.

A unique type of dengaku called "quick dengaku" is prepared in some tofu shops after the master finishes making the day's supply of grilled tofu. He broils both sides of an entire 12-ounce cake of tofu, spreads one surface with sweet white miso, broils the miso until it is fragrant, then sits down to enjoy a hefty treat.

There are a great many varieties of dengaku in Japan. Although the most popular are generally prepared using regular tofu, others are made with grilled tofu, thick agé, ganmo, or agé. Occasionally, tofu is even replaced by skewered pieces of eggplant, *konnyaku*, *mochi*, *shiitake* mushrooms, green peppers, fresh or deep-fried wheat gluten, sweet or Irish potatoes, bamboo shoots, *daikon*, or boiled quail eggs.

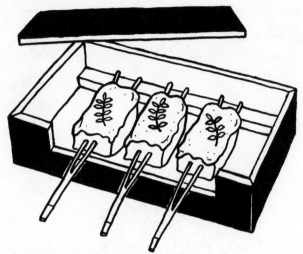

Fig. 45. Skewered Tofu Dengaku

Miso Topping: Use a total of ¼ to ½ cup of one or more of the following types of Sweet Simmered Miso
    Red- or White Nerimiso
    Yuzu- or Lemon Miso
    Kinome- or Egg Yolk Miso
    Sesame- or Walnut Miso; or a Nut Butter Topping (p. 47)
12 to 24 ounces tofu, pressed (p. 96)
Garnishes (optional):
    Kinome sprigs
    Slivered *yuzu* or lemon rind
    Poppy or roasted sesame seeds
    Hot mustard

Prepare the miso toppings in advance and allow to cool. In a large skillet or pan, heat water to about the temperature of a hot bath. Drop in the tofu, then cut into pieces as large as 2½ by 1 by ¾ inch or as small as 1¼ by ¾ by ½ inch. Pierce each of these under water using either 2 round bamboo skewers or 1 flat skewer as shown in figure 46. Cover a cutting board or flat tray with a dry dishtowel and raise one end of the board. Carefully place the pieces of skewered tofu on the cloth and allow to stand for about 15 minutes, or until tofu is firm.

Holding 3 to 4 pieces of skewered tofu at a time side by side over a gas burner, broil for about 30 seconds or until tofu is lightly speckled; or broil tofu on one side over a charcoal brazier or barbeque. Turn tofu over and coat broiled side with a 1/8-inch-thick layer of topping, then broil second side. Turn tofu again and broil miso topping until it too is speckled, then arrange garnishes, if used, atop miso. Repeat with remaining ingredients; if desired, use a different miso topping with each set of tofu pieces. Serve Dengaku hot with the meal or as an hors d'oeuvre.

VARIATIONS

*Deep-fried Dengaku: Cut well-pressed tofu into Dengaku-sized pieces and pierce each piece with 10-inch-long bamboo skewers. Deep-fry with or without batter until golden brown. Spread on the topping and serve hot. When deep-fried in a bound breading, this dish has an excellent crunchy texture.
*Butter-fried Dengaku: Prepare Butter-fried Tofu (p. 128). Skewer each piece and coat one surface with Sweet Simmered Miso or Miso-Sesame Butter Topping (p. 41) sprinkled with toasted wheat germ. Serve as an hors d'oeuvre.

*Oven-broiled Dengaku: Preheat oven broiler to its highest temperature. Place unskewered tofu pieces into a baking dish in one snug layer, then pour in water to a depth of ¼ inch. Broil tofu as near the flame as possible until speckled. Turn tofu over with a spatula and broil the second side. Spread with miso topping about 1/8 inch thick, and broil once again until topping is lightly speckled. Insert skewers or small forks into the end of each tofu piece before serving.
*Oven-baked Dengaku: Spread the pieces of tofu with topping and bake on a cookie sheet at 350° until lightly browned.
*Skewered, Charcoal-broiled Dengaku: In this method used at the Nakamura-ro restaurant, the tofu is broiled over a bed of live coals in a rectangular brazier about 24 by 3½ by 4 inches deep. Cut tofu into Dengaku-sized pieces and pierce with small bamboo skewers so that the skewer tips extend about ½ inch out the front of each piece. Lay skewered tofu across mouth of brazier and broil as in the basic recipe above. Spread with Kinome Miso (p. 43) and serve each piece topped with a sprig of *kinome*.

*Preparing Dengaku in old Japan
(from Hokusai's sketchbooks)*

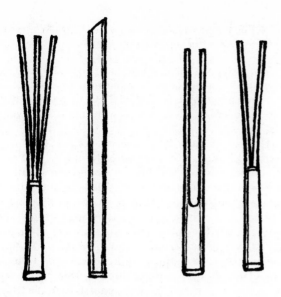

Fig. 46. A variety of skewers

*Simmered Dengaku: Prepare Simmering Tofu (p. 142). Remove tofu from the hot water, cut into dengaku-sized pieces, and insert skewers. Spread on topping and serve. Or the tofu may be skewered before it is simmered; invite each guest to hold one end of skewer as tofu cooks.

*Unheated, Unskewered Dengaku: Drain tofu well, then cut into Dengaku-sized pieces. Arrange on a platter and top each piece with a dollop of Sweet Simmered Miso.

Tofu Teriyaki

SERVES 4

24 ounces regular or grilled tofu, drained and pressed (p. 96;
    sliced tofu method)
2/3 cup Teriyaki Sauce (p. 48)

Combine tofu and sauce in a shallow pan; marinate tofu pieces for 30 minutes on each side. Grill tofu over a barbeque or broil in an oven (or on a Japanese-style broiling screen; see p. 36), basting with the sauce from time to time. Serve hot, accompanied by the remaining sauce for dipping, or by a mixture of 1/3 cup grated *daikon* and 1½ teaspoons shoyu. Also delicious served topped with a sprinkling of *sansho* pepper.

For variety, roll the pressed tofu in *kuzu* or arrowroot and deep-fry before marinating.

Additional Suggestions for Serving Tofu Broiled

*Barbequed Tofu: Press whole 12-ounce cakes of tofu until quite firm (p. 96). Barbeque until both sides are lightly speckled. Cut tofu horizontally into halves and barbeque the uncooked surfaces. Serve topped with a few drops of shoyu, a Shoyu Dipping Sauce (p. 40), or Sweet Simmered Miso (p. 41).

*Broiled Tofu Patties: Prepare Tofu-Brown Rice Croquettes (without bread crumbs) (p. 132), Tofu Burgers (p. 127), or Homemade Ganmo (p. 186). Broil like hamburger patties until richly browned. Serve topped with your favorite sauce.

TOFU SIMMERED IN ONE-POT COOKERY AND SEASONED BROTHS

In *nabe* (pronounced nah-bay) "one-pot" cookery, the food is prepared right at the table in a large earthenware casserole or tureen placed on top of a charcoal brazier, table-top burner, electric coil, or alcohol burner. An electric skillet can also be used, or the food may be prepared in the kitchen and brought steaming hot to the table. The *nabe* contains the entire meal, and each guest serves himself from the bounty of its many delicacies. Usually served during the cold months, *nabe* dishes almost always contain tofu together with a wide range of vegetables. The tofu is cooked for only a few minutes, since overcooking gives it an undesirably firm and porous structure.

The tradition of Japanese *nabe* cookery probably had its origins in the various Chinese "firepots" or "chafing pots," of which there are two main types. The Mongolian firepot *(huo kuo)*, typical of northern China, consists of a large brass or pewter bowl 9 to 12 inches in diameter. Through its center rises a hollow, vertical funnel containing a grating set at the same level as the bottom of the pot. Live coals lowered onto the grating from the mouth of the chimney-funnel heat the water or broth in the surrounding bowl (fig. 47). The second type of pot resembles a traditional American chafing dish. A large, shallow basin resting on a brass stand is heated by a small alcohol burner. As the flames from the burner dance up through the latticework in the collar of the stand, they take on a greenish hue from the copper in the brass. Placed at the center of the large round dining table found in most Chinese homes, the firepot itself becomes a warm and friendly centerpiece for the communal dinner on chilly evenings from about November to March. Each person cooks his own ingredients in the pot's simmering broth.

As in most Japanese *nabe* dishes, tofu is one of the key ingredients in Chinese firepots. The Sandy Pot of Chekiang, for example, is a close relative of Japan's famous Simmering Tofu, with tofu serving as the main ingredient. Prepared in the kitchen rather than at the table, the tofu is cooked in a chicken-base stock together with long rice noodles, Chinese cabbage, black mushrooms, bean sprouts, water chestnuts, various seafoods, and thin slices of meat. Deep-fried tofu is used in the *Huichou* Pot, the Ten Varieties Pot, and the Chrysanthemum Pot. In the latter preparation, the ingredients simmer in a light fish broth in a large chafing dish and receive a topping of white chrysanthemum petals just before being served. In the Porcelan Pot of Yunan, the food is steamed in the covered bowl by means of a perforated funnel rising through the bowl's center. Like *nabe* dishes, each of these dishes is served accompanied by a dipping sauce (see p. 263).

Fig. 47. Chinese firepots

Simmering Tofu
(Yudofu or Tofu no Mizutaki)

SERVES 4 TO 6

One of Japan's three or four most popular tofu dishes, Simmering Tofu is the simplest of the many *nabe* dishes. The wintertime counterpart of Chilled Tofu, it brings out the delicate flavors of fine tofu and allows them to be enjoyed to their utmost.

The early history of Simmering Tofu centers in two Zen temples in the ancient capital of Kyoto. According to one tradition, this dish was first served in Japan about 500 years ago at Tenryu-ji temple. At that time, the abbot of Myochi-in, a subtemple of Tenryu-ji, was invited by a Chinese high prince to the Imperial Court at Peking to study Ming dynasty culture. The abbot was apparently well received at the capital, where he was introduced to the finest of Chinese cuisine, including the tradition of firepot cookery. Upon his return to Japan, he is said to have introduced Simmering Tofu to the monks at his temple. Several centuries later, the temple became the well-known restaurant Nishiyama Sōdo (p. 312), where to this day Simmering Tofu remains the specialty of the house.

According to another tradition, Simmering Tofu was invented by the monks at Nanzen-ji temple in the eastern part of Kyoto. It is said that since "ancient times" the dish has been served each year on the evening of December 8, at the end of the intensive one-week meditation period held annually to commemorate the enlightenment of Shakyamuni Buddha. Nanzenji's Simmering Tofu is now famous throughout Japan. It is served within the temple compound at the Okutan *Shojin-ryori* restaurant (p. 308) and at a number of other restaurants in the vicinity. Each restaurant has its own type of heating and serving container (fig. 48).

Fig. 48. A Simmering Tofu serving container
heated by coals from within

Thus, Japan's finest Simmering Tofu is still to be found in Kyoto where it is typical of the simple, delicate flavors characterizing Kyoto cuisine. Since the tofu—like the melted cheese in fondue—retains a remarkable amount of heat, it is often served outdoors on chilly winter nights; the bright fire, bubbling pot, and feeling of warm conviviality that accompany it all lend a special magic to this do-it-yourself delicacy.

Tosa-joyu Dipping Sauce (p. 41)
2 leeks or 4 scallions, sliced into very thin rounds
1 teaspoon 7-spice red pepper
1 tablespoon grated gingerroot
1 sheet of *nori*, toasted and cut into thin strips (or crumbled)
A 5- to 6-inch square of *kombu*, wiped clean; or substitute ½ teaspoon salt
6 cups boiling water
3 pounds tofu, cut into 1¼-inch cubes or 2-inch squares ¾-inch thick

Bring the sauce to a boil and pour into a heat-resistant cup. Arrange the leeks, red pepper, gingerroot, and *nori* on a platter and place on the table. Set a charcoal brazier or gas burner at the center of the dining table. Atop heat source place a large casserole, tureen, chafing dish, or copper pot. Place *kombu* at the bottom of casserole and set the cup of dipping sauce atop the *kombu*. Now fill the casserole with boiling water, return to the boil, and drop in tofu.

Invite each guest to ladle some of the dipping sauce into a small dish provided for this purpose and add to it his choice of garnishes and seasonings. After 2 or 3 minutes, or as soon as the tofu begins to sway in the simmering water or float to the surface, each guest uses a slotted spoon or pair of chopsticks to lift out the tofu. Dip tofu into sauce-and-garnish mixture before eating.

VARIATIONS
*Chinese-style Dipping Sauce:
    1 egg yolk
    2 tablespoons shoyu
    2 tablespoons sake or white wine
    1 tablespoon minced leek greens
    1 tablespoon bonita flakes

Place all ingredients in the heat resistant cup, and heat in the *nabe*. Stir occasionally until mixture is quite thick, then remove from *nabe* and serve as above.
*Use Mirin-Shoyu, Lemon-Shoyu or Shoyu Dipping Sauces (p. 40) in place of Tosa-joyu.
*Any of the following garnishes may also be used: Grated *wasabi*, bonita flakes, grated *daikon*, grated *yuzu* or lemon peel, *sansho* pepper, finely minced garlic, or lemon juice. The combination of leeks, gingerroot, and lemon juice is a tangy favorite. Western-style garnishes which may be mixed with shoyu include diced hard-boiled egg, diced or grated cheese, chives, garlic, or sesame butter.
*Add 2 to 4 tablespoons of sake or white wine to the water in the casserole.
*Use kinugoshi or grilled tofu.
*Add any of the following to the simmering broth several minutes before adding the tofu:
    8 to 10 mushrooms (Western-style, *shiitake*, cloud-ear, or *enokidake*)
    8 ounces chrysanthemum leaves
    4 leaves of Chinese cabbage cut into 3-inch-wide strips
    2 celery stalks, cut into matchsticks

Four Nabe Dishes Containing Tofu

Each of the following popular *nabe* dishes is prepared in basically the same way as Simmering Tofu. After the broth is brought to a boil in the *nabe* pot, however, each guest adds to it his choice of ingredients which are arranged on large platters. After the foods have been cooked for 2 or 3 minutes or until tender, they are removed from the simmering broth one piece at a time and dipped into the garnished dipping sauce. *Nabeyaki Udon* features whole-wheat or buckwheat noodles, often freshly prepared by the head cook just before mealtime. *Yosenabe* means "a gathering of everything." In the countryside, Chinese cabbage and leeks are its basic ingredients, while in the cities and particularly along the seacoasts, this dish generally includes lobster, fish, clams, prawns, and sometimes chicken and pork. *Mizutaki* means "cooked in water." The main ingredient here is usually chicken and the broth is a chicken stock. *Chirinabe* is very similar to *Mizutaki* except that it usually contains chunks of white fish rather than chicken. Each of these *nabe* dishes serves 6.

Nabeyaki-udon, Nabeyaki-soba, and Udon-tsuki

Basic Ingredients:
    1 pound *(udon)* whole-wheat noodles or *(soba)* buck-
       wheat noodles, cooked (p. 50)
    6 eggs, poached in the broth
    6 mushrooms and ½ pound sliced bamboo shoots pre-
       simmered in Sweetened Shoyu Broth (p. 40)
    1 pound Chinese cabbage leaves, cut into 3-inch-wide
       strips
    ½ pound spinach leaves
    24 ounces tofu, cut into 1-inch cubes
    6 cakes of dried wheat gluten
    6 pieces of vegetable tempura (optional)
    6 small ganmo balls (optional)
Broth:
    9 cups dashi (p. 39), stock, or water
    ¾ cup shoyu
    ¼ cup *mirin* or natural sugar
Garnishes:
    Thinly sliced leeks
    Grated *yuzu* or lemon peel
    Crumbled, toasted *nori*
    7-spice red pepper

Sprinkle garnishes over broth in casserole just before serving. Since dipping sauce is not ordinarily used, invite each guest to ladle garnished broth into individual serving bowls to be used for the purpose.

Yosenabe

Basic Ingredients:
    4 Chinese cabbage leaves, cut into 3-inch-wide strips
    2 leeks (including green stems), cut into 2-inch lengths
    6 chrysanthemum or spinach leaves
    1 carrot, cut diagonally into thin ovals and parboiled
    2 ounces dry transparent noodles
    12 small mushrooms
    4 ounces dry noodles
    24 ounces tofu, cut into 1-inch cubes
    6 cakes of dried wheat gluten
    3 small ganmo balls (optional)
    3 eggs, poached in the broth
Dipping Sauce:
    Tangy Shoyu Dipping Sauce (p. 41)
Broth:
    6 cups dashi (p. 39), stock, or water
    2 teaspoons shoyu
    2 teaspoons sake
    ¾ teaspoon salt

Mizutaki

Basic Ingredients:
    4 carrots, cut diagonally into thin ovals
    2 leeks, cut into 4-inch-long matchsticks
    ½ pound bamboo shoots, cut into thin half moons
    12 mushrooms

    1½ pounds Chinese cabbage (if desired, parboil leaves,
       roll into tight cylinders, and cut into 1-inch lengths)
    12 sprigs of watercress
    24 ounces tofu, cut into 1-inch cubes
    9 ounces ganmo cut into thin strips, used as a substitute
       for the chicken
Broth:
    4 cups dashi (p. 39), stock, or water, seasoned with a
       5-inch square of *kombu*
Dipping Sauce:
    ¾ cup Lemon-Shoyu (p. 40); or 6 tablespoons each
       lemon juice and vinegar, and ½ cup shoyu
Garnishes:
    Grated *daikon*
    Sliced leeks or scallions
    7-spice red pepper

Chirinabe

Prepare as for *Mizutaki* but use Vinegar-Shoyu (p. 40), Sweetened Vinegar-Shoyu (p. 41), or Tangy Shoyu Dipping Sauce (p. 41) instead of Lemon-Shoyu. Additional ingredients include transparent noodles and trefoil.

Chinese-style Firepots with Tofu

    Although generally more elaborate and complex than Japanese *nabe* dishes, and containing a number of distinctly Chinese ingredients, Chinese-style firepots are prepared in basically the same manner as their Japanese counterparts. Dipping sauces, which often contain red doufuru, may be either a mixture of up to ten spicy ingredients (p. 263), or a raw egg mixed with a little soy sauce and some of the cooking broth (p. 143). Detailed recipes for the Chrysanthemum Chafing Pot, Ten Varieties Pot, *Huichou* Pot, and Sandy Pot are given in Buwei Yang Chao's delightful *How to Cook and Eat in Chinese* (see Bibliography).

Miso Oden
                  SERVES 3

Gingerroot-Miso Dipping Sauce (p. 46), Rich Red Nerimiso
    (p. 42), or Yuzu Miso (p. 42)
12 ounces tofu or grilled tofu, cut into 1- by 3- by ½-inch
    strips
1 cake of *konnyaku*
4 inches large *daikon*, cut into ½-inch-thick half moons
A 5-inch square of *kombu*, wiped clean; or substitute ½ tea-
    spoon salt

Place the miso sauce into a small heat-resistant cup. Spear each tofu strip with two (6-inch bamboo) skewers or a fork. Rub *konnyaku* well with salt, rinse, cut crosswise into ½-inch-wide strips, and skewer each piece. Parboil *daikon*, then skewer each piece.

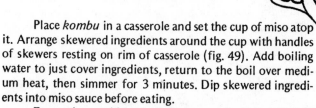

Fig. 49. Miso Oden

Place *kombu* in a casserole and set the cup of miso atop it. Arrange skewered ingredients around the cup with handles of skewers resting on rim of casserole (fig. 49). Add boiling water to just cover ingredients, return to the boil over medium heat, then simmer for 3 minutes. Dip skewered ingredients into miso sauce before eating.

For variety, add parboiled skewered pieces of cauliflower, potato, sweet potato, yam, or turnip. This dish may also be prepared at the table as for Simmering Tofu.

Yukinabe *(The Snow Pot)*   SERVES 2

This dish derives its name from the fact that the grated *daikon* turns snow white after it has been thoroughly cooked.

¼ cup shoyu
½ cup grated *daikon*
1 cup boiling water
12 ounces tofu, cut into 1¼-inch cubes
½ leek, cut into thin rounds, rinsed and pressed (p. 37)
1 tablespoon bonita flakes or crumbled, toasted *nori*

Pour the shoyu into a small heat-resistant cup and place in the center of a casserole set atop a tabletop brazier. Surround the cup with the grated *daikon* mixed with the boiling water, and return to the boil over high heat. Reduce heat to low and simmer for 3 minutes, or until *daikon* starts to become transparent. Place tofu on surface of *daikon*, return to the boil, and serve. Invite each guest to ladle a little hot shoyu and *daikon* into his or her individual serving dish, and garnish with leeks and bonita flakes; use as a dipping sauce.

Other possible garnishes include grated gingerroot, 7-spice red pepper, and grated *yuzu* peel.

Tofu & Miso Stew   SERVES 4

1½ onions, cut into thin rounds or wedges
4 mushrooms, cut into halves
1½ cups cubed sweet potatoes, yams, or potatoes
½ small carrot, cut into thin rounds
¼ cup green peas or thinly sliced green peppers
2 cups water or stock
¼ cup ketchup
1½ tablespoons butter
¼ cup red, barley, or Hatcho miso
12 ounces tofu, cut into 14 small rectangles (p. 37)
¼ cup grated cheese (optional)

Combine the first six ingredients in a large pot and bring to a boil over high heat. Reduce heat to low, cover, and simmer for 15 to 20 minutes. Stir in ketchup, butter, and the miso thinned in a few tablespoons of the hot broth. Cover and simmer for 15 minutes more. Add tofu and simmer, covered, for 5 more minutes. Stir in the cheese, if used. Serve hot or cold.

If desired, add chunks of deep-fried tofu, *daikon*, burdock root, cabbage, or broccoli; season with curry powder.

VARIATION

*Jibu-ni *(Country-style Tofu & Miso Stew):* In a heavy pot combine 2 cups water or dashi, ¼ cup each barley miso and bonita flakes, and 12 ounces thinly-sliced, parboiled tofu. Cover and bring to a boil, then reduce heat and simmer for about 1 hour. Serve steaming hot. Nothing better for chilly winter nights!

Niyakko   SERVES 2

This popular dish is the simmered counterpart of *Hiya-yakko* or Chilled Tofu. In both preparations the tofu is cut into large cubes called *yakko* (see p. 105).

2/3 cup dashi (p. 39) or stock
1½ tablespoons shoyu
2 teaspoons *mirin*
12 ounces tofu, cut into 6 cubes
¼ cup sliced leeks (very thin rounds)
3 tablespoons bonita flakes
Dash of *sansho* pepper (optional)

Combine the first three ingredients in a small saucepan and bring to a boil. Add tofu, return to the boil, and simmer for 3 minutes, or until tofu is just warmed through. Add sliced leek and remove from heat. Divide among serving bowls and serve immediately, topped with a sprinkling of bonita flakes and *sansho* pepper.

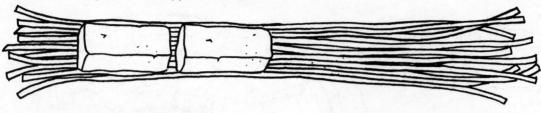

Fig. 50. Tofu wrapped in rice straw

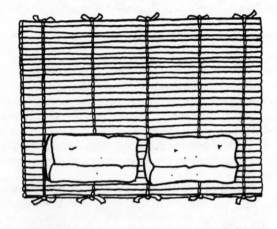

Simmered Tofu Wrapped in Rice Straw
(Tsuto-dofu or Komo-dofu)

A *tsuto* is a wrapper made of rice straw; a *komo* is a piece of straw or rush matting. Traditionally, both were used throughout Japan for wrapping foods. This tofu preparation is a favorite in the countryside, especially on Japan's southern island of Kyushu. Fresh rice straw imparts its tasty aroma and subtle flavor to the tofu, and lengthy simmering expels excess water from the tofu and gives it the porous texture that makes it more absorbent when simmered in seasoned broths. In urban areas, where fresh rice straw is not available, the tofu is often wrapped in a *(sudare)* bamboo mat while being simmered.

Cut a 12-ounce cake of tofu lengthwise into halves. Place 16 to 20 strands of fresh rice straw, each 20 inches long, side by side on a cutting board. Lay the tofu pieces end to end on top of the straw near one end (fig. 50). Fold the other end of straw over top of tofu, and tie with a single strand. Now bind straw around tofu from end to end, wrapping tofu 8 to 10

times with a long strand of rice straw to form a cylindrical bundle about 1½ inches in diameter. (If using a bamboo mat, lay the tofu pieces end to end across one end of the mat, roll up the mat to form a cylinder, and tie in several places with string.)

Combine the wrapped tofu and 1 to 2 quarts water in a large pot. Bring to a boil and simmer for 20 minutes. Unwrap and serve with your choice of Shoyu Dipping Sauces (p. 40) and garnishes, or simmer for 20 to 30 minutes more with vegetables in a broth of dashi or stock seasoned with shoyu. Also delicious in Clear Soups (p. 119) or Oden (p. 175).

For a more elaborate variety of *tsuto-dofu*, mash the tofu and mix with chopped vegetables, ground sesame, and slivered mushrooms. Shape mixture into cylinders and wrap in rice straw.

TOFU STEAMED

Any Japanese or Chinese family kitchen can get along fine without an oven—but not without a good steamer. In the few Chinese homes which have ovens, they are used for baking pastries' only. In Japan, foods are usually steamed in a bamboo steamer *(seiro)* set over a wok (p. 35). But a collapsible French steamer or a plate set on top of a bowl in a lidded pot or pressure cooker are both satisfactory substitutes. For instructions on preparing a steamer see page 38.

Tofu Steamed in Chinese Lotus Spoons SERVES 2 OR 3

---

12 ounces tofu, pressed (p. 96) and mashed
3 1/3 tablespoons milk
1 egg white
½ teaspoon natural sugar
½ teaspoon salt
¾ cup Gingerroot Sauce (p. 49)

Combine the first five ingredients, mixing well. Press the mixture into 8 Chinese porcelan "lotus spoons" (the kind with the flat bottom used for serving Chinese soups), or into large Western-style serving spoons. Steam tofu in the spoons for 10 minutes in a preheated steamer (p. 38). Remove firm tofu from spoons, invert, and arrange on a large serving plate. Serve topped with the hot sauce and accompanied by the spoons, which are now used to eat the tofu.

Tofu Chawan-mushi
(Steamed Egg-Vegetable Custard)

SERVES 4

6 ounces tofu, cut into ½-inch cubes
4 small mushrooms, cut into thin strips
¼ onion, thinly sliced
4 slivers of lemon peel
4 ginkgo nuts (optional)
4 lilly bulb sections (optional)
4 small cakes of dried wheat gluten (optional)
2 cups dashi (p. 39) or stock, cooled to room temperature
1 tablespoon shoyu
2 teaspoons *mirin*
3 eggs, lightly beaten
½ teaspoon salt
4 trefoil or spinach leaves

Divide the first seven ingredients among 4 custard cups with lids or 4 *chawan-mushi* cups. Combine the dashi, shoyu, *mirin*, eggs, and salt, and pour through a strainer into the four cups. Set a trefoil leaf on surface of liquid in each cup. Place cups into a large pot and pour water into pot until water comes halfway up the sides of the cups. Cover cups with individual lids, aluminum foil, or a large sheet of paper (figure, p. 38). Now cover pot and bring to a boil over high heat. Reduce heat and simmer for about 13 minutes, or until custard is firm but not porous. Serve hot or cold.

VARIATIONS

*Simmer the mushrooms in Sweetened Shoyu Broth (p. 40) before placing them in the custard cups.
*Substitute soymilk for all or part of the dashi.
*Add to or substitute for the vegetables used one or more of the following: snow peas, fresh corn, parboiled cubes of sweet potato, yam or potato, chestnuts, small rolls of fresh or dried yuba, green peas, or turnip cubes.

Nanzen-ji Wrapped Tofu

SERVES 4

24 ounces tofu
¼ to ½ cup Yuzu Miso (p. 42) or any Sweet Simmered Miso (p. 41)

Cut tofu into four pieces. With the sharp point of a knife, cut a section 2 inches square and 1 inch deep from the surface of each piece, and lift out carefully (fig. 51). Fill the well that remains with 1 to 2 tablespoons of the miso, then replace the small piece of tofu atop the miso. Wrap each piece of tofu in strong, absorbent paper (the Japanese use *washi* for this purpose) or in aluminum foil.

Bring water to a boil in a steamer (p. 38). Place wrapped tofu in steamer and steam for 5 to 10 minutes, or until miso is well heated. Serve hot, inviting each guest to unwrap his portion just before eating.

Other Ways of Serving Tofu in Steamed Dishes

*Yuzu Treasure Pot *(Yuzu-gama):* Cut a large *yuzu* horizontally into halves and hollow out the insides. Place 1 or 2 teaspoons Yuzu Miso (p. 42) in the bottom of each half, then pack firmly with squeezed tofu (p. 97). Spread a thin layer of the miso on top of tofu and rejoin the *yuzu* halves. Place in a heated steamer and steam for about 13 minutes. Serve hot or cold.
*Tofu Spiral in Butterbur Leaves *(Naruto-dofu):* Soak 2 small butterbur leaves overnight in a mixture of 5 cups water and 1 tablespoon baking soda. Parboil drained leaves, then drain again. Mix 2 parts squeezed tofu (p. 97) with 1 part grated glutinous yam and season lightly with salt. Spread this mixture in an even layer on each of the leaves, then roll up. Steam until firm. Cut into ½-inch sections to serve.
*Use tofu in Shinoda-maki (p. 195).

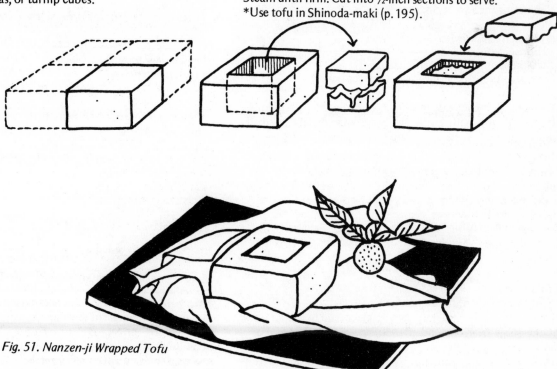

Fig. 51. Nanzen-ji Wrapped Tofu

TOFU DESSERTS

Tofu can be adapted to fresh fruit purées, whipped cream toppings, puddings, dessert soufflés, Japanese-style confections—even cheese cake.

Uncooked Desserts

In each of these preparations, nigari tofu gives by far the best flavor and consistency. Most take only a few minutes to prepare and, containing little sweetening, can also be used as side dishes at any meal.

Tofu Whipped Cream or Yogurt
MAKES 1½ CUPS

This delicious dish can be used like whipped cream or, as the basis of desserts, like yogurt.

12 ounces tofu
2 tablespoons honey or natural sugar
Dash of salt (optional)
½ teaspoon vanilla extract (optional)

Combine all ingredients in a blender and purée until smooth. To serve as yogurt, top with a sprinkling of slivered almonds or walnut meats, shredded coconut, and raisins. Or reduce the sweetening by one-half and top with Okara Granola (p. 84).

Tofu-Fruit Whips
SERVES 2 OR 3

These refreshing summertime desserts can be transformed into high-protein breakfast dishes by reducing or eliminating the sweetening.

½ pound fresh strawberries or peaches
12 ounces tofu, chilled
2 tablespoons honey or natural sugar
Chopped nutmeats or sunflower seeds (optional)

Combine all ingredients in a blender and purée until smooth. If desired, top with nutmeats. Serve immediately in small dessert dishes or use as a topping for pancakes, crêpes, or waffles.

VARIATIONS: Prepare as in the basic recipe:

*Banana-Lemon Whip
    2 small bananas
    6 ounces tofu
    Juice of ½ lemon
    1 to 2 tablespoons honey
    ½ teaspoon sesame butter (optional)
    Dash of nutmeg (optional)

*Coconut-Raisin Whip
    ½ cup shredded coconut
    ¼ cup raisins
    12 ounces tofu
    3 tablespoons marmalade

*Banana-Raisin Whip
    2 bananas
    ¼ cup raisins
    6 ounces tofu
    1 teaspoon honey
    ¼ cup toasted wheat germ
    Dash of nutmeg (optional)
*Honey-Lemon Whip
    1 tablespoon lemon juice
    ¼ to ½ teaspoon grated lemon rind (optional)
    1 tablespoon honey
    6 ounces tofu

Chunky Tofu-Pineapple Purée
SERVES 3

1½ cups pineapple chunks, drained
12 ounces tofu, drained (p. 96)
1½ teaspoons honey (optional)

Combine 1 cup pineapple chunks with the tofu and honey in a blender and purée until smooth. Served topped with remaining pineapple chunks.

Tangy Tofu-Prune Purée
SERVES 2

1½ cups stewed prunes
8 ounces tofu
3 tablespoons lemon juice

Combine all ingredients in a blender and purée until smooth. For best flavor, chill for several hours before serving. Delicious also as a breakfast fruit dish or topping for buttered toast.

Tofu-Orange Juice Purée with Tangerines
SERVES 4

12 ounces tofu, pressed (p. 96)
1 cup orange juice
1 tablespoon honey
1 cup tangerine or orange sections, drained

Combine the first three ingredients in a blender and purée until smooth. Stir in the tangerine sections, spoon into dessert cups, and chill for several hours.

Fruit Cocktail Chilled Tofu
SERVES 2

This refreshing summertime dish is a close relative of Chinese-style Annin-dofu (p. 268) in which mock tofu is prepared from milk jelled with agar.

6 to 8 ounces tofu or kinugoshi, chilled and cut into ½-inch cubes
1 to 2 cups canned fruit cocktail or sections of fresh mandarin oranges, cherries, peaches and/or chunks of pineapple

Combine all ingredients, mixing lightly, and chill for about 6 hours. Serve in small bowls or shrimp cocktail dishes.

Banana-Sesame Cream

SERVES 4

12 ounces tofu
2 tablespoons honey
2 bananas
¾ cup milk (soy or dairy)
1 to 1½ tablespoons sesame butter, *tahini*, or ground roasted
    sesame seeds (p. 38)

Combine all ingredients in a blender and purée until smooth.
Serve chilled as a dessert, or use as a topping for pancakes,
waffles, crêpes, or Nut Crunch (see below).

Banana Dessert with Tofu Whipped Cream

SERVES 4 TO 6

4 bananas, cut into long ovals
½ cup peanut or sesame butter
2 tablespoons honey
½ cup raisins
1½ cups Tofu Whipped Cream (p. 148)
¼ to ½ cup toasted wheat germ or Okara Granola (p. 84)

Arrange banana slices on a large platter. Combine peanut
butter and honey and mix until smooth. Spread mixture over
each banana slice, dot with raisins, and top with a spoonful of
the whipped cream. Serve sprinkled with wheat germ.

Banana-Tofu Milkshake

SERVES 3 TO 4

6 ounces (nigari) tofu
3 small frozen bananas, or fresh bananas and 3 ice cubes
1 tablespoon honey
¼ cup toasted wheat germ
¼ teaspoon nutmeg
¼ cup cold milk (soy or dairy)

Combine all ingredients in a blender and purée until smooth.
Serve immediately. When milk is omitted, this preparation
has the texture of banana ice cream.

Nut Crunch with Tofu Whipped Cream

SERVES 6

2 bananas, cut into thin rounds; or 2 apples, cut into wedges
¼ cup chopped almond meats
¼ cup chopped walnut meats
¼ cup sunflower seeds
¼ cup raisins
¼ cup chopped pitted dates
¼ cup shredded coconut
1½ cups Tofu Whipped Cream (p. 148) or Banana-Sesame
    Cream (p. 149)
3 tablespoons toasted wheat germ (optional)

Combine the first seven ingredients in a large bowl; mix well.
Serve in individual bowls topped with the whipped cream and
a sprinkling of wheat germ.

Tofu-Strawberry Dessert

SERVES 4 TO 6

24 ounces tofu, chilled and mashed
4½ tablespoons honey
2 teaspoons vanilla extract
12 to 15 strawberries, cut vertically into halves
¼ cup sliced hazel or almond nutmeats

Combine the tofu, honey, and vanilla in a large serving bowl;
mix well with a fork. Dot the surface with strawberries, then
sprinkle with sliced nutmeats.

Tofu Cream Cheese Dessert Balls

MAKES 6 TO 8

1 cup Tofu Cream Cheese (p. 109)
2 tablespoons shredded coconut
2 tablespoons chopped dates or raisins
¼ teaspoon cinnamon
½ teaspoon grated lemon or orange rind
½ teaspoon vanilla extract
½ cup chopped almonds

Combine the first six ingredients and 2 tablespoons chopped
almonds in a large bowl. Mix well, shape into 1½-inch balls,
and roll in remaining almonds. Serve chilled.

Tofu Icing

MAKES 1 CUP

12 ounces tofu, squeezed (p. 97); or 1 cup Tofu Cream
    Cheese (p. 109)
2 or 3 tablespoons sugar; or 2 tablespoons honey
½ teaspoon vanilla
Dash of salt
2 tablespoons powdered milk (optional)
1½ teaspoons grated lemon or orange rind (optional)

Combine all ingredients in a blender and purée for 30 seconds; refrigerate until just before serving on cake or cupcakes.

Tofu Ice Cream

SERVES 3 OR 4

18 ounces tofu, well chilled
3 tablespoons honey
¼ teaspoon vanilla extract
1/8 teaspoon salt

Combine 12 ounces tofu, honey, vanilla, and salt in a blender
and purée for about 1 minute. Transfer to a covered container
and place in the freezer overnight.

Purée remaining 6 ounces tofu in the blender until
smooth. Cut the frozen tofu into small chunks. While puréeing at high speed, add a few chunks at a time to the tofu in the
blender until all has been added and the mixture is smooth
and thick. Serve immediately.

For variety, add toward the end of puréeing: 1 egg
yolk, 2 to 4 tablespoons each chopped almonds or shredded
coconut, and your choice of fresh or frozen fruits. Serve
topped with chopped nutmeats. Or add 1 teaspoon powdered
green tea *(matcha)* and 1 additional tablespoon honey; omit
vanilla.

Cooked and Baked Desserts

Tofu can be used like dairy products to add plenty of protein and a rich, creamy texture to your favorite desserts. Apples, raisins, and small amounts of honey make delicious natural sweeteners.

Tofu Cheesecake   SERVES 6 TO 8

Filling:
        24 ounces tofu, well drained or pressed (p. 96)
        1½ tablespoons natural sugar or honey
        ¼ cup raisins, minced
        1 tablespoon lemon juice
        ½ teaspoon grated lemon rind
        1 tablespoon *tahini* or sesame butter
        ½ teaspoon vanilla
        1/8 teaspoon salt
        1 or 2 eggs (optional)
        1 teaspoon white wine or sake (optional)
        ¼ cup walnut meats, minced (optional)
2 teaspoons butter
Crust:
        1 cup crunchy granola
        2 teaspoons honey
        2 teaspoons lemon juice

Preheat oven to 350°. Combine all filling ingredients in a blender and purée until smooth. Coat an 8-inch pie tin with the butter. Combine ¾ cup granola with the honey and lemon juice, mix well, and press into the tin to form a crust. Spoon filling over crust, smooth filling surface, and sprinkle with remaining ¼ cup granola. Bake for about 25 minutes or until surface is lightly browned. Allow to cool for at least 6 to 8 hours before serving.

This filling also works well with conventional cheesecake crusts. If desired, served topped with applesauce or Tofu Whipped Cream (p. 148).

Tofu-Rice Pudding   SERVES 4

12 ounces tofu, mashed
1 cup cooked Brown Rice (p. 50)
1 cup milk (soy or dairy)
3 tablespoons honey
¼ teaspoon salt
¼ teaspoon cinnamon
¼ cup raisins
1 teaspoon oil
3 tablespoons crushed corn flakes or cracker crumbs
2 tablespoons butter

Preheat oven to 350°. Combine the first seven ingredients in a large bowl; mix well. Coat a casserole or bread pan with the oil, spoon in the tofu-rice mixture, sprinkle with corn flakes, and dot with butter. Bake for 25 minutes, or until set. Or omit the corn flakes and simmer all ingredients in a large saucepan over low heat for 10 to 15 minutes, or until firm.

Apple-Raisin Dessert with Tofu Whipped Cream   SERVES 4

¼ cup water
3 apples, cut into thin wedges
¼ to ½ cup raisins
4 teaspoons lemon juice (optional)
1 tablespoon butter (optional)
¼ teaspoon cinnamon
Tofu Whipped Cream (p. 148)

Combine water and apple in a small saucepan. Simmer, covered, stirring occasionally, for 10 to 15 minutes until apples are tender and the water has mostly evaporated. Stir in remaining ingredients and cook for several minutes more. Spoon into serving bowls, sprinkle with cinnamon, and serve hot or cold topped with whipped cream.

For variety, core the apples and fill with raisins, brown sugar, and cinnamon. Wrap in aluminum foil and bake in a 350° oven for about 20 minutes. Cut vertically into halves and serve topped with the whipped cream.

Crêpes with Apple-Whipped Cream Filling   MAKES 12 TO 15

1½ cups (whole-wheat) flour, sifted
1 cup milk (soy or dairy)
2 eggs, lightly beaten
¼ teaspoon salt
2 tablespoons oil or butter
Apple-Raisin Dessert with Tofu Whipped Cream (above)

Combine the first four ingredients in a large bowl; mix just until smooth. Heat a skillet and coat very lightly with oil. Add just enough batter to cover bottom of skillet in a very thin layer. Cook over medium-high heat on both sides until golden brown. Repeat until all batter is used. Top each crêpe with the apple-raisin dessert.

Tofu Dessert Soufflé   SERVES 4

2 tablespoons oil
2½ tablespoons whole-wheat flour
¾ cup milk (soy or dairy)
6 ounces tofu, mashed
½ cup chopped roasted soybeans or chopped peanuts
¼ teaspoon salt
3 tablespoons honey
½ cup raisins
4 egg yolks
4 egg whites, beaten until stiff
½ teaspoon butter

Preheat oven to 350°. Heat a skillet and coat with the oil. Add 2 tablespoons flour and cook until lightly browned and fragrant. Add the milk gradually, stirring constantly, to form a thick sauce; turn off heat. Add the next six ingredients; mix well. Carefully fold mixture into egg whites. Coat a soufflé dish lightly with butter, then dust with remaining flour. Place soufflé mixture into dish and bake for 30 to 40 minutes, or until set.

Tofu Mincemeat

MAKES 5¼ CUPS

4 (tart) apples, peeled, cored, and diced
½ cup apple juice
1½ cups raisins
Grated rind of 1 orange
Juice of 1 orange
24 ounces tofu, pressed (p. 96) and mashed; or 10 ounces thick agé or ganmo, diced
½ to 1 cup nutmeats
½ teaspoon cinnamon
½ teaspoon cloves, allspice, or coriander (optional)
¼ cup Hatcho miso

Combine the first five ingredients in a heavy pot, bring to a boil, and simmer for 30 minutes. Add tofu, return to the boil, and simmer for 5 minutes more. Add the next three ingredients and miso creamed in a little of the cooking liquid; mix well and remove from heat. Allow to cool to room temperature, then cover and refrigerate for at least 8 hours. Use as a filling for mince pie or turnovers. Also delicious as a spread for buttered toast or served like chutney with curried dishes.

Tofu-Pineapple Sherbet

SERVES 3

¼ cup pineapple juice
1½ tablespoons lemon juice
1 tablespoon natural sugar or honey
1 egg, lightly beaten
½ cup crushed pineapple
1 cup finely-diced apple
¼ cup raisins
6 ounces tofu, rubbed through a sieve or puréed in a blender

Combine the first four ingredients in a saucepan. Simmer, stirring constantly, over very low heat for 4 to 5 minutes, or until thickened; allow to cool for 30 minutes. Stir in remaining ingredients, pour into a mold, and freeze for 1 hour, or until as firm as sherbet.

Tofu-Banana-Raisin Jelled Dessert

SERVES 3

½ stick of agar (4 gm), reconstituted and torn into small pieces (p. 37)
¾ cup milk
1 banana, sliced into thin rounds
1/3 cup raisins
6 ounces tofu, rubbed through a sieve or puréed in a blender
Dash of salt
¾ cup Honey-Lemon Whip (p. 148)

Combine the agar and milk in a saucepan and bring to a boil. Simmer, stirring constantly, for 3 to 4 minutes, or until agar dissolves. Mix in the next four ingredients and remove from heat. Pour into cups or a mold and allow to cool. Cover and refrigerate until firm. Serve chilled, topped with the whip.

Tofu-Peanut Butter Cookies
(High Protein)

MAKES 20

36 ounces tofu, crumbled (p. 98)
½ cup peanut butter
¼ cup brown sugar, sifted
¼ cup butter, beaten until soft
1 egg, lightly beaten
¼ teaspoon salt

Preheat oven to 350°. Combine all ingredients, mixing well to form a smooth dough. Roll dough into small balls, place balls on an oiled cookie tin, and press flat with a fork. Bake for about 15 minutes. Or press the dough into a loaf pan, bake, and serve cut into squares.

Tofu-Brown Rice Cookies

MAKES 15 TO 20

12 ounces tofu, squeezed (p. 97)
1 cup cooked Brown Rice (p. 50)
3 tablespoons natural sugar
1 tablespoon honey
¼ cup raisins
Cinnamon
¼ cup shredded coconut

Preheat oven to 350°. Combine the first five ingredients in a large bowl; mix well. Form mixture into small patties and arrange on a lightly-oiled cookie tin. Top with a sprinkling of cinnamon and the coconut. Bake for 15 to 20 minutes, or until nicely browned.

Marbled Tofu & Banana Delight

SERVES 2 OR 3

24 ounces tofu, crumbled (p. 98)
3 bananas, mashed
½ cup walnut meats (optional)
Dash of nutmeg
¼ teaspoon salt
1 tablespoon oil

Preheat oven to 350°. Combine the first five ingredients in a large bowl and mash together. Press the mixture into a small bread pan lightly coated with the oil, and bake for 20 to 30 minutes until lightly browned. Cool to room temperature before serving.

Tofu-Orange-Almond Dessert

SERVES 3

1 cup fresh orange juice
2 tablespoons honey or sugar
1½ teaspoons grated orange rind (optional)
1/8 teaspoon almond extract (optional)
12 ounces tofu, drained (p. 96) and cut into ½-inch cubes
1 cup tangerine sections, drained
3 tablespoons (toasted) sliced almonds

Combine orange juice and honey in a small saucepan and simmer uncovered until reduced to about ¾ cup. Stir in orange rind and almond extract, then combine with tofu and tangerine sections in a serving bowl. Cover and chill for at least 2 hours. Serve in dessert cups topped with sliced almonds.

Deep-fried Tofu Balls with Peanut Butter and Honey

SERVES 2 OR 3

6 ounces tofu, squeezed (p. 97)
¼ cup raisins
Dash of salt
Oil for deep-frying
1 tablespoon honey
2 tablespoons peanut butter
1 banana, sliced into thin rounds
2 tablespoons chopped peanuts

Combine tofu, raisins, and salt in a large bowl. Mix for several minutes to develop cohesiveness. Shape into 1-inch balls and allow to dry for 5 to 10 minutes.

Heat the oil to 350° in a wok, skillet, or deep-fryer. Drop in the balls and deep-fry until golden brown (p. 130); drain and allow to cool to room temperature. Arrange in a snug layer on a serving dish. Combine honey and peanut butter, mixing well, and pour mixture over deep-fried balls. Top with banana slices and peanuts. Chill in a freezer for 30 minutes, or until firm.

Tofu Custard Pudding

SERVES 3

12 ounces tofu
1 egg
2 to 2½ tablespoons honey
½ teaspoon salt
½ teaspoon vanilla extract
½ cup Tofu Whipped Cream (p. 148)

Combine first five ingredients in a blender and purée until smooth. Spoon the puréed mixture into 3 custard cups with tops. Cover cups, place in a heated steamer, and steam over low heat for 12 to 14 minutes, or until just firm. Or set the cups in a pan of hot water and bake at 325° for about 20 minutes. Serve hot or cold topped with the whipped cream.

Tofu also gives a delicious creamy texture to chocolate puddings.

Fig. 52. Gisei-dofu

Gisei-dofu
(Tofu Cheesecake-Like Dessert)

SERVES 8

Gisei means "fictitious or imitation." Traditionally, *Gisei-dofu* was any tofu preparation made to resemble a food prohibited by the precepts of Buddhism, like *ganmodoki* (p. 184) made to resemble the flavor of wild goose, and *yuba-no-kabayaki* (p. 245) designed to resemble the taste of broiled eels. In Zen Temple Cookery, regular Gisei-dofu was prepared in imitation of the flavor and texture of eggs, which the monks of most Japanese sects were forbidden to eat.

Gisei-dofu may also refer to any tofu preparation which contains—or rather conceals—a prohibited food. Whenever Buddhist monks drank sake, they referred to it as *hanya-to*, meaning "warm elixir of transcendental wisdom." When they dined on wild boar, they asked for some *yama kujira*, or "mountain whale." Likewise, they referred to eggs mixed with tofu as *Gisei-dofu*, or "mock tofu."

Gisei-dofu is one of the few representatives of tofu cuisine prepared in some traditional tofu shops. It usually contains no eggs and is broiled in sturdy copper pans over a charcoal brazier (fig. 86, p. 217).

24 ounces tofu, parboiled (p. 96) and squeezed (p. 97)
1 egg
¼ cup natural sugar

2 teaspoons shoyu
½ teaspoon (sesame) oil
3½ teaspoons *mirin*, sake, or white wine

Preheat oven to 350°. Combine the first four ingredients in a large bowl; mix well, stirring for about 5 minutes to develop cohesiveness. Press the mixture to a depth of 1 to 1½ inches into a small baking pan or pie tin coated with the oil. Place the bottom of a pan of equal size directly on top of the tofu mixture to serve as a pressing lid, then place an 8-ounce weight or 1 cup water in the upper pan. Bake for about 30 minutes, or until sides of tofu are a deep golden brown.

Remove from oven and immediately invert. Lift off upper pan so that tofu rests on top of the pressing pan. Brush and rub top and sides of tofu with *mirin*, then allow to cool. Cut into eighths to serve (fig. 52).

VARIATIONS

*Gisei-dofu Cookies: After mixing the first four ingredients in the basic recipe, shape mixture into cookies and bake on a lightly oiled tin for about 15 minutes. Brush with the *mirin* and allow to cool before serving.

*To the basic recipe add 2½ tablespoons ground roasted sesame seeds (p. 38), sesame butter, or *tahini*. Increase sweetening to 5 tablespoons honey or sugar, add ½ teaspoon salt, and omit *mirin*. Serve topped with a sprinkling of *sansho* pepper.

*Omit the egg and *mirin*. Increase sweetening to 5 tablespoons honey or sugar. This is the traditional recipe used in temple cookery.

*Sauté in (sesame) oil or simmer in Sweetened Shoyu Broth (p. 40) about ¼ cup slivered carrots, cloud-ear or *shiitake* mushrooms, green peas, or diced lotus root. Combine with 2 to 3 tablespoons diced walnut meats, ground roasted sesame seeds or roasted hemp seeds. Add to the tofu mixture before baking.

*Skewered Gisei-dofu: Cut the baked tofu into pieces 1½ by 1 by 1 inch. Pierce each piece from one end with a food-pick or a 2-pronged bamboo skewer 6 inches long. Sprinkle tofu with a dash of *sansho* pepper and garnish with 6 to 8 beefsteak seeds *(shiso-no-mi)*. Serve with shavings of *konnyaku* topped with Sweet Simmered Miso (p. 41). Or serve on a green beefsteak leaf garnished with pickled red ginger-root *(beni shoga)*.

Tofu-Egg Roll *(Datémaki)* SERVES 4

5 eggs, lightly beaten
12 ounces tofu, drained (p. 96)
¼ cup natural sugar
¼ teaspoon salt
1½ tablespoons oil

Preheat oven to 350°. Combine the first four ingredients in a blender and purée until smooth. Spread purée in a ¼-inch-thick layer over the bottom of a large baking pan (8 by 12 inches) lightly coated with oil. Bake for about 15 minutes until well set.

Using a large spatula, carefully remove freshly baked mixture from pan and transfer onto a dishtowel. Using the towel like a *sudare* (bamboo mat), roll the omelet from one end into a compact cylindrical spiral (fig. 57, p. 171). Fold both ends of towel over top of omelet to prevent spiral from unrolling, and allow to cool to room temperature. Cut roll into 1½-inch lengths and serve on small dishes with the cut spiral surface facing upward.

Additional Suggestions for Serving Tofu in Desserts

*Prepare cream puffs according to your favorite recipe. Fill with Tofu Whipped Cream (p. 148) topped with small strawberries.

*Use Sweetened Tofu Cottage Cheese (p. 109) in place of dairy cottage cheese or goat cheese in your favorite cheesecake recipe.

*Try tofu in applesauce cake or lemon pie.

9
Deep-fried Tofu

THREE TYPES of deep-fried tofu are prepared in most Japanese (and many American) tofu shops: *thick agé* (pronounced *ah-gay*), whole cakes of regular tofu which have been pressed and deep-fried; *ganmo*, deep-fried burger-shaped patties or small balls of firmly-pressed tofu containing minced vegetables and sesame seeds; and *agé*, small pouches or puffs of deep-fried tofu that can be filled with salads, grains, cooked vegetables, or other stuffings. We will begin by discussing the properties common to all three types and giving recipes in which they can be used interchangeably. In the sections that follow, we will speak more of their unique individual qualities.

Many Japanese chefs and tofu masters are of the opinion—with which we agree—that of the various types of tofu, deep-fried tofu may be most suited to Western tastes and cooking. All three varieties have a distinct, hearty flavor, golden-brown color, and firm, meaty texture that remind some of fried chicken. In fact the word *ganmo* actually means "mock goose," and this tasty tofu was originally developed by chefs who longed for the flavor of wild goose meat, a delicacy once forbidden to all but the Japanese nobility.

Deep-fried tofu can be used as a delicious and inexpensive substitute for meat in a remarkably wide variety of recipes. Grilled or broiled, it has a savory barbequed aroma; added to casseroles, sautéed vegetable dishes, or curry and spaghetti sauces, it adds body, texture, and plenty of protein; served in sandwiches, egg dishes, or atop pizzas, it may be used like cold cuts or bacon; and when frozen, its structure undergoes a total change, making it even more meatlike, tender, and absorbent.

Because the processes of pressing and deep-frying greatly reduce the water content in this tofu, it will stay fresh for long periods of time without refrigeration. Thus it is well suited for use in lunch boxes or on picnics and hikes, even during the warm summer months. Perhaps more important, it can serve as a basic daily food in tropical regions such as India or Africa where facilities for cold storage are not widely available. And, in fact, deep-fried tofu comprises a relatively large proportion of the tofu prepared in semi-tropical Taiwan and the warmer, southernmost provinces of China and Japan.

In addition to imparting a rich flavor and aroma to tofu, the process of deep-frying also adds highly digestible polyunsaturated fats, usually from either

Fig. 53. Serving freshly deep-fried agé

154

Fig. 54. The deep-frying area in a traditional tofu shop

rapeseed or soy oil. Thus when deep-fried tofu is used in place of meat, it serves as a source of the fatty acids necessary for a balanced diet and simultaneously helps to reduce the intake of saturated fats.

All varieties of deep-fried tofu are rich in protein: thick agé, ganmo, and agé contain respectively 10.1, 15.4, and 18.6 percent protein by weight. Thus both ganmo and agé have a higher percentage of protein than either eggs or hamburger (which have 13 percent each). A typical 5-ounce serving of thick agé, for example, provides about one-third of the daily adult requirement of usable protein.

Deep-fried tofu—like most deep-fried foods—is at its very best just after being prepared, while still crisp and sizzling (fig. 53). And each of the three basic types can easily be prepared at home from regular tofu using recipes given in the following three sections. Deep-fried tofu purchased commercially may be served as is, without reheating or further cooking, seasoned with any of the toppings or dipping sauces described on page 40. Or it may be lightly broiled to impart added flavor and aroma, then served in salads or other quick-and-easy preparations.

Deep-fried tofu is used in virtually every style of Japanese cuisine. Approximately one-third of all tofu served in Japan is deep-fried, and each day tofu makers prepare more than ten million pieces of agé alone!

In most Japanese tofu shops, the highly skilled work of preparing deep-fried tofu is entrusted entirely to the tofu maker's wife. She and her husband generally work side by side since, in most traditional shops, the cauldron in which the soymilk is prepared is located next to the deep-frying area (fig. 54). Two containers of deep-frying oil are used in the preparation of ganmo and agé; one is kept at a moderate temperature and used for the initial, slow cooking; the other is kept at a high temperature, which causes the tofu to expand and imparts a handsome, golden-brown coating to each piece. Only the simplest tools are necessary to prepare fine deep-fried tofu: long chopsticks, two small skimmers, and a draining basket set over an earthenware container (fig. 55). The crisp, freshly-prepared tofu is transferred to attractive, handmade trays of woven bamboo (fig. 56) where it is allowed to cool.

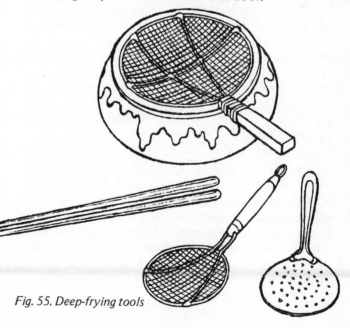

Fig. 55. Deep-frying tools

In each of the following recipes, an equal weight of any of the three basic types of deep-fried tofu may be used interchangeably. However, since the texture and flavor of one type often seems to go best with each dish, that type will generally appear in the recipe title and be listed first in the ingredients, followed by the second and third choices. Because the size and weight of individual pieces of the basic types of deep-fried tofu differ widely from shop to shop and area to area, we have listed the total weight of tofu to be used in each recipe rather than the number of pieces. In our recipes we actually used pieces with the following weights and sizes:

Thick agé: 5¼ ounces (150 grams), 4 by 2¾ by 1¼ inches.

Ganmo patties: 3½ ounces (100 grams), 4¾ inches in diameter by 3/8 inch thick.

Agé pouches: 1 ounce (28 grams), 6 by 3¼ by ¼ inch.

PREPARATORY TECHNIQUES

Dousing

Dousing removes excess oil from the surface of deep-fried tofu, making the tofu lighter, easier to digest, and more absorptive of dressings and seasoned broths. In some dishes, dousing is also used to warm the tofu. Some cooks always douse deep-fried tofu, while others find the results are not worth the time and effort. Generally, we hold to the latter point of view. But if you are on a low-fat diet, douse!

Place uncut pieces of deep-fried tofu in a strainer or colander. Bring 2 or 3 cups of water to a boil in a saucepan. Douse first one, then the other side of the tofu. Allow to drain for about 1 minute before using.

Or, holding individual pieces of tofu with chopsticks or tongs, dip tofu quickly into boiling water, then drain in a strainer.

Broiling

This technique, too, rids the tofu of some of its excess surface oil, while imparting a crispier texture and savory aroma to it. If you broil, do not douse beforehand. Some cooks like the broiled texture and aroma so much that they use this technique as a prelude to most deep-fried tofu preparations.

*If using a *stove-top burner* or bed of *live coals*, skewer tofu with a long-tined fork and hold just above the flames until lightly browned on both sides and fragrant.
*If using a regular *bread toaster*, simply drop in the deep-fried tofu and toast. Fast and easy. Serve immediately.
*If using an *oven broiler*, place tofu on a sheet of aluminum foil and broil under a high flame until lightly browned on both sides.

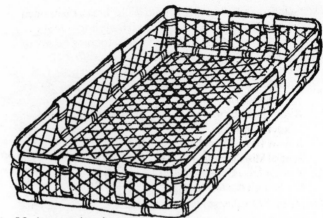
Fig. 56. A woven bamboo tray

*If using a grill over a *barbeque* or *brazier*, or a Japanese-style broiling screen over a stove-top burner (p. 36), broil tofu over high heat for 30 to 60 seconds on each side until speckled and fragrant. Turn with chopsticks or tongs. In our opinion, this method—used with a charcoal fire—gives the finest flavor and aroma.

*If using a *dry skillet*, preheat skillet over medium heat and drop in tofu. Pressing tofu down with chopsticks or fork, rub tofu over entire bottom of skillet until tofu is fragrant and lightly browned. Turn and brown second side.

DEEP-FRIED TOFU—QUICK AND EASY

The three basic types of deep-fried tofu are ready to serve in the form in which they are purchased or prepared at home. Thus, the following dishes require no cooking and can be prepared in less than 2 or 3 minutes.

Crisp Deep-fried Tofu   SERVES 1

This is our favorite recipe for serving deep-fried tofu, especially agé. If you live near or visit a tofu shop, the master may invite you to sample his sizzling, freshly deep-fried tofu served in this simple way.

4 to 5 ounces homemade agé, ganmo, or thick agé, freshly deep-fried; or storebought varieties lightly broiled (p. 156)
1 to 1½ teaspoons shoyu or Shoyu Dipping Sauces (p. 40)
½ teaspoon thinly sliced leeks or scallions, grated gingerroot, minced garlic, or any of the garnishes served with Chilled Tofu (p. 105)

Cut the hot tofu into bite-sized pieces and serve topped with the shoyu and garnish.

VARIATIONS
*Chilled Deep-fried Tofu: Serve as above using deep-fried tofu which has been well chilled. In Japan, this is a popular summertime lunch or dinner preparation. If the tofu is cut with chopsticks at the table, it will absorb the flavors of seasonings and garnishes more readily.
*Deep-fried Tofu with Miso Topping: Use either crispy hot

or well-chilled tofu. If using ganmo balls, break them open and fill with a little of the miso. Cut thick agé into thin slices. Spread one surface of the tofu with a thin topping of any of the following:

Sweet white, red, barley, or Hatcho miso
Yuzu Miso, Red Nerimiso, or any variety of Sweet Simmered Miso (p. 42)
Kinzanji miso, moromi miso, or any variety of Finger Lickin' Miso (p. 31)
Any variety of Miso Sauté (p. 43)
Special Miso Toppings (p. 45)
Vinegar Miso Dressings (p. 46)
Nut & Seed Butter Toppings (p. 47)

*Deep-fried Tofu Topped with Sauces: Serve any of the following hot or cold over crisp or chilled deep-fried tofu:

Ketchup-Worcestershire Sauce (p. 49), plain ketchup, or Worcestershire sauce
All Basic Sauces (p. 48)
Chinese Oyster Sauce
Chili Sauce or Barbeque Sauces
Mango or Apple Chutney

*Serve thick agé cubes (hot or cold) topped with maple syrup or honey. Chinese laborers enjoy this dish as a snack.

Grilled Thick Agé with Korean Barbeque Sauce

SERVES 2

5 ounces thick agé, ganmo, or agé
¼ cup Korean Barbeque Sauce (p. 49)

Broil the tofu over a barbeque fire, in a broiler, or in a hot unoiled skillet. Remove from heat and cut crosswise into sixths. Dip pieces briefly in the sauce and broil lightly once again. Serve topped with the remaining sauce.

Mock Peking Duck

SERVES 2

4 *tortillas*, cut into halves and warmed in a steamer
Butter
10 ounces thick agé or ganmo, cut into 4-inch-long-strips
2 or 3 tablespoons Peking Duck Dipping Sauce (p. 45)
1 leek or 3 green onions, cut into 4-inch slivers, soaked in water for 5 minutes and drained

Butter warmed *tortillas* lightly on one side. Divide tofu among *tortillas*, placing the strips in the center of each *tortilla*-half perpendicular to the *tortilla's* cut edge. Spread the dipping sauce on the tofu, then top with a sprinkling of the leek slivers. Roll up the tofu in the *tortilla* and, if desired, secure with a foodpick. Serve while still warm.

DEEP-FRIED TOFU HORS D'OEUVRE

Homemade deep-fried tofu served crisp and hot, or storebought tofu when lightly broiled, make hors d'oeuvre preparations with a wonderful flavor, aroma, and texture. During the summer the tofu can be served chilled.

Thick Agé with Curry Dip

SERVES 3

¼ cup cream cheese
2 teaspoons warm water
½ teaspoon shoyu
¼ teaspoon curry powder
10 ounces thick agé, ganmo, or agé, cut into thin strips

Combine the first four ingredients in a small bowl, mixing until smooth. Spread on tofu strips or use as a dip.

Thick Agé with Sesame-Cream Cheese Dip

SERVES 3

1 teaspoon sesame butter or *tahini*
5 tablespoons cream cheese
1 tablespoon warm water
1 teaspoon shoyu; or 1½ teaspoons red or barley miso
Dash of tabasco sauce or 7-spice red pepper
10 ounces thick agé, ganmo, or agé, cut into thin strips

Combine the first five ingredients, mixing until smooth. Spread on tofu slices or use as a dip.

Deep-fried Tofu Appetizers

MAKES 16

4 teaspoons Sweet Simmered Miso (p. 41), Miso Sauté (p. 43), or Finger Lickin' Miso (p. 31)
10 ounces thick agé, ganmo, or agé, cut into 16 bite-sized pieces
Toppings: Cut to fit on top of each piece of tofu
Cheese
Cucumbers
Tomatoes
Fresh mushrooms
Bananas

Spread miso on one surface of each piece of tofu, cover with one or two slices of the toppings and, if desired, secure with a foodpick. Combinations with cheese are delicious if broiled until the cheese begins to melt.

Deep-fried Tofu Teriyaki Hors D'oeuvre

MAKES 12

10 to 14 ounces thick agé, ganmo, or agé, doused (p. 156) and cut into 1-inch-wide strips
2/3 cup Teriyaki Sauce (p. 48)
2 tablespoons (ground) roasted sesame seeds (p. 38)
Dash of (7-spice) red pepper (optional)

Cut shallow slits in the deep-fried surfaces to aid absorption of the sauce. Marinate, broil, and serve as for Tofu Teriyaki (p. 141), sprinkling each sizzling piece with the sesame seeds and, if desired, the red pepper.

For variety, add 2 teaspoons cornstarch to the sauce, bring to a boil, and simmer briefly until thick. Use hot as the marinade.

Spicy Broiled Ganmo Hors D'oeuvre   SERVES 2

7 ounces ganmo, thick agé, or agé
1 teaspoon shoyu
Dash of 7-spice red pepper

Broil ganmo lightly (p. 156), brush with the shoyu, and sprinkle with the red pepper. Cut into bite-sized pieces and serve hot or cold. If desired, pierce each piece with a foodpick.

Thick Agé Hors D'oeuvre with Cheese   SERVES 2

1 teaspoon oil
2 teaspoons butter
5 ounces thick agé, ganmo, or agé, cut crosswise into ½-inch strips
8 slices of cheese, each 1 by 3 by ¼ inch
¼ teaspoon salt

Heat a skillet and coat with the oil and butter. Add thick agé and fry on both cut faces until lightly browned. Lay a piece of cheese on top of each piece of tofu, cover skillet, and cook for 1 minute more. Salt lightly and serve hot.

For variety, top with a slice of green pepper or cucumber. Serve on small pieces of lettuce-covered bread, toast, or crackers.

VARIATION

*Cut and fry tofu as above. Omit cheese, and add 1 teaspoon shoyu and 1½ teaspoons sake or white wine to the skillet. Stir tofu into the seasoning liquid, then turn tofu over and simmer until liquid is absorbed. Top with a sprinkling of minced parsley and a mixture of 1 teaspoon each lemon juice and shoyu.

Marinated Thick Agé Hors D'oeuvre   SERVES 2

5 ounces thick agé, ganmo, or agé, doused (p. 156) and cut into six equal cubes
6 green *togarashi* peppers, or 1 green pepper cut lengthwise into sixths
2 tablespoons shoyu
½ clove garlic, crushed or minced
¼ teaspoon grated gingerroot
¾ teaspoon (sesame) oil
¾ teaspoon vinegar
2 teaspoons natural sugar

Combine all ingredients in a small bowl and marinate for 5 minutes. Heat an unoiled skillet, remove tofu and green peppers from marinade, and fry over medium heat until fragrant. Dip tofu and green peppers in marinade, then fry again for about 30 seconds. Place a piece of green pepper on top of each piece of tofu, secure with a foodpick, and serve piping hot.

This dish is also delicious if the ingredients are broiled over a charcoal brazier or barbeque fire, or in an oven broiler. For variety try the following marinade: 2 tablespoons shoyu,

1 tablespoon sugar, 1 teaspoon each sesame oil and *mirin*, ¼ teaspoon 7-spice red pepper.

Deep-fried Tofu Fondue   SERVES 2 TO 4

4 ounces Swiss or Gruyere cheese, grated or diced
2 teaspoons flour
1 teaspoon crushed garlic
5 to 7 tablespoon dry white wine or sake
2 teaspoons shoyu
1 teaspoon lemon juice
10 ounces thick agé or ganmo, cut into 1-inch cubes
Spices: your choice of grated gingerroot or powdered ginger, minced onion, pepper, paprika, nutmeg, or cloves

Mix cheese and flour in a small cup and set aside. Rub a small, heavy enamel pot (or a fondue pot) with the garlic, leaving garlic in pot. Add wine, shoyu, and lemon juice and bring almost to a boil over medium heat. Add floured cheese a little at a time, stirring constantly with a wooden spoon in a figure eight motion, until cheese melts and fondue is smooth. When fondue starts bubbling, stir in tofu and your choice of spices.

To serve: if you have a fondue table set with a warmer, place the pot on the warmer in the center of your serving table accompanied by long (fondue) forks. Invite each guest to spear the tofu while it's hot. Or serve the pot set in or over a container of hot water.

Tofu fondue may also be served cold or as a main dish.

DEEP-FRIED TOFU IN SALADS

Sliced, cubed, or diced, deep-fried tofu adds flavor, texture and protein to salads and harmonizes nicely with a wide range of popular dressings. The various Tofu Mayonnaise Dressings (p. 107) and Miso Salad Dressings (p. 46) also go nicely over salads containing deep-fried tofu. Thick agé may be substituted for regular tofu in all recipes where the tofu is served cubed or reshaped in salads. In most recipes, the flavor of the salad is greatly enhanced if the tofu is lightly broiled (p. 156). Roasted soybeans may be used with good results sprinkled lightly over the top of most deep-fried tofu salds. For a description of the differences between Western- and Japanese-style salads, see pages 111 and 114.

Western-style Salads

Ganmo-Tomato-Mayonnaise Salad   SERVES 2

3½ ounces ganmo, thick agé, or agé, lightly broiled (p. 156) and cut into ½-inch strips or squares
1 large tomato, diced fine
2 or 3 tablespoons (tofu) mayonnaise (p. 107)
¼ teaspoon salt or 1 tablespoon sweet white miso
Dash of white pepper
½ to 1 teaspoon lemon juice (optional)
¼ cup diced cheese or pieces of torn lettuce (optional)

Combine all ingredients in a large bowl; toss lightly.

Thick Agé Salad with Tangy Tofu Cottage Cheese

SERVES 4

10 ounces thick agé, ganmo, or agé
Shoyu
7-spice red pepper or paprika
Tangy Tofu Cottage Cheese (p.109)
4 large lettuce leaves
1 tomato, cut into thin wedges
1 cucumber, sliced into thin diagonals
¼ to ½ cup raisins

Broil thick agé lightly (p. 156) and cut crosswise into thin strips. While still hot, dip into shoyu and sprinkle with the red pepper, then combine with the tofu cottage cheese, mixing well. Arrange lettuce leaves in individual salad bowls, mound with the tofu cottage cheese, and serve topped with tomato and cucumber slices and a sprinkling of raisins.

Fresh Sea-vegetable Salad with Thick Agé and Miso-Mayonnaise

SERVES 4

7½ ounces thick agé, ganmo, or agé, lightly broiled (p. 156) and cut crosswise into thin strips.
1 cucumber, thinly sliced
1 green pepper, thinly sliced
1 cup fresh or refreshed *wakame* (p. 37), cut into 2-inch lengths
½ cup raisins
Miso-Mayonnaise Dressing:
    5 teaspoons red, barley, or Hatcho miso
    3 tablespoons mayonnaise
    3 tablespoons lemon juice
    Dash of pepper (optional)
1 tomato, cut into thin wedges
4 lettuce leaves

Combine the first five ingredients and the dressing; mix lightly. Arrange tomato wedges on lettuce leaves in a large salad bowl. Top with the salad mixture and chill for several hours before serving.

    If *wakame* is unavailable, substitute 1 large diced apple or tomato.

Thick Agé & Brown Rice Salad with Mushrooms

SERVES 3 OR 4

1 teaspoon oil
1/3 cup minced onion
¾ cup minced mushrooms
1¼ cups cooked Brown Rice (p.50)
1 tablespoon shoyu
Dressing:
    3 tablespoon mayonnaise
    2 tablespoons lemon juice
    ¼ teaspoon curry powder
5 ounces thick agé or ganmo, diced
3 or 4 lettuce leaves

Heat a skillet or wok and coat with the oil. Add onion and one-half the mushrooms and sauté for 3 to 4 minutes. Remove from heat and stir in rice and shoyu; allow to cool to room temperature. Now add the remaining mushrooms, dressing, and thick agé, mix lightly and, for best flavor, allow to stand for several hours. Serve mounded on lettuce leaves.

    Also delicious as a filling for Agé Pouches (p. 192).

Thick Agé-Kabocha Salad with Miso Mayonnaise Dressing

SERVES 4

10 ounces *kabocha*, pumpkin, or squash
½ teaspoon salt
10 ounces thick agé, ganmo, or agé, doused (p. 156) and cut into small bite-sized cubes
Miso Mayonnaise:
    4 tablespoons (tofu) mayonnaise (p. 107)
    2 tablespoons red, barley, or Hatcho miso
    1 tablespoon vinegar
    1½ tablespoons natural sugar
8 lettuce or Chinese cabbage leaves (optional)
4 teaspoons slivered Vinegared Gingerroot (p. 51) (optional)

Cut *kabocha* into large bite-sized cubes, sprinkle with the salt, and steam for about 20 minutes, or until soft (p. 38). Combine *kabocha*, tofu, and miso mayonnaise in a large bowl; mix lightly. Arrange lettuce leaves in salad bowls, mound with the *kabocha*-tofu mixture, and top with gingerroot slivers.

    This salad is also delicious dressed with Mustard-Vinegar Miso Dressing (p. 46).

Buckwheat Noodle Salad with Miso Mayonnaise

SERVES 4

3 ounces *(soba)* buckwheat noodles (or spaghetti), cooked (p. 50)
5 ounces thick agé, ganmo, or agé, diced
1 large tomato, diced
1½ cucumbers, cut into thin rounds
2/3 cup diced celery
½ cup grated cheese or walnut meats; or 2 diced hard-boiled eggs (optional)
Dressing:
    ¼ cup mayonnaise
    1½ tablespoons red, barley, or Hatcho miso
    1 teaspoon lemon juice
    Dash of pepper
4 lettuce leaves
¼ cup parsley

Combine the first five (or six) ingredients with the dressing; mix lightly. Arrange lettuce leaves in individual bowls, mound with the salad, and top with a sprinkling of parsley.

    Delicious served in Agé Pouches (p. 192).

Agé-Noodle Salad

SERVES 3 OR 4

4 ounces agé, ganmo, or thick agé, cut into thin strips
1½ cups cooked transparent noodles *(harusame)*, soba, or
   macaroni
2 small celery stalks, diced
2 teaspoons Sesame Salt (p. 51) or ¼ teaspoon salt
5 tablespoons (tofu) mayonnaise (p. 107)
Dash of pepper

Combine all ingredients in a large bowl; mix lightly. To serve,
divide among individual salad bowls.

Mock Tuna Salad with Deep-fried Tofu

SERVES 3 OR 4

1 tablespoon oil
1 small onion, thinly sliced
3 mushrooms, thinly sliced
2 green peppers or 12 green beans, slivered
3 eggs, lightly beaten
2 ounces of agé, ganmo, or thick agé, thinly sliced
¼ cup mayonnaise
2 teaspoons shoyu or 1 tablespoon red miso
Dash of pepper
1½ tablespoons minced parsley
2 or 3 lettuce leaves, torn into small pieces

Heat a skillet and coat with the oil. Add the next three ingredients and sauté for 4 to 5 minutes. Add eggs and agé, and
scramble until eggs are firm. Remove from heat and allow to
cool to room temperature. Combine mayonnaise, shoyu, and
pepper to make a dressing, then mix with the eggs. Just before serving, add parsley and lettuce; mix lightly.

Macaroni-Parsley Salad with Thick Agé

SERVES 4

4 lettuce leaves
¾ cup dry macaroni, cooked
2/3 cup chopped parsley
1 cup chopped celery
7½ ounces thick agé, ganmo, or agé, cut into small cubes
Dressing:
    2 tablespoons mayonnaise
    2 tablespoons vinegar
    1½ tablespoons lemon juice
    1½ tablespoons red miso or 1 tablespoon shoyu
    1 tablespoon oil
    1 tablespoon minced onion

Line 4 individual salad bowls with the lettuce. Combine the
next four ingredients and the dressing in a large bowl; mix
well. Spoon onto the lettuce leaves.

Thick Agé with Marinated Vegetables

SERVES 2

5 ounces thick agé, ganmo, or agé, diced
2 cucumbers, slivered
½ carrot, finely diced
1 tomato, finely diced
15 green beans, parboiled and diced
Dressing:
    3 tablespoons vinegar
    2 tablespoons sesame oil
    1 tablespoon salad oil
    3 tablespoons shoyu
    1 tablespoon sugar
    2 tablespoons ground roasted sesame seeds (p. 38),
       sesame butter, or *tahini* (optional)
    ¼ teaspoon salt
    Dash of 7-spice red pepper

Combine the first five ingredients and the dressing; marinate
overnight (or for at least 3 to 4 hours).

Garbanzo Bean Salad with Thick Agé

SERVES 6

2 cups garbanzo beans, rinsed, soaked overnight in 3 cups
   water, and drained
10 ounces thick agé, ganmo, or agé, cut into ½-inch cubes
2 stalks of celery, diced
½ onion, diced
¼ cup minced parsley or chives
½ cup diced green pepper, tomato, or carrot (optional)
Dressing:
    ¼ cup salad oil
    1½ teaspoons sesame oil
    2 tablespoons lemon juice or vinegar
    ½ cup Sesame Salt (p. 51) or 1 tablespoon salt
    1½ teaspoons shoyu
    ¼ teaspoon hot mustard
    1½ teaspoons powdered or 1 teaspoon grated gingerroot
    1 clove garlic, crushed
    Dash of pepper

Combine beans with 3 cups fresh water and bring to a boil.
Reduce heat to low, cover, and simmer for 2½ hours, or
until all liquid has been absorbed. Combine hot beans and
next five ingredients in a large flat-bottomed pan and add
dressing; mix well. Allow to stand for about 1 hour, or until
cool, before serving.

Japanese-style Salads
(Aemono)

Ganmo-Cucumber Salad with Miso Dressing

SERVES 2

3½ ounces ganmo, thick agé, or agé, cut into 1-inch squares
1 cucumber or *uri* melon, sliced into thin rounds
½ cup Mustard-Vinegar Miso Dressing (p. 46)

Combine all ingredients, mixing lightly. Serve chilled.

Vinegared Cucumber-Wakame Salad with Ganmo

SERVES 4

2 cucumbers, sliced into thin rounds
1½ cups fresh or refreshed *wakame* (p. 37) or slivered *kombu*
7 ounces ganmo or 4 ounces agé, cut into thin strips, each 1½ inches long
Dressing:
   2 tablespoons shoyu
   6 tablespoons vinegar
   2 tablespoons natural sugar
   3 tablespoons sesame butter

Combine the first four ingredients with the dressing, mix lightly, and serve.

Or try a *Sambaizu* dressing using 3 tablespoons each shoyu and vinegar, and 2 tablespoons sugar.

Pressed Salad with Agé and Sesame-Vinegar Dressing

SERVES 2 TO 3

2 ounces agé, ganmo, or thick agé, lightly broiled (p. 156) and cut crosswise into thin strips.
7 ounces *daikon*, cut into 2-inch matchsticks
¼ small carrot, cut into matchsticks
1 cucumber, cut diagonally into thin slices
2 teaspoons salt
2 tablespoons ground roasted sesame seeds (p. 38)
2 tablespoons (rice) vinegar
2 tablespoons natural sugar
1 teaspoon shoyu

Combine the first four ingredients in a small bowl; rub with 1½ teaspoons salt, rinse, and press (p. 37). Combine ½ teaspoon salt with remaining ingredients in a small bowl and mix well. Place pressed vegetables and tofu in a large bowl, sprinkle with the vinegar mixture, and mix lightly. Serve immediately.

Also delicious with *kombu*, fresh *(shiitake)* mushrooms, *konnyaku* noodles, or green beans.

DEEP-FRIED TOFU WITH SANDWICHES AND TOAST

These preparations are as delicious as they are easy to prepare. Lightly broiled, deep-fried tofu serves as a savory sandwich ingredient or may be used as a substitute for bacon or meat slices. The use of any variety of Finger Lickin' Miso (p. 31), Sweet Simmered Miso (p. 41), or regular miso in sandwiches with deep-fried tofu gives added flavor. Due to protein complementarity (p. 25), serving tofu and whole-wheat bread together can yield up to 32 percent additional protein.

Deep-fried Tofu Sandwiches

Use 2 ounces agé, ganmo, or thick agé, lightly broiled (p. 156), if desired, and cut lengthwise into 1-inch-wide strips. Place between 2 slices of buttered (whole-grain) bread or toast with any of the following combinations of ingredients:

   *Miso, Miso Toppings (p. 41), or salt; cheese, cucumber, lettuce, tomato, mayonnaise, mustard, ketchup.

   *1 egg fried in butter (see Fried Eggs with Deep-fried Tofu; p. 164) miso, ketchup, pepper, grated cheese, and parsley. Serve on toast.

   *Lettuce, mayonnaise, pepper
   *Cream cheese, tomato, lettuce
   *Nut Butter Spreads (p. 47), grated cheese, alfalfa sprouts
   *Cheese, *nori*, lettuce, miso
   *Grilled cheese, mayonnaise, tomato, lettuce, miso
   *Deep-fried Tofu Salads (p. 158), lettuce, tomato and mayonnaise; serve on toast.
   *Deep-fried tofu in onion sauce (p. 165) or with Fried Rice (p. 168); serve hot or cold on toast.
   *Deep-fried tofu simmered in seasoned broths (p. 174), cooled; serve on toast.

Pizza Toast with Deep-fried Tofu

MAKES 5

Use thin slices of deep-fried tofu in place of salami, sausage, or anchovies in your favorite pizza toppings. This variation on the traditional motif, now popular in many Japanese pizza parlors, can be prepared quickly and easily at home.

5 large, fairly thick slices of (whole-wheat or French) bread, buttered on one side
5 large, thin slices of (mozzerella) cheese
1¼ cups Tomato & Cheese Sauce (p. 49)
5 ounces thick agé or ganmo, thinly sliced

3 to 4 mushrooms, thinly sliced
1 to 2 green peppers, thinly sliced
½ tomato, thinly sliced
Olive oil
¼ cup minced parsley (optional)
Oregano and/or thyme
1 cup grated cheese (optional)
Parmesan cheese
Tabasco sauce

Preheat oven to 350°. Cover the buttered side of each piece of bread with a slice of cheese, and spread with the sauce. Arrange on top: slices of tofu, mushrooms, green peppers, and tomatoes, then sprinkle lightly with oil. If desired, top with grated parsley, herbs and cheese. Bake for 10 to 15 minutes, or until toast is nicely browned. Serve hot, topped with Parmesan cheese and tabasco sauce.

Tofu & Wakame Open-faced Toasted Sandwich

MAKES 6

7 ounces ganmo or thick agé, diced
2 cucumbers, thinly sliced
½ cup fresh or refreshed *wakame* (p. 37), thinly sliced
Dressing:
    3 tablespoons mayonnaise
    ½ cup walnut meats, mashed, ground, or minced
    2 tablespoons red, barley, or Hatcho miso
    1 tablespoon water
    Dash of pepper
6 pieces of buttered whole-grain toast

Combine the first three ingredients with the dressing; mix lightly. Spread in an even layer on the pieces of toast and serve immediately.

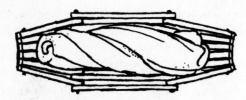

DEEP-FRIED TOFU IN SOUPS

Thin strips or bite-sized cubes of deep-fried tofu can add a tender, meaty texture and savory aroma to your favorite soups. Seasoning the soup with a small amount of miso or shoyu will often give it a delicious, distinguishing accent. Try broiling the tofu lightly before adding it to split pea, lentil, or tomato soups. Deep-fried tofu may also be substituted for regular tofu in most of the recipes beginning on page 117, or used in soymilk soups such as Creamy Corn (p. 207). Agé is also popular in Gôjiru (p. 74) and Kenchin-jiru (p. 120).

Onion Soup with Thick Agé

SERVES 4 OR 5

2 tablespoons oil
4 large or 6 medium onions, thinly sliced
10 ounces thick agé, ganmo, or agé, thinly sliced
1 tablespoon butter
¼ cup red miso (or 3 tablespoons shoyu) thinned in 1 to 2 cups warm water
2 ounces cheese, grated or diced

Heat a large casserole and coat with the oil. Add onions, cover, and simmer over lowest possible heat for 3½ hours, stirring the bottom once every 20 minutes. Add the thick agé, butter, and thinned miso; mix well. Allow to cool to room temperature, then refrigerate overnight. Add the cheese, bring just to a boil and, stirring constantly, simmer for 1 minute, or until cheese melts. Serve hot or, for a richer flavor, allow to cool to room temperature before serving. Or use as the basis for Baked Onion Soup (p. 165).

For variety, add 2 to 3 lightly beaten eggs and/or ½ cup thinly sliced lotus root 15 minutes before adding miso.

Thick Agé in Rich Kabocha Soup

SERVES 6

30 ounces *(kabocha)* pumpkin or winter squash, cut into 1-inch cubes
2½ cups water
10 ounces thick agé, ganmo, or agé, thinly sliced
¼ cup red or barley miso (or 3 tablespoons shoyu) thinned in 1 cup hot water
2 tablespoons butter

Bring the *kabocha* and 1 cup water to a boil in a large casserole or heavy pot. Reduce heat to low, cover, and simmer for 1 hour. Add tofu and 1½ cups water, and simmer for 1 hour more. Stir in thinned miso and butter and simmer for 10 minutes. Serve hot, or for a richer, sweeter flavor, allow to cool for 6 to 8 hours.

For an even meatier texture, use thick agé which has been frozen overnight and then thawed in warm water. Simmer ½ cup thinly sliced onions with the *kabocha*, and add 2 to 4 tablespoons sesame butter and a dash of pepper together with the butter.

Agé-Miso Soup with Wakame

SERVES 2 OR 3

This is one of Japan's favorite traditional ways of serving miso soup. The *wakame* supplies an abundance of calcium and other minerals, while the agé and miso supply protein and unsaturated oils. Requiring less than 3 minutes to prepare, this soup is particularly popular at breakfast, and is renowned for its fine aroma and flavor.

1¾ cups dashi (p. 39) or stock
¼ to 1/3 cup fresh or refreshed *wakame* (p. 37), cut into 1-inch lengths
1 to 2 ounces agé or ganmo, cut crosswise into thin strips
2 tablespoons red, barley, or Hatcho miso
1 tablespoon thinly sliced leeks or a dash of 7-spice red pepper

Bring dashi to a boil in a saucepan. Add *wakame* and agé and cook for 1 minute. Add miso creamed in a little of the hot broth and return just to the boil. Serve immediately, garnished with the leeks.

Thick Miso Soup with Onions and Agé

SERVES 2

1½ cups dashi (p. 39), stock, or water
1 onion, thinly sliced
2 ounces agé, ganmo, or thick agé, lightly broiled (p. 156) and cut into thin strips
2 tablespoons red, barley, or Hatcho miso
1 tablespoon minced parsley

Combine dashi and onion in a small saucepan and bring to a boil. Reduce heat to low, cover, and simmer for 10 minutes. Add agé, then the miso creamed with a little of the hot broth. Simmer for 1 minute more and serve garnished with parsley.

Although the Japanese almost always serve miso soup

piping hot, we find this dish to be just as tasty if served at room temperature or even chilled.

VARIATION

*Ozoni: This popular New Year's dish is prepared by adding *mochi* to any variety of miso soup. In the above recipe, use 2½ cups dashi and 3 tablespoons miso. Just before serving, add 3 cakes of *mochi* (each 2 by 2 by ½ inch) which have been broiled until they swell to twice their original size and are crisp and nicely browned. Serves 3.

Picnic Miso Soup with Agé   SERVES 3

3 tablespoons red, barley, or Hatcho miso
2 tablespoons bonita flakes or grated cheese
Dash of pepper (7-spice, red, or black)
1 to 2 ounces agé or ganmo, cut crosswise into thin strips
12 inches dry *wakame*, cut into 1-inch lengths; or 3 cakes of dried wheat gluten
2 to 3 tablespoons sliced leeks, minced chives, or minced parsley
2 cups hot or boiling water

Combine miso, bonita flakes, and pepper, mixing well, then shape into 3 balls. Skewer and broil each ball over a burner (as for Broiled Miso, p. 46) until it is well browned and fragrant. Place balls and the next three ingredients into a picnic container. Take the hot water in a thermos or heat water at the picnic site: To serve, divide all solid ingredients among 3 bowls, pour in the hot water, and mix until miso dissolves. Cover and allow to stand for several minutes before serving.

Other Ways of Serving Deep-fried Tofu in Miso Soups

In Japan, entire books and round-the-year calendars suggest hundreds of tasty ways to serve deep-fried tofu in miso soups. The following combinations containing deep-fried tofu appear on one such calendar. The first mentioned is the principal ingredient followed by its complements, the type of miso, and the garnish or seasoning. In the basic pattern for preparation, the fresh vegetables and deep-fried tofu are simmered together in dashi until the vegetables are just tender. The thinned miso is then added and the soup returned just to the boil before being served sprinkled with a garnish topping.

*Spring, Sunday morning: agé, chrysanthemum leaves, sweet white miso, slivered *yuzu* rind
*Spring, Tuesday evening: grilled tofu, agé, burdock root, red miso, grated gingerroot juice
*Spring, Thursday evening: *kampyo* (shaved dried gourd), agé, red miso, *fuki* buds *(fuki-no-to)*
*Spring, Friday morning: bracken or Osmund fern fronds, agé or ganmo, light-yellow miso, *sansho* pepper
*Summer, Sunday evening: tiny eggplants, agé, red miso, 7-spice red pepper

*Summer, Tuesday morning: snow peas, agé, sweet white miso and light-yellow miso, ground roasted sesame seeds
*Summer, Thursday evening: taro *(satoimo)*, agé, *shiitake* mushrooms, carrot, light-yellow miso, 7-spice red pepper
*Summer, Saturday morning: leeks, agé, red miso, *sansho* pepper
*Fall, Sunday morning: *hijiki*, thick agé, red miso, 7-spice red pepper
*Fall, Tuesday morning: cabbage, agé, light-yellow miso, pepper
*Fall, Wednesday morning: sweet potato, agé, light-yellow miso, pepper
*Fall, Friday morning: *kabocha*, fresh *shiitake* mushrooms, thick agé, red miso, beefsteak seeds *(shiso-no-mi)*
*Winter, Tuesday morning: small turnip, agé, red miso, hot mustard
*Winter, Wednesday morning: Chinese cabbage, agé, light-yellow miso, pepper

Noppei Soup *(Noppei-jiru)*   SERVES 3

This hearty vegetable soup is a traditional wintertime favorite in Japan's cold northwest provinces.

2 ounces agé, ganmo, or thick agé, cut into small rectangles
½ small carrot, cut into small rectangles
1 cup small rectangles of *daikon*
½ cake *konnyaku*, cut into small rectangles
3 *(shiitake)* mushrooms, thinly sliced
1½ cups half moons of sweet potatoes or taro
2 cups dashi (p. 39), stock, or water
5½ teaspoons shoyu
1 teaspoon salt
2 teaspoons sake
Dash of 7-spice red pepper (optional)
¼ cup slivered leeks

Combine all but the last two ingredients in a large pot or casserole and bring to a boil. Reduce heat to low, cover, and simmer for 30 minutes. Divide among 3 soup bowls and garnish with red pepper and leek.

For variety, simmer the agé in a mixture of dashi, shoyu, and sugar before combining it with the soup's other ingredients, or use grilled tofu in place of agé. This soup is also very tasty if it is allowed to cool for 4 to 6 hours before being served.

DEEP-FRIED TOFU IN BREAKFAST EGG DISHES

Use any variety of deep-fried tofu like bacon in your favorite egg dishes. Most Japanese tofu-and-egg preparations are lightly seasoned with a mixture of shoyu (or miso) and sugar. Or substitute diced deep-fried tofu for regular tofu in omelet recipes (p. 122).

Fried Eggs with Deep-fried Tofu

SERVES 2

2 tablespoons butter
2 eggs
5 ounces thick agé, ganmo, or agé, cut crosswise into very thin slices
¼ teaspoon salt or 1 teaspoon shoyu
Dash of pepper
1 tablespoon minced parsley (optional)

Melt the butter in a skillet. Break in the eggs and cover with tofu slices. Cover skillet, reduce heat to very low, and cook for 6 minutes. Season with salt and pepper, re-cover, and cook for 2 minutes more. Serve topped with a sprinkling of parsley.

For variety, butter-fry the tofu before breaking in the eggs.

Scrambled Eggs with Thick Agé and Onions

SERVES 3 OR 4

10 ounces thick agé or ganmo, cut into 1½-inch squares, each ½ inch thick
2 eggs, lighty beaten
½ onion, minced; or ½ cup chopped chives or wild onions
1 to 2 teaspoons shoyu
¼ teaspoon salt
1 tablespoon oil

Combine the first five ingredients, mixing lightly. Heat the oil in a large skillet. Pour in the egg-and-tofu mixture and scramble gently for 2 or 3 minutes, pressing tofu occasionally with back of spatula until each piece is golden brown and fragrant. Serve hot or cold.

Thick Agé & Scrambled Eggs with Mushrooms and Cheese

SERVES 2

5 ounces thick agé, ganmo, or agé, lightly broiled (p. 156) and cut into ½-inch cubes or thin slices
4 mushrooms, thinly sliced
1 tablespoon shoyu
1½ tablespoons natural sugar
1 tablespoon sake or *mirin* (optional)
2 eggs
3 tablespoons grated cheese or ¼ teaspoon *sansho* pepper

Combine the first five ingredients in a skillet and simmer, covered, for about 8 minutes. Break in the eggs and, stirring constantly, scramble until eggs are firm. Serve topped with the cheese or *sansho.*

If desired, sauté the mushrooms in butter before adding other ingredients. Or simmer the tofu and mushrooms in the sweetened shoyu broth used with Inari-zushi (p. 194), then add eggs after most of broth has been absorbed or evaporated.

Thick Agé Scrambled Eggs with Miso and Bonita Flakes

SERVES 3

2 eggs
2½ tablespoons red, barley, or Hatcho miso
1½ teaspoons bonita flakes
2 tablespoons minced onion
10 ounces thick agé or ganmo, cut into 1-inch squares, each ½ inch thick
4 teaspoons oil

Combine the first four ingredients, mixing until miso is well dissolved. Stir in the thick agé. Heat one-half the oil in a large skillet. Pour in one-half the egg-tofu mixture and scramble gently for 2 or 3 minutes, pressing tofu occasionally with back of spatula until each piece is golden brown and fragrant. Repeat with remaining oil and egg-tofu mixture. Serve hot or cold.

Swirled Eggs with Thick Agé and Onion

SERVES 3 OR 4

1½ cups dashi (p. 39) or stock
1 onion, thinly sliced
10 ounces thick agé or ganmo, cut into bite-sized pieces
3 tablespoons red, barley, or Hatcho miso; or 2 tablespoons shoyu
1½ tablespoons natural sugar
2 eggs, lightly beaten

Bring dashi to a boil in a small saucepan. Add onion, return to the boil, and simmer for 2 minutes. Add thick agé and return to the boil. Stir in miso (creamed in a little of the hot broth) and sugar, and return to the boil over high heat. Stir in eggs and remove immediately from heat. Serve hot or cold.

Poached Eggs with Deep-fried Tofu

SERVES 2

1 piece of thick agé, cut horizontally into 2 thin slices; 2 large ganmo patties; or 2 pieces of agé
1 teaspoon shoyu
2 eggs, poached
Dash of salt and pepper

Broil tofu lightly (p. 156), then sprinkle with shoyu. Serve topped with the poached eggs and seasoned with salt and pepper.

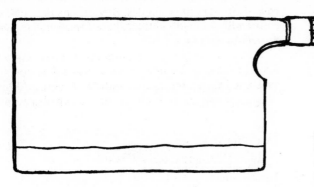

DEEP-FRIED TOFU BAKED

Diced or cut into thin strips, deep-fried tofu may be substituted for regular tofu in most baked preparations (p. 123). Ganmo and agé provide the chewiest, meatiest texture, while thick agé combines the soft tenderness of regular tofu with the savory deep-fried firmness of agé. To add extra flavor to your favorite baked dishes, simmer tofu cubes or slices in Sweetened Shoyu Broth (p. 40) for about 5 minutes before combining with your other ingredients.

Cheese-Onion Casserole with Thick Agé
SERVES 3 OR 4

3 tablespoons butter
3 tablespoons whole-wheat flour
1½ cups milk
1 to 1½ tablespoons red miso or 1 tablespoon shoyu
1 clove garlic, crushed
Dash of pepper
10 ounces thick agé or ganmo, cut into bite-sized pieces
½ cup grated cheese
1 onion, thinly sliced
1 carrot, grated
½ cup cracker or bread crumbs

Preheat oven to 350°. Melt butter in a skillet, stir in flour, and brown for about 1 minute. Stir in milk, reduce heat to low, and simmer for several minutes to form a thick sauce. Add miso, garlic, and pepper, mixing until miso is well dissolved. Add tofu, cheese, onions and carrot; turn off heat and mix thoroughly. Pour into a bread pan or casserole, sprinkle surface with cracker crumbs, and bake for about 25 minutes.

Baked Onion Soup with Thick Agé

Prepare Onion Soup with Thick Agé (p. 162). Place in a casserole and cover surface with large pieces of whole-wheat bread. Sprinkle liberally with grated cheese and bake in a moderate oven until cheese just begins to brown.

Or pour 2 or 3 lightly beaten eggs over the bread before adding cheese.

DEEP-FRIED TOFU SATUÉED, STIR-FRIED, OR TOPPED WITH SAUCES

Deep-fried tofu makes an excellent substitute for regular tofu in most tofu sauces (especially Sesame, Spaghetti, Onion-Curry, and Onion & Raisin White Sauce). It is also delicious topped with any of the Soymilk Sauces (p. 207) or Basic Sauces such as Onion, Gingerroot, Teriyaki, Sweet & Sour, or Tomato & Cheese (pp. 48-49).

Onion Sauce with Agé
SERVES 2 OR 3

1 1/3 cups Onion Sauce (p. 48)
3 ounces agé, ganmo, or thick agé, cut into small rectangles
1 tablespoon shoyu
¼ cup water
2½ ounces cheese, grated or finely diced
1 egg, lightly beaten

Combine Onion Sauce, agé, shoyu, and water in a casserole or heavy pot and, stirring constantly, bring just to a boil over medium heat. Now cover pot and simmer for 3 minutes. Add cheese and simmer, covered, for 10 minutes more. Mix in egg, increase heat to high and cook, stirring constantly, for 1 minute, or until egg becomes firm. Allow to cool for 5 to 6 hours, then serve as is or as a topping for brown rice or (soba) buckwheat noodles.

Or combine all ingredients in a casserole, sprinkle surface with cheese (and bread crumbs), and bake at 350° until nicely browned. Serve seasoned with sansho pepper.

Deep-fried Tofu with Barbeque Sauce
SERVES 4

10 ounces thick agé
7 ounces ganmo or agé, or substitute more thick agé
Sauce:
    2 tablespoons ketchup
    2 tablespoons shoyu
    1 tablespoon sake or white wine
    1 tablespoon melted butter
    ¼ small onion, diced
    1½ teaspoons sugar
    Dash of chili pepper or 7-spice red pepper
    ½ clove garlic, crushed

Heat an unoiled skillet and broil the thick agé and ganmo lightly on both sides until fragrant. Remove from pan and cut thick agé crosswise into 8 equal rectangles and ganmo into 12 equal wedges.

Combine all sauce ingredients in a small bowl; mix well. Mix sauce and tofu in the skillet and cook over medium heat for about 1 minute. Serve hot or cold.

Ganmo Sautéed with Green Pepper, Garlic, and Miso

SERVES 2

7 ounces ganmo, thick agé, or agé, cut into ½-inch strips
½ cup dashi (p. 39), stock, or water
3 tablespoons barley, red, or Hatcho miso
2 tablespoons natural sugar
2 teaspoons sake
2 tablespoons oil
1½ teaspoons crushed or minced garlic
5 green peppers, cut lengthwise into sixths
2/3 teaspoon shoyu

Combine ganmo, dashi, miso, sugar, and sake in a saucepan and bring to a boil. Cover and simmer for 5 minutes; set aside.

Heat a skillet or wok and coat with the oil. Add garlic and sauté for 1 minute. Increase heat to high, add green peppers and sauté for 1 minute more. Add ganmo, any remaining cooking liquid, and the shoyu. Stirring constantly, cook for 1 minute more. Serve hot or cold.

Apple & Onion Curry Sauce with Deep-fried Tofu

SERVES 3 OR 4

Any type of tofu may be used with excellent results in your favorite curry sauce. We like the tender yet meaty texture of deep-fried tofu in this richly-flavored preparation.

7½ ounces thick agé, ganmo, or agé, diced
1 apple, diced
2 potatoes, diced (1¾ cups)
1 cup water or stock
3 tablespoons butter
1 clove of garlic, crushed
1 teaspoon grated or 1½ teaspoons powdered gingerroot
1½ onions, minced
5 to 6 mushrooms, thinly sliced
1½ to 2 teaspoons curry powder
2 tablespoons whole-wheat flour
3 to 3½ tablespoons red miso or 2 tablespoons shoyu
1 tablespoon honey or natural sugar
2 tablespoons ketchup
Sambals: Sliced bananas, grated coconut, raisins, diced apples, peanuts or almonds, chopped hard-boiled eggs, and chutney

Combine the first four ingredients in a heavy pot or casserole and bring to a boil. Cover and simmer over low heat. Meanwhile melt the butter in a skillet. Add garlic and gingerroot, and sauté for 30 seconds. Add onions and mushrooms, and sauté for 5 to 6 minutes more. Mix in curry powder and flour, and cook, stirring constantly, for 1 minute. Cream miso with about 1/3 cup broth removed from the pot, then stir into the curried mixture together with the honey and ketchup to form a smooth, thick sauce. Now mix sauce into contents of pot, cover, and simmer for 20 to 30 minutes, stirring occasionally. Serve over brown rice or buckwheat noodles, topped with the *sambals.*

For a more elaborate sauce, add diced lotus root, cooked lentils, sweet potatoes, *kabocha*, or squash. To serve as an entrèe without grains, reduce the amounts of miso and curry powder by about one-fifth.

Thick Agé with Pineapple-Sweet & Sour Sauce

SERVES 4 TO 5

2 tablespoons oil
1 clove garlic, crushed or minced
1 small onion, thinly sliced
1 green pepper, cut into 1-inch squares
2 small tomatoes, diced; or 1 cup cherry tomatoes, cut into halves
Pineapple-Sweet & Sour Sauce:
    1¼ cups pineapple chunks, drained
    1½ tablespoons natural sugar
    3 tablespoons vinegar
    ½ cup water
    2 tablespoons shoyu or 3 tablespoons red miso
    2 tablespoons ketchup
    ½ teaspoon grated gingerroot or 1 teaspoon powdered ginger
    1 tablespoon cornstarch
7½ ounces thick agé, ganmo, or agé, cut into 1-inch cubes

Heat the oil in a large skillet or wok. Add garlic and onion and stir-fry over high heat, stirring constantly, for 2 minutes. Add green pepper, tomatoes and sauce ingredients, and cook, stirring contantly, for about 1 minute until thick. Mix in thick agé and remove from heat. Serve chilled. (To serve hot, increase amount of sugar and vinegar in sauce by 1 tablespoon each.)

Agé with Hijiki and Carrots

SERVES 5 TO 6

1 tablespoon oil
1/3 cup dried *hijiki*, reconstituted (p. 37)
2 ounces agé, ganmo, or thick agé, cut into thin strips
¼ small carrot, cut into matchsticks
4 teaspoons shoyu
4 teaspoons natural sugar or honey
¼ cup water
Dash of salt

Heat a skillet or wok and coat with the oil. Add all ingredients and sauté over low heat for about 15 minutes. Allow to cool or, for best flavor, chill for several hours before serving.

For a spicer taste, add 1 teaspoon grated gingerroot, ¼ to ½ cup diced lotus root, and 1 to 2 tablespoons ground roasted sesame seeds (p. 38) or sesame butter to the *hijiki*-agé mixture before sautéing. Or substitute ½ ounce dried-frozen tofu for 1 ounce agé.

Thick Agé with Zesty Steak Sauce

SERVES 2

1½ teaspoons butter
2 tablespoons finely chopped green onions
2 tablespoons ketchup
5 teaspoons Teriyaki Sauce (p. 48)
1 teaspoon mustard (optional)
Dash of black pepper
5 ounces thick agé, ganmo, or agé, cut into 1-inch cubes

Melt butter in a skillet. Add onions and sauté until tender. Stir in ketchup, Teriyaki Sauce, mustard, and pepper, and simmer for 1 minute. Arrange thick agé in bowls and top with the sauce. Serve hot or cold.

Sautéed Carrots with Agé, Wheat Germ, and Sunflower Seeds

SERVES 2

1 tablespoon oil
1 carrot, cut into matchsticks or thin rounds (1¾ cups)
3 ounces agé, ganmo, or thick agé
2 tablespoons water
3½ teaspoons shoyu or ½ teaspoon salt
2 or 3 tablespoons toasted wheat germ
2 or 3 tablespoons sunflower seeds or almonds

Heat a skillet and coat with the oil. Add carrots and sauté over high heat until just tender. Add next four ingredients, and reduce heat to low; cover and simmer for 4 to 5 more minutes. Remove from heat and mix in wheat germ and sunflower seeds. Serve hot or cold.

For variety, substitute 1¾ cups of 1-inch cubes of yam for the carrots. Serve with sunflower seeds or with wheat germ and walnuts.

Chinese-style Sweet & Sour Thick Agé

SERVES 4

2 tablespoons oil
½ carrot, cut into half moons
1 large onion, thinly sliced
½ small bamboo shoot (3 ounces), cut into half moons
5 mushrooms, cut into quarters
2 inches of lotus root, cut lengthwise into sixths
3 green peppers, cut lengthwise into sixths
15 ounces thick agé, ganmo, or agé, cut into ½-inch cubes
1½ tablespoons vinegar
3 tablespoons soy sauce
2 tablespoons sugar
1 tablespoon cornstarch dissolved in 3 tablespoons water

Heat a wok or skillet and coat with the oil. Add the vegetables consecutively, stir-frying each over high heat for about 1 minute. Mix in tofu, vinegar, soy sauce, and sugar, reduce heat to medium and cook, stirring constantly, for several minutes more. Stir in dissolved cornstarch and cook for 1 minute more. Serve hot or cold, as is, or as a topping for rice or (buckwheat) noodles.

Other Suggestions for Serving Deep-fried Tofu Sautéed

*Agé with Carrots and Burdock Root (Kinpira): Use 1½ cups each slivered carrots and burdock root, 1 tablespoon each sesame oil and salad oil, 2 ounces agé, ganmo, or thick agé cut into thin slices, 1 tablespoon shoyu and 2 tablespoons roasted sesame seeds. Sauté vegetables in oil over high heat for 5 minutes, or until almost tender. Add tofu and shoyu, reduce heat to medium, and sauté for 5 minutes more. Mix in sesame seeds and serve (hot or cold) seasoned with 7-spice red pepper.

*Tofu Sautéed with Vegetables: Sauté deep-fried tofu with any of the following: chard, spinach, Chinese cabbage or cabbage, wild greens or chrysanthemum leaves; green beans and almonds; winter squash or (kabocha) pumpkin. If desired, top with Ankake or Gingerroot Sauce (p. 49).

DEEP-FRIED TOFU DEEP-FRIED

Deep-frying chilled commercial thick agé, ganmo, or agé with any of the batters or coatings described on page 130 gives them a crisp texture similar to that of freshly deep-fried tofu. Try using deep-fried tofu in any of the recipes for deep-fried regular tofu.

Thick Agé Tempura with Miso Sauce

SERVES 2 OR 3

Orange-Sesame Miso Sauce:
  3 tablespoons barley, red, or Hatcho miso
  1 tablespoon sesame oil
  3 tablespoons boiling water
  ½ teaspoon grated orange rind
Oil for deep-frying
Tempura Batter (p. 134)
10 ounces thick agé or ganmo, cut into 1½-inch cubes

Combine all sauce ingredients in a small bowl; mix well. Heat oil to 350° in a wok, skillet, or deep-fryer. Dip tofu cubes in tempura batter and deep-fry until crisp and golden-brown (p. 130); drain briefly. Serve hot, topped with the sauce.

Breaded Thick Agé Cutlets

SERVES 2 OR 3

10 ounces thick agé, ganmo, or agé, frozen and thawed (p. 230) if desired
¼ cup flour
1 egg, lightly beaten
½ cup bread crumbs or bread crumb flakes
Oil for deep-frying
Worcestershire or Worcestershire-Ketchup Sauce (p. 49)

Dust uncut thick agé with flour, dip in eggs, and roll in bread crumbs. Place on a rack and allow to dry for 5 to 10 minutes.

Heat oil to 350° in a wok, skillet, or deep-fryer. Drop in tofu and deep-fry until golden brown (p. 130); drain briefly. Serve topped with the sauce.

Crispy Thick Agé in Miso Sauce

SERVES 3

6 tablespoons cornstarch or arrowroot
1 cup water
1 tablespoon oil
1 tablespoon red, barley, or Hatcho miso
1 tablespoon natural sugar
2 tablespoons sake or white wine
White of 1 egg
10 ounces thick agé or ganmo, cut into 1½-inch cubes
Oil for deep-frying
6 lettuce leaves

Mix the cornstarch and water in a bowl; allow to stand for 5 to 10 minutes until cornstarch settles and becomes firm. Meanwhile, heat the oil in a skillet. Add the miso and sugar, and sauté over medium heat for 2 or 3 minutes. Mix in the sake, cook for 1 minute more, and remove from heat.

Carefully pour off water from cornstarch. Mix egg white with cornstarch in bowl, then add thick agé cubes, mixing until each cube is covered with batter. Heat the oil to 350° in a wok, skillet, or deep-fryer. Slide in the tofu cubes and deep-fry until crisp and golden brown (p. 130); drain.

Reheat miso sauce, stir in the deep-fried tofu and cook for 1 minute. Serve in individual bowls, mounded on the lettuce leaves.

DEEP-FRIED TOFU WITH GRAINS

Combining soy and grain proteins gives a substantial increase in the total protein content of each of these preparations, as explained on page 25. Deep-fried tofu mixed with sauces (Sweet & Sour, Curry, Spaghetti, etc.) makes delicious toppings for brown rice, noodles, or other cooked grain dishes. Try also using deep-fried tofu in Chop Suey or Chow Mein (p. 67), or in grain salads (pp. 111 and 158).

Fried Buckwheat Noodles with Deep-fried Tofu (Yaki-soba)

SERVES 3 OR 4

2 tablespoons oil (used tempura oil is excellent)
1 clove garlic, crushed or minced (optional)
½ cup slivered carrot
1 small onion, thinly sliced
1 green pepper, diced
2 thinly sliced mushrooms or ½ cup thin rounds of lotus root
¼ cup raisins
3½ ounces ganmo, agé, or thick agé, thinly sliced
4½ to 5 ounces (soba) buckwheat noodles, cooked (p. 50)
1 tablespoon shoyu or ½ teaspoon salt
3 tablespoons ketchup (optional)
½ teaspoon salt
4 Paper-thin Omelets (p. 51), cut into thin strips; or substitute ¼ cup diced cheese
Crumbled toasted nori

Heat a wok or skillet and coat with the oil. Add the next six ingredients and sauté for about 4 minutes. Add ganmo and sauté for 1 minute more. Add the next four ingredients and cook, stirring constantly, for 1 minute more. Divide among deep bowls and top with the omelet strips and nori. Serve hot or, for a richer flavor, allow to stand for 4 to 6 hours before serving.

For variety, add 2 lightly beaten eggs together with the shoyu. Add ¼ to ½ cup thinly sliced lotus root, snow peas or Chinese cabbage together with the mushrooms. Season with curry powder or black pepper. Serve topped with ¼ cup roasted soybeans or peanuts or Sweet Simmered Miso (p. 41). Serve in Agé Pouches (p. 192) or Inari-zushi Pouches (p. 194).

Sizzling Rice with Deep-fried Tofu (Chahan or Yaki-meshi)

SERVES 3 OR 4

This recipe may also serve as a simple and delicious way of using leftover vegetables.

2 tablespoons oil
1 or 2 cloves of garlic, crushed or minced
1 small onion, diced; or ¼ cup minced chives or nira
5 to 10 ounces thick agé, ganmo, or agé, cut into bite-sized pieces
2 to 4 eggs, lightly beaten
2 cups cooked Brown Rice (p. 50)
2 to 3 tablespoons ketchup (optional)
2½ teaspoons shoyu
½ teaspoon salt
Dash of pepper
2 Paper-thin Omelets (p. 51), cut into thin strips (optional)
¼ cup crumbled toasted nori

Heat the oil over high heat in a wok or skillet. Add garlic and stir-fry for 1 minute. Reduce heat to medium-high, add onion, and stir-fry for 3 minutes. Add thick agé and stir-fry for 2 minutes more. Add egg and cook, stirring occasionally, for about 1 minute until egg becomes firm and bubbly. Mix in rice and stir-fry for 1½ to 2 minutes more, using spatula to cut egg into small pieces. (If using a wok, hold the wok handles and flip the cooking foods into the air 3 or 4 times to create a drier texture.) Mix in the ketchup, shoyu, salt, and pepper and sauté for 2 to 3 minutes more. Transfer to serving bowls, top with a sprinkling of the omelet strips and nori, and serve hot or cold.

VARIATIONS

*Add ¼ to ½ cup of any of the following chopped vegetables together with the onion: green peppers, green or snow peas, fresh corn, celery, bamboo shoots, Chinese cabbage, or takuan pickles. Add 3 (shiitake) mushrooms together with the thick agé.
*Serve topped with a dab of Sweet Simmered Miso (p. 41) or miso pickles.
*Serve on buttered toast or in Agé Pouches (p. 192).

Curried Buckwheat Noodles with Thick Agé

SERVES 4 TO 6

2 tablespoons oil (used tempura oil is excellent)
1 carrot, sliced into thin rounds
1 onion, thinly sliced
1/3 cup raisins
½ apple, diced
¼ cup water
1½ teaspoons curry powder
1 teaspoon salt
2 teaspoons shoyu or 1 tablespoon red or barley miso
10 ounces thick agé or ganmo, cut into thin 1-inch squares
4½ to 5 ounces buckwheat noodles, cooked (p. 50)
Dash of pepper
¼ cup roasted soybeans or peanuts (optional)
¼ cup diced or grated cheese (optional)
¼ cup chutney (optional)

Heat the oil over high heat in a skillet or wok. Add carrots and stir-fry for 2 minutes. Add onions and stir-fry for 2 minutes more. Add raisins and apple and stir-fry for 3 minutes. Stir in water, curry powder, salt, shoyu, and thick agé; reduce heat to medium and cook for 3 minutes. Stir in noodles, season with pepper, and remove from heat. Serve hot or cold. If desired, top with roasted soybeans, peanuts, cheese, and/or chutney.

Crumbly Agé Soboro with Brown Rice

SERVES 4

Soboro refers to dishes which have the texture of sautéed hamburger.

5 ounces agé, ganmo, or thick agé, doused (p. 156) and diced fine (and, if desired, ground in a meat grinder or *suribachi*)
1 cup dashi (p. 39), stock, or water
2 tablespoons shoyu
1½ tablespoons natural sugar
2 tablespoons sake
2 teaspoons minced gingerroot
1½ cups brown rice, cooked (p. 50)
1 tablespoon roasted sesame seeds (p. 38)
1 tablespoon minced parsley
1½ tablespoons diced red pickled gingerroot (beni shoga) (optional)

Combine the first six ingredients in a small saucepan and bring to a boil. Reduce heat to low and simmer for 5 to 6 minutes. Stirring constantly with 4 or 5 chopsticks held in the fist of one hand, simmer until all liquid has been absorbed or evaporated.

Divide hot brown rice among large individual bowls, top with the *soboro*, and serve garnished with sesame, parsley, and gingerroot.

Soboro may also be served as an entrèe.

Five-color Sushi Rice with Agé (Maze-gohan or Gomoku-zushi)

SERVES 3

This dish is served each year during Japan's week-long spring and autumn equinox celebrations. Known also as *Kayaku Gohan*, it is a close relative of *Chirashi-zushi* which is served at *sushi* shops and generally contains fish. Since the weeks of the equinox are considered sacred seasons, fish is traditionally omitted.

½ cup water
1½ tablespoons shoyu
2 tablespoons natural sugar
4 (shiitake) mushrooms, thinly sliced
½ carrot, cut into matchsticks
2 ounces agé, ganmo, or thick agé, thinly sliced
1 green pepper, thinly sliced
2 tablespoons ground roasted sesame seeds (p. 38) (optional)
1½ cups Sushi Rice (p. 50; made from 2/3 cup raw brown rice)
2 Paper-thin Omelets (p. 51), cut into thin strips
¼ cup crumbled toasted *nori*
12 to 15 snow peas, parboiled (p. 37)
2 to 4 tablespoons diced trefoil (optional)

Combine water, shoyu, and sugar in a small saucepan and bring to a boil. Add mushrooms, carrots, and agé, cover pan, and simmer for about 5 minutes. Increase heat to medium and simmer, stirring constantly, for 3 to 5 minutes more, or until all liquid has been absorbed or evaporated. Set aside and allow to cool.

Combine cooked vegetables, green pepper, sesame, and rice in a large wooden salad bowl or sushi tray; mix well. Sprinkle with the omelet strips, *nori*, snow peas, and trefoil; place at the center of the dining table.

Substitute or add any of the following to the cooked vegetables: green beans or peas, lotus root, bamboo shoots, or *kampyo*. Four ounces of lotus root may also be simmered separately in a mixture of 1½ tablespoons vinegar, 1 tablespoon sugar, and ½ teaspoon salt. Or add sliced cucumber or *udo* which has been marinated in equal parts vinegar and sugar. Other toppings include slivered red pickled gingerroot or parsley. Serve in Agé Pouches (p. 192) or Inari-zushi Pouches (p. 194).

Chinese-style Thick Agé and Bean Sprouts

SERVES 2

2 tablespoons oil
1½ teaspoons crushed or minced garlic
2 cups bean sprouts
¼ cup thinly sliced chives, *nira*, or green onions
5 ounces thick agé, ganmo, or agé, cut into 1-inch cubes
1 teaspoon grated gingerroot
1 teaspoon sake or white wine
¾ teaspoon salt
3 tablespoons soy sauce
½ teaspoon cornstarch or arrowroot, dissolved in 2 table-spoons water

Heat a skillet and coat with the oil. Add garlic and sprouts and stir-fry over high heat for about 1 minute. Mix in chives and agé and stir-fry for 1 minute more. Reduce heat to medium, stir in gingerroot, sake, salt, and soy sauce and sauté briefly. Mix in dissolved cornstarch and cook for 1 minute more. Serve hot.

VARIATIONS

*Omit the garlic and chives. Sauté the sprouts in 1 tablespoon sesame oil. Add the tofu together with ¼ cup water, 1 teaspoon vinegar, 4 teaspoons each soy sauce and sugar, and ¾ teaspoon grated gingerroot. Simmer for 5 minutes, then stir in 1 teaspoon cornstarch dissolved in 1 tablespoon water.

Crisp Tortillas with Taco Sauce and Deep-fried Tofu

SERVES 5

Taco Sauce:
    2/3 cup ketchup
    1¼ cups grated cheese
    2 tablespoons red miso
    2 tablespoons minced onion or leek
    1 teaspoon grated gingerroot
    1 teaspoon sake or white wine
    Dash of tabasco sauce or pepper
    1 tablespoon water
2½ cups shredded lettuce or cabbage
15 ounces thick agé, ganmo, or agé, thinly sliced
10 seven-inch *tortillas*
Butter

Place taco sauce, lettuce, and tofu in separate serving bowls. Heat *tortillas* in a medium oven for 5 to 7 minutes until lightly browned and crisp, then butter immediately and arrange on a large serving platter. Invite each guest to spread *tortillas* with sauce, sprinkle with lettuce, and top with sliced tofu.

    Or, use Mushroom Sauce (p. 48) in place of the taco sauce.

Deep-fried Tofu Gruel with Leftovers

Combine plenty of deep-fried tofu with leftover cooked grains and vegetables. Add enough leftover soup, stock, or water to give the consistency of a thick stew; bring to a boil and simmer for 5 to 10 minutes. Add shoyu or creamed miso and, if desired, curry powder or ketchup to unify the flavors. To thicken, stir in lightly roasted whole-wheat or barley flour and cook for several minutes more. Serve hot or cold. To use leftover gruel as the basis for full-bodied breads, knead in flour to earlobe consistency, allow to rise overnight, and bake in a slow oven for several hours.

Thick Agé with Gingerroot Miso

SERVES 2 OR 3

1½ tablespoons oil
10 ounces thick agé, ganmo, or agé, cut into ½-inch-thick, bite-sized rectangles
2 tablespoons red, barley, or Hatcho miso
2 to 2½ tablespoons natural sugar
1 teaspoon grated gingerroot
Minced parsley or lettuce leaves

Heat a skillet or wok and coat with the oil. Add thick agé and sauté over high heat for 3 to 4 minutes until slightly crisp and well browned. Add miso, sugar, and gingerroot, and cook, stirring constantly, for about 2 minutes more, or until all ingredients are well mixed. Serve hot or cold, garnished with parsley or placed on individual lettuce leaves.

Nori-wrapped Sushi with Agé (*Norimaki-zushi*)

SERVES 3 OR 4

3½ tablespoons vinegar
2 tablespoons natural sugar
3 ounces agé, ganmo, or thick agé, doused (p. 156)
3 sheets of *nori*
3½ cups Sushi Rice (p. 50)
½ cucumber, cut into long, 1/8-inch-square strips
3 tablespoons shoyu

Combine vinegar and sugar in a small saucepan and bring to a boil. Add agé, cover pan, and reduce heat to low; simmer for 3 to 4 minutes. Uncover pan and simmer over medium heat, stirring constantly, until all liquid evaporates. Set aside to cool, then cut agé lengthwise into very thin strips.

Place 1 sheet of *nori* on a *sudare* or small dry dishcloth. Spread one-third of the rice evenly over the *nori*, leaving a 1-inch-wide strip uncovered along the far edge (fig. 57). Place one-third of the agé and cucumber strips in a row about 2 inches from the near edge of the *nori*. Now roll up *nori* and moisten edge of *nori* with water to seal. With a sharp knife, cut the roll crosswise into 10 small discs. (Wipe knife with a moist cloth to prevent sticking.) Repeat with remaining ingredients until all are used. Serve the shoyu in small dishes for dipping.

For variety, add or substitute for the cucumber: thin strips of Paper-thin Omelets (p. 51), Walnut Miso (p. 42), or slivered walnuts simmered in a mixture of honey, shoyu, and sugar; *kampyo* or *hijiki* simmered in Sweetened Shoyu Broth (p. 40).

Fig. 57. Making Nori-wrapped Sushi with Agé

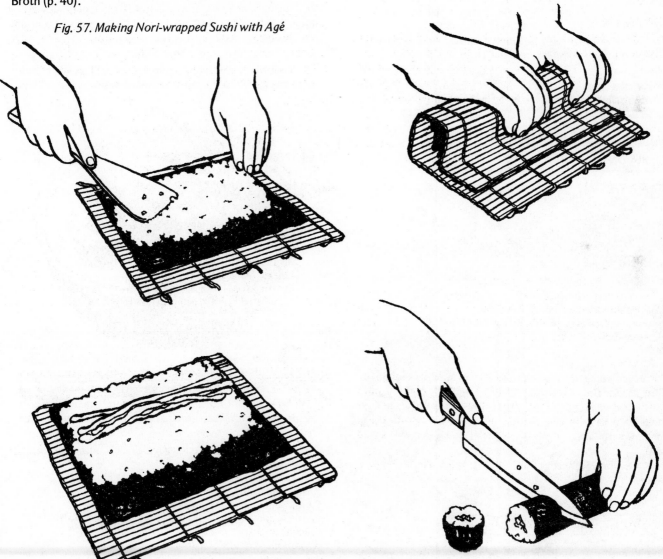

Fox Domburi (Kitsune Domburi)

SERVES 4

This and the following dish are named after foxes which, in Japan, are said to be very fond of agé. A *domburi* is a deep serving bowl, usually heaped high with rice. Fox Domburi is one of the most popular dishes served in the many thousands of *soba* shops throughout Japan.

1 cup water, stock, or dashi (p. 39)
3 tablespoons shoyu
3 tablespoons natural sugar
1 tablespoon *mirin* (optional)
4 ounces agé, ganmo, or thick agé, cut into ½-inch-wide strips
1 onion, thinly sliced
1 cup brown rice, cooked (p. 50)
Dash of *sansho* pepper (optional)

Combine the first four ingredients in a saucepan and bring to a boil. Add agé and onion, then simmer for 7 minutes. Divide cooked rice among bowls and pour on hot broth, onions, and agé. Serve seasoned with the pepper.

If desired, top with crumbled toasted *nori* or slivers of Sweet Vinegared Gingerroot (p. 51).

Fox Noodles (Kitsune Soba or Udon)

SERVES 3

3 pieces of agé or ganmo, doused (p. 156) and each cut into 4 equal triangles or diagonal ½-inch-wide strips
1 cup dashi (p. 39), stock, or water
1½ to 2 tablespoons natural sugar
1 tablespoon shoyu
2 teaspoons *mirin* (optional)
Dash of salt
2¼ cups Noodle Broth (p. 40)
1 onion, cut into very thin wedges
4½ ounces *soba* or *udon* noodles, cooked (p. 50) and drained
7-spice red pepper

Combine the first six ingredients in a small saucepan and bring to a boil. Reduce heat to low and simmer uncovered, stirring occasionally, until all liquid has been absorbed or evaporated.

Meanwhile, combine Noodle Broth and onion in a large pot and bring to a boil. Add cooked noodles and agé and return to the boil. Serve in deep bowls, inviting each person to season his portion to taste with red pepper.

Buckwheat Noodles with Grated Glutinous Yam and Agé (Yamakake Soba)

SERVES 3

4½ ounces *(soba)* buckwheat noodles, cooked (p. 50)
2¼ cups Noodle Broth (p. 40)
Grated Glutinous Yam with Agé (p. 174)

Divide the cooked noodles among 6 deep bowls. Pour in the hot broth and top with the yam-and-agé. Serve hot or cold.

Noodles & Deep-fried Tofu in Chilled Broth (Hiyashi-soba)

SERVES 4 TO 6

A popular summertime recipe in both China and Japan, *Hiyahsi-soba* is often prepared with slivers of ham rather than ganmo.

6 to 7 ounces *(soba)* buckwheat noodles, cooked (p. 50) and doused with cold water
7 ounces ganmo, thick agé, or agé, slivered
½ cucumber, slivered
½ tomato, cut into thin wedges
4 Paper-thin Omelets (p. 51), slivered
Broth:
    2/3 cup dashi (p. 39) or stock
    2½ tablespoons shoyu
    3 tablespoons vinegar
    ½ teaspoon sesame oil
    Dash of 7-spice red pepper
    ¼ cup slivered leeks, rinsed and pressed (p. 37)
Crumbled toasted *nori* (p. 38) (optional)

Place the first five ingredients in separate bowls, cover, and chill. Bring the dashi to a boil in a saucepan. Add shoyu and return just to the boil. Remove from heat and allow to cool. Stir in remaining broth ingredients, cover, and chill.

To serve, mound noodles on individual plates or in bowls. Arrange tofu, cucumber, tomato, and omelet slivers in equal portions atop each serving. Pour on the chilled broth and, if desired, top with a sprinkling of *nori*.

Eating noodles in old Japan (from Hokusai's sketchbooks)

Ganmo Simmered with Homemade Noodles and Miso *(Nikomi Udon)*

SERVES 6

This dish is a favorite in the village of Uehara, which is renowned for its many vigorous centenarians. They claim the key to their long life is eating unrefined barley and vegetables, little or no animal foods, and plenty of miso. In this nutritious dish, the water in which the noodles are cooked is not discarded but is used as the basis for a thick miso sauce that closely resembles a Western white sauce. For best flavor, allow this dish to stand overnight so that the noodles further contribute to the thickening of the sauce. Then serve either cold or reheated.

2 cups flour, half of which is whole-wheat
8½ cups warm water
¼ teaspoon salt
6 tablespoons sweet white miso
5 tablespoons red or barley miso
10½ ounces ganmo, thick agé, or agé, cut into bite-sized pieces
3 large leeks, cut diagonally into 2-inch lengths
1½ small leeks or green onions, cut into thin rounds
7-spice red pepper
Crumbled toasted *nori* (optional)

Put the 2 cups flour into a large bowl and, adding ½ cup water a little at a time, mix and knead to form a heavy dough. Roll out dough on a floured board to 1/8-inch thickness, sprinkle surface lightly with flour, and fold lengthwise accordion fashion into quarters (fig. 58). Now cut crosswise into 1/8-inch-wide strands to make noodles. Spread noodle strips on the floured board to dry briefly.

Bring remaining 8 cups water to a boil in a large pot. Drop in noodles and salt, and simmer until noodles float to surface. Cream the miso with a little of the hot cooking water and add to the pot. Add ganmo and large leeks and simmer for 10 minutes. Serve garnished with thin rounds of leeks, red pepper, and *nori.*

Use about 10 ounces dried noodles in place of the homemade variety.

Deep-fried Tofu with Tabbouli *(Lebanese Grain Salad)*

SERVES 4

¾ cup raw bulgur wheat
2 2/3 cup boiling water
10 ounces thick agé, agé, or ganmo, diced; or 24 ounces regular tofu, crumbled (p. 98)
½ cup minced mint
1 cup minced parsley
½ cup minced scallions
2 tomatoes, diced
3 tablespoons olive oil
6 tablespoons lemon juice
1 teaspoon salt
1 clove of garlic, crushed
Dash of pepper
4 large lettuce or (Chinese) cabbage leaves

Combine bulgur and boiling water in a saucepan, cover, and allow to stand for 2 hours. Drain bulgur, press between the palms to expel excess water, then mix with all remaining ingredients except the lettuce. Chill for 1 hour. Serve mounded on the lettuce leaves.

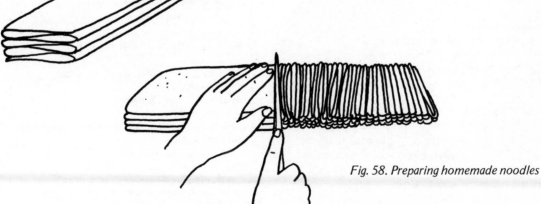

Fig. 58. Preparing homemade noodles

DEEP-FRIED TOFU BROILED

Try using your favorite barbeque sauces with deep-fried tofu. When cooked over a bed of live coals, the tofu develops a delicately crisp texture and savory barbequed aroma.

Grilled Thick Agé with Korean Barbeque Sauce
SERVES 2

5 ounces thick agé, ganmo, or agé
¼ cup Korean Barbeque Sauce (p. 49)

Broil the tofu over a barbeque fire, in an oven broiler, or in a hot unoiled skillet (p. 156). Remove from heat and cut cross-wise into 6 equal pieces. Dip briefly in the sauce and broil lightly once again. Serve in bowls, topped with the remaining sauce.

Savory Thick Agé with Broiled Miso
SERVES 1 OR 2

5 ounces thick agé, ganmo, or agé
1½ to 3 teaspoons red, barley, or Sweet Simmered Miso (p. 41)

Pierce thick agé from one end with a large fork or 2 chopsticks. Holding tofu just above a strong flame (or use an oven broiler), broil quickly on both sides until lightly browned. Spread both sides of the tofu with a thin layer of miso and re-broil for about 15 seconds per side, or until miso is fragrant and speckled. Cut tofu into bite-sized pieces and serve immediately.

Or cut thick agé or ganmo crosswise into fourths, skewer, and prepare as for Tofu Dengaku (p. 139); use Egg Yolk Miso (p. 43) or any variety of Sweet Simmered Miso for the topping. If using agé, spread one surface of each piece with miso, then roll from one end to form a tight cylinder. Insert skewers from the side, fastening the roll; broil (fig. 100, p. 245).

Agé Mock Broiled Eels
(Kabayaki or Yaki-Shinoda)
SERVES 4

2 tablespoons shoyu
2 tablespoons natural sugar
2 green peppers, cut lengthwise into quarters
1 tablespoon oil
8 ounces agé, ganmo, or thick agé, cut into bite-sized triangles
Dash of *sansho* pepper

Combine shoyu and sugar in a small bowl for use as a dipping sauce. Brush peppers lightly with the oil. Place peppers and tofu over a charcoal brazier or barbeque, or in an oven broiler, and grill on both sides until lightly browned and fragrant. Set peppers aside. Dip tofu into sauce, then broil again lightly and sprinkle with the pepper. Serve tofu and peppers on small plates accompanied by the remaining dipping sauce.

Thick Agé Shish Kebab
SERVES 4

Ingredients for skewering: (Use four or more)
    5 ounces thick agé or ganmo, cut into bite-sized cubes
    4 green peppers, cut into 2-inch triangles
    8 mushrooms
    1 apple, cut into bite-sized chunks or rounds
    8 chunks of firm pineapple
    4 firm small tomatoes
    4 small blanched onions
    1 celery stalk or cucumber, cut into bite-sized sections
2/3 cup Teriyaki Sauce (p. 48)

Place basic ingredients in a shallow pan and pour on sauce. Marinate for 1 hour, turning ingredients serveral times. Skewer pieces on 4 to 8 skewers and broil for 2 to 3 minutes, basting occasionally, until nicely speckled and fragrant.

VARIATIONS

*Broil tofu without basting. Substitute ½ teaspoon grated gingerroot and/or 2 teaspoons grated *daikon* for the sugar in the dipping sauce. Serve broiled tofu accompanied by sauce garnished with thinly sliced leeks (or scallions) and 7-spice red pepper.
*While broiling, baste tofu with a mixture of 2 tablespoons shoyu and 1½ teaspoons *mirin*. Serve garnished with a mixture of ¼ cup grated *daikon* and ½ teaspoon grated gingerroot.

DEEP-FRIED TOFU SIMMERED
IN SEASONED BROTHS

Deep-fried tofu absorbs simmering liquids or broths best if first doused (p. 156). Avoid simmering for too long, lest a chewy, web-like structure and many small bubbles form in the tofu. Most of these dishes attain their peak of flavor if served 4, or as much as 48, hours after they have been prepared. During this time they should be allowed to stand in the remaining broth, covered and refrigerated. If thick agé is frozen overnight, then thawed in warm water, it develops a very absorbent texture somewhat like tender meat (p. 230) and makes an excellent replacement for regular thick agé in most of the following recipes, or for regular tofu in Sukiyaki (p. 224) and other *nabe* preparations.

Grated Glutinous Yam with Agé
SERVES 3

1 2/3 cups dashi (p. 39), stock, or water
4 tablespoons shoyu
2 tablespoons natural sugar
1 tablespoon *mirin*
4 ounces agé, ganmo, or thick agé, doused (p. 156) and cut into thin strips
1 cup grated glutinous yam
3 eggs
¼ cup thinly sliced rounds of leek or scallion
Dash of 7-spice red pepper or *sansho* pepper
Crumbled toasted *nori*

In a saucepan combine the dashi, 2 tablespoons shoyu, sugar and *mirin*, and bring to a boil. Add agé and reduce heat to low. Cover pan and simmer for 10 minutes, then transfer agé from pan and allow agé to cool separately.

Stir 1½ tablespoons shoyu into cooled broth. Divide the grated yam among 3 deep bowls and break an egg into each. Top with the agé and seasoned broth, and garnish with leeks, pepper, and *nori*. Invite each guest to beat the ingredients together with chopsticks or fork before eating.

This dish also makes a delicious topping for buckwheat noodles or brown rice. Or use in Yamakake Soba (p. 172).

Deep-fried Potatoes & Thick Agé in Seasoned Broth

SERVES 6

Oil for deep-frying
7 small potatoes, quartered
2 cups water or dashi (p. 39)
5 tablespoons shoyu
5½ tablespoons natural sugar
10 ounces thick agé, ganmo, or agé, cut into 1-inch cubes

Heat the oil to 350° in a wok, skillet, or deep-fryer. Drop in the potatoes and deep-fry until golden brown (p. 130); drain well.

Combine water, shoyu, and sugar in a saucepan and bring to a boil. Add potatoes, cover pan, and simmer for 30 minutes. Add thick agé, return to the boil, and remove from heat. Cover pan and allow to stand for 6 to 8 hours. Serve cold.

Deep-fried Tofu Simmered in Seasoned Broth

SERVES 2

5 ounces thick agé, ganmo, or agé, cut into bite-sized pieces
Basic Seasoned Broth:
   ½ cup water, stock, or dashi (p. 39)
   1½ tablespoons shoyu or 2 tablespoons red miso
   1 to 1½ tablespoons natural sugar
   1½ teaspoons sake or white wine (optional)

Combine all ingredients in a small saucepan and bring to a boil. Reduce heat to low and simmer for about 10 minutes, then set aside to cool. Divide thick agé and broth among serving bowls. Garnish with a sprig of *kinome*, a dab of grated gingerroot or mustard, or a dash of *sansho* pepper.

VARIATIONS
*Agé Simmered with Vegetables: In the basic broth simmer 2 ounces agé, ganmo, or thick agé cut into small rectangles and 2 cups of any of the following vegetables cubed or diced: *kabocha*, sweet potatoes, small yams or taro, celery, butterbur, bracken ferns, or green beans. Prepare as above and serve cold, sprinkled with ground roasted sesame seeds or sesame salt.
*Ganmo Treasure Balls with Snow Peas: In the basic seasoned broth above simmer 2 Homemade Ganmo Treasure Balls (p.

188) or 3 ounces agé and 4 to 5 ounces (1½ cups) snow peas. Serve chilled. Use deep lacquerware bowls for greater aesthetic effect.
*Thick Agé Sandwiches: Cut a 5-ounce cake of thick agé horizontally into halves and simmer in the seasoned broth as above. Place each half on a plate, cover with a slice of cheese and mound with sautéed onions, carrots, green beans, and burdock root. Serve like open-faced sandwiches.
*Mother's Favorite (Ofukuro no aji): In the basic seasoned broth, simmer bite-sized pieces of thick agé, ganmo, lotus root, *daikon*, carrot, and *konnyaku*. Meanwhile prepare finely diced green beans, burdock root, and carrots; mix with thick tempura batter and deep-fry as for Kaki-agé (p. 136). Arrange deep-fried patties in deep bowls with the simmered tofu and vegetables. Serve topped with a little of the seasoned broth.

Agé Simmered with Shredded Dried Daikon

SERVES 4 TO 6

1½ cups (2½ ounces) shredded dried *daikon (kiriboshi)*
2 ounces agé, ganmo, or thick agé, cut lengthwise into halves, then crosswise into ½-inch-wide strips
3 tablespoons natural sugar or honey
2 tablespoons shoyu
1 tablespoon sake or white wine

Pour 1½ cups water into a large bowl. Rinse *daikon* quickly in the water, then press *daikon* lightly between the palms of both hands so that water is returned to the bowl. Rinse and press 3 more times. Combine *daikon* and 1 cup of the pressing water in a small saucepan. Cover and simmer over low heat for about 40 minutes, or until *daikon* is quite soft. Mix in the agé, sugar, shoyu, and sake; cover and simmer for about 30 minutes more, stirring well every 10 minutes. Set aside uncovered and allow to cool to room temperature before serving.

Deep-fried Tofu in Western-style Stews

All three varieties of deep-fried tofu make excellent additions to your favorite stews, as well as tasty meat substitutes. Try using deep-fried tofu in place of regular tofu in Tofu-Miso Stew (p. 145). To give the stew a meatier flavor, season with miso or shoyu. Use lightly roasted whole-wheat or barley flower as a thickener. Add curry powder or ketchup, if desired, to help marry the various flavors.

Oden (Japanese Stew)

SERVES 4 TO 8

When October nights grow chilly, Oden carts become a familiar and welcome sight along Tokyo's streets. Each old-fashioned wooden stall, mounted on two bicycle wheels, is equipped with a gaslight lantern illuminating a compact, self-contained kitchen. Two pans of foods simmering in a fragrant, dark broth are heated by a small charcoal brazier. Large bottles of shoyu, sake, and water stand ready to replenish the steaming bubbling liquid, and a knife and pair of long chopsticks are kept busy serving the many customers who gather around this little oasis of warmth for a quick night meal or snack. Here you can find tofu and deep-fried tofu of all types simmering together with as many as twenty other different foods. In nearby suburban neighborhoods, the "Oden man" roams the night streets at dinnertime, pulling his cart behind him and ringing his familiar bell. Stopping at homes when someone hails him from the doorway, he provides one of Japan's oldest ready-made meals and leaves a wake of savory aromas floating in the cold air behind him as he goes on his way (fig. 59).

Fig. 59. The "Oden man"

Throughout Japan, huge red papper lanterns hung outside the doorway of working class taverns and bars bear the name Oden in bold jet-black brushstroke letters. Each evening throughout the year—but especially during the cold months—steaming hot Oden is served inside as the favorite accompaniment to hot sake. And in fine Kyoto Oden shops such as *Takocho* (p. 308) or Kyoto-style shops in Tokyo such as *Otako* (p. 312), Oden is served in an atmosphere of quiet refinement. Seated at high, square stools along a simple but elegant counter made of thick, unfinished wood, each customer orders his favorite items from the wide selection of ingredients cooking in a brightly polished one-by-three-foot copper tray located just behind the counter. As the guest refreshingly wipes hands and face with a hot, damp towel, the cheery, white-clad shopkeepers whisk his order onto a small plate, cut the tofu, *daikon*, or potatoes into smaller pieces with quick strokes of a razor-sharp knife, pour a little of the hot broth over the food, add a dab of mustard, and place the dish before the guest with no time lost. As the evening progresses, the shopkeeper keeps a running tally of what was ordered on an inconspicuous card behind the counter. Each item has its own, very reasonable price.

In Japanese farmhouses, Oden is one of the most ancient and most popular forms of *nabe* cookery. Prepared in a heavy iron pot hung over the coals of the living-room open-

hearth fireplace (fig. 69, p. 186), the Oden is simmered slowly and leisurely, which allows fullest development of its fine flavors.

The name Oden is an abbreviation of *Nikomi Dengaku* or "Dengaku simmered in seasoned broth." Tofu Dengaku (p. 139) was originally made of grilled tofu topped with a layer of miso. After about 1750, *konnyaku* began to be prepared in somewhat the same way. At a later stage, instead of being broiled, the *konnyaku* was cut into large triangles and simmered in a broth seasoned with miso. Gradually other ingredients such as potatoes, *daikon* and various types of fish sausage were added to the stew, and the miso was replaced by a topping of tangy hot mustard.

The name Oden seems to have first been used in a well-known play called *Keian Taiheki*, written about 1850. In it, one character says, "It looks like they're enjoying Nikomi Oden with their sake." Oden itself originated in the Tokyo area where it was generally served together with hot sake in working class and lower class bars. The broth was quite dark and richly seasoned with shoyu and *mirin* or sugar; the ingredients were simmered for many hours until they turned a deep amber. As Oden spread to then more aristocratic Kyoto area, it underwent some basic transformations. Served as a high-class food in fine shops, it contained a much wider variety of ingredients. The relatively light-colored broth was conservatively seasoned with pale (*usukuchi*) shoyu, salt, and sake. After the great earthquake of 1923, the new Kyoto style was brought back to Tokyo where it now co-exists with its lower-class, but none the less delicious, progenitor as well as an increasingly popular blend of the two styles.

Oden's ingredients, broth, and manner of preparation are closely related to Nishime (p. 178), except than Oden is a cold weather dish usually served hot with plenty of broth and various toppings and seasonings. Using a pressure cooker, both dishes can be prepared in about 20 minutes. Like Nishime, Oden is very delicious if allowed to stand overnight and then served cold or reheated the next day. In the following recipe, the basic ingredients are listed in order of popularity in Japan.

Broth:
> 5 cups dashi (p. 39), stock, or water
> 7 to 8 tablespoons shoyu
> 2 to 3 tablespoons natural sugar
> 1½ tablespoons sake or white wine (optional)

Basic Ingredients: choose about 8
> 10 inches of *kombu*, wiped clean with a damp cloth and cut crosswise into 2-inch-wide strips
> 1 cake of *konnyaku*, cut into 4 triangles
> 3 to 4 small potatoes, cut into quarters or halves
> 5 to 10 ounces regular or frozen thick agé, cubed; or thick agé cubes
> 4 to 8 small taro, cut into halves
> 5 to 6 ounces lotus root, cut into half moons
> 12 ounces *daikon*, peeled and cut into ½-inch-thick half moons
> 2 large ganmo patties, quartered; 4 ganmo treasure balls (p. 188) or 8 small ganmo balls
> 4 hard-boiled eggs, peeled
> 4 Kinchaku Agé Pouches (p. 196)
> 12 ounces tofu, grilled tofu, or kinugoshi, quartered
> 4 cabbage rolls (see below)
> 4 *kombu* rolls (see below)
> 4 agé rolls (see Shinoda Maki, p. 197)
> 4 *konnyaku* noodle bundles (see below)
> 4 prepared skewers (see below)
> 1 carrot, cut into large irregular chunks
> 4 rolls of *Oharagi* yuba (p. 241)
> 10 ounces bamboo shoots, cut into large irregular pieces
> 2 sweet potatoes, quartered
> 2 turnips, quartered

Seasonings:
> 2 teaspoons hot mustard
> 4 tablespoons thinly sliced leek or scallion
> Dash of 7-spice red pepper

Pour dashi into a large pot or casserole. Tie 4 of the *kombu* strips into simple overhand knots, and arrange remaining *kombu* pieces over bottom of pot. Chose about 7 more basic ingredients from the list. Arrange those which require the longest cooking *(daikon, konnyaku)* atop *kombu* and bring dashi to a boil over high heat. Reduce heat to low and simmer for 10 minutes. Add remaining uncooked vegetables (potatoes, taro, lotus root) and simmer for 10 minutes more. Stir in shoyu, sugar, and sake, then add tofu ingredients. Return broth to the boil, then reduce heat to very low and cover pot. Simmer for at least 40 to 60 minutes, lifting pot and shaking it gently every 20 minutes to mix broth. Do not change the order of layering. For best flavor, allow Oden to stand for at least 6 to 8 hours, then serve reheated or as is. Divide the ingredients and broth among individual serving bowls and invite each guest to top his portion to taste with mustard and, if desired, other seasonings.

TO MAKE:

Cabbage Rolls: Dip a large cabbage leaf into boiling water until pliable. On the concave surface place 2 to 4 tablespoons of any of the following: diced or slivered onions, carrots, lotus root, *shiitake* or cloud-ear mushrooms (fresh or sautéed); cooked transparent or rice flour noodles, or yuba.

Roll the cabbage leaf from one end, tucking in the sides, then tie with a piece of *kampyo* which has been soaked for a few minutes in water until pliable.

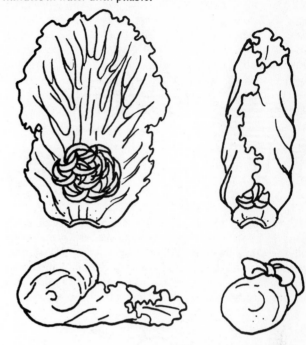

Kombu Rolls: Refresh a large piece of *kombu* until pliable by soaking in water, then cut into a piece about 6 inches square. Cut eight 6-inch-long strips of carrot, burdock, lotus root, or butterbur and arrange in a bundle at the center of *kombu*. Roll up cut vegetables in the *kombu*, tie in 4 places with refreshed *kampyo*, and cut crosswise to form 4 rolls about 1½ inches long.

Konnyaku Noodle Bundles: Wrap about 10 *konnyaku* noodles around the tips of 2 fingers, then tie in the center with a single *konnyaku* noodle.

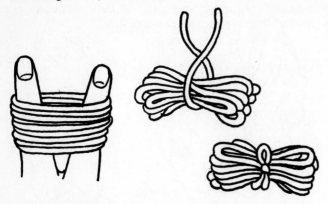

Prepared Skewers: Skewer 4 ginkgo nuts or green beans on a foodpick or small bamboo skewer. Or make tiny balls or dumplings of glutinous rice flour or wheat flour kneaded with a little water, and skewer. Or mix grated lotus root and grated carrot with a little whole-wheat flour and salt; deep-fry, and skewer alternately with brussel sprouts.

Other Ingredients: Additional ingredients may include dried wheat gluten cakes, tempura, eggplants, deep-fried fresh wheat gluten or any of the following commonly used sea foods: fish sausage *(tsumire, hanpen, satsuma agé, chikuwa, kamaboko)*, octopus or squid, *sakura* shrimp, or shark marrow *(suji)*. Alternative seasonings include: grated gingerroot, grated orange peel, or a few drops of *yuzu* juice.

Fig. 60. Making konnyaku "twists"

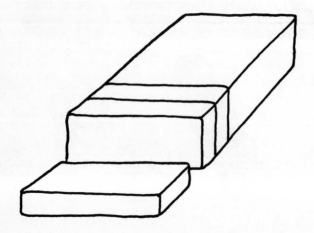

Nishime

A popular dish at equinox rituals or ceremonial occasions and national holidays, *Nishime* is also frequently included in picnic box lunches as a special treat. At New Year's, grilled tofu is generally used in place of or together with the usual deep-fried tofu. Enough *Osechi* (New Year's) *Nishime* is made on the last day of the "old year" to last throughout the following week of festivities, and the flavor is said to improve with each passing day.

Many recipes include only 3 or 4 of the vegetables listed below, so omit or substitute according to what is available. Adjust the amount of cooking liquid accordingly. Some cooks prefer to cook each of the ingredients separately for a different length of time in a broth seasoned to match the food's unique character. Each cooked ingredient is allowed to marinate overnight in its own broth, but is served without broth in a bowl together with all the other ingredients.

If Nishime is simmered in a relatively small amount of broth until all is absorbed and a soft luster forms on each ingredient, the dish is called *Uma-ni.* If the vegetables are first cooked in unseasoned dashi, to be seasoned toward the end of the cooking and served with a large amount of broth, the dish is called *Fukume-ni.* All three of these types of popular *Ni-mono,* or "foods simmered in seasoned broths," include tofu.

3 cups dashi (p. 39), stock, or water
7 tablespoons shoyu
7 to 9 tablespoons natural sugar or *mirin*
3 tablespoons sake or white wine
½ teaspoon salt
1 cake of *k̓onnyaku,* cut crosswise into ¼-inch-thick pieces
1 carrot, cut into large random chunks
½ burdock root, cut lengthwise into halves, then into 1½-inch lengths and parboiled for 10 minutes
1 large taro or potato, cut into eighths
2 inches *daikon,* cut into half moons
½ lotus root, cut into half moons
8 inches *kombu,* wiped clean with a moist cloth and cut crosswise into 1-inch-wide strips
1 small bamboo shoot, cut into large random chunks
3 *(shiitake)* mushrooms, cut into quarters
10½ ounces ganmo (patties or small balls), thick agé, or agé, doused (p. 156) and cut into bite-sized pieces
10 ounces grilled tofu, cut into large triangles (optional)
8 sprigs of *kinome*

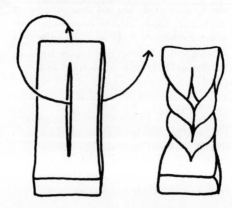

Combine the first five ingredients in a large pot or casserole and bring to a boil. Meanwhile, cut a slit lengthwise down the center of each small piece of *konnyaku* and thread one end up through the slit and back again (fig. 60). Add *konnyaku* and next 8 ingredients to the broth, and return to the boil. Reduce heat to low, cover pot, and simmer for about 40 minutes. Add tofu, stir vegetables so that uppermost ones are transferred to bottom of pot, re-cover, and continue simmering until all but about ¾ cup of broth has been absorbed or evaporated. Remove from heat and allow to cool for at least 5, preferably 24 hours. Divide ingredients among individual serving bowls, pour on remaining liquid, and garnish with a sprig of *kinome*.

For variety, add or substitute a small amount of frozen-, or dried-frozen tofu, or frozen thick agé.

DEEP-FRIED TOFU DESSERTS

In these tasty treats, the combination of apples and agé makes healthful and satisfying desserts. Other treats using agé pouches are found beginning on page 196.

Cooked Apples with Agé and Tofu Whipped Cream

SERVES 4

---

3 apples, cut into thin wedges
¼ cup raisins
1 cup water
1½ tablespoons natural sugar
2 ounces agé, ganmo, or thick agé, cut into small triangles
¼ teaspoon cinnamon
12 ounces tofu made into Tofu Whipped Cream (p. 148)

Combine 2 apples, raisins, water, and sugar in a pressure cooker. Bring to full pressure, reduce heat to low, and cook for 15 minutes. Remove from heat and let stand under pressure for 10 minutes. Add tofu and remaining apple, and simmer uncovered over low heat for 15 minutes more. Sprinkle with cinnamon and allow to cool. Serve topped with Tofu Whipped Cream.

Cooked Apples with Agé and Creamy Topping

SERVES 3 TO 4

---

2 apples, thinly sliced
1½ tablespoons natural sugar
2 ounces agé, cut crosswise into fourths
¼ cup water
¼ teaspoon cinnamon
Soymilk Thick Sweet Cream (p. 206)

Combine the first four ingredients in a small saucepan and simmer until apples are just tender and most of the liquid has evaporated. Allow to cool, then sprinkle with cinnamon and serve topped with soymilk cream.

For variety, add 1 to 2 teaspoons lemon juice before cooking.

Thick Agé
(Deep-fried Tofu Cutlets)

IN JAPAN thick agé, whole deep-fried cakes of tofu, are referred to both as *nama-agé*, meaning "fresh or raw deep-fried tofu," and as *atsu-agé*, meaning "thick deep-fried tofu." Both names are used interchangeably, and the former is used frequently in the United States. The word "thick" is used to contrast thick agé with agé and ganmo, which are usually made in fairly thin sheets or patties, while the words "fresh" or "raw" refer to the fact that only the surface of the tofu cake is affected by the quick deep-frying in very hot oil; the center remains almost as tender and soft as firmly-pressed regular tofu.

Of the many and varied types of Japanese and Chinese tofu, we feel that thick agé is perhaps the best suited to Western tastes and cuisine. We use more thick agé in our daily cookery than any other type of tofu. It is unique in combining the softness and substantial quality of regular tofu with the crisp firmness and deep-bodied flavor and aroma acquired from deep-frying. Costing no more on a protein basis than regular tofu, it keeps its form better during cooking and tossing in salads, and works better in casseroles and most other baked dishes due to its lower water content and tender, meaty texture. It is also easier to transport, maintains freshness longer and, due to its lower water content, absorbs seasoned broths and other flavors more readily than regular tofu. When frozen, it becomes more porous and tender than ganmo or agé and is therefore particularly delicious in sauces, stews, and sautéed vegetable preparations.

In most parts of Japan, thick agé is prepared from whole, 12-ounce cakes of regular tofu. (In some cases, day-old tofu is used.) The cakes are arranged on bamboo mats placed on top of large boards. Several layers of boards, mats, and tofu are combined to form a sort of "sandwich" that is placed (with one end raised) on a barrel and topped with two buckets filled with water (fig. 61). The tofu is pressed for 20 to 40 minutes in order to reduce its water content and make it suitable for deep-frying. The firm, individual cakes are then dropped into high-temperature oil and deep-fried (without batter) for several minutes until crisp and golden brown (fig. 62). The resulting thick agé contains all of the protein from the original 12 ounces of tofu, but now weighs only 5¼ ounces (44% of its original weight) and is slightly reduced in size.

All of the thick agé in Japan, like its Chinese predecessor, was originally made in triangular form. It is said that Tokyo craftsmen first changed to rectangular pieces because they were easier to prepare and to cut into cubes. However, in the Kyoto area, most thick agé is still sold in the original design and is called "three-cornered agé" (*sankaku-agé*). These triangles, as thick as the rectangular variety, have sides which range from 2 to 3½ inches in length. In most semi-traditional or modern tofu shops, 20 to 30 triangles are arranged on each of several large screen trays during deep-frying (fig. 63).

In both Tokyo and Kyoto, many shops also cut pressed cakes of regular tofu into fourths—each piece being about 2 by 1½ by 1½ inches—then deep-fry these to make "agé cubes" (*kaku-agé*). Sometimes these cubes are only 1 inch on a side and, when that small, are excellent for use in soups or as hors d'oeuvre.

Fig. 61. Pressing tofu for thick agé

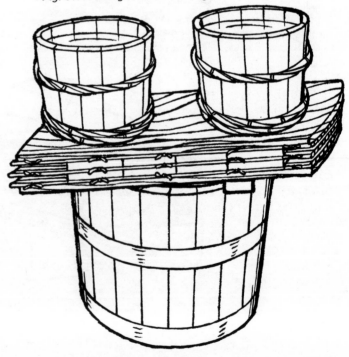

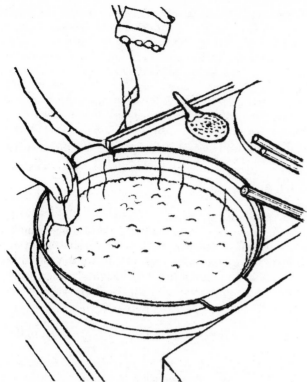

Fig. 62. Deep-frying tofu for thick agé

A fourth and rarer type of thick agé, called "five-color agé" (*gomoku-agé*), contains ingredients such as green peas, sesame seeds, minced carrots, burdock root, mushrooms, *kombu*, or *hijiki*. These are stirred gently into the soymilk curds just before the curds are ladled into the settling boxes. After this tofu is pressed and deep-fried, it has a unique flavor and texture somewhat resembling that of ganmo.

In Taiwan and China, where ganmo and agé are rarely if ever seen, most of the deep-fried tofu is made from very firm Chinese-style Pressed Tofu (p. 251) and sold as triangles each 2 inches on a side and 3/8 inch thick (see Chapter 15). In some areas small cubes of thick agé are eaten as a snack served with maple syrup or honey.

In Western-style cookery, thick agé is particularly delicious cooked whole, grilled, broiled, or barbequed like a steak. If you have a small charcoal brazier, try preparing the tofu indoors. Connoisseurs say it tastes best if the surface is lightly scored during cooking, then sprinkled with shoyu and served sizzling hot as an hors d'oeuvre.

In traditional Japanese cuisine, thick agé is most commonly used in *nabe* dishes, where it is simmered with a variety of vegetables in a seasoned broth. Thick agé triangles are always found in Oden, Japan's favorite wintertime potpourri, and are the most commonly used variety of tofu in the popular Nishime (p. 178). Thick agé holds its shape well even after many hours of simmering, adds its own fine flavor to the cooking broth, and absorbs and retains the flavors of each of the many other ingredients with which it is cooked. It will absorb flavors even better if first doused with boiling water to remove excess surface oil.

In the United States at present, thick agé is available at many stores that sell regular tofu. The Japanese-style cakes are golden-brown and about 3 by 2 by 1 inch in size. From 3 to 8 cakes are generally sold in a small polyethylene tub covered with an airtight seal of transparent film. Chinese-style thick agé cubes are sold by the dozen in sealed plastic bags.

Most of the recipes in this book using thick agé are included in the previous section. The few recipes that follow are those in which thick agé is used in unique ways and cannot be replaced by ganmo or agé.

Fig. 63. Deep-fried thick agé triangles on screen trays

Homemade Thick Agé

SERVES 2 TO 4

Use fresh or day-old regular tofu. Tofu that is just beginning to spoil is rendered fresh and tasty by deep-frying. When short on time, pat the tofu with a dry dishtowel instead of pressing it to remove excess surface moisture. A 12-ounce cake of tofu usually weighs about 5¼ ounces after pressing and deep-frying. Consequently, the protein content by weight increases from 7.8 to about 15 percent.

2 cakes of tofu (12 ounces each), pressed (p. 96)
Oil for deep-frying

Heat the oil to 375° in a wok, skillet, or deep-fryer (p. 130). Carefully slide in both cakes of tofu. Deep-fry for about 2½ to 3 minutes, or until tofu is floating on surface of oil. Stir occasionally to prevent tofu from sticking to pan. Turn tofu over and deep-fry for 30 seconds more, or until crisp and golden brown. Drain on a wire rack for several minutes, then pat dry with absorbent paper. For best flavor, serve immediately, topped with a few drops of shoyu and garnished with grated gingerroot (or *daikon*) and thinly sliced leek or scallion rounds. Or serve as for Crisp Deep-fried Tofu (p. 156).

To store, allow to cool, then refrigerate in an airtight cellophane bag.

VARIATIONS

Thick-Agé Triangles or Cubes: After pressing, cut each cake of tofu diagonally into halves or into 4 equal cubes before deep-frying. Serve hot with shoyu, honey, or maple syrup. Or simmer with vegetables in *nabe* cookery or Sweetened Shoyu Broth (p. 40).
Five-Colored Deep-fried Tofu: Prepare any of the various types of Five-Colored Tofu (p. 105). Cut into 12-ounce cakes, press, and deep-fry. Serve immediately with shoyu and desired garnish, or simmer with vegetables in Sweetened Shoyu Broth (p. 40).

Chinese-style Thick-Agé Net: Press a 12-ounce cake of tofu until very firm. Score the tofu diagonally to half its depth about 6 to 8 times (fig. 109, p. 254). Turn cake over and score other side in exactly the same way. Holding the tofu with one hand at each end, gently pull and twist the two ends to open the cuts slightly into a coarse net. Now deep-fry the tofu as above. After deep-frying, recut each of the original cuts with a knife. Simmer the entire cake of deep-fried tofu with vegetables in Sweetened Shoyu Broth (p. 40) or use in place of thick agé in any of the recipes on pages 156 to 179.

Thick Agé Pouches

These pouches are an excellent substitute for regular agé pouches which are difficult to prepare at home and are not yet widely available in the West. They can be filled with cooked grains, vegetables, eggs, or noodles and served like luncheon sandwiches. Or they may be coated with batter and deep-fried, or simmered in Sweetened Shoyu Broth (p. 40). Start with either homemade or storebought thick agé.

To make *two pouches,* cut a (4- by 3- by 1-inch) piece of thick agé crosswise into halves. Carefully spoon out most of the soft white tofu inside each half and reserve for use in other cooking. Use the hollow pouches in recipes calling for Agé Pouches (p. 192).

To make *one large pouch,* cut a 1/8-inch-thick slice from one end of a piece of thick agé, then spoon out the tofu.

Stuffed Thick Agé Triangles

SERVES 2 TO 4

This preparation is similar to Stuffed Agé Pouches (p. 192), except that the soft tofu scooped from within the thick agé is mixed with other ingredients and used as a filling. Any of the fillings used with agé pouches may also be used with thick agé cut and hollowed out this way.

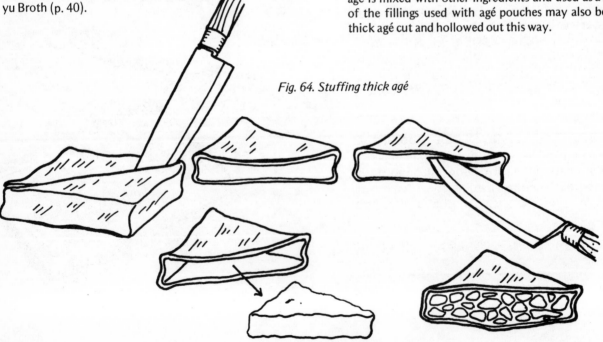

Fig. 64. Stuffing thick agé

2 cakes of thick agé (5 ounces each), lightly broiled (p. 156)
and cut diagonally into halves
2 hard-boiled eggs, minced
¼ cup mayonnaise
2 tablespoons minced onion
1 tablespoon red, barley, or Hatcho miso
Dash of pepper

Cut the thick agé halves as shown in fig. 64; using a knife or two fingers, cut or scoop out the soft white tofu from the deep-fried covering. Combine this soft tofu with remaining ingredients and mash well, then use mashed mixture to stuff the 4 triangular pouches.

Homemade Frozen Thick Agé

When we freeze thick agé, we transform its internal structure. Like frozen tofu, it becomes highly absorbent and acquires a firm texture similar to that of tender meat or gluten meat. Reconstituted, frozen thick agé may be cut into cubes or thin slices and then deep-fried like Frozen Tofu Cutlets (p. 232). Or it may be substituted for regular thick agé in dishes simmered in seasoned broths (pp. 174 to 179).

Frozen Thick Agé Cutlets   SERVES 4 TO 6

18 ounces thick agé, frozen (p. 230), reconstituted (p. 229), and cut crosswise into ½-inch-thick strips
6 tablespoons flour
2 eggs, lightly beaten
½ cup bread crumbs or bread crumb flakes
Oil for deep-frying
Salt
Lemon wedges or Tofu Tartare Sauce (p. 109)

Dust tofu strips with flour, dip into beaten egg, and roll in bread crumbs; place on a rack and allow to stand for 10 minutes. Heat oil to 350° in a wok, skillet, or deep-fryer. Slide tofu into oil and deep-fry until crisp and golden brown (p. 130). Serve sprinkled with salt and garnished with lemon wedges.

VARIATIONS

*Omit salt and serve with shoyu, topped with a small mound of grated gingerroot or a few drops of lime or lemon juice
*Substitute 9 ounces thick agé or frozen thick agé for the tofu in Frozen Tofu Cutlets (p. 232).

Crisp and Crunchy Thick Agé Cubes   SERVES 2 TO 4

Cut 9 ounces thick agé into 1½-inch cubes. Roll each cube in *kuzu* (or, for a less crisp texture, substitute arrowroot powder); deep-fry and serve as for Frozen Thick-Agé Cutlets (see above).

Thick Agé Stuffed with Onions   SERVES 2 TO 4
(Horoku-yaki)

2 cakes of thick agé (5 ounces each), cut diagonally into halves
¼ onion, thinly sliced
1 teaspoon oil
3/8 cup White Nerimiso, Rich Red Nerimiso or Yuzu Miso (p. 42)
Dash of *sansho* pepper

Cut a deep slit from end to end of the cut surface of each piece of thick agé (fig. 65). Open this slit to form a pouch and stuff with the sliced onion. Heat a skillet and coat with the oil. Sauté the thick agé on both sides for 3 minutes, or until fragrant. Serve topped with the miso and seasoned with the *sansho* pepper. Or top with shoyu and grated *daikon* or gingerroot.

Fig. 65. Thick Agé Stuffed with Onions

Ganmo
(Deep-fried Tofu Burgers)

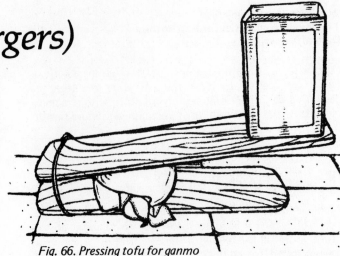

A T DAITOKU-JI, one of the great, centuries-old temples in Kyoto, an entire ceiling is covered with the monochromatic, writhing coils of a Chinese dragon. Portrayed with spiky whiskers and sharp horns, it races through a dark sky among swirling clouds. Two thick, whip-like whiskers stream back from flaring nostrils along its long snout. In one scaly claw, this fierce creature clutches the precious wish-fulfilling gem of Complete Perfect Enlightenment. Zen masters say that the awakening to one's true nature is like the shock of seeing the True Dragon.

The Zen dragon of enlightenment also appears in the world of tofu. Each morning in shops throughout Japan, the tofu maker's wife places all tofu remaining from the previous day into a coarse-weave sack, twists the sack's mouth closed, and presses the tofu between two boards arranged like a kind of nutcracker (fig. 66). After several hours, during which time all excess moisture has been expelled, she mixes sesame seeds and finely-slivered vegetables into the tofu (fig. 67), then kneads the mixture in a large basin or bowl as if she were kneading bread. Finally she kneads in a little grated glutinous yam and, sometimes, salt. After shaping the mixture into burger-sized patties or 2-inch balls, she deep-fries them, first in moderate and then in hot oil, until they

Fig. 66. Pressing tofu for ganmo

puff up and turn golden brown (fig. 68). For some reason, deep-frying causes the slivered vegetables to stick out helter-skelter from the surface of the tofu. Seeing this, the Japanese are reminded of the terrifying Chinese sky dragons with their bristling whiskers and spiky horns. Thus, in the Kyoto area, the unassuming little balls or patties are commonly given the awesome name "Flying Dragon's Heads" (*Hiryozu*).

Fig. 68. Deep-frying ganmo

Fig. 67. Adding seeds and vegetables

The method for preparing deep-fried tofu is thought to have originated in Buddhist temples and monasteries about 500 years ago. At that time, the rarest, most expensive, and most sought-after food of the nobility was wild goose (*gan*). The story is told that when these freshly deep-fried tofu creations were first served to the monks, they praised their flavor as surely being equal to that of the finest wild goose. As a result, in all parts of Japan (except Kyoto) these patties are still most frequently known as *gan-modoki*, or simply *ganmo*, which means "mock goose."

Although most scholars believe that ganmo were first developed by the Japanese, there are several other interesting theories concerning their origin. The first suggests that they were an adaptation of the Portuguese skewered meatballs (called *hirosu*) which became popular in Japan during the 15th century. Since the Japanese word *gan* can mean "ball" as well as "goose," and since the names *hirosu* and *hiryozu* are very similar and are still used interchangeably to refer to Kyoto's round ganmo, this theory seems quite plausible. The second theory suggests that ganmo were first developed by the Chinese, who still prepare a similar type of homemade deep-fried tofu containing ground meat instead of minced vegetables. This tofu, however, is not available in most Chinese or Taiwanese tofu shops.

In the Tokyo area, and throughout most of Japan (except Kyoto), ganmo are prepared in the shape of patties ranging from 3½ to 5 inches in diameter. A typical patty weighs 3½ ounces, about the same as a good-sized hamburger. The flavor and chewy texture of ganmo are also quite similar to those of hamburger. Only the price is different: in 1975 one thick patty cost only 19 cents. Indeed, ganmo makes an excellent replacement for meat in hefty, Western-style cheeseburgers and hamburgers; who, we wonder, will be the first to start a chain of ganmo-burger restaurants?

Probably the most famous ganmo in Japan are the Ganmo Treasure Balls prepared at the Morika tofu shop and others in the Kyoto area. Each 2-inch-diameter ball contains seven different vegetable ingredients including ginkgo nuts and lilly bulb sections. These delicacies are a popular ingredient in the *nabe* dishes served at many of Kyoto's finest restaurants.

Most tofu shops presently use only two or three vegetable ingredients in ganmo, the favorites being grated carrots, slivered *kombu*, and burdock root. Many shops, in addition to patties or balls, also prepare Small Ganmo Balls which swell up to no larger than 1½ inches in diameter and are often served stuffed with minced vegetables and nuts. Some shops prepare firm ganmo ovals containing a large proportion of varied ingredients; these are sometimes said to be Japan's earliest form of ganmo. To please children and for use in one-pot cookery and Dengaku, the tofu craftsman will occasionally use a cookie cutter to make ganmo in the shape of tiny gourds, flowers, or maple leaves.

Each year as the weather turns cold, ganmo makes its appearance in various *nabe* dishes. Since earliest times, the Japanese have believed in heating the body, not the house. The methods they use for doing so, developed out of necessity in a country where fuel and other energy resources have always been scarce, could serve as practical models for ecological living in generations to come. Able to absorb and retain heat unusually well, tofu, and especially deep-fried tofu, is served in the winter as much for its ability to warm the body as to please the palate.

Beginning in about November, Japanese homemakers bring out their earthenware, casserole-shaped *nabe* (pronounced nah-bay; p. 176). A good *nabe* may be many generations old, and is usually rustically beautiful, simple, and rugged. Its heavy lid fits snugly down inside the pot's lips to prevent boiling over—a necessary precaution when cooking over wood fires. The earliest Japanese *nabe*—still found in many farmhouses—was a heavy iron pot that hung suspended from a large overhead hook above an open-hearth fireplace located at the center of the main room of the house (fig. 69). During the long winter months, when the thick straw roofs of the farmhouses were heaped with snow, the small fire or bed of live coals and the bubbling *nabe* became a center of warmth and brightness. Since the rest of the house was dark and cold, the family gathered around the *nabe* while its steam danced and delicious aromas curled into the cold night air. Here one could feel that ancient and primitive magic of conviviality. We moderns, children of the electric lightbulb and central heating, easily forget that for most of man's several million years on this planet, he has cooked over wood fires and had no other source of light and heat at his table. This was not fire from slender white candles or a flame neatly contained in the glass chimney of a kerosene lamp. Rather, it crackled, spit sparks, and sent smoke up into the dark, arching roofbeams. The *nabe* and the many fine deep-fried tofu dishes associated with it were developed during this earlier age.

Today, the context has changed. The *nabe* has acquired a sense of elegance that makes it the featured dish in many of Japan's finest restaurants. Set over a portable burner at the family dining table, it is associated with celebration: holding a large family reunion, welcoming an old friend or an honored guest, or even bringing home the monthly paycheck. Yet the *nabe* and tofu—and especially ganmo—have maintained their centuries-old association. Because they serve as the focus of an atmosphere filled with good cheer, they are always warmly welcomed. Best known and most widely used in Oden (p.175), ganmo is indeed one of Japan's favorite wintertime foods.

Ganmo also makes an excellent addition to many Western-style dishes. It combines the substantial quality of thick agé with the firm and meaty texture of agé pouches. Lower in water content than thick agé, it stays fresh longer and therefore is ideal for use on picnics and short hiking trips. Ganmo patties, cut into small cubes and seasoned with a miso topping, make very tasty hors d'oeuvre, while small ganmo balls make a creative addition to vegetarian shish kebab. If you have tried making soyburgers and were disappointed to find that they were heavy and hard to keep from falling apart, try preparing homemade ganmo patties instead.

Ganmo is made by relatively few tofu shops in America today. However, since it can be prepared easily at home from regular tofu and your choice of nuts, seeds, and minced vegetables, anyone can enjoy this special treat served fresh and crisp, at its peak of flavor.

Fig. 69. A farmhouse open-hearth fireplace with nabe kettle

Homemade Ganmo

MAKES 8 PATTIES OR 12 BALLS

Ganmo can be prepared quite easily at home. Experiment with different combinations of ingredients to suit your taste. The various vegetables, nuts, and seeds used should comprise about 15 to 20 percent of the total volume of the ganmo mixture. In tofu shops, ganmo is usually deep-fried, first in low or moderate oil and then in hot oil, and contains grated glutinous yam as a binding agent. Ganmo balls seem to hold together better than large patties and, having a smaller surface area, they absorb less oil during deep-frying. Patties are better for use in Ganmo Burgers (p. 188).

30 ounces tofu, squeezed (p. 97)
2 tablespoons grated carrots
2 tablespoons diced onions, scallions, leeks, or gingerroot
2 tablespoons slivered or diced mushrooms
2 tablespoons green peas (use only with ganmo balls)
2 tablespoons sunflower seeds, peanuts or chopped nut meats
2 tablespoons roasted sesame or poppy seeds, whole or ground
2 tablespoons raisins
¾ teaspoon salt
Oil for deep-frying

Combine the first eight ingredients in a large shallow bowl; mix well. Knead the mixture for about 3 minutes, as if kneading bread. Add the salt and knead for 3 minutes more until "dough" is smooth and holds together.

Fill a wok, skillet, or deep-fryer with 2 to 2½ inches of oil and heat to 300° (p. 130). Moisten your palms with a little oil or warm water and shape the dough into 8 patties 3 to 3½ inches in diameter or 12 balls about 1½ inches in diameter. Deep-fry patties or balls for 4 to 6 minutes, or until they float high in the oil. Turn patties over and deep-fry for several minutes more until crisp and golden brown; drain ganmo on a wire rack or absorbent paper. Serve sprinkled with a little shoyu as Crisp Deep-Fried Tofu (p. 156), or in any of the ganmo recipes in Chapter 9.

Fig. 70. Preparing homemade ganmo

Refrigerated in an airtight container, ganmo will keep for up to 1 week; frozen, it will last indefinitely.

VARIATIONS

*When preparing large patties, add 1½ tablespoons grated glutinous yam or lightly beaten egg to the ganmo mixture to serve as a binding agent.

*Sauté vegetables lightly in oil before combining with the tofu. For a richer flavor, simmer the sautéed vegetables in Sweetened Shoyu Broth (p. 40) until all the liquid is absorbed or evaporated.

*For lighter, airier ganmo, heat two woks filled with oil, one to 340° and the other to 385°. Deep-fry patties or balls in the moderate oil for 2 to 4 minutes until they float to the surface. Now transfer them to the hot oil and deep-fry both sides for 30 seconds each.

* **Small Ganmo Balls:** Form the dough into balls about 1 inch in diameter and deep-fry as in the basic recipe. Serve as Stuffed Ganmo Balls (below) or Crisp Deep-fried Tofu (p. 156). Or use in Oden (p. 175), Udon-tsuki (p. 144), or Nishime (p. 178).

* **Japanese-Style Ganmo:** Combine 2 cups squeezed tofu, 1½ tablespoons grated carrots, 3 tablespoons refreshed shredded *kombu*, 1½ teaspoons whole roasted sesame seeds, ¾ teaspoon salt, and 1 tablespoon grated glutinous yam. Prepare as for the basic recipe.

* **Simple Hokkaido-style Ganmo:** Make ganmo patties using only squeezed tofu, salt and, if desired, grated glutinous yam. Pat a sprinkling of sesame seeds into both surfaces of each patty and deep-fry. Quick, easy, and delicious.

*Make ganmo balls using only squeezed tofu. Before deep-frying, fill the center of each ball with 1 teaspoon Yuzu Miso (p.42), Sweet Simmered Miso (p. 41), or sweet white miso.

*Form the ganmo dough into cylinders 10 inches long and 1½ inches in diameter. Wrap each cylinder in 2 pieces of agé opened into flat sheets (p. 191). Deep-fry in 340° oil for 8 to 10 minutes. Cut cylinders crosswise into 1-inch lengths and simmer for 5 minutes in Sweetened Soy Broth (p. 40). Cool and serve topped with a sprig of *kinome*.

Ganmo Treasure Balls *(Hiryozu)* MAKES 6

This popular traditional recipe comes from the Morika tofu shop located in the countryside town of Arashiyama west of Kyoto.

36 ounces tofu, squeezed (p. 97)
1 tablespoon matchsticks of carrot
1½ teaspoons whole roasted sesame seeds (p. 38)
1 refreshed cloud-ear mushroom, cut into ¼-inch-wide strips
1½ teaspoons paper-thin half moons of burdock root
1½ teaspoons flax or hemp seeds
2 tablespoons grated glutinous yam
6 shelled ginkgo nuts, boiled for 30 minutes
30 thin sections of lilly bulbs
Oil for deep-frying

Combine the first six ingredients in a large bowl; mix well, then knead for 3 minutes. Add yam and knead for 2 minutes more. With moistened hands, shape dough into 6 balls. Press a ginkgo nut and 5 lilly bulb sections into the center of each ball; seal hole. Deep-fry at 240° for 10 minutes, or until balls float high in the oil, then increase heat to 350° and deep-fry for 1 or 2 minutes more, or until balls are crisp and golden brown. Drain on a wire rack or absorbent paper. Serve as Crisp Deep-Fried Tofu (p. 156).

Ganmo in a draining tray

Stuffed Ganmo Ball Hors D'oeuvre

Cut a small slit in one side of regular or small ganmo balls and fill with any of the following: Applesauce or diced apples (fresh or cooked), cinnamon and raisins; sliced bananas, nutmeg, and raisins; Tofu Whipped Cream (p. 148) and fresh strawberries; a dab of Yuzu Miso (p. 42), Sweet Simmered Miso (p. 41), or sweet white miso; peanut butter or peanuts, raisins, and honey; regular or Tofu Cream Cheese (p. 109), chopped dates and grated lemon rind; diced cheese and cucumbers with Tofu Mayonnaise (p. 107).

Ganmo Cheeseburger MAKES 1

1 toasted hamburger bun or 2 slices of whole-wheat bread
1 tablespoon (tofu) mayonnaise (p. 107)
2 teaspoons butter
1 tablespoon ketchup
1 teaspoon mustard
1½ teaspoons miso or ½ teaspoon shoyu
1 ganmo patty—4 to 4½ inches in diameter—lightly broiled (p. 156)
1 large, thin slice of onion
1 large slice of tomato
1 large slice of cheese
1 lettuce leaf

Cut the bun horizontally into halves and spread with mayonnaise, butter, mustard, and ketchup. Spread the miso on one side of the ganmo pattie, then place pattie on the lower half of the bun. Stack onion, tomato, cheese, and lettuce on top of ganmo. Top with upper half of bun.

For variety, douse ganmo in boiling water (p. 156), then simmer for 5 minutes in Sweetened Shoyu Broth (p. 40). Drain briefly before assembling burger. Substitute cucumber pickles or relish for the miso.

Agé
(Deep-fried Tofu Pouches)

THE MORIKA tofu shop, located in the country-side west of Kyoto, is spacious and quiet, with the well-ordered look that comes from a long tradition of careful craftsmanship. Early one morning, we visited the shop to watch agé being prepared. Sunlight streamed in through the shop's tall windows falling on the large sinks filled with cold, clear well water and on the glistening hand-cut granite blocks making up the shop's floor. By 4 o'clock in the morning, the first batch of tofu was ready and cooling in the sinks. Now the master's wife would use this specially-prepared tofu to make agé.

She carefully lifted one large block of tofu out of the water on a thick cutting board. Using a long, wide-bladed knife which she wielded with stacatto swiftness, she sliced off thin pieces of the tofu, trimmed their tops to precisely the same thickness, then scooped them up with the knife and placed them carefully on a bamboo pressing mat (fig. 71). The tofu seemed to come alive, each small piece dancing with the knife, leaping onto the shining blade.

After the sandwiched layers of thinly-sliced tofu—called *kiji*—had been pressed under heavy weights for several hours (as in the preparation of thick agé; p.180), they were taken to the deep-frying area. A grandmother, wearing a blue kerchief and traditional Japanese apron, worked with a pair of long chopsticks in front of two deep-fryers filled with bubbling, golden-brown oil. She carefully explained to us each step in the process of making agé, her gold teeth sparkling whenever she laughed.

Into the first container of moderate oil, she lowered a flat screen tray neatly spread with 16 thin tofu kiji, each about 5½ by 2½ by ½ inch thick. The oil hissed and steamed as the kiji sank out of sight. After several minutes, they began to reappear, slowly floating upward until their soft white edges were just above the surface of the oil. The woman carefully turned over each piece, and soon they were floating high and light. Lifting up the screen tray, she transferred it and all of the kiji into the second container of hot oil. The oil came alive, crackling and filling the air with steam. In an instant, as if by magic, each kiji had puffed up and swelled to almost twice its original size. Light, airy, and golden-brown, the little "fleet" bobbed in the sunlight on the surface of the deep-brown oil (fig. 72). The whole room filled with agé's deep aroma, and all the cats in the neighborhood awoke, stretched, and sniffed the suddenly-fragrant morning air.

After turning the agé twice more, lifting it out of the oil on the screen, and allowing it to drain briefly, our new friend said that we must try a piece right away while it was crisp, light, and steaming hot. That morning, sizzling-crisp agé, served topped with a few drops of shoyu, became one of our favorite ways of enjoying tofu.

Tofu makers say that it is only when a young

Fig. 71. Cutting tofu to make agé kiji

Fig. 72. Deep-frying agé

189

apprentice is able to prepare fine agé that he may call himself a full-fledged craftsman and receive permission to leave his master in order to start his own shop. Making agé takes more time and skill than making any other type of tofu. The tofu from which agé is prepared is treated somewhat differently from regular tofu: the soymilk is cooked for only a short time and then cooled quickly by adding a large amount of cold water to it; the curds, solidified with nigari, are broken up very fine and a relatively large amount of whey is removed; the curds are then pressed with heavy weights for a long time in the settling boxes. This complex procedure is designed to make the tofu swell during deep-frying so that, when cooled, the agé can be cut crosswise into halves and the centers opened to form small pouches.

A typical tofu shop prepares about 300 pieces of agé each morning. These come in three different sizes; in general, most pieces are about 6 by 3¼ by 3/8 inch thick; some shops make 2½-inch-square pieces which are specially used as Inari-zushi; and Kyoto shops make pieces up to 9 inches long and 3½ inches wide.

All agé has a tender, slightly chewy texture and much less body than either of the other types of deep-fried tofu. Since it has a high oil content (31%) and is the most expensive type of deep-fried tofu on a weight basis, it is generally used in fairly small quantities. Yet its remarkable versatility makes it popular in almost the entire panorama of Japanese cuisine, where it is used in three basic forms: as pouches, flat sheets, and thinly-sliced strips.

Agé pouches may be filled with almost any fresh or cooked ingredients and served as light hors d'oeuvre or hearty main dishes. Leftovers placed in agé pouches are transformed instantly into new and tasty dishes which may be used in lunch boxes in much the same way as a sandwich. In Japan, pouches are often filled with grains, noodles, or vegetables and simmered in stews or *nabe* dishes. Stuffed pouches are also very delicious when deep-fried with batter. The most popular way of using agé pouches in Japanese cookery is with Inari-zushi; the pouches are simmered in a sweetened shoyu broth, filled with vinegared rice, and served as a favorite lunch-box ingredient at picnics and special occasions.

If a piece of agé is used as is, or is cut along three sides and opened to form a flat sheet, foods such as cucumbers and strips of cheese seasoned lightly with miso or shoyu may be rolled up inside. The roll can be pierced with food picks, cut crosswise, and served as an hors d'oeuvre.

Sliced into thin strips, agé may be used interchangeably with thick agé and ganmo. It is partic-

ularly popular in miso soups, especially in combination with *wakame*, and may also be used like bacon or ham in breakfast egg dishes, or sautéed like thinly-sliced beef with a wide variety of vegetables.

It seems likely that the Japanese invented agé, since it is not presently found in Taiwan or China. While most of the agé in Japan is still made in neighborhood tofu shops, an increasingly large proportion is prepared in huge, mechanized factories (the largest of which produces 200,000 pieces daily!) and sold at supermarkets for about two-thirds the price of traditional agé.

Traditional masters say that there are four requirements for making the most delicious agé: the tofu must be solidified with nigari from soymilk cooked in a cauldron; the agé must be made to expand without the addition of chemical agents; each slab of tofu used must be sufficiently thick so that the agé has body and can be opened easily to form pouches; and the agé must be deep-fried (by hand) in rapeseed oil. Unfortunately, the tofu used to prepare agé in most factories is solidified with calcium sulfate from soymilk cooked in a pressure cooker, and the agé is made to expand with a chemical agent consisting primarily of calcium carbonate (a white powder found in limestone, chalk, and bones) and phosphate salts. The tofu is cut into very thin slabs (which sometimes tear upon opening) and is deep-fried in inexpensive soy oil using an automatic conveyorized machine. The difference in quality is readily apparent.

Japan's most unique variety of agé is Crisp Agé (*Kanso Aburagé*), which comes in light crisp sheets that are mild in flavor, golden-brown in color, and about 6 by 8 by ¼ inch in size. Rich in protein (24%) and natural oils (64%), it has a very low water content (4½%) which allows it to be stored for more than 3 months at room temperature without spoiling. Like its two long-lasting relatives (dried-frozen tofu and dried yuba), Crisp Agé is very well suited for areas such as Africa and India where spoilage is a major problem. A traditional, natural food, it has been prepared for several hundred years in the city of Matsuyama on the large island of Shikoku, as well as on Okinawa. (It is often sold as Milk Agé, since 1 part of dairy milk curds [resembling cottage cheese] is mixed with 5 parts of soymilk curds to give the tofu additional calcium and amino acids). The curds are ladled into shallow, cloth-lined trays which are then stacked and pressed under a hydraulic press until the tofu is very thin. These tofu sheets are then deep-fried in 5 temperatures of oil ranging from 250 to 392° F until the agé is almost as crisp as a light biscuit. Crisp Agé is generally served in miso soups or sautéed and simmered with vegetables. In Western-style preparations it may be topped with various spreads and crisp vegetables like canapés, used like croutons in salads and soups, or mounded with lettuce and cheese like *tacos* or *tortillas*.

At present, two unique varieties of agé are made and sold in the United States. The first—which we call Agé Puffs—is prepared at most Japanese tofu shops. Made from pressed tofu shaped like a small square rod, this variety puffs up during deep-frying until it looks like a golden-brown sausage 4½ inches long and 2 inches in diameter. Unlike Japanese agé, it stays puffed up even after it cools. Some varieties also puff up to form triangular shapes. Three Agé Puffs (weighing a total of 1½ ounces) are often sold in plastic bags under such names as Fried Soybean Cakes, Fried Tofu, or simply Agé. Each puff is meant to be slit open at one end. Unlike Japanese agé, these puffs are not easily opened into flat sheets.

The second variety—which we call Hollow Agé Cubes—is made in many Chinese tofu shops. Like agé puffs, these 1-inch cubes stay puffed up after deep-frying and can therefore be stuffed with other foods and cooked or served as hors d'oeuvre. One or two dozen cubes are generally sold at Chinese markets in plastic bags under such names as Nama-agé or Raw-fried Bean Curd.

Imported, canned Japanese agé is now sold in Japanese markets as Shinoda-maki and Inari-zushi no Moto, or Prepared Fried Bean Curd. Filled with vinegared rice, the latter may be served without further preparation as Inari-zushi.

Opening Agé into Pouches, Puffs, and Large Sheets

In the recipes that follow, the word agé refers to pieces 6 by 3¼ by 3/8 inches. One piece of agé makes 2 pouches. Agé Puffs sold in the U.S. may be slightly smaller, so when using them, decrease the filling proportionally.

*Agé pouches: Cut agé crosswise into halves. To open the center, carefully work your thumbs between the two deep-fried surfaces (fig. 73).

*Large agé pouches: Cut a thin slice from one end of

each piece of agé, then open the center by working your thumbs between the deep-fried surfaces.

*Agé puffs: One piece of hollow (Western-style) agé makes one sausage-shaped puff about 4½ inches long and 2 inches in diameter. With the point of a sharp knife, cut a slit across one end of each agé puff. If desired, pull or scoop out any tofu which may remain inside.

*Large sheets: Using a knife or pair of scissors, open agé into a sheet 6 inches square by cutting into 1 long and 2 short sides.

Homemade Agé Pouches
(from Storebought or Homemade Tofu)   MAKES 4 TO 6

This is the quick and easy way to prepare homemade agé pouches although they will not expand quite as much as when you use the lengthier process starting with whole soybeans described below. Twelve ounces of unpressed tofu will yield 5 ounces of agé pouches.

12 to 20 ounces tofu
Oil for deep-frying.

Cut tofu horizontally into ½-inch-thick slices, 4 to 6 inches long and 3 to 3½ inches wide. Press slices using the sliced tofu method (p. 97), except place a cutting board and a 5- to 10-pound weight on the tofu and press for about 40 minutes.

Fill a wok, skillet, or deep-fryer with 2 inches of oil and heat to 240°. Slide in the pressed tofu and deep-fry over high heat until temperature of oil reaches 310°. Reduce heat to medium-high and continue to deep-fry until agé pieces float on the surface of oil. Return heat to high, turn agé with chopsticks, and deep-fry until oil reaches 385°. Reduce heat to medium and deep-fry until agé are crisp and golden brown. Remove agé from oil, drain briefly on a wire rack or absorbent paper, and allow to cool for about 10 minutes.

Cut a thin slice from the end of each piece of agé. Carefully insert the point of a knife between the deep-fried surfaces from the cut end and separate the surfaces to form a pouch. Using a small spoon, scoop out any tofu remaining inside the pouch. (To make 2 small pouches, cut each piece of agé crosswise into halves, then proceed to open as above.)

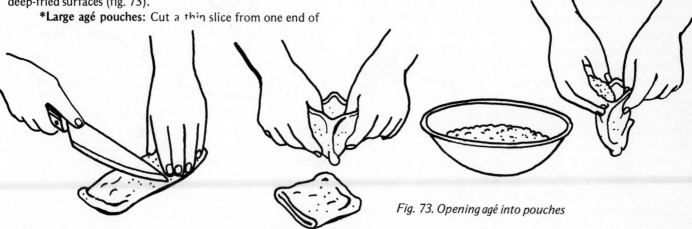

Fig. 73. Opening agé into pouches

Homemade Agé Pouches
(from Storebought or Homemade Thick Agé)

If thick agé is available at your local market, it can easily be transformed into agé pouches by following the method for Homemade Thick Agé Pouches (p. 182).

Homemade Agé Pouches *(from Whole Soybeans)*

This recipe should be attempted only after you have mastered the process for Homemade Tofu (p. 99). Although quite time consuming, it yields excellent agé which expands nicely and is light and crisp.

1½ cups whole dry soybeans
18 cups water
¾ teaspoon baking powder or calcium carbonate
Solidifier as for Homemade Tofu
Oil for deep-frying

Prepare the tofu for homemade agé as for Homemade Tofu but with the following modifications: 1) Begin by heating 5¼ cups water in cooking pot. 2) Rinse pressed okara with 1½ cups warm water. 3) Bring soymilk to a boil and simmer only 3 minutes; turn off heat and immediately stir 6 cups (unheated) water into soymilk. 4) Add baking powder to solidifier solution before stirring solution into soymilk. 5) After removing whey, stir curds slowly, then set colander or strainer back on curds, place ½-pound weight into colander, and ladle off any remaining curds which settle in colander. 6) Ladle curds quickly and rather roughly into settling container. 7) Press curds in the container with a 3- to 4-pound weight for about 30 minutes.

Remove tofu from container and proceed to cut and deep-fry it as for Homemade Agé Pouches (from storebought or homemade tofu; p. 191).

Homemade Agé Slices
(from Storebought or Homemade Tofu)

Many of the recipes in Chapter 9, Deep-fried Tofu, call for regular pieces of agé which do not need to be opened into pouches or large sheets. This type of agé can be quickly and easily prepared at home as described in the recipe for Crisp Agé Slices (p. 131).

AGÉ POUCHES, PUFFS, AND HOLLOW AGÉ CUBES

Agé pouches, puffs, or hollow cubes may be stuffed with fresh vegetables, salads, fruits, or a wide variety of cooked foods and served instead of sandwiches or as finger foods. The pouches may first be simmered in a sweeten-ed shoyu broth, then filled with sushi rice or other cooked grains. Once filled, pouches can be simmered (in seasoned broths), deep-fried, baked, steamed, or even smoked to create a rich variety of flavors and textures. To create a dappled, felt-like exterior, turn pouches inside-out before filling. Leftovers can be rejuvenated and transformed when used as fillings.

In most of the following recipes 4 to 6 hollow agé cubes may be substituted for 1 pouch or puff.

Fresh Vegetable Salads in Agé Pouches   SERVES 2

½ tomato, diced
¼ cucumber, diced
¼ onion, diced
¼ cup diced cheese
3½ ounces ganmo or thick agé, diced (optional)
1½ tablespoons (tofu) mayonnaise (p. 107)
1½ tablespoons ketchup
Dash of pepper
4 agé pouches or puffs (p. 191), broiled (p. 156) if desired

Combine the first eight ingredients in a small bowl; toss lightly. Spoon the mixture into agé pouches until each is one-half to two-thirds full. Fold over mouth of each pouch and fasten with a foodpick (fig. 74).

Or substitute 2 teaspoons red miso for the ketchup and add 2 thinly sliced lettuce, cabbage or Chinese cabbage leaves, and ½ teaspoon hot mustard to the ingredients listed above. Serve on a piece of hot buttered toast.

VARIATIONS: Use any of the following as filling for the agé pouches:
*1 cup fresh mung, soy, or alfalfa sprouts, 1 tablespoon red miso, ½ diced tomato and ¼ diced cucumber.
*Waldorf Salad, Potato Salad, Tossed Green Salad, Tomato-Mayonnaise Salad, or any of the various tofu (p. 111) or deep-fried tofu salads (p. 158).
*Grain or noodle salads made with deep-fried (p. 159) or regular tofu (p. 111).

Agé Treasure Pouches

Fruits in Agé Pouches

SERVES 2

2 bananas, cut into thin rounds
½ teaspoon nutmeg
½ cup yogurt or cottage cheese
½ cup raisins
¼ cup walnut meats
4 agé pouches or puffs (p. 191), broiled (p. 156) if desired

Mix the first five ingredients and spoon into agé pouches. Fold over mouth of each pouch and fasten with a foodpick (fig. 74).

VARIATIONS

*Cut 2 bananas into thin slices and fry in plenty of butter until slightly soft. Season with nutmeg and serve hot as a filling.
*Use only sliced fresh bananas mixed with 1 tablespoon sweet white miso.
*Substitute apple wedges for the bananas, and cinnamon for the nutmeg. If desired, add sesame or peanut butter and 2 teaspoons lemon juice.

Cooked Grains and Noodles in Agé Pouches

SERVES 3

In the following recipe for Sizzling Rice, the use of green peppers, carrots, mushrooms, bean sprouts, or lotus root sautéed with the onions will give a variety of flavors. Or mix into the cooked rice: ground roasted sesame seeds, sunflower seeds, nutmeats, or diced cheese.

2 tablespoons oil
1 small onion, diced
2 eggs, lightly beaten
2 cups cooked Brown Rice (p. 50)
3 tablespoons ketchup
½ teaspoon salt
Dash of pepper
9 agé pouches or puffs (p. 191), lightly broiled (p. 156) if
    desired

Heat a wok or skillet and coat with the oil. Add the onion and sauté over high heat for 2 minutes, or until lightly browned. Add beaten eggs and stir briefly until light and dry, then immediately add rice. Reduce heat to medium-high and fry rice for 3 to 4 minutes, stirring constantly. Add ketchup, salt, and pepper and fry for 2 minutes more; turn off heat. Spoon 3 to 4 tablespoons of the rice mixture into each pouch. Fold over mouth of pouch to form a flap and fasten with a foodpick (fig. 74). Serve hot or cold.

VARIATIONS

*Fried Buckwheat Noodles with Vegetables: In 1 tablespoon oil sauté ½ onion cut into thin wedges and 1 small carrot grated or cut into matchsticks. When carrot is tender, add 2 cups cooked buckwheat noodles (soba), 2 tablespoons each roasted sesame seeds and shoyu, ¼ cup diced cheese, and a dash of salt. Sauté for several minutes more, then cool briefly.

Fig. 74. Agé pouches sealed with foodpicks

If desired, mix with a little crumbled toasted nori. Use to fill pouches; broil pouches (p. 156) before serving.
*Grain Fillings with Sauces: Prepare Curry Sauce (p. 121), Onion Sauce (p. 48), Mushroom Sauce (p. 48), Spaghetti Sauce (p. 121), or your favorite and combine with brown rice or noodles. If using curry sauce, just before filling the pouches, add peanuts, raisins, coconut, diced hard-boiled eggs, sliced bananas or diced apples. With the other sauces, you may wish to add diced or Parmesan cheese. Serve cold.
*Adzuki Rice (Sekihan): Soak 1 cup brown rice and 2 tablespoons adzuki beans over night in 1¾ cups water. Pressure cook for 40 minutes, then season with Sesame Salt (p. 51). Use as filling.

Tofu Dishes in Agé Pouches

Use any of the following as filling for agé pouches: Shira-ae (p. 114), Iri-dofu (p. 128), all sautéed okara dishes (p. 80), Okara Salad with Rice-flour Noodles (p. 79), Tofu with Onion Sauce (p. 116), Tofu with Mushroom Sauce (p. 127), Vinegared Okara (p. 83).

Eggs in Agé Pouches

SERVES 3

4 hard-boiled eggs, diced
4 tablespoons (tofu) mayonnaise (p. 107)
2 teaspoons red miso or ½ teaspoon salt
¼ cup minced parsley
6 agé pouches or puffs (p. 191)

Mix the first four ingredients, then spoon into pouches. Fold over the mouth of each pouch to form a flap. Scrambled eggs work well too.

Agé Treasure Pouch with Egg and Onion

SERVES 2 OR 3

3 eggs, lightly beaten
1 small onion, diced
¼ teaspoon salt
1½ cups water
2 tablespoons shoyu
2 tablespoons natural sugar
6 agé pouches or puffs (p. 191)

Combine eggs, onion, and salt; mix well. Combine water, shoyu, and sugar in a small saucepan and bring to a boil. Meanwhile spoon the egg and onion mixture into each of the agé pouches, fold over the mouth of each pouch, and seal with a foodpick (fig. 74, p. 193). Place pouches into shoyu broth, return to the boil and cook over medium heat for 5 10 minutes. Pierce each pouch in several places with a fork or chopsticks and simmer for 30 to 40 minutes more, or until most of the liquid is absorbed or evaporated. Serve hot or cold.

For variety, add diced carrots, mushrooms, snow peas, green peppers, and/or cubes of deep-fried tofu to the filling.

Treasure-Pouch Poached Egg

SERVES 1

1 egg
1 agé pouch or puff (p. 191)
Shoyu, or salt and pepper

Fill a small saucepan with several inches of water and bring to a boil. Break egg into pouch without breaking yolk. Seal mouth of pouch with a foodpick (fig. 74 p. 193) and place pouch in water. Return to the boil and simmer for 2 or 3 minutes, or until egg is just firm. Using a mesh skimmer, remove pouch and any egg white in the water. Serve hot, seasoned with a sprinkling of shoyu.

Cooked Vegetables in Agé Pouches

SERVES 3

2 cups small cubes of steamed *kabocha*, winter squash, or
    pumpkin
2 tablespoons minced onion
3 tablespoons (tofu) mayonnaise (p. 107)
2 teaspoons red, barley, or Hatcho miso
2 tablespoons ground roasted sesame seeds (p. 38)
6 agé pouches or puffs (p. 191), broiled (p. 156) if desired

Mix the first five ingredients, then spoon into the pouches. Fold over the mouth of each pouch to form a flap and fasten with a foodpick (fig. 74, p. 193). For variety omit the onion, mayonnaise, and miso; and 1½ tablespoons butter and ¼ teaspoon salt.

VARIATIONS: Use any of the following combinations as a filling for agé pouches; serve topped with a sprinkling of shoyu:

*½ cup diced steamed sweet potato or yam, ¾ cup cubes of steamed cauliflower, 3 tablespoons mayonnaise, ¼ teaspoon salt and a dash of pepper.
*Steamed, baked, or boiled sweet potatoes or yams and any of the following: yogurt, sunflower seeds, sautéed onion, and shoyu; butter, salt, pepper, cinnamon, orange juice, and grated orange rind; raisins, butter, and salt or miso.
*Baked or boiled potatoes, sour cream, salt, pepper, butter, crushed garlic, and grated cheese.
*Hashed brown potatoes seasoned with a little shoyu or salt.

Agé Pouches Served in Thickened Sauces

Fill agé pouches with cooked (or stir-fried) brown rice, noodles, buckwheat groats, or millet. Seal each pouch with a foodpick. Prepare Sweet & Sour, Ankake, or Gingerroot Sauce (p. 49). Arrange 2 or 3 pouches in individual serving bowls and serve with a topping of the hot sauce.

Inari-zushi (*Vinegared Sushi Rice in Sweetened Agé Pouches*)

SERVES 5

In Japan, the most popular way of serving agé is in the form of *Inari-zushi*. Packed into lightweight wooden boxes and topped with thin slices of vinegared gingerroot, Inari-zushi are often found at picnics and outings of all kinds where they play much the same role as do sandwiches in the West. Served at most sushi shops, they are very inexpensive and are prepared in a different way by each chef.

Inari-zushi is said to have originated in Tokyo about 1848, the creation of one Jiro Kichi, chef at the *Jukkenten* restaurant. Kichi peddled his new culinary treats at night through the streets of Tokyo carrying a four-sided paper lantern called an *andon*. On this he painted a red Shinto *torii* gateway, the hallmark of the Inari shrine where the Goddess of rice is said to abide. Since foxes are said to be very fond of agé, and since the fox is the patron animal of Inari shrines, this pictorial symbolism and its curious logic seemed natural and appropriate; Inari-zushi soon spread throughout Japan.

20 agé pouches or puffs, doused with boiling water (p. 156)
1 2/3 cups water
7½ tablespoons sugar
5 tablespoons shoyu
2 teaspoons *mirin* (optional)
3¾ cups Sushi Rice (p. 50)
20 slices Sweet Vinegared Gingerroot (p. 51)

Combine the first five ingredients in a large saucepan, cover, and bring to a boil. Reduce heat to low and simmer for 20 minutes. Set aside and allow to cool overnight. (Meanwhile begin soaking the rice for Sushi Rice.)

The next morning while cooking the rice, simmer the agé until just heated through. Drain pouches thoroughly in a strainer set over a bowl and allow to cool to room temperature. Reserve the remaining broth for use as a cooking liquid for potatoes or other vegetables.

Using your fingertips, gently form 2½ to 3 tablespoons of the rice into egg-shaped ovals. Place one oval into each agé pouch so that the pouch is 1/3 to ½ full. Fold over the mouth of each pouch, and arrange pouches on a serving tray or place in Japanese-style wooden lunch boxes. Top each sushi pouch with a slice of the gingerroot.

VARIATIONS

*Add 4 to 8 tablespoons ground or whole roasted sesame seeds (black or white), flax seeds, or hemp seeds to the hot rice just before cooling. Or mix ¼ cup toasted okara with the rice.

*Add any or all of the following diced vegetables: mushrooms, carrots, burdock root, *kampyo*, green beans, or green peas. Simmer vegetables in Sweetened Shoyu Broth (p. 40), drain and add to the rice before cooling. Or use Five-Colored Sushi (p. 169) as the filling for the pouches.

*Turn each pouch inside out before simmering. Tie each filled pouch with a strip of *kampyo* that has been soaked for 20 minutes in the broth used to simmer the pouches.

*Cut each piece of agé diagonally into halves to form 2 triangular pouches. Starting from the short side, roll up the filled pouch along the diagonal.

*Prepare Inari-zushi pouches, but instead of filling them with sushi rice, use plain cooked buckwheat noodles, brown rice (plain, seasoned with sesame salt, or sautéed with vegetables), or Sushi Okara (p. 83).

*Lima Ohsawa's Inari-zushi: This recipe uses no sugar or vinegar. Simmer 8 agé pouches in a mixture of ½ cup water and 1 tablespoon each shoyu and *mirin* until all of the liquid has evaporated or been absorbed. Simmer ½ cup diced lotus root and 2 minced *umeboshi* in ¼ cup water for about 5 minutes or until liquid has been absorbed. Sauté ¼ cup slivered or grated carrot and 3 tablespoons reconstituted *hijiki* seaweed in 2 teaspoons oil, then season with a dash of salt and a little shoyu. Mix all of the vegetables and the juice of ½ lemon with 1 cup of hot cooked brown rice; allow to cool to room temperature. Divide this mixture among the agé pouches and proceed as above.

Agé Treasure Pouches with Crunchy Vegetables (*Fuku-bukuro*)

SERVES 4

Small agé pouches loaded with vegetables and tied with *kampyo* are known as "bags of wealth and good fortune" (*fuku-bukuro*) or "treasure sacks" (*takara-zutsumi*).

½ cake of *konnyaku*, cut into small rectangles
1 small carrot, cut into matchsticks
4 inches of lotus root, cut into thin quarter moons
4 (*shiitake*) mushrooms, cut into thin strips
¼ cup reconstituted, diced cloud-ear mushroom (optional)
2 tablespoons green peas
8 agé pouches or puffs (p. 191), turned inside-out
8 strips of *kampyo*, each 13 inches long, reconstituted (p. 37)
3 cups dashi (p. 39), stock, or water
4 tablespoons shoyu
2 tablespoons natural sugar
2 tablespoons sake

Heat an unoiled skillet. Put in *konnyaku* and cook over medium heat for several minutes, or until surface of *konnyaku* is dry. Transfer to a large bowl and combine with the next five ingredients. Spoon *konnyaku*-and-vegetable mixture into each of the agé pouches. Fold over the mouth of each pouch, then tie with *kampyo* (fig. 75).

Combine the last four ingredients in a small saucepan and bring to a boil. Add agé pouches, cover, and simmer for 20 to 25 minutes; allow to cool. Now divide pouches among individual serving bowls, top with any remaining broth, and serve hot or cold.

For variety, add to each pouch: 1 ginkgo nut, 3 thin sections of lilly root, or 1 small roll of yuba.

VARIATIONS

*Sacks of Gold (*Takara-zutsumi*): Combine cooked buckwheat groats, millet, or transparent noodles with sautéed onions, carrot, lotus root, mushrooms, and burdock root (all diced). Spoon the mixture into long agé pouches (p. 191) and tie the mouth of each pouch with *kampyo*, or seal with a foodpick. Simmer in a sweetened shoyu broth, as above.

*Matchstick Vegetables Wrapped in Agé Pouches (*Shinoda-maki*): Cut burdock root, *daikon*, carrot, or butterbur into matchsticks 3 inches long. Use the vegetables individually or in combination to completely fill agé pouches. Tie each pouch with *kampyo*. Simmer in sweetened shoyu broth as above until vegetables are tender. Or cook in Oden or *nabe* dishes.

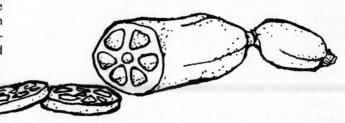

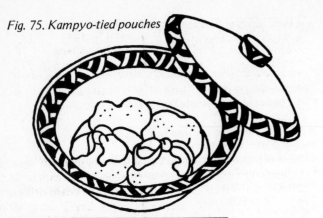

Fig. 75. Kampyo-tied pouches

Drawstring Purses and Treasure Bags
(Kinchaku and Takara-bukuro)

SERVES 4

Also known simply as "bags" (fukuro) or "bags of wealth and good fortune" (fuku-bukuro), these handsome preparations are most widely used in Kyoto-style Oden (p. 175) and occasionally in Nishime (p. 178). Prefilled, uncooked kinchaku are often sold in Kyoto's bustling outdoor markets.

4 agé pouches or puffs (p. 191)
Fillings: konnyaku noodles or threads, carrots, cabbage, cubes of fresh or dried wheat gluten, small balls of mochi, transparent noodles, bean sprouts, cubes of thick agé or ganmo, shiitake mushrooms, burdock root, Osmund fern, lotus root, quail egg, daikon, diced konnyaku, snow peas, bamboo shoots (all diced or slivered)
4 pieces of kampyo, each 13 inches long, reconstituted (p. 37)

Turn the agé pouches inside-out, then fill each pouch with your choice of 6 to 8 of the different filling ingredients. Tie each pouch closed with kampyo (fig. 75), then use the pouches as one of the ingredients in Oden or Nishime.

Deep-fried Agé Apple Turnover

SERVES 2

1½ small apples, cut into thin wedges
¼ cup raisins
1 tablespoon natural sugar
3 tablespoons water
¼ teaspoon cinnamon
4 agé pouches or puffs (p. 191)
1 tablespoon whole-wheat flour
Oil for deep-frying

In a small saucepan simmer apples, raisins, sugar, and water for 6 to 8 minutes until apples just begin to soften. Sprinkle with cinnamon, then spoon mixture into agé pouches. Fold over the mouth of each pouch and fasten with a foodpick. Combine flour with just enough water to make a thick paste and use to seal the mouth of each pouch.

Heat the oil to 350° in a wok, skillet, or deep-fryer. Slide in the pouches and deep-fry until crisp and golden brown (p. 130). Remove foodpick, drain, and serve piping hot.

Or dip each pouch into tempura batter (p. 134) and roll in bread crumbs (or dust with flour, dip in lightly beaten eggs, and roll in bread crumbs) before deep-frying.

Mashed Potatoes Deep-fried in Agé Pouches (Hasami-agé)

SERVES 3 OR 4

1½ tablespoons oil
¼ onion, diced
1 green pepper, diced
1¼ potatoes, boiled and mashed
1 tablespoon butter
¼ teaspoon salt
8 agé pouches or puffs (p. 191)
2 tablespoons whole-wheat flour, combined with enough water to form a thick paste
Oil for deep-frying
Dipping Sauce:
    2 tablespoons ketchup
    1 tablespoon Worcestershire sauce
    ½ teaspoon salt

Heat a wok or skillet and coat with the oil. Add onions and green pepper and sauté until onions are transparent. Transfer onions and pepper to a large bowl and combine with potatoes, butter, and salt. Spoon mixture into agé pouches. Fold over the mouth of each pouch and seal with the flour paste.

Heat the oil to 350° in a wok, skillet, or deep-fryer. Slide in the pouches and deep-fry until crisp and golden brown (p. 130); drain. Serve hot, accompanied by a small dish of dipping sauce.

Baked or Steamed Agé Pouches

SERVES 2

1 large mushroom, diced
½ onion, diced
2 tablespoons diced cheese
2 eggs, lightly beaten
1 tablespoon shoyu
4 agé pouches or puffs (p. 191)

Preheat oven to 350°. Combine the first five ingredients in a bowl; mix well. Place agé pouches on a well-oiled baking tin and fill with equal portions of the egg-and-vegetable mixture. Fold over the mouth of each pouch and fasten with a foodpick. Bake for 15 to 20 minutes, or until egg is just firm.

VARIATIONS
*Add first these ingredients, then carefully break 1 egg into each pouch (do not break yolk). Proceed as above, and serve topped with a sprinkling of shoyu. This method helps prevent the egg from leaking from the pouch.
*Use as fillings any of your favorite casserole mixtures or the ingredients used for stuffing baked green peppers or other vegetables.
*Steam the prefilled pouches for about 15 minutes. Or begin by frying the filled pouches in a well-oiled skillet, then add a little water, cover, and steam for about 10 minutes.

Smoked Tofu

SERVES 4

Smoked tofu is now sold commercially as a canned food in Japan.

24 ounces tofu, well pressed (p. 96)
¾ cup chopped mushrooms, chestnuts, or walnut meats
½ teaspoon salt
4 large agé pouches (p. 191)
Oil for marinating

Combine the tofu, mushrooms, and salt in a large bowl; mix until cohesive. Spoon the mixture into the agé pouches, then seal the mouth of each pouch with 2 foodpicks. Place the pouches on a *(sudare)* bamboo mat, screen, or grill. Place a cutting board on top of the pouches, and a 5- to 10-pound weight on top of the board; press for 30 minutes. Remove weight and board, and transfer mat and pouches to a smoke-house or place above a barbeque, wood-burning stove, or fireplace; smoke for 2 or 3 hours.

Cut smoked tofu crosswise into slices 3/8 inch thick and marinate for several hours in salad oil. Serve as hors d'oeuvre on crackers or toast, or in tossed green salads.

FOODS ROLLED IN AGÉ AND LARGE AGÉ SHEETS

Fresh crisp vegetables or cheeses may be rolled up in a single piece of agé and served as hors d'oeuvre. Or the agé may be opened into large sheets and used to wrap various ingredients into a compact roll which may then be simmered in seasoned liquids, steamed, or deep-fried.

Shinoda-maki *(Agé-Cabbage Rolls)*

SERVES 4

The name *Shinoda* is given to numerous dishes in which a large sheet of agé is used as a wrapper for a cylindrical core of other ingredients. This name—like the name *Inari*— is connected with foxes, an animal whose favorite food is said to be agé. In a well-known *kabuki* play, a fox turns into a lovely woman—as foxes often do in Japan to deceive gullible men—marries, and has a child. Eventually the time comes when she must turn back into a fox. At the difficult moment of parting from her child she says: "If you miss me and long to be together, come to the forest of Shinoda in Izumi." Thus Shinoda became known as a favorite hangout for foxes, and the name soon came to be used with agé rolls. Shinoda-maki are often used as an ingredient in Oden (p. 175) or other *nabe* dishes. Fasten the rolls with foodpicks if *kampyo* is not available.

4 large leaves of Chinese or regular cabbage
4 pieces of agé, opened into large sheets (p. 191)
6 carrot strips, 3/8 inch square and 6 inches long
8 strips of *kampyo*, each 12 inches long, refreshed (p. 37)
1½ cups water
2 tablespoons shoyu
1½ tablespoons natural sugar
½ teaspoon salt
4 slivers of *yuzu* or lemon rind

Trim the stems of cabbage leaves smooth, then dip leaves in boiling water until pliable. Place 1 sheet of agé with its deep-fried surface facing downward on a cutting board or *sudare*. Cover agé sheet with 2 cabbage leaves. Lay 3 carrot strips crosswise near one end of the leaves, and top with a second sheet of agé with its deep-fried surface facing downward. With the carrot strips as the core, roll up the layered preparation and tie with *kampyo* in 4 places (see p. 177). Repeat with remaining ingredients to form a second roll.

Combine the water, 1 tablespoon shoyu, and ¾ tablespoon sugar in a 2-quart saucepan and bring to a boil. Add the rolls (*kampyo* bow facing down) and simmer for 15 minutes. Add remaining shoyu and sugar, and the salt, and simmer for 10 minutes more; allow to cool. Cut each roll crosswise into fourths and divide among 4 deep bowls. Serve topped with the remaining broth, garnished with a sliver of *yuzu*.

VARIATIONS

*Single Sheet Rolls: Wrap 8 to 10 long strips of any of the following vegetables in one sheet of agé: carrot, burdock root, bracken fern, *daikon*, butterbur, or celery. Tie as above and cook in the seasoned broth until tender.

*Fragrant Agé-Cabbage Roll: Roll up 1 large cabbage leaf in 1 large sheet of agé and fasten with foodpicks. Make 2.

In a skillet, combine 2 tablespoons shoyu, ½ clove of crushed garlic, 2 teaspoons natural sugar, and ¼ teaspoon each grated gingerroot, vinegar, and sesame oil. Bring just to a boil, then add the cabbage rolls and 6 green *togarashi* peppers (or 1 green pepper cut lengthwise into strips). Sauté over low heat until cabbage is tender. Serve hot or cold as hors d'oeuvre.

Rolled Agé Hors D'oeuvre

SERVES 2

2 pieces of agé, lightly broiled (p. 156) if desired
Vinegar-Miso Spread:
    2 teaspoons vinegar
    1 teaspoon red, barley, or Hatcho miso
    1 tablespoon natural sugar
    Dash of *sansho* green pepper (optional)
½ cucumber, cut into 3-inch-long matchsticks

Coat the surface of each piece of agé with the spread. Lay cucumber matchsticks at one end of the coated surface, then roll up agé (fig. 76). Secure each roll with 3 foodpicks. Cut rolls crosswise into thirds to serve.

Or use 4 strips of cheese, 6 parboiled green beans, and 6 strips of cucumber for the core of each roll. Substitute red, barley, or Sweet Simmered Miso (p. 41) for the miso spread used above. Sauté the rolls briefly in butter before cutting them into thirds.

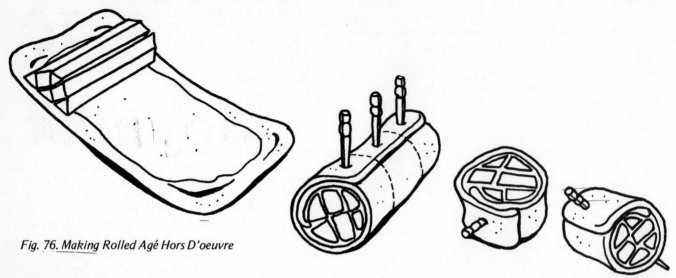

Fig. 76. *Making Rolled Agé Hors D'oeuvre*

Steamed Agé Roll with Tofu and Vegetables (*Shinoda-mushi*)

SERVES 3 OR 4

2 small mushrooms, diced
¼ cup diced carrots
¼ cup water
2 tablespoons natural sugar
2½ teaspoons shoyu
12 ounces tofu, well pressed (p. 96) and mashed
3 2/3 tablespoons cornstarch
1 teaspoon salt, approximately
1 egg, separated into white and yolk
1 teaspoon oil
3 pieces of agé, doused in boiling water (p. 156) and opened into large sheets (p. 191)
2 tablespoons green peas, parboiled in lightly salted water (p. 37)
12 seven-inch strips of *kampyo*, reconstituted (p. 37)
¾ cup dashi (p. 39), stock, or water
1 tablespoon sake

In a small saucepan combine carrots, mushrooms, ¼ cup water, 2 teaspoons sugar, and 1 teaspoon shoyu. Cover and bring to a boil, then reduce heat to low and simmer for 3 minutes. Uncover, simmer until all liquid is absorbed, then set aside to cool briefly.

In a large bowl combine tofu, 2 tablespoons cornstarch, 1 tablespoon sugar, ½ teaspoon salt, and the egg white. Mix well, then stir in the carrots and mushrooms.

Heat a skillet and coat with the oil. Scramble the egg yolk with a dash of salt; set aside to cool.

Spread the 3 agé sheets on a cutting board with the deep-fried surface facing downward and 1 piece resting on a *sudare* bamboo mat (if available). Sprinkle 1 teaspoon cornstarch evenly over each of the 3 sheets. Spread the tofu mixture in an even layer over the 3 sheets. Arrange the green peas and scrambled eggs in a line about 1 inch from one edge of each of the layers of tofu. With the aid of the bamboo mat, roll up each of the sheets firmly from this edge so that the peas and eggs form the core of the roll. Tie each roll in 4 places with *kampyo* strips (see p. 177), place in a preheated steamer, and steam over high heat for 10 minutes.

In a small saucepan combine ¾ cup dashi, 1½ teaspoons shoyu, 1/3 teaspoon salt, 1 tablespoon sake, 1 teaspoon sugar, and 2 teaspoons cornstarch. Stirring constantly, heat until thick. Cut the steamed rolls crosswise into 4 sections, divide among the bowls and serve hot or cold, topped with the thick sauce.

For variety, add a little grated *yuzu* or lemon rind to the sauce, and garnish with a sprig of *kinome* and several parboiled green beans. And/or substitute diced burdock root for the mushrooms and use a core of fresh wheat gluten *(fu)* in place of the scrambled eggs.

10
Soymilk

ON A CLEAR cold morning in late October, Akiko and I paid out first exploratory visit to a Japanese tofu shop. Above the shop's steam-matted windows was written its name, San-gen-ya, in bold, black characters. The shop's master, Mr. Toshio Arai, greeted us cheerfully, accepted our gift of crisp autumn apples, then quickly returned to the bubbling cauldron behind him. Into it he ladled some 25 gallons of freshly-ground gô (fig. 77) and on top of it he placed a 3-foot cedar lid, all the time explaining that he was preparing soymilk later to be made into kinugoshi tofu. After about 10 minutes, steam billowed up from beneath the lid, filling the shop with a delightful aroma. The master uncovered the cauldron and with a specially-made split bamboo rod, stirred down its swelling contents just before they were about to overflow (fig. 78). Lowering the

flame, he continued to simmer the bubbling gô for about 10 minutes more, stirring it down from time to time. As he worked, he explained that there were four basic requirements for preparing the very finest soymilk: first, the soybeans used had to be bestgrade whole beans, and the water well water; second, a relatively small amount of water had to be used to give the resulting soymilk a thick, rich consistency; third, the gô had to be cooked in a cauldron and, ideally, over a wood fire to evoke its full flavor; and finally, the gô had to be simmered long enough to ensure lasting freshness and make best use of its potential nutrients (see p. 70).

When the gô had finished cooking, he ladled it into a large, coarsely woven sack set into a cedar barrel next to the cauldron. He raised the sack with a hand-turned hoist and allowed the soymilk to drain

Fig. 77. Ladling gô into the cauldron

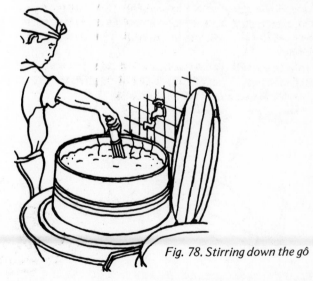

Fig. 78. Stirring down the gô

into the barrel through a layer of finely-woven silk cloth. Lowering the sack onto a sturdy rack placed across the mouth of the barrel, he then pressed it thoroughly (below) until the okara had yielded its last drop of precious soymilk.

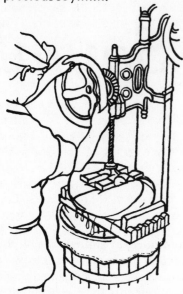

Pressing soymilk from okara

Now, from the deep wooden barrel, he scooped out a large ladleful of this steaming soymilk and used it to fill seven earthenware mugs (fig. 79): one for each of his three children, his wife, his visitors and, of course, for himself. Into each mug he spooned a little wildflower honey—chunks of the honeycomb still suspended in it. A tiny pinch of salt and *kampai*— "bottoms up."

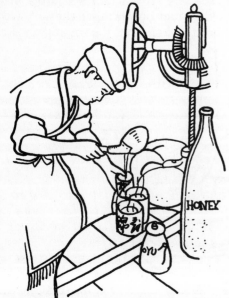

Fig. 79. Serving fresh soymilk

Within the space of less than 40 minutes, we had witnessed a truly remarkable process: the transformation of soybeans into milk. Its consistency and appearance resembling that of creamy, fresh dairy milk, this delicious drink had a natural full-bodied flavor, a mellow aroma, and a subtle, mild sweetness. Highly nutritious and low in cost, it soon became a regular part of our daily meals; we picked up a bottle each morning together with our day's supply of tofu.

Nutritionally, soymilk compares very favorably with dairy milk, as will be seen by comparing the following figures showing the composition of a 100 gram portion of soy, dairy, and mother's milk:

	SOYMILK	DAIRY MILK	MOTHER'S MILK
Water (grams)	88.6	88.6	88.6
Protein	4.4	2.9	1.4
Calories	52	59	62
Fat	2.5	3.3	3.1
Carbohydrates	3.8	4.5	7.2
Ash	0.62	0.7	0.20
Calcium (mg.)	18.5	100	35
Sodium	2.5	36	15
Phosphorous	60.3	90	25
Iron	1.5	0.1	0.2
Thiamine (B_1)	0.04	0.04	0.02
Riboflavin (B_2)	0.02	0.15	0.03
Niacin	0.62	0.20	0.2

(SOURCE: *Standard Tables of Food Composition* [Japan])

When prepared with the same precentage of water as that found in dairy milk (it is usually made with less), soymilk contains 51 percent more protein, 16 percent less carbohydrate, 12 percent fewer calories (18 percent fewer calories per gram of protein), and 24 percent less fat (48 percent less saturated fat). At the same time, it contains 15 times as much iron, many of the essential B vitamins, and no cholesterol. Finally it contains one-tenth the amount of dangerous agricultural chemicals (DDT among them).

(Unlike some varieties of commercial soymilk or that described above for the sake of comparison, the rich kinugoshi soymilk sold in most tofu shops and described in the recipe for Homemade Soymilk [p. 204] contains an average of 5.5 percent protein and, in some cases, as much as 6.3 percent; its complement of minerals and vitamins is also, of course, about 25 percent higher.)

Because it contains only 52 percent as much calcium as mother's milk (18 percent as much as found in dairy milk), soymilk is often enriched with calcium or calcium lactate when used in baby formulae. But whereas 7 to 10 percent of all American babies—as well as many adults—are allergic or otherwise sensitive to dairy milk (an even larger percentage find that it creates digestive difficulties), there is no evidence of similar reactions to regular or enriched soymilk.

Although various types of "vegetable milks" can be prepared from nuts (almonds, peanuts, walnuts, coconut) and seeds (sunflower and sesame), the soybean is, perhaps, the only plant known to man capable of yielding milk in large quantities at reasonable cost. And it strikes us as a deeply mysterious coincidence that the substance of a simple seed, ground and cooked with water, should be so similar to the life-giving milk produced in the bodies of mammals and used to suckle their young.

Soymilk has been used for centuries throughout East Asia in much the same way that dairy milk is now used in the West. Today many people who could not possibly afford cow's milk find that soymilk's greatest appeal lies in its remarkably low cost. Whether prepared at home or in tofu shops, specialty shops, or factories, it can be produced for about one-half to one-third the cost of cow's milk. Thus, in many parts of the world where dairy milk is not generally consumed and does not give promise of ever being able to meet the needs of growing populations, soymilk could serve as a practical source of high-quality, essential nutrients both for infants and growing children in their crucial formative years, and for adults of all ages. Moreover, it is already finding popular appeal in the affluent West, especially among the many people interested in natural, health, and diet foods, and in a growing number of communities that find they can produce their own soymilk fresh each morning for a fraction of the price they would have to pay for dairy milk. *The Farm* (see p. 316), a community of seven hundred, for example, has recently started its own soy dairy capable of producing 80 gallons of rich soymilk every day at a cost of only 7½ cents per quart. *Farm* spokesmen report that the community's "babies love soymilk" and that most of its 250 children have been weaned onto it directly. And many tofu shops in America now sell bottled soymilk (available plain, or sweetened with honey or honey-carob) to a growing number of patrons.

As we studied the tofu-making process in Taiwan, we noticed a continuous stream of people, each bringing a teapot or kettle to the local tofu shop to purchase several quarts of fresh soymilk. We learned that this is commonly served as part of the family breakfast and is considered an essential source of protein for babies and young children. Here, as well as on the mainland, soymilk is also bottled on a large scale by shops and factories and is delivered each morning to regular customers: workmen are said to consider it an excellent source of energy and stamina. We found that most tofu makers took special pride in the flavor of their own preparation; in every shop we visited, we were unfailingly offered a large cup of hot soymilk, generally sweetened with a little brown sugar. And almost every block in the city of Taipei seemed to have at least one shop or cafe specializing in spicy hot soymilk soups and sweetened soymilk drinks available from early morning until well after midnight.

In the 1950s, soymilk appeared in a new form, as a bottled, non-carbonated soft drink produced on a large scale by industrial methods. Aimed at replacing the empty calories of conventional soft drinks with protein and other essential nutrients, this product has been given an up-dated image by means of modern advertising techniques and slogans emphasizing health and nutrition. *Vitasoy*, the first beverage of its kind, was developed by Mr. S.K. Lo, an idealistic Hong Kong businessman, whose primary motivation was to provide nourishment for the masses at a price they could afford. Each 6½-ounce bottle contains 3 percent protein (6.8 grams) and retails for less than 3½ U.S. cents, or about two-thirds the cost of the same sized bottle of Coca Cola. Sold from sampans, sidewalk stands, and grocery stores, it is enjoyed ice cold in summer and piping hot in winter. By 1974, *Vitasoy's* sales had skyrocketed to more than 150 million bottles per year, making it Hong Kong's best selling soft drink.

Soon after *Vitasoy* caught on in Hong Kong, *Vitabean*, a similar beverage marketed by the Yeo Hiap Seng Company, came on the scene in Singapore and Kuala Lumpur (Malaysia). Pasteurized and packaged in decorative, aseptic tetrapak cartons containing 10 fluid ounces (284 cc), *Vitabean* can stay fresh for weeks without refrigeration. By the late 1960s, America's Monsanto Corporation had formed a joint venture with the Vitabean Company to market a variety of soymilk beverages (among them, *Puma*) in South America. Not long thereafter, the Coca Cola Corporation, apparently deciding to join rather than fight, opened its own soymilk soft drink plant in Rio de Janeiro, where it is producing *Saci*. And in India, Africa, and a growing number of other areas, protein-rich soymilk drinks flavored to suit local tastes (malt, orange, coffee, cinnamon, and vanilla) are now being sold for about one-fourth the price of cow's milk.

Recognizing the nutritive value of these soymilk beverages, prestigious international organizations such as UNICEF and the Food and Agricultural Organization (FAO) have recently given them their endorsement. The World Health Organization (WHO) has gone so far as to build a one-million-dollar soymilk factory in Indonesia and smaller plants in the Philippines (Manila) and other areas where soymilk has long been a traditional breakfast drink. Perhaps the world's most modern soymilk plant, privately owned by a Mr. Cheng, is located in Bangkok, Thailand; it is fully automated from the time the beans are dehulled until the finished product is bottled and packed for distribution. A product comprised of a mixture of soymilk and ordinary skim milk is also being marketed here.

In the West, the growing recognition of the value of soymilk has been greatly stimulated by the work of Dr. Harry W. Miller, now a resident of Southern California. Strong, alert, and very active at age 95, he is a living testimony to the health-giving virtues of soymilk. In 1936, while working as a medical missionary in Shanghai, Dr. Miller started the first soy dairy where soymilk was prepared on a large scale, sterlized in bottles, and distributed daily. Largely through Dr. Miller's efforts, soymilk fortified with vitamins and minerals has finally come to be used in the United States, too, primarily for feeding infants. His life's dream has been to see soymilk made available to people throughout the world, especially to the increasing number of children suffering from malnutrition.

The research work of Dr. Miller and other nutritionists around the world, based on experiments with large numbers of infants and young children, shows clearly and conclusively that soymilk can be used as a complete and effective substitute for dairy or human milk. When fortified with sulphur-containing amino acids, calcium, and vitamins A,B,C, and D, the nutritional balance of the product approaches its ideal as a baby food. In 1937, when Dr. Miller patented the first such formulated drink, he was advised that if he called it by its common and obvious name, soymilk, he would be fought by the dairy industry; so he latinized the name to *Soyalac*. The actual cost of preparing this milk in the United States is about one-half the cost of obtaining dairy milk (before bottling and distribution). Reports in various publications suggest that, for this reason, the American dairy industry may be growing increasingly concerned about the use of soymilk and other soy products to extend, or even replace, dairy products.

In Japan, soymilk is prepared by a number of large companies and sold in tetrapak cartons or, in condensed form, in cans. Now available in a variety of flavors (plain, honey, barley-malt, strawberry, or chocolate) at virtually all natural and health food stores and at most supermarkets, some types are even dispensed from vending machines or delivered door to door. (Many Japanese tofu makers used to deliver a bottle of soymilk each morning to a large number of their regular customers, but the tradition has gradually declined with the increasing availability of commercial soymilk and the post-war trend toward drinking dairy milk.) A formulated, canned soymilk for infants (and those allergic or sensitive to dairy milk) and at least four varieties of powdered, spray-dried soymilk packaged in cartons are available at most pharmacies or natural food stores. Plain powdered soymilk contains 44 to 52 percent protein, 28 percent fat (mostly polyunsaturated), and 12 percent carbohydrates; stored at room temperature, it will keep its flavor indefinitely and is an excellent lightweight ingredient for use on camping trips or picnics. One type of powdered soymilk, called *Bonlact*, is especially formulated for infants and growing children. Another, used primarily as a health food by adults on low-fat or reducing diets, is fortified with lecithin and linoleic acid, methionine, fruit sugar, plus vitamins and minerals. The most popular spray-dried soymilk is packaged together with a small envelope of lactone solidifier and sold at most food markets as instant homemade tofu.

Soymilk is well thought of by medical practitioners as well as laymen. Many Japanese doctors view it as an effective natural medicine and prescribe it as a regular part of the diet for diabetes (because it is low in starch); heart disease, high blood pressure, and hardening of the arteries (because it is free of cholesterol, low in saturated fats, and rich in lecithin and linoleic acid); and anemia (because it is rich in iron and is thought to stimulate the production of hemoglobin). It is also used to strengthen the digestive system (since health-giving lactic acid bacteria thrive and multiply in its presence) and alkalize—hence fortify—the bloodstream (since it is among the most alkaline sources of protein).

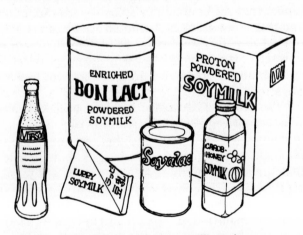

Commercial Japanese soymilk products

In his full-length book, *The Wonders of Soymilk*, Mr. Teisuke Yabuki carefully documents case after case where doctors or patients attribute the cure of various diseases to soymilk. Some prescribe it as an effective remedy for chronic nosebleed or bruises that won't heal; others find that it alleviates arthritis, softens corns, or restores healthy black hair. Some doctors assert that since soymilk contains an abundance of water-soluble vitamins (some of which dissolve in the whey during the tofu-making process), they actually prefer soymilk to tofu for use in diets related to vitamin-deficiency diseases.

Tofu makers have frequently told us that a number of their customers order soymilk daily for use as a medicine as well as a tasty beverage. Many Japanese claim that soymilk helps bring out the natural luster of the skin, and, in fact, people who work in tofu and yuba shops are well known for their fine complexions. Many a tofu maker has told us how, when his nursing wife's milk supply decreased or failed, she fed the baby soymilk, often using it as a basic food until weaning time. And even today, many pregnant and nursing women drink soymilk to increase the quality and flow of their milk. Soymilk is also thought to be effective in curing constipation and intestinal disturbances in children.

In Japanese tofu shops, soymilk is the source of each of the six types of tofu. The rich soymilk served as a drink is generally used to make kinugoshi tofu, while regular tofu is made from soymilk with a much thinner consistency. The secret of delicious soymilk lies above all in its thickness, which varies widely from shop to shop.

The point can well be made that soymilk is a better and more convenient way of using soybeans as a food than tofu: it is considerably easier to make, takes less than one-half the time, requires less fuel and equipment, and therefore costs less; it contains 83 percent of the protein originally present in the soybeans (tofu contains only 73½ percent due to losses in the whey and soaking water); it is a simpler food since no solidifier need be added in its manufacture; it contains the full, subtle sweetness of the soybeans, which gradually diminishes in proportion to the length of time the resultant kinugoshi or regular tofu is soaked in water; and it can be fed even to babies who are too young to eat tofu.

In recent years, a number of large commercial manufacturers of soymilk have developed methods for producing soymilk with a flavor quite similar to that of dairy milk. The characteristic soy flavor, which is found in water-soluble soybean enzymes rather than in the protein or oil, is removed by dehulling the beans, washing and draining them thoroughly several times before and after soaking, and cooking the gô for a fairly long time at a high temperature (about 8 minutes at 238°). Some makers then pasteurize the soymilk at 293° for a few seconds and package it in foil-lined tetrapak cartons in which it will keep for up to 1 month without refrigeration. Although this mild-flavored, modern product is said to have a wider appeal than its traditional counterpart, we—like almost all people in China and most Japanese tofu makers—definitely prefer the flavor of the natural product.

Used for centuries to make doufu-ru, a soft Chinese cheese-like product fermented in brining liquor (p. 262), soymilk can also be used to make Western-style cheeses (p. 88). Furthermore, it can be fermented with the same starters as dairy milk to make delicious and inexpensive homemade yogurt (p. 205). In Western-style cookery, soymilk may be used in any recipe calling for dairy milk.

The soymilk used in the recipes that follow may be the type freshly prepared at home (you can prepare excellent soymilk in a blender in less than 20 minutes) or any one of the varieties of fresh, powdered, or canned soymilk now available throughout the United States at most natural- and health food stores, many Japanese and Chinese markets, and a growing number of supermarkets.

"Kids love soymilk" (The Farm)

Homemade Soymilk

The recipe given below is the traditional one used in Japanese tofu shops. This rich, thick soymilk contains 5.5 percent protein (vs. 3% for dairy milk). Using storebought soybeans, it can be prepared at home for less than one-half the cost of dairy milk and should be ready to serve 20 minutes after you start. If you are not preparing homemade kinugoshi or yuba and desire a slightly larger yield of soymilk, heat 1 (instead of ½) cup water in the cooking pot initially. The utensils you will need are included among those required for preparing Homemade Tofu (p. 99).

1 cup soybeans, washed and drained 3 times, soaked in 2 quarts water for about 10 hours (see graph; p. 289), then rinsed and drained twice
4 cups water, approximately

Prepare pressing pot and sack in advance as for Homemade Tofu.

1) Heat ½ cup water over very low heat in covered cooking pot. While water is heating, combine beans and 2 2/3 cups water in a blender and purée at high speed for about 3 minutes, or until very smooth. (If using a grain mill, food mill, or meat grinder, grind beans without adding water and add 2 2/3 cups more water to cooking pot.)

2) Add soybean purée to water heating (or boiling) in cooking pot, rinsing out blender with ¼ cup water to retrieve any purée that may cling to blender's walls. Increase heat to medium-high and continue cooking, stirring bottom of pot constantly with a wooden spatula or spoon to prevent sticking (fig. 34b, p. 101). When foam suddenly rises in pot, quickly turn off heat and pour contents of pot into pressing sack (fig. c). Using a rubber spatula, retrieve any soybean purée that may still cling to sides of cooking pot and transfer to pressing sack. Quickly fill cooking pot with water and set aside to soak.

3) Twist hot sack closed. Using a glass jar or potato masher, press sack against colander, expressing as much soymilk as possible (fig. d). Open sack, shake okara into one corner, close and press again. Now open sack wide in colander and stir okara while blowing on it to hasten cooling, then allow okara to stand for 3 to 5 minutes while you wash cooking pot. Sprinkle ½ cup water over surface of okara. Close sack and press well as before, then squeeze sack by hand to express last of soymilk (fig. e). Empty okara into any large container and set aside.

4) Pour soymilk into cooking pot and bring to a boil over medium-high heat, stirring bottom constantly to prevent sticking. Reduce heat to medium and cook for 5 to 7 minutes, then turn off heat.

Serve soymilk hot or cold as Rich Soymilk (p. 205). To serve chilled, stir desired sweeteners and seasonings into hot soymilk, cover pot, and set into cold water for 10 minutes. Pour into a bottle, cover, and refrigerate.

Substitute soymilk for dairy milk in all cooking, or use to prepare Homemade Kinugoshi (p. 215) or Yuba (p. 242).

The leftover okara is especially rich in nutrients; be sure to use it (Chapter 6).

VARIATIONS

*For soymilk with a refreshing but subtle citrus fragrance and a slightly richer creaminess, add a very thin wedge of lemon, lime, or *yuzu* to soymilk at the beginning of step 4, and remove wedge just before serving.

*For soymilk with a milder flavor (more like that of dairy milk), remove hulls from soaked beans by rubbing under water, then skimming off with a mesh skimmer.

Homemade Chinese-style Soymilk
(Doufu-chiang)

Chinese-style soymilk is usually thinner than the Japanese variety and, in our opinion, considerably more difficult to prepare. Moreover, since unheated purée does not pass as easily through the pressing sack, this method gives a 10 percent lower yield of nutrients. If the okara is to be used in other recipes, be sure to cook it thoroughly since it is not cooked with the soymilk.

1 cup soybeans, washed and drained 3 times, soaked in 2 quarts water for 10 hours, then rinsed and drained twice
5½ to 6 cups water

Combine beans with 3½ cups (warm) water in a blender and purée at high speed for 3 minutes. Empty purée into a moistened cloth pressing sack lining a colander set over a large pot. Twist sack closed and squeeze sack gently but thoroughly to expel as much soymilk as possible. Remove okara and return to blender with 2 to 2½ cups more (warm) water; purée for about 1 minute. Return okara to pressing sack and squeeze again.

Bring soymilk to a boil over high heat, stirring constantly. Reduce heat to low and simmer for 5 to 7 minutes. (If foam begins to rise, remove with a skimmer.) Serve hot or cold with sweetening, as for Rich Soymilk (p. 205).

Homemade Soymilk
(from Powdered Soymilk)

Although soymilk prepared from powder is somewhat more expensive than (and not quite as delicious as) that made from whole soybeans, the process is naturally much faster since it is unnecessary to grind the beans or press the milk from okara. The soymilk will be ready less than 10 minutes after you start. This recipe is good for use on camping trips or when the soymilk is blended with other ingredients. Powdered soymilk is now available at many natural food stores and Japanese markets and when prepared according to the following recipe can be used to prepare Homemade Kinugoshi (p. 215).

1 cup powdered soymilk
3 cups water

Combine powder and water in a 3 to 4 quart saucepan and whisk well until dissolved. Bring to a boil over high heat, stirring constantly. Reduce heat to low and simmer for 3 minutes. Serve hot or cold.

Homemade Soymilk
(from Soy Flour)

MAKES 4¼ CUPS

Here is a recipe you can use if you are unable to obtain whole soybeans or powdered soymilk, or if you do not have a blender or grinder.

1 cup soy flour
3½ cups water

Combine soy flour and 3 cups water in a small saucepan and bring to a boil over medium heat, stirring constantly. Proceed as for Homemade Soymilk (p. 204), pressing soymilk through a cloth sack; rinse okara with ½ cup water and re-press. Now bring soymilk to a boil and simmer for 5 minutes before serving.

For variety, the soymilk may be cooked in a double boiler for about 50 minutes; omit the second cooking.

Soymilk Yogurt

MAKES 3¼ CUPS

Since soymilk ferments faster than dairy milk, soymilk yogurt takes less time and less starter, and involves much less trouble than dairy yogurt. Soymilk yogurt requires no special incubating and heating equipment and can be prepared at room temperature. When prepared from homemade soymilk, the cost is about one-sixth that of commercial dairy yogurt, while the protein content is often twice as high. The bacteria in the starter—fresh plain yogurt—produce lactic acid which acts as a protein solidifier in much the same way as nigari.

3¼ cups Homemade Soymilk (p. 204)
1 teaspoon yogurt

Allow freshly made soymilk to cool to slightly warmer than body temperature (105° to 110°). Remove thin yuba film from surface of soymilk and reserve. Stir yogurt into soymilk, then pour innoculated milk into a clean jar. Cover and allow to stand at room temperature (70°F or above) for 14 to 18 hours. When ready, set aside several tablespoons of the new yogurt to use as a starter for the next batch. Serve yogurt as is, sweetened with a little honey, or mixed with sliced bananas, raisins, toasted wheat germ, grated coconut, apple wedges, chopped nuts, sunflower seeds, or granola. Serve yuba sprinkled with a few drops of shoyu.

If cultured for too short a time, the tang and subtle sourness of fine yogurt will not develop; if cultured for too long, the yogurt will sour and separate into curds and whey.

Storebought soymilk can be made into yogurt by simply mixing in starter at room temperature and proceeding as above. To decrease fermentation time, add 1 teaspoon honey before innoculation, or use a little more starter or an incubator set at 100° to 110°.

SOYMILK QUICK AND EASY

Chilled soymilk can be served just as is, like dairy milk, on your favorite dishes such as hot or cold applesauce, crunchy granola, or fresh strawberries.

Rich Soymilk

SERVES 1

This is the most popular way of serving soymilk throughout East Asia. Generally soymilk is served steaming hot out of the tofu shop cauldron; but during the summer it is also served chilled. The latter has a richer, creamier consistency, a deeper natural sweetness, and a flavor more like that of dairy milk. In China and Taiwan, a well-known breakfast drink called *tento-chiang* or *tien-chiang* (sweet soymilk) consists of soymilk sweetened with sugar or molasses. It is usually served with deep-fried bread sticks wrapped in a *chapati*.

Serve Homemade Soymilk plain, or stir into 1 cup, hot or cold:
*1 to 2 teaspoons honey, natural sugar, molasses, *mizuame*, or barley sugar; and a dash of salt or several drops of shoyu. (The latter may also be used without the sweetening.)
*1 egg yolk. This greatly improves the drink's nutritional value.
*2½ teaspoons carob powder, 1 tablespoon honey or sugar, and a dash of salt. If desired, add several teaspoons malt and a few drops of vanilla to make malted milk or malted carob cocoa.
*2 teaspoons honey or sugar, ¼ teaspoon grated ginger-root (or 1/8 teaspoon powdered ginger), and 1/8 teaspoon each nutmeg and salt.
*1 tablespoon honey or *mizuame*, 2 tablespoons ground roasted sesame seeds and, if desired, 1 tablespoon grated glutinous yam.
*Cream ¼ cup nut butter (cashew, almond, peanut), 1½ teaspoons honey or natural sugar, and a dash of salt with a small amount of the warm milk, then stir in remainder of milk.

Sesame Soymilk for Children

MAKES 1 CUP

Soymilk is richer than dairy milk in almost every nutrient except calcium, a mineral which is essential for babies and growing children. The world's richest source of calcium is the sesame seed which contains over six times as much calcium by weight as dairy milk. Since soy and sesame proteins are complementary, their combination yields an abundance of high quality protein.

1 cup (warm) soymilk
1½ to 2 tablespoons *tahini* or sesame butter
1 to 1½ teaspoons honey or natural sugar
Dash of salt
1 egg yolk (optional)

Combine all ingredients, mixing well.

PURÉED SOYMILK BEVERAGES, FRUIT-WHIPS, AND DRESSINGS

Frothy Soymilk with Honey

MAKES 2 CUPS

2 cups chilled soymilk
1½ tablespoons honey or natural sugar

Combine ingredients in a blender and purée for 1 minute at high speed until light and frothy. Serve immediately in chilled mugs, over ice if desired.

Whipped Creamy Soymilk

SERVES 3

The lemon juice partially solidifies the soy protein which, when puréed, gives this beverage a thick, rich texture; the lemon adds a tasty tang. If a blender is not available, use an egg beater or whisk.

3¼ cups fairly hot soymilk, preferably homemade (p. 204)
1½ tablespoons honey
1½ teaspoons lemon juice and/or 2 tablespoons oil

Combine soymilk and honey in a blender and purée for 15 seconds. Slowly add lemon juice while continuing to purée for 30 seconds more. Allow mixture to stand for at least 1 minute, then purée again briefly just before serving.

Banana-Raisin Whip

MAKES 2 CUPS

½ cup chilled soymilk
2 chilled or frozen bananas
1/3 cup raisins
1 teaspoon lemon juice

Combine all ingredients in a blender and purée until smooth.

Healthy Banana Milkshake

MAKES 2 CUPS

1 cup chilled soymilk
¼ cup toasted wheat germ or Okara Granola (p. 84)
1 raw egg
1 or 2 chilled or frozen bananas
1 to 2 teaspoons honey or natural sugar
Dash of nutmeg

Combine all ingredients in a blender and purée until smooth. For variety, add a few dried fruits or nuts.

Nutty Soymilk

MAKES 2½ CUPS

2 cups soymilk
½ cup nutmeats, sunflower seeds, or roasted sesame seeds
1½ teaspoons honey or natural sugar
Dash of salt (if nuts are unsalted)

Combine all ingredients in a blender and purée until smooth. For extra sweetness, add a few dates, bananas, or raisins before puréing. Substitute nut butters, *tahini,* or sesame butter for the whole nuts. Serve chilled as a drink or topping for crunchy granola, or serve warm as a topping for cooked vegetables.

Fresh Fruit Whip

MAKES 2½ CUPS

2 cups chilled soymilk
½ to 1 cup fresh or frozen fruits or berries

Combine all ingredients in a blender and purée until smooth.

Thick Sweet Cream

MAKES 2½ CUPS

1 cup soymilk
12 ounces tofu
2 tablespoons honey or natural sugar

Combine all ingredients in a blender and purée until smooth. Serve over desserts, salads, cooked vegetables, or Cooked Apples with Agé (p. 179).

Soymilk Mayonnaise Dressing

MAKES 1 CUP

½ cup soymilk
½ cup oil
Juice of 1 lemon or 2½ tablespoons vinegar
½ teaspoon salt

Combine soymilk and ¼ cup oil in a blender and purée for 1 minute. Slowly add remaining oil in a thin stream. When mixture is fairly thick, add lemon juice and salt, and purée for 30 seconds more. For variety add minced onions, garlic, grated gingerroot, paprika, or your choice of herbs or seasonings. Or add any of the combinations of ingredients used in the variations to Tofu Mayonnaise (p. 107).

SOYMILK IN SOUPS OR SAUCES, WITH EGGS, AND IN OVEN COOKERY

Use soymilk as you would dairy milk in cream soups or scrambled eggs. It lends a creamy rich quality to casseroles, quiches, soufflés, and other baked dishes. In white, cheese, and cream sauces, soymilk may be used as either milk or cream depending on the soymilk's thickness.

Creamy Soymilk-Corn Soup with Thick Agé

SERVES 4 OR 5

Kernels from 1 ear of fresh corn
1 potato, diced
½ small carrot, diced
1½ small onions, minced
1¾ cups water
¾ teaspoon salt or 2 tablespoons red miso
¾ cup soymilk
1 tablespoon butter
Dash of pepper
10 ounces thick agé, ganmo, or agé, cubed (optional)
¼ cup minced parsley

Combine the first six ingredients and bring to a boil over medium heat. Reduce heat to low, cover pot, and simmer for 30 minutes. Allow to cool for a few minutes, then combine with soymilk in a blender and purée until smooth. Return mixture to pot and bring to a boil over medium heat. Add butter, pepper, and thick agé, and return to the boil. Serve hot or chilled, garnished with parsley.

Chinese Breakfast Soymilk Soup
(Siento-chiang)

SERVES 5

This soup is served morning and night in small shops throughout the cities and towns of Taiwan and China. It is given a special name if the raw egg is mixed with the soymilk before the various garnishes are added.

5 cups soymilk
Seasonings and Garnishes:
    Diced *cha-t'sai* or *takuan* salt pickles
    "Bits" of *yu-chiao* deep-fried bread sticks
    Grated *yuson* dried shrimp
    Bonita flakes or fish meal
    Diced leeks
    Sesame oil
    Salt
    Soy sauce
    Minced or 7-spice red pepper
    Raw egg (optional)

Heat the soymilk but do not bring to a boil; serve in individual bowls. Arrange small dishes filled with garnishes and allow each guest to select garnishes to taste.

Rich and Creamy Potatoes

SERVES 4

3 tablespoons butter
4 potatoes, cut into ½-inch cubes
2 small onions, cut into thin wedges
2½ cups soymilk
½ teaspoon salt
Dash of pepper
2 tablespoons natural sugar
¼ cup diced parsley

Melt the butter in a skillet. Add potatoes and onions, and sauté until onions are transparent. Add soymilk, salt, and pepper and simmer until potatoes are thoroughly cooked. Mix in sugar and simmer for several minutes more, then remove from heat and allow to cool. Serve topped with parsley.

Lemon-Miso White Sauce

SERVES 2

2 tablespoons butter or oil
2 tablespoons (whole-wheat) flour
1 cup soymilk
4 teaspoons red or barley miso; 2½ teaspoons shoyu; or 2/3 teaspoon salt
2 teaspoons lemon juice
¼ teaspoon grated lemon rind (optional)
12 ounces tofu or 7½ ounces thick agé, cut into bite-sized cubes
Dash of pepper, paprika, or cayenne
1 tablespoon minced parsley (optional)

Use the first four ingredients to prepare a White Sauce (p. 48). When sauce is partially thickened, add lemon juice (and rind) together with tofu. Continue to cook, stirring gently, for about 2 minutes more, or until sauce is well thickened. Stir in pepper and, if used, the parsley, and remove from heat.

VARIATIONS

*Soymilk-Mushroom Sauce: After adding milk, add ¼ diced onion and 6 thinly-sliced mushrooms. Simmer over low heat, stirring constantly, for 4 to 5 minutes, then add 1 teaspoon lemon juice, a dash of pepper, and 1 tablespoon white wine or sake. Add tofu or substitute 5 ounces thick agé, ganmo, or agé. Finish cooking as above.

*Soymilk-Cheese Sauce: Sauté 1 clove crushed garlic in the butter for 15 seconds, then add flour, soymilk, and miso as above. Omit lemon juice. Stir in pepper and ½ teaspoon powdered hot mustard. Simmer, stirring constantly, for 2 minutes, or until sauce has thickened. Stir in ½ to 1 cup (1½ to 3 ounces) grated cheese and 5 ounces deep-fried tofu (or 12 ounces regular tofu) cut into cubes. Serve hot or cold.

*Herb Sauce: Use 2 teaspoons each minced chives and parsley, and 1/8 teaspoon marjoram. Sauté chives and parsley for 3 minutes, then add marjoram with flour and proceed as for basic recipe.

SOYMILK WITH GRAINS

Use soymilk as you would dairy milk in pancakes or waffles, breads, French toast, or muffins, and as a topping for hot breakfast cereals such as rolled oats or oatmeal.

Buckwheat Noodles Cooked in Soymilk   SERVES 2

1½ cups soymilk
1 small onion, diced
2 tablespoons shoyu or 2½ tablespoons red miso
2 tablespoons butter
½ cup grated cheese or 2½ tablespoons sesame butter
3½ ounces *(soba)* buckwheat noodles, cooked (p. 50) and
    well drained
Dash of pepper
2 tablespoons minced parsley or ground roasted sesame seeds
    (p. 38)
Crumbled toasted *nori* (optional)

Combine soymilk and onion in a large saucepan and bring to a boil over medium heat, stirring constantly. Mix in the next three ingredients, add noodles, and return to the boil. Season with pepper and remove from heat. Allow to stand until soymilk clabbers. Serve garnished with parsley and, if desired, the *nori*.

SOYMILK IN COOKED DESSERTS AND STEAMED DISHES

Use soymilk in puddings, cakes, ice cream, and other treats, or as a base for delicately-flavored Japanese-style steamed custards.

Soymilk Custard Pudding   SERVES 4

2 tablespoons melted butter
1½ to 2 cups soymilk
3 tablespoons honey or natural sugar
Dash of salt
½ teaspoon vanilla (optional)
4 eggs, well beaten
1 cup Tofu Whipped Cream (p. 148)

Preheat steamer (p. 38) or oven to 300°, and use the butter to coat 4 custard cups. Combine soymilk, honey, and salt in a small saucepan and heat to body temperature. Add vanilla and stir well.

Place eggs in a large bowl and stir vigorously with a whisk. Add the warm soymilk while stirring, then pour mix-

ture through a strainer into the 4 custard cups. Cover cups with paper and lid (p. 38) and steam over low heat for 13 to 15 minutes. (Or, if using an oven, place cups in a pan of hot water and bake for 20 to 30 minutes.) Chill thoroughly and serve topped with Tofu Whipped Cream.

For variety, add a little grated lemon rind or 2 teaspoons minced raisins to the custard just before steaming. Or omit eggs and substitute 6 tablespoons cornstarch, arrowroot, or *kuzu*.

Brown Rice Pudding   SERVES 4 TO 6

1¼ cups cooked Brown Rice (p. 50)
2 cups soymilk
2½ tablespoons honey
2 tablespoons butter
½ cup raisins
½ teaspoon salt
½ teaspoon cinnamon

Combine rice and soymilk in a small pan and bring to a boil over low heat. Add remaining ingredients and simmer, stirring constantly, for 10 minutes or until soymilk is completely absorbed. Serve chilled.

For variety, add 2 thinly sliced bananas and substitute ½ teaspoon nutmeg for the cinnamon. Or add ¼ cup *tahini*, 2 eggs, and 1 teaspoon vanilla. Any of these dishes may be baked at 350° for 20 minutes.

Oatmeal Pudding   SERVES 3 TO 4

2½ cups soymilk
½ cup oatmeal
½ cup raisins
1½ cups chopped apple
2 or 3 tablespoons brown sugar
¼ to ½ teaspoon cinnamon
½ teaspoon salt

Bring soymilk to a boil over medium heat in a small pan. Slowly stir in the oatmeal, then the remaining ingredients. Reduce heat to low and simmer, stirring constantly, for about 10 minutes, or until thick. Serve chilled.

Apple Soymilk Dessert

SERVES 2

In this Chinese dish, the natural acid from the apple clabbers the soymilk to yield a pudding consistency.

1 cup soymilk
½ cup water
1 to 2 tablespoons natural sugar or honey
Dash of salt
1 teaspoon cornstarch or arrowroot dissolved in 1 tablespoon water
1 small apple, peeled and grated

Combine the first four ingredients in a saucepan and bring to a boil over medium heat. Stir in dissolved cornstarch and grated apple, and return just to the boil. Serve chilled.

For variety, add 1 tablespoon butter, 3 tablespoons raisins, and a dash of cinnamon.

Soymilk Egg Tofu

SERVES 2

Soymilk gives this richly-textured tofu a creamier, more custard-like quality than its close relative, Egg Tofu (p. 267).

¾ cup (homemade) soymilk, cooled to room temperature
1 egg, lightly beaten
¼ teaspoon shoyu

Combine all ingredients in a small bowl; mix well. Divide the mixture among 2 custard cups, cover, and place in an unheated steamer (p. 38). Bring steamer to a boil, reduce heat to low and steam for 13 to 15 minutes. (Oversteaming will create tiny bubbles in the tofu and spoil its delicate texture.) Serve as is or topped with a few drops of shoyu.

For a richer flavor, include an additional egg, 1 tablespoon butter, and 1 teaspoon *mirin*. Or add 2 tablespoons peanut butter. This dish may also be steamed in a rectangular pan (as for Egg Tofu, p. 267) or baked in a 300° oven for 20 minutes (as for custard).

Soymilk Chawan-mushi

SERVES 4

2 cups soymilk
1 egg, lightly beaten
2½ tablespoons shoyu
2 mushrooms, thinly sliced
1/8 onion, thinly sliced
¼ cup green peas or fresh corn, parboiled
½ ounce agé, thinly sliced; or 4 small ganmo balls (p. 188) (optional)
2 tablespoons diced sweet potatoes (optional)

Combine the first three ingredients in a small bowl; mix well. Divide the remaining ingredients among 4 Chawan-mushi or custard cups, then pour in the soymilk mixture. Steam for 15 minutes as for Chawan-mushi (p. 147).

For variety, add small amounts of fresh or deep-fried yuba, chestnuts, cubes of fresh wheat gluten, or sections of lilly bulbs and ginkgo nuts.

JELLED AND MOLDED SOYMILK DISHES
(Yose-dofu)

A number of dessert or semi-dessert dishes can be prepared from soymilk jelled with agar, *kuzu*, or arrowroot starch.

Soymilk Kuzu Mochi

SERVES 4

3¼ cups soymilk
½ cup powdered *kuzu*
¼ cup brown sugar
¼ cup kinako

Combine soymilk and *kuzu* in a small saucepan and cook over medium heat, stirring constantly, until the mixture begins to thicken. Reduce heat to low and stir vigorously for 2 or 3 minutes or until mixture thickens and becomes transparent. Smooth surface of mixture with a wooden spatula, then remove from stove and allow to cool thoroughly. Cut jelled mixture into small triangles or break into bite-size pieces and arrange on 4 plates. Mix the sugar with enough water to form a thick syrup, and pour over each serving. Serve topped with a sprinkling of kinako.

For variety, add the sugar (or 2 teaspoons powdered green *matcha* tea) to the soymilk with the *kuzu*. Serve topped with Sweet Peanut Sauce (p. 91).

Banana Blancmange

SERVES 4 TO 6

1¼ cups soymilk
¼ cup powdered *kuzu*
1 banana
2 tablespoons honey
1 tablespoon lemon juice
Tofu Whipped Cream (p. 148)

Combine the first four ingredients in a blender and purée until smooth. Transfer to a small saucepan and cook, stirring constantly, over medium heat until mixture begins to thicken. Reduce heat to low and stir for 2 or 3 minutes more, until mixture becomes partially transparent. Stir in lemon juice and spoon the mixture into a mold partially immersed in cold water; allow to cool to room temperature, then refrigerate until well chilled. Serve topped with Tofu Whipped Cream.

VARIATIONS

*Egg Blancmange: Substitute 1 egg for the banana.
*Egg-Lemon Blancmange: Combine in a blender: ¾ cup soymilk, 2 tablespoons *kuzu*, 1 egg, 2 teaspoons lemon juice, and 1 tablespoon honey; prepare as above but serve without the whipped cream.

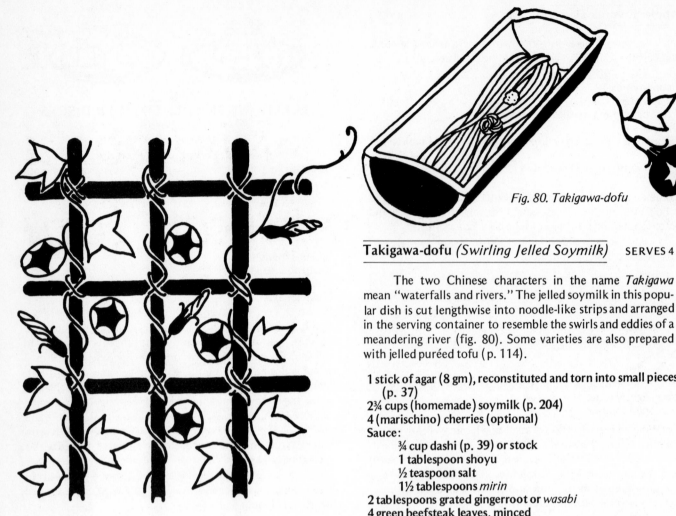

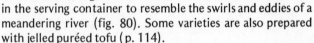

Fig. 80. Takigawa-dofu

Takigawa-dofu (Swirling Jelled Soymilk) SERVES 4

The two Chinese characters in the name *Takigawa* mean "waterfalls and rivers." The jelled soymilk in this popular dish is cut lengthwise into noodle-like strips and arranged in the serving container to resemble the swirls and eddies of a meandering river (fig. 80). Some varieties are also prepared with jelled puréed tofu (p. 114).

1 stick of agar (8 gm), reconstituted and torn into small pieces (p. 37)
2¾ cups (homemade) soymilk (p. 204)
4 (marischino) cherries (optional)
Sauce:
    ¾ cup dashi (p. 39) or stock
    1 tablespoon shoyu
    ½ teaspoon salt
    1½ tablespoons *mirin*
2 tablespoons grated gingerroot or *wasabi*
4 green beefsteak leaves, minced

Combine agar and soymilk in a large saucepan. Stirring constantly, bring soymilk to a boil over medium heat, then simmer for 3 minutes, or until agar dissolves. Pour through a strainer into a shallow rectangular pan so that soymilk fills the pan to a depth of about 1½ inches. Allow to cool to room temperature, then cut into 4 equal rectangular pieces. Cut each piece lengthwise and horizontally to form thin noodle-like strips (or press each piece through a *tentsuki* or *konnyaku* noodle slicer available at Japanese markets or hardware stores). Place 1 cherry at the center of each of four serving dishes (or in large hollow sections of fresh bamboo), then arrange strips around cherries so that they seem to swirl around them. Chill.

Combine dashi, shoyu, salt, and *mirin* in a saucepan and bring just to a boil. Allow to cool to room temperature, then refrigerate. Pour over each serving of tofu, then top with dabs of gingerroot and beefsteak leaves.

VARIATIONS

*Substitute ¼ cup Yuzu Miso (p. 42) for the sauce.

*Gohoji-dofu: Cook ¼ cup parboiled green soybeans together with the soymilk and agar; serve without cutting into strips. Top with shoyu and grated gingerroot.

Jelled Soymilk Dessert with Bananas and Raisins SERVES 4

1 banana, sliced into thin rounds
1/3 cup raisins
¼ cup chopped walnut or almond meats
2 tablespoons honey
1½ cups soymilk
1 stick of agar (8 gm), reconstituted and torn into small pieces (p. 37)
Nutmeg

Divide the banana slices, raisins, and nutmeats among 4 (custard) cups. Combine honey, soymilk, and agar in a saucepan and bring to a boil. Simmer, stirring constantly, for 3 minutes, or until agar dissolves. Pour soymilk-agar mixture through a (warmed) strainer into the cups. Top each serving with a pinch of nutmeg and allow to cool. Chill thoroughly before serving.

Or substitute 1½ cups fresh strawberries for the first three ingredients and omit nutmeg.

11

Kinugoshi or Silken Tofu

K INU MEANS "silk"; *kosu* means "to strain": well-named, *kinugoshi* tofu has a texture so smooth that it seems to have been strained through silk. Soft and white, it melts in the mouth like custard or firm yogurt. Made from thick soymilk, kinugoshi has a subtle bouquet (especially when prepared with nigari) and natural sweetness resembling that of rich, fresh cream.

The Japanese language contains an abundance of words used to describe nuances of feeling, texture, and taste. *Shita-zawari*, for example, refers to the particular feeling that a food makes as it touches the tongue, and *nodo-goshi* to the gentleness with which it goes down the throat: kinugoshi is the epitome of exquisite *shita-zawari* and *nodo-goshi*. Free of even the fine-grained structure and internal cohesiveness of regular tofu, kinugoshi is so delicate that a chopstick slices—almost glides—evenly and effortlessly through it, leaving behind a nearly smooth surface.

At the tofu shop or market, a cake of kinugoshi is almost indistinguishable from one of regular tofu. Their shape and proportions appear the same, but the kinugoshi is usually slightly smaller, its color is a bit whiter, and its surface is smoother and less porous. The two types are made from the same basic ingredients and sell for about the same price.

Nevertheless, kinugoshi is prepared by a fundamentally different process, one characterized above all by its use of relatively thick soymilk. The boxes used to give form to the kinugoshi have neither draining holes nor lining cloths. While still hot, kinugoshi soymilk is simply poured in (fig. 81) and, in most neighborhood shops, solidified with calcium sulfate placed at the bottom of the boxes just before the soymilk is added. (Traditionally, kinugoshi was prepared by carefully stirring a solution of nigari and water into the soymilk just after it had been poured into the box [fig. 82]). The kinugoshi is allowed to stand in the boxes for 20 to 30 minutes until it becomes firm. *The curds and whey never separate and the tofu is never pressed.* Finally, the tofu is trimmed away from the sides of each box with a long knife (fig. 83), the box and tofu are immersed in cold water, and the tofu is carefully removed and cut into 12-ounce cakes.

When making regular tofu, some of the protein, vitamin B, natural oils, and sugars dissolve in the whey and are removed with it. Since whey is never removed from kinugoshi, the latter contains more of the nutrients originally in the soybeans. At the same time, it has a slightly higher water content, hence a somewhat lower percentage of protein than that contained in regular tofu (5.5% vs. 7.8%). It is this higher water content that gives kinugoshi its softer consistency. Its homogenous, fine-grained structure prevents the loss of natural sugars (as well as solidifier) when the tofu is soaked in water, so that kinugoshi generally retains more of the soymilk's sweetness. However, because of its delicate, fine grain, kinugoshi cannot be pressed and firmed, and when simmered with sauces or in seasoned broths, it does not readily absorb other flavors. Although its versatility in cooking is, therefore, limited, its sensuous texture and creamy sweetness make it a much favored delicacy.

In Japan, kinugoshi, like cool silk, is associated with summer. When served chilled, it can be as lus-

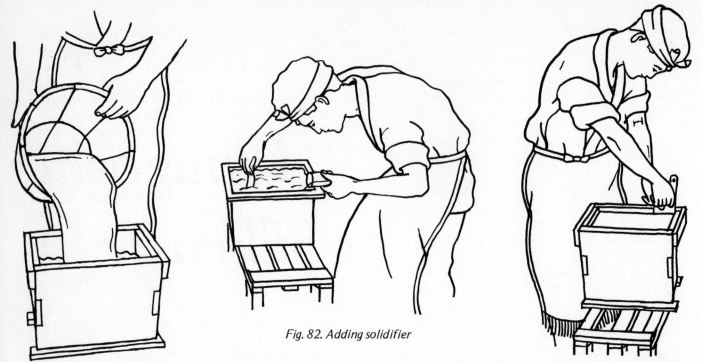

Fig. 81. Pouring the soymilk

Fig. 82. Adding solidifier

Fig. 83. Trimming kinugoshi from sides of box

cious as a succulent melon. Refreshingly light, it quenches thirst and cools both body and spirit while providing the energy to carry one through a hot day's work. During the hottest months, most kinugoshi in Japan is served as Iceberg Chilled Tofu, a simple refreshing dish designed to bring to life and celebrate the tofu's flavor.

With the first autumn colors on the maple leaves, kinugoshi begins to appear in the second of its most popular roles, Simmering Tofu, the cold-weather equivalent of Chilled Tofu and one of Japan's most popular *nabe*, or one-pot cookery, dishes. At many fine restaurants, the *nabe* is heated over a charcoal brazier and served outdoors, with no sources of light or heat other than the glowing coals, perhaps a paper lantern, and the piping-hot tofu.

Other main uses of kinugoshi are in miso soups, clear soups, and dishes served with various shoyu dipping sauces or miso toppings. Regular tofu can always be substituted for kinugoshi, but keep in mind that the texture of the dish may not be quite as soft and smooth. Kinugoshi, however, *cannot* always be substituted for regular tofu, particularly if the recipe calls for the tofu to be pressed, skewered, broiled, or sautéed in cube form. Kinugoshi is also not generally used in dishes such as scrambled eggs, omelets, or casseroles since it may contribute more water than is desirable. Kinugoshi yields good results when steamed or puréed to make cream sauces, spreads, dips, dressings, or foods for babies or elderly adults.

In many Japanese tofu shops, kinugoshi is prepared only during the warm months from about May until October and, during this time, the demand is often greater than that for regular tofu. In some shops, a little freshly-grated *yuzu* (or lime) rind or gingerroot is mixed into the soymilk before adding the solidifier to impart a light fragrance.

At present, there are five different types of kinugoshi sold in Japan. The primary factors determining the quality of each are the thickness of the soymilk and the type of solidifier used. The most traditional varieties, those solidified with nigari, were probably first developed in Japan. However, since the preparation of this tofu required a great deal of skill, and since nigari kinugoshi was too fragile to be easily transported, it was made at only a small number of Japan's finest tofu shops. Hence it was considered a rare delicacy—which most Japanese never had an opportunity to taste.

The earliest form of nigari kinugoshi, *shikishi-dofu*, was prepared in about 30 to 50 tiny wooden kegs, each about 4 inches deep, 4 inches in diameter, and coated inside with lacquer. Hot soymilk was poured into each container, nigari stirred in, and the kinugoshi allowed to form. The individual kegs were then immersed in water and the tofu removed, to be sold in its cylindrical form.

Beginning in the year 1703, a second form of nigari kinugoshi came to be prepared in Japan at Tokyo's Sasa-no-yuki tofu shop and restaurant. Today, as far as we now, no other shop in Japan makes nigari kinugoshi, primarily for lack of a sufficiently talented master. (The present master asserts that it took him six years to learn the process.) Sasa-no-yuki's delicious kinugoshi, with its unmatched nigari-evoked sweetness, is the delight of tofu connoisseurs throughout Japan. The words *sasa-no-yuki* mean "the snow on small bamboo leaves," a precise description of the delicate softness of this tofu from which the shop took its name. For three centuries, the terms "nigari kinugoshi" and "Sasa-no-yuki" have been almost synonymous, and today, too, the restaurant offers 12 separate dishes, each featuring its kinugoshi. (Many of these recipes and the method for preparing homemade nigari kinugoshi are included in this chapter.)

The transformation of kinugoshi from a rare and somewhat aristocratic food into one that was truly democratic came about through a quirk of history. At the beginning of World War II, the Japanese government siezed all of the nigari from the country's salt fields to use as a source of magnesium to build lightweight aircarft. Tofu makers were suddenly forced to switch to calcium sulfate solidifier. Although considered at the time to make less delicious tofu, it required less skill and less time to use and produced firmer tofu that was easier to transport. This made it possible for virtually every craftsman in the country to begin making kinugoshi. Thus most Japanese first tasted kinugoshi in the 1950s. And although it is now as common as regular tofu, and takes less time and effort to make, even calcium sulfate kinugoshi retains a sense of its aristocratic origins, being sold in equally priced but slightly smaller cakes than regular tofu. This second type of kinugoshi, which is still the most popular variety in Japan, has been prepared in China using gypsum (natural calcium sulfate) since ancient times.

The third type of kinugoshi is made with lactone (glucono-delta lactone or GDL), an organic acid that solidifies soymilk in much the same way that lactic acid or a yogurt starter is used to curdle dairy milk. A newly discovered solidifier made from natural gluconic acid, lactone makes it possible for the first time to solidify very thin soymilk, and even cold soymilk, by simply heating it to somewhat below the boiling point. When used in neighborhood tofu shops, lactone is generally combined with calcium sulfate. It is also included with the powdered soymilk in the packages of instant homemade tofu now sold in most Japanese supermarkets.

The fourth type of kinugoshi available in Japan, Packaged Lactone Kinugoshi, is also solidified with lactone, but the chilled soymilk is mixed with the solidifier right in the plastic container in which

the tofu is eventually sold. The top of the container is covered with a sheet of plastic film, sealed thermally, and immersed in hot water at the factory for about 50 minutes during which time the tofu solidifies. (In some cases the tofu is solidified in sausage-shaped plastic bags [fig. 84].) This method allows the tofu to be mass-produced in highly automated factories, the largest of which have a daily output of 60,000 cakes (fig. 85). Japan's least expensive tofu, the 10½-ounce packaged cakes are distributed over an area of several hundred miles and sold at supermarkets at about 68 percent the cost (on a usable protein basis) of regular tofu and 60 percent the cost (on an equal weight basis) of the kinugoshi sold in neighborhood tofu shops. Furthermore, since the tofu is sterilized and sealed in the container, it stays fresh for up to 1 week if refrigerated. In many cases, however, the low price of the tofu only too faithfully reflects the thinness of the soymilk from which it is made. Although its flavor is often rather weak and the use of lactone gives it a texture somewhat like that of jello, however, it presently retails for as low as 15 cents per pound and consequently has found a very large market. Recently a number of higher quality (and slightly higher priced) varieties of Packaged Lactone Kinugoshi have become available. Made with richer soymilk (containing 5.5 rather than the typical 4.4 percent protein), they are solidified with a combination of lactone and calcium sulfate.

The fifth type of kinugoshi, and the most recently developed, is called Sealed Lactone Kinugoshi. The soymilk-lactone mixture is funneled into thick-walled polyethylene containers through a very small opening. The opening is then pinched closed and thermally sealed so that (unlike the previous type of kinugoshi) absolutely no air can enter. After being heated and solidified as above, this tofu (which contains no preservatives) stays fresh for 2 to 3 months. Moreover, the sturdy container makes it

Fig. 84. Modern lactone kinugoshi

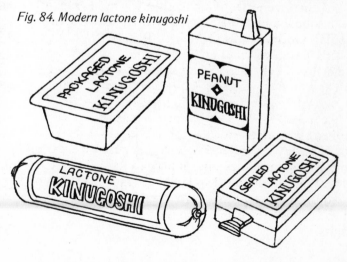

possible to carry the tofu (in box lunches, for example) without fear of leakage or crushing the delicate curd structure. Although the cost of the container makes the retail price of this tofu about 85 to 90 percent higher than the previous variety, it is still relatively inexpensive and its convenience is winning it wide acceptance. Sealed Lactone Kinugoshi is now sold in three different flavors: regular, peanut, and egg. In the peanut type, nuts are ground together with the soybeans and made into soymilk; in the egg type, eggs are stirred into the chilled soymilk and the mixture reheated slightly before it is funneled into the containers. These two varieties contain up to 26 percent more protein than regular kinugoshi and are popular items at many natural- and health food stores.

Another type of modern tofu, closely resembling but nevertheless different from kinugoshi, is called "soft tofu." Like kinugoshi, it is solidified using calcium sulfate without the separation of curds and whey. But it is solidified in the curding barrel rather than in the kinugoshi box, and the solidified curds, ladled into the settling boxes used for regular tofu, are pressed with heavy weights until the tofu is firm. Soft tofu has almost the same smooth, homogeneous texture as kinugoshi, plus some of the internal strength and cohesiveness of regular tofu. Very fine-grained and difficult to press, it is generally used in recipes calling for kinugoshi.

It has been estimated that during the summertime in Japan, the total consumption of regular tofu is only about one-fourth that of the five types of kinugoshi plus "soft tofu."

Kinugoshi is now prepared by many Japanese and Chinese tofu shops in the United States. Sold in 12-ounce cakes in the same type of containers as regular tofu, it is commonly called Kinugoshi Soft Tofu or, in some Chinese shops, *Sui-dofu*. It is usually solidified with either lactone (GDL) or calcium sulfate. Some Japanese markets and co-op stores now

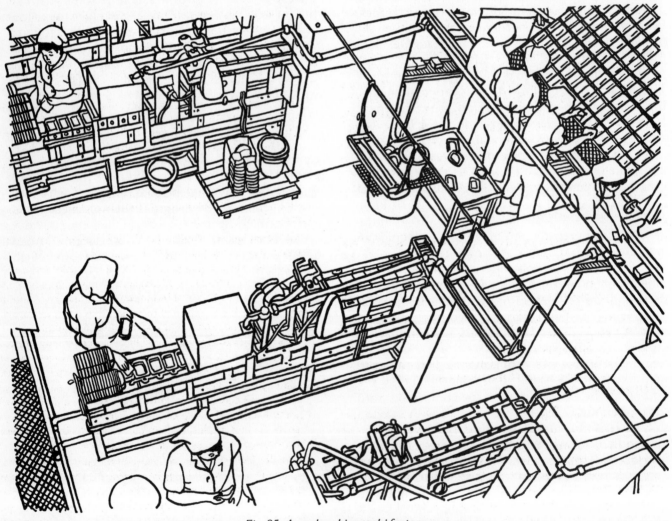

Fig. 85. A modern kinugoshi factory

also sell an instant homemade kinugoshi consisting of powdered soymilk and a small envelope of lactone solidifier. One package makes about 21 ounces and takes 15 to 20 minutes to prepare; directions are given on the package. A high-priced, canned kinugoshi is available in some Japanese markets but, in our opinion, its flavor does not meet up to expectation. Fortunately, fresh kinugoshi is very easy to prepare at home, even using nigari-type solidifier.

HOMEMADE KINUGOSHI

Homemade Kinugoshi (from Whole Soybeans)	MAKES 27 OUNCES

Kinugoshi is easier and faster to prepare than regular tofu and requires no special settling container. The yield is also considerably greater—1 pound of beans makes about 4½ pounds of tofu—and only half as much solidifier is required. We feel that kinugoshi made with natural nigari or magnesium chloride nigari is the most delicate and delicious. However, kinugoshi made with calcium sulfate is the firmest and easiest to prepare. Kinugoshi is usually ready to serve about 50 minutes after you start to prepare soymilk. In the following method, the kinugoshi is served like a custard or molded salad. In the last variation, the kinugoshi is first removed from the settling container so that it can be cut into cakes, as is usually done in Japan. This latter procedure is a bit difficult to master. For information about solidifiers, see pp. 282-285.

3¼ cups Homemade Soymilk (p. 204)
Solidifier:
1) For delicate, subtly-sweet nigari kinugoshi: ½ teaspoon magnesium chloride or calcium chloride; 3/8 teaspoon granular or powdered natural nigari; 1/3 to 1 teaspoon liquid natural nigari from (home-processed) sea salt; or ½ to 1½ teaspoons liquid natural nigari from a salt refinery
2) For firm, mild kinugoshi: ½ teaspoon Epsom salts (magnesium sulfate) or calcium sulfate; or 1 teaspoon lactone (GDL)
3) For firm, subtly tart kinugoshi: 4 teaspoons lemon or lime juice, or 1 tablespoon (apple cider) vinegar
2 tablespoons water

Prepare Homemade Soymilk (p. 204). Place a 1½- to 3-quart serving bowl or a casserole on a firm surface (where it will not be jiggled or disturbed for 20 minutes) and pour in the freshly-made hot soymilk; cover. In a small cup quickly mix the solidifier with 2 tablespoons water and stir until dissolved. Stir soymilk back and forth briskly for 3 to 5 seconds, then quickly pour in all of the solidifier solution. Continue stirring soymilk for 3 to 5 seconds more, making sure to stir to bottom of container. Now stop spoon upright in center of soy-

milk and wait until turbulence ceases; lift out spoon. Let soymilk stand uncovered and undisturbed for 20 to 30 minutes while it cools and solidifies. Now cover with plastic wrap and refrigerate, or float bowl in cold water until chilled. To serve, bring the bowl to the table or ladle the kinugoshi into individual serving dishes. Serve as for Chilled Tofu (p. 105).

VARIATIONS

*Fragrant Kinugoshi: Just before adding the solidifier, stir any of the following into the hot soymilk: ¼ teaspoon grated rind of *yuzu*, lemon, or lime; ¼ to ½ teaspoon grated ginger-root; 10 to 15 minced mint leaves; 10 green beefsteak leaves which have been soaked in water for 10 minutes, drained, squeezed gently in a dry towel, and minced. Serve the latter garnished with 2 teaspoons *benitade*.

*Peanut Kinugoshi: Cream 2 or 3 tablespoons smooth peanut butter with a little of the hot soymilk, then stir into the soymilk just before adding solidifier. Or purée 3 to 4 tablespoons whole peanuts with the soybeans when preparing soymilk, and increase the amount of solidifier used by about 25 percent.

*Kinugoshi with Eggs: Whisk 2 lightly beaten eggs into the hot soymilk just before stirring in solidifier.

*Jade-Green Kinugoshi: Just before adding solidifier, stir 1 tablespoon powdered green tea *(matcha)* and 3 tablespoons honey into the soymilk. Serve chilled without topping or garnish.

*Sweet Kinugoshi: Stir 1 tablespoon honey or natural sugar into the hot soymilk just before adding the solidifier.

*Subtly-Sweet & Firm Kinugoshi: Solidify the soymilk with a combination of ¼ teaspoon Epsom salts (or calcium sulfate) and ¼ teaspoon magnesium chloride (or calcium chloride) nigari.

*Gelatinous Kinugoshi: Solidify 3¼ cups soymilk with a combination of ½ teaspoon lactone (GDL) and ¼ teaspoon calcium sulfate (or Epsom salts).

*Reheated Lactone Kinugoshi: Mix 3¼ cups soymilk at room temperature (below 86°) with 1 teaspoon lactone. Pour into one or more heat-resistant containers (plastic tubs serve well) and seal or cover. Float or partially immerse containers in water at about 185° for 50 minutes until solidified. Cool in water below 68° for 50 minutes more. This method is used commercially to prepare Packaged Lactone Kinugoshi.

*Tofu Shop-style Kinugoshi: In place of a large bowl or casserole, use a 5- to 7-inch diameter, 1½-quart saucepan or box (wooden or metal) as a settling container. After 15 to 20 minutes, when kinugoshi is quite firm, float the pan in a large basin or sink filled with cold water for several minutes more. Carefully separate kinugoshi from walls of container using a narrow spatula or knife, then cut kinugoshi into quarters. Slowly press one edge of container under water so that it gradually fills with water. Wait several minutes as tofu cools further and firms. If kinugoshi quarters do not float, use spatula to carefully separate each quarter from bottom of container. Wait 5 to 10 minutes until center of tofu is firm. Now slip a small plate under each piece, lift out, drain, and serve. Or store in a cool place.

Kinugoshi Custard (Shikishi-dofu)   SERVES 3 OR 4

The earliest kinugoshi made in Japan was prepared in this simple but attractive way. If possible, use calcium sulfate solidifier: it curdles the soymilk slowly, and the curds and whey do not separate while the soymilk-solidifier mixture is being poured into the serving cups.

Prepare Homemade Soymilk (p. 204). Place 3 or 4 custard or coffee cups where they will be undisturbed. Mix the solidifier with 2 tablespoons water as for Homemade Kinugoshi (p. 215), then stir quickly into hot soymilk in the cooking pot. Immediately pour this soymilk-solidifier mixture into the cups. Cool and chill as for Homemade Kinugoshi. Serve in the cups seasoned with shoyu, or top with Ankake Sauce (p. 49), or any of the dipping sauces or toppings used with Chilled Tofu (p. 105).

VARIATIONS

*Kinugoshi Custard with Crisp Vegetables: This dish bears a close resemblance to *Chawan Mushi*. Dice or sliver any or all of the following: lotus root, carrot, mushroom, ginkgo nuts, green peas, trefoil, burdock root. Simmer in Sweetened Shoyu Broth (p. 40) until just tender. Place 3 tablespoons of the vegetables in the bottom of each custard cup before pouring in the soymilk-solidifier mixture; wait several minutes. Poke a few vegetable pieces into the surface of the solidifying curds and sprinkle a few pieces on top.
*Sweetened Kinugoshi with Fruits: Fill each of 5 custard cups about two-thirds full with fresh strawberries, thinly-sliced peaches, bananas, or apples. Prepare one-half of the regular recipe for Homemade Soymilk (p. 204). Stir quickly into the hot soymilk: 1 to 2 tablespoons honey, ¼ teaspoon vanilla extract, and 3/8 teaspoon calcium sulfate solidifier. Pour the mixture immediately into the cups to cover the fruits. Allow to cool, then cover with plastic wrap and chill before serving.
*Rich Kinugoshi Custard Dessert: Add ½ cup powdered milk (soy or dairy) to 3¼ cups hot soymilk just before stirring in ¾ teaspoon calcium sulfate solidifier. Pour mixture immediately into cups. Serve chilled as is, or top with a small amount of honey, dark brown sugar, maple syrup, or crunchy granola. Or serve accompanied by any of the shoyu dipping sauces and garnishes used with Chilled Tofu (p. 105).

Homemade Soft Tofu   MAKES 23 TO 25 OUNCES

"Soft Tofu" is made by pressing kinugoshi in a cloth-lined settling container. The result is firmer, more cohesive, and less delicate than kinugoshi, but softer, smoother, and higher-yielding than regular tofu. Always use calcium sulfate solidifier.
Prepare Homemade Soymilk (p. 204), but heat 2½ (rather than ¼) cups water in the cooking pot and rinse the okara with ½ (rather than ¼) cup water. Solidify as for Homemade

Kinugoshi (p. 215), using ½ teaspoon calcium sulfate. After stirring in solidifier, allow tofu to stand for about 8 minutes, then carefully ladle the soft curds in large, unbroken scoops into the cloth-lined settling container (as for regular Homemade Tofu, p. 99.) Avoid leaving gaps between adjacent scoops of curds. Put on the lid and press with a ½-pound weight for about 5 minutes, then add 1½ pounds more and press for an additional 20 minutes, or until whey no longer drips from the settling container. Cool under water for 10 to 15 minutes before removing cloths from tofu. Serve as for Chilled Tofu (p. 105).

Homemade Kinugoshi   MAKES 25 OUNCES
(from Powdered Soymilk)

This is a good way to make tofu on a camping trip since the ingredients are lightweight and the only utensils required are a 2-quart pot and a measuring cup. The tofu takes only 8 to 10 minutes to prepare and 20 minutes more to cool and firm. We find the flavor of the tofu is greatly improved by the addition of any of the ingredients mentioned in the variations for Kinugoshi Custard (p. 216), or the first 5 variations to Homemade Kinugoshi (p. 215).

Using 1 cup powdered soymilk, prepare Homemade Soymilk (p. 204). Using any of the solidifiers in the same amounts listed in the recipe for Homemade Kinugoshi (p. 215), quickly combine the solidifier with 2 tablespoons water in a small cup, stirring until dissolved. Now stir the solidifier solution into the hot soymilk. If calcium sulfate solidifier is used, the soymilk-solidifier mixture may be poured into cups to make Kinugoshi Custard (p. 216).

Rich Kinugoshi with Milk   MAKES 24 OUNCES
(Mineoka-dofu)

Using 1 cup powdered soymilk, 1½ cups dairy milk, and 1½ cups water, prepare Homemade Soymilk (from powdered soymilk, see above). Solidify with ¾ teaspoon calcium sulfate and allow to cool and firm either in a pot or in individual cups (as for Kinugoshi Custard). Serve chilled as is, or top with a little honey, maple syrup, or dark brown sugar.

Modified Kinugoshi

True kinugoshi is solidified with a salt (such as nigari or calcium sulfate) or an acid (such as lactone or lactic acid) each of which coagulates soybean protein. But soymilk can also be solidified with other jelling agents to create tofu with a soft, homogeneous texture similar to kinugoshi. To solidify 3¼ cups (homemade) soymilk use any of the following: 2 sticks (16 gm) of agar, as for Takigawa-dofu (p. 210); ½ cup *kuzu*, arrowroot, or cornstarch, as for Kuzu Mochi (p. 209); a mixture of ½ teaspoon each calcium sulfate and cornstarch; 3 or 4 well beaten eggs, as for Egg Tofu (p. 267).

KINUGOSHI DISHES FROM SASA-NO-YUKI

The following ten recipes come from Tokyo's famous *Sasa-no-Yuki* restaurant (p. 307) where the kinugoshi is made "on the spot."

Chilled Kinugoshi *(Hiya-yakko)*   SERVES 1

Most of the kinugoshi served in Japan is prepared in this simple way, which makes possible the full enjoyment of the kinugoshi's subtly sweet flavor and delicate texture. The kinugoshi at Sasa-no-Yuki is so soft that you can just barely pick it up with chopsticks. This and the recipe that follows are the owner's favorites.

6 to 8 ounces fresh kinugoshi
1 to 2 tablespoons shoyu
1 tablespoon thinly sliced rounds of leeks, soaked in cold water for 1 minute and drained
½ teaspoon grated gingerroot

Cut kinugoshi into 1-inch cubes and float with ice cubes in a shallow bowl of iced water. Serve accompanied by 2 tiny dishes (2½ inches in diameter and ¾ inch deep), one containing shoyu and one containing the leeks and gingerroot. Add condiments to shoyu to taste, then transfer several kinugoshi cubes into shoyu using a slotted spoon. For best flavor, cut and eat tofu with chopsticks.

Kinugoshi with Yuzu-Miso *(Yuzumiso-dofu)*   SERVES 2

6 ounces kinugoshi
2 teaspoons Yuzu Miso (p. 42)

Parboil tofu (p. 37), then cut into four ½-inch-thick pieces. Divide tofu pieces between 2 small, shallow bowls. Top each piece with a dab of the miso. Serve immediately, while still warm.

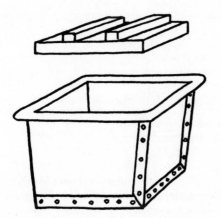

Fig. 86. Sasa-no-Yuki's Gisei-dofu container

Kinugoshi Gisei-dofu   MAKES 25 SERVINGS

At Sasa-no-Yuki—as at many traditional tofu shops—this tasty dish is cooked in a specially designed copper container into which fits a 1-inch-thick wooden pressing lid (fig. 86). The Sasa-no-Yuki container is 6 inches deep, 7½ inches square at the bottom, and 8½ inches square at the top. This recipe may also be prepared in an 8-inch skillet or baking tin: when doing so, omit paper and reduce oil by one-half.

5 tablespoons oil
3 pounds kinugoshi, ground (p. 98) (about 4½ cups)
1 3/8 cup sugar
4 2/3 tablespoons shoyu
8 2/3 tablespoons *mirin*
3 eggs

Heat copper container or skillet over a burner for 30 seconds, then coat bottom and lower walls of container with 2 tablespoons oil. Line bottom with a sheet of white *(washi)* stationery paper cut to just cover the entire surface. Brush paper with 1½ teaspoons oil.

In a large pot, combine tofu, sugar, shoyu, and 6 2/3 tablespoons *mirin*. Mix for 2 minutes with a large wooden paddle or spoon to develop cohesiveness. Cook over medium heat, stirring constantly, for about 5 minutes. Remove from heat, break in eggs, and stir for 2 minutes more.

Spoon tofu-egg mixture into the paper-lined container, press firmly into the corners with backs of fingers, and smooth surface with fingertips. Cover with a wooden pressing lid and a 6- to 8-pound weight. Cook over low heat for 15 minutes, turning container ¼ turn every 5 minutes to ensure even heating. Now and then, run a metal spatula down the walls of the container to help release steam and prevent cracks from forming in center of tofu.

Remove from heat. Pressing lid against tofu with one hand and holding container in the other, invert container and lift off, leaving tofu inverted on lid. Now place a second pressing lid on top of tofu and invert again so that tofu is upright on the second lid. Remove used paper, re-oil bottom of container with 2 tablespoons oil, and re-line bottom with a fresh piece of paper. Brush paper with remaining 1½ teaspoons oil. Holding cooking container with one hand and pressing lid topped with tofu in the other, invert container over lid. Pressing tofu against bottom of container, quickly return container to upright position leaving tofu with uncooked surface facing downward. Re-weight and cook for 10 minutes over medium heat. Invert tofu on pressing lid once again and remove from container. Brush top and sides of golden brown tofu with 2 tablespoons *mirin* and allow to cool. Cut tofu into 25 equal squares, cut each square into halves, and serve 2 halves on a small plate to each person (fig. 52, p. 152).

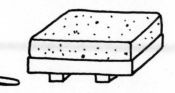

Fig. 87. Kinugoshi with Ankake Sauce

Warm Kinugoshi with Ankake Sauce SERVES 2
(Ankake-dofu)

From the year 1704, when Sasa-no-Yuki first began to make and serve tofu, until 1926, this was the only dish offered at the restaurant. The story is still told that many generations ago a famous samurai, having enjoyed one dish of Ankake-dofu, asked if he might be permitted to order another. In memory of that occasion, two small dishes of this speciality have been offered to each guest ever since (fig. 87).

12 ounces kinugoshi
1¼ cups Mild Ankake Sauce (p. 49), well warmed
½ teaspoon hot mustard

Parboil tofu (p. 96). Cut tofu horizontally, then crosswise into halves. Divide among 4 small bowls and top with warm sauce and a dab of mustard. Offer each guest 2 servings.

Warm Kinugoshi with Shoyu, SERVES 1
Mustard, and Leeks (Kijoyu)

4 ounces kinugoshi
1 tablespoon shoyu, warmed
1/8 teaspoon hot mustard
1½ teaspoons thinly-sliced rounds of leek, soaked in cold
    water for 1 minute and drained

Parboil tofu (p. 96), then cut tofu into halves and place in a small bowl. Mix shoyu with mustard and pour over tofu. Serve topped with leeks.

Chiri-mushi SERVES 1
(Kinugoshi Steamed with Egg in Lemon-Shoyu)

3 ounces kinugoshi
1 egg
1 thin slice of white fish meat (2 by 3 inches), or substitute
    1 large mushroom
1 tablespoon shoyu
A thin half-moon of lemon

Place tofu in a small—4½-inch-diameter, 2½-inch-deep—heat resistant bowl. Break in the egg and place the fish on the tofu. Place bowl in a heated steamer (p. 38) or over a pan of hot water in an oven. Steam for 10 minutes or until egg is just firm. Pour on shoyu and top with lemon. Serve hot.

Kinugoshi-Egg Custard with Ankake SERVES 4
(Kuya-dofu or Kuya-mushi)

8 ounces kinugoshi
1 egg
2 teaspoons shoyu
1½ teaspoons sugar
1 cup dashi (p. 39), stock, or water
¼ cup Mild Ankake Sauce (p. 49)
2 tablespoons cooked hamburger (optional)
Dash of pepper
15 to 20 strips of toasted nori, each 1½ by 1/8 inch

Cut tofu into fourths and divide among 4 custard or Chawan-mushi cups. Combine egg, shoyu, sugar, and dashi in a bowl, mixing well, then divide among the 4 cups filling each ½ to 2/3 full. Place cups in a heated steamer (p. 38), and steam for about 10 minutes or until custard is firm. Pour in warm Ankake Sauce to a depth of about 3/8 inch. Divide hamburger among the 4 cups and top with a sprinkling of pepper and the "pine needles" of nori. Cover with a small lid and serve while still hot.

Scrambled Kinugoshi (Iridofu) SERVES 4 TO 6

½ cup thinly sliced shiitake mushrooms
1 tablespoon bamboo shoots, cut into thin ginkgo leaves (p. 37)
1 tablespoon diced chicken (optional)
2 tablespoons sugar
½ teaspoon salt
2 teaspoons shoyu
2 tablespoons water, stock, or dashi (p. 39)
2 cups ground kinugoshi (p. 98) (use about 2 pounds fresh kinukoshi)
2 eggs, lightly beaten
2 tablespoons green peas, parboiled (p. 37)

Combine the first seven ingredients in a skillet; simmer, stirring occasionally, for about 5 minutes. Meanwhile combine ground tofu and eggs in bowl, mixing well. Stir tofu-and-egg mixture into cooking vegetables and simmer, stirring constantly, for about 10 minutes, or until mixture is light, dry, and crumbly. Allow to cool. Divide among small bowls and serve topped with green peas.

Kinugoshi Miso Soup

SERVES 6

The following is a description of how miso soup is prepared each morning at Sasa-no-Yuki; the amounts have been reduced to about one-eighth their actual figures.

1½ cups (5 ounces) dried *shiitake* mushrooms, soaked overnight in 2 cups water
½ cup (¾ ounce) round-herring flakes *(urume iwashi)*
½ cup (medium salty) light-yellow miso
1/3 cup Hatcho miso
5½ cups water
60 (canned) *nameko* mushrooms
12 ounces kinugoshi, cut into 3/8-inch cubes
18 trefoil leaves (including stems)

Pour mushrooms into a colander set over a pot. Press mushrooms gently but firmly against bottom of colander to expel remaining liquid, then reserve mushrooms for use in other cooking. Bring mushroom soaking water to a boil over high heat. Skim off any foam that may develop, then add herring flakes and return to the boil. Reduce heat to low, simmer for 5 minutes, and turn off heat.

Meanwhile, combine light-yellow and Hatcho miso with ¾ cup warm water in a mixing bowl. Mix well until miso is dissolved. Pour herring dashi through a fine-mesh strainer set over the mixing bowl and press the herring flakes (in the strainer) to expel all remaining liquid.

Combine herring flakes with 2 cups water in a saucepan to make a Number 2 Dashi (p. 39). Bring dashi to a boil, reduce heat to low, cover pan, and simmer for 5 minutes.

While Number 2 dashi is simmering, pour miso-dashi mixture through a fine-mesh strainer set over the pot. Remove particles of miso grain left in strainer, and mix with 2 cups warm water. Pour mixture back through strainer into pot, reserving miso grain particles for use in other cooking.

Pour Number 2 dashi through strainer into pot; discard herring flakes remaining in strainer. Bring the dashi in pot just to a boil, then add *nameko* mushrooms and tofu. Serve piping hot, garnished with trefoil leaves.

OTHER WAYS OF SERVING KINUGOSHI

Kinugoshi can be used in place of regular tofu in many preparations. It is particularly delicious in Fruit Cocktail Chilled Tofu (p. 148), on toast and sandwiches, with fried eggs, in soups, and topped with sauces. In Japan, during the wintertime, it is very popular in Simmering Tofu (p. 142) and many of the various tofu *nabe* dishes (p. 143).

Deep-fried Kinugoshi

SERVES 2 OR 3

Although kinugoshi's delicate texture and high water content make it somewhat difficult to deep-fry, it can be done, and the results are well worth the effort. Its crisp breaded crust enfolds a soft, creamy texture.

12 ounces kinugoshi, cut into 1½-inch-squares about ½ inch thick
2 tablespoons sweet white miso
1½ teaspoons natural sugar
Dash of *sansho* pepper (optional)
¼ cup flour
1 egg, lightly beaten
Oil for deep-frying
Shoyu

Arrange tofu squares on a large plate. Combine miso, sugar, and pepper, mixing well, then use the mixture to coat the upper surface of each tofu square. Matching their coated surfaces, gently press the pieces together, two at a time, to form "sandwiches." Carefully dust each sandwich with flour, dip in beaten egg, and deep-fry until golden brown (p. 130). Serve topped with a few drops of shoyu.

12
Grilled Tofu

As morning and evening cool and late summer turns into early fall, many tofu shops gradually stop making kinugoshi and shift their attention to grilled tofu (*yaki-dofu*). Easily recognized by its speckled brown surface and distinctive barbecue-broiled flavor and aroma, a cake of grilled tofu is a little longer and thinner than one of regular tofu. And unlike regular tofu, which is so soft and yielding, grilled tofu is firm and compact, its texture resembling that of Chinese-style doufu. Simmered in Sukiyaki and other types of *nabe* cookery, or skewered and broiled to make Dengaku, it always keeps its shape. And because it contains relatively little water, it readily absorbs the flavors of seasoned broths, soups, or casseroles.

Grilled tofu is prepared from the same curds used to make regular tofu. However, to create a strong, cohesive structure, the tofu maker stirs these curds in the curding barrel until they break into fine particles. Then, after ladling off more whey than usual, he places the curds quickly (and rather roughly) into the settling box and presses them with a heavy weight (10 to 12 pounds) for a relatively long time (40 to 50 minutes). Finally, he cuts the finished tofu into cakes about 5 inches long, 3 inches wide, and 2 inches thick, and these he presses for about one hour between alternate layers of bamboo mats sandwiched between large wooden boards (as when pressing tofu to make thick agé; fig. 61, p. 180). At each step in the process, the tofu becomes firmer and more compact so that it will hold together when skewered and grilled over a charcoal fire.

A traditional master grills tofu with the effortless precision of a circus juggler and the speed of a chuckwagon flapjack cook. Sitting squarely in front of a small, round charcoal brazier, he places two iron bars on opposite sides of its glowing mouth. Using a sturdy, metal skewer about 12 inches long, he then pierces a cake of well-pressed tofu to the hilt and sets it over the hot coals (fig. 88). Quickly skewering a second cake, he flips over the first and slides it to the opposite side of the brazier, while setting the second in its place and skewering a third. At just the right instant—a second too long and the tofu will burn, too short and it will lack the proper color and aroma—the master snatches the first cake from the fire, checks to see that its surfaces are nicely browned, and plunges it into a tub of cold water, withdrawing the skewer. He then flips over the second cake, sets a third in its place, and skewers the next piece. With a small paper fan, he sends several quick strokes of air down into the live embers. The charcoal-broiled fragrance of the sizzling tofu fills the shop and a thin curl of white smoke rises through a shaft of morning sunlight.

(In the spirit of traditional craftsmanship, nothing is wasted. When the work is done, the coals—which were originally scooped from the dying fire under the cauldron—will be placed in a charcoal brazier and used to warm the living room and boil the morning tea.)

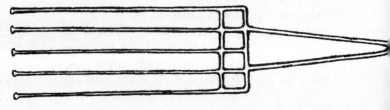

220

Fig. 88. Traditional master making grilled tofu

Grilled tofu may have been one of the earliest ways of preparing tofu in Japan. Since it is not found at all in present-day Taiwan or mentioned in writings on Chinese tofu, this variety may be another Japanese invention. In many Japanese farmhouses, regular tofu was generally broiled around a bed of coals in the open-hearth fireplace. Country-style tofu, made very firm (see p. 271), lent itself well to skewering without the need for additional pressing. And broiling the tofu—especially during long winter evening—gave the family a chance to come together near the warmth and light of the fire. Skewered on specially-cut pieces of bamboo (below), the freshly-

grilled tofu was either served sizzling hot, seasoned with a little miso or shoyu, or used as a basic ingredient in miso soups, Nishime, Oden, or Simmering Tofu.

Even today, many of Japan's rural festivals are not considered complete unless they end with a fireside feast featuring grilled tofu. We've witnessed one such feast in a small village in Japan's snowy northeast provinces. At its conclusion, a large bonfire was built and all the members of the village gathered round. After each person had prepared a 2-foot-long bamboo skewer, the village tofu makers passed around cakes of freshly prepared tofu. With flames

leaping and everyone singing and clapping in time to the rhythmic beating of huge drums, the skewered tofu was stuck upright in the ground as near to the fire as possible, then snatched back when done. The grilled tofu, together with hot sake, was served late into the night.

Grilled tofu's ancient ancestor may have been prepared without skewers on a lightly oiled, hot iron griddle—a method still used in a few rural tofu shops and farmhouses. Apparently, the predecessor of the present round charcoal brazier used in tofu shops was an oblong brazier about 2 feet long. We have watched one highly-skilled tofu maker prepare five cakes of grilled tofu at once on such a brazier using an elaborate version of the method described earlier (fig. 89). On the whole, the use of live coals and the traditional skewers is rapidly disappearing. Most Japanese shops now arrange cakes of well-pressed tofu on metal trays or thick wooden boards and broil them under the flame of a hand-held, propane blow torch. In more modern shops, the tofu-containing metal tray is placed on rollers and passed slowly under several rows of propane burners. This modern variety of grilled tofu—recognizable by the absence of skewer holes—is similar in appearance to traditional grilled tofu, but lacks the latter's charcoal aroma and some of its ability to absorb flavors during cooking.

Open-hearth grilling

Fig. 89. An early method of elaborate grilling

in a dish called New Year's Nishime (p. 178), grilled tofu is said to reach its peak of goodness several days after it has been cooked, when the flavors of the broth and fresh vegetables have mellowed and permeated it.

The tofu maker spends the last few days of the old year working from morning until night trying to fill all his orders for grilled tofu. At the end of the year's work, as the great temple bells throughout Japan sound the midnight hour, the master may use his freshly-made grilled tofu to prepare a special type of Dengaku. He spreads one entire surface of the cake with a thin layer of miso, then broils the miso quickly until it is fragrant and flecked with brown. This steaming hot Dengaku, a small feast in itself, is meant to welcome in the new year.

Many of our fellow Westerners have been surprised to learn that tofu is one of the indispensable ingredients in Japan's most famous overseas dish: Sukiyaki. If you have ever tasted real Sukiyaki, you have also tasted grilled tofu. Indeed, in Japan, more grilled tofu is used in Sukiyaki than in any other type of cuisine.

In Western cookery, grilled tofu is particularly suited to the barbeque and broiler. You can prepare your own over the live coals of an outdoor barbeque, a small indoor Japanese-style brazier, or in an oven broiler. Or try cooking pre-grilled tofu in these various ways, treating it almost as if it were a large steak and basting it with a favorite sauce. Grilled tofu can also be substituted in most recipes calling for regular tofu and is especially delicious in Western-style egg dishes.

Grilled tofu is usually about 10 percent more expensive than regular tofu since each cake is larger, contains less water, and requires additional time, effort, and fuel to prepare. In Japan, its season usually comes to an end in March or April, when the tofu maker packs away his charcoal brazier and begins to prepare kinugoshi.

At present in the United States, fresh grilled tofu is available in only a few areas. An imported, canned variety called *yaki-dofu* or Baked Bean Curd is sold at some Japanese markets, but the tofu loses much of its flavor and fine texture in canning and after lengthy storage. For best results, make your own.

Grilled tofu is one of the featured ingredients in Japan's New Year's cuisine. In accordance with an ancient custom, no fresh food is cooked during the first three—and sometimes the first seven—days of the new year. Thus, during the last two days in December, most housewives are busy from morning until night preparing the New Year's food and setting it aside in special layered, lacquerware boxes reserved for the occasion. Since the basic New Year's dishes were standardized in the centuries before refrigeration, the only foods used traditionally were those which could be kept fresh for a fairly long time. Since grilled tofu stayed fresh longer than regular tofu (due in part to its low water content and in part to the effects of broiling) it was chosen as the ideal variety for use in the holiday menu. Moreover, since it was very firm, grilled tofu could be simmered in sweetened shoyu broths—which acted as a natural preservative—without losing its form so that it looked attractive when served. Today used most widely

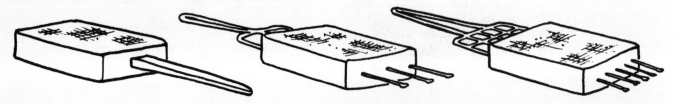

Homemade Grilled Tofu

Grilled tofu can be prepared quickly and easily at home.

Preparing the Tofu: Firm Chinese-style doufu may be grilled without additional preparation. Regular commercial tofu should be thoroughly pressed between layers of toweling or bamboo mats (p. 97) before skewering, but may be broiled in an oven broiler without pressing if you are in a hurry or want a softer texture. When preparing Homemade Tofu (p. 99) to be made into grilled tofu, use a nigari-type solidifier if possible, ladle the curds into the settling container rather quickly and roughly, and press the curds with a fairly heavy weight for a longer time than usual. Cut the finished tofu into 2-inch-thick pieces and press again in toweling or between bamboo mats.

Grilling or Broiling: The appropriateness of the cooking method depends first on whether or not the tofu is to be skewered, and second on the nature of your heat source. A charcoal or wood fire gives the best flavor.

Skewered Tofu

1. *Charcoal Brazier:* Skewer 12-ounce cakes of pressed tofu from one end using a pronged metal skewer, two metal shish kebab-type skewers, two sturdy bamboo skewers which have been soaked in (salted) water, or a large fork with tynes longer than the tofu. Place 2 parallel bars across the brazier to support both ends of the skewers. Grill each piece of tofu for about 15 to 30 seconds on each side, or until nicely browned.

2. *Open-Hearth Fireplace or Campfire* (planted skewer style): Prepare skewers 12 to 18 inches long by sharpening both ends of a flat, 1-inch-wide piece of bamboo or wood; skewer tofu from one end. Plant the base of the skewer upright in the ashes or ground near the bed of coals so that the tofu leans slightly over the coals and each side of the tofu browns in 1 to 2 minutes.

3. *Open Fire or Stove-Top Burner* (marshmallow style): Skewer the tofu with a long metal fork or forked stick. Hold just above the flames or coals and brown on both sides.

Unskewered Tofu

1. *Oven Broiler:* Place 12-ounce cakes of tofu (pressed or unpressed) on a lightly-oiled baking sheet or sheet of aluminum foil and broil for 3 to 5 minutes on both sides until nicely browned.

2. *Barbeque or Brazier:* Place well-pressed tofu on the grill or grating like a steak. When one side is nicely browned, turn over with a large spatula or fork.

3. *Griddle:* Heat a heavy griddle and coat lightly with oil. Fry each cake of tofu on both sides until golden brown. Turn with a wide-blade knife or spatula. Country-style grilled tofu is still prepared in this way.

Serving or Storing Grilled Tofu: Grilled tofu is most delicious when served still hot and fragrant, as in the following recipe. However if you wish to save some homemade grilled tofu for later use, plunge the hot tofu into a large container of (circulating) cold water as soon as the tofu is removed from the fire. Allow tofu to cool thoroughly, then place in a covered container and refrigerate. If tofu is to be stored for more than 24 hours, refrigerate in cold water to cover.

Sizzling Grilled Tofu *(Quick and Easy)*

These simple serving suggestions are for connoisseurs who prepare their own grilled tofu at home and want to enjoy it "fresh from the fire" when its flavor and aroma are at their peak.

***Grilled Tofu with Miso:** Cut the cake of freshly grilled tofu horizontally into halves. Place each half on a plate with the grilled side up. Coat with your favorite variety of Sweet Simmered Miso (p. 41) or Finger Lickin' Miso (p. 31). Serve immediately.

***Country-style Tofu Dengaku:** Prepare grilled tofu skewered and grilled over a bed of coals. When tofu is golden brown, spread both large surfaces with a thin coating of red, barley, or Hatcho miso; broil for about 1 minute more on each side until miso is fragrant. Invite each guest to hold the tofu "popsicle-style" while eating.

***Grilled Tofu Steak:** Marinate tofu for 30 to 60 minutes before grilling, using Teriyaki (p. 48) or your favorite steak sauce. Grill slowly, basting lightly with the marinade. Serve topped with marinade or Ketchup-Worcestershire Sauce (p. 49).

*Serve the hot tofu with any of the dipping sauces and garnishes used with Chilled Tofu (p. 105). Cut tofu as for Grilled Tofu with Miso, above.

*Serve cubes of freshly grilled tofu topped with Ankake Sauce (p. 49) and a little slivered gingerroot; or with grated *daikon* and a little shoyu.

Sukiyaki

A Japanese cookbook written over 350 years ago contains the following recipe for *Sukiyaki:* "Obtain either wild goose, wild duck, or antelope, and soak the meat in *tamari shoyu*. Heat a well-used Chinese plow *(kara-suki)* over an open fire. Place the meat on the plow, garnish with thin rounds of *yuzu*, and broil on both sides until the color changes. Serve and be happy."

The word *sukiyaki*—pronounced skee-ya-kee—means "broiled on the blade of a plow." Although the modern preparation generally features beef as the basic ingredient, sukiyaki was traditionally prepared with wild game, fowl, fish, or shellfish. Wild boar was also a favored ingredient, and seafoods such as tuna, yellowtail, whale, wreath shells, and scallops were and, in areas such as Kyoto, still are widely used in the dish.

Before reaching its present form, sukiyaki passed through a number of unusual historical transformations. The earliest preparation was undoubtedly developed by farmers, hunters, and fishermen who broiled their catch over an open fire using a plow or whatever other utensil was available. Since the earliest plow, the predecessor of the present *nabe*, was nothing but a flat iron plate, it was unable to hold cooking liquids. It was probably for this reason that the meat came to be marinated or basted with tamari shoyu, a technique that is still practiced in some Japanese restaurants. Gradually, sake or *mirin* came to be used in the marinade, various vegetables and grilled tofu were broiled with the meat, and the traditional flat plow or griddle became inadequate to hold the juices of this cornucopia of new ingredients. A new container was needed, and at this point, the ancient tradition of broiling wild meat on a plow merged with the newly-imported tradition of *shippoku*, a type of beef-*nabe* cookery which originated about 300 years ago, just after the first contact with Western traders and missionaries.

Developed in the international port town of Nagasaki, *shippoku* was said to have its historical culinary roots in Holland, Portugal, China, and Korea. As a result of the merger, the original sukiyaki ingredients eventually came to be cooked in heavy iron or Korean-style stone pots, and the dish was served as a one-pot meal prepared at the table. Consequently "sukiyaki" became a misnomer, for the new dish was neither broiled nor prepared on a griddle-like plow. But neither was the new sukiyaki a true *nabe* dish, since its ingredients were not simmered in a seasoned broth. Rather, this unique Japanese creation straddled three categories: it was a broiled dish insofar as the meat was first cooked in a sizzling-hot pan; it was a *nabe* dish since it was a one-pot dish prepared at the dining table; and it was a *nimono*, or simmered dish, insofar as the meat and vegetables were simmered together in a rich mixture of shoyu, sake, and dashi.

Up until this time, the Japanese had never apparently considered using beef or other livestock in sukiyaki. According to a popular legend, *kamado-gami*, the god of the kitchen hearth, is said to have instructed the Japanese people in ancient times to refrain from eating the meat of all four-legged animals, especially of livestock. This admonition was reinforced by the nation's emperors and the vegetarian teachings of Buddhism, so that for about 1200 years—from the 8th until the 19th century—most Japanese did not eat meat. However with the arrival of Christianity in the 16th century, and the public knowledge that missionaries considered meat important in the diet, some Japanese—and particularly Christian converts—came to know its taste. But with the expulsion of Christianity from Japan in the late 16th century, the eating of beef was also forbidden, and sukiyaki was once again prepared exclusively with seafood, wild game, or poultry. Those who developed a longing for broiled meat, but who were not allowed to prepare it in the family's common pot or in the presence of those who kept the faith, were compelled as a last resort to prepare their sukiyaki in the traditional way, substituting a plow or mattock for the kettle and enjoying the forbidden delicacy alone and in secret in the barn, field, or forest. This tradition of "underground sukiyaki" is said to have continued until about 1900.

With the opening of Japan to the West in the mid 19th century and the relaxation of traditional prohibitions, meat eating gradually became fashionable in the cities. Yet most Japanese tasted their first beef with considerable trepidation, having been warned by priests and traditionalists that their action was an affront to their ancestors and that dire consequences would befall them. Little by little, however, beef sukiyaki came to be accepted.

The first Japanese who worked up the courage to actually eat beef did not prepare it Western-style as steak or roast beef. Rather, they cut the meat into paper-thin slices, employing the same method they had used for centuries to prepare *sashimi*, or raw fish. And they seasoned this meat with shoyu in much the same way they would season simmered vegetable or tofu dishes. Many Japanese probably ate their first beef in the form of sukiyaki, and different parts of the country soon developed unique styles of serving it. To this day in the Kyoto area, restaurants place dispensers of shoyu, *mirin*, and sugar on the table and allow each guest to season his food to taste, whereas restaurants in Tokyo have developed their own unique mixtures of these ingredients to form standard cooking liquids.

Throughout the world people now associate sukiyaki with fine Japanese cookery. In a sense, this is ironic because Japanese cuisine still makes relatively little use of meat, and much of sukiyaki's historical influence came from abroad. The ancient delicacy of Japanese hunters and the imported *nabe* preparation have now been totally transformed to become Japan's most famous international dish. And although tofu plays a relatively inconspicuous role in creating the flavor of this dish, sukiyaki has nevertheless been the vehicle whereby thousands of Westerners have had their first taste of "soybean curd."

Although most present-day sukiyaki uses beef as the featured ingredient, our recipe uses ganmodoki—mock goose—in deference to the earliest traditions of using wild fowl. Homemade frozen tofu and frozen thick-agé, the textures of which resemble that of tender beef, make excellent substitutes. Although regular tofu is occasionally used in sukiyaki, grilled tofu is generally preferred for its ability to absorb the flavors in the rich broth; its substantial, almost meaty texture; its ability to keep its form during the frequent stirring; and its barbeque flavor. In Japan, more grilled tofu is used in sukiyaki than in any other type of cuisine.

3 tablespoons oil
12 ounces ganmo; or 4 pieces of frozen or dried-frozen tofu (p. 229); or 12 ounces (frozen) thick-agé or gluten cutlets, cut crosswise into ¾-inch-thick strips
12 ounces grilled tofu, cut into ¾-inch cubes
4 leeks, including green portions, cut diagonally into 2-inch lengths; or 10 green (or 4 regular) onions, thinly sliced
4 ounces trefoil or spinach leaves
8 ounces *konnyaku* noodles, parboiled and cut into thirds
8 small cakes of dried wheat gluten, reconstituted (p. 37) (optional)
8 *(shiitake)* mushrooms, thinly sliced
4 ounces chrysanthemum leaves, watercress, or Chinese cabbage, cut into 2-inch-wide strips
2 small bamboo shoots, thinly sliced and parboiled (p. 37)
Sukiyaki-Shoyu Mixture:
    ¼ cup dashi (p. 39), stock, or water
    ½ cup shoyu
    ¼ cup sake
    ¼ cup *mirin* or 3 tablespoons natural sugar
4 eggs

Arrange tofu and vegetables on a large platter. Preheat a 10- to 12-inch skillet set on a tabletop burner, or set an electric skillet to 350°. Coat skillet with the oil, add about one-third of each of the tofu and vegetable ingredients, and sprinkle with one-third of the shoyu mixture. Cook over medium heat for 5 to 6 minutes, turning ingredients gently from time to time. Using chopsticks or long-handled forks, serve from the skillet an ingredients become done. Replenish the sauce and each ingredient, and continue cooking while the guests eat.

To serve, each person breaks a raw egg into his serving bowl and beats it lightly with chopsticks. The tofu and vegetables are dipped into the egg, then eaten. The usual accompaniment for sukiyaki is plain rice. Reserve any leftover sauce to use when sautéing other vegetable dishes, or as a broth for noodles.

Alternate ingredients and seasonings include celery stalks, bean sprouts, green peppers, thinly sliced carrots or *daikon*, and slender white *enokidake* mushrooms. Season with pepper and hot mustard, and garnish with a little parsley.

Other ways of Serving Grilled Tofu

Grilled tofu may be used in place of regular tofu with excellent results on sandwiches and toast, in egg dishes and soups, and in sautéed vegetable and grain dishes. In Japan it is particularly popular in Tofu Dengaku (p. 139), Simmering Tofu (p. 142) and most other *nabe* cookery, Oden or Nikomi Oden (p. 175), New Year's *Osechi* Nishime (p. 178), Noppei Soup (p. 163), and Miso Soup (p. 118).

In country farmhouses grilled tofu is used in a Nishime stew in which it is combined in a large iron pot with *daikon*, potatoes, *konnyaku*, seasonal vegetables, and an unsweetened miso broth which may include dried fish. The stew is simmered for at least 30 minutes and served steaming hot on winter evenings.

Farmhouse Sukiyaki with grilled tofu

13

Frozen and Dried-frozen Tofu

THE METHOD for preparing frozen tofu was first discovered in the cold mountainous regions of northern China about 1,000 to 1,500 years ago. It was found that if regular tofu was cut into ½-inch-thick slabs, arranged on boards or bamboo mats, and then set out in the snow overnight until frozen solid, the structure and basic character of the tofu underwent a radical transformation. All the water in the tofu—about 86 percent of the tofu's total weight—turned to ice, and the protein and other solids congealed into a lacy but firm network. When the frozen tofu was later placed in warm water, the ice thawed, leaving only the network of protein and solids; this network looked like a beige, fine-grained natural sponge or a zwieback biscuit. With the loss of water, the tofu became a highly concentrated source of protein and energy. Like a delicate sponge, it was resilient, highly absorbent, and cohesive enough to hold together when pressed or cooked. Its soft texture was appealing and, in some types of cooking, seemed remarkably similar to that of very tender meat. This tofu had its own special flavor, which was enhanced by the flavors it so readily absorbed when simmered or sautéed.

As well as showing a way to transform regular tofu into a completely new food with unique uses in cooking, the discovery of frozen tofu also made it possible to preserve tofu—otherwise highly perishable—for long periods of time. After the arrival of frozen tofu in Japan over 1,000 years ago, it became possible for families in country farmhouses or monks in snowbound temples to make a large quantity of tofu, freeze what wasn't eaten, and then enjoy tofu daily for as long as the supply lasted, or until the snows melted. In rural areas, where there were no tofu shops, this saved the time and fuel required to make a small batch of fresh tofu every few days. Since it was almost impossible to obtain fish or other seafoods during the winter in the snowy mountain provinces, frozen tofu became a popular element in the daily diet and was soon known throughout much of Japan as "one-night frozen tofu."

Made almost exclusively in rural farmhouses and temples, frozen tofu has never been sold at neighborhood tofu shops. At present, many people make it at home by placing fresh tofu into the freezing compartment of their refrigerator. And it is sold on a limited scale in the frozen foods section of some department stores as six ½-inch-thick slices sealed in a cellophane bag. However, it is no longer a common commercial food in Japan, because modern, lightweight, dried-frozen tofu is now available at low prices in the dry goods section of most markets.

For us in the West, though, the process of freezing tofu can be an easy way to ensure a ready supply, either after making a large batch of homemade tofu or after purchasing a large quantity from a store. Homemade frozen tofu will generally have a better flavor than, but will not be quite as light, fine-grained and expansive as, the commercial dried-frozen variety. Since storebought dried-frozen tofu is generally permeated with ammonia gas, baking soda, or other chemical agents which cause the tofu to expand during cooking, homemade frozen tofu will be more natural. The less water the tofu contains and the faster it freezes, the finer will be the grain structure and the more delicate the texture of the finished product. Good quality frozen tofu can be prepared with less than 12 hours of freezing, and may be used immediately or stored under refrigeration indefinitely. It makes an excellent, low-cost replacement for gluten meat or cutlets in vegetarian menus. Thick agé and kinugoshi can also be used to make frozen tofu: the first develops a firm, meaty texture; the second, a fine, delicate consistency.

Dried-frozen Tofu

But preserving tofu by freezing it outdoors had two basic limitations: first, the tofu could only be stored in its frozen form for as long as the air temperature remained below freezing; and, second, the tofu was very heavy and susceptible to thawing when transported from place to place. The Japanese, therefore, began to experiment with drying frozen tofu to create a lightweight, staple food that could be preserved well into springtime. Since this idea seems never to have occurred to the Chinese, dried-frozen tofu is thought to have originated in Japan. Two different traditional methods of freezing and drying arose independently in the snowy, mountainous regions of the nation.

The home of the first experiment, Mount Koya, stands high and solitary in a vast forest of cedars south of Kyoto, Japan's ancient capital. Kobo Daishi, one of Japan's great Buddhist saints, founded a monastery there in 816, and it continues to serve as the headquarters of the Shingon sect of esoteric Buddhism. Tradition has it that the method for making dried-frozen tofu was first discovered there some 750 years ago by a Shingon priest.

The priests and monks living in Mount Koya's snowbound temples chose a day for making tofu when the night temperatures were expected to be bitterly cold and there were winds to help hasten the freezing process in order to give the tofu the desired fine-grained texture. Beginning work in the late afternoon, they prepared a large quantity of firm tofu, cut the cakes into ½-inch-thick slabs, and pressed these in layers between bamboo mats or boards to expel excess water. Waking at about 3 a.m., the coldest hour, they set the tofu out in the snow on the mats or boards in a place that received no direct sunlight during the day.

The next morning, after the tofu slabs had been out in the cold for about 8 hours and were frozen solid, the monks took them into a specially built shed, arranged them on shelves, and allowed them to stand undisturbed (out of direct sunlight) at temperatures below freezing for about one to three weeks. During this second freezing, the tofu slabs developed an even finer grain and firmer structure and became more resilient. They were then thawed in warm water and pressed lightly to expel the melted ice. The entire shed was then heated in much the same way as a sauna (using large charcoal braziers) and each slab was dried until it turned light beige and was as hard and crisp as a zwieback biscuit. It was found that if this dried tofu was stored in a cool, dry place, it could be preserved for about 4 months after the last snows had melted.

Farm villages in the area learned the technique from the monks, and many large freezing and drying sheds were built in the mountain valleys. "Koya-dofu" soon came to be made on a fairly large scale as a communal wintertime occupation and source of income during the lean months. In some areas, an entire village would turn out on cold days and work together, freezing and drying the tofu. By the Edo period (1600-1868) Koya-dofu was known throughout Japan. In 1911, it started to be made on an even larger scale throughout the year using artificial refrigeration.

The second traditional experiment with dried-frozen tofu began about 400 years ago in the cold mountains of Nagano north of Tokyo. A famous samurai warrior, Takeda Shingen, thought of drying frozen tofu to make a lightweight, nutritious food that his soldiers could carry in their backpacks. The soldiers apparently learned how to prepare the tofu, then taught the method to local farmers. After the pieces of well-pressed tofu had been placed overnight in the snow and frozen solid, they were wrapped in straw mats, placed in the shade in a barn or tool shed, and left at below-freezing temperatures for about one week. Then five pieces of tofu at a time were tied together with several pieces of rice straw (fig. 90), and these strands were hung from poles under the eaves of farmhouses (where they received no direct sunlight). After several weeks of thawing during the day and freezing again at night, the tofu became completely dry and crisp.

This technique, which obviated the special drying shed and equipment used on Mount Koya, was simple and inexpensive, so that most tofu of this type came to be made on a small scale by individual farmers. Carrying the light tofu in backpacks, these farmers often walked from village to village selling it as a source of wintertime income. To this day, strands of drying tofu can be seen hanging under the verandas of farmhouses and the eaves of temples throughout the Nagano area (fig. 91).

Today, dried-frozen tofu is produced year round in huge automated factories (most of which are still located in the Nagano area.) Since the tofu is neither perishable nor fragile, it is well suited to centralized, large-scale production and nationwide (or worldwide) distribution. If kept sealed in the airtight cellophane bag in which it is sold, and if stored at room temperature, it has a shelf life of 6 to 8 months during the colder seasons and 4 to 6 months during the warmer ones. Each package is stamped with the date of manufacture to encourage quick use. If stored for too long, dried-frozen tofu loses its softness, freshness, and ability to expand and absorb cooking liquids.

In 1928, it was found that if thawed tofu was steeped in a solution of baking soda before being dried, it swelled during cooking and become softer and more absorbent than the traditional dried-frozen variety. In 1929 it was discovered that thoroughly dried tofu, when permeated with ammonia gas, became even softer and swelled even more than the tofu containing baking powder. Moreover, if the tofu was reconstituted in hot water before use in cooking, the odor and flavor of the ammonia completely disappeared. (The ammonia was not intended as a preservative and, in fact, if the tofu was not treated with ammonia, it stayed fresh longer.)

At present the largest dried-frozen tofu factory employs about 250 workers and over 23 tons of soybeans daily. The only ingredients used are whole soybeans, well water, and calcium chloride nigari solidifier—plus ammonia gas added at the end of the process. The tofu is made in a continuous production line that takes about 25 days from start to finish. The basic techniques are essentially the same as those developed for making Koya-dofu 750 years ago. The first freezing is carried out in a very cold refrigerated room with strong winds provided by huge electric fans. The frozen tofu is then stored in a refrigerated warehouse for 20 days. Finally it is placed on a wide conveyor belt, thawed under a spray of warm water, pressed between heavy rollers, and dried in a 100-yard-long tunnel dryer. Permeated with ammonia in large vacuum chambers, it is

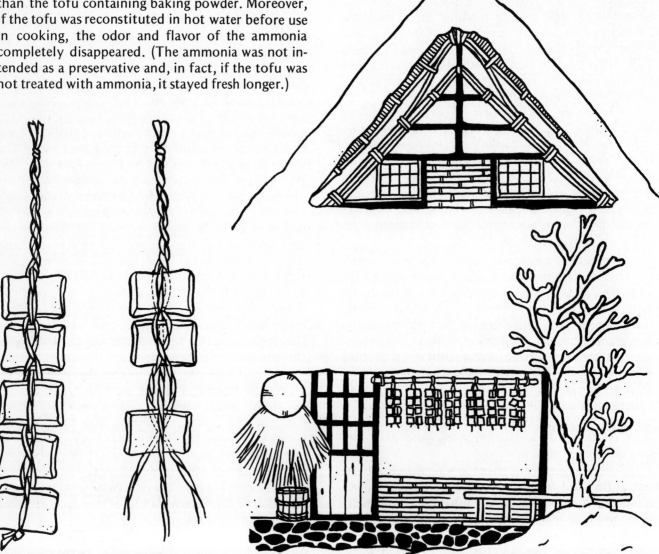

Fig. 90. Tying frozen tofu with rice straw   Fig. 91. Drying farmhouse frozen tofu

sealed 5 to 10 pieces at a time in airtight cellophane bags, packaged in small paper boxes, stamped with the date, and shipped throughout Japan. A small portion of the tofu is also cut into ½-inch cubes for use as soup croutons or ground into meal for use in baked or sautéed dishes. Some of the large factories still make strands of dried tofu tied with rice straw, which are sold mostly as a tourist item.

Present-day dried-frozen tofu differs from both its traditional counterpart and from homemade frozen tofu in that it has a very fine, firm grain structure, and is much softer and more absorbent. When reconstituted, it swells by about 26 percent, as compared with 7 percent in the case of tofu containing no ammonia. Dried-frozen tofu has relatively little flavor of its own: it is used mostly for its texture and ability to acquire flavor from seasoned broths and sauces.

Dried-frozen tofu is also highly valued as a concentrated source of nutrients. It contains 53.4 percent protein and 26.4 percent natural oils, and is only 7 percent carbohydrate and 10 percent water. An excellent energy source, it provides 436 calories per 100 grams, and contains more than 7 times the amount of protein and energy as an equal weight of regular tofu. In Japan, it is advertized as providing both the highest percentage of protein and the least expensive energy of any known food. The economies of large-scale production make it possible to produce dried-frozen tofu at about 96 percent the cost (on a usable protein basis) of regular tofu made in small shops. Its relatively low cost has been a major factor in its growing popularity and, combined with its durability even when not refrigerated, would make it an excellent food for use in developing areas such as India, Africa, and South America.

In Japan, a carton containing ten pieces of dried-frozen tofu (each 2½ by 2 by 5/8 inches thick) weighs only 5.8 ounces (165 grams). The same amount of protein in the form of fresh tofu would weight about 6 times as much. Thus, its light weight and ease of preservation obviously make dried-frozen tofu an ideal back-packing food, now available in the West at prices far below those of most freeze-dried camping foods.

Highly versatile and requiring only a few minutes of cooking, dried-frozen tofu is well suited to a wide variety of Western-style dishes. We have found it preferable to regular tofu in a number of sautéed vegetable preparations, egg dishes, and casseroles. Preliminary experiments in Japan indicate that it can be flavored to resemble meat and can therefore be used in many of the same ways as textured soybean protein.

In Japanese cookery, it is commonly used in *nabe* cookery, Sukiyaki, simmered and sautéed dishes, and sushi rice preparations. Properly seasoned, dipped in tempura batter or eggs, then rolled in bread crumbs and deep-fried, it makes an excellent cutlet. While still dry, it can be grated, and the gratings added to almost any dish. It is also, of course, a popular ingredient in Zen Temple Cookery.

At present in the United States, dried-frozen tofu is available at most Japanese markets and some co-op stores at very reasonable prices. It can also be prepared quite easily at home.

Reconstituting Frozen and Dried-frozen Tofu

IMPORTANT: In the following recipes, "1 piece of frozen tofu" refers either to 5 or 6 ounces of tofu made into Homemade Frozen Tofu (p. 230), or an equivalent weight of regular tofu which has been frozen and sold commercially. The phrase "1 piece of dried-frozen tofu" refers to a standard ½ ounce (16.5 gram) piece of the commercial variety, measuring about 2½ by 2 by ½ inches. In many recipes the two types can be used interchangeably.

Frozen Tofu (or natural dried-frozen tofu): Remove tofu from freezer and place in a large pan or bowl. Add several quarts boiling water, cover, and allow to stand for 5 to 10 minutes until completely thawed. (If a large cake of tofu was frozen initially, cut crosswise into ½-inch-thick slices after cake is partially thawed to hasten the process.) Pour off hot water and add lukewarm or cold water. Gently but firmly press tofu several times between the palms of both hands to expel all hot water. Lift tofu out of water and press firmly before using (fig. 92). This last pressing makes the tofu light and dry so that it will readily absorb liquids during cooking.

Dried-frozen Tofu (containing ammonia or baking soda): The stronger the smell of ammonia when the tofu package is opened, the fresher the tofu. When reconstituted, the volatile ammonia gas disappears and the tofu becomes soft and absorbent as it expands.

Remove dried tofu from airtight package, place in a pan

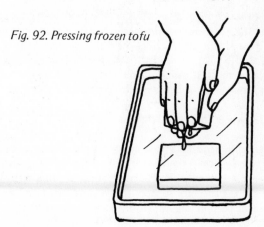

Fig. 92. Pressing frozen tofu

or bowl, and add just enough hot water (175°) to cover. (Do not pour water directly onto tofu.) Cover pan and allow to stand for 3 to 5 minutes while tofu swells. Do not allow to stand for too long, lest the tofu fall apart. Pour off hot water and cover with lukewarm or cold water. Press tofu several times under water gently but firmly between the palms of both hands to expel hot water and milky ammonia residue. Discard soaking water and add fresh water. Repeat pressing and discarding of water twice more, or until water pressed from tofu is no longer whitish. Lift tofu out of water and press very firmly once more before using.

Some Japanese chefs insist that dried-frozen tofu should be reconstituted by placing it in cold (rather than hot) water for 5 to 10 minutes and then pressing it repeatedly in clear cold water until the milky liquid no longer emerges. This technique is said to produce a softer texture and prevent the tofu from falling apart during lengthy simmering.

Grated Dried-frozen Tofu: Grate dried-frozen tofu on a metal grater to give a fine, granular texture. Place gratings in a bowl, cover with hot water (175°), and soak for 2 minutes. Pour into a dishcloth set over a strainer, allow to drain, then squeeze or press to expel excess water. Rinse twice with cold water, squeezing after each rinsing. Squeeze very firmly the last time to expel as much water as possible.

Storing and Cooking Dried-frozen Tofu

During summer, use commercial dried-frozen tofu within 4 months of the production date printed on the package; during winter, use within 6 months. After opening the airtight cellophane package, try to use all of the tofu as soon as possible, preferably within several days, to prevent it from losing its ability to expand and soften. Any tofu not used immediately should be placed in a small polyethylene bag sealed with a rubber band.

If fresh tofu is simmered for too long or over very high heat, it will begin to fall apart. If too much shoyu is used in the cooking broth, the tofu may shrink somewhat and become firmer than desirable.

Homemade Frozen Tofu   MAKES 2 "PIECES"

Although regular tofu is generally used as the basis for frozen tofu, both kinugoshi and whole cakes of thick agé may also be used. Due to freezing, the latter develops a texture remarkably similar to tender meat. If using homemade tofu (p. 99), make it as firm as possible by pressing with a heavy weight for a long time in the settling container.

10 to 12 ounces tofu, cut crosswise into halves

Arrange tofu pieces on a plate, leaving at least ½ inch between pieces, then place in the freezer with the temperature turned down as cold as possible. (Or place outdoors on a very cold winter night.) Its color turned from white to dark amber, the tofu will be completely transformed and ready to use after 48

hours; the most porous and resilient texture, however, is attained after 1 week of freezing. If you do not wish to use the tofu immediately, seal it in a polyethylene bag and store in the freezer. Lengthy storage actually improves the texture.

VARIATIONS
*For tofu with a very soft texture but little resiliency, freeze for only 24 hours. Use in soups and simmered dishes.
*For tofu with a very fine-grained structure similar to that of commercial dried-frozen tofu: Press tofu (p. 96), then cut crosswise into ½-inch-thick pieces. (For an even finer grain, press again briefly using the sliced tofu method, p. 97). Place pieces on a porous surface—such as a bamboo mat (sudare) or colander (zaru)—or on a large plate or tray, leaving at least ½ inch between pieces. Freeze as in the basic recipe.

Homemade Dried-frozen Tofu   MAKES 10 TO 20 PIECES

For a description of the traditional methods of preparing *Kori-dofu* and *Koya-dofu* see page 227. During winter, we have had good results using the former method, which requires no special equipment. Our 20-ounce batch of tofu was ready and well-dried after about 1 week.

To prepare homemade dried-frozen tofu in any season for use in camping or traveling, try the following:

10 to 20 pieces of (homemade) frozen tofu, reconstituted (p. 229) and cut crosswise into ¼-inch-thick slices

Preheat oven to 170°. Arrange the thin, slightly moist tofu slices on large baking sheets, leaving at least ½ inch between slices. Place in oven for about 2 hours, or until tofu color has turned from amber to light beige and slices are crisp and dry. Remove and allow to cool. Seal in polyethylene bags and store in a cool dry place. Use within 2 to 3 months.

Scrambled Eggs with Frozen Tofu   SERVES 2

Because of its excellent ability to absorb flavors and its tender, almost meaty texture, frozen tofu makes an excellent addition to many egg dishes. Frozen kinugoshi may be used to lend a soft, delicate texture to the dish, while frozen thick agé adds a substantial, hearty quality similar to that provided by ham or bacon.

1 piece of frozen or dried-frozen tofu, reconstituted (p. 229) and torn into small pieces
2 eggs
2 teaspoons shoyu
1 tablespoon natural sugar
1/3 cup dashi (p. 39), stock, or water

Combine all ingredients in a small bowl; beat lightly. Pour into a skillet and scramble without oil over medium heat until just firm. Serve hot or cold, seasoned lightly with Sesame Salt (p. 51) or ketchup, if desired.

Frozen Tofu in Scrambled Egg Salad with Tofu Dressing

SERVES 4

1 piece of frozen or dried-frozen tofu, reconstituted (p. 229) and torn or diced into very small pieces
4 eggs
¼ teaspoon salt
½ teaspoon butter or oil (optional)
2 cucumbers, cut into thin strips
2 tomatoes, cut into thin wedges
½ cup Tofu Mayonnaise Dressing (with onion) (p. 107)

Combine tofu, eggs, and salt in a small bowl; mix well. Heat a skillet and, if desired, coat with the butter or oil. Add tofu-egg mixture and scramble until dry and crumbly. Arrange cucumber and tomato pieces in serving bowls, sprinkle on the eggs-and-tofu, and top with the mayonnaise.

Frozen Tofu & Scrambled Eggs with Ankake

SERVES 2

2 teaspoons oil
1 piece of frozen or dried-frozen tofu, reconstituted (p. 229) and torn into small pieces
1 onion or leek, diced
1 clove of garlic, crushed
1 tablespoon grated gingerroot
2 eggs
2 teaspoons shoyu
Dash of salt and pepper
Ankake Sauce (p. 49)

Heat a skillet and coat with the oil. Add tofu, onion, garlic, and gingerroot, and sauté until onion is lightly browned. Add eggs, shoyu, salt, and pepper and scramble until egg is just firm. Serve topped with the sauce.

Or omit the sauce and use as a filling for Gyoza (p. 232).

Frozen Tofu & Egg Casserole with Cheese and Raisins

SERVES 4

Frozen tofu makes an excellent substitute for regular tofu in many baked dishes, but because the tofu is so absorbent, it may be necessary to increase the amount of liquid in the recipe slightly. Use the tofu cubed, grated, or cut into thin strips to create a variety of textures. Especially delicious in *gratin* preparations (p. 124).

2 pieces of frozen or dried-frozen tofu, reconstituted (p. 229) and torn into small pieces
2 ounces cheese, chopped fine or grated
¼ cup raisins
¼ cup milk (soy or dairy)
½ to ¾ teaspoon salt
Dash of pepper
2 tablespoons butter

Preheat oven to 350°. Combine the first six ingredients in a large bowl; beat lightly. Pour into a lightly oiled casserole and dot with butter. Bake for 25 minutes or until firm.

Frozen Tofu with Eggs and Onions (Tamago-toji)

SERVES 2 OR 3

1 piece of frozen or dried-frozen tofu, reconstituted (p. 229) and cut into ½-inch cubes; or 7 ounces (frozen or regular) deep-fried tofu, cut into strips
½ cup dashi (p. 39), stock, or water
2 tablespoons natural sugar
1½ tablespoons shoyu
1 tablespoon oil
1 onion or leek, thinly sliced
1 egg, lightly beaten

Combine tofu, dashi, sugar, and shoyu in a bowl; beat lightly. Heat a skillet and coat with the oil. Sauté onion for about 1 minute, then add tofu-dashi mixture and simmer, stirring occasionally, for 7 to 10 minutes. Turn heat to high, mix in egg, and cook, stirring constantly, for about 1 minute more, or until egg is just firm.

Frozen Tofu & Onion Sauce with Eggs and Cheese

SERVES 4

Frozen tofu makes a good addition to most sautéed or stir-fried dishes, especially when seasoned with shoyu or miso. Try substituting it for regular tofu in the recipes beginning on page 126. It is also delicious used in (or topped with) sauces such as Mushroom (p. 48), Spaghetti (p. 121), Onion-White (p. 207), or Curry (p. 166). Or try the following:

2 tablespoons oil
6 onions, thinly sliced
3 pieces of frozen or dried-frozen tofu, reconstituted (p. 229) and torn into ½-inch pieces
3 tablespoons red or barley miso; or 2 tablespoons shoyu
2 or 3 eggs
2 ounces cheese, cut into small cubes
2/3 cup water

Using the oil and onions, prepare an Onion Sauce (p. 48); simmer for 1½ hours. Stir in tofu and remaining ingredients and simmer for about 15 minutes more, or until sauce is well thickened. For best flavor, allow to cool to room temperature. Serve either cold or reheated.

For variety, omit eggs and cheese. Add ½ cup lotus root (cut into gingko leaves, p. 37) to the sauce together with the tofu.

Frozen Tofu in Soups

The addition of cubes, thin strips, or gratings of frozen tofu to any soup means added protein and body. Add reconstituted tofu about 10 minutes before the soup is done to allow it time to absorb the soup's unique flavors. In Japan, frozen tofu is popular in wintertime miso soups, especially in combination with white miso, hot mustard, and various greens.

Gyoza

We use frozen tofu rather than hamburger in this famous Chinese dish.

2½ tablespoons oil
1 piece of frozen or dried-frozen tofu, grated and reconstituted (p. 229)
1 onion or large leek, minced
1 clove garlic, crushed
1 tablespoon grated gingerroot
1 teaspoon shoyu
¼ teaspoon salt
Dash of pepper
1 teaspoon cornstarch, arrowroot, or *kuzu*, dissolved in 2 tablespoons water
¼ cup dashi (p. 39), stock, or water
½ cup flour
Dipping Sauce:
    1½ tablespoons shoyu
    1 teaspoon (rice) vinegar
    ½ teaspoon sesame oil
    ¼ teaspoon hot mustard

Heat a skillet and coat with 1 tablespoon oil. Add the next seven ingredients and sauté over low heat for 10 minutes. Stir in dissolved cornstarch and dashi, simmer for 30 seconds more, and set aside to cool.

Add enough water to the flour to prepare a stiff dough. Divide dough into sixths and roll out on a floured breadboard into thin rounds about 3½ inches in diameter. Divide the tofu filling into sixths and place a dollop of the filling at the center of each round. Fold rounds in half and seal with the tynes of a fork, like a turnover. Heat a large skillet and coat with remaining 1½ tablespoons oil. Add the *gyoza* and fry over high heat for about 1 minute on each side. Add 2½ tablespoons water, reduce heat to low, cover pan, and steam for 5 minutes more. Serve hot with the dipping sauce.

Or use Frozen Tofu & Scrambled Eggs (p. 231) as the gyoza filling, or substitute Crumbled Tofu (p. 98) for frozen tofu. Gyoza may also be deep-fried (with or without batter).

Frozen Tofu Cutlets

One of our favorite tofu recipes, these cutlets often bear a remarkable resemblance to fish or veal cutlets, depending on the type of sauce with which they are served.

2 tablespoons grated gingerroot
4 tablespoons shoyu
1½ cups water
4 pieces of frozen or dried-frozen tofu, reconstituted (p. 229) and cut into large 3/8-inch-thick slices
½ cup flour
1 egg, lightly beaten
½ cup bread crumbs or bread crumb flakes
Oil for deep-frying
1 lemon, cut into 4 wedges

Combine gingerroot, shoyu, and water in a large saucepan and bring to a boil. Reduce heat to low, add tofu, and simmer for 15 to 20 minutes. Lift out tofu, allow to cool slightly, then press each piece lightly with your fingertips to expel about one-fourth of the liquid. Dust well with flour, dip in egg, and roll in bread crumbs. Heat the oil to 375° in a wok, skillet, or deep-fryer. Drop in tofu and deep-fry until golden brown (p. 130). Serve hot or cold with lemon wedges.

To lend more of a seafood flavor, serve with Tofu Tartare Sauce (p. 109) or Tangy Ketchup & Lemon Sauce (p. 109). To give the feeling of breaded veal, serve with Worcestershire or Ketchup- Worcestershire Sauce (p. 49).

VARIATION
*Frozen Tofu Tempura: Simmer the tofu as above, then dip in Tempura Butter (p. 137) and deep-fry. Serve as above or with a Tempura Dipping Sauce (p. 137).

Frozen Tofu in Breads

Adding reconstituted frozen or dried-frozen tofu to breads is an easy way to add plenty of inexpensive protein. Use 2 to 3 pieces of grated (or diced), reconstituted tofu for each loaf of bread.

Dried-frozen Tofu French Fries

1 piece of dried-frozen tofu, reconstituted (p. 229) and cut into pieces the size of French-fried potatoes
¼ cup *kuzu*, arrowroot, or cornstarch
Oil for deep-frying
¼ teaspoon salt
2 lemon wedges

Dust tofu pieces liberally with *kuzu* or arrowroot and set aside on a rack to dry briefly. Heat the oil to 375° in a wok, skillet, or deep-fryer. Drop in the tofu and deep-fry until crisp and golden brown (p. 130). Drain briefly, sprinkle with salt, and serve garnished with lemon.

Or omit the salt and lemon and sprinkle with a little shoyu or Lemon-Shoyu (p. 40).

Deep-fried Frozen Tofu with Chinese Sauce

1½ pieces of frozen or dried-frozen tofu, reconstituted (p. 229) and torn into 12 pieces
6 tablespoons *kuzu*, arrowroot, or cornstarch
Oil for deep-frying
Chinese Sauce:
    1 teaspoon grated gingerroot
    2 tablespoons water or stock
    3 tablespoons natural sugar
    2 tablespoons soy sauce or shoyu
    1 tablespoon ground roasted sesame seeds (p. 38)
    1 tablespoon vinegar
15 snow peas, parboiled (p. 37) and cut crosswise into halves

Roll tofu in 4 tablespoons *kuzu* or arrowroot, then set aside briefly to dry. Heat oil to 350° in a wok, skillet, or deep-fryer. Drop in tofu and deep-fry until golden brown (p. 130); drain briefly.

Combine all sauce ingredients and bring just to a boil. Stir in 2 tablespoons *kuzu* or arrowroot dissolved in 3 tablespoons water. Add snow peas, then simmer for 30 seconds more. Divide tofu pieces among two serving bowls and serve topped with the hot sauce.

You can also serve this dish as a topping for deep-fried noodles or fried rice.

Deep-fried Frozen Tofu & Chinese Sauce with Fried Noodles

SERVES 4

1½ pieces of frozen or dried-frozen tofu, reconstituted (p. 229) and cut into 20 thin rectangles or triangles
6 tablespoons cornstarch
Oil for deep-frying
1 onion, diced
½ carrot, cut into matchsticks
3 mushrooms, sliced
1 green pepper, thinly sliced
10 to 15 snow peas or green beans
Tangy Chinese Sauce:
    3 tablespoons soy sauce or shoyu
    2 tablespoons vinegar
    1 clove crushed garlic
    1 teaspoon grated gingerroot
    2 tablespoons water or stock
    3 tablespoons natural sugar
2 cups cooked noodles (p. 50), well drained

Dust tofu with cornstarch and deep-fry as in the previous recipe. Heat 2 tablespoons oil in a skillet, add all the vegetables and sauté for 4 to 5 minutes until carrots are just tender. Combine all the sauce ingredients in a small saucepan and bring just to a boil. Stir in 2 tablespoons cornstarch dissolved in 3 tablespoons water. Add tofu and vegetables and simmer for 30 seconds more. Deep-fry the noodles (without batter) until crisp in oil heated to 350°, then drain well. Serve hot or cold, topped with the vegetables-and-sauce.

Deep-fried Frozen Tofu with Sweet Miso

SERVES 4

1 piece of frozen or dried-frozen tofu, reconstituted (p. 229) and cut into 4 equal cubes
2 tablespoons Yuzu Miso (p. 42) or Sweet Simmered Miso (p. 41)
2 tablespoons cornstarch, arrowroot, or *kuzu*
Oil for deep-frying
4 tablespoons kinako
2 tablespoons natural sugar
Dash of salt

Cut a ¾-inch-deep, 1-inch-square piece out of one surface on each piece of tofu (see fig. 51, p. 147). Fill this "well" with 1½ teaspoons of the miso. Trim bottom of square and replace

on top of miso. Roll filled tofu pieces in cornstarch. Heat oil to 350° in a wok, skillet, or deep-fryer. Drop in tofu and deep-fry until golden brown (p. 130); drain briefly.

Combine kinako, sugar, and salt in a small bowl; mix well. In a saucepan, bring 2 cups water to a boil. Dip tofu into boiling water, drain briefly, then roll in the sweetened kinako. Serve with the meal, or as an hors d'oeuvre or dessert.

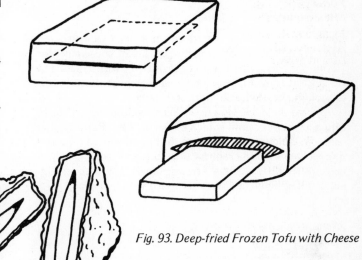

Fig. 93. Deep-fried Frozen Tofu with Cheese

Deep-fried Frozen Tofu Stuffed with Cheese

SERVES 2

2 pieces of frozen or dried-frozen tofu, reconstituted (p. 229)
1 tablespoon shoyu
½ cup water
2 slices of cheese, each 3 by 2 by ¼ inch
2 tablespoons flour
1 egg, lightly beaten
¼ cup bread crumbs or bread crumb flakes
Oil for deep-frying
Tofu Tartare Sauce (p. 109), Ketchup-Worcestershire (p. 49), or ketchup

Combine tofu, shoyu, and water in a small saucepan and bring to a boil. Reduce heat and simmer for 5 minutes, pressing tofu occasionally to aid absorption of the liquid. Remove tofu and allow to cool briefly.

Make a horizontal slit from one end of each piece of tofu to the other, leaving about ¼ inch of uncut tofu along each side so that tofu can be opened like a tube (fig. 93). Slide the cheese into the slit tofu.

Combine flour and egg in a small bowl and mix lightly to form a thick batter. Dip stuffed tofu into batter, then roll in bread crumbs. Heat oil to 350° in a wok, skillet, or deep-fryer. Drop in tofu and deep-fry until golden brown (p. 130). Drain briefly, then cut each piece diagonally into halves. Serve hot or cold topped with the sauce.

Deep-fried Frozen Tofu in Lemon Sauce (Oranda-ni)

SERVES 3

3 pieces of frozen or dried-frozen tofu, reconstituted (p. 229)
1 cup water, stock, or dashi (p. 39)
3 tablespoons natural sugar
2 tablespoons shoyu
½ cup cornstarch, arrowroot, or *kuzu*
Oil for deep-frying
3 lemon slices
3 sprigs of parsley

Combine the first four ingredients in a small saucepan and bring to a boil. Reduce heat to low, cover pan, and simmer for 10 minutes, pressing the tofu once or twice with a spatula to aid absorption of the cooking liquid. Remove tofu and allow to cool, then dust liberally with cornstarch.

Heat oil to 350° in a wok, skillet, or deep-fryer. Drop in tofu and deep-fry until golden brown (p. 130). Return initial cooking liquid to a boil, drop in the hot deep-fried tofu, and simmer for 1 minute more. Cut tofu pieces diagonally into halves, then divide among 3 serving bowls. Top with remaining cooking liquid and serve garnished with lemon and parsley.

Onion-Sauce Flavored Frozen Tofu Cutlets

MAKES 18

We like to prepare a large batch of these cutlets and freeze the leftovers for use on hiking trips.

2 tablespoons oil
7 onions, thinly sliced
¼ cup red, barley, or Hatcho miso
2 tablespoons shoyu
2½ cups water
Dash of pepper
9 pieces of Homemade Frozen Tofu (p. 230), reconstituted (p. 229) and cut into ½-inch-thick slices
½ cup flour
2 eggs, lightly beaten
½ cup bread crumbs or bread crumb flakes
Oil for deep-frying
Ketchup-Worcestershire Sauce (p. 49) or lemon wedges

Heat the oil in a casserole or heavy pot. Add onions, cover, and simmer over very low heat for 2 hours, stirring occasionally, to form an Onion Sauce (p. 48). Mix in miso, shoyu, water, and pepper, and return to the boil. Add tofu, cover, and simmer for 40 to 60 minutes more. Now remove tofu and allow to cool briefly. Press tofu lightly between your fingers to expel about one-fourth of the liquid it contains.

Dust cutlets with flour, dip in egg, and roll in bread crumbs; set aside briefly to dry. Heat oil to 350° in a wok, skillet, or deep-fryer. Drop in tofu and deep-fry until golden brown (p. 130). Serve topped with Ketchup-Worcestershire Sauce or garnished with lemon wedges; or top with remaining Onion Sauce.

VARIATIONS

*Shish Kebab Cutlets: Cut frozen tofu into bite-sized cubes before simmering in the onion sauce. On 6-inch bamboo or metal skewers place 1 tofu cube, a piece of vegetable (onion, carrot, green pepper) and finally another tofu cube. Dust all ingredients with flour, dip in beaten egg, and roll in bread crumbs. Deep-fry and serve as above, placed on a bed of slivered cabbage.

*Serve cutlets on buttered whole-wheat bread or toast with mustard, shredded cabbage, and Ketchup-Worcestershire Sauce. Add thin slices of tomato, cheese, or onion, if desired.

Deep-fried Frozen Tofu Dengaku

SERVES 2

2 pieces frozen or dried-frozen tofu, reconstituted (p. 229)
1 cup dashi (p. 39), stock, or water
2 tablespoons natural sugar
¼ cup cornstarch, arrowroot, or *kuzu*
Oil for deep-frying
Sweet Simmered Miso (p. 41)

Combine tofu, dashi, and sugar in a small saucepan; bring to a boil and simmer for 5 minutes. Remove tofu and allow to cool briefly, then cut into 6 rectangular pieces. Roll pieces in cornstarch.

Heat oil to 350° in a wok, skillet, or deep-fryer. Drop in tofu and deep-fry until golden brown (p. 130). Pierce each piece of tofu from one end with 1 or 2 small bamboo skewers (fig. 46, p. 141). Spread the upper surface of each piece with the miso and serve.

Soboro (Grated Frozen Tofu Rice Topping)

SERVES 2 OR 3

2 teaspoons oil
1 onion, minced
3 pieces of frozen or dried-frozen tofu, grated and reconstituted (p. 230)
1 tablespoon shoyu
¾ teaspoon salt
1 carrot, grated
15 to 20 green beans, parboiled (p. 37)
2 to 3 cups cooked Brown Rice or Sushi Rice (p. 50)

Heat a skillet and coat with the oil. Add onion and sauté until transparent. Add tofu and sauté for 2 minutes more. Season with shoyu and ¼ teaspoon salt, and simmer for 30 seconds more; set aside.

Reheat skillet and add grated carrot. Stirring constantly, parch for about 1 minute. Season with ¼ teaspoon salt and cook for 1 minute more, or until just tender; set aside.

Cut beans diagonally into thin strips and sprinkle with remaining ¼ teaspoon salt. Divide cooked rice among 3 individual serving bowls or lunch-box compartments. Cover one-third of surface of rice in each bowl with each of the three cooked vegetables to form an attractive pattern.

Deep-fried Frozen Tofu Sandwich
(Hakata-agé)

SERVES 2

An *hakata obi* is a brightly colored woman's belt or sash with a horizontal stripe design from which this dish takes its name.

2 pieces of dried-frozen tofu, reconstituted (p. 229)
½ cup water
1 tablespoon shoyu
1 tablespoon natural sugar
2 teaspoons red, barley, or Hatcho miso (optional)
3 ounces cheese
1 sheet of *nori*, cut crosswise into fourths
¼ cup (whole-wheat) flour
Oil for deep-frying

Before pressing water from reconstituted tofu, cut each piece crosswise into halves, then horizontally into thirds. Now, using your fingertips, firmly press out any remaining water.

Combine tofu, water, shoyu, and sugar in a small saucepan, and bring to a boil. Reduce heat to low, cover, and simmer for 5 minutes. Uncover pan, increase heat to medium and cook for 2 or 3 minutes more, or until all liquid has been absorbed or evaporated. Set aside to cool.

Cut cheese into eight 1/3-inch-thick slices the size of each piece of tofu, and coat one side of each slice with miso. Combine 2 pieces of cheese and 3 pieces of tofu to form a double-layer sandwich (fig. 94). Wrap each sandwich with a strip of *nori*, leaving the sandwich ends exposed and sealing the ends of the *nori* with water.

Mix the flour with just enough water (about ¼ cup) to form a thick batter. Heat the oil to 350° in a wok, skillet, or deep-fryer. Dip each sandwich in batter, drop it into the oil, and deep-fry until golden brown (p. 130). Drain and allow to cool briefly. Cut each sandwich crosswise into thirds and serve with the cut surface facing up.

Or substitute for the cheese thinly-sliced carrots which have been simmered in the shoyu broth. Cut each sandwich diagonally into halves and serve standing on end. Garnish with parsley.

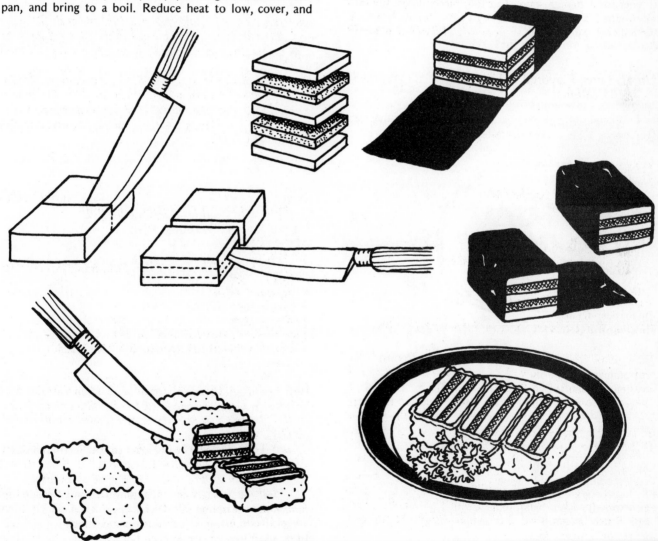

Fig. 94. Making deep-fried frozen tofu sandwiches

Fig. 95. Frozen Tofu Wrapped in Kombu

Frozen Tofu Wrapped in Kombu
(Koya-dofu no Kombu-maki)

SERVES 3

3 pieces frozen or dried-frozen tofu, reconstituted (p. 229) and cut lengthwise into halves
6 pieces of *kombu*, each 2½ by 8 inches, wiped with a moist cloth
6 strips of *kampyo*, each 12 inches long, reconstituted (p. 37)
1 cup dashi (p. 39), stock, or water
1½ tablespoons shoyu
2 tablespoons natural sugar
3 tablespoons *mirin* or sugar (p. 322)

Wrap each piece of tofu with a piece of *kombu* and tie around the middle with a piece of *kampyo* as shown in figure 95. Combine in a pressure cooker with the dashi, shoyu, sugar, and *mirin* and bring to full pressure (15 pounds). Simmer for 10 minutes, then remove from heat and allow pressure to come down naturally. Chill rolls and broth before serving.

Three-color Brown Rice
(Sanshoku Gohan)

SERVES 3

2 teaspoons vegetable oil
1 teaspoon sesame oil
2 pieces of frozen or dried-frozen tofu, grated and reconstituted (p. 229)
2 mushrooms, diced
½ cup dashi (p. 39), stock, or water
3 tablespoons shoyu
3 tablespoons natural sugar
1 tablespoon sake or white wine
1 tablespoon grated gingerroot
3 tablespoons Sesame Salt (p. 51)
2 eggs, lightly beaten
Dash of salt
8 green beans, parboiled (p. 37)
3 cups cooked Brown Rice or Sushi Rice (p. 50)

Heat a skillet and coat with the vegetable and sesame oil. Add the next eight ingredients and sauté for 3 to 5 minutes, or until dashi has been absorbed or evaporated. Set aside.

Using eggs and salt, prepare 1 Paper-thin Omelet (p. 51). Allow omelet to cool, then cut into 2-inch-long, thin strips.

Cut beans diagonally into thin strips and season lightly with salt. Place the rice into 3 individual bowls or lunch-box compartments. Cover one-third of the surface of the rice in each container with a sprinkling of each of the toppings: tofu, omelet, and beans.

Frozen Tofu Simmered in One-Pot Cookery and Seasoned Broths

Frozen and dried-frozen tofu are used widely in Yosenabe and Mizutaki (p. 144), and Sukiyaki (p. 224), as well as in most other types of one-pot cookery. The tofu may be either simmered in Sweetened Shoyu Broth (p. 40) for 10 to 15 minutes and added to the *nabe* at the last minute, or simmered in the *nabe* together with the other ingredients. If homemade frozen tofu is used in Sukiyaki, it adds a texture and flavor resembling tender meat to the dish.

Frozen tofu is often added to Chinese-style Happosai (p. 249), simmered with vegetables in Nishime (p. 178), or topped with Ankake Sauce (p. 49).

Frozen Tofu Simmered in Sweetened Broth (Fukuyose-ni)

SERVES 2

Probably the most popular way Japanese restaurants serve frozen tofu, the following recipe is that provided us by Tokyo's Sasa-no-Yuki. There the tofu is served with young butterbur, tiny "maiden" bamboo shoots, and a roll of deep-fried, fresh yuba which has been simmered in a lightly seasoned broth.

2 pieces of frozen or dried-frozen tofu, reconstituted (p. 229)
1 cup water
3 tablespoons sugar
1 tablespoon shoyu
Vegetables: butterbur *(fuki)*, carrot slivers, tiny bamboo shoots, *(shiitake)* mushrooms, green beans, snow peas, *konnyaku* rectangles, wheat gluten cakes, or deep-fried fresh yuba rolls

Combine tofu, water, sugar, and shoyu in a saucepan and bring to a boil. Reduce heat to low, cover pan, and simmer for 15 to 20 minutes. Remove tofu and allow to cool, then cut into bite-sized cubes.

Add your choice of vegetables to the remaining cooking liquid and simmer until tender. Arrange tofu and vegetables in individual bowls, pour any remaining cooking liquid over the top of each portion, and serve cold or chilled.

For variety, garnish each serving with a sprig of *kinome*.

VARIATIONS

*Try the following cooking liquid: 1 cup dashi (p. 39), 1½ teaspoons shoyu, 2 tablespoons sugar, 1½ teaspoons each sake and *mirin*, and a dash of salt. For added richness, mix in 2 to 3 tablespoons sesame butter.

*Simmered Frozen Tofu Wrapped in Agé and Kampyo *(Shinoda-maki):* Cut each piece of reconstituted tofu lengthwise into thirds. Using 6 pieces of agé, cut each piece along 3 sides, then open to form flat sheets. Roll up one piece of tofu in each of the sheets and tie in two places with pieces of refreshed *kampyo*. Simmer rolls for 15 minutes in the dashi described in the recipe above. Cut rolls crosswise into halves and serve with the simmered vegetables.

*Add 1 piece of reconstituted frozen or dried-frozen tofu cut into thin rectangles to Agé with Hijiki and Carrots (p. 166), and simmer together with the other ingredients.

Deep-fried Frozen Tofu Dessert with Apples

SERVES 2

Two of our favorite recipes for frozen tofu are dessert preparations. Reconstituted frozen tofu can also be substituted for regular tofu in Tofu-Rice Pudding (p. 150). Or it can be grated and added in small amounts to cookies, cakes, or muffins.

1 apple, cut into thin wedges
3 tablespoons raisins
1 teaspoon natural sugar
½ cup water
1 piece frozen or dried-frozen tofu, reconstituted (p. 229)
¼ cup flour mixed with 3 tablespoons water
½ cup bread crumbs or bread crumb flakes
Oil for deep-frying
¼ teaspoon cinnamon
½ to 1 cup milk (soy or dairy)

Combine the first four ingredients in a small saucepan and simmer for about 5 minutes. Cut tofu into 6 or 8 equal pieces, add to the cooking apples, and continue to simmer until apples are tender and most of the liquid is absorbed or evaporated. Set aside and allow to cool briefly.

Mix the flour and water to form a thick batter. Remove tofu pieces from the cooked apples, dip into the batter, and roll in bread crumbs. Heat the oil to 350° in a wok, skillet, or deep-fryer. Drop in the tofu and deep-fry until golden brown (p. 130). Divide drained tofu between 2 serving bowls and top with the apples, a sprinkling of cinnamon, and the milk.

VARIATIONS

*Use 2 pieces of dried-frozen tofu. After reconstituting, cut each piece horizontally into 4 thin sheets. Cook with the apples as above; allow to cool. Spread the cooked apple mixture on 4 of the tofu sheets, then top with remaining sheets to make 4 "sandwiches." Cover each sandwich with a thick batter prepared by mixing flour with lightly beaten eggs. Sprinkle with bread crumbs, then carefully deep-fry until golden brown. Serve as is, or top with applesauce or cooked apples, a dash of cinnamon, and 1 cup milk.

*Combine the first four ingredients in the above recipe and 1 tablespoon butter in a pressure cooker. Bring to full pressure (10 pounds) and cook for 10 to 15 minutes. Cool under running cold water to release pressure. Cut tofu into 12 equal rectangles, mix into the cooked apples, and return to full pressure. Cook for 5 minutes more, then release pressure. Chill the tofu-apple mixture and serve topped with (soy or dairy) milk and a pinch of cinnamon.

Abekawa-dofu
(Frozen Tofu Rolled in Sweetened Kinako)

SERVES 2

This dish takes its name from *Abekawa Mochi,* a popular New Year's confection made by rolling moist, freshly-made *mochi* (pounded rice cakes) in a mixture of roasted soy flour and sugar.

1 piece frozen or dried-frozen tofu, reconstituted (p. 229)
¼ cup dashi (p. 39), stock, or water
3 tablespoons natural sugar
¼ cup *kuzu*, arrowroot, or cornstarch
Oil for deep-frying
3 tablespoons kinako
Dash of salt

Cut tofu crosswise into sixths. Combine with dashi and 1 tablespoon sugar in a small saucepan and bring to a boil. Reduce heat to low, cover pan, and simmer for about 10 minutes. Remove tofu and allow to cool, then roll in the *kuzu* or arrowroot.

Heat oil to 350° in a wok, skillet, or deep-fryer. Drop in tofu and deep-fry until golden brown (p. 130). Drain and allow to cool briefly. While tofu is cooling, combine kinako, 2 tablespoons sugar, and the salt in a bowl, mixing well. Bring 2 cups water to a boil in a saucepan. Dip cooled tofu into the boiling water, drain, then roll in the sweetened kinako. Serve immediately.

Or cut the tofu horizontally into 2 thin sheets, then cut each sheet crosswise into thirds. Proceed as above, but roll in a mixture of 3 tablespoons ground roasted sesame seeds, 2 to 3 tablespoons sugar, and a dash of salt.

14

Yuba

IF YOU HAVE ever simmered a pot of milk over very low heat or set a bowl of hot milk aside to cool, you have no doubt noticed the thin, delicate film that soon forms on the milk's surface. The longer it is allowed to set, the firmer and thicker it becomes. And if you have ever tried lifting this film off and tasting it, you may well have found it to be soft, warm, and delicious. In the same way, if fairly thick soymilk is gently heated, a thin film soon covers its surface. In Japan this film is called *yuba*, and since ancient times it has been considered a true delicacy. It is easily prepared at home, and since it is best when fresh and warm, yuba made in your own kitchen and served as an hors d'oeuvre or as part of a meal will have a tenderness and fragrant richness that can far surpass that of the yuba ordered from even the finest traditional shops.

Yuba in its commonly-sold dried form is a nutritional treasure-trove containing a remarkable 52.3 percent high-quality protein. This makes it one of the richest natural sources of protein known to man. Easy to digest, yuba also contains 24.1 percent natural oils (mostly polyunsaturated), 11.9 percent natural sugars and, in its dried form, 8.7 percent water. Thus it is extremely lightweight and easy to carry. Furthermore, a 100-gram portion contains some 432 calories, making it a highly concentrated energy source that is ideal for camping. Finally, yuba is rich in minerals, as shown in figure 5 on page 24. Because of its nutritional excellence, yuba is a popular item at Japanese natural food and health food stroes. Recommended to mothers before and after childbirth, it has been said for centuries to stimulate the flow of milk. Widely used in Japanese hospitals as a concentrated source of protein, doctors also recommend it to patients suffering from high blood pressure (it is believed to aid in the removal of cholesterol) and diabetes.

In spite of its nutritional excellence, yuba is appreciated primarily for its unique flavor and texture. The Japanese say that the natural sweetness and the subtle richness of yuba remind them of the flavor of fresh cream. Like cream, yuba rises to the surface of the soymilk from which it is made and embodies the condensed essence or elixir of the soymilk's flavor and nutrients. The most popular way of enjoying yuba's fine flavor is also the simplest: a delicate half-done sheet is lifted with the fingertips from the surface of steaming soymilk and placed in a small bowl; sprinkled with a few drops of shoyu, it is served immediately. Soft and warm, it melts on the tongue—and is gone.

Fresh yuba looks like a diaphanous veil of creamy silk and is usually sold in single sheets about 15 by 17 inches. When dried, it turns beige and has a crisp, brittle texture. yet it softens as soon as it is refreshed or added to soups, stocks, egg dishes, or the like. In Japan, the dried form is also popular as a deep-fried hors d'oeuvre; it turns as crisp and crunchy as a potato chip.

The art of making yuba was transmitted from China to Japan about 1,000 years ago. During the following centuries, yuba developed a well-established role as one of the indispensable delicacies in both Zen Temple and Tea Ceremony Cookery. Today, in restaurants serving these two varieties of haute cuisine, yuba will often appear in more than half the dishes in a typical six-course meal. The beau-

238

tiful *Sorin-an* restaurant (p. 311), which specializes in yuba cuisine, features homemade fresh yuba in a selection of more than 15 delectable dishes. Likewise, many Chinese restaurants—including those in the United States—generally have a special section on the menu devoted solely to yuba or "bean curd skin" preparations.

In Japan, yuba is (and has traditionally been) served largely as a gourmet food. A special product of the ancient capital, Kyoto, where most of the country's yuba shops are still located, it gradually acquired an aura of aristocracy, refinement, and elegance through its close association with the Imperial Court. And because it is made by slow traditional methods on a small scale, most of Japan's yuba is quite expensive. In Taiwan, China, and Hong Kong, on the other hand, yuba is a very popular food sold at prices anyone can afford. Although much of the yuba there, too, is still made in tiny cottage shops, modern methods have also been developed for preparing good-quality yuba on a large scale. This yuba, in its dried form, is now sold throughout the world.

Although, strictly speaking, yuba is not a type of tofu and is not made or sold at neighborhood tofu shops, it is nevertheless grouped together with tofu in most books on Japanese foods and cooking. This is partially because yuba, like all tofu, is made from soymilk; partially because its history parallels that of tofu; and partially because the two foods have closely related flavors and are therefore used in many of the same types of cookery.

Yuba and tofu shops have a great deal in common. And although yuba is made commercially only in special shops, a small amount is produced inadvertently each day at neighborhood tofu shops when soymilk cools in the curding barrel just before it is solidified into curds. This yuba is picked off to prevent it from entering the tofu, where it could form an interface and cause a large block of tofu to split apart. It is either eaten fresh at the tofu shop by the tofu maker and his family, served to guests or visitors as a special treat, or set aside and dried to be used later in cooking.

Like tofu shops, virtually all of Japan's yuba shops are run by a single family whose home adjoins the shop. Many of Kyoto's 23 shops have been in the family for centuries. Yuba Han, for example, is a beautiful example of classical Kyoto architecture; the building itself is 120 years old with massive rafters arching below a 20-foot-high ceiling. Here one can find a unique collection of all the ancient tofu-making tools still in daily use: large granite grinding stones, an iron cauldron heated by a wood fire, and a lever press weighted by heavy granite pendants. This historic shop and its tools were used as the basis for the drawing on the cover of this book. The Yuba-cho shop is run by a master (now assisted by his two sons) who has been making yuba in the same shop for fifty years. This cheerful old man, now a Living National Treasure, prepares his yuba for the Imperial Household.

In most shops, yuba is prepared in large copper or stainless steel steaming trays supported by a sturdy brick dais. One steaming table mav be 8 to 10 feet long and 3 feet wide (fig. 96); most shops will have at least two such tables. Thick soymilk, prepared with the same tools and in the same way as in tofu shops, is poured into the trays to a depth of about 1½ inches. Each tray is divided into rectangular compartments by removable wooden frames. The soymilk is heated from below by steam or low flames until it is steaming but not bubbling (about 175°F). After 5 to 7 minutes, when a firm film has formed in each compartment, the master makes his or her rounds, lifting off each sheet with a 2-foot-long bamboo skewer, then hanging the yuba-draped skewer in a rack over the steaming table. Here the yuba drains and begins to dry.

Fig. 96. Steaming table in a yuba shop

To visit Kyoto's yuba shops early in the morning and watch the craftsmen at work is an unforgettable experience. Sunlight shines from the high windows down through the steam rising from heating soymilk and makes pinpoint rainbows in the air. Falling on the sheets of translucent yuba, the light renders them shimmering white. The delicious fragrances of fresh soymilk and wood-smoke are everywhere. At times, the entire shop can suddenly take on a surrealistic, almost unreal appearance as through this hushed world, half-visible figures move slowly along the steaming white pools. Hundreds of sheets of pale yuba teem and hover in the thick mist like the frail ghosts of a vision and flutter in the magical netherworld light like silken banners on the lances of dream knights. As the day warms or the sun's position shifts, the visual reverie can vanish as quickly as it came, leaving us in a world only slightly less enchanted.

Types of Yuba

Yuba is commonly sold in three different states: fresh, half-dried, and dried. The first pieces of yuba to be lifted off the steaming soymilk are considered to be the best grade: their color is creamy white, their flavor mild and light with relatively little sweetness, and their texture firm. This yuba stays relatively soft and flexible even when dried. After about half of the yuba sheets have been removed from the soymilk, the remaining sheets begin to have a faintly reddish tinge and a sweeter flavor. Having less internal cohesiveness, they tear more easily and become somewhat brittle when dried. This yuba is regarded as second grade.

Fresh yuba (Nama-yuba), served as soon as possible after it has been made, is usually thought to be the most delicious. Highly perishable, it keeps, for only 2 to 4 days in summer and 3 to 5 days in winter, even when refrigerated. To prevent molding, it must be kept dry and well sealed. In yuba shops, it is allowed to drain and begin to dry in the moisture-laden air over the steaming tables before it is wrapped, five pieces at a time, in paper-thin, shaved wood, placed in airtight plastic bags, and whisked away on dry ice to the finest restaurants and Japanese inns.

Half-dried yuba (Nama-gawaki or Han-gawaki) keeps longer than its fresh counterpart but not nearly as long as dried yuba. It is usually prepared by inserting a bamboo skewer under the center of a sheet of yuba in the steaming tray and lifting it up so that the two halves of the sheet hang down on each side of the skewer and stick together. The resulting half-sized piece, having a double thickness and firm exterior, is then cut from the skewer when it has dried enough so that it is no longer moist but is not yet brittle. Packed in an airtight plastic bag and stored on regular or dry ice, it is used mostly in restaurants.

Dried Yuba (Kanso- or Hoshi-yuba) is the most common of the three forms sold in Japan; its five most popular varieties (flat sheets, long rolls, small rolls, large spirals, and Oharagi), are illustrated below. Thoroughly dried yuba will last for 4 to 6 months if stored in a cool dry place and sealed tightly to prevent the entry of moisture. Since the flavor diminishes with time, dried yuba should be used as soon as possible. The various rolled or folded forms of yuba are usually prepared when the yuba is half-dried and still pliable; they are then dried thoroughly. All types of commercial yuba are understood to be dried unless the name specially states that they are fresh or half-dried.

At present in the United States, Chinese-style dried yuba is available at most Chinese dried-goods markets in two forms: dried yuba sheets (called Dried Bean Curd, Bean Curd Sheets, or Bean Curd Skin) and u-shaped rolls (called Bamboo Yuba or Bean Curd Sticks). Five varieties of Japanese dried yuba (flat sheets, long rolls, small rolls, large spirals, and Oharagi) are available at some Japanese markets and natural food stores. We know of no yuba shops in the United States nor of any commercial sources of fresh yuba. The latter, however, is easy to make at home. And its fine flavor can always be enjoyed when preparing homemade soymilk, for then yuba inevitably appears of its own accord.

The Varieties of Yuba

Fresh Yuba Sheets (Nama-yuba): A typical yuba sheet is 12 to 15 inches wide and 14 to 17 inches long. In recipes calling for "large sheets of fresh yuba," use sheets with the larger dimensions, if possible. Each sheet weighs about 0.8 ounces or 23 grams. When fresh sheets are gathered like a cloth, draped over individual skewers to drain, and then packaged, the yuba is called "fresh gathered sheets" (hikiage).

Flat Yuba Sheets (Hira- or Taira-yuba): These are prepared from fresh yuba sheets, usually folded into thirds before being dried. In some cases, yellow food coloring is added to the soymilk to make "yellow yuba sheets" (kiyuba), often used as a colorful topping in sushi shops.

Fresh Yuba Rolls (*Maki-yuba*): A "long roll of fresh yuba" is about 16 inches long and 1 inch in diameter. It is made by folding a piece of fresh or sweet yuba lengthwise into halves, laying it lengthwise on a second sheet together with fresh yuba trimmings, and rolling the second sheet up lengthwise. "Small rolls of fresh yuba" are prepared by cutting this long roll into 1½-inch lengths.

Long Yuba Roll (*Komaki*): About 1 inch in diameter and 15 inches long, *komaki* are prepared by rolling fresh yuba trimmings in several fresh yuba sheets. After partial drying, the roll is wrapped in still another sheet of fresh yuba, dried again, and then trimmed at both ends.

Small Yuba Rolls (*Kiri-komaki*): Prepared by cutting a long yuba roll into 1½- to 2-inch lengths, these delicate rolls are used in thin soups, one-pot cookery, or with sautéed vegetables.

Tied Yuba (*Musubi-yuba*): Prepared from a piece of regular or yellow fresh yuba about ½ inch wide and 5 inches long, *musubi-yuba* is tied into a simple loop and used in thin soups.

Large Yuba Spirals (*Omaki-, Futomaki-,* or *Uzumaki-yuba*): To make yuba spirals, about 40 sheets of half-dried yuba are rolled up to form a long cylinder 1½ to 2 inches in diameter and 1½ feet long. This is wrapped in a single sheet of fresh yuba, dried until crisp, then cut crosswise into discs about ½-to 1-inch thick. They are used widely in thin soups, one-pot cookery, and seasoned broths.

Ginkgo-leaf Yuba: Prepared by cutting fresh yellow or regular fresh yuba sheets with a cookie cutter, these dried pieces resemble 3-inch-diameter ginkgo leaves and are used as a garnish in thin soups and on top of sushi.

Oharagi Yuba: This slightly-flattened yuba roll, tied with a thin piece of *kombu*, is about 2½ inches long, 2 inches wide, and ¾ inch thick. It is prepared by loosely rolling one sheet of half-dried yuba inside a sheet of fresh yuba, tying the oval-shaped roll with 5 strips of *kombu*, then cutting the roll crosswise into fifths. (This variety derives its name from the large bundles of firewood tied around the center with a length of rope which the women of Ohara village near Kyoto are famous for carrying on their heads.)

Sweet Yuba (*Amayuba*): This is the last sheet of yuba lifted (and often partially scraped) from the bottom of the steaming tray. It has a sweet rich flavor and slightly reddish color. Thicker and less delicate than most yuba, its edges are often ragged and uneven. Eaten fresh and warm at the yuba shop, it is ambrosial. It is usually dried and sold in large pieces of various sizes in sealed cellophane bags. The least expensive of all types of yuba, sweet yuba is, in our opinion, the most delicious, especially when deep-fried, lightly salted, and served like potato chips. Dried pieces may be added to soups, egg dishes, or sautéed vegetable preparations.

Fresh Yuba Trimmings (*Kirehashi*): These small pieces and scraps, left over after trimming the ends of yuba rolls or sheets, serve as an excellent ingredient in fillings for other rolls or pouches. When dried, they are called yuba flakes.

Yuba Flakes (*Kuzu-yuba* and *Mimi*): These dried yuba trimmings, sold in sealed bags at a very low price, are used in many of the same ways as sweet yuba. They are also served in many hospitals as an inexpensive source of high-quality protein.

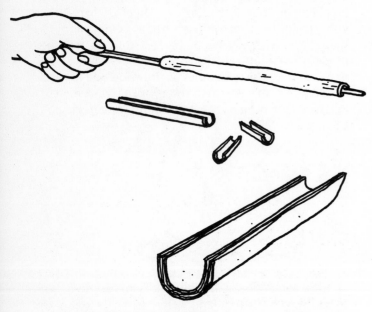

Trough-shaped Yuba (*Toyuba*): When dried sheets of yuba are cut off their bamboo skewers, the part of the yuba that was in contact with the top and sides of the skewer remains attached in the form of a long, inverted trough. After 8 to 10 sheets of yuba have been cut away, the "trough" is about 1/8 inch thick and composed of 8 to 10 layers of dried yuba. Pried off the skewer with a knife, it is cut into 2-inch lengths. Often served deep-fried, it is also used in Sukiyaki, one-pot cookery, and all types of Zen Temple Cookery.

Reconstituting Dried Yuba

Since dried yuba is very brittle, before being used in cooking it is briefly reconstituted in water or dashi until it becomes soft and pliable. It should be added to most dishes just before they are served, and should never be simmered for much more than a minute lest it begin to fall apart and lose its delicate flavor. When unrefreshed dried yuba is added to a dish, it tends to absorb a large amount of liquid; be sure to use enough stock or water to cover this loss. Reconstituted dried yuba may be substituted for fresh yuba in any of the following recipes.

Dried Yuba Rolls: Dip rolls into a bowl of water, or place on a plate or bamboo colander and sprinkle lightly with water. Moisten a dish towel, arrange the yuba atop one half of it, and fold the other half over to rest atop the yuba. Allow to stand for 5 to 10 minutes.

Dried Yuba Sheets: Dip sheets into a bowl of water. Place on a cutting board or other flat surface, roll up, and cut into 1½-inch lengths. Soak in the water for 5 to 10 minutes.

Homemade Fresh Yuba   MAKES 12 TO 14 SHEETS

This dish takes about an hour to make, but it's worth it. Prepare yuba while you have other work to do in the kitchen. For the steaming container, use either a shallow enamel pan (about 9 by 12 inches) or a heavy iron skillet about 12 inches in diameter. Be sure that the steaming container is at least 1½ but no more than 3 inches deep. Two different steaming arrangements may be used: 1) Place the steaming container on a broiling screen, perforated metal plate, or asbestos pad set directly over a low flame. 2) Use a double boiler arrangement with a large pot on the bottom at least one-half full of rapidly boiling water, and a shallow pan on top that fits into the lower pot. Since each piece of yuba takes about 7 minutes to form, you can save time by using more than one steaming container at the same time.

Prepare Homemade Soymilk (p. 204) and pour into steaming containers to a depth of 1 to 1½ inches. Skim off foam with a spatula. Heat soymilk to about 175° (until steaming but not quite boiling). Wait about 7 minutes until a firm yuba film has formed over entire surface of soymilk. Trim film away from walls of steaming container with the tip of a knife. Using your fingertips, lift up one edge of yuba film, and insert a long moistened chopstick, skewer, or knitting needle under center of yuba sheet (fig. 97). Carefully lift yuba away from soymilk, drain for a few seconds over steaming container, then set chopstick across the mouth of a deep pot allowing yuba to drain and cool for 4 to 5 minutes. Slide yuba off chopstick and arrange on a small plate. Serve immediately as hors d'oeuvre seasoned with a dash of shoyu, or reserve and serve with other yuba during the meal.

Continue lifting off yuba sheets at 7-minute intervals until all soymilk has evaporated from steaming containers and only a thick reddish film remains on bottom of pan. This is "sweet yuba" *(amayuba),* a true delicacy. Carefully scrape

Fig. 97. Lifting yuba away from soymilk

it off with a spatula and arrange with the other yuba. Place any crisp scraps or soft scrapings into a small bowl and serve together with the yuba as Warm Fresh Yuba (p. 243).

VARIATIONS

*Half-formed Yuba *(Tsumami-agé):* Using your fingertips, lift the delicate yuba sheets off the surface of the steaming soymilk at about 4 to 5 minute intervals, just before the yuba has had a chance to become attached to the sides of the container. Place yuba directly into a small cup and serve immediately.

*Large Sheets of Fresh Yuba: Prepare homemade fresh yuba, however when lifting yuba off surface of soymilk, insert moistened chopstick or skewer along one edge of sheet (rather than under the center) so that sheet hangs like a flag from chopstick. Allow yuba to drain as above for 15 to 20 minutes until it is no longer moist; carefully remove chopstick and lay flat sheet on a dry cutting board. Use as called for in the following recipes. For larger sheets use a 12- by 15-inch pan.

*Fresh Yuba Rolls *(Maki-yuba):* After yuba has dried on the chopstick for 4 to 5 minutes, place the flat yuba sheet on a cutting board or other flat surface and roll into a cylinder; then cut into 1-inch lengths. Use in recipes calling for small yuba rolls.

*Dried Yuba: Prepare yuba sheets or rolls. Leave sheets drying on chopsticks and put rolls into a screen basket. Place in a warm dry place—such as over a hot water heater or in a very low temperature oven—for 10 to 20 hours, or until dry and crisp. Store in an airtight bag in a cool dry place until ready to use.

YUBA HORS D'OEUVRE

In Japan, yuba is prized for its use in delicate and ambrosial hors d'oeuvre. The variety of shapes, textures, and flavors which you can offer your guests is almost unlimited.

Warm Fresh Yuba

SERVES 3

If you prepare your own yuba at home, this is the only recipe you need to know. Here is how most yuba masters offer fine yuba to their guests. The simpler, fresher, and warmer the yuba, the more completely your guests will enjoy it.

12 sheets of homemade fresh yuba, half-formed yuba, or fresh yuba rolls
3 tablespoons shoyu, Wasabi-Shoyu, or Yuzu-Shoyu (p. 40)

Serve the yuba warm and fresh in small bowls or arranged on a serving platter accompanied by tiny dishes containing the dipping sauce. Or serve with any of the following mixtures:

*Honey- Vinegar Dipping Sauce
    3 teaspoons honey or sugar
    2 teaspoons (rice) vinegar
    1 teaspoon *mirin*, sake, or white wine

*Honey-Lemon Dipping Sauce
    3 teaspoons honey
    4 teaspoons lemon or lime juice

*White Miso Dipping Sauce
    1½ teaspoons sweet white miso
    1 teaspoon sugar or honey
    1 teaspoon vinegar

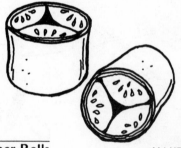

Yuba-Cucumber Rolls

MAKES 8 TO 10

1 small cucumber, cut lengthwise into quarters and crosswise into 4-inch lengths
2 or 3 sheets of fresh yuba
Wasabi-Shoyu, Yuzu-Shoyu (p. 40), or shoyu

Arrange cucumber pieces in groups of 3 and wrap with a sheet of fresh yuba. Cut crosswise into 1-inch rounds (above) and serve with the dipping sauce.

Yuba-Nori Rolls

MAKES 8 TO 10

4 sheets of *nori*
4 sheets of fresh yuba
Shoyu

Arrange equal-sized sheets of *nori* and fresh yuba on top of each other in alternate layers. Roll up lengthwise, secure with foodpicks, and cut into 1-inch lengths. Serve topped with a sprinkling of shoyu.

Yuba Canapés

12 Fresh Yuba Rolls (p. 243)
12 bite-sized pieces of (lightly buttered) toast or crackers
Shoyu
Sweet White miso, Yuzu Miso, or Red Nermiso (p. 42)

Arrange yuba rolls on toast and crackers. Sprinkle one-half the rolls with a few drops of shoyu and top the remainder with a dab of the miso.

Fresh Yuba Sashimi   SERVES 1

2 sheets of (homemade) fresh yuba (p. 242)
¼ cup slivered *daikon* or fresh *daikon* threads
2 green beefsteak leaves
Wasabi-Shoyu (p. 40), Vinegar-Shoyu, Gingerroot-Shoyu,
   or shoyu garnished with crumbled *nori;* or plain shoyu

Fold the yuba from one end to form a many-layered, 4-inch-wide sheet; cut diagonally into ¾-inch-wide strips (fig. 98). Arrange strips on a mound of the *daikon* slivers or threads, garnish with the beefsteak leaves, and serve accompanied by the dipping sauce.

   Served this way, fresh yuba bears a close resemblance to *sashimi*, or Japanese-style raw fish.

Fig. 98. Yuba Sashimi

Crunchy Sweet-Yuba Chips

   This is one of our very favorite yuba preparations. The crisp texture resembles that of potato chips, but the flavor and aroma are truly unique.

Oil for deep-frying
10 to 15 sheets of dried sweet yuba (p. 241)
Salt

Heat the oil to only 275° in a wok or skillet. Drop in yuba and Deep-fry for about 3 to 5 seconds, until yuba turns reddish golden brown and is covered with tiny bubbles. Drain thoroughly, salt lightly and serve immediately. Also delicious served with a dip of Tofu Mayonnaise (p. 107) seasoned with a little extra lemon juice and sweetened with sugar.

VARIATIONS
Deep-fried Trough-shaped Yuba (Toyu Yuba): Deep-fry yuba pieces without batter for about 1 minute, salt lightly and serve like yuba chips. This crisp hors d'oeuvre is especial-

ly prized in Zen temple cookery where it is sometimes referred to as "Flowers of Kyoto." It is also served in high-grade restaurants and bars as an accompaniment to beer or sake, sprinkled as a topping over rice, or floated in soups.
Deep-fried Dried Yuba Trimmings, Rolls, and Flakes: Prepare and serve as in either of the above two recipes. This is the least expensive way to enjoy deep-fried yuba hors d'oeuvre. They also make a nice addition to scrambled eggs, tossed green salads, and soups, lending a bacon-like flavor and texture.

Kaori Yuba   MAKES 6
(Sweet Miso Deep-fried in Fresh Yuba)

1 large sheet of fresh yuba, cut into six 4½-inch squares
9 tablespoons fresh yuba trimmings
3 tablespoons Yuzu Miso or Red Nerimiso (p. 42)
Oil for deep-frying
Shoyu or Wasabi-Shoyu (p. 40)

In the center of each yuba square layer 1 tablespoon fresh yuba trimmings, 1½ teaspoons Yuzu Miso, and ½ teaspoon yuba trimmings, in that order. Fold over the four corners of the yuba to form an envelope (fig. 99). Deep-fry at 350° for about 40 seconds, turning from time to time with chopsticks. Drain briefly, place on absorbent paper, and serve with dipping sauce.

VARIATIONS
*Omit yuba trimmings and use 1 tablespoon Mushroom Miso Sauté (p. 43) as the filling for each yuba "packet."
*On a large sheet of fresh yuba, spread a thin layer of Yuzu Miso, sweet white miso, or Sweetened Tekka Miso (p. 44). Roll up the sheet to form a cylinder, cut crosswise into 1-inch lengths, and deep-fry. Serve with shoyu and a mixture of equal parts grated *daikon* and grated gingerroot.

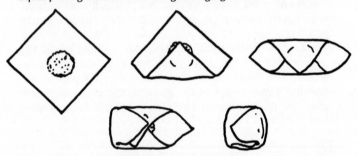

Fig. 99. Yuba envelopes

Deep-fried Yuba Dengaku   MAKES 6

1 large sheet of fresh yuba, cut crosswise into thirds
Oil for deep-frying
Sweet white miso or Red Nerimiso (p. 42)
Roasted sesame seeds

Fold each yuba piece into thirds, then roll up from the folded end to form a cylinder (fig. 100). Wrap each cylinder with a second yuba piece moistened along one edge to seal. Pierce

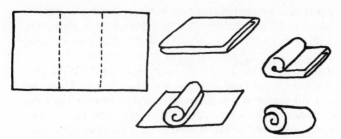

yuba cylinder from one end with a (green) bamboo dengaku skewer (or two foodpicks) and deep-fry for about 1 minute until golden brown. Spread tops of rolls with the miso and top with a sprinkling of sesame seeds. Serve while crisp and hot.

The freshly deep-fried rolls —called *Agé-maki* Yuba— may also be served as is, sprinkled with a little shoyu. Simmered in Sweetened Shoyu Broth (p. 40), they make a tasty addition to soups and *nabe* dishes.

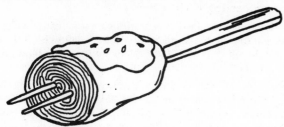

Fig. 100. Deep-fried Yuba Dengaku

Yawata-maki *(Yuba-Burdock Root Roll)*   MAKES 6

8 to 10 strips of burdock root (or carrot), each 12 inches long
    and 1/8-inch square
Sweetened Shoyu Broth (p. 40)
2 large sheets of fresh yuba, each 12 by 14 inches
5 to 6 fresh yuba trimmings, each 12 inches long
Oil for deep-frying

Soak burdock root strips in cold water for 15 minutes; drain. Combine with the broth in a saucepan and simmer, covered, for 1 to 2 hours. Place 1 yuba sheet congruently atop the other. Arrange burdock and yuba strips in a bundle crosswise at one end of the sheets. Roll to form a cylinder 1½ inches in diameter and 12 inches long. Deep-fry in 350° oil until crisp and golden brown; drain well. Cut roll crosswise into thirds, then cut each third diagonally into halves. Serve upright (below).

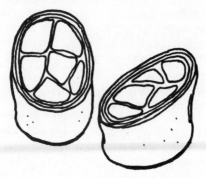

Toji Yuba *(Deep-fried Yuba*   MAKES 6
with Ginkgo Nuts and Lilly Bulbs)

1 large sheet of fresh yuba, cut into six 6-inch squares
3 teaspoons refreshed cloud-ear mushroom
10 tablespoons fresh yuba trimmings
6 ginkgo nuts
18 small sections of lilly bulbs
Oil for deep-frying
Wasabi-Shoyu (p. 40) or shoyu

Arrange the yuba squares on a cutting board or other flat surface. Divide the next four ingredients evenly among the squares, placing them in a small mound at the center of each square. Fold over the two opposing corners (below), then roll up lengthwise from one end. Secure with a foodpick and deep-fry in 350° oil until golden brown. Serve with the dipping sauce or use as an ingredient in one-pot cookery.

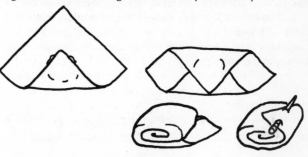

Deep-fried Yuba-Nori Rolls   MAKES 10

10 pieces of fresh yuba, each 2½ inches square
10 pieces of *nori*, each 2½ inches square
10 tablespoons grated glutinous yam or 10 teaspoons Red
    Nerimiso (p. 42)
Oil for deep-frying
Shoyu (optional)
Parsley sprigs

Place each of the *nori* pieces congruently on top of a piece of yuba. Spread the surface of each piece of *nori* with either 1 tablespoon yam or 1 teaspoon miso. Roll each square into a tight cylinder, and deep-fry until golden brown. Serve with shoyu and garnish with parsley.

Yuba-Mock Broiled Eels   MAKES 12
(Yuba no Kabayaki)

1 small roll of fresh yuba, cut crosswise into 1-inch lengths
Oil for deep-frying
Sweetened Shoyu Broth (p. 40)
Sansho pepper

Deep-fry yuba rolls until crisp and golden brown, drain briefly, then simmer in the broth for 10 minutes. Drain well and gently press out excess broth. Now broil rolls over a low flame (on a screen) until lightly browned and fragrant. Serve topped with the pepper.

Or simply baste fresh or trough-shaped yuba with shoyu while broiling over charcoals.

Buddha's Chicken

SERVES 4

1½ tablespoons soy sauce
¼ teaspoon salt
2 teaspoons sugar
1½ teaspoons sesame oil
½ cup stock or water
6 large sheets of fresh yuba
Oil for deep-frying
Parsley and radish roses

Combine the first five ingredients in a small saucepan, bring just to a boil, and remove from heat; allow to cool briefly. Place 1 yuba sheet in a baking pan and coat with a little of the warm sauce. Continue to add sheets in layers, coating each, until all ingredients are used. Roll up sheets from one end to form a compact sylinder. Wrap in cheesecloth, place into a preheated stemer (p. 38), and steam for 10 minutes; remove cheesecloth. (Or bake over a pan of water in a 350° oven.)

Heat oil to 350° in a wok, skillet, or deep-fryer. Drop in yuba roll and deep-fry until golden brown (p. 130). Cut diagonally into ½-inch-thick rounds and serve garnished with parsley and radish roses.

Homemade Buddha's Ham
(Suhuo-t'ui)

SERVES 3 OR 4

3 tablespoons oil
2 cups dried yuba flakes and trimmings, well-packed
¼ cup grated carrot
1 tablespoon grated gingerroot
2½ tablespoons soy sauce

Heat a skillet and coat with the oil. Add the remaining ingredients and sauté over low heat for about 5 minutes. Remove from heat and allow to cool for several minutes, then press ingredients into a 3- by 8-inch mold, or tupperware container of comparable size. Cover with a pressing lid, and press with a 6- to 8-pound weight for 1 hour. Cut into thin slices and serve like ham as an hors d'oeuvre.

In China, another variety of Buddha's Ham is prepared as follows: Spread one surface of a large sheet of fresh (or refreshed) yuba with sesame oil. Roll the sheet into a tight cylinder and tie with string in 3 or 4 places (p. 177); steam for 30 to 40 minutes. When cut crosswise into slices, this preparation looks remarkably like rolled meat. It is often used as a key ingredient in an elaborate vegetarian dish known as the Arhat's Feast or Monk's Dish (p. 261).

Chinese Smoked Yuba Sausage
(Su-tsang or Su-shiang tsa)

MAKES 6

The aroma and the deep red filling of this savory hors d'oeuvre make it resemble a high-grade sausage. Used widely in Chinese vegetarian restaurants, these mock sausages are also sold in most traditional marketplaces.

1 cup red fermented rice (ang-tsao)
¼ cup sake lees (chu-tsao)
¼ cup each sliced mushrooms and wheat gluten, simmered until tender in a mixture of wine, brown sugar, salt, and dashi
6 large sheets of fresh yuba

Combine the red rice, sake lees, mushrooms, and wheat gluten; mix well. Spread in a thin layer over the yuba sheets. Roll up each sheet to form a tight cylinder 9 inches long and ½ inch in diameter. Deep-fry until golden brown, then wrap from end to end with a single strand of rice straw. Now smoke over a wood fire for about 3 hours.

Chinese-style Deep-fried Yuba Hors D'oeuvre

Each of these tasty preparations are sold ready-made in many traditional marketplaces and some modern food stores in Taiwan and China (p. 257). Many are illustrated in figure 111.

*Yuba Chicken (Ssu-chi): Mix diced fresh yuba trimmings with a little soy sauce, salt, sugar, sesame oil, and minced mushrooms. Spread the mixture on a large sheet of fresh yuba, roll into a tight cylinder and cut into 4-inch lengths. Wrap each roll tightly in a 6-inch square of cotton cloth, tying both ends and the middle with string to form a sausage-like shape. Simmer rolls for 15 to 30 minutes in Sweetened Shoyu Broth (p. 40), or steam for the same time in a preheated steamer. Remove cloth, wrap each roll with a sheet of *nori*, and deep-fry until golden brown.

*Deep-fried Buddha's Yuba: Cut Buddha's Ham, Fish, or Chicken (above) diagonally into 3/8-inch-thick strips and deep-fry without batter until crisp. Serve with sautéed mushrooms and topped with a sprinkling of soy sauce.

*Yuba-Nori Roll: Simmer diced carrots, cabbage, and bamboo shoots in Sweetened Shoyu Broth, then roll in sheets of fresh yuba to form cylinders 9 inches long and ¾ inch in diameter. Wrap cylinders in *nori* and deep-fry. Cut into 1-inch lengths and serve with soy sauce.

*Yuba Drumstick (Sso-tsai): On a sheet of fresh yuba place a mixture of diced yuba trimmings, minced carrots, cabbage, *konnyaku*, mushrooms, bamboo shoots and hot spices. Roll the yuba to form a cone about 6 inches long and 2 inches in diameter at the mouth. Tuck in the edge of the yuba at the mouth of the cone to hold in the filling. Simmer cone in sweetened shoyu broth for 15 minutes, then drain well. Deep-fry without batter and serve with a sprinkling of soy sauce. The yuba may also be folded as a pouch rather than a cone.

*Glutinous Rice Roll: On a large sheet of fresh yuba, spread a mixture of cooked glutinous rice combined with diced carrots which have been simmered in sweetened shoyu broth. Roll up tightly to form a cylinder 9 inches long and ¾ inch in diameter. Deep-fry and cut into 1-inch lengths. Serve with soy sauce.

YUBA IN SALADS, SOUPS, AND SAUCES

Add yuba trimmings or sweet yuba to tossed green salads just before adding the dressing. Or deep-fry the yuba and allow to cool before adding. Use yuba in Shira-ae (p. 114) or other *Aemono* (Japanese-type salads) in the recipes described in the chapters on tofu and deep-fried tofu cookery. Or serve yuba with thinly-sliced fresh cucumbers, carrots, and mushrooms marinated with Vinegar-Miso (p. 46) or Sambai-zu (p. 41).

Flakes or trimmings of dried or sweet yuba make a delicious addition to most thick soups. For thinner soups, add small yuba rolls, large yuba spirals, or *Oharagi*-yuba.

Yuba trimmings and flakes go well in all types of sauces. In China and Taiwan, yuba is often served in gravy or thick brown sauces generally seasoned with plenty of red pepper and other fiery spices. Favorite combinations of ingredients in the sauces include: yuba and mushrooms; yuba, bamboo shoots, and mushrooms; yuba, green soybeans, leeks, and cabbage. The yuba is added shortly before the sauce is ready to be served.

Yuba in Miso Soups

Yuba is most commonly used in thick miso soups made with sweet white miso. Add 1 or 2 small yuba rolls per serving to the broth when you add the miso. In Zen Temple Cookery, trough-shaped yuba is floated on miso soups as a savory granish or is crumbled and used as a replacement for bonita flakes. Ingredients which combine well with yuba in sweet white miso soups are *mochi*, wheat gluten, trefoil, and slivered *yuzu* or lemon rind. Try adding yuba to any of the miso soups beginning on page 118.

Yuba in Clear Soups

Place several pieces of yuba —fresh or dried, flat or rolled— into a soup bowl, then carefully pour in Clear Broth (p. 40). Allow to stand for about 5 minutes before serving. The following combinations make nice garnishes: *(shiitake)* mushrooms, (Japanese) spinach, and slivered *yuzu* rind; green beans, mushrooms simmered in Sweetened Shoyu Broth (p. 40), and several drops of *yuzu* or lemon juice; trefoil, crumbled *nori*, and *junsai* (water shield).

YUBA IN SANDWICHES, EGG DISHES,
AND OVEN COOKERY

Sheets of fresh yuba lightly seasoned with shoyu are delicious served on lightly-buttered pieces of hot toast or with fresh vegetable slices on open-face sandwiches.

Add yuba trimmings and flakes, or sweet yuba to your favorite casseroles, quiches, gratin dishes, or vegetable pies, using about ¼ cup yuba to each cup of casserole ingredients.

Mixed with a little milk, yuba makes a good addition to scrambled eggs and omelets. Deep-fried dried or sweet yuba may be used with excellent results to lend a bacon-like flavor and texture to all egg dishes. Yuba Ham and Smoked Yuba Sausage (p. 246), too, are delicious with most breakfast egg preparations.

Tamago-toji Yuba　　　　　　　　　　　SERVES 1
(Raw Eggs Cooked Over Hot Yuba)

3 to 4 small yuba rolls or 2 large yuba spirals
¼ to ½ cup Sweetened Shoyu Broth (p. 40)
1 egg, lightly beaten

Combine yuba rolls and broth in a small saucepan and simmer for 3 to 4 minutes. Place rolls steaming hot into a small bowl. Quickly mix egg with 1 tablespoon hot broth, then pour over yuba. Serve as is, or use as a topping for hot brown rice or noodles.

YUBA SAUTÉED AND DEEP-FRIED

Add yuba trimmings and flakes, or sweet yuba, to vegetable dishes near the end of sautéeing, or use in Okara with Vegetables (p. 80).

Yuba is always deep-fried without batter in moderate oil for a very short time. For deep-fried yuba hors d'oeuvre see pp. 244-246.

Simmered Roll of Deep-fried Fresh Yuba　SERVES 1

1 large yuba spiral, 1½ inches in diameter and 1 inch thick,
　　containing about 30 layers of rolled yuba
Oil for deep-frying
½ cup water
1½ tablespoons sugar
1 teaspoon shoyu
1 tiny "princess" bamboo shoot (2 inches long and 3/8 inch
　　in diameter)
2 cubes of dried-frozen tofu, each 1 inch on a side
3 sections of butterbur stem, each 2 inches long

Deep-fry the yuba roll until very lightly browned; drain. Now drop into boiling water and simmer for 5 minutes to remove excess oil. Rinse twice in cold water, then soak for 5 minutes in circulating cold water.

Combine the water, sugar, and shoyu in a small saucepan and bring to a boil. Add the yuba, vegetables and frozen tofu, return to the boil, and simmer for about 7 minutes. Allow yuba and vegetables to cool, then arrange in a bowl (fig. 87, p. 218). Serve topped with a little of the cooking liquid.

This preparation is a specialty at Tokyo's *Sasa-no-Yuki* restaurant (p. 307).

Deep-fried Yuba in Ankake Sauce
(Tamago Yuba)   SERVES 4

4 large sheets of fresh yuba
Oil for deep-frying
1½ cups Ankake Sauce (p. 49)
2 teaspoons grated gingerroot or 1 teaspoon hot mustard

Fold each yuba sheet lengthwise into thirds, then fold in
2-inch lengths from one end to form compact bundles (fig.
101). Secure each bundle with a foodpick and deep-fry in
350° oil until golden brown. Divide yuba bundles among 4
deep bowls and top with the sauce and a dab of grated gingerroot or mustard.

Kenchin-maki   MAKES 2
(Large Yuba Rolls with Tofu and Vegetables)

¼ cup green peas
¼ cup diced or grated carrots
¼ cup sliced mushrooms
¼ cup diced burdock root, soaked for 15 minutes in water
   and drained
2 cups Sweetened Shoyu Broth (p. 40)
24 ounces tofu, pressed (p. 96)
2 large sheets of fresh yuba
Oil for deep-frying

Combine the first five ingredients in a saucepan and bring
to a boil; simmer, covered, for 20 minutes. Drain vegetables,
reserving broth, and combine vegetables with tofu; mash together thoroughly. Lay yuba sheets on *sudare* bamboo mats.
Cover each sheet with a ½-inch-thick layer of the tofu-vegetable mixture, then roll up yuba as for Nori-wrapped Sushi (p.
170) to form a 1½-inch-diameter, 10-inch-long cylinder.
Deep-fry yuba rolls until golden brown (p. 130); drain well.
Return rolls to the Sweetened Shoyu Broth and simmer for 5
minutes. Cut rolls crosswise into 1-inch lengths to serve.

VARIATIONS
*Shinoda-maki: Across one end of a large sheet of fresh yuba,
lay a long bundle of Osmond fern fronds and butterbur stems.
Roll up yuba, secure in several places with foodpicks, and
deep-fry. Now simmer in the shoyu broth. Serve as above.
*Chinese-style Yuba Spring Rolls *(Yuba Harumaki):* In a
large bowl combine thinly sliced leeks, bamboo shoots, mushrooms, and minced gingerroot. Season with salt, sugar, sake,
pepper, and sesame oil. Mix in 1 egg and cornstarch. Place ¼
cup of the mixture in the center of each of a number of fresh
yuba rectangles, then fold over edges to form envelopes (fig.
99). Seal edges with a thick paste of flour and water. Deep-fry
in moderate oil, first with the seam-side down. Cut crosswise
into 1-inch-wide strips and serve with the cut surface facing
upwards accompanied by Mustard-Shoyu Dipping Sauce (p.
40).

    For variety, add or substitute diced onion, sweet pota-
toes, carrots, slivered burdock root or green peas. After deep-
frying, dip in hot water to remove surface oil, then simmer in
Sweetened Shoyu Broth (p. 40). Serve as is or top with Gingerroot Sauce (p. 49).

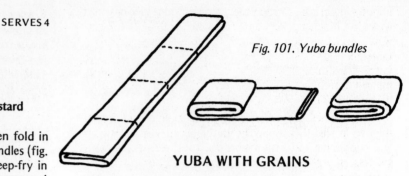

Fig. 101. Yuba bundles

YUBA WITH GRAINS

    When used as a topping for grain dishes, yuba adds rich
flavor, delicate sweetness, and plenty of protein. In China,
Bamboo Yuba (p. 259) is often added to or sprinkled on top
of breakfast rice gruel.

Yuba with Noodles

*Lay several pieces of *Oharagi* yuba or small yuba rolls atop
buckwheat or whole-wheat noodles in a deep bowl. Pour on
Noodle Broth (p. 40) and serve hot.
*Sauté onions and cabbage until just tender. Add thinly-
sliced Buddha's Ham (p. 246) and sauté for 1 minute more.
Stir in several cups of cooked noodles and season to taste with
shoyu and Sesame Salt. Serve topped with a sprinkling of
crumbled toasted *nori.*
*Serve cooked buckwheat noodles topped with a mixture of
thinly-sliced, parboiled green beans, carrot matchsticks sautéed in lightly salted oil, slivers of uncooked leeks, and fresh
yuba rolls which have been simmered for several minutes in
Sweetened Shoyu Broth (p. 40). Top with hot Noodle Broth
(p. 40) and season with 7-spice red pepper.

Yuba with Rice and Sushi

*Deep-fry dried yuba flakes, trough-shaped yuba, or dried
sweet yuba. Sprinkle with salt, break into small pieces, and
serve as a topping over hot rice.
*Sliver fresh yuba and use as one of the toppings for Five-
color Sushi (p. 169). Prepared in this way, the yuba is called
"threads of gold."
*Simmer yuba in Sweetened Shoyu Broth (p. 40) then use
with or in place of agé as the core of Nori-wrapped Sushi (p.
170). Yellow yuba is often used in this preparation.

YUBA IN ONE-POT COOKERY
AND SEASONED BROTHS

    In Japan, all varieties of yuba are used widely in the
various *nabe* dishes described on pages 143 to 144, and in
Sukiyaki (p. 224). Add the yuba toward the end of cooking.
Yuba is also preserved as *tsukudani* by simmering it for a long
time in a mixture of shoyu and a little sugar, grated gingerroot, and water.
    Fresh or refreshed yuba is delicious simmered for 10

minutes in a broth of 1 cup water, 2 tablespoons sake or white wine. In Chinese cookery a more potent broth is used: ½ cup water, 4½ tablespoons soy sauce, 1½ tablespoons sugar, and 1 tablespoon sake. Simmer vegetables in the broth with the yuba. Garnish with slivers of *yuzu* or lemon peel and/or minced trefoil leaves. Yuba-rolled vegetables are also delicious when simmered in seasoned broths.

In Chinese-style *Happosai,* yuba is simmered for 10 minutes in a lightly seasoned broth thickened with cornstarch and containing lotus root, burdock root, carrots, bamboo shoots, *(shiitake)* mushrooms, green peas, and cloud-ear mushrooms.

YUBA STEAMED

Yuba is a favorite addition to Chawan-mushi (p. 147). Use small yuba rolls, fresh yuba trimmings, or a small square of fresh yuba folded around a dab of slivered vegetables and secured with a foodpick. If desired, simmer any of these forms of yuba in Sweetened Shoyu Broth (p. 40) before adding to the Chawan-mushi.

Yuba Kenchin-maki (p. 248) is often prepared by steaming rather than deep-frying yuba rolls before simmering them in Sweetened Shoyu Broth.

Yuba Shinjo *(Yuba Steamed with Eggs)* SERVES 2

1 cup fresh yuba trimmings, ground in a meat grinder or *suribachi*
2 eggs, lightly beaten
2 tablespoons shoyu
4 teaspoons natural sugar

Combine all ingredients and divide among 2 custard or Chawan-mushi cups. Cover and steam as for Chawan-mushi (p. 147). Serve hot or cold.

Chinese-style Steamed Yuba

*Yuba-filled Steamed Buns: Combine equal volumes of diced yuba trimmings, mushrooms, and carrots, and simmer until tender in Sweetened Shoyu Broth (p. 40). Place 1 heaping tablespoon of the drained vegetables at the center of 2-inch diameter patties of leavened dough. Fold dough around filling and seal to form a bun, then steam in a pre-heated steamer for 30 minutes. Serve hot, topped with a sprinkling of soy sauce.
*Pressed Yuba with Peanut Sauce: Dice fresh yuba trimmings and press into a mold the shape of a bun. Steam until firm, then serve topped with a sauce made from a mixture of peanut butter, miso, sugar, and vinegar.

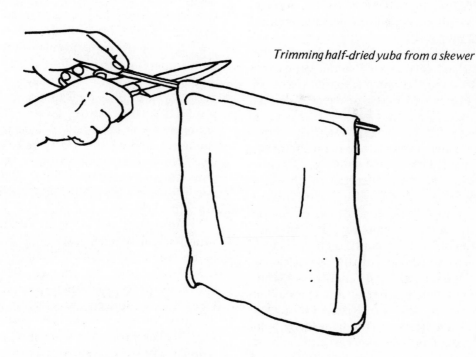

Trimming half-dried yuba from a skewer

15
Tofu and Yuba in China, Taiwan, and Korea

TOFU ORIGINATED in China over two thousand years ago and today serves as one of the most popular basic foods of that nation's more than 800 million people. Costing only about 8 cents per pound—roughly one-third the price of regular Japanese tofu (which has a lower protein content)—firm Chinese-style tofu plays a crucial nutritional role in the life of most Chinese. The average Taiwanese, for example, is said to eat as much as 64 pounds of tofu every year.

The subject of Chinese tofu is so vast, and the varieties of tofu and tofu cuisine so numerous and unusual, that this short chapter actually merits an entire volume. For every Chinese province makes its own varieties of tofu and has its own names (and pronunciations) for the many varieties found throughout the other provinces. This proliferation of titles, combined with the presence in China of numerous dialects and the difficulties of phonetic translation from Chinese into English, has resulted in the fact that these various types of tofu often appear in cookbooks and other contemporary literature under differing and sometimes contradictory names. Fortunately, even though each of the basic varieties is referred to in speech differently by the Mandarin-speaking people of Peking, the Cantonese-speaking residents of the south, and the citizens of Taiwan, each is nevertheless written with the same ideographic characters by all. Thus we have learned (the hard way) that the easiest way to make ourselves understood by Chinese chefs or tofu masters—whether in Japan, Taiwan, or America—is to carry a list of the names of all the different types of tofu written in Chinese!

In what follows, we have consistently used the standard Mandarin, which is slowly becoming China's national language. The word "tofu" will be used as a general term to refer to all varieties of tofu, Japanese or Chinese. In Mandarin, the word for tofu is *doufu*, with the first syllable pronounced like a combination of the two English words "doe" and "toe." It is called *dowfu* (also spelled *dow-foo*) in Cantonese, with the first syllable being pronounced like the "Dow" of Dow Jones.

At present, many excellent Chinese tofu shops are in operation throughout the United States (see Appendix B). Most produce several varieties of Japanese-style tofu as well as uniquely Chinese tofu products such as doufu, pressed tofu, savory tofu, white *doufu-ru*, and hollow agé cubes. In addition, Chinese grocery stores carry red *doufu-ru*, Chinese dried yuba, and bamboo yuba. A list of the size, shape, and Chinese name(s) of each of these products together with the types of stores at which they are sold can be found on page 22.

Although many more varieties of tofu are found in China and Taiwan than in Japan, a number of common Japanese varieties (such as grilled and dried-frozen tofu, agé, ganmo, and kinugoshi cakes) are rarely if ever seen there. China's southern provinces have produced the greatest number of tofu products, possibly because of the necessity to find ways to keep the tofu from spoiling in their semi-tropical climate.

Three Varieties of Tofu

Regular Chinese tofu can be divided into three basic types according to moisture content and texture: *doufu*, which is about as firm as Japanese-style grilled tofu; *pressed tofu*, which is even firmer; and *Chinese kinugoshi*, which is often so much softer than Japanese kinugoshi that it cannot be cut into cakes.

Doufu: Known in the West as Chinese-style firm tofu, *doufu* is the most common variety of tofu found in China. It is closely related to regular Japanese tofu, although it has a firmer texture and contains less water (about as much as does Japanese tofu after being pressed). By using doufu in all recipes calling for pressed Japanese tofu, or in stir-fried or sautéed dishes, you can be assured of excellent results while saving the time otherwise needed for pressing. (Substitute 9 ounces of doufu for 12 ounces of regular Japanese tofu.) Having a firm, cohesive texture, doufu keeps its form well—when transported over China's back roads as well as during the vigorous process of stir-frying. In semitropical areas such as Canton and Taiwan, its low water content helps it to stay fresh for up to several days without refrigeration or the addition of preservatives; thus doufu is especially well suited for tropical or semitropical areas such as India, Africa, and South America. Its protein content averages about 10 percent (versus Japanese tofu at 7.8 percent and ground beef at about 13 percent).

As it spread throughout East Asia, doufu was transmitted first to Japan where it became known as tofu. Its close relative can still be found in Japanese farmhouse tofu which, like its Chinese progenitor, is so firm it can be tied with rope and carried hanging from one hand (fig. 112, p. 271). In the Philippines, this variety of Chinese tofu was to become known as *tojo* or *tokua;* in Indonesia as *tahu.*

Since doufu is often solidified with a mixture of nigari and calcium sulfate, and since (like farmhouse tofu) it is not generally soaked in water after being removed from the settling box, it has a rich, subtly sweet flavor. Whereas Japanese tofu is prepared in large, deep settling boxes, then cut into 12-ounce cakes sold individually by the tofu maker at his shop and in the neighborhood, doufu is prepared in the form of 5½ pound "flats" about 10 to 12 inches square and 1½ inches thick. Each flat is cut to yield 16 squares, each square weighing about 4½ ounces and measuring 2½ to 3 inches on a side and 1½ inches thick. Venders buy entire flats from the maker, place them on wooden pallets for easy transport, then sell the doufu in marketplaces or by the roadsides. The flat is usually cut into individual squares for each customer (fig. 102).

Although most doufu is quite firm, a less com-

Fig. 102. Cutting doufu at the marketplace

mon variety with about the same water content as regular Japanese tofu can also be found in parts of China and Taiwan. In the West, fresh doufu is now widely available at Chinese food markets, natural food stores, and some supermarkets, where it is sold immersed in water in sealed plastic tubs.

Pressed Tofu: The firmest variety of Chinese tofu, pressed tofu or *doufu-kan*, contains about 22 percent protein and only 62 percent water. It can be prepared at home from Japanese tofu by means of the reshaping process described on page 98. The character *kan* means "dry" or "containing little water." In the actual process of making pressed tofu, cloth-lined trays or small cloth-wrapped bundles of firm curds are pressed in multiple layers under a large hand-turned screw press until as much whey and water as possible have been expelled (fig. 103). The finished tofu has a chewy, meaty texture like that of smoked ham, sausage, or firm cheese. The use of nigari, or a mixture of nigari and calcium sulfate solidifiers, adds to the tofu's solidity.

Regular pressed tofu is sold in individual squares about 3 inches on a side and ¾ inch thick. Although many squares are sold as is, with their natural white color and subtly-sweet flavor, others are simmered in solutions of water and either burnt millet sugar, molasses, turmeric, or tea to create a variety of colors and flavors and to further help preserve them. Thus, some squares are dark chocolate brown and others are brilliant saffron yellow. The latter, stamped with a vermilion red Chinese character, are used as offerings at household altars.

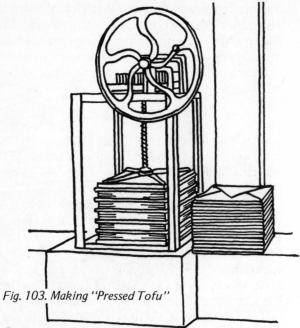

Fig. 103. Making "Pressed Tofu"

Pressed tofu is usually cut into thin strips, shredded, or diced. It is stir-fried with vegetables, used in thickened Chinese sauces, added to soups, marinated with fresh (or cooked) vegetables and nuts in salads, or served in thin slices like cuts of cold meat. Its firm texture and high protein content make it an excellent meat replacement in many Western-style preparations including casseroles and breakfast egg dishes.

Savory Pressed Tofu (Wu-hsiang kan): This variety of pressed tofu is prepared by simmering pressed tofu squares in a mixture of soy sauce, oil, and seasonings. The latter, which vary widely from maker to maker and from province to province, include anise, garlic, minced scallion, cinnamon, cloves, peppermint, and bay leaves as well as a number of spices which have no English equivalent. The name *wu-hsiang kan* means literally "five fragrances dry" indicating that a combination of five or more spices and seasonings is generally used. This tofu ranges in color from light to dark brown and has a texture and flavor resembling smoked ham. In the San Francisco area it is freshly prepared daily and sold as Flavored Bean Cake. Savory Pressed Tofu is served as an hors d'oeuvre, thinly sliced like cold cuts, and is often accompanied by drinks. Or it is sometimes used as a side dish or topping for rice gruel, or in salads with peanuts and a sesame oil dressing.

Soy-sauce Pressed Tofu (Chiang-yu doufu-kan): Sold in most market places and tofu shops in China and Taiwan (but not yet available in the West), these 1½-inch squares, pressed to a thickness of only

3/8 inch, are simmered in a mixture of soy sauce and water until they turn dark brown. Some varieties, prepared at delicatessens, are simmered (whole or diced) in a chicken or pork broth seasoned with soy sauce and red peppers. Others are smoked after being simmered and served as an hors d'oeuvre, like smoked ham, or used as a seasoning for rice dishes.

Pressed Tofu Sheets (Pai-yeh): Perhaps the most unusual variety of pressed tofu, *pai-yeh* is written with the characters meaning either "one hundred pages" or "one hundred leaves." Sometimes called bean curd "sheets" or "wrappers" in Chinese cookbooks, each sheet looks like a 6- to 12-inch square of canvas with a clothlike pattern imprinted on both sides, and each has a soft flexible texture. They are prepared by ladling a thin layer of firm curds onto each of about 100 pieces of cloth stacked consecutively in a tall wooden frame. The alternate layers of cloth and curds are then pressed for several hours beneath a very heavy weight. Most of the finished sheets are sold in outdoor marketplaces and are generally used in cooking as wrappers for various steamed or deep-fried foods, just like *wonton,* spring-roll (*harumaki*), or egg-roll skins. Since the sheets resemble and are used in many of the same ways as Chinese yuba (*tou-p'i*), they are sometimes called by the same name. Sheets which have been cut (by hand or with a noodle-cutting machine) into very thin strips are known as "pressed tofu noodles" or "beancurd shreds" (*doufu-ssu* or *kan-ssu*), and sheets which have been cut into ½-inch-wide strips that are tied into simple overhand knots are known as "pressed tofu loops" or *pai-yeh chieh* (fig 104). These preparations are very popular in soups, *nabe* dishes or firepots, and in simmered or sautéed vegetable dishes.

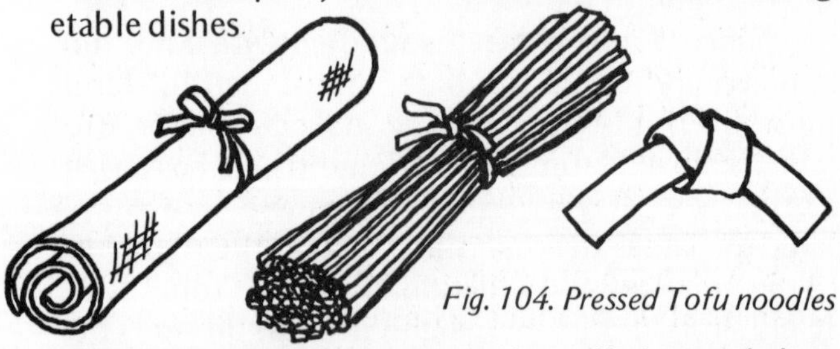

Fig. 104. Pressed Tofu noodles

Pressed tofu sheets are also rolled up tightly to form a cylinder, wrapped and bound in a piece of cloth, and simmered in water until they are tender yet maintain their form when unwrapped. Sold in Chinese markets as varieties of Buddha's Chicken (*su-chi*) or Buddha's Ham (*suhuo-t'ui*), this firm tofu is generally used like rolled meat. It is usually either simmered in sweetened soy broth or stir-fried with vegetables, or it is sometimes allowed to mold for several days, and is then deep-fried in sesame oil

Buddha's Chicken

to give it a flavor resembling that of fried chicken. Another preparation, also called Buddha's Chicken, is made by first softening pressed tofu sheets in a solution of natural soda and water, then coating each sheet with sesame oil and pressing a number of sheets into individual molds. After being steamed, the "chicken" is cut into ½-inch-thick slices and deep-fried until crisp and golden brown. (A third variety of Buddha's Chicken is prepared in a similar way from pressed fresh yuba.)

Salted-Dried Tofu (*Doufu-kan*): This variety is prepared from squares of regular pressed tofu which are rubbed with salt, tied together with rice straw like the dried-frozen tofu made in Japanese farmhouses (p. 228), and hung in sunlight until thoroughly dried. Very similar to Japanese *rokujo-dofu* (p. 94), salted-dried tofu is dark brown and has a consistency resembling that of a very firm dry cheese. It is generally shaved or sliced into paper-thin strips and used in vegetable soups, in dashi as a substitute for bonita flakes, or as an hors d'oeuvre with drinks. Although the Chinese name is pronounced exactly like the *doufu-kan* meaning "pressed tofu," it is written with a different character for *kan*, one meaning "to dry thoroughly."

Chinese Soft Kinugoshi (*Shui-* or *Sui-dofu*): Not nearly as common in China or Taiwan as is kinugoshi in Japan, this product has a very soft texture due largely to the thinness of the soymilk from which it is made and to the practice of storing it under water to prevent spoilage. Two varieties are available in the Far East, both solidified with calcium sulfate. The first is prepared like Japanese kinugoshi and is sold in cakes which are only slightly softer than the average Japanese-style product. The second, which is more common, is curded in a large kettle and is too soft to be cut and sold as individual cakes. Rather, it is scooped like pudding into large bowls brought by each customer to the tofu shop and is generally eaten with a spoon, topped with a little soy sauce or sugar, or served in soups and delicate sautéed dishes. Both varieties are also known as "young" or "soft" tofu (*nen-* or *nan-doufu*) in contrast to firm doufu and pressed tofu, both of which are known as "old" tofu (*lao-doufu*); the word "old" being used here in the figurative sense to indicate that lack of softness and flexibility often connected with old age. Chinese kinugoshi is often referred to as "calcium sulfate tofu" (*shin-kao doufu* or *sekko-dofu*) to contrast it with most traditional firm tofu which was solidified with nigari.

Warm Soymilk Curds

A popular delicacy throughout China and Taiwan, curds play a much more important role in the nutritional life and cookery of these countries than they do in Japan.

Chinese Smooth Curds (*Doufu-nao* or *Dou-nao*): A close relative of the softer variety of kinugoshi, this product's Chinese name means "tofu brains": when ladled into a bowl, the warm curds apparently remind the Chinese of their namesake. Most widely served in southern China, Taiwan, and Nanking, smooth curds are now available in the West as Tofu Pudding or Fresh Soybean Pudding. In China, they are made in special shops and hawked along city streets early each morning by men who either carry the curds in wooden buckets dangling from shoulder poles or who sell the curds out of small pushcarts (fig. 105). In some areas the venders chant the name of their product as they roam the awakening streets. Customers seat themselves at stools around the cart and get ready for a hearty breakfast (costing less than 5 cents). The vender ladles out scoops of custard-like curds into deep bowls, tops them with a warm syrupy sauce (*hung t'ang*) containing peanuts and brown sugar, and places them (together with porcelain spoons) on the edge of the cart, which serves as a table. In some areas the curds

Fig. 105. Selling soymilk curds

are mixed with *cha-t'sai* pickles, tiny dried shrimp, soy sauce, and a dash of sesame oil, then served as a thick soup. In others, they are mixed with sweet oil, vinegar, finely chopped meat, or spices.

Most smooth curds are prepared at special soymilk shops rather than at tofu shops. Soymilk is cooked in a large kettle over a very hot fire and is solidified in the kettle; the hot fire imparts a fragrant, slightly nutty flavor to the curds. When solidified with nigari, the curds have an extremely soft texture, more delicate than that of yogurt; when calcium sulfate or natural gypsum is used, they have much the same texture as soft Japanese kinugoshi.

Curds-in-Whey (*Doufu-hua*): The Chinese name for this variety of curds means "tofu flowers," since the curds have somewhat the same appearance as eggs swirled in hot broth to make egg-flower soup. Although most varieties are identical to Japanese *oboro* (p. 86), in some areas they are prepared by simmering smooth curds over a low fire to give them a firmer texture.

Deep-fried Tofu

Deep-fried tofu is not as readily available in China and Taiwan as it is in Japan, and the art of deep-frying has not reached the level of sophistication in Chinese tofu shops that it has in their Japanese counterparts. This may be partly because many Chinese chefs and housewives prefer to deep-fry their tofu at home so as to serve it hot and crisp. All Chinese deep-fried tofu is called *yu-dofu* ("oil tofu") or *cha-dofu* ("frying-tofu"). Chinese thick-agé triangles, the most common variety, are prepared by

pressing curds very firmly under a weighted lever (fig. 106), then cutting the sheets of finished tofu into triangles 1½ inches thick and 1½ inches on a side. These are deep-fried in a single large pot of very hot oil (fig. 107). Another popular variety now available in the West is hollow agé cubes (*doufu-kuo*) prepared from 1-inch cubes of doufu which swell up during deep-frying and can later be stuffed with meats or vegetables; they are often added to thickened sauces or soups. Thick agé cubes (*cha-dofu*) or agé balls are sometimes sold strung on a loop of bamboo fiber (fig. 108) and are eaten with syrup like fritters by Chinese laborers as a popular lunchtime snack. In some tofu shops, entire cakes of medium-firm doufu may be cut on both sides in a criss-cross pattern, opened up by pulling gently on both ends to create a netlike structure, and deep-fried (fig. 109). When simmered in seasoned broths or sauces, this structure helps the netlike thick agé to absorb flavors and is quite attractive when served. Neither agé nor ganmo are generally prepared in Chinese tofu shops; the technique of deep-frying in moderate and then hot oil to make the tofu expand has apparently not yet been developed. Sautéed Tofu (*kuo-lao doufu*), a cross between Japanese thick agé and grilled tofu, is thinly sliced doufu fried in oil until it turns a rich brownish yellow.

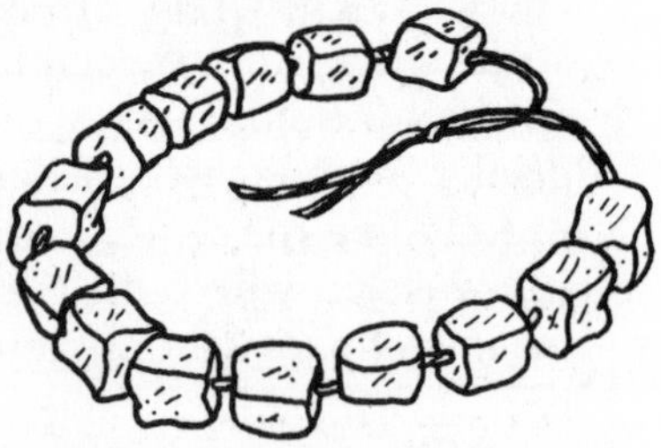

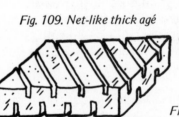

Fig. 109. Net-like thick agé

Fig. 108. Threaded thick-agé cubes

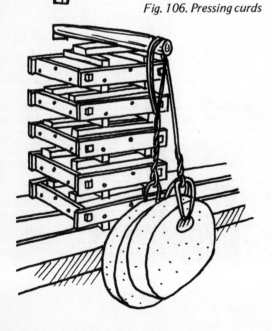

Fig. 106. Pressing curds

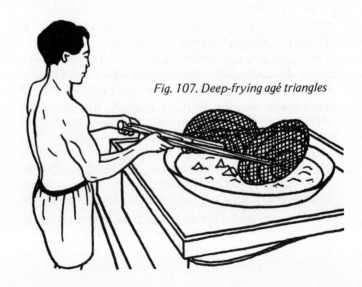

Fig. 107. Deep-frying agé triangles

Frozen Tofu

Frozen tofu, called *tung-doufu* or *ping-doufu*, has been prepared in China since ancient times by setting firm tofu out in the snow overnight. It is the exact counterpart of the "one-night frozen tofu" traditionally prepared in the Japanese countryside. However, dried-frozen tofu, a Japanese invention, has come into production only very recently in China and does not yet play an important role in Chinese cookery. It is sold in small paper boxes as Dried Bean Curd.

Doufu-ru

Surely the most distinctive genre of tofu prepared in China is *doufu-ru*, or fermented tofu. Doufu-ru, in its many forms, is completely unlike anything prepared in Japan or, for that matter, any food familiar to most Westerners. Known in English as Chinese cheese, tofu-, bean curd-, or soybean cheese, or preserved- or pickled bean curd, it is called *doufu-ru*, *furu*, *rufu*, or *dou-ru* in Mandarin, *fuyu* or *funan* in Cantonese (and in most Western tofu shops run by Cantonese masters), and *sufu* or *dou-sufu* in Shanghai and in most scientific literature. The latter terms, which mean "molded milk," are not at all familiar to most Chinese.

Doufu-ru has a soft—almost creamy—consistency and strong flavor and aroma reminiscent of Camembert cheese. Most varieties, seasoned with minced red peppers, are quite sharp and hot on the tongue, so that a little bit goes a long way. Widely enjoyed as a relish and seasoning, doufu-ru is prepared and sold in special Chinese pickle-and-miso shops rather than in neighborhood tofu shops. Traditionally, it was also prepared in many homes and farmhouses. The process of fermentation and preservation in a brining liquor enables this variety of tofu to last for as long as one to two years, even in semitropical climates, and its low cost makes doufu-ru especially popular among the poorer classes. Like cheese, wines, miso, shoyu, and many other fermented foods, doufu-ru gradually improves in flavor, aroma, and texture as it ages. As mold enzymes break down and digest the protein in the tofu, the latter's sharp flavors mellow and its consistency softens: well-aged doufu-ru virtually melts on the tongue. After the tofu has ripened for 6 to 8 months, its color turns from yellowish white to a soft light-brown, and the wine-and-salt brining liquor, too, grows richer and mellower.

Fermented tofu is the only traditional soybean product made in the manner of Western cheeses, that is, by ripening tofu with a mold. Although one would think that soymilk could easily be made into cheeses similar to those prepared from dairy milk, repeated attempts to produce such cheeses—even in modern Western laboratories—have until very recently met with failure. But unlike Western cheeses, doufu-ru is immersed in an alcoholic brine during ripening and is generally sold still immersed in the brining liquor in pint bottles or small cans. To prepare doufu-ru, ¾- to 1¼-inch cubes of doufu or firm tofu are innoculated with spores of a mucor-type mold, then incubated in a warm place for about 3 to 7 days until each cube is covered with a dense mat of fragrant white mycelium. The molded cubes are immersed in the brine, which generally contains Chinese rice wine and red peppers (or other spices and seasonings). After ripening for one to two months in the brining liquor, the bottled tofu is shipped to Chinese markets where it is often allowed to age for another two to four months before being placed on sale. It is said that if the doufu-ru remains motionless when the jar is spun quickly on its axis, it has been properly aged and is ready to use.

In China, the most popular ways of serving doufu-ru are as a seasoning for *congee* (hot breakfast rice porridge) or rice, as an appetizer or hors d'oeuvre with drinks, or as an ingredient in stir-fried dishes or simmered sauces, used to add zest and flavor. The brining liquor is also used in many of these preparations. In Western cookery, doufu-ru is delicious used like Camembert or Roquefort cheese in dips, spreads, dressings, and casseroles. Recipes for each of these preparations are given at the end of this chapter.

The ideographic character for *fu* in doufu-ru (also used in the word doufu) means "spoiled." The character for *ru* means "milk." These characters have an unusual and very ancient etymology. Although the Chinese had a highly developed civilization long before the beginning of the Christian era, they never developed the art of dairy farming or, consequently, of making cheese. But their northerly neighbors, the Mongols, whom the Chinese regarded as uncivilized barbarians, were quite skilled in the preparation of fine goat's cheese. The Chinese called this cheese *furu*, or "spoiled milk." Centuries later, the Chinese learned how to prepare their own variety of fermented cheese, but from soy rather than dairy milk, probably with some help (or at least inspiration) from the Mongols. And the name which they had used derogatorily for the Mongolian cheese gradually came to be used for their own tofu cheese: their insult boomeranged and remains with them to this day. Consequently some modern Chinese and

Japanese—especially those operating expensive restaurants—write the character *fu* in the words tofu, doufu, and doufu-ru with a different character which, although pronounced "fu," means "affluent, ample, or abundant."

Records show that doufu-ru was being produced in China by the fifteenth century and that it may have originated much earlier. The technique for making fermented tofu spread from China to Vietnam (where similar a food called *chao* is now prepared) and to the East Indies (where *tao tuan* is made.) A type of fermented tofu called *tahuri* is also produced in the Philippines by packing large (4- by 4- by 2½-inch) cakes of firm molded tofu into cans with a large quantity of salt. Neither sake nor brine is used in the process. After ripening for several months, the tofu is yellowish brown and has a distinctive salty flavor.

The four basic types of Chinese fermented tofu are white doufu-ru, red doufu-ru, *tsao*-doufu ("tofu fermented in sake less"), and *chiang*-doufu ("tofu fermented in miso or soy sauce"). The brining liquor used for each is also a popular ingredient in many Chinese recipes, especially in dipping sauces. Called doufu-ru *chih*, it often contains various spices or minced red peppers which make it a zesty seasoning.

White Doufu-ru (*Pai doufu-ru*): In most of China and in the West, this is the most popular type of fermented tofu. Unless it is specifically being contrasted with the red variety, it is generally called simply doufu-ru. The tofu's flavor, color, and aroma can be modified either by changing the salt or alcohol composition of the brining liquor or by adding different combinations of spices and seasonings. The most common brine contains about 10 percent alcohol and 12 percent salt; some contain little or no alcohol, while others may contain more than twice as much alcohol as salt. One brine of the latter type yields "drunken cheese" (*tsui-fang*) and another yields "small cheese cubes" (*chih-fang*).

At least five different varieties of white doufu-ru are sold in markets and marketplaces throughout Taiwan and China. The most popular is red pepper doufu-ru (*la doufu-ru, la-chiao furu*, or *la furu*). Available in the West as Fermented Bean Curd, it contains a hearty portion of minced red peppers which make the flavor hot and spicy while also serving as a natural preservative. When sesame oil is added to this type of fermented tofu it is known as sesame-red pepper doufu-ru (*mayu-la* foufu-ru). Some milder and particularly delicious types of doufu-ru are made in liquors containing only rice wine, salt, and water plus an occasional small amount of sesame oil. Other seasonings include anise, cinnamon, lemon juice, slivered lemon peel, tiny dried shrimp, and diced ham. Spiced, fermented tofu with five seasonings is called *wu-hsiang furu*, and a variety of fermented tofu called *hsia-tsu* doufu-ru is dried after brining, then sold in paper cartons.

Red Doufu-ru (*Hung doufu-ru, Nanru*, or *Nanyu*): This product is prepared in basically the same way as its white counterpart except that Chinese red fermented rice (*ang-tsao*) is added to the brining liquor (to give it a deep-red color, thick consistency, and distinctive flavor and aroma) and soy sauce is generally used in place of rice wine. The liquor may or may not contain minced peppers. Red doufu-ru is now available in the West packed in a hot red sauce in small (4- to 6-ounce) cans labeled Red Bean Curd. One popular variety is "rose-essence doufu-ru" (*mei-kui doufu-ru, mei-kui hung nanru*, or *nanyu*), made in a brining liquor similar in appearance to ketchup and seasoned with small amounts of rose essence, caramel, and natural sugar. The seasonings lend a distinctive fragrance to any dish in which it is served. Red doufu-ru is especially popular in spicy hot sauces served with *nabe* dishes, meats, and fresh or even live "dancing" shrimp.

Tsao-doufu: Prepared by aging either fresh or molded tofu in rice wine and its lees (*chu-tsao*), this product has a heady alcoholic flavor and aroma. Green tsao-doufu (*ch'ou doufu*), a popular Taiwanese food, is prepared in homes and marketplace stalls by placing pressed tofu squares into a crock containing sake less, crushed leaves, and a green mucor mold. After the tofu has fermented for 12 hours or more, venders peddle it in the streets. *Ch'ou doufu* means "foul-smelling tofu." While many Chinese themselves dislike its strong aroma and flavor, slippery texture, unusual color, and aftermath of bad breath, its devotees claim that once a taste is acquired for this unique food, it is for evermore regarded as a great delicacy.

Chiang-doufu: Prepared by pickling firm cubes of tofu for several days in either Chinese-style miso (*chiang*) or soy sauce (*chiang-yu*), this product has a reddish-brown color and a salty flavor. In some cases it is dried briefly or fermented with mold before being pickled; sake lees are occasionally mixed with the *chiang*. This tofu often has much the same rich sweetness as Japanese Finger Lickin' Miso (p. 31). Chiang-doufu sauce (*chiang-doufu chih*) is prepared by mixing the pickled tofu with its pickling brine, then grinding the mixture until it is smooth; it is used as a condiment for Chinese lamb or beef dishes.

Soymilk

Chinese-style soymilk (*doufu chiang, dou-chiang, dou-nai,* or *dou-ru*) has been an essential source of protein for Chinese infants, children, and adults since long before the Christian era and continues to play a much more important role in the nutritional life of the people than does soymilk in Japan. It is widely enjoyed as a spicy hot breakfast soup or warm, sweetened beverage (pp. 204 and 207). Every morning many Chinese bring large containers to the local tofu shop to purchase their family's daily supply of soymilk. Whereas the Japanese drink only the rich, thick soymilk used to make kinugoshi tofu, the Chinese drink the thinner soymilk used to make regular tofu, since neither thick soymilk nor Japanese-style kinugoshi are prepared in Chinese tofu shops. Many small shops and some large factories are engaged solely in the production of soymilk and most of the shops serve their specialty from early morning until late at night in adjoining streetside cafes or restaurants. Accompanied by 18-inch-long deep-fried bread sticks and Chinese wheat *tortillas,* the soymilk serves as the basis of a snack or light meal. In some cities, it is bottled and sold by street venders (fig. 110).

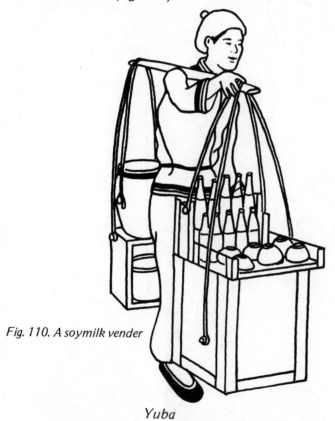

Fig. 110. A soymilk vender

Yuba

Yuba is much more popular and much less expensive in China and Taiwan than it is in Japan. There are hundreds of yuba shops throughout Taiwan and probably thousands in China, and yuba plays an important role in the nutritional life of the people in home and restaurant cookery. Called bean curd "skin" or "sheets" in most Chinese cookbooks, yuba is known in Mandarin as *doufu-p'i,* "tofu skin," or *doufu-i,* "tofu robes." In any public market, especially in the old quarter of many cities, there will be a number of special shops or stalls selling only yuba in a variety of forms. In two of Taiwan's largest cities, Taipei and Taichung, for example, we saw more than 35 different types of fresh, dried, or pre-cooked yuba for sale.

One of the most obvious differences between the uses to which yuba is put in China as compared to Japan is the remarkable ingenuity and inventiveness employed by the Chinese in giving yuba the semblance of meat. Imagine walking by the display case of an attractive restaurant or marketplace yuba shop and seeing perfect replicas of plucked hens, roosters and ducks, light-brown fish (complete with fins, gills, eyes, and mouth) juicy hams, tripe, liver and rolled meats—all made from yuba (fig. 111)! Rich red sausage links hang in rows and deep-fried drumsticks are handsomely arranged on a large platter—together with a lifesized pig's head. Most of these imitation meat dishes are prepared by pressing fresh yuba into a hinged (wooden or aluminum) mold, then placing the well-packed mold in a steamer until the yuba's shape is fixed. In some cases the finished products are deep-fried or simmered in a sweetened or seasoned soy broth (in the same way the Chinese "whole-cook" many fish and other animals). Served at *su-tsai* restaurants which specialize in Buddhist vegetarian cookery, each has its own well-known name: Buddha's Chicken (*suchi*), Buddha's Fish (*suyu* or *sushi*), Buddha's Duck (*suya*), Vegetarian Tripe (*taoto*) or Liver (*sukan*); Molded Pig's Head (*tutao*), and Molded Ham (*suhuo*). The Sausage Links (*enchan*) are made of a mixture of fresh yuba, agar, and Chinese red fermented rice (*angtsao*) packed into real sausage skins. Buddha's Drumsticks (*sutsai tsui*) are prepared by rolling fresh yuba into a conical shape which is filled with minced mushrooms and then deep-fried. Deep-fried Duck (*suya*) is made by pressing together sheets of soft fresh yuba, then tearing these into irregular pieces about 6 to 8 inches across; finally the pieces are deep-fried. Each of these dishes is served at fine restaurants or family banquets as part of eleborate cold plates. Occasionally they are served whole in soups and *nabe* dishes, or sliced and deep-fried. Recipes for a number of these basic preparations are given in Chapter 14.

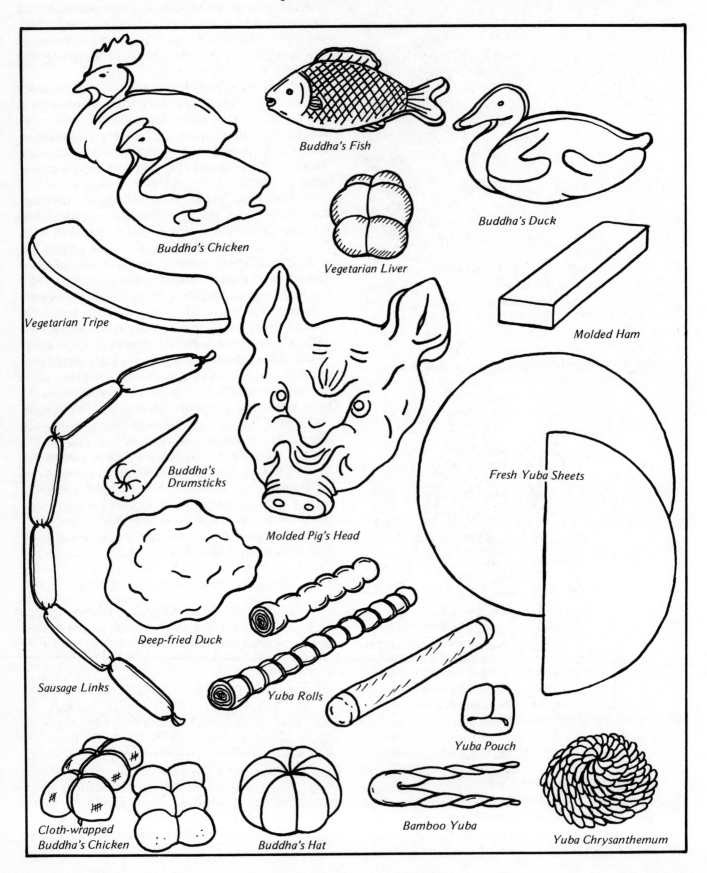

Fig. 111. Yuba mock meats

Buddha's Fish

Buddha's Duck

Buddha's Chicken

Vegetarian Liver

Vegetarian Tripe

Molded Ham

Buddha's Drumsticks

Molded Pig's Head

Fresh Yuba Sheets

Deep-fried Duck

Sausage Links

Yuba Rolls

Yuba Pouch

Cloth-wrapped Buddha's Chicken

Buddha's Hat

Bamboo Yuba

Yuba Chrysanthemum

Yuba in China and Taiwan is remarkably inexpensive. Most fresh yuba sells for as little as 27 cents per pound; higher quality varieties cost about 40 cents. Dried yuba, containing 53 percent protein, sells for about the same prices. In Japan, comparable yuba is roughly 15 *times* as expensive! Consequently, in China, yuba is available to everyone, whereas in Japan, since ancient times, it has been enjoyed mostly by the affluent. Chinese yuba is sold in particularly large amounts to temples, Buddhist laymen, vegetarians, and the nutrition-conscious.

Fresh Yuba: About 90 percent of all yuba made in Taiwan and China is sold fresh, while in Japan, the majority is sold dried. The most common form of fresh yuba is sheets, some of which are round or semi-circular since the yuba is often prepared in large (16-inch-diameter) steaming pots (fig. 112). Some sheets are so thin they are almost transparent,

Fig. 112. Yuba steaming pots

and others, sold by weight, are as thick as cotton cloth. Whole or cut sheets are folded into many forms and sizes to make rolls and pouches later simmered in sweetened soy broths, deep-fried, steamed, or smoked. Long rolls are often bound with a strand of rice straw to hold them together during deep-frying. One particularly delicious variety of roll is filled with Chinese red fermented rice, sake lees or glutinuous rice, and minced pickles; it is wrapped with a sheet of *nori* before being deep-fried or smoked. Pouches are generally filled with diced bamboo shoots, mushrooms, or other vegetables. Fresh yuba sheets, often in combination with pressed tofu sheets, are shaped into different forms by wrapping them in cloth, tying the bundle with twine, and steaming or boiling until set. Cloth-wrapped Buddha's Chicken (*suchi*) is prepared this way and may bo sold either wrapped in the cloth or a sheet of *nori*, or simmered in a sweetened or seasoned broth. Buddha's Hat (*taobo*) is prepared by mixing diced mushrooms with the yuba before cloth-wrapping and steaming.

Dried Yuba (*Kan doufu-p'i*): Much of the dried yuba sold in Taiwan and Hong Kong is prepared in the world's most modern yuba factories using completely natural methods to make a high-quality, low-priced product that can be stored for up to 6 months. The great majority of dried yuba is sold in plain sheets—either round or rectangular—in 1¼-pound bundles. Sweet yuba (*amayuba*) and deep-fried yuba sheets and rolls are also available. Most Chinese rolled dried yuba is sold as Bamboo Yuba (*fuchu*), so called because the color and form of the u-shaped rolls resemble a pair of young bamboo shoots. This variety is now available in many Chinese food markets in the West. Yuba Chrysanthemums are one of the most elaborate and decorative of the many yuba forms; to make them, fresh yuba is folded and twisted into a three-dimensional spiral about 4 inches in diameter and 4 inches high. Many thin slits are then cut along the yuba's perimeter to resemble chrysanthemum petals. After the flowers have dried, they are painted with natural red, yellow, and green food dyes, then deep-fried to be used as ingredients in soups and *nabe* dishes. One of the most famous dried yuba preparations is a variety of Buddha's Ham (*suhuo-t'ui*) made by sautéing crumbled dried yuba with grated gingerroot, soy sauce, and (diced or grated) carrots, pressing the warm mixture into a rectangular mold, and allowing it to cool. Served in thin slices as an hors d'oeuvre, it is as juicy and delicious as its meat counterpart.

Tofu and Yuba in Chinese Cookery

Gourmets have long recognized Chinese cuisine to be one of the finest in the world, and in it, tofu and yuba are highly esteemed foods which form an integral part of each of the main schools of Chinese cookery. In Canton, China's culinary capital, tofu is used to create the light and subtle flavors and textures which characterize Cantonese cookery. In Shanghai, tofu is used in dishes prepared by the technique known as "red cooking," wherein foods are simmered in a rich mixture of soy sauce, stock, anise, and other seasonings to yield hearty, robust flavors. In the Imperial cuisine of Peking, firm tofu is a favorite ingredient in stir-fried dishes and in the many powerfully-flavored sauces with contrasting seasonings: sweet-and-sour or hot-and-sour. In Szechwan and Taiwan, the mild flavor of fine tofu makes an excellent base for the fiery and exciting flavors created by *fagara* red peppers and spicy sauces. In the boldly-seasoned, hot cookery of Hunan, the famous firepots of Mongolia, and the distinctive red broths of Fukien, too, tofu is a popular ingredient. And tofu is widely used in *Mandarin* cooking as well, "*Mandarin*" referring not to a regional cooking style but to a level of quality suitable for the emperor and the members of the court. Thus, a fine tofu dish prepared in any of the regional styles may bear the proud Mandarin title; it need not be prepared in the Peking or northern style.

Tofu is also popular in the thousands of Chinese restaurants in Japan where dishes such as Mabo-doufu (p. 128), and Oyster Sauce Tofu (p. 129) are particularly popular. In America's many Chinese restaurants—a majority of which are Cantonese—tofu can be enjoyed in traditional Chinese preparations as well as dishes modified to Western tastes and expectations. On the menu of virtually every Chinese restaurant in the world is a section entitled "bean curd," which generally contains at least five, and often as many as ten or fifteen dishes. Tofu also appears in soups, firepots and sandpots, vegetable, meat or seafood dishes, and even hors d'oeuvre and desserts. And in many Chinese delicatessens, ready-made preparations such as Oyster Sauce Tofu and Marinated Pressed Tofu are available.

In Japan, the great majority of tofu dishes contain no meat at all and tofu is honored in and of itself; in China, however, and particularly in restaurants, tofu is often cooked together with or used in conscious imitation of seafoods and meats. Since most varieties of Chinese tofu have the firm texture of ham or smoked sausage, they lend themselves well to their role as meat substitutes in a way the softer, more delicate Japanese varieties cannot match. In many Chinese cookbooks and restaurants, more than three-fourths of all tofu dishes contain shrimp, fish, pork, chicken, or beef. Studying restaurant menus and cookbooks, one could easily get the impression that the Chinese eat meat as a regular part of their diet. In fact, however, most Chinese—including the pre-revolution affluent—have traditionally eaten only small quantities of meat (see fig. 2, p. 18). The Chinese nutritional equilibrium has become a source of great interest to nutritionists and doctors, and should serve as a source of data and inspiration for the growing number of Westerners who are now moving away from a meat-centered diet.

For most Chinese farmers, laborers, and office workers, meals of rice and tofu, cabbage, a hearty soup and, perhaps, soymilk epitomize daily home cooking. In many homes in China, as in Japan, tofu is served at all three meals. At breakfast it accompanies the course of *congee* (rice porridge), and at lunch and dinner it appears most commonly in stir-fried dishes, sauces, soups, and/or steamed preparations. In this diet, in which 95 percent of all protein comes from vegetable sources, tofu plays a role worthy of the name "meat of the fields." And since most Chinese do not drink cow's milk or use other dairy products, tofu (solidified with calcium sulfate) and soymilk also serve as essential sources of calcium.

Whereas the Japanese delight in the simple light flavors of the tofu itself, and generally give tofu the leading role in any particular dish, the Chinese often serve their tofu as an extender in dark-brown, cornstarch-thickened sauces generally made from a meat, chicken, or oyster-sauce base and seasoned with plenty of sesame oil. Many of these "red broiled" sauces (*hong-sao*)—especially those in the cookery of Szechwan and Taiwan—are fiery hot, peppery, and spicy, and in restaurants will often contain small pieces of meat, chicken, or seafood. A crisp texture may be supplied by such exotic delicacies as water chestnuts, bamboo shoots, tiger lillies, bean sprouts, "wood-ear" mushrooms, Chinese cabbage, or hairlike black seaweeds. In some cases these rich tofu sauces are served over noodles or fried rice, a practice almost never met with in Japan.

Over a period of several thousand years, Chinese tofu has been adapted to the unique tools and cooking techniques used in a typical Chinese kitchen: especially stir-frying. In preparation for the actual cooking, the Chinese chef or housewife first uses a razor-sharp cleaver to mince tofu and vegetables on massive chopping blocks set near a great black stove—which is actually more like a forge or blast furnace—holding three or four different-sized woks. Neatly arranged on a long table near the stove are at least 16 open-top bowls or crocks, each containing a commonly-used oil, sauce, or seasoning. After the ingredients are assembled and the wok to be used is surrounded by a cushion of dancing flames, oil is scooped in to sizzle and crackle for an instant as the brisk fire leaps higher. Tofu and vegetables are then added, stirred, and flipped with such dexterity and split-second timing that not a single piece is broken. Scooped from their respective crocks with a large metal ladle and measured by eye, red-pepper oil, miso sauce, salt, and/or minced gingerroot are then added to season the tofu dish to perfection. A half-ladleful of water, and the wok's contents are tossed lightly into the air three, four, five times. At just the right instant—and fast as magic—the wok is snatched from its nest of fire and the stir-fried tofu-and-vegetables transferred to elegant serving platters. The tofu's firm texture enables it to retain its form during this vigorous process.

At certain times each month and year, the average family's meals contain no meat or fish at all. Since ancient times, many Chinese—especially orthodox Buddhists—have refrained from eating such foods on the first and fifteenth days of each lunar month. And during the entire sultry sixth month, the hottest period of summer, many people also take no wine, eggs, or cooked foods, a practice which gives a rest to both the cook and the digestive system (and one related perhaps to the ancient Christian tradition of fasting or eating more simply during Lent). At these times, a great deal of imagination is expended in using tofu and yuba in daily family meals or banquets at which many of the dishes bear all of the appearance of delicately layered or rolled meats, fresh fowl, or fish. One popular main dish served on meatless days is called The Arhat's (Buddhist Saint's) Fast or the Vegetarian's Ten Varieties. Containing hollow agé cubes, pressed tofu sheets, plus eight varieties of land and sea vegetables, it is a large stew or soup said to improve in flavor for up to one week. Tofu also plays an important part in the large repasts served in connection with funerals and memorial services, meals in which meat and eggs are generally not allowed.

The many *Su-tsai* or *Shojin Ryori* restaurants throughout China and Taiwan which specialize in Buddhist or Taoist vegetarian cookery are filled to capacity on Sundays and during those periods when people eat no meat. Laymen and house-holders—as well as the usual monks and nuns with their shaved heads, rosary beads, and long gray robes—enjoy sumptuous meals featuring dishes such as "baked ham," "roast duck," or "sliced chicken breast." Tofu, yuba, and wheat gluten (*mien tien*) are indispensable foods which appear in more than half the dishes on the menu. In each of the *su-tsai* restaurants we visited in Taiwan, the large rooms were bustling with activity. Bare neon lights, large linoleum tables, canned foods, and white plaster walls created an atmosphere in sharp contrast to that of the lovely Japanese Zen temple restaurants where the guests are served in a garden setting of rocks, sand, water, bamboo, and trees, and each dish is served with a sense of refined simplicity and artfulness. Tofu is also served to the guests and visitors in China's temples, but many temples are so improverished that the monks only rarely enjoy the tofu themselves.

In most places in China and on most occasions when tofu is served, yuba is also to be found. Most Chinese restaurants, including those in the West, will generally offer 10 to 15 dishes featuring yuba. Any of the different types of yuba may be sautéed or stewed with vegetables, topped with thickened sauces, deep-fried, or added to soups or *nabe* dishes. Recipes for many of these preparations are given in Chapter 14.

Since most of the basic varieties of Chinese tofu, soymilk, and yuba available in the West are closely related to their Japanese counterparts, we have included Chinese-style recipes in many of the preceeding chapters. However, since fermented tofu is not found in Japan, we have presented recipes for its use in the pages that follow.

The Chinese Tofu Shop

In most Chinese tofu shops, the gô is cooked in a cut-off drum can (fig. 113) using steam from a coal-heated boiler. It is then run into a cloth-lined cone set over a curding barrel into which the soymilk filters before being solidified, usually with a mixture of calcium sulfate and nigari. Using this simple, inexpensive equipment, large batches of tofu can be prepared in rapid succession (at intervals of about 17 minutes) and the finished product sold at a very low price (about one-third that of Japanese tofu). Although the tofu lacks some of the subtle flavor of traditional Japanese tofu and the work is often done rather hastily, the basic process (described in detail in the companion volume to this work) could provide an excellent model for use in developing countries.

Fig. 113. A steam-heated drum-can cooker

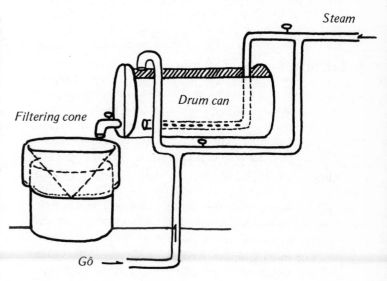

Steam

Drum can

Filtering cone

Gô

Tofu in Korea

Although tofu is an important staple in Korean cookery, it does not play quite the essential role that it does in China, Taiwan, and Japan. Koreans eat about one-third as much tofu as do the Japanese. This tofu is made at the more than one thousand small tofu shops (*tubu kong jang*) scattered throughout the country, 150 of which are located in the capital city of Seoul. Most shops use a fire-heated cauldron and calcium sulfate solidifier. A great deal of tofu is still prepared at home in farmhouses, especially on festive occasions.

Regular Korean tofu, called *tubú*, is slightly firmer than its Japanese counterpart but not as firm as Chinese tofu (*doufu*). This tofu is widely sold in outdoor marketplaces. Shopkeepers and venders buy flats of tofu from tofu shops in returnable wooden boxes, each 10 by 13 by 2 inches deep. The tofu is placed on wooden pallets, then cut into cakes weighing 12 to 16 ounces. Tubu is the only traditional variety of Korean tofu.

During the Japanese occupation, the Koreans developed a number of varieties of deep-fried tofu (*tofu kuii* or *twigin tubu*). Agé strips (*yubu*) are pieces of deep-fried tofu about 7 by 1 by ¾ inches. Ten strips are sold together in a sealed plastic bag. This food is unlike any deep-fried tofu in Japan or China. Agé pouches (*fukuro*) are similar to Japanese agé but are sold in different sizes; the smallest is 2½ inches square, the medium size is 4½ by 2½ inches, and the largest size is 8½ by 3 inches. Each variety can be opened and filled with various stuffings, and many are used to make Inari-zushi (p. 194) or Oden Kinchaku (p. 196).

Okara (*piji*), soymilk curds (*sun tubu*), and whole soybeans (*kung kong*) are used widely in Korean cookery. Fermented tofu (*tubu kuppa*), available mostly in Chinese food markets, is not. Kinugoshi, grilled tofu, soymilk, and yuba are rarely if ever seen.

Korean cuisine is extremely hot and spicy. Tofu serves to soften the flavors of red peppers and other strong seasonings while lending body and protein to soups, stews, and sautéed vegetable dishes. The most famous Korean tofu dish is *Tubu Chige* or "tofu soup," a fiery preparation containing tofu cubes, thin slices of beef, and shellfish seasoned with red and green hot peppers, ground red peppers, Korean soybean miso (*kotsu jang*), and soy sauce. The soup is served bubbling hot in a small iron pot set on a wooden platter. When it contains miso as the dominant seasoning and is served with rice, it becomes the popular *Tenjang Chige Pekpen*. When seasoned with *kimchi* pickles, it is known as *Kimchi Chige*, and when it contains more broth and is prepared with less salt, it is known as *Tubu Kuk*. Tofu is also sautéed in oil until golden brown, then cooked with vegetables for 5 to 10 more minutes to create the favorite household preparation *Tubu Puchim*. Sautéed with bean sprouts, tofu becomes the dish known as *Konamul Kuge Tubu*.

DOUFU-RU DRESSINGS, SPREADS, DIPS, AND HORS D'OEUVRE

Tangy and flavorful, rich and zesty, these are some of our favorite recipes. If you like Roquefort or Camembert, Cream Cheese or Sour Cream, try some of the following.

Doufu-ru Salad Dressing

3 small cubes of white or 2 large cubes of red doufu-ru
1 teaspoon doufu-ru brining liquor
6 ounces tofu
3 tablespoons lemon juice
¼ cup oil
¼ teaspoon salt

Combine all ingredients in a blender and purée until smooth. Serve over a salad of fresh vegetables. Or simply blend or mash the dofu-ru and brining liquor with ¾ cup mayonnaise.

Tangy Doufu-ru & Cream Cheese Spread

MAKES ¾ CUP

6 cubes of doufu-ru, well drained (about 4 ounces)
4 ounces cream cheese
2 teaspoons sake or white wine
½ small onion, grated or minced
1 tablespoon softened butter
1½ teaspoon Worcestershire sauce

Combine all ingredients and mash together until smooth. For best flavor, refrigerate in a covered container for at least 2, preferably 7 days. Serve on crackers, potato chips, toast rounds, cucumber slices, or celery stalks.

Cream Cheese & Doufu-ru Dip

MAKES 1 CUP

3 cubes of white doufu-ru
6 ounces cream cheese
2 tablespoons mayonnaise
2 teaspoons shoyu; or 1 teaspoon Worcestershire sauce and ¼ teaspoon salt
1½ teaspoons minced onion

Combine all ingredients and mash together until smooth. Serve as a dip for crackers, potato chips, toast rounds, or crisp vegetables; or as a sandwich spread. Also good as a stuffing for celery stalks.

Sour Cream & Doufu-ru Dip

MAKES 1¼ CUPS

1 cup sour cream (dairy or tofu, p. 109)
2 or 3 cubes of white doufu-ru
1 tablespoon minced chives
1 tablespoon minced parsley
¼ teaspoon salt
Dash of curry powder
Dash of paprika or 7-spice red pepper

Combine all ingredients and mash together until smooth. Serve chilled as a dip or sandwich spread.

Oriental Doufu-ru & Sour Cream Dip

MAKES ¾ CUP

2 cubes of white doufu-ru
½ cup sour cream (dairy or tofu, p. 109)
1 tablespoon grated gingerroot
1½ teaspoons shoyu
¼ cup minced leeks, onions, or scallions
2 tablespoons minced parsley
¼ teaspoon fresh coriander (optional)

Combine all ingredients and mash together until smooth. Serve chilled as a dip for crackers.

Doufu-ru & Egg Spread

MAKES ½ CUP

1 or 2 cubes of doufu-ru
2 hardboiled eggs, minced
1 teaspoon Worcestershire sauce
1 tablespoon cream cheese (dairy or tofu, p. 109)
1 tablespoon cucumber pickles (optional)

Combine all ingredients and mash together until smooth.

Doufu-ru Hors D'oeuvre

Place a single cube of white or red doufu-ru on a tiny dish and serve with other hors d'oeuvre, appetizers, or drinks, or as a side dish or relish with the main meal. Each guest uses the tips of his chopsticks to take a tiny piece of the doufu-ru from time to time between sips of the drinks, bites of grain or vegetables, or courses of the meal.

In some Chinese restaurants in Japan, the doufu-ru cube is served topped with 1 tablespoon sesame oil and ½ teaspoon sugar.

Doufu-ru Spread

Use doufu-ru like Camembert or Roquefort cheese as a spread for crackers, canapés, or small pieces of toast. If desired, garnish with a small slice of cheese, hard-boiled egg, tomato, cucumber, or a sprig of parsley.

DOUFU-RU IN SAUCES, EGG DISHES, AND WITH GRAINS

Creamy and mellow Western sauces; fiery Chinese dipping sauces. In scrambled eggs and with steaming hot rice, doufu-ru can bring any dish to life.

Spicy Red Doufu-ru Dipping Sauce

SERVES 2 TO 4

1 cube of red doufu-ru
½ teaspoon doufu-ru brining liquor
2 tablespoons sake or white wine
½ teaspoon soy sauce
1 teaspoon grated gingerroot
Dash of salt
¼ teaspoon minced fresh coriander (optional)

Combine all ingredients and mix together until smooth. Serve as a dipping sauce with lightly roasted strips or cubes of deep-fried tofu, tempura, or, as in China, with live "dancing shrimp" or shrimp cocktail.

In Szechwan, a simplified version of this sauce is prepared using only 1 tablespoon each doufu-ru brining liquor and soy sauce, 1 teaspoon sake, and ¼ teaspoon sesame oil.

Simmering Tofu Dipping Sauce a là Chinois

Doufu-ru
Chinese rice wine or cooking wine
Chinese vinegar
Minced chives
Sesame oil
Sesame butter (or sesame jam)
Pickled garlic
Fresh coriander, minced
Hot pepper oil
Shrimp Sauce

Arrange all of the ingredients on separate plates or in bottles at the dining table. Invite each guest to combine the ingredients to taste in the small saucer provided at his place setting.

A somewhat simpler version of the above sauce is used as a dipping sauce for lamb.

Doufu-ru White Sauce

SERVES 2

2 cubes of white doufu-ru
¼ teaspoon doufu-ru brining liquor
Dash of salt
Dash of Pepper
1 cup milk (soy or dairy)
2 tablespoons butter
2 tablespoons (whole-wheat) flour

Combine the first four ingredients and mash together. Slowly stir in the milk, mixing until smooth. Melt the butter in a skillet. Add the flour and proceed as for White Sauce (p. 48). Serve as a topping for deep-fried tofu or cooked vegetables.

Stir-fried Thick agé and Greens with Doufu-ru Sauce

SERVES 2 OR 3

2 tablespoons oil
7 ounces spinach, Chinese cabbage, or *komatsuna*, cut into 2-inch lengths
Dash of salt
½ cup stock or water
1 tablespoon soy sauce
3 tablespoons natural sugar
2 teaspoons sake or white wine
1¼ teaspoons sesame oil
10 ounces thick agé, cut crosswise into ½-inch-wide strips
1 large or 3 small cubes of doufu-ru, preferably red
1 tablespoon doufu-ru brining liquor
1 teaspoon cornstarch or arrowroot, dissolved in 2 tablespoons water

Heat a wok and coat with the oil. Add the greens and stir-fry for 1 or 2 minutes until just tender. Add salt and stock and cook for 2 minutes more. Remove wok from heat and transfer only the greens to a large bowl. Add the next five ingredients to the liquid remaining in the wok, return to the boil, and simmer over low heat for 5 minutes. Meanwhile combine doufu-ru and brining liquor in a cup and mash together until

smooth. Remove only the thick agé from the wok and transfer to the bowl with the greens. To the broth in the wok, add the mashed doufu-ru thinned in a few tablespoons of the hot broth. Mix well, then stir in the dissolved cornstarch and cook for about 30 seconds, or until thickened. Return the greens and thick agé to the thickened broth in the wok. Mixing gently, cook for 1 minute. Serve hot in large bowls.

Brining Liquor Dipping Sauce

MAKES 3/8 CUP

The brining liquor remaining in the bottle or can after the doufu-ru has been served can be used in sauces, dips, or dipping sauces.

2½ tablespoons doufu-ru brining liquor
2½ tablespoons shoyu
2 teaspoons sake or white wine
¼ teaspoon sesame oil
1 to 2 tablespoons thinly sliced leeks (optional)

Combine all ingredients, mixing well. Serve as a dipping sauce for deep-fried tofu or barbequed foods.

Tangy Ketchup & Lemon Sauce with Doufu-ru

SERVES 2 TO 4

1/3 cup ketchup
5 tablespoons lemon juice
2 cubes of doufu-ru, preferably red
½ teaspoon shoyu
1 teaspoon minced onion

Combine all ingredients and mash or blend until smooth. Serve with deep-fried tofu, tempura, or shrimp cocktail.

Doufu-ru with Hot Rice

SERVES 2

This is the most popular way of serving doufu-ru in China. The dish is generally served for breakfast. Some people prefer to use the tips of their chopsticks to take a tiny piece of doufu-ru with each bite, whereas others like to mix the doufu-ru with the hot rice or rice porridge *(congee)* before starting the meal.

2½ cups freshly cooked Brown Rice or Rice Porridge (p. 50)
2 to 4 cubes of doufu-ru (white or red)
2 tablespoons thinly sliced scallions or leeks (optional)

Place the hot rice in large individual serving bowls and top with doufu-ru cubes and, if used, sliced scallions.

A street-side doufu vender

16
Special Tofu

SESAME-, peanut-, walnut-, and egg tofu are subtly flavored tofu-like preparations served with traditional Japanese cuisine. Since these dishes have somewhat the same appearance and custard-like texture as real tofu, each bears the tofu name. However they are all fundamentally different from tofu: they are not made from soybeans or solidified by curding; they are never stored under water; and they are not made or sold in tofu shops. Sesame-, peanut-, and walnut tofu are prepared by blending or mixing the respective ground nuts or seeds with water, simmering the mixture with *kuzu* (Japanese arrowroot) or other starches until thick and transparent, and then cooling it in a mold until firm. These dishes are usually served with various shoyu dipping sauces or miso toppings. Egg tofu looks like and is made in somewhat the same way as rich egg custard.

Sesame tofu, the most popular variety of special tofu, is served at the beginning of the meal in most restaurants featuring Zen Temple Cookery or Tea Ceremony Cuisine. Each chef has his own unique (and highly secret) way of preparing both it and the sauce that accompanies it. All four types of special tofu are available at large food markets and some natural food stores in Japan. They are usually sealed in plastic containers accompanied by a separate container of dipping sauce.

In China and Taiwan another type of special tofu, Annin-dofu, is a popular dessert. Made with milk, sugar, and a little almond extract, and jelled with agar (*kanten*), it is cut into small cubes and served with sections of mandarin oranges and other sweet fruits.

Recipes for Western-style sesame tofu have recently appeared in a number of natural food cookbooks in America. Often made with sesame butter (or *tahini*), honey, and *kuzu*, and generally containing nuts, dried fruits, and coconut, it is a delicious innovation on the more subtly flavored, unsweetened Japanese sesame tofu.

Most of the following recipes may be served as side dishes, desserts, or hors d'oeuvre.

TOPPINGS AND SAUCES

The various types of special tofu are often served with the following toppings and sauces.

Shoyu-Wasabi Topping   FOR 1 SERVING

Place each serving of special tofu in a deep bowl, sprinkle with about 1 teaspoon of shoyu, then top with a small dab (about ¼ teaspoon) of *wasabi*. Freshly grated *wasabi* —which is mixed with water just before use— is more readily available and less expensive.

Rich Shoyu Sauce   FOR 6 TO 8 SERVINGS

5 tablespoons dashi (p. 39), stock, or water
2 tablespoons shoyu
2 teaspoons natural sugar or honey
1 teaspoon sake or white wine
2 teaspoons *wasabi* (grated or powdered)

Combine the first four ingredients in a saucepan and bring to a boil. Reduce heat to low and simmer for 1 minute. Cover and set aside to cool, or refrigerate. Pour over individual serving of special tofu and top with a small dab of *wasabi*.

Thickened Shoyu Sauce

FOR 4 SERVINGS

1 cup dashi (p. 39), stock, or water
¼ cup shoyu
3 tablespoons natural sugar or honey
5 teaspoons *kuzu*, cornstarch, or arrowroot
1 teaspoon *wasabi*

Combine the first four ingredients in a small saucepan and, stirring constantly, bring to a boil. Reduce heat and simmer until transparent and quite thick. Cover pan and set aside to cool, or refrigerate. Pour over individual servings of special tofu and top with *wasabi*.

Sweet Miso Topping

FOR 8 SERVINGS

5 tablespoons red, barley, or Hatcho miso
1½ teaspoons *mirin*
2 tablespoons natural sugar or honey
1½ teaspoons sake or white wine
¼ cup dashi (p. 39), stock, or water

Combine all ingredients in a small saucepan and simmer, stirring constantly, until mixture becomes almost as thick as the original miso. Set aside to cool. Serve in large dabs atop individual portions of special tofu. Refrigerated, unused portions will last indefinitely.

Shoyu-Mirin Sauce

FOR 4 SERVINGS

2½ tablespoons shoyu
4 teaspoons *mirin*
2 teaspoons sake
½ cup dashi (p. 39), stock, or water

Combine all ingredients in a small saucepan, cover, and bring just to a boil. Allow to cool before serving over Egg Tofu (p. 267).

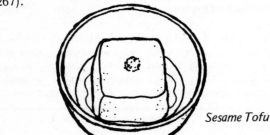

Sesame Tofu

Sesame Tofu *(Goma-dofu)*

SERVES 6 TO 8

In the following basic recipe, the tofu is prepared in a blender using whole roasted sesame seeds. Roasting gives the tofu a rich brown color and delicious, nutlike fragrance, while the blender makes the process quick and easy. Some Japanese chefs prefer to use either unroasted or only lightly roasted sesame to obtain a subtler, more delicate flavor. The seeds are generally ground by hand in a *suribachi* (p. 34) until they turn into a smooth, slightly oily paste. In shops making com-

mercial sesame tofu, the seeds are ground by machines for about 5 hours to obtain the ideal consistency. The finest sesame tofu is solidified with genuine *kuzu*, now available in the West in many natural food stores. Powder from the root of the bracken fern *(warabiko)* may also be used. Arrowroot or cornstarch are fair substitutes; add about 25 percent more than if using *kuzu*. The longer the tofu is stirred while thickening, the finer the texture: shops and restaurants often mix large quantities vigorously for up to 30 minutes.

6 tablespoons (white) sesame seeds
2½ cups water
5½ tablespoons *kuzu*, or 7 tablespoons arrowroot or cornstarch
½ teaspoon salt
Shoyu-Wasabi Topping (p. 265)

Roast sesame seeds over medium heat in a heavy skillet, stirring constantly, until they are well browned and begin to pop. Place in a blender with ¼ cup water and purée for 20 to 30 seconds, gradually increasing blender's speed. Turn off blender, rinse down walls with ½ cup water, and purée again. Rinse off walls and lid of blender with 1½ cups water, add *kuzu* and salt, and purée for about 3 minutes more. Immediately pour contents of blender into a fine-mesh strainer set over a small saucepan. Using your fingertips, rub as much of the solids as possible through the strainer, then douse the sesame seeds hulls in the strainer with the remaining ¼ cup water. Again rub sesame residue against strainer, then discard any remaining seed hulls.

Heat contents of saucepan over medium heat, stirring constantly with a wooden spoon, until mixture begins to thicken. Reduce heat to low and stir for about 12 minutes more. Pour sesame mixture into a metal or glass mold —preferably one with square corners and a flat bottom— and smooth surface of mixture with moistened fingertips. Partially immerse mold in cold water and allow to cool, then cover with a sheet of plastic wrap and refrigerate until thoroughly chilled and firm. Cut into individual portions with a moistened knife, apportion among deep (lacquerware) bowls or individual serving dishes, and top with shoyu and *wasabi*.

If a mold is not available, the sesame mixture may be cooled in the saucepan.

VARIATIONS

*Any of the following topping may also be used:
   Rich Shoyu Sauce (p. 265)
   Thickened Shoyu Sauce (p. 266)
   Sweet Miso Topping (p. 266)
   Red Nerimiso (p. 42) garnished with a sprig of *kinome*
   Gingerroot Sauce (p. 49)
   Ankake Sauce (p. 49) topped with a dab of grated gingerroot or hot mustard
   Mustard-Shoyu Dipping Sauce (p. 40)
   Yuzu Miso (p. 42)
   Any variety of Finger Lickin' Miso (p. 31)
   A mixture of 1 cup dashi, ¼ cup shoyu, several drops of grated gingerroot juice, and a pinch of grated *yuzu* rind

*Tahini Tofu: Substitute 4 tablespoons *tahini* for the whole sesame seeds in the basic recipe. Mix all ingredients thoroughly using a spoon, egg beater or blender, before cooking. Or, for a richer version, use 2½ cups water or dashi, ½ cup *tahini*, 6 tablespoons *kuzu*, 2 tablespoons sake, and ½ teaspoons each salt and sugar.

*Sesame Butter Tofu: Substitute 3 tablespoons sesame butter for the sesame seeds in the basic recipe. Prepare as for Tahini Tofu.

*Use almonds, cashews, filberts, Brazil nuts, sunflower or poppy seeds, substituting 6 to 8 tablespoons of any one of these for the sesame seeds in the basic recipe.

Sweet & Crunchy Sesame Tofu   SERVES 3 OR 4

This Western dessert-style adaptation of the traditional Japanese favorite has a rich and hearty flavor.

3 tablespoons sesame butter or ¼ cup *tahini*
2½ cups water
5½ tablespoons *kuzu*, or 7 tablespoons arrowroot or cornstarch
¼ cup natural sugar
½ cup raisins
2/3 cup shredded coconut
½ cup walnut meats

Combine sesame butter, water, *kuzu*, and sugar in a large bowl or blender and mix or purée until smooth. Pour into a saucepan, add raisins, and cook as for Sesame Tofu. Sprinkle one-half the coconut over the bottom of a mold or shallow pan, and spoon in the sesame-*kuzu* mixture. Smooth surface of mixture, press in the walnut meats, and sprinkle on the remaining coconut. Serve chilled.

If using honey instead of sugar, increase the amount of *kuzu* by ½ tablespoon.

Peanut Tofu   SERVES 4 TO 6

½ cup peanuts or ¼ cup peanut butter
2½ cups water
5½ tablespoons *kuzu*; or 7 tablespoons arrowroot or cornstarch
¼ to ½ teaspoon salt; or 2 to 4 tablespoons honey or natural sugar

Combine peanuts and 1 cup water in a blender and purée at high speed for about 2 minutes, or until smooth. Without turning off blender, rinse off inside walls with remaining water, add *kuzu*, and purée for 30 seconds more. Pour mixture quickly into a small saucepan and proceed as for Sesame Tofu. Serve chilled, topped with Shoyu-Wasabi (p. 265) or, if preparing the sweetened version, top with a sprinkling of shredded coconut and chopped nutmeats.

If using peanut butter, the ingredients may be mixed with a spoon rather than a blender.

VARIATION

*For **Walnut Tofu** (*Kurumi-dofu*), substitute ½ cup chopped walnut meats for the peanuts in the above recipe. Do not use sweetening. Serve topped with *Wasabi*-Shoyu. This delicious preparation is a specialty at many fine Japanese temple restaurants.

Egg Tofu (*Tamago-dofu*)   SERVES 4

Resembling a mild and delicate custard, Egg tofu is a Japanese summertime favorite, whether sold packaged in food stores or prepared at the finest restaurants. The only type of special tofu not solidified with *kuzu*, this dish made with dashi should not be confused with Soymilk Egg Tofu (p. 209) which is prepared with soymilk and sold commercially in Japan. It is very important to steam Egg Tofu for just the right length of time; oversteaming causes it to develop internal bubbles and a porous structure, spoiling its delicate texture.

4 large eggs
¾ to 1 cup dashi (p. 30), stock, or water
½ teaspoon shoyu
1 teaspoon *mirin* or honey
1½ teaspoons sake or white wine
Shoyu-Mirin Sauce (p. 266)
1½ teaspoons *wasabi* or grated gingerroot
4 sprigs of *kinome* (optional)

Break eggs into a measuring cup and add an equal volume of dashi. Pour egg-and-dashi mixture into a large bowl and combine with shoyu, *mirin*, and sake. Mix well with chopsticks, trying to make as few bubbles as possible. Strain through a fine-mesh strainer or piece of cheesecloth into a small pan (one 5 inches in diameter is ideal) so that egg mixture fills pan to a depth of 1½ to 2 inches. Skim off any bubbles, then cover pan with a cloth or piece of paper and place in a preheated steamer (p. 38). Steam over high heat with lid slightly ajar for about 5 minutes until tofu surface is just firm. Reduce heat and steam for 5 to 10 minutes more, checking frequently to see that bubbles have not formed within the tofu. When a chopstick or foodpick inserted into tofu comes out dry, remove pan from steamer and allow to cool. Cut tofu into fourths and serve in deep (lacquerware) bowls, topped with the sauce, a dab of *wasabi*, and a sprig of *kinome*.

Other garnishes include slivers of *yuzu* or lemon peel, a mixture of grated *wasabi* and gingerroot, or a combination of grated *yuzu* rind and thin rounds of cucumber.

VARIATIONS

*Add ½ cup refreshed *wakame* cut into 3-inch lengths. Mix into the strained egg mixture just before steaming.
*Cut Egg Tofu into 1½- by 2-inch pieces and serve in Clear Soup (p. 119) in place of regular tofu.
*Serve topped with hot or chilled Ankake Sauce (p. 49).

Emerald Tofu *(Uguisu-dofu)*   SERVES 3 TO 4

Made from fresh green soybeans, this tofu is a brilliant emerald green, as green as the *uguisu,* the Japanese nightingale.

10¼ cups water
1¼ teaspoons salt
2½ to 3 cups green soybeans in their pods
5½ tablespoons *kuzu;* or 7 tablespoons arrowroot or cornstarch

Bring 8 cups water to a boil in a large pot and add 1 teaspoon salt. Drop in the soybeans, return to the boil, and simmer for 4 minutes. Rinse beans in a colander under cold running water; drain. Remove pods and measure out ½ cup green soybeans, reserving any remaining beans. Combine the ½ cup beans, 2½ cups water, *kuzu,* and remaining ¼ teaspoon salt in a blender, and purée for 3 minutes, or until smooth. Pour into a saucepan and proceed as for Sesame Tofu. Serve chilled, topped with Thickened Shoyu Sauce (p. 266).

Kinako Tofu   SERVES 4 TO 6

This recipe is the result of our experiments using Kinako Butter (p. 65) to develop an easy-to-make special tofu similar in flavor to Sesame Tofu but richer in protein and less expensive.

10½ tablespoons kinako (roasted soy flour)
3 tablespoons oil
2½ cups water
5½ tablespoons *kuzu;* or 7 tablespoons arrowroot or cornstarch
¾ teaspoon salt
Sweet Miso Topping (p. 266) or Shoyu-Wasabi Topping (p. 265)

Combine kinako and oil in a small bowl, mixing well, then stir in water, *kuzu,* and salt. Pour through a fine-mesh strainer into a saucepan. Bring just to a boil over high heat, reduce heat to medium, and cook, stirring constantly, for 3 to 4 minutes after mixture thickens. Proceed as for Sesame Tofu (p. 266). Serve chilled with the miso topping.

VARIATION

*Prepare like Sweet & Crunchy Sesame Tofu (p. 267) but substitute the kinako-and-oil mixture in the above recipe for sesame butter.

Annin-dofu   SERVES 4 OR 5
(Milk & Almond Tofu with Fruit Cocktail)

This famous Chinese-style dessert preparation is often called Almond Bean Curd in Western-style Chinese cookbooks. In Japan, where it is sold in cans or prepared fresh in Chinese-style restaurants, it is known variously as *Kyonin-, Chinden-* or *Shinrin-dofu.*

1 stick of agar (8 gm), reconstituted and torn into small pieces (p. 37)
2/3 cup milk
2/3 cup water
1 tablespoon honey
½ teaspoon almond extract
3 cups fruit cocktail

Combine agar, milk, and water in a small saucepan. Stirring constantly, bring to a boil over medium heat, then simmer for 3 minutes or until agar is completely dissolved; stir in honey and almond extract. Pour through a strainer or fine cheesecloth into a flat-bottomed container (one about 9 inches in diameter is ideal) and allow to cool. Cover container and chill. Cut tofu into 1½-inch-long diamond-shaped pieces and mix with the fruit cocktail. For best flavor, chill for about 6 hours before serving.

Milk Tofu   MAKES 8 OUNCES

Dairy milk can be solidified with an acid, as when preparing cottage cheese, then shaped and pressed in a mold like homemade tofu. Although the flavor and texture are good, the yield is only about one-third that obtained from an equal volume of powdered soymilk.

1 cup powdered (non-fat) dairy milk
6 cups water
Solidifier:
        1 tablespoon vinegar
        1¼ tablespoons fresh lemon juice

Prepare as for Homemade Tofu (from powdered soymilk) (p. 99), except 1) stir bottom of pot constantly while heating milk and 2) omit 3 minute simmering and stir in solidifier as soon as milk comes to a boil. Serve cubed in tofu salads with or in place of regular tofu, or serve as for Chilled Tofu (p. 105) topped with any variety of Sweet Simmered Miso (p 41) or Finger Lickin' Miso (p. 31).

PART III

Japanese Farmhouse Tofu: Making Tofu for More and More People

Why have we failed to realize our Buddha Nature? It is only because our practice has not been based on the true method. We know, for example, that doufu can be made from soybeans. Yet knowing this and actually making the doufu are two completely different things. First we must grind the beans and add the purée to boiling water. Removing the lees from the soymilk, we must then stir in the correct amount of gypsum. In this way we will certainly get doufu.
—From a sesshin lecture
by the Chinese Zen Master Shu Yun;
Ku Shan Monastery, 1930

17

The Quest

COUNTRY-STYLE tofu has become something of a legend in Japan, a legend that has arisen not just from the deep reverence the Japanese feel for their rich cultural heritage, nor simply from the feeling of separation from a life which was rooted for millenia in the earth and surrounded by the mystical dance of the four seasons. Perhaps the memory is being romanticized as the reality becomes more and more remote, yet many modern Japanese speak with a sense of profound nostalgia of a way of life characterized by the fragrance of woodsmoke and freshly harvested sheaves of rice, a way of life which helped men to grow strong on grandma's cooking and strenuous work under a vast sky, and which made people want to sing and dance together in celebration of the birth of new life into the world, of sons and daughters being given in marriage, of house-building, rice-planting, and village festivals: a way of life both simple and sacred, partially lost forever, partially vanishing, and partially dissolving into yet another dream.

For fine tofu craftsmen who sustain and nourish the legend, country-style tofu-making represents both a pure and early stage of their art and a standard of excellence for which they continually strive. "Once you have enjoyed the satisfying flavor of homemade country tofu," they say, "you will never forget it." They tell how, in the old days, farmhouse tofu was made so firm it could be tied into a package with rice-straw rope and carried over long distances without breaking apart (fig. 114). One piece was two to four times the size of the present 12-ounce cake and was always solidified with nigari, which the farmers extracted from natural salt. Fine craftsmen praise the farmhouse tofu-making art for its simplic-

ity (its use of only basic natural ingredients and hand-crafted tools) and elegance—its mastery of the art of simplicity itself. The closer one comes to the perfection of this art, it is said, the more one has the heart and mind of a true beginner.

But when we asked the tofu craftsmen with whom we studied where we might go to observe this tofu being made, no one seemed to know. Some surmised that we might find it in remote villages where the traditional culture was still alive. Although we inquired about country-style tofu during our travels in the towns and villages of rural Japan, however, we met again and again with disappointment.

Fig. 114. Traditional farmhouse tofu

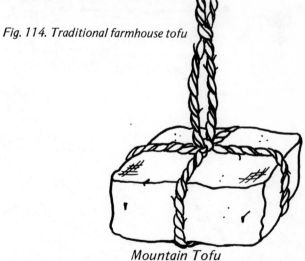

Mountain Tofu

Finally, on the suggestion of friends, we set out one spring for the picturesque mountain village of Shirakawa-go. It is believed that the survivors of the defeated Heike clan, immortalized in the epic

271

Tale of Genji, took refuge in this village at the end of the twelfth century when chased from Kyoto, Japan's early capital, by the victorious Genji family. After the Heike fled, they were never seen or heard of again. The village's unique, aristocratic architecture, its well-preserved ancient traditions, and its history of genetic inbreeding all serve as evidence in support of it's unusual origin. If the traditional way of making tofu had been preserved in this isolated village, we realized we might catch a glimpse of the way tofu was first prepared when it came to Japan's capital from China more than 1,000 years ago.

Carrying backpacks and feeling an inevitable kinship with the many wanderers who have fallen victim to the power of Japan's spring, we began our journey, walking and hitch-hiking. As we followed the Nagara River higher and higher into the mountains, it seemed as if its bright cold headwaters and a strong current of life from traditional Japanese culture flowed down from a single distant source. As we left the murky cities behind, we felt that we were moving back through time. The roofs on the houses turned from tile to thatch, the windows from glass to paper, the people's clothes from Western-style suits to well-worn farming attire. The air grew radiant, creeks cascaded down the steep mountainsides, flowers and birds were more abundant, and people's faces seemed more and more expressive of the shaping forces of wind, snow, and sun.

When we finally arrived at the village, its surrounding ridges were still crowned with snow and the mountain cherry trees were in brilliant full bloom. We spent the night at a traditional farmhouse inn (fig. 115) and immediately inquired of the old woman who ran it whether or not she knew of any-

Fig. 115. Shirakawa-go farmhouses with water-powered rice-husker in foreground

one in Shirakawa-go who still made old-fashioned tofu. She replied that while she and many other women her age had made tofu when they were younger, everyone had stopped during the last decade, either because they were no longer able to turn the heavy grinding stones or because they could no longer obtain unrefined salt from which to make nigari. She also pointed out that it had become possible to buy ready-made tofu from a shop that had opened in a neighboring village. The next day, though, she introduced us to Kidoguchi-san, an energetic old woman with laughing eyes, and together these two women led us to the village temple's attic museum. Showing us the tools they had once used, they described in detail how traditional country-style tofu was made. To our disappointment, however, no one in the village under 70 knew how to make tofu, and no one over 70 was making it any more. What's more, no one knew where we might continue our search.

We left Shirakawa-go somewhat downhearted, but our spirits were immediately lifted by the first man who offered us a ride. He informed us that one old woman who lived in his village still made the kind of tofu we were looking for. Excited, we asked that he drop us off at her home. We waited there until evening, when Ozawa-san returned from the rice fields. Kindly but firmly, she explained that we had come at a bad time—she was too busy with her rice planting to make tofu for us—but she spent several hours showing us the traditional tools she used and the small shed behind her house specially built for preparing tofu. After describing her method in detail, she invited us to return after the harvest in late fall when, she said, she would be happy to prepare farmhouse tofu for us. Unfortunately, she, too, knew of no one else in the area who could help.

We took to the road again next morning and, after walking quite a ways, met a solitary woman working in the fields. She told us of Kaminonomata, a small village nearby, where she thought a number of villagers still made tofu on special occasions. Kaminonomata was so small it wasn't even listed on our map! Undaunted, we headed out in the direction the woman had indicated and, after tramping for several hours, arrived and were directed to the home of one Watanabe-san, a 72-year-old grandmother. To our surprise, we found that we had arrived at just the right moment. Watanabe-san ushered us into her home just as she and a friend were about to make tofu in commemoration of the seventh anniversary of the passing of a former member of the village. We felt blessed.

Watanabe-san and her friend seemed as pleased as they were surprised at our sudden, yet timely, arrival. Soon the four of us were laughing and joking together as the transmission of the ancient art of farmhouse tofu-making began to take place. We watched the beans ground into gô between hand-turned stones, then cooked in a wide-mouthed iron pot set over a wood fire. We noticed how rice bran was sprinkled into the pot and how the head of foam that formed on the cooking gô was stirred down with a bamboo rod. Once transferred to a pressing sack set on a rack made of tree limbs and placed across the mouth of an old wooden barrel, the cooked gô was pressed with one of the heavy grinding stones. The soymilk in the barrel was solidified with (store-bought) nigari and the curds were then pressed in a homemade settling box under a lid weighted by a large rock. Without soaking the tofu in water, Watanabe-san cut it into small pieces for us all to sample.

The flavor of this tofu was graced with the faintest aftertaste of woodsmoke. Country-style pressing had given it a firmness and slight coarseness of texture quite unlike the soft, smooth tofu common to the cities. By not placing the tofu in water after it was pressed, a shade of beige and a fine edge of bouquet had been preserved; these we had never seen or experienced before. Beneath the subtle sweetness and fragrance of home-grown soybeans was a faint and even subtler bitterness left by the nigari. Somehow this tofu seemed to embody and share completely in the total configuration out of which it had been born. The wine-sweet morning air, the water drawn from the deep farmhouse well, the pleasure of communal down-home craftsmanship all participated in its essence. Wholesome, rustic, and deeply satisfying, this tofu seemed imbued with a genuine warmth that was the heart's warmth; and this was the loveliest flavor of all.

Seawater Tofu

Having recorded three detailed accounts of how nigari tofu was traditionally made in the mountain villages of central Japan, we decided to travel to Kyushu, Japan's southernmost main island, to see if the same method was employed there. In Kyushu, too, we found that only elderly women seemed to know about farmhouse tofu-making and that the traditional method in the south was basically the same as that used farther north. But several of the women mentioned to us in passing that they had heard of a rather simple way of preparing tofu which made use of seawater as the solidifier rather than nigari, the seawater's concentrated essence. We were advised that if this method were still being practiced any-where, it would probably be on some of the tiny, sparsely-populated islands that extend in a chain from the southern tip of Kyushu as far south as Okinawa. We had already planned a visit to the Banyan Ashram located on Suwanose island, one of the smallest islands in the chain. The ashram (which has been described by the poet Gary Snyder in *Regarding Wave* and *Earth Household*) is a commune founded by the Japanese wanderer-poet Nanao Sasaki together with numerous other young people. Devoted to a simple life-style based on farming and meditation, Suwanose is 17 hours by boat from the mainland.

Upon our arrival at Suwanose, we asked the native farmers and fishermen if they had ever heard of solidifying tofu with seawater. We were surprised to find that not only was the tofu made in the small village always solidified with it, but that the ashram's members had already learned the process, built or acquired the necessary tools, and were now making their own tofu once or twice a week! Within a few days we were—with a little help from our friends—making seawater tofu for the whole ashram. Fortunately, the island, surrounded by a spectacular coral reef and presided over by its own active volcanoe, is set like a tiny jewel in a vast expanse of remarkably clear water. At night, after starting the soybeans to soak, we walked several miles to the ocean along dirt

paths, making our way by moonlight. At the shore, we filled large sake bottles with foaming brine dipped from the dark waves. Next morning we ground the beans between hand-turned stones, cooked the gô outdoors over a wood fire (fig. 116), and served the tofu for lunch at long, rustic tables under the nodding bamboos. Its fine flavor, firm texture, and down-home feeling closely resembled the nigari tofu we had enjoyed so much in the mountains.

"Long-Life" Tofu

Just one and a half years after visiting Suwanose, we traveled to the northernmost tip of Japan's main island to study Ugemura, one of the nation's many "long life" villages, where people regularly live past the age of 90. We had recently heard that these snowy northeast provinces were one of the few places in Japan where the traditional culture was still very much alive and where farmhouse tofu was still prepared in many homes. When we arrived at this small village situated high in the mountains of Iwate prefecture, the family to whom we had been introduced by letter had just finished preparing their day's supply of firm nigari tofu. The woman of the house had skewered a number of cakes and was preparing farmhouse-style grilled tofu (see p. 221)

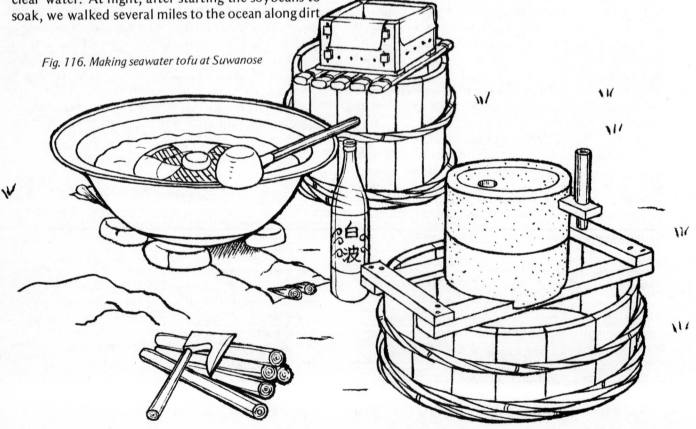

Fig. 116. Making seawater tofu at Suwanose

which she served to her family and to us in the form of Dengaku as a mid-morning treat. We soon learned that every home in the village was equipped with a small-scale tofu shop and that each family prepared country-style tofu on a regular basis. Furthermore, each batch of tofu was about 5 times as large as that prepared at Suwanose or most of the other villages we had visited, so that tofu could be served three meals a day to a large family for several days. An illustrated description of this tofu-making process is given on page 288. Here, we felt, was an historic link between the earliest farmhouse tofu and the traditional tofu shop.

Village Tofu

In villages throughout Japan, tofu and tofu makers have traditionally had their own special place in a tightly interwoven pattern of social relationships and the yearly cycle of festivals. In most villages, tofu has been regarded as a delicacy served on no less than ten to fifteen special occasions each year, and it was largely because a single batch (made from 8 cups of dry soybeans) could serve 15 to 20 people that tofu became a communal as well as a family treat. In most villages, the soybeans were never purchased and the tofu was never sold. Rather, the beans were gathered from the local fields and given to the tofu makers who, in turn, offered the fruits of their craft gratis to the community. The resulting tofu was usually served at the feast accompanying most of the year's major events, including the week of New Year's celebrations, the week of *Obon* (the Buddhist All-Souls' Festival), weddings, funerals and memorial services, *Sekku* Holidays (such as the third day of the third month or the fifth of the fifth), the various agricultural and religious festivals, and other special times of shared communal life. In the ancient chronicles of the village of Shirakawa-go, it is recorded that gifts of tofu were often brought to the ceremony that followed the completion of a new house or thatch roof. Served at most religious events held in the village temple or shrine, a portion of tofu was usually placed on the temple altar by a priest before the rest was enjoyed by the villagers. In remote villages, these customs still perservere.

During the winter months, tofu was prepared by individual families and served around an open-hearth fireplace. From about the beginning of May until the end of October, most villagers were busy from sunrise until sunset working in the fields; except on holidays, therefore, there was little time to make tofu. But after the crops had been harvested and the world had filled with snow, there was more free time. The new crop of soybeans was as its peak of flavor, and the clear water's low temperature would help to keep the tofu fresh. Now, even if there were no festival or special occasion to use as an excuse, a farmer's wife might take the time to prepare a batch of tofu for family and friends.

Farmhouse tofu was—and in villages where it is still made continues to be—served in relatively simple preparations: country people seem to find the greatest pleasure in the unmasked flavor and bouquet of the tofu itself. During the cold months, tofu will often be served sizzling hot as grilled tofu or Dengaku, prepared on skewers around a huge communal bonfire or over the dying embers of the family's open-hearth fireplace. Or the tofu may be served in Oden, Nishime, Miso Soup, or Simmering Tofu, prepared in a heavy iron *nabe*, or kettle, suspended over the living-room fire. Wrapped in fresh rice straw, the tofu may be simmered to make Komo-dofu. And during the summer months, it is most widely served as Chilled Tofu.

The history of the art of preparing farmhouse tofu has several interesting parallels with that of homemade bread-baking in America. In both cultures, the art was first practiced primarily by women. In Japanese communities, there were as many as 10 to 15 women, all in different households, who had their own grinding stones and a complete set of tofu-making tools. Sometimes working in pairs, these women often began the slow, difficult work of grinding the beans in the wee hours in order to have the tofu fresh and ready to serve by mid-morning. And just as home-baked bread started to disappear from American culture as soon as commercial bakeries were established and mass-produced bread became available at local stores, so did the practice of making tofu at home tend to die out in Japan shortly after tofu shops spread into rural areas. Since there are now about 38,000 commercial shops throughout the country, farmhouse tofu has survived only in the most remote villages. And finally, just as there has been a revival in America of the traditional art of baking bread among people who have re-discovered the beauty of the work and the superior flavor and nutritional quality of the end product, so in Japan, too, among people seeking to re-establish a simpler, more natural way of life and to revive ancient Japanese crafts, there is now a growing interest in making country-style tofu.

In many villages, especially after motor-driven grinding wheels came into use, either a widow or a poor farmer's wife would open a small shop as a means of augmenting the family income. These shops not only supplied tofu on a regular basis but were also known as favorite places to sit and gossip. In some rural areas, several families lived in farmhouses which were too far apart to be called a village and were also a long distance from the nearest tofu shop. These families often made tofu on a rotating basis, each family delivering it to the other families in turn. Gradually in these and other ways, farmhouse tofu makers began to practice their art as a profession. Tofu which was once shared was now sold. Yet, no doubt, the villagers were happy to have a readily available source of fresh, inexpensive tofu, and the craftsman was glad to have a source of income.

Traditionally, the tofu shops that grew up in both the cities and villages of Japan used the same ingredients and methods. The differences between country-style and city-style tofu first began to appear in the postwar period. Needless to say, in villages where farmhouse tofu is still prepared, it is considered incomparably superior to its modern, commercial counterpart, and we would have to agree. Thus we have asked every village tofu maker we have met what she or he considers the most important elements in preparing fine tofu. The following, listed in order of priority, are believed to be the essentials of the farmhouse process:

1. Use nigari or seawater as solidifier.
2. Press the tofu in the settling boxes with a heavy weight for a long time to create a firm texture and rich, dense flavor.
3. Do not soak the finished tofu in water; serve it as soon as possible.
4. Use a wood fire.
5. Use high-quality, organically-grown whole soybeans, preferably a Japanese variety.
6. Use a moderately coarse pressing sack so that a small amount of very fine-grained okara enters the tofu to give it a more substantial texture and slightly increase the yield.
7. Use pure water, from a deep well or clear stream if possible.
8. Prepare the tofu in a heavy iron pot or cauldron (rather than in a pressure cooker or aluminum container).
9. Learn to work with single mindedness and care, giving life to each ingredient and each action, wasting nothing, preparing tofu as a festive offering for the delight of both gods and men.
10. Use simple tools, make them yourself, treat them with respect.
11. Grind the soybeans with slowly-turning granite stones which yield a fine-textured, smooth purée.
12. Serve the tofu in the simplest possible way to allow full appreciation of its flavor.

Mortar and pestle for pounding mochi

18
Making
Community Tofu

L EARNING TO make country-style tofu and bringing this fine tradition to the West can be as easy—and joyous—as learning to bake bread. Only about 1½ hours of work are required from the time the beans are ground until the curds are ladled into the settling container. An additional hour or more is then necessary for the curds to settle and the tofu to cool. If the soybeans are purchased inexpensively in bulk, the following recipe can be prepared for about one-sixth the cost of the same amount of commercial tofu. Since tofu will stay fresh if kept under cold water, a single batch of farmhouse tofu will feed a family of four for 3 or 4 days. For best results, be sure you have mastered the method for preparing Homemade Tofu (p. 99) before starting to make the farmhouse variety.

The finest flavor will be obtained by following the traditional farmhouse method as closely as possible. (Be assured, however, that a blender or handmill can be used in place of the grinding stones with no loss in quality.) The basic recipe that follows is a description of the easy-to-use "island method" practiced at Suwanose. The "mainland method" used in most mountain villages and tofu shops is explained as a variation.

Frequent variations and adaptations to both the traditional tools and method have been suggested so that the recipe can be followed easily in any Western kitchen. Although it is always easier to make country-style tofu if two or more people work together, one person working alone can do the job.

This method, which uses simple, traditional tools and natural ingredients, is also well suited to people living in even primitive conditions, such as in the villages of Africa, India, or South America, or in Western communities or communes practicing voluntary (or involuntary) poverty. In either situation, the method might be used as the basis for a new vocation, craft, or small family-based enterprise which can be started easily in one's home or community with little or no initial investment. If a person begins work at 6 o'clock in the morning, he or she should be able to make 4 batches (about seventy 12-ounce cakes) of this tofu by noon.

The following recipe (and the scale of the tools) is designed for making each batch of tofu from 8 cups of dry soybeans. While this size batch is the most common in Japan, some farmhouse craftsmen use 16 (or in large families as much as 40) cups of soybeans at a time. If you have a large enough cooking pot and can assemble the other utensils you will need, it is much faster to prepare one large batch than two or three small ones. In either case, however, the method is the same.

Use the same basic ingredients as for homemade tofu, giving special attention to the quality of the soybeans and water. Contact your nearest tofu shop (p. 313) to learn more about the best available soybean varieties, and ask the craftsman or a local natural foods dealer about prices for bulk (100 pound) purchases. Using the latter (at about 17 cents per pound), you can produce tofu costing about 6 to 7 cents per pound.

Tools and Utensils

The basic tools needed to prepare country-style tofu resemble those used for homemade tofu; most are simply larger. Those which cannot be made at home are easily obtainable and relatively inexpensive.

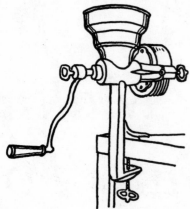

Blender, Foodmill, Grinder, or Grinding Stones: If electricity is available, use a fairly large electric blender, mill, or grinder. The former is now used in many Japanese farmhouses for recipes of this size. A small electric grinder with 6-inch-diameter, vertically mounted stone wheels is used in farmhouses where slightly larger batches of tofu are made on a regular basis. A good grinder is the key to the tofu-making process since the most difficult and time consuming step is the grinding of the beans. If electricity is not available, use a handmill (such as the inexpensive Corona Hand Mill or a Quaker City

Hand Grain Grinder) or a meat grinder with a hopper on top and a fine blade attachment.

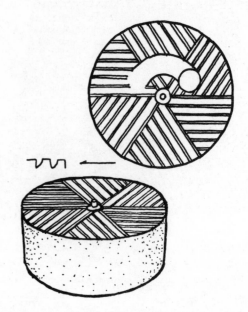

Traditionally, farmhouse tofu makers grind their soybeans with hand-turned granite grinding stones. Each of the two granite stones, weighing about 40 to 50 pounds, is about 13 inches in diameter and 4 to 5 inches thick. In the concave upper surface is a 2-inch-diameter hole into which the soaked beans are ladled. A metal rod in the center of the upper face of the bottom stone fits into a metal sleeve in the center of the lower face of the top stone to hold the stones in place while they are turning. Both grinding faces are cut with 1/8-inch-deep grooves beveled as illustrated. For the preparation of smooth, fine-grained gô, it is essential that the two stones be well balanced and aligned and that the grooves be well cut and sharpened once every 3 to 6 months.

During grinding, the lower stone remains stationary while the upper stone is turned by means of its vertical wooden handle. Larger stones, used for making larger batches of tofu, can be turned more easily by the push-pull action of a 3½-to 4-foot-long handle supported at one end by a rope from the ceiling (fig. 16, p. 70). The craftsman stands in one place while turning the stones. A grinding platform, which supports the stones, usually rests directly on top of a sturdy wooden catch-barrel about 22 inches in diameter and 10 to 12 inches deep. If the catch-barrel is not sturdy enough to support the weight of the stones, or if you wish to remove the barrel without moving the platform, set the stones on a platform supported by four sturdy legs, as in the design shown on the cover of this book.

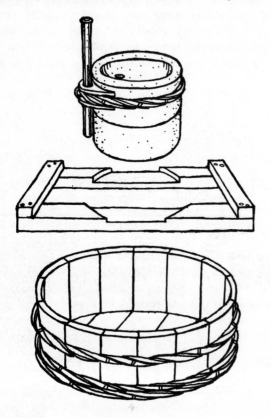

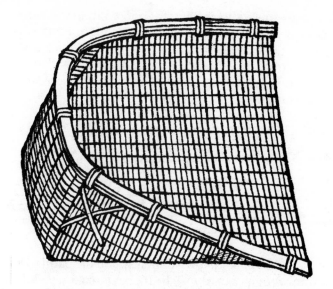

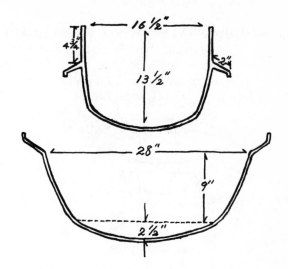

Colander: Any metal or plastic colander, sieve, or large strainer will work well. It should be at least 10 inches in diameter but smaller than the diameter of the cooking pot. Farmhouse tofu makers generally use a shallow, round colander made of tightly woven bamboo. In some farmhouses the soaked beans are rinsed in the colander; in others, they are rinsed in a large scoop-shaped basket made of woven, split bamboo and used for winnowing grains.

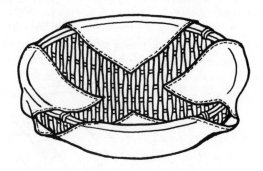

Colander Cloth: A piece of cotton cloth 18 to 24 inches square is used to cover the underside of the colander to prevent tiny particles of curd from entering and being ladled off with the whey.

Colander Weight: Use a clean stone or half brick weighing about 1 pound.

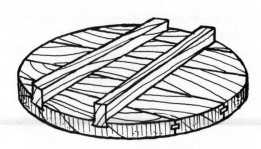

Cooking Pot and Lid: Use a heavy metal (or earthenware) pot with a capacity of at least 6, and preferably 8 to 10, gallons to minimize spilling. If the pot is to be used over an open wood fire, the lid should be thick enough so that its edges will not burn.

Farmhouse tofu makers prefer a pot with a rounded bottom made of fairly thick iron or steel. Two designs commonly used are shown above. The upper design, with its flaring mouth and lower center of gravity, is excellent for use over an open wood fire or drum-can cooker. The lower design, similar to the cauldron used in most tofu shops, is meant to be placed over a large wood-burning stove or firebox. In some farmhouses where large batches of tofu are made regularly, the pot is built into a brick dais and

may be as large as 20 inches deep and 36 inches in diameter. It is essential that the pot be thoroughly washed with hot water before each use since the slightest amount of oil it may contain can interfere with the action of nigari-type solidifiers.

Heat Source: All farmhouse craftsmen agree that the most delicious tofu is that prepared over a wood fire. However, 1 or 2 large (gas or electric) stovetop burners also give good results. In farmhouses, four different systems are used to support the cooking pot over the fire: 1) It is placed on top of 4 solid rocks set 2 on each side of a shallow trench located outdoors (fig. 116, p. 274) or in a small shed; 2) It is set into the mouth of a 2-foot-high cut-off drum can which has a 10-inch-square opening cut out at the bottom of one side for feeding in firewood and letting out woodsmoke (see above); 3) It is placed over the typical earthen stove located in most farmhouse kitchens; 4) It is built into a permanent brick dais (similar to that in many tofu shops) that has a chimney in the rear and firebox door at the lower front (see p. 279).

Hot Water Pot: Use a large tea kettle or covered pot with a capacity of at least 5 quarts.

Ladle: Any small saucepan works well. Farmhouse craftsmen prefer a ladle similar to that shown here. The 12- to 24-inch handle makes it easy to reach over the fire into the large pot, and the rounded bottom and 5- to 6-inch-diameter mouth aid in handling the curds gently. The ladle used with a Chinese wok (p. 35) is also satisfactory.

Measuring Utensils: Use one container having each of the following capacities: 1 gallon, 1 quart, 1 cup, 1 tablespoon. When measuring whole dry soybeans, most farmhouse craftsmen use a standard 1 *sho* wooden box (fig. 10, p. 56) which holds 1800 cc, or about 8 cups.

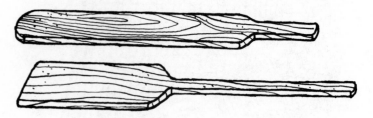

Paddle: Any large wooden spoon or spatula, or a thin wooden board may be used. Or make a paddle from a piece of wood about ¾ inch thick, 4 to 6 inches wide, and 2½ to 3 feet long.

Purée Container (Gô Catch Barrel): Use any container with a capacity of at least 3 gallons to hold the freshly-puréed gô or to catch the gô beneath the grinding stones.

Pressing Pot or Barrel: Use any sturdy pot, barrel, or tub made of wood or metal and having a capacity of 6 to 8 gallons. If using the mainland method (p. 287), try to use a wooden container in order to help keep the soymilk hot. Typical farmhouse pressing barrels, 18 to 22 inches in diameter and 16 to 18 inches deep, are made of sturdy cedar staves bound together with 2 or 3 hoops of plaited bamboo or twisted wire.

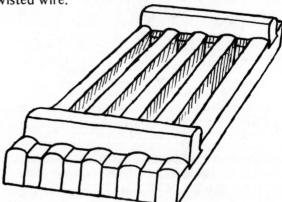

Pressing Rack: The simplest design consists of about 5 strong wooden rods or boards (broom-, shovel-, or axe-handles can also be used) placed across the mouth of the pressing barrel with a space of several inches between each rod. A sturdier, more permanent rack can be made either by notching the ends of the rods and tying them together with rope or by joining the rods or other sturdy boards with wooden cross pieces at both ends.

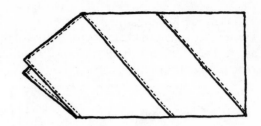

Pressing Weight and Lever: For a weight, use any clean object or objects weighing at least 50, and preferably 80 to 100 pounds. A large rock with at least one flat surface is ideal. In Japan, a grinding stone is often employed for this purpose (see above). A slightly more complicated but more effective design for pressing the okara is the simple lever press. The pressing lever is a 2-by-4 board about 3½ feet long. Some farmhouse craftsmen simply place the paddle they are using across the top of the closed pressing sack and press with the weight of their body (p. 288).

Pressing Sack: Use a rectangular sack (such as a small flour sack) about 24 inches long and 13 to 15 inches wide made of rather coarsely-woven, undyed cotton, hemp, nylon, or other strong fabric. If the weave of the cloth is too fine, the okara will be difficult to press and a large quantity of it will be left in the sack, causing a decline in the tofu yield and a lack of that certain substantial quality in the tofu cherished by farmhouse tofu makers. Furthermore, the mesh opening in such a sack will also gradually become clogged after 8 to 10 batches of tofu. However, if the weave of the sack is too coarse, too much okara will pass through the sack into the tofu. The strongest homemade pressing sacks are prepared with the seams running diagonally.

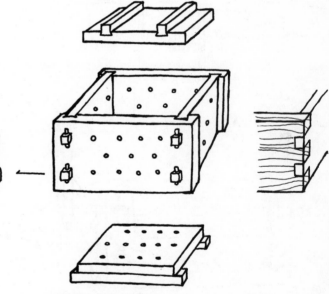

Settling Container: For best results, prepare a container with a capacity of 1½ to 2 gallons, using the design shown here, or any of the 3 designs in figure 33 on page 100. Use ¾-inch-thick (cedar or oak) boards, and make the box about 4 to 5 inches deep and 10 to 12 inches square (inside dimensions). Drill about eleven 3/8-inch-diameter holes in each of the four sides and about 13 holes in the bottom. The lid may be made with or without holes and the sides joined with or without nails, using either of the two designs shown in the inset. A box of this size will hold the curds made from 8 cups of dry soybeans. A large flat or round-bottomed colander may also be used as the settling container.

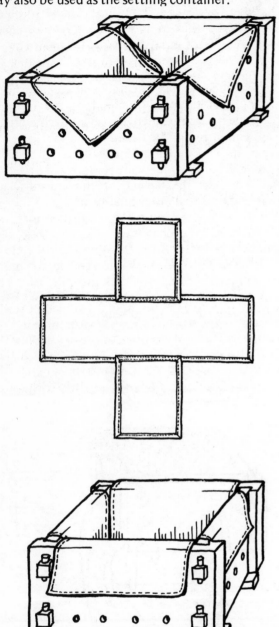

Settling Container Cloths: The simplest design is a piece of cheesecloth or a light cotton dishtowel about 20 to 24 inches square which can be arranged diagonally into a square (or round) settling container. A design that allows for slightly better drainage and gives the tofu a smoother surface is made by sewing the cloths to form a square and arranging them in the settling box as illustrated. Sew the cloth to fit your box and seam the edges to prevent fraying.

Wooden boxes and barrels should be dried in the sun after use and stored in a clean dry place. Cloths and sacks should be thoroughly scrubbed in hot whey or hot water as soon as possible after use to prevent soymilk from gradually clogging the mesh; rinse well, dry in the shade, and store in a dry, well-ventilated place to prevent molding.

Solidifiers

Farmhouse tofu makers in Japan have traditionally used either seawater or natural nigari to solidify their tofu. At present, the refined forms of nigari (magnesium chloride or calcium chloride) are also widely used and give virtually the same fine flavor. Although we, like most traditional craftsmen, prefer to use and recommend simple, natural ingredients, the level of contamination of seawater in most parts of the world makes it necessary for us to advise caution in the use of natural seawater or nigari and suggest the use of their refined forms. Nevertheless, for people who still have access to clean seawater, and in the hope that man's large-scale pollution of the environment will soon stop, we would like to give detailed information concerning the composition, preparation, and use of the traditional farmhouse solidifiers. In the process, we will try to explain why the refined forms of nigari make good substitutes.

Seawater: Clean seawater is highly recommended as a solidifier because it is easy to use, makes delicious tofu, requires no further processing or preparation and, if taken directly from the ocean, is available at no cost. Whenever possible, collect the seawater shortly before it is to be used and store it in a clean bottle or other non-corrosible container; it gradually loses its potency as a solidifier the longer it is stored. Do not collect the seawater from near the mouth of a stream or river since it will be relatively dilute and impotent. Do not use water which is cloudy or unclear.

The composition of seawater varies somewhat from place to place throughout the world. A typical sample has the following composition by weight. The remainder is water (H_2O):

	Percent
Sodium chloride (common salt)	2.72
Magnesium chloride	0.38
Magnesium sulfate	0.17
Calcium sulfate	0.13
Potassium chloride	0.09
Magnesium bromide	0.01

Seawater also contains over 60 trace elements, all of which are of nutritional value. In approximate order of abundance are strontium, boron, silicon, nitrogen, aluminum, rubidium, lithium, phosphorous, barium, and iodine, among others.

It is interesting to note that magnesium chloride, magnesium sulfate (Epsom salts), and calcium sulfate are each effective tofu solidifiers used (separately) in modern tofu shops. By using seawater to solidify tofu, their combined action seems to bring out a wide range of complementary flavors and ensure more complete solidification of the different types of soy protein.

Since all seawater contains approximately the same concentration of nigari, it is easy to specify exactly how much seawater will be necessary to solidify tofu made from a given quantity of soybeans. By remarkable coincidence, the required volume of seawater is just equal to the volume of dry soybeans used. Since the concentration of liquid nigari, on the other hand, varies widely and is difficult to measure, it is not easy to specify exactly how much to use in a given recipe.

Tofu prepared with seawater does not taste "salty" because all the salt dissolves in the whey as the latter separates from the curds. However, since a very small amount of whey is inevitably contained in the tofu, even after thorough pressing, the salt contained therein serves as a seasoning, further enhancing the tofu's flavor. Thus, if you have a supply of clean seawater, by all means use it to solidify your tofu. Only if you wished to make your own natural salt would it make sense to first extract salt from seawater, then extract nigari from the salt.

Natural Nigari: Called "bittern" or "bitterns" in the West, *nigari* is the mineral-rich mother liquor that remains after salt is extracted from seawater. All natural sea salt contains some nigari, which gives the salt its hygroscopic propensity to absorb and retain water from the air and imparts to it a subtle bitterness, a slightly gray color, and a concentrated flavor that makes natural salt taste "saltier" and more potent than refined salt. In fact, the refining process is basically the removal of nigari from natural salt to create a pure-white product that is about 99 percent sodium chloride. Generally containing magnesium carbonate additive, refined salt bears about as much resemblance to natural salt as do white bread, white rice, or white sugar to their whole, natural counterparts. The Japanese call natural salt *nami-no-hana*, "the flowers of the waves." It has been regarded as a symbol of purity and is used in a wide array of sacred ceremonies and rituals.

Anyone can make natural salt: to do so, take a large, wide-mouth pot to a clean stretch of ocean, use seawater to fill the pot two-thirds full, then simmer its contents over a driftwood fire until all of the water has evaporated and only moist solids remain. Transfer the solids to a glass jar and cover. (This is a beautiful and fruitful way to spend a day at the ocean!) One gallon of seawater (weighing 8¼ pounds) yields about ¼ pound natural sea salt, almost one-fourth of which consists of minerals other than sodium chloride. Containing all of the trace elements found in seawater, its composition on a moisture-free basis is:

	Percent
Sodium chloride	77.8
Magnesium chloride	9.5
Magnesium sulfate	6.6
Calcium sulfate	3.4
Potassium chloride	2.1
Magnesium bromide	0.2

Using your moist salt (or natural sea salt available at most natural foods stores) you can now prepare your own nigari. For small-scale production, place the salt into a fine-mesh bamboo (or plastic) colander set over the mouth of a non-corrosible (earthenware, glass, wood, or plastic) container (fig. 117). If the salt is dry, sprinkle it lightly with water,

Fig. 117. Making nigari with bamboo colander

then place the salt and container in a cool, damp place. (Or, for faster results, place a large bowl filled with water next to the container and cover the salt, bowl, and container with a large plastic bag or box to form a simple humidifier.) As the salt absorbs moisture from the air, the nigari, a slightly reddish, concentrated liquid, will begin to drip into the empty container. After several days, depending on the amount of salt and the humidity, there should be enough nigari to solidify the tofu made from 8 cups of soybeans.

For larger-scale production, obtain at least 10 pounds (or as much as 50 to 100 pounds) of sea salt. Place the salt in a moistened sack (such as a flour or gunney sack) or on a piece of cotton or linen cloth which is then gathered at the corners to form a sack. Suspend the sack above a large container or, if the container is sturdy and has a wide mouth, place the sack on top of several boards resting across the container's mouth. Set in a cool damp place and allow the nigari to factor out.

In traditional Japanese farmhouses, about 100 pounds of unrefined sea salt were placed in a sack 3 feet long and 2½ feet wide made of woven rice straw. This was either set directly on top of a specially-made wooden container called a "salt boat" (fig. 118) or suspended from the farmhouse rafters over an empty wooden barrel. These sacks could be seen

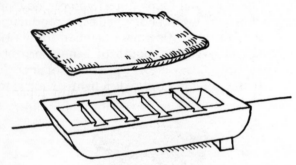

Fig. 118. A "salt boat"

working throughout the year as farmers "refined" their own salt while simultaneously collecting the valuable nigari: thus, full use was made of the natural salt purchased from oceanside salt fields, nothing was wasted, and no energy was consumed in the refining process. The nigari was used for solidifying homemade tofu. The well-drained topmost portions of the salt were used in the preparation of farmhouse miso and shoyu, and for seasoning foods at the dinner table. The lowermost portions, which still contained a small amount of nigari, were used for pickling, since farmers found that the nigari gave vegetables (such as *daikon*) and fruits (such as the *ume*) a crisper texture, firmer skin, and better flavor. Over a period of several weeks during the warm, humid months when nigari could be collected most rapidly, 100 pounds of unrefined (grade 5) natural salt yielded about 10 to 20 quarts of the liquid usually with the following composition (not including its water content):

	Percent
Magnesium chloride	31
Magnesium sulfate	2
Potassium chloride	2
Sodium chloride	1

It will be seen why refined magnesium chloride and natural nigari produce almost identical flavors in tofu.

Natural nigari is also available from salt refiners (such as Leslie Salt in the U.S.) using natural salt fields. Enormous quantities of bittern are produced as a byproduct of the salt refining process. Although this bittern has not been approved for use in foods by the Food and Drug Administration, it is purified by natural processes; algae eat any organic matter in the salt fields, brine shrimp are introduced to eat the algae, and the shrimp are carefully removed before the brine is made into salt. Most of this nigari is sold for commercial use in tank-truck quantities to produce magnesium chloride, magnesium metal, Epsom salts, potash, or bromine, or to remove the ice from frozen road surfaces. Weighing 10.7 pounds per gallon (specific gravity 1.28 at 60°F), a typical sample of the solids in this nigari shows the following composition by weight:

	Percent
Magnesium chloride	11.8
Sodium chloride (common salt)	6.9
Magnesium sulfate	6.7
Potassium chloride	1.8
Potassium bromide	0.2

For over 1,000 years, up until the beginning of World War II, almost all the tofu made in Japanese farmhouses and tofu shops, and much of the tofu made near the seacoast in China, was solidified with natural nigari. The word "nigari" is composed of the two characters meaning "bitter" and "liquid." Unlike the word "bittern" in the West, "nigari" is well known and widely used in Japan due to its long-standing association with natural sea salt and salt-pickled vegetables as well as with tofu. Magnesium chloride, the main active ingredient in nigari, coagulates the soy protein in soymilk to form curds; in chemical terms, the double-bonded, positive magnesium ion (Mg^{++}) combines with a double-bonded negative ion in the protein to form a fruitful and happy marriage.

Until the postwar period, most of Japan's nigari and natural salt were produced by the solar evaporation of seawater in small salt farms located on the seashore in areas with low rainfall, plenty of sunshine, and a high average temperature. Using the ancient "raised beach" method, the salt maker carried sea water from the ocean in large wooden buckets suspended from the ends of a shoulder pole. On hot, sunny days, he scattered this water over the surface of a small, level field consisting of clean sand spread several inches thick over a base of hard clay. (In the early part of the twentieth century, the salt fields came to be built at sea level, and the water was run in by a type of irrigation system.) The salt water in the wet sand rose to the surface of the field by capillary action. Here it evaporated and salt crystals formed. These were raked up and placed in a double-level draining vat. The latter consisted of a shallow wooden tub on top of which was mounted a slightly deeper wooden vat with a slatted bamboo bottom covered with a matting of woven rice straw. The sand (in which was deposited the crystallized salt) was placed in the upper vat. Sea water was then poured over it so that the salt dissolved and drained into the lower tub as a concentrated brine. The well-drained sand was scattered back over the field and raked smooth. The brine was then transferred to a large cauldron in which it was further evaporated (simmered) over a wood fire. As the concentration of the brine increased, sodium chloride (common salt) reached its saturation point and crystallized on the bottom of the pot. The crystals were scooped up with a shallow strainer and placed in a tightly-woven bamboo basket. The basket was set on a draining board attached to the edge of the cauldron so that the liquid (nigari) in the salt drained back into the cauldron. The well-drained salt was then put into a 6-foot-deep double-level draining vat—similar in design to but larger than the one used to wash the sand—and was allowed to drain for one week. The liquid remaining in the cauldron, "fresh nigari," was set aside and conserved. The well-drained salt was then sorted into 5 grades. That at the top of the vat, which drained best and contained the least nigari, was considered top-grade and sold at the highest price. That at the bottom of the barrel, grade 5, was relatively moist and bitter; it was sold at the lowest price and was widely used in farmhouses where it was further refined, as described above.

The nigari that remained in the cauldron after all the salt had been removed was cooled, placed into well-seasoned cedar shoyu vats (fig. 9, p. 32), and shipped to tofu shops throughout the country. In some cases it was condensed (by simmering) to twice its concentration or even until it became a solid. Because of its light weight, concentrated (or solid) nigari was easier to transport and was therefore often sold to tofu makers at a lower price.

As the simple salt farms throughout the country were gradually replaced by large scale, industrial salt factories, the lower grades of salt gradually disappeared. By 1931, grades 4 and 5 were no longer available, and by the end of World War II all salt made in Japan was either grade 1 or 2. This meant that farmers could no longer produce their own nigari. Although some farmhouse tofu makers began to order nigari from commercial sources, country tofu gradually started to disappear from the culture.

Food-grade natural nigari is now available at low prices from natural food distributors in both the United States and Japan (see p. 315). It is usually sold in its solid form, which has a coarse, granular texture resembling sea salt, is tan to reddish gray in color, and will dissolve in cold water in less than 1 minute. The solid form is preferable to liquid nigari primarily because the amount necessary to solidify a given quantity of tofu can be specified exactly, whereas with liquid nigari the amount required depends on the concentration. One pound of solid nigari will solidify about the same amount of tofu as 6½ cups of typical liquid nigari or 114 pounds (14 gallons) of seawater. It is obvious from these figures why nigari rather than seawater has been used in most farmhouses and tofu shops in Japan.

Refined Nigari: Because of the present level of contamination in the oceans and the difficulty of obtaining food-grade natural nigari, most Japanese farmhouse craftsmen and many tofu shops throughout East Asia and the United States now use refined nigari—either magnesium chloride or calcium chloride. Although both evoke much the same delicate natural sweetness and bouquet as natural nigari, magnesium chloride gives tofu that is slightly closer in flavor to the traditional, natural product, while calcium chloride is valued for yielding tofu that is rich in calcium. On a farmhouse scale, both solidify the tofu more quickly and are easier to use than the two solidifiers listed below. Both are sold in the form of a granular or crystalline white solid.

Calcium Sulfate and Magnesium Sulfate: When used with soymilk cooked in a metal pot over a wood fire, both of these solidifiers yield delicious, though rather mild-flavored, soft tofu. Natural calcium sulfate (gypsum) has been used to solidify farmhouse and commercial tofu in China for about 2,000 years. Although it has never been used by Japanese farmhouse craftsmen, it is now the most widely used solidifier in tofu shops throughout the world. Its recent popularity is due primarily to its ability to give a slightly larger bulk yield (by incorporating more water into the tofu) and to the ease and speed with which it can be used on a commercial scale. (Keep in mind, however, that nigari gives tofu with the same yield of solids and nutrients as calcium or magnesium sulfate.) Although present-day natural gypsum is about 97 percent pure, the remaining portions may contain lead or other impurities. To be safe, therefore, use only natural gypsum certified as a food ingredient.

Regardless of the variety of solidifier, use the *minimum amount necessary* to curdle the soymilk. If too much is added, the bulk yield (but not the yield of solids or nutrients) will drop, and the end product will be relatively hard, coarse, and crumbly. Its surface will be less smooth and glossy and contain tiny holes or air pockets. It may also have a slightly bitter taste (which can be alleviated by soaking in cold water as soon as the tofu is removed from the settling container). If the curds forming in the cooking pot separate from the pot's walls and the space in between fills with yellow whey, you have probably added too much solidifier.

Country Farmhouse Tofu   MAKES 15 TO 20 SERVINGS

8 cups soybeans
5 gallons water, approximately
Solidifier:
    For subtly sweet nigari tofu use: 3 tablespoons solid granular magnesium chloride or calcium chloride; or 2½ to 4 tablespoons granular or powdered natural nigari; or 2½ to 5 tablespoons homemade liquid nigari, or 3 to 8 tablespoons commercially prepared liquid nigari; or 8 cups clean seawater (freshly collected)

    For mild soft tofu use: 3 tablespoons Epsom salts (magnesium sulfate) or calcium sulfate

    For subtly tart or slightly sour tofu use: 1¼ cups lemon or lime juice (freshly squeezed), or 1 cup (apple cider) vinegar

Prepare in advance:
    On the evening of the previous day: Place beans in pressing pot and rinse with water, stirring vigorously with paddle or hands. Drain in colander, rinse again, and re-drain. Combine beans and 1½ gallons water in pressing pot and soak for 8 to 10 hours (or in very cold weather for as long as 15 to 20 hours).[1]
    If using a wood fire, gather firewood, preferably oak or other fragrant hardwood. Prepare cooking site and lay (but do not light) a small fire.
    Rinse out pressing pot, sack, and rack. Place sack and rack in pressing pot and set pot 6 to 8 feet away from fire.

Moisten settling-box cloths and use to line bottom and sides of settling container. See that cloths fit closely against all inside edges and corners of container and are free of large wrinkles. Set container aside for later use.
    Pour soaked beans into colander, rinse well under running water, and allow to drain.

After making the above preparations, proceed as follows:

    1) Light fire and begin to heat 4¾ gallons water in covered cooking pot. While water is heating, combine about 2½ cups soaked beans with 2 2/3 cups water in blender and purée at high speed for 2 to 3 minutes or until smooth. Transfer purée (gô) to purée container and repeat until all beans are used. (If using a foodmill or meat grinder, grind beans without adding water, and add 5½ quarts more water to cooking pot. If using grinding stones, see Note 2.)
    2) When water in cooking pot comes to a boil, transfer 1 gallon to hot water pot. Add soybean purée to water in cooking pot, rinsing out purée container and blender with a little water from hot water pot to retrieve any remaining purée. Taking care that pot does not boil over, heat over high heat, stirring bottom of pot frequently with wooden paddle to prevent sticking. When foam suddenly rises in pot, quickly lift pot off fire (or use tongs or a shovel to remove fire from under pot) or turn off heat.
    3) Place pressing pot next to cooking pot. While a second person holds sack down inside pressing pot with mouth of sack open, ladle and then pour hot purée into sack. Rinse out cooking pot with a little water and pour into sack. Lift sack out of barrel, quickly place pressing rack across barrel's mouth, and set sack on top of rack. Twist hot sack closed and fold neck across top of sack. Balance a heavy pressing weight directly on top of neck in center of sack and press for 2 to 3 minutes. (Or press sack with lever press.) Adding your full body weight, press for about 1 minute more to expel as much soymilk as possible.
    4) Remove weight and bounce sack on rack to loosen pressed okara. Open sack on rack and pour in 1 gallon hot water from hot water pot, dampening entire surface of okara. Stir okara briefly with paddle or ladle, then twist sack closed and re-press for 2 to 3 minutes. Open sack, shake okara into one corner of sack, twist closed again, and press for 1 to 2 minutes more. Adding your full body weight, press for several minutes more, or until soymilk no longer drips into pressing pot. Bounce sack on rack to loosen okara, then empty okara into purée container and set aside. Dry hot water container thoroughly, measure in solidifier, and set aside.
    5) Scrub out and rinse cooking pot, return it to the fire and pour in soymilk. Stoke fire, increasing heat to medium-high. Bring soymilk to a boil, stirring bottom of pot frequently to prevent sticking. Reduce heat to medium and cook for 5 minutes, then turn off heat. (Or place lid on pot, then rake or shovel all burning wood and coals out from under pot.)
    6) Add 1½ quarts water to solidifier in hot water container. (Do not add additional water to seawater.) Using paddle or ladle, stir soymilk clockwise to form a swift whirlpool, stop paddle abruptly near side of cooking pot with blade

broadside to swirling soymilk, and pour 2 cups solidifier solution down upstream side of paddle.[3] (Pour from a height of 1 foot above surface of soymilk so that solidifier penetrates to bottom of pot.) Stir soymilk 1 turn counter clockwise, bring paddle to a halt upright in soymilk and wait until all turbulence ceases; lift out paddle. Sprinkle 2 cups more solidifier solution over surface of soymilk, cover pot, and wait for 4 minutes while curds form. Stir remaining 2 to 3 cups solidifier solution, uncover pot, and sprinkle solution over surface of soymilk.[4]

7) Very slowly stir the upper 1-inch-thick layer of the curdling liquid for 30 to 40 seconds, then cover pot and wait for 5 to 6 minutes. (Wait 8 to 10 minutes if using Epsom salts or calcium sulfate.) Uncover and stir surface layer again for 30 to 40 seconds, or until all milky liquid curdles.

(White "clouds" of delicate curd should now be floating in the whey, a clear, pale yellow liquid. If any milky, uncurdled liquid remains, wait for 3 minutes, then gently stir until it has curdled. If milky liquid persists, dissolve a small amount of additional solidifier [about ¼ of the original amount] in 2 cups water and pour directly into the uncurdled portions; stir gently until curdled.)

8) Set pressing pot next to cooking pot. Place pressing rack across mouth of pressing pot and set cloth-lined settling container in center of rack. Cover outside surface of colander with colander cloth, and set colander on surface of liquid in cooking pot, allowing colander to sink until it is half-filled with whey. Ladle all of this whey into the settling container to remoisten the lining cloths. Place the 1-pound colander weight at center of colander. After about 1 minute, when colander is almost filled with whey, remove weight and ladle whey into pressing pot. Move colander to a place in cooking pot where whey still remains, replace weight, and repeat ladling off whey. When most of whey has been removed from surface of curds, remove colander and set aside.

9) Smooth out any wrinkles in cloths. Now, working rather quickly, ladle curds —and any remaining whey— into settling container one layer at a time. Rinse out pot with a little water to retrieve any remaining curds, and pour into settling container. Fold edges of cloths neatly over curds, place settling container lid on top of cloths, and set a 4- to 6-pound weight on top of lid for about 5 minutes. Increase weight to about 10 pounds and press for 30 to 40 minutes more, or until whey no longer drips from settling container.

10) Remove weight and lid from atop tofu. If using settling box with removable bottom, lift off sides, leaving cloth-wrapped tofu resting on bottom of box. (If bottom is not removable, leave lid resting atop tofu and invert box, leaving cloth-wrapped tofu resting on lid as in figure 35, p. 104.) Allow tofu to cool for 10 to 15 minutes more, then carefully unwrap cloths. Tofu may be served immediately, allowed to cool to room temperature, or chilled before serving. Serve (or reserve) tofu and use okara and whey as described at Homemade Tofu (p. 99).

VARIATIONS

*The Mainland Method: This method, used in most Japanese farmhouses (and virtually all tofu shops), may be thought of as the major tradition of country-style tofu making; the is-land method comprises a minor —even esoteric— tradition in the sense that even most professional tofu makers in Japan are not aware of its existence.

The main differences between the two methods can be summarized as follows:

Island Method	Mainland Method
1. Cook gô partially in pot	1. Cook gô throughly in pot
2. Omit use of bubble extinguisher (see below)	2. Stir in bubble extinguisher 3 times
3. Extract soymilk, return soymilk to pot, and cook throughly	3. Extract soymilk and leave in pressing barrel
4. Solidify soymilk in pot while soymilk is very hot	4. Solidify soymilk in pressing barrel while soymilk is only fairly hot

For people who are just learning to make tofu and who wish to prepare only one cauldronful at a time, there are three basic advantages to using the island method: 1) It obviates the need for bubble extinguisher; 2) A smaller-sized cooking pot may be used; 3) The soymilk can be solidified more quickly and easily with the use of a smaller quantity of solidifier. The main advantage of the mainland method is that it permits the preparation of additional batches of tofu while the soymilk from the first batch is being solidified in the pressing barrel. (In the island method too, however, the soymilk can be returned to the pressing barrel before it is solidified.) Seawater or nigari can be used as the solidifier with either method, although the former is of course generally used with the island method and the latter with the mainland method.

Any of three types of bubble extinguisher may be used to prevent foam from rising and overflowing as the gô cooks: most farmhouse craftsmen use either rice bran (nuka), which is rich in natural oils, or cold water. Professional craftsmen use 1 part cooking oil—preferably thick oil which has been used several times for deep-frying tofu—and 1 part finely-ground natural limestone or its refined counterpart, calcium carbonate.

When preparing tofu with the mainland method, use the same tools as for the island method except make sure to use a pot with a thick bottom and a capacity of at least 8 gallons, and use a wooden (or split-bamboo) rod about 1 inch in diameter and 18 inches long for stirring in bubble extinguisher (see page 301). If possible, use a wooden pressing barrel. Use the same ingredients and methodology but:

1. Do not remove 1 gallon hot water from cooking pot before adding gô; cook gô in 4 ¾ gallons boiling water.

2. After gô first comes to a boil in cooking pot, reduce heat immediately to low. When foam rises, sprinkle 1 to 2 cups water or 1 to 2 tablespoons rice bran over surface of foam while stirring slowly with paddle or large spoon. (Or dip the wooden stirring rod into a mixture of limestone and oil until 1 inch of the tip is coated, then stir down.) Return to a boil twice more, stirring down foam each time, then simmer over very low heat for about 5 minutes.

3. Ladle cooked gô into pressing sack and press okara thoroughly. Omit rinsing and re-pressing of okara.

4. Increase amount of solidifier used by about 15 percent to compensate for soymilk's lower temperature. Dissolve solidifier in 2 quarts warm or hot water, then add immediately to soymilk as in basic method.

5. After all solidifier has been added, let curds stand in covered barrel for 10 to 20 minutes before ladling off whey.

*Large-scale Farmhouse Tofu Making: In some farmhouses (as in the village of Ugemura described earlier), a typical batch of tofu is made from 40 cups of dry soybeans, or 5 times the amount used in our basic recipe. A cooking pot about 3 feet in diameter at the mouth and 20 inches deep is used. Either traditional push-pull grinding stones (fig. 119a) or small electric grinders are employed to grind the soaked soybeans into gô. Using the mainland method, the cooked gô is ladled into the pressing sack (fig. b). A wicker or bamboo support is used to hold open the sack's mouth obviating the need for a co-worker. The okara is pressed in the sack using the bubble-extinguisher rod (fig. c). Nigari, (diluted only slightly) is stirred into the soymilk in the pressing barrel (fig. d). After the whey has been removed, the curds are ladled into the settling box set on the pressing rack over the cauldron (fig. e) and are then pressed with a 6- to 8-pound weight for about 1 hour (fig. f).

Fig. 119. Making farmhouse tofu

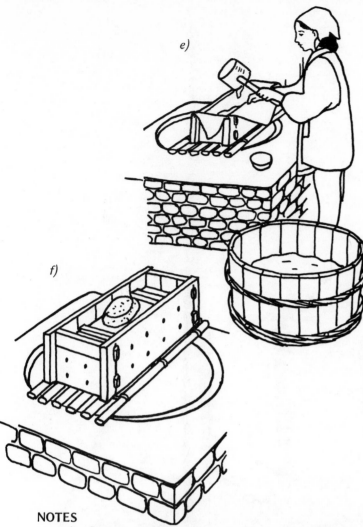

e)

f)

NOTES

1. *Soaking Time for Soybeans:* The correct soaking time varies with the air temperature, as shown in figure 120. If tiny bubbles have begun to form on the surface of the soaking water, the beans have been soaked too long. Examine

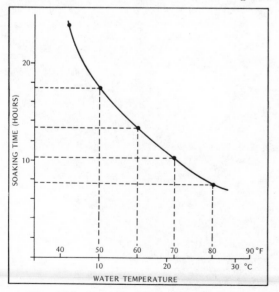

Fig. 120. Soaking Time for Soybeans

the inside of a bean by breaking it lengthwise into its two halves with your fingertips. If the faces of the two halves are flat and the same color in the center as at the edges, and if each half can be easily broken crosswise into halves, the soaking time has been correct. However, if the faces of the two halves are slightly concave and a little more yellow at the center than at the edges, and if the halves are flexible and rubbery, the beans have not been soaked long enough.

2. *Using Hand-turned Grinding Stones:* If one person turns the stone and another person ladles in the beans and water, the work of grinding goes more quickly and easily. Proceed as follows: place well-washed grinding stones on grinding platform over gô catch-barrel. Place colander containing soaked, rinsed soybeans together with a pot of water next to catch-barrel. Using a small cup or ladle, pour about ½ to ¾ cup soybeans into hole in top stone so that entire hole and part of concave upper surface of stone are filled with beans. Pour about 1/8 to ¼ cup water from pot over beans and begin to turn top stone counter clockwise at about 1 revolution every 1 to 2 seconds. After 8 to 10 revolutions (or when almost all soybeans in the hole have been ground), add another dose of beans and water.

Watch for the following: If too much water is added, the gô will be thin and will contain chunks of unground beans. If too little water is added, the gô will be thick and pasty, making it difficult to turn the stones. If the hole in the upper wheel is too small or if too little water is used, the beans may get clogged in the hole; poke them down by hand. The smoother and finer the gô's texture, the higher the yield of tofu. If the gô contains chunks of soybeans, it may be worth the time and effort to regrind (without adding more water). Grinding 8 cups soybeans generally takes about 45 minutes. Light the fire under the pot 5 to 10 minutes before you have finished.

3. *Adding Solidifier to Soymilk:* Each farmhouse (and commercial) tofu maker has his own unique way of adding solidifier. Some stir in a circle and some stir back and forth across the pot; some stir rapidly, some slowly; some add all of the solidifier at once, some in two or three installments; some pour in the solidifier from 6 to 12 inches above the soymilk surface, some sprinkle it gently over the soymilk surface, and some do both; many add liquid nigari in concentrated form without first diluting it in water. Some craftsmen using the mainland method return the soymilk to the cauldron, bringing it to a boil, before adding the solidifier. Craftsmen using the island method, but wishing to prepare a number of tofu batches in quick succession, transfer the heated soymilk to the pressing barrel just before stirring in the solidifier.

4. *Making Softer Tofu with a Higher Yield:* The use of magnesium sulfate or calcium sulfate will generally give yields 10 to 20 percent larger than other solidifiers: remove less whey from the curds; ladle the curds slowly and carefully into the settling container; after all curds are in the box, wait for about 5 minutes before pressing; press with a 1- to 2-pound weight during the first 5 minutes, then double the weight and press for 15 to 20 minutes more. Remove tofu from box underwater (see Homemade Tofu), cut into cakes, and allow to cool underwater for 15 to 20 minutes before serving.

PART IV

The Practice of Making Tofu:
The Traditional Tofu Shop

"Tofu-making possesses that stillness so cherished by one who wishes to practice. Daily work is a moment by moment apprenticeship in stillness."
                                           — *A Tofu Master*

19

The Traditional Craftsman

IN TRADITIONAL Japan, the daily work of the craftsman was regarded as a spiritual path or *sadhana* that had as its goal self-realization, liberation, and the expression of inner awakening in artistic perfection. The *sumi-e* painter realized this state of Being when, in complete selflessness, he became one with the bamboo and the bamboo effortlessly painted itself. The archer approached mastery of his practice when he in no way interfered with the arrow releasing itself from the bow and flying to its true destination at the center of the target. It was the same with the swordsmith, the potter, the calligrapher, the martial artist, and others—including the tofu master.

In Japanese, each of the traditional disciplines—which Westerners usually refer to as "arts"—is called a "Way": *Sado,* the Way of Tea; *Kado,* the Way of Flowers; *Butsudo,* the Way of the Buddha, or of meditation. More broadly, however, the Chinese character that means "Way" also refers to the *Tao,* the fundamental ordering principle of the universe, the ineffable Logos. Thus, although each Way has its own unique outward form, all are united by a single underlying principle and animated by a common spirit: the spirit of *practice.*

Practice is a way of working that transforms work into art. Paradoxically, he who is engaged in practice is not primarily concerned with an explicit result—striking the bull's eye, painting the bamboo—but rather with the moment to moment realization of selflessness; through selflessness, supreme beauty is enabled to express itself.

For the true tofu master, practice is a living reality, giving energy and an ungraspable, deep meaning to daily work. To watch such a master at work is a rare and beautiful experience. His every gesture seems to emerge from a deep, still center. Grace and economy of movement give a feeling of dance to even the most mudane of his actions. A sense of rhythm, alertness, and precision shows the result of years of patient training and untiring striving for excellence. A panoramic awareness allows the master to be wholly concentrated on the one activity before him while being simultaneously attentive to the full field of activity around him.

Work done in the spirit of practice is its own fulfillment and reward. Moment to moment, the true craftsman touches reality and gives it life. In each moment, through practice, he dies and is reborn, continually reborn in the giving of selfless service. When a craftsman learns to work with his whole body and mind, time becomes for him an unbroken Being-in-Nowness. Repetition is no longer repetition, but perpetual new creation. Everything extra falls away in the direct contact with the wellspring of living reality.

Entering into his work wholeheartedly, the craftsman loses himself. He discovers a silence that cannot be broken by sounds and finds a new home at the very center of his work. The work flows freely through him into the world, finding its own way. In the midst of the world of time, he becomes free of time, and so he neither hurries nor wastes his precious moments. Through constant and patient practice, the mysteries and inner harmonies of his calling are revealed to him. Like a fish in the great ocean or a bird in the air, he reaches a clear and boundless space. Here he discovers humility. Then others may see that a fine tofu master has appeared in the world.

Master, Disciple, and Lineage

In traditional Japan, a young man's decision to enter a craft meant, initially, becoming the disciple of a master and undertaking practice as an apprentice. If the young man came from a family of tofu makers, which was often the case, the master would be his father, and he would eventually inherit his father's work. If he were bold and determined enough to start out on his own, he would probably have to obtain an excellent recommendation to a tofu master from an influential person. In either case, his relationship with his master was bound to be a trying experience. Japanese masters, whether in the arts, the crafts, or the spiritual disciplines, were known to express their kindness and compassion in what appeared at first sight to be a harsh, sudden, and unexpected manner. The story is told, for example, of a boy who, having apprenticed himself to a master swordsman, was told to chop wood, carry water, and pound rice all day. At every opportunity, the old master would sneak up behind him and whack him with a broom, a pot lid, or a stick of firewood. At first the boy was continually caught off guard, and retired each night dejected and covered with bruises. But he quickly developed a hair-trigger alertness and catlike agility which began to permeate all his work. This new sixth sense gradually deepened until his master could no longer touch him. When, after five years of housework apprenticeship, the boy was finally given a sword for the first time and showed how to hold it, he was actually well on his way to absorbing the spirit of his mentor.

In being required to become as dust before the master, the disciple learned humility. The master, by demanding complete and unquestioning obedience, self-effacement, and self-surrender, compelled the disciple to "let go" of everything he identified with himself—all old habits of thought and behavior—and thus realize selflessness. By requiring the disciple to give of himself again and again with no expectation of reward, the teacher helped him realize that only the perfect servant could eventually become the perfect master. This was the essential background or underlying spirit of all the arts, crafts, and practices. The teaching of particular forms, techniques, or methodology—the foreground—was either left until the very end of the apprenticeship or, as was generally the case in tofu shops, allowed to take place as an inevitable result of prolonged contact with the master.

As an apprentice's skill and understanding developed, he advanced through stages corresponding roughly to those designated in the West as journeyman, craftsman, and, finally, master. But the process went slowly—the average apprenticeship lasted about 8 years—since no true master wished to place his seal of approval on an apprentice with whom he was not well pleased. Of course, the master benefitted from the presence of a strong, semi-skilled helper receiving only subsistence wages. In addition, he was generally hesitant to part with the hard-earned secrets of his profession. Young apprentices, meanwhile, were expected to keep busy washing pots and tidying the shop. They peddled most of the shop's tofu and were generally allowed to keep about 10 percent of their receipts. Many apprentices were allowed to use leftover okara to prepare special treats sold to earn them a little pocket money.

Although they were never taken by the hand and instructed—especially in the master's secrets, which often had to be learned almost surreptitiously—apprentices were gradually taught fundamentals: placement of the feet, distribution of the weight when ladling or lifting to conserve energy, use of the body's inherent momentum and natural rhythms to give ease to each movement. They learned shop ecology: regard for each drop of precious hand-pumped well water, each bit of hand-cut firewood, each soybean. Principles of recycling were stressed: the mixing of used deep-frying oil and sifted ashes to make bubble-extinguisher, the use of live coals at the end of each morning for preparing grilled tofu and then for heating the home.

When each disciple was finally approved by the master as a full-fledged craftsman, he was often expected to work for one more year in the shop as a token of gratitude for having received his training. If he planned to starts his own shop—rather than take over his master's—he would receive the treasured gift of his master's lineage name, which he would inscribe in bold letters above his shop door, on his lapel and apron, and on certain tools. The Sangen-ya lineage, my master's, for example, was started more than 200 years ago and now includes about 30 shops, all in Tokyo. Most of these shops take pride in continuing to use traditional methods; their masters meet monthly for business and fraternizing. At the Sasa-no-yuki shop, the lineage has remained in the one shop for 270 years; each master transmitted his knowledge to only one disciple who then succeeded him.

Quality

The traditional craftsman placed great importance on the quality of his work and the quality of his tofu. He was first and foremost a craftsman, not a businessman or merchant. As the tofu sold, it provided sufficient income but, like all true craftsmen, he wasn't in it primarily for the money. He worked in a shop that was simple, well-ordered and immaculate; a perfect union of the aesthetic and the practical. His tools had their own character and charm. He honored them, cared for them, made them his friends, and they helped him. Work was the movement of the body in space, the feeling of water on the hands and arms, the fragrance of woodsmoke, the exertion of lifting, grinding, and pressing. Work had an intrinsic richness that was life itself. Through work, the spirit of the craftsman found concrete expression in the world of forms—as tofu. And the quality of a master's tofu bore living witness to the depth of his understanding and practice.

Each year, throughout Japan, tofu-making contests were held among master craftsmen. First on the city, then on the provincial, and finally on the national level, master craftsmen met for a period of several days and were judged by retired masters on the speed and accuracy of their cutting, their ability to grind smooth thick gô or make agé that expanded well, and, above all, on their ability to make tofu with fine flavor, texture, bouquet, and appearance.

Balance and the Middle Way

The tofu craftsman is involved in a dynamic process whose central principal is balance. Throughout the day, he must constantly seek the optimum middle way between the two extremes: he must soak the beans for neither too long nor too short; grind the gô neither too thick nor too thin; have the fire neither too high nor too low; cook the gô for neither too long nor too short a time; add neither too much nigari nor too little. To continually find the precise point of balance or perfection requires sustained attention, careful observation, and considerable experience. Furthermore, this point of balance is constantly changing with the weather and air temperature, the type and freshness of the beans, the concentration of the nigari, and the flavor and texture of the tofu desired at a particular season or on a particular day. Fine traditional craftsmen with over twenty years of experience have said that of the 25 or 30 batches of tofu they make each week, there are usually no more than one or two with which they feel completely satisfied. Such a statement points not only to the high personal standards of these men but also to the depth and subtlety of the process itself.

The Cycles and Rhythms of the Day and Year

In Japan's neighborhood tofu shops, it is the tradition for the tofu maker and his wife to rise together early in the morning. At that hour, except for the light in the tofu shop, the streets are usually dark. Although most craftsmen begin work at about 5 or 6 o'clock, those who make a large quantity of tofu—and especially those using a cauldron and the slower, traditional methods—may rise as early as 2 or 3 o'clock. In Taiwan and China, most shops start work at about 10 o'clock at night and work straight through until morning.

Upon awaking, the tofu maker begins to heat the water in the cauldron for the first batch of tofu. He then fills the sinks with cold water, rinses off his tools, and begins to prepare at least three consecutive batches of tofu: one of regular tofu that can also be made into thick agé, grilled tofu, or ganmo; one of kinugoshi made from relatively thick soymilk; and one of agé, made from very thin soymilk. As soon as the first batch has been completed and is cooling in the water-filled sinks, the tofu maker is joined by his wife who has finished her morning housework. She cuts and begins pressing the fresh tofu to prepare it for deep-frying, then gathers up any tofu leftover from the previous day and begins pressing it to make ganmo. Working together in the confined space of the small shop, the skilled tofu maker and his wife develop a dance-like sense of harmonious movement and a close feeling of cooperation and sensitivity to each other's work.

By about 7 or 8 o'clock, housewives from the neighborhood begin stopping by to purchase fresh tofu for their breakfast miso soup (fig. 121). Since the neighborhood markets are not open at this early hour, many tofu shops also sell miso, eggs, sea vegetables, dried mushrooms, and other breakfast food staples as a service to their customers as well as a means of supplementing their income. At about this same time, the tofu maker may cut the freshly-made tofu into 12-ounce cakes and make quick early morning deliveries to local markets, restaurants, hospitals, or school cafeterias. At times, he also fills special orders for meetings or other large gatherings. Returning to the shop, he will continue work if there is more tofu to be made for that day.

Since the craftsman's wife usually has complete responsibility for all deep-frying, her work continues after her husband has finished washing the tofu-making tools and cleaning up the shop. She waits on customers who come to the shop's window and, at the end of the morning's work, enjoys a leisurely breakfast with her husband.

Fig. 121.
Morning shopping

At about 3 o'clock in the afternoon, the tofu maker resumes his deliveries. He carefully immerses the tofu in cold water in a special wooden delivery box placed on the back of a bicycle or motor bike, then drives through the streets of those neighborhoods which are a long walk from his shop. When housewives hear the sound of his small, trumpet-like horn, they come quickly into the street, usually carrying their own containers, and buy their choice of the five or six types of tofu being offered.

During the afternoon or evening, depending on the season and the air temperature, the tofu maker washes and begins soaking the beans for the following day's tofu; a typical shop uses 70 pounds of soybeans daily. In deciding how much tofu he will prepare, the craftsman must first try to predict the coming day's weather: if it rains, many housewives will not leave their homes to go shopping and sales will drop; if it is a hot summer's day, people will probably eat a lot of Chilled Tofu; if it is a cold winter's day, people will want to gather around a tabletop brazier to enjoy Simmering Tofu or other types of one-pot cookery. The tofu maker must also consider the day of the week (tofu is often served at large elaborate meals on the weekend), the time of the month (tofu sales rise shortly after payday), and the season (peak sales are in June, the hottest month).

Since the busiest time of the day for selling tofu at the shop window is in the evening, most shops stay open for several hours after dinner, or until all of the day's tofu has been sold. The craftsman and his wife take turns waiting on customers. The family ordinarily goes to bed quite early.

Most tofu makers take a one-day vacation in the middle of each week. On either the previous or following day, the shop will be cleaned and scrubbed with even more care than usual; all wooden boxes and barrels are dried in the sun, and brass barrel hoops and the cauldron's rim are polished until they shine. The wooden barrels and boxes are then stacked as usual on top of the cauldron where they continue to dry during the night. Japanese tofu shops have a long history of the highest standards of cleanliness which, in recent times, the government health department has helped to maintain by strict, periodic inspections.

For the tofu maker, the year, too, like the day, has its inborn rhythms. January and February are ideal months for making tofu. Ice cold water helps keep the tofu fresh for long periods, and the air in the shop is brisk but not too chilly, being warmed slightly by the fires under the cauldron and deep-fryer. The windows steam up and the shop becomes a small, cozy world unto itself. With the advent of

spring, many shops begin to prepare silken-smooth kinugoshi. By mid-March, at the time of school graduations, the tofu maker works from morning until night to fill orders for agé which are made into Inari-zushi, the little rice-filled pouches so popular at graduation-day picnic lunches. As summer approaches, masters begin work even earlier than usual while the pre-dawn air is still cool. As the demand for tofu increases, so do working hours. During the warm months, additional care is required to keep the tofu fresh and the shop up to hygenic standards. By September, the blessed cool of fall ushers in Japan's most welcomed season. Kinugoshi is replaced by grilled tofu as the nights become chilly and families start to prepare *nabe* dishes. Restaurants, bars, and small pushcart venders order different types of tofu for use in steaming-hot Oden, and families use grilled tofu in Sukiyaki and other dishes which are warming and satisfying. In some parts of Japan, tofu makers hold a public festival each September in honor of the God or Spirit of water, *Suijin-sama*, who provides an abundant supply of pure cold water to each shop's well. Their parade begins at the local shrine, winds through the town, and concludes at a warm tavern for an evening of fraternizing. (It is said that from the earliest of these gatherings grew Japan's first tofu unions.)

In late fall, the new crop of soybeans arrives, and the tofu suddenly has a sweetness, softness, and bouquet that sends customers hurrying to their neighborhood shops. Shops also begin to sell more okara, which keeps well when the air is cold. With the coming of the New Year's season, the demand for grilled tofu reaches its peak. During the two or three days preceding the last day of the year, the tofu maker is busy from early morning until late at night grilling tofu that will be used in the traditional New Year's cuisine. (Up until the postwar era, tofu makers also prepared a variety of special tofu treats for New Year's Day and other ceremonial occasions.) On New Year's Eve, all of Japan's tofu shops close and, like most Japanese, the tofu maker and his family spend at least three, and as many as seven, days resting and celebrating the most important holiday of the year. Masters from the same shop lineage often gather at large parties. Few true masters are unhappy, however, when the vacation ends and they can get back to their work and practice—and once again have fresh tofu at family meals.

Basic Characteristics of the Traditional Shop

The traditional shop is characterized by the use of an iron or steel cauldron, a wood fire, nigari solidifier, whole (Japanese-grown) soybeans, and a simple lever press or hand-turned screw press for pressing the okara. Most of these shops use well water; their settling boxes and curding barrels are made of wood. Some have also preserved the use of granite grinding stones driven by a small motor, and homemade bubble-extinguisher prepared from finely-ground natural limestone or wood ash mixed with thick oil used previously for deep-frying. Of course, no preservatives or other chemical additives are used. The tools in the shop are generally simple, inexpensive, and beautiful. The atmosphere is quiet, and work is done slowly and carefully with little waste and a feeling of genuine craftsmanship.

The traditional shop is a small-scale family enterprise or "cottage industry." The master and his wife often receive help from one of their elder sons, or from their parents who share the home. Workers hired from outside the family are almost never found in traditional shops. Most of the tofu is sold either from the shop window or in the nearby neighborhood rather than through a middleman or other retail outlets. This system helps keep the price of the tofu low and encourages decentralization, since each neighborhood has its own tofu shop. At present over 95 percent of Japan's 38,000 tofu shops are small neighborhood outlets, although very few of these have all the characteristics of a traditional shop.

The traditional workshop itself is generally quite small—often no larger than 12 by 15 feet—and almost always adjoins the tofu maker's home. The front of the shop usually faces the street so that tofu can be sold from the store-front window and customers may look into the shop to see what varieties of fresh tofu are in the sink or cold storage unit ready for sale. In many shops there is a view from the family kitchen or living room to the shop front so that the master and his wife can see when customers arrive. A small shop is advantageous in that is saves unnecessary movement during work, allows the shop to fit easily into the architecture of the home, and keeps building and remodeling costs to a minimum. The floor plan of a typical traditional shop is shown in figure 122. The spatial relationships between each of the main pieces of equipment have been determined during centuries of experimentation with different layouts and designs. Like the cabin of a small boat (or a Japanese garden), the traditional tofu shop is a model of compactness and utility.

The traditional shop has a low rate of energy consumption and causes almost no pollution. For these reasons, Japanese neighborhood tofu shops are given the same zoning status as family dwellings. Although the traditional process is not as fast as its modern counterparts—which utilize a pressure cooker, a boiler heated by fuel oil, and an hydraulic

press—only about 90 minutes are required between successive batches of tofu, each consisting of 120 twelve-ounce cakes.

The traditional shop is particularly well suited for two types of social and economic environments. First, those in which people have a genuine interest in high-quality, natural foods and desire the very finest tofu, and where the tofu maker places importance on the feeling and quality of the work. Second, areas where there is a critical need for inexpensive sources of protein, a lack of capital for investment in expensive equipment, and a shortage of energy and high level technology. Thus the traditional tofu shop can serve both the post-industrial nations where many people are seeking meaningful work and a return to simpler, more independent and decentralized life-styles, and the great majority of mankind who have always lived simply and are now in need of both protein and employment.

A typical shop can be built and equipped at a relatively low cost. The only two pieces of equipment that cannot be easily built or inexpensively purchased are the cauldron and the grinding stones (or grinder). The total cost of setting up a small traditional shop can be less than $1,500 if you improvise and do the construction work yourself. In Japan, a complete neighborhood shop with all new tools installed cost about $2,900 in 1975. Yet as described in Part III, a farmhouse-style tofu shop using large pots, a sturdy blender, and other tools found in most homes can be started at virtually no expense and slowly expanded into a small-scale traditional shop.

Fig. 122. A tofu-shop floor plan

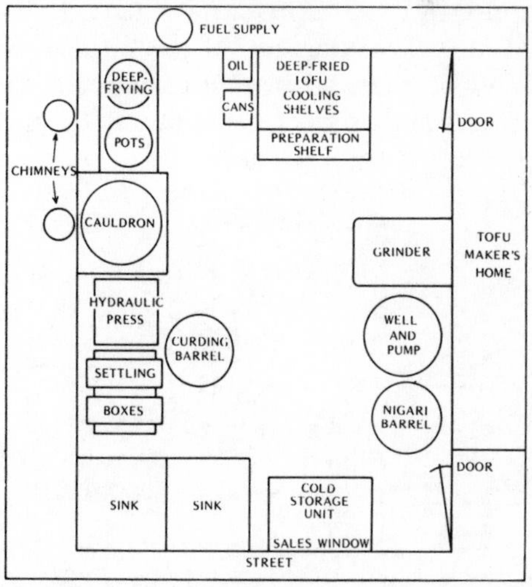

The Traditional Shop in the Modern World

The basic tools, ingredients, methodology, and spirit which characterize the traditional shop remained almost unchanged from the time that tofu was first introduced into Japan over 1,000 years ago up until the outbreak of World War II. Unlike much of the rest of Japanese society, the traditional arts and crafts—and especially that of tofu-making—were surprisingly unaffected by the period of Westernization and modernization that began in 1868. Only after World War II did traditional shops feel the full impact of the industrial revolution, which led to their gradual modernization—and decline.

With this late coming of the industrial revolution, a new consciousness began to replace the traditional one. Work came to be seen primarily as an economic enterprise and, for many, producing tofu became just another job or business. The spirit of craftsmanship was gradually diluted or largely forgotten as emphasis shifted to productivity, efficiency, cost reduction, and growth. Profits took on a new importance as commercialism became the order of the day. The master-disciple relationship was eventually reduced to a 3-month training period or eliminated altogether, and tofu-making contests were gradually discontinued. With the decline in the perceived value of the work itself and the importance of daily practice came an inevitable decline in the quality of the tofu.

During the 1960s Tokyo's prestigious Food Research Institute did the first scientific study of the tofu making process with the intent of increasing yields, reducing production times, and replacing traditional methods based on personal intuition and experience with modern methods arrived at rationally and objectively. Hoping to standardize tofu making throughout the country, the institute urged makers to use calcium sulfate (to yield tofu with high water content) and pressure cookers (to reduce cooking time). The question of the tofu's flavor was never raised. Replete with graphs and scientific data, the institute's final report played a major role in the modernization of traditional shops.

As simple tools and natural ingredients were replaced by machines and a number of new synthetic ingredients, the traditional tofu shop evolved into its modern form. Cauldrons were replaced by boilers and high-speed pressure cookers (fig. 123), wood fires by fuel-oil burners, simple lever presses or hand-turned screw presses by centrifuges and hydraulic presses (fig. 124), natural nigari by refined calcium sulfate, and whole soybeans in part by defatted soybean meal. In many shops, well water, contaminated by industrial pollution, was replaced by municipal water, wooden boxes and barrels by their aluminum counterparts, stone grinding wheels by higher-speed grinders, and charcoal braziers by propane burners. During the decade of the 1960s the traditional tofu shop reached its lowest ebb and its very existence was threatened by the new shops and factories, with their faster production time and higher output. By 1970, the wood fire, granite grinding stones, lever press, and charcoal brazier were still being used in only a very few shops throughout the country. It was estimated that a mere 1 percent of all tofu makers used only nigari solidifier (although some 14 percent used a mixture of nigari and calcium sulfate). About 60 percent continued to use cauldrons (heated by fuel-oil burners) and 55 to 60 percent used hand-turned screw presses.

Fortunately, however, the crisis seems to be passing. In Japan, as in many other industrialized nations, an appreciation of high-quality natural foods and traditional craftsmanship is re-emerging. Nigari is coming into wider use, as are many of the other traditional ingredients and tools. The small number of masters who have weathered the storm now hold the key to a rejuvenation, the promise of a potential renaissance.

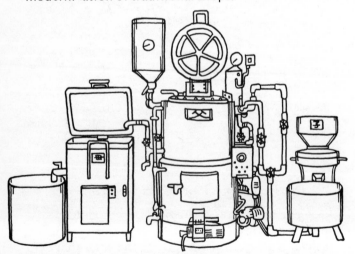

Fig. 123. A modern pressure cooker with hydraulic press

Fig. 124. A modern centrifuge with 3 soymilk barrels

20

Making Tofu in the Traditional Way

"H OW WOULD you prepare tofu to serve the Emperor?" is a question we asked of every master we met, and each responded only after careful deliberation. Our question allowed each craftsman to go directly to the heart and essence of his art, leaving aside all consideration of cost, time, and economic profitability. And almost all tofu makers, both young and old, both modern and old-fashioned, answered our question quite simply: "To make the very finest tofu, we would use the traditional method."

This chapter briefly describes that method in words and pictures. An in-depth discussion of the basic principles and practical techniques for starting your own tofu plant and making all the different types of tofu and soymilk on any of six different scales (from community and traditional shops up to a modern factory) is given in our book *Tofu & Soymilk Production: The Book of Tofu, Volume II* (see inside back cover). To the best of our knowledge, the process has never before been committed to writing since, traditionally, it was seen as a living transmission, handed down from master to disciple in relative secrecy.

Making Tofu for the Emperor

The basic ingredients required to make one batch (or cauldronful) of tofu yielding 120 twelve-ounce cakes are:

13¼ quarts (7 *sho*) whole Japanese soybeans (22.5 pounds)
30½ gallons well water, approximately (191 pounds)
4½ cups natural liquid nigari solution (relative density 1.14)
Natural bubble extinguisher
Hardwood firewood (preferably oak)

In the afternoon or evening, the tofu maker uses a handsome 1-*sho* box to measure dry soybeans into a large cedar barrel. Adding fresh water, he churns the beans vigorously with a wooden paddle to rinse them thoroughly, then pours off the water. After repeating this process several times, he adds 10 to 12 gallons of fresh water and allows the beans to soak overnight. Before retiring, the craftsman ladles about 22½ gallons of water into the cauldron; this will save him time next morning—and serve as an emergency reservoir in case of fire in the neighborhood.

Early the next day, the tofu maker dresses in the traditional garb of his craft. His raised wooden *geta* keep his feet high and dry above the shop's wet stone floor; his cloth apron bears the name of his shop and lineage; in Japan, his headband, which keeps his brow free of perspiration during the hot summer, has long been a symbol of exertion.

When the water in the cauldron has come to a boil, the tofu maker ladles about 1½ gallons into a separate container for later use. The gô catch-barrel is moved next to the cauldron, into which the craftsman now ladles most of the gô.

Lifting the catch-barrel onto the lip of the cauldron, all remaining gô is poured and scooped in.

After lighting a large wood fire under the covered cauldron, the tofu maker washes his hands thoroughly, then scrubs out and fills the sinks with cold water. He transfers the soaked beans into a bucket with a perforated bottom. After draining the beans briefly, he then pours them into the hopper above the grinding stones (or grinder) and runs in a steady trickle of water. The beans are transformed into gô which runs into the cedar catch-barrel.

The gô is brought to a boil a total of three times and is stirred down each time with a little bubble extinguisher; it is then simmered for about 5 minutes. While the gô simmers, the tofu maker rinses out the cedar curding barrel, the straining bag, and the pressing sack. The straining bag is used to line the barrel; the sack is hung down inside the bag. When the gô has finished cooking, the craftsman removes the cauldron's wooden rim, fits a special wooden trough just inside the mouth of the pressing sack,

Held over the cauldron, the ladle is then rinsed with some of the hot water set aside previously. A small dipper is used for this purpose.

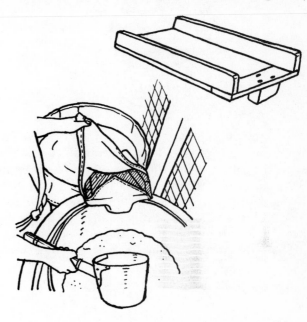

and hangs the sack and trough on the cauldron's lip. Now, holding the sack open with one hand, he ladles in the cooked gô.

The tofu maker now cooks the gô over high heat, placing a wooden rim on the lip of the cauldron to prevent the gô from overflowing. (The cauldron lid is set aside during cooking so that the fragrance of the woodsmoke can permeate the gô.) When a head of white foam rises in the cauldron, the craftsman dips the tip of a split bamboo rod into a container of bubble extinguisher, then uses the coated rod to briskly stir down the rising foam.

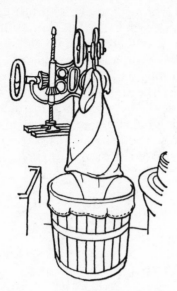

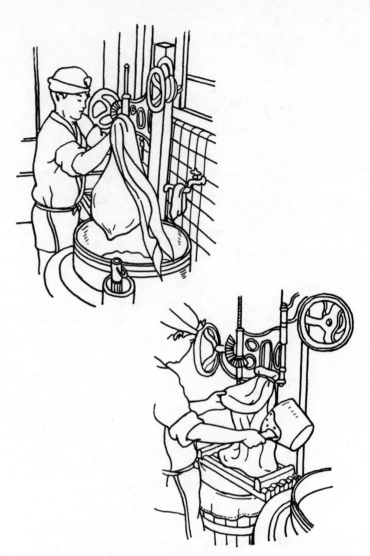

After rinsing out the cauldron with a few dippersful of hot water and transferring all gô into the sack, the tofu maker refills the cauldron with about 9½ gallons of fresh well water and stokes the fire. Using the cable from a hand-turned cogwheel winch located just above the curding barrel, he hoists the heavy sack into the air: soymilk drains into the curding barrel; okara remains in the sack.

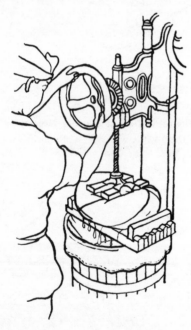

After several minutes, the craftsman places a wooden pressing rack across the mouth of the barrel directly below the sack, then lowers the sack onto the rack. After twisting closed the sack's neck and folding it across the top of the sack, he presses the sack for about 4 to 5 minutes using either a simple lever press or a hand-turned screw press.

The master now opens the pressing sack and empties the okara into the water heating in the cauldron. A small amount of fine-grained okara has found its way into the straining bag; this okara, too, is drained briefly, then emptied into the cauldron. The heavy wooden lid is now placed on the cauldron to hasten the reheating process. The tofu maker meanwhile stretches a rinsed, fine-weave straining cloth over the mouth of the curding barrel and sets the pressing rack on top of it. He places the sack on top of the rack, drapes one edge of the sack's mouth over the hanging-bar, and secures it with a piece of rope. When the okara comes to a boil in the cauldron, it is stirred briefly with the bamboo rod, then ladled into the sack. The cauldron is rinsed out with a little hot water, the rinsings are ladled into the sack, and the cauldron is then refilled with water for the next batch of tofu. The okara is re-pressed, then emptied into a special container and put outside the shop to be picked up later by a local dairyman.

The master covers the curding barrel with the cauldron lid to keep the soymilk from cooling, then ladles 4½ cups of nigari solution from the sturdy cedar nigari barrel into a wooden bucket, where it is diluted with about 3 gallons of warm water.

Another one-third of the nigari is sprinkled over the surface of the soymilk, poured first onto the paddle to give a finer spray. The curding barrel is re-covered and the curding soymilk allowed to stand for 10 minutes. The master then sprinkles the remaining one-third of the nigari over the surface of the curding soymilk and slowly stirs the upper 2 inches of the surface of the curds for about 20 seconds; the barrel is re-covered and allowed to stand for 10 minutes more.

Using the paddle, the tofu maker stirs the soymilk into a swift clockwise whirlpool. Stopping the paddle suddenly and holding it against the side of the barrel with its face broadside to the soymilk's flow, he uses the dipper to pour about one-third of the nigari solution down the upstream side of the paddle.

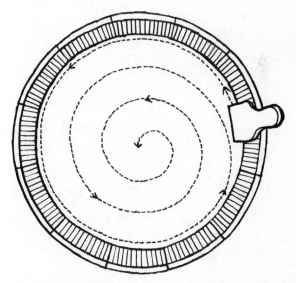

Removing the barrel's lid, the tofu maker now uses the paddle to cut a slow, deep spiral through the curds, thereby helping any unsolidified soymilk at the bottom of the barrel to rise to the surface, where it will curdle.

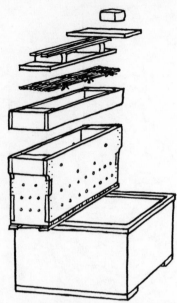

The master moistens the settling-box cloths and uses them to line the settling boxes. He then covers a large bamboo colander with a cloth, and places the cloth-lined colander into the liquid in the curding barrel. The colander fills with whey which is ladled off into the whey catch-box located beneath the settling boxes. Weighting the colander with a brick or stone, he allows it to fill with whey several more times.

If the settling boxes are too small to hold all the curds initially, the tofu maker places a special frame atop each box to increase its depth. When all of the curds are in the boxes, the settling-box cloths are folded over the top of the curds, and a bamboo pressing mat and wooden pressing lid are set atop the cloths. Across the tops of the lids is laid a small board; atop this board is placed an 8- to 10-pound weight.

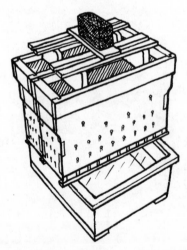

Removing the colander, the tofu maker carefully ladles the soymilk curds into the cloth-lined settling boxes. He tilts the barrel to one side to reach the curds at the very bottom.

After 4 or 5 minutes the curds will have settled several inches in the boxes. The pressing apparatus and frames are removed, the cloths on all four sides of each box are gently pulled up to smooth out any wrinkles that may have formed, and the pressing apparatus is replaced, this time topped with a 20- to 25-pound weight; the curds are pressed for 10 to 15 minutes more, or until whey no longer drips from the boxes. The pressing apparatus is once again removed, the cloths are unfolded, and the boxes carried to the water-filled sinks.

Immersed in the water, each settling box is inverted, then lifted out, leaving the cloth-wrapped tofu resting on the bottom of the sink.

About one-half of the tofu remains in the sinks until it is sold to customers at the shop window; the rest is sold in the neighborhood. In many shops, up until the end of World War II, the tofu was placed in special water-filled wooden containers and carried throughout the neighborhood by means of a shoulder pole.

The tofu maker unwraps the cloths, slips a wooden cutting board under the tofu, and cuts the tofu (under water) crosswise into fifths. Each fifth is then cut lengthwise into halves, and each half crosswise into sixths. The resulting 12-ounce cakes (120 in all) are allowed to cool under water.

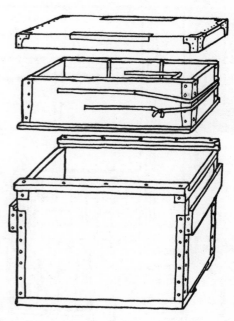

At present the tofu is placed in a large double-layer wooden box. The bottom compartment (which is lined with rustproof metal) is partially filled with water, into which is placed regular tofu, kinugoshi, and grilled tofu; the top compartment holds deep-fried tofu.

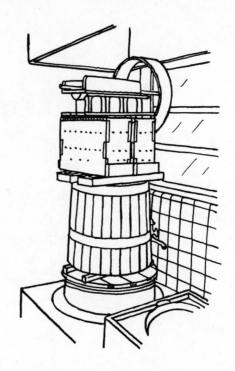

The entire box is strapped onto the back of a bicycle or motorbike which the tofu maker rides through the neighborhood as he sells the fruits of his labor.

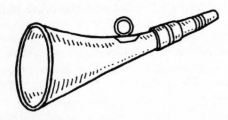

Whenever he makes his rounds, the craftsman carries a small horn tied around his neck; he blows it to announce his arrival.

At the end of work each day, the tofu maker washes all his tools with hot whey, rinses them with well water, then stacks them neatly above the cauldron to dry.

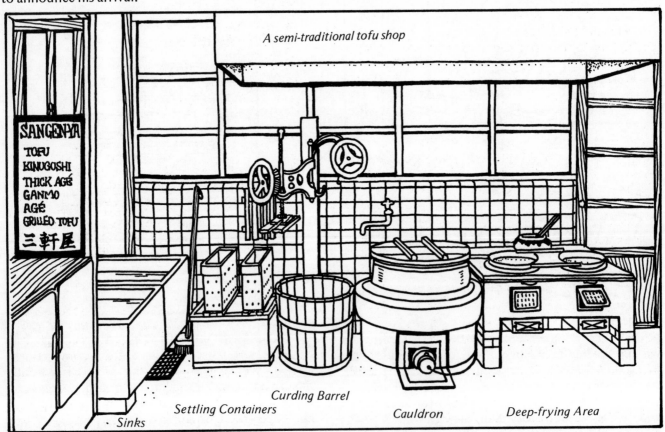

A semi-traditional tofu shop

SANGENYA
TOFU
KINUGOSHI
THICK AGÉ
GANMO
AGÉ
GRILLED TOFU
三軒屋

Curding Barrel

Settling Containers

Sinks

Cauldron

Deep-frying Area

Appendix A
Tofu Restaurants in Japan

THIS SECTION has been included first, to give Western readers a sense of the key role tofu plays and the excellent reputation it enjoys in the most distinguished traditions of East Asian cuisine; second, to provide creative suggestions for Westerners who might like to start tofu restaurants or include tofu on the menu of restaurants now in operation; and finally, to serve as a guide for those living or traveling in Japan who wish to enjoy tofu restaurant cookery. A listing of each of the restaurants mentioned in the following pages is given at the end.

Some of Japan's oldest and finest restaurants have built their reputation around tofu cuisine. If you ask a Japanese to recommend one restaurant where you can enjoy tofu cookery at its best, though, he will probably suggest Sasa-no-yuki. Founded in 1703, Sasa-no-yuki has been managed by one family for twelve generations and has long been known throughout Japan for its unequalled nigari kinugoshi, its delicious variety of tofu dishes at democratic prices, and its warm and friendly atmosphere. The name of the restaurant is proudly displayed in flowing characters written on two cloth *noren* that hang in front of the doorway. As you duck under these into the traditional Japanese entrance room, two doormen greet you with a hearty welcome. They check your shoes as you step onto long, thick beams of smoothly polished wood. Their loosely fitting blue coats—resembling *Happi* coats—give an added taste of old Japan. Perhaps the true genius of Sasa-no-yuki is that everyone feels welcome and at home here: aristocrat or working man, country grandmother or schoolboy. As in the Japanese tea house, where all are asked to come together as equals and friends, the charm here is found in refined simplicity. This book began, quite unexpectedly, with the first evening we enjoyed tofu at Sasa-no-yuki. We ended up trying one dish of every type on the menu!

The Nakamura-ro restaurant, too, has a long and distinguished history. Said to be the oldest of all existing Japanese restaurants, it began about 400 years ago as a simple tea shop serving travelers, pilgrims, and townspeople who came to pay homage at the revered Yasaka Shrine in Kyoto's Gion Quarter. Over the centuries, the shop grew into a restaurant and became famous for its "Gion-dofu." In front of the shop, kneeling behind small wooden tables and wearing distinctive kimonos and elaborate hairdos (fig.125), women cut cakes of tofu into thin slices with a speed and synchopated rhythm that have become legendary. Visitors were entertained by a *shamisen* player who took her rhythms from the beat of

Fig. 125. Cutting tofu for Dengaku (from the "Tofu Hyaku Chin")

the knives. Each small piece of tofu was pierced with bamboo skewers, spread with miso, broiled over a charcoal fire, and served piping hot as Dengaku (fig. 126).Gradually the shop's spirited atmosphere and its savory tofu became the subject of poem and song, and its spacious interior gradens attracted writers, poets, and other distinguished figures throughout the four seasons. The present master and head chef, Mr. Shigemitsu Tsuji, is famous throughout Japan as

Fig. 126. Busy Making Dengaku (from the "Tofu Hyaku Chin")

a cook, lecturer, and author. He has recently published an entire volume devoted solely to tofu cuisine, his specialty. In the seven rooms adjoining the famous old gardens, he and his staff offer both a moderately-priced luncheon of tofu dishes and an expensive but exquisite meal of Tea Ceremony Cuisine, served in the banquet style and featuring tofu in many of the dishes. The original tea shop at Nakamura-ro retains the charm and familial warmth of old Japan. In one corner of the room is the original stone grill where Dengaku used to be broiled (fig.

Fig. 127. Nakamura-ro

127).Two gracefully-curved tea kettles with elegant wooden lids fit down into the raised stone hearth at the center of the room; here hot *amazake* (thick sweet sake) is kept simmering. In one corner of the room, an old, hand-carved bucket and pulley hang from the ceiling above an indoor well. This is a delightful setting for enjoying Dengaku considered by many to be the best in Japan.

Another of Japan's oldest and most well-known tofu restaurants is Okutan, founded over 300 years ago and now in its twelfth generation. Started originally as a tea house inside the spacious grounds of Nanzenji temple in Kyoto, Okutan soon began serving Zen Temple Cookery and Simmering Tofu to the many pilgrims, worshippers, and visitors who came to the famous temple from throughout Japan. The restaurant continues to preserve an atmosphere of quiet serenity which reflects the spirit of Zen. While strolling along Kyoto's historic tree-lined "Philosopher's Path," hungry students, statesmen, poets, and gourmets have for centuries entered Okutan's rustic front gate and stopped to enjoy a light meal. Today, for many Japanese, the name Nanzenji is associated just as much with Simmering Tofu as it is with Zen. At Okutan, lunch and early dinner are served both indoors in teahouse-style rooms or outdoors on raised *tatami* mats set among the trees and greenery around a large, meandering pond. In summer the shaded garden is cool and filled with the rock-splitting sound of a thousand cicadas. In winter the trees are bare and the only sound to be heard is the bubbling of Simmering Tofu in the earthenware *nabe* set over a tabletop charcoal brazier (fig. 128).

Like Sasa-no-yuki with its kinugoshi tofu, Nakamura-ro with its Dengaku, and Okutan with its Simmering Tofu, many of Japan's oldest and finest tofu restaurants have a single specialty, the preparation of which is a carefully guarded secret. Takocho, perhaps the most famous place in Kyoto to enjoy Oden, is no exception to this rule. Founded in 1888, Takocho is known for the savory broth that makes this Oden a true delicacy. A generations-old secret of the shop, it has a fragrance that fills the shop's single cozy room and makes passers-by want to step inside and see "what's cooking." More than 15 separate Oden ingredients (including five types of tofu) simmer in a shiny brass pot behind the thick, natural-wood counter. The elegant, dark beams and white plaster walls create something of the same convivial atmosphere found in the inns of Old England.

Tofu is one of the key ingredients used in both of Japan's main schools of haute cuisine: Tea Ceremony Cuisine (*Kaiseki Ryori*) and Zen Temple

Fig. 128. The garden at Okutan

Cookery (*Shojin Ryori*). Often called Buddhist Vegetarian Cookery, the *Shojin* school began to flourish in Japan in the thirteenth century and served as one of the first vehicles for introducing laymen to the many tofu dishes prepared by monks in monasteries and temples. Restaurants soon opened in the major temples of Japan's larger cities and led the way in developing much of the tofu cookery now famous throughout the country. Today, many of Japan's best known centers of tofu cuisine are located in or near major temples. At one of Kyoto's largest temples, Daitokuji, the *Shojin* restaurant Izusen is known for its attractive garden atmosphere, its selection of more than eight different tofu dishes, and its reasonable prices. Tenryuji, an active Zen temple in Arashiyama near Kyto, is surrounded by about eight restaurants specializing in tofu cookery, and Nanzenji temple in eastern Kyoto by at least this many tofu restaurants. *Shojin* Cookery is said to be the art of simplicity raised to perfection. From it have originated almost all of the basic principles which characterize the best in Japanese cuisine. Rich in protein, inexpensive, and highly-versatile, tofu serves as the backbone of the *Shojin* meatless diet.

Tea Ceremony Cuisine, an offshoot of Zen Temple Cookery, was taken to the level of a fine art during the sixteenth century by the great tea master Sen-no-Rikyu. Though originally the school of gourmets who cherished the life of tasteful frugality, *Kaiseki* is now among the most elegant and expensive types of cookery served in Japan. And tofu will often appear in over half the dishes on the menu. The Nishiki restaurant in Kyoto offers a type of modified *Kaiseki* cuisine at prices available to everyone. Yet a full *Kaiseki* banquet can serve as an unforgettable introduction to the finest in Japanese culture and tofu cookery, an aesthetic experience that will refresh the senses, delight the intellect, and nourish the soul.

Closely related to *Kaiseki* and *Shojin* cookery are *Fucha Ryori*, the tea ceremony cookery developed in Chinese temples, and *Sansai Ryori*, the tradition which features edible wild plants gathered fresh from the mountains throughout the four seasons. When the great Chinese priest Ingen came to Japan in 1661 to found Manpukuji temple and transmit the Zen teachings of the master Huang Po, he also introduced the Japanese to *Fucha* cuisine and to Chinese-style Pressed Tofu (*doufu-kan*). The headquarters of this school is at the attractive Hakuun-an restaurant located next to Ingen's temple; and here they still serve Pressed Tofu and a wide variety of other tofu dishes. *Sansai* restaurants, usually located in rural areas, offer more than 30 different varieties of tasty mountain vegetables and numerous tofu preparations. Many of these restaurants are located in temples and reflect the finest of the spirit of Zen Temple Cookery.

In many Japanese tofu restaurants, the beauty of the setting is considered as important as the food itself. In most cases, the setting is one of natural beauty permeated by a sense of the season, which is also reflected in the ingredients appearing on the menu. The Rengetsu tofu restaurant, set snugly at the foot of Kyoto's eastern mountains, is composed of a number of private dining rooms opening onto a lovely courtyard beneath the spreading branches of an 800-year-old tree. Rengetsu means "lotus moon," and these two Chinese characters are written in weather-worn brush strokes on a plank of wood that hangs before the restaurant's welcoming gate. In the evening, each room seems filled with the same warm and golden light that glows in the paper-covered windows of the large stone lantern near the entranceway, while on balmy summer nights, Rengetsu becomes a harbor of coolness. A cedar dipper, set across the mouth of a stone basin overflowing with water, invites guests to drink and rinse their hands. The young bamboos in the garden and the flat, natural stones underfoot are kept moist and glistening with an occasional sprinkling of water. Along one side of the courtyard, a tiny stream emerges from a grotto of rushes and ferns, and flows around both sides of a large granite grinding stone (once used in a tofu shop) which now serves as a stepping stone. Crossing the brook, guests step onto a large, flat rock at the entranceway to their room, where they remove their shoes before entering.

In restaurants such as the Dengaku in Kamakura, the atmosphere is contained entirely within the walls of a single room no larger than 12 feet square. In the center of a floor made of jet-black river pebbles is a large open-hearth fireplace similar to that found in country farmhouses but raised several feet above floor level. Four massive timbers form the edges of the hearth and serve simultaneously as the dining table for guests seated around the perimeter on low stools with seats of woven rice straw. In the rectangular hearth, partially filled with black sand, glows a small charcoal fire. Several wooden platters are piled with neatly-arranged pieces of grilled tofu, three varieties of deep-fried tofu, and numerous fresh vegetables. Antique pottery bowls are filled with three varieties of Sweet Simmered Miso. The hostess pierces each guest's choice of foods with a foot-long bamboo skewer, daubs on his or her choice of miso with a wooden spatula, and sticks the base of the skewer firmly into the sand at a slant so that the tofu or vegetables are close to the live coals. Now and then she pours out water for tea from an iron pot suspended near the fire on a rustic hook hanging from the ceiling. The sizzling hot Dengaku is as delicious as the mood is warm.

In temple restaurants the atmosphere is one of utter simplicity: the uncluttered *tatami* room with its single scroll and flower; the garden of raked sand broken by a single outcropping of rocks; the fragrance of incense and perhaps the sound of a bamboo flute that helps us, in its pauses, to hear the silence. The simplicity of tofu seems to harmonize perfectly with this atmosphere.

In most tofu restaurants, the menu changes continually with the seasons, creating both a challenge for the chef and a delightful sense of variety for the regular customer. During the peak of winter, a piece of dried-frozen tofu in white miso soup may bring to mind the image of a snowbound temple. In the spring, Chilled Tofu may be garnished with a sprig of *kinome* from the tree in the garden. It has been rightly said that, in the finest Japanese cuisine, the right food is honored at the right season in the right setting. In fact, many Japanese tofu cookbooks arrange their recipes according to the four seasons rather than by types of food. It is precisely tofu's adaptability and versatility that allows it to be used throughout the year as host to an unending parade of seasonal delicacies.

In most of the restaurants mentioned above, great attention is given to the way in which the food is served and the care with which each guest is treated. The Japanese believe that a dish must please the eye as well as the palate. Thus chefs have made an art

of cutting and slicing so that each ingredient is given added character. Generally, a meal is composed of a large number of small courses, each served in a distinctive container, each a work of art in itself, carefully arranged and meticulously prepared. The colors, shapes, and textures are as carefully balanced as the flavors. Each ingredient is honored in and of itself; the chef works to enhance and bring to life its innate natural flavors. Thus Japanese cookery is an excercise in nuance and subtlety, the use of restraint and reserve in the highest sense to do full honor to every food.

At the Sagano restaurant in western Kyoto, for example, guests are ushered into private rooms facing a large and carefully manicured garden of emerald moss, inlaid with several clusters of large rocks and set against a background of towering bamboos. The rooms are decorated with original woodblock prints, earthenware sake jugs, and antique Japanese lutes. The waitress serving each room is dressed in a kimono of hand-dyed indigo *kasuri* cloth. A *tasuki*, or band of bright red cloth, passes over both shoulders and crosses in front to tie up the kimono's sleeves as she works. An *obi*, or wide brocade sash, is wrapped firmly around her waist, and white *tabi*, or Japanese socks, make her feet look light and cool. First she brings in a large cup of tea, then chopsticks which she rests upon a small coral support, then a moist towel for refreshing each guest's hands and face. In summer, Chilled Tofu is served floating with chunks of ice in a handsome wooden container, and a variety of fresh and colorful garnishes are served in tiny dishes. The tofu dessert, Gisei-dofu, is presented on handmade square ceramic plates and decorated with a sprig of maple.

At the tofu restaurant Goemon, located in the center of a busy section of Tokyo, the guests enter down a long path lined on both sides with stone lanterns lit with candles. An unexpected oasis of beauty and quiet amid the cacophony of modern Tokyo, the restaurant garden surrounds a small stream. A large cauldron—the type used in tofu shops—is filled with water from a bamboo pipe and overflows to form the stream's headwaters. The sound of a windbell fills the spacious rooms. In the winter, guests are seated at low tables, each containing a charcoal brazier filled with live coals. The hostess places an earthenware *nabe* over the brazier and invites guests to add their choice of several types of tofu and other carefully cut ingredients arranged on a large platter. Tofu and yuba are served in various forms in many of the delicate portions accompanying the main dish. In summer, Chilled Tofu is served in handsome lacquerware boxes accompanied by a thin crescent of watermelon and surrounded by chunks of ice. In a half section of fresh bamboo, a single red cherry is surrounded by strips of Takigawa-dofu arranged to swirl like a meandering river.

Most tofu restaurants bear living witness to tofu's remarkable versatility. At Hisago in Tokyo, over 200 tofu dishes are served throughout the four seasons and more than 85 are available at any one time. The inspirational source of many of these recipes is a two-volume book of tofu cusine written about 200 years ago. The *Tofu Hyaku Chin*, which combines the virtues of a travel and restaurant guide-book and a cookbook, was written to introduce the Japanese people to about 230 different varieties of tofu cuisine served in the different provinces. The famous novelist Tanizaki Junichiro is said to have personally prepared each of the 100 tofu recipes described in the first volume. Ms. Fukuzawa, the founder of Hisago, worked with these traditional vegetarian recipes to develop much of her present repertoire.

At Sorin-an, located in a temple surrounded by rice fields in the countryside west of Kyoto, home-made yuba is the featured ingredient in each of the restaurant's 15 dishes. Likewise, at Sasa-no-yuki, each of the twelve dishes on the menu, several of which are also available on a "take out" basis, has kinugoshi tofu as its main ingredient. In many Zen temple restaurants, tofu will be used in more than half of all dishes made throughout the four seasons. And in Japan's most famous book on *Shojin* Cookery, more than one-quarter of the recipes use tofu and many more use yuba.

One might well expect that at most of the restaurants described here, the cost of a meal would be relatively high. Yet because tofu itself is so inexpensive, most restaurants featuring tofu can offer very reasonable prices—especially considering the beautiful setting, gracious hospitality, and elegant service that invariably accompany the fine food. At Sasa-no-yuki, for example, the average price in 1975 for any of the 12 dishes on the menu was only 41 cents. In many Zen temple restaurants, a full 7-course meal costs between $2.50 and $3.50.

Most of these restaurants purchase their tofu wholesale from a nearby tofu shop, often going out of their way to obtain tofu made with nigari and prepared in the traditional way. The many excellent tofu restaurants of Arashiyama, west of Kyoto, have grown up around the famous Morika tofu shop and built their reputations on Morika tofu's fine flavor. Sasa-no-yuki is the only tofu restaurant we know of that prepares its own tofu. The restaurant's owner, Mr. Takichi Okumura, is himself a master of the tofu-making process; he learned it when he was a boy from the former master, his father. A distinguished restauranteur and tofu connoisseur, he feels strongly that the flavor of the tofu itself is the indispensable foundation for fine tofu cuisine: "Unless the tofu exhibits its own natural sweetness and bouquet, it can never become a dish worthy of the Japanese cuilinary tradition, not even in the hands of the most talented chef." Thus he insists on serving tofu made with nigari and the best-grade Japanese soybeans, prepared fresh each day in the shop located in the basement of the restaurant.

In addition to restaurants specializing in tofu cookery, there are many more which serve tofu regularly in dishes such as Sukiyaki, Miso Soup, Nishime, Chilled Tofu, or Simmering Tofu. Each of Japan's Chinese restaurants has a special section devoted to tofu cookery, and most of the thousands of *soba* shops use deep-fried tofu in a variety of noodle dishes. In the large number of restaurants specializing in Inari-zushi and in most sushi shops, agé is one of the main ingredients. And in the shops, bars, and winter-time street stalls featuring Oden, tofu is found in its many forms.

Japan's most bizarre—indeed barbaric—restaurant tofu dish is called Yanagawa-dofu. Several small, live loaches (fresh-water eels) are placed in a large tureen containing cold water and a cake of tofu. The pot is placed over a tabletop burner in front of the diners and the water is slowly brought to a boil. The loaches frantically burrow into the soft, cool tofu, trying to escape the heat. Once inside, they are cooked.

Tofu is also one of the main items on the menu at the many natural food restaurants which have opened throughout Japan in recent years. Most of these restaurants make a special point of advertizing the tofu as nigari-based and using it in both traditional Japanese and Western-style preparations. Surely, tofu salads, soups, egg dishes, sauces, sandwiches, and burgers would make excellent additions to the menus of many natural food and other restaurants in the West, as well.

TOKYO AND ENVIRONS

SASA-NO-YUKI: *Tofu Cuisine*
67 Kaminegishi Machi
Daito-ku, Tokyo
Uguisudani Station
Tel: 03-873-1145

GOEMON: *Tofu Cuisine*
Hongomagome 1-1-26
Bunkyo-ku, Tokyo
Sugamo Station
Tel: 03-811-2015

SANKO-IN: *Zen Temple Cookery*
Honcho 3-1-36
Koganei-shi, West Tokyo
Musashi Koganei Station
Tel: 0423-81-1116

SHINODA-ZUSHI: *Inari-zushi*
25 restaurants in Tokyo
For information call:
03-666-4561

TOFUYA: *Tofu Cookery*
Akasaka 3-5-8
Minato-ku, Tokyo
Akasaka Mitsuke Station
Tel: 03-582-1028

TENMI: *Natural Foods Restaurant*
Sakuragaoka 4-3
Shibuya-ku, Tokyo
Shibuya Station
Tel: 03-461-7988

MISUZU: *Tofu Cuisine*
Kogawa-cho 3-3, Kawasaki-ku
Kawasaki City (south of Tokyo)
Tel: 044-244-6845

DENGAKU: *Dengaku Cuisine*
Komachi 1-6-5
Kamakura (South of Tokyo)
Kamakura Station
Tel: 0467-23-2121

KYOTO AND ENVIRONS

OKUTAN: *Simmering Tofu*
Nanzenji Keidai, Fuji-cho
Sakyo-ku, Kyoto
Tel: 075-771-8709

JUNSEI: *Tofu Cuisine*
Nanzenji Keidai, Fuji-cho
Sakyo-ku, Kyoto
Tel: 075-761-2311

NAKAMURA-RO: *Dengaku and Kaiseki Cuisine*
Yasaka Jinja-nai
Higashiyama-ku, Kyoto
Tel: 075-561-0016

RENGETSU: *Tofu Cuisine*
Chion-in, Kitaohairu
Higashiyama-ku, Kyoto
Tel: 075-561-4589

IZUSEN: *Zen Temple Cookery*
Daitokuji-nai
Kita-ku, Kyoto
Tel: 075-4891-3806

TAKOCHO: *Oden*
Miyazawa-suji 1-237
Higashiyama-ku, Kyoto
Tel: 075-525-0170

SORIN-AN: *Yuba Cuisine*
Higashi-no-kuchi-cho 45
Kami-katsura, Ukyo-ku, Kyoto
Hankyu Line, Katsura Station
Tel: 075-381-7384

NISHIYAMA SODO: *Simmering Tofu*
Tenryuji-nai
Ukyo-ku, Kyoto
Arashiyama Station
Tel: 075-861-1609

SAGANO: *Tofu Cuisine*
Susuki-no-baba 45
Saga, Tenryuji
Ukyo-ku, Kyoto
Arashiyama Station
Tel: 075-861-0277

NISHIKI: *Kaiseki Cuisine*
Nakanoshima Koen
Ukyo-ku, Kyoto
Arashiyama Station
Tel: 075-871-8888

OHARA: *Simmering Tofu and Kaiseki*
Torii-moto, Saga
Ukyo-ku, Kyoto
Arashiyama Station
Tel: 075-871-1788

TAKEMURA: *Simmering Tofu*
Tenryu-ji, Hokuzoji-cho 48
Ukyo-ku, Kyoto
Arashiyama Station
Tel: 075-861-1483

HAKUUN-AN: *Fucha Cuisine*
Obaku, Manpuku-ji
Uji-shi (South of Kyoto)
Obaku Station
Tel: 0774-31-8017

Appendix B
Directory of Tofu Manufacturers

This directory has been updated to 22 February 2001

UNITED STATES

ALAKSA

99517 Anchorage—
Northland Soy Products, 2905 Tanglewood Place. Ph: 907-248-2326. Bernie Souphanavong

ARKANSAS

72701 Fayetteville—
Summercorn Foods, 1410 West Cato Springs Rd. Ph: 501-521-9338. David Druding

CALIFORNIA

90012 Los Angeles—
Visoy, 111 West Elmyra. Ph: 213-221-4079. David Ma

90022 Los Angeles—
Mighty Soy Inc., 1227 S. Eastern Ave. Ph: 213-266-6969. Maung Myint

90032 Los Angeles—
American Food Co. / AFC Trading, 4738 Valley Blvd. Ph: 213-223-7738. Jackson Wu

90249 Gardena—
Sumiyoshi-ya Foods USA, 1429 West 134th St. Ph: 310-538-2626. Seizo "Bob" Tanibata

90280 Southgate—
Pulmuone U.S.A, Inc., 4585 Firestone Blvd. Ph: 213-564-3000.

92020 El Cajon—
San Diego Soy Dairy, 1330 Hill St., Suite B. Ph: 619-447-0129. Gary Stein

92683 Westminster—
Tan Tan Tofu, 15084 Weststate St. Ph: 714-895-3565. Kim Lai

92841 Garden Grove—
House Foods America Corp., 7351 Orangewood Ave. Ph: 714-901-4350.

93706 Fresno—
Louie Foods International, 471 So. Teilman Ave. Ph: 209-264-2745. Jay Louie

93706 Fresno—
Tofuji, 664 "F" St. Ph: 559-696-0838. Fujie Robesky

94080 South San Francisco—
Quong Hop & Co., 161 Beacon St. Ph: 650-553-9900. J. Frank Stephens.

94124 San Francisco—
Golden Gate Tofu Inc., 1265 Griffith St. Ph: 415-822-5618. Robert Chen

94124 San Francisco—
Vitasoy USA Inc.-Azumaya, 1575 Burke Ave. Ph: 415-285-8500 Factory.

94510 Benicia—
North Coast Distributors (Tofu Life), 4860 East 2nd St. Ph: 707-747-1482. Hanan Onn

94544 Hayward—
China Tofu, 1781 Addison Way. Ph: 510-782-9728. Po Hsiang Lin

94545 Hayward—
Pure Land Co., 3456 Depot Rd. Ph: 510-670-8621. Jim Pong

94587 Union City—
China Tofu, 3222 Whipple Rd. Ph: 510-489-7288. Po Hsiang Lin

94806 San Pablo—
Ahimsa Gourmet, 1520 International Marketplace (1520 El Portal Dr.). Ph: 510-235-8343. Van Thi Dang

95062 Santa Cruz—
Wildwood Natural Foods of Santa Cruz, Inc., 1560 Mansfield Ave. Ph: 831-476-4448 SC or 800-499-8638 Fairfax. Jeremiah Ridenour

95111 San Jose—
Hung Vuong Tofu #2, 4138 Monterey Rd. Ph: 408-229-9255. Scott Truong

95112 San Jose—
San Jose Tofu Co., 175 E. Jackson St. Ph: 408-292-7026. Chester & Amy Nozaki

95122 San Jose—
Binh Minh Tofu Manufacturing, 1180 Tully Rd., Unit B. Ph: 408-279-3655. Binh Tran

95521 Arcata—
Tofu Shop Specialty Foods Inc., 100 Erickson Court, Suite 150. Ph: 707-822-7401. Matthew Schmit

95822 Sacramento—
Wa Heng Dou-Fu Soy Sauce, 2451 26th Ave., #1. Ph: 916-737-0545. Martin Peng-Xiang Lin

95826 Sacramento—
Sacramento Tofu Mfg. Co., 8300 Belvedere Ave. Ph: 916-383-0725. Alvin Kunishi

95928 Chico—
California Kitchen, 1919 Park Ave. Ph: 530-342-1405. Cal Parrot

COLORADO

80205 Denver—
Denver Tofu Co., 3825 Blake St. Ph: 303-298-8638 (298-TOFU). Mr. Haruhisa Yamamoto

80301 Boulder—
White Wave, Inc., 1990 North 57th Court. Ph: 303-443-3470. Steve Demos

DISTRICT OF COLUMBIA

20002 Washington—
Superfoods, 1257 4th St. Ph: 202-546-5205. Tom Lee

FLORIDA

33138 Miami—
Fully Foods, 400 N.E. 67th St., Bay D. Ph: 305-758-3880. Manny Wong

33567 Plant City—
Marjon Specialty Foods, Inc., 3508 Sydney Rd. Ph: 813-752-3482. John & Marcia Miller

GEORGIA

30324 Atlanta—
W & W Bean Products, Inc., dba Valco of Atlanta, Inc., 2059 Manchester St. N.E. Ph: 404-874-3650. Eric Wang

HAWAII

96720 Hilo, Hawaii—
Oshiro Tofu Products Inc., 738 Kinoole St. Ph: 808-935-6903. Masayuki Oshiro

96720 Hilo, Hawaii—
Tomori's Tofu Factory, 909 West Kawailani St. Ph: 808-959-8516. Albert Tomori

96746 Kapaa, Kauai—
Kapaa Poi Factory, 1181 Kainahola Rd. Ph: 808-822-5426. Kembo & Sophie Fujinaga

96749 Keaau (near Hilo), Hawaii—
Natural Pacific Tofu, 15-205 Wiliama Place. Ph: 808-966-9579. Tyler Katibah

96766 Lihue, Kauai—
Matsumoto Tofu Shop, 3469 Maono St. Ph: 808-245-6141. Mr. Matsumoto

96786 Wahiawa, Oahu—
Hawaii Tofu, 322-A Palm St. Ph: 808-621-6949. Donald Akiyama

96786 Wahiawa, Oahu—
Rural Food Products, 117 Mango St. Ph: 808-621-5603. Mr. Haruo Honda

96793 Wailuku, Maui—
Tamashiro Tofu Shop, 326 Alahee Dr. Ph: 808-244-5215. Mr. Tokusaburo Tamashiro

96793 Wailuku, Maui—
Teruya Tofu Factory, 1830 Mill St. Ph: 808-244-5313. Mr. Takeshi (Walter) Teruya

96814 Honolulu, Oahu—
Kanai Tofu Factory (RMR Inc.)., 515 Ward Ave. Ph: 808-538-1305. Richard K. Kaneda

96817 Honolulu, Oahu—
Aala Tofu Co., 513 Kaaahi St. Ph: 808-845-0221. Mr. Shojin Yamauchi

Honolulu, Oahu—
Aloha Tofu Factory, 961 Akepo Ln. Ph: 808-845-2669. Jack & Kazu Uehara

ILLINOIS

60616 Chicago—
Mei Shun Tofu Products Co., 523 W. 26th St. Ph: 312-842-7000. Louis Hong

60616-1803 Chicago—
Nomura Tofu Co., 2904 W. Fullerton St. Ph: 718-791-9111. William Woo

60626 Chicago—
MU Tofu Shop, 1735 W. Greenleaf Ave. Ph: 773-743-1339. Rebecca & Yoshiharu Uchida

IOWA

50112 Grinnell—
Midwest Harvest Corp., 3635 Hwy 146. Ph: 515-236-5170. Tom Lacina

52556 Fairfield—
American Pride Soyfoods Inc., P.O. Box 524, 1603 N. Fourth St. Ph: 515-472-4881. Alex Green

KANSAS

66044 Lawrence—
Central Soyfoods, 11 West 14th St. Ph: 785-843-0653. Jim Cooley

LOUISIANA

70072 Marrero—
Mai Tofu, 4025 Cypress St. Ph: 504-347-7784. Tung Dac Ho

MARYLAND

21045 Columbia—
Wen's Food, Inc., 9179-E Red Branch Rd. Ph: 410-730-6699. Ting-yi Wen

21075 Elkridge—
Natural, Inc., 6650 Santa Barbara Rd. Ph: 888-868-2858. William Tsai

21750 Hancock—
Takoma Soy Inc., 11 South Pennsylvania Ave. Ph: 301-678-5283. Ed Mueller

MASSACHUSETTS

01230 Great Barrington—
Smoke & Fire Natural Foods, Inc., P.O. Box 743. Ph: 413-528-6891. Jose Antunes

01432 Ayer—
Nasoya Foods, One New England Way. Ph: 1-800-229-8638 (TOFU). Fred Eaton

02142-1511 Cambridge—
Chang Shing Tofu, 37-39 Rogers St. Ph: 617-628-2224 PL. Cathy & Albert Huynh

02154 Waltham—
Yah Kee, Inc., 108 Clematis Ave. #G. Ph: 781-642-8999. James Wong

MICHIGAN

48067 Royal Oak—
Michigan Soy Products, 1213 N. Main St. Ph: 248-544-7742. Dorothy Hwang

48103 Ann Arbor—
Tree Town Tofu, 396 West Washington St. Ph: 313-663-8429 (TOFU). John Gingrich

48108 Ann Arbor—
Rosewood Products, Inc., 738 Airport Blvd., Suite 6. Ph: 734-665-2222. Bruce Rose

MINNESOTA

55331 Excelsior—
Organic Foods, Inc., 534 Smithtown Ct. Ph: 612-474-3989. Tom & Donna Stacey

MISSOURI

64141 Kansas City—
Chunco Foods Inc., 1400 E. 2nd St., P.O. Box 883. Ph: 816-283-0716. Peter Chun

NEW JERSEY

08221 Linwood—
Clofine Dairy & Food Products, Inc., P.O. Box 335, 1407 New Road. Ph: 800-441-1001. Richard Eluk

NEW YORK

10474 Bronx—
MSB Food Enterprises, Inc., 710 Longfellow Ave. Ph: 718-617-4105. Michael Lee

10960 Nyack—
Local Tofu, 203 Main St. Ph: 914-358-2309. Sam Weinreb

10989 Valley Cottage—
Global Protein Foods, 707 Executive Blvd., Bldg. E. Ph: 914-268-8100. Anson Wong

14611-2424 Rochester—
Northern Soy Inc., 545 West Ave. Ph: 716-235-8970. Andy Schecter

14850 Ithaca—
Ithaca Tofu, 23 Cinema Dr. Ph: 607-266-0336. Michael Pan

OHIO

43338-1019 Mt. Gilead—
Soytein Inc., 408 Douglas St. Ph: 614-766-0688. Y.K. "Bill" Lui

45896 Waynesfield—
VitaLite Foods, 103 S. Westminster St., P.O. Box 10. Ph: 419-568-8638. Frederick J. Osheskie

OREGON

97214 Portland—
Dae Han, Inc., 737 S.E. Alder St. Ph: 503-233-8638. Yeun Mo Koo

97214 Portland—
Ota Family Tofu, 812 S.E. Stark St. Ph: 503-232-8947. Eileen Ota

97401-2524 Eugene—
Surata Soyfoods Cooperative, 325 West 3rd Ave., Bldg. A. Ph: 541-485-6990. Steve Shevah Lambert

97520-1883 Ashland—
Ashland Soy Works, 225 Water St. Ph: 541-482-1865. James & Diana Muhs

PENNSYLVANIA

18103 Allentown—
Fresh Tofu Inc., 1101 Harrison St. Ph: 610-433-4711. Gary Abramowitz

19123 Philadelphia—
Sun Kee, 448-452 North 12th St. Ph: 215-625-3818. Yatsun Wen

TENNESSEE

38483 Summertown—
FarmSoy Company, 96C The Farm. Ph: 931-964-2411. Tom Elliott

TEXAS

75212 Dallas—
Dallas Calco, 2726 Barge Lane Ph: 214-331-6122. Louis Wang

77003 Houston—
Houston Calco Inc., 2400 Dallas St. Ph: 713-236-8668. Kent Wang

77099 Houston—
Banyan Foods, Inc., 10940 S. Wilcrest Dr. Ph: 281-575-8801. Carol Chiu

UTAH

84104 Salt Lake City—
Nature Jim's, 2119 W. Alexander St. Ph: 801-972-9767. George Reynolds

VIRGINIA

22902 Charlottesville—
Sunergia Soyfoods, P.O. Box 1186. Ph: 804-970-2798. Jon Kessler

WASHINGTON

98070 Vashon—
Island-Spring, Inc., P.O. Box 747. Ph: 206-463-9848. W.M. Luke & Suni Lukoskie

98402 Tacoma—
Tacoma Soyfoods, 1302 Martin Luther King Jr. Way. Ph: 206-627-5085. Jim Van Wie

98499 Tacoma—
Han Yang Oriental Food Manufacturing, 3819 94th St., S.W. Ph: 253-588-7303. John Choi

98814 Carlton—
Methow Valley Foods, P.O. Box 247. Ph: 509-996-2372. Joyce Campbell

99156 Newport—
Small Planet Soyfoods, 330112 Hwy 2. Ph: 509-447-5146. Phil Spiegel

WEST VIRGINIA

25276 Spencer—
Spring Creek Natural Foods, 212-C East Main St. Ph: 304-927-1815. Mark Bossert

WISCONSIN

53216-0677 Milwaukee—
Simple Soyman (The), 3901 N. 35th St., P.O. Box 16677. Ph: 1-888-588-8638. R. Jay and Barbara Gruenwald

CANADA

ALBERTA

T2E 6W3 Calgary—
Kinmen Food, Bay 8, 2219, 35 Ave. North East. Ph: 403-291-4991.

T2G 1N2 Calgary—
Norman Leong Tofu, 1034-21 Avenue South East. Ph: 403-264-1911. Norman Leong

T5H 2N4 Edmonton—
Ying Fat Food Products Ltd., 10512 - 98 St. Ph: 403-425-9489.

T5L 0X4 Edmonton—
Yat Sun Food Products, 12531 - 126 St. Ph: 403-455-8787. Kenson Quan

BRITISH COLUMBIA

V0E 2G0 Lumby—
Vibrant Health Products (Silver Hills Bakery), P.O. Box 1052. Ph: 250-547-2000.

V5L 2G1 Vancouver—
Superior Tofu Ltd., 1469 Venables St. Ph: 604-251-1888. Percy & Rita Chan

V6A 1H5 Vancouver—
Sunrise Markets Inc., 729 Powell St. Ph: 604-254-8888. Peter Joe

V6A 1P4 Vancouver—
Yet Chong Bean, 440-E Hastings St. East. Ph: 604-254-2515.

V6A IH5 Vancouver—
Sunrise Soya Foods, 729 Powell Street. Ph: 604-254-8888. Peter Joe.

V6P 5Z2 Vancouver—
Nagasawa Enterprises Ltd., 20 954 South West Marine Drive. Ph: 604-325-9511.

V6V 2J4 Richmond—
May Lian Foods Company, 150 - 13911 Maycrest Way. Ph: 604-273-1365.

V8K 2C8 Salt Spring Island—
Soya Nova Tofu Shop, 1200 Beddis Road. Ph: 604-537-9651. Debbie Lauzon

V8X 2N2 Victoria—
Islands West, 4247 Dieppe Rd. Ph: 250-727-0744.

V9A 3L4 Victoria—
Dayspring Soyacraft Corp., 5-626 Esquimalt Road. Ph: 250-382-5115. Michael Hsieh

MANITOBA

R3B 3H4 Winnipeg—
Yee's/Chung Ku, 330 King Street, Unit E. Ph: 204-947-9327. Philip Yee

NOVA SCOTIA

B0P 1M0 Grand Pre—
Acadiana Soy Products, P.O. Box 34. Ph: 902-542-5511.

B2G 2L2 Antigonish—
Maritime Soycraft, R.R. #4, Harbour Centre. Ph: 902-863-3978. Sian Newman-Smith

ONTARIO

K0G 1K0 Lanark—
Pulse Foods, R.R. 2. Ph: 613-256-6638.

K1B 4E4 Ottawa—
Fung's (Meliwa Food Products), 2555 Blackwell St., Bay 103. Ph: 613-745-8225.

K1G 3N2 Gloucester—
Kitchen Sprouts Farm (Capital Bean Products Company), 8-4095 Belgreen Drive. Ph: 613-737-1095.

K1Z 5M3 Ottawa—
Pine River Bean Products Company, 309 Athlone Avenue. Ph: 613-798-8110.

K4M 1A5 Manotick—
Guilt-Free Fine Foods, P.O. Box 553. Ph: 613-692-7001.

L3R 9W5 Markham—
Yin On Food Products Inc., 8392 Kennedy Rd., Unit A-16. Ph: 905-948-0325.

L4L 8Z3 Woodbridge—
Summer Fresh Salads Incorporated, 181 Sharer Rd. Ph: 905-856-8816.

M1B 3J5 Scarborough—
Veg-A-King Food, 33 Casebridge Court, Units 5 & 6. Ph: 416-283-8328.

M1B 5P3 Scarborough—
Pak Fok Food Products Inc., 50 Thornmount Drive, Unit 24. Ph: 416-208-7050. Simon Kwan

M1J 1A2 Scarborough—
Full Fortune Foods Inc., 489 Brimley Rd., Unit 20. Ph: 416-266-9113.

M1R 3C7 Scarborough—
Wing Loon Food Products Company Ltd., 105 Howden Rd. Ph: 416-755-1050.

M1V 5B6 Scarborough—
Heng Lee Food Products Company Ltd., 605 Middle Field Rd., Unit 11. Ph: 416-299-6086.

M4M 2T4 Toronto—
Hollend Enterprises Inc., 388 Carlaw Ave., Unit 102. Ph: 416-466-9777.

M4T 2S8 Toronto—
Loblaw Brands Limited, 22 St. Clair Ave. East. Ph: 416-967-2501.

M5J 2S7 Toronto—
Tofu Berry Inc., 33 University Ave., Suite 505. Ph: 416-363-1900.

M5T 1L1 Toronto—
Yet Sing Co., 11 Baldwin St. Ph: 416-977-3981. Tony Wong

M5T 2K1 Toronto—
Fong On Food Limited, 46 Kensington Avenue. Ph: 416-598-7828.

M6N 1X8 Toronto—
Pyung Hwa Food Co., 115 McCormack St. Ph: 416-767-7604. Mr. Jhasun Koo

M6N 3P1 Toronto—
Tofu Superior Co., 175 Weston St. Ph: 416-766-3332.

M6P 1Y6 Toronto—
Soy City Foods, Div. of The Golden Age Food Ltd., 2847 Dundas Street West. Ph: 416-762-3927.

M8W 2T7 Etobicoke—
New Chao Phong Food Processing Ltd., 486 Evans Ave., Unit 1A. Ph: 416-252-8228.

M8Y 2V9 Etobicoke—
Wah Chong Tofu, 31 Windsor St., Unit 10. Ph: 416-251-9310. Chiu Ping

M8Z 2R6 Etobicoke—
Samson Produce Inc., 11 Lockport Avenue. Ph: 416-239-1276.

M8Z 5Y2 Etobicoke—
Sunrise Food Products, Inc., 30 Titan Rd., Unit 15. Ph: 416-239-7232.

N8X 2A9 Windsor—
Ruey Feng Trading Co. Ltd., 1519 Crawford Avenue. Ph: 519-258-4112.

QUEBEC

H2S 3K2 Montreal—
Produits Alimentaires Oriental Food Products Inc., 6909 Marconi St. Ph: 514-272-9580.

H2V 1K1 Montreal—
Wah Hoa Eng., 1169 Van Horne Ave. Ph: 514-277-5394.

H2Z 1G5 Montreal—
Epicerie Kein Vinh Corporation, 1062—1066 St-Laurent. Ph: 514-393-1030.

H4C 2Z3 Montreal—
Les Aliments Horium Foods Inc., 1050 rue Lacasse, C1-18. Ph: 514-933-4605. Mr. Chong-Hong Ho

H4C 3N8 Montreal—
Les Aliments Panda Foods Inc., 4800 St. Ambroise, Suite 111. Ph: 514-846-0824.

H4P 1J3 Montreal—
Les Aliments Din Ho, Inc., 5475 Royal Mount, Suite 123. Ph: 514-735-9502.

H7S 2G2 Laval—
Hannah Foods, 1995 Francis-Hughes. Ph: 514-629-3900.

J0L 2A0 St-Isidore, Co. Laprairie—
Unisoya Inc., 185 Boyer St. Ph: 514-454-5123. Real & Bernard Beaulieu

J2S 8K4 St. Hyacinthe—
Nutrisoya Foods, Inc., 4050 Pinard St. Ph: 514-796-4261. Nick Feldman

J4Y 2R2 Brossard—
Les Aliments Tarasoy Ltée, 3455 Local D, rue Isabelle. Ph: 514-659-6586. Helen Wan

J7H 1M6 Boisbriand—
Les Mets Du Commensal Inc., 3737 Grande-Allee. Ph: 514-949-3311.

J8Y 3S2 Hull—
La Soyarie, Inc., 94 Adrien Robert St. Ph: 819-777-6716. Koichi & Francine Watanabe

OUTSIDE NORTH AMERICA

AUSTRALIA, Kilsyth, VIC 3137—
Blue Lotus Foods, 9/83 Canterbury Road. Ph: (03) 728 6011. Beng Eu

AUSTRALIA, Sheffield, Tasmania—
7306 P.O. Box 157. Trishala Shub

AUSTRIA, A-2514 Traiskirchen—
Sojarei Vollwertkost GmbH, Roemerstrasse 14. Ph: (02252) 559 01. Guenter Ebner

BELGIUM, B-2320 Hoogstraten—
Benelux Soya N.V., Industrieweg 3. Ph: 03-314-5632. J. Singh

BELGIUM, B-9830 Sint-Martens-Latem—
Lima n.v. / Lima Foods, P.O. Box 59, Edgar Gevaertdreef 10. Ph: 91-82-4176. Lydia Verkelten

BRAZIL, Nova Friburgo, RJ—
Centro Ecobiotico do Brasil Ltda., Rua Apolinario Correa da Silva, 30 Conejo / CEP 28620.

BURKINA FASO, Ouagadougu—
Total Texaco Burkina, B.P. 359.

COLOMBIA, Santafe de Bogota—
Delisoya, Calle 78 No. 12-03. Ph: +57 1-346-2178 OF. Nestor and Cecilia Santacruz M.

CROATIA, 51215 Kastav (near Rijeka)—
Anyo, Skolska Ulica 43A. Ph: 051-274-527. Ivan Jugovac

CROATIA, Zagreb-Horvacanski zavoj 15—
Medielektronik Zagreb, d.o.o. za promet 1 usluge. Mr. Slavko Maric

CROATIA, Zagreb—
SoyaLab, Nad Miljenko

CZECH REPUBLIC, 272 00 Kladno—
Tofu Company, Dalimilova 1730. Ph: 0312/5065. Pavel Petracek

CZECH REPUBLIC, 27 00 Kladno—
VETO, Tr. Sportovcu. Mr. Pavel Petracek

DENMARK, DK-1454 Copenhagen—
Scandinavian Soya, Larsbjoernstrade 20. Ph: 02-85-9669. Thomas Andersen

DOMINICAN REPUBLIC, Santo Domingo—
UFIESA. Div. of Productos Nutrisoya, Calle 33, #9-A, Villa Carmen Este. Ph: 809-590-3418. Mr. Leonidas R. Ubiera

EGYPT, Giza—
National Agricultural Research Project (NARP) 263-0152, Agricultural Research Center, 9 El Gamma St. Dr. Neil Patrick

EGYPT, 6th of October City, Giza—
Egyptian American Dairy Prods. Est., Albasoy, Lot 15, Block 6, Industrial Area #1. Ph: 711-816. Aladin S. Hassan

EL SALVADOR, San Salvador—
Soya, Vida y Nutricion S.A. de C.V., Calle del Marmara y Av. Rio Lempa No. 44, Colonia Jardines de Guadelupe, La Libertad, Antiguo Cuscatlan. Mr. Bruno Claeys

FINLAND, SF-10601 Ekenas—
Oy Makrobios Ab, P.B. 86.

FRANCE, F-04210 Valensole—
Marinus Janssen Tofu Shop, Le Grand Villars. Marinus Janssen

FRANCE, F-26560 Sederon—
Tofoulie, St. Pierre. Ph: 7528.5505. Joel Pichon

FRANCE, F-31250 Revel (near Toulouse)—
Nutrition et Soja S.A., Z.I. de la Pomme, B.P. 33. Ph: +33 62 18 72 50. Bernard Storup

FRANCE, F-35531 Noyal-sur-Vilaine-Brittany
Sojasun Technologies / Affiliate of Laiterie Triballat, 2, rue Julien Neveu, B.P. 21. Ph: +33 299 041104. Jean & Francoise Clanchin

FRANCE, F-68500 Issenheim—
Sojinal (Soja Innovation Alimentaire), Div. of B & K Holdings, 8 rue Merxheim. Ph: +33 389-74.5353 or 389.74.1707. Maurice Rochet

FRANCE, F-75013 Paris—
Le Bol en Bois, 35 Rue Pascal. Ph: 707-2724. Noboru Sakaguchi

GERMANY, D-22607 Hamburg—
Tofumanufaktur Christian Nagel GmbH, Osdorfer Landstrasse 4. Ph: 040-89 4937. Christian Nagel

GERMANY, D-27572 Bremerhaven—
Geestland, An der Packhalle V, Nr. 1. Ph: (0471) 971 20 63. Paul E. Bremer

GERMANY, D-34127 Kassel—
Kassel Tofu Kato, Angersbachstr. 2. Ph: 0561-844-81. Heike Hellerung

GERMANY, D-53881 Euskirchen-Kuchenheim—
Viana Naturkost GmbH, Willi Graf Str. 88,. Ph: 02251-94460 OF. Bernd Drosihn

GERMANY, D-55413 Trechtingshausen—
Sojafarm, Im Paradis. Ph: 06721-6470. Lothar Stassen

GERMANY, D-59269 Beckum—
Berief Feinkost GmbH, Kerkbrede 3 (Roland). Ph: +49 2521 18081. Hermann Berief

GERMANY, D-6078 Neu Isenburg—
Hanyang Sojaprodukte GmbH, Hermannstr. 31. Ph: 06102/21956.

GERMANY, D-6719 Lautersheim—
Das Tofuhaus, Hauptstrasse 13. Ph: 06351-43718. Albert Hess

GERMANY, D-78052 Villingen—
Naturkost Zollhaeusle, Zollhausleweg 5. Ph: +49 07721-21289. Harmut Rainer Hauser

GERMANY, D-79108 Freiburg—
Life Food GmbH, Taifun-Produkte, Bebelstrasse 8. Ph: 0761 / 15210-0. Wolfgang Heck

GERMANY, D-83254 Breitbrunn am Chiemsee—
Soto Tofu, Wolffbergerstr. 47. Ph: 08054/1283. Rolf Barthof (Prabuddha)

GUATEMALA, Amatitlan—
Rey Sol, Colonia el Recreo, Lote No. 9. Ph: +502 633-0971. Mario Cesar Jimenez

GUATEMALA, Solola, San Bartolo—
Alimentos de San Bartolo, Lecheria de Soya, Apartado Postal 118. Ph: 502-514896.

HONG KONG, Tai Po, N.T.—
Amoy Industries (International) Ltd., Tai Po Industrial Estate, Whole Bldg., 11-15 Dai Fu Street. Ph: 665-6633.

HUNGARY, 1095 Budapest—
Interprotein Feherje es Biotechnologiani kft, Soroksari ut 58. Mrs. Zsuzsanna Rak

INDIA, Allahabad 211 002—
Shayam Biri Works (P) Ltd., 44, Thornhill Rd. Ph: 53608. Shyama Charan Gupta

INDIA, Bombay—
Mishra Soya Food Products Pvt. Ltd., Vasudeo Nagar, Parsi Panchayat Rd., Andhieri (East). Ph: 632-0627. P.K. Mishra

INDIA, Indore, MP 452 001—
General Foods Ltd., 101, Mahakosh House, 7/5 South Tukoganj, Opp. Nathmandir. Ph: +91 0731 22135.

INDIA, K. Pudur, Madurai 625 007—
Palaami Food Products India (P) Ltd., I 1/C Sidco Industrial Estate. Ph: 91+ 452-43224. Mr. Prem Palanivel

INDIA, Kanpur 208 001—
Tofu India, 58/4 Ram Sadan, Birhana Road. Ph: 66566. Mr. M.S. Grewal

INDIA, Lucknow 226 019—
Gyan Food Products, 5 Ashok Nagar, Gautam Budh Marg. Ph: 52 24 9494. Praveen Chandra

INDIA, New Delhi 110 016—
Soyami Foods, Z-6, Haug Khas. S.P. Aggrawal

INDIA, Secunderabad 500 003—
Supreme Proteins & Oils Ltd., Chency Trade Centre, 116 Park Lane. Ph: 823 253. Ms. Naidu

INDONESIA, Surabaya 60223—
Halim Jaya Tofu Industries, Jalan Mastrip 183-B. Handoko Halim

IRELAND, Malahide, Co. Dublin—
Molly Turner Tofu & Tempeh, The Hill. Ph: 01-845-3853. Molly Turner

ISRAEL, Dimona 86000—
Nature's Gate Ltd., Mivne Taaseya Haradash 76, P.O. Box 029. Ph: 972-7-655-7774.

ISRAEL, M.P. Mercaz 73188—
High Design, Moshav Shilat. Eli Ben-Gad

ISRAEL, 96 Tal-shachar 76805—
Kafri-Bari Mashak-Wyler, Ph: 972-8-349-263. David Wyler

ISRAEL, Hofit 40295—
Tiltan Ha Argaman, P.O. Box 76. Ph: 972 (0)53-607435. Asher Roy

ISRAEL, Jerusalem 90885—
Jerusalem Tofu, Moshav Aminadav. Ph: 02-642-6981. Simha / Susan Ergas

ISRAEL, Jerusalem 93272 —
Tasty Tofu, Kannhai Hagalil 25. Iris & Eli Mor

ISRAEL, Kfar-Saba—
Tiltan Haargaman, Ph: +972-53-607-435. Roy Grant

ITALY, 36061 Bassano del Grappa (Vicenza)—
Defontaine s.n.c., di Mattiello R. & Congedo A, Via Torreselle, 24.

ITALY, 34170 Gorizia—
Biolab, Via dei Grabizio, 11. Ph: +39 0481 533522. Massimo Santinelli

ITALY, 90139 Palerno
Giacomo Tofu. Via Onorato N. 46. Ph: 091-325-813. Mr. Riccobono Giacomo

JAMAICA, Kingston 20—
Country Farmhouse Soya Products Co., Ltd., Affiliate of the Country Farmhouse Lifeline, 12 Faulkner Ave., Duhaney Park. Ph: +98 1809-983-2244. Marlon B. D'Aguilar

JAPAN, Aisaka Towada City, Aomori Prefecture 034—
Wadaken Food Co., Ltd., 1163 Aza Takashimizu. Ph: +81 176/252111.

JAPAN, Fujisawa-shi 251—
Maruka Shokuhin, Kanagawa-ken, Fujigaoka 2-10-2. Ph: 046-626-3261.

JAPAN, Fukuoka-ken 822-01—
Taiyo Shokuhin, Wakamiya-cho, Shimofujiwara 400-1 Oaza. Ph: 094-952-3141.

JAPAN, Fukuoka-ken 838—
Okay Shokuhin, Miwa-cho. Ph: 094-622-7131.

JAPAN, Isezaki-shi 372—
Nihon Beans, Gunma-ken, Kita Senmoku-cho 1435. Ph: 027-024-8111.

JAPAN, Itami-shi, Hyogo-ken—
Tajimaya, Ikejiri 7-139. Ph: (0727) 77-3939.

JAPAN, Kanagawa-ken—
Home Shokuhin Co., 1090 Kosono Ayase-shi. Ph: 046-777-6621. Tokusaburo Osawa

JAPAN, Kobe 652—
Fuji Oil Co. Ltd (Kobe Factory), Hamanaka-cho 2-18-24, Hyogo-ku. Ph: +81 078-652-3215. Yukio Miyazawa

JAPAN, Kobe Hyogo-ken—
Nada Kobe Seikyo, Higashi 5-1-9, Higashinada-ku Sumiyoshi. Ph: 078-811-0001.

JAPAN, Okazaki-shi— Aichi-ken 444-21—
Marusan-Ai Co. Ltd., 1 Arashita, Niki-cho, (P.O. Box 444-21). Ph: +81 056427 3710.

JAPAN, Sapporo-shi 062—
Nichiryo Daily Shokuhin, Hokkaido, Higashi X 148 Toyohira-ku. Ph: 011-851-1364.

JAPAN, Tokyo 130—
Tengu Tofu, Kotobashi 4-29-16, Sumida-ku. Ph: 03-653-4411.

JAPAN, Tokyo 166—
Yamato Tofu, Horinouchi 3-16-45, Suginami-ku. Ph: 03-312-1101.

JAPAN, Tokyo 170—
Asahi Food Processing Co. Ltd., No. 3 Kinzumen Bldg., 4-21-6 Higashi Ikebukuro, Toshima-ku. Ph: +81 3-3987-2176. Hiromu Morita

LEBANON, Beirut—
Inoshi, P.O. Box 175360. Ph: 0366-7678. Helen Marale Emmian

MEXICO, Guadalajara— Jalisco
Valencia Martin Tofu. Avenida Ninos Heroes #1633-307. Jaimie Valencia Martin

MEXICO, Veracruz, VER 91700—
Organica-ecotienda, Xicotencatl 653-18, Col. Centro. Ph: 29-31-30-83. Pat Hayward

NEPAL, Kathmandu—
Nepal Tofu Factory, P.O. Box 5250, 20/321 Naya Bazar. Ph: 4-13101. Mr. T.B. Gubhaju

NETHERLANDS, 6374 AG Landgraaf—
Heuschen-Schrouff B.V., Sperwerweg 7-9. Ph: +31 45-5323700. Mr. Wil Puik

NETHERLANDS, 2521 BB Den Haag—
Vanka-Kawat B.V., 3e van de Kunstraat 18. Ph: 070-388-8804. Mr. G.L. Van Kasteren

NETHERLANDS, 6381 BW Ubach over Worms—
Heuschen-Schrouff B.V., Reeweg 137. Ph: 31-045-311998. Mr. Wil Puik

NETHERLANDS, 6468 EJ Kerkrade—
Tempe Produkten B.V., Tunnelweg 107. Ph: 045-45-5803. J. Singh

NEW ZEALAND, Auckland—
Tofu Shop Ltd., 89 Dominion Road, Mt. Eden. Mr. Ron Hoy Fong

NEW ZEALAND, Motueka 7161—
Soy Works, 205A High St. Ph: +64 3 528-6361. LeeAnn Brereton

NEW ZEALAND, Penrose, Auckland—
Bean Supreme Ltd., 14 Hugo Johnston Dr., P.O. Box 12082. Ph: 09 5710-0592. Trevor Johnston

PHILIPPINES, Buhangin, Davao City 8000—
Lotus Food Products, Km. 6, Diversion Rd. Andrew Rawlings

POLAND, 05-830 Rozalin
Polsoja, ul. Parole 36A. Ph: +48 (22) 729-9100. Piotr Poninski

PORTUGAL, 4970-249 Arcos de Valdevez—
Nutrideias - Industria Alimentar, L.da, Loteamento Industrial de Paco, Lote 20. Ph: +351 258-480 040. Roy Kamiki

RUSSIA, 350063 Krasnodar—
Soya, Inc., Affiliate of ASSOY, Distributor for ProSoya, Inc., ul. Mira 28. Ph: +7 8612/523366, 525614. A. Podobedov

SINGAPORE, Singapore 2261—
Fortune Food Manufacturing Pte. Ltd., 348 Jalan Boon Lay. Ph: +65 266 4188.

SINGAPORE, Singapore 2263—
Fraser & Neave (Singapore) Pte., Ltd., 457 Jalan Ahmad Ibrahim. Ph: +65 861-7600. Kain Sze Kwok

SINGAPORE, Singapore 2263—
Fraser & Neave (Singapore) Pte., Ltd., 457 Jalan Ahmad Ibrahim. Ph: +65 861-7600. Melvin Wee

SINGAPORE, Singapore 758089—
Unicurd Food Co. Pte. Ltd., 18, Senoko South Road. Ph: +65 759-2855. Francis N.K. Goh

SLOVAKIA, 913 03 Drietoma 85—
Sojaprodukt, Ph: +42 31 99 283.

SPAIN, E-01001 Vitoria-Gasteiz—
Zuaitzo Proteinas Vegetales, Plaza Santa Maria, 2 Bajo 1 Izda. Ph: 945-28-8630. Javier Arocena Aramburu

SPAIN, E-08180 Moia (Barcelona)—
La Sojeria, S.C., Carretera de Vic Km. 30. Ph: (93) 830 1123. Mario Rimoldi

SPAIN, E-08183 Castellcir (Barcelona)—
Vegetalia, S.L. / Productos Naturales, Plaza de l'Era S/N, Ph: 93-866 6161. Salvador Sala

SPAIN, E-08183-Castelltercol, Barcelona—
Natursoy, Josep Galles 36-52. Ph: 93.866.60.42. Sra. Carmen Asensio

SPAIN, E-18015 Granada—
Tofu Company, Avda. de Andalucia 99 5 D. Juan del Castillo Lopes

SPAIN, Granada Capilerilla—
Pitres 18414. Sra. Jane A. Garbutt

SWEDEN, S-37482 Karlshamn—
Carlshamn Mejeri AB, Vastra Kajen. Ph: +46 454-82500.

SWITZERLAND, CH-3123 Belp—
Galactina AG., Birkenweg 1-6. Ph: 031-81-1111. Conrad Seewer

SWITZERLAND, CH-3714 Frutigen—
Berner Tofurei, Obere Bahnhofstrasse. Ph: 33-671-3090.

SWITZERLAND, CH-8909 Zwillikon—
Genossenschaft Tofurei Engel, Hoftbachstr. 21. Ph: 01-761-2349.

SWITZERLAND, CH-8952 Schlieren—
Soyana, Turmstrasse 6. Ph: 01-731-1200. Walter Daenzer

TAIWAN, Kaohsiung Hsien—
Herng Yih Food Industrial Co., No. 110-6 Lung Mu Road, Ta Su Hsiang. Ph: 07-651-5511.

TRINIDAD AND TOBAGO—
Tofu Co., 240 Waterloo Road. Ph: 868-673-1476. Peter Ngai

TURKEY, Izmir 35230—
Key Gilda Inc., Sehitler CAD No. 18-6, Alsancak. Ataman Bukey

UNITED KINGDOM (ENGLAND), Portishead, Bristol BS20 9BF—
Cauldron Foods Ltd., Affiliate of Hero-Rayners & Company Ltd., Units 1-2, Portishead Business Park. Ph: +44 275 818448. Philip Marshall

UNITED KINGDOM (ENGLAND), Manchester M13 0NN—
L.S. Foods, Ltd., No. 14 Birch Lane, Longsight. Ph: 161-225-3098. George Long

UNITED KINGDOM (ENGLAND), Manchester M17 1AU—
Soya Health Foods Ltd., Unit 4, Guinness Rd., Trafford Park. Ph: 061-872-0549. Mr. Arora

UNITED KINGDOM (ENGLAND), Lewes, E. Sussex BN7 1YT—
Full of Beans, The Old Bottling Store, Castle Ditch Lane. Ph: +44 273-472627. John & Sara Gosling

UNITED KINGDOM (ENGLAND), London E1 5LP—
Clean Bean Tofu, 37e Princelet St. Ph: 0171 247 8349. Neil McLennan

UNITED KINGDOM (ENGLAND), London N1 9PD—
8Dragon & Phoenix Ltd., 15-18 White Lion St. Ph: 01-837-0146. Donald Lyen

UNITED KINGDOM (ENGLAND), Melton Mobray, Leics. LE13 1PD—
Paul's Soyfoods Ltd., 66 Snow Hill Estate. Ph: 01664 60572. Paul Jones

UNITED KINGDOM (ENGLAND), Newport Pagnell, Bucks., MK16 9PY—
Haldane Foods Group Ltd., Howard Way. Ph: +44 1 908 211311. Peter Fitch

UNITED KINGDOM (ENGLAND), York YO4 1AU—
R&R Tofu, Fold Court, Home Farm, Buttercrambe. Ph: +44 7593 72979. Ron Malarney

UNITED KINGDOM (WALES/CYMRU), Flint, Flintshire CH6 5UY—
Clark Foods, Unit 13, Manor Industrial Estate. Ph: 01352 73-5522. John Clark

Appendix C
Table of Equivalents

TEMPERATURE

$C = 5/9 (F-32)$
$F = 9/5C + 32$
$350°F = 177°C$
$375°F = 191°C$

VOLUME

1 tablespoon = 3 teaspoons = 14.75 cc.
1 cup = 236 cc = 16 tablespoons
1 quart = 4 cups = 0.946 liters
1 U.S. gallon = 4 quarts = 3.785 liters = 231 in³ = 5/6 Imperial gallon.
1 bushel = 8 gallons = 4 pecks
1 *sho* = 10 *go* = 1800 cc = 7.63 cups

WEIGHT

1 ounce = 28.38 grams
1 pound = 16 ounces = 454 grams
1 ton (U.S.) = 2,000 pounds = 0.907 metric tons

NATURAL EQUIVALENTS

1 gallon of water weighs 8.33 pounds
1 quart of soybeans weighs 1.69 pounds
1 bushel of 1st grade soybeans weighs 56 pounds

Bibliography

PUBLICATIONS ON TOFU

Additional publications relating to the manufacture of tofu and soymilk will be found in *Tofu and Soymilk Production* by Shurtleff and Aoyagi.

Abe, K. 1964. Outlook for fewer tofu producers, more production. *Soybean Digest.* May. p. 48.

Abe, Koryu. 1972. *Tofu Hyakuchin to Zokuhen.* Tokyo: Shinshu Shorin. (Original edition, 1782).

Abe, Koryu and Tsuji, Shigemitsu. 1974. *Tofu no Hon.* Tokyo, Japan: Shibata Shoten. 328 p.

Adolph, W.H. and Kiang, P.C. 1919. The nutritive value of soy bean products. *National Medical J. of China* 5:40-49.

Adolph, W.H. 1922. How China uses the soy bean as food. *J. of Home Economics* 14:63-69.

Agricultural Research. 1968. Better sufu. Nov. p. 6.

Aihara, Cornellia. 1972. *The Chico-san Cookbook.* Chico, CA: Chico-san Inc. Reissued as *Macrobiotic Kitchen* by Japan Publications in 1982. 140 p.

Aihara, H. 1974. *Soybean Diet.* Oroville, CA: George Ohsawa Macrobiotic Foundation, 164 p.

Andersen, J. 1980. *The Tofu Primer.* Berkeley, CA: Creative Arts Communications. 41 p.

Andersen, J. 1981. *Juel Andersen's Tofu Kitchen.* New York: Bantam Books. 211 p.

Andersen, Juel. 1982. *Tofu Fantasies: A Cookbook of Incomparable Desserts.* Berkeley, CA: Creative Arts. 88 p.

Anson, M.L. 1958. Potential uses of isolated oilseed proteins in foodstuffs. In *Processed Plant Protein Foodstuffs,* A.M. Altschul, ed. New York: Academic Press. p. 279.

Asahimatsu Shokuhin. 1981. *Asahimatsu Sanju-nen no Ayumi.* Iida-shi, Nagano-ken, Japan: Asahimatsu. 290 p.

Bannar, R. 1980. Let's talk tofu. *Food Engineering.* May. p. 126-28.

Barrett, C. 1982. The Hilton Hotel's gourmet tofu dishes. *Vegetarian Times.* Oct. p. 32-36.

Bauer, C. and Andersen, J. 1979. *The Tofu Cookbook.* Emmaus, PA. Rodale Press. 188 p.

Belenki, D.E. and Papowa, N.N. 1933. Soy cheese. Russian Patent 32,907 and 32,908. Oct. 31. C.A. 28:3808 (1934).

Beltzer, F.J.G. 1911. Extended utilization of soya bean products: Milk, cheese, and a variety of other products from a vegetable seed. *Scientific American Supplement.* 72(1859): 115. Aug. 19.

Beltzer, Francis J.G. 1911. Le lait vegetal, la caseine vegetale. *Revue de Chimie Industrielle et le Moniteur Scientifique Quesneville* 22(259):209-215, 22(260):241-51.

Blasedale, W.C. 1899. Some Chinese vegetable food materials. USDA OES Bull 68:32-36.

Bloch, A. 1906. Quelques mots sur la fabrication et la composition du Teou-Fou. *Bulletin des Sciences Pharmacologiques, Paris.* 13:138-143. Also in the 1906 *Archives d'Hygiene et de Medicine Coloniales.* p. 298.

Bloch, A. 1907. Le Soja. Sa culture, sa composition, son emploi en medecine et dans l'alimentation. *Bulletin des Sciences Pharmacologiques, Paris* 14:536-51, 593-606. Sept.-Oct.

Boyd, B.R. 1980. Tofu in public schools. *East West Journal.* June. p. 46-50.

Bretschneider, Emilii Vasilevich. 1881-95. *Botanicon Sinicum.* Notes on Chinese Botany from Native and Western Sources. London: Trübner & Co. 3 Vols. Issued originally in the Journal of the Royal Asiatic Society, North China Branch. Series 2, Vols. 16, 25, 29.

Bui, Quang Chieu. 1905. Les cultures vivrieres au Tonkin. *Bulletin Economique de l'Indo-Chine.* New Series 2. No. 48. p. 1152-53, 1157-68.

Bulkeley, W.M. 1979. Good old bean curd; It's suddenly popular but you call it tofu. *Wall Street Journal.* April 12. p. 1-2.

Bulkeley, W.M. 1979. The Americanization of bean curd. *Washington Post.* May 24. p. E1, E11, E26.

Burkill, I.H. 1935. *A Dictionary of the Economic Products of the Malay Peninsula.* London: Crown Agents. p. 1080-86. (The work is 2 volumes, 2400 p.)

Champion, P. 1866. Sur la fabrication du fromage de pois en Chine et au Japon. *Bull. de la Societe d'Acclimatization.* p. 562-65.

Champion, Paul. 1869. *Industries Anciennes et Modernes de l'Empire Chinois.* (Translated by Stanislas Julien.) Paris: Eugene Lacroix. p. 185-89.

Champion, P. and Lhôte, M. 1869. *Fabrication du fromage de pois. In* Julien and Champion. p. 185-89.

Chang, I.C.L. and Murray, H.C. 1949. Biological value of the protein and the mineral, vitamin, and amino acid contents of soy milk and curd. *Cereal Chemistry* 26:297-305.

Chang, K.C. ed. 1977. *Food in Chinese Culture.* New Haven, CT: Yale University Press. 429 p.

Chen, P.S. 1956. Soybeans for Health, Longevity, and Economy. Revised ed. 1973. *Soybeans for Health and a Longer Life.* New Canaan, CT: Keats Publ. Co. 178 p.

Cherniske, S.S. 1980. *Tofu: Everybody's Guide.* East Woodstock, CT: Mother's Inn Center for Creative Living. 90 p.

Chiang, Cecelia S. 1974. *The Mandarin Way.* Boston: Little, Brown and Co.

Chiu, W.C.L. 1960. Soy curd can add variety to diet. *Soybean Digest.* June. p. 8.

Chiu, W.C.L. and Van Duyne, F. 1961. Soybean curd. *Illinois Research* (Univ. of Ill. Ag. Expt. Station). Fall. p. 6-7.

Chiu, W.C.L. 1961. *The Calcium Content and Palatability of Soybean Curd from Field and Vegetable Varieties.* MSc thesis, University of Illinois, Dept. of Home Ec.

Church, M.B. 1920. Laboratory Experiments on the Manufacture of Chinese Ang-Khak in the United States. *J. of Industrial and Engineering Chemistry* 12:45-46.

Church, M.B. 1923. Soy and related fermentations. USDA Department Bulletin No. 1152, May 12. 26 p.

Clarke, Christina. 1981. *Cook with Tofu.* New York: Avon Books. 223 p.

Cohen, Richard L. 1981. Local tofu makers and sellers trying to stir up interest within food market. *San Francisco Business Journal.* Oct. 20. p. 18-19.

Colchie, E.S. 1981. Light, low calorie, and versatile tofu. *Bon Appetit.* Aug. p. 52-55.

Concepcion, I. 1943. Significance of soybean in the dietary of Filipinos. *Proceedings of the Sixth Pacific Science Congress of the Pacific Science Assoc.* July 24-Aug. 12, 1939. Vol VI. p. 437-47. Berkeley, CA: Univ of Calif. Press.

Coville, F.W. 1929. Soybean cheese. *Science* 70(1812):282-83. Sept. 20.

Cummins, J.S. 1962. *Travels and Controversies of Friar Domingo Navarrete 1618-1686.* Hakluyt Soc. Ser. 2. No. 118, Cambridge.

Dänzer, A.W. 1982. *Tofu, die Einladung ins Schlaraffenland.* Zurich: Verlag Bewusstes Dasein. 97 p.

Dänzer, A.W. 1982. *Tofu, l'Invitation au pays de cocagne.* Zurich: Editions Bewusstes Dasein. 107 p.

Dänzer, A.W. 1982. Tofu—Ein neues altes produkt aus Asien. *Reform + Diät.* June. p. 2.

Deroin, N. 1980. Tofu. *Cuisine* (Cover story). June. p. 32-38, 40, 73-75.

Dittes, F. 1929. The calcium content of soybean cheese. *J. of Home Economics.* October:779.

Dittes, Frances Linda. 1935. *Food For Life.* Madison, Tennessee: Associated Lecturers, Inc. 332 p.

Dominguez, Blanca. 1978. *Alimentacion Integral Para Una Vida Plena: Los Mil Usas de la Soya.* San Angel, Mexico: Editorial Posada. 232 p.

Drown, M.J. 1943. *Soybeans and Soybean Products as Food.* USDA Misc. Publ. No. 534. 14 p.

319

Dukess, K. 1981. Tofu, tofu everywhere. *New York Times*. Aug. 2.

DuSablon, Mary Anna. 1981. *Cooking with Tofu*. Charlotte, VT: Garden Way Publishing. 32 p.

Dyson, G.M. 1928. Mould food of the Far East. *The Pharmaceutical Journal and Pharmacist* 121:375-77. (Oct. 20, London).

Ebine, Hideo et al. 1965. *Daizu cheezu no seizoho* (Preparation of a soy cheese.) Japanese Patent 16,737. July 30.

Escuenta, E.E. 1979. *Effect of Boiling Treatment and Gata (Coconut Cream) Addition to Soymilk on the Chemical, Rheological, and Sensory Properties of Tofu*. Cornell University. PhD thesis. 155 p.

Family Circle. 1979. Tofu—The Oriental way to high-protein, low-calorie meals. July. p. 140, 157, 164.

Farm, The. 1974. *Hey Beatnick*. Summertown, TN: The Book Publishing Co. 100 p.

Farm, The. 1974. *Yay Soybeans*. Summertown, TN: The Book Publising Co. 14 p.

Farm, The. 1975. *The Farm Vegetarian Cookbook*. Summertown, TN: The Book Publishing Co. 128 pp. Revised edition by L. Hagler. 1978. 223 p.

Farm, The. 1977. *Vegetarian Prenatal Nutrition and High Protein Recipes*. Summertown, TN: The Book Publishing Co. 14 p.

Farm, The. 1979. Soybean project in Guatemala Highlands. *Plenty News* 1(2):1-3.

Farm, The. 1981. Soy Demonstration Program: *Introducing Soyfoods to the Third World*. Summertown, TN. 16 p.

Fesca, M. 1898. Die Sojabohne. *Tropenpflanzer* 2(8):233-46.

Fillip, J. 1981: The amazing tofumobile. *East West Journal*. May. p. 38-40.

FIND/SVP. 1981. *The Tofu Market: Overview of a High-Potential Industry*. New York: FIND/SVP. The Information Clearinghouse, 500 Fifth Ave., 10110. 140p.

Forbes, R.M. et al. 1983. Bioavailability of zinc in coagulated soy protein (tofu) to rats and effects of dietary calcium at a constant phytate:zinc ratio. *J. of Nutrition* 130(1):205-10.

Ford, R. 1981. *Soy Foodery Cookbook*. Santa Barbara, CA: Self published. 78 p.

Fox, Chloe and Abraham. 1983. *The Au Naturel Tofu Manual: Modern Jewish Tofu Cooking*. Montreal QUE, Canada: Au Naturel, 6110 Monkland Ave., H4A 1H4. 47 p.

Fox, M. 1980. Tofu and special diets. *Soyfoods*. Summer. p. 9.

Fox, M., O'Connor, K. and Timmins, J. 1981. *Delights of Tofu*. Greenfield, MA: Soy to the World Publishing Co. 42 p.

Fuerstenberg, Maurice. 1917. *Die Soja*. Berlin: Paul Parey. 43 p.

Gibbs, H.D. and Agcaoili, F. 1912. Soy-bean curd, an important Oriental food product. *Phillipine J. of Sci.* (A) 7:47-51.

Giraud-Gillet, J. 1942. *Le Soja: Aliment d'Avenir*. Saigon: SIDI Anct. C. Ardin. 282 p.

Goldman, S. 1977: Charles Atlas versus the Bodhisattva: An Interview with Bill Shurtleff and Akiko Aoyagi. *East West Journal*. Jan. p. 32-35.

Gurafusha. 1973. *Tofu no Ryori* (Tofu Cookery). Tokyo: Gurafusha, My Life Series, No. 15.

Haberlandt, Friedrich. 1878. *Die Sojabohne: Ergebnisse der Studien und Versuche über die Anbauwürdigkeit dieser neu einzufuhrenden Culturpflanze*. Vienna: Carl Gerold's Sohn. 119 pp.

Hagler, Lousie, ed. 1978. *The Farm Vegetarian Cookbook*, revised ed. Summertown, TN: The Book Publishing Co., 156 Drakes Ln., 38483. 223 p.

Hagler, L. 1982. *Tofu Cookery*. Summertown, TN: The Book Publishing Co., 156 Drakes Ln., 38483. 160 p.

Hall, Janice. 1981. *A Taste for Tofu*. Avalon, CA: A Marjanal Publication (P.O. Box 1363; 90704) 50 p.

Harris, R.F. et al. 1949. The composition of Chinese foods. *J. of the American Dietetic Association* 25:28-38.

Hayashi, S. 1957. Tofu takes large volume of soybeans. *Soybean Digest*. Aug. p. 26-27.

Hayashi, S. 1960. A visit to a leading tofu factory. *Soybean Digest*. May. p. 26.

Heartsong, Toni & Bob. 1977. *The Heartsong Tofu Cookbook*. Miami, FL: Banyan Books. 80 p. Revised 1978.

Hepburn, J.S. and Sohn, K.S. 1930. Do fu: An Oriental food. *American J. of Pharmacy* 102(10): 570. Oct.

Hesseltine, C.W. and Wang, H.L. 1972. Fermented soybean food products. In A.K. Smith and S.J. Circle. 1972. *Soybeans: Chemistry and Technology*. Westport, CT: AVI Publ. Co. p. 389-419.

Hoffman, J. and Keough, C. 1981. *Home Soyfood Equipment*. Emmaus, PA: Rodale Press. 80 p.

Holthaus, Fusako. 1982. *Tofu Cookery*. Tokyo: Kodansha International. 159 p.

Hommel, Rudolph P. 1937. *China at Work*. New York: John Day. p. 105-09.

Honcamp, F. 1910. Die sojabohne und ihre verwertung. *Tropenpflanzer* 14(12):613-634.

Horvath, A.A. 1927. The soybean as human food. Peking: Chinese Government Bureau of Economic Information. *Bulletin Series No. 3*. 86 pp. Also published as a series in *Chinese Economic Journal*. Sept. 1926 to April 1927.

Hosie, A. 1901: *Manchuria: Its People, Resources, and Recent History*. London: Methuen & Co. (or 1910, Boston: J.B. Millet Co.)

Hymowitz, T. and Newell, C.A. 1981. Taxonomy of the genus Glycine, domestication and uses of soybeans. *Economic Botany* 35(3):272-88.

Immegart, M. and Dansby, P.J. 1981. *The Incredible Tofu Cookbook: California Style*. P.O. Box 1146, Yorba Linda, CA 92686. 128 p.

Inouye, M. 1895. The preparation and chemical composition of tofu. *Bulletin of the College of Agriculture, Tokyo* 2(4):209-15.

Jackobs, S.L. 1983. Company finds a niche selling frozen foods made with tofu. *Wall Street Journal*. Jan. 24. p. 23.

Japanese National Tofu Assoc. 1972. *Tofu Shusetsu*. Tokyo. 20 p. Tools and techniques for making tofu in the traditional way.

JDAC: Japan Dietetic Assoc. Corp. 1964. *Standard Composition of Japanese Foods*. Tokyo: Daiichi Shuppan K.K. Bilingual: Japanese/English.

Jones, D.V.G. 1963. *The Soybean Cookbook*. New York, NY: Arco Publ. Co. 240 p.

Jordan, S. 1918. Soy beans from soup to nuts. *Country Gentleman* 83(39):7, 34, Sept 28.

Julien, S. and Champion, P. 1869. *Industries Anciennes et Modernes de L'Empire Chinois, d'Apres des Notices Traduites du Chinois*. Paris: Eugene Lacroix. p. 185-89.

Kano, S. and Iishima, S. 1899. Digestion experiments with single food materials. *Gun-i Gakko Gyofu (Bul. Army Medical College)*, Tokyo. No. 3, p. 101.

Katayama, T. 1906. On the preparation of a vegetable cheese from the protein of the soy bean. *Bulletin of the College of Agric. Tokyo Imp. Univ.* 7(1):117-119.

Kato, Yogoro. 1909. Physico-chemical studies on tofu. Chem. La. Higher Tech. School, Tokyo. *Mem. Coll. Sci. Eng.*, Kyoto. 1:325-31.

Kellner, O. and Mori. Y. 1887. Beiträge zur Kenntniss de Ernährung der Japaner. *Mitteilungen der Deutschen Gesellschaft für Natur and Völkerkunde Ostasiens, Tokyo*. 4(37):305-21.

Kellner, O. and Mori, Y. 1889. Untersuchungen über die Ernährung der Japaner. *Zeitschrift für Biologie* 25:102-22.

Kellner, O.J. 1889. Tofu Cakes. *Bulletin of the College of Agriculture. Tokyo Imperial University* 1(4):24-25.

Kellner, O., Nagaoka, M. and Kurashima, Y. 1889. Researches on the manufacture and composition of "miso." *Bulletin of the College of Agriculture, Tokyo Imperial University* 1(6):1-24.

Kempski, Karl E. 1923. *Die Sojabohne: Geschichte, Kultur und Verwendung unter besonderer Berucksichtigung der Verhältnisse in Niederländisch-Indien*. Berlin: Paul Parey. 88 p.

Kikuchi, Grace. 1974. *Tofu Recipes*. Ann Arbor, MI: Mrs. Chihiro Kikuchi, 260 Sumac Ln., 48105. 47 p.

Kinch, E. 1879. (About tofu and kori-dofu). In *A Classified and Descriptive Catalog of a Collection of Agricultural Products*, Tokyo.

Kinderlehrer, J. 1979. Tofu, Food of 10,000 flavors. *Prevention*. Jan. p. 111-23.

Krieger, V. 1981. Gestern steak, morgen tofu. *Tages Anzeiger Magazin*. Aug. 22. p. 6-12.

Krieger, V. 1982. Die tausend talente von tofu. *Naturlich* 2(5):69-73.

Kudo, S. 1976. Kori-dofu. *Shoku no Kagaku*. No. 29. p. 122-27.

Lager, Mildred. 1942. *Soy Bean Recipes: 150 Ways to Use Soy Beans as Meat, Milk, Cheese & Bread*. Los Angeles: House of Better Living. 44 p.

Lager, M. 1945. *The Useful Soybean: A Plus Factor in Modern Living*. New York, NY: McGraw-Hill. 295 p.

Lager, M. 1946. The meat without a bone. *Soybean Digest*. April. p. 22.

Lager, Mildred. 1955. *How to Use the Soybean: A Plus Factor in Modern Nutrition*. Burbank, California. Self published. 115 p.

Lager, M. and Jones, D.V.G. 1963. *The Soybean Cookbook*. New York, NY: The Devin-Adair Co. 240 p.

Landgrebe, G. 1978. *Tofu Goes West*. Palo Alto, CA: Fresh Press. 114 p.

Landgrebe, G. 1981. *Tofu at Center Stage*. Palo Alto, CA: Fresh Press. 114 p.

Langgaard, A. 1878. Bemerkungen ueber den naehrwerth des tofu nach analysen von J. Schimoyama. *Mitteilungen der Deutschen Gesellschaft fur Natur- und Volkerkunde Ostasiens* 2:268-69, 271.

Langworthy. C.F. 1897. Soybeans as food for man. *USDA Farmers Bulletin* No. 58. p. 20-23. Revised 1899.

Lappe, F.M. 1971. *Diet for a Small Planet*. New York: Ballantine Books. 410 p. Revised 1975 and 1982.

L'aurore. 1979. *La Cuisine au Tofu: Un Art Japonais*. Montreal, QUE, Canada. 191 p. Based on *The Book of Tofu* by Shurtleff & Aoyagi.

Leviton, R. 1979. The soy delicatessen. *Soyfoods*. Summer. p. 12-18.

Leviton, R. 1980. Soyfoods and the media. *Soyfoods*. Winters: 56-59.

Leviton, R. 1981. Putting tofu in the lunch boxes of America. *Soyfoods*. Winter. p. 54-61.

Leviton, R. 1981. The world's best tofu cheesecake. *Vegetarian Times* No. 52. Nov. p. 74-77.

Leviton, R. 1982. *Tofu, Tempeh, Miso and Other Soyfoods*. New Canaan, CT: Keats Publishing Inc. 26 p.

Leviton, R. 1982. Tofu for institutions. Recipes for 225. *Soyfoods*. Winter. p. 66-67.

Leviton, R. 1983. Jack's Beanstalk: The American tofu dream on trial in Salt Lake City. *Soyfoods*. Winter. p. 18-27.

Leviton, R. 1983. Profile: Hinode Tofu Company. *Soyfoods*. Winter. p. 33-36.

Li, Ch'iao-p'ing. 1948. The Chemical Arts of Old China. Easton, PA: *Journal of Chemical Education*.

Li, Shih-chen. 1597. *Pen ts'ao kang mu*. 1965 ed. Hong Kong: Commercial Press (in Chinese). p. 360-371.

Li, Yu-ying. 1910. *Vegetable milk (from soya beans) and its derivatives*. English Patent 30,275. Dec. 30.

Li, Yu-ying. 1910. *Ta Tou: Le Soja*. Paris: Societe biologique de l'Extreme Orient. 65 p.

Li Yu-ying and Grandvoinnet, L. 1912. *Le Soja. Sa Culture. Ses Usages Alimentaires, Therapeutiques, Agricoles et Industriels*. Paris, France: A. Challamel. 141 p.

Li Yu-ying and Grandvoinnet, L. 1911-12. Le soja. *L'Agriculture Pratique des Pays Chauds* 11:177-96, 270-94, 360-75, 459-74. 12:28-38, 120-32, 213-23, 302-08.

Lin, H.Y. Shia, C.L. and Shia, C.M. 1975. *Chinese soybean curds*. Chun Wen Hsueh Publisher. Taipei, Taiwan.

Lin, Hai-ying et al. 1975. *Chung-kuo toufu (Chinese Tofu)*. Taipei, Taiwan: Wen-hsueh ch'u-pan-she. 249 p.

Linder, U.V. 1912. Soybean cheese. *J. of Industrial and Engineering Chemistry* 4(12):897-98.

Liu, P.W. 1932. Hakko-dofu no koso ni tsuite (About the enzymes of fermented tofu). *Nippon Nogei Kagaku Kaishi* (J. of the Agricultural Chemical Socy. of Japan) 8(3):273-79.

Lockwood, L.B. and Smith, A.K. 1952. Fermented Soy Foods and Sauce. *Yearbook of Agri*. 1950-51. p. 357-361.

Loetterle, F. 1977. Tonyu to tofu. *California Living*. April 17. p. 40, 42, 44.

Loew, O. 1904. Ueber die anwendung des frostes bei herstellung einiger japanischer nahrungsmittel. *Mitteilungen de Deutschen Gesellschaft fur Natur- und Volkerkunde Ostasiens* 10(1):75-76.

Loew, O. 1906. Ueber einige sonderbare Japanische nahrungsmittel. *Mitteilungen der Deutschen Gesellschaft fur Natur- und Volkerkunde Ostasiens* 11(1):109-11.

Loomis, H.M. 1914. Food products from the soy bean. *American Food Journal*. 9(8):472-74.

Loureiro, Juan de. 1793. *Flora Cochinensis*. Vol. 2. p. 537-38.

MacCormack, H. 1982. The place of small tofu shops in the industry. *Soyfoods*. Summer. p. 28-29.

MacCormack, H. 1982. *The Soy Dairy: A Way to Save the Small Farm*. P.O. Box 229, Philomath, OR: Sunbow Publishing. 26 p.

Madison Food Co. ca. 1933. *Madison Soy Cheese*. Madison, TN. 6 p.

Madison Health Messenger. 1939-44. Early articles on tofu at Madison College. 1939, Vol. 2(3): 1944. Vol 6(1) and 7(1).

Madison Survey. 1929-32. Early articles on tofu at Madison College. 1929: May 15, June 19, Oct. 23; 1932: Dec. 7. Madison, TN: Madison College Press.

Madison Health Foods. ca. 1934. *Vegetable Milk and Cheese*. Madison, TN. 21 p.

Makino, Magotaro. 1918. *Soy-bean Food*. U.S. Patent 1,258,427. Mar. 5.

Maruhi. 1972. *Tofu Ryori, Hyaku-sen* (Tofu Cookery, One Hundred Favorites). Tokyo: Sankosha Katei Buhen, Maruhi.

McGruter, P.G. 1979. *The Great American Tofu Cookbook*. Brookline, MA: Autumn Press. 124 p.

Melhuish, W. J. 1913. *Artificial milk from soy beans*. British Patent No. 24,572. Oct. 29.

Miller, C.D. 1933. Japanese foods commonly used in Hawaii. *Hawaii Agric. Exp. Station. Bulletin* No. 68. p. 1-10, 28-43.

Miyashita, A. 1962. *Kori-dofu no Rekishi (History of Dried-frozen Tofu)*. Tokyo: Japanese National Frozen Tofu Association. 571 p.

Moore, Karen. 1979. Tofu, a Far East import offers potential as meat, fish, cheese substitute. *Food Product Development* 13(5): 24. May.

Moriyama, Yukiko. 1982. *Quick & Easy Tofu Cookbook*. Tokyo: Joie. c/o J.P. Trading Inc., 300 Industrial Way, Brisbane, CA 94005. 104 p.

Morse, W.J. 1918. The soybean industry in the United States. *USDA Yearbook* (1917):101-111. (Separate No. 740).

Morse, W.J. 1929-31. *Log of the Dorsett-Morse Expedition to East Asia*. Typewritten manuscript in 17 volumes and handwritten notebooks. Only copy located at offices of American Soybean Assoc., St. Louis, Missouri. 6,000 p.

Motoyama, T. 1958. *Inshoku Jiten* (Encyclopedia of Food and Drink). Tokyo: Heibonsha. 604 p.

Murakami, Kamekichi. 1916. *Bean curd and process of making same*. U.S. Patent 1,195,843. Aug. 22.

Nakano, M., Ebine, H. and Ota, T. 1967. *Hakko Shokuhin* (Fermented Foods). Tokyo: Korin Shoin.

Nakayama, Tokiko. 1973. *Chugoku Meisaifu* (Chinese Cuisine: Famous Recipes). Tokyo: Shibata Shoten. 4 Vols.

Nasoya Foods. 1981 *Nasoya Tofu Cookbook*. P.O. Box 841, Leominster, MA. 28 p.

Natural Foods Merchandiser. 1981. Soyfoods report. Sept. 16 p.

Nelson, J.H. and Richardson, G.H. 1967. Molds in flavor production. In *Microbial Technology* (H.J. Peppler, ed.). New York: Reinhold.

New York Times Magazine. 1917. Woman off to China as government agent to study soy bean. June 10, Section VI, p. 9.

New Yorker. 1982. Tofu 'n Tab (cartoon). May 3, p. 44.

Newman, Marcea. 1975. *Sweet Life*. Boston: Houghton Mifflin.

Ng Sock Nye, 1979. *Soya Bean—Nutritious Food for the People*. Malaysia: Institut Masyarakat Berhad, 9 Lorong Kucing, Pulau Tikus, Penang. 19 p.

NHK. 1979. *Tofu Ryori* (Tofu Cookery). Tokyo: Nihon Hoso Kyokai. 128 p.

Nordquist, Ted, and Öhlund, Tim. 1981. *Tofu-Boken*. Orsundsbro, Sweden: Aros Sojaprodukter. 52 p.

Norinsho. 1964. *Nihon Shokuhin Hyojun Seibunhyo*. (Standard Composition of Japanese Foods). Tokyo: Norinsho (Japanese Ministry of Agriculture and Forestry).

Norton, R. and Wagner, M. 1980. *The Soy of Cooking: A Tofu and Tempeh Recipe Book*. Eugene, OR: White Crane, P.O. Box 3081, 97403. 24 p. 1983 revised ed. 58 p.

Ochomogo, M.G. 1974. *An unfermented cheese from soy-cow's milk mixture.* Thesis. Louisiana State University.

Ochse, J.J. 1931. *Vegetables of the Dutch East Indies.* Buitenzorg (Bogor), Java: Archipel Drukkerij. p. 366, 372, 389-93, 398, 407-08, 732, 943-71.

Ohsawa, Lima. 1971. *Makurobiotiku Ryori* (Macrobiotic Cookery). Tokyo: Nihon CI Kyokai. 199 p.

Ohsawa, Lima. 1974. *The Art of Just Cooking.* Brookline, MA: Autumn Press. 216 p.

Okada, K. et al. 1976. *Method of Manufacturing an aseptic soya bean curd.* Morinaga Milk Industry Co. Ltd. U.S. Patent 4,000,326.

Olszewski, N. 1978. *Tofu Madness.* Vashon, WA: Island Spring. 64 p.

Omura, Y. 1981. *The Tofu-Miso High Efficiency Diet.* New York: Arco Publishing Inc. 221 p.

Orosa, Maria Y. 1932. Soybeans as a component of a balanced diet and how to prepare them. *Popular Bulletin 13*, Science Bureau, Manila. 53 p.

Osawa, K. and Ueda. 1887. Digestion experiment with tofu. *Chugai Iji Shimpo* (Medical News, Foreign and Domestic), Tokyo. No. 177. p. 16.

Osawa, K. 1889. Shoka shiken tsuika ("additional investigations on digestion"). *Chugai Iji Shimpo* 211:6-8.

Osbeck, Peter. 1771. *A Voyage to China and the East Indies.* (Trans. by J.R. Forseter; original edition publ. 1757 in Swedish). London: Benjamin White. pp. 218, 253, 305 (Vol. 1).

Oshima, Kintaro. 1905. A digest of Japanese investigations on the nutrition of man. *USDA OES Bulletin* 159. p. 23-33, 145-53, 168-73.

Paillieux, A. 1880. Le soya, sa composition, chimique, ses varietes, sa culture et ses usages. *Bulletin de la Societe d'Acclimatization* 27 (or 3rd Series vol. 7):414-71, 538-96.

Piper, C.V. and Morse, W.J. 1923. *The Soybean.* New York: McGraw-Hill. 329 p.

Poirier, Marie. 1982. *Le Plaisir de la Cuisine au Tofu.* Prevost, Quebec, Canada: Unisoya Inc. 52 p.

Pontecorvo, Aldo J. and Bourne, M.C. 1978. Simple methods for extending the shelf life of soy curd (tofu) in tropical areas. *J. of Food Science* 43:969-72.

Prinsen-Geerligs, H.C. 1895. Eenige Chineesche voedingsmiddelen uit Soja boonen bereid. *Pharmaceutisch Weekblad Voor Nederland* 32(33):1-2. Dec. 14.

Prinsen-Geerligs, H.C. 1896. Einige chinesische Sojabohnenpraparate. *Chemiker-Zeitung* 20(9):67-69 (Jan. 29).

Rein, J.J. 1899. *The Industries of Japan.* London: Hodder and Stoughton. pp 105-07. A translation of volume II of his *Japan nach reisen und studien.* publ. 1886.

Richard, C. 1959. Le chao. Fromage de soja fermente, sale, et alcoolise. *Societe des Etudes Indochinoises, Bulletin* (Saigon) 34:317-24.

Ritter, D. 1874. Tofu, yuba, ame. *Mitteilungen der Deutschen Gesellschaft fur Natur- und Volkerkunde Ostasiens* 1(5):3-4.

Rose, M.S. and MacLeod, G. 1925. Maintenance values for the proteins of milk, meat, bread and milk, and soy bean curd. *J. of Biological Chemistry* 66:847-67.

Rouest, L. 1921. *Le Soja et son Lait Vegetal: Applications Agricoles et Industrielles.* Carcassonne (Aude), France: Lucie-Grazaille. 157 p.

Rovira, E. ed. 1979. *The What to Do with Tofu Cookbooklet.* Philadelphia, PA: The Grow-cery, 6526 Landsdowne Ave, 19151. 28 p.

Rudzinsky, Russ. 1969. *Japanese Country Cookbook.* San Francisco: Nitty Gritty Productions. 192 p.

Ruhräh, John. 1909. The soy bean in infant feeding. Preliminary report. *Archives of Pediatrics* 26:496-501. (July).

Saio, K., Sato, I. and Watanabe, T. 1974. Food use of soybean 7S and 11S proteins. High temperature expansion characteristics of gels. *J. of Food Science* 39:777-82.

Saio, K., Terashima, M. and Watanabe, T. 1975. Food use of soybean 7S and 11S proteins. Heat denaturation of soybean proteins at high temperature. *J. of Food Science* 40:537-40.

Sass, L.J. 1980. A couple on a tofu mission in the West. *New York Times.* Sept 24.

Sass, L.J. 1981. Soyfoods: Versatile, cheap and on the rise. *New York Times.* Aug. 12. p. C1, C6. Widely syndicated.

Satow, E.M. 1900. The Voyage of Captain John Saris to Japan, 1613. *Hakluyt Society*, London. Vol. 5, Series 2. p. 124.

Schmit, Matthew. 1978. *Peaking Out on Tofu.* Telluride, CO: Self published. 16 p.

Schroder, D.J. and Jackson, H. 1972. Preparation and evaluation of soybean curd with reduced beany flavor. *J. of Food Science* 37:450-51.

Science News Letter. 1943. Soybean curd makes good cottage cheese substitute. Dec. 4:360.

Senft, E. 1872. Untersuchung von chinesischen Oelbohnen. *Chemische Ackersmann.* p. 122-25.

Senft, E. 1907. Ueber einige in Japan verwendete vegetabilische nahrungsmittel mit besonderer beruecksichtigung der japanischen militaerkonserven. *Pharmazeutische Praxis* 6(3):81-89; 6(4):122-24, 131-32.

Shaw, Norman. 1911. *The Soya Bean of Manchuria.* Shanghai: Statistical Dept. of the Inspectorate General of Customs. II. Special Series No. 31. 32 p.

Sheppard, Sally. 1981. *Tofu Cookbook.* Salt Lake City, UT: Jack's Beanstalk. 99 p.

Shih, Chi-yien. 1918. *Beans and Bean Products.* Shanghai: Soochow Univ. Biology Dept. 13 p.

Shinoda, Osamu. 1971. Tofu-ko ("Thoughts on Tofu"). *Sekai.* p. 30-37.

Shinoda, Osamu. 1974. *Chugoku Shokumotsu-shi ("History of Chinese Foods").* Tokyo: Shibata Shoten. 389 p.

Shufu-no-tomo. 1972. *Ryori Hakka* (Encyclopedia of Japanese Cookery). Tokyo: Shufu-no-tomo.

Shurtleff, W. and Aoyagi, A. 1975. *The Book of Tofu.* Brookline, MA: Autumn Press. 336 p.

Shurtleff, W. and Aoyagi, A. 1977. *The Book of Kudzu.* Lafayette, CA: The Soyfoods Center. 104 p.

Shurtleff, W. and Aoyagi, A. 1979. *The Book of Tempeh: Super Soyfood from Indonesia.* New York: Harper & Row. Paperback 160 p. Professional hardcover 248 p.

Shurtleff, W. and Aoyagi, A. 1979. *Tofu & Soymilk Production.* Lafayette, CA: The Soyfoods Center. 336 p.

Shurtleff, W. and Aoyagi, A. 1979. *The Book of Tofu.* New York: Ballantine Books. 434 p. Extensively revised.

Shurtleff, W. and Aoyagi, A. 1981. *Das Tofu Buch.* Soyen, W. Germany: Ahorn Verlag. 286 p.

Shurtleff, W. and Aoyagi, A. 1981. La Soya y Sus Derivados: Tofu, Miso, Tempeh. *Quadernos de Natura.* No. 20. 87 p.

Shurtleff, W. and Aoyagi, A. 1982. *Using Tofu, Tempeh & Other Soyfoods in Restaurants, Delis & Cafeterias.* Lafayette, CA: The Soyfoods Center. 116 p.

Shurtleff, W. and Aoyagi, A. 1983. *The Book of Miso.* Berkeley, CA: Ten Speed Press. 256 p.

Shurtleff, W. and Aoyagi, A. 1983. *Soyfoods Industry and Market: Directory and Databook.* Lafayette, CA: The Soyfoods Center. 116 p.

Simonds, N. 1979. Chinese cuisine: Bean curd. *Gourmet.* Sept., p. 28-29, 84-91.

Sinclair, P. et al. 1974. Soybean in family meals. *USDA Home and Garden Bulletin* No. 208. 26 p.

Smith, A.K. and Beckel, A.C. 1946. Soybean or vegetable milk. *Soybean Digest* 6(7):18-23 or *Chemical and Engineering News.* 24:54-56.

Smith, A.K. 1949. Oriental use of soybeans as food. *Soybean Digest.* Feb:15-17, March:26-34, April:23-31, May:24-30, June:15-22.

Smith, A.K. 1949. *Oriental methods of using soybeans as food with special attention to fermented products.* USDA, AIC-234. June. 40 p. Reissued as ARS-71-17, July 1961. 65 p.

Smith, A.K. 1958. Use of U.S. soybeans in Japan. *USDA Bulletin* ARS-71-12. 36 p.

Smith, A.K., Watanabe, T. and Nash, A. 1960. Tofu from Japanese and United States Soybeans. *Food Technology.* July:332-36.

Smith, A.K. 1961. *Oriental Methods of Using Soybeans as Food. With Special Attention to Fermented Products and Notes on Oriental Farming Practices.* USDA/ARS-71-17. 65 p.

Smith, A.K. 1962. Problems involved in increasing world-wide use of soybean products as foods—technical assistance in developing soybean markets. In *Proceedings of Conference on Soybean Products for Protein in Human Foods.* USDA-NRRC, Peoria, IL, Sept 13-15, 1961. p. 214-16.

Smith, A.K. 1963. Foreign uses of soybean protein foods. *Cereal Science Today* 8(6):196, 198, 200, 210.

Smith, A.K. and Circle, S.J. eds. 1972. *Soybeans: Chemistry and Technology.* Vol 1, Proteins. Westport, CT: AVI Publishing Co. 470 p. Slightly revised, 1978.

Soyanews. 1978-83. Articles about tofu in Sri Lanka. Colombo, Sri Lanka. P.O. Box 1024. Feb. 1978; Aug., Sept. 1980; Feb., June 1981; April, May, Oct. 1982.

Soybean Digest. 1950. Soy foods from a unique college (Madison). Nov. p. 14-15.

Soybean Digest. 1960. USDA research may put more U.S. soybeans in Japanese foods. Feb. p. 20-21.

Soybean Digest. 1965. Research leads to a new food market for soybeans. June. p. 16.

Soyfoods magazine. 1979 to date. Every issue has articles about tofu. 100 Heath Rd., Colrain, MA 01340.

Stahel, G. 1946. Foods from fermented soybeans as prepared in the Netherlands Indies. I. Taohoo, a cheese-like substance, and some other products. *J. of the New York Botanical Garden* 47:261-67.

Standal, B.R. 1963 Nutritional value of proteins of Oriental soybean foods. *J. of Nutrition* 81:279-85.

Steiman, H. 1980. Tofu: Trader Vic Americanizes an Asian staple. *San Francisco Examiner.* Sept 3. p. B7-8.

Stein, E. 1978. Making money making tofu. *Whole Foods.* Jan. p. 32-37.

Steinberg, Raphael, 1969. *The Cookery of Japan.* New York: Time-Life Books.

Stern, Arthur M. 1952. *Studies on the Physiology of Mucor mucedo and its Role in the fermentation of Soybean Curds.* Univ. of Illinois Thesis. (from University Microfilms, 3150).

Strayer, G.M. 1956. Japanese tofu makers don't like green beans or foreign material. *Soybean Digest.* March. p. 20, 22.

Stuart, G.A. 1911. *Chinese Materia Medica:* Vegetable Kingdom. Shanghai: American Presbyterian Mission Press. p. 189-96.

Suchi, T. 1888. Digestion experiments with rice and tofu. *Tokyo Igakkai Zasshi* (J. of the Tokyo Medical Socy.) 2:457, 511.

T'ao Ku. 10th century A.D. *Ch'ing I Lu.* Earliest known Chinese reference to tofu.

Time magazine. 1980. Climbing curd. Feb. 25. p. 62.

Timmins, T. 1978. New England's tofu shop. *Soycraft Newsletter* 1(2):1-3. Winter.

Tremblay, Yvon and Boyte, Frances. 1982. *La Magie du Tofu.* Montreal and Paris: Stanké Ltee. 101 p.

Trimble. H. 1896. Recent literature on the soja bean. *American J. of Pharmacy* 68:309-13.

Tseng, R.Y.L., et al. 1977. Calcium and phosphorous contents and ratios in tofu as affected by the coagulants used. *Home Economics Research Journal* 6(2):171-75.

Tsuda, Tadao et al. 1974. *Shojin Ryori* (Zen Temple Cookery). Tokyo: Fujokai Shuppansha. 242 p.

Tsuji, Kaichi. 1962. *Tofu Ryori* (Tofu Cookery). Tokyo: Fujin Gaho.

Tsuji, Kaichi. 1971. *Zen Tastes in Japanese Cooking.* Tokyo: Kodansha. 207 p.

USDA Weekly News Letter. 1918. Cooking soy beans. 5(21):6. Soy beans as food. 5(34):6. Soy beans, used like navy kind, make valuable food. 5(42).

U.S. Dept. of Health, Education, and Welfare. 1972. *Food Composition Table for Use in East Asia.* Nutrition Program, Center for Disease Control, HEW, Atlanta, GA 30333. 334 p.

Van Gundy, Dorothea. 1936. *La Sierra Recipes.* Ontario, CA: Self published. 47 p.

Vitale, E. and Brock T. 1977. Plowboy interview with Shurtleff and Aoyagi. *Mother Earth News.* No. 44. March-April. p. 8-18.

Waggoner, D. 1980. With his *Book of Tofu* William Shurtleff hopes to bring soy to the world. *People* magazine. Oct. p. 57-58.

Wai, Nganshou. 1929. A new species of mono-mucor, *Mucor sufu,* on Chinese soybean cheese. *Science* 70:307-08.

Wai, Nganshou. 1964. Soybean cheese. *Bulletin of the Institute of Chemistry* (Taiwan). Academia Sinica 9. July. p. 75-94.

Wai, Nganshou. 1968. *Investigation of the various processes used in preparing Chinese cheese by the fermentation of soybean curd with mucor and other fungi.* Final Technical Report. Institute of Chemistry, Academia Sinica, Taiwan.

Wai, N. 1968. *Final Technical Report: Chinese Cheese.* USDA Grant No. FG-Ta-100, Project No. UR-A6-(40)-1. 90 p.

Wang, H.L. 1967. Products from soybeans. *Food Technology* 21:115-16.

Wang, H.L. 1967. Release of protease from mycelium of *Mucor hiemalis. J. of Bacteriology* 93:1794-99.

Wang, H.L. and Hesseltine, C.W. 1970. Sufu and lao-chao. *J. of Agricultural and Food Chemistry* 18(4):572-75.

Wang, H.L., Ellis, J.J. and Hesseltine, C.W. 1972. Antibacterial activity produced by molds commonly used in Oriental food preparations. *Mycologia* 64(1):218-21.

Wang, H.L. et al. 1977. *An Inventory of Information on the Utilization of Unprocessed and Simply Processed Soybeans as Human Food.* Peoria, IL: USDA Northern Regional Research Center. AID AG/TAB-225-12-76. 197 p.

Wang, H.L. and Hesseltine, C.W. 1979. Mold-modified foods. In *Microbial Technology,* 2nd ed. Vol. II, H.J. Peppler ed. New York: Academic Press. p. 95-129.

Watanabe, T. et al. 1960. Tofu seizo kotei no hyojunka ni taisuru kenkyu. (Research into the standardization of the tofu making process.) *Report of the Food Research Institute No. 14B.* Tokyo. Part 1, regular tofu; part 2, silken tofu; part 3, bagged lactone silken tofu. p. 6-30.

Watanabe, T. 1969. Industrial Production of Soybean Foods in Japan. Presented at *Expert Group Meeting on Soya Bean Processing and Use,* Peoria, IL 17-21 No. 1969. United Nations Industrial Dev. Org. 38 p.

Watanabe Tokuji, Ebine Hideo, and Ota Teruo. 1971. *Daizu Shokuhin* (Soyfoods). Tokyo: Korin Shoin. 270 p.

Watanabe, T., Ebine, H. and Okada, M. 1974. New protein food technologies in Japan. In *New Protein Foods. Vol. 1A. Technology.* (A.M. Altschul, ed.). New York: Academic Press. p. 414-53.

Watt, B.K. and Merrill, A.L. 1963. *Composition of Foods.* USDA, Food Economics Research Div., Agriculture Handbook No. 8. 190 p.

Wells, P. 1978. What is this thing called tofu? *New York Times,* May 3, p. 19-20.

Whiteman, Elizabeth F., and Keyt, Ellen K. 1938. *Soybeans for the Table.* USDA Leaflet No. 166. 6 p.

Whole Foods. 1979. The soyfoods revolution (Cover story). Jan. 44 p.

Winarno, F.G. et al. 1976. *The Present Status of Soybean in Indonesia.* Bogor, Indonesia: FATEMETA, Bogor Agricultural University. 128 p.

Women's College of Nutrition. 1969. *Tofu, Mame, Miso Ryori: Ju-ni Kagetsu* (Tofu, Soybean, and Miso Cookery Throughout the Twelve Months). Tokyo: Joshi Eiyo Daigaku.

Wood, B.J.B. and Hounan, L.L. 1981. 'Dairy' products from soya beans. *Proceedings of Dairy Symposium at the Food Industries Exhibition, London.* 19 p.

Wu, Ch'i-chun. 1848. Ta Tou (the soy bean). In *Chih wu ming shih t'u k'ao.* T'ai-yuan-fu, Shansi, China. 98 p. Translated into English and indexed by W.J. Hagerty, USDA, Washington, D.C. 1917. With photocopies of plates.

Yamaguchi, H.S.K. 1934-50. *We Japanese.* Yokohama, Japan: Yamagata Press. 590 p.

Yao, M.Y. and Peng, A.C. 1979. New chemical coagulant for making soybean curd. *Ohio Report* 64(1):11.

Yeo, V. and Wellington, G.H. 1974. Effects of soy curd on the acceptability and characteristics of beef patties. *J. of Food Science* 39:288-92.

The three most important works are starred.

Berg, Alan. 1973. *The Nutrition Factor*. The Brookings Institute, 1775 Massachusetts Ave., N.W., Washington, D.C. 20036. A nutrition expert on the staff of the World Bank, Berg discusses the way hunger in the Third World is linked to underdevelopment and malnutrition.

Borgstrom, Georg. 1974. *The Food/People Dilemma*. New York: Duxbury Press.

_____. 1973. *World Food Resources*. New York: Intext.

_____. 1972. *The Hungry Planet*. New York: Collier-Macmillan. A professor at Michigan State Univ., Borgstrom examines the food/population problem from an environmentalist's point of view, focusing on the effects of uneven food distribution between the rich and poor nations.

Brown, Lester R. 1974. *By Bread Alone*. New York: Praeger. One of the best books on the world food crisis. Head of the newly formed Worldwatch Institute in Washington, D.C., Brown is a highly articulate agricultural economist with a clear vision of the present problem and its solutions. His other recent writings include *In the Human Interest* (1973), *World Without Borders* (1972), and *Seeds of Change* (1970).

*Brown, Lester R. 1978. *The Twenty-Ninth Day: Accommodating Human Needs and Numbers to the Earth's Resources*. New York: W.W. Norton, 363 p. Outstanding!

Brown, Lester R. 1981. *Building a Sustainable Society*. New York: W.W. Norton & Co. 433 p. A great work.

George, Susan. 1977. *How the Other Half Dies: The Real Reasons for World Hunger*. Montclair, NJ: Allanheld, Osmun & Co. 308 p.

Lappé, Frances M. 1982. *Diet for a Small Planet* (Revised Edition). San Francisco: Ballantine/Friends of the Earth. 498 p. A two million-copy bestseller and one of the most influential books ever written concerning the world food crisis and basic nutrition. Emphasis on protein complementarity, meatless meals, and the wisdom of eating low on the food chain.

*Lappé, F.M., and Collins, J. 1978. *Food First: Beyond the Myth of Scarcity*. New York: Ballantine Paperback. Revised edition. 619 p. The finest and most up-to-date book on the world food crisis. A must! Available at reduced rates from the Institute for Food and Development Policy, 2588 Mission Street, San Francisco, Calif. 94110.

Lerza, Catherine, and Jacobson, Michael, ed. 1975. *Food for People Not for Profit*. New York: Ballantine. This official handbook for Food Day 1975 contains a wealth of information concerning every aspect of the food crisis; each chapter written by an authority in the field.

Manocha, Sohan L. 1975. *Nutrition and Our Overpopulated Planet*. Springfield, Ill: Charles C. Thomas. An extensive and up-to-date treatment of the population/food crisis and means for its solution.

*Mesarovic, M., and Pestel, E. 1974. *Mankind at the Turning Point: The Second Report to the Club of Rome*. New York: Signet. The successor to *The Limits of Growth*, this highly readable and condensed book, based on sophisticated computer models, spells out clearly what we can and must do to avoid worldwide famine and catastrophe in the near future.

Miller, G. Tyler. 1975. *Living in the Environment*. Belmont, CA: Wadsworth. An excellent ecology textbook with extensive material concerning the population/food crisis and the means of its solution.

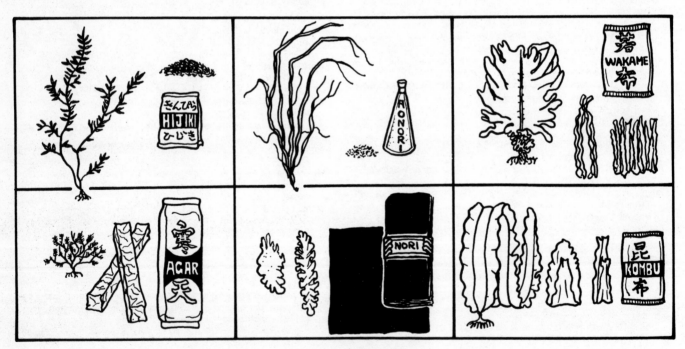

Japanese sea-vegetables

Glossary

The following Japanese-style ingredients, referred to in the recipe sections of this book, are generally available in the West at Japanese food markets and at a growing number of natural and health food stores. For local addresses look in the Yellow Pages under Japanese (or Chinese) Food Products or Oriental Goods.

AGAR *(kanten):* A sea vegetable gelatin made from the genera *Gelidium* and *Gracilaria.* Sold in the form of flakes, bars, powder, and strands.

AMAZAKÉ: Literally "sweet sake." A creamy thick drink with a rich, sweet flavor and virtually no alcohol content. Made from rice *koji* or steamed rice overgrown with a fragrant white mycelium of *Aspergillus oryzae* mold.

AZUKI BEANS: These small red beans *(Vigna angularis)* are cooked with glutinous rice or used to make a sweet filling for confections.

BEEFSTEAK PLANT *(shiso):* This fragrant herb *(Perilla nankinensis)* is prized for its versatility: beefsteak buds and blossoms *(mejiso and hojiso)* are garnishes, beefsteak seeds *(shisonomi)* are a condiment, green beefsteak leaves *(aojiso)* can be used like mint, and red beefsteak leaves *(shisonoha)* are used in making salt plums, pickles, and confections.

BENI-TADÉ: Also called *akamé* or "red bud," these tiny purple leaflike sprouts are used as a garnish for chilled tofu.

BONITO FLAKES *(Hana katsuo):* A popular garnish and basis for soup stocks made by shaving hard-as-wood, dried fermented bonito *(katsuobushi).*

BRACKEN FERN *(warabi):* The olive green young fiddlenecks of *Pteridium aquilinum.* Parboiled and served as a delicacy.

BREAD CRUMB FLAKES *(panko):* Similar to bread crumbs except that each particle has been rolled under pressure to form a tiny, thin flake. Used in deep-fried breadings.

BURDOCK ROOT *(gobo):* *Arctium lappa* has a long, dark-brown tapering root ½ to 1 inch in diameter and 18 to 24 inches long.

BUTTERBUR *(fuki):* The 4-foot-long, ½-inch-diameter stem of this spring vegetable, *Petasites japonicus,* has a flavor resembling that of celery.

CHILIES *(togarashi):* Japanese chilies *(Capsicum annum),* usually sold dried, are 2½ inches long and fiery hot. See also 7-spice chili powder.

CHINESE CABBAGE *(hakusai):* Splendidly tight and crisp heads of *Brassica pekinensis* are as delicious as they are inexpensive.

CHIVES: Popular Japanese varieties include *asatsuki (Allium ledebourianum)* and *nira (Allium tuberosum).*

CHRYSANTHEMUM LEAVES *(shungiku):* The fragrant greens of *Chrysanthemum coronarium* resemble spinach or trefoil.

CLOUD-EAR MUSHROOM *(kikuragé):* A delicate variety with a wavy cap, *Auricularia auricula-judae* grows on trees and has virtually no stem. Solid dried, it is also known as Dried Black Fungus or Wood Ear.

DAIKON: The marvelously versatile Japanese giant white radish *(Raphanus sativus)* is often as thick as a man's arm and 18 to 24 inches long.

EGGPLANT *(nasu):* The Japanese variety *(Solanum melongena),* sweeter and more tender than its American counterpart, averages 4½ inches in length and 1½ inches in diameter, and weighs 2 ounces.

ENOKIDAKÉ: This pale white mushroom *(Flammulina velutipes),* has a 5-inch-long stem and a tiny 3/8-inch-diameter cap. Usually sold fresh.

GINGERROOT *(shoga):* The 4-inch-long knobby tan root of *Zingiber officinale* is peeled and freshly grated. Two parts by volume of powdered ginger may be substituted for 1 part fresh grated gingerroot. Gingerroot shoots *(shin shoga)* are a popular soup garnish and red pickled gingerroot *(beni-shoga)* is thinly sliced and served with Inari-zushi.

GINKGO NUTS *(ginnan):* These tender ½-inch-long delicacies from the giant *Ginkgo bilboa* tree are sold fresh or canned.

GLUTINOUS RICE *(mochigomé):* Used to make mochi and a variety of treats, *Oryzae sativa glutinosa* contains no amylase, and therefore cooks to a sticky, moist consistency. Occasionally known in the West as sweet rice.

GLUTINOUS YAM *(tororo imo):* When rubbed on a fine metal grater, these yams (all of the Genus *Dioscorea)* develop a highly cohesive, glutinous quality. Available fresh in many varieties, including *jinenjo* and *yamanoimo.*

GREEN NORI FLAKES *(aonoriko):* A sea vegetable seasoning made by crumbling the fragrant, bright-green fronds of dried *Enteromorpha prolifera.* Delicious on noodles.

HEMP SEEDS *(asanomi):* The tiny light green seeds of *Cannabis sativa,* about the size of sesame or poppy seeds, are widely used in Japanese deep-fried tofu burgers.

HIJIKI: A stringy black sea vegetable *(Hizikia fusiforme)* sold in pieces about 1½ inches long. Often misspelled "hiziki" in the West.

JUNSAI: A "water shield" *(Brasenia purpurea),* this tiny wild pond plant, surrounded by a slippery gelatinous coating, is used in soups.

KABOCHA: Also called Hokkaido pumpkin, this delectable fall vegetable *(Cucurbita moschata),* with its dark-green edible skin, looks like a 6-to-8-inch-diameter acorn squash. Substitute winter squash or pumpkin.

KAMPYO: Strips shaved from the dried *yugao* gourd or calabash *(Lagenaria siceraria)* are used for tying food into bundles or rolls.

KATAKURIKO: Japan's most popular, low-cost cooking starch. Often synonymous with potato starch.

KINAKO: Roasted soy flour; see Chapter 4.

KINOMÉ: The fragrant, bright green sprigs of the *sansho* tree *(Zanthoxylum piperitum)* are plucked in the spring and used as a garnish.

KOMBU: A sea vegetable *(Laminaria* species) somewhat resembling kelp and sold as leathery olive brown fronds. 3 to 6 inches wide and 2½ to 6 feet long. Used to make soup stocks and in stews.

KONNYAKU: Eight-ounce gray, firm jellylike cakes made from the starch of *Amorphallus konjac,* the devil's tongue plant, a relative of the sweet potato. Konnyaku threads *(ito konnyaku)* and noodles *(shirataki)* are used in one-pot cookery.

KUDZU POWDER *(kuzu-ko):* The white, starchlike powder extracted from the roots of the kudzu vine *(Pueraria lobata),* which grows abundantly in the southeast U.S., is a high quality cooking starch and natural medicine widely used in East Asia. For details see *The Book of Kudzu* by Shurtleff and Aoyagi.

LEEK *(negi):* The Japanese leek *(Allium fistulosum)* or Welsh onion is somewhat sweeter, mellower, and faster cooking than its Western counterpart.

LILLY BULB *(yuriné):* These fresh roots, about the size and shape of a bulb of garlic, have a mild flavor and are used in tofu treasure balls. The bulb of the tiger lily *(oni yuri; Lilium lancifolium)* is most widely used but those of the Maximowicz's lily *(L. maximowiczii)* and star lily *(L. concolor)* are also used.

LOTUS ROOT *(renkon):* The sausage shaped roots of the lotus *(Nelumbo nucifera),* which grow in the mud at the bottom of ponds, are 2 to 3 inches in diameter and 5 to 8 inches long. Prized for their crisp texture, they are best when fresh.

MANDARIN ORANGE *(mikan):* Japan's most popular and least expensive domestic fresh fruit, it is available from November until March. Delicious.

MATCHA: Powdered green tea, widely used in the tea ceremony.

MATSUTAKÉ: The most expensive and most delicious of Japanese mushrooms, *Trichloma matsutaké* grows a cap up to 8 inches in diameter.

MIRIN: Sweet sake used only for cooking. For each tablespoon of mirin called for, you may substitute ½ teaspoon honey or 2 teaspoons sake or pale dry sherry. Or you may substitute 1½ teaspoons honey and 2½ teaspoons water.

MISO: Fermented soybean paste; see Chapter 4.

MIZUAMÉ: A natural grain sugar extracted from rice, millet, or barley, it looks like a solid, pale-amber resin and may be softened by heating. Also sold as Millet Jelly, Amé, or Rice Honey. Close relatives are barley malt syrup and sorghum molasses.

MOCHI: Cakes of steamed, pounded glutinous rice, each about 3 by 2 by ½ inches.

MUSHROOMS: See Cloud-ear mushroom, *enokidaké, matsutaké, nameko, shiitaké,* and *shimeji.*

MYOGA: The pinkish white buds of the *Zingiber mioga* that emerge from the plant's base each August are a popular garnish.

NAMEKO: Tiny yellowish-brown mushrooms with a slippery coating, *pholiota namcko* are sold fresh or canned.

NATTO: Fermented whole soybeans; see Chapter 4.

NIGARI: Bittern or bitterns. The traditional Japanese tofu coagulant extracted from clean seawater. See Chapter 8.

NOODLES *(menrui):* See rice-flour noodles, ramen, soba, somen, and udon.

NORI: A sea vegetable sold in paper-thin purplish-black sheets about 8 inches square and packaged in bundles of ten. The Japanese presently consume about 9 *billion* sheets each year. Other *Porphyra* species are known in the West as laver.

OSMUND FERN *(zenmai):* The slender young fiddlenecks of *Osmunda japonica* are a springtime delicacy.

PICKLES *(tsukemono):* Salt pickled vegetables *(shiozuké),* miso pickles *(misozuke),* and rice-bran pickles *(nukamiso-zuké)* are widely used as seasonings in Japan. Famous varieties include *Narazuké* (Uri melons pickled in sake lees) and *Takuan* (dried daikon pickled in nuka-miso).

RAMEN: Crinkly yellowish-white Chinese noodles now widely used in Japan, especially in the form of Instant Ramen.

RICE FLOUR *(joshinko):* Finely ground white rice widely used in the preparation of steamed desserts and dumplings *(dango).*

RICE FLOUR NOODLES: Slender, round, white noodles about 10 inches long; popular in salads.

SAKÉ: Japanese rice wine containing about 15 percent alcohol and widely used in cooking. The lees *(sake-no-kasu)* are used in dressings and soups and for pickling other foods.

SALT PLUM *(umeboshi):* The partially ripe fruit of the *Prunus mumé* (which is actually more like an apricot than a plum), is salt pickled, usually with red beefsteak leaves, and used as both a tart seasoning with rice or in salad dressings, or as a highly alkaline natural medicine.

SANSHO PEPPER *(kona zansho):* A fragrant and spicy brownish-green pepper made from the seedpods of the *sansho* tree *(Zanthoxylum piperitum),* the same tree that bears *kinomé* sprigs.

SEA VEGETABLES *(kaiso):* See agar, green nori flakes, hijiki, kombu, nori, and wakame.

SESAME SEEDS *(goma):* The delicious calcium-rich seeds come in white and black varieties and are usually lightly roasted and ground before use. Substitute one half the amount of sesame butter or tahini.

SEVEN-SPICE CHILI POWDER *(shichimi togarashi):* A zippy blend of ground dried chilies and other spices including sesame, *sansho,* grated dried orange peel, green nori flakes, and white pepper.

SHIITAKÉ: Japan's most popular mushroom, *Lentinus edodes* is sold fresh or dried and widely sauteed or used as a basis for stocks.

SHIMEJI: Small mushrooms with tan caps 1 to 1½ inches in diameter, *Lyophyllum aggregatum* are usually sold fresh.

SHOCHU: A popular and very potent type of inexpensive spirits related to gin and often made from sweet potatoes.

SHOYU: Japanese all-purpose soy sauce; see Chapter 4.

SNOW PEAS *(saya endo):* Also called edible-pod peas, these are the paper-thin type widely associated with Chinese cookery.

SOBA: Japanese buckwheat noodles. A great food.

SOMEN: Very slender wheat-flour noodles, usually served chilled in summertime. Substitute vermicelli.

SPINACH *(horenso):* *Spinacia oleracea* is milder and slightly sweeter than its Western counterpart. Delicious.

SUDARÉ: A bamboo mat about 10 inches square used for rolling sushi and other foods.

SURIBACHI: An earthenware grinding bowl or mortar with a serrated interior surface, the usual suribachi is 10 inches in a diameter and 3½ inches deep, and is accompanied by a wooden pestle *(surikogi).*

SWEET POTATO *(satsuma imo):* One of Japan's most beloved and tastiest foods, *Ipomoea batatas* has no exact counterpart in the West. About 1½ to 2½ inches in diameter and 4 to 8 inches long, it has a pale red skin and a light-yellow, richly-flavored meat.

TAHINI: A smooth creamy paste made from unroasted or very lightly roasted, hulled white sesame seeds. Due to the removal of the calcium-rich hulls, tahini is not as nutritious as sesame butter, and some commercial varieties use caustic soda in the cleaning and dehulling process. Contains 19 percent protein.

TAMARI: A type of soy sauce resembling shoyu; see Chapter 4.

TARO: A 2½-inch-diameter root vegetable also known in the West as dasheen or albi; the most popular of the many Japanese varieties are *sato imo (Colocasia antiquorum), yatsugashira,* and *akame imo.* Rich, creamy, and delicious. Used to make Hawaii's *poi.*

TOGAN: Also known in English as "white gourd," *Benincasa hispida* is a mild flavored vegetable.

TRANSPARENT NOODLES *(harusamé):* This slender vermicelli, made from mung beans or sweet potatoes, is also popular in Chinese cookery.

TREFOIL *(mitsuba):* Prized for its unique pungent aroma and handsome green leaves. *Cryptotaenia japonica* is most widely used as a garnish.

TURNIP *(kabu):* The Japanese *Brassica rapa* is a heart-shaped white root about 3 inches in diameter having a mild, slightly sweet flavor.

UDO: Neither quite celery nor asparagus, *Aralia cordata* is a crisp and tender oddity with a unique hint of lemon flavor that is enjoyed fresh or cooked. The best varieties grow wild.

UDON: Fat, white, wheat-flour noodles similar to a No. 2 spaghetti.

URI MELON *(shirouri):* Also called "white melon," "white gourd melon," or "Oriental pickling melon," *Cucumis melo* var. *conomon* is a pale green fruit shaped like a cucumber about 12 inches long and 3 inches in diameter. Widely pickled in sake lees or miso.

WAKAME: A dark-green sea vegetable *(Undaria pinnatifida)* with fronds about 3 inches wide and 12 to 18 inches long, it is sold both fresh and dried; widely used in soups and salads.

WASABI: A hot green horseradish-like paste made from the grated root of the *wasabi* plant *(Wasabia japonica)* which is cultivated in terraced mountain stream beds. Sold fresh or powdered.

WHEAT GLUTEN *(fu):* Both fresh and dried varieties, sold in a multitude of shapes, are widely used in Japanese cookery.

YUZU: A citrus fruit similar to a citron, lime, or lemon, the fruit of the *yuzu* tree *(Citrus junos)* has a green to yellow, refreshingly fragrant rind which is slivered or grated and widely used in soups, sauces, and tofu or miso preparations.

Note: Monosodium glutamate (MSG), a flavor intensifier also known as Aji-no-moto or Accent, is a highly refined white crystalline powder that differs in structure from natural glutamic acid. When used in more than very small quantities, it is well known to produce in some people the "Chinese Restaurant Syndrome" characterized by headaches, burning sensations, a feeling of pressure in the chest, and other discomforting symptoms. Originally extracted from kombu, it is now produced by fermentation or hydrolysis of molasses or glucose from tapioca, cornstarch, potato starch, etc. We and many others interested in natural healthy foods strictly avoid use of this product.

Index

SOYFOODS CENTER

THE SOYFOODS CENTER, founded in 1976 by William Shurtleff and Akiko Aoyagi, has offices in California. Our basic goals and activities are related to soyfoods and world hunger.

Soyfoods: Our center is, above all, a source of information about soyfoods, especially tofu, soymilk, tempeh, and miso, about which we have done extensive research and written books and recipe pamphlets. Like a growing number of people, we feel that soybeans will be one of the key protein sources of the future on planet Earth, and that both traditional and modern soyfoods from East and West will serve as important sources of delicious, high-quality, low-cost protein in the diets of people everywhere, regardless of their income. We are interested in each of the following soyfoods, listed here in what we consider to be their approximate order of potential worldwide importance: tofu (soybean curd), soy flour, soymilk, tempeh, shoyu (natural soy sauce), textured soy protein (TVP), miso, whole dry soybeans, soy protein isolates and concentrates, roasted soybeans or soy nuts, fresh green soybeans, roasted full-fat soy flour (*kinako*), soy sprouts, yuba, and natto. We have developed hundreds of tasty and nutritious Western-style recipes for the use of these foods and compiled extensive, up-to-date information on their nutritional value, history, and production.

World Hunger: Presently more than 15,000,000 people die each year of starvation and malnutrition-caused diseases; three fourths of these are children. We constantly relate our work to this urgent problem of world hunger by studying and developing creative, low-cost, village-level methods for soyfood production using appropriate technology, by traveling and speaking in less developed countries, and by sending complementary copies of our publications to and communicating with key soyfoods researchers and producers in these countries.

Meatless Diets: Over half of all agricultural land in the United States is now used to grow crops (such as corn, soybeans, oats, and wheat) that are fed to animals. The affluent American diet is emerging as a major cause of world hunger as well as of degenerative diseases such as heart disease and cancer. Soyfoods, which are low in cost, high in protein, low in saturated fats, free of cholesterol, and relatively low in calories, can be used as delicious replacements for meats and dairy products as part of meatless or vegetarian diets. We encourage the adoption of such diets which help to make best use of the planet's precious food resources, are conducive to the development of a healthy body and clear mind, kind to animals, economical, and ecologically sound.

Commercial Soyfood Production: We encourage and aid people throughout the world in starting community or commercial production of soyfoods by providing technical manuals, technical advice, materials, and equipment. We have helped to establish the *Soyfoods Association of North America (*SANA*)* and its international publication *Soyfoods*, to found *Bean Machines, Inc.* (a company selling tofu and soymilk equipment), and to develop catalogs of large and small scale equipment. We have compiled various technical manuals and presently serve as consultants for a wide variety of companies.

Lecture Demonstrations: We have done more than one hundred programs relating to soyfoods for natural food groups, research scientists, food technologists, nutritionists, commercial producers, university audiences, international symposia, home economists, and cooking schools. We have also done numerous television and radio programs and cooking classes throughout the world. We welcome invitations.

Soyfoods Center Network: Our main Center in California is devoted primarily to research and publication about soyfoods. We have the world's largest library (more than 3,500 documents) on soyfoods. Our growing International Soyfoods Center Network, with branches around the world, is helping to introduce soyfoods around the world.

New Lifestyles: Our work is deeply involved in the development of lifestyles conducive to the welfare and survival of all beings on planet Earth. Thus we encourage voluntary simplicity, self-sufficiency (particularly food self-sufficiency on personal, regional, and national levels), right livelihood, a deeper understanding of selfless service, and of daily life and work as a spiritual practice, ecological awareness, holistic health, appropriate technology, the rapid development and adoption of solar energy, and the phasing out of nuclear energy.

Publications and Catalog: Our Center has published a number of full-sized specialty books on soyfoods including Tofu & Soymilk Production, Miso Production, Tempeh Production, Soyfoods Industry and Market: Directory and Databook, and History of Soybeans and Soyfoods. We also provide a free catalog listing our other widely distributed books on tofu, miso, and tempeh, materials such as pamphlets, tofu kits, and slide shows related to soyfoods, and a list of soyfoods manufacturers in North America and Europe.

Your Financial Support and Help: Our work, now reaching people throughout the world, is not supported by government or corporate funds. We do, however, welcome contributions of any size from individuals and private foundations to aid us in furthering the soyfoods revolution and helping to put an end to world hunger. We have established Friends of the Center for supporters willing to contribute $35.00 or more; smaller contributions are also welcomed. If you would like to contribute your time and energy to our work, please contact us. See the next page for our address and phone number.

ABOUT THE AUTHORS

William Shurtleff and Akiko Aoyagi spent their formative years on opposite sides of the Pacific. Born in California on 28 April 1941, Bill received degrees in engineering, honors humanities, and education from Stanford University. He taught physics for two years in Nigeria in the Peace Corps and has lived and traveled extensively in East Asia and Third World countries. He speaks seven languages, four fluently, including Japanese.

Akiko Aoyagi, born in Tokyo on 24 January 1950, received her education there from the Quaker-run Friends' School and the Women's College of Arts. She has worked as an illustrator and designer in Japan's modern fashion industry and America's emerging soyfoods industry.

Starting in October 1972, Bill and Akiko began working together, doing research and writing books about soyfoods. They worked together for six years in East Asia, mainly Japan, studying with top soyfoods researchers, manufacturers, nutritionists, historians, and cooks. Over 750,000 copies of their 53 books on soyfoods are now in print. The titles and publishers of some of these are listed on the copyright page at the beginning of this book.

In April 1976, Bill and Akiko founded the Soyfoods Center, and since that time they have worked to introduce soyfoods, especially traditional low-technology soyfoods, to the Western world. They feel that soyfoods can play a key role in helping to solve the world food crisis while providing high-quality, low-cost protein and healthier diets for people everywhere. Their work has led to the establishment of hundreds of soyfoods businesses making tofu, soymilk, miso, tempeh, and other soyfoods, and to the publication by others of more than 50 books about these foods. Their nationwide tours and many lectures, demonstrations, and media appearances have drawn widespread acclaim.

Soyfoods Center also produces SoyaScan, the world's largest bibliographic database on soybeans and soyfoods, containing more than 55,000 records (publications, original interviews, unpublished archival documents, and commercial soy products) from 1100 B.C. to the present. And the Soyfoods Center Library and Archives houses more than 50,000 documents—many unique.

Their global view and uniquely holistic, interdisciplinary approach are aimed at presenting the best of both traditional lore and modern scientific knowledge about soyfoods in a language accessible to both laymen and professionals.

By constantly addressing the problems of world hunger, the suffering of human beings and animals, and the perennial longing for good health and liberation, they hope to make their work relevant everywhere and a force for planetary renaissance.

As of 1998, William Shurtleff is director of Soyfoods Center. Akiko Aoyagi is a freelance illustrator and graphic designer. She runs her own art business in Walnut Creek, California.

If you would like to help in the larger work related to soyfoods and world hunger, if you have any questions or suggestions related to this book, or if you would like to receive a free copy of the Soyfoods Center Catalog, please contact or send a self-addressed, stamped envelope to Soyfoods Center.

SOYFOODS CENTER
P.O. Box 234
Lafayette, CA 94549 USA
(Phone: 925-283-2991)

Many men and women throughout the world today are in search of meaningful work. In industrial and post-industrial societies, "alienated labor" is fast losing its appeal as respect for traditional craftsmanship revives and demand for its products grows steadily. In developing nations, where hunger is often a basic fact of daily life, countless individuals are in need of truly productive labor, labor which serves the fundamental needs of society. Whether in a rural village or bustling megalopolis, the traditional tofu shop could serve as a practical yet revolutionary means toward the satisfaction of all these crucial needs.

In any setting, the tofu shop can be set up and operated with a minimum of capital and technical know-how. To make the very best tofu, after all, requires only the simplest ingredients, tools, and workshop to make: soybeans which are or can be made available in bulk at relatively low prices almost everywhere; tools which can be handmade or purchased inexpensively; and a shop which need be no bigger than 12 by 15 feet and which, situated near or even adjacent to one's home, can be operated as a cottage industry, with the work and income shared by the members of one's family or community. Retailed directly or through secondary outlets, tofu products can be attractively priced anywhere in the world, and demand for these high-quality foods is bound to grow rapidly over the months and years ahead.

In Boulder or Boston, New Delhi or New Guinea, the daily practice of the traditional tofu-making art offers more than just the challenges and benefits of self-employment and independence. In its subtlety and depth, it can be an enriching exercise in concentration, heightened sensitivity, and creative self-expression. And like Gandhi's spinning, it can serve as the center of a regular pattern of daily life conducive to clear-mindedness, meditation, and peaceful living.

The obstacles to learning the tofu-making art are perhaps greatest in areas such as India, Africa, and South America, where tofu could make its most immediate contribution to human welfare. These obstacles can best and perhaps only be met on the national level. The Japanese government is presently taking an increasingly active role in aiding less developed nations. But only very recently have the Japanese themselves begun to recognize the unique treasure they possess in their traditional technologies for utilizing soybeans as food. We would urge the Japanese government to initiate a program whereby Japan's knowledge and experience in this field would be shared with receptive, protein-short countries around the world. A pilot program could be modeled on those the Japanese are now using effectively for other technologies: it might include the invitation of teams of foreign representatives to Japan to learn the tofu-making process in detail; the sponsoring of Japanese craftsmen in setting up schools abroad; and the subsidizing (where necessary) of private entrepreneurs invited to developing nations to open shops operated by host nationals. Similarly, we would urge the governments of developing nations to educate and encourage their citizens to incorporate tofu products into their daily diet.

Since 1976 over 185 new (Caucasian-run) tofu shops and soy dairies have been started throughout North America to bring the present total to 115. In 1978 representatives from these shops plus producers of tempeh, miso, shoyu, and other soyfoods established the Soyfoods Association of North America (SANA), a trade association to serve the burgeoning new industry. To aid in the establishment of tofu shops and soy dairies, we have written *Tofu & Soymilk Production: The Book of Tofu, Volume II* which is now available exclusively from our Soyfoods Center, P.O. Box 234, Lafayette, California, 94549. An easy to follow technical manual, it is based on over five years of research. In cooperation with Takai Tofu & Soymilk Equipment Co., Japan's largest and best known manufacturer, we have developed an illustrated English-language equipment catalog which is now available from The Soyfoods Center.

These developments now make it relatively easy for people everywhere to start their own tofu shops and soy dairies—and to send these fine foods to the four directions.

THE BOOK OF MISO

**Praise for
THE BOOK OF MISO**

"A CONTEMPORARY CLASSIC."
East West Journal

"Crammed full of historical information,
traditional and Western recipes, explicit instructions
for homemade miso in Japanese life."
Library Journal

"The most impressive single book on food that I have ever seen."
*Dr. Eugene N. Anderson, Jr.
Professor of Anthropology (Chinese food and nutrition)
University of California, Riverside*

"Numerous excellent illustrations…Useful as a
guide for food technologists, home economists, dieticians,
and others interested in fermented soybean products."
Food Technology

"WONDERFULLY ENTERTAINING
AND COMPREHENSIVE."
Mother Earth News

"THE DEFINITIVE SOURCE ON THE SUBJECT."
Alternatives

Putting Hatcho Miso to Bed

THE BOOK OF
MISO

Savory, High-Protein Seasoning
VOLUME I

WILLIAM SHURTLEFF & AKIKO AOYAGI
Illustrated by Akiko Aoyagi

Ten Speed Press
Berkeley • Toronto
A Soyfoods Center Book

*For all the world's children
whose lives are filled with hunger...
and can't understand why.*

*And for all beings
who are dedicated to doing something about it.*

Contents

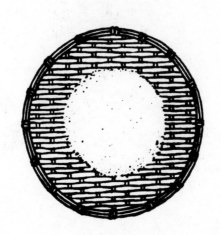

PART I

Miso: Savory, High-Protein Seasoning

PART II

Cooking with Miso

PART III

The Preparation of Miso

What is Miso?

MISO (pronounced MEE-so, and also known as "fermented soybean paste") is a savory, high-protein seasoning made from soybeans, grain (usually rice or barley), salt, water, and *Aspergillus oryzae* culture. Miso has no equivalent in the West—which may be one reason it has caught on here so quickly. Its range of flavors and colors, textures and aromas is as varied as that of the world's fine cheeses and wines. Miso's texture resembles that of a soft peanut butter. Its many warm colors range from deep chocolate browns, reddish browns, and russets, through ambers, clarets, and cinnamon reds, on up to creamy beiges and sunlight yellows for some sweeter, more modern varieties. To the sensitive palate, no two of the many miso varieties taste the same. The darker, more traditional types have flavors and aroms that are deep, rich, and hearty, almost meaty at times, making them ideal for the preparation of savory meatless dishes; the lighter, more modern misos are subtly sweet and delicately refreshing. The wonderfully fragrant aroma of traditional miso has been compared with that of freshly ground coffee.

Miso is one of East Asia's most important soyfoods. In Japan, over 70 percent of the population starts each day with a health-giving, nutritious, and warming cup of miso soup instead of coffee. Its alkalizing effect wakes up the body and mind, providing it with a steady supply of high-quality energy that lasts all morning. Miso can be used as an all-purpose seasoning in many of the same ways as salt, yet because it contains only 5.5 to 13 percent sodium chloride (versus 99 percent in table salt) it can serve as the key seasoning in moderate- or low-salt diets that are still rich in flavor. But miso is much more than just a seasoning. Highly nutritious, it is such a concentrated source of protein, vitamin B-12, and other essential nutrients, that the Japanese consider it to be a basic staple and full-fledged "food," although typically only several tablespoons are used per person each day. Moreover, like yogurt, miso is a living, cultured food containing lactic acid-forming bacteria (such as *Pediococcus halophilus* and *Lactobacillus delbrueckii*) plus other health-giving microorganisms and digestion-aiding enzymes. Traditional misos can be stored for months without refrigeration. And in 1983, a month's supply of natural miso for a person in North America using it twice daily (1½ tablespoons a day) costs as little as $2.55.

Miso is prized by cooks for its almost unlimited versatility. It can be used like bouillon or a rich meat stock in soups, meatless gravies, or stews; like soy sauce or *shoyu*, Worcestershire sauce, or ketchup in sauces, dips, and dressings; as an unmatched thickener in barbecue sauces; like cheese in casseroles and spreads; like chutney or relish as a topping for grains, fresh vegetable slices or open-faced sandwiches; as a gravy base with sauteed or steamed foods; or even like vinegar as a pickling medium. Used in many of these ways for centuries in Japanese kitchens, it has set its distinctive mark of fine flavor on the entire panorama of Japanese cuisine and added zest and variety to a diet that has long consisted primarily of grains, land-and-sea vegetables, and tofu.

There are six basic types of miso among which are found more than 28 distinctly different varieties. The three basic traditional types are rice, barley and soybean miso, the first two made from soybeans, salt and the respective grain, the last made from soybeans and salt alone. Two "special" types, finger lickin' and sweet simmered miso, contain bits of chopped vegetables, nuts and/or seasonings and are delectably sweet and chunky. Finally, there are a number of "modern" misos developed since 1959, including dehydrated and low-salt/high-protein varieties.

The progenitor of present-day miso originated in China some 2,500 years ago. Called *chiang* (pronounced jang), it was brought to Japan during the 7th century by Buddhist priests. During the following centuries, Japanese craftsmen transformed *chiang* into miso and shoyu (all-purpose Japanese soy sauce), two unique and distinctive foods which are now quite different from their Chinese counterparts. Indeed the word "miso" was first coined in Japan and its many varieties were created and developed there. *Chiang* or Chinese-style miso continues to be widely used throughout its mother country and at least five varieties are now available in the West, as are a number of types of *jang* or Korean-style miso.

First introduced to America on a small scale in the early 1960s, miso is now becoming better known and appreciated. High-quality varieties are available throughout the United States at reasonable prices in most natural and health food stores, co-op markets, Japanese and Chinese grocery stores, and a growing number of supermarkets. Some stores carry as many as 15 different varieties sold in both bulk and prepackaged 1- to 2-pound quantities. Various types of American-made miso are now being marketed, and many people—especially those in communities—have taken to preparing their own at home.

We feel that miso has come to the West to stay, and that in the near future it will come to be considered an essential element in America's evolving cuisine, a basic seasoning, of which several varieties will be found in well-stocked kitchens throughout the country. It can—and should—play an increasingly important role in the cookery and nutrition of people around the world.

Preface

To the Second Edition

SINCE THE publication of the first edition of *The Book of Miso* in September 1976 there have been many promising developments in the work to introduce this fine fermented soyfood to America. That month we bought a large Dodge van, painted a sign on one side reading "Tofu and Miso America Tour," then traveled 15,000 miles around America presenting 70 public programs for groups that had invited us. At each we talked about miso, showed color slides, and served samples—usually peanut miso on apple slices.

Increasingly we received letters from people interested in making miso on a community or commercial scale, so in August 1977 our Center published *Miso Production: The Book of Miso, Volume II.* Many new factors joined in helping to make miso more popular: the burgeoning macrobiotic, natural foods, and vegetarian movements; the sustained media interest which produced eleven major articles between 1976 and 1972; the many new cookbooks and cooking articles that included miso recipes; the rapid rise of emigration from East Asia during the 1970s; the active Soyfoods Association of North America, founded in July 1978; and *Soyfoods* magazine.

Soon a new generation of miso companies grew up in North America, led by Japanese-owned Miyako Oriental Foods in Los Angeles (1976), but soon followed by North America's first Caucasian-run miso operations: Ohio Miso Co. in Monroeville, Ohio (1979), Shin-Mei-Do on Denman Island, B.C., Canada (1979), American Miso, Inc. in Rutherfordton, North Carolina (1981), South River Miso Co. in Conway, Massachusetts (1982), Imagine Foods/Moniteau Farm in Jamestown, Missouri (1982), and General Oriental Foods in Holmdale, New Jersey (1982). Note that most of these new miso companies are located in rural areas, following an ancient East Asian tradition.

The American miso market has grown dramatically in the years since 1975, with both imports and domestic miso production expanding. Between 1975 and 1982, imports rose 109 percent, from 459 to 959 tonnes (metric tons), while production in the continental U.S. jumped a remarkable 525 percent from 120 to 750 tonnes and production in Hawaii grew 18 percent from 543 to 640 tonnes. Thus by early 1983 Americans are consuming an estimated 2,349 tonnes of miso, more than twice as much (and in the continental U.S. three times as much) as eight years earlier.

In 1976 most of the miso was purchased as miso itself, but by the late 1970s a rapidly growing proportion came to be sold as an ingredient in other popular American foods such as dehydrated instant miso soups, miso-flavored seasonings for dips and salad dressings, bottled miso dressings, brown rice pilaf seasoned with miso, miso-seasoned corn chips, and the like. These new products helped miso to reach a broad spectrum of Americans, who were formerly unaware of this savory seasoning.

The growing concern with excess salt consumption that began in the late 1970s led to a shift toward lower salt misos. In the process many people came to realize that

miso, containing an average of only 12 percent salt (versus 99 percent for straight table salt) plus a host of natural flavor enhancers, is an excellent way to help *reduce* salt intake with no sacrifice in flavor.

In July 1980 our book was published in a handsome German edition, *Das Miso Buch.* Then in March 1981, based on the popularity of the first edition of our work, Ballantine Books published an updated mass-market edition; by late 1982 the two American editions had sold more than 70,000 copies, helping to spread the good word.

With all these changes that have taken place, combined with the extensive additional research that we have done on the history of miso (it was first mentioned by a Westerner in 1597!) as well as on its nutritional value, biochemistry, production, cookery, etc., we and our new publisher felt that it was time for a second edition. Changes and updates have been made throughout the book, but the most extensive ones are to be found in the chapters on History of Miso (Appendix A), Chinese, Korean, and Indonesian Misos (Appendix B), People and Institutions Connected with Miso (Appendix C), Miso Companies in the West (Appendix D), the Bibliography, and Soybeans, Protein, and World Hunger (Chapter 1).

We are happy to see that miso is finding its rightful and enriching place in America's evolving new cuisine—more natural, healthful, light, traditional, and diverse.

The Soyfoods Center
Lafayette, California
February 1983

Preface
To the First Edition

*I*RECEIVED MY first introduction to fine miso while working as a cook at California's Tassajara Zen Mountain Center. It was there that I first participated in the preparation of miso—we made a 50-gallon vatful once each year—and learned its many uses as a seasoning. But it was only while living in Japan and working together with Akiko on *The Book of Tofu* that we both really discovered the enormous wealth and variety contained in the world of miso and began to recognize the great value this savory soyfood has to offer the world. This learning experience was an adventure and not the least of its many pleasures was shopping for the different varieties of miso needed to prepare our recipes.

Throughout Japan, thousands of small shops specialize in the sale of miso (and miso pickles), and a sampling of forty to fifty varieties will generally be available. Each is displayed in a 5-gallon cedar keg ringed with broad hoops of braided bamboo and marked in bold black characters with the miso's name, price, and province of origin. The hues and shades create a festival of autumn-maple colors, and the total atmosphere has all the warmth and rustic beauty of a Florentine cheese shop or a small wine cellar in the French countryside.

We enjoyed learning the names of Japan's traditional favorites and their distinguished makers, and slowly developed the ability to judge quality and character. Using miso as a seasoning in our daily cookery, we found it made many of our Western-style dishes even more delicious. Its versatility seemed almost unlimited and its deep, rich flavors served to enrich and add variety to our meatless diet. In fine restaurants, we enjoyed a wide variety of different dishes featuring miso and found that it had long been important in the two main schools of Japanese haute cuisine: Zen Temple Cookery and Tea Ceremony Cuisine. I soon came to understand that, for many Japanese, miso is the very epitome of the satisfying flavors and aromas of home cooking; the mere mention of mother's or grandma's miso soup can evoke all the warm feelings that come to most Westerners at the thought of a loaf of home-baked bread, piping hot from the oven.

As our interest deepened, we began to visit, learn from, and eventually become friends with a number of the more than 2,400 master craftsmen who make Japan's miso. Working in shops which are usually located adjacent to their homes, many of these men honored the traditional spirit of fine craftsmanship in a way that transformed daily work into an art and spiritual practice. We were drawn to their handsomely crafted tools, their high-roofed shops with massive arching rafters, and their huge cedar vats—often more than 150 years old—that stand taller than a man. In the morning air, billows of steam would rise from the great iron caldron and large cedar steamer in which half a ton of soybeans and rice were being cooked. When

freshly harvested *koji* (rice or barley covered with a cottony mycelium of fragrant white mold) was removed from its granite-hewn incubation room, it would fill the entire shop with an incomparable lingering aroma, rich and subtly sweet, like that of freshly-roasted chestnuts or coffee.

I was eventually given the opportunity to do an informal apprenticeship with Mr. Kiyoshi Tsujita, an exemplary miso master living quite near our home. A strong traditionalist and purist at heart, he made the most delicious miso—and the *only* brown-rice miso—that we had ever tasted. Studying with him and watching him at work, I began to appreciate the mysteries of the fermentation process, the complexities of its chemistry and microbiology, and the harmony of its interaction with the great movements of the four seasons. He stressed that the essence of his art could not be transmitted in words, for it was linked to one's local climate and the soil in which soybeans, rice, and barley grow; embodied in the strains of microorganisms which for generations had permeated the air, wood, and rock walls of a shop; half hidden in the muscles and bones, feeling and intuition of each craftsman. It was a total understanding, rooted in a particular place and in a man who becomes imbued with it like one who, unbeknownst to himself, becomes wet by walking through a mist. As in the ancient wine chateaux throughout Europe, it reflected a tradition and culture that took centuries to mature.

Nevertheless, he wanted to help both Akiko and me to understand his craft and convey its fundamentals to people in the West. He therefore encouraged us to begin making our own miso and helped us get started. Under his tutelage, we prepared many small batches and, for more than a year, patiently endured the suspense of waiting, wondering how they would turn out. When we seemed pleased with the results, he teased us with the Japanese proverb saying that, naturally, every person likes his own homemade miso best!

Over a period of some four years, Akiko and I had the opportunity to visit miso shops throughout Japan and study the preparation of most of the main traditional varieties. Though ordinarily quite protective of their traditional secrets, the shops' masters were pleased to see our sincere interest in their work and, without exception, spared no time or effort in showing us everything we wanted to see, answering all our questions, and in some cases, later carrying on a detailed correspondence.

Early in the spring of 1973, we made our first contact with country-style miso, a tradition started hundreds of years ago by Buddhist priests in their temples and rural peasants in their farmhouses, and which still accounts for an estimated 17 percent of all Japanese miso production. At the Banyan Ashram, a community of young people living a simple life of meditation and farming on tiny Suwanose Island, we learned how to make barley koji (mold barley) in the ancient way by "catching" natural wild mold spores floating in the air. Invited one sunny April morning to join in the work, we used a large wooden mortar and heavy pestles to mash koji and cooked soybeans together. In an atmosphere of down-home merriment, everyone lent rhythm to the pounding by clapping, stomping, and chanting. The women packed the mashed ingredients into tall earthenware crocks, which were then ceremoniously sealed. We were urged to return for the grand opening when the fermentation had finished, but warned not to be late, since even fifty gallons of homemade barley miso wouldn't last long in a large community of hungry, hardworking men and women.

As our book began to take form, we traveled to Taiwan and Korea to visit local miso makers at their work, study new varieties of Chinese- and Korean-style miso in sprawling outdoor marketplaces, and sample miso cuisine at restaurants representing the full gamut of provincial cooking styles.

In the fall of 1974, we traveled deep into the mountains of the northeast provinces to visit one of Japan's "long-life" villages, where many people live past the age of ninety and most families still prepare their own miso using an ancient method. Upon arrival we were invited to join our host family in a light meal featuring farmhouse-style *Dengaku*; fresh homemade tofu was pierced with bamboo skewers, coated on both sides with homemade miso, and grilled around a bed of live coals in the open-hearth fireplace. We were deeply touched to discover that both the miso and tofu had been made entirely from soybeans grown in the village fields, and the mere fragrance of that sizzling *Dengaku* made our 600-mile trip well worthwhile. As we studied the miso-making process, we could not help but notice how vigorous and healthy the villagers seemed, and how this simple life close to nature had made each person the master of many useful arts. Here we first came to realize how miso could make a major contribution to the life of self sufficiency.

While Akiko worked with miso in day-to-day cookery, I spent considerable time studying Western and Japanese literature on miso fermentation and visiting Japan's most modern research institutes and factories. I discovered that during the past few decades a revolution has taken place in miso manufacturing as the use of large-scale, automatic machinery, quick fermentation in heated rooms, and high-speed polyethylene packaging have made it possible to mass-produce miso at low cost and distribute it throughout the nation and even the world. The uniqueness and character of traditional provincial varieties are gradually being lost and the new factories have become a threat to the very existence of Japan's many small shops and their high-quality natural products.

Continuing our daily experimentation with miso cookery, we eventually prepared more than 600 recipes, from which we chose our favorites for use in this book. In the mornings and evenings we practiced meditation; our days were given over to writing and research, artwork and cookery.

Despite the joy we found in our work, though, one almost unbearable reality has been constantly before us: in a world blessed with an abundance of food, indeed more than enough for everyone, millions of people are now faced with perpetual hunger, severe protein malnutrition, and starvation. Yet the use of miso allows each of us to do our small part in making better use of the earth's precious food reserves by enjoying soy and grain proteins directly and thereby avoiding the colossal waste inherent in the Western pattern of feeding these proteins to livestock. How fortunate, we feel, that miso offers us its fine flavor and remarkable nutritional value together with a time-tested promise to help make the world a better home for all.

Tokyo, Japan
June 1976

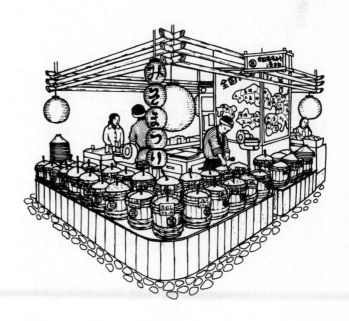

9

Acknowledgments

ALL BEINGS, past and present, have shared in the creation of this book, yet to some we wish to express special thanks: Mr. Kiyoshi Tsujita, mentor and friend, who taught us the art of traditional miso making and supplied us with the finest brown-rice miso we have ever tasted; Mr. Wataru Kawamura, Japan's "miso sensei," who introduced us to the romance of miso history and its place in the heart of the people; Messrs. Hideo Ebine, Masahiro Nakano, Kazuo Shibasaki, Clifford W. Hesseltine, and Ms. Hwa L. Wang, miso researchers from East and West, who have pioneered the way in scientific exploration of the mysteries of miso fermentation; Messrs. Kiyoshi Kaneko and Choichi Kato, directors of Japan's two Hatcho miso companies; Messrs. Shigeru Honda and Keinosuke Ishino, owners of Kyoto's two famous sweet white miso shops; Messrs. Kojiro Ikeda and Yanosuke Kanemitsu, makers of fine barley miso; Messrs. Soichi Nishida, Nobushi Takeyama, and William Higa, makers respectively of red, sweet red, and mellow white miso; Messrs. Shigeo Sasaki, Kenichiro Sasaki, and Hiroshi Haga, of the Sendai Miso Co.; Mr. Yojuro Watanabe, production manager at Japan's largest miso factory; Messrs. Yasu Niimi and Akira Chiba, makers of fine koji starter; Messrs. Denei Fujimori and Zenichi Matsushita of the Japanese National Miso Association; Mr. Kinichiro Shibata, producer of commercial miso pickles;

Mmes. Saiyo Miura and Kazuko Shinya, who taught us how to make farmhouse *tama-miso* in remote Ugemura village; the members of Banyan Ashram, who taught us the preparation of sweet-potato miso using wild mold spores; Mr. Akiyoshi Kazama who kept us well informed on the world of international miso trade; Mr. Masahiro Miyashita of Kikkoman International, who provided us with extensive information about shoyu; Bob Gerner and Gordon Bennett who gave us support and advice; Messrs. Junsei Yamazaki, Noboru Muramoto, Wally Gorell, Thom Leonard and Blake Rankin, who have helped to get the word out; and makers of *chiang* and *jang* throughout Taiwan and Korea who gave generously of their time and experience.

Finally, we would like to give particular thanks to: Herman and Cornellia Aihara, Michio and Aveline Kushi, and Pierre Gaevert, who were instrumental in preparing the way; Frances Moore Lappé, Lester R. Brown, E. F. Schumacher, and Stephen Gaskin, whose teachings have inspired our work; Ty Smith and Paul Discoe, whose initial encouragement gave birth to this book; Bobbie and Lawton, Fumio and Kinjiro, for their love and generosity; Beverly, for her inspired design; and Nahum Stiskin, our friend and publisher, whose vision and ceaseless striving for excellence have won our deepest admiration.

PART I

Miso:
Savory, High-Protein
Seasoning

1
Soybeans, Protein and World Hunger

DURING THE past decade, the population/food crisis has suddenly emerged as the most serious problem facing mankind. We are now experiencing the greatest famine in history and the situation is clearly getting worse. Experts estimate that starvation and malnutrition-caused diseases are now taking the lives of between five and 20 million people each year (15,000 to 60,000 *daily*), and half of the victims are children under five. According to the United Nations Food and Agricultural Organization (FAO), an additional 400 to 500 million children (more than twice the population of the United States) living in the sixty poorest countries suffer from such severe chronic malnutrition that their growth and mental capacity are permanently retarded. And more than one-quarter of the earth's present four billion inhabitants confront inescapable hunger during some part of each year. At this turning point in history, we have, for the first time, rounded the bend on three dangerous exponential curves—population, resource-and-energy consumption, and pollution—and are heading almost vertically upward at a dizzying pace. These cold statistics add up to immense human suffering, which is quickly becoming the dominant reality of daily life for poor people throughout the world.

In the least developed nations, where population generally doubles every 20 to 25 years and most of the good land is already intensively cultivated, food supplies cannot possibly keep up with demand. As the gap between the poor and rich nations widens, and the latter use increasingly large quantities of already scarce corn, soy, wheat, and oats to fatten their livestock, the price of these basic foods is pushed out of reach of the destitute and hungry. What once were local short-term famines now threaten to engulf entire nations, leading to social and political chaos. Already millions find themselves trapped in unimaginable squalor. And poverty, illiteracy, and malnutrition transferred from generation to generation in an accelerating downward spiral continually degrades the quality of individual lives and must soon have grave consequences for all people everywhere.

We in the affluent West have been fortunate. We have forgotten how it *feels* to be always hungry, for hunger has remained a news item from faraway countries. Most of us have been spared—perhaps unfortunately—the terrible and unforgettable experience of witnessing firsthand a death by starvation. And slowly many of us have allowed ourselves to become numbed—even apathetic—to the painful reality of what is happening all around us in the world. Often quite unconsciously, many have already given up the situation as hopeless, and this attitude has emerged as one of the primary forces allowing the problem to grow worse. Some feel there is not enough room in the lifeboat to save the drowning, not realizing that the earth presently produces more than enough food for everyone. Others believe it is already too late and that there is nothing they could do to make a difference, forgetting that the way they eat—which only they can change—may be one of the basic causes of worldwide food shortages. Still others argue pessimistically that to help in any way would only stimulate snowballing population growth which would ultimately make the problem even worse and simply delay the day of reckoning; they fail to understand that the easiest—if not the only—way to lower birth rates is to ensure adequate food supplies and improve living standards.

Discarding false or unexamined myths and assumptions can lead from a sense of hopelessness and helplessness to a genuine, realistic commitment to change. The present food/population crisis, if neglected, will not somehow work itself out or gradually go away. It will only get worse and worse. In our small and increasingly interdependent global village, the burden of suffering will eventually be visited upon everyone. Will we continue to live as a privileged and wealthy minority, consuming vastly more than our share of precious food (and energy) resources, until we are a tiny island in a sea of hunger, compelling the deprived, in desperation, to force us to stop? Or will we start now to really care and, thus, to work for change? These are life and death matters on which the balance of this century will turn.

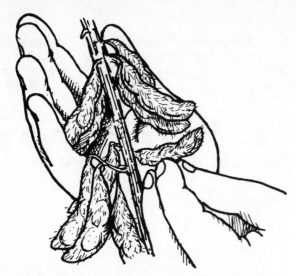

Soybeans: Protein Source of the Future

Experts studying the world food crisis are quick to emphasize that the key nutrient in shortest supply is protein. World hunger is primarily protein hunger and most starvation—especially among children—is caused not by a lack of calories but of this relatively costly and scarce nutritional component. Thus it is often said that the food crisis is more specifically a protein crisis, and that if the protein gap could be filled, the most difficult part of the problem would be solved. While these experts agree that the situation admits of no easy solution, they also are virtually unanimous in their opinion that soybeans will be the protein source of the future. Why? Because soybeans can produce more usable protein per acre of land than any other known crop—33 percent more on the average (360 percent more under ideal conditions) than second-place rice and twenty *times* as much as if the land were used to raise beef cattle or grow their fodder. This fact becomes increasingly important as farmland grows more and more scarce.

Soybeans have served as the protein backbone of the East Asian diet for over 2,000 years and today—used in the form of tofu, miso, shoyu, soymilk, tempeh, fresh green soybeans and a host of other delicious foods—they are an integral part of the diet of more than one billion people. Containing 34 to 36 percent high-quality protein—more than any other plant or animal food—plus all of the eight essential amino acids, they are rightfully known throughout the Orient as "the meat of the fields." From the body's point of view, the amount of usable protein contained in ½ cup dry soybeans (1 cup cooked) is no different from that contained in 5 ounces of steak. And low-cost, low-calorie soybean foods contain no cholesterol and almost none of the saturated fats so abundant in most animal-derived products.

Americans are often surprised to learn that their country is the world's largest soybean producer, accounting for about 67 percent of the planet's total yearly output. In 1975, over 600,000 U.S. soybean farmers planted a total of 54 million acres and sold their crop for $7.5 billion. Soybeans are one of our largest and most important farm crops, second only to corn (and ahead of wheat) in total dollar value, and third in total acreage. Exporting about half of the domestic crop, America is the largest international supplier, providing 70 percent of the total trade. These beans are our biggest farm export, worth over $5 *billion* in 1975.

Institutionalized Protein Waste

But what happens to all these soybeans and the 18 *million* tons of protein they contain? Virtually all of the non-exported crop is sent to huge factories where the soy oil—which contains no protein—is extracted with hexane solvent. Then, approximately 95 percent of the protein-rich meal left over is fed directly to livestock. The soybeans exported to Russia, Europe, Poland, Iran, and other countries now building up their livestock herds follow the same route. Only in East Asia are large quantities of soybeans transformed into high-protein foods. If all of this U.S. soy protein were used directly, it could fulfill about 25 percent of the yearly protein requirements of every person on the planet.

The system responsible for this immense waste is the feedlot, which was designed after World War II in an era of huge farm surpluses as a way of transforming excess grains and soy into more "profitable" meat. Although we now live in an era of famine with reserves at a precariously low level, an astonishing 50 percent of all U.S. farmland is still used to grow crops that end up being fed to animals. In addition to soybeans, we feed livestock a full 78 percent of our cereal grains including about 90 percent of our corn, oats, and barley, and 24 percent of our wheat, all of which could, of course, serve as foods for human beings. As a result, the average American now consumes the equivalent of 2,000 pounds of grain and soybeans annually, 200 pounds of which is used directly, while the remaining 90 percent is consumed in the form of meat, poultry, dairy products, and eggs. But the average person in developing countries consumes only 400 pounds per year, virtually all of which is used directly in meatless diets. Thus, the birth of one typical American baby has *five* times the adverse effect on precious world food reserves (not to mention water, fertilizer, energy, and land resources) as the birth of a child in Asia, Africa, or Latin America.

And as other countries become affluent, they quickly follow the American pattern. Resource geographer Georg Borgstrom estimates that the developed world, with 28 percent of the world's population, consumes some two-thirds of world grain production and three-fourths of the world's fish catch (much of which is purchased from protein-starved Latin America and used to feed cats and dogs as well as livestock). In fact, the rich use practically as much cereal grains to feed animals as the poorer half of mankind eats directly as food. The 6 percent of the world's population who live in the United States eat 30 percent of the world's meat and drink half its milk. Our beef consumption has jumped from 50 pounds per capita in 1950 to 124 pounds in 1975, and our total intake of beef, pork, and poultry averages 11 ounces daily (254 pounds a year). Moreover, we consume $25 billion worth of alcoholic beverages (made largely from grains) at an annual cost of $120 per person. Thus, while population still accounts for the major part of rising food demand, it is often said that a ravenous new rival, affluence, has emerged to further increase food shortages.

As a result, livestock and pets in wealthy countries are in direct competition for basic foods with hungry people throughout the rest of the world. On the international grain markets, U.S. livestock farmers, supported by the growing demand for meat, can always outbid representatives from poor grain-eating countries. Thus, basic foods go to cows and pigs, chickens and turkeys, instead of to the people who need them most. America's 90 million dogs and cats alone consume an annual $1.5 billion worth of pet food containing enough protein to feed 4 million human beings. In his authoritative *Nutrition and our Overpopulated Planet*, Sohan Monocha concludes that "animals in developed countries eat a better, more nutritionally balanced diet than two-thirds of the human population in poorer countries." Until quite recently, though, cattle were grazed on land unfit for farming or fed vegetable refuse (such as cornstalks) that could not be eaten by people; at present only 30 percent are still raised in this way. Every effort (legal, political, and personal) should be made to return to this system as soon as possible, and consumers who feel they need beef should insist on the grass-fed variety.

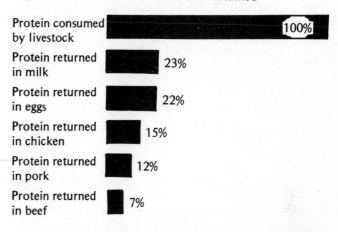

Food Energy

Food is a form of energy, and in a sense, the fundamental energy crisis is getting human beings enough food calories and protein. All food is ultimately derived from plants, which do the primary work of energy transformation that makes other life forms possible. Without plants we would have sunlight, water, air, and earth—but no food. As energy flows through a food chain, about 80 to 90 percent is degraded to useless heat at each step of the chain as explained by the second law of thermodynamics and illustrated here. The shorter the food chain between plants and man, the less the energy lost as heat and the greater the food calories available. Most people in the world—and especially those living in areas which have long been densely populated—eat low on the food chain, avoiding meat and eating plants directly. About 70 percent of the world's protein presently comes from plants and only 30 percent from animal-derived products, yet in affluent countries, these figures are often reversed. In developing countries, cereal grains alone generally provide 65 to 70 percent of the protein intake and 70 to 80 percent of the calories. This traditional grain-centered diet will support about seven times the population as its meat-centered counterpart.

The process of running grains and soybeans through animals and then eating the animals is so inefficient, uneconomical, and energy-expensive as to be virtually inexcusable. Clearly, the earth cannot support this level of waste. On the average, it takes about 7 pounds of grain- or soy protein to make 1 pound of livestock protein, but in the case of the feedlot steer, the least efficient converter, it takes a full 15 pounds. In other words, 93 percent of the protein fed to a steer is lost to human consumption, being used instead to support the animal's metabolism or build inedible parts of its body. The "return on investment" for other livestock products is shown below:

Fig. 1. Protein Consumed vs. Protein Returned

Protein consumed by livestock	100%
Protein returned in milk	23%
Protein returned in eggs	22%
Protein returned in chicken	15%
Protein returned in pork	12%
Protein returned in beef	7%

In her incisive million-copy best seller, *Diet for a Small Planet*, Frances Moore Lappé describes the basic situation vividly: "To imagine what this means in practical everyday terms, simply set yourself at a restaurant in front of an 8-ounce steak and then imagine the room filled with 40 to 50 people with empty bowls in front of them. For the 'feed cost' of your steak, each of their bowls could be filled with a full cup of cereal grains."

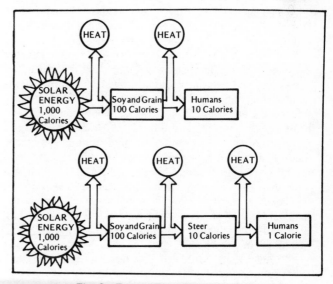

Fig. 2. Energy Flow through Food Chains

Soy Protein for a Hungry Planet

Experts studying the world food crisis generally agree that the easiest and quickest way that we in affluent countries can do something concrete to help is to greatly reduce our consumption of livestock products—especially meat. Each person that cuts his or her consumption of grain-fed beef by only one pound frees 15 pounds of grains and soybeans to be used directly as food. And a reduction in American meat consumption of only 10 percent would free 12 million tons of these basic foods per year, enough to meet the annual grain requirements of about 60 million people in less developed countries.

The key to making the transition toward a balanced meatless diet while still maintaining an adequate intake of high-quality protein lies in the use of soy products served together with the very grains that are now fed to livestock. Cereal grains have been the staff of life in virtually every traditional society, and the god of food has usually been more specifically the god of grain, as with the Roman deity Ceres, from whom we derive the word "cereal." Throughout most of East Asia, rice has long been the primary food. It was wheat in Europe, corn in North and South America, sorghum in Africa and parts of Asia, barley in Tibet, oats in Scotland, millet in northern China and Japan, rye in Mediterranean countries, and buckwheat in Russia. To this day, wheat and rice remain the primary foods for two-thirds of the human population, followed in importance by corn, sorghum, and barley in that order. Cereal grains and soy are the most democratic of foods, for nature produces them in such abundance that there is enough to go around at prices everyone can afford. And because soy products—such as miso—contain an abundance of the very amino amino acids lacking in grains, their use as a regular part of a grain-based diet can raise the quality of the protein combination to the same level as that found in most meats, while boosting the total available protein by as much as 40 percent (see p. 23). For these reasons, it is particularly important that people in protein-scarce developing countries learn to use soy.

Relying more on plant protein and less on meat can do wonders for your food budget, health, weight, conscience and ecological environment, which is perhaps why an estimated 10 million Americans have now turned to meatless diets and why the number is rapidly increasing. Since plant foods have no cholesterol and very little saturated fats or harmful environmental contaminants (DDT, etc.), your intake of these substances will be greatly reduced, as will your susceptibility to heart disease and cancer (see p. 24–26). In a world plagued by malnutrition and starvation, 67 percent of all Americans report that they are trying to lose weight, and a recent Public Health Survey shows that 25 to 45 percent of all U.S. adults are more than 20 percent overweight (i.e., "obese"); vegetarians, on the other hand, are found to be 20 pounds below the national average. Animals will be grateful to you for not eating them and hungry people everywhere will thank you for taking no more than your share.

While their American counterparts have sold their beans to be used for oil and fodder, farmers throughout East Asia have long used homegrown soybeans as a basic daily protein source. Recently, however, a Tennessee-based new-age community called *The Farm* has taken the historic step of cultivating soybeans for use primarily as a food staple in the vegetarian diet of its 850 members. The 200 acres they planted yielded 65 tons, most of which was made into soymilk at their soy dairy or tempeh in their incubators; some of the crop, however, was shared with people in famine-stricken areas around the world in an attempt not only to help but also to educate them in the many wonders of soy. Thanks to *The Farm's* ongoing efforts to teach other Americans about soybeans, small communities across the country are starting to grow them for home consumption.

South American nations have recently turned to soy farming on a massive scale. In 1974, Brazil (with extensive financial and technical aid from Japan) passed China to become the world's second largest producer, and Argentina is actively following Brazil's lead. In Mexico, soy imports jumped from 2 million bushels in 1971 to 30 million in 1975. Until recently most of the beans have been used for fodder or exported, but in 1975, representatives from numerous Latin American countries met in Mexico with experts from around the world to discuss ways of using soy proteins directly to help feed local populations. The first conference of its kind, this historic event will undoubtedly have important implications for people in all developing countries.

Soybeans and Agriculture

Food production can be increased either by expanding farm acreage or by increasing per-acre yields. Virtually all advances during the past quarter century have come in the latter area, largely through the use of genetically engineered hybrid seeds and fossil fuels in the form of mechanization, irrigation, chemical fertilizers, pesticides, and herbicides. The result has been a 60 percent increase in U.S. farm output since 1950. However in developed countries, the intensive use of agrichemicals is now considered to have reached a point of diminishing returns. This represents a basic change in the nature of the food problem and, as agricultural economist Lester R. Brown says, "points to the urgency of a radical shift in the traditional approach to its solution—the need to concentrate much more effort than in the past on slowing the growth in world *demand* for food." With all the major resources used to produce food—water, fertilizer, energy, and land—now scarce, and the worldwide demand from burgeoning populations of people and livestock unceasing, it is believed that food prices will continue to skyrocket.

A related question that many farmers in developed countries now raise is no longer "How much food can we produce?" but "What are the environmental consequences of doing so?" Large corporations, determined to apply the principles of industry to agriculture, have been grossly negligent of the health of our soil. Believing they have emancipated themselves from dependence upon nature, agribusiness technologists have come to view soil simply as a mixture of nitrogen, phosphorous, and potassium rather than as a living, fragile substance replete with microorganisms, humus, and organic matter. Corporate executives involved in large-scale farming seem not to take the time to understand the needs of the land and its natural cycles. A growing number of farmers, however, prompted by soaring energy costs (the price of nitrogen fertilizer alone more than quadrupled between 1971 and 1980) and a solid intuition that we can't remain insensitive to the quality of our soil without eventually suffering the consequences, are taking new interest in traditional organic techniques.

Chemical fertilizers, now applied at the average level of 150 pounds per acre, were virtually unused before 1940. Up until that time, farmers practiced crop rotation, planting legumes—such as soybeans—every three years to regenerate soil nutrients and help control monoculture insect populations. Rhizobia bacteria living in the legumes' root nodules capture atmospheric nitrogen and "fix" it in the soil; this nitrogen (the main component in protein) serves as a source of free natural fertilizer that nourishes the plant and future crops. When chemical fertilizers (anhydrous ammonia or amonium nitrate) are applied to the soil, plants utilize only about 50 percent of their nitrogen, the rest being lost to seepage and runoff which often pollute local waterways. Yet the nitrogen fixed by bacteria is used completely and there is no resulting pollution. Soybeans can fix about 100 pounds of nitrogen per acre, the chemical equivalent of which would cost about $30. The American Indians apparently recognized the soil enriching value of legumes, for they generally planted beans in alternate rows with corn. The corn, which has a hearty appetite for nitrogen, sucks up the excess nitrogen as fast as the legumes can produce it, thereby signalling the latter to produce much more total nitrogen than if there were no intercropping. Some farmers and gardeners now use soy to yield a triple bonus: first, free fertilizer; second, high-protein beans; and finally, humus-forming organic matter when the plants are turned under in the fall as green manure. Most important, organic gardeners using natural fertilizers (manure and compost) find they can obtain soybean yields of 50 bushels or more per acre, almost twice the national average, accompanied by substantial savings from not using chemicals. And soybeans have such a hardy resistance to disease and insects, that avoiding the use of toxic pesticides often makes little or no difference in crop yields, while not using herbicides helps keep the root bacteria alive and vital.

Throughout the world, there is a movement away from the energy-expensive, environmentally damaging agricultural methods now popular in industrial countries. The fact that it often costs *ten times* as much to grow an acre of "green revolution" rice as an acre of the traditional crop is bringing this lesson home to poor farmers everywhere. Soybeans thrive in virtually any climate from tropical Brazil to Japan's snowy Hokkaido, and they are as well suited for use in small vegetable gardens as on huge farms. Due to their unique ability to nourish both the soil and human beings, they are bound to play a key role in the planet's emerging agriculture.

Soyfoods: Modern and Traditional

We in the West must learn to use soybeans directly as foods. And with soy oil now facing severe competition from low-cost Malaysian and African palm oil, with growing popular resistance to the wasteful and expensive feedlot system, and with the expanding need for low-cost protein foods in developing countries, the time is ripe for the influential American Soybean Association, the food industry, and concerned inivividuals to begin to take a serious interest in developing these foods.

Advanced Western technology is already being used to manufacture a number of new fabricated soy products: protein concentrates, isolates, spun fibers, and textured vegetable proteins (TVP). The latter are now widely used as meat extenders or, in combination with numerous artificial coloring and flavoring agents, as simulated meats: sausages, bacon bits, chicken, and the like. Although these products still utilize less than 2 percent of all United States soy protein, their domestic consumption is expected to increase 10-fold from 500 million pounds in 1972 to 5 billion pounds by 1985. Yet the technology and cost required to produce such products places them out of reach of the poor in developing countries who need them most, while their synthetic qualities generally limit their appeal to the growing number of Westerners interested in natural foods.

In both the developed and developing nations, there is a growing interest in methods of production employing decentralized, small-scale technology and simple, honest craftsmanship. Mass production and heavily centralized technology have created work that is mechanical and monotonous, overcrowded cities to the point of breakdown, caused severe industrial pollution, and led in many cases to massive unemployment. Most of East Asia's soyfoods are still produced in small shops which use little energy and require a minimum of capital investment to start. Traditional miso-making is a fine example of such a craft, providing truly enjoyable work that nourishes and enlivens; a beautiful mode of self expression, self discipline, and self sufficiency. Compatible with the basic needs and aspirations of human beings, it is well suited to be a model of craftsmanship for future generations.

Deeper Causes of World Hunger

We have seen in the above discussion how soybeans offer great promise to meet great needs as a key protein source for the future on our small planet, and how each of us, by moving away from meat-centered diets that support the highly wasteful feedlot system, can take a significant first step toward alleviating world food shortages. Yet we must understand that this is only a first step. As Frances Moore Lappé says so well in *Diet for a Small Planet* (Ballantine Books, 1982, revised edition) the notion of "meatless, guiltless" can be a seductively simple escape preventing further involvement. For even if the practice of feeding basic foods to animals were abandoned altogether, there would be no automatic guarantee that the vast amounts of grains and soybeans thereby released for direct consumption would actually become available to the poor at prices they could afford. Thus, if we are really serious about bringing an end to hunger and starvation on our planet, we must make an even deeper commitment to understand the larger forces that cause hunger and to do something, each in our own way, to stop them. What *are* these forces causing hunger and what *can* we do?

Population: At the present population growth rate of 1.64 percent, the population of the planet will double every 43 years. Many of the poorer nations, with growth rates of 3 percent, double every 23 years and therefore (theoretically) increase a staggering nineteenfold every century. During the 1970s, the rate of increase began to slow, perhaps for the first time in history—a promising sign. Yet each morning 178,000 new faces appear at the breakfast table and each year there are 64 million more passengers on spaceship earth. Roughly 85 to 90 percent of all new babies are born in the have-not countries, and the fastest growing populations are the ones that are the most miserable. In 1789, the English clergyman-economist Thomas Malthus accurately foresaw our predicament: "The power of population is so superior to the power of earth to provide subsistence" that man will succumb to "gigantic inevitable famine." In his excellent book *The Twenty-Ninth Day*, Lester Brown, president of the Worldwatch Institute, shows how population growth is putting increased stresses on the earth's four major biological systems that support all life: croplands, oceanic fisheries, grasslands, and forests. In each area, as demand exceeds sustainable yield, populations begin to undercut their own well being and threaten their future survival. In economic terms, they consume principal as well as interest. Brown urges governments to make a multi-pronged attack on the population problem by making family planning services universally available, liberating women from traditional roles, meeting basic social needs such as health care, nutrition, and illiteracy that are usually associated with reduced fertility, educating people about the consequences of rapid population. Brown points out that governments such as China and Singapore that have moved on all these fronts at once have been extremely successful in slowing population growth. And, of course, each of us can make a vital contribution to population control by limiting our own family size to two children or less.

Many citizens in the affluent nations tend to think of the population problem as being confined primarily to developing countries where the increase in human numbers is the highest. Yet in terms of resource consumption and pollution, the problem is actually *more* severe in the industrial nations with slower populations growth. Twenty-five percent of the passengers on spaceship earth traveling in the first class and tourist compartments consume 80 percent of the yearly supply of food, energy, and mineral resources, while contributing 75 percent of the pollution. The remaining 75 percent of the passengers traveling in the hold without adequate food, water, or shelter are beginning to get upset. It should be clear, then, that as a precondition to helping the third-class passengers, those traveling in the luxurious quarters should take all possible measures to bring their own population growth to zero while sharply limiting their consumption and waste.

While virtually all experts agree that every effort must be made on every level by almost every country to reach zero population growth as soon as possible, not all agree that high birth rate is a primary cause of hunger. In their brilliant and pioneering work, *Food First* (Ballantine Books, 1979), Frances Moore Lappé and Joseph Collins make a strong case that both hunger and population growth, rather than being causes, are symptoms of the same deeper disease—the insecurity and poverty of the majority resulting from the control over national productive resources by a small and wealthy power elite. High birth rates are seen as symptomatic of the failures of a social system, reflecting people's need to have many children in an attempt to provide laborers to increase their meager family income, to provide old-age food security, and to compensate for the high infant death rate, the result of inadequate nutrition and health care. Thus parents who are in a tragic double bind—acting quite rationally in having large families yet knowing full well they may not be able to feed them—often have no interest in birth control programs. As Lappé and Collins point out: "To attack high birth rates without attacking the causes of poverty that make large families the only survival option is not only fruitless, it is a tragic diversion our planet simply cannot afford."

Affluence: We have seen above how people (including the upper classes in less developed countries), as they become more affluent, tend to increase their consumption of foods derived from animals. In 1979, to produce these products, roughly 35 percent of the world's grain harvest (including 79 percent of the U.S. grain harvest) was fed to livestock, yet could have been used as human food. Thus while population growth accounts for about two-thirds of the annual growth in world food demand, this affluent pattern of feeding livestock grain and soy via the feedlot system accounts for the remaining one-third.

Narrow Focus on Increasing Productivity: The standard analysis that hunger is a result of food scarcity has inevitably led to programs to increase food production, generally through technological modernization. Yet when new agricultural technology enters a system based on severe economic and power disparities, it selectively benefits the rich and powerful, who have the money, land, intelligence, credit worthiness, and political influence to take fullest advantages of the new opportunities. In the end, the rich get richer and the poor poorer. A major study by the International Labor Organization (confirmed in a similar study by the United Nations Institute for Social Development) documents that in seven South Asian countries comprising 70 percent of the rural population of the nonsocialist world, while there has been a rise in per capita grain production, the food consumption of the rural poor is less than it was ten to twenty years ago; more people are more hungry and poorer than ever before. In many cases the so-called Green Revolution, expected to abolish hunger, has actually made it worse. Farm mechanization has left large numbers of farm workers without jobs and the high cost of the "inputs" necessary to grow the special new hybrid seeds —inputs such as irrigation, chemical fertilizers and pesticides, farm machinery, and the seeds themselves—have caused small farmers to go bankrupt or forced them to sell their farms to the landed elite. Not only are the poor left without a source of income, the large landowners often move the land out of basic food production and start to grow export cash crops such as grapes for wine or even flowers, which greatly increase per-acre profits.

International Food Exploitation: Large agribusiness corporations from the industrialized countries have recently begun to buy up huge quantities of basic foods from the less developed countries to sell in supermarkets at home. They have turned the planet into a Global Farm to supply a Global Supermarket, where the poor must compete with affluent foreigners for food grown in their own countries. By 1976 over 50 percent of the winter and early spring fruits and vegetables sold in U.S. supermarkets were grown in Latin America on land formerly used to feed local people. This system also puts U.S. farm workers out of work.

Land Monopolization and Misuse: In many less developed countries a small and wealthy percentage of the population owns most of the land. Based on a study of 83 developing countries, slightly more than 3 percent of all landowners controlled almost 80 percent of the farmland. The landed elite prevent land reform and redistribution by using their great political power. Yet where land redistribution has taken place, farmers who own their land are found to produce two to three times as much food per acre as tenant farmers and sharecroppers, who have no incentive to make long-term agricultural improvements on the land. All efforts must be made to give farmers control over their own land and to remove the obstacles that prevent them from growing the food they need.

Cash Crop System of Export Agriculture: The finest land in less developed countries is now widely used to grow export cash crops (coffee, sugar, cocoa, bananas, etc.) instead of growing food for the people. This system generally benefits the rich, while the poor go hungry. Clearly, agriculture must become, first and foremost, a way for people to produce the food they need and only secondly a source of foreign exchange.

An in-depth discussion of each of these problems and their complex interrelationships is given in *Food First.* Read this book! Called "One of the most stimulating books in years" by the *New York Times Book Review,* it has been highly praised by the emerging American hunger movement and by Third World leaders alike as offering a penetrating new perspective and dispelling traditional myths that prevent us from grasping how hunger is generated. While challenging the basic assumption that the main causes of hunger are too many people and not enough food, the authors show that hunger exists in the face of plenty and is caused primarily by social, economic, and political structures that block development and prevent people from democratically controlling the resources that would allow them to produce

their own food. An important part of our work is to see that our own government stops its support of foreign elites and their partners, multinational corporations, that increasingly represent primary causes of the problem, then commits itself, as we each must commit ourselves, to putting an end to worldwide hunger and starvation at the same time that we put an end to the proliferation of nuclear weapons, nuclear power, and deadly environmental chemicals. Our work is cut out for us, and it will not be short or easy. But what joy in such a great and noble challenge.

Going Beyond Ourselves

An ancient Chinese proverb reminds us that "A time of crisis is a time of great opportunity." Outmoded lifestyles and patterns of thought are beginning to crack under the strain of change so rapid it borders on discontinuity, and overlapping crises are forcing us to totally re-evaluate the very basis of our being. At the still point within us all a new vision of reality, richly detailed yet strikingly simple, is beginning to take form. In part it is the holistic and contemporary view of ecology, mother of all the sciences, that sees the perfect interconnectedness of all things, the jewelled matrix form-and-energy body of the world. In part it is the holy and ancient understanding of the spiritual paths that points to an underlying oneness in which the impossible union of opposites is made real. Our expanding vision must inevitably be a call to action, and it is abundantly clear that nothing less than selfless service and loving kindness—which accord with the truth of our oneness—are suited to the immense task we face. The child wasting in the forgotten village is our child; thus do we realize that we are all brothers and sisters. We must bring food. Watch in the years to come how selflessly soybeans offer themselves to help us feed a hungry world.

2 *Miso as a Food*

LTHOUGH SOYBEANS are a treasure trove of high-quality protein and other nutrients, only a portion of these are available to the body when the whole beans are served in their baked, boiled, or roasted forms. However through the process of natural fermentation, soybeans undergo a total biochemical transformation in which virtually all of their complex protein, carbohydrate, and lipid (oil or fat) molecules are broken down into readily digestible amino acids, simple sugars, and fatty acids. Most important, the process of leisurely fermentation unfolds a panorama of delicious new flavors and aromas.

Rich in High-quality Protein

The 21 amino acids which constitute all protein are the building blocks of the body: in children and adolescents they are essential for providing new tissue for growth, while in adults they supply the material for routine body maintenance. Eight (or occasionally ten) of these amino acids are termed "essential" because if they are available from the food a person eats, the body can manufacture the others. Because soybeans—and miso—contain the eight essential amino acids, they are known as sources of "complete protein."

The protein value of a food depends on both the quantity and quality of the protein in that food: Miso is unusually high in both.

Protein *quantity* is a measure of the percentage by weight of the protein actually present in a food. The average of all miso varieties is about 12 to 13 percent, and certain types (such as Hatcho) containing a large percentage of soybeans exceed 20 percent. These figures compare very favorably with common Western protein sources such as chicken (21%), beef or cottage cheese (20%), hamburger or eggs (13%), and whole dairy milk (3%).

Protein *quality* is a measure of the percentage of pro-

tein in a food that can actually be utilized by the body. Usually expressed in terms of Net Protein Utilization (NPU), it depends primarily on the configuration of essential amino acids in the food and on the food's digestibility. It is now becoming widely recognized that there is no fundamental difference between animal and vegetable protein: it is simply a question of degree. All foods, animal and vegetable, can be ranked on a simple scale which shows their protein quality or NPU. Generally speaking, animal foods have relatively high NPU ratings. Eggs, for example, with an NPU of 94, have the highest quality protein of any known food. This means that of the 13 grams of protein present in 100 grams of eggs, 94 percent (12.2 grams) can actually be utilized by the body. Other animal foods with high NPU ratings are milk (82), fish (80), cottage cheese (75), cheeses (70), beef and hamburger (67), and chicken (65). But a number of plant foods are also high on the scale. Rice, with an NPU of 70, contains the highest quality protein of any basic plant food. Soybeans (NPU = 61) and barley (NPU = 60) are also both relatively high. Miso, however, has NPU ratings of up to 72, *higher than any of its constituent ingredients!* This is largely because in the production of miso, rice (or barley) and soybeans are *combined*. Due to the fact that soy and grain proteins *complement* each other, the NPU of the resultant combination is higher than that of either of the individual foods, and the final product contains all of the eight essential (plus nine non-essential) amino acids in a configuration which is highly utilizable by the human body (fig. 4). Moreover, the process of fermen-

Fig. 4. Amounts of Essential Amino Acids and Their Percentages of Minimum Daily Requirements in 100 Grams of Miso (Source: *Japanese Scientific Research Council*)

Amino Acids	MDR (gm)	Red (Rice) Miso (gm)	MDR (%)	Barley Miso (gm)	Hatcho (Soybean) Miso (gm)
(Methionine-Cystine)	1.10	.29	26	.27	.45
Lysine	.80	.57	71	.65	1.36
Tryptophan	.25	.19	76	.16	.33
(Phenylalaline-Tyrosine)	1.10	1.09	99	1.23	2.10
Valine	.80	.80	100	.79	1.21
Methionine	.20	.20	100	.17	.25
Leucine	1.10	1.37	125	1.28	1.68
Isoleucine	.70	.92	131	.94	1.18
Threonine	.50	.71	142	.74	1.03
Phenylaline	.30	.57	190	.63	1.25
Protein	61.5	13.5	22	12.8	21.0

Note: Amino acids in shortest supply are listed first. Those in parentheses are important combinations of essential and semi-essential amino acids with common properties. Thus 100 grams (5½ tablespoons) of red miso (13.5% protein) contains .29 grams of the sulfur-containing amino acids (methionine-cystine), or 26 percent of the minimum adult daily requirement of 1.10 grams.

tation renders each of the basic component foods more digestible and, therefore, increases their individual NPUs. Because red miso, the most common variety (made with rice and soybeans), contains 13.5 percent protein and has an NPU of 72, one hundred grams of this product can supply us with 9.7 grams of usable protein—more than from an equal weight of hamburger (13% protein; NPU = 67).

Miso has long been a key source of protein in the Japanese diet. It presently accounts for up to 25 percent of the protein consumed in some inland rural areas and more than 8 percent for the population as a whole. The average Japanese enjoys about 16 pounds of miso each year, or about 19 grams (3½ teaspoonsful) per day.

A Powerful Protein Booster

We saw above how the combination of two foods whose proteins are complementary—such as soybeans and grains—can lead to an increase in NPU and therefore create extra usable protein at no extra cost. Yet miso *itself* is also ideal for use in combining proteins. Because it contains an abundance of precisely the amino acids lacking in other basic foods (especially wheat, corn, sesame, and even rice), the addition of as little as several teaspoons of miso to preparations containing these foods can result in large increases in usable protein. Thus miso is not only a good source of pro-

tein, but also a protein booster. Herein lies one of its basic advantages over salt as a daily seasoning.

Miso has long been considered an important nutritional complement to rice in East Asia's grain-based diet. Similarly, the use of miso with whole-wheat bread in the form of a spread, for example, or with noodles, pizza, bulgur, or other Western-style grain dishes, can increase the sum of the protein available by as much as 30 to 40 percent.

Aids Digestion and Assimilation

Miso is prized for its ability to aid in the digestion and assimilation of other foods. At least four digestive agents are contained in all non-pasteurized miso: natural digestive enzymes, lactic acid-producing baceris (*Lactobacillus* and *Pediococcus* species), salt-resistant yeasts, and the mold and other microorganisms present in koji. Only the very heartiest microorganisms are able to survive the rigors of several years' fermentation in the presence of salt. Thus they and their enzymes are well suited to continue their work in the large and small intestines where they break down or digest complex proteins, carbohydrates, and fats into simpler, more easily assimilable molecules. In Japan, commercially available digestive enzymes are often made from the same type of koji used to make miso.

Pasteurization of miso, however, destroys most of the beneficial, digestion-aiding lactic-acid forming bacteria and their enzymes, while also decreasing some of miso's natural flavor and aroma. Most of the miso (except most Hatcho miso and a few natural imports) sold in sealed plastic bags has been pasteurized to stop the natural fermentation and its production of carbon dioxide, which would cause the bag to swell and eventually burst. Most miso sold in small plastic cottage-cheese style tubs with a pop-off lid or in bulk is *not* pasteurized. In each case, check the label to be sure . . . if you care.

Lactic acid bacteria play the key role in making both yogurt and miso aids to digestion. Studies in the early 1900s by Metchnikoff and many recent studies by Japanese scientists have suggested that either the beneficial effects of the lactic acid bacteria in aiding digestion or the effect of the lactic acid they produce in altering the pH in the intestines may be a basic cause for the association of yogurt with long life and good health. It is well known that the use of penicillin or other antibiotics kills the beneficial microflora that ordinarily live in the human digestive tract. A quick, easy, and healthful way to replenish them after use of antibiotics is by drinking a cup of miso soup.

The process of lengthy aging in cedar vats—in effect, "external" digestive systems—breaks down 80 to 90 percent of miso's basic nutrients into their simpler forms. When the human system tries to do the same job (in a much shorter time) it is not as successful: roasted soybeans are only 60 percent digestible and whole boiled soybeans 68 percent. By eating miso, the body's energy ordinarily needed to digest soybeans is freed to work on other foods. The fermentation process also serves to eliminate the factors in whole

Fig. 5. Composition of Nutrients in 100 grams of Miso*

Sources: Standard Composition of Japanese Foods (Norinsho 1964; JDAC 1964), the Japanese National Miso Association Nutrient Tables, and Data Supplied by Miso Producers.

Type of Miso	Food Energy	Moisture	Protein	Fat	Carbo-hydrates (incl. fiber)	Fiber	Ash	Sodium Chloride	Calcium	Sodium	Phosphorous	Iron	Vit. B1 (Thiamine)	Vit. B2 (Riboflavin)	Vit. B3 (Niacin)
	Calories	Percent	Percent	Percent	Percent	Percent	Percent	Percent	Mg	Mg	Mg	Mg	Mg	Mg	Mg
Red Miso	153	50	13.5	5.8	19.1	1.9	14.8	13.0	115	4600	190	4.0	0.03	0.10	1.5
Light-yellow Miso	155	49	13.5	4.6	19.6	1.8	12.8	12.5	90	4100	160	4.0	0.03	0.10	1.5
Mellow Red Miso	162	42	11.2	4.2	27.9	1.3	14.5	13.0	81	3200	135	3.5	0.04	0.10	1.5
Mellow Beige Miso	165	44	13.0	4.2	29.1	1.2	8.5	7.0	80	2500	133	3.5	0.04	0.10	1.5
Mellow White Miso	215	57	12.3	1.4	27.5	1.3	4.9	9.1	31	3200	138	1.3	0.03	0.10	1.5
Sweet Red Miso	168	46	12.7	4.0	31.7	1.4	8.1	6.0	75	2100	134	3.0	0.03	0.08	3.0
Sweet White Miso	178	47	11.1	1.9	35.9	1.0	7.5	5.5	70	2100	120	4.0	0.04	0.10	1.5
Barley Miso	154	48	12.8	5.0	21.0	1.9	14.9	13.0	116	4600	190	3.5	0.04	0.10	1.5
Mellow Barley Miso	160	46	11.1	5.0	29.8	1.3	14.6	10.0	86	3500	139	3.6	0.04	0.10	1.5
Hatcho Miso	224	40	21.0	10.2	12.0	1.8	16.8	10.6	154	4100	264	7.1	0.04	0.13	1.3
Soybean Miso	180	48	19.4	6.9	13.2	2.2	13.0	11.2	140	3800	240	6.5	0.04	0.12	1.2
Tamari Miso	160	61	16.3	5.7	11.4	1.6	11.7	9.8	138	3600	220	6.3	0.04	0.11	1.1
Kinzanji Miso	172	58	11.3	2.0	30.1	2.1	5.1	8.0	95	2800	131	3.5	0.04	0.10	1.5
Peanut Miso	432	17	16.1	27.6	37.1	1.3	4.8	7.0	80	3100	180	5.6	0.04	0.10	1.3
Akadashi Miso	169	44	16.0	4.1	31.9	1.4	10.8	8.0	75	2800	135	3.6	0.05	0.10	1.4
Dehydrated Miso	303	5	32.2	9.0	35.8	3.6	26.6	18.5	180	7500	320	8.0	0.05	0.15	2.0
Low-salt/High-protein Miso	140	53	17.6	6.4	24.0	1.9	13.1	6.3	112	4600	180	4.0	0.03	0.11	1.6

Note: Values for each product vary widely depending on the maker; many of those listed are averages. The Standard Tables of Food Composition contain detailed data for red, light-yellow, sweet white, soybean, and dehydrated varieties. The Miso Association tables contain moisture, protein, fat, carbohydrate, and ash data for barley, mellow barley, mellow red and beige, and sweet red. Hatcho, peanut, and mellow white data were obtained from the makers. All other figures were derived by interpolation.

soybeans that may cause flatulence, and to inactivate trypsin inhibitors, substances found in all fresh and uncooked dried soybeans which prevent the full utilization of soy nutrients by the body.

Adds Flavor to Low-Salt Diets

A growing number of Western doctors and nutritionists are coming to favor a relatively low-salt diet as one of the simplest ways of combatting high blood pressure, hypertension and, in some cases, obesity. Most people use salt to accentuate the flavors inherent in foods. But, because miso, which contains an average of only 12 percent salt, has its own rich flavor, it can actually impart all of the desired taste and aroma with the addition of considerably *less* salt than would ordinarily be used if the food were seasoned with salt alone.

In our ongoing study of American eating patterns, we have noticed repeatedly that Americans tend to be extremists. For example, they consume either a high-salt diet or a salt-free or low-salt diet. Yet common sense and an abundance of scientific evidence show that *moderation* in the use of salt (as of many other ingredients and nutrients) is the healthiest way. Mankind's traditional diet based on grains and vegetables, when prepared with little or no added salt is simply too bland to be enjoyed day after day. Equally important is the *quality* of the salt we use. Natural sea salt supplies us with an abundance of trace elements (micronutrients) so essential for good health and metabolic balance. Moreover, recent experiments suggest that the fermentation process actually changes the effect of salt on the human body: rats have been shown to be able to tolerate a considerably higher salt intake in the form of miso than in the form of table salt. The Japanese, who may have developed an intuitive understanding of these phenomena during their long contact with fermented soybean seasonings, now obtain less than 10 percent of their total salt intake from table salt; miso supplies 20 percent, shoyu 30 percent, and *tsukemono* (salt-pickled vegetables) 40 percent.

People on a very low salt diet might consume 1 tablespoon per day of red, barley, or Hatcho miso (the equivalent of ½ teaspoon salt): an average intake is 4 tablespoons (equivalent to 2 teaspoons salt). Low-salt/high-protein miso (p. 44) lends itself particularly well to salt-restricted diets.

Miso's salinity is four times that of sea water, but because the salt is mellowed by the presence of amino acids and natural oils, miso does not taste particularly salty. And if the salt is removed, what remains tastes remarkably sweet.

A Key to Low-fat Cookery

Miso contains an average of 5 percent natural oils—mostly unsaturated and completely free of cholesterol. These give miso its savory flavor and aroma. And because they are primarily soy oils, unrefined and unprocessed, they are rich in lecithin and linoleic acid which help disperse accumulations of cholesterol and other fatty acids in the circulatory system.

In the West, our total intake of fats (a high proportion of them saturated) is about three times that of Japan. The fact that the Japanese have fewer problems with heart disease, high blood pressure, arterio- and atherosclerosis, and overweight than people in any other part of the world has often been attributed to their low consumption of fats. One of the keys to this low-fat cookery lies in the use of miso (and shoyu) in place of salt. Since we in the West generally use salt as our basic seasoning, we tend to also use fairly large amounts of oil or butter—as in dressings, sauces, or sautéed dishes—to soften the salt's intrinsic sharpness. Yet miso's saltiness is mellowed by the natural (unsaturated) oils and amino acids already present in it, and by the slow process of fermentation. Thus miso can be used in place of salt to prepare a host of delicious Western-style dishes—ranging from miso French dressings to savory white sauces—each using less than one-half the amount of fats called for in standard recipes.

An Excellent Seasoning for Weight-watchers

A welcome addition to the diet of weight watchers, miso has one of the highest known ratios of protein to calories found in any natural food: a typical portion (1 tablespoon) contains a total of only 27 calories or as little as 11 calories per gram of protein. By comparison, brown rice contains 45, bread 34, and eggs 12 calories per gram of protein. Stated slightly differently, a 100-gram portion of red miso (containing 150 calories) will fulfill 30 percent of the daily male adult protein requirement while costing only 5 percent of the typical calorie allotment. And we saw above how using miso in place of salt can help to reduce fat intake; this is an additional aid in helping us watch our weight, since the reduction of only 1 tablespoon of oil from a dish means a decrease of some 153 calories.

While carbohydrates are a food's main source of "fattening" calories, those same calories also provide us with energy. As a result of the process of fermentation, miso's carbohydrates are largely in the form of simple, easily digestible sugars and contain relatively little fiber or cellulose. Thus miso can serve as a concentrated source of stamina.

A Vegetarian Source of Essential Vitamin B-12

B-12 is one of the vitamins most commonly deficient in the diets of those vegetarians who exclude dairy products as well as meat from their diet. Until as recently as 1977, many nutritionists believed that *only* foods of animal origin contained vitamin B-12, the most concentrated sources being beef liver, tuna, eggs, and Swiss cheese. Recent research, however, has shown that there are a number of excellent vegetarian sources of vitamin B-12 including fermented soyfoods (tempeh, natto, miso, and shoyu), sea vegetables, and some single-cell proteins. By far the best soyfood source is *tempeh* (see our *Book of Tempeh*,

Harper & Row, 1979); a typical 100-gram (3½-ounce) serving of tempeh sold in the U.S. contains from 3.9 to 8.8 micrograms of vitamin B-12. Since the official U.S. recommended daily allowance (RDA) of B-12 for adults is 3 micro grams (National Academy of Sciences, 1980) one serving the tempeh can provide 130 to 294 percent of the RDA. A study in Japanese by Dr. Jusaku Takahashi in 1955 showed that light-yellow miso contained 0.17 micrograms of vitamin B-12 per 100 grams, or 2.8 percent of the RDA. A typical serving of 1 tablespoon (18 gm) of this miso would provide 0.5 percent of the RDA.

In each of the above foods, vitamin B-12 is produced by certain bacteria or molds, as it is in the rumen of livestock from which most people who are not complete vegetarians obtain their daily allotment in the form of meat or dairy products. It is important to note that many nutritionists feel that the U.S. RDA for vitamin B-12 of 3 micrograms per day is too high. The corresponding figure set by the prestigious United Nations Food and Agricultural Organization is 2 micrograms. An intake of 0.6 to 1.2 micrograms per day is generally considered sufficient for normal blood formation and good health but it will not replenish liver stores if they are depleted. We must also recall that, for centuries, Japanese Buddhist monks, who consume no foods of animal origin but obtain their vitamin B-12 from miso, natto, shoyu, and sea vegetables, have been renowned for their good health, vigor, and longevity.

Low in Phytic Acid

Raw soybeans (like most cereal grains) contain a relatively large amount (1.4 percent on a dry basis) of phytic acid, the principal source of the phosphorus in most seeds. Phytic acid and its phytate salts can have adverse nutritional effects because of its ability to chelate or bind various important minerals (especially calcium, zinc, and iron), reducing their availability to the body and thereby leading to possible nutritional deficiencies in humans and other nonruminants. Fortunately cooking the soybeans destroys some (14 percent) of the phytic acid, and the phytase enzymes, produced by the *Aspergillus* mold during the fermentation, break down much (35 percent) of the rest of the phytic acid into inositol and phosphorus, both useful nutrients. The result is that the miso's nutritional value is doubly enhanced (Wang et al. 1980; Cheryan 1980).

May Protect from Cancer

In September 1981 the *Asahi Shimbun,* Japan's equivalent of *The New York Times,* published a front page story entitled "Unexpected Virtue of Miso Soup: It lowers the Death Rate from Cancer, Heart Disease, and Liver Disease." The article was based on a major study conducted on 265,000 people over a period of 13 years by Dr. Hirayama and the prestigious and impartial National Cancer Center. The study showed that Japanese who drink miso soup every day have 32 to 33 percent less stomach cancer

mortality than those who do not drink it at all (the most likely group to develop stomach cancer) and 8 to 18 percent less than those who drink it "sometimes" (*Asahi Shimbun* 1981; see also English translation, Shurtleff 1982). MacDonald and Deuck (1976) similarly found that shoyu apparently protects rats from stomach cancer.

Promotes Long Life and Good Health

In the following sections we will introduce a number of personal and cultural testimonies from Japan concerning the health-promoting value of miso. Because most of these lack scientific verification they should not be accepted uncritically, yet they may provide promising leads for further scientific investigation.

Although the Japanese are well aware that miso is an excellent source of essential nutrients, they prize it even more for properties which are not easily defined or measured, but which are believed to promote good health and long life. After centuries of experimentation using intuitive and systematic methods based on a holistic view of life, people have found that eating miso together with a diet low in animal foods is an effective way to improve one's physical constitution and internal environment.

In his delightful and remarkably comprehensive *We Japanese,* written in 1937, Mr. Atsuharu Sakai begins his chapter on miso by saying: "It is generally believed in Japan that miso (bean paste) is responsible in great measure for the generally sound physical health of the Japanese." In recent years, scientific studies have been conducted in order to isolate the causes of longevity in Japanese communities where many of the inhabitants live to be over one hundred. One finding that has received considerable publicity concerns the high correlation between long life and the regular consumption of miso—most of which is homemade and served in soups. One well-known researcher, Dr. Akitani Kondo, found a village near Mount Fuji where the people drank an average of six bowls of miso soup daily; the per capita miso consumption was 200 grams, a national record! When we visited a "long-life" village located deep in the mountains west of Tokyo and asked a number of the villagers what they felt were the secrets of health and long life, the most frequent responses were: hard work in the fields, clean mountain air, a diet of grains and vegetables—and plenty of miso soup. (It is interesting to note that the centenarians living in the Balkans and Eastern Europe give almost the same advice except that they recommend another fermented food: yogurt.)

Recent Western laboratory experiments offer scientific explanations for the fact that traditional Oriental cultures have shown such a strong resistance to disease. Of the 161 strains of aerobic bacteria isolated in miso, almost all have been found to be antagonistic to *Escherichia coli* and *Staphylococcus aureus*—two organisms responsible for food poisoning. And specific miso bacteria are thought, by analogy, to be useful as controllers of disease-causing agents. In 1972, Drs. H. L. Wang and C. W. Hesseltine of the Northern Regional Research Center of the U.S. Department of Agriculture (p. 259) demonstrated that the molds of tempeh, shoyu, and wine-fermented tofu (doufu-ru), each fermented soybean products, inhibited the growth of harmful bacterial cultures. Yokotsuka and others in Japan have likewise shown that the compounds produced by the miso mold, *Aspergillus oryzae,* also have antibacterial activity.

Countless laboratory tests have checked for the existence of mycotoxins and especially aflatoxins (toxins caused by harmful molds) in miso. None have been found (Manabe and Matsuura 1968; Matsuura 1970; Manabe et al. 1972; Wang and Hesseltine 1979). Likewise the extremely low levels of nitrosamines in miso and shoyu (generally less than 1 part per billion) are of no conern (Nagahori 1980). For more on aflatoxins and nitrosamines, see Appendix A.

The Perfect (Alkaline) Coffee Substitute

We consider a morning cup of miso soup to be the perfect coffee substitute. Coffee hits the nervous system with a jolt of acidic caffeine (often amplified in effect by white sugar) that snaps open droopy eyes and provides a quick shot of speedy energy, followed, unfortunately, by a depressing drop in energy and further sleepiness that requires more coffee to stave it off. Miso soup, on the other hand, as well as being a source of abundant nutrients, wakes up the nervous system gently yet effectively by alkalizing the blood stream, then providing a steady flow of energy throughout the morning. We have many friends who have kicked the coffee habit with miso soup and discovered how great it feels to be *really* awake.

Throughout East Asia, miso's alkalizing (and cleansing) effect are considered to be extremely important in the development of an alkaline constitution, which is widely believed to promote resistance to disease. In standard East Asian nutritional sourcebooks, basic foods are categorized as either alkaline or acidic. This information is common knowledge throughout the culture since it is considered one of the basic principles of maintaining good health. Most of the foods which we moderns consider special treats (sweets, alcohol, meat) are listed as acidic; taken in excess, they are said to weaken the constitution. With the consumption of sugar and liquor climbing to dangerously high levels in many affluent nations, the use of alkaline miso could at least provide a counterbalance until better eating patterns are resumed; thereafter, it could be used to promote good health.

A well-known Japanese proverb states that a bowl of miso soup each day keeps the doctor away, and traditional folk wisdom abounds with sayings about the value of miso as a medicine used to cure colds, improve metabolism, clear the skin, and help develop resistance to parasitic diseases. Miso soup is often used quite specifically in the same way Westerners use Alka-Seltzer or milk of magnesia to settle an upset stomach, ameliorate a hangover, or get rid of acid indigestion.

May Prevent Radiation Sickness

In recent years, Japanese doctors and scientists have begun to consider the possibility that miso may also be an effective agent in preventing radiation sickness. Interest in this subject was stimulated by a book called *Physical Constitution and Food* written in 1965 by Dr. Shinichiro Akizuki, director of the Saint Francis Hospital in Nagasaki. Born with a congenitally weak constitution, Dr. Akizuki has devoted his career to researching the use of food as preventive medicine, placing special emphasis on a holistic (rather than symptomatic) approach to healing, and on traditional natural foods native to Japan. Throughout his intensive experimentation and research—which included the study of Japanese folk medicine, "long life" villages, and modern nutritional science—he continually applied the findings to his own life in an attempt to develop a strong physical constitution or *taishitsu.* This latter concept, which in Japanese means literally "the quality of the body" and has a somewhat deeper meaning than its English equivalent, soon became the key to his work. As miso soup and brown rice became the central foods in his diet, he experienced a steady rejuvenation accompanied by physical strength, vigor, and resistance to disease. Soon not only his family but also his entire hospital staff and patients were including miso soup and brown rice in their daily meals. A lengthy and detailed examination of the results led him to write:

> I feel that miso soup is the most essential part of a person's diet...I have found that, with very few exceptions, families which make a practice of serving miso soup daily are almost never sick ... By enjoying miso soup each day, your constitution will gradually improve and you will develop resistance to disease. I believe that miso belongs to the highest class of medicines, those which help prevent disease and strengthen the body through continued usage... Some people speak of miso as a condiment, but miso brings out the flavor and nutritional value in all foods and helps the body to digest and assimilate whatever we eat... I use and have deep respect for modern medicines such as antibiotics and modern surgical techniques, yet they must only be employed when absolutely necessary. Of prime importance is the development of a strong constitution through proper eating. The basic condition of a person's constitution determines whether or not he will be only mildly and temporarily affected by diseases, or be seriously and chronically affected.

In 1945, when the atomic bomb fell on Nagasaki, Dr. Akizuki's hospital—located only one mile from the epicenter of the blast—was left in ruins. Fortunately, he and his nurses and co-workers were not in the building and were uninjured. Throughout the following two years, though, Dr. Akizuki and his staff worked daily in prolonged close contact with fallout victims in areas of Nagasaki which were heavily damaged and highly radioactive. Nevertheless, neither he nor his associates suffered from the usual and expected effects of radiation. Dr. Akizuki was extremely interested in this phenomenon, which he hypothesized may well have been due to the fact that he and his staff had been drinking miso soup regularly. But he felt that only a thorough scientific study of the phenomenon could provide the full answer.

In 1972, a number of Japanese scientists, including Dr. Morishita Keiichi (p. 256) doing agricultural research stimulated by Dr. Akizuki's writings, discovered that miso contained dipicolinic acid (*zybicolin* in Japanese). Produced by miso and natto yeasts, it is an alkaloid which chelates (grabs onto) heavy metals such as radioactive strontium and discharges them from the body. The discovery received front-page coverage in Japan's major newspapers.

In 1978, we received the following letter from a woman in America:

My mother just underwent six weeks of radiation treatments for cancer. The doctors told me she would be very ill and uncomfortable from the aftereffects of the radiation. I gave her miso soup and other miso recipes and she experienced almost no aftereffects. The doctors couldn't believe it. When I told them about the miso they laughed it off—but I'm convinced.

We feel that phenomena such as this deserve careful study by doctors in America, a country where over 25 percent of the population now dies of cancer.

Neutralizes the Effects of Smoking and Air Pollution

There is a traditional saying in Japan that smokers should drink miso soup, and some authorities contend that the amino acids contained in miso are effective in neutralizing the harmful influences of tobacco and in eliminating them from the bloodstream. In her book *Miso Cookery*, Tatsumi Hamako relates the following story:

Since I was a little girl, my grandmother emphasized repeatedly that each morning's miso soup and pickles should be carefully and tastefully prepared, especially if they were to be served to someone who smokes. She said that miso is a solvent for nicotine and helped to carry it out of the body.

One day she placed 2 or 3 drops of miso soup in the small, ½-inch-deep metal bowl of a clogged, long-stemmed Japanese pipe (*kiseru*). She held the metal bowl over a charcoal fire until we could hear the sound of the miso soup simmering. After about one minute, all of the liquid had evaporated and only the nicotine which had dissolved in the miso soup was left in the bowl. This condensed into a small pellet and suddenly jumped out. When we placed the pipe to our lips, we found that it now drew freely and easily. But at other times, when we tried using water or *bancha* tea in place of miso soup to clear the congested pipe, the nicotine refused to dissolve. Even if we blew vigorously on the pipe, we could not clear it. I realized that what grandmother had been saying was true.

A kiseru

It is said to be common knowledge among Japanese traffic policemen that the consumption of miso soup each day ameliorates the effects on the body of auto exhaust pollutants. Even today, in many areas where the police department provides communal lunches, a conscientious effort is made to include miso soup.

So if you have to smoke or breathe polluted air, at least protect yourself by drinking miso soup too.

A Seasoning of Unlimited Versatility

Even if there were only one variety of miso, its uses would invite endless experimentation. Yet each of the many miso varieties has its own unique flavor and aroma, color and texture, and each can lend the crowning touch to a wide variety of your favorite Western-style and Oriental dishes. The more than 400 recipes in the following pages give only an inkling of the many possibilities.

In a vegetarian diet, often characterized by the simple, light flavors of grains, land and sea vegetables, and soyfoods, miso has long served to add depth of flavor and savory richness.

A Traditional Natural Food

Capable of being stored without refrigeration, even in semitropical climates, miso is a traditional, natural food. Many commercial varieties are still prepared in small-scale shops using traditional technologies and without chemical additives.

An Inexpensive Delicacy

Miso is a remarkably inexpensive food, even in the West where prices of the best imported varieties are of necessity higher than they are in Japan. The per capita cost of a month's supply of top-quality miso (1½ tablespoons per day) in San Francisco, Boston, or New York need not exceed a few dollars. And if the miso is prepared at home using ingredients now readily available throughout the United States, it will cost only a fraction as much.

A Key to the Vegetarian Transition

Polls taken in 1980 show that there are ten million people in the United States who eat no meat, and that the number is rapidly increasing. Recently, doctors and nutritionists have joined the bandwagon. Their arguments:

1. **Physiology:** Man's digestive system, like that of the anthropoid apes, is fundamentally different from that of carnivores. The latter have very short bowels (3 times the body's length) for rapid expulsion of putrefying meat, stomachs with ten times as much hydrochloric acid as non-carnivores for processing saturated fats and cholesterol, and sharp elongated canines for tearing flesh. Man, however, has a long bowel (12 times the body's length) ideal for the slow diges-

tion of plant foods; his dental structure is that of a strictly herbivorous animal with molars designed for grinding grains and nuts and his incisors for slicing vegetables and fruits.

2. **Heart Disease:** Over 54 percent of all deaths in the United States are caused by cardiovascular illnesses which are practically unknown in societies where meat consumption is low. About 40 percent of the fat in our diet comes from meat, and 40 percent of this is the saturated, cholesterol-producing type. A recent study of Seventh Day Adventist vegetarians showed that they had only 40 percent the incidence of heart disease as the general population, and those that ate neither eggs nor dairy products had only 23 percent. Heart specialists estimate that if we were to reduce our saturated fat intake by 35 to 50 percent, our heart attack rate could be cut in half.

3. **Cancer:** The graph (Fig. 6) reprinted from the prestigious *Scientific American* magazine, shows the striking relationship between cancer of the large intestine and meat consumption among women in 23 countries; the writers explain that "an alternative explanation attributes cancer . . . to a low consumption of cereals. The two hypotheses are hard to distinguish from each other because high meat consumption and low cereal consumption tend to go together." Large studies of Mormons (who characteristically eat little meat) show an incidence of cancer 50 percent below the norm.

4. **Longevity:** Repeated studies by anthropologists throughout the world show that vegetarians live longer and are generally healthier than meat eaters. The long-lived Hunzas are almost total vegetarians.

5. **Arthritis:** Widely recommended dietary cures for this painful ailment call for strict avoidance of meat.

6. **Obesity:** Vegetarians in America are 20 pounds below the national average weight, while those following a standard meat-centered diet are 12 to 15 pounds above their ideal weight. Obesity is now considered a major cause of heart disease and many other illnesses.

7. **Stamina:** Numerous studies of athletes show that vegetarians have much more stamina than meat eaters, are able to perform endurance tests several times longer before exhaustion, and take less than one-fourth the time to recover from fatigue. A growing number of world record and Olympic medal holders are vegetarians. And for strength — look at the elephant, the bull, or the gorilla.

But . . . in the face of all this evidence, many people still ask, where will I get that meaty flavor I love?

From miso.

Fig. 6. Intestinal Cancer vs. Meat Consumption Among Females (*Sources: Scientific American, Nov. 1975*)

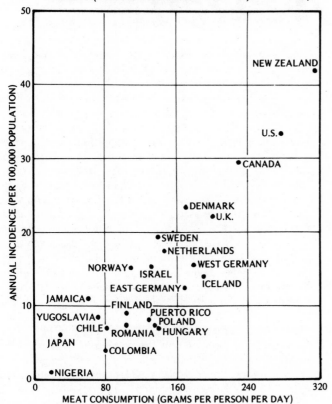

3
The Miracle of Fermentation

THE KEY TO the art of making fine miso lies in the process of fermentation, a process which, throughout its long and varied history around the world, has served three fundamental purposes: the improvement of a food's digestibility; the transformation of its flavor and aroma, color and texture; and its preservation without refrigeration. Watching the drama enlarged a thousandfold and presented in time-lapse color photography, one witnesses a near-miraculous world in which tiny spores burst into blossom like elegant and complex flowers, enzymes reach out inquisitively like long fingers melting solid particles at their touch, and populations of mold explode until they have totally enveloped the foods—or "substrates" —which support their life.

Just as Western craftsmen have fermented milk to form cheese and yogurt, or grapes to form wine, Eastern craftsmen have fermented soybeans and grains to form miso, shoyu, and tempeh. In each case, the *dramatis personae* are myriads of microorganisms which serve as the vital essence and force of the living fermentation process. These tiny creatures work best at their own unhurried pace, timed by the great rhythmic movements of the four seasons and the delicate biochemical changes occurring in their "household." Man serves his highest function by understanding the laws of change written into these life processes and providing the optimum conditions for their natural unfoldment. He thus becomes a partner with the Master Alchemist in creating a masterpiece of fine flavor.

All natural miso is prepared in basically the same way, using a two-part fermentation process. *To prepare rice miso, for example, rice is soaked overnight, drained, and then steamed. Cooled to body temperature, it is mixed with a small amount of "koji starter" consisting of spores of the mold *Aspergillus oryzae (Ass-per-JIL-us oh-RAI-zee)*. Every craftsman prizes and guards his favorite strains of this

*For a more detailed discussion of the microbiology and biochemistry of miso fermentation, see Appendix C.

mold, since they are essential to imparting a unique character to his miso. Some strains have been in the custody of family-run shops for generations: they permeate the tools, the vats, the very air. Molds are used in East Asia to activate the fermentation for miso, soy sauce, rice wine, and vinegar, just as they are used in the West to make Brie, Roquefort, Camembert, Bleu, and other mold-ripened cheeses.

The inoculated rice is spread in shallow wooden trays and incubated in a warm, humid room for about 45 hours. Here it becomes bound together by a bloom of fragrant white mold. This mold-covered grain is called *koji*. The function of the koji molds is to produce enzymes that will later break down proteins, starches, and fats into more readily digestible amino acids, simple sugars, and fatty acids.

The first fermentation complete, the koji is crumbled to break up the mat-like mycelium, thereby giving the koji an appearance similar to rice crispies that have been dusted with flour. It is then combined with cooked soybeans, a little of the soybean cooking liquid, salt, and a small amount of mature miso from a previous fermentation. This "seed miso" introduces distinctive yeasts and bacteria from the shop's miso lineage while making it possible to complete the next step in a shorter time.

The ingredients are mashed together (traditionally underfoot, like grapes for wine, in shallow wooden tubs), then packed into 6-foot-deep cedar vats. Covered with a layer of sheeting and a wooden pressing lid topped with heavy weights, they now begin their second fermentation. While enzymatic digestion gets underway, a small amount of liquid rises to the surface creating a sealed, airtight environment that prevents the entry of contaminating microorganisms. Once the complex soy and grain nutrients have been broken down into their simpler forms, yeasts and bacteria propagate. The bacteria, primarily lactic acid-formers such as *Pediococcus halophilus* and *Lactobacillus delbrueckii*, transform simple sugars into various organic acids which impart a unique flavor to the miso and help prevent spoilage. The yeasts react with sugars to produce alcohols, contributing to the miso's aroma. Eventually, alcohols and acids react with one another to produce esters, which become the chief components of the miso bouquet. Time mellows the sharpness of the salt and harmonizes it with the other deepening flavors. Slowly the color of the mixture turns from its initial light tan or yellow to rich shades of brown.

The character of a miso is determined largely by the proportions of koji and salt to soybeans. Misos made from a mixture in which koji predominates tend to be sweet since the koji enzymes break down the abundant grain carbohydrates into simple sugars. The use of a relatively large proportion of salt slows down the fermentation process and the resulting lengthy aging yields a product having a dark color and deep, rich flavor. By contrast, a miso low in salt and rich in koji requires only a short fermentation and its sweet flavor is usually accompanied by a light color.

In large tile-roofed, almost window-less buildings that serve to insulate the miso from extremes of heat and cold, fermentation continues throughout the year with the greatest activity during the warm months and almost none at all during the dead of winter. When, after one to three summers, the miso has come to maturity, it contains an immense number of vital and very beneficial microorganisms and enzymes. These are present in the natural miso you serve, ready to continue their work of aiding digestion within the human body.

Miso Aging (from Miso Daigaku)

4

The Varieties of Miso

THE MOST COMMON classification divides the world of miso into three basic groups: *regular miso*, consisting of three types—rice, barley, and soybean—is used primarily in cooking and, in Japan, particularly in soups; *special miso*, consisting of two types—finger lickin' and sweet simmered miso—is used primarily as a topping for grain dishes, fresh vegetable slices and tofu, and is usually not cooked; and *modern miso* consisting of a group of products developed since the end of World War II. Each type is represented by a number of unique varieties (fig. 7), for every batch of miso differs according to the proportions of ingredients used, the cooking methods employed, and the duration and temperature of fermentation. Each craftsman, professional or amateur, produces miso which is an expression of his tradition, his mastery of the craft and, in the case of natural miso, the dominant and subtle climatic factors affecting the environment in which he lives. As is the case with the world's fine cheeses or wines, individual representatives of the same miso variety, each often bearing the name of its birthplace, differ according to their region and year of origin: a red (rice) miso made in Sendai, for example, is not the same as one made in Tokyo, while one shop's barley miso of 1980 "vintage" may be distinctly different from that made the year before using identical ingredients.

In recent years, the number of miso varieties has steadily increased. Many unknown several generations ago outside the immediate region in which they have traditionally been prepared are now available throughout the country and even in the West.

An Overview

Before we go on to a discussion of the classical varieties and their major subdivisions, it might be best to begin with an overview. The world of miso lends itself to just such a perspective since all varieties share six principle attributes: method of fermentation, flavor, color, texture, cost, and region of origin.

Natural vs. Quick Miso: Natural miso, universally regarded as having the finest flavor, is prepared in the traditional way and has three basic characteristics: it is fermented slowly and leisurely (usually for six months to three years) at the natural temperature of its environment; it is made from only natural ingredients and contains no defatted soybean meal (an inexpensive substitute for whole soybeans) or chemical additives (except, in some cases, ethyl alcohol, p. 265); and it is never pasteurized. Most natural misos have a distinctive texture imparted by clearly visible chunks of whole soybeans and koji. About 97½ percent of Japan's miso is made with whole beans, 70 percent contains no chemical additives, 50 percent is not pasteurized, and 35 percent is fermented under natural conditions. Since some of the varieties which are not pasteurized *do* contain additives, only about 25 percent of Japan's total output is estimated to be *completely* natural. The three varieties most widely prepared in the traditional way (red, barley, and Hatcho) are called for in the majority of recipes in this book.

When measuring the age of natural miso, the Japanese (and Chinese) use an unusual system which has caused some confusion in the West. In the Orient, the age of miso—and of people— is calculated in the same way we reckon the age of race horses; regardless of the actual date of production or "birth," the miso becomes one year older on the first day of each new year. Thus New Years, the most important holiday of the year in East Asia, is everyone's and everything's birthday. And miso started in the fall of one year and harvested 12 months later is called "two-year-miso," since it has been in existence during two calendar years. "Three-year" barley and Hatcho miso are often actually aged for only 18 months.

Quick miso, a 20 to 30 percent less expensive modern product, is fermented for a short time (generally about three weeks but sometimes for as little as three days) in a temperature-controlled, heated environment. The short fermenta-

Fig. 7. The Varieties of Miso

GROUP	TYPE	VARIETY	FLAVOR	COLOR	FRAGRANCE AND AROMA	NATURAL AGING TIME	JAPANESE NAMES AND SUB-VARIETIES	PLACE OF PRODUCTION	PROTEIN %	CARBO-HY-DRATE %	SALT %	INGREDIENTS PER 10 LBS. SOYBEANS	
												DRIED KOJI (LBS.)	SALT (LBS.)
REGULAR MISO	Rice Miso	Red Miso (incl. Brown-rice Miso)	Deep rich saltiness	Reddish brown to russet	Deep fermented aroma	6 to 12 months	Aka-miso, Genmai Miso, Sendai, Sado, Echigo, Tsugaru	Tohoku, Niigata, Sado, Hokkaido, Hokuriku, Chugoku	13.5	19.1	13.0	8.5	4.4
REGULAR MISO	Rice Miso	Light-yellow Miso	Mature rounded saltiness with subtle tartness	Bright light yellow	Light refreshing fragrance	1 to 2 years	Shinshu Miso, Akita Miso	Nagano, Tokyo Area, Akita	13.5	19.6	12.5	7	4.1
REGULAR MISO	Rice Miso	Mellow Red Miso	Deep semi-sweetness	Yellowish red	Rich fragrance	3 to 6 months	Amakuchi Aka-miso, Gozen Miso	Urban Centers	11.2	27.9	13.0	14	4.0
REGULAR MISO	Rice Miso	Mellow Beige Miso	Light semi-sweetness	Yellow to tan	Light mild fragrance	5 to 20 days	Amakuchi Tanshoku Miso, Aijiro Miso, Mochigomé Miso	Nagano, Tokyo Area, Urban Centers	13.0	29.1	7.0	12	4.7
REGULAR MISO	Rice Miso	Mellow White Miso	Rich, heady mellowness	Light beige	Subtly sweet, fermented fragrance	4 weeks	Shiro-koji Miso	Hawaii	12.3	27.5	9.1	15	3.4
REGULAR MISO	Rice Miso	Sweet Red Miso	Rich, deep sweetness	Lustrous reddish brown	Savory and sweet	10 to 30 days	Edo Ama-miso	Tokyo	12.7	31.7	6.0	13	2.2
REGULAR MISO	Rice Miso	Sweet White Miso	Light, rich dessert-like sweetness	Ivory to yellowish white	Light, sweet springtime fragrance	1 to 4 weeks	Shiro Miso, Saikyo Miso, Fuchu Miso, Sanuki Miso	Kyoto, Hiroshima, Takamatsu	11.1	35.9	5.5	20	2.4
REGULAR MISO	Barley Miso	Barley Miso	Deep rich saltiness	Dark reddish brown	Prominent barley aroma	1 to 3 years	Karakuchi Mugi Miso	Kyushu, Saitama	12.8	21.0	13.0	10	4.6
REGULAR MISO	Barley Miso	Mellow Barley Miso	Deep, rich subtle sweetness	Yellowish brown to russet	Subtle barley fragrance	10 to 20 days	Amakuchi Mugi Miso	Kyushu, Chugoku, Shikoku	11.1	29.8	10.0	17	4.8
REGULAR MISO	Soybean Miso	Hatcho Miso	Mellow richness, subtly tart	Chocolate brown	Distinctive rich, deep aroma	18 to 36 months	Hatcho Miso, Waka-Hatcho, Sanshu Miso	Aichi, Okazaki	21	12	10.6	0	2.0
REGULAR MISO	Soybean Miso	Soybean Miso	Mellow saltiness	Dark reddish brown	Prominent soy aroma	1 year	Ichi-nen Mamé Miso, Nagoya Miso	Aichi, Mie, Gifu	19.4	13.2	11.2	0	2.1
REGULAR MISO	Soybean Miso	Tamari Miso	Deep saltiness	Dark brown	Deep, heavy soy aroma	1 year	Tamari Miso	Aichi, Mie, Gifu	20	12.3	11.3	0	2.4
SPECIAL MISO	Finger Lickin' Miso	Kinzanji Moromi Hishio Namémiso Natto Goto	Rich fermented sweetness	Golden brown to dark amber	Deep barley fragrance	20 to 60 days	Namémiso	All Japan	11	30	8	20	3
SPECIAL MISO	Sweet Simmered Miso	Peanut Walnut Sesame Yuzu Kinomé Red-snapper Tekka	Sweet and varied	Varied	Varied		Nerimiso	All Japan, Homes, Restaurants	14	37	7	–	–
MODERN MISO	Modern Miso	Akadashi Miso	Rich, mellow sweetness	Dark reddish brown	Savory sweet aroma		Akadashi Miso	Aichi, Kyoto	16	31.9	10	–	–
MODERN MISO	Modern Miso	Dehydrated Miso	Varied	Varied	Varied		Kanso Miso, Kona Miso	Tokyo	32.2	35.8	18.5		
MODERN MISO	Modern Miso	Low-salt/High-protein Miso	Mild saltiness	Tan	Mild aroma		Gen-en Miso	Tokyo	17.6	14.0	6.3		

tion does not allow it to develop the full mellowness of flavor and aroma, deep color, and long-lasting properties characteristic of natural miso. Hence, various chemicals and synthetics (bleaches, food colorings, sweeteners, vitamins, and monosodium glutamate) are occasionally added together with preservatives (ethyl alcohol or sorbic acid). Most quick miso is also pasteurized to prevent its microorganisms from producing carbon dioxide which would cause the plastic bags in which it is packaged to swell and sometimes explode. Pasteurization, like overcooking, causes a further decline in the miso's flavor and aroma, and, by killing the microorganisms which would otherwise aid digestion in the human body, lowers the miso's nutritional value. Most quick miso has a smooth texture since the soybeans and koji are ground together usually twice, once in the vats to shorten the fermentation time and again later during pasteurization. Prepared with a large proportion of koji and small amount of salt to further accelerate fermentation, quick miso is also usually quite sweet. First manufactured on a large scale during the 1960s, it is now mass-produced in modern factories, as described in Chapter 10.

Like quick miso, naturally fermented varieties are also now available in 1- to 2-pound polyethylene bags which allow for better distribution. To prevent swelling, virtually all miso (except Hatcho) sealed in bags is pasteurized and/or contains ethyl alcohol or sorbic acid preservative. If packed in bulk

kegs or cottage cheese-type containers, pasteurization and additives become unnecessary.

Salty vs. Sweet Miso: All misos can be grouped according to their salt content as shown in figure 8.

Varieties containing 10½ to 14 percent salt are generally low in carbohydrates (20% or less) and have a savory, rather salty flavor. At the other extreme, those containing less than 7 percent salt are generally rich in carbohydrates (30 percent or more) and enjoy a heady sweetness. Note that all misos are assumed to be salty unless specifically designated otherwise. When thinned in ½ cup water, 2 teaspoons of salty miso produce about the same strength broth as 3 to 4 teaspoons mellow or 5 to 6 teaspoons sweet miso. (Mellow red miso, which contains 13 percent salt, falls outside its proper domain; due to its abundant carbohydrates, it actually has a flavor similar to that of mellow barley miso.)

Japan's sweetest misos are found in Kyoto, her ancient capital, and Tokyo, her present-day metropolitan center. As one moves from modern urban areas to more traditional farming and fishing districts, the preferred miso grows saltier and more of it is made at home. Consumption patterns demonstrate that urban office workers, young people, and the upper classes prefer the sweeter varieties, whereas farmers, laborers, and elderly adults prefer the saltier. As one might expect, the consumption of sweet miso has increased and that of salty miso has decreased since the end of World War II, paralleling Japan's rapid urbanization and industrialization. The Western pattern of sugar consumption (now over 14 tablespoons per person daily in the U.S.) has also strongly affected Japanese tastes. And the shorter fermentation time needed by the sweet misos has been an added incentive for manufacturers to emphasize their production.

Sweet miso is most commonly used in toppings, spreads, sauces, and vegetable side dishes; salty miso is preferred in soups, as a pickling agent for vegetables, and with seafoods. One tablespoon of sweet miso and 1½ teaspoons of salty miso each contain approximately ¼ teaspoon of salt.

Because the natural sugars with which it abounds tend to ferment quite quickly, forming alcohols, sweet miso has a short shelf life and is therefore difficult to export. Salty miso, on the other hand, can be stored indefinitely even at room temperature.

The sweetness or saltiness of a miso has no hard-and-fast relationship to its color. Generally, though, saltier varieties tend to be darker since both salinity and depth of color are directly related to length of fermentation.

Red vs. White Miso: Like wines, all misos can be divided into reds (actually russets and warm chestnut browns) and whites (soft light-yellows and creamy beiges). Most red miso, like red wine, obtains its coloration from natural changes requiring lengthy aging, whereas white miso is generally prepared by quick, temperature-controlled fermentation. In general, rice miso tends to be lighter in color than barley miso, and barley miso tends to be lighter than soybean miso.

The great majority of Japan's white miso is made with rice koji and contains a large proportion of carbohydrates and

Fig. 8. The Percentage of Salt in Different Miso Varieties

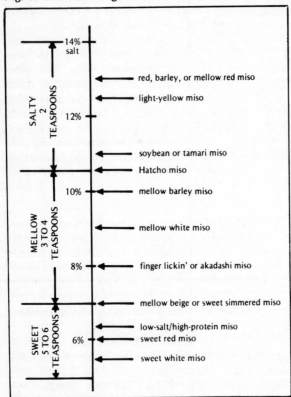

relatively little salt; hence, most white miso is rather sweet. The soybeans used are carefully selected to exclude dark varieties, dehulled to give them an even lighter coloration, and then pressure cooked under water (rather than in steam) for a relatively short time; in some cases a small amount of bleach is added to the cooking and/or soaking water. After cooking, all water is immediately expelled (with the loss of valuable nutrients), and the beans are cooled rapidly in a partial vacuum inside the pressure cooker to further minimize oxidation and browning. Yellow riboflavin food coloring (vitamin B_2) is sometimes added before fermentation to give the bleached end-product a more natural-looking luster. Packed into vats and well sealed, the miso is fermented quickly in a warm environment. Very light-colored sweet varieties are often shipped to retailers before the end of fermentation; they come to maturity en route and on the shelves in order to minimize darkening and spoilage. Varieties sealed in bags may have bleach added just before packaging.

Most white miso is a very modern product. The ancient sweet white miso of Kyoto was not nearly as white as its present descendants, since it was prepared by natural fermentation without bleaches or pressure cooking, and contained less carbohydrates. Recently, the consumption of light-colored miso has grown rapidly with the increase in the number of large-scale miso factories which find it more profitable to produce, and under the influence of modern advertising which has worked to create the image that "white" (as in white rice, white bread, and white sugar) is beautiful. Like most sweet miso, and for the same reasons, white varieties have a short shelf life and are difficult to export.

NOTE: In Japan, the term "red miso" (*aka* miso), used in its usual narrow sense, refers only to salty red rice miso. However, in its broad sense it may refer to any miso with a reddish or dark brown color. The term "white miso" (*shiro* miso) usually refers only to Kyoto-style sweet white miso; "light-colored miso" (*tanshoku* miso) is generally used to refer to all yellowish or whitish varieties. Occasionally the term "black miso" is used to refer to the darker varieties of soybean miso.

Chunky and Koji vs. Smooth Miso: Chunky miso (*tsubu miso*) is any variety in which the shape of the soybeans (and usually of the koji grains) is still visible. It is the oldest form of miso and comprised virtually all that made before 1945. During the mixing and mashing of ingredients before the fermentation of natural miso, almost all of the koji and at least half of the soybeans were left in their natural form. The koji gradually dissolved as the miso aged, but the beans generally retained their individual form, even after three years of fermentation, thereby lending the finished miso a distinctive, flavor-enhancing texture.

In koji miso, the form and texture of the koji grains are still visible. Prepared by mashing the cooked soybeans thoroughly before they are combined with the koji and salt, koji miso, with its distinctive texture, is usually quite young (12 to 18 months). It nevertheless retains a strong appeal among miso connoisseurs.

Smooth miso is that which has been blended or ground to a homogeneous purée. First prepared after 1945, it now comprises about 80 percent of all miso sold in Japan. It derives much of its appeal from the fact that the Japanese have traditionally ground their miso with a little water before adding it to soups; smooth miso saves modern cooks the time and trouble. In factories making quick miso, this smooth-textured product is an inevitable result of the production process since all of the ingredients are ground anyway, once to shorten the fermentation time and then again to reinforce the effects of pasteurization.

Expensive vs. Inexpensive Miso: In Japan, miso varieties sold in polyethylene bags through supermarkets and grocery stores are the least expensive. The same miso automatically rises in price when it is sold out of open-top kegs at traditional miso retail outlets. To avoid pasteurization and the use of preservatives, much natural miso is still sold in the latter way, but many varieties of even natural (unpasteurized) miso now contain ethyl alcohol preservative and can be found in natural food stores for relatively low prices packaged in polyethylene bags.

In general, rice miso is less expensive than barley miso, and barley miso is less expensive than soybean miso. The least expensive misos, often characterized by a soft texture due to the addition of extra water, are usually quick misos made by large-scale production methods. More expensive misos are frequently natural varieties made by small, tradition- and quality-oriented companies.

In February 1983 miso prices in Japan ranged from about $0.51 per pound for quick light-yellow miso to about $1.35 per pound for Hatcho, sweet white, and other fine natural misos. The average price per pound of quick miso was $0.57 compared with $0.82 for natural varieties. At the same time in the United States, imported natural miso packaged in polyethylene bags sold at natural food stores for the following average prices per pound: red miso $1.77, brown-rice miso $2.11, barley miso $1.96, Hatcho miso $2.35, and finger lickin' miso (including natto miso) $2.36.

Miso from the Provinces: In Japan, the many varieties of miso are often grouped according to the provinces or regions in which they are produced. Like many of the world's wines and cheeses, the majority of Japan's traditional misos bear the name of their birthplace as shown in figure 9a. A miso having a history deeply rooted in the provinces is often called *tochi* miso, or "miso of the land," and is especially prized.

If one travels the entire length of the Japanese archipelago from southwest to northeast—a distance of about 1,360 miles—one would find that as the climate changes from warm to cold, the preferred miso generally changes from sweet to salty and consumption tends to increase. In the southern third of Japan, barley miso is preferred; in the central third, soybean miso; and in the northern third, rice miso (fig. 9b).

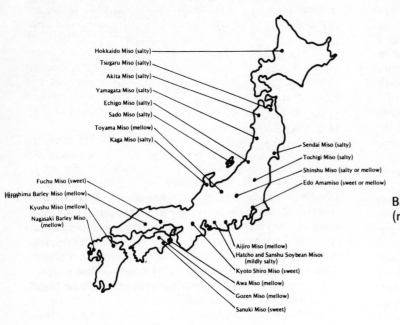

Hokkaido Miso (salty)
Tsugaru Miso (salty)
Akita Miso (salty)
Yamagata Miso (salty)
Echigo Miso (salty)
Sado Miso (salty)
Toyama Miso (mellow)
Kaga Miso (salty)

Sendai Miso (salty)
Tochigi Miso (salty)
Shinshu Miso (salty or mellow)
Edo Amamiso (sweet or mellow)

Fuchu Miso (sweet)
Hiroshima Barley Miso (mellow)
Kyushu Miso (mellow)
Nagasaki Barley Miso (mellow)

Aijiro Miso (mellow)
Hatcho and Sanshu Soybean Misos (mildly salty)
Kyoto Shiro Miso (sweet)
Awa Miso (mellow)
Gozen Miso (mellow)
Sanuki Miso (sweet)

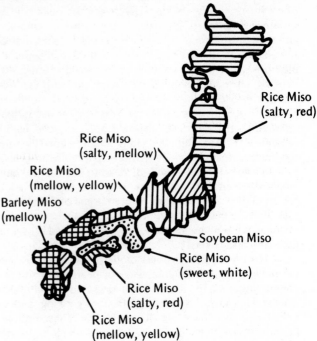

Rice Miso (salty, red)

Rice Miso (salty, mellow)

Rice Miso (mellow, yellow)

Barley Miso (mellow)

Soybean Miso

Rice Miso (sweet, white)

Rice Miso (salty, red)

Rice Miso (mellow, yellow)

REGULAR MISO

Our overview complete, let us proceed to the three major groupings outlined at the start of this chapter. The first group, regular miso, constitutes about 90 to 95 percent of all commercial miso prepared in Japan. The three basic types—rice, barley, and soybean miso—are classified according to the basic raw material or substrate used for the koji. The production of rice miso predominates (81% of yearly output in this category), followed by barley (11%) and soybean (8%). Each type may be further divided on the basis of flavor into sweet, mellow, and salty, and then subdivided on the basis of color into red, light-yellow, and white varieties (fig. 7, p.31).

The following three types and 12 varieties of miso are widely available throughout Japan. Within each variety are hundreds of sub-varieties which differ according to the maker, process, ingredients, and locality of origin.

Rice Miso (Komé Miso)

Prohibitively expensive as recently as 50 to 100 years ago, rice miso now accounts for 81 percent of the miso sold in Japan. In fact, today all miso is assumed to fall under this classification unless otherwise stated, just as all miso is assumed to be salty-tasting unless specifically called sweet; hence salty red rice miso is simply called "red miso." Very rich in glucose and other natural sugars, rice serves as the basis of the koji used in most of Japan's sweet, quick, and white misos. The finest salty rice misos have traditionally been produced in the cold provinces north of Tokyo noted for yield-

ing high-quality rice.

The scarcity of rice miso in traditional Japan is thought to be due to the fact that rice — and especially the polished or milled rice from which most rice miso has always been made — was a food reserved for the aristocracy and samurai. Feudal peasants were required to send the rice they grew to their lords, leaving them with only barley, although in some areas, the farmers were allowed to collect broken rice kernels to prepare their miso. Thus, part of the present popularity of rice miso in Japan is an expression of the ancient tendency to regard rice and rice miso as foods of the upper classes.

Variety	Native Region	Soy-beans	Rice	Salt	Natural Fermentation
Red Miso (incl. Brown-rice miso)	Northeast provinces	10	8.5	4.4	1-3 years
Light-yellow	Shinshu	10	7.0	4.1	1-3 years
Mellow Red	Urban centers	10	14.0	4.0	4-7 weeks*
Mellow Beige	Urban centers	10	12.0	4.7	3-4 weeks*
Mellow White	Hawaii	10	15.0	3.4	4-6 weeks
Sweet Red	Tokyo (Edo)	10	13.0	2.2	2-5 weeks
Sweet White	Kyoto	10	20.0	2.4	1-4 weeks
					*Quick fermentation only

Red Miso *(Aka Miso):* Fermented naturally for one to three years or by temperature-controlled methods for three to four months, red miso has a rich-and-savory salty flavor with subtly sweet undertones. Deeply fragrant, its color ranges from lustrous russet to dark reddish brown; its texture from chunky-and-soft to smooth-and-firm. It takes its Japanese name *(Sendai miso)* from the city in the northeastern provinces which has served as the center of red miso production since ancient times.

Of all types of regular miso, whether rice, barley or soybean, red miso has the lowest proportion of carbohydrates (19.1%), the second highest proportion of protein (13.5%), and the highest proportion of salt (13%). Thus the natural product can be stored for several years at room temperature and, in most cases, the flavor will actually improve over time. A popular and versatile miso, it is well suited for use in all types of cookery. An estimated 75 percent of all the rice miso now sold commercially in Japan, and virtually all the rice miso prepared in farmhouses, is red (or light-yellow, as described below).

Well known sub-varieties of red miso are listed in figure 10; their places of origin are shown on the map on page 34. Of particular historical interest is the delicious Sado miso, which was developed about 350 years ago on Sado Island in the Japan Sea far to the north of Tokyo. Centuries ago, a famous shipping route led from Osaka around the southern tip of Honshu to Sado Island, and then on to Japan's northernmost island, Hokkaido. Ships transported Sado miso to Hokkaido where it was too cold to make a local variety, and on the return voyage brought back high-quality Hokkaido soybeans, which were used in subsequent batches of Sado miso. Sado islanders now grow their own fine beans, and their miso is known for its subtly-sweet flavor and koji texture.

A sub-variety of rice miso that has recently won considerable favor in the West is brown-rice miso. It has a delectable natural flavor, deep and mellow, and a satisfying fragrance. This miso is endowed with real character, is loaded with nutrients found in the rice's bran layers, and is priced quite reasonably. Its fermentation time is 6 to 18 months. At present a number of Japanese producers make brown-rice miso (see Appendix E); the product most widely sold in America is made by Sendai Miso-Shoyu. Most red miso has always been made with white rice because: 1) the surface layers of brown rice are so nutritious that alien microorganisms as well as the koji mold spores tend to thrive and produce off-flavors; 2) preventing this phenomenon requires delicate temperature control during koji preparation; 3) the koji mycelium has difficulty penetrating the bran layers and therefore in breaking down the central portions of the rice kernels; 4) most modern Japanese prefer the flavor of white to brown rice. The rice used to make brown-rice koji is polished very slightly to aid penetration of the mycelium; about 2½ pounds of bran are removed from each 100 pounds of unpolished grain as compared with 10 pounds when making white rice. In some cases, the rice is also split before being steamed. The preparation of the koji is identical to that using white rice except that the temperature is kept within a narrower range of the ideal at each step in the process.

Light-Yellow Miso *(Shinshu Miso):* Shinshu refers to the ancient province north of Tokyo—now Nagano prefecture—where this popular variety was first developed. Originally resembling Sendai red in proportion of basic in-

gredients, color, and flavor, Shinshu contained slightly less salt and therefore enjoyed a subtle and highly prized tartness. Whereas Sendai miso was generally chunky, Shinshu was smooth, and some varieties were prepared with black soybeans. Traditional Shinshu, usually fermented for at least one year, is still made in farmhouses in its native locality but is no longer widely available on a commercial basis. Akita miso, its close relative, has a sweeter flavor and lighter color (see chart below).

Modern Shinshu, which we call light-yellow miso, is a quick miso the best examples of which have a mature and mellow salty flavor, and a subtle tart quality. Light and refreshing in aroma, its color ranges from light yellow to yellowish brown, and its firm texture is almost always smooth. Low in carbohydrates (19.6%) and quite high in both salt (12.5%) and protein (13.5%), it keeps for up to two months at room temperature, but for longer storage must be refrigerated. Prepared by temperature-controlled fermentation in only three to four weeks, light-yellow miso is Japan's least expensive variety. Some varieties may contain bleach and vitamin B_2 food coloring.

According to popular tradition, the original Shinshu miso was developed about 450 years ago by Takeda Shingen, a great and powerful samurai living in the Nagano area. This progenitor of modern Shinshu was prepared commercially in farmhouses as early as 1924 (using sodium sulfite bleach), but large-scale production and distribution did not start until after 1945. Most light-yellow miso is still produced in Nagano, although 95 percent of it is shipped throughout the rest of Japan and accounts for over 20 percent of all miso consumed in the nation. Especially popular in Tokyo and central Japan, it is used in all types of cooking. The most widely available miso presently produced in the United States falls under this category. Light-yellow miso may be substituted for red or barley miso in any of the recipes in this book.

Fig. 10 Famous Sub-varieties of Salty Rice Miso

	Japanese Name	Koji (% by wt. of soybeans)	Salt (% by wt. of miso)	Characteristics
Red miso	Sendai	60	13.6	Chunky texture, soybeans cracked coarsely, deep-red color, long aging
	Echigo	60-65[1] 80-120[2]	14.0 12.2	Chunky texture with white koji mosaic on fine-grained soybean base
	Sado	60-65	15.4	Chunky or smooth texture, long aging
	Tsugaru	50	14.6	Deep-red color, long aging
Light-yellow miso	Shinshu	60-90	13.0	Radiant light-yellow color, smooth texture
	Akita	80-100	12.3	Yellowish gold color midway between Shinshu and Sendai; relatively low salt content
				1) Niigata type 2) Joetsu type

Mellow Red Miso *(Amakuchi Akamiso):* A close relative of red miso, this variety is prepared with exactly the same amount of salt (13.0%) but a much larger percentage of koji and thus of carbohydrates (27.9% vs. 19.1%), resulting in a slightly sweeter flavor. The traditional representative of this category is Gozen miso, a specialty of the city of Tokushima on Shikoku Island. Fermented naturally for six to 12 months, it attains a deep reddish-brown color. Since World War II, a number of quick varieties have been developed, which are prepared with pressure-steamed ingredients and fermented without the use of additives in a temperature-controlled environment for three to six months.

Mellow Beige Miso *(Amakuchi Tanshoku Miso):* This broad category is a catch-all for the many quick, light-colored misos developed as imitations of modern Shinshu but forbidden by law to use the Shinshu name. *Amakuchi* means "moderately sweet" and *Tanshoku* means "light-colored," indicating that these products are midway in flavor between sweet and salty, and in color between red and white. By 1969 this miso (together with its close relatives mellow red miso and light-yellow Shinshu) accounted for a full 70 percent of all misos sold in Japan, but its popularity is now waning as traditional varieties return to favor.

Mellow beige miso was explicitly designed to use proportions of raw materials that would minimize both the fermentation time and the cost of ingredients, and thereby maximize profits. Thus, typical products are relatively rich in carbohydrates (29.1%), and low in salt (7.0%) and protein (13.0%). The light color is produced by pressure-boiling and short fermentation (3 to 4 weeks) in a temperature-controlled environment, often together with the use of bleach and food coloring.

The traditional representatives of this category are Aijiro miso and Kyushu miso, neither of which is now widely available. Aijiro, made only in Shizuoka prefecture, was first created about 350 years ago as an imitation of Kyoto's sweet white miso, but it is not quite as sweet.

A unique sub-variety of mellow beige miso is Glutinous-Rice Miso *(mochigomé miso).* Prepared with 3 parts soybeans and 7 parts glutinous rice, it has a thick smooth texture, light yellow color, and fairly sweet flavor. First developed during the 1970s, it is sold only by the Hinode Miso Co.

Mellow White Miso *(Shiro Koji Miso):* The rich natural flavor of this variety is nicely harmonized with a subtly sweet fermented fragrance, reminiscent of *amazaké.* Unlike its slightly sweeter relative, sweet white miso, this mellow miso is a completely natural product, fermented at the temperature of its environment and prepared without pasteurization, preservatives, or bleach. Made only in Honolulu, it is now widely available on the American mainland where it is reasonably priced ($1.29 per pound) and generally sold in white cottage cheese-type containers bearing the name "Shiro White Miso." It is not available in Japan.

Midway between red and sweet white miso in salt content, it is highly versatile and can be substituted for either in most recipes in this book; use twice as much mellow white as red miso or two-thirds as much as the sweet miso called for. A good approximation of sweet white miso's flavor can be obtained by mixing ½ teaspoon honey with 4 teaspoons mellow white miso. By using a pinch of salt instead of the honey you can approximate the flavor of light-yellow miso.

Sweet Red Miso *(Edo Miso* or *Edo Ama-miso):* Endowed with a rich, slightly savory aroma and a deep, mellow sweetness, Edo miso contains a large proportion of carbohydrates (32%) and is relatively low in salt (6%) and protein (12.7%). Ranging in color from light reddish brown to lustrous russet, its traditional texture was always chunky, but many contemporary products are smooth and soft. Because virtually all varieties, even though they now contain preservatives, begin to change flavor after two to four weeks unless refrigerated, Edo miso is difficult to export.

Edo, the ancient name of modern Tokyo, is also the title of an era which began in 1603. It is said that Ieyasu Tokugawa, Japan's ruling shogun at the time, developed Edo miso in order to combine the best features of Hatcho miso, his hometown favorite, and Kyoto's sweet white miso, very popular at the time among the upper classes. In the days before the Japanese had access to sugar, Edo miso was a widely used sweetening agent. Today it is most popular in soups, where it is often mixed with red miso. Mixed with *azuki* beans, it becomes the filling for *Kashiwa Mochi* (p. 155), a famous confection served each year on Boy's Day. It is also used in Dengaku (p. 144), Nuta (p. 96), Sweetened Tekka Miso (p. 67), and nabé dishes such as Doténabé (p. 142). In Western-style preparations, it is delicious in spreads, dips, and dressings.

Most of Japan's sweet red (Edo) miso is still produced and consumed in the Tokyo area. To this day, it is made by an ingenious method of natural temperature-controlled fermentation: the miso is packed into vats while the soybeans are still hot, and the vats are wrapped with heavy rice-straw mats to keep in the heat. Although fermented for as few as ten to 20 days in summer and four to five weeks in winter, this miso enjoys a deep reddish color thanks to a unique cooking method in which the beans are boiled for a long time, allowed to stand overnight in the cauldron, then reheated before going into the vat.

A fairly good approximation of Edo miso's flavor can be obtained by mixing 3 parts red miso with 1 part honey.

Sweet White Miso *(Shiro Miso, Kyoto Shiro Miso,* or *Saikyo Miso):* Also known as "Kyoto white miso" or simply "white miso," this variety is made by combining as much as 4 parts by weight of rice koji with only 2 parts soybeans and 1 part salt. Deliciously sweet, it is so smooth it can be spread like butter on pancakes or bread. Its light refreshing flavor goes well with fresh fruits and crisp vegetables, and lends a rich, mellow quality to desserts. Ranging in color from ivory to light yellow, its fragrance is reminiscent of springtime.

Highest of all misos in carbohydrates (36%) and lowest in salt (5.5%) and protein (11.1%), its abundance of natural sugars hastens the fermentation process so that the average *natural* aging period is only three weeks, becoming as short as one week during the summer and as long as one to two months during winter. Many makers now calculate the fermentation time to include the time in transit to food stores and sitting on the shelves. If allowed to stand unrefrigerated for more than one week in summer or one month in winter, it develops a slightly alcoholic or sour flavor and reddish color. Refrigerated, however, it will keep for two months or more. Difficult to export, many varieties—whether sold in open-top kegs or sealed polyethylene bags—have been pasteurized and contain preservatives plus small amounts of bleach; some contain 2 to 3 percent added sweeteners from refined grain sugars (*mizuamé*).

Costing 63 to 83 cents per pound, this is one of Japan's most expensive misos. It is used as a pickling agent for fish and vegetables, as a topping for the grilled tofu dish Dengaku, in a special New Year's soup, Ozoni (p. 105), in Japanese confections (mixed with *adzuki* beans), and in a wide variety of *aemono* or salad dressings, sauces and spreads. Except in the Kyoto area, it is used rather infrequently in soups.

For centuries a famous product of Kyoto, it is a featured ingredient at many of the city's restaurants offering Zen Temple Cookery or Tea Ceremony Cuisine. Two large, well-known Kyoto companies, Honda and Ishino (p. 258), account for most of the nation's production. One delicious variety sold as "Hanabishi Shiro Miso" is now widely available in the United States. Produced by Nakamuraya & Co., it is pasteurized and contains preservatives and bleach. Well known sub-varieties of sweet white miso include Hiroshima's Fuchu Miso and Takamatsu's Sanuki Miso.

The commercial preparation of sweet white miso involves a rather complex process which is said to be a well guarded secret of its Kyoto manufacturers. Many Tokyo shops have tried to duplicate it but none have succeeded. Due to its short shelf life, this miso was traditionally prepared in shops only during the cold months (from October until March) without preservatives or bleaches. It is still made in farmhouses in Wakayama prefecture, especially during March and April. In modern factories, it is prepared in the general manner described previously for white miso except that, like sweet red (Edo) miso, it is packed into the fermentation vats while the mixture is still quite hot.

Since this miso can be prepared very quickly, it is an excellent variety to try making at home. A fairly good approximation of its flavor can be obtained by mixing 2 parts by volume of light-yellow miso, 1 part honey, and 1 part water.

Barley Miso
(*Mugi Miso*)

Most barley miso is darker, saltier, and aged longer than rice miso. Generally sold in the traditional chunky or koji form, its distinctive texture is one of its preferred characteristics. Each barley grain has a clearly visible dark line—known in Japanese as its "loincloth"—running the length of the kernel: this line gives the miso a unique appearance. The koji is prepared from polished or pearled barley—either the regular (*O-mugi*) or "naked" (*Hadaka-mugi*) varieties—which are higher in protein (11% vs. 7.5%) and lower in carbohydrates (67% vs. 73%) than polished rice. Therefore barley miso is generally not as sweet as its rice counterpart and takes a longer time to ferment.

At present, barley miso comprises only 11 percent of the miso sold in Japan. Nevertheless, since low-cost barley was once widely grown throughout the warmer parts of the country, and since the Chinese ideograph for the word *koji* is composed of characters meaning "barley" and "chrysanthemum," many miso scholars believe that barley miso was Japan's most popular variety from ancient times up until 50 to 100 years ago. Other authorities contend, however, that miso has always been made using the predominant grain of each region and that in most areas rice and rice miso have always been produced in greater quantities. In any event, although a large amount of farmhouse miso is still made with barley koji and many farmers believe that barley and barley miso are foods which promote long life and good health, barley miso has nevertheless gradually decreased in popularity during the past century.

Barley miso's decline has been most pronounced among urbanites and young people. Japanese miso makers, scholars, and cooks suggest a number of possible reasons for this phenomenon: 1) Barley, which even now sells for only 40 percent the cost of rice, has long been considered a poor man's grain. The miso made from it seems to have acquired low-class associations, and as people move upward socially and economically, they tend to use less and less of it, preferring rice miso instead; 2) Barley miso's heady flavor and earthy aroma, its high salt and low sugar content, no longer suit the more refined tastes and needs of urbanites; and its dark color is considered to be outdated; 3) Its chunky texture makes it inconvenient for use in creamy-smooth miso soups since it must be hand-ground and strained before use; 4) Koji-textured barley miso, made from regular barley rather than the softer "naked" barley, is said to leave a slight residue on the tongue from the firm "loincloth" line.

Yet, in parts of Japan where barley fields are still more common than rice paddies and the traditional culture has retained its vitality, barley miso continues to be produced and enjoyed in large quantities. In urban areas, mellow barley miso is swiftly taking the place of its saltier traditional counterpart; a typical Tokyo miso retail store offering 40 varieties of miso will generally have only one barley miso, and it will likely be mellow.

An estimated 80 percent of all Japan's barley miso is still prepared by natural fermentation, and most of the salty varieties are made only during the cold months, from November to April, when the new-crop barley is at its best flavor, the water is clear and delicious, and the air is cold and free of contaminating microorganisms.

The traditional home and present center of barley miso production is the southern third of the Japanese archipelago, and particularly the southernmost main island, Kyushu, where barley miso became popular in about 1600 and 75 percent of Japan's total output new originates. In the various provinces of Kyushu, the following percentages of all miso produced are barley miso: Kagoshima 100, Kumamoto 80, Nagasaki, Saga and Oita 70, and Fukuoka 50. Likewise in Yamaguchi and Hiroshima prefectures located at the southern end of Japan's main island in the Chugoku region, the proportion of miso which is barley miso is respectively 50 and 30 percent. Two of the traditional barley miso areas, Saitama prefecture located near Tokyo and Shikoku island, now produce only small amounts.

Variety	Native Region	Soy-beans	Barley	Salt	Fermen-tation
Barley Miso	Southern Japan	10	10	4.6	1-3 years
Mellow Barley Miso	Southern Japan	10	17	4.8	10-14 days

Barley Miso *(Karakuchi Mugi Miso):* Although the name of this particular variety is identical to that of the larger category described above, the "barley miso" called for in recipes always refers specifically to this product. Its relatively high salt content (13% or more) is mellowed by lengthy natural fermentation and harmonized by the barley's underlying subtle sweetness to give the miso a deep rich flavor. Many connoisseurs in fact contend that fine barley miso actually tastes *sweeter* than Sendai rice miso! Low in carbohydrates (21%) and high in protein (13%), it is fermented naturally for at least one full year, at the end of which time it has acquired its characteristic reddish-brown color, chunky texture, and prominent fragrance. When aged for three years, the color turns a deep chocolate brown, the texture becomes more homogeneous, and the flavor grows richer, subtler, and more elaborate. Although barley is generally less than one-half as expensive as rice, lengthy fermentation makes this miso more expensive than most varieties of rice miso: natural three-year barley miso *(sannen-miso),* at more than $1 per pound, is one of Japan's most expensive varieties.

Most of the natural barley miso now exported to the United States is this salty product. It is strongly favored by the American macrobiotic community, which has been one of the main influences working to popularize the use of miso in the West. Barley miso is used in soups and a wide variety of other types of cookery.

Mellow Barley Miso *(Amakuchi Mugi Miso):* Although this variety has a pleasant sweetness, the koji from which it is prepared demands a fairly high minimum level of salt for proper fermentation. Hence it is impossible to make this miso as sweet as the sweet white or sweet red rice misos. Compared with the latter variety, mellow barley miso contains almost twice as much salt (10.0% vs. 6.0%), and a little less carbohydrates (30% vs. 32%) and protein (11.0% vs. 12.6%). The color ranges from light yellow for the quick varieties to reddish brown for those produced naturally. The texture is usually chunky. It has a distinctive flavor characteristic of both the koji and soybeans, and a light fermented aroma.

Popular on the island of Kyushu—and especially in Nagasaki and Kumamoto—for over 350 years, it is known in some areas as "10-day miso" due to its short natural fermentation time of one to two weeks. At present, most mellow barley miso is prepared on a large scale using temperature-controlled fermentation, typically for 20 to 35 days in a warm room and then 15 to 20 days at room temperature, or in some cases for as few as four to six days. Although it generally contains preservatives and bleach (some varieties also contain 1% honey), this quick miso spoils rather quickly and changes color unless refrigerated. It is therefore difficult to export. Used mostly in cooked vegetable dishes and as a topping for Dengaku (p. 144), it is also combined with salty barley miso in the preparation of soups.

Soybean Miso
(Mamé Miso)

Soybean miso is fundamentally different from rice and barley miso in that it contains no grain; its koji is made exclusively from soybeans. Due to a consequent lack of carbohydrates and a moderately high salt content, soybean miso requires lengthy aging, most of which is still done in the slow, natural way.

Much of Japan's earliest farmhouse and commercial miso was probably of this type. In the clear, cold uplands of northern Japan, it is still prepared in the ancient way, with wild mold spores and cooked soybeans that are crushed and shaped into large balls *(miso-dama).* The balls are wrapped or tied with rice straw and hung outdoors under the eaves or indoors over an open-hearth fireplace or wood-burning kitchen stove. After a month or so when the balls are covered with mold, they are crushed, mixed with salt and water, and fermented in kegs or crocks (p. 193).

Commercial soybean miso was developed and is still most widely prepared and consumed in central Japan, in Aichi, Mie, and Gifu prefectures. It presently constitutes 8 percent of all miso sold in the nation as a whole. Since it is impossible to vary the ratio of grains in the basic ingredients, the different varieties have a relatively narrow range of flavors and aromas. All are fermented naturally for at least one year. The darker ones are occasionally called "black miso" *(kuro miso),* and all are frequency called Sanshu miso, the ancient name of central Japan.

Variety	Native Region	Soy-beans	Salt	Fermentation
Hatcho Miso	Okazaki near Nagoya	10	2.1	18-36 months
Soybean Miso	Central Japan	10	2.1	8-12 months
Tamari Miso	Central Japan	10	2.5	10-12 months

Hatcho Miso *(pronounced hot-cho):* No other miso in Japan is endowed with such a lofty and aged tradition. For centuries, Japanese poets, connoisseurs, and statesmen have celebrated Hatcho's ineffable savory aroma, deep mellow sweetness, and uniquely astringent flavor, each faintly reminiscent of chocolate; these lend the miso a sense of what the Japanese call *shibui*, a term which in its broader aesthetic usage refers to subdued yet refined tastefulness which borders on subtle, almost severe beauty. Other "shibui" things include a Zen brush painting, a sparse haiku, a tart—almost puckery—autumn persimmon.

Dark cocoa brown, Hatcho has a slightly chunky texture that in most cases is so firm you can cut it with a knife. Higher in protein (21.0%) and lower in carbohydrates (12.0%) and water (40%) than any other miso, it nevertheless contains less salt than either red or barley miso (10.6% vs. 13%).

Although any maker of Hatcho-type miso is legally allowed to use the traditional name for his product, only two companies, Hayakawa and Ota (p. 256), both of which claim to have been founded over 600 years ago (p. 223), are generally recognized as Japan's originators and present manufacturers of the real thing. Both are located in the same block, or *cho*, on the banks of the Yahagi River in the town of Okazaki near the bustling city of Nagoya (see map, frontispiece). Hat-cho, or "Eighth-street" miso, takes its name from this location. The Tokugawa family, which founded Japan's feudal shogunate in 1603 and moved its capital to Edo (now Tokyo), originally resided in this area. Very fond of their native miso, they imported it by boat to their new capital where, as it happens, it never became widely popular.

八丁味噌

In making Hatcho miso, a unique species of mold, *Aspergillus hatcho* said to flourish in the Okazaki area, was traditionally used in place of the regular *Aspergillus oryzae*. The fermented soybean koji is mixed with salt and a relatively small amount of water (see p. 210), then packed into huge cedar vats, some of which are 150 to 200 years old. Their thick cedar staves bound together with wide and beautifully woven hoops of braided bamboo, typical vats are 6 feet deep and 7 feet in diameter, with a capacity of 4 to 5 tons (1,600 gallons). A heavy wooden pressing lid is placed on top of the miso, and at least 100 large rocks, equal in their total weight to the weight of the miso, are then piled on (see frontispiece). Even with this enormous pressure, however, the mixture contains so little moisture that virtually no liquid (*miso-damari*) rises to the surface!

Because all Hatcho miso must age through at least two full summers, the youngest batches, which start to ferment in the late spring, are about 16 months old; older batches, begun in early fall, have been aged for at least 24 months. Hatcho makers say that the miso begins to reach its best flavor only after 24 months and peaks at three *full* years, but miso this old is very uncommon at present. Yet due to the unusual Japanese way of measuring a miso's age, Hatcho which is actually only 18 to 24 months old is often sold as "three-year" miso.

Since all Hatcho is prepared by lengthy natural fermentation, it costs about 79 cents per pound, or roughly 40 percent more than most rice miso. The oldest batches, which have had a large proportion of their protein broken down into amino acids, are valued for their medicinal properties. Only about 1 to 2 percent of the miso produced each year in Japan is Hatcho, and about half of the total is employed in the production of akadashi miso (see below). Most often used in soups, Hatcho is usually mixed with 3 parts red, light-yellow, or sweet rice miso to soften its astringent qualities. It is also the key ingredient in Tekka Miso (p. 66), and small chunks of the well-aged product can be served as is, to be enjoyed as a rich and mellow hors d'œuvre. When used in place of red or barley miso—as called for in most of the recipes in this book—the quantity should be increased by 15 to 20 percent to impart the equivalent degree of saltiness.

In recent years a product called "Young Hatcho Miso" (*Waka-Hatcho*) has begun to be sold. Prepared by the traditional Hatcho companies, it differs from the true Hatcho in that it is aged through only one full summer (usually for a total of 12 to 14 months) and has a lighter weight on the vat's pressing lid. Slightly less mellow in flavor, lighter in color, softer in texture, and about 15 percent less expensive, it is often preferred to true Hatcho by students of macrobiotics who feel that the latter is too *yang* due to its lengthy aging in such a warm climate.

Hatcho is said to be the Emperor's favorite miso, and he takes it with him on overseas trips. Formerly certain fine producers of miso, shoyu, and other foods received the honor of being supplier to the Imperial Household, but recently a more democratic approach has been adopted. No company is allowed to be a special supplier to the Emperor, even if they offer their goods for free, since the resulting publicity is considered to give them an unfair advantage over competitors. The Emperor must buy and pay for his beloved Hatcho miso just like everyone else.

Hatcho has been taken on all six Japanese expeditions to the South Pole, and is considered an essential food by many athletes and mountain climbers who use it as a condensed source of protein and energy. Regarded also as a key ingredient in Tea Ceremony Cuisine (*kaiseki ryori*), it is now widely available in the West and is the only miso sold in sealed bags that is not pasteurized and contains no alcohol.

Fig. 11. Supplier to the Imperial Household

Soybean Miso (*Mamé Miso* or *Ichi-nen Mamé Miso*): Also called "one-year" or "regular" soybean miso to distinguish it from other soybean misos, this variety is prepared like Hatcho except that the minimum aging requirement is one year rather than two and the usual *Aspergillus oryzae* mold is used to make the koji. Compared to Hatcho, its flavor is less rich; its color is redder; its texture is softer due to its higher water content (48% vs. 40%); and its price is about 30 percent lower. Much of this miso is used as a substitute for Hatcho in akadashi (see below). About 80 to 90 percent of the soybean miso made in Japan is of this type. The term "Nagoya Miso," the name of the most popular brand, is often used as a synonym for "soybean miso."

Tamari Miso: Prepared in miso- and shoyu shops in central Japan since 1500, this is the miso-like residue that remains after producing tamari-shoyu, an early prototype of modern shoyu. (Tamari-shoyu is made from a pure soybean koji, while modern shoyu is made with a koji consisting of equal parts soybeans and roasted wheat.)

In making tamari miso, soybean koji prepared as for Hatcho or regular soybean miso is mixed with the usual amount of salt plus about five times as much water. The resulting mash, called *moromi*, has a consistency like that of applesauce; it is placed into a huge cedar vat in the center of which is stacked a series of inverted, bottomless wooden kegs which form a hollow cylinder (fig. 12). The base of the cylinder is joined to an inverted V-shaped trough that is permeated with small holes and connected at one end to a spigot at the bottom of one side of the keg. Liquid tamari from the moromi mash quickly collects in and fills the cylindrical core. Each day some of this tamari is ladled over the surface of the moromi to stimulate fermentation and, since the usual pressing lid is not used, to prevent the formation of mold. After 10 months or more of natural fermentation, the spigot is opened and the thick, richly-flavored tamari runs out. Traditionally it was the well-drained *moromi* remaining in the vat that was sold as tamari miso. At present, however, most of the moromi is ladled into cloth sacks and hydraulically pressed to extract its full content of liquid tamari; the pulpy dry residue is then discarded or used as cattle fodder. Hence, tamari miso is now quite rare, although not extinct.

Long regarded as a very high-class food, tamari miso has a subtle natural sweetness and a distinctive flavor similar to that of fine, natural Chinese soy sauce. However, because it contains no grain koji and is fermented for a relatively short period of time, it has rather little aroma. Generally used in miso soups, it is also popular as a relish-like topping or dip for fresh vegetable slices. For a description of the liquid tamari, see pages 184 and 222.

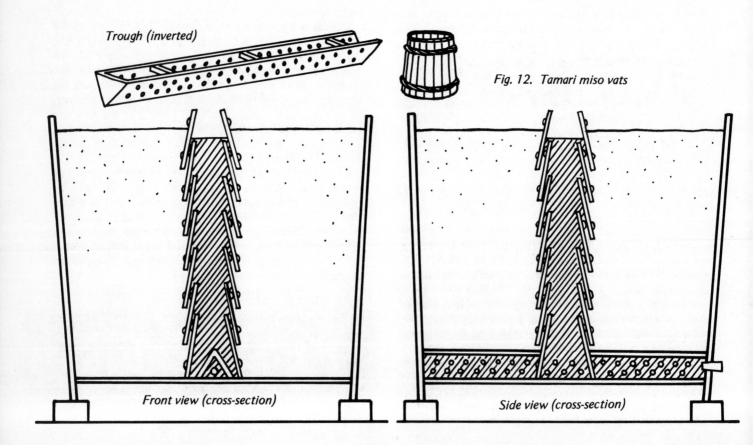

Trough (inverted)

Fig. 12. Tamari miso vats

Front view (cross-section)

Side view (cross-section)

SPECIAL MISO

Special misos are different from their regular counterparts in four basic ways: 1) In addition to the usual miso ingredients (soybeans, koji, and salt), they contain chopped vegetables, nuts, seeds, seafoods, or natural seasonings and spices which impart a distinctive chunky texture; 2) They are generally quite sweet and, unless refrigerated, have a relatively short shelf life; 3) Generally served at the dining table for use as a topping or seasoning, they never appear in miso soups and are further cooked in only a few special dishes such as Dengaku (p. 144) and Broiled Miso (p. 71); 4) They are usually sold in small quantities (200 grams) from 2-quart crocks rather than large kegs at prices slightly higher than even the most expensive regular misos. The two basic types are finger lickin' miso and sweet simmered miso.

Finger Lickin' Miso
(Namémiso)

Each variety of namémiso—a word derived from the verb nameru meaning "to lick"—is prepared by fermenting a small amount of finely-chopped salt-pickled vegetables and spicy seasonings (about 10%) with whole cooked soybeans (15%) and a large proportion (75%) of a unique whole-grain koji usually containing barley or wheat. The resulting consistency is similar to that of apple sauce but slightly chunkier, and the color is generally a warm light brown. The high proportion of grain carbohydrates which are broken down into sugars gives this miso its characteristic rich sweetness and heady, delectable aroma.

Now available in different parts of the United States, finger lickin' miso seems particularly well suited to Western tastes. In Japan, the different varieties are favorite toppings for crisp vegetable slices, hot rice or rice porridge, Ochazuke, regular or deep-fried tofu, crackers and canapés, rice balls and mochi, baked potatoes and other root vegetables, and even some aemono salads. Finger lickin' miso is also delicious in Western-style sauces and dressings, especially with sesame tahini and seasonings such as orange juice, garlic, onion, gingerroot, shoyu, and/or honey. The following varieties, which retail for an average of $1.50 per pound in Japan, are listed in order of their availability and popularity there: refrigerated, each will keep for three to six months.

Kinzanji Miso: Kinzanji is made from a special koji containing both whole-grain barley and soybeans. (In most misos, it will be remembered, either grains or soybeans but never both are used in the koji.) The individual barley grains are abundant and clearly visible, and the soybeans, which have been roasted, cracked and dehulled, give the finished product a slightly nutty aroma and chunky texture. Most Kinzanji contains minced eggplant, gingerroot, white uri melon, kombu and burdock root; some varieties may contain daikon and cucumbers, plus green beefsteak leaves and seeds, sansho green pepper, and slivered togarashi red peppers used to enhance the fragrance. These vegetables and seasonings are added either at the start of or halfway through the natural six-month fermentation process. Traditional Kinzanji contained equal portions by weight of soybeans and barley, but many modern varieties contain four times as much barley as soybeans in order to give a sweeter product, and reduce the cost, time, and difficulty of preparation. For even greater sweetness some makers add rice koji to the original mixture, and mizuamé (barley- or millet jelley) at the end; the mizuamé also improves luster. Modern varieties may contain brown food coloring, and pasteurization or preservatives are often used to increase shelf life. Two types of Kinzanji are available, one quite sweet and the other rather mild.

Several theories are offered to account for this miso's origin. The first traces it to Kinzanji, the Temple of the Golden Mountain, one of China's five great Sung dynasty Zen centers. According to popular oral tradition, the Zen priest Kakushin brought a prototype back with him from China in 1255 A.D. and taught the method of its preparation to the people of Yuasa in Wakayama prefecture, where the same ancient technique is employed to this day. Yuasa has since become a famous center of shoyu production as well, and legend has it that shoyu's earliest progenitor was discovered as the dark, fragrant liquid left over at the bottom of the Kinzanji barrel! The Osaka-Wakayama area is the present center of Kinzanji production, yet manufacturers in Shizuoka prefecture to the north have developed ten new varieties plus a ready-made dried koji for use in preparing a homemade type.

A second theory suggests that some of the earliest types of Chinese chiang (see Appendix A), containing pieces of fish or meat fermented with grains and soybeans, were actually prototypes of Kinzanji, and that all the devotedly vegetarian Japanese had to do was substitute vegetables and seasonings for the meat and fish. In fact, the earliest hishio (the progenitor of Japanese shoyu; see below) was probably very similar to Kinzanji. The basic method for preparing this Kinzanji is believed to have been transmitted not by a priest but by a book, the Ch'imin Yaoshu, written in China about 550 A.D., which when translated and circulated widely in Japan had a profound influence on Japanese fermented food preparation and agricultural methods. This theory places the origin of Kinzanji 400 years after the time of Kakushin and fails to establish its famous link with the origin of shoyu. A third theory suggests that Kinzanji originated from the practice of soaking vegetables in hishio to make "vegetable hishio" (kusa hishio).

Four close relatives of Kinzanji are Sakura Miso, Shiina Miso, Hamana Miso, and Bonito Miso. Sakura — which means "cherry" —has a deep red color and is prepared from barley koji plus mizuamé and sugar; a modern miso with the same name is described on page 43. Shiina— which means "China," in honor of the fact that most finger lickin' miso originated there—and Hamana contain soybeans, wheat-(or barley-) and rice koji, plus diced eggplants, beefsteak seeds, and gingerroot. Some varieties contain amazaké (p. 162). Fermented for 20 days during the winter, they are prepared and sold mostly in Fukui prefecture. Bonito (Katsuo) Miso, a specialty of Tosa City on the island of Shikoku, substitutes chunks of raw bonito for the usual vegetables. It is occasionally used in soups.

Moromi Miso: Moromi is the mash from which shoyu is made. It consists of a koji made of soybeans, cracked roasted wheat, salt, and water. After a natural fermentation period of one year, it is ordinarily ladled into cloth sacks and pressed to yield the liquid shoyu.

The earliest moromi miso, developed during the 16th century in Kyushu and Shikoku by shoyu makers, was simply shoyu moromi (made with whole rather than cracked roasted wheat) taken from the fermentation vats either before or after the shoyu was filtered off. To develop their own version, all that miso makers had to do was reduce the amount of water used in the mash, add chopped, salt-pickled vegetables, and substitute miso starter (*Aspergillus oryzae* mold) for the shoyu starter to activate the fermentation. The resulting product, from which the liquid was never filtered or pressed, was dark brown and had a consistency like that of applesauce.

Today, most moromi miso contains chopped eggplants, cucumbers, and gingerroot; Nagasaki's delicious Batten Moromi also contains short sections of *wakame* midrib (*kuki-wakame*). Two varieties of moromi, prepared by miso makers, are available; one is quite sweet and slightly pink, the other tan and mild. Retailing for about 80 cents per pound, both are most widely served on fresh cucumber slices.

Hishio: The word *hishio* (pronounced HEE-shee-oh) is the Japanese pronunciation of the Chinese character *chiang*, and the present-day product is thought to bear a close resemblance to this progenitor of all Japanese miso and shoyu (see Appendix A). Commercial hishio is generally prepared from drained, unpressed shoyu moromi to which are added salt-pickled vegetables (eggplant, white *uri* melon, and gingerroot); the mixture is then further fermented by natural methods for 20 to 60 days, usually during the months of March and April. Traditional farmhouse hishio—still widely prepared in the Osaka, Chugoku, and Shikoku areas (see map, inside cover) where it is also known as *namémono* or *o-namé*—is generally prepared by fermenting the vegetables together with a barley koji from the beginning, and often contains soybeans which have been split and dehulled. Both commercial and farmhouse hishio, prized as gift items in Japan, are now available at only the best miso shops.

Namémiso: Closely related to the three varieties described above, namemiso is characterized by the presence of 3-inch-long strips of *kombu* together with diced pickled eggplants, gingerroot, and *uri* melons. Some varieties contain only wheat or barley koji and no soybeans.

Natto Miso: Prepared in the area of Nagasaki since the 1700s, natto miso contains a relatively large proportion of soybeans which gives it an appearance similar to the famous sticky fermented soybeans called *natto*, although there are no real *natto* in natto miso. Containing whole soybeans, barley koji, slivered kombu, gingerroot, and, in some modern varieties, *mizuamé* (a natural honeylike sweetener extracted from rice, millet, or barley), this miso is ferment-

ed at the natural temperature for about 30 days. One delicious and very popular variety, now widely available in the United States, is free of preservatives, artificial or refined sweeteners, and all other additives—proving that it can still be done. We would prefer to see this and all similar misos labeled as "Finger Lickin' Miso;" we feel the general term is more appealing and less confusing.

Goto Miso: A *to* is a Japanese unit of measure equal to 4¾ gallons, and the word *go* means "five." This miso is prepared by combining one *to* of each of the following five ingredients: cooked soybeans, rice koji, sake lees, salt, and sugar. The fermentation requires only ten days.

Relatives of finger lickin' miso: The numerous varieties of farmhouse miso enriched or extended with potatoes, sweet potatoes, *kobocha* or corn (or with koji made from these foods), and the farmhouse miso in which vegetables are buried and pickled are closely related to finger lickin' miso (see p. 192).

Sweet Simmered Miso
(*Nerimiso*)

Sweet simmered miso is prepared by combining regular miso with a mixture of sweetening (sugar, honey, or *mizu-amé*), a little water or sake, and nuts, seeds, minced vegetables, seafoods, or seasonings. The mixture is cooked in a skillet and stirred constantly until it attains the same degree of firmness as regular miso. The most widely available commercial variety is peanut miso, which is chock full of whole peanuts, roasted sesame seeds and, in special cases, raisins; the use of *mizuamé* imparts a thick taffy-like consistency and deep amber color, while the peanuts and sesame boost the protein level to over 16 percent. Commonly sold in 3½-ounce sealed polyethylene bags or rectangular containers, it is now also available commercially and at school cafeterias in tiny ¾-ounce packets which provide a single serving for only 5 cents and are used as a sandwich spread as well as a topping for rice, tofu, and fresh vegetable slices. Other readily available commercial varieties include walnut, sesame, *yuzu*, *kinomé*, and red snapper. Since these and numerous other varieties are also prepared non-commercially in homes and restaurants, a detailed discussion of sweet simmered miso is given in the recipe section (p. 60).

MODERN MISO

Three varieties of miso, all developed since 1945, fall under this classification. They are composed of traditional misos processed or mixed in unique ways. When two or more varieties of miso are combined, the resulting commercial product is designated as "mixed miso" (*chogo-* or *awasé miso*), the best known example of which is akadashi, described below. Modern miso represents about 5 percent of all miso consumed today in Japan.

Akadashi Miso: This dark reddish-brown and rather sweet miso is prepared by combining 1 part Hatcho miso with 2 parts of various other misos (mellow beige, sweet white, and/or one-year soybean). Many varieties also contain caramel syrup, *mizuamé*, refined sugar, monosodium glutamate, shoyu, and sorbic acid preservative. The mature misos and other ingredients are simply mixed, puréed or blended, pasteurized, and packaged; the process takes less than two days since no additional fermentation is required. Hatcho akadashi miso, the finest variety, is guaranteed to contain authentic Hatcho miso, whereas less expensive varieties often substitute regular soybean miso. *Sakura* (cherry) and *Kyozakura* are types of akadashi containing about two-thirds sweet white miso.

Some Japanese say that the word *akadashi* originated in Kyoto and initially referred to any soybean miso that had a strong aroma; it is said that geishas would grind the soybean miso finely in a *suribachi* (serrated earthenware mortar), then rub it through a sieve to make a tasty miso soup. In Kyoto, the soybean miso first came to be mixed with sweet white miso to make the forerunner of today's akadashi.

Richly fragrant and hearty-tasting, akadashi is very popular in most Japanese urban centers even though its price is fairly high (48 to 73 cents per pound). Its name—literally "red dashi"—comes from a traditional, deep-red miso soup prepared with Hatcho miso, often containing oysters, and highly prized for its wonderful flavor (see p. 104).

Dehydrated Miso (Freeze-dried or Spray-dried): Called *Kanso Miso* or *Kona Miso* in Japan, this variety, developed in 1959, has become quite popular since the late 1970s, especially as the main ingredient in instant miso soups (now available at natural food stores and supermarkets throughout the U.S.), and also in the soup for instant Miso Ramen noodles. One popular natural instant miso soup, brand-named Miso Cup, contains a mixture of dehydrated onions, parsley, sea vegetables (wakame), and miso. In Japan, the most popular varieties contain slivered freeze-dried leeks, plus dried wakame and wheat gluten (or deep-fried tofu); many Japanese and supermarket products also contain chemical additives such as monosodium glutamate, sodium succinate, and inosinic acid. The mixture is sealed in tiny one-or-two serving packets (9 grams make an 8-ounce cup of instant miso soup) and five to ten packets are sold together in a foil package or box. At least three varieties are available to make red, white, or akadashi miso soup. The soup, prepared by simply mixing the contents of one packet with hot water, is ready in less than a minute at a very small cost per serving. Ideal for backpacking and camping, this miso also makes an excellent seasoning; we like to keep some in a shaker and sprinkle it on salads, sandwiches, brown rice, noodles, or crisp-fried tempeh, or to mash it with tofu for use as a spread or dip.

Of the 560,000 metric tons of miso made in Japan in 1979, no more than 2½ to 3½ percent end up dehydrated. Of the 10,000 to 15,000 tons of dehydrated product, an estimated 80 percent is freeze dried and 20 percent is spray dried. Yamajirushi is the largest maker of freeze-dried miso and Marukome and Nagatani-en are the biggest makers of spray-dried miso.

Initially, most of the dehydrated miso in Japan was made by spray drying. Miso (containing 50 percent solids) is mixed with enough water to give a slurry containing only 10 percent solids; this is blown in a fine spray from an atomizer into the top of a 150-foot-tall tower filled with circulating hot air. The miso dries as it falls. The spray inlet temperature is 482°F (250°C) and the exit temperature is 167 to 176°F (75-80°C). In recent years, freeze-drying has come to be more widely used than spray drying. Regular miso is spread to a depth of about 1 inch (2-3 cm) on large stainless steel trays, which are slid into shelves in a large vacuum chamber. First the miso is quick frozen at a very low temperature (-22°F or -30°C), then dried using a strong vacuum (0.5 to 0.8 mm of mercury or torr) at a relatively low drying temperature (104°F or 40°C) for 10 to 15 hours, to yield dehydrated miso containing only 4 to 5 percent moisture, but 32.2 percent protein, 18.5 percent salt, and 35.8 percent carbohydrates. Though slightly more expensive, freeze-drying gives a finished product with a noticeably better flavor and aroma (some of which are lost at the high temperatures used for spray drying), that is slightly more nutritious and dissolves more readily in water. Freeze-drying is labor intensive, has a long drying time, and uses expensive, complex equipment with a small capacity but low noise level. Spray-drying is easy to mechanize, has a short drying time, and uses simple, inexpensive equipment with a large capacity, but which is very noisy.

Low-salt and Salt Free Miso *(Gen-en Miso and Mu-en Miso):* Typical low-salt miso is made by pressure-steaming dehulled, defatted soybeans, hydrolizing them with enzymes, then mixing them with an equal weight of mature red or light-yellow miso and fermenting the mixture at 86°F to 95°F for three to five days. First developed in 1959 the resulting product contains only 5.1 percent sodium chloride together with 17.6 percent protein and 53 percent moisture. Since its low salt content requires that the fresh miso be stored at below 50°F, it is usually freeze-dried and sold in 7-ounce bottles for about $1.70. Generally used as a health food, the dehydrated form contains 14 percent sodium chloride, 26.4 percent protein, and 6 percent moisture.

Some varieties, typically containing 5 percent salt and prepared like light-yellow miso using an 80-day fermentation, contain 3 to 3.5 percent alcohol as a preservative and are sold pasteurized in cans. Other methods of making low-salt miso include substituting ethyl alcohol for part of the salt (2 to 5 percent), adding *Saccharomyces rouxii* yeasts to

generate natural alcohol as in wine, or reducing the moisture content to 40 percent (Koyama 1976).

Salt free miso, which typically contains 3.5 percent alcohol, has a very noticeable alcohol flavor and aroma that we find unappetizing, except when it is masked by seasonings as for use in dressings or sauces. A canned salt-free red miso contains 53.7 percent moisture, 13.9 percent protein, 6.7 percent fats, and 24.2 percent carbohydrates including the 3.5 percent ethanol (ethyl alcohol), and 189 calories per 100 grams. Nagano Miso Co. in Japan reportedly holds the only patents on salt-free miso. Made by sterilizing koji, then mixing it with a little ethyl alcohol and cooked soybeans (without subsequent fermentation), the product, called JEPRON, contains 3 times the free amino acids of regular miso and costs about 50 percent more. Protein content ranges from 12 to 20 percent. Gold in color and rich in flavor, it can be used like miso in many recipes—yet is totally salt free. In 1982 some 250 metric tons a month were being made in Japan.

Total production of both these types of miso is still very limited, but the appeal is growing since the Japanese per-capita salt consumption is the highest in the world, 30 grams per capita in northern Japan and 18 grams in the rest of Japan, as compared with 11 grams in the United States. It is now well known that excess salt consumption can cause high blood pressure (hypertension). These products may eventually even find a market in the West.

New American Misos: American miso makers in homes, communities, and commercial shops have had good results making new types of miso using peanuts, garbanzo beans (chickpeas), black soybeans, azuki beans, common beans *(Phaseolus vulgaris,* incl. pinto, navy, kidney, great northern, etc.), *natto* (fermented soybeans), okara (soy pulp), green lentils, or green peas, as the protein source in place of regular soybeans. They have also made koji from corn (dent or flint), millet, wheat, or buckwheat. In 1982 Imagine Foods in Missouri introduced a miso in which kelp replaces some of the usual salt. Who, we wonder, will be the first to introduce miso in cubes like bullion or powdered miso in a shaker, perhaps mixed with herbs and/or spices.

A product resembling miso, produced in America by Loma Linda Foods and widely used by Seventh-day Adventists, is called *Savorex*. Made from extract of brewer's yeast, vegetable flavoring, and salt, it imparts a rich and meaty flavor. In 1983 it was sold in 9-ounce plastic containers for the equivalent of $3.61 per pound, or almost twice as much as popular natural misos.

PART II

Cooking with Miso

Getting Started

5

VIRTUALLY ALL OF THE basic types of Japanese miso described in Chapter 4, plus several new American-style misos (such as corn-soy miso or peanut miso) are now available at reasonable prices in most parts of the United States. Look for them at natural and health food stores, Japanese or other Oriental food stores, and at some supermarkets. As the amount of miso imported and made domestically continues to grow, new types continue to appear. Most miso is presently sold in 1-to 2-pound sealed polyethylene bags, cottage cheese-type containers, or small plastic tubs, although at many natural food stores it is sold in the traditional way out of wooden kegs (fig. 14). Occasionally it is sold in jars or even plastic squeeze tubes. Dehydrated miso—generally in the form of instant miso soups—are packaged in foil envelopes. If your local store does not carry miso, you may wish to give the manager the name and address of one of the makers or importers listed in Appendix D.

Buying and Storing Miso

What are the most important things to look for when buying miso? First, buy small quantities of a number of different varieties in order to become familiar with their flavors and colors, textures and aromas. Compare imported and domestic products and learn to recognize which types go best with your favorite recipes. People interested in natural foods will probably prefer traditional natural un-

pasteurized misos, which now compare very favorably in price with the more modern, quick varieties. Labels such as the one below should contain all the basic information relevant to natural miso:

Variety	Red Miso *(Sendai Akamiso)*
Type (optional)	Rice Miso *(Komé Miso)*
Texture	Chunky
Ingredients	White rice and whole soybeans
(incl. additives)	organically grown, unrefined sea salt, well water, alcohol, miso culture
Pasteurization	No
Temp.-controlled Fermentation	No
Age	At least 12 months
Weight	16 ounces
Maker	Nakamura Miso Co. 160 Westlake Blvd. Berkeley, CA 94706

Fig. 14. Miso packaging

All varieties should be stored in a cool, dark place. Sweet misos should always be refrigerated; during warm weather, it is best—but not absolutely necessary—to also refrigerate other varieties in order to prevent the growth of surface mold. Miso purchased in polyethylene bags should be kept tightly closed; expel all air from the bag, fold over the mouth, and secure with a rubber band. Miso purchased in bulk out of kegs can be packed firmly into an earthenware, glass, or tupperware container with plastic wrap, wax paper, or butcher paper pressed firmly over the entire miso surface; or it can be stored tightly enclosed in plastic wrap bound with a rubber band, or simply left in the store's small paper carton and refrigerated. During warm weather, a thin layer of harmless, almost tasteless mold may form on the air-exposed surfaces of unrefrigerated natural misos—those which contain no preservatives and are not pasteurized. Don't worry; simply scrape off the mold and discard it just before use or mix it into the body of the miso. Sweet misos may develop an alcoholic fragrance, and light-colored misos may darken, if allowed to stand open for too long; light cooking will remove the alcohol, and the darkening in no way affects the flavor.

Using Miso as a Seasoning

Miso may be used in place of salt or shoyu in most recipes. It has a more mellow and varied flavor than shoyu, and imparts added body to broths and sauces. The following quantities impart approximately the same "saltiness" and can therefore be used interchangeably as explained on page 32:

½ teaspoon salt
2 teaspoons shoyu
1 tablespoon salty miso (see chart p. 32)
1½ to 2 tablespoons mellow miso
2½ to 3 tablespoons sweet miso

To use miso sold in a polyethylene bag, cut across one of the bag's upper corners to make a ¾-inch-long opening. Then simply squeeze the bag (as you would apply icing to a cake using a pastry bag) to give a neat, smooth bead.

One tablespoon of miso weighs 17.3 gm.

Remember that natural miso is a living food containing many beneficial microorganisms which are easily killed by prolonged cooking. Whenever possible add the miso to soups or other preparations just before they are removed from the heat or use the miso in ways that require no cooking.

Basic Ingredients

We recommend the use of whole, natural foods. Since cans and bottles tend to contribute to environmental clutter, the recipes in this book call for ingredients which can be purchased free of non-biodegradable packaging. The rarer ingredients used in Japanese-style recipes are defined in the Glossary at the end of this book. Many basic Oriental foods are now widely available at natural food stores and supermarkets, as well as at Japanese and Chinese markets. Or contact the Japan Food Corporation with offices in San Francisco, Los Angeles, New York, Chicago, Houston, Columbia (Md.), and Sacramento (Calif.). The following ingredients, listed alphabetically, are those we consider basic to miso cookery:

Flour: Since all-purpose white flour contains only about 75 percent of the protein, 36 percent of the minerals, and 25 percent of the vitamins found in natural whole-wheat flour, we generally prefer to use the latter for baked goods, sauces, and the like. However, in tempura batters and pie crusts where lightness is essential, we recommend the use of unbleached white flour or a mixture of equal parts whole-wheat and white flours.

Honey and Sugar: Most of the recipes in this book that use sweetening call for honey, used in the minimum amounts we consider necessary to create the desired flavor and "balanced" by the miso's salt. One teaspoon honey imparts the same sweetness as 2 teaspoons of sugar, and in most recipes the two can be used interchangeably. Since honey is about twice as expensive as sugar, the net cost ends up being the same. But honey is a whole, natural food with a mild flavor, whereas natural unrefined sugar (available in Japan but not in America) has a dominant molasses taste and white sugar is now widely recognized as being bad for both body and mind. (We feel it is important that decreases of meat in the diet be accompanied by proportional decreases of sugar usage, and that in general, grains, vegetables, and fruits be used as natural sweetening agents.)

The first sugar arrived in Japan in 753 A.D., brought by the Chinese Buddhist priest Ganjin on the same boat said to have brought the first Chinese miso. Yet sugar was virtually unknown in Japan until the late 1500s, and not until 1776 was the first sugar refinery established. Although Japan still has the lowest sugar consumption of any industrialized country in the world, the per capita figure jumped from 28.5 pounds in 1955 to 64.0 pounds in 1975. (The latter figure is only 57 percent of America's 112 pounds—14 tablespoons per day—for the same year.) In Japan, sugar is used mostly in cooking, where it is balanced by the saltiness of miso or shoyu; its use in desserts, treats, and "junk foods" is now rapidly increasing as Western dietary patterns become popular. Honey is only rarely used in Japanese cookery.

Oil: For best flavor, use natural vegetable oils. For sautéing and salad dressings, we prefer soy, corn, or "salad" oil—often mixed with small amounts of sesame oil; for deep-frying, rapeseed or soy oil. Olive oil works well in Western-style dressings. Sesame oil, especially popular in Chinese dishes, is now widely available in the West. No recipes require the use of hydrogenated oils or animal fats.

Rice: Polished or white rice contains an average of only 84 percent of the protein, 53 percent of the minerals, 38 percent of the vitamins and 30 percent of the dietary fiber found in natural brown rice. We prefer the flavor, texture, and nutritional superiority of the natural food. Yet brown rice is not flawless. Compared to white rice, it takes more time and fuel to cook (unless it is pressure cooked), and contains more mineral-binding phytic acid, and has extra oils which grow rancid faster in tropical climates.

In Japan, virtually everyone (including Zen monks) now eats white rice. The trend began in the early 1600s when it became a status symbol enjoyed first by the aristocracy and finally, in the early 1900s, by everyone. During World War II, time and energy could not be spared for polishing and, therefore, everyone ate brown rice. Today, however, the thought of un-polished rice triggers in most adults an almost Pavlovian response recalling the horrors of the war. Yet, the Japanese macrobiotic community has done excellent work in promoting the many virtues of brown rice and now, especially among the alternative lifestyle-sector of the younger generation, it is the symbol of a new, more natural and healthful way of living and eating.

Salt: Natural, unrefined sea salt contains an abundance of essential minerals which are lost during the refining process. Its flavor is richer and more concentrated than that of pure-white, refined table salt.

Shoyu and Soy Sauce: The skillful use of authentic shoyu and miso is the key to most Japanese cookery. An all-purpose seasoning, shoyu contains 6.9 percent protein and 18 percent salt; natural shoyu has been a mainstay of Japanese cooking for more than 500 years. We use shoyu, the Japanese word for "soy sauce," to distinguish this fine product from the modern nonfermented chemical or synthetic soy sauces now widely used in the West. There are five different varieties of Japanese shoyu; their composition of nutrients and relative importance in Japan are shown in the table below. Two of these varieties, regular shoyu (which includes natural shoyu) and tamari shoyu, bear special mention.

Natural Shoyu: This traditional product is always brewed using a natural (rather than temperature-controlled) fermentation process, generally for 12 to 18 months. The finest varieties are prepared from whole soybeans, natural salt, and well water fermented together in huge cedar vats. All types also contain *koji* starter *(Aspergillus oryzae)* and roasted cracked wheat. All natural shoyu presently available in the West—some of which is sold as *Tamari*—is imported from Japan. Actually, Japanese *tamari*, the progenitor of shoyu, is a different product (see below).

Shoyu: At present, this is the standard regular shoyu sold in Japan. A high quality product now produced on a large scale in the U.S., its flavor, aroma, and color are quite similar to those of the finest natural shoyu, and its price is considerably lower. Using techniques based on the traditional method but first developed during the 1950s, it is generally prepared from defatted soybean meal and brewed in large tanks for about 4 to 6 months under conditions of strictly controlled temperature and humidity.

Tamari Shoyu: This type of shoyu, a close relative of Chinese soy sauce, is made with a large percentage of soybeans (85-100 percent) and little or no wheat (0-15 percent). Produced and consumed mostly in Central Japan (Aichi, Mie, and Gifu prefectures), it constitutes only 2.2 percent of all Japanese shoyu. Tamari shoyu has a slightly darker color, richer consistency, and distinctively deeper flavor than regular shoyu, though its aroma is more subdued; since it contains little or no wheat it lacks the subtle alcohol bouquet found in regular shoyu. Many Westerners and some Japanese producers distinguish between *tamari shoyu,* which contains a small amount of wheat, and *tamari,* which contains no wheat (but may contain up to 0.15 percent roasted barley flour). According to some reports, the koji used to make tamari or tamari shoyu uses *Aspergillus tamarii* rather than *A. oryzae* as the primary microorganism. In Japan, the production of tamari shoyu is over five times as great as that of tamari. Whereas some 3,500 compaines make regular shoyu, only about eight make tamari shoyu (or tamari).

Varieties, Compositions, and Production of Japanese Shoyu

English Name	Japanese Name	Be	NaCl % (W/V)	Total nitrogen % (W/V)	Reducing sugar % (W/V)	Alcohol % (V/V)	pH	Color	Annual production %
Regular shoyu	Koikuchi shoyu	22.5	17.6	1.55	3.8	2.2	4.7	Deep brown	85.4
Light-colored shoyu	Usukuchi shoyu	22.8	19.2	1.17	5.5	0.6	4.8	Light brown	11.7
Tamari shoyu	Tamari shoyu	29.9	19.9	2.55	5.3	0.1	4.8	Dark brown	2.2
Clear shoyu	Shiro shoyu	26.9	19.0	0.50	20.2	Trace	4.6	Yellow to tan	0.4
Rich shoyu	Saishikomi shoyu	26.9	18.6	2.39	7.5	Trace	4.8	Dark brown	0.3

Source: Adapted from Fukushima, 1979

By an unusual quirk and accident of history, the word "tamari" has come to be widely known in the West, where it is frequently misused to refer to natural shoyu. In about 1960, when the Lima Foods company of Belgium started importing the first natural shoyu from Japan, they asked Georges Ohsawa, leader of the international Macrobiotic movement, what they should call the product to distinguish it from both regular commercial shoyu and from "chemical soy sauce," an inexpensive unfermented product described below. Ohsawa suggested that Lima Foods call the new product "natural shoyu," since that was its name in Japan. Lima Foods said the word "shoyu" seemed somewhat difficult to pronounce (in French and Dutch) and asked for alternative names. Ohsawa mentioned that words like "tamari" and "murasaki" were also used to refer to soy sauce in Japan. Lima Foods liked the word "tamari," finding it short, distinctive, and easy to pronounce. So they decided to call their natural shoyu "tamari." Ohsawa eventually came to use this terminology in his teaching and writing, and it was picked up and popularized by the Western Macrobiotic movement that has played a key role in introducing the product to the West. Little did any of them foresee the confusion that would result from this misnomer as people in the West became familiar with both natural shoyu and real tamari, and as distributors began to sell both of these fine seasonings.

In Japan, tamari is now rarely used in its natural form, being generally made into *sashimi-damari* by mixing it with miso-damari (see below), *mizuamé*, cane sugar, caramel, and often preservatives. Although not widely used in Japan, it remains fairly popular in Kyoto and central Japan, where it is used as a seasoning for *sashimi* (raw fish). In ancient times, tamari was widely used in its natural form and highly prized as a fine seasoning, having much the same flavor as best-grade Chinese soy sauce. Today, an increasing amount is made synthetically.

A close relative of tamari shoyu is *miso-damari*—also called *uwahiki* which is the tamari-like liquid that accumulates in *any* variety of miso during fermentation. Thicker and richer than tamari, it is gathered only in very small quantities and is not sold commercially. A delicious by-product of most homemade miso (it rises to the surface in summer and settles in winter), it may be used like shoyu and is especially delicious with hors d'oeuvres.

Chinese Soy Sauce: This traditional Chinese product, which has a stronger and saltier flavor than shoyu, is also made by natural or temperature-controlled fermentation. Although some varieties are excellent, they are not widely available in the West. Our Chinese recipes call for this product. If unavailable, substitute shoyu.

Chemical or Synthetic Soy Sauce: This domestic product, sold under various Chinese brand names, is what most Westerners mean when they speak of soy sauce. It is not brewed or fermented but is prepared from hydrolyzed vegetable protein (HVP) by the reaction of defatted soybeans with hydrochloric acid. Its flavor and coloring come from additives such as corn syrup and caramel. Since it takes only a few days to prepare, the production costs are quite low. Some varieties may contain sodium benzoate or alcohol preservatives.

Soybeans: Inexpensive, whole dry soybeans are now available in the West at most natural and health food stores; buy in bulk for substantial savings. For detailed information, see *The Book of Tofu.*

Tempeh: A cake of cultured soybeans with a flavor and texture remarkably similar to that of Southern fried chicken. Tempeh has twice as much protein as hamburger and is the world's best source of vegetarian vitamin B-12. For details, see our *Book of Tempeh* (Harper & Row, 1979).

Tofu: Also known as soybean curd, this delicious protein backbone of the traditional Oriental diet is low in cost, calories and fats, and entirely free of cholesterol. Remarkably versatile, tofu is now available throughout America in more than 10 different forms, all of which are described in detail in *The Book of Tofu.* The main varieties called for in the following recipes are:

Tofu: The most widely available product sold in waterpacked 12-ounce cakes containing 7.8 percent protein.

Firm Tofu (Chinese-style Doufu or Dow-foo): A firm product resembling Japanese tofu that has been pressed (p. 55). Good for use in deep-frying, stir-frying, and salads.

Deep-fried Tofu Cutlets(Thick Agé): Whole cakes of tofu that have been pressed and deep-fried until golden brown; 10 percent protein.

Deep-fried Tofu Burgers (Ganmo): Tofu-and-vegetable patties that look like large hamburgers; 15 percent protein.

Deep-fried Tofu Pouches (Agé): Each 6- by 3- by ¼-inch-thick pouch can be opened and stuffed with fillings; 19 percent protein.

Silken Tofu (Kinugoshi): A custard-like variety made without the separation of curds and whey; 5½ percent protein.

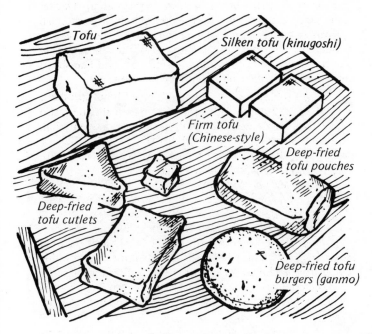

Tofu

Silken tofu (kinugoshi)

Firm tofu
(Chinese-style)

Deep-fried
tofu pouches

Deep-fried
tofu cutlets

Deep-fried tofu
burgers (ganmo)

Vinegar: Use either Western-style cider or white wine vinegar, or the milder, subtly-sweet Japanese rice vinegar *(su)*. The latter is especially tasty in salad dressings, sweet-sour sauces, and sushi rice. For 1 teaspoon rice vinegar, substitute ¾ teaspoon cider or mild white vinegar.

NOTE: Monosodium glutamate—also known as MSG or *ajinomoto*—is a crystalline, pure-white powder widely used to intensify the flavor of protein foods by exciting the taste buds. But MSG's ability to overexcite nerve endings may also cause brain damage, especially in infants, who do not have a well-developed blood-brain barrier to inhibit MSG from travelling freely to the brain. A committee of scientists selected by the U.S. Food and Drug Administration has advised that MSG should not be given in any amount to children under 12 months of age, and U.S. baby food manufacturers have recently agreed to omit MSG from their products.

In 1968 Dr. Ho Man Kwok, reporting in the prestigious *New England Journal of Medicine*, found MSG to be responsible for what has come to be known as the Chinese Restaurant Syndrome, characterized by headaches, a burning sensation at the back of the neck, chest tightness, and nausea, experienced by some people after eating foods highly seasoned with MSG.

This highly refined chemical additive, which is the sodium salt of glutamic acid, differs in chemical structure from natural glutamic acid. Originally extracted from the sea vegetable kombu *(Laminaria)* it is now generally produced by fermentation and hydrolysis of molasses or of glucose from tapioca, cornstarch, potato starch, etc. We and many other people interested in healthful, natural foods, strictly avoid use of this controversial substance. It does not appear in any of the recipes in this book.

Oriental Kitchen Tools

The Japanese chef (like most Japanese craftsmen) uses only a small number of relatively simple tools in his work. While the recipes in this book can be prepared using only the utensils found in most Western kitchens, the following tools may make cooking with miso somewhat easier and more enjoyable. Most of these tools are inexpensive and are available at many Japanese and Chinese hardware stores, as well as at some large Japanese markets.

Bamboo colander: Usually round and slightly concave, a typical *zaru*, made of thin strips of woven bamboo, is about 12 inches in diameter. It is used for draining and straining, and as a serving tray for such foods as tempura.

Broiling screen: This double-layer, 8-inch-square screen rests atop a stove burner and is used for broiling. Both layers are made of thin metal sheets, the bottom one perforated with 1/8-inch, and the top with 3/8-inch holes. The top layer slides out for easy cleaning. Broils foods faster and with less fuel than a Western oven broiler.

Charcoal brazier: Made of baked earthenware, the *konro* or *shichirin* is used for grilling and broiling, as well as for heating *nabé* dishes (p. 139) or the family teapot. When preparing *nabé*, you may substitute a tabletop gas burner, heating coil, or chafing-dish warmer.

Chinese bamboo steamer: Although most varieties of *seiro* are round and are set into a *wok* during steaming, some types are rectangular. They are made of slatted or woven bamboo with ¼-inch gaps between the bottom slats. This design allows steam to rise through the steamer's lid and prevents it from collecting and dripping on the steaming foods. Two to four steaming compartments may be stacked in layers during steaming.

Cutting board: A board about 19 by 9 by 1 to 2 inches thick, the *manaita* is designed to be set across the kitchen sink and hung on the wall when not in use.

Japanese grater: A metal tray about 9 inches long, the *oroshi-gané* has many sharp teeth protruding from its upper surface. Since there are no holes in the grater, the grated foods collect in the trough at one end.

Japanese vegetable knife: One of the finest knives ever designed for cutting vegetables, the *hocho* makes the art of cutting and slicing a true joy. Most varieties are quite inexpensive. The finest of these knives are handmade and bear the stamp of the craftsman on the blade near the knife's wooden handle.

Pressing sack: A simple cloth sack about 15 inches wide and 15 inches deep made of coarsely woven cloth is very helpful in squeezing and crumbling tofu.

Sudaré: A bamboo mat about 10 inches square used for rolling sushi and other foods. A small bamboo table mat makes a good substitute.

Suribachi: An earthenware grinding bowl or mortar with a serrated interior surface, the usual *suribachi* is 10 inches in diameter and 3½ inches deep, and is accompanied by a wooden pestle *(surikogi)*.

Tawashi scrub brush: Made of natural palm fiber, the *tawashi* is the perfect utensil for scrubbing root vegetables or

Fig. 15. Oriental Kitchen Tools

Bamboo colander

Broiling screen

Charcoal brazier

Chinese bamboo steamer

Cutting board

Japanese grater

Tawashi

Hocho

Pressing sack

Paddles & spoons

Lid

Wok

Draining rack

Sudaré

Wok support

Ladle & spatula

Suribachi

Cooking chopsticks

Mesh skimmer

Thermometer

washing pots. It is inexpensive and outlasts most synthetic brushes.

Wok set: Popular now in the West, the wok is the Orient's standard utensil for deep-frying, stir-frying, steaming, and sautéing.

1. *The wok:* The wok itself is a metal pan about 13 inches in diameter and 3½ inches deep. When placed atop a special circular support, it may be used with electric ranges. Surprisingly low in cost and now widely available in the West, its design has numerous advantages over that of a regular flat-bottomed skillet, especially when deep-frying: a) It provides the maximum oil surface and depth with the minimum necessary oil volume (3 to 5 cups); b) Each piece of food can be slid gently down the wok's sides rather than dropped with a splash into the oil; c) Freshly-fried foods can be drained into the pan on an inobtrusive rack which saves oil and allows more thorough draining when the foods are later placed on absorbent paper; d) The wok's rounded bottom and thin metal sides allow for quick heating and oil temperature adjustment; e) During stir-frying and sautéing, the wok's large surface area allows each piece of food to have maximum contact with the bottom of the pan, yielding crisp-textured foods in minimum cooking time; f) Cooked foods can be scooped out easily and thoroughly and, when all is done, the wok is easier to clean or wipe free of oil than angular, flat-bottomed pots. After sautéing or stir-frying, wash the hot wok immediately with water and a scrub brush (do not use soap), place it back on the fire until the inside is just dry, then wipe it quickly with a dry dishtowel.

2. *Wok support:* Used in most Chinese kitchens to give the wok stability and focus the strong fire at its base.

3. *Stir-frying ladle and spatula:* In Chinese kitchens, these large, sturdy tools are used during stir-frying. The ladle is employed to measure (by eye) and add all liquids and seasonings to foods cooking in the wok.

4. *Long cooking-chopsticks:* Shaped like regular Japanese wooden chopsticks but about 10 to 14 inches long and often joined with a string at one end, these *saibashi* are used mostly during deep-frying for turning foods in the hot oil or transferring cooked foods to the draining rack. Substitute a pair of long cooking tongs.

5. *Draining rack:* A semi-circular rack, the *hangetsu* is attached to the wok during deep-frying so that excess oil from the draining foods drips back into the wok.

6. *Mesh skimmer:* Used for skimming debris from the surface of the hot oil during deep-frying and for removing very small deep-fried foods.

7. *Wooden lid:* Used when simmering foods, the lid fits inside the wok's rim.

8. *Deep-frying thermometer:* Use a regular Western-style deep-fat thermometer that measures temperatures up to 380°.

Wooden spatulas, rice paddles, and spoons: These utensils make the work of sautéing, stirring, and serving easier and more enjoyable.

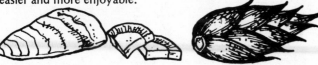

BASIC PREPARATORY TECHNIQUES

The following preparatory techniques will be referred to in many of the recipes in this book. We list them all here for easy reference.

Salt-rubbing

This process softens and seasons vegetables (and *konnyaku*) without cooking.

Place thinly sliced vegetables into a bowl and sprinkle with salt. Rub the salt into the vegetables with your fingertips until the vegetables are fairly soft, then let stand for 15 to 20 minutes. Fill the bowl with water and rinse away the salt. Empty vegetables into a strainer or colander and drain briefly. Wrap vegetables in a clean cloth and squeeze gently to expel excess moisture.

Rinsing and Pressing Leeks or Onions

This is a quick and easy method for neutralizing the harsh and evoking the mild, sweet flavors of these vegetables. Slice leeks or onions into thin rounds or slivers. Combine with several cups water in a small bowl and soak for 2 or 3 minutes. Pour into a cloth-lined strainer, gather the cloth's corners to form a sack, and press vegetables gently between your palms. Use immediately or refrigerate in a covered container.

Soaking Burdock Root

Burdock root has a slightly harsh, alkaline flavor that is easily removed by proper cutting and soaking. If unsoaked, burdock will lose its white color and turn a dark reddish brown soon after it is cut and exposed to the air.

Holding the root under running cold water, scrape off its dark peel with a knife or scrub it off with a scrub brush (*tawashi*). Cut the root into 2-inch lengths and submerge the lengths in cold water. Cut one section at a time into matchsticks and return these immediately to the water. Soak for about 10 minutes, then change the water and soak for 20 to 40 minutes more. Soaking time can be decreased by using warm or hot water, but some of the burdock's flavor will be lost. Drain quickly before sautéing.

Reconstituting Dried Sea Vegetables, Wheat Gluten, and Kampyo

Dried Hijiki: Immerse in several cups (warm) water and allow to soak for 20 to 30 minutes. Stir gently, then lift *hijiki* carefully out of water so that any grit stays at bottom of bowl. Place *hijiki* in a colander or strainer and press lightly to rid it of excess moisture. Note: ¼ cup (27 gm) dry *hijiki* yields 1 cup (200 gm) reconstituted.

Dried Wakame: Rinse *wakame* once, then soak for 15 to 30 minutes. Strain, reserving the nutritious liquid for use in stocks. Remove the midrib of each leaf only if it is unusually large. Squeeze *wakame* firmly, place in a compact mound on a cutting board, and cut at ½-inch intervals. (Place fresh *wakame* in several quarts of water, rinsing and squeezing 2 or 3 times to rid it of excess surface salt.) Note: 25 gm dried *wakame* yields 1 cup (125 gm) reconstituted.

Agar *(Kanten):* Tear agar bar crosswise into halves and soak in 1 quart water for several minutes. Lift out agar and squeeze firmly. Change water and resoak briefly. Squeeze again, then tear into small (1-inch) pieces.

Dried Wheat Gluten: Soak for several minutes in water. Press lightly with fingertips to expel excess moisture before use.

Kampyo: Soak for 15 minutes in water to cover seasoned with a pinch of salt. Drain briefly, then rub lightly with salt.

Parboiling

To parboil vegetables, drop them into more than enough boiling water to cover, and cook until just tender. When parboiling green vegetables, add about ¼ teaspoon salt for each 2 cups water to help the vegetables retain their color. Vegetables that are easily overcooked may be plunged into cold water as soon as they are done. Length of cooking depends both on how finely the ingredients have been cut and on whether they will be cooked again. Shredded or slivered vegetables, or leaves that will be simmered again in a seasoned liquid, may be parboiled for 30 to 60 seconds; boil for 30 to 60 seconds more if they will not be recooked. Small rectangles of *konnyaku* and root vegetables should be parboiled for 1 to 2 minutes. Larger pieces may be boiled for as much as 3 to 4 minutes.

Cutting Vegetables

Most of the cutting techniques used in the recipes presented in this book are familiar to any Western cook. A few, however, deserve special mention. The Japanese pay great attention to the way in which each ingredient is cut, because careful cutting not only lends beauty to the preparation when it is served but also assures that each uniform piece will be cooked to precisely the desired degree of tenderness.

Cutting vegetables into small rectangles: Cut thick vegetables (carrots, *daikon*, etc.) into 1½-inch lengths, then cut each section vertically into thirds. Now place each piece on its largest surface and cut lengthwise into small rectangles about 1/8 inch thick.

Cutting into matchsticks: This technique is used with long, thin root vegetables. Cut crosswise into 2-inch lengths; then stand each piece on end and cut vertically into 1/8-inch-thick pieces. Stack these on top of one another and cut lengthwise into 1/8-inch-wide strips the size of wooden matchsticks. Slivering or cutting *julienne* are variations on this basic technique.

Cutting into half moons: Use with long, thick roots or

tubers. Cut lengthwise into halves, then cut each half crosswise into pieces about ½ to ¼ inch thick.

Cutting into ginkgo leaves: Cut lengthwise into quarters, then cut crosswise into thin pieces.

Using Sesame Seeds

When roasted and ground, sesame seeds have a wonderful nutty flavor and aroma, and almost every Japanese kitchen is equipped with a *suribachi* and *surikogi* (a serrated earthenware bowl and wooden pestle, p. 51) used for grinding them. Small quantities of seeds can also be ground in a pepper grinder, a spice or coffee mill, or a special grinder that fits over the mouth of a jar of sesame seeds and is sold at Japanese hardware stores. If you are using ½ cup or more of seeds, you can grind them in a hand mill or meat grinder, or, in some cases, purée them in a blender with a dash of oil or shoyu. You may wish to make enough to last for several days or to use in Sesame Salt (p. 58). Grind the seeds with a firm but light touch until they are well crushed but not oily.

Two parts of ground roasted seeds impart about the same flavoring as 1 part pre-packaged sesame butter or *tahini*.

(Proper care of the *suribachi* is very important. Before use, scrub the suribachi with hot water and douse with boiling water. Dry with a dishcloth, then turn the bowl upside down and dry thoroughly with one edge raised to allow air to circulate. After use, fill the *suribachi* with hot water and soak for 1 hour; then scrub and dry as above.)

Heat a heavy skillet until a drop of water flicked across its surface evaporates instantly. Add seeds and reduce heat to low. Shaking the pan and stirring seeds constantly, roast for about 3 minutes or until seeds are fragrant and light brown and just begin to pop. (A seed pressed between the thumb and little finger should crush easily.) Transfer about ½ cup seeds at a time to the *suribachi* and grind with the pestle until no more than 10 to 15 percent of the seeds remain whole. For best flavor and aroma, use seeds immediately. To store, allow leftover seeds to cool, then seal in an airtight container in a cool, dry place. Prepare just enough for a week.

Toasting Nori

Wave a sheet of *nori* over medium heat for about 30 seconds or until crisp and slightly green.

Preparing a Steamer

Chinese Bamboo Steamer: Set the steamer over a wok filled with water to a depth of about 1½-inches. Bring water to a boil over high heat, then reduce heat to medium. Place the food in the steamer, cover with the bamboo lid, and steam for the required length of time. The woven bamboo lid prevents dripping by allowing steam to pass out. With this tool, several layers of food can be steamed at one time.

Covered Pot Steamer: Fill a 10- to 12-inch-diameter pot with water to a depth of about 1 inch. Bring to a boil over high heat, then reduce heat to low. Into the pot place a collapsible French steamer, a colander, or a plate set on top of an inverted bowl. Now put in the food to be steamed. (In many cases, tofu will be wrapped in a *sudaré* bamboo mat before insertion.) Place a single layer of absorbent toweling or paper over the mouth of the pot to prevent moisture from dripping onto the food, then cover the pot. Steam as directed.

PREPARING TOFU

The following procedures are used regularly in cooking with tofu. Try to master them from the outset, since each gives the tofu a unique consistency and texture.

Draining Tofu

Place the tofu in a 1- or 2-quart flat-bottomed container. Cover well and refrigerate for 1 to 2 hours or, for a firmer texture, overnight.

If set on a small colander or folded towel placed into the container beforehand, the tofu will drain even more thoroughly.

If two cakes are stacked one on top of the other, the one on the bottom will be almost as firm as if it were pressed (see below).

If the tofu was purchased in a sealed plastic tub, prick a tiny hole in bottom of tub, drain out any water, and place tofu and tub in container as described above.

Pressing Tofu

*Towel and Fridge Method: Wrap the tofu firmly in a small terry-cloth or cotton towel folded into fourths, and set on a plate in a refrigerator for 1½ to 2 hours or overnight. To decrease the pressing time, drain the tofu beforehand, place a 2- or 3-pound weight on top of the tofu, and replace the damp towel with a dry one after about 30 minutes. Or cut the cake horizontally into halves before pressing and place in the towel as illustrated.

*Slanting Press Method: Wrap the tofu in a towel or bamboo mat *(sudaré)* (or sandwich the tofu between bamboo mats) and place on a cutting board, tray, or large plate next to the sink; raise the far end of the board several inches. Set a 2- to 4-pound weight on the tofu and let stand for 30 to 60 minutes.

*Sliced Tofu Method: Cut the tofu crosswise into ½- to ¾-inch-thick slices and arrange on two towels placed on a raised cutting board. Cover the slices with a double layer of towels and pat lightly to ensure even contact. Allow to stand for 30 to 60 minutes. This method is commonly used when preparing tofu for deep-frying. For faster results, top with a cutting board and 5-pound weight and change the towels after 10 minute intervals.

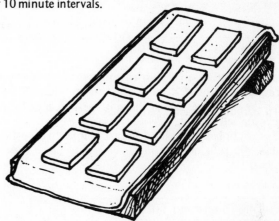

Squeezing Tofu

Place drained, parboiled, or pressed tofu (or doufu) at the center of a large dry dishtowel and gather its corners to form a sack. (Or use a tofu pressing sack [p. 51] if available.) Twist sack closed, then squeeze tofu firmly, kneading it for 2 or 3 minutes to expel as much water as possible. Squeeze lightly enough so that no tofu penetrates the sack. Empty the squeezed tofu into a mixing bowl.

Scrambling Tofu

Place tofu in an unheated skillet. Using a (wooden) spatula, break tofu into small pieces. Now cook over medium heat for 4 to 5 minutes, stirring constantly and breaking tofu into smaller and smaller pieces until whey separates from curds. Pour contents of skillet into a fine-mesh strainer; allow curds to drain for about 15 seconds if a soft consistency is desired, or for about 3 minutes for a firmer consistency. Spread curds on a large plate and allow to cool to room temperature.

Crumbling Tofu

Combine 12 ounces tofu and 1 cup water in a saucepan. With a wooden spoon or spatula, break the tofu into very small pieces while bringing the water to a boil. Reduce heat and simmer for 1 to 2 minutes. Place a colander in the sink and line with a large cloth (or a tofu pressing sack). Pour the contents of the pan onto the cloth, gather its corners to form a sack, then twist closed. Using the bottom of a jar or a potato masher, press the tofu firmly against the bottom of the colander to expel as much water as possible. Empty the pressed tofu into a large bowl and allow to cool for several minutes. Now break the tofu into very small pieces, using your fingertips or a spoon.

Dousing Deep-fried Tofu

Place uncut pieces of deep-fried tofu in a strainer or colander. Bring 2 or 3 cups of water to a boil in a saucepan. Douse first one, then the other side of the tofu. Allow to drain for about 1 minute before using.

Or, holding individual pieces of tofu with chopsticks or tongs, dip tofu quickly into boiling water, then drain in a strainer.

Broiling Deep-fried Tofu

*If using a *stove-top burner* or bed of *live coals*, skewer tofu with a long-tined fork and hold just above the flames until lightly browned on both sides and fragrant.
*If using a regular *bread toaster*, simply drop in the deep-fried tofu and toast. Fast and easy. Serve immediately.
*If using an *oven broiler*, place tofu on a sheet of aluminum foil and broil under a high flame until lightly browned on both sides.
*If using a grill over a *barbecue* or *brazier*, or a Japanese-style broiling screen set over a stove-top burner, broil the tofu over high heat for 30 to 60 seconds on each side until speckled and fragrant. Turn with chopsticks or tongs. In our opinion, this method—used with a charcoal fire—gives the finest flavor and aroma.
*If using a *dry skillet*, preheat skillet over medium heat and drop in tofu. Pressing tofu down with chopsticks or fork, rub tofu over entire bottom of skillet until tofu is fragrant and lightly browned. Turn and brown second side.

The following stocks, sauces, toppings, dressings, rice and noodle dishes, and other basic preparations are often served with miso. They play important supporting roles in miso cookery, so we have grouped them all together here. They will be called for frequently in later recipes.

The different varieties of fresh *dashi* (Japanese soup stock) serve as the basis for a wide variety of miso preparations and are easily made from natural ingredients. An instant dried dashi (dashi-no-moto) is now available in the West. Refrigerated in a sealed container, fresh dashi will last for 2 to 3 days without appreciable loss of flavor. Western-style vegetable or vegetable bullion stocks make satisfactory substitutes.

Number 1 Dashi *(Ichiban Dashi)*   MAKES 3 CUPS

This preparation is a cornerstone of Japanese cooking. The amount and variety of bonito flakes used vary slightly from chef to chef, as does the (often highly secret) method of preparation. For best flavor use flakes which have been shaved just before use.

3 cups water, Kombu Dashi, or Niboshi Dashi
¼ to 1 cup bonito flakes (15 to 30 grams)

Heat the water until quite hot in a small saucepan. Add bonito flakes and bring to a boil. Turn off heat and allow to stand for 3 minutes, or until flakes settle; skim off foam. Filter the dashi through a (cloth-lined) strainer placed over a saucepan. Press flakes with the back of a spoon to extract remaining dashi, then reserve flakes. (Some cooks add fine-textured flakes to simmered broths, *nabé* dishes, and miso soups together with the dashi, or simply omit straining.)

For a richer flavor, use a relatively large amount of flakes, simmer flakes for 2 or 3 minutes, and allow the dashi to stand (covered) for 15 to 30 minutes before straining.

Number 2 Dashi *(Niban Dashi)*   MAKES 2½ CUPS

The basic dashi ingredients are generally reused at least once to make a milder-flavored "Number 2" dashi. Thereafter the kombu may be slivered and simmered in shoyu and *mirin* to make *tsukudani* (a garnish for rice), pressure cooked with brown rice (p. 57), or cut into strips, each of which are tied into a simple loop and simmered in Oden (p. 141) or Nishimé (p. 143); whole pieces are sometimes used to prepare vinegar- or *nukamiso* pickles.

Whereas Number 1 Dashi is featured primarily in Clear Soups, this stock is generally used when simmering vegetables, with miso soups, or in noodle broths.

2½ cups water
Bonito flakes and *kombu* reserved from Number 1 Dashi

Combine all ingredients in a small saucepan and bring just to a boil. Remove *kombu* immediately, then simmer for 1 more minute. Strain and allow to cool.

Two tablespoons of fresh bonito flakes may be added to the boiling water after removing the *kombu;* reduce heat to lowest point and simmer for 5 minutes before straining. Leftovers may be reboiled in 1¼ cups water to make Number 3 Dashi.

Kombu Dashi *(Kombu Stock)*

MAKES 3 CUPS

Used in many homes as the basis for Number 1 Dashi (see above), this stock is featured in its own right in Zen Temple Cookery. *Kombu's* flavoring components (such as glutamic acid) reside mostly on its surface; be careful not to remove them by washing. Since they and the *kombu's* nutrients pass quickly into the stock, lengthy cooking is unnecessary, and actually leads to a decline in flavor.

1 strip of *kombu,* **about 3 by 7 inches, wiped lightly with a moistened, well-wrung cloth**
3 cups water

Combine *kombu* and water in a saucepan and bring just to a boil. Turn off heat, remove *kombu,* and reserve for use in other cooking. Use dashi as required or, if preparing Number 1 (or *Niboshi*) Dashi proceed to add bonito flakes (or *niboshi*) immediately.

For a more pronounced flavor but somewhat more viscous consistency, score *kombu* surface across grain at ½-inch intervals; simmer for 3 to 5 minutes before removing; double the amount of *kombu* if desired.

VARIATIONS

*Cold Water Method: Combine water and *kombu* and allow to stand for at least six hours, and preferably overnight. Remove *kombu* and use dashi as required. (Some cooks bring the stock just to a boil before removing the *kombu.*) The lengthy soaking is often said to make best use of the *kombu's* nutrients and give the finest flavor.
*Shiitake & Kombu Dashi: Select 2 or 3 *shiitaké* mushrooms, preferably ones having thick, partially opened caps and whitish (rather than darkish or yellowish) gills. (Or use ¼ cup dried stems or broken pieces.) Rinse briefly under running water, then soak either in cold water with the *kombu* or for 30 minutes in hot, freshly prepared Kombu Dashi. Strain dashi before use; do not squeeze *shiitaké* to extract absorbed dashi lest stock turn a dark brown.

Soybean Stock

MAKES 1 QUART

Prepare Pressure Cooked Soybeans (p. 129) doubling the amount of water used. (At the end of cooking, about 1 quart cooking liquid should remain for each cup soybeans.) Strain stock before serving beans.

Shiitaké Dashi *(Mushroom Stock)*

The preparation of Shiitaké Dashi as an integral part of the process for making miso soup is described on page 105. In Chinese Buddhist vegetarian restaurants and temples, a soybean & *shiitaké* stock is prepared by adding 1 to 2 cups washed and drained *shiitaké* stems or pieces to the ingredients for Soybean Stock (see above). The *shiitaké* are usually removed before serving the beans.

Niboshi Dashi *(Sardine Dashi)*

MAKES 3 CUPS

3 cups water or Kombu Dashi (p. 57).
¼ to ½ cup tiny (2-inch-long) dried sardines

Combine ingredients and bring to a boil over medium heat. Reduce heat to low and simmer for 3 to 5 minutes, skimming off any foam that rises to the surface. Strain through a (cloth-lined) sieve, reserving fish for use in other cookery. Use dashi as required or, if preparing Number 1 Dashi, proceed to add bonita flakes immediately.

Brown Rice

MAKES 4 CUPS

The Japanese say that when cooked, both regular and *sushi* rice are at their peak of flavor when the rice at the bottom of the pot is golden brown and slightly crisp. And even moderns prize the aroma of rice cooked in a heavy iron pot over a wood fire.

2 cups brown rice, rinsed and soaked overnight in 2 2/3 cups water

In a heavy covered pot, bring water and rice to a boil over high heat. Reduce heat to low and simmer for 45 to 50 minutes, or until all water is absorbed or evaporated. Uncover pot, remove from heat, and stir rice thoroughly with a wooden spoon. (If a slightly drier consistency is desired, transfer rice to a wooden bowl before stirring). Allow to cool for several minutes, then cover pot (or bowl) with a double layer of cloth until you are ready to serve.

To pressure cook: Rinse and drain 1 cup rice. Without soaking, combine in a pressure cooker with 1 cup water. Bring to pressure (15 pounds), reduce heat to low, and simmer for 25 minutes. Allow pressure to come down naturally for 10 to 15 minutes. Open pot and mix rice well. Allow to stand uncovered for 3 to 5 minutes, then cover with a cloth as above.

Brown Rice Porridge

SERVES 2 OR 3

Called *Congee* in China and *Okayu* in Japan, this is a popular main course at breakfast in many homes and temples. Easy to digest, rice porridge is considered the ideal food for sick people, and nursing mothers sometimes skim the creamy liquid from the porridge's surface to feed their babies as a breast milk supplement. In China, rice porridge is often served garnished or seasoned with *chiang* (p. 242), as are the hundreds of varieties of rice gruel. The latter, a close relative of Japan's *Zosui* (p. 122), is prepared by cooking vegetables (often leftovers) with rice porridge and seasoning the mixture with miso or soy sauce.

½ cup brown rice, soaked overnight in 4½ cups water

Prepare as for brown rice, setting lid slightly ajar and simmering for about 90 minutes, or until rice develops a porridge-like consistency. Serve immediately, seasoned with Sesame Salt (p. 58) or salt- or miso-pickled vegetables. If desired, add crumbled *nori* and minced leeks.

Or combine 1¼ cups (leftover) cooked rice with 3½ cups water and, without soaking, proceed as above.

To pressure cook: Rinse and drain ½ cup rice. Without soaking, combine in a pressure cooker with 2½ cups water. Bring to pressure (15 pounds), reduce heat to low, and simmer for 45 minutes. Allow pressure to come down naturally for 10 to 15 minutes. Open pot and mix porridge well. Allow to stand uncovered for 3 to 5 minutes before serving.

Sushi Rice
(Rice in Vinegar Dressing)
MAKES 2½ CUPS

1 cup (brown) rice, soaked in 1½ cups water overnight in
　a heavy 2- to 4-quart pot
Vinegar Dressing:
　2½ tablespoons (rice) vinegar
　1½ teaspoons honey
　2 teaspoons *mirin* (optional)
　½ teaspoon salt

Bring soaked rice to a boil in a covered pot. Reduce heat to low and simmer for 40 to 50 minutes, or until all water has been absorbed and rice is quite light and dry. (If using white rice, simmer for only 15 to 20 minutes). Remove rice from heat and allow to stand for 5 minutes. Transfer hot rice to a large wooden bowl, platter, or other non-metallic container and immediately sprinkle on the dressing. With a wooden spoon, chopsticks, or a wide fork in one hand, and a fan or flat pot lid in the other, mix the rice vigorously while fanning to cool it as quickly as possible. Fan and stir for about 3 minutes, then allow rice to cool to room temperature.

For variety, prepare Unsweetened Sushi Rice by omitting the honey and *mirin* in the dressing, and by increasing the vinegar to 4 tablespoons and the salt to 1½ teaspoons.

Paper-thin Omelets
MAKES ABOUT 8

These omelets may be made into an envelope or purse (*chakin*) used to contain Sushi Rice or they may be cut into thin strips called "threads of gold" and scattered over the top of Sushi Rice.

4 eggs
¼ teaspoon salt
1 teaspoon ground roasted sesame seeds (p.54) (optional)
1 to 2 teaspoons oil

In a small bowl, combine eggs, ¼ teaspoon salt and sesame; mix well. Heat a small skillet and coat lightly with oil, pouring off any excess. Pour about one-eighth of the egg mixture into the skillet, swishing it around quickly so that it just covers the bottom of the pan. Cook over high heat for about 20 to 30 seconds on one side only to form a thin omelet. Transfer omelet to a plate and allow to cool. Prepare 8 omelets, oiling the pan lightly after every 3 or 4. Sliver to use as a garnish.

Noodles
SERVES 2 OR 3

4½ to 5 ounces dry buckwheat or whole-wheat noodles (*soba* or *udon*)

Bring 2 to 3 quarts of water to a rolling boil over high heat. Scatter noodles slowly over surface of water and return to the boil. Lower heat until water is boiling actively but does not overflow. Cook uncovered for about 5 minutes, or until noodles are tender but not soft. Pour noodles into a colander placed in the sink and drain briefly, then transfer to a large container filled with circulating cold water. Stir noodles with chopsticks for several minutes until they cool to temperature of water, then transfer noodles back into colander; drain well and serve.

Sesame Salt (Gomashio)
MAKES ABOUT ½ CUP

A delicious all-purpose seasoning for grains, salads, beans, eggs, cereals, and sautéed vegetables, Sesame Salt is generally made with about 7 parts whole sesame seeds to 1 part salt. Please begin by studying instructions for preparing ground roasted sesame seeds (p. 54).

2 teaspoons sea salt
5 tablespoons white or black sesame seeds

Heat a heavy skillet. Pour in the salt and roast, stirring constantly, for about 1 minute. Add the sesame seeds and roast until done. Grind the salt-sesame mixture in a *suribachi* or hand mill as for Ground Roasted Sesame Seeds (p. 54). Store in an airtight container.

Ketchup-Worcestershire Sauce
MAKES 6 TABLESPOONS

¼ cup ketchup
2 to 3 teaspoons Worcestershire sauce

Combine ingredients, mixing well.

6
Recipes
from East & West

MISO'S EXQUISITE flavor and deep aroma, complex orchestrations brought to perfection over the centuries, evoke and accentuate the subtlest nuances of taste. Its warm colors have long been artfully used in a cuisine which demands that the eye as well as the palate find satisfaction. Its yielding texture has been prized for being gentle on the tongue.

Our 400 recipes hope to demonstrate that miso is, indeed, an all-purpose seasoning. *Arranged with our personal favorites at the beginning of each section,* they are meant to serve as an introduction to basic principles. The possibilities are limitless, as are the wonderful flavors you will discover as you begin to create new recipes based on your own favorite dishes.

FAVORITE MISO RECIPES

Among the many recipes in this book, there are certain ones we enjoy again and again, and like to serve to guests as an introduction to miso cookery. Most take little time to prepare and use readily available ingredients. This chart gives suggestions for their use in a weekly menu.

	Breakfast	Lunch	Dinner
Sun.	• Basic Miso Soup (p. 110)	• Floating Cloud Miso Dressing (p. 83) on your favorite salad • Mushroom Casserole with Miso, (p. 133)	• Peanut Miso (p. 62) or Walnut Miso (p. 61) on brown rice or on Apple Slice Hors D'oeuvres (p. 75) • Miso Mushroom Saute (p. 65)
Mon.	• Eggs Cooked Over Brown Rice with Miso (p. 151)	• Gaucamole with Miso (p. 74) as a dressing or dip; or • Miso-Sesame-Avocado Spread (p. 79)	• Baked Potatoes in Miso Gravy (p. 133) or • Potatoes with Miso White Sauce au Gratin (p. 134)
Tues.	• Deep-fried Tofu & Wakame Miso Soup (p. 102)	• Cucumber Slices Topped with Finger Lickin' Miso (p. 77) • Grilled Cheese Sandwich on Miso-Garlic Brean (p. 81)	• Miso Spaghetti Sauce (p. 114) • Grilled Corn-on-the Cob with Miso (p. 144)
Wed.	• Instant Miso (Better 'n Coffee) Soup (p. 109)	• Velvet Zucchini Miso Soup (p. 110) • Miso-Cream Cheese Dip (p. 74)	• French Onion Soup with Miso (p. 107) or • Miso Onion Soup Casserole au Gratin (p. 133) .
Thurs.	• Brown Rice or Brown Rice Porridge with Miso Toppings (p. 119)	• Miso Onion Sauce or Mushroom Sauce (p. 113) or Miso White Sauce (p. 114) over cooked vegetables or potatoes • Miso Paté (p. 79)	• Stir-fried Rice with Almonds and Miso (p. 120) • Miso Barbecue Sauce (p. 118) on tofu burgers or tempeh burgers
Fri.	• Scrambled Eggs with Miso, Onions, (p. 151)	• Stir-fried Buckwheat Noodles with Miso (p. 123) • *Amazaké* (p. 162) or Potato Salad with Sour Cream and Miso (p. 86)	• Rich Noodle Casserole with Miso-Sour Cream & Chives (p. 133) • Baked Apples Filled with Sesame-Raisin Miso (p. 153)
Sat.	• Thick Winter Squash Soup with Miso (p. 107)	• Tabbouli with Miso (p. 126) • Miso French Dressing (p. 84) with your favorite salad	• Miso & Nutritional Yeast Gravy (p. 113) over cooked grains or vegetables, or fried tempeh or tofu • Dengaku (p. 144)

Miso Toppings

Together with miso soup and *aemono*, the following are among the most popular ways of using miso in Japanese cookery. As versatile as they are delicious, Sweet Simmered Miso, Sautéed-, Mixed-, Broiled-, and Yubeshi Miso are each easy to prepare and well suited for use in a wide variety of Western-style dishes. All varieties make excellent toppings for grain, tofu, and fresh or cooked vegetables.

SWEET SIMMERED MISO
(*Nerimiso*)

Nerimiso derives its name from the verb *neru* which means "to simmer, stirring constantly, until smooth and thick." Prepared by combining miso with honey or sugar, water or dashi, seasonings and/or sake, and in most cases, nuts, diced vegetables, or seafoods, some varieties—such as peanut, walnut, and *yuzu*—are sold commercially, but most are made at home or in Zen temple restaurants, where they are said to have originated. Sweet Simmered Miso is generally prepared as a preserved food meant to be served over a period of several weeks. One or two cups are usually prepared at a time and are kept in a small attractive container, often an earthenware crock. At mealtimes, it is served as a seasoning at the table and used as a convenient topping for rice or rice porridge, chilled or deep-fried tofu, *mochi*, curries (it replaces chutney), oatmeal and other hot breakfast cereals, sweet or Irish potatoes (baked, broiled, mashed, or tempura), fresh vegetable slices, and a variety of cooked vegetables. The sweeter varieties make delicious spreads for toast or sandwiches, waffles, crêpes and pancakes, and steamed vegetables (such as cauliflower or broc-

coli). Small (1-teaspoon) portions are served on tiny ceramic dishes as accompaniments for Japanese-style tea and cakes, or as hors d'oeuvres together with sake or beer. Sweet Simmered Miso is also used as an ingredient in cooked preparations such as Miso Oden (p. 141), Eggplants Shigiyaki (p. 146), Dengaku (p. 144), and Aemono (p. 91). Unlike regular miso, it is never used in soups.

In restaurants, Sweet-Simmered Miso is often prepared in quantities of several quarts or more; cooked in a double boiler, it is stirred for as long as 1 to 2 hours to develop cohesiveness and luster, and improve its shelf life and flavor. After cooling, it becomes somewhat firmer than regular miso, often developing a consistency similar to that of peanut butter; some makers use *mizuamé* as the sweetener to create an even firmer consistency, closer to that of taffy.

Since imported varieties are relatively expensive, several natural food companies in the United States are now beginning to prepare their own Sweet Simmered Misos (using peanuts, walnuts, or cashews as the main ingredient) packaged in small transparent cottage cheese-type containers for nationwide distribution. Actually, any natural food store could offer its own varieties prepared fresh, refrigerated and sold in bulk. A sample large-scale recipe for Peanut & Sesame Miso is given on page 62.

We generally keep a cup of each of 3 or 4 types of Sweet Simmered Miso in the refrigerator at all times. Their flavors seem to marry and improve over a period of several weeks, and they keep their peak for a month or more if well sealed after each use.

Vary the amount of sweetening to taste. If *mirin* is unavailable, use a mixture of honey and sake (or white wine).

Red Sweet Simmered Miso   MAKES ½ CUP

This is the simplest and most basic form of Sweet Simmered Miso; all other recipes may be thought of as variations or elaborations on this fundamental theme. By adding different ingredients and seasonings (sesame, gingerroot, grated lemon rind, etc.) to those listed below, you can create a wide array of delicious toppings.

5 tablespoons red or barley miso
1½ to 2½ tablespoons honey
1 tablespoon water; or 1½ teaspoons each water and white wine (or sake or *mirin*)

Combine all ingredients in a small earthenware pot or a skillet and bring to a boil. Simmer for 2 to 3 minutes over low heat, stirring constantly with a wooden spatula or spoon, until mixture begins to thicken. Remove from heat and allow to cool to room temperature before serving. Cover and refrigerate unused portions.

VARIATIONS: Prepare as above

*Rich Red Sweet Simmered Miso: A favorite for use in Miso Oden (p. 141)
   6 tablespoons red, barley, or Hatcho miso
   2 tablespoons honey
   ¼ cup *mirin*
   2 tablespoons sake
*Chinese-style Sweet Simmered Miso: Topping for the popular noodle dish *Cha-chiang Mien*
   3 tablespoons red or barley miso (preferably chunky)
   1½ tablespoons soy sauce
   1 to 1½ tablespoons honey
   1 teaspoon (peanut or salad) oil
   ½ teaspoon sesame oil
   1 tablespoon sake or white wine
   2 tablespoons ground roasted seasame seeds (p. 54) or
       1½ tablespoons sesame butter (optional)
*Hatcho Sweet Simmered Miso: Use Hatcho miso and reduce the amount of sweetening by about one-third. This preparation has a deep, chocolate-brown color and savory aroma.
*Sake Lees Sweet Simmered Miso: Add 3 to 4 tablespoons sake lees; reduce the honey to 1½ teaspoons and omit the water.
*Crunchy Granola Miso: Prepare ½ cup Red Sweet Simmered Miso (using a relatively small amount of honey) and allow to cool to room temperature. Combine with ½ to 2/3 cup granola, mixing well.

Thyme

*Herb Sweet Simmered Miso: Just before removing miso from heat, stir in ½ to 1 teaspoon of any of the following fresh or dried herbs: thyme, basil, oregano, *sansho* pepper, rosemary, or mint.
*For use in Dengaku (p. 144), divide Red Sweet Simmered Miso into two equal portions. To one portion add ½ to 1 teaspoon hot mustard or ½ teaspoon *sansho* pepper.

White Sweet Simmered Miso   MAKES 1¼ CUPS

This recipe, a specialty of Kyoto's 400-year-old Nakamura-ro restaurant, is used as the topping of Japan's most famous Tofu Dengaku. In springtime, ground *kinomé* is mixed with the miso, or individual sprigs of *kinomé* are used to garnish the Dengaku portions. The use of egg gives White Sweet Simmered Miso a rich, smooth texture.

1 cup sweet white or 2/3 cup mellow white miso
3 tablespoons *mirin*
1½ tablespoons sake
1 egg yolk
3 tablespoons ground roasted sesame seeds (p. 54) or 1½ tablespoons sesame butter or *tahini*

Prepare as for Red Sweet Simmered Miso (see above).

VARIATION: Prepare as above

*Sweet White Sweet Simmered Miso (Makes ½ cup)
   ¼ cup sweet white or 2½ tablespoons mellow white miso
   1½ to 2 teaspoons honey
   2 teaspoons *mirin*
   1 egg yolk
   Dash of *sansho* pepper (optional)
For use in Dengaku (p. 144) or hors d'oeuvres (p. 76), or as a topping for deep-fried foods, divide the prepared miso into two equal portions. To one, add any of the following: ½ to 1 teaspoon grated gingerroot; 2 to 3 tablespoons thinly sliced leeks or green onions; 3 to 4 tablespoons ground roasted sesame seeds (p. 54) or sesame butter; 1 to 2 tablespoons bonito flakes and 1½ teaspoons water.

Walnut Miso   MAKES 1 CUP

One of our favorite miso preparations, Walnut Miso is often served in Zen temple restaurants and is sold commercially in Japan. Delicious as a topping for crisp apple slices (p. 75).

1 cup walnut meats, preferably large pieces
¼ cup red, barley, or akadashi miso
2 to 3 tablespoons honey or *mizuamé*
1 tablespoon water or 1½ teaspoons each water and white wine (or sake)

Prepare as for Red Sweet Simmered Miso (see above).

VARIATIONS

*Sauté walnuts in 1 tablespoon oil for 1 minute before adding remaining ingredients. Or pre-roast walnuts until fragrant in a dry pan or oven and, if desired, add ¼ cup sesame butter to the ingredients listed above.
*Cashew-, Almond-, or Pecan Miso: Substitute ¾ to 1 cup of any one of these for the walnuts.
*Sunflower Seed Miso: Sauté ½ cup sunflower seeds in 1 teaspoon oil for 1 to 2 minutes; then add miso and other ingredients and proceed as above.

Peanut Miso

MAKES ½ TO ¾ CUP

1 cup peanuts, lightly roasted, if desired
¼ cup red, barley, or Hatcho miso
1½ to 3 tablespoons honey or *mizuamé*
2 tablespoons water; or 1 tablespoon each water and sake,
    wine, or *mirin*

Prepare as for Red Sweet Simmered Miso (see above).

VARIATIONS

*Peanut & Raisin Miso: Use ¼ cup each peanuts and raisins,
and 2 to 3 teaspoons honey. Add 1 to 2 tablespoons (whole or
ground) roasted sesame seeds, if desired. This delicious product is sold commercially in Japan and America.
*Use akadashi miso and reduce the honey to 1½ teaspoons.
*Sauté peanuts briefly in oil before adding the remaining
ingredients; serve garnished with a sprig of *kinomé*.
*Use ¼ cup sweet white miso, omit the honey and add ¼ to ½
teaspoon salt.

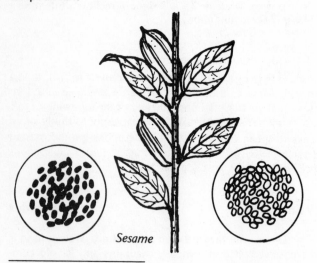

Sesame

Peanut & Sesame Miso

MAKES 1 GALLON

Here is a sample recipe that could be used by natural food
stores, restaurants, or communities that would like to begin
commercial production of Sweet Simmered Miso.

16 cups whole roasted peanuts, or substitute walnuts,
    cashews, or sunflower seeds
4 cups red or barley miso
1 cup roasted sesame seeds (whole or ground)
1 to 2½ cups honey
½ to 1 cup malt syrup
½ cup water

Combine all ingredients in a heavy 1½- to 2-gallon pot and
bring to a boil. Simmer, stirring constantly for 5 to 10
minutes, or until mixture begins to thicken. Pour into a large
crock or wide-mouth jar and allow to cool to room temperature. Cover and refrigerate.

For variety, add 2 cups raisins and reduce the honey to
taste.

Sesame Miso

MAKES ¾ CUP

The use of freshly-ground roasted sesame seeds gives
the finest flavor and aroma. If desired, use black seeds with
Red or Hatcho Sweet Simmered Miso, but always use white
seeds with White Sweet Simmered Miso. Excellent as a topping for sauteed or steamed vegetables such as *daikon*, turnips, eggplants, or burdock root. Sesame Miso thinned in
water during cooking also makes a delicious sauce.

¼ cup sesame butter, *tahini*, or ground roasted sesame seeds
    (p. 54)
1/3 cup red, barley, or Hatcho miso
1 to 2 tablespoons honey
1 tablespoon water; or 1½ teaspoons each water and sake
    (or white wine)
1 to 2 teaspoons grated orange, lemon, or *yuzu* rind
    (optional)

Prepare as for Red Sweet Simmered Miso (see above).

VARIATIONS

*For the sweet, chocolate-like flavor of Chinese *T'ien Mien
Chiang* or Peking Duck Dipping Sauce (p. 70), use akadashi
instead of the red miso.
*To the basic recipe add ¼ cup whole or chopped nutmeats
(almonds, walnuts, etc.)
*To ¼ cup Red or White Nerimiso, add 1 to 2 tablespoons
ground roasted sesame seeds or sesame butter, and ½ to 1
teaspoon grated gingerroot.

Yuzu

Yuzu Miso

MAKES 1 CUP

This recipe comes from Tokyo's 370-year-old tofu
restaurant, Sasa-no-Yuki, where the miso is served over
warm pieces of silken tofu and also sold in small ceramic
jars for home use. The fragrant rind of the *yuzu* (citron) is
preserved for about 1 year in *shochu*—a popular and very
potent type of spirits related to gin—before being used in
the miso. The chefs prepare about 35 pounds of *yuzu* miso
at a time, stirring the mixture in a heavy pot for 1½ to 3
hours over low heat to develop a dark lustrous color. Some
commercial varieties, most of which are a creamy beige,
contain *yuzu* rind which has been immersed for 1 year in a
crock of sugar before being diced and simmered with sweet
white miso. In grating fresh *yuzu* at home, it is important
to use only the yellow or green surface layers of the well-
washed rind. If the deeper white layers are used, the miso
may become bitter.

½ cup (light) red or barley miso
6 to 6½ tablespoons sugar or 3 tablespoons honey
6 tablespoons water
½ teaspoon grated *yuzu* rind, or substitute 1 to 2 teaspoons
grated lemon, lime, or orange rind

Prepare as for Red Sweet Simmered Miso (p. 60) except add the *yuzu* rind just before removing miso from heat.

For a darker color, simmer for a longer time. For a lighter color, substitute sweet white miso for the red and reduce sugar to 1½ tablespoons. The addition of 1 tablespoon *mirin* gives a nice luster without lengthy cooking.

VARIATIONS

*Tipsy Wintertime Yuzu Miso: Prized for its subtle bitterness, this preparation makes a fine topping for cooked vegetables and broiled tofu. In traditional Japanese homes, the *yuzu* and sake are simmered in a small earthenware teapot set over the mouth of a large iron tea kettle heated by a charcoal fire in the living room *hibachi* brazier.

During December or January, choose a well-ripened, yellow *yuzu*, wash well, and cover with sake or white wine in a small lidded pot. Place pot over a double boiler and simmer until *yuzu* dissolves. (If double boiling is inconvenient, use a mixture of equal parts sake and water and simmer over low heat, stirring occasionally.) Remove *yuzu* seeds, then stir in sweet white miso and a little sugar. Simmer over low heat, stirring occasionally, until well thickened.

Lemon or Lime Miso

MAKES ¼ CUP

¼ cup red, barley, or Hatcho miso
1½ to 3 teaspoons honey
1 tablespoon water
1 teaspoon lemon (or lime) juice
1 teaspoon grated lemon (or lime) rind

Combine the first three ingredients in a skillet and proceed as for Red Sweet Simmered Miso (p. 60). After removing from heat, stir in lemon juice and rind, allow to cool to room temperature. Delicious with sliced bananas, apples, and most deep-fried foods.

A softer version can be prepared by mixing 2 teaspoons lemon juice with 2 tablespoons Red Sweet Simmered Miso. Or prepare as for Tipsy Wintertime Yuzu Miso (above).

Tangy Mustard Miso

MAKES 1 CUP

2 tablespoons red, barley, or Hatcho miso
2 tablespoons vinegar
½ teaspoon hot mustard
1 tablespoon oil
Dash of pepper (optional)

Prepare as for Red Sweet Simmered Miso (p.60) but simmer for only 30 to 60 seconds. For variety, add 1 tablespoon ground roasted sesame seeds.

Kinomé

Kinomé Miso
(Miso with Fresh Sansho Leaves)

Also called *sansho* miso, this green and refreshingly fragrant miso is a springtime favorite. When *kinomé*, the fresh sprigs of the *sansho* tree, emerge early each April, this miso is widely enjoyed as a topping for Tofu Dengaku (p.144), in *aemono* (p. 91) or on butter-fried mushrooms.

¼ cup (about 60) *kinomé* leaves (not sprigs)
5 tablespoons sweet white miso
1½ teaspoons honey
2 tablespoons water
1 teaspoon shoyu (optional)
1½ teaspoons *mirin* or sake (optional)
Dash of *sansho* pepper (optional)

Place leaves in a strainer, douse with boiling water, and drain well. Grind leaves thoroughly in a *suribachi* (or mortar), or mince with a knife. Combine the next five ingredients in a small saucepan and prepare as for Red Sweet Simmered Miso (p. 60). Add contents of saucepan and pepper, if desired, to ground *kinomé* in *suribachi*; mix well.

VARIATION

*Jade-Green Miso: Collect 4 ounces of the tender tips of (*horenso*) spinach and/or *daikon* leaves. Mince thoroughly, then grind almost to a paste in a *suribachi* or mortar. Pour in 1 cup water and, using your fingertips, free the ground leaves from the grooves in the bowl. Now pour the contents of the *suribachi* into a fine sieve set over a small saucepan and rub the leaves through the sieve with the back of a large spoon. Heat contents of saucepan over high heat until puréed leaves float to the surface, then reduce heat to low and simmer for 1 minute. Pour contents of pan into a cloth-lined strainer; drain well. Using a small spoon, carefully remove green purée (called *aoyosé*) from cloth. Add 1 teaspoon *aoyosé* to Kinomé Miso, stirring well, until the miso has turned a delicate green.

A simpler version of *aoyosé* may be prepared by parboiling and draining the greens, then pressing them with your fingertips; grind in a *suribachi* or rub through a strainer, then mix with the miso.

In many recipes *aoyosé* is used together with *kinomé* to give the miso a richer color. It is stirred into the miso just before the miso is mixed with the *kinomé*.

Egg Yolk Miso

MAKES 1 CUP

6 tablespoons sweet white or ¼ cup mellow white miso
2 egg yolks
1 tablespoon honey
5 tablespoons dashi (p.56), stock, or water
Dash of *sansho* pepper (optional)

Prepare as for Red Sweet Simmered Miso (p. 60)

For use in Tofu Dengaku (p. 144), divide the prepared miso into 2 equal portions. To one add 1 teaspoon *aoyosé* (see preceeding recipe) and 60 *kinomé* leaves prepared as for Kinomé Miso. Stir in these ingredients just after removing miso from the heat.

Garlic Miso

MAKES ¼ CUP

Often cooked without thinning the miso with water or sake, this preparation has a very firm texture: refrigerated, it will stay fresh for several months. Considered by many Japanese to promote good health, it is usually served as a topping for hot rice; the heat gives it a softer consistency.

3 cloves of garlic, thinly sliced or crushed
¼ cup red, barley, or Hatcho miso
2½ to 4 teaspoons honey
2 teaspoons sake, white wine, or water (optional)

Prepare as for Red Sweet Simmered Miso (p. 60), but simmer over very low heat for 8 to 10 minutes, or until quite firm.

Gingerroot Miso

MAKES ½ CUP

2 to 3 teaspoons grated gingerroot
5 tablespoons red, barley, or Hatcho miso
1 to 1½ tablespoons honey
2 teaspoons sake, white wine, or water

Prepare as for Red Sweet Simmered Miso (p. 60). Serve with Dengaku (p. 144), as a cracker spread, with deep-fried foods, or as a topping for rice.

To obtain a somewhat similar flavor, simply mix ½ teaspoon grated gingerroot juice with ¼ cup Red Sweet Simmered Miso.

Leek or Onion Miso

MAKES ½ CUP

This miso is especially popular in Japanese villages where it is used as a topping for baked potatoes—and as a cure for colds.

6 tablespoons barley or red miso
6 tablespoons diced or grated leek, scallion or onion
2 tablespoons bonito flakes (optional)

Prepare as for Red Sweet Simmered Miso (p. 60) but cook for only 1 to 2 minutes. Or simply mix all ingredients without cooking.

VARIATIONS

*For a sweeter version of the above, mix 1 part Red Sweet Simmered Miso (p. 60) with 1 part minced leeks or onions. Excellent as a topping for Dengaku (p. 144).
*Red-Pepper & Leek Miso: This popular Korean preparation called *doen jang* is usually prepared with Red Pepper Miso (*kochu jang;* p. 231) and served as a zesty topping for cooked rice. Omit the bonito flakes in the basic recipe above and add ¼ teaspoon red pepper or tabasco sauce and 1 teaspoon (sesame) oil.

Beefsteak Leaf Miso *(Shiso Miso)*

MAKES ½ CUP

1 tablespoon butter
3 tablespoons red or barley miso
1 tablespoon honey
4 tablespoons water
¼ teaspoon 7-spice or minced red pepper
¼ cup minced green beefsteak leaves

Melt the butter in a skillet. Add the next four ingredients and cook, stirring constantly, for 3 to 5 minutes or until fairly thick. Mix in the beefsteak leaves and cook for 1 minute more.

Or, substitute ¾ cup beefsteak seeds for the leaves. Sauté in the butter for 1 minute before adding remaining ingredients.

Vinegar Miso

MAKES 3/8 CUP

This miso is generally prepared without cooking and used in various forms as a dressing for *aemono* (p. 91). Only when the miso is heated or cooked is Vinegar Miso considered a type of Sweet Simmered Miso.

3 tablespoons red or barley miso
3 tablespoons vinegar or lemon juice
1 tablespoon honey

Heat the miso until just warm in a small saucepan. Remove from heat and mix in vinegar and honey, stirring until smooth.

Allow to cool before serving. Use as a topping for fresh or cooked vegetables, or deep-fried foods, or as a dressing for *aemono*.

Variations containing sweet white miso, *mirin*, mustard, sesame, walnuts, peanuts, or chives may be prepared as above using the ingredients found in the recipes beginning on page 91.

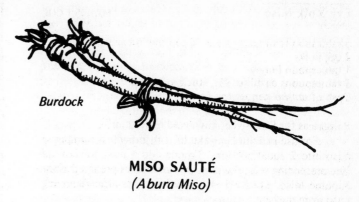

Burdock

Sweetened Mustard Vinegar Miso   MAKES ½ CUP

3 tablespoons red, barley, or Hatcho miso
1½ teaspoons honey
1 tablespoon oil
¼ cup water
1 tablespoon vinegar
½ teaspoon hot mustard

Combine the first four ingredients in a saucepan or skillet and bring to a boil. Simmer, stirring constantly, for 3 to 4 minutes, or until as firm as regular miso. Remove from heat, stir in vinegar and mustard, and allow to cool. Delicious with Chilled Noodles (p. 126).

Kanro Hishio   MAKES ½ CUP

Kanro means "sweet morning dew." This product, sold commercially in Japan, is a specialty from the city of Choshi, famous for its fine shoyu and hishio.

½ cup hishio (p. 43)
2 tablespoons *mizuamé* or honey
1 teaspoon sake or white wine (optional)

Prepare as for Red Sweet Simmered Miso (p. 60).

Red Pepper-Miso with Burdock Root   MAKES ¾ CUP

At Tokyo's famous *Yabusoba* noodle restaurant, a dab of this tangy miso is served on a tiny wooden dish as an accompaniment for green tea.

1 teaspoon oil
6 tablespoons minced burdock root, soaked for 10 minutes in water, and drained
2½ tablespoons red miso
2½ tablespoons sweet red miso
2 tablespoons sugar or 1 tablespoon honey
2 tablespoons water or the starchy water remaining after boiling *soba* buckwheat noodles
1/8 to ¼ teaspoon 7-spice red pepper, minced chili peppers, or tabasco sauce

Heat a skillet and coat with the oil. Add burdock root and sauté for 2 or 3 minutes. Add remaining ingredients and cook over low heat, stirring constantly, for about 5 minutes. Allow to cool before serving.

If sweet red miso is unavailable, substitute red or barley miso and increase the amount of sugar by 1½ tablespoons.

MISO SAUTÉ
(Abura Miso)

Originally a Chinese-style preparation featuring fresh vegetables sautéed in sesame oil, Miso Sauté serves as a delicious topping for brown rice or rice porridge, fresh or cooked vegetable slices, and chilled or deep-fried tofu. Refrigerated and well-sealed, unused portions will keep for up to 1 week. In each of the following recipes, up to one half of the oil may be sesame, which lends a nutty flavor and savory aroma. Experiment with other vegetables and nuts, or even with fruits.

Plain Miso Sauté   MAKES ¼ CUP

1½ tablespoons (sesame) oil
4½ tablespoons red, barley, or Hatcho miso

Heat a skillet and coat with the oil. Add miso and sauté over low heat for about 1 minute, or until miso just begins to stick to skillet. Allow to cool before serving. Delicious on cucumber slices.

Mushroom Miso Sauté   MAKES ½ CUP

2 tablespoons oil
10 mushrooms, thinly sliced
1 tablespoon red, barley, or Hatcho miso
1 teaspoon honey

Heat a skillet or wok and coat with the oil. Add mushrooms and sauté over medium heat for about 1 minute or until tender. Reduce heat to low, add miso and honey, and cook, stirring constantly, for about 1 minute more, or until mushrooms are evenly coated with miso. Allow to cool to room temperature before serving.

For variety, substitute butter for one-half of the oil, and sauté over low heat adding ¼ cup chopped walnut meats. Or use sweet white miso and reduce the honey to ½ teaspoon.

OTHER TYPES OF VEGETABLE MISO SAUTÉ

Each of the following recipes is prepared in basically the same way as Mushroom Miso Sauté. Use 1½ to 2 tablespoons oil, 1 to 1½ tablespoons miso, and 1 to 1½ teaspoons honey.

*Lotus root: Sauté 1½ cups ginkgo leaves of lotus root over low heat for about 5 minutes, or until tender but still crisp. Proceed as above.

*Kabocha: Use ¼ onion cut into thin wedges and 1½ cups thinly sliced pieces of *kabocha*, squash, or pumpkin. Sauté over medium-high heat for 4 to 5 minutes, or until softened. Add 1 tablespoon sesame butter, *tahini*, or ground roasted sesame seeds (p. 54) together with the miso and honey.

*Eggplant: Use 1 diced onion and 1½ cups 2-inch matchsticks of eggplant. Sauté just until all oil is absorbed, then add miso and honey.

*Sweet potato: Use 1¼ cups of sweet potato, yam, or Irish potato cubes. Sauté over high heat for 3 to 5 minutes until softened. If desired, sauté ½ diced onion and ½ thinly sliced carrot for 3 to 4 minutes before adding potatoes.

*Burdock root: Use 1½ to 2 cups matchsticks of burdock root, soaked (p. 53), and 1 carrot cut into matchsticks or grated. Sauté burdock root over high heat for 8 to 10 minutes, or until softened. Add carrot and sauté for 5 minutes more, or until both vegetables are tender. If desired, add 1 to 2 tablespoons roasted sesame seeds together with the miso and honey.

*Onion: Use 2 onions, cut into thin wedges, and 1 carrot, thinly sliced, slivered, or grated. Sauté both vegetables together over medium heat for 5 to 6 minutes, or until carrot is tender. Proceed as for Mushroom Miso Sauté.

*Gingerroot: Sauté 2 tablespoons grated gingerroot for about 1 minute.

*Celery: Sauté 1 cup diced celery or celery root for 2 minutes over high heat, or until softened. Add miso and honey and proceed as above.

Lemon-Walnut-Mushroom Miso Sauté

MAKES ¾ CUP

1½ teaspoons oil or butter
4 (*shiitaké*) mushrooms, thinly sliced (about 1/3 cup)
1 tablespoon minced lemon, lime, or *yuzu* rind
¼ to ½ cup chopped walnut meats
1/3 cup red, barley, or Hatcho miso
1½ to 2 tablespoons honey
2 to 3 tablespoons water

Prepare as for Mushroom Miso Sauté (p. 65) but sauté mushrooms for 2 minutes, then add lemon rind and walnuts, and sauté for 1 minute more.

Crumbly Tekka Miso

MAKES 1½ CUPS

The word *tekka* is composed of the Chinese characters for "metal" and "fire": this all-purpose condiment was traditionally simmered for a long time on a metal griddle or in a heavy iron pot. A favorite topping for brown rice, rice porridge, rice patties, and regular or deep-fried tofu, it is also served as is, as an hors d'œuvre with sake, beer, or wine. Several commercial varieties are now available at Japanese natural food stores and miso retail stores, and every good chef

has his or her own unique recipe. Crumbly Tekka Miso is prepared without sweetening and generally features chunky Hatcho miso and finely shaved burdock root; it is sautéed in sesame oil, often for as long as several hours, to create its dry, crumbly texture. Most varieties also contain roasted soybeans.

In Japan, this preparation is known formally as *Konjo Tekka Miso*. The word *konjo* means "root nature" and refers to those qualities in a great man which carry him through the most difficult situations. It is said that this miso was first developed during World War II for use as a seasoning with brown rice—which took the place of the usual white rice since it was less expensive, more nourishing, and did not require the time, energy, and manpower necessary for polishing. Eating this miso was believed to help a man develop his "root character". Today, tekka is widely regarded as one of Japan's finest and most high-class miso preparations, prized for its flavor and aroma, its long lasting qualities and versatility, and its medicinal properties (which make it a popular gift to friends who are sick). In Zen temples, it is often served as a condiment with each meal of the day.

3 tablespoons sesame oil
½ cup minced burdock root, soaked in cold water for 15 minutes and drained
6 tablespoons minced carrot or slivered, reconstituted *kombu*
¼ cup minced lotus root or whole peanuts
1 teaspoon grated gingerroot
¼ cup roasted soybeans (optional)
1 cup Hatcho, red, or barley miso
Dash of (7-spice) red pepper (optional)

Heat a large skillet or wok and coat with the oil. Add burdock root and sauté over high heat for 1 minute. Reduce heat to medium, add carrot and lotus root, and sauté for 2 to 3 minutes. Mix in gingerroot, miso and, if used, soybeans and red pepper: sauté for 2 minutes more. Reduce heat to low and cook, stirring constantly with a wooden spatula, for 20 to 30 minutes, or until miso is crumbly and fairly dry. Allow to cool before serving. Refrigerate unused portions in an airtight container.

VARIATION

*If roasted soybeans are unavailable, wash ¼ cup whole soybeans and soak in water for 30 minutes. (Or, for a firmer texture, omit soaking.) Drain beans thoroughly, then pat dry with a towel. Dry-roast in a heavy skillet until lightly browned and speckled, then add ¼ cup water and steam over low heat for 15 minutes. Add soybeans to miso together with carrots, and proceed as above.

Fine-textured Crumbly Tekka Miso

MAKES 2 CUPS

3 to 4 tablespoons (unrefined) sesame oil
¼ cup grated carrot
¼ cup grated lotus root
¼ cup grated burdock root
¼ cup black sesame seeds, ground to a paste; or sesame butter
¼ cup bonita flakes
2½ teaspoons minced gingerroot
1 cup (chunky) Hatcho miso

Heat a skillet and coat with the oil. Add the next six ingredients and sauté for about 5 minutes. Add miso, stirring well until evenly mixed with other ingredients. Reduce heat to very low and cook, stirring occasionally, for 20 to 30 minutes, or until miso is quite dry and slightly crumbly.

Moist Tekka Miso with Orange Rind

MAKES 3½ CUPS

5 tablespoons sesame oil
2 cups minced onion
2/3 cup minced burdock root
2/3 cup minced lotus root
2/3 cup minced or grated carrot
1 cup red, barley, or Hatcho miso
1 cup water
1 tablespoon grated gingerroot
1 teaspoon grated orange rind

Heat a heavy skillet and coat with the oil. Add onions and sauté for 5 minutes. Add consecutively burdock root, lotus root, and carrot, sautéing each lightly as you add it. Thin miso with the water and add, then stir in gingerroot and orange rind. Reduce heat to low and cover pan. Simmer, stirring occasionally, for 30 to 40 minutes, or until firm.

Sweetened Tekka Miso

MAKES 1¼ CUPS

The most popular form of *tekka* miso, this sweetened variety generally contains the same ingredients as Crumbly Tekka Miso plus honey; the miso is cooked only until smooth and firm.

1 tablespoon oil
2/3 cup thin rounds or matchsticks of burdock root, peeled, soaked in cold water for 15 minutes, and drained
½ carrot, cut into matchsticks
½ cup diced or slivered lotus root (optional)
1/3 cup Hatcho, red, or akadashi miso
2 tablespoons honey
1 tablespoon sake or white wine
2 tablespoons ground roasted sesame seeds (p. 54), sesame butter or *tahini*; or ¼ cup poppy or hemp seeds
¼ cup roasted soybeans (or see the variation to Crumbly Tekka Miso, p. 66)

Heat a wok or skillet and coat with the oil. Add burdock root and carrot, and sauté over medium-high heat for 3 or 4 minutes. Reduce heat to low, then stir in the next four ingredients and sauté for 3 or 4 minutes more. Stir in soybeans and remove from heat. Transfer to a bowl and allow to cool. Use as an all-purpose condiment or topping.

VARIATION

*Tekka Miso from Hatcho Sweet Simmered Miso
   ¼ cup soybeans
   1 tablespoon sesame oil
   ½ cup thin rounds or matchsticks of burdock root, prepared as above
   ¾ cup Hatcho Sweet Simmered Miso (p. 61)
   1 tablespoon ground, roasted sesame seeds
   1 tablespoon *mirin*

Roast soybeans as described in the variation under Crumbly Tekka Miso (p. 66). Sauté burdock in oil for 4 minutes, then add cooked beans and sweet simmered Miso, and sauté for 3 or 4 minutes more. Stir in sesame and *mirin*, and remove from heat.

Carrot & Red Pepper Miso Sauté

MAKES ¾ CUP

Many delicious varieties of Miso Sauté may be prepared without the use of sweetening using the basic techniques given in the following two recipes.

3 tablespoons sesame oil
¼ teaspoon minced red peppers, Chinese red-pepper *chiang*, or tabasco sauce
1 carrot, grated fine
1 tablespoon grated gingerroot
¼ cup red, barley, or Hatcho miso

Heat a wok or skillet and coat with the oil. Add the red pepper and sauté for 15 seconds. Add grated carrot and gingerroot and sauté for 1 minute more. Stir in miso and sauté for 6 more minutes. Remove from heat and allow to cool before serving.

Onion-Sesame Miso Sauté

MAKES ½ CUP

1 tablespoon sesame oil
½ cup minced wild onions, scallions, leeks, or onions
3 to 4 tablespoons sweet red miso
Dash of 7-spice red pepper, tabasco sauce, or paprika

Heat the oil over high heat in a wok or skillet. Add onions and sauté for about 1 minute. Stir in the miso and red pepper, reduce heat to low, and sauté for 2 or 3 minutes more.

Onion Miso Sauté with Orange

MAKES 1½ CUPS

2 tablespoons sesame oil
4 onions, thinly sliced
3 tablespoons red, barley, or Hatcho miso
¼ cup water
1 teaspoon grated orange rind
¼ cup grated cheese (optional)

Heat a skillet and coat with the oil. Add onions and sauté for 5 minutes. Stir in miso and water, cover, and simmer for 8 to 10 minutes. Add orange rind and, if used, grated cheese; remove from heat. For best flavor, allow to stand for 6 to 8 hours. Delicious on brown rice, tofu, or toast.

Sesame-Leek Miso Sauté

MAKES 1¼ CUPS

2 tablespoons sesame oil
2 cups chopped leeks or scallions, separated into whites and greens
6 tablespoons water or stock
4 tablespoons red, barley, or Hatcho miso

Heat a skillet or wok and coat with the oil. Add greens and sauté for 30 seconds. Add whites and sauté for 30 seconds more. Add 4 tablespoons water, cover pan, and simmer for 5 minutes. Thin miso in remaining 2 tablespoons water, add to vegetables, and simmer for 2 or 3 minutes.

Spicy Eggplant-Miso Sauté

MAKES 1½ CUPS

2 tablespoons oil
1¾ cups unpeeled, diced eggplants
3 tablespoons red, barley, or Hatcho miso
2½ teaspoons honey
2 tablespoons water
2/3 cup leeks or scallions, cut into ½-inch lengths
¼ teaspoon (7-spice) red pepper or tabasco sauce

Heat a skillet or wok and coat with the oil. Add eggplants and sauté over low heat for 3 to 4 minutes. Add miso, honey, and water and cook, stirring constantly, for 2 to 3 minutes. Mix in leeks, season with red pepper, and cook for 1 minute more.

　　For variety, omit leeks and serve skewered on foodpicks as a hot or cold hors d'œuvre.

Garlic & Green Pepper Miso Sauté

MAKES ½ CUP

1 tablespoon oil
½ clove garlic, crushed or minced
1 or 2 green peppers, thinly sliced
2 tablespoons barley, red, or Hatcho miso
1½ teaspoons honey
3 tablespoons water

Heat a wok or skillet and coat with the oil. Add garlic and sauté over high heat for about 15 seconds. Add green peppers and sauté for 1 minute more. Reduce heat to medium, stir in

remaining ingredients and cook, stirring constantly, for 2 more minutes. Allow to cool before serving.

Spicy Burdock Miso Sauté

MAKES 1¼ CUPS

1 tablespoon sesame oil
1¼ cups shaved or slivered burdock root
1 teaspoon grated gingerroot; or ½ teaspoon grated lemon rind; or 1 tablespoon minced *umeboshi*
3 tablespoons red, barley, or Hatcho miso
1 tablespoon sesame butter or *tahini*
5 tablespoons water
Dash of (7-spice) red pepper

Heat a skillet or wok and coat with the oil. Add burdock and sauté for 5 minutes. Combine the next four ingredients, mixing well, then add to contents of skillet. Cover and simmer for 15 minutes over very low heat, stirring occasionally. Season with the red pepper and allow to cool. Serve as a topping for cooked Brown Rice (p.119).

Green Pepper Miso Sauté

MAKES 2/3 CUP

1 tablespoon oil
1 green pepper, diced
¼ cup red, barley, or Hatcho miso
2 tablespoons sake or white wine
3 to 4 tablespoons water
1½ teaspoons honey
1 teaspoon grated *yuzu*, lime, or lemon rind (optional)

Heat a wok or skillet and coat with the oil. Add green pepper and sauté for 1 minute. Mix in the next four ingredients and sauté for about 1 minute more. Remove from heat and stir in grated citrus peel. Serve as a sauce for croquettes, tofu (regular or deep-fried), baked potatoes, or sautéed vegetables.

　　For variety, substitute *sansho* pepper or beefsteak seeds for the citrus peel.

Beefsteak Seed Miso Sauté
(Shisonomi Abura Miso)

MAKES ½ CUP

1 teaspoon oil
¼ cup beefsteak seeds or buds, rubbed with salt, then rinsed well
¼ cup red, barley, or Hatcho miso
1¼ to 1½ tablespoons honey
1 teaspoon shoyu
1 tablespoon water or dashi (p. 56)

Heat a skillet and coat with the oil. Add beefsteak seeds and sauté for 1 minute. Add remaining ingredients and proceed as for Mushroom Miso Sauté (p. 65), sautéing for 9 to 10 minutes more.

Banana Miso Sauté

MAKES 2 CUPS

1 tablespoon butter or oil
2 bananas, cut into thin rounds
½ cup chopped walnut or almond meats (optional)
1 tablespoon sweet white or 2 teaspoons mellow white miso
½ teaspoon honey (optional)

Prepare as for Mushroom Miso Sauté (p. 65), sautéing the walnuts, if used, with the bananas.

For richer color and flavor, use 1 tablespoon red or barley miso and 1½ teaspoons honey.

Spicy Korean Miso Sauté

MAKES ¾ CUP

2 tablespoons sesame oil
1 clove of garlic, crushed
1 tablespoon grated gingerroot
2 green peppers, minced
½ small onion, diced
Dash of minced red pepper, tabasco sauce, or 7-spice red pepper
3 tablespoons red, barley, or Hatcho miso
2 teaspoons soy sauce
1 tablespoon sake or white wine

Heat a wok or skillet and coat with the oil. Add the next five ingredients and sauté for 2 minutes. Stir in the miso, soy sauce, and sake, return just to the boil, and remove from heat. Allow to cool before serving. Delicious as a topping for fresh cucumber, celery, or tomato slices; for noodles or deep-fried tofu.

Vinegar Miso Sauté (Abura-su Miso)

MAKES ½ CUP

The addition of vinegar to many varieties of Miso Sauté gives a tangy flavor which is particularly well suited to deep-fried foods.

1 tablespoon oil
1 small onion or leek, thinly sliced
1 clove of garlic, crushed or minced
1½ tablespoons red, barley, or Hatcho miso
1½ teaspoons honey
1 tablespoon vinegar

Heat a wok or skillet and coat with the oil. Add onion and garlic and sauté over high heat for 2 minutes. Reduce heat to low, mix in miso and honey, and simmer for 1 minute more. Remove from heat, mix in vinegar, and allow to cool.

VARIATIONS

*Mustard-Vinegar Miso Sauté: Add ½ teaspoon hot mustard together with the vinegar.
*Substitute for the onions an equal volume of thinly sliced green peppers, mushrooms, or bamboo shoots.
*Add vinegar to taste to any of the previous recipes for Miso Sauté.

Oregano

MIXED MISO
(Awasé Miso)

These simple but delicious recipes, requiring no cooking, are quick and easy to prepare. A number of closely related dishes are given at Vinegar Miso Dressings (p. 91). Unseasoned mixed misos are described on page 44.

Mixed Red Miso Toppings

MAKES ABOUT ¼ CUP

In Japan, many of the following mixtures, prepared with shoyu rather than miso, are widely used as dipping sauces. The simplest of all types of miso recipes, these are extremely versatile, adapting themselves readily to experimentation with your favorite herbs and spices. All varieties may be served as toppings for rice or rice gruel, regular or deep-fried tofu, fresh vegetable slices, *mochi*, and baked or broiled potatoes.

Combine ¼ cup red, barley, or Hatcho miso with any one of the following, mixing well. Cover and refrigerate unused portions.
  *Garlic: 2 cloves of garlic, grated or crushed
  *Bonito: ¼ cup bonito flakes and, if desired, 1½ tablespoons *mirin*
  *Umeboshi Salt Plums: 1½ tablespoons minced *umeboshi* (about 10) and, if desired, 2 tablespoons bonito flakes
  *Wasabi: 1 teaspoon freshly grated *wasabi*, *wasabi* paste, or Western-style horseradish and, if desired, 1½ teaspoons honey
  *Gingerroot: 2 teaspoons grated gingerroot
  *Daikon: 4 to 6 tablespoons grated *daikon* and, if desired, 2 tablespoons bonito flakes
  *Leek: ¼ cup diced or grated leeks or scallions and, if desired, 1½ tablespoons bonito flakes
  *Citrus: 1 to 2 teaspoons grated or slivered lemon, lime, or *yuzu* rind
  *Herb: ½ to 1 teaspoon dill, marjoram, oregano, thyme, basil, or tarragon
  *Mustard: ½ to 1 teaspoon hot mustard and 2 tablespoons *mirin*, sake, or white wine
  *Lemon: 2 to 2½ tablespoons lemon (or lime) juice or vinegar and, if desired, 2 tablespoons sake or white wine
  *Sesame: 1½ tablespoons sesame or nut butter and, if desired, 1½ tablespoons honey and 4 teaspoons sake or white wine
  *Sesame-Bonito-Citrus: 1 tablespoon each sesame butter and bonito flakes (or grated cheese) and ¼ teaspoon grated lemon rind; serve in a hollowed half-lemon rind

Mixed White Miso Toppings
MAKES ABOUT ¼ CUP

¼ cup sweet white or 2½ tablespoons mellow white miso
½ to 1 teaspoon honey
Seasonings (optional): Choose one

    ¼ teaspoon grated lemon or orange rind and 1 teaspoon
      lemon juice
    1 tablespoon finely minced mint or green beefsteak
      leaves and ½ teaspoon water
    1 tablespoon each Parmesan cheese and parsley, and 1
      teaspoon water

Combine all ingredients, mixing well. Try with thinly sliced cucumbers or tomatoes, canapés or crackers, apple wedges or banana rounds.

Subtly Sweet Leek Miso
MAKES 1 CUP

1 cup leeks, sliced into very thin rounds
¼ cup barley or red miso

Combine ingredients, mixing well (with chopsticks) for several minutes. For best flavor, refrigerate for 1 to 2 days before serving. Excellent as a topping for Furofuki Daikon (p. 140) or baked potatoes. Or serve in small portions as an hors d'œuvre with drinks. A favorite in Japanese farmhouses where it is said to warm the body while providing strength and stamina.

    For a richer flavor, use ¼ cup each leeks and miso, and 1½ tablespoons bonita flakes.

Natto-Miso Topping
SERVES 2

½ cup *natto* (fermented soybeans)
2½ tablespoons red, barley, or Hatcho miso
1½ tablespoons bonito flakes
1½ tablespoons thinly sliced leeks, minced onions, or *daikon* leaves
1/3 teaspoon hot mustard
1½ tablespoons green *nori* flakes or crumbled toasted *nori* (p. 54) (optional)

Combine all ingredients, mixing well (with chopsticks) for several minutes to develop cohesiveness. Serve as a garnish for brown rice or rice porridge, or as a spread for crackers or canapés.

Homemade Akadashi Miso
MAKES ¼ CUP

2 tablespoons Hatcho miso
2 tablespoons red or light-yellow miso
1 tablespoon honey or *mizuamé*
½ to 1 teaspoon shoyu

Combine all ingredients, mixing well. For a smoother texture, rub through a sieve.

Cheese Miso
MAKES ¼ CUP

¼ cup finely grated (firm) cheese or Parmesan
1 tablespoon red, barley, or Hatcho miso
1 tablespoon butter (optional)
Seasonings (optional): Choose one
2 teaspoons minced onion, leek, or chives
1 to 2 tablespoons bonito flakes
½ clove crushed garlic
Dash of pepper, 7-spice red pepper, or tabasco sauce

Combine the cheese, miso and, if desired, the butter and seasoning. Mix lightly so that grated cheese retains its texture. Serve as a topping (or filling) for broiled or baked potatoes, sliced cucumbers, canapés, *mochi*, brown rice, or deep-fried tofu.

Peking Duck Dipping Sauce
(Homemade T'ien Mien Chiang)
MAKES ½ CUP

    This recipe, used by many Chinese-style restaurants in Japan, yields a sauce closely related to Sweet Wheat-flour Chiang (*t'ien mien chiang*), but with a slightly sweeter flavor and softer consistency. It is often used as an all-purpose cooking seasoning in sauces and stir-fried dishes, as well as with Peking Duck and Pancake Rolls.

¼ cup Hatcho miso
1½ teaspoons sesame oil
½ teaspoon vegetable oil
¾ teaspoon sake or white wine
1 teaspoon shoyu
1½ tablespoons honey
2 tablespoons water

Combine all ingredients, mixing until smooth. Refrigerate unused portions in a sealed container.

Peking Duck Dipping Sauce
(from Sweet Wheat-flour Chiang)
MAKES 3/8 CUP

¼ cup Sweet Wheat-flour Chiang (*t'ien mien chiang*)
1 teaspoon sesame oil
1½ teaspoons honey
1 teaspoon *mirin*, sake, or white wine

Combine all ingredients, mixing well.

Homemade Korean Red-pepper Miso (*Kochu jang*)

MAKES 3/8 CUP

¼ cup Hatcho or red miso
½ teaspoon powdered red pepper or tabasco sauce
1 tablespoon soy sauce
1 tablespoon honey
1 teaspoon sesame oil

Combine all ingredients, mixing well. A favorite with Korean-style five-color rice (*Bibimpap*, p. 123).

Rich & Savory Bonito-Miso Topping

MAKES 3 TABLESPOONS

2 to 3 tablespoons bonita flakes
1 to 1½ tablespoons red, barley, or Hatcho miso
1 tablespoon minced leeks or scallions
¼ teaspoon grated gingerroot

Combine all ingredients, mixing well. A favorite topping for tofu or deep-fried foods.

Savory Broiled Miso

SERVES 1

Use 1 to 2 teaspoons of any of the following:
  A chunky, natural Hatcho, barley or red miso
  Any dark-colored Sweet Simmered Miso (p. 60)
  Any variety of Mixed Miso, especially varieties containing bonito flakes (p. 69)
  Subtly Sweet Leek Miso (p. 64)
  Cheese Miso (p. 70)

If using a stove-top burner, charcoal brazier, or bed of live coals: Spread miso in a layer about 1/8 inch thick on a thin cedar plank, the lid of an earthenware bowl, in a clam or scallop shell, or in the concave surface of a large wooden or metal spatula or spoon (fig. 16). Holding the miso (with tongs) 1 to 2 inches above the open fire and moving it back and forth slowly, broil for 15 to 30 seconds (checking miso every 5 seconds) until it is fragrant and lightly speckled. If broiling miso on a lid, place lid on its matching (empty) cup or bowl to help retain miso fragrance. If using a shell, serve in the shell. Or scrape miso from the plank, spatula, or spoon into a small shallow dish. Serve immediately.

If using an oven broiler: Spread miso as above on a piece of aluminum foil or directly onto canapés, buttered crackers, toast, thinly-sliced, steamed potatoes, deep-fried tofu, or eggplants. Broil and serve as above.

Fig. 16. Broiling Miso

BROILED MISO
(*Yakimiso*)

When broiled or grilled over an open fire, miso develops a delightful aroma and flavor, and in Japan, the use of cryptomeria or Japanese cedar *(sugi)* as the broiling plank imparts an additional subtlety to the fragrance. Served as a topping for hot rice or rice gruel, regular or deep-fried tofu, canapés, broiled potatoes or cucumber slices, broiled miso transforms the simplest dishes into gourmet delights. It may also be served as is, as an hors d'œuvre with sake or beer, or added to chilled summertime soups.

VARIATIONS

*Skewered Broiled Miso: Shape miso into 1½-inch-diameter balls, adding bonito flakes or grated cheese if necessary to give a firmer texture. Pierce with a skewer, chopsticks, or a fork, and broil over an open fire.
*Broiled Citrus Miso: Prepare Yuzu- or Lemon Miso (p. 62) and pack firmly into a hollowed half yuzu or lemon rind. Broil slowly over a bed of live coals until fragrant.
*Broiled Miso & Leek Broth: This preparation is a Japanese folk remedy said to cure colds and fevers. Combine broiled red miso with 1 tablespoon thinly sliced leeks. Stir in ½ cup boiling water, adding a little at a time until smooth. Serve hot.

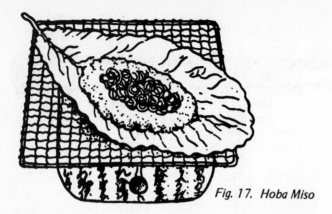

Fig. 17. Hoba Miso

Hoba Miso (Miso & Vegetables Broiled on Magnolia Leaves)

SERVES 2

The word *hoba* refers to the huge oval leaves of the wild *ho* tree *(Magnolia hypoleuca)*. Often attaining a length of over 16 inches, the dried leaves have a delightful aroma that permeates the miso as the latter broils. This preparation is famous in and around Japan's mountain village of Takayama. In restaurants, it is usually prepared over a small tabletop charcoal brazier (fig. 17); in farmhouses, over the dying coals in the open-hearth fireplace located at the center of the main room. The fragrance of the woodsmoke is said to be one of the keys to its fine flavor.

1 large dry magnolia leaf, at least 12 inches long and 5 inches wide
2 to 3 tablespoons red, barley, or Hatcho miso
2 to 4 tablespoons grated *daikon*
½ leek, sliced into very thin rounds
4 (fresh *shiitaké*) mushrooms, thinly sliced
Seasonal wild vegetables, thinly sliced; or nuts (optional)
1 teaspoon oil (optional)

Place leaf with concave side facing upward atop a glowing charcoal brazier or barbecue, then place other ingredients at center of leaf. Broil, stirring occasionally with chopsticks, for 5 to 6 minutes, or until miso begins to simmer. While continuing to broil, transfer hot miso-vegetable mixture a little at a time from leaf and use as a topping for cooked Brown Rice, Rice Patties (p. 121), thin cucumber slices, or Ochazuké (p. 123). Or eat as is in small amounts as an hors d'œuvre with drinks.

A fairly good facsimile of this dish can be prepared using aluminum foil in place of the leaf and broiling in an oven broiler. In some parts of Japan, dry buckeye leaves are also used.

Kaiyaki-miso

Kaiyaki-miso (Miso Sautéed with Vegetables in Scallop Shells)

SERVES 4

This close relative of Hoba Miso is ideal for use at barbecues or campfire dinners.

4 teaspoons (sesame) oil
2 green *(togarashi)* peppers, minced
¼ cup diced eggplant
8 green beans, slivered
¼ cup slivered burdock root or carrot
2 teaspoons minced or grated gingerroot or garlic
2 green beefsteak or fresh basil leaves, slivered
4 to 6 tablespoons Hatcho, red, or barley miso
¼ cup bonito flakes (optional)

Place 4 scallop shells over a charcoal brazier, on a barbecue grill, or directly atop the dying coals of a campfire. Divide the oil among the shells and heat, then add equal amounts of the next six ingredients to each shell. Sauté, stirring occasionally, for 4 to 6 minutes, or until all vegetables are tender. Stir in miso (and bonito flakes) and cook for 2 minutes more. Without removing shells from fire, transfer hot miso-vegetable mixture a little at a time from shell and use as a topping as for Hoba Miso.

Fuki-no-to Miso (Butterbur-buds Broiled Miso)

MAKES 1¼ CUPS

The butterbur or bog rhubarb *(Petasites japonicus)* is an edible wild mountain plant whose budding forth from the frozen earth heralds the coming of spring. While the mature stems also make a delicious food, the young buds which emerge from the base of the plant close to the ground are used to create the unique, subtly bitter flavor and aroma of this popular preparation.

½ cup red or barley miso
½ cup bonito flakes
¼ cup minced walnuts or sesame butter
1½ tablespoons honey or mirin (optional)
5 butterbur buds, with outer layers carefully removed and reserved
1½ tablespoons honey or *mirin* (optional)

Combine the first three (or four) ingredients, mixing well, and divide into two equal portions. Dice buds and mix with one portion of the miso, then use the mixture to prepare Broiled Miso (p. 71). (For a mellower flavor, allow the miso-buds mixture to stand in a cool place for 10 days before broiling.)

Divide second portion of miso mixture into fifths, shape into small balls, and wrap each in butterbur's outer layers. Place into a preheated steamer and steam for 15 minutes, then set in a cool dry place and allow to stand for 6 months. Remove leaves and discard. Cut miso balls into thin rounds and serve as hors d'œuvres, in miso soups, or as a topping for Ochazuké (p.123) or brown rice.

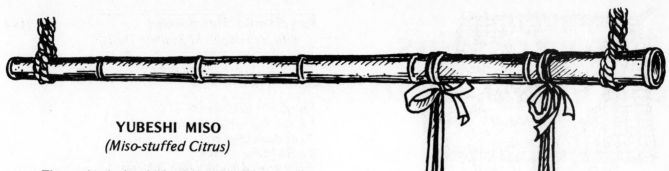

YUBESHI MISO
(Miso-stuffed Citrus)

The word *yubeshi*, which originated in China, is written with three ideographic characters: the first means *yuzu* (the fragrant East-Asian citron); the second refers either to a treat or confection or, more specifically, to *mochi* (steamed and pounded glutinous rice); the third means child. *Yubeshi* has long been made in Japanese farmhouses during the cold months, especially just before New Year's. *Yuzu* (or lemon) halves are stuffed with a miso mixture, steamed, and hung in the shade to dry. The miso and citrus gradually become permeated with each other's fragrance, and the finished product is firm enough to be sliced into thin rounds. There are two basic types of *yubeshi:* that which contains *mochi* has a relatively mild and sweet, rather spicy flavor, and is excellent for use as an hors d'œuvre or confection; that which contains mostly miso is generally used as a topping, but can also be served in very thin slices as an hors d'œuvre. The preparation of the former, less common variety, will be described under hors d'œuvres (p. 76).

Yubeshi Miso Topping

MAKES ½ CUP

½ cup red, barley, or Hatcho miso
2 tablespoons bonito flakes, or substitute grated cheese
2 tablespoons sesame butter, minced walnuts, or ground roasted sesame seeds
2 large *yuzu* or lemons, washed, cut crosswise (or vertically) into halves, the fruit scooped out and reserved

Combine the first three ingredients, mixing well, and use to stuff the yuzu or lemon halves. Rejoin halves and tie with 4 long strips of cloth (or rice straw) as shown in figure 18. Place into a pre-heated steamer and steam for 40 minutes. Hang (under the eaves) in a shady, well-ventilated place and allow to dry for at least 1, preferably 3 to 4 weeks. Cut crosswise into ¼-inch-thick rounds (or scoop out the miso filling) and serve as a topping for grain or tofu dishes, thinly sliced cucumbers, tomatoes, or apples, crackers or canapés.

VARIATIONS

*Quick Yubeshi: Add ½ teaspoon grated *yuzu* or lemon peel to the above ingredients. Omit steaming. Wrap miso-stuffed citrus with plastic wrap and refrigerate for 1 or 2 days. To serve, scoop out fragrant miso and discard citrus halves.
*Use as the filling: miso, grated gingerroot, (7-spice) red pepper and, if desired, minced walnuts. For a sweeter version, add a little honey.

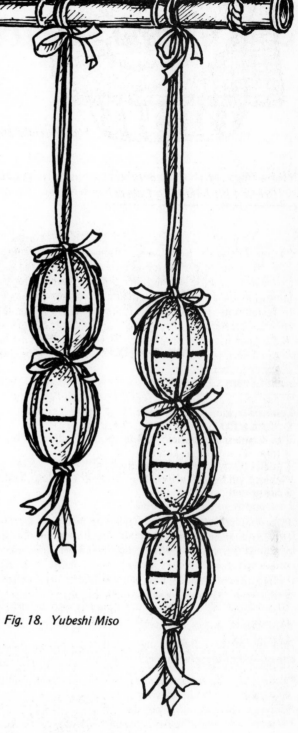

Fig. 18. Yubeshi Miso

Miso in Dips
& Hors D'oeuvres

Most of the recipes in this section make use of nut butters and dairy products, are uniquely Western and, we feel, exemplify miso's delicious versatility.

MISO IN DIPS

Miso-Cream Cheese Dips

MAKES ¾ CUP

4 ounces cream cheese, softened with 1½ to 3 tablespoons warm water
2 teaspoons red or barley (or 4 teaspoons mellow white) miso
½ small onion, grated or minced
1 tablespoon butter, softened
¼ cup grated cheese
2 teaspoons sake or white wine

Combine all ingredients, mixing well until thoroughly blended and smooth. For best flavor, refrigerate in a sealed container for 5 to 7 days. Serve with crackers, chips, fresh vegetable slices, celery stalks, or apple wedges. Also delicious as a spread for sandwiches or canapés.

VARIATIONS

Add any of the following ingredients to the softened cream cheese and miso; serve immediately:

*Tangy: 2 tablespoons grated cheese, 1 teaspoon minced onion, and 4 teaspoons mayonnaise
*Curry: ½ teaspoon curry powder
*Sesame: 1½ tablespoons sesame butter or *tahini* and a dash of tabasco sauce or red pepper
*Lemon: 2 to 3 teaspoons lemon juice plus 1 tablespoon warm water to soften the cream cheese, ½ teaspoon grated lemon rind, 3 tablespoons mayonnaise, 1 tablespoon minced parsley, and a dash of pepper
*Sweet Miso and Sesame: See Miso-Stuffed Celery (p. 77)

Guacamole with Miso

MAKES 1 CUP

1 well-ripened avacado, peeled and seeded
¼ tomato, diced
2 teaspoons lemon juice
½ clove garlic, crushed
1½ tablespoons red or barley (or 2½ tablespoons mellow white) miso
2 tablespoons sesame butter or *tahini* (optional)
2 tablespoons minced onion
Dash of paprika or ¼ teaspoon tabasco sauce
1 to 2 tablespoons minced parsley

Combine the first eight ingredients; mash together with a fork until smooth. Serve as a dip, spread, or dressing; garnish with the parsley. Flavor improves if sealed and refrigerated for one hour or more.

Miso-Cottage Cheese Dip

MAKES ½ CUP

6 tablespoons cottage cheese
1½ teaspoons red or barley (or 1 tablespoon mellow white) miso
2 teaspoons minced parsley
Dash of pepper
1 tablespoon minced onion, or ½ clove of garlic, crushed (optional)

Combine all ingredients, mixing well. Excellent on hors d'œuvre crackers or as a sandwich spread.

Cream Cheese-Miso Dip with Nuts and Raisins

MAKES 1 CUP

4 ounces cream cheese softened with 1 tablespoon warm water
4 tablespoons sweet white or 2½ teaspoons red miso
2 tablespoons butter
¼ cup chopped walnuts or almonds
¼ cup raisins

Combine all ingredients, mixing well. Serve with crackers, tomato and cucumber slices, or celery stalks. Good also as a sandwich spread.

Tofu-Miso-Sour Cream Dip

MAKES 1½ CUPS

12 ounces tofu, drained and mashed
1½ tablespoons red or barley (or 3 tablespoons mellow white) miso
5 tablespoons sour cream
1 teaspoon lemon juice or vinegar
1 tablespoon minced parsley or chives
Dash of pepper

Combine all ingredients, mixing well. Delicious with crackers or fresh vegetable slices.

Soy Jalapeño with Miso

MAKES 1¼ CUPS

1 cup cooked soybeans (p.129), well drained and mashed
¼ onion, minced
2 tablespoons red, barley, or Hatcho miso
1 teaspoon oil
½ clove garlic, crushed
1 tablespoon lemon juice or vinegar
½ to ¾ teaspoon tabasco sauce or powdered red pepper

Combine all ingredients and mash until smooth or run through a hand mill or meat grinder. Serve as a dip or spread. Especially good with taco chips.

For variety, substitute pinto beans for one-half the cooked soybeans.

Tangy Miso-Tahini Dip

MAKES 1 CUP

2 teaspoons red, barley, or Hatcho miso
½ cup tahini or sesame butter
¼ cup lemon juice
1½ cloves garlic, crushed
¼ cup water

Combine all ingredients, mixing well. For a sweeter flavor, add 2 teaspoons honey. To make a sauce, add ¼ cup more water.

MISO IN HORS D'ŒUVRES

Miso is perhaps at its best when used in the preparation of Western-style hors d'œuvres. See also Dengaku (p. 144), Eggs Pickled in Sweet White Miso (p. 159), and other miso pickles (p. 156). Finger Lickin' Miso (p. 41) and Sweet Simmered Miso (p. 60) are often served in quantities of 1 to 2 teaspoons on a small dish as an accompaniment for drinks.

Miso Walnuts, Cashews, or Almonds

SERVES 3 TO 4

½ cup unsalted walnut, cashew, or almond meats
1½ teaspoons red or barley miso, dissolved in 3 tablespoons water

Heat a heavy skillet, drop in nuts, and dry-roast over medium heat, stirring constantly, for about 3 minutes, or until fragrant. Add dissolved miso and sauté for 30 seconds, or just until all liquid has evaporated. (Slight overcooking may cause the miso to burn.) Allow to cool before serving.

For a crunchier texture, toast in a medium oven for about 20 minutes, or until fragrant.

Crackers with Cream Cheese, Egg & Miso Topping

MAKES 10 TO 15

2 hard-boiled eggs, separated into yolks and whites
2 ounces cream cheese
1½ teaspoons red or barley (or 3 teaspoons mellow white) miso
1 tablespoon minced parsley
Dash of pepper or paprika
10 to 15 hors d'œuvre crackers

Combine egg yolks with the cream cheese, miso, parsley, and pepper; mash well. Slice egg whites into thin rounds and place one round on each cracker. Top with a dab of the cream cheese-miso mixture.

Mushroom Hors D'œuvre with Miso Marinade

SERVES 2 TO 4

1 tablespoon red, barley, or Hatcho miso
2½ to 3 tablespoons (rice) vinegar
1½ teaspoons honey
1 tablespoon sesame butter (optional)
20 (shiitaké) mushrooms, washed and drained

Combine the first four ingredients in a shallow pan, mixing until smooth. Broil mushrooms for 1 minute on each side, or until speckled and fragrant, then add immediately to miso-vinegar mixture; marinate for 30 minutes. Serve skewered on foodpicks or mounded on lettuce leaves with a little marinade poured over the top.

Apple Wedges with Miso Toppings

SERVES 4

2 apples, cut into thin wedges
¼ cup Peanut Miso (p. 60), Orange-Sesame Miso (p. 115), Walnut Miso (p. 61), Sesame Miso Spread (p. 81), or your favorite variety of Finger Lickin' Miso (p. 41)

Arrange apple slices on a serving platter and top each with a ½ teaspoon dollop of the miso.

Apple & Banana Hors D'œuvre with Miso Topping

SERVES 4 TO 6

1 banana, cut diagonally into 1-inch-thick ovals
1 apple, cut into thin wedges
Sweet Miso & Tahini Topping:
    2 tablespoons *tahini* or sesame butter
    1 teaspoon honey
    1 teaspoon red, barley, or Hatcho miso
    2 to 3 tablespoons raisins
    2 to 3 tablespoons chopped almonds or walnuts

Arrange fruit slices on a serving platter. Mix topping ingredients and spoon in dollops (or spread) onto slices.

Sliced Bananas with Peanut Butter-Miso Topping

SERVES 2

2 bananas, cut diagonally into long, thin ovals
1½ tablespoons peanut butter
1 teaspoon red or 2 teaspoons sweet white miso
2 tablespoons wheat germ
1½ tablespoons raisins

Arrange banana slices on a serving platter. Combine peanut butter and miso, mixing well, and place in dabs atop bananas. Sprinkle with wheat germ and dot each dab with 3 or 4 raisins just before serving.

    For added richness, combine 1 tablespoon each grated coconut and minced nutmeats with the peanut butter and miso.

Canapés with Miso Spreads

MAKES 30

30 pieces of buttered (whole-grain) bread or toast, each 2 inches square
Spreads: About 2 to 3 tablespoons each
    Sweet Simmered Miso (pp. 60 to 65; Sesame, Peanut, Red Pepper, or Subtley Sweet Leek Miso)
    Finger Lickin' Miso (p. 42)
    Miso Mayonnaise (p. 84)
    Sweet White Miso & Butter Spread (p. 80)
    Cheese Mixed Miso (p. 10)
Canapé Toppings:
    ½ cucumber, sliced into thin ovals
    1 green pepper, cut lengthwise into quarters
    1 hard-boiled egg, thinly sliced
    1 tomato, thinly sliced
    ½ carrot, sliced into thin ovals
    8 green peas, parboiled (optional)
    1 small potato or sweet potato, boiled and thinly sliced

Use each of the five types of miso as a spread for one-fifth of the bread slices. Place the toppings individually or in combinations on the bread to form canapés. If desired, pierce each canapé with a foodpick. Arrange on large serving platters.

VARIATION

*Deep-fried Tofu & Miso Hors d'œuvre: Cut any variety of deep-fried tofu into thin strips or bite-sized pieces. For best flavor, broil quickly until speckled and fragrant. Top each piece with any of the above miso spreads and canapé toppings. Serve skewered with foodpicks.

    The ingredients may also be rolled up in an opened deep-fried tofu pouch, fastened in 3 or 4 places with foodpicks, and cut crosswise into small cylinders.

Tomato Hors D'œuvre with Sesame Miso

SERVES 8 TO 12

¼ cup sesame butter or *tahini*
2 teaspoons red, barley, or Hatcho miso
2 tablespoons mayonnaise
1 clove of garlic, crushed
½ teaspoon honey
1 teaspoon sake or white wine
1 to 2 teaspoons water (optional)
3 tomatoes, cut into ½-inch-thick rounds

Combine the first seven ingredients, mixing well. Arrange tomato slices on a serving platter and top each slice with a dollop of the sesame miso.

    This topping is also delicious on other fresh vegetable slices and canapés; or use as a sandwich spread.

Spicy Yubeshi Miso Hors D'œuvre

MAKES 1 CUP

    Please begin by reading about Yubeshi (p. 76). This traditional preparation, a specialty of Japan's southernmost main island, Kyushu, is now sold commercially throughout Japan and looks remarkably like a 5-inch-long sausage. Whereas the traditional product was steamed in bamboo leaves and packed (and occasionally sold) in the joined halves of a citrus, its modern counterpart is plastic-wrapped, but is still very delicious.

6 tablespoons glutinous rice flour (*shiratama-ko*)
2½ tablespoons water
3 tablespoons red, barley, or Hatcho miso
1 tablespoon honey
Dash of (7-spice) red pepper or tabasco sauce
½ teaspoon grated gingerroot
2 teaspoons sesame butter or *tahini;* or 3 to 4½ teaspoons minced walnuts
¼ teaspoon grated *yuzu*, lemon, or orange rind

Combine the flour and water, and mix for several minutes to develop a smooth dough of earlobe consistency. Mix in remaining ingredients and knead with a rubber spatula (or your hands) for several minutes more. Form mixture into a 1½-inch-diameter sausage shape and wrap in corn leaves or celophane. (Or pack into a cup or small bowl and cover with cellophane.) Place into a preheated steamer and steam for 20 minutes, then allow to cool to room temperature. Slice into thin rounds (or serve in cup accompanied by a small knife or spoon). Use like cold cuts as an hors d'œuvre topping for crackers, thin vegetable slices, or canapés, or as a garnish for rice.

For variety, wash 2 *yuzu* or lemons, cut into halves, scoop out the fruit and reserve. Fill with the (unsteamed) miso mixture and proceed as for Yubeshi Miso (p. 73).

Cucumber and/or Jicama Slices Topped with Finger Lickin' Miso

SERVES 4

Crisp, juicy, and unbelievably delicious, *jicama* is a root vegetable from Latin America now widely available in the United States and quite inexpensive. Heart-shaped and 5 to 7 inches in diameter, its peel is the color of a potato's. Best fresh, it may also be cooked lightly.

1 large cucumber, cut into diagonal slices and/or
¼ jicama, cut into sticks for dipping
3 to 6 tablespoons finger lickin' miso

Top each slice with a dab of the miso. Serve chilled, arranged on a platter. As delicious as they are easy to prepare.

Fresh Cucumber Slices with Miso Topping

SERVES 2

In Japan, a popular hors d'œuvre called *Morokyu* is prepared by slicing fresh cucumbers on the diagonal to form thin ovals, then spreading one surface of each with moromi miso. Other varieties of Finger Lickin' or Sweet Simmered Miso may also be used. The following cooked topping takes longer to prepare but is well worth the time and effort.

1 tablespoon oil
2 inches of leek or ¼ onion, thinly sliced
1 tablespoon red, barley, or Hatcho miso
1 tablespoon grated gingerroot
1 (*shiitaké*) mushroom, thinly sliced
1 large cucumber, cut into thin diagonal slices

Heat a wok or skillet and coat with the oil. Add the next four ingredients and sauté over low heat, stirring constantly, for 3 to 4 minutes. To serve, allow to cool, then spread on sliced cucumbers.

Stuffed Eggs with Miso and Sesame

MAKES 8 HALVES

4 eggs, hard-boiled and cut lengthwise into halves
2 teaspoons red, barley, or Hatcho miso
4 teaspoons sesame butter or grated cheese
2 tablespoons minced onion
Paprika (optional)

Remove egg yolks and mash together with the miso, sesame butter, and onion. Form the mixture into 8 balls, and use as a stuffing for the egg halves. If desired, top with paprika.

Hors D'œuvre with Miso-damari

SERVES 4

2 hard-boiled eggs, shelled and cut lengthwise into halves
1 cucumber, cut into long, thin diagonals
1 small tomato, cut into ½-inch-thich rounds
2 deep-fried tofu cutlets or burgers, cut into bite-sized pieces
2 tablespoons miso-damari (pp. 50 and 219)

Arrange the first four ingredients on a serving platter, then top each with a sprinkling of the *miso-damari*.

Miso-Stuffed Celery Hors D'œuvre

Peanut Butter & Miso:
    2 tablespoons peanut butter
    2 to 3 teaspoons red, barley, or Hatcho miso
    1 teaspoon grated onion and juice
Cream Cheese, Sweet Miso & Sesame:
    2 tablespoons cream cheese
    2½ tablespoons sweet white miso
    ½ teaspoon shoyu
    1 tablespoon ground roasted sesame seeds (p. 54) or sesame butter
Cream Cheese, Miso & Lemon:
    2 tablespoons cream cheese
    1 tablespoon red, barley, or Hatcho miso
    1 teaspoon lemon juice
    2 tablespoons mayonnaise
6 large celery stalks

Combine the ingredients for each of the three stuffings, mixing until smooth. Stuff celery stalks, then cut stalks into 2-inch lengths and serve as hors d'œuvres. If desired, top with a sprinkling of paprika.

Celery stalks are also delicious served with most types of Sweet Simmered Miso (p. 60), Vinegar Miso (p. 91), Peanut Butter-Miso (p. 80), Sesame Miso Spreads (p. 81), or Cream Cheese-Miso Dips (p. 74).

Crunchy Miso - Soynut Butter Balls

MAKES 12

1/3 cup Miso-Soynut Butter (p. 80), cooled to room temperature
¼ cup raisins
¼ cup (roasted) sunflower seeds, chopped nuts, or ground roasted sesame seeds
2 tablespoons roasted soy flour *(kinako)* or ¼ cup shredded coconut

Combine the first three ingredients, mixing well. Shape mixture into 12 small balls, then roll each in roasted soy flour. Chill briefly before serving.

Lotus Root Hors D'œuvre Stuffed with Miso-Cream Cheese

MAKES 12

1 lotus root, 4 inches long and 2 inches in diameter, peeled
1 ounce cream cheese
1 teaspoon red, barley, or Hatcho miso
1 teaspoon minced onion
½ teaspoon minced parsley
1/8 teaspoon curry powder

Trim both ends of lotus root, revealing hollow tubules. Cut into 2-inch lengths and simmer in water to cover for 15 to 20 minutes, or until tender; then drain and allow to cool to body temperature. Combine remaining ingredients, mixing well. Press mixture into tubules using your finger tips or a spatula. Cut each section of lotus root crosswise into 6 thin discs and spread any remaining filling in a thin layer over one surface of each disc. Serve chilled.

For variety, substitute 1 mashed hard-boiled egg for the cream cheese. Omit curry powder, and add a dash of pepper and 2 teaspoons mayonnaise.

Nori-wrapped Cucumbers with Sour Cream & Miso

MAKES 12

¼ cup sour cream
1 teaspoon red, barley, or Hatcho miso
Dash of pepper
3 sheets of *nori*, toasted (p. 54)
1 cucumber, cut into long slivers

Combine the first three ingredients, mixing well, and spread in an even layer over one surface of each *nori* sheet. Now arrange cucumber slivers in a row along the near edge of each sheet. Roll up from the near edge so that the cucumbers form the central core. Cut the rolls crosswise into fourths; serve immediately.

For variety, use slivers of cheese and agé (deep-fried tofu) together with the cucumbers.

Miso-filled Beefsteak Leaf Hors D'œuvre

SERVES 2

This popular Japanese hors d'œuvre, now available commercially, is prepared with red beefsteak leaves which have been salt-pickled (p. 158) to give them a softer flavor and texture. The filling may be made with Peanut Miso (p. 62).

1½ tablespoons sweet white miso or 2 teaspoons red miso
1½ tablespoons sesame butter or whole roasted peanuts
½ teaspoon honey
6 green beefsteak leaves

Combine the first three ingredients, mixing well, and divide into six equal portions. Place one portion at the center of each leaf near one end, then roll up leaf firmly so that miso-sesame mixture fills rolled cylinder. Skewer with foodpicks, if desired, and serve arranged on small plates.

Sashimi Konnyaku

SERVES 4

Cut and served in this way, *konnyaku* is made to resemble one of Japan's culinary specialties, *sashimi*, or fresh uncooked fish cut into thin slices and served with a dipping sauce or topping. In Zen temples and *shojin* temple restaurants, the *konnyaku* is prepared in prefect resemblance of fresh squid.

10 to 12 ounces *konnyaku*, cut crosswise into ¼-inch-thick strips and parboiled in lightly-salted water
¼ cup Tangy Mustard Vinegar Miso (p. 92), or 2 to 3 tablespoons Wasabi Mixed Miso (p. 69)

Arrange *konnyaku* strips in a flower-petal pattern on a serving platter. Place the dipping sauce and a serving spoon in a cup at center of platter. Invite each guest to serve himself.

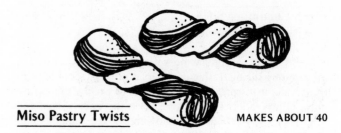

Miso Pastry Twists

MAKES ABOUT 40

Made with unsweetened pie crust, these have a slightly salty flavor; serve as you would potato chips, or use as the accompaniment for sweet fruits or desserts.

3 tablespoons red, barley, or Hatcho miso
6 tablespoons water
5 ounces butter, chilled
2¼ cups flour, approximately
1 egg yolk

Combine miso and water, mixing well. Cut butter into 2 cups flour until butter pieces are the size of peas. Gently stir in thinned miso to form a moist dough. Wrap in a very lightly dampened towel and refrigerate for 1 hour.

Roll dough out thin, and fold into thirds. Sprinkle lightly with flour, and repeat 4 times to give a 12-layer pastry dough. Finally, roll dough into a long rectangle ¼ inch thick and about 3 inches wide. Cut crosswise into ¾-inch-wide strips. Twist each strip once and brush with egg yolk. Arrange strips on lightly oiled baking pans. Bake in a 390° oven for 4 minutes, then reduce heat to 300° and bake for 8 to 10 minutes more, or until strips are nicely browned.

For variety, replace one-half the miso with grated cheese. Sprinkle ¼ cup minced walnuts over dough before final folding.

Miso in Spreads & Sandwiches

Whether used with nut butters or dairy products, creamy avocados or butter, high-protein tofu or cooked soybeans, miso adds richness of flavor to many of your favorite sandwich fixin's. Thinned slightly, miso spreads make excellent dips; creamed with hot stock or broth, they make savory sauces.

MISO IN SPREADS

Miso Paté
MAKES 1½ CUPS

Remarkably similar in flavor and texture to its liver-based counterpart, this recipe combines wheat, sesame butter, and miso to yield maximum protein value (p. 23).

2 cups broken pieces of (dry) whole-wheat bread
½ cup water or stock
½ cup sesame butter
1½ tablespoons red, barley, or Hatcho miso
1 small onion, minced
1 tablespoon (sesame) oil
1 clove of garlic, crushed or minced
¼ cup minced parsley
Dash each of thyme, rosemary, and sage

Combine bread and water, mashing well with fingers. Mix in remaining ingredients and allow to stand for at least 1 hour, preferably 1 full day. Serve as a spread on crackers, canapés, or bread.

For a firmer consistency, bake in a loaf pan at 350° for 1 to 1½ hours, or until surface is nicely browned.

Tofu-Miso Paté
MAKES 1¾ CUPS

12 ounces tofu, lightly pressed (p. 55)
5 teaspoons red, barley, or Hatcho miso
¼ cup sesame butter or ½ cup ground roasted sesame seeds (p. 54)
3 tablespoons minced parsley
1 tablespoon dill seeds, minced
2 tablespoons chopped green onion
1 clove of garlic, crushed
¼ teaspoon nutmeg

Preheat oven to 350°. Combine all ingredients, mixing well, and press into a loaf pan. Bake for 15 to 20 minutes, or until lightly browned. Serve as a spread. Also delicious unbaked.

Hard-boiled Egg & Miso Spread
MAKES ½ CUP

2 hard-boiled eggs, mashed with a fork
1 teaspoon red or barley (or 2 teaspoons mellow white) miso
2 tablespoons mayonnaise
1 tablespoon minced parsley
Dash of pepper or paprika

Combine all ingredients, mixing well. For variety, add ½ teaspoon curry powder.

Miso-Sesame-Avocado Spread
MAKES ¾ CUP

2 teaspoons red, barley, or Hatcho miso
6 tablespoons sesame butter
½ avocado, peeled and seeded
¼ tomato, minced
1 tablespoon minced onion
1 tablespoon lemon juice
½ clove of garlic, crushed
1 tablespoon minced parsley or ¼ cup alfalfa sprouts

Combine the first seven ingredients; mash together until smooth. Serve topped with a sprinkling of the parsley or sprouts.

Sweet Carob-Sesame-Miso Spread

MAKES 1/3 CUP

1 tablespoon carob powder
4 to 5 teaspoons water
2 to 3 tablespoons sesame butter or *tahini*
2 teaspoons sweet white or 1½ teaspoons mellow white miso
1 teaspoon honey

Combine carob powder with water, mixing until smooth, then stir in remaining ingredients. Nice on toast or unsalted crackers.

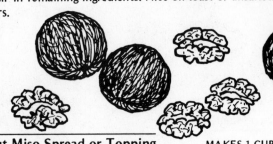

Walnut Miso Spread or Topping

MAKES 1 CUP

1 cup walnut meats, lightly roasted and ground to a paste
¼ cup red, barley, or Hatcho miso
3 to 4 tablespoons water

Combine all ingredients, mixing well. Serve as a spread with sandwiches or crackers, or as a topping with cooked vegetables or tofu.
For variety, add ½ teaspoon grated orange or lemon rind.

Miso - Soynut Butter

MAKES ½ CUP

This delicious spread tastes like a cross between sesame and peanut butter but is less expensive and higher in protein. Produced commercially, it would surely sell well at natural- and health food stores.

2½ tablespoons oil or butter
½ cup roasted soy flour *(kinako)*
1 teaspoon red, barley, or Hatcho miso
1 tablespoon honey
1½ to 2 tablespoons water

Heat the oil in a skillet, then turn off heat. Add remaining ingredients, mixing until smooth. Delicious on crackers, canapés, or fresh vegetable slices.

Sweetened Peanut Butter-Miso Spread

MAKES ¾ CUP

¼ cup peanut butter
1 tablespoon red, barley, or Hatcho miso
1 tablespoon honey
¼ cup diced apples
2 tablespoons sunflower seeds or minced nutmeats
2 tablespoons raisins
1 teaspoon sake or white wine (optional)

Combine all ingredients, mixing well. Serve on buttered whole-wheat bread.

VARIATION

*Omit raisins, sunflower seeds, and apple. Use 4 teaspoons miso; serve in vegetable sandwiches with lettuce, cucumbers, tomatoes, sprouts, and cheese. For more zest, add 1 table-spoon diced onion and/or parsley; nice on canapés. For more tang, add 2½ tablespoons vinegar.

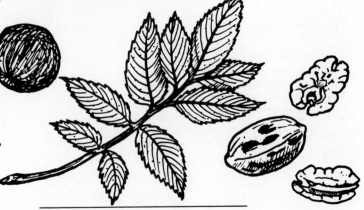

Savory Peanut Butter-Miso Spread

MAKES ½ CUP

¼ cup peanut butter
2 teaspoons red, barley, or Hatcho miso
1 teaspoon Worcestershire sauce
2 tablespoons butter, softened

Combine all ingredients, mixing well.

Miso Cheese Spread

MAKES 1 CUP

1 tablespoon butter
1 tablespoon red, barley, or Hatcho miso
6 ounces grated cheese
¼ cup milk (soy or dairy)
1 egg, lightly beaten
Dash of mustard
¼ teaspoon crushed garlic or 1 tablespoon minced parsley (optional)

Melt butter in a skillet. Stir in miso, then add remaining ingredients, mixing well. Cook, stirring constantly, for 1 to 2 minutes, or until cheese just melts. Serve on buttered toast or canapés. Brown under a broiler, if desired.

Sweet White Miso & Butter Spread

MAKES 3/8 CUP

2 tablespoons butter
¼ cup sweet white or 2½ tablespoons mellow white miso

Combine butter and miso, mixing well. Serve as a spread for hors d'œuvre crackers and sandwiches topped with fresh vegetables and cheese, or as a topping for pancakes and waffles.

Sesame-Miso Spread

MAKES ½ CUP

4 or 5 tablespoons sesame butter
1 tablespoon red, barley, or Hatcho miso
½ teaspoon grated lemon or *yuzu* rind (optional)
3 tablespoons water

Combine all ingredients, mixing well. Nice on freshly sliced cucumbers, crackers, or open-faced sandwiches.

Sweetened Sesame-Miso Spread

MAKES ½ CUP

¼ cup sesame butter or *tahini*
2 to 4 teaspoons red, barley, or Hatcho miso
1½ to 2 tablespoons honey
Dash of cinnamon, (7-spice) red pepper, or tabasco sauce
1 to 1½ tablespoons water

Combine all ingredients, mixing well. Serve on bread, toast, or deep-fried tofu. Or use as a topping for Dengaku (p. 144).

Tahini-Miso Spread

MAKES ABOUT ¼ CUP

¼ cup *tahini*
1 tablespoon red, barley, or Hatcho miso
1 teaspoon honey
¼ to ½ teaspoon grated orange or lemon rind

Combine all ingredients, mixing well. Serve as a sandwich spread.

Tangy Soybean-Sesame-Miso Spread

MAKES 1½ CUP

1 cup cooked soybeans (p.129), drained and mashed
1/3 cup sesame butter
1½ tablespoons red, barley, or Hatcho miso
2 tablespoons lemon juice
1/3 cup diced raw onion
1 clove of garlic, crushed or minced
1 tablespoon honey
Dash of pepper

Combine all ingredients, mashing together until smooth. For best flavor allow to stand for at least 8, preferably 24, hours before serving.

VARIATIONS

*Rich and Crunchy Spread: Omit lemon juice, onion, and garlic. Add several tablespoons each sunflower seeds, raisins, and diced apple, and ½ teaspoon grated orange peel.
*Garbanzo or Navy Bean Spreads: Substitute an equal volume of either of these cooked beans for the soybeans in the basic recipe or variation.
*Lentil-Miso Spread: Prepare lentils as in thick Lentil-Miso Soup (p. 111). For a smoother texture, purée in a handmill or blender. To each cup of purée add 2 teaspoons red miso, a

pinch of nutmeg and minced parsley and, if desired, sesame butter or ground roasted sesame seeds. Mix well and chill to thicken. Serve on buttered whole-wheat bread or toast.
*Azuki-Miso Spread: Prepare Azuki-Vegetable Soup with Miso (p. 111) except use only 2½ cups water. Serve on Chapaties (p. 128) or as a sandwich spread.

MISO IN SANDWICHES

The many spreads we've described above can serve as the makings for a sandwich in themselves. Any of the following types of miso or miso mixtures can be used with thinly sliced vegetables, cheese, sprouts, or (deep-fried) tofu on buttered whole-grain bread or toast. Try using ketchup, mayonnaise, and/or mustard together with the miso. Or use Finger Lickin' Miso or diced miso pickles like relish.
   *All types of regular red or white miso
   *Sweet Simmered Miso (p.60), Finger Lickin' Miso (p. 41), Miso Sauté (p. 65), Mixed Miso (p. 69) or Broiled Miso (p. 71)
   *2 parts sesame or nut butter and 1 part miso
   *6 parts red or barley miso and 1 part grated gingerroot (or diced leeks or scallions)

Grilled Cheese Sandwich on Miso-Garlic Bread

SERVES 4

Miso-Garlic-Butter Spread:
   1½ teaspoons red, barley, or Hatcho miso
   ¼ teaspoon crushed garlic
   ¼ cup melted butter
   ½ teaspoon grated lemon peel or grated onion (optional)
4 large slices of French or sourdough bread
½ cup grated or ¼ cup Parmesan cheese
4 teaspoons minced parsley

Combine spread ingredients, mixing well, then brush onto surface of bread. Top with a sprinkling of the cheese and parsley. Toast in a medium broiler or oven until nicely browned.

For variety arrange tomato (and deep-fried tofu) slices on the bread before sprinkling with cheese. Or soften the butter, mix with the other spread ingredients, and serve on canapés.

Grilled Cheese and Tomato Sandwich

MAKES 5

½ cup grated cheese
1 tablespoon red, barley, or Hatcho miso
1 tablespoon minced onion
1 tablespoon minced parsley
1 clove of garlic, crushed
5 pieces of buttered (whole-grain) bread
2 tomatoes, cut into thin rounds

Combine the first five ingredients, mixing well, and spread on the buttered bread. Top with tomato slices and broil under medium heat for 4 to 5 minutes, or until fragrant and nicely browned. Serve sizzling hot.

Fried Egg Sandwich with Deep-fried Tofu and Miso

MAKES 1

4 teaspoons butter
2½ to 3 ounces deep-fried tofu, cut into thin strips
1 egg
Dash of pepper
1 teaspoon red, barley, or Hatcho miso
1½ teaspoons ketchup (optional)
1 large piece of (whole-wheat) toast

Melt 1 tablespoon butter in a skillet. Arrange tofu strips in a single layer on bottom of skillet, then break egg over the top. Cover and fry until egg is firm, season with pepper, cover, and remove from heat. Combine remaining 1 teaspoon butter with miso and, if desired the ketchup; mix well and spread on one surface of toast. Top with the tofu-fried egg placed sunny side up and serve immediately.

For added color and flavor, top with a sprinkling of minced parsley or grated cheese.

Deep-fried Tofu Burger

MAKES 1

Spread both surfaces of a 3- to 4-ounce deep-fried tofu burger with a thin layer of red, barley, or Hatcho miso. Broil tofu briefly on both sides if desired, then use in place of meat in a hamburger or cheeseburger, accompanied by all of your favorite trimmings.

Miso Dressings with Salads

Smooth sour-cream dressings and nut-butter favorites; tangy French- or citrus dressings; thick and creamy tofu- or yogurt dressings. Miso makes each of them a little more delicious, and can help to keep your intake of fats to a minimum as explained on page 25.

WESTERN-STYLE DRESSINGS

Floating Cloud Miso Dressing — MAKES ABOUT 1 CUP

One of our very favorites; the key to the flavor lies in the miso-sesame oil-garlic combination.

6 tablespoons vegetable oil
¼ teaspoon sesame oil
2 tablespoons (rice) vinegar or lemon juice
2 tablespoons red, barley, or Hatcho miso
¼ cup water
½ clove of garlic, crushed
Dash of powdered ginger
Dash of dry mustard

Combine all ingredients; whisk or shake well. Good on all tossed green salads, especially those with Chinese cabbage. Tomatoes and (deep-fried) tofu make excellent accompaniments. Try marinating hot green beans or artichoke hearts overnight in this dressing, then serving them drained and chilled on lettuce. Also great on cooked broccoli.

Miso-Cheese Dressing — MAKES ABOUT 1 CUP

½ cup oil
3 tablespoons vinegar
1½ tablespoons red, barley, or Hatcho miso
2 tablespoons Parmesan cheese
2 tablespoons water
1 tablespoon minced onion
1½ tablespoon minced green pepper
1 clove of garlic, crushed
¼ teaspoon (7-spice) red pepper or tabasco sauce

Combine all ingredients and allow to stand for at least 1 hour. Shake thoroughly before serving.

Lemon-Mustard-Miso Dressing — MAKES ½ CUP

3 tablespoons red, barley, or Hatcho miso
2 tablespoons oil
1 tablespoon lemon juice
1/8 teaspoon lemon rind
½ teaspoon hot mustard
1½ teaspoons honey
1½ teaspoons minced onion (optional)

Combine all ingredients, mixing well. Delicious with 1 small head of torn butter lettuce and 6 thinly-sliced fresh mushrooms; serves 2.

Miso-Sour Cream Dressing — MAKES ¾ CUP

3 tablespoons sour cream
1 tablespoon red or barley (or 2 tablespoons mellow white) miso
1½ tablespoons cream cheese or Roquefort cheese, softened
¼ cup oil
2 tablespoons lemon juice
1 tablespoon minced onions or chives

Combine all ingredients, mixing well. Good on steamed cauliflower or green beans. Or try on tossed green salads with thinly sliced beets.

Cream Cheese-Miso Mayonnaise Dressing — MAKES ABOUT ½ CUP

¼ cup mayonnaise
1 tablespoon red or barley (or 2 tablespoons mellow white) miso
2 tablespoons lemon juice
1½ tablespoons cream cheese, softened
1 tablespoon sesame or peanut butter
1½ teaspoons grated onion and juice

Combine all ingredients, mixing well. Especially good with asparagus, cauliflower, broccoli, or artichoke hearts salads.

83

Tangy Peanut Butter-Miso Dressing

MAKES ¼ CUP

2 tablespoons peanut butter
4 teaspoons vinegar
1 tablespoon red, barley, or Hatcho miso
2 tablespoons oil
1½ teaspoons honey

Combine all ingredients, mixing well.

White Sesame-Miso Dressing

MAKES 3/8 CUP

2 tablespoons sweet white or 1½ tablespoons mellow white
   miso
2 tablespoons sesame butter or *tahini*; or 3 tablespoons
   ground roasted sesame seeds (p. 54)
2 teaspoons *mirin*, sake, white wine, or water
½ teaspoon honey
1 teaspoon shoyu or ¼ teaspoon salt

Combine ingredients, mixing well. Try with (1 pound) par-boiled spinach, or an apple-and-raisin salad.

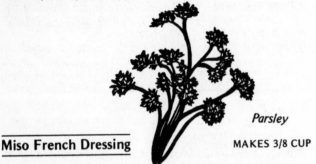

Parsley

Miso French Dressing

MAKES 3/8 CUP

The use of miso, which has a much mellower saltiness than plain salt, makes it possible to reduce the proportion of oil in the traditional recipe and also to take full advantage of the fine miso flavor. Good for those who like their salads with plenty of dressing but must still watch their intake of fats.

4 tablespoons oil
2 tablespoons lemon juice or vinegar
2½ to 3 teaspoons red, barley, or Hatcho miso
1 teaspoon minced parsley
½ teaspoon dill or caraway seeds
Dash of pepper

Combine all ingredients, whisking or shaking well just before dressing salad.

VARIATIONS

*Substitute for the miso 1½ tablespoons any variety of Sweet Simmered Miso (pp. 60 to 65), or 2 tablespoons sweet white miso.
*For zest, add ½ clove of crushed garlic and a dash of dry mustard or gingerroot.
*For richness and variety, add small amounts of your favorite herbs, Roquefort cheese, Worcestershire or chili sauce, or chutney.

Tangy Miso-French Dressing

MAKES ¾ CUP

4 tablespoons oil
3½ tablespoons red, barley, or Hatcho miso
3½ tablespoons vinegar
2½ tablespoons lemon juice
¾ teaspoon hot mustard
½ clove of garlic, crushed (optional)
Dash of pepper

Combine all ingredients, mixing well. Use in small amounts. Especially tasty with a salad of lettuce, jicama, cucumbers, and deep-fried tofu.

Miso-Vinegar Dressing with Gingerroot

MAKES 1/3 CUP

2 tablespoons red, barley, or Hatcho miso
2 tablespoons vinegar
2 teaspoons (sesame) oil
1 tablespoon juice pressed from grated gingerroot
Dash of (7-spice) red pepper or tabasco sauce

Combine all ingredients, mixing well. Delicious served over fresh tomato and cucumber slices, with parboiled bean sprouts, or with *wakame* and deep-fried tofu.

Miso-Mayonnaise Dressings

MAKES 1/3 TO ½ CUP

The combination of miso, mayonnaise, and lemon juice (or vinegar) yields a wide variety of dressings and sauces. Experiment using the following guidelines to develop your own combinations, or try a few of our favorites listed below.

To ¼ cup mayonnaise add:
  Miso: Choose one
    1 teaspoon red, barley, or Hatcho miso for tossed
     green salads. Use 1 to 2 tablespoons with fresh
     vegetable slices and as much as 3 tablespoons with
     noodle salads.
    2 to 3 teaspoons sweet white or mellow white miso,
     Sweet simmered Miso (p. 60), Finger Lickin' Miso
     (p. 42), or Miso-Nut Butter Spreads (p. 80).
  Vinegar or Lemon Juice: Use 2 parts for every 3 parts
    miso.
  Pepper: A dash of white, black, or red is essential.
  Other Seasonings: ½ to 2 teaspoons of minced onion, hot
    mustard, crushed garlic, grated gingerroot, or your
    favorite herbs or spices.
  Sesame or Nut Butters: Use 1 part to every 1 part red
    miso.
  Dairy Products: 1 to 2 tablespoons cream cheese, sour
    cream, or grated cheese adds richness and flavor.
  Sweetenings: The occasional use of 1 to 2 teaspoons
    honey goes nicely with red miso.

We have found the following combinations to go particularly well with certain salad ingredients. Mix miso and other ingredients with ¼ cup mayonnaise; dress salad just before serving. Serves 4 to 6.

*Basic: Use with your favorite tossed green salads or cooked vegetables (asparagus, broccoli, cauliflower, bean sprouts)

> 1 teaspoon red, barley, or Hatcho miso
> 1 teaspoon lemon juice
> 1 to 2 teaspoons water or stock
> Dash of paprika or pepper

*Cheese-Garlic: Try with lettuce-cucumber-and-tomato salads

> 2 to 3 teaspoons red miso, or 4 to 6 teaspoons Sesame Miso (p. 62)
> 2 to 3 teaspoons lemon juice
> 2 tablespoons grated cheese
> ½ clove of garlic, crushed
> Dash of pepper
> ½ teaspoon caraway or dill seeds (optional)

*Tangy Onion: Nice with buckwheat noodle or macaroni salads

> 3 tablespoons red, barley, or Hatcho miso
> 3 tablespoons lemon juice
> 4 tablespoons vinegar
> 2 teaspoons minced onion
> 1 to 2 tablespoons oil (optional)

*Sweetened: Delicious with salads of chilled cooked vegetables, especially pumpkin, squash or *kabocha*, potatoes, asparagus, or deep-fried tofu

> 2 tablespoons red, barley, or Hatcho miso
> 1 tablespoon lemon juice or vinegar
> ½ to ¾ teaspoon honey

*Sesame: Nice over lettuce-egg-and-tomato salads

> 1 tablespoon red, barley, or Hatcho miso
> 1 tablespoon sesame butter, *tahini*, or ground roasted sesame seeds (p. 54)
> 2 tablespoons vinegar or lemon juice
> ½ teaspoon honey

*Rich & Creamy Nut Butter: Often prepared from leftover Miso-Nut Butter spreads; try with apple or tomato wedges, or fresh cucumber slices

> ¼ cup Miso-Nut Butter Spread (any variety) (pp. 80 to 81)
> 3½ tablespoons lemon juice
> Dash of pepper

Creamy Tofu Dressings & Dips with Miso

MAKES ABOUT 1 CUP

Here is a wonderful way to introduce both tofu and miso into your daily menu served with salads, hors d'œuvres, or even as a sandwich spread. Quick and easy to prepare, the possible variations are virtually unlimited. Each is thick, rich, and full of flavor, yet remarkably low in fats and calories. The perfect answer for those who love dressings but dislike their typical oily qualities.

6 ounces tofu
1½ to 2 tablespoons lemon juice or vinegar
2 tablespoons oil
1 tablespoon red, barley, or Hatcho miso; or 2 tablespoons mellow white miso
Choice of seasonings (see below)

Combine all ingredients in a blender and purée for 20 seconds, or until smooth. (Or mash all ingredients and allow to stand for 15 to 30 minutes before serving.) If desired, serve topped with a sprinkling of minced parsley or a dash of pepper. Refrigerated in a covered container, these preparations will stay fresh for 2 to 3 days; the consistency will thicken (delectably).

SEASONINGS: Use any one of the following

*Curry: ½ teaspoon curry powder and 2 tablespoons minced onion. Top with a sprinkling of 1 tablespoon minced parsley.

*Dill: ¼ to ½ teaspoon dill seeds. If desired, add 1 clove of minced garlic. Top with a sprinkling of parsley.

*Onion: ¼ cup diced onion. Excellent on all types of deep-fried tofu and with many vegetable dishes.

*Cheese and Garlic: ¼ cup Parmesan or grated cheese and ½ clove of garlic (or ¼ onion), minced. Serve topped with a sprinkling of minced parsley.

*Gingerroot: 1 teaspoon grated or 1½ teaspoons powdered gingerroot and a dash of (7-spice) red pepper or tabasco sauce. Try over tomato & cucumber salad. Top with a sprinkling of parsley.

*Avocado: 1 well-ripened avocado, peeled, seeded, and mashed. For tang, add a few drops of tabasco and 2 tablespoons minced onion.

*Carrot: ¼ cup grated carrot and 2 teaspoons minced onion. Top with a sprinkling of parsley.

*Sesame: 2 tablespoons sesame butter or *tahini* and, if desired, 1 clove of crushed garlic.

*Walnut: ¼ cup each walnut meats and ketchup. Try over a salad of hard-boiled eggs, asparagus, and tomato wedges.

*Sweetened: Use white miso plus 1½ to 3 teaspoons honey. Nice with tomatoes.

*Herb: ½ teaspoon fresh or dried herbs (oregano, marjoram, caraway, basil).

Basil

Tofu Mayonnaise with Miso

MAKES ABOUT 1 CUP

At last a delicious homemade mayonnaise that is low in fats and calories, entirely free of cholesterol-rich eggs, and takes only a minute to prepare. Commercial mayonnaise, by comparison, is required by law to contain at least 65 percent fats—and most homemade varieties have even more. The following recipe, which serves 4 to 6, contains a total of only 466 calories, whereas an equal weight (9.1 ounces) of commercial mayonnaise contains 1820 calories, or *four* times as many!

6 ounces tofu, drained and pressed (p. 55) if desired
1½ to 2 tablespoons lemon juice or vinegar
2 tablespoons oil
2 tablespoons sweet white miso; or 4 teaspoons mellow
    white miso; or 1 tablespoon light-yellow miso; or 1½ tea-
    spoons red miso and ¼ teaspoon salt
Dash of pepper (optional)

Combine all ingredients in a blender and purée for about 20 seconds, or until smooth. Store as for Creamy Tofu Dressings (above).

Soymilk Mayonnaise Dressing

MAKES 1 CUP

½ cup soymilk
½ cup oil
3 tablespoons lemon juice or 2½ tablespoons vinegar
2 tablespoons sweet white miso; or 4 teaspoons mellow
    white miso; or 1½ teaspoons red miso and ¼ teaspoon
    salt

Combine soymilk and ¼ cup oil in a blender and purée for 1 minute. Slowly add remaining oil in a thin stream. When mixture is fairly thick, add lemon juice and miso, and purée for 30 seconds more. For variety add minced onions, garlic, grated gingerroot, paprika, or your choice of herbs or seasonings. Or add any of the combinations of ingredients used in the variations to Creamy Tofu Dressings (above).

Miso-Yogurt Dressing

MAKES ABOUT ½ CUP

½ cup yogurt
4 teaspoons red or 8 teaspoons sweet white miso
1 tablespoon orange juice
2 tablespoons (olive) oil
Dash of pepper
½ teaspoon fresh herbs (tarragon, basil, thyme) (optional)

Combine all ingredients; whisk well. Good with both tossed green and fruit salads.

Sweet Mustard-Vinegar Miso Dressing

MAKES ½ CUP

2 tablespoons sweet white or 4 teaspoons mellow white
    miso
2 tablespoons vinegar or lemon juice
3 tablespoons oil
½ teaspoon powdered hot mustard
Dash of paprika or (7-spice) red pepper

Combine all ingredients, mixing well. Try with a salad of (Chinese) cabbage, apples, raisins, and walnuts.

Sweet Miso Marinade

MAKES ¾ CUP

6 tablespoons sweet white or ¼ cup mellow white miso
2 tablespoons ketchup
2 tablespoons lemon juice
2 tablespoons oil
1 tablespoon grated or minced onion
Dash of (7-spice) red pepper

Combine all ingredients, mixing well. Use as a marinade for fresh vegetables.

WESTERN-STYLE SALADS

Potato Salad with Sour Cream and Miso

SERVES 3 OR 4

4 small potatoes, boiled or steamed in the skins until tender,
    cubed (2 cups)
2 tablespoons butter
¼ cup chives
½ cup sour cream
1½ tablespoons red, barley, or Hatcho miso
1½ cucumbers, sliced into very thin rounds
Dash of pepper or paprika

Place hot cubed potatoes into a bowl and top with butter and chives; mix lightly until butter has melted. Combine sour cream and miso, mixing well, then use to dress potatoes. Allow to cool, then mix in cucumbers. Serve chilled, topped with a sprinkling of pepper.

Carrot, Raisin & Walnut Salad
with Tofu and Miso

SERVES 4

1 cup grated carrots; or diced apple or celery
½ cup raisins
½ cup (roasted) walnut meats, diced
1½ tablespoons red, barley, or Hatcho miso
1 teaspoon honey
1 teaspoon white wine or sake
2 tablespoons sesame butter
4 lettuce leaves (optional)

Combine all ingredients, mixing well. If desired, serve mounded on lettuce leaves.

For a milder, slightly sweeter flavor, substitute for the red miso and honey: 3 to 4 tablespoons sweet white miso and ½ teaspoon shoyu.

Carrot & Raisin Salad
with Miso-Mayonnaise Dressing

SERVES 5

2 carrots, grated
¾ cup raisins
¾ to 1 cup diced apple or persimmon (optional)
½ cup walnut meats
1/3 cup mayonnaise
2 tablespoons sweet white miso; or 1 tablespoon red miso
    and 1 teaspoon honey

Combine all ingredients, mixing lightly.

Fresh Vegetable Slices
with Tofu-Miso Dressing

SERVES 3

3 tablespoons red, barley, or Hatcho miso
2½ tablespoons vinegar or lemon juice
1 tablespoon honey
2 tablespoons oil
2 tablespoons minced parsley
Dash of paprika
12 ounces tofu
3 large lettuce leaves
2 tomatoes, cut into thin wedges
2 cucumbers, cut into thin diagonals
2/3 cup peanuts

Combine the first seven ingredients and mash together well (or purée in a blender). Place lettuce leaves in individual salad bowls, arrange sliced tomatoes and cucumbers on leaves, and spoon on the dressing. Top with peanuts just before serving.

Crispy Sprout Salad
with Tofu-Miso Dressing

SERVES 3 TO 4

2 cups alfalfa sprouts
1 carrot, grated
¼ cup (roasted) sunflower seeds
¼ cup raisins
1 cup Creamy Tofu Dressing with Miso (p. 85)

Combine the first four ingredients, toss lightly, and serve topped with dollops of the dressing.

Cucumbers with Walnut-
Vinegar Miso Dressing

SERVES 2

1 cucumber, sliced into thin rounds; or 20 to 30 green beans,
    parboiled
Dressing:
    1½ teaspoons red, barley, or Hatcho miso
    1 teaspoon vinegar
    ¼ cup chopped (roasted) walnut meats
    1 tablespoon *tahini* or sesame butter

Combine the cucumber rounds and dressing; mix lightly. Serve immediately.

Tomato-Cucumber Salad
with Tangy Miso Dressing

SERVES 3 OR 4

This simple but delicious salad shows how Japanese-style *aemono* dressings can be used with fresh Western-style salads.

1 tomato, cut into ½-inch cubes
2 cucumbers, sliced into thin rounds
6 tablespoons Sweet Sesame-Vinegar Miso Dressing (p. 93)

Combine all ingredients, mixing lightly. Serve immediately.

For variety, add fresh mushrooms, green beans, grated carrot or reconstituted *wakame*.

Tomatoes with Sesame-Miso
Mayonnaise

SERVES 4

2 tomatoes, cut into wedges
2 tablespoons mayonnaise
1 to 1½ tablespoons red, barley or Hatcho miso
½ clove of garlic, grated or crushed
1 tablespoon sesame butter or *tahini*
1 teaspoon honey or lemon juice

Arrange tomato wedges on individual plates. Combine the next 5 ingredients, mixing well, then spoon over tomatoes. Serve topped with a sprinkling of parsley.

For a milder dressing, use ¼ cup mayonnaise, 3 to 4 teaspoons Sweet Simmered Miso (p. 60), 2 tablespoons sesame butter, 2 teaspoons water, and a dash of pepper.

Tofu-Miso Salad
with Walnuts and Apple

SERVES 4 TO 5

8 ounces tofu pressed (p. 55); or 7 ounces firm tofu
1 tablespoon red miso
2 tablespoons sesame butter
1 tablespoon lemon juice
2 tablespoons honey
½ cup raisins
1 cup walnut meats
1 apple, diced

Combine the first five ingredients, mashing and mixing well. Add the raisins, walnut meats, and apple, mixing lightly. Serve as is, or chill for several hours.

Fruit Salad
with Miso-Cream Cheese Balls

SERVES 3

3 ounces cream cheese
2½ tablespoons sweet white miso
¼ cup minced walnut meats or sunflower seeds
2 lettuce leaves
1 apple or pear, cut into ½-inch cubes
3 tablespoons raisins
2 tablespoons mayonnaise
2 tablespoons lemon juice

Combine the first three ingredients, mixing well, and shape into about 25 small balls. Arrange lettuce leaves on plates and mound with apples, raisins, and cream cheese-miso balls. Combine mayonnaise and lemon juice to make a dressing; pour over salad and serve immediately.

Fruit Salad
with Sweet Miso-Mayonnaise Dressing

SERVES 4

1 grapefruit, sectioned
1 orange, sectioned
1 apple, cut into ½-inch cubes
1 banana, sliced into thin rounds
6 prunes, seeded and minced
Dressing:
   1 tablespoon sweet white miso
   2 tablespoons mayonnaise
   1 tablespoon grapefruit- or apple juice

Combine the fruits in a serving bowl; toss lightly with the dressing.

Apple-Raisin Salad
with Sesame-Miso Dressing

SERVES 4

1½ to 2 large apples, cut into thin wedges
3 tablespoons raisins
¼ cup chopped walnuts
¼ cup chopped celery or sliced cucumber (optional)
3/8 cup White Sesame-Miso Dressing (p. 84)

Combine all ingredients, mixing lightly.

Macaroni Salad
with Miso Mayonnaise

SERVES 4 TO 5

5 to 6 ounces (1¼ cups) dry macaroni, cooked (3 cups)
2 cucumbers, sliced into thin rounds
2 small tomatoes, cut into wedges
White Miso & Mustard Mayonnaise Dressing:
   ¼ cup sweet white miso
   ¼ cup mayonnaise
   1½ tablespoons lemon juice
   ½ teaspoon hot mustard
   1 tablespoon finely minced or grated onion
   Dash of pepper
4 lettuce leaves
Parsley sprigs

Combine the first three ingredients with the dressing; mix lightly. Chill for several hours, then serve mounded on lettuce leaves and garnished with parsley.

For variety, add 9 ounces cubed deep-fried tofu, ½ cup raisins, and 3½ ounces fresh or reconstituted *wakame* (or grated carrot); double the amount of dressing. Or substitute for the macaroni an equal weight of noodles (whole-wheat, buckwheat, rice-flour, or transparent).

Buckwheat Noodle Salad
with Miso Mayonnaise

SERVES 4

3 ounces (*soba*) buckwheat noodles (or spaghetti), cooked (p. 58), cooled, and cut into 3-inch lengths
1 large tomato, diced
1½ cucumbers, cut into thin rounds
2/3 cup diced celery
½ cup grated cheese or walnut meats; or 2 diced hard-boiled eggs (optional)
Dressing:
   ¼ cup mayonnaise
   1½ tablespoons red, barley, or Hatcho miso
   1 teaspoon lemon juice
   Dash of pepper
4 lettuce leaves
¼ cup parsley

Combine the first four (or five) ingredients with the dressing; mix lightly. Arrange lettuce leaves in individual bowls, mound with the salad, and top with a sprinkling of parsley.

For variety, add 5 ounces diced deep-fried tofu.

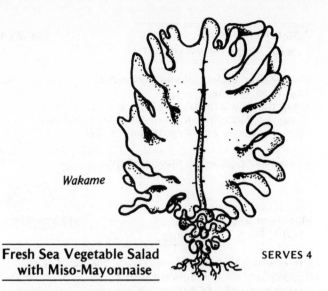

Wakame

Fresh Sea Vegetable Salad with Miso-Mayonnaise

SERVES 4

1 cup fresh or reconstituted *wakame* (p. 54), cut into 2-inch lengths
1 green pepper, thinly sliced
1 cucumber, thinly sliced
7 ounces deep-fried tofu, lightly broiled if desired, cut crosswise into thin strips
Rich Miso-Mayonnaise Dressing:
    ¼ cup mayonnaise
    6 tablespoons red, barley, or Hatcho Miso
    ¼ cup lemon juice
    Dash of pepper
1 tomato, cut into thin wedges
4 lettuce leaves

Combine the first five ingredients and the dressing; mix lightly. Arrange tomato wedges on lettuce leaves in a large salad bowl. Top with the salad mixture and chill for several hours before serving.

    If *wakame* is unavailable, substitute 1 large diced apple or tomato.

Wakame Salad with Miso-Cream Cheese Dressing

SERVES 4

1 cup fresh or reconstituted *wakame* (p. 54), chopped
1 cucumber, thinly sliced
4 lettuce leaves, torn into small pieces
Dressing:
    2 teaspoons red, barley, or Hatcho miso
    2 ounces cream cheese mixed with 2 tablespoons warm water
    ¼ cup mayonnaise
    1 tablespoon lemon juice
    ½ teaspoon grated lemon rind
    Dash of pepper
1 small tomato, cut into thin wedges
¼ cup sunflower seeds

Combine the first three ingredients and the dressing; toss lightly and place into individual bowls. Garnish with tomato wedges and top with a sprinkling of sunflower seeds.

Land-and-Sea Vegetable Salad with Mustard Lemon-Miso Dressing

SERVES 3

1 cup fresh or reconstituted *wakame* (p. 54), cut into 1½-inch lengths
1 cucumber, cut into thin rounds
1 tomato, cut into thin wedges
1¼ cups thin rounds of jicama, turnip, *daikon*, or celery root
2 ounces deep-fried tofu, broiled if desired, thinly sliced
Dressing:
    2 tablespoons sweet white miso
    3 tablespoons lemon juice
    1 teaspoon honey
    ¼ teaspoon hot mustard

Combine the first five ingredients with the dressing, mixing lightly; serve immediately.

Green Beans with Miso-Sour Cream

SERVES 2 OR 3

1½ cups green beans (stringed, split lengthwise into halves, and cut diagonally into 2-inch lengths)
¼ cup water
2 tablespoons sour cream
1 tablespoon red, barley, or light-yellow miso
Dash of pepper

Combine beans and water in a small saucepan and bring just to a boil. Reduce heat to low, cover, and cook for about 10 minutes, or until liquid has evaporated and beans are just tender; remove from heat. Combine sour cream, miso and pepper, mixing well. Stir in green beans. Serve cold as a salad or hot as a dinner vegetable.

    Any of the following, steamed until tender, make excellent substitutes for the green beans: *(kabocha)* pumpkin, winter squash or zucchini seasoned with a little dill; Irish or sweet potatoes, celery, bean sprouts, or eggplant.

Fresh Vegetable & Raisin Salad with Mustard Vinegar-Miso Dressing

SERVES 3

2 tomatoes, diced
1½ cucumbers, cut into thin rounds
1 cabbage leaf, shredded
½ cup diced celery
2 to 4 ounces deep-fried tofu, diced (optional)
¼ cup raisins
Dressing:
    2 tablespoons red or barley miso
    2 tablespoons vinegar
    1½ tablespoons lemon juice
    ½ teaspoon mustard
    1 tablespoon oil (optional)
    Dash of pepper
3 lettuce leaves

Combine the first six ingredients with the dressing; mix lightly. Serve immediately, mounded on the lettuce leaves.

Refreshing Potato Salad
with Miso Dressing

SERVES 5 OR 6

1¼ pounds potatoes, halved or quartered and steamed for
    30 minutes
1½ tablespoons red, barley, or Hatcho miso
¼ cup lemon juice
Dash of pepper
¼ cup mayonnaise
1 tablespoon honey
1½ to 2 cucumbers, sliced into thin rounds
¼ cup chopped parsley
1 cup mandarin orange or tangerine sections, chopped
    apples, or tomato wedges
¼ cup raisins (optional)

Break or cut freshly steamed potatoes into bite-sized pieces
and place in a serving bowl. Combine miso, lemon juice and
pepper, mixing well, then pour over the pototoes. Toss lightly
and allow to cool for 20 to 30 minutes. Mix mayonnaise and
honey, then stir into the potatoes together with the cucumbers and parsley. Add orange sections and, if used, the raisins;
mix gently. Chill before serving.

Tofu & Tomato Salad
with Walnut-Lemon Miso

SERVES 3

12 ounces tofu, scrambled (p. 55)
1½ tablespoons Lemon-Walnut-Miso (p. 66) or Sesame Miso
    (p. 62)
3 tablespoons mayonnaise
3 tablespoons minced parsley
1 tomato, cut into thin wedges
¼ cup chopped walnut meats (optional)
Dash of pepper

Combine tofu, miso, and mayonnaise in a serving bowl; mix
well. Add parsley, tomato and nutmeats, mixing lightly.
Season with a sprinkling of the pepper. Chill before serving.

Cottage Cheese & Tomato Salad
with Miso Dressing

SERVES 3 OR 4

1 cup cottage cheese
1 small tomato, cut into wedges
1 cucumber, cut into thin rounds
3½ cups sprouts (parboiled mung or soy; or fresh alfalfa)
Dressing:
    ¼ cup oil
    2 tablespoons vinegar
    2 tablespoons red, barley, or Hatcho miso
    Dash of (7-spice) red pepper or tabasco sauce
    1 clove of garlic, crushed (optional)
3 or 4 lettuce leaves

Combine the first four ingredients and the dressing; mix lightly. Serve mounded on lettuce leaves, if desired.

Quick Potato Salad
with Miso Dressing

SERVES 2

2 potatoes or sweet potatoes (12 ounces), boiled or steamed
    and cut into 1-inch cubes
½ cup Sweetened Miso Mayonnaise Dressing (p. 85)
½ cup parsley

Combine potatoes and miso mayonnaise, mix lightly and chill
for at least 1 hour. Served topped with the parsley.

Tomato Slices Mounded with
Miso-Cottage Cheese

SERVES 3

2 tomatoes, cut into ½-inch-thick rounds
½ cup cottage or ricotta cheese
5 tablespoons sweet white miso or White Nerimiso (p. 61)
2 to 2½ tablespoons lemon juice
Dash of pepper or paprika
Minced parsley or chives (optional)

Arrange tomato slices on a serving plate. Combine the next
three ingredients, mixing well, then mound on the tomato
slices. Serve topped with a sprinkling of the pepper and
parsley.

Vegetable & Tofu Salad
with Peanut Butter-Miso Dressing

SERVES 2 OR 3

½ carrot, cut into large matchsticks and steamed
15 green beans, steamed and cut diagonally into halves
4 to 5 ounces deep-fried tofu, cut into thin bite-sized
    rectangles
¼ cup Tangy Peanut Butter-Miso Dressing (p. 84)

Combine all ingredients, mixing lightly. If tofu is unavailable
use 1¼ carrots and 35 green beans.

Fresh Vegetable Salad
with Miso Mayonnaise

SERVES 4

1 tomato, cut into wedges
2 cucumbers, sliced into thin rounds
1/3 cup raisins
1 green pepper, thinly sliced
3 lettuce leaves, torn into small pieces
Mustard-Miso Mayonnaise Dressing:
    ¼ cup mayonnaise
    1½ tablespoons lemon juice
    ¼ teaspoon hot mustard
    1½ tablespoons red, barley, or Hatcho miso

Combine the first five ingredients with the dressing; toss lightly. For best flavor, chill for several hours before serving.

AEMONO AND THEIR DRESSINGS

Next to miso soups, *aemono* are the most popular way of using miso in Japanese cookery. These unique preparations are a favorite among most Western visitors to Japan, not only because of their fine flavor and the artistic way in which they are served, but also because of the way in which they make creative use of the tastiest and freshest seasonal vegetables, including those from wild upland meadows and the sea. Aemono trace their origins to the two schools of Japanese haute cuisine: Zen Temple Cookery *(Shojin Ryori)* and Tea Ceremony Cuisine *(Kaiseki Ryori)*, which were founded and developed by men who treasured a life of elegant simplicity and refined frugality. Early temple cooks, monks, and tea masters knew of no better union of joy and economy than to roam Japan's mountains early each spring in search of edible wild buds and fronds, tender sprigs, and leafy shoots. These became the ingredients and garnishes for the finest of Japan's many *aemono*.

The word *aemono* means "dressed things," and these preparations might be described as Japanese-style salads of mixed foods in thick, rich dressings. Whereas the vegetables in Western-style salads are often light, crisp and fresh, those in aemono generally have a softer texture imparted by parboiling, simmering in sweetened shoyu broths, or rubbing with salt. Fresh vegetables, *konnyaku*, deep-fried tofu, and various seafoods are also used.

In Japanese, aemono dressings are known as *ae-goromo*, a word derived from *koromo*, the robes worn by Buddhist priests. Whereas many Western-style dressings are light "negligee" which help to preserve the crisp quality of tossed green salads, the Japanese "robes" generally have plenty of body. This helps them to unite and bind various soft vegetable pieces while simultaneously evoking and harmonizing their individual flavors.

The most common ingredients in aemono dressings are miso, vinegar, nut-and-seed butters, tofu and, in some cases, relatively large amounts of sweetening. In the many dressings that contain vinegar, use rice vinegar for a milder, gentler flavor and Western-style fruit-based vinegar for additional tang and zest. Since oil is virtually never used in aemono dressings, they are low in calories and highly digestible. Dairy products—such as mayonnaise, cottage, cream-, or regular cheese—so widely used in Western dressings are virtually never employed. Yet because of the richness of the dressing, aemono are typically served in very small portions (often no more than 3 or 4 tablespoons) and are meant to accompany main dishes which they complement in color, taste, and texture. On Western menus they may be served either as first courses or as salads. Moreover, many aemono dressings, sometimes seasoned with herbs and spices, go well with Western-style salads, too.

There are fourteen basic aemono dressings which feature miso (and a number of others in which shoyu or salt provide the seasoning). Most are closely related to Sweet Simmered Miso except that they are almost always prepared without cooking. Each aemono preparation takes its name from the name of its dressing: thus, a lotus root salad with vinegar-miso dressing would be called Lotus Root Vinegar-

Miso Ae. The basic dressings are listed here in the approximate order of their popularity.

Red Miso Dressing   MAKES ¼ CUP

This and the following preparation are known collectively in Japanese as *awasé-miso* or "uncooked mixed miso." They contain almost the same ingredients in the same proportions as their close relatives red and white *nerimiso*. Rather than being used directly as *aemono* dressings, they are generally mixed with vinegar, mustard, sesame, and other ingredients, thereby serving as the foundation for a wide variety of dressings.

2½ tablespoons red or barley miso
1 to 2 tablespoons (natural) sugar or 1 to 3 teaspoons honey
1½ to 3 teaspoons water or dashi (p. 56)
1 teaspoon sake, white wine, or *mirin*

Combine all ingredients, mixing well.

White Miso Dressing   MAKES ¼ CUP

3 tablespoons sweet white miso
½ teaspoon sugar or ¼ teaspoon honey
2 teaspoons water or dashi (p. 56)
2 teaspoons sake, white wine, or *mirin*

Combine all ingredients, mixing well.

Vinegar Miso Dressing *(Sumiso)*   MAKES ¼ CUP

These tangy preparations are delicious with almost all varieties of aemono as well as with Western-style salads, thin slices of fresh vegetables, and even deep-fried foods. Experiment adding your favorite herbs and spices. For a more vivid flavor use a slightly smaller quantity of cider vinegar or lemon juice in place of the traditional rice vinegar. In each preparation, the trick is to use just enough vinegar to give the desired tang, but not so much as to make the consistency too thin. All vinegar miso dressings can be divided into two basic types: those which contain more miso than vinegar have a richer flavor and more body, while those containing more vinegar are tangy and more delicate in consistency.

2 tablespoons red, barley, or Hatcho miso
1 tablespoon vinegar or 2½ teaspoons lemon juice
2 to 3 teaspoons (natural) sugar or 1 to 1½ teaspoons honey
2 teaspoons *mirin* or 1 teaspoon sake (or white wine) (optional)

Combine all ingredients, mixing well.

VARIATIONS

*Tangy: A favorite with sea and wild mountain vegetables

2 tablespoons vinegar
1 tablespoon red, barley, or Hatcho miso
1 to 2 tablespoons dashi (p. 56), stock, or water
*Sweet White Vinegar Miso Dressing: Nice with steamed cauliflower
2 tablespoons sweet white miso
1½ tablespoons vinegar or lemon juice
1 teaspoon sugar or ½ teaspoon honey
*Miso Sambaizu: Sweet and zesty
2 tablespoons red miso
5 tablespoons vinegar
2½ tablespoons dashi (p. 56), stock, or water
2½ tablespoons (natural) sugar or 4 teaspoons honey
*Mix ¼ cup Red Miso Dressing (p. 91) with 1 tablespoon vinegar

Mustard-Vinegar Miso Dressing
(Karashi Sumiso)

MAKES ½ CUP

This preparation is generally made with sweet white miso, and may or may not contain sugar, sake or *mirin*. Various forms can be prepared simply by adding a small amount of hot mustard to any of the different recipes for Vinegar Miso Dressing given above. This dressing is a favorite with sea vegetables (such as *wakame*), green beans, eggplants, cabbage, steamed (*kabocha*) squash or pumpkin sprinkled with minced parsley, thinly sliced *konnyaku*, and deep-fried tofu.

3 tablespoons sweet white or 2 tablespoons mellow white miso
3 tablespoons vinegar
1½ to 3 teaspoons (natural) sugar or ¾ to 1 teaspoon honey
1 teaspoon *mirin* (optional)
¼ teaspoon hot mustard

Combine all ingredients, mixing well.

VARIATIONS

*Tangy Mustard Vinegar Miso: Made with red miso, this is a popular topping for *Sashimi Konnyaku* (p. 78)
2 tablespoons red miso
1 tablespoon vinegar
4 teaspoons (natural) sugar or 2 teaspoons honey
½ teaspoon *mirin*
¼ teaspoon mustard
*To 5 tablespoons Vinegar Miso Dressing add ½ to 1 teaspoon hot mustard.

Sesame, Walnut, or Peanut Miso Dressings
(Goma Miso or Kurumi Miso)

MAKES 6 TABLESPOONS

In Japan these dressing are generally prepared by grinding roasted seeds or nuts to a paste in a *suribachi*, then adding the remaining ingredients and mixing them together with the pestle until smooth. White sesame seeds should be used with white miso; either white or black seeds with red miso. Although freshly roasted and ground sesame yields the best flavor and aroma, sesame butter or *tahini* may be more convenient. This dressing goes well with spinach, chrysanthemum leaves, boiled *daikon*, turnips, celery, or even apples.

2 tablespoons sweet white or 4 teaspoons mellow white miso
3 tablespoons ground roasted sesame seeds (p. 54), sesame butter, or *tahini*
1 teaspoon sugar or ½ teaspoon honey
1 tablespoon sake, *mirin*, water, or dashi (p. 56)
¼ teaspoon salt

Combine all ingredients, mixing well.

For variety substitute for the sesame seeds: ground walnuts or peanuts, or your choice of nut butters. In Japan, Walnut Miso Dressing is especially popular.

Sesame-Vinegar Miso Dressing
(Goma Sumiso)

MAKES 3/8 CUP

This preparation and its popular relatives, containing walnuts or peanuts in place of sesame, combine the tangy flavor of vinegar miso with the richness of nut butters. In some preparations the sesame flavor is featured, while in others the miso is accentuated. One of Japan's most widely-used dressings for *aemono*, it goes especially well with green beans, cucumbers, mushrooms, deep-fried tofu, and all sea vegetables. Or try it with Western-style apple-walnut-celery salads.

2 tablespoons red, barley, or Hatcho miso
2 tablespoons vinegar
2 tablespoons ground roasted sesame seeds (p. 54), sesame butter, *tahini*, or walnuts
1 tablespoon (natural) sugar or 1½ teaspoons honey

Combine all ingredients, mixing well.

VARIATIONS: Prepare as above

*Peanut-Vinegar Miso Dressing:
1 tablespoon sweet white or 2 teaspoons mellow white miso
2 tablespoons vinegar
20 peanuts, chopped fine; or 3 tablespoons peanut butter
2 teaspoons honey
½ teaspoon shoyu

*Sweet Sesame-Vinegar Miso Dressing: Nice with Western-style green salads.

> 3 tablespoons sweet white or 2 tablespoons mellow white miso
> 1½ tablespoons vinegar
> 1 tablespoon sesame butter or *tahini*, or 1½ tablespoons ground roasted sesame seeds (p. 54)
> ¼ teaspoon honey

*Try reversing the proportions of miso and sesame.

Tofu Miso Dressing
(Shira-ae and Shirozu-ae)

SERVES 4

In *shira-ae*-type *aemono*, the dressing itself often forms the basis and bulk of the salad, and the vegetables are used subordinately to add texture, flavor and color. Tofu plays the leading role, supported by white miso, ground roasted sesame seeds and, sometimes, vinegar. This dressing goes especially well with cooked carrots, *konnyaku*, and mushrooms. Or use lotus root, burdock, sweet potatoes, eggplants, or your favorite wild mountain vegetables. The vegetables are often simmered in a sweetened shoyu broth before being mixed with the dressing. The amounts of sweetening, *mirin*, and vinegar should be adjusted carefully to suit the flavoring given to the vegetables and other basic ingredients. A well-made Tofu Miso Dressing has a texture similar to that of very firm cottage cheese.

> 3 to 6 tablespoons roasted sesame (p.54), or 1½ to 3 tablespoons sesame butter or *tahini*
> 6 ounces tofu, pressed or squeezed (p. 55)
> 3 tablespoons sweet white or 2 tablespoons mellow white miso
> 1 to 3 tablespoons sugar or 1½ to 4½ teaspoons honey
> 1 to 2 teaspoons *mirin* (optional)

Place the hot, freshly roasted sesame seeds into a *suribachi* and grind to a smooth paste. Add tofu and re-grind. Add miso, sugar and *mirin*, and grind for several minutes more to develop cohesiveness. Then add the cooked vegetables to be used, mixing lightly. Serve immediately.

To prepare Tangy Tofu & Miso Dressing *(Shirozu-ae)*, add 2 tablespoons vinegar or lemon juice and 2 to 3 drops of shoyu to the completed dressing just before mixing in the vegetables.

If using sesame butter or *tahini* in place of sesame seeds, the dressing may be prepared by simply combining all ingredients in a bowl and mixing with a (wooden) spoon for about 3 minutes to develop cohesiveness.

Egg Yolk-Vinegar Miso Dressing
(Kimi Sumiso)

MAKES ½ CUP

This rich, light-yellow dressing is generally used with the same ingredients as Tofu Miso Dressing or with light-colored foods such as white mushrooms, asparagus, okra, or shrimp.

> 2 hard-boiled eggs, separated into yolks and whites
> 1 tablespoon sweet white or 2 teaspoons mellow white miso
> 2½ teaspoons vinegar or lemon juice
> ¼ teaspoon honey
> 2 teaspoons dashi (p. 56) stock, or water

Press firm egg yolks through a sieve, then combine with all remaining ingredients except the egg whites, which are diced and used in the salad itself. Try with 5 grilled *(shiitaké)* mushrooms, and top with 1 tablespoon minced parsley.

Gingerroot Miso Dressing

MAKES 2 TABLESPOONS

> 1½ tablespoons red, barley, or Hatcho Miso
> 1 teaspoon grated gingerroot or its juice
> 2 teaspoons (natural) sugar or 1 teaspoon honey (optional)

Combine all ingredients, mixing well. Excellent with green beans, snow peas, crisp green vegetables, or deep-fried tofu.

Kinomé Miso Dressing

MAKES 1/3 CUP

> 10 to 15 individual *kinomé* leaves (not sprigs)
> 5 tablespoons sweet white or 3 tablespoons mellow white miso
> 1 teaspoon sugar or ½ teaspoon honey (optional)
> 1 teaspoon *mirin*

Place *kinomé* in a strainer or colander and douse with boiling water. Drain well, then transfer to a *suribachi* and grind thoroughly. Add the remaining ingredients and grind to a smooth paste. For a richer green, add 1 to 2 teaspoons *aoyosé* (p. 63). Try with regular or deep-fried tofu, celery cut into very thin diagonals, bamboo shoots, or turnips cut into paper-thin rounds.

Chive-Vinegar Miso Dressing

MAKES ¾ CUP

2 tablespoons red or barley miso
2 tablespoons vinegar
¼ cup minced chives, *nira*, or *asatsuki*
2 to 3 teaspoons sugar or 1 to 1½ teaspoons honey

Combine all ingredients, mixing well.

Leek Miso Dressing

MAKES ¼ CUP

4 tablespoons thinly-sliced leeks
1 tablespoon barley, Hatcho, or red miso

Combine ingredients, mixing well. For best flavor, cover and refrigerate for 1 to 2 days. Goes nicely with 2 cups steamed and cubed potatoes, sweet potatoes, or *kabocha*; or try with deep-fried tofu, steamed green beans, or spinach.

Yuzu Miso Dressing *(Yuzu Miso Ae)*

Prepare Yuzu Miso (p. 62) or Lemon Miso (p. 63), and allow to cool thoroughly. Use as is, or mix 3 parts with 1 part vinegar. Serve as for Kinomé Miso Dressing.

Sake Lees & Miso Dressing *(Kasumiso)*

MAKES ¼ CUP

2 tablespoons sake lees
2 teaspoons red or 4 teaspoons mellow white miso
1 teaspoon honey or 2 teaspoons (natural) sugar
2 tablespoons water

Combine all ingredients, mixing well. Delicious with par-boiled or steamed *(horenso)* spinach or chrysanthemum leaves; use 10 ounces fresh.

AEMONO THEMSELVES

When preparing *aemono*, be sure that your vegetables contain no excess surface moisture when mixed with the dressing; drain them well and pat lightly with a dry cloth just before they are to be dressed. Parboil vegetables for only as long as is necessary to make them tender while still preserving some of their crispness (and most of their vitamins). Use lightly salted water for green vegetables, and plunge into cold water immediately after parboiling to preserve their emerald color. Use the seasoning quantities in the basic dressing recipes as guidelines, adjusting them to suit your ingredients and taste. Use seasonal ingredients and whatever is on hand. In Zen temples, even trimmings and peelings are sometimes creatively incorporated.

Cucumber Salad with Vinegar-Miso Dressing *(Sunomono)*

SERVES 4

3 cucumbers, sliced into thin rounds
1 teaspoon salt
3 tablespoons (rice) vinegar
2 teaspoons red, barley, or Hatcho miso
2 teaspoons (natural) sugar or 1 teaspoon honey
¼ teaspoon grated gingerroot

Place cucumber slices in a bowl, sprinkle with the salt, and allow to stand for 1 to 2 hours. Drain and squeeze out excess liquid. Combine vinegar, miso, sugar, and gingerroot in a serving bowl; add cucumbers and mix well. Serve chilled.

For variety, add to the dressing 1/3 cup reconstituted *wakame*, raisins, or cooked transparent noodles.

Pumpkin or Squash with Mustard-Vinegar Miso Dressing

SERVES 2 OR 3

9½ ounces *(kabocha)* pumpkin or squash, steamed and cut into 1-inch cubes
Mustard Vinegar-Miso:
  1½ tablespoons red, barley, or Hatcho miso
  2 tablespoons vinegar
  1 teaspoon (natural) sugar or ½ teaspoon honey
  ¼ teaspoon hot mustard
  ½ teaspoon *mirin*, sake or white wine
  2 tablespoons minced parsley

Combine well-cooled squash with the dressing, mixing lightly. Refrigerate for several hours before serving.

Refreshing Wakame Salad with Lemon

SERVES 4

1 cup fresh or reconstituted *wakame* (p. 54), cut into 1-inch lengths
Dressing:
  1½ teaspoons red, barley, or Hatcho miso
  1 tablespoon vinegar
  1 tablespoon dashi (p. 56), stock, or water
  ¼ teaspoon grated lemon rind

Combine *wakame* and dressing, mixing lightly; serve immediately.

Wakame & Cucumber Salad with Peanut-Vinegar Miso Dressing

SERVES 2 OR 3

2 tablespoons vinegar
1 tablespoon red, barley, or Hatcho miso
2 tablespoons peanut, sesame, or walnut butter
1 cucumber, sliced into thin rounds
1/3 cup fresh or reconstituted *wakame* (p. 54), cut into 1½-inch lengths

Combine the first three ingredients in a serving bowl, mixing well. Add cucumbers and *wakame*, mixing lightly. Serve immediately.

Wakame Salad with Vinegar Miso Dressing

SERVES 3

½ cup fresh or reconstituted *wakame* (p. 54), thinly sliced
½ large tomato, cut into thin wedges, or 2 Chinese cabbage leaves, thinly sliced
1 cucumber, cut into thin rounds
1 to 2 ounces deep-fried tofu, thinly sliced
3/8 cup Sesame-Vinegar Miso Dressing (p. 92), or ¼ cup Vinegar Miso Dressing (p. 91)

Combine all ingredients, mixing lightly. For best flavor, allow to stand for several hours before serving.

Konnyaku & Carrot Salad with Tofu Miso Dressing *(Shira-ae)*

SERVES 4

1 piece of *konnyaku*, cut into small rectangles and par-boiled
1 carrot, cut into small rectangles
½ cup dashi , stock, or water
3 tablespoons sugar
½ teaspoon salt
½ teaspoon shoyu
¼ cup sesame seeds, roasted and ground to a paste (p. 54), sesame butter, or *tahini*
4 ounces tofu, pressed (p. 55), or 3 ounces firm tofu
2 tablespoons sweet white or 4 teaspoons mellow white miso
4 sprigs *kinomé* (optional)

Combine *konnyaku*, carrots, dashi, 1 tablespoon sugar, salt and shoyu in a small saucepan. Simmer until all liquid has been absorbed or evaporated, then allow to cool to room temperature. To the ground sesame seeds (in a *suribachi*), add tofu, miso and the remaining 2 tablespoons sugar; mix together (with a wooden pestle). Stir in the vegetables and serve each portion garnished with a sprig of *kinomé*.

Carrot-Daikon-Konnyaku Salad with Tofu Miso Dressing *(Shira-ae)*

SERVES 4

¼ carrot, cut into matchsticks
4 ounces *daikon*, cut into small rectangles
½ piece of *konnyaku*, cut into small rectangles
1¼ teaspoons salt
3 (*shiitaké*) mushrooms, cut into thin strips
2 teaspoons shoyu
4 teaspoons *mirin*
1 tablespoon roasted sesame seeds, sesame butter or *tahini*
8 ounces tofu, pressed (p. 55), or 6 ounces firm tofu
3 tablespoons sweet white or 2 tablespoons mellow white miso
1 teaspoon (natural) sugar or ½ teaspoon honey

Combine carrot, *daikon* and *konnyaku* in a small bowl. Rub with 1 teaspoon salt, rinse and press (p. 53). Heat an unoiled skillet or wok, drop in *konnyaku* and cook for several minutes, stirring constantly, until it becomes quite dry and begins to shrink; set *konnyaku* aside and allow to cool.

Combine mushrooms, shoyu and 1 teaspoon *mirin* in a small saucepan. Simmer until most of the liquid has been absorbed or evaporated, then drain and allow to cool to room temperature.

Combine sesame seeds and ¼ teaspoon salt in a *suribachi* and grind until seeds are slightly oily (p. 54). Add tofu, miso, sugar and 1 tablespoon *mirin*, and mix with the sesame using the wooden pestle. Stir in the *daikon*, carrot, *konnyaku* and mushrooms just before serving.

Vinegared Shira-ae *(Shirozu-ae)*

SERVES 2

6 ounces tofu, pressed (p. 55) and mashed
1 tablespoon sesame butter or *tahini*
1 tablespoon lemon juice
1½ tablespoons vinegar
1 tablespoon red or 2 tablespoons mellow white miso
1 teaspoon sake or white wine
1 cucumber or small carrot, sliced into thin rounds
2 hard-boiled eggs, chopped
¼ cup walnut meats
¼ cup raisins
2 tablespoons minced cucumber pickles (optional)

Combine the first six ingredients, mixing until smooth. Gently stir in the remaining ingredients. Serve immediately.

Green Beans and Carrots with Tofu-Miso Dressing *(Shira-ae)*

SERVES 4 TO 5

16 green beans, parboiled (p. 54) and cut into thin strips
1 carrot, cut into matchsticks and parboiled (p. 54)
4 teaspoons shoyu
4 teaspoons (natural) sugar or 2 teaspoons honey
4 tablespoons sesame butter, *tahini*, or ground roasted sesame seeds (p. 54)
12 ounces tofu, well pressed (p. 55), or 9 ounces firm tofu
4½ tablespoons sweet white or 3 tablespoons mellow white miso
1 tablespoon sake, white wine, or *mirin*

In a small saucepan combine green beans, carrots, shoyu, and sugar. Simmer over low heat until liquid has been absorbed or evaporated, then cool to room temperature. To the sesame butter (or ground sesame seeds in the *suribachi*), add tofu, miso and sake. Grind all ingredients together with the wooden pestle, or mix together with a spoon. Stir in the green beans and carrots. Serve immediately.

Green Beans with Vinegar Miso Dressing

SERVES 2

1½ tablespoons red, barley, or Hatcho miso
1 tablespoon vinegar
1½ tablespoons (natural) sugar or 2½ teaspoons honey
1 clove of garlic (or *myoga*), crushed or minced
25 green beans, parboiled (p. 54), and sliced diagonally into thin strips; or substitute 70 whole, parboiled snow peas

Combine the first four ingredients to make a dressing and mix lightly with the freshly cooked beans; allow to cool before serving.

Green Bean & Tofu Salad with Gingerroot Miso Dressing

SERVES 3

5 ounces green beans, parboiled (p. 54) and cut crosswise into halves; or substitute whole, parboiled snow peas
5 ounces deep-fried tofu, cut into small rectangles
2 tablespoons Gingerroot Miso Dressing (sweetened; p. 93)
1/3 cup peanuts or roasted soybeans

Combine crisp green beans, deep-fried tofu, and the dressing in a serving bowl; mix lightly. Top with peanuts just before serving.

Spinach with Sesame Miso Dressing

SERVES 4

1 pound (*horenso*) spinach
3 tablespoons sweet white or 2 tablespoons mellow white miso
1½ tablespoons sesame butter or *tahini*, or 3 tablespoons ground roasted sesame seeds
1 tablespoon (natural) sugar or 1½ teaspoons honey
1 to 3 teaspoons water

Bring 1 quart lightly salted water to a boil. Drop in spinach, return to the boil, and simmer for 1 to 2 minutes. Drain spinach briefly in a colander and douse with cold water. Press spinach firmly in one hand to form a compact cylinder then cut crosswise into 1-inch lengths.

Combine miso with remaining ingredients in a large bowl, mixing well. Now stir in spinach. For best flavor, allow to stand for several hours before serving.

Leek & Wakame Nuta

SERVES 2

Nuta is such a popular type of *aemono* that many Japanese actually use the two words interchangeably. *Wakame* and leeks (preferably the tender young variety known as *wakegi*) are used in most versions. Other popular ingredients include short-necked clams, sardines, squid, yellowtail, tuna, and a number of wild mountain vegetables such as *udo* and bracken ferns. Moist, cool and refreshing, *nuta* is generally prepared with a Miso Vinegar Dressing or occasionally with Sweet Simmered Miso.

2 leeks or 6 scallions, cut into ½-inch lengths
½ cup fresh or reconstituted *wakame* (p. 54), cut into 1½-inch lengths
2 ounces deep-fried tofu (*agé*), lightly broiled if desired and thinly sliced
Sweet White Vinegar-Miso Dressing (p. 92)

Cut leek pieces lengthwise into halves and parboil very briefly. Drain well, pat dry with a towel, and combine with the *wakame*, agé, and dressing; mix lightly. Serve immediately.

Onion Sesame-Miso Ae

SERVES 3 OR 4

3 onions, cut into thin wedges
¼ teaspoon salt
1½ tablespoons red, barley, or Hatcho miso
1½ tablespoons sesame butter or *tahini*

Bring ½ cup water to a boil in a small saucepan. Drop in the onions, season with the salt, and simmer for 5 minutes. Pour contents of saucepan into a strainer set over a bowl, and allow onions to drain well. In a large bowl combine miso, sesame butter, and 4½ tablespoons of the drained cooking liquid; mix well. Add onions and toss lightly. Serve immediately.

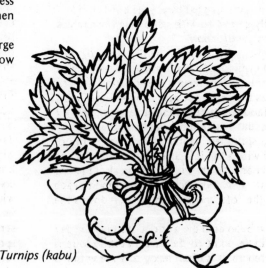

Turnips (kabu)

Miso in Soups & Stews

The great majority of Japan's miso (an estimated 80 to 85 percent of total yearly production) is used in the preparation of miso soup, and a recent survey showed that 73 percent of all Japanese—whether rich or poor, farmers or urbanites—enjoy miso soup at least once a day. Indeed, for most Japanese, the words miso and miso soup are practically synonymous.

Generally called *miso shiru* or *o-miotsuké*, but also known in better restaurants as *miso-jitaté*, miso soup became popular in Japan about 700 years ago, when samurai warriors who had siezed power from the traditional nobility developed a national cuisine reflecting the simplicity and frugality of their new life-style. Grains were given the leading role at each meal, supported by miso soup, cooked vegetables, tofu, and occasionally fish and shellfish. Today, miso soup is an indispensable element in the traditional Japanese breakfast, where it is accompanied by a large bowl of rice or rice porridge, usually garnished with salt-pickled vegetables, *umeboshi* (salt plums), and/or *nori*.

To prepare miso soup, fresh (or lightly sautéed) vegetables are simmered until just tender in dashi, the all-purpose soup stock; ingredients such as regular or deep-fried tofu and *wakame* are added as the vegetables near completion. Finally the miso is added (about 1 tablespoon per serving), and the soup reheated until the first bubble appears. Poured into lacquerware bowls, sprinkled lightly with a seasoning or garnish and covered with a lid, it is generally served steaming hot, while its aroma and flavor are at their peak. Plucking them out of the bowl with chopsticks (never a spoon), each person first enjoys the tofu and vegetables, then downs the warming broth.

One of the few peoples in the world to start off the day with soup, the Japanese point to the fact that miso soup is quick and easy to prepare; it is often ready to serve within 5 minutes after the cook starts work—a key factor during the busy morning meal. Almost any ingredient goes well in it and, being cooked only briefly, they all retain their health-giving vitamins, crispness, and delicate flavor. For the Japanese, the hearty aroma of this filling soup is as appetizing as that of coffee for many Westerners, while its mellow, subtly pungent flavor and low-calorie warmth help to start the day off right. By alkalizing the blood, miso soup is said to wake up the nervous system and offer abundant nourishment, stamina, and energy that last all morning. An aid to digestion and assimilation, it is also said to relieve acid indigestion and settle an upset stomach. Sake-lovers are unanimous in their assertion that miso soup does wonders for a hangover.

True enough, a typical serving is remarkably rich in essential nutrients. The tofu and miso together provide about 9 to 12 grams of protein (roughly one-sixth of the adult daily requirement), plus important polyunsaturated oils. The *wakame* and tofu supply abundant calcium and other minerals; the fresh vegetables offer vitamins; and the miso supplies salt.

In most rural farmhouses, a large kettle of miso soup is prepared each morning and reheated before lunch and dinner. This practice simplifies the work of the housewife in preparing meals, and many claim that as the flavors intermingle and marry, the soup becomes even more delicious. On winter evenings, the family will often have dinner around the open-hearth, sunken fireplace at the center of the main room, with the pot of simmering soup, suspended above the live coals from an overhead hook, serving as the center of conviviality and warmth. Miso soup is one of the most commonly served foods in Japan's many "long-life" villages where it is considered essential to good health and longevity; in some areas, the villagers are reported to consume an average of 4 to 6 cups daily. In most of Japan's Zen temples, miso soup is served with each meal, often using miso prepared by the monks; at breakfast and lunch it accompanies rice or rice porridge and cooked or salt-pickled vegetables, while at dinner it is mixed with leftovers to make a richly flavored gruel.

One of Japan's truly seasonal preparations, miso soup is served throughout the year. By using fresh vegetables, sprouts, sprigs and even flowers, the sensitive cook is able to reflect in a dark lacquerware soupbowl the great rhythms and cycles of the natural world. And by choosing from and com-

97

bining the multitude of different types of fine miso, giving each combination the perfect accent with the proper choice of seasonings and garnishes, it is quite easy to prepare a different type of miso soup every day of the year. In fact, a number of Japanese cookbooks contain easy-to-follow charts suggesting ingredients for breakfast and dinner each day of the week throughout the four seasons (see p. 101), and cookbooks devoted exclusively to the preparation of miso soups group recipes as spring, summer, fall, and winter preparations. In Japan's most popular book on miso cookery, 76 of the 131 pages describe the preparation of miso soups. Several of Japan's largest miso makers have gone so far as to provide a free service whereby any cook can dial a widely advertised phone number and listen to a recording of "the miso soup of the day," featuring seasonal ingredients and the miso with which they best harmonize.

Likened to a haiku in a lacquerware bowl, miso soup is surrounded by a veritable mystique. It has been noted that in the writings of almost every great Japanese author and poet, there can be found a section of reminiscences about its ineffable aroma filling the air on unforgettable childhood mornings. Mr. Wataru Kawamura, Japan's best known writer on the subject, whose works include *An Encyclopedia of Miso Soups* and *Miso Soups Throughout the Provinces*, feels that it epitomizes Japanese character and culture. Describing himself as "a scholar not of miso, but of miso soup," Mr. Kawamura points out that even the thought of the piping hot broth has the power to touch Japanese heartstrings. The contemporary wanderer and poet Nanao Sasaki has written: "Everything starts from miso soup in good morning. Miso soup is made of shiny spider web..." The Japanese National Miso Association now uses as the motto for its letterhead: "A Happy Family is One that Starts the Day with Miso Soup." And many writers — both Japanese and foreign — have commented on the similarity between its essence and that of Zen: a certain simple yet deeply satisfying flavor that can be enjoyed day after day. Of course, miso soup is an integral part of the life of monks in their temples and tea masters in their hermitages, who delight in the flavor of a soup prepared with homemade miso and seasonal delicacies gathered wild from nearby mountains.

Japan's great master of Tea Ceremony Cuisine, Mr. Kaichi Tsuji, writes eloquently about miso soup: "Its taste must be subtle, complex, and compact—all within what is appropriate to the tea ceremony. A fine *misoshiru* is like the trailing reverberations of a great temple bell. Its goodness lies in its aftertaste, which invites the guest to a second bowl ... Its flavor is indeed the flavor of Japan."

A well-known Japanese proverb says that only when a young woman has mastered the art of making fine miso soup is she ready to become a bride. For although it is remarkably simple to follow the basic recipe and come up with a tasty result, to learn to prepare the very finest miso soup is deceptively difficult and requires years of practice. Yet many find that the joy lies in the learning, and claim that each day's effort allows the cook to express culinary mastery and love while serving as a nutritional key-stone for a healthy family.

Numerous Japanese restaurants specialize in the preparation of miso soup (p. 240), and virtually every restaurant

offers at least several varieties as standard fare. In recent years, modern technology has yielded a number of new forms, some sold through coffee-like vending machines and others in sealed foil packages as "instant miso soup," now widely available even in the West. The latter contain either regular or dehydrated miso (p. 44), plus dehydrated dashi, *wakame*, and tofu with freeze-dried vegetables. These lightweight, inexpensive products are ready to serve as soon as they have been mixed with hot water and are well suited for back packing, camping, and picnicking.

Although miso is used to season soups in China and Korea, too, the resulting dishes are completely different from Japanese miso soup and play a much less important role in the national cuisine. The Chinese variety, *chiang t'sang*, is usually made with a chicken broth and contains fish and vegetables sautéed in sesame oil. The fiery Korean *daen jang chigé* contains diced tofu, leeks, chunks of beef, and plenty of red pepper.

Since the 1960s, miso soup has come to be widely enjoyed in the West, particularly among those interested in natural foods. New variations on the traditional Japanese motif are beginning to appear using Western ingredients matched to Western tastes: some like to substitute cottage cheese for tofu or drop in an egg, add their favorite herbs or serve the soup chilled on hot summer afternoons. Winning growing acceptance among doctors and nutritionists alike, miso soup is rapidly finding a new home in America.

Basic Ingredients

Every miso soup is composed of four principal elements: dashi, miso, vegetables or other solids, and garnishes or seasonings.

Dashi: The Japanese consider a richly-flavored, fragrant dashi to be the indispensable foundation of a fine miso soup. Most dashi is prepared with *kombu* (dried kelp) together with either freshly-shaved bonita flakes or tiny dried sardines *(niboshi)*. In Zen Temple Cookery, the dashi is made with either *kombu* or a combination of *kombu* and *shiitaké* mushrooms (p. 57). In the West, vegetable or vegetable bouillon stocks are also used. Surprisingly delicious flavors result from the combination of 1 part stock with 1 part herb or peppermint teas or (home-extracted) vegetable juices (carrot, tomato, cabbage, etc.).

Miso: All varieties of regular miso are used in miso soups. Red, barley, and Hatcho miso are by far the most popular. Broiled miso is sometimes used to add savory aroma to chilled soups; sweet white and sweet red varieties are used only on special occasions. (Finger Lickin' and Sweet Simmered Miso are never used.) In most home cookery only one type of miso is used at a time, although restaurant chefs and cookbooks often call for the simultaneous use of two or occasionally even three types. Just as in the blending of fine coffees, the combination of fundamentally different misos (red and white, sweet and salty, rice and barley, etc.) produces delightful harmonies of flavor and aroma. The five most popular mixtures are:

4 parts red or light-yellow and 1 part Hatcho
3 parts red and 2 parts sweet white
1 part red and 9 parts sweet white
1 part light-yellow and 1 part sweet barley
1 part red and 1 part barley

For each cup of dashi or stock, use about 1 to 1½ tablespoons red, barley, or Hatcho miso; 2 tablespoons mellow miso; or 2 to 3 tablespoons sweet white or sweet red miso.

Vegetables, etc.: The English language has no good equivalent for the Japanese term *mi*—literally "fruits"—which refers to all of the basic solids in a soup. One of Japan's largest food and housekeeping magazines recently conducted a nationwide survey to find out which "fruits" were used most frequently in daily miso soups. The top 25 favorites, with relative popularity, are listed below. Note the total absence of meat, fish, or poultry, and the low position of two types of shellfish:

Daikon	19.6	Onion	3.7
Leek	19.1	Burdock root	3.4
Tofu pouches	16.2	Eggplant	3.2
Wakame	15.7	Mushrooms	3.1
Tofu	13.8	Turnip (kabu)	2.9
Chinese		Lotus root	2.5
Cabbage	8.5	Bean sprouts	2.4
Potato	7.7	Wild vegetables	2.3
Spinach	5.8	Corbicula (shellfish)	2.0
Cabbage	4.3	Sweet potato	1.6
Wheat gluten	4.2	Spring chrysanthemum	1.1
Carrot	3.9	Short-necked clams	0.8

Other popular ingredients are listed in the chart on page 101. Unlisted ingredients which are also used include:

Yuba (fresh or dried)
Tempura dumplings and skimmings
Snow peas
Noodles (all types)
Natto and *Hamanatto*
Cottage cheese
Ginkgo nuts

Most soups contain a combination of two or three of these "fruits", with one given the leading role and others used to complement and support it. All are sliced or diced fine so that they will cook quickly. An average serving contains about 1 to 1½ ounces (30 to 40 grams) of solids, and a thick soup 2½ times this much. In choosing ingredients, a skilled cook considers:

What locally grown vegetables are fresh and in season?
Which of these will harmonize best with the color and flavor of the miso to be used?
How much should be used together with a given amount of a particular miso?
Will they sink or float on the surface to complement the garnish?
Should they be cut into tree-leaf (maple, ginkgo) or blossom (cherry, plum) shapes to express the sense of the season; or do they lend themselves to cutting into loops, interlocking rings, pine-needle, or fan shapes?
Does the color and shape of the vegetable suit the color and design of the bowl to be used?

Seasonings and Garnishes: The proper seasoning or garnish provides the crowning touch. True to their name, many Japanese seasonings are strictly seasonal; they are used fresh and prized for their transiency. Many of the favorites are shown in the chart on page 101.

Although Western herbs and spices are not widely used in Japan, we have found them remarkably well suited for use in miso soups. For best fragrance, use them freshly picked, crushed, or ground. Parmesan and grated cheeses as well as sesame- and nut-butters also add delicious flavor and richness. Occasionally miso soups are spiked with a little sake or white wine, and thickened with *kuzu* (kudzu powder) or arrowroot.

Principles of Preparation and Serving

*Miso is always mixed with hot broth and sometimes puréed or ground before being added to a soup. In the following recipes, for the sake of brevity, we will simply call for the miso to be creamed. However any of the following four techniques may be used:

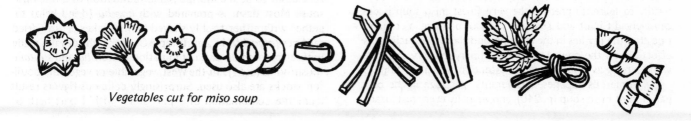

Vegetables cut for miso soup

1. *Creaming:* Place miso in a small cup. Remove about ½ cup hot dashi or stock from the saucepan and, adding a little at a time, stir into the miso; then add the cream back into the soup. Dip the cup into the soup to retrieve all the miso. This quick-and-easy technique allows the texture of the miso to appear in the soup.

2. *Puréeing:* Place miso in a small sieve or woven bamboo miso strainer (below). Partially immerse sieve in

Miso-koshi

broth and press miso through sieve with the back of a (wooden) spoon. If desired, add to the soup any particles of koji or soybeans remaining in the sieve. This technique yields a satin-smooth soup even when made from chunky miso.

3. *Grinding:* Combine miso and a small amount of hot broth in a *suribachi* (mortar) and grind to a smooth paste with a wooden pestle. Pour through a sieve (or directly) into the hot broth. Using a rubber spatula or wooden spoon, retrieve any miso remaining in *suribachi*, then rinse out *suribachi* with a little of the hot soup. This technique is used with (home-made) miso containing firm chunks of koji or soybeans.

Mad monks grinding miso

4. *Mincing:* Place very firm miso in a small mound on a cutting board and mince with a sharp knife. This technique, used exclusively with Hatcho miso, is usually followed by puréeing or creaming.

*Overcooking spoils the miso's prized aroma while also destroying microorganisms and enzymes which aid digestion. Remove soup from heat just before it comes to a boil and, for best flavor, serve immediately.

*For breakfast miso soup or when the ingredients are primarily vegetables, the Japanese use a relatively large amount of red or barley miso to create a rich, hearty broth. At dinnertime or when the ingredients are primarily tofu or seafoods, less miso is generally used to yield a more delicately flavored broth which allows the character of the individual ingredients to shine forth. Better restaurants generally serve a dinner miso soup prepared with a somewhat mild broth containing relatively few solid ingredients; the dinnertime miso soup served in private homes, however, can often resemble a hearty Western-style stew, served at the table in a casserole, earthenware *nabé*, or cast iron pot.

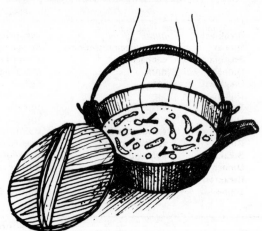

*During the warm half of the year (April to September), red or barley miso is generally used and the total amount of solid ingredients is kept relatively small; in midsummer, chilled miso soup is a favorite at lunch or dinner. During the cold seasons, the amount of solid ingredients increases and thick, sweet miso soups are served more frequently: in midwinter, a thick-as-a-stew miso soup may serve as the main course. During March-April and September-August, the months preceeding and following the equinoxes, mixtures of salty and sweet miso are enjoyed.

*Miso soup is generally served at the end of formal Japanese meals.

Fig. 19. Miso Soups Throughout the Four Seasons   (FROM: *Miso Cookery Throughout the Twelve Months*)

Spring

Day	Meal	Main Ingredient	Supporting Ingredient	Miso	Seasoning
Sunday	Breakfast	deep-fried tofu	chrysanthemum leaves	sweet white miso	*yuzu* or lemon rind
	Dinner	egg tofu	*junsai*	red miso	*sansho* pepper
Monday	Breakfast	small turnips	chrysanthemum leaves	sweet white miso	mustard
	Dinner	mackerel or sardines	leek or wild onion	red miso	*sansho* pepper
Tuesday	Breakfast	onions	*wakame*	red miso	mustard
	Dinner	grilled tofu	burdock & deep-fried tofu	red miso	gingerroot juice
Wednesday	Breakfast	fish sausage	trefoil	sweet white miso	horsetails
	Dinner	bamboo shoots	*wakame*	sweet white miso	*kinomé*
Thursday	Breakfast	egg & dry sardines	trefoil	red miso	*yuzu* or lemon rind
	Dinner	*kampyo*	deep-fried tofu	red miso	butterbur sprouts
Friday	Breakfast	Osmund fern	deep-fried tofu	light-yellow miso	*sansho* pepper
	Dinner	young burdock	pork	light-yellow miso	gingerroot juice
Saturday	Breakfast	clams	*udo* or *nanohana*	red & white miso	*sansho* pepper
	Dinner	eggs	leeks	sweet white miso	curry powder

Summer

Day	Meal	Main Ingredient	Supporting Ingredient	Miso	Seasoning
Sunday	Breakfast	eggplant	*wakame*	red miso	cucumber or myoga
	Dinner	loach	burdock root	red & white miso	*sansho* pepper
Monday	Breakfast	egg	fresh greens	white & yellow miso	gingerroot juice
	Dinner	white gourd-melon	chicken	red & yellow miso	*sansho* pepper
Tuesday	Breakfast	green beans	deep-fried tofu	white & yellow miso	ground sesame
	Dinner	tomato & milk	green pepper & onion	sweet white miso	minced parsley
Wednesday	Breakfast	*kabocha*	*wakame*	red miso	7-spice red pepper
	Dinner	ground sesame	cucumber	broiled miso	7-spice red pepper
Thursday	Breakfast	cabbage	*tororo kombu*	sweet white miso	red pepper powder
	Dinner	taro	fried tofu, *shiitaké* & carrot	light-yellow miso	7-spice red pepper
Friday	Breakfast	potato	*daikon* & *wakame*	red miso	*daikon* leaf tips
	Dinner	corbicula (shellfish)	leeks	light-yellow miso	beefsteak leaf
Saturday	Breakfast	cucumber	beansprouts	Hatcho miso	hot mustard
	Dinner	fresh *shiitaké*	rice-flour dumplings	sweet white miso	hot mustard

Fall

Day	Meal	Main Ingredient	Supporting Ingredient	Miso	Seasoning
Sunday	Breakfast	*hijiki*	deep-fried tofu	red miso	7-spice red pepper
	Dinner	*matsutaké* mushrooms	*myoga* buds	red miso	*yuzu*
Monday	Breakfast	cabbage	deep-fried tofu	light-yellow miso	pepper
	Dinner	pork	grilled eggplants	sweet white miso	*myoga* or beefsteak buds
Tuesday	Breakfast	tofu	*nameko* mushrooms	Hatcho miso	hot mustard
	Dinner	taro	chicken	white & red miso	*sansho* pepper
Wednesday	Breakfast	cucumber	tomato	sweet white miso	*wasabi*
	Dinner	*shimeji* mushrooms	tofu & chrysanthemum leaves	white & red miso	*yuzu*
Thursday	Breakfast	sweet potato	deep-fried tofu	light-yellow miso	pepper
	Dinner	grilled eggplant	roasted sesame	sweet white miso	trefoil
Friday	Breakfast	*kabocha*	fried tofu & *shiitaké*	red miso	beefsteak seeds
	Dinner	fish	burdock root	white & red miso	*sansho* pepper
Saturday	Breakfast	*nira* chives	egg	white & red miso	gingerroot juice
	Dinner	mackerel	spinach & *wakame*	red miso	*sansho* pepper

Winter

Day	Meal	Main Ingredient	Supporting Ingredient	Miso	Seasoning
Sunday	Breakfast	*mochi*	*daikon*, carrot & *shiitaké*	red miso	*yuzu*
	Dinner	*junsai*	glutinous yam	Hatcho miso	green *nori* flakes
Monday	Breakfast	tofu	milk & *asatsuki* chives	light-yellow miso	pepper
	Dinner	peanuts	*aona* greens	red miso	crumbled *wakame*
Tuesday	Breakfast	small turnips	deep-fried tofu	red miso	hot mustard
	Dinner	dried-frozen tofu	chrysanthemum leaves	white & red miso	hot mustard
Wednesday	Breakfast	Chinese cabbage	deep-fried tofu	light-yellow miso	pepper
	Dinner	taro & *konnyaku*	burdock, leek, & sake lees	light-yellow miso	7-spice red pepper
Thursday	Breakfast	*daikon*	leeks	sweet white miso	butter or red pepper
	Dinner	pork	*konnyaku*	red miso	*sansho* pepper
Friday	Breakfast	tofu	bean sprouts	red miso	slivered leeks
	Dinner	tofu	salmon roe	sweet white miso	Mandarin orange peel
Saturday	Breakfast	oyster & tofu	leeks	red miso	*sansho* pepper
	Dinner	dried slivered *daikon* & *shiitaké*	chrysanthemum leaves	red miso	*sansho* pepper

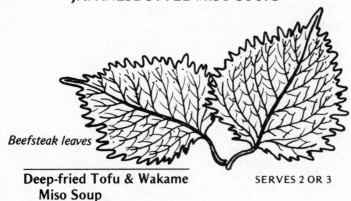

Beefsteak leaves

Deep-fried Tofu & Wakame Miso Soup SERVES 2 OR 3

This is one of Japan's favorite and most traditional miso soups. The *wakame* supplies an abundance of calcium and other minerals, while the deep-fried tofu and miso provide protein and unsaturated oils. Requiring less than 3 minutes to prepare, this soup is particularly popular at breakfast.

1¾ cups dashi (p. 56) or stock
¼ to 1/3 cup fresh or reconstituted *wakame* (p. 56), cut into 1-inch lengths
1 to 2 ounces deep-fried tofu, cut crosswise into thin strips
2 tablespoons red, barley, or Hatcho miso
1 tablespoon thinly sliced leeks and/or a dash of 7-spice red pepper

Bring dashi to a boil in a saucepan. Add *wakame* and deep-fried tofu, and simmer for 1 minute. Add miso creamed in a little of the hot broth and return just to the boil. Serve immediately, garnished with the leeks.

White Miso Soup with Tofu, Nori & Spinach SERVES 2

This recipe is a specialty of Fugetsu, a Japanese natural-food restaurant in Berkeley. The key is the combination of sweet white miso with a little salt. The broth is kept warm in a double boiler and simply poured over the other ingredients in a bowl for each new serving.

1½ cups Number 1 Dashi (p. 56)
¼ cup sweet white miso
¼ teaspoon salt
1½ to 2 ounces tofu, cut into 3/8-inch cubes
3 to 4 tablespoons steamed or parboiled spinach, well drained
2 tablespoons thinly sliced green onions
2 pieces of *nori*, each 1½ inches square

Bring the dashi to a boil in a saucepan. Add the creamed miso and salt and return just to the boil. Divide the tofu, spinach, and green onions among individual warmed bowls and pour on the hot broth. Float a square of *nori* in the soup and serve immediately.

Nori & Deep-fried Tofu Miso Soup SERVES 2

1¼ cups dashi (p. 56)
1½ ounces deep-fried tofu, cut into 3/8-inch cubes
¼ cup thinly sliced rounds of leek
1½ tablespoons red, barley, or Hatcho miso
½ sheet of *nori*, torn into small pieces; or 2 tablespoons rinsed and diced fresh *nori*

Bring dashi to a boil in a small saucepan. Add tofu, leeks, and miso creamed in a little of the hot broth; return to the boil. Stir in *nori*, return just to the boil, and serve.

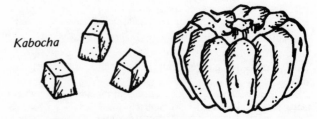

Kabocha

Refreshing Pumpkin Miso Soup SERVES 2

1¼ cups (*kabocha*) pumpkin or squash (1-inch chunks)
2 cups dashi (p. 56), stock, or water
2 tablespoons akadashi or red miso
1 green beefsteak leaf, thinly sliced

Combine pumpkin and dashi in a small saucepan and bring to a boil. Cover and simmer for about 15 minutes, or until pumpkin is tender. Stir in miso creamed in a little of the hot broth and return just to the boil. Serve garnished with the beefsteak leaf.

Miso Soup with Sake Lees (Sakenokasu-jiru) SERVES 2

Available in the West at most Japanese food markets, sake lees may be added to any miso soup to impart a rich flavor, heady aroma, and thick texture: use 2 to 3 parts (by volume) lees to 3 parts miso, or about 1 tablespoon per serving.

1½ cups dashi (p. 56), stock, or water
2 Chinese cabbage leaves, thinly sliced
2/3 cup diced sweet potatoes, yams, or Irish potatoes
1 to 2 ounces deep-fried tofu (optional)
2 tablespoons red, barley, or Hatcho miso
1½ to 2 tablespoons sake lees

Bring dashi to a boil in a small saucepan. Add Chinese cabbage, sweet potatoes and, if used, the tofu. Return to the boil and simmer for 5 minutes. Combine the miso and sake lees, cream with a little of the hot broth, and stir into the soup. Return just to the boil. Serve piping hot.

For a softer texture and lower alcohol content, simmer the lees with the vegetables before adding the miso.

Miso Soup with Potato, Wakame & Tofu

SERVES 4

4 cups water or stock
¼ cup bonito flakes
1 small potato, cut into ½-inch cubes
¾ cup fresh or reconstituted *wakame* (p. 54), cut into 1½-inch lengths
2 ounces deep-fried tofu, thinly sliced (optional)
5 tablespoons red, barley, or Hatcho miso
¼ cup thinly-sliced leeks

Bring water to a boil in a small saucepan. Add bonito flakes, turn off heat and allow to stand for 3 to 4 minutes. (Strain if flakes are coarse.) Return broth to a boil, add potatoes and cook for 8 to 10 minutes, or until potatoes are tender. Add *wakame*, tofu, and miso creamed in a little of the hot broth. Return just to the boil and remove from heat. Top with a sprinkling of the leeks and serve hot or cold.

Gingerroot-Onion Miso Soup

SERVES 3

2 teaspoons oil or butter
½ clove of garlic, crushed or minced
1 onion, thinly sliced
2 cups water or stock
2 tablespoons sweet white or 4 teaspoons mellow white miso
1 tablespoon red, barley, or Hatcho miso
½ teaspoon grated gingerroot

Heat a small pot or saucepan and coat with the oil. Add garlic and sauté for 30 seconds, then add onion and sauté for 5 minutes more. Add water and bring to a boil; cover and simmer for 3 minutes. Add both varieties of miso dissolved in a little of the hot broth, stir in gingerroot, and return just to the boil. Serve piping hot.

Picnic Miso Soup

SERVES 3

3 tablespoons red, barley, or Hatcho miso
2 tablespoons bonito flakes or grated cheese
Dash of pepper (7-spice, red, or black)
1 to 2 ounces deep-fried tofu, cut crosswise into thin strips
12 inches dry *wakame*, cut into 1-inch lengths; or 3 cakes of dried wheat gluten
2 to 3 tablespoons thinly-sliced leeks; or minced chives or parsley
2 cups hot or boiling water

Combine miso, bonito flakes, and pepper, mixing well, then shape into 3 balls. Skewer and broil each ball over a burner (as for Broiled Miso, p. 71) until well browned and fragrant. Place balls and the next three ingredients into a picnic container. Take the hot water in a thermos or heat water at the picnic site. To serve, divide all solid ingredients among 3 bowls, pour in the hot water, and mix until miso dissolves. Cover and allow to stand for several minutes before serving.

Curried White Miso Soup with Onion and Egg

SERVES 2

1¼ cups dashi (p. 56) or stock
1 small onion, sliced very thin
¼ cup sweet white or 2½ tablespoons mellow white miso
½ teaspoon curry powder
1 egg, lightly beaten

Combine dashi and onion in a small saucepan, bring to a boil, and simmer, covered, for 3 minutes. Add miso and curry powder creamed in a little of the hot broth; return to the boil. Stir in egg a little at a time. Remove from heat and serve immediately.

Natto & Chinese Cabbage Miso Soup

SERVES 2 OR 3

1¼ cups dashi (p. 56), stock, or water
2 (Chinese) cabbage leaves, cut lengthwise into halves, then crosswise into 1½-inch-wide strips
1 tablespoon red, barley, or Hatcho miso
2 tablespoons sweet white or 4 teaspoons mellow white miso
½ cup *natto*
¼ cup thin rounds of leek or scallion
Dash of 7-spice red pepper

Bring dashi to a boil in a saucepan. Add Chinese cabbage, cover, and simmer for 2 or 3 minutes. Add miso creamed in a little of the hot broth. Add *natto* and return just to the boil. Sprinkle on leeks and remove from heat. Serve seasoned with a sprinkling of the red pepper.

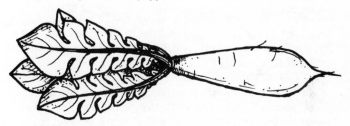

Daikon & Onion Miso Soup

SERVES 3 TO 4

2 to 3 teaspoons oil
1 onion, thinly sliced
1 cup thin half-moons of *daikon* (p.54)
2 cups water, stock, or dashi (p.56)
4 tablespoons red, barley, or Hatcho miso
2 tablespoons thinly sliced leek or scallion greens (optional)

Heat a skillet or casserole and coat with the oil. Add onion and sauté for 3 minutes. Add *daikon* and water, and bring to a boil. Reduce heat to low and simmer, covered, for 15 minutes. Add miso creamed in a little of the hot broth and return to the boil. Serve garnished, if desired, with a sprinkling of leek slices.

Akadashi Miso Soup with Tofu and Mushrooms

SERVES 2 OR 3

Akadashi or "red dashi" was originally the name of a miso soup containing a mixture of soybean (usually Hatcho) miso and one or two rice misos. It originated in central Japan and was prepared in either of two ways: 1) The firm soybean miso was minced on a bread board, mixed with the softer rice miso(s) and tied in a small piece of coarsely-woven cloth to form a sack, which was then immersed in hot dashi until the miso flavor and color had permeated the broth; 2) The red and minced soybean misos were combined with bonita flakes in a *suribachi* and ground until smooth; hot water was stirred in and the mixture allowed to stand until strained for use as the broth. After World War II, "akadashi" came to refer to a new variety of miso (p. 44). Yet the colorful and tasty soup is still a favorite in many of Japan's finest restaurants, where it may be prepared with either the modern or traditional misos. Since the basic ingredients are added to the broth *after* the miso, only those requiring very little cooking are used.

1¼ cups dashi (p. 56) or stock
2 teaspoons Hatcho miso
1 tablespoon red miso
1 teaspoon sweet white miso (optional)
6 ounces tofu, cut into 3/8-inch cubes
1/3 cup *nameko* mushrooms and their liquid
3 sprigs of trefoil, cut into 1-inch lengths

Bring dashi to a boil in a small saucepan. Add misos creamed in a little of the dashi and return to the boil. Add tofu and mushrooms, and return again to the boil. Serve garnished with trefoil.

If *nameko* mushrooms are not available, sauté 6 thinly sliced fresh mushrooms in butter until tender and add to dashi together with tofu. If desired, substitute dry wheat gluten cakes for the tofu; season with *sansho* green pepper.

Hiyashi-jiru
(Broiled Miso in Chilled Soup)

SERVES 2 OR 3

1½ cups dashi (p. 56) or stock, cooled
1½ to 2 tablespoons Savory Broiled Miso (p. 71; use red miso)
½ cup thinly sliced cucumber
½ cup diced tomato
2 green beefsteak or mint leaves, minced (optional)

Cream the miso in a little of the dashi, then add remaining dashi, stirring until smooth; cover and refrigerate until chilled. Refrigerate vegetables in separate containers. Divide vegetables among individual bowls and pour on the chilled broth. Serve immediately.

Tororo-jiru with Sweet White Miso

SERVES 5 TO 6

This unusual Japanese delicacy bears some resemblance to a chilled Western-style consommé. The ingredients are traditionally mixed in a *suribachi* rather than a blender.

2½ cups dashi (p. 56) or stock, cooled to room temperature
7½ tablespoons sweet white or 5 tablespoons mellow white miso
10½ ounces glutinous yam, peeled and grated
1 egg
1 sheet of *nori*, toasted (p. 54) and crumbled (optional)

Combine the first four ingredients in a blender and purée for about 1 minute. Serve as is or chilled, topped with a sprinkling of *nori*.

Onion-Miso Soup with Tofu and Eggs

SERVES 3

2 cups dashi (p. 56), stock, or water
1 onion, thinly sliced
2½ to 3 tablespoons red, barley, or Hatcho miso
4 to 6 ounces regular or deep-fried tofu, cut into 3/8-inch cubes
2 or 3 eggs, lightly beaten if desired (optional)
Dash of black or 7-spice red pepper

Combine dashi and onion in a small saucepan, bring to a boil, and simmer, covered, for 4 to 5 minutes. Add the miso creamed in a little of the hot broth, then the tofu and eggs. (For an egg-flower soup, swirl broth while adding lightly beaten eggs.) Return just to a boil over high heat, season with pepper, and serve immediately. Or allow to cool to room temperature and serve topped with 1 tablespoon minced parsley.

Miso Soup with Buckwheat Noodles and Eggs

SERVES 2

2 teaspoons (sesame) oil
1 small onion, thinly sliced
1½ cups water, stock, or dashi (p. 56)
2 ounces *(soba)* buckwheat noodles, broken into 4-inch lengths and cooked (p. 58)
3 tablespoons red, barley, or Hatcho miso
2 eggs
1 tablespoon minced parsley (optional)

Heat a skillet and coat with the oil. Add onion and sauté for 5 minutes, then add water and bring to a boil. Add cooked noodles and return to the boil. Stir in miso creamed in a little of the hot broth. Now increase heat to medium-high and carefully break in the eggs, keeping the yolks whole. Cook for 1 minute more, or until whites are just firm. Serve immediately, garnished with parsley.

Miso Ozoni
SERVES 3

Ozoni is a soup containing *mochi* (pounded rice cakes) served daily in Japan during the week of festivities that begins on New Year's Day. Neither the usual cooked rice nor miso soup are served throughout this period; Ozoni takes their place and is eaten with special, thick chopsticks *(zoni-bashi)* which help to pluck out the soft mochi while also serving as a symbol of the holiday season. In the Kyoto area, freshly-prepared *mochi* dumplings are served in a rich soup made with sweet white miso and generally containing taro, *daikon*, carrot, grilled tofu, and a garnish of grated bonita flakes. The *mochi* partially melts in the hot soup, imparting to it a thick, almost creamy consistency. In country farmhouses, the *mochi* is often broiled and—to prevent its dissolution—added at the last minute to soups prepared with red miso. Fresh or broiled *mochi* may be added to many of the miso soups given in this section. Or try this country-style preparation:

2 cups dashi (p. 56) or stock
1 leek, cut diagonally into ½-inch-thick ovals, separated into greens and whites
7 ounces deep-fried tofu, thinly sliced
3 tablespoons red, barley, or Hatcho miso
3 cakes of *mochi* (each 2 by 1½ by ½ inches), broiled until speckled then pierced in several places with a chopstick or fork

Combine dashi, leek greens, and deep-fried tofu in a saucepan and bring to a boil. Add leek whites and stir in miso creamed in a little of the hot broth; return just to the boil. Pour into individual bowls, add *mochi*, and serve immediately.

Red & White Miso Soup with Swirled Eggs and Chives
SERVES 2

1¼ cups dashi (p. 56) or stock
1 teaspoon butter or oil
2/3 cup chopped chives or *nira*
1 tablespoon red, barley, or Hatcho miso
1½ tablespoons sweet white or 1 tablespoon mellow white miso
1 egg, lightly beaten
¼ to ½ teaspoon grated gingerroot or ½ teaspoon powdered ginger

Heat dashi in a small saucepan over medium heat. Meanwhile heat a skillet and coat with the butter. Add chives and sauté for 20 to 30 seconds. Add to dashi and bring to a boil. Add miso creamed in a little of the hot broth and return to the boil. Stir in eggs a little at a time, then remove from heat. Serve immediately, topped with a dab of gingerroot.

For a richer flavor and thicker consistency, combine with the eggs before stirring into the soup: 1½ teaspoons sake or white wine and 1 teaspoon *kuzu* (kudzu powder) or cornstarch, dissolved in 1 tablespoon water.

Mushroom Miso Soup
SERVES 2

1½ tablespoons butter
6 mushrooms, thinly sliced
1 small onion, thinly sliced
2 cups dashi (p. 56), stock, or water
3 tablespoons akadashi or 2½ tablespoons red miso
2 tablespoons minced parsley or thinly sliced leeks

Melt the butter in a heavy skillet. Add mushrooms and onion, and sauté until onions are just transparent. Add dashi and bring to a boil. Add miso creamed in a little of the hot broth and return just to the boil. Serve hot garnished with parsley.

Mushroom & Tofu Miso Soup
SERVES 6

The following is a description of the method used to prepare the daily miso soup in a large, well-known Japanese restaurant. Each ingredient has been reduced to about one-eighth its usual quantity. Notice the integrated preparation of both Number 1 and Number 2 Dashi along with a basic *shiitaké* dashi.

1½ cups (5 ounces) dried *shiitaké* mushrooms, soaked for 10 hours (overnight) in 2 cups water
½ cup (¾ ounce) round-herring flakes *(urume iwashi)*
½ cup (medium salty) light-yellow miso
1/3 cup Hatcho miso
5½ cups water
60 (canned) *nameko* mushrooms
12 ounces silken (or regular) tofu, cut into ½-inch cubes
18 trefoil leaves (including stems)

Pour mushrooms into a colander set over a pot. Press mushrooms gently but firmly against bottom of colander to expel remaining liquid, then reserve mushrooms for use in other cooking.

Bring mushroom soaking water *(shiitaké dashi)* to a boil over high heat. Skim off any foam that may develop, then add herring flakes and return to the boil. Reduce heat to low, simmer for 5 minutes, and turn off heat.

Meanwhile, combine light-yellow and Hatcho miso with ¾ cup warm water in a mixing bowl. Mix well until miso is dissolved. Pour herring-*shiitaké* dashi through a fine-mesh strainer set over the mixing bowl and press herring flakes in strainer to expel all liquid.

Now combine herring flakes with 2 cups water in a saucepan to make a Number 2 Dashi. Bring this dashi to a boil and reduce heat to low; cover pan and simmer for 5 minutes.

While Number 2 Dashi is simmering, pour miso-dashi mixture through a fine-mesh strainer set over the pot. Remove particles of miso grain left in strainer and combine with 2 cups warm water. Mix well, then pour back through strainer into pot, reserving grain particles for use in other cooking.

Pour Number 2 Dashi through strainer into pot, discarding herring flakes. Now bring dashi in pot just to a boil, add *nameko* mushrooms and tofu, and remove from heat. Serve piping hot, garnished with trefoil leaves.

Butter & Lemon Soup
with Sweet Miso

SERVES 3 OR 4

2½ tablespoons butter
1 onion, minced
½ cup corn or green peas, parboiled
2 cups hot water or stock
2 teaspoons lemon juice
6 tablespoons sweet white or ¼ cup mellow white miso
Dash of pepper (optional)

Melt the butter in a heavy skillet. Add onion and corn, and sauté for 4 to 5 minutes. Stir in the hot water and bring to a boil. Add lemon juice and miso, creamed in a little of the hot broth, and return just to the boil. Serve hot, seasoned with pepper.

Sweet White Miso Potage

SERVES 2 OR 3

2 tablespoons butter
½ cup minced onion
1½ tablespoons whole-wheat flour
2 cups dashi (p. 56), stock, or water
6 tablespoons sweet white or ¼ cup mellow white miso
Dash of pepper
1 tablespoon minced parsley

Melt butter in a skillet. Add onion and sauté for 4 to 5 minutes. Reduce heat to low, add flour and sauté for 1 minute more. Add dashi a little at a time, stirring constantly until smooth. Mix in miso dissolved in a little of the hot broth, season with pepper, and return just to the boil. Serve topped with a sprinkling of parsley.

JAPANESE-STYLE MISO STEWS

In addition to its daily use in soups, miso is also employed as the essential seasoning in a number of stew-like preparations, most of which are made with soybeans or tofu and have enough body and protein to serve as a main course. Kenchin-jiru, Tanuki-jiru, and Gôjiru are the three most famous representatives of these dinnertime specialties.

Kenchin-jiru

SERVES 5

1½ tablespoons sesame oil
18 ounces tofu, pressed (p.55) and broken into small pieces
½ cup shaved burdock root
1 cup half-moons of *daikon*
5 *shiitaké* or cloud-ear mushrooms, thinly sliced
1 to 1¼ cups large irregular chunks of sweet potato, yam, or taro
½ cup carrot (cut into ginkgo leaves; p. 54)
½ cake of *konnyaku*, broken into small pieces and lightly salted
2¼ cups dashi (p. 56), stock, or water
5 tablespoons red, barley, or Hatcho miso
¼ teaspoon salt
2 teaspoons sake or *mirin*
Garnishes: 7-spice red pepper, slivered leeks, crumbled *nori*, and/or grated lemon or *yuzu* rind

Heat the oil in a heavy-bottomed saucepan. Add consecutively: tofu, burdock root, *daikon*, mushrooms, sweet potato, carrot, and *konnyaku*, sautéing each over medium heat for about 1 minute. Reduce heat to low, and add broth, miso, salt, and sake. Cover pan and simmer for 30 to 40 minutes, or until *daikon* is transparent. For best flavor, allow to stand for 6 to 8 hours, then serve individual portions topped with a sprinkling of the garnishes.

VARIATION

Tanuki-jiru (Badger's Soup): Omit all vegetables except the burdock root and carrot, and triple the amounts of both of these. Use barley miso.

Gôjiru

SERVES 4 TO 6

This thick miso soup prepared with *gô*, a purée of well-soaked soybeans, is a wintertime favorite in Japan's snowy northeast provinces. It can be prepared using a wide range of vegetables, seasonings, and garnishes; experiment with whatever is available, in season, or simply appealing.

½ cup soybeans, rinsed and soaked for 8 to 10 hours in 1 quart water
4½ cups water, stock, or dashi (p. 56)
2 tablespoons oil
1 onion, thinly sliced; or 1 leek, cut into 2-inch lengths
½ carrot, cut into thin half moons
2 ounces deep-fried tofu, cut into thin strips
3 mushrooms, thinly sliced
2 inches *daikon*, cut into half moons; or ½ cup chopped celery
1 potato, sweet potato, yam, or taro, diced
5 to 6 tablespoons red, barley, or Hatcho miso

Rinse, then drain beans in a colander. Combine beans and ¾ cup water in a blender and purée at high speed for about 3 minutes, or until smooth.

Heat a heavy pot and coat with the oil. Add the next six ingredients and sauté for 5 to 10 minutes, or until potatoes are softened. Add soybean purée and remaining 3¾ cups water, bring to a boil, and simmer uncovered for 10 to 15 minutes, stirring occasionally. Add miso thinned in a few tablespoons of the hot broth and simmer for 1 minute more. Serve immediately or, for a richer, sweeter flavor, allow to cool for at least 6 hours.

VARIATIONS

*Any of the following garnishes or seasonings may be added to the soup with the miso or sprinkled on top of individual servings: 7-spice red pepper, green *nori* flakes, *sansho* pepper; minced trefoil, sake lees, slivered *yuzu* or lemon rind; pepper, crushed garlic, croutons, sage, or thyme.
*Experiment using other vegetables such as green beans, celery (including leaves), snow peas, *kombu*, or shelled green soybeans. For extra richness, try adding 2 lightly beaten eggs or 2 thinly sliced, deep-fried potatoes together with the miso.

WESTERN-STYLE SOUPS AND STEWS

Miso can be used to combine the functions of a hearty bouillon- or meat broth and a savory seasoning. Try substituting about 1 tablespoon of red, barley, or Hatcho for each ½ teaspoon salt in your favorite recipes. To keep the miso aroma, flavor, and nutrients at their peak of goodness, remember to add the creamed miso just before the end of cooking.

Thick French Onion Soup with Miso
MAKES 4 CUPS; SERVES 4

Our favorite Western-style soup with miso, this dish reaches its peak of flavor after lengthy cooking and when allowed to stand overnight for the flavors to marry. It can, however, be served before the marriage night, while piping hot, and is still guaranteed to delight the senses of even Monsieur Brillat-Savarin.

2 tablespoons oil
6 onions, thinly sliced
3 tablespoons red, barley, or Hatcho miso, dissolved in 2 cups warm water
1 tablespoon butter
2 ounces cheese, grated or minced

Heat a large casserole or heavy pot and coat with the oil. Add onions, cover, and simmer over very low heat for 3½ hours, stirring every 20 to 30 minutes. Mix in dissolved miso and butter, return just to the boil, and remove from heat. Allow to cool, then refrigerate overnight. Stir in the cheese, bring to a boil and simmer, stirring constantly, for about 1 minute, or until cheese melts. Serve hot or, for a richer, sweeter flavor, allow to cool to room temperature.

For variety, add 10 ounces diced deep-fried or regular tofu, 1 more tablespoon miso and, if desired, 2 lightly beaten eggs 15 minutes before adding miso.

Thick Winter Squash Soup with Miso
SERVES 4 OR 5

1½ tablespoons oil
1 pound seeded *(kabocha)* pumpkin, squash, or zucchini, cut into ½-inch squares
2 onions, thinly sliced
2 cups water or stock
¼ teaspoon nutmeg or cinnamon
1 clove garlic, minced
4 tablespoons red, barley, or Hatcho miso
3 tablespoons parsley, minced
½ cup croutons or dry bread pieces
2 tablespoons ground roasted sesame seeds (p. 54) (optional)

Heat the oil in a casserole or large pot. Add pumpkin and onion, and sauté for 3 minutes. Add water, cover, and bring to a boil. Reduce heat to low and simmer for 25 minutes. Stir in nutmeg, garlic, and miso thinned in a little of the hot soup, and return just to the boil; remove from heat. For best flavor, allow to cool to room temperature, then serve cold or reheated, topped with parsley, croutons and, if used, the sesame seeds. Also nice pureed in a blender.

For a slightly richer flavor, add 2 tablespoons butter and/or finely-shaved bonito flakes together with the miso.

Tomato & Cottage Cheese Soup with Miso
SERVES 2

1 tablespoon butter
2 small tomatoes, peeled and thinly sliced
½ onion, thinly sliced
1 green pepper, seeded and diced
1 bay leaf (optional)
1 cup water or stock
1½ tablespoons red, barley, or Hatcho miso
6 tablespoons cottage cheese
Dash of pepper
Dash of oregano (optional)
3 to 4 tablespoons Parmesan cheese

Melt butter in a skillet. Add the next four ingredients and sauté for 3 minutes, or until tomato dissolves. Add water and bring to a boil. Stir in miso dissolved in a little of the hot broth. Add cottage cheese, mixing lightly, and return just to the boil. Remove from heat. Remove bay leaf and serve hot, seasoned with the pepper and oregano and topped with a sprinkling of the cheese.

Thick Corn & Tomato Soup with Miso

SERVES 2

1 tablespoon oil
1½ small onions, thinly sliced
½ cup corn kernels
1 large tomato, diced
1 cup milk (soy or dairy)
2½ tablespoons red, barley, or Hatcho miso
Dash of pepper or a dab of mustard
¼ teaspoon oregano or marjoram
1 tablespoon minced parsley

Heat a pot and coat with the oil. Add onion and corn and sauté for 4 minutes. Add tomato and sauté for 2 to 3 minutes more. Stir in the milk and miso, and season with pepper and oregano. Cook for about 1 minute, whisking or stirring constantly, but do not bring to a boil. Remove from heat and allow to cool to body temperature. Transfer to a blender and purée until smooth. Return to the pot and bring just to a boil. Serve hot or cold, topped with a sprinkling of parsley.

Creamy Corn & Cheese Soup with Miso

SERVES 3

1 tablespoon oil
1 onion, minced
1 cup grated carrot
1 cup fresh corn kernels
2 cups water or stock
1 cup grated cheese
2 tablespoons red, barley, or Hatcho miso
1½ tablespoons sweet white or 1 tablespoon mellow white miso
Dash of pepper
1 tablespoon minced parsley

Heat a heavy pot or deep skillet and coat with the oil. Add consecutively: onion, carrot and corn, sautéing each for 3 minutes. Stir in water, cover, and bring to a boil; simmer for 10 minutes. Add cheese and both varieties of miso creamed in a little of the hot broth. Return just to the boil, then season with pepper and top with parsley. Serve hot or cold.

For extra protein and flavor, add 5 to 10 ounces diced tofu (deep-fried or regular) together with the miso, increasing the miso by 1½ to 3 teaspoons.

Refreshing Yogurt Soup with Miso

SERVES 2

1 tablespoon butter
1 small onion, thinly sliced
1 green pepper, sliced into thin rings
1 cup dashi (p. 56) or stock
1½ tablespoons red, barley, or Hatcho miso
¼ cup yogurt
Dash of pepper

Melt the butter in a skillet. Add onion and green pepper, and sauté for 3 minutes. Add dashi and bring to a boil. Stir in miso creamed in a little of the hot broth, then mix in yogurt and return to the boil. Season with pepper and serve immediately.

Vichyssoise with Miso

SERVES 4

2 tablespoons butter
1 cup minced leek whites and/or (wild) onions
2 potatoes, thinly sliced
2 cups water or stock
2 tablespoons red, barley, or Hatcho miso
1½ cups cream or rich soymilk
Dash of pepper
Chopped chives or watercress (optional)

Melt the butter in a skillet. Add leeks or onions and sauté for 3 minutes. Add potatoes, water and miso (creamed in a few tablespoons of the water). Simmer, covered, for 15 minutes, then cool briefly. Purée in a blender until smooth. Add cream and pepper and purée again. Chill thoroughly. Serve topped with the chives.

Potato & Onion Soup with White Miso

SERVES 2

4 small potatoes (2½-inch diameter), peeled and cut into halves
1 small onion, thinly sliced
2 cups water or stock
1 bay leaf
5 tablespoons sweet white or 3 tablespoons mellow white miso
2 tablespoons Parmesan cheese
Dash of pepper
1 tablespoon parsley

Combine the first four ingredients in a saucepan and bring to a boil. Cover and simmer over low heat for 1 hour. Remove bay leaf, add miso creamed in a little of the hot broth, and stir in Parmesan. Season with pepper and return just to the boil. Serve chilled, topped with a sprinkling of parsley.

For variety, substitute sweet potatoes, *kabocha*, squash, or lentils for the potatoes.

Potato, Cottage Cheese & Chive Soup with Miso

SERVES 2

The cottage cheese in this dish works somewhat like tofu in traditional Japanese miso soups, but since some of the cottage cheese melts, it gives the soup a rich, slightly creamy consistency.

1 tablespoon butter
2 small potatoes, cut into thin rectangles (1¼ cups)
5 tablespoons chives, *nira*, or wild onions, chopped
1¼ cups water or stock
2 tablespoons red, barley, or Hatcho miso
½ cup cottage cheese

Melt the butter in a skillet. Add potatoes and ¼ cup chives, and sauté for 2 minutes. Add water and simmer for about 7 minutes. Stir in miso creamed in a little of the hot broth. Add cottage cheese, mix lightly, and return just to the boil. Serve immediately, garnished with the remaining 1 tablespoon chives.

Potato & Miso Soup with Milk, Cheese & Tofu

SERVES 3

1½ tablespoons butter
1 potato, cut into pieces 3 inches long and ½ inch square
5 ounces deep-fried or 12 ounces regular tofu, cut crosswise into thin slices
1 cup dashi (p. 56), stock, or water
2 to 2½ tablespoons red, barley, or Hatcho miso
1 cup milk (soy or dairy)
2 tablespoons minced leeks, scallions, or onions
Dash of pepper
¼ cup grated cheese or parboiled green peas (optional)

Melt the butter in a skillet. Add potato pieces and sauté for 5 minutes, then transfer to a separate container. Add tofu to skillet, sauté for 3 minutes, and remove from heat.

Bring dashi to a boil in a small saucepan. Add the miso creamed in a little of the hot dashi, then add potatoes, tofu and milk. Return just to the boil before removing from heat. Sprinkle on leeks, pepper, and cheese. Serve immediately.

Instant Miso (Better 'n Coffee) Soup

SERVES 1

½ cup very hot or boiling water
Miso: Choose one
    2 teaspoons red, barley, Hatcho, or light yellow
    4 teaspoons mellow white
    6 teaspoons sweet white

Place miso in a cup or small bowl and add hot water a little at a time, stirring until smooth. Serve immediately; a good way to start the day off right!

Cream of Mushroom Soup with Miso

SERVES 3

2 tablespoons butter
2 cups diced mushrooms (about 16)
½ cup thinly sliced onion
¼ cup chopped celery
1 cup water or stock
2 tablespoons minced parsley
5 to 6 teaspoons red, barley, or Hatcho miso
1½ tablespoons white wine or sake
Dash of pepper
½ cup Miso White Sauce (p. 114)

Melt the butter in a saucepan. Add mushrooms and sauté for 2 to 3 minutes. Add onion, celery, water, and 1 tablespoon parsley; cover and bring to a boil. Simmer over low heat for 20 minutes. Remove from heat, uncover, and allow to cool briefly. Transfer to a blender, add miso, white wine and pepper, and purée until smooth. Return to saucepan, stir in white sauce, and bring just to a boil. Serve hot or chilled, garnished with the remaining 1 tablespoon parsley.

For variety, add 12 ounces diced regular tofu or 5 ounces deep-fried tofu together with the white sauce. For best flavor, allow to stand overnight, then serve chilled.

Mushroom & Onion Soup with White Miso

SERVES 2

2 tablespoons butter
6 mushrooms, diced (½ cup)
½ onion, thinly sliced
1¼ cups water or stock
2 tablespoon sweet white or 4 teaspoons mellow white miso
1 tablespoon red, barley, or Hatcho miso
2 tablespoons Parmesan cheese
Dash of pepper
1 tablespoon minced parsley

Melt the butter in a skillet. Add mushrooms and onions, and sauté for 4 minutes. Add water and bring to a boil. Add miso creamed in a little of the hot broth, then stir in Parmesan; season with pepper and return just to the boil. Serve topped with a sprinkling of parsley.

Almost Pudding Soup with Miso

SERVES 3

1½ teaspoons butter
½ cup minced onion
1½ cups diced whole-wheat bread
2 cups milk (soy or dairy)
2½ tablespoons red, barley, or Hatcho miso
1 small egg
Dash of freshly-grated nutmeg
1 tablespoon minced parsley

Melt the butter in a skillet, add onions and sauté for 5 minutes. Add bread pieces and 1½ cups milk, and bring just to a boil. Remove from heat, cover, and allow to stand for 20 minutes. Mix well with a whisk or fork to give a smooth texture. Combine miso and egg with remaining ½ cup milk, mixing well, then stir into soup. Return to heat and bring just to a boil, whisking constantly. Mix in nutmeg and serve hot or cold, topped with a sprinkling of parsley.

For use as a dessert, add ¼ to ½ cup raisins together with the nutmeg.

Tomato Juice & Onion Soup with White Miso

SERVES 3

1 tablespoon oil
1 small onion, thinly sliced
2 mushrooms, thinly sliced
¾ cup tomato juice
1 cup dashi (p. 56), stock, or water
2 tablespoons sweet white or 4 teaspoons mellow white miso
1 teaspoon red, barley, or Hatcho miso
1 tablespoon minced parsley

Heat a saucepan and coat with the oil. Add onion and mushrooms, and sauté for 5 minutes. Add dashi and tomato juice, bring to a boil, and simmer for 3 minutes. Add creamed miso and return just to the boil. Serve hot or chilled topped with a sprinkling of parsley.

Carrot Juice Soup with Miso

SERVES 2 OR 3

2 teaspoons oil
¼ onion, thinly sliced
¼ cabbage leaf, shredded
¼ carrot, grated or cut into thin rounds
1 small potato, yam, or sweet potato, diced into ¼-inch cubes
¾ cup carrot- or tomato juice
¾ cup water or stock
4 teaspoons red, barley, or Hatcho miso
3 tablespoons Parmesan cheese
Dash of oregano or pepper
1 tablespoon minced parsley

Heat a skillet and coat with the oil. Add the next four ingredients and sauté for 2 minutes. Add juice and water, bring to a boil, and simmer, covered, for 20 minutes. Add miso creamed in a little of the hot broth; stir in Parmesan, season with oregano, and return just to the boil. Serve topped with a sprinkling of parsley.

Chilled Cucumber & Yogurt Soup with Miso

SERVES 2

1 cucumber, sliced into thin rounds
2 tablespoons minced onion
1½ cups stock or water
1½ tablespoons red, barley, or Hatcho miso
Dash of pepper
2 tablespoons flour
½ bay leaf or 1 clove
½ cup yogurt
½ teaspoon caraway seeds or 1½ teaspoons grated lemon rind, dill, or chives

Combine cucumber, onion, and ½ cup stock in a saucepa
Bring to a boil, cover, and simmer for 15 minutes. Allow i
cool for 10 minutes. Stir in miso and pepper, transfer to blender, and purée until smooth.

Combine flour and ¼ cup stock, mixing well, then gradually add the remaining ¾ cup stock, stirring until smooth. Combine with the cucumber purée in a saucepan, add bay leaf, and bring to a boil. Cover and simmer for 2 to 3 minutes. Cool to room temperature and remove bay leaf. Mix in yogurt and caraway. Serve chilled.

Chilled Cucumber & Tahini Soup with Miso

SERVES 2

1¼ cups dashi (p. 56) or stock
1 tablespoon red, barley, or Hatcho miso
1½ tablespoons sweet white or 1 tablespoon mellow white miso
1 tablespoon *tahini* or sesame butter
1 cucumber, sliced into thin rounds
Dash of (7-spice) red pepper or tabasco sauce (optional)

Bring dashi to a boil in a small saucepan. Add miso and *tahini*,

both creamed in a little of the hot broth. Add cucumber and return to the boil. Serve chilled, seasoned with the red pepper.

VARIATION

*Chilled Cucumber & Tomato White Miso Soup. Omit red miso and *tahini*. Use ¼ cup sweet white miso. Add 1 small tomato (cut into wedges) together with cucumber. Season with black pepper and garnish with minced parsley.

Basic Miso Soup

SERVES 4 TO 6

Featuring the most widely used and inexpensive vegetables, this easy-to-make recipe is a favorite year-round, day after day.

2 teaspoons oil
1 cup sliced onions
1 cup sliced carrots
2 cups chopped cabbage
4 cups water or stock
3½ tablespoons red, barley, or Hatcho miso
2 tablespoons minced parsley or scallions

Heat the oil in a wok or heavy pot. Add onion and carrots and sauté for 3 to 4 minutes. Add cabbage and sauté for 2 minutes more. Add water, cover, bring to a boil, and simmer for 15 minutes. Stir in miso creamed with a little of the broth, then remove from heat. Serve topped with a sprinkling of parsley. Delicious hot or cold. Chilled, pureed leftovers are especially tasty.

For variety, add 1 cup diced potatoes together with the carrots.

Velvet Zucchini Miso Soup

SERVES 4

A wonderful way to make use of the summer garden's overflowing zucchini crop and to cool and refresh the body on hot summer afternoons or evenings. Leftovers may be frozen indefinitely.

1 tablespoon oil
½ onion, sliced
1¼ cups chopped celery (2 stalks)
2½ cups diced zucchini
3 cups water or stock
3½ tablespoons red, barley, or Hatcho miso
2 tablespoons minced parsley

Heat the oil in a wok or heavy pot. Add onion and sauté for 2 to 3 minutes. Add celery and zucchini and sauté for another 2 to 3 minutes. Add the water or stock, cover, and simmer for 5 minutes, then remove from heat. Stir in miso creamed with a little of the cooking broth. Allow to cool briefly, then puree in a blender until smooth. Serve chilled, topped with a sprinkling of the parsley. In colder months, this recipe is also nice served unpureed and piping hot.

Onion Soup with Ketchup & Miso   SERVES 2 OR 3

1 tablespoon butter
1 onion, thinly sliced
1¼ cups water or stock
4 teaspoons red, barley, or Hatcho miso
3 tablespoons ketchup or tomato paste
Dash of pepper
2 tablespoons Parmesan cheese
1 tablespoon minced parsley

Melt the butter in a skillet. Add onion and sauté for 5 minutes, then add water and bring to a boil. Stir in miso creamed with ketchup, add pepper and cheese, and return just to the boil. Serve topped with a sprinkling of parsley.

Quick Cream of Onion Soup   SERVES 3
   with Miso

2 tablespoons oil
3 onions, thinly sliced
2½ cups water or stock
3 tablespoons whole-wheat flour
3 tablespoons red, barley, or Hatcho miso
Dash of pepper
1 tablespoon minced parsley

Heat a pressure cooker and coat with the oil. Add onions and sauté for 3 minutes. Add 2 cups water, cover, and bring to full pressure (15 pounds). Reduce heat and cook for 5 minutes, then allow pressure to come down naturally.

Meanwhile, heat a skillet and coat with remaining 1 tablespoon oil. Add flour and sauté for 2 minutes, or until fragrant. Slowly add ½ cup water, stirring constantly, to make a thick sauce. Add miso and pepper, mixing until smooth. Open pressure cooker, mix sauce into onions, and bring just to a boil. Serve hot or, for a richer flavor, allow to stand overnight and serve reheated or cold, garnished with parsley.

Azuki-Vegetable Soup with Miso   SERVES 4 TO 6

1 cup azuki beans, rinsed and drained
3 cups water
1 tablespoon oil
1 onion, thinly sliced
1 small carrot, cut into matchsticks or grated
4 tablespoons red, barley, or Hatcho miso
2 tablespoons honey
2 tablespoons sesame butter
¼ teaspoon cinnamon or nutmeg

Combine beans and water in a pressure cooker. Bring to full pressure (15 pounds), reduce heat to low and cook for 40 minutes. Remove from heat and allow to stand for 15 minutes while pressure comes down naturally.

Heat a skillet and coat with the oil. Add onions and carrot, and sauté for 5 minutes; remove from heat. Add miso, honey, sesame butter, cinnamon, and several tablespoons hot cooking liquid from the beans. Mix thoroughly, then stir miso-vegetable mixture into the beans in the cooker. For best flavor, allow to cool, then refrigerate for at least 8, preferably 24, hours. Serve cold or reheated.

Thick Lentil or Split Pea Soup   SERVES 4 OR 5
   with Miso

1 cup lentils or split peas, rinsed and drained
5 to 5½ cups water or stock
2 tablespoons oil
½ cup thinly sliced onions
½ cup thinly sliced carrots or diced yams
¾ cup chopped celery (with leaves)
1 clove of garlic, crushed
3½ tablespoons red, barley, or Hatcho miso, creamed with
   ¼ cup water
2 tablespoons butter
½ teaspoon oregano, thyme, or rosemary
Dash of black or red pepper; or ½ teaspoon nutmeg
2 to 4 tablespoons ground roasted sesame seeds (p. 54)
   (optional)
1 tablespoon minced parsley

Combine lentils and water in a large pot and soak overnight. Bring to a boil and simmer for about 2 hours, stirring occasionally, until quite thick. (Or reduce water to 2½ cups and pressure cook at 15 pounds for 20 minutes.)

Meanwhile, heat a skillet and coat with the oil. Add onions, carrots, celery and garlic, and sauté for about 5 minutes. Add ¼ cup water, cover, and simmer for 10 to 15 minutes, or until water has been absorbed or evaporated.

When soup has finished cooking, stir in miso, butter, oregano, and sautéed vegetables. Cover and allow to stand for at least 10 minutes; serve topped with a sprinkling of sesame and parsley. (For a richer flavor, refrigerate overnight and serve as is or reheated.)

Creamy Cauliflower & Tofu Soup with Miso

SERVES 4

1 tablespoon oil
1 onion, thinly sliced
1½ to 2 cups cauliflowerets, parboiled (p. 54)
2 tablespoons butter
2 tablespoons whole-wheat flour
1 cup milk
½ cup water
2 ounces cheese, grated or finely diced
12 ounces regular or 5 ounces deep-fried tofu, cut into small rectangles
2 tablespoons light-yellow or red miso
Dash of pepper

Heat a casserole and coat with the oil. Add onion and sauté for 3 minutes, or until lightly browned. Add cauliflower and sauté for 1 minute more, then turn off heat.

Using the butter, flour, and milk, prepare a white sauce (p. 114). Add the sauce and water to the casserole, cover, and simmer over low heat for 5 minutes. Add cheese and tofu, increase heat to medium, and cook for 3 minutes. Stir in the miso thinned in a little of the cooking broth, season with pepper, and return just to the boil. Serve hot or, for a richer, sweeter flavor, allow to cool before serving.

Miso Stew

SERVES 4 TO 5

This hearty dish resembles a very thick miso soup prepared with sautéed vegetables.

1½ tablespoons sesame oil
3 onions, cut into thin wedges
½ carrot, cut into half moons
2 potatoes or 4 taro cut into irregular chunks (1½ cups)
1½ cups sliced (Chinese) cabbage or 1 cup thin rounds of *daikon*
3 cups water or stock
5½ tablespoons red, barley, or Hatcho miso
2 tablespoons minced parsley (optional)

Heat a heavy pot or skillet and coat with the oil. Add the four vegetables consecutively, sautéing each for about 1 minute. Add the water and bring to a boil. Reduce heat to low, cover, and simmer for 15 minutes. Stir in miso creamed in a little of the hot broth and return just to the boil. For best flavor, allow to cool for 6 to 8 hours. Serve as is or reheated, garnished with the parsley.

For added body and protein, substitute for the potatoes 12 to 18 ounces regular or 5 to 7 ounces deep-fried tofu. Use other seasonal vegetables.

Open-hearth fireplace

Miso in Sauces

Whether Western-style or Oriental, Near Eastern or Latin American, any sauce is enhanced by the presence of miso. Creamy Tofu Dressings also work well, especially with grains and vegetables.

Miso & Nutritional Yeast Gravy FOR 2 to 3 SERVINGS

¼ cup butter or margarine
¼ cup nutritional yeast (we prefer the good-tasting Red Star brand)
¼ cup whole-wheat flour
2 tablespoons red miso, dissolved in 1½ to 1¾ cups hot water

Melt the butter in a skillet. Add nutritional yeast and mix well for 30 seconds. Add flour and sauté for 1 minute. Add the hot miso-water mixture a little at a time, stirring constantly to create a thick, creamy consistency. When all is added, bring just to the boil, then remove from heat. Delicious served over cooked grains (brown rice, noodles, millet), baked potatoes, cooked vegetables (broccoli, cauliflower, etc.), or fried tempeh or tofu.

Miso Onion Sauce SERVES 4

3 tablespoons (sesame) oil
4 onions, thinly sliced
2½ to 3 tablespoons red, barley, or Hatcho miso, thinned in 2/3 cup water

Heat the oil in a large, heavy skillet. Add onions and sauté for 5 minutes. Add thinned miso, cover pan, and simmer for 30 minutes, or until most of the liquid has been absorbed or evaporated. For best flavor, allow to stand for 6 to 8 hours. Serve as is or reheated. Delicious over grain dishes, toast, steamed vegetables, or tofu. Or serve as a side dish.

This sauce may also be prepared by starting with Thick French Onion Soup (p. 107); add the miso dissolved in 3 tablespoons (rather than 2 cups) warm water.

VARIATION

*Seasoned Onion Sauce with Nut Butters: Thin your favorite nut butter with a small amount of water or stock and, if desired, some lemon or orange juice, and add to 2 parts Onion Sauce. Season with herbs, 7-spice red pepper, shoyu, or miso.

Garnish with thinly sliced green onions or parsley. For variety, add large chunks of nuts, diced cheese, or sprouts.

Miso-Gingerroot Ankaké Sauce MAKES 1 CUP

2/3 cup dashi (p. 56), stock, or water
4 to 4½ tablespoons red, barley, or Hatcho miso
1 tablespoon honey or 2 tablespoons (natural) sugar
2 teaspoons arrowroot, cornstarch, or *kuzu* (kudzu powder) dissolved in 2 tablespoons water
2 teaspoons freshly grated gingerroot

Combine dashi, miso, and honey in a small saucepan. Bring to a boil, then stir in dissolved arrowroot and gingerroot. Cook for about 1 minute or until thick.

Miso-Lemon Ankaké Sauce MAKES 1¼ CUPS

1 cup dashi (p. 56), stock, or water
2½ tablespoons red, barley, or Hatcho miso
1½ teaspoons honey or 1 tablespoon (natural) sugar
2 teaspoons cornstarch, arrow root, or *kuzu* (kudzu powder), dissolved in 1½ tablespoons water
½ teaspoon grated lemon rind

Combine dashi, miso, and honey in a small saucepan, mixing well. Bring to a boil, stir in dissolved cornstarch and lemon rind, and cook for about 1 minute more until thick. Serve over cooked vegetables, tofu, or broiled *mochi*.

Miso-Mushroom Sauce FOR 3 SERVINGS

1½ tablespoons butter
½ teaspoon minced or crushed garlic
1 tablespoon minced onion
½ teaspoon grated gingerroot
5 mushrooms, thinly sliced
1/3 cup ketchup
1 tablespoon red, barley, or Hatcho miso
Dash of pepper

Melt the butter in a skillet. Add garlic, onion and gingerroot, and sauté for 1 minute. Add mushrooms and sauté for 2 minutes. Stir in ketchup and miso, season with pepper, and sauté for 1 minute more. Delicious with most grain dishes, especially *tacos* or *tortillas*, and with deep-fried or barbecued foods.

Miso White Sauce

MAKES 1 CUP

Also known as Cream- or Béchamel Sauce, this traditional Western favorite acquires a distinctive flavor and creaminess when seasoned with miso. Season lightly for use with vegetables and more prominently for use with tofu dishes.

2 tablespoons butter or oil
2 tablespoons (whole-wheat) flour
1 cup milk (soy or dairy) or stock
3 to 4 teaspoons red, barley, or Hatcho miso; or 2 to 2½
    tablespoons sweet white or mellow white miso
Dash of pepper, paprika, or cayenne
1 tablespoon minced parsley (optional)

Melt the butter (or heat oil) in a skillet. Add flour and, stirring constantly, cook over low heat for 1 to 2 minutes, or until four is well blended and its raw taste has vanished. Add ½ cup milk (or stock) a little at a time, continuing to stir, then mix in the miso and slowly add the remainder of the milk. Increase heat to medium and cook, whisking or stirring, for 3 to 4 minutes more, or until sauce develops a smooth, thickened consistency. Stir in pepper (and parsley) and remove from heat.

VARIATIONS

*Cheese-Miso White Sauce: Sauté 1 clove of crushed garlic in butter for 30 seconds before adding flour. Add ½ teaspoon dry mustard and ½ cup grated cheese several minutes before removing from heat.
*Lemon-Miso White Sauce: Add 2 teaspoons lemon juice (and ¼ teaspoon grated lemon rind) about 1 minute before removing from heat.
*Herb Sauce: Add or substitute for the parsley any of the following, preferably fresh: thyme, basil, oregano, or beefsteak leaves.
*Mushroom-Miso White Sauce: Just after adding the last of the milk, add ¼ diced onion and 6 thinly-sliced mushrooms. Stirring constantly, simmer over low heat for 4 to 5 minutes. Then add 1 teaspoon lemon juice, the pepper, and 1 tablespoon white wine or sake.
*Sesame-Miso White Sauce: Add 1 tablespoon sesame butter or *tahini* several minutes before removing from heat. Delicious over steamed cauliflower, mushrooms, chard, Brussels sprouts, or celery. Serve topped with a sprinkling of parsley.
*Tofu-Miso White Sauce: Use 4 teaspoons red miso. Add 12 ounces regular tofu (mashed) or 7½ ounces deep-fried tofu (diced) about 2 minutes before removing from heat.
*Brown Sauce: Prepare as for a white sauce except cook the flour until it is lightly browned and fragrant.

Miso-Spaghetti Sauce

SERVES 3 OR 4

2 tablespoons oil
2 small onions, thinly sliced
1 clove of garlic, crushed
10 mushrooms, thinly sliced
5 tomatoes, diced,
3 green peppers, diced
½ carrot, grated or thinly sliced
2 cups water or stock
2 bay leaves
4½ tablespoons red, barley, or Hatcho miso
1 tablespoon butter
Dash of pepper
Dash of oregano and/or basil
1/3 cup grated or Parmesan cheese

Heat a heavy pot and coat with the oil. Add onions and garlic and sauté for about 3 minutes. Add the next four ingredients and sauté for 4 minutes more. Add water, drop in bay leaves, and bring to a boil. Simmer uncovered for 10 minutes. Mix in miso and next three ingredients; simmer, stirring every 5 minutes, for 1 hour. For best flavor, allow to stand for 6 to 8 hours. Remove bay leaves and serve hot or cold over buckwheat noodles or spaghetti. Top with cheese.

VARIATIONS

*With Soybeans: Add together with the miso in the basic recipe: 1 cup stock (soybean cooking liquid or mushroom soaking water), 1½ tablespoons additional red miso, and 2¼ cups cooked soybeans (p. 129). Proceed as above; serve topped with an additional 3 tablespoons grated or Parmesan cheese. Also delicious served chilled as a dish in its own right.
*With Tofu: Add 12 to 24 ounces diced regular tofu (or 5 to 10 ounces deep-fried tofu) together with the miso; simmer covered. Mix in ½ cup additional grated cheese just before removing from heat.

Miso Taco or Pizza Sauce

MAKES 1¼ CUPS

2/3 cup ketchup
1¼ cup grated cheese
2 tablespoons red, barley, or Hatcho miso
2 tablespoon minced onion, leek, or scallion
1 teaspoon grated gingerroot (optional)
1 teaspoon sake or white wine
Dash of tabasco sauce
Dash of pepper
1 tablespoon water

Combine all ingredients, mixing well. For best flavor, allow to stand for at least several hours before serving. Spread 3 to 4 teaspoons on each of 12 crisp buttered tortillas before topping with shredded lettuce, diced tomatoes, grated cheese, and your choice of other ingredients. Or use with pizza.

Quick Spaghetti Sauce with Miso & Tofu

SERVES 3 OR 4

1½ tablespoons oil
1 clove of garlic, crushed or minced
2 onions, diced
2 leaves of (Chinese) cabbage, thinly sliced
1 tomato, diced
1 cup ketchup
¼ cup water
2 green beefsteak leaves, minced, or 1 teaspoon grated
    gingerroot
10 ounces deep-fried or regular tofu, cubed
½ cup chives or *nira*
1/3 cup grated cheese
3 tablespoons butter
Dash of pepper
2 tablespoons red, barley, or Hatcho miso
½ cup Parmesan cheese
¼ cup minced parsley

Heat oil in a pot. Add the next four ingredients and sauté for 5 to 7 minutes, or until soft. Add ketchup, water, and beefsteak leaves, and simmer for 5 minutes. Add tofu, chives, and grated cheese, and simmer for 4 minutes more. Stir in the butter, pepper and the miso creamed in a little of the hot sauce. Stirring constantly, simmer for 1 more minute. For best flavor, remove from heat and allow to stand for 6 to 8 hours. Serve reheated or as is, topped with the cheese and parsley.

Pineapple Sweet & Sour Sauce with Miso

MAKES 1½ CUPS

1¼ cup pineapple chunks, drained
2½ teaspoons honey
3 tablespoons vinegar
½ cup water
3 tablespoons red, barley, or Hatcho miso
2 tablespoons ketchup
½ teaspoon grated gingerroot or 1 teaspoon powdered ginger
1 tablespoon cornstarch

Combine all ingredients in a saucepan, mixing well. Bring to a boil and cook, stirring constantly, for about 1 minute, or until thick. Delicious served over vegetables sautéed with a little garlic, or over brown rice, buckwheat noodles, or deep-fried tofu.

Orange-Sesame Miso Sauce

MAKES ½ CUP

3 tablespoons red, barley, or Hatcho Miso
1½ tablespoons sesame butter
1½ to 2 teaspoons honey
1 tablespoon sake or white wine
2 tablespoons water or dashi (p. 56)
¼ to ½ teaspoon grated orange rind
1 egg yolk (optional)

Combine all ingredients in a small saucepan or skillet. Simmer for 2 to 3 minutes over low heat, stirring constantly with a wooden spoon or spatula, until mixture has a slightly firmer consistency than that of regular miso. Serve hot or cold. Delicious as a topping for Furofuki Daikon (p. 140), fried eggplant slices, or crisp apple wedges; a dipping sauce for Miso Oden (p. 141); or slightly thinned as a sauce for potatoes, (kabocha) pumpkin, okra, or squash.

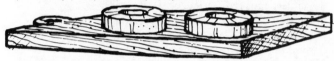

Garbanzo-Tahini Sauce with Miso (*Hummus bi Tahina*)

MAKES 4 CUPS

1 cup garbanzo beans, soaked for 3 hours in 3½ cups water
½ cup tahini
1 to 2 cloves of garlic, minced or crushed
2½ tablespoons lemon juice
2 tablespoons red or barley (or ¼ cup mellow white) miso
Dash of pepper and/or tabasco sauce
3 tablespoons minced parsley and/or a dash of paprika

Combine beans and soaking water in a pressure cooker, bring to full pressure (15 pounds), and simmer for 30 minutes. Remove from heat and allow to stand for 10 minutes while pressure returns to normal. Combine hot beans and remaining cooking liquid in a blender with the next five ingredients; purée until smooth. Serve hot or cold, topped with a sprinkling of parsley and/or paprika. Excellent served over rice, millet, buckwheat groats, or steamed greens. Also makes a delicious dip.

Sweet White Miso Sauce

MAKES 1 CUP

½ cup sweet white miso
½ cup water, stock, or dashi (p. 56)
1 tablespoon honey
¾ teaspoon sesame oil
¾ teaspoon tapioca, arrowroot, or cornstarch, dissolved in 1
    tablespoon water
1 teaspoon sake or white wine (optional)

Combine all ingredients in a heavy saucepan, bring to a boil, and simmer, stirring constantly, for 3 minutes, or until slightly thick. Delicious served over Grilled Tofu & Vegetables (p. 146) or Brussels sprouts.

Miso-Cream Cheese Sauce

MAKES ½ CUP

4 ounces cream cheese
2 teaspoons red or barley (or 4 teaspoons mellow white) miso
1 tablespoon Worcestershire sauce
3 tablespoons water or milk

Combine all ingredients and beat or blend together until smooth. Delicious over cooked vegetables such as broccoli, squash, or cauliflower.

Miso Gravy

MAKES 1½ CUPS

2 tablespoons butter
1 small onion, minced
3 tablespoons (whole-wheat or barley) flour
1½ tablespoons red, barley, or Hatcho miso
1 cup water
Dash of pepper

Melt 1 tablespoon butter in a skillet. Add onion and sauté for 5 minutes, or until soft and lightly browned. Add remaining 1 tablespoon butter; when melted, add flour and sauté for 2 to 3 minutes. Add miso and sauté for 30 seconds more. Now add the water a little at a time, stirring constantly; bring to a boil, season with pepper, and simmer for 1 minute. Delicious over steamed cauliflower or broccoli.

For a richer flavor use 2½ tablespoons miso. Serve as a topping for brown rice or deep-fried tofu.

Spicy Indoneisan Peanut Sauce with Miso (Gado-gado Sauce)

MAKES 2 CUPS

3 tablespoons oil
1 cup roasted (unsalted) peanuts
1 clove of garlic, crushed or minced
¼ to ½ teaspoon (7-spice) red pepper or tabasco sauce
1½ teaspoons honey
2½ tablespoons red, barley, or Hatcho miso
1½ cups stock, water, or (coconut) milk
¼ onion, minced
1 teaspoon minced parsley

Heat a wok or skillet and coat with 2 tablespoons oil. Add peanuts and sauté for 3 to 5 minutes, or until browned and fragrant. Mix in the next five ingredients and bring to a boil, then remove from heat and allow to cool briefly. Meanwhile, heat the remaining 1 tablespoon oil in a skillet. Add onion and sauté for 5 minutes, or until well browned. Transfer cooled peanut sauce to a blender and purée until smooth. Pour into a serving container, mix in sautéed onion, and top with a sprinkling of parsley. Serve hot or chilled over cooked rice or noodles, or lightly steamed vegetables (especially cabbage, cauliflower, or broccoli).

If Indonesian spices (kenchur, asam, or danjelpur) are available, add together with the red pepper.

Korean-style Miso Dipping Sauce

MAKES ¼ CUP

1½ tablespoons red, barley, or Hatcho miso
½ teaspoon sesame oil
¼ teaspoon crushed or minced garlic
1 tablespoon water
Dash of (7-spice) red pepper or tabasco sauce

Combine all ingredients, mixing well. Serve with broiled or deep-fried foods. Excellent with vegetarian Shish Kebab (p. 144).

Tangy Miso Chirizu Dipping Sauce

MAKES 1/3 CUP

2 tablespoons red, barley, or Hatcho miso
4 teaspoons lemon juice
2½ tablespoons grated daikon
2½ tablespoons thin rounds of leek or scallion
Dash of 7-spice red pepper or tabasco sauce

Combine all ingredients, mixing well. Serve with regular or deep-fried tofu, all nabé preparations, tempura, or croquettes.

Apple & Onion Curry Sauce with Deep-fried Tofu and Miso

SERVES 3 OR 4

7½ ounces deep fried tofu cutlets, burgers, or pouches, diced; or 18 ounces regular tofu
1 apple, diced
2 potatoes, diced (1¾ cups)
1 cup water or stock
3 tablespoons butter
1 clove of garlic, crushed
1 teaspoon grated or 1½ teaspoons powdered gingerroot
1½ onions, minced
5 to 6 mushrooms, thinly sliced
1½ to 2 teaspoons curry powder
2 tablespoons whole-wheat flour
3 to 3½ tablespoons red, barley, or Hatcho miso
1 tablespoon honey
2 tablespoons ketchup
Sambals: Sliced bananas, grated coconut, raisins, diced apples, peanuts or almonds, chopped hard-boiled eggs, and chutney

Combine the first four ingredients in a heavy pot or casserole and bring to a boil. Cover and simmer over low heat. Meanwhile melt the butter in a skillet. Add garlic and gingerroot, and sauté for 30 seconds. Add onions and mushrooms, and sauté for 5 to 6 minutes more. Mix in curry powder and flour, and cook, stirring constantly, for 1 minute. Cream miso with about 1/3 cup broth removed from the pot, then stir into the curried mixture together with the honey and ketchup to form a smooth, thick sauce. Now mix sauce into contents of pot, cover, and simmer for 20 to 30 minutes, stirring occasionally. Serve over brown rice or buckwheat noodles, topped with the sambals.

For a more elaborate sauce, add diced lotus root, cooked lentils, sweet potatoes, *kabocha*, or squash. To serve as an entrèe without grains, reduce the amounts of miso and curry powder by about one-fifth. Try substituting 1½ cups cooked soybeans for the tofu.

Tangy Miso, Ketchup & Lemon Sauce
MAKES ¾ CUP

½ cup ketchup
2 tablespoons red, barley, or Hatcho miso
1½ tablespoons lemon juice
1 tablespoon minced onion
1 tablespoon minced parsley
Dash of pepper

Combine all ingredients, mixing well. Serve with deep-fried, broiled, or barbecued foods. Also good with shrimp cocktail or seafoods.

For variety add any of the following: ¼ teaspoon hot mustard, 1 teaspoon horseradish, ½ teaspoon crushed anise or ground roasted sesame seeds, or 1 tablespoon minced parsley.

Sesame-Miso Sauce
MAKES 2/3 CUP

This recipe is good for use with vegetables such as cauliflower, spinach or turnips; use the hot cooking water as the basis of the sauce.

2 tablespoons red, barley, or Hatcho miso
1 tablespoon sesame butter
½ cup hot vegetable cooking liquid, stock, or dashi (p. 56)
½ teaspoon grated lemon or *yuzu* rind

Combine the first three ingredients, mixing until smooth. Pour over cooked vegetables and top with a sprinkling of the lemon rind.

Miso-Sesame Lyonnaise Sauce
MAKES 1½ CUPS

2 tablespoons sesame oil
2 onions, minced
2 tablespoons whole-wheat flour
1 cup stock, water, or dashi (p. 56).
¼ cup white wine or sake
3 tablespoons red, barley, or Hatcho miso
Dash of pepper
1 tablespoon minced parsley

Heat a skillet and coat with the oil. Add onions and sauté for 5 minutes, or until lightly browned. Stir in flour and sauté for 2 minutes more. Add stock a little at a time, stirring until smooth. Stir in wine and cook, stirring constantly, for 3 minutes. Add miso creamed in a little of the hot sauce, season with pepper, and return just to the boil. Serve topped with a sprinkling of parsley.

Sesame, Onion & Miso Sauce
MAKES 2/3 CUP

2 to 3 teaspoons sesame oil
1 onion, minced
2 tablespoons sesame (or peanut) butter
2 tablespoons red, barley, or Hatcho miso, thinned in 2½ tablespoons water
1 teaspoon white wine, sake, or *mirin* (optional)

Heat a skillet or wok and coat with the oil. Add onion and sauté for 4 to 5 minutes. Combine sesame butter and thinned miso, mix briefly, and stir into onion. Add wine (if used), mix well, and remove from heat. Serve as a topping for Brown Rice (p. 57), Rice Patties (p. 121), or steamed vegetables.

Creamy Sesame-Miso Sauce
MAKES ½ CUP

3 tablespoons sweet white or 2 tablespoons mellow white miso
1½ tablespoons sesame butter or *tahini*
3 tablespoons milk (soy or dairy)
1½ tablespoons vinegar

Combine all ingredients, mixing well. Serve with cooked vegetables (especially good with spinach, cauliflower, chard, or broccoli).

Peanut Butter-Miso Sauce
MAKES ½ CUP

1 to 1½ tablespoons red, barley, or Hatcho Miso
2 tablespoons peanut butter
2 to 3 tablespoons hot vegetable cooking liquid, stock, or dashi (p. 56)
1 teaspoon grated lemon or *yuzu* peel, or ½ teaspoon lemon juice

Prepare and serve as for Sesame-Miso Sauce, above. If desired, reduce the amount of water and use as a cracker spread or filling for celery stalks.

Tomato & Cheese Sauce with Miso
MAKES 1¼ CUPS

2 tablespoons butter
1¼ cups chopped fresh tomatoes
½ onion, minced
1½ tablespoons red, barley, or Hatcho miso
¾ cup grated cheese
¼ teaspoon oregano or basil
¼ teaspoon paprika
Dash of pepper

Melt the butter in a skillet. Add tomatoes and onion and sauté for 2 minutes, then cover and simmer for 3 minutes. Uncover and continue to simmer, stirring occasionally, for 15 minutes more, or until sauce is well thickened. Add miso creamed in a little of the hot sauce, then stir in remaining ingredients and remove from heat.

Miso-Gingerroot Sauce
MAKES 2 CUPS

5 tablespoons red, barley, Hatcho miso
3 to 4 teaspoons honey
1 cup dashi (p. 56), stock, or water
2 teaspoons arrowroot, cornstarch or *kuzu* (kudzu powder),
    dissolved in ¼ cup water
1 tablespoon grated gingerroot
Dash of (7-spice) red pepper

Combine the first three ingredients in a small saucepan and bring to a boil. Stir in dissolved arrowroot and grated gingerroot and cook for about 1 minute, or until thickened. Season with red pepper. Delicious with steamed or sautéed vegetables (cauliflower, cabbage, chard, broccoli, squash), deep-fried foods, or tofu.

Gingerroot-Miso Barbecue Sauce
MAKES ½ CUP

1½ teaspoons oil
½ teaspoon minced gingerroot
3½ tablespoons red, barley, or Hatcho miso
¼ cup water, stock, or dashi (p. 56)
2½ teaspoons honey
1½ tablespoons *mirin*, dry sherry, or white wine
Dash of 7-spice red or *sansho* pepper (optional)

Heat a wok or skillet and coat with the oil. Add gingerroot and sauté for 1 minute, or until just fragrant. Add the next four ingredients and cook, stirring constantly, for 3 minutes, or until mixture has the consistency of a thick sauce. Stir in the pepper, if used, and remove from heat. Allow to cool before serving with deep-fried tofu, barbecued foods, tempura, or fresh vegetable slices.

Korean-style Miso Barbecue Sauce
MAKES ¼ CUP

3 tablespoons red, barley, or Hatcho miso
1 tablespoon honey
1 clove of garlic, crushed
1 tablespoon diced leeks or onions
1 tablespoon ground roasted sesame seeds (p. 54), or 2 teaspoons sesame butter or *tahini*
2 teaspoons sesame oil
¼ teaspoon (7-spice) red pepper or tabasco sauce
Dash of white pepper

Combine all ingredients, mixing well. Delicious with (grilled) deep-fried tofu.

Miso Shish Kebab (or Barbecue) Sauce
MAKES ¼ CUP

In Japan, a close relative of this preparation is used with the popular chicken shish kebab called *yakitori*.

2 tablespoons red, barley, or Hatcho miso
1 teaspoon oil
½ teaspoon honey
¼ teaspoon grated gingerroot
¼ to ½ clove garlic, crushed
2 tablespoons water

Combine all ingredients, mixing well. Use as a marinade and/or basting sauce with your favorite preparations, or with Shish Kebab (p. 144).

Miso-Ketchup Barbecue Sauce
MAKES ½ CUP

2 tablespoons red, barley, or Hatcho miso
2 tablespoons ketchup
¼ small onion, diced
1 tablespoon melted butter
1 tablespoon sake or white wine
½ clove of garlic, crushed
¾ teaspoon honey
Dash of (7-spice) red pepper or tabasco sauce

Combine all ingredients in a skillet, mixing well. Cook over medium heat for about 1 minute. Serve hot or cold. Excellent over croquettes or deep-fried tofu.

Miso Teriyaki Sauce
MAKES 1 CUP

Generally used in Japan to baste broiled fish, this savory sauce is now used by many Westerners with shish kebab and other barbecued preparations. Also good as a dip for fresh vegetables or a topping for deep-fried tofu.

6 tablespoons red, barley, or Hatcho miso
3 tablespoons sake or white wine
1 tablespoon sesame or vegetable oil
1 teaspoon grated gingerroot or 1½ teaspoons powdered ginger
2 cloves of garlic, crushed
3 tablespoons brown sugar or 1½ tablespoons honey
¼ teaspoon dry mustard (optional)

Combine all ingredients, mixing well. Marinate foods (green peppers, onions or leeks, deep-fried tofu, tomatoes, mushrooms, etc.) for at least 1 hour before skewering and broiling. Use remaining sauce to baste.

Miso with Grains, Beans & Tofu

Miso evokes and accentuates the simple, satisfying flavors of grains and beans (pulses), mankind's most basic foods. Inexpensive and easy to prepare, these dishes can be enjoyed day after day and serve as the center of a healthful diet. Using miso and soybean products together with grains can increase the total protein content of each dish by more than 30 percent (p. 23). See also Miso in Baked Dishes (p. 133) and Miso in Sandwiches (p. 81).

MISO WITH BROWN RICE

For most of recorded history, unpolished rice has served as the staff of life for more than one-half of the world's population. Fortunately, its health-giving virtues are now gaining greater and greater recognition in the West.

Brown Rice or Rice Porridge with Miso Toppings

MAKES 1 SERVING

In Japan, this is the most popular way of serving rice seasoned with miso. Quick and easy to prepare, the many variations of this tasty dish can be enjoyed daily throughout the four seasons.

1 to 1½ cups cooked Brown Rice or Rice Porridge (p. 57; unseasoned)
1 to 2 teaspoons of any one of the following:
    Red, barley, or Hatcho miso
    Finger Lickin' or akadashi miso
    Sweet Simmered Miso (p. 60)
    Miso Sauté (p. 65)
    Mixed Miso (p. 69)
    Broiled Miso (p. 71)
    Yubeshi Miso (p. 73)
    Soybean & Miso Garnish (p. 130)
    Miso pickles, minced or thinly sliced (p. 156)

Place rice in a bowl and top with a bead or dab of the miso. Mix well or, if using chopsticks, take a small piece of miso together with each biteful of rice. Chew well for best flavor and nutrition.

Brown Rice Topped with Miso Sauces

Serve cooked hot or cold brown rice topped with any of the miso sauces and garnishes listed on page 124 for use with noodles.

Rice Jambalaya with Miso

SERVES 3 OR 4

3 tablespoons butter
3 ounces mushrooms, thinly sliced
5 ounces deep-fried tofu, cubed; or substitute an equal weight of sliced mushrooms
½ onion, thinly sliced
2 green peppers, thinly sliced
¼ cup diced celery
1 tomato, diced
1½ tablespoons red, barley, or Hatcho miso
Dash of (7-spice) red pepper or tabasco sauce
¼ teaspoon paprika
½ cup brown rice, cooked (p. 57); or use 1¼ cups leftover rice
2 tablespoons minced parsley

Preheat oven to 300°. Melt 1½ tablespoons butter in a skillet. Add mushrooms and deep-fried tofu, and sauté for 2 minutes. Add the next four ingredients and sauté for 2 minutes more. Mix in miso, red pepper, and paprika, then remove from heat. Combine with cooked rice, 1 tablespoon parsley, and the remaining 1½ tablespoons butter. Mix well and spoon into an oiled casserole or loaf pan. Cover and bake for 45 to 60 minutes. Serve hot or cold, topped with the remaining 1 tablespoon parsley.

119

Deep-fried Miso-Rice Balls with Sweet & Sour Sauce

SERVES 3 OR 4

1 cup brown rice, cooked (p. 57) and cooled to body or
   room temperature
¾ cup chopped leeks or scallions
2 tablespoons red, barley, or Hatcho miso
¼ cup sesame butter or *tahini*
2 teaspoons grated gingerroot
1 clove of garlic, crushed
½ cup cornstarch, arrowroot, or *kuzu*
Oil for deep-frying
1½ cups Pineapple Sweet & Sour Sauce (p. 115)

Combine the first six ingredients, mixing well. Shape into
1½-inch-diameter balls (20 to 25) and roll in cornstarch. Heat
the oil to 350° in a wok, skillet, or deep-fryer. Drop in balls (8
to 10 at a time) and deep-fry until crisp and golden brown (p.
147). Drain well, then top with the hot sauce. Serve immediately or, for a richer, sweeter flavor, allow to stand for 6
to 8 hours.

Stir-fried Rice with Almonds and Miso

SERVES 4

2 tablespoons oil
1 clove of garlic, minced
½ cup almonds, slivered
½ leek, chopped fine
2 eggs, lightly beaten
1 cup brown rice, cooked (p. 57) and cooled
2 tablespoons red, barley or Hatcho miso, creamed with 1
   tablespoon water
Dash of pepper (optional)

Heat 1 tablespoon oil in a wok or large skillet. Add garlic and
almonds, and sauté for 2 to 3 minutes until browned. Add
leeks, sauté for 1 minute more, then remove from heat and
transfer to an empty bowl. Re-heat wok and coat with remaining 1 tablespoon oil. Add eggs and scramble for 1 minute
until just firm. Mix in rice and sauté for 1 minute, then add
almond-leek mixture and sauté for 2 minutes more, or until
crumbly. Mix in miso and pepper and cook for 2 minutes.
Delicious hot or cold.

Brown Rice Porridge with Miso and Vegetables

SERVES 3 OR 4

½ cup brown rice
4½ cups water
1 tablespoon (sesame) oil
½ onion, thinly sliced
½ small carrot, slivered or diced
½ cup diced or slivered celery or *daikon*
1 tablespoon red or barley miso, dissolved in ¼ cup water
½ cup fresh or reconstituted *wakame* (p. 54), thinly sliced
   (optional)
Miso Pickles (p. 156) or Sesame Salt (p. 58)
Crumbled toasted *nori* (optional)

Combine rice and water in a heavy pot, cover, and bring to a
boil. Reduce heat to very low, and simmer for 90 minutes
with lid set slightly ajar.

    Meanwhile, heat a skillet and coat with the oil. Add
onion and sauté for 2 minutes. Add carrot and celery, and
sauté for 5 minutes more. Add dissolved miso together with
wakame, if used. Bring just to a boil, turn off heat, and cover.

    When porridge is ready, stir in miso-vegetable mixture
and simmer for 5 minutes. Serve individual portions seasoned
with miso pickles or sesame salt and, if desired, the *nori*.

VARIATIONS

*Pressure Cooked Porridge: Combine rice with 2½ cups
water in a pressure cooker and bring to full pressure (15
pounds). Reduce heat to very low and simmer for 45 minutes.
Turn off heat and allow to stand for 10 minutes while pressure returns to normal. Open cooker and stir in miso and
vegetables. Allow to stand for 5 to 10 minutes. Mix well
before serving.

*Porridge with Miso and Soybeans: Combine rice with 2¾
cups water and ¼ cup dry soybeans, soaked for at least 3
hours in water to cover, then drained. Proceed as for Pressure
Cooked Porridge, above. After opening cooker, stir in 1½
tablespoons red miso, 1 tablespoon butter, and 1 tablespoon
minced parsley. Let stand for several minutes before serving.

Creamy Rice Porridge with White Miso and Broccoli

SERVES 4

2 tablespoons butter
1 onion, minced
1½ cups cooked Brown Rice (p. 57)
2 cups water
2 cups chopped broccoli (4½ ounces)
¼ cup sweet white or 2½ tablespoons mellow white miso,
   dissolved in 3 tablespoons water

Melt the butter in a heavy (earthenware) pot. Add onion and
sauté for 3 minutes. Add brown rice and water, and bring to a
boil. Add broccoli and return to the boil, then simmer, covered, for 15 minutes, stirring occasionally. Stir in creamed miso
and return just to the boil. Delicious hot or cold.

Sang Chu

SERVES 3 TO 5

One of Korea's most popular national dishes, Sang Chu is composed of rice and a spicy garnish wrapped in a crisp lettuce leaf; held in the fingers, it is eaten like a sandwich. In the following recipe, we substitute tofu (or scrambled eggs) for the usual hamburger or pork miso.

1 tablespoon sesame oil
1 clove of garlic, minced
12 ounces tofu, crumbled (p. 56); or 3 eggs, scrambled (without salt)
3 tablespoons red, barley, or Hatcho miso
1 teaspoon juice pressed from grated gingerroot
1/3 cup chopped leeks or scallions
¼ teaspoon red pepper powder
12 to 15 (butter) lettuce leaves
3 to 5 thin lemon wedges
6 to 10 thin tomato wedges, sprigs of parsley, spring chrysanthemum leaves, or cheese slices
2 to 2½ cups cooked Brown Rice (p. 57)

To prepare garnish, heat a skillet and coat with the oil. Add garlic and sauté for 30 seconds. Add tofu (or eggs) and sauté for 2 minutes. Add gingerroot juice and miso, sauté for 30 seconds more, and remove from heat. Stir in leeks and red pepper, mash all ingredients together thoroughly, and spoon into a small bowl.

Place bowl at the center of a large serving plate and surround with lettuce leaves. Top leaves with lemon and tomato wedges. Serve as a main course or hors d'œuvre accompanied by a serving bowl mounded with the rice.

Hold a lettuce leaf in the palm of one hand, spoon about 2 tablespoons of rice onto the leaf's center, and top the rice with a tablespoon of garnish. Squeeze a little lemon juice over the garnish and/or top with a tomato wedge. Fold ends and sides of leaf over filling.

Other popular Korean garnishes include Red-Pepper & Leek Miso (doen jang; p. 64) and Red-pepper Miso (kochu jang; p. 71). Try also Finger Lickin' Miso.

Egg & Miso Domburi

SERVES 4 TO 5

1 tablespoon oil
2/3 cup grated carrot
1 small onion, minced
1 cup green peas or minced green peppers
3 tablespoons red, barley, or Hatcho miso, thinned in ¼ cup water
2½ teaspoons honey or 1½ tablespoons natural sugar
1½ cups brown rice, cooked (p. 57).

Heat a skillet or wok and coat with the oil. Add carrot, onion

and green peas, and sauté for 4 to 5 minutes. Add thinned miso and honey, and cook, stirring constantly, until most of the liquid has been absorbed or evaporated. Add eggs and cook, stirring constantly, for about 2 minutes, or until firm. Divide hot rice among large individual bowls and spoon on the egg-and-miso topping. Serve hot or cold.

Fig. 20. Rice Patties

Rice Patties with Miso
(O-musubi or O-nigiri)

MAKES 9

1½ tablespoons red, barley, or Hatcho miso
6 umeboshi salt plums, pitted and minced (optional)
3 tablespoons bonito flakes or grated cheese (optional)
2 cups brown rice, cooked (p. 57), then cooled for 5 minutes; or use 5 cups leftover rice
3 sheets of nori, toasted (p. 54) and each cut into 6 squares

Combine the first three ingredients, mixing well. (Or use only the miso.) Add to the rice, mixing lightly with a wooden spoon or spatula. Moisten hands in cold water (to prevent sticking) and shape rice into 9 triangular wedges or patties, pressing each firmly as shown in figure 20. Lay a nori square over both of the large surfaces of each pattie, then press edges and corners of nori against rice. (Keep your hands lightly moistened at all times.) Serve patties arranged on a large platter garnished with parsley sprigs or use in box lunches.

VARIATIONS

*Substitute for the red miso mixture ¼ cup Sesame Miso (p. 62), Sweet Simmered Miso (p. 60), or Finger Lickin' Miso (p. 41). If desired, mix with 10 to 15 minced green beefsteak leaves.
*Omit nori and roll patties in roasted (whole or ground) sesame seeds.
*Form the miso or miso mixture into 9 small balls and press one ball into the center of each rice pattie.
*Broiled Rice Patties (Yaki-musubi): Make rice patties using the crisp, golden-brown rice from the bottom of the cooking pot. Spread the surface of each pattie with a thin layer of miso (omitting nori), then broil quickly over an open flame until miso is fragrant.
*Crisp Rice Patties: Deep-fry or pan-fry patties in hot oil until crisp and golden brown (p. 147). Serve hot or cold.

Fried Miso-and-Rice Patties

SERVES 4

4 cups cooked (or leftover) Brown Rice (p. 57)
¼ cup diced leeks or scallions
¼ cup red, barley, or Hatcho miso
2 tablespoons oil

Combine the first three ingredients, mixing well, and shape into eight patties. Heat one-half the oil in a large skillet. Add four patties and fry on both sides until golden brown and fragrant. Repeat with remaining ingredients.

For variety, roll patties in 2 tablespoons roasted sesame seeds (or mix 2 tablespoons sesame butter into the miso) before frying.

Brown Rice with Mushrooms and Miso (*Chameshi*)

SERVES 3 OR 4

Also called *Takikomi-gohan*, this richly-flavored, popular dish is frequently prepared with chestnuts, chicken, crab, or shrimp used in place of the mushrooms and green peas.

1½ cups brown rice, rinsed and drained
12/3 cups water or green tea
5 (*shiitaké* or *matsutaké*) mushrooms, thinly sliced
½ cup fresh green peas
2 tablespoons red, barley, or Hatcho miso
2 teaspoons *mirin*, sake, or white wine
Minced parsley or trefoil (optional)

Combine all ingredients in a pressure cooker; mix briefly. Proceed as for Brown Rice (p. 57). Serve hot, topped if desired with a sprinkling of parsley.

For a simpler preparation, combine 1½ tablespoons red miso with the rice and water, and proceed as for Brown Rice.

VARIATION

*Brown Rice with Chestnuts and Miso (*Miso Kuri Kinton*): Substitute ½ cup whole or halved fresh or dry chestnut meats for the mushrooms and peas.

Thick Miso Shake with Brown Rice

SERVES 3

2 cups carrot-, tomato-, or mixed vegetable juice
¾ cup cooked Brown Rice (p. 57)
1 tablespoon red, barley, or Hatcho miso
Dash of pepper or oregano
¼ cup (toasted) wheat germ (optional)
1 teaspoon lemon juice (optional)

Combine all ingredients in a blender and purée for 2 to 3 minutes, or until creamy and thick. If desired, chill before serving.

Zosui or Ojiya (Rice Gruel)

SERVES 1 OR 2

Zosui, which means "a variety of things cooked together," is a popular way of using leftover rice (or rice porridge) and miso soup or clear soup served daily in most Japanese homes. In times of war or famine when rice was scarce, Zosui was daily fare; prepared with a large proportion of broth, it served to fill the belly and ward off hunger. Today, in times of abundance, thick Zosui served piping hot is still a wintertime favorite, prized for its ability to warm body and soul.

Known colloquially (and in Tokyo) as *Ojiya*, it originated at an early date in China, where more than 100 varieties were developed as part of that country's elaborate Congee or Rice Porridge Cuisine. During the 15th century, it became a popular dish throughout Japan, served on January 7, the last day of the New Year's season. Its preparation, using the "seven spring herbs," "newly drawn water," and miso, was transformed into a lovely ceremony linked to the zodiacal hours. One who added each freshly gathered wild herb at its propitious hour and served the dish "before the Chinese white eagle flies overhead" (a euphemism for diseases feared brought to Japan from the Chinese mainland), was said to be given by the gods an additional 8,000 years of happy life — and made instantaneously 70 years younger. To this day it is thought to be good insurance against colds and the flu, even in the midst of the influenza season. The proportions of rice and soup can be varied considerably depending on the amounts of leftovers.

1½ cups Miso Soup (p. 97)
1 cup cooked Brown Rice (p. 57) or Rice Porridge (p. 57)

Bring miso soup to a boil in a saucepan. Mix in the rice and return to the boil. Cover and simmer for 15 to 30 minutes, or until rice is soft.

For variety, just before removing from heat, stir in diced tofu, leftover vegetables or tempura, and/or eggs. Season to taste with 7-spice red pepper or grated gingerroot. Garnish with crumbled, toasted *nori*, green *nori* flakes, slivered leeks or citrus rind, or minced parsley. Serve immediately.

Miso Gruel with Leftovers

Gruel is an ancient preparation designed to create continually new and tasty combinations of foods while simultaneously preventing waste.
Combine all leftover cooked grains, vegetables, and tofu or other soybean foods in a large, heavy pot. Add enough leftover soup, stock, or water to give the consistency of a thick stew; bring to a boil and simmer for 5 to 10 minutes. Add creamed miso and, if desired, curry powder or ketchup to unify the flavors. To thicken, stir in lightly roasted whole-wheat flour or barley flour and cook for several minutes more. Serve hot or cold. To use leftover gruel as the basis for full-bodied breads, knead in flour to earlobe consistency, allow to rise overnight, and bake in a slow oven for several hours.

Ochazuké with Miso Toppings   MAKES 1 SERVING

If you're in a hurry or want to make a quick, light meal (or when there is leftover rice which you don't have time to reheat), this impromptu dish is ideal. In Japan, some people also like to make Ochazuké using the rice remaining in their bowls toward the end of a meal, and many restaurants even feature Ochazuké as their specialty. Its most popular accompaniments are *takuan* (or other salt-pickled vegetables) and *tsukudani* (slivers or 1-inch squares of *kombu*, beefsteak seeds, tiny dried fish, etc., which have been simmered in a salty mixture of shoyu and *mirin*). Various types of miso are used as toppings. Although each person prepares Ochazuké at the table, using ingredients and proportions to taste, the method might look like this in recipe form:

½ to 1 cup cooked (leftover) rice
Miso Toppings (listed in order of popularity): Use 1 to 2
    teaspoons of any one of the following
        Thinly sliced Miso Pickles (p. 156)
        Broiled Miso (p. 71)
        Finger Lickin' Miso (p. 42)
        Sweet Simmered Miso (p. 60)
        Miso Sauté (p. 65)
        Hoba Miso (p. 72)
¼ to 1 cup very hot green tea
1 tablespoon crumbled, toasted *nori* (p. 54) or bonito
    flakes (optional)

Place rice in individual bowls and top with miso. Pour on hot tea, then press miso into rice with tips of chopsticks. Cover and allow to stand for several minutes. Sprinkle with *nori*, then sip the broth alternately with bites of rice.

Bibimpap   SERVES 6

This famous Korean rice dish, seasoned with fiery hot Red-pepper Miso *(kochu jang)* and topped with sautéed vegetables, is served on special occasions in much the same way as its relative, Five-Color Sushi, is served in Japan. Since the method of preparation is quite detailed and varies widely from chef to chef, we will present it here in a concise outline form.

Prepare 2 paper-thin omelets (p. 58) and reserve.
    Cut 2 cucumbers into thin rounds and rub lightly with salt. Allow to stand for 20 minutes, then rinse. Sauté rounds for 3 minutes in sesame oil together with a little minced leek, ground sesame seeds, and red pepper.
    Parboil 3 cups soybean sprouts for 10 minutes in lightly salted water. Drain sprouts, then sauté for 4 minutes in the same mixture of ingredients used with the cucumbers.
    Sauté 9 thinly sliced mushrooms (or Osmund ferns) in the same mixture to which has been added a little natural sugar and crushed garlic.
    Place 5 cups cooked brown rice in a large, shallow bowl. Atop rice arrange sautéed vegetables, slivered omelets, slivered almonds, and crumbled deep-fried *kombu* or toasted *nori*. Accompany rice with a small cup filled with (homemade) Red-pepper Miso (p. 71). Invite each guest to transfer his choice of vegetables and rice to his individual plate, then top the combination with a small dab of the miso.

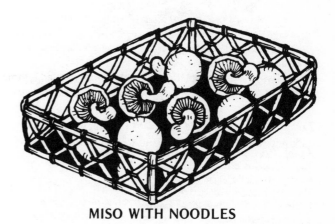

MISO WITH NOODLES

Noodles are among the most easily digestible of all foods and can serve as a central element in a meatless diet. For best nutritive value, look for noodles rich in whole-wheat, unrefined buckwheat, or soy flours.

Richly-flavored *soba* or fat *udon*; Italian spaghetti or crinkly Chinese *ramen*; winter noodles steaming hot or summer noodles in chilled broth; stir-fried noodles in savory sauces, and deep-fried noodles, brittle, crisp, and golden brown; homemade or leftover noodles in soups, sauces, and casseroles. Oodles of possibilities, each made more tasty and nutritious by the use of miso.

Stir-fried Buckwheat Noodles   SERVES 4
with Miso

3 tablespoons oil, preferably used deep-frying oil
5 eggs, lightly beaten
¼ teaspoon salt
Pepper
1 onion, thinly sliced
10 ounces Chinese cabbage
3½ tablespoons red, barley, or Hatcho miso
6 to 7 ounces (soba) buckwheat noodles, cooked (p. 58)
¾ cup grated or Parmesan cheese (optional)

Heat 1 tablespoon oil in a wok or skillet. Add eggs, salt and a dash of pepper; scramble until eggs are fairly dry and crumbly, then transfer to a separate container and reserve.

Heat the remaining 2 tablespoons oil in the wok. Add onion and cabbage, and sauté for 3 minutes. Add miso and cook, stirring constantly, for 1 minute more. Mix in cooked eggs, noodles and, if desired, the cheese. When noodles are heated through, remove from heat. Serve hot or cold.

For variety, substitute 10 ounces diced deep-fried tofu for the eggs. Sauté until nicely browned and increase the miso to 5 tablespoons.

Bamboo noodle-tongs

Soybeans, Miso, and Sautéed Vegetables with Noodles

SERVES 4

2½ cups Pressure Cooked Soybeans (p. 129; unseasoned),
    drained
3 tablespoons red, barley, or Hatcho miso
2 tablespoons oil
1 clove of garlic, minced or crushed
1½ cups shredded cabbage
1 cup thinly sliced leeks or onions
½ cup grated carrot
6½ ounces (buckwheat or Chinese) noodles, cooked (p. 58)
1½ tablespoons shoyu
Dash of pepper

Combine cooked soybeans and miso, mixing well and mashing half the beans; set aside. Heat a large wok or skillet and
coat with the oil. Add garlic and sauté for 30 seconds. Add
cabbage, onions and carrot, sauté for 4 minutes more, and
turn off heat. Add soybeans, mixing until evenly distributed.
Stir in noodles, sprinkle with shoyu, and season with pepper;
mix lightly. Delicious hot or cold.

Buckwheat Noodles in Miso-Soymilk Sauce

SERVES 2

1½ cups milk (soy or dairy)
1 small onion, diced
1 tablespoon red, barley, or Hatcho miso
2 tablespoons sweet white miso or 1 tablespoon red miso
2 tablespoons butter
½ cup grated cheese or 2½ tablespoons sesame butter
3½ ounces (soba) buckwheat noodles, cooked (p. 58) and
    well drained
Dash of pepper
2 tablespoons minced parsley or ground roasted sesame
    seeds (p. 54)
Crumbled toasted *nori* (optional)

Combine milk and onion in a large saucepan and bring to a
boil over medium heat, stirring constantly. Stir in miso
creamed in a little of the hot liquid. Add butter, cheese and
noodles, and return to the boil, then season with pepper and
remove from heat. For best flavor, allow to stand for several
hours. Serve as is or reheated, garnished with parsley and, if
used, the *nori*.

    For variety, combine all ingredients in a casserole and
bake at 350° for about 20 minutes, or until nicely browned.

Noodles Topped with Miso Sauces

SERVES 4

7 to 8 ounces buckwheat or whole-wheat noodles, cooked
    (p. 58)
Miso Sauce: Use 2 to 4 cups of any of the following (pp.113
    to 118):
        Miso Onion Sauce
        Miso Mushroom Sauce
        Miso Spaghetti Sauce
        Miso White Sauce
        Miso Curry Sauce
        Miso Gravy
        Spicy Indonesian Peanut Sauce
        Sesame Miso Sauce
Garnishes and seasonings:
        Crumbled, Toasted Nori (p. 54)
        Sambals (p. 116)
        Roasted (whole or ground) sesame seeds (p. 54)
        Thinly sliced Miso Pickles (p. 156)
        7-spice red pepper

Arrange hot or cold noodles in individual or serving bowls.
Spoon on the sauce and serve accompanied by garnish.

Deep-fried Noodles with Miso Sweet & Sour Sauce

SERVES 4

6 ounces noodles
Oil for deep-frying
3 cups Pineapple Sweet & Sour Sauce (p. 115)

Cook noodles (p. 58), then drain in a colander for about 1
hour. Heat the oil to 350° in a wok, skillet, or deep-fryer.
Place about ¼ cup noodles on a spatula and slide into the oil.
Deep-fry for about 30 seconds (p. 147), then turn and deep-
fry for 30 seconds more, or until crisp and golden brown;
drain well. Repeat until all noodles are used. Divide noodles
among individual plates, top with the sauce, and serve immediately.

    Also good with most of the sauces enumerated in
Noodles Topped with Miso Sauces (above).

Noodles Cooked with Miso & Milk

SERVES 2

1½ cups milk (soy or dairy)
3½ ounces (*soba*) buckwheat noodles, cooked (p. 58)
2 tablespoons butter
1/3 cup grated cheese (optional)
3½ tablespoons red, barley, or Hatcho miso
2 tablespoons minced parsley or ground roasted sesame
    seeds (p. 54)
Crumbled, toasted *nori* (optional)

In a large pot, bring milk just to a boil over medium heat,
stirring constantly. Add cooked noodles, butter, cheese, and
miso creamed with a little of the hot milk. Return to the boil,
then set aside to cool until milk clabbers. Serve garnished
with the parsley and *nori*.

    For variety, combine ¼ cup diced onion with the milk
in the pot before heating.

Buckwheat Noodles with Miso Dipping Sauce

SERVES 5 OR 6

2 tablespoons sweet white miso
4 tablespoons shoyu
1 tablespoon honey
2 tablespoons *mirin*, dry sherry, or white wine
2 tablespoons sesame butter or ¼ cup ground roasted sesame seeds (p. 54)
2 cups dashi (p. 56), stock, or water
1/3 cup thinly sliced leeks or scallions
Dash of (7-spice) red pepper
8 to 10 ounces (*soba*) buckwheat noodles, cooked (p. 58)

Combine the first five ingredients in a pot or large skillet and cook, stirring constantly, for about 1 minute, or until smooth. Stir in dashi and bring to a boil. Remove from heat and allow to cool, then divide among individual bowls. Place noodles on plates or in a large bamboo colander. Invite guests to garnish dipping sauce to taste with leeks and red pepper. Dip noodles into sauce to serve.

VARIATION

*Miso Tanuki Soba: Prepare the dipping sauce using 9 to 10 tablespoons red miso, 4½ cups dashi and, if desired, 1 tablespoon natural sugar and 2 tablespoons sake, white wine, or *mirin*. Pour hot broth over noodles in individual bowls, garnish and season as above, then top each portion with ¼ cup of *agédama*, tiny particles of deep-fried tempura batter skimmed off during the deep-frying process or specially prepared for this dish.

Nikomi-udon
(Homemade Noodles Simmered in Miso)

SERVES 6

In this popular miso preparation, the water in which the noodles are cooked is not discarded, but is used as the basis for a thick miso sauce that closely resembles a Western-style white sauce. For best flavor, allow this dish to stand overnight so that the noodles further contribute to the thickening of the sauce. Serve either cold or reheated.

2 cups flour, half of which is whole-wheat
8½ cups warm water
¼ teaspoon salt
5 tablespoons sweet white or 3 tablespoons mellow white miso
3 tablespoons red, barley, or Hatcho miso
3 large leeks, cut diagonally into 2-inch lengths
1½ small leeks or scallions, cut into thin rounds
7-spice red pepper
Crumbled, toasted *nori* (optional)

Put the 2 cups flour into a large bowl and, adding ½ cup water a little at a time, mix and knead to form a heavy dough. Roll out dough on a floured breadboard to 1/8-inch thickness, sprinkle surface lightly with flour, and fold lengthwise accordion fashion into quarters. Now cut dough crosswise into 1/8-inch-wide strands to make noodles. Spread noodle strips on the floured board to dry briefly.

Bring the remaining 8 cups water to a boil in a large pot. Drop in noodles and salt, and cook until until noodles float to surface. Add miso creamed with a little of the hot water, then add large leeks and simmer for 10 minutes. Remove from heat and allow to stand as long as overnight. Serve garnished with thin rounds of leeks, red pepper, and *nori*.

To save time, use about 10 ounces dried noodles in place of the homemade variety. In some parts of Japan, *daikon*, mushrooms, taro, carrots, and deep-fried tofu are parboiled or simmered in sweetened shoyu broth, then added to the noodles together with the miso. Result: A thick noodle-and-vegetable stew.

Homemade noodles

Miso Ramen

SERVES 2 OR 3

A favorite at Japan's thousands of small restaurants specializing in Chinese-style *ramen* noodles, this preparation is usually made with a chicken-based broth and served steaming hot. Sapporo Miso Ramen, the most famous variety, is named after the city in Hokkaido, Japan's northernmost island, where this dish is said to have originated.

3½ ounces (Chinese) noodles
1 tablespoon sesame oil
1 clove of garlic, minced or crushed
1½ cups bean sprouts
½ cup thinly sliced leeks or onions
3 tablespoons red, barley, or Hatcho miso
1 tablespoon shoyu
2½ cups stock or dashi (p. 56)
Dash of (7-spice) red pepper or tabasco sauce
1 tablespoon dry (cloud-ear) mushroom, reconstituted (p. 54) and minced

Cook noodles (p. 58), drain, and reserve. Heat a skillet or wok and coat with the oil. Add garlic and sauté for 30 seconds. Add bean sprouts and leeks and sauté for 3 minutes more. Dissolve miso and shoyu in ½ cup stock and add to skillet together with red pepper and mushrooms; bring to a boil. Add remaining dashi and return to the boil, stirring constantly.

Place noodles in a strainer and dip briefly into boiling water until warmed through. Mound in deep bowls, then pour on the vegetables-and-broth.

Noodles Cooked with Miso
(*Misoyaki Udon*)

SERVES 4

6 tablespoons sweet white miso or 3 tablespoons red miso
7 tablespoons dashi (p. 56), stock, or water
1 tablespoon shoyu
2½ tablespoon *mirin*, sake, or white wine
1½ tablespoons oil
1 small onion, thinly sliced
2 to 3 ounces deep-fried tofu or 4 to 6 mushrooms, thinly sliced
1½ teaspoons grated or minced gingerroot
3½ ounces (*udon* or *soba*) whole-wheat or buckwheat noodles, cooked (p. 58) and drained

Combine the first four ingredients, mixing well. Heat the oil in a pot or large skillet. Add onion, deep-fried tofu and gingerroot, and sauté over medium-high heat for 2 to 3 minutes. Stir in the miso-dashi mixture and cooked noodles, cover, and return to the boil. Lower heat and simmer for 10 to 15 minutes. Serve hot or cold.

Chilled Noodles with Mustard-Vinegar Miso (*Sumiso Udon*)

SERVES 4

7 ounces noodles, cooked (p. 58), drained and chilled
½ cup Sweetened Mustard Vinegar Miso (p. 65)
1 cucumber, slivered
1 tomato, cut into thin wedges
1 egg, hard-boiled and cut into thin wedges

Place chilled noodles into a large serving bowl. Spoon miso into a mound at center of noodles, then arrange garnishes around miso. Invite guests to serve themselves.

Cha-chiang Mien

SERVES 4

One of the most popular ways of using miso in Chinese-style cookery, this tasty dish is usually prepared with chiang (Chinese miso) mixed with bits of pork (or occasionally ground beef) fried in oil and served over crinkly noodles together with a wide variety of toppings and garnishes.

3½ ounces (Chinese or buckwheat) noodles, cooked (p. 58)
Garnishes: Any or all of the following
    2 cups bean-sprouts, quickly parboiled
    2 cucumbers, slivered
    2 eggs made into paper-thin omelets, cooled and slivered (p. 58)
    6 mushrooms or 2 leeks, thinly sliced and sautéed in butter
Chinese-style Nerimiso (p. 61)

Place noodles, individual garnishes and the miso in separate serving bowls. Invite each guest to serve himself with noodles and preferred garnish, then miso. Mix well.

MISO WITH OTHER GRAINS

Miso with bulgur wheat and tortillas, *mochi* and French toast; miso toppings with oatmeal, cornmeal, and cream of wheat. All offer many delicious possibilities. For corn-on-the-cob, see page 144.

In Japan, miso rice crackers (*miso senbei*) and sweet miso rolls topped with sesame seeds (*miso pan*) are both sold commercially. In each case, red miso is simply mixed with a sweetened rice-flour or wheat-flour dough and then baked.

Curried Bulgur Pilaf with Cheese and Miso

SERVES 2 OR 3

Bulgur wheat—also known as couscous—is prepared by partially cooking, drying, and then cracking whole-grain wheat. A popular ingredient in Near Eastern and North African cuisines, it needs little cooking and has a pleasant, nutty flavor. In the West, it is now widely known as Ala.

2 tablespoons butter
½ cup bulgur wheat
1 small onion, thinly sliced
1 small carrot, slivered or diced
1 cup water or stock
½ teaspoon curry powder
1½ tablespoons red, barley, or Hatcho miso
2½ tablespoons Parmesan or grated cheese
1 tablespoon minced parsley

Melt the butter in a skillet. Add bulgur and onion, and sauté for 4 to 5 minutes. Add water and curry powder, cover, and bring to a boil. Simmer for 15 minutes, or until all liquid has been absorbed. Stir in miso and cheese, and remove from heat. Serve hot or cold, garnished with parsley.

Tabbouli with Miso (*Bulgur Salad with Mint and Lemon*)

SERVES 4 TO 6

1 cup bulgur wheat or couscous
¾ cup lemon juice
¾ cup very finely minced parsley
2 tablespoons minced fresh mint, or 3 tablespoons dried mint flakes reconstituted in 2 tablespoons hot water
3 tomatoes, minced
½ green pepper, chopped fine
6 to 8 tablespoons olive oil
1 teaspoon red, barley, or Hatcho miso, dissolved in 2 teaspoons warm water

Combine the bulgur and lemon juice, mix lightly, and allow to stand for 1 hour. Stir in the remaining ingredients and, for best flavor, allow to stand for at least several hours, preferably 2 to 3 days. Delicious served chilled.

French Toast with White Miso & Raisins

SERVES 2

½ cup milk (soy or dairy)
1 egg, lightly beaten
2 tablespoons sweet white or 4 teaspoons mellow white miso
1½ teaspoons honey
¼ cup raisins
2 large slices of whole-wheat bread, cut into fourths
2 tablespoons butter
Dash of cinnamon

Combine the first five ingredients in a shallow pan, mixing until smooth. Add bread and allow to stand for 3 to 5 minutes. (For very firm or unyeasted bread, soak for 1 hour.) Melt the butter in a large skillet. Add bread, spoon on any raisins remaining in pan, and cook for 2 to 3 minutes on each side, or until nicely browned. Serve topped with a sprinkling of cinnamon.

Cornmeal Spoonbread with Miso

MAKES 1 LOAF

Rich as cheesecake, this delicious loaf separates into three decorative layers. The miso lends its own savory flavor while the combination of soy, corn, and milk boosts the total protein content by up to 13 percent.

½ cup cornmeal
¼ cup whole-wheat flour
1 teaspoon baking powder
1½ cups milk (soy or dairy)
1 egg, lightly beaten
1 tablespoon honey
1½ tablespoons red or barley (or 3 tablespoons mellow white) miso
¼ cup raisins
2 tablespoons butter

Preheat oven to 375°. Combine the first three ingredients, sifting or mixing well. Combine 1 cup milk with the next four ingredients, mixing until miso is dissolved, then stir into the flour mixture and beat until well blended. Melt butter in a loaf pan. Pour in batter and top with the remaining ½ cup milk. Bake for 45 minutes. Serve buttered, piping hot or, for a richer sweeter flavor, chilled.

Hot Cereals with Miso Toppings

MAKES 1 SERVING

1 to 1½ cups freshly cooked rolled oats, oatmeal, cornmeal, rice cream, or cream of wheat
1 to 1½ tablespoons of any of the following (pp. 61–62):
    Peanut- or Peanut & Raisin Miso
    Sesame Miso
    Walnut-, Cashew-, or Sunflower Seed Miso

Dash of salt
1 tablespoon butter (optional)
¼ cup nuts, raisins, and/or granola (optional)
¼ to ½ cup warm milk (soy or dairy) (optional)

Serve hot cereal in a large bowl, topped with a dab of miso and seasoned with salt. Add butter, nuts, and milk if desired; mix lightly.

Broiled Mochi with Sweet Miso and Nori

SERVES 2 TO 4

8 cakes of *mochi*, each about 3 by 2 by ¾ inches
8 teaspoons butter
4 teaspoons honey (optional)
2 teaspoons grated gingerroot (optional)
8 teaspoons of any one of the following:
    Sweet Simmered Miso (p. 60)
    Finger Lickin' Miso (p. 41)
    Sweet White Miso
8 pieces of *nori*, each 3 by 6 inches

Broil *mochi* cakes on both sides in an oven broiler or on a grill until cakes are crisp, nicely browned, and puffed to twice their original thickness. Slit one end of each cake and fill with butter, honey and gingerroot. Spread both sides of cakes with the miso, wrap in a sheet of *nori* (fig. 21) and serve hot.

If *nori* is not available, use miso as part of the filling. Or omit honey and grated gingerroot, and fill *mochi* with 8 teaspoons Gingerroot Mixed Red Miso (p. 69) combined with ¼ cup grated *daikon*.

VARIATION

*Mochi in Miso-Ankaké: Broil *mochi* cakes as above. Place 2 cakes in each of four bowls and top with about ¼ cup of any of the following: Miso-Gingerroot Ankaké Sauce (p. 113), Miso-Lemon Ankaké Sauce (p. 113), Miso-Gingerroot Sauce (p. 118).

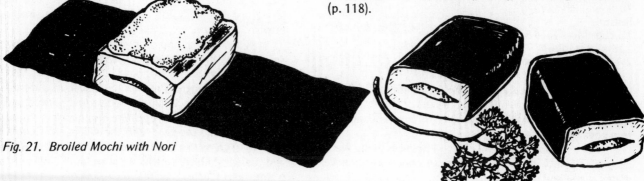

Fig. 21. Broiled Mochi with Nori

Millet or Buckwheat Pilaf

SERVES 4

3 tablespoons butter
½ cup millet or buckwheat groats (kasha)
1 onion, minced
1 tablespoon red miso, dissolved in 1 cup boiling water
¼ teaspoon oregano
Dash of pepper

Melt the butter in a heavy skillet. Add millet and onion, and saute until golden brown. Add remaining ingredients, cover, and bring to a boil. Reduce heat and simmer for 30 to 35 minutes. Delicious topped with Garbanzo-Tahini Sauce (p. 115) or Gado-Gado (p. 116).

Buckwheat Groats Medley with Miso

SERVES 4

1 cup buckwheat groats (kasha)
1 tablespoon oil
1 carrot, diced, slivered, or grated
¼ cup chopped hazel- or Brazil nuts
¼ cup sunflower seeds
¼ cup roasted sesame seeds
1 banana, sliced into thin rounds
1 apple, diced
1 pear, diced
Seeds from 1 cardamom, crushed
Dash of cinnamon
1 tablespoon red or barley miso; or 2 tablespoons mellow white miso
½ cup apple juice

Dry roast buckwheat groats until fragrant and nicely browned. Heat a skillet and coat with the oil. Add groats and the next ten ingredients and sauté for 10 minutes. Dissolve miso in apple juice, add to contents of skillet, and sauté for 1 minute more. Serve hot or chilled topped with applesauce, yogurt, kefir, or ricotta cheese. Or use as is like granola.

Crisp Tortillas with Taco Sauce
(*Tostadas*)

SERVES 5

Miso can serve as a delicious complement to the simple, natural flavors of these grain-based "platters" so widely used throughout Latin America and India.

10 seven-inch *tortillas*
Butter
1¼ cups Miso Taco Sauce (p.114)
2 tomatoes, diced
2½ cups shredded lettuce, sprouts, or cabbage

Heat *tortillas* in a medium oven for 5 to 7 minutes, or until lightly browned and crisp. (Or deep-fry in hot oil.) Butter one side of each *tortilla*, then spread with the sauce and top with tomatoes and lettuce.

For a meatier flavor, mix 10 to 15 ounces thinly sliced deep-fried tofu with the lettuce. Serve topped with a little grated cheese and tabasco sauce.

OTHER PREPARATIONS WITH *TORTILLAS, CHAPATIES, TACOS,* OR *PURIES*

*With Butter and Mixed Miso: Butter warm *tortillas* well, then coat one surface with a thin layer of Finger Lickin' Miso, sweet white miso, Mixed White Miso Topping with Parmesan (p. 69), or Mixed Cheese Miso (p. 70).
*Miso-filled Puries: Deep-fry *tortillas* (or puri dough) in hot oil until they swell and turn golden brown. Fill with butter, honey, gingerroot, and miso as for Broiled Mochi (p. 127).
*Tacos with Miso & Salads: Bake or deep-fry *tortillas* until crisp. Top with thinly sliced lettuce, tomatoes, deep-fried tofu and grated cheese. Spoon on Floating Cloud (p. 83) or your favorite miso dressing.
*With Miso Spreads: Top individual (warm) *tortillas* with ¼ to ½ cup Azuki-Miso (p. 81) or Soybean-Sesame-Miso (p. 81), or any of your other favorite miso spreads. Roll before eating.
*Serve miso-seasoned vegetable or grain dishes atop *tortillas*.

Chinese Pancake Rolls with Miso Sauce

SERVES 4

This recipe is closely related to the famous Peking Duck also served with miso (*t'ien mien chiang*) in tender, thin pancake rolls. In China, these *chapati*-like pancakes are usually prepared in the kitchen, fried in a dry skillet and steamed in large bamboo steamers. Since the process is complex, this recipe calls for ready-made *tortillas*.

4 teaspoons oil
4 eggs, lightly beaten
1 cup thinly sliced leek rounds
1½ cups bean sprouts
2 green peppers, thinly sliced
Miso Sauce:
    3½ tablespoons red, barley, or Hatcho miso
    4 teaspoons honey
    2 tablespoons sesame oil
    1 teaspoon soy sauce
    2 tablespoons water
½ large tomato, cut into thin wedges
½ small onion, minced
12 wheat-flour *tortillas*, warmed (preferably steamed)

Heat a skillet and coat with 1 tablespoon oil. Add eggs and leeks, and scramble until firm. Transfer to a small serving bowl.

Reheat skillet and coat with remaining 1 teaspoon oil. Add sprouts and green peppers, and sauté for 2 to 3 minutes. Transfer to a second serving bowl.

Combine ingredients for the sauce in a third (small) bowl; mix well. Place tomato wedges and minced onions on small plates. Fold warm *tortillas* into quarters and place on the dining table together with the sauce and fillings. Invite each guest to open a pancake, coat upper surface with sauce, and top with fillings. Roll pancake around fillings and eat like a sandwich or *taco*.

Mock Peking Duck

MISO WITH SOYBEANS AND TOFU

The use of miso (or shoyu) is one of the keys to seasoning soybeans and the more than eight varieties of Japanese and Chinese tofu described in *The Book of Tofu*. Tofu and soybeans are also used in a number of recipes throughout the preceding sections of this book. Topped with or added to Miso Sauces, especially Sweet & Sour-, Gingerroot- or White Sauce, deep-fried or regular tofu is at its very best. For miso with high-protein soybean spreads, see page 81.

Miso-filled Rolled Breads
MAKES 2 LOAVES

Dough for 2 loaves of bread (reduce salt content to 1 teaspoon)
¼ cup red, barley, or Hatcho miso
¼ cup honey
2 tablespoons butter or sesame butter
¾ cup raisins
1 apple, cut into very thin wedges; or 1 large banana, cut into thin rounds
½ cup chopped nutmeats (walnut or almond)

Roll out dough into two long rectangles, each about 8 inches wide and 3/8 inch thick. Combine miso, honey, and butter, mixing well, then spread in an even layer over upper surface of each rectangle. Top with a sprinkling of raisins, apple wedges and, if used, nutmeats. Roll each rectangle from one end to form a compact cylinder. Place into oiled loaf pans and bake at 350° for about 45 minutes, or until nicely browned. Allow to cool thoroughly. Serve with butter.

Mock Peking Duck
SERVES 2

This delicacy is the prized creation (and most expensive item) in many fine Chinese restaurants. Thin slices of duck with lacquer-crisp skin are rolled up in paper-thin wheat-flour "doilies" (each 6 inches in diameter) or folded in steamed *litus* buns together with slivered leeks (or scallions) and *t'ien mien chiang* (or *hoishin* sauce). The following is a vegetarian version of the original using ingredients more readily available in the West.

4 *tortillas*, cut into halves and warmed in a steamer
Butter
10 ounces deep-fried tofu cutlets, cut into 4-inch-long strips
2 or 3 tablespoons *t'ien mien chiang* (homemade, p. 70 or commercial, p. 243)
1 leek or 3 green onions, cut into 4-inch slivers, soaked in water for 5 minutes and drained

Butter warmed *tortillas* lightly on one side. Divide tofu among *tortillas*, placing the strips in the center of each *tortilla* half perpendicular to the *tortilla's* cut edge. Spread the *t'ien mien chiang* on the tofu, then top with a sprinkling of the leek slivers. Roll up and, if desired, secure with a foodpick. Serve while *tortillas* are still warm.

Pressure Cooked Soybeans with Miso
MAKES 2¼ CUPS

---

1 cup dry soybeans, rinsed and soaked for 2 to 3 hours in 2 quarts water
2 cups water
A thin wedge of lemon or lime (optional)

Drain and rinse soaked beans, and combine with 2 cups water is a pressure cooker. Bring to full pressure (15 pounds) and simmer for 45 minutes. Remove from heat and allow to stand for 10 to 15 mnutes as pressure returns to normal. Cool lid under cold running water and open.

Return cooker to stove, stir in any of the ingredients listed below, and simmer uncovered for 10 to 15 minutes, or until flavors are nicely married. If necessary, add ¼ cup water during simmering. Stir from time to time. Serve hot or cold.

*2 tablespoons red, barley, or Hatcho miso (creamed with a little of the cooking liquid). If desired, add 1 teaspoon lemon juice and/or 1 tablespoon butter. For a deliciously rich flavor, add 1 (sautéed) minced onion together with the miso and stir in ½ cup grated cheese or ¼ cup Parmesan just before removing from heat.

*1½ tablespoons red miso, 3 tablespoons sesame butter or *tahini*, 3 to 4 tablespoons dry *hijiki* or slivered *kombu* (reconstituted, p. 54), and 1 onion or ¾ cup carrot (pre-sautéed in 1 tablespoon oil, if desired). For extra sweetness, add 1½ teaspoons honey or natural sugar.

*1 to 1½ tablespoons red miso and 2 to 3 tablespoons molasses or honey.

*1 tablespoon red miso and ¼ cup sesame butter or *tahini*.

*1 tablespoon red miso and ½ to 1 cup total of the following (added alone or in combination): diced tomatoes, onions, carrots, celery, mushrooms, lotus root, burdock root, sprouts, fresh or dried *daikon*, or *kombu*. For variety add ½ teaspoon curry powder and/or 1 clove of crushed garlic.

*In any of the above recipes, after the beans and seasonings have finished cooking, try sautéing the mixture for a few minutes in a little (sesame) oil.

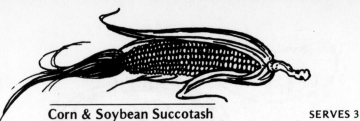

Corn & Soybean Succotash

SERVES 3

Here's a delicious, high-protein favorite of the American Indians with soybeans used in place of the traditional lima beans, and miso in place of salt.

2 tablespoons butter or oil
1 cup cooked soybeans (p. 129; unseasoned)
1 cup cooked fresh corn
1 tablespoon red, barley, or Hatcho miso
1/8 teaspoon paprika
1 tablespoon minced parsley

Melt the butter in a heavy skillet or pot. Add corn and beans, and sauté over low heat for 5 minutes. Mix in miso, season with paprika, and remove from heat. Top with a sprinkling of parsley.

For variety, sauté ½ minced onion together with the corn and/or add ¼ cup grated cheese together with the miso.

Boston Baked Soybeans
   with Brown Rice & Miso

SERVES 3

1 cup cooked soybeans (p. 129), drained
2 cups cooked Brown Rice (p. 57)
¼ cup minced onion
2½ tablespoons ketchup
5 teaspoons red, barley, or Hatcho miso
1½ teaspoons honey
2 teaspoons dry mustard
½ cup soybean cooking liquid
¾ teaspoon curry powder
½ teaspoon vinegar
2½ teaspoons Worcestershire sauce

Preheat oven to 250°. Combine all ingredients, mixing well. Place into a lightly oiled baking dish and bake covered for 30 minutes, then uncovered for 30 minutes more. Delicious hot or chilled.

Miso also makes an excellent substitute for salt in your favorite recipe for Boston Baked Beans.

Soybean & Miso Garnish

MAKES 1 CUP

2 tablespoons sesame oil
1 cup cooked soybeans (p. 129), well drained
2 tablespoons red, barley, or Hatcho miso
½ teaspoon grated gingerroot
Dash of 7-spice red pepper (optional)

Heat a skillet or wok and coat with the oil. Add soybeans and sauté for 2 to 3 minutes. Reduce heat to low, add remaining ingredients, and sauté for 2 minutes more. Allow to cool to room temperature. Serve as a garnish with brown rice or rice porridge.

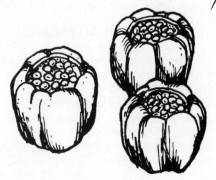

Green Peppers Stuffed with
   Miso-Soybeans

SERVES 6

1 cup dry soybeans, cooked (p. 129) and drained
2 tablespoons red, barley, or Hatcho miso
¼ cup ketchup
½ onion, minced
2 tablespoons dark brown sugar
1½ to 2 teaspoons mustard
½ cup grated cheese
3 green peppers, seeded and parboiled in salted water for 5 minutes
1 tablespoon oil

Preheat oven to 350°. Combine the first seven ingredients, mixing well, then use to fill green pepper shells. Rub shells lightly with oil, place in an oiled pan, and bake for 20 minutes. Serve hot or chilled.

Other delicious fillings for green pepper shells include Refried Pinto Beans (p. 132), and Boston Baked Soybeans.

Savory Soybean, Corn
   & Miso Casserole

SERVES 4

1¼ cups cooked soybeans (p. 129), drained
1¼ cups cooked corn
1 tomato, diced
¼ cup ketchup
1½ tablespoons red, barley, or Hatcho miso
½ teaspoon honey
¼ onion, minced
¼ cup chopped peanuts or bread crumbs

Preheat oven to 350°. Combine the first seven ingredients, mixing well. Place into a lightly oiled baking dish and top with a sprinkling of peanuts. Bake covered for about 45 minutes. Serve hot or chilled.

Also delicious as a topping for plain or stir-fried brown rice (pp. 119 and 120).

Tofu with Miso Toppings

SERVES 1

6 to 8 ounces regular or 3 to 5 ounces (lightly-broiled) deep-fried tofu

Miso Toppings: Use any of the following
    1 to 2 teaspoons red, barley, or Hatcho miso
    1 tablespoon Sweet Simmered Miso (p. 60). Finger Lickin' Miso (p. 41), Miso Sauté (p. 65), Mixed Miso (p. 69), or Broiled Miso (p. 71); or, for use only with deep-fried tofu, Vinegar Miso (p. 64) or Daikon Mixed Miso (p. 69)
    1½ tablespoons sweet white or red miso

Garnishes: Use ½ to 1 teaspoon of any of the following (optional)
    Thinly sliced leeks
    Grated gingerroot
    Minced or crushed garlic
    Wasabi
    Slivered lemon, lime, or *yuzu* rind

Place tofu on a plate and coat its upper surface with your choice of topping. If desired, cut into bite-sized pieces and serve topped with the garnish.

Tofu with Miso-Onion Sauce and Cheese

SERVES 4 TO 6

2 tablespoons oil
6 onions, thinly sliced
6 tablespoons red, barley, or Hatcho miso
1½ teaspoons honey
1 tablespoon sake or white wine
24 ounces tofu, cut into bite-sized cubes
2 ounces grated cheese
2 eggs, lightly beaten
2 to 3 tablespoons Parmesan cheese (optional)

Heat a large casserole or pot and coat with the oil. Add onions, cover, and cook over very low heat for 1½ hours, stirring occasionally. Mix in miso, honey and sake, then carefully add tofu cubes, covering them by spooning onion sauce over the top. Cover pot and simmer for 10 minutes. Gently mix in grated cheese and pour egg over the top. Re-cover and simmer for 5 minutes more, or until egg is firm. Sprinkle with Parmesan if desired and allow to stand, covered, overnight. Serve as is or reheated.

Fig. 22. Steamed Tofu

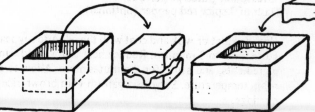

Tofu with Miso White Sauce Au Gratin

SERVES 3

1 tablespoon oil
1 clove of garlic, crushed or minced
2 small onions, thinly sliced
1/3 cup grated cheese
7½ ounces deep-fried tofu, cubed; or 18 ounces regular tofu, pressed (p. 55) and cubed
1 cup Miso White Sauce (p. 114; season with 2 tablespoons red miso)
2 tablespoons Parmesan cheese
1 tablespoon bread crumbs

Preheat oven to 350°. Heat the oil in a skillet or wok. Add garlic and sauté for 15 seconds. Add onions and sauté for 3 minutes more. Remove from heat, stir in grated cheese and tofu, then spoon into a loaf pan or casserole. Pour on the white sauce and top with a sprinkling of Parmesan and bread crumbs. Bake for about 20 minutes, or until nicely browned. Delicious either hot or cold.

Steamed Miso-filled Tofu
(*Nanzenji no Tsutsumi-dofu*)

SERVES 4

24 ounces tofu
¼ to ½ cup Yuzu Miso (p. 62) or any Sweet Simmered Miso (p. 60)

Cut tofu into four 6-ounce pieces. With the sharp point of a knife, cut a section 2 inches square and 1 inch deep from the larger surface of each piece, and lift out carefully (fig. 22). Fill the "well" that remains with 1 to 2 tablespoons of the miso, then replace the small piece of tofu atop the miso. Wrap each piece of tofu in strong, absorbent paper (the Japanese use *washi* for this purpose) or in aluminum foil.

    Bring water to a boil in a steamer. Place wrapped tofu in steamer and steam for 5 to 10 minutes, or until miso is well heated. Serve hot, inviting each guest to unwrap his or her portion just before eating.

Deep-fried Tofu with
Gingerroot Miso

SERVES 2 OR 3

1½ tablespoons oil
10 ounces deep-fried tofu, cut into bite-sized rectangles ½-
    inch thick
2 tablespoons red, barley, or Hatcho miso
1 tablespoon honey
1 teaspoon grated gingerroot
Minced parsley or whole lettuce leaves

Heat a skillet or wok and coat with the oil. Add deep-fried
tofu and sauté over high heat for 3 to 4 minutes until slightly
crisp and well browned. Add miso, honey, and gingerroot and
cook, stirring constantly, for 2 to 3 minutes, or until all ingredients are well mixed. Serve hot or cold garnished with the
parsley or placed on individual lettuce leaves.

Making tortillas

Mexican-style Pinto Beans with
Miso (*Frijoles de Olla*)

SERVES 6 TO 8

2 cups pinto beans, washed and soaked overnight in 9 cups
    water
1 onion, minced
3½ tablespoons red, barley, or Hatcho miso
Dash of cumin seeds and/or red pepper (optional)
½ to 1 cup grated or Parmesan cheese

Place beans and water in a casserole or heavy pot and bring to
a boil. Reduce heat to very low, cover, and simmer for 1½
hours. Add onion, miso and cumin seeds, then simmer for 30
minutes more, or until beans are tender. Serve in soup bowls,
topped with a sprinkling of the cheese.

Refried Pinto Beans with Sour Cream
and Miso (*Frijoles Refritos*)

SERVES 3

In Mexico, the leftovers from a large pot of *Frijoles de
Olla* (above) are usually served at the next meal prepared in
the following manner:

2 tablespoons oil
1 clove of garlic, minced or crushed
½ onion, minced
2 cups *Frijoles de Olla* (without cheese), drained of excess
    liquid
¼ to ½ cup grated cheese
½ cup sour cream
2 teaspoons red, barley, or Hatcho miso

Heat a skillet and coat with the oil. Add garlic and onion, and
sauté for 1 minute. Add beans, mash well with a fork, and
sauté for about 3 minutes, or until slightly dry and crisp.
Combine cheese, sour cream and miso, mixing well, then stir
into the beans and remove from heat. Delicious served as a
side dish, in *tortillas* or as a spread.

Miso in Baked Dishes

More of our very favorite recipes appear among the following than in any other section of this book. Almost all are Western-style preparations and many contain grains as the basic ingredient.

Rich Noodle Casserole with Miso-Sour Cream and Chives

SERVES 5 TO 6

1 cup sour cream
3 tablespoons red, barley, or Hatcho miso
2 eggs, lightly beaten
6 tablespoons minced chives
1½ cups cottage cheese
4¼ ounces (*soba*) buckwheat noodles, cooked, drained and cooled (p. 58)
2 to 3 tablespoons butter

Preheat oven to 350°. Combine the first five ingredients, mixing well, then gently stir into the cooked noodles. Place into a buttered casserole and top with dabs of the remaining butter. Bake covered for 20 minutes, then uncover and bake for about 15 minutes more, or until nicely browned.

Miso-Onion Soup Casserole Au Gratin

SERVES 5 TO 6

2½ to 3 cups bread cubes (fresh, stale, or croutons)
4 cups Thick French Onion Soup with Miso (p. 107)
6 tablespoons Parmesan or grated cheese

Combine bread and soup, mixing well, and spoon into a lightly oiled or buttered loaf pan or casserole; allow to stand for 1 to 2 hours. Preheat oven to 350°. Sprinkle casserole with cheese and bake for about 20 minutes, or until nicely browned. Serve hot or cold.

Mushroom Casserole with Miso

SERVES 5

3 tablespoons butter
4 cups sliced mushrooms (12 ounces)
6 slices of whole-wheat bread, buttered and broken into bite-sized pieces
½ cup minced onion
½ cup minced green pepper
½ cup minced celery
3½ tablespoons red, barley, or Hatcho miso
1 cup milk (soy or dairy)
4 eggs, lightly beaten
¼ cup mayonnaise
Dash of pepper

Melt the butter in a skillet. Add mushrooms and sauté for 3 minutes, then transfer to a large buttered casserole. Add bread and minced vegetables. Cream miso with a little milk, then combine with the remaining ingredients, stirring vigorously until smooth. Add to casserole and mix with vegetables and bread. Smooth surface of ingredients, cover, and refrigerate for 6 to 8 hours. Bake in a preheated 325° oven for 50 minutes.

Baked Potatoes in Miso Gravy

SERVES 6 TO 8

3¾ pounds potatoes (6 to 8), each peeled and cut into fourths
1 cup vegetable stock or water
3½ tablespoons butter
3½ tablespoons red, barley, or Hatcho miso
3½ tablespoons honey
1 tablespoon shoyu (natural soy sauce)

Preheat oven to 450°F. Place potatoes in a greased casserole. Mix remaining ingredients in a bowl or blender and pour over the potatoes. Cover and bake for 30 minutes. Mix well. Re-cover and bake for 30 minutes more. Serve hot or cold.

Potatoes with Miso White Sauce Au Gratin

SERVES 3

1½ teaspoons oil
1 onion, thinly sliced
1 cup Miso White Sauce (p. 114), seasoned with dill if
    desired
3 potatoes, boiled and cubed (2 to 2½ cups)
¼ cup grated cheese
1½ teaspoons butter
1½ tablespoons bread crumbs
1½ tablespoons Parmesan cheese

Preheat oven to 400°. Heat a skillet and coat with the oil. Add
onions and sauté for 3 minutes. Prepare Miso White Sauce,
then mix in the potatoes, onions, and grated cheese. Spoon
into a buttered loaf pan or casserole, dot with butter, and
sprinkle with bread crumbs and Parmesan cheese. Bake for 10
to 15 minutes, or until nicely browned. Serve hot or, for a
richer flavor, refrigerate overnight and serve cold.

For variety, substitute squash or (*kabocha*) pumpkin
for the potatoes.

Potatoes Baked in Miso Gravy Au Gratin

SERVES 3 OR 4

4 small potatoes, boiled in their skins until tender and cut
    into bite-sized pieces
2½ cups Miso Gravy (p. 116)
2 tablespoons Parmesan cheese

Preheat oven to 350°. Combine potatoes and gravy in an oiled
loaf pan or casserole and top with a sprinkling of cheese. Bake
for about 20 minutes, or until nicely browned. Delicious hot
or cold.

Quiche Nicoise with Miso

SERVES 6

A 9-inch pie shell
6 tablespoons (olive) oil
1 onion, minced
4 tomatoes, diced
2 large cloves of garlic, minced
1 teaspoon basil
1 teaspoon thyme
1½ teaspoons red, barley, or Hatcho miso
Dash of pepper, coarsely ground
3 eggs
3 tablespoons tomato paste
¼ cup chopped parsely
Dash of cayenne or tabasco sauce
8 black olives, thinly sliced (optional)
½ cup Parmsan cheese

Bake pie shell at 425° for 7 minutes until partially done, then
set aside. Heat a skillet and coat with 4 tablespoons oil. Add
onions and sauté for 4 minutes, or until tender. Add the next
six ingredients, cover, and cook over low heat for about 5

minutes. Uncover and cook 5 minutes more, or until liquid
has evaporated, then set aside to cool for 10 minutes. Meanwhile, combine the eggs in a mixing bowl with the last four
ingredients plus 2 tablespoons olive oil; beat until smooth.
Gently stir in cooked ingredients, then spoon mixture into
pie shell. Decorate, if desired, with olive slices, sprinkle with
cheese, and dribble the remaining 1 tablespoon oil over the
top. Bake at 375° for about 25 minures, or until quiche has
set. Delicious hot or cold.

Quick Cheese & Onion Quiche with Miso

SERVES 6

2 teaspoons oil
¾ onion, thinly sliced
A 9-inch pie shell, uncooked
4 eggs, one of which is separated into yolk and white
6 ounces Swiss cheese, grated
¾ cup half-and-half cream
1½ teaspoons red miso, creamed in 1 tablespoon hot water
Dash of nutmeg

Preheat oven to 350°. Heat a skillet and coat with the oil. Add
onions and sauté for about 3 minutes, or until limp. Line a
9-inch pie pan with the pastry shell, then brush lightly with
egg white. Place alternate layers of onion and cheese in shell
until both ingredients are used up. Mix together remaining
eggs, cream, and softened miso; pour over cheese-and-onions,
then top with a sprinkling of nutmeg. Bake for 45 minutes.

Miso-Noodle Gratin

SERVES 4 TO 6

5 tablespoons butter
2/3 onion, thinly sliced
4 small mushrooms, sliced
5 ounces deep-fried tofu, thinly sliced (optional)
2½ tablespoons red, barley, or Hatcho miso
7 ounces (*soba*) buckwheat noodles or macaroni, cooked
Dash of pepper
3 tablespoons whole-wheat flour
2 cups milk (soy or dairy)
2 tablespoons grated cheese
2 tablespoons bread crumbs or bread crumb flakes
2 tablespoons minced parsley

Preheat oven to 350°. Melt 4 teaspoons butter in a skillet.
Add onion and sauté for 1 minute. Add mushrooms and deep-
fried tofu, and sauté for 2 minutes more. Stir in 1½ teaspoons
miso, the cooked noodles, and pepper; sauté for 1 minute
more and remove from heat.

Using 3 tablespoons butter, the flour, 2 tablespoons
miso and the milk, prepare a Miso White Sauce (p.114). Stir
in the noodle-vegetable mixture, then transfer to a lightly
buttered gratin dish, casserole, or baking pan. Sprinkle with
cheese and bread crumbs, and dot with the remaining 2 teaspoons butter. Bake for 15 minutes, or until lightly browned.
Serve topped with a sprinkling of minced parsley.

Noodles & Eggs with Miso White Sauce Au Gratin

SERVES 3

2 tablespoons butter
1 onion, thinly sliced
1 cup Miso White Sauce (p. 114; seasoned with 1½ table-spoons miso)
3 ounces (buckwheat) noodles, cooked (p. 58), drained, and cut into 4-inch lengths
3 hard-boiled eggs, shelled and cut lengthwise into halves
2 tablespoons Parmesan cheese
2 tablespoons minced parsley

Preheat oven to 350°. Melt the butter in a skillet, add onion, and sauté for 4 minutes. Remove from heat, combine with noodles and one-half the white sauce, and spoon into an oiled casserole or loaf pan. Arrange egg halves atop noodles, top with remaining white sauce, and sprinkle with Parmesan; bake for 20 minutes or until nicely browned. Delicious either hot or chilled, topped with a sprinkling of parsley.

Tomatoes Stuffed with Eggs and Miso

SERVES 4

2 large, firm tomatoes, unpeeled
2 hard-boiled eggs, diced
¼ cup bread crumbs
1 tablespoon red, barley, or Hatcho miso
1 tablespoon minced parsley
1 tablespoon butter
Dash of pepper
3 tablespoons Parmesan cheese

Preheat oven to 350°. Slice off tops of tomatoes and scoop out insides, reserving one half of the latter for use in other cooking. Combine the remaining scooped-out portion with the diced eggs and the next five ingredients. Add 1 tablespoon Parmesan cheese and mix well, then use mixture to stuff tomatoes. Place tomatoes in an oiled loaf pan, sprinkle with the remaining 2 tablespoons Parmesan, and bake for 20 minutes. Cool to room temperature before serving.

For variety, pour 1 cup Miso White Sauce (p. 114; seasoned with 4 teaspoons red miso) over tomatoes in loaf pan. Top with the Parmesan and 2 tablespoons bread crumbs, then bake until nicely browned.

Miso-Creamed Celery Casserole

SERVES 4 TO 6

2 cups sliced celery stalks and leaves
2 cups water or stock
6 tablespoons butter
6 tablespoons flour
¼ cup red, barley, or Hatcho miso
2 cups milk (soy or dairy)
Dash of pepper
4 slices whole-wheat bread (preferably several days old)
¼ cup grated or Parmesan cheese; or ¼ to ½ cup sherry, sake, or white wine

Combine celery and water in a saucepan, bring to a boil, and simmer uncovered for 10 to 12 minutes. Cool briefly, then purée in a blender until smooth.

Preheat oven to 350°. Melt ¼ cup butter in a large saucepan, then use the flour, 2 tablespoons miso, milk, puréed celery, and pepper to make a Miso White Sauce (p. 114); remove from heat.

Spread 2 tablespoons each butter and miso over one surface of each piece of bread. Break bread into small chunks and place into a lightly buttered casserole. Pour in white sauce and allow to stand for 1 to 2 hours. Top with the cheese or sherry, and bake uncovered for 30 minutes, or until nicely browned.

Cooked rice or noodles may be substituted for the bread, and the 2 tablespoons miso and butter may be added directly to the white sauce.

Curried Green Rice Casserole with Miso

SERVES 3

2 eggs, lightly beaten
¾ cup milk (soy or dairy)
2½ to 3 tablespoons red, barley, or Hatcho miso
2 cups cooked Brown Rice (p. 57)
½ cup minced parsley
½ cup grated cheese
1 onion, minced
¼ teaspoon curry powder
1 clove of garlic, crushed or minced
1 tablespoon butter

Preheat oven to 325°. Combine the eggs, milk and miso, mixing well, then stir in the next six ingredients. Coat a casserole or baking tin with the butter and spoon in the curried-rice mixture. Bake for about 40 minutes, or until nicely browned. For best flavor, allow to cool for 6 to 8 hours. Serve hot or cold.

For variety, sauté onion for several minutes before use and/or substitute ½ cup corn kernels for one-half the onion.

Baked Potatoes with Miso

2 potatoes, baked in their skins
2 tablespoons butter
2 teaspoons of one of the following:
    Red, barley, or Hatcho miso
    Finger Lickin' Miso (p. 42)
    Leek or Onion Miso (pp. 64 and 70)
    Cheese Miso (p. 70)
Sour cream or Creamy Tofu Dressing (with Cheese & Garlic, p. 85) (optional)
Minced chives, grated cheese, or parsley (optional)

Cut open the hot potatoes and spoon in butter and miso. Mix lightly, and, if desired, top with sour cream and chives. Serve hot or cold.

Or, substitute 4 teaspoons mellow white miso for the miso above.

Miso Sautéed & Simmered with Vegetables

The recipes that follow are only a few of many delicious possibilities. Experiment using our basic techniques applied to your favorite vegetable cookery.

SAUTÉED PREPARATIONS

Most types of Japanese-style miso toppings—especially Sesame Miso (p. 62), Walnut Miso (p. 61), and Miso Sauté (p. 65)—make excellent additions to sautéed vegetable dishes. Note the use of miso in the cooking technique called *nitsuké* wherein vegetables are first sautéed until just barely tender, then steamed or simmered in a little water—and miso —until done.

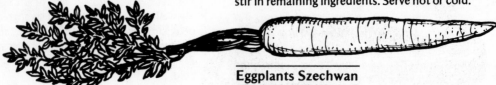

Mushrooms Sautéed in Miso   SERVES 2 OR 3

1 tablespoon oil
12 fresh (*shiitaké*) mushrooms, cut into halves or quarters
1 tablespoon red, barley, or Hatcho miso
1 to 1½ teaspoons honey
1 teaspoon shoyu
¼ teaspoon freshly grated or ½ teaspoon powdered ginger-root (optional)
1 tablespoon ground roasted sesame seeds (p. 54) (optional)

Heat a skillet and coat with the oil. Add mushrooms and sauté for 2 to 3 minutes. Stir in the next three (or four) ingredients and sauté for 1 minute more. Serve hot or cold, topped, if desired, with a sprinkling of sesame seeds.

VARIATION

*Eggplants Sautéed in Miso. Use 4 small Japanese eggplants, cut lengthwise into halves, then diagonally into 3/8-inch-thick slices. Sauté in 2 tablespoons oil over medium heat for 5 minutes, then reduce heat to low and proceed as above.

Miso-Cooked Carrots   SERVES 2 OR 3
with Wheat Germ and Nuts

2 tablespoons oil
1 carrot, sliced into thin rounds (1½ cups)
4 teaspoons red, barley, or Hatcho miso, thinned with 3 tablespoons water
¼ cup (toasted) wheat germ
¼ cup sunflower seeds or chopped nutmeats
½ teaspoon grated orange rind (optional)

Heat the oil in a wok or skillet. Add carrots and sauté for 3 minutes. Mix in creamed miso and cook for 4 minutes, or until liquid is absorbed or evaporated. Remove from heat and stir in remaining ingredients. Serve hot or cold.

Eggplants Szechwan   SERVES 4

3 tablespoons oil
4 small eggplants (about 12 ounces total), cut into ½-inch cubes
1 clove of garlic, minced or crushed
1½ teaspoons minced gingerroot
3 tablespoons chopped leek greens or green onions
Dash of (7-spice) red pepper or tabasco sauce
½ cup stock or water
2 tablespoons red, barley, or Hatcho miso
½ teaspoon honey
1½ teaspoons sesame oil
1½ teaspoons vinegar

Heat a skillet and coat with the oil. Add eggplants and sauté for 3 minutes, then drain briefly over skillet and transfer to a separate container. Now add to the skillet: garlic, gingerroot, 2 tablespoons chopped leek greens, and enough red pepper to give a spicy hot flavor; sauté for 15 seconds. Mix in stock, miso and honey, and bring to a boil. Add eggplants, simmer for 1 minute, and turn off heat. Sprinkle with sesame oil and vinegar, and garnish with the remaining 1 tablespoon chopped leek greens.

Eggplant with Sesame & Miso Sauce

SERVES 4

6 tablespoons oil
2½ to 3 cups eggplant (¾-inch cubes)
3 tablespoons red, barley, or Hatcho miso
2 tablespoons sesame butter
1 tablespoon honey
1 tablespoon white wine, sake, or *mirin*
6½ tablespoons stock or water
½ teaspoon grated or 1 teaspoon powdered gingerroot
4 lettuce leaves

Heat a wok or skillet and coat with 5 tablespoons oil. Add eggplants and sauté for 3 to 4 minutes, then transfer to a separate container.

Reheat skillet and coat with remaining 1 tablespoon oil. Add miso and the next 5 ingredients. Cook, stirring constantly, for 1 to 2 minutes to form a smooth sauce. Mix in cooked eggplant and remove from heat. For best flavor, serve chilled, mounded on lettuce leaves.

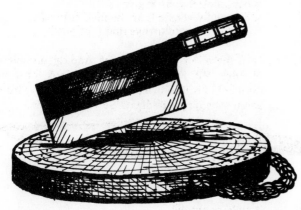

Cauliflower & Carrots with Miso & Cheese

SERVES 2 OR 3

2½ tablespoons butter
½ cup thin rounds of leek or scallion
2 tablespoons red, barley, or Hatcho miso
½ cauliflower, separated into flowerets, steamed for 10 minutes
1 carrot, cut into thin half moons and steamed for 15 minutes
3 tablespoons grated cheese
2 tablespoons minced parsley
Dash of pepper

Melt the butter in a skillet. Add leek rounds, miso and steamed vegetables, and sauté for 2 to 3 minutes. Turn off heat and top immediately with cheese and parsley. Season with pepper. Serve hot.

Sautéed Leeks & Carrots with Sesame Miso

SERVES 3 OR 4

¼ cup sesame butter
3 tablespoons red, barley, or Hatcho miso
2 tablespoons water
2 teaspoons oil
2½ cups thinly sliced leeks or onions
1 cup slivered or grated carrots

Combine the first three ingredients, mixing well. Heat oil in a skillet or wok. Add leeks and carrots and sauté for 4 to 5 minutes. Add sesame-miso mixture and cook, stirring constantly, for 1 minute more. Serve as is, or as a topping for grain dishes or tofu.

Green Peppers & Tofu Sautéed with Miso

SERVES 2

3½ tablespoons red, barley, or Hatcho miso
½ cup stock or water
2½ to 3 teaspoons honey
2 teaspoons sake or white wine
7 ounces deep-fried tofu, cut into ½-inch strips
2 tablespoons oil
1½ teaspoons minced garlic
5 green peppers, cut lengthwise into sixths
1 large onion, thinly sliced

Combine the first five ingredients in a saucepan and bring to a boil. Cover and simmer for 5 minutes, then remove from heat.

Heat a wok or skillet and coat with the oil. Add garlic and sauté for 30 seconds. Increase heat to high, add green peppers and onion, and sauté for 3 minutes more. Add deep-fried tofu and any remaining cooking broth, then cook, stirring constantly, for 1 minute. Serve hot or cold.

Green Beans & Onions in Spicy Miso Sauce

SERVES 3

1 tablespoon oil
1 clove of garlic, minced or crushed
½ onion, thinly sliced
20 green beans, parboiled until just tender
1½ tablespoons red, barley, or Hatcho miso, dissolved in ½ cup water or stock
¾ teaspoon honey
1½ teaspoons sake or white wine
Dash of (7-spice) red pepper or tabasco sauce
2 teaspoons cornstarch, arrowroot, or *kuzu*, dissolved in 3 tablespoons water

Heat a wok or skillet and coat with the oil. Add garlic and sauté for 30 seconds, then add onion and sauté for 4 minutes. Add green beans and sauté for 1 minute more. Stir in the next four ingredients and bring to a boil. Add dissolved cornstarch and simmer, stirring constantly, for about 1 minute, or until thick. Serve as a side dish or as a topping for (deep-fried) noodles.

Potatoes Sautéed with Miso

SERVES 4

1½ to 2 tablespoons oil
6 small potatoes, sliced into thin rounds (3½ cups)
½ cup water
2 tablespoons red, barley, or Hatcho miso
Dash of pepper
2 tablespoons minced parsley and/or grated cheese

Heat a large skillet or wok and coat with the oil. Add potatoes and sauté for 4 minutes. Add water, cover, and simmer for 5 to 6 minutes. Mix in miso and cook, stirring constantly, for 1 to 2 minutes, or until most of liquid has evaporated. Serve seasoned with pepper and topped with parsley.

Sweet & Sour Cabbage with Miso

SERVES 2 OR 3

1½ teaspoons oil
1 red pepper, seeded and minced
11 ounces cabbage, chopped into 1½-inch squares
2½ tablespoons red, barley, or Hatcho miso
1 teaspoon honey
2 teaspoons vinegar
2 teaspoons sesame oil

Heat a wok or skillet and coat with the oil. Add red pepper and sauté for 30 seconds, or until color changes. Add cabbage and sauté for 3 to 4 minutes, then add the next three ingredients and sauté for 1 minute more. Sprinkle with the sesame oil and remove from heat. Serve hot or cold.

Land & Sea Vegetables with Miso

SERVES 4

2 tablespoons sesame oil
1 large onion, thinly sliced
1 carrot, grated or slivered
1 cup thin half-moons of lotus root
¾ cup dry *hijiki*, soaked for 15 minutes in water to cover, rinsed and drained
2½ tablespoons red, barley, or Hatcho miso
¾ cup water

Heat a skillet or wok and coat with the oil. Add onion, carrot, and lotus root and sauté for 4 minutes. Add *hijiki* and sauté for 3 minutes more. Stir in miso and water and bring to a boil. Cover and simmer for 10 minutes. Serve hot or cold.

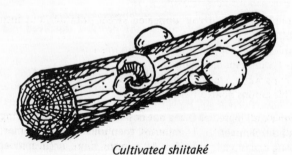

Cultivated shiitaké

FRIED AND STIR-FRIED PREPARATIONS

Fried Eggplants Shigiyaki
(*Nasu no Nabé Shigiyaki*)

SERVES 4

One of Japan's favorite miso recipes, this is a close relative of the equally popular Grilled Eggplants Shigiyaki described on page 146. The key to the fine flavor lies in choosing tender young eggplants.

4 Japanese eggplants, each 1¼ inches in diameter, or 2 small Western eggplants
2 tablespoons red, barley, or Hatcho miso
1 tablespoon honey
1½ teaspoons sake or white wine
¼ teaspoon grated gingerroot
1 tablespoon water
3 to 4 tablespoons oil
1 to 2 teaspoons roasted sesame seeds or Parmesan cheese

Peel eggplants lengthwise so that ½-inch-wide peeled strips alternate with ½-inch-wide unpeeled strips. Soak in water for 10 minutes.

Meanwhile combine miso, honey, sake, gingerroot and water in a small skillet and simmer over low heat, stirring constantly, for 3 to 4 minutes until smooth and slightly thickened. Remove from heat.

Pat eggplants dry with a dishtowel. Cut Japanese eggplants lengthwise into halves, Western eggplants into ½-inch-thick diagonal sections. Heat the oil in a skillet. Add eggplant slices, cover, and fry for 2 minutes or until golden brown. Turn and repeat on second side. Arrange slices on a large serving plate, spread with the miso sauce and sprinkle with sesame seeds. For best flavor, serve chilled.

For variety, cut eggplants into ¾-inch-thick rounds and pierce each side in 2 or 3 places with chopsticks or a fork. Fry in oil as above, then serve topped with White Nerimiso (p. 61) or Kinomé Miso (p. 63) and, if desired, a sprinkling of roasted sesame seeds.

Fried Eggplants with Sweet Simmered Miso (Yaki-nasu)

SERVES 4

4 small eggplants, each about 4 inches long
1½ tablespoons sesame oil
2 tablespoons Sesame-(p. 62) or Walnut Miso (p. 61)

Cut eggplants lengthwise into halves and score the outer surfaces in a checkerboard pattern to a depth of 1/3 inch. (If using larger Western eggplants, cut into ¾-inch-thick half moons.) Heat a skillet and coat with the oil. Add eggplants and fry over low heat on both sides until nicely browned. Coat flat surface with a thin layer of miso. Serve hot or cold.

Deep-fried Tofu and Vegetables with Miso-Sweet & Sour Sauce

SERVES 4 TO 5

2 tablespoons oil
1 clove of garlic, crushed or minced
1 small onion, thinly sliced
2 tomatoes, diced; or 1 cup cherry tomatoes, cut into halves
1 green pepper, cut into 1-inch squares
1½ cups Pineapple Sweet & Sour Sauce (p. 115)
7 ounces deep-fried tofu, cut into 1-inch cubes

Heat the oil in a large skillet or wok. Add garlic and onion, and stir-fry over high heat for 2 minutes. Add tomatoes, green pepper and sauce. Cook, stirring constantly, for about 1 minute until thick. Mix in deep-fried tofu and remove from heat. Serve chilled. (To serve hot, increase amount of honey and vinegar in sauce by 1 tablespoon each.)

Fried Sweet Potatoes with Sesame Miso

SERVES 2 OR 3

1 sweet potato (6 inches long)
2 teaspoons oil
2½ to 3 tablespoons Sesame Miso (p. 62)

Steam sweet potato for 30 minutes, then cut into ½-inch-thick rounds. Heat oil in a large skillet. Add rounds and fry for 2 minutes on each side, or until nicely browned. Transfer onto absorbent paper (or a large plate) and allow to cool for several minutes. Coat one surface of each round with the miso. Serve as a side dish or hors d'œuvre.

NABÉ AND SIMMERED PREPARATIONS

Miso is used as the basis for the dipping sauce in a number of Japan's famous *nabémono*, the do-it-yourself one-pot cookery prepared at the table. In dishes known as *Miso-ni*, vegetables (or seafoods) are simmered slowly in a rich, slightly sweet miso sauce. Most Miso Sauces (p. 113) or Toppings (p. 60) can be used with excellent results over vegetables simmered until tender in dashi or stock.

Kabocha Simmered in Miso (Kabocha no Miso-ni)

SERVES 4

2 tablespoons sesame oil
2 onions, thinly sliced
1 pound *kabocha*, pumpkin, or squash, cubed
1 cup water
¼ cup red, barley, or Hatcho miso, thinned in ½ cup warm water

Heat a wok or skillet and coat with the oil. Add onions and sauté for 5 minutes. Add pumpkin and sauté for 3 minutes more. Stir in water and bring to a boil. Cover and simmer for 30 minutes, or until tender. Stir in thinned miso and simmer uncovered for about 5 minutes, or until liquid has been absorbed or evaporated.

VARIATION

*Other Types of Miso-ni: Substitute for the *kabocha* in the above recipe an equal weight of any of the following: potatoes or sweet potatoes, red radishes, turnips, bamboo shoots, butterbur. Serve hot or cold.

Taro or Sweet Potatoes Simmered in Miso

SERVES 4

1 pound peeled taro or unpeeled sweet potatoes, cut into bite-sized pieces
3 tablespoons red, barley, or Hatcho miso
1 to 1½ tablespoons honey
1¼ cups water, stock, or dashi (p. 56)
3 tablespoons bonito flakes

Combine all ingredients in a pot or saucepan, cover, and bring to a boil. Simmer for 15 minutes, then uncover and simmer, stirring occasionally, for 5 to 10 minutes more, or until most of the liquid has evaporated. Allow to cool before serving.

Pumpkin Simmered in Sweetened Miso

SERVES 3 OR 4

14 ounces *kabocha*, pumpkin, or squash, seeded and cut
 into 1½-inch squares
¾ cup water, stock, or dashi (p. 56)
1½ to 2 tablespoons red, barley, or Hatcho miso
2 to 3 teaspoons honey
1½ tablespoons bonito flakes (optional)

Combine *kabocha* and water in a saucepan and bring to a boil.
Cover and simmer for 10 minutes. Stir in remaining ingredients and simmer for about 8 minutes more, or until *kabocha* is tender and all but ¼ cup liquid has been absorbed or
evaporated. For richest flavor, serve chilled.

 For variety, omit bonita flakes and add 1½ tablespoons
butter and a dash of nutmeg. Serve topped with Tofu Mayonnaise (p. 86) and a little minced (fresh) basil or parsley.

Sautéed Potatoes Simmered in Sweet Miso

SERVES 2

1 tablespoon oil
4 small potatoes, cut crosswise into halves, then into thin
 wedges (1¾ cups)
1 tablespoon sweet white or 2 teaspoons mellow white miso
1½ teaspoons red or barley miso
½ teaspoon honey
2½ teaspoons sake or white wine
¾ teaspoon minced gingerroot
¼ cup water, stock, or dashi (p. 56)

Heat a skillet and coat with the oil. Add potatoes and sauté
for 3 minutes. Mix in remaining ingredients and bring to a
boil. Cover and simmer over low heat for 10 minutes. Serve
hot or cold.

 For variety, substitute eggplants or 5 ounces deep-fried
tofu for the potatoes.

Turnips with Sesame Miso Sauce

SERVES 4

6 small (*kabu*) turnips, with greens
3 cups dashi (p. 56), stock, or water
2/3 cup Sesame Miso Sauce (p. 117)

Cut turnip roots lengthwise into halves, combine with dashi
in a saucepan, and bring to a boil. Cover and simmer for 15
minutes, or until tender. Remove from heat and drain, reserving liquid for use in sauce.

 Parboil turnip greens for 2 to 3 minutes in lightly salted
water; drain in a colander. Squeeze to remove excess liquid,
then cut into 1-inch lengths. Divide leaves and turnip halves
among individual bowls and top with the sauce.

 Daikon, radishes, and other root vegetables may be
substituted for the turnips.

Furofuki Daikon

SERVES 4

8 *daikon* rounds, each 2½ to 3 inches in diameter and ¾ inch
 thick
½ cup Orange-Sesame Miso Sauce (p.115) or
 Subtly Sweet Leek Miso (p. 70)

Combine *daikon* rounds with water (or dashi; p. 56) to cover
in a saucepan, bring to a boil, and simmer for 20 to 30
minutes, or until *daikon* is very tender. Drain well and
arrange rounds on serving plates. Place a large dollop of the
miso atop each round. Serve hot or cold.

 For variety, prepare as for Miso Oden (p. 141). Cook 4
daikon rounds together with 4 taro and 4 *konnyaku* triangles
in a *nabé* pot. Place the miso sauce in a cup at the center of
pot and use for dipping.

Daikon Rounds with Orange-Onion Miso

SERVES 2 OR 3

4 teaspoons oil, one of which may be sesame
6 *daikon* or turnip rounds, each 1 inch thick and 2½ inches
 in diameter
1 cup water or stock
¼ teaspoon salt
1 onion, minced
1½ tablespoons red, barley, or Hatcho miso
1 tablespoon sesame butter (optional)
½ teaspoon grated orange rind

Heat a large skillet and coat with 1 tablespoon (regular) oil.
Add *daikon* and fry for about 2½ minutes on each side, or
until nicely browned. Add water and bring to a boil. Cover
and simmer for 30 minutes, or until only several tablespoons
of liquid remain. Sprinkle rounds with salt and transfer to
serving plates; reserve liquid in skillet.

 Heat a second small skillet and coat with 1 teaspoon
(sesame) oil. Add onion and sauté for 5 minutes, then transfer
to the first skillet. Mix in miso and, if used, sesame butter.
Bring to a boil and cook, stirring constantly, for about 1
minute. Spoon this sauce over *daikon* rounds and top with a
sprinkling of orange rind. Serve hot or cold. Also delicious on
toast.

Miso Oden

In Japan, this popular wintertime dish is sold by street venders out of pushcarts or prepared in homes, particularly on special occasions.

Choose one of the following sauces:
    Orange-Sesame Miso Sauce (p. 115)
    Gingerroot-Miso Barbecue Sauce (p. 118)
    Rich Red Nerimiso (p. 61)
    Yuzu Miso (p. 62)
12 ounces tofu (regular or grilled), cut into 1- by 3- by ½- inch strips
1 cake of *konnyaku*
4 inches large *daikon*, cut into ½-inch-thick half moons
A 5-inch square of *kombu*, wiped clean; or substitute ½ teaspoon salt

Place the miso sauce into a small heat-resistant cup. Spear each tofu strip with two (6-inch bamboo) skewers or a fork. Rub *konnyaku* well with salt, rinse, cut crosswise into ½-inch-wide strips, and skewer each piece. Parboil *daikon*, then skewer each piece.

Place *kombu* in a casserole and set the cup of miso atop it. Arrange skewered ingredients around the cup with handles of skewers resting on rim of casserole (fig. 23). Add boiling water to just cover ingredients, return to the boil over medium heat, then simmer for 3 minutes. Dip skewered ingredients into miso sauce before eating.

For variety, add parboiled skewered pieces of cauliflower, potato, sweet potato, yam, or turnip.

Eggplants & Corn Simmered in Miso

2 tablespoons oil
4 small (Japanese) eggplants, uncut and unpeeled; or 1 medium-sized Western eggplant, cut lengthwise into fourths
1 cup fresh corn kernels
1½ tablespoons red, barley, or Hatcho miso, dissolved in ¾ cup water
1 teaspoon honey
Dash of (7-spice) red pepper or tabasco sauce

Heat a heavy pot or casserole and coat with the oil. Add eggplants and fry over low heat for 7 to 8 minutes on each side. Add remaining ingredients and bring to a boil. Re-cover and simmer for 5 minutes. Serve hot.

If using Western eggplants, increase oil to 3 tablespoons. Place pieces in pot with skin down and fry for 8 minutes, then fry for 2 minutes on each of the cut surfaces. Add remaining ingredients and proceed as above.

Spinach with Miso White Sauce

¼ cup water
1 pound spinach or *horenso*, washed, tough stems removed
3½ tablespoons butter
4½ tablespoons whole-wheat flour
2 tablespoons red, barley, or Hatcho miso
1½ cups milk (soy or dairy)
Dash of pepper

Combine water and spinach in a large skillet. Bring to a boil, stirring constantly, and cook for 3 to 4 minutes, or until spinach is just tender. Drain briefly and chop into 1-inch lengths.

Using the butter and remaining ingredients, prepare a Miso White Sauce (p. 114). Add spinach to the sauce and serve hot or cold.

Fig. 23. Miso Oden

Doténabé

SERVES 4

In Japanese, a *doté* is an earthen embankment or "shoulder." The reddish-brown miso in this preparation resembles an embankment around the *nabé's* rim until, that is, it dissolves into the simmering broth. The most famous Doténabé contain oysters, for which we substitute deep-fried tofu.

2½ cups dashi (p. 56) or stock
1 small potato, cut into quarters
1/3 cup shaved burdock root, soaked (p. 53) and drained
4 *daikon* rounds, each 2 inches in diameter and ½ inch thick
¼ cup red, barley, or Hatcho miso
1 to 1½ tablespoons honey
2½ tablespoons sake, white wine, or *mirin*
1 tablespoon bonito flakes (optional)
½ cake of *konnyaku*, torn into small pieces and rubbed lightly with salt
5 ounces deep-fried tofu, cut into 8 pieces
2 hard-boiled eggs, shelled; or 4 quail eggs
1 Chinese cabbage leaf, cut crosswise into 1½-inch-wide strips
1 leek, cut diagonally into 2-inch lengths
2 to 3 teaspoons hot mustard
Dash of *sansho* pepper
1 cup cooked noodles (optional)

Combine the first four ingredients in a saucepan and bring to a boil. Cover and simmer for 15 minutes. Meanwhile combine the miso, honey, 1 tablespoon sake and, if used, the bonita flakes in a skillet. Cook over low heat, stirring constantly, for 2 to 3 minutes, or until firm.

Ring the inner rim of an 8- to 10-inch diameter casserole or *nabé* pot with a thin, 1-inch-wide layer of the miso. Transfer cooked vegetables to casserole together with *konnyaku* and the next four ingredients. Add remaining 1½ tablespoons sake and enough of the dashi to fill casserole to ¼ inch above bottom of miso ring. Place casserole on a tabletop burner, cover, and bring to a boil. Simmer for about 15 minutes, or until flavors are well married and miso has melted into broth. Invite each guest to remove ingredients with chopsticks and transfer them to an individual bowl. (Cut egg lengthwise into halves.) Spoon on a little of the hot broth and serve topped with a dab of mustard and a sprinkling of *sansho* pepper.

Toward the end of the meal, drop cooked noodles into broth remaining in casserole and simmer until heated through. Serve in individual bowls, topped with the remaining broth.

For a richer flavor, allow cooked ingredients to stand in *nabé* overnight, then serve the next day, chilled or reheated.

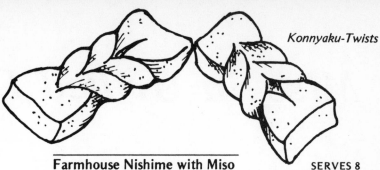

Daikon

Farmhouse Nishime with Miso

SERVES 8

A tasty Japanese vegetable stew, Nishime is a popular dish at New Year's, equinox celebrations, and other national holidays. Farmhouse Nishime often employs homemade miso as the basic seasoning, whereas in restaurants and city homes, shoyu is generally used. Both varieties are usually prepared in large enough quantities to last for up to one week, during which time the flavors marry and improve.

Many recipes include only 3 or 4 of the vegetables listed below, so omit or substitute according to what is available. Adjust the amount of cooking liquid accordingly. Some cooks prefer to cook each of the ingredients separately for a different length of time in a broth seasoned to match the food's unique character. Each cooked ingredient is allowed to marinate overnight in its own broth, but is served without broth in a bowl together with all the other ingredients.

3 cups dashi (p. 56), stock, or water
8 to 10 tablespoons red, barley, or Hatcho miso
3½ to 4½ tablespoons honey or *mirin*
3 tablespoons sake or white wine
½ teaspoon salt
1 cake of *konnyaku*, cut crosswise into ¼-inch-thick pieces
1 carrot, cut into large random chunks
½ burdock root, cut lengthwise into halves, then into 1½-inch lengths and parboiled for 10 minutes
1 large taro or potato, cut into eighths
2 inches *daikon*, cut into half moons
½ lotus root, cut into half moons
8 inches *kombu*, wiped clean with a moist cloth and cut crosswise into 1-inch-wide strips
1 small bamboo shoot, cut into large random chunks
3 (*shiitaké*) mushrooms, cut into quarters
10½ ounces deep-fried tofu, doused (p. 56) and cut into bite-sized pieces
12 ounces tofu, cut into large triangles (optional)
8 sprigs of *kinomé*

Combine the first five ingredients in a large pot or casserole and bring to a boil. Meanwhile, cut a slit lengthwise down the center of each small piece of *konnyaku* and thread one end up through the slit and back again (above). Add *konnyaku* and next eight ingredients to the broth, and return to the boil. Reduce heat to low, cover pot, and simmer for about 40 minutes. Add tofu, stir vegetables so that uppermost ones are transferred to bottom of pot, re-cover, and continue simmering until all but about ¾ cup of broth has been absorbed or evaporated. Remove from heat and allow to cool for at least 5, preferably 24 hours. Divide ingredients among individual serving bowls, pour on remaining liquid, and garnish with a sprig of *kinomé*.

Boiled Potatoes with Onion Miso

SERVES 2

4 small potatoes, boiled in their skins until tender
¼ cup Leek or Onion Miso (p. 64 or 70)
Butter or Parmesan Cheese (optional)

Cut potatoes into bite-sized pieces (or mash). Serve hot or cold, topped with the remaining ingredients. A favorite in Japanese farmhouses.

Potatoes Simmered in Miso

SERVES 4

10 small potatoes (1 pound), peeled and cut into halves
1¾ cups water
1½ tablespoons bonito flakes
3½ tablespoons red, barely, or Hatcho miso
1 tablespoon honey
1 tablespoon *mirin*, sake, or white wine

Combine the first three ingredients in a large saucepan and bring to a boil. Cover and simmer for 20 minutes, or until potatoes are tender. Mix in the last three ingredients and simmer, uncovered, for 10 minutes more. Cover and allow to stand for at least 4 hours, preferably overnight. Serve cold or reheated.

For variety, deep-fry potatoes (without batter) before simmering. Or substitute for the potatoes 5 small taro (whole) and 2 inches lotus root, the latter cut into 3/8-inch-thick rounds.

Miso in Grilled Dishes

Dengaku Hoshi

The process of broiling or grilling miso—especially over a barbecue, campfire, or charcoal brazier—imparts a heart-warming, savory aroma and flavor to both the miso and the food it coats. Why not start by trying a traditional Western favorite, corn-on-the-cob, then move on to shish kebab and Japan's famous Dengaku? See also Broiled Miso Toppings (pp. 71—72).

Grilled Corn-on-the-Cob with Miso   SERVES 2

This savory dish, generally prepared with shoyu rather than miso, is a favorite throughout Japan where it is served freshly grilled from small, sidewalk vending booths.

2 ears of fresh corn
2 teaspoons red, barley, or Hatcho miso
4 teaspoons butter

Grill, broil, or barbecue ears of corn until nicely speckled. Spread on miso using a small rubber spatula or a butter knife, then rebroil for about 1 minute until fragrant. Butter corn and serve piping hot.

If you prefer to steam the corn, spread on miso and butter just before serving. For variety, mix about ¼ teaspoon crushed garlic with the miso.

Shish Kebab with Miso Sauce   SERVES 4

Ingredients for Skewering: Use four or more
      5 ounces deep-fried tofu, cut into bite-sized cubes
      4 green peppers, cut into 2-inch triangles
      8 mushrooms
      1 apple, cut into bite-sized chunks or rounds
      8 chunks of firm pineapple
      4 small blanched onions
      4 small firm tomatoes
      1 celery stalk or cucumber, cut into bite-sized sections
¾ cup Miso Shish Kebab Sauce (p. 118) or 2/3 cup Teriyaki Sauce (p. 118)

Place basic ingredients in a shallow pan and pour on sauce. Marinate for 1 hour, turning ingredients several times. Skewer pieces on 4 to 8 skewers and broil for 2 to 3 minutes, basting occasionally, until nicely speckled and fragrant.

Dengaku   SERVES 4

Dengaku, one of Japan's oldest and most famous types of miso cuisine, is prepared by charcoal broiling skewered, bite-sized pieces of various foods. Each piece is then coated on one or both sides with a thin layer of miso and the skewers are rebroiled briefly until the miso is speckled and fragrant. Although the best known type of Dengaku is prepared with small pieces of firmly-pressed tofu, other varieties are made with eggplants, taro, sweet potatoes, mushrooms, and a host of other tasty ingredients listed below. In restaurants, the foods are generally pierced with tiny bamboo skewers, broiled over a charcoal brazier, and topped with one or more types of Sweet Simmered Miso. In farmhouses, the tofu or vegetables are skewered on 18-inch-long slats of bamboo, which are poked at a slant into the ashes around a bed of glowing coals in the living room open-hearth fireplace. A hand's width above the embers, the foods imbibe the fragrance of woodsmoke as they sizzle and broil. Here homemade barley or red miso is often used as the topping.

The two Chinese characters which form the word *Dengaku* mean "rice paddy" and "music." It is said that the name originated about 600 years ago when an ancient form of folk drama consisting of music and dance was popular in Japan's rural villages. In one famous play using a rice paddy as its setting, a Buddhist priest mounted a single stilt (resembling a pogo stick) which was called a "heron's leg." Precariously balanced, this character was called Dengaku Hoshi, and he did a dance known as the *dengaku* or "music in the rice

144

paddy." The newly conceived grilled cuisine, initially prepared by piercing each tofu cake with a single skewer, apparently reminded the people of the dengaku dancer, and the tasty preparation soon became known as Dengaku.

Dengaku first became popular throughout Japan in the early 1600s, and by 1775 it had become fashionable for tea shops and way stations in Tokyo and Kyoto to serve this delicacy, often together with Tea Ceremony Cuisine. Until the late 1900s, many tofu shops prepared and delivered Dengaku to order.

The basic recipe that follows is that for grilled Tofu Dengaku. The use of other basic ingredients and cooking techniques are discribed as variations. Additional variations on the basic Tofu Dengaku method can be found in *The Book of Tofu.*

Miso Topping: Use a total of ¼ to ½ cup of one or more of the following types of Sweet Simmered Miso (p. 60):

>   Red or White Sweet Simmered Miso
>   Yuzu or Lemon Miso
>   Kinomé or Egg Yolk Miso
>   Seasame or Walnut Miso; or a Nut Butter Topping

12 to 24 ounces tofu, pressed (p. 55)
Garnishes (optional):
>   Sprigs of *kinomé*
>   Slivered *yuzu* or lemon rind
>   Poppy seeds, roasted sesame seeds, or wheat germ
>   Hot mustard

Prepare the miso topping(s) in advance and allow to cool. In a large skillet or pan, heat water to about the temperature of a hot bath. Drop in tofu, then cut into pieces about 2 by 1 by ¾ inches. Pierce each piece under water from one end using either 2 round bamboo skewers or 1 flat skewer. Cover a cutting board or flat tray with a dry dishtowel and raise one end of the board. Carefully place skewered tofu on cloth and allow to stand for 15 minutes, or until tofu is firm.

Holding 3 to 4 pieces of skewered tofu at a time side by side over a gas burner, broil for about 30 seconds, or until tofu is lightly speckled. (Or broil tofu on one side over a charcoal brazier or barbecue.) Turn tofu over and coat broiled side with a 1/8-inch-thick layer of topping, then broil second side. Turn again and broil miso topping until it too is speckled, then arrange garnishes, if used, atop miso. Repeat with remaining ingredients. If desired, use a different miso topping with each set of tofu pieces. Serve hot with the meal or as an hors d'oeuvre.

Tofu Dengaku is also prepared with grilled or deep-fried tofu.

OTHER INGREDIENTS AND METHODS OF PREPARATION

*Eggplant: Cut small Japanese eggplants into ½-inch-thick rounds (or larger Western eggplants into bite-sized half moons or wedges). Soak for 5 to 10 minutes in lightly salted water, drain well, and pat dry with a towel. Pierce both sides in several places with a fork or chop-stick, then brush with (sesame) oil. Skewer and proceed as above. Top with Sesame (or Gingerroot) Miso and garnish with sesame or poppy seeds. Or use White Sweet Simmered Miso, Egg Yolk Miso, or Kinomé Miso and garnish with *kinomé* sprigs.

*Sweet Potato, Taro, Daikon, Bamboo Shoots, or Irish Potato: Cut vegetables into ½-inch-thick ovals or rounds and steam or parboil until just tender. Top with Sesame Miso or Miso Sauté (p. 65).

*Mushroom: Skewer large, whole (fresh *shiitake*) mushrooms and broil. Spread both sides with Sweet Simmered Miso, rebroil, and garnish with roasted sesame seeds.

*Fresh Wheat Gluten: Cut into tofu-sized rectangles or ½-inch-thick rounds. Broil and top with Sweet Simmered Miso or Kinomé Miso; garnish with *kinomé*.

*Hard-boiled Eggs, Mochi, Konnyaku, or Green Peppers: Use (chicken or quail) eggs and uncut *mochi* cakes. Cut *konnyaku* and peppers into bite-sized triangles. Skewer individually or in combinations like shish kebab. Top with Sweet Simmered Miso.

*Leeks: Parboil whole leeks for 2 to 3 minutes, cut into 1¼-inch sections, and skewer four sections crosswise. Broil using Walnut Miso.

*Unskewered Dengaku: Broil any of the above-mentioned ingredients on both sides until speckled in an oven broiler. Spread upper surface with miso and rebroil briefly.

*Deep-fried Dengaku: All varieties of tofu, yuba, and wheat gluten are most commonly prepared in this way, but other ingredients may also be used. Roll pieces in flour, dip in lightly beaten egg, and roll in bread crumbs. Skewer and deep-fry until crisp, then serve topped with Sweet Simmered Miso. Or skewer first, dip into tempura batter (or leave uncoated), and deep-fry.

*Sautéed and Butter-fried Dengaku: Sauté eggplant rounds on both sides and serve topped with Sesame Miso. Or butter-fry mushrooms or tofu on both sides and serve like eggplant.

Tofu Dengaku

Grilled Tofu & Vegetables with Miso White Sauce

SERVES 3 TO 4

At Fugetsu, a Japanese natural-food restaurant in Berkeley, this delicious preparation is served either as an hors d'oeuvre or a main course. The sauce is prepared and kept hot in a double boiler.

2 tender eggplants, cut into ¾-inch-thick rounds and brushed with oil
6 large mushrooms
12 ounces tofu, drained or pressed (p. 55)
1 cup Sweet White Miso Sauce (p. 115)
Dash of green *nori* flakes
Dash of *sansho* pepper
1 to 2 teaspoons roasted sesame seeds

Barbecue or grill eggplants, mushrooms, and tofu for about 3 minutes on each side, or until eggplants are tender and other ingredients are nicely browned. Arrange barbecued ingredients on individual plates, spoon on the hot sauce, and top with a sprinkling of green *nori*, *sansho*, and sesame seeds.

Broiled Sweet Potatoes with Miso Topping

SERVES 2

4 sweet potatoes, steamed until just tender and cut lengthwise into 3/8-inch-thick slices
2 tablespoons butter
2 tablespoons Sweet Simmered Miso (p. 60) or Finger Lickin' Miso (p. 42)

Broil sweet-potato slices until lightly speckled and just fragrant. Spread each slice with butter and a thin layer of the miso. Serve hot or cold.

Grilled Eggplants Shigiyaki (*Nasu no Shigiyaki*)

SERVES 4

The word *shigiyaki* means "grilled snipe." Old cookbooks show that this now famous eggplant dish was originally prepared by stuffing a pickled eggplant with snipe meat, capping the eggplant with a persimmon leaf, and simmering the tender morsel in a seasoned broth. The present version is a close relative of Eggplant Dengaku (p.145) and Fried Eggplants Shigiyaki (p. 138)

4 tender, young Japanese eggplants, cut lengthwise into halves (unpeeled)
1 tablespoon sesame oil
2½ tablespoons of one of the following types of Sweet Simmered Miso (pp. 60 to 65):
    Red or White Sweet Simmered Miso
    Egg Yolk, Kinomé, or Gingerroot Miso
    Sesame or Walnut Miso
Dash of *sansho* pepper

Pierce eggplant halves crosswise with metal skewers, spread cut surface with sesame oil, and broil over a charcoal fire (or stove-top burner) on both sides until nicely speckled. Spread each cut surface with a thin layer of the miso and rebroil quickly until miso is fragrant and speckled. Remove skewers, arrange on individual serving dishes, and top with a sprinkling of the pepper. Serve as a side dish or hors d'œuvre.

VARIATIONS

*Deep-fried Shigiyaki: Cut eggplants into ½-inch-thick rounds, deep-fry, and drain well. Skewer, spread one side with sweet white miso, and score miso in a crisscross pattern with a wet knife. Grill on both sides.

*Savory Shigiyaki: Cut eggplants into ½-inch-thick rounds before skewering, then score both surfaces with a knife or poke with a fork or chopstick. (If using large Western eggplants, cut into bite-sized wedges of an equivalent thickness.) Brush surfaces with oil, skewer, and proceed as above.

Miso in Deep-fried Dishes

Sweet Simmered Miso (p. 60) and most other Miso Toppings are delicious served in small quantities atop tempura or other deep-fried foods. The different varieties of deep-fried Dengaku are described on page 145.

ABOUT DEEP-FRYING

Although deep-fat frying has long been a part of Western cookery, it has never attained the degree of popularity or artistry that it enjoys throughout the Orient, and particularly in Japan. Deep-frying is as common in the typical Japanese kitchen as baking is in the West, while it is faster and uses much less fuel. In only a few minutes, it transforms the simplest fresh vegetables, pieces of tofu, and even leftovers into prize creations. The art of deep-frying is a joy to practice.

For the Japanese, whose diet is still very low in meats, deep-fried foods are an important source of both savory flavor and essential (unsaturated) oils. Some Westerners still have the image of deep-fried foods as being necessarily "greasy," while others believe that heating the oil to high temperatures impairs its nutritional value. Yet anyone who has lived in Japan or dined on tempura knows that deep-frying can yield foods that are remarkably crisp and light. And keeping the oil at its proper temperature, at 350° or less, guarantees its health-giving benefits.

In Japanese, the verb *ageru* means "to deep-fry," and *agé-mono* or "deep-fried things" are the many foods that make up this vast world. The simplest form of deep-frying is called *kara-agé* or "deep-frying without a coating or batter." The three basic types of deep-fried tofu are each prepared in this way. After mastering this technique, you should find no difficulty in preparing fine, crisp tempura.

If you wish to make deep-frying a permanent part of your repertoire of cooking techniques, it is best to start with the proper tools. Most important is the deep-frying pot. While many Westerners use a heavy 3- to 4-quart kettle, or an electric deep-fryer, most Japanese use either a wok (see p. 53) or a heavy-bottomed skillet 2½ to 3 inches deep and 10 to 12 inches in diameter.

For best results use a simple vegetable oil. Japanese prefer rapeseed oil, but Western cooks use soy, corn, or cottonseed oil. Some chefs specializing in vegetable tempura prefer a combination of oils. If 10 to 30 percent sesame oil is added to any of the above basic oils, it will give the foods a delicious, nutty flavor. Other popular combinations are: peanut or corn (70%) and sesame (30%); peanut (75%), sesame (20%), and olive (5%); cotton-seed (85%), olive (10%), and sesame (5%). For a light, crisp texture, avoid the use of animal fats in deep-frying.

Used deep-frying oil should be kept in a sealed jar and stored in a cool, dark place. When sautéing vegetables or frying eggs, you may use some of this oil to impart added flavor to the foods and help use up the oil. When deep-frying, try to use about one part fresh oil and one part used. Dark or thick used oil has a low smoke point and imparts a poor flavor. Foods deep-fried in used oil only are not as light and crisp as they could be. Pour oil from the storage jar into the deep-fryer carefully so that any sediment remains at the bottom of the jar. Then add fresh oil to fill the wok or skillet to a depth of 1½ to 2 inches.

Maintaining the oil at the proper temperature is the most important part of deep-frying. At first it may be easiest to measure the temperature with a deep-frying thermometer. More experienced chefs judge the oil's temperature by its appearance, aroma, and subtle crackling sound. If the oil begins to smoke, it is too hot. Overheating shortens the life of the oil—Japanese say it "tires" the oil— and imparts a bad flavor to the foods cooked in it. Tempura chefs drop a little batter into hot oil to test its temperature. If the batter submerges slightly, then rises quickly to the surface where it browns within about 45 seconds, the temperature is just right. If the batter sinks to the bottom and rises only slowly to the surface, the oil is not hot enough; if it remains on the surface and dances furiously, the oil is too hot. Oil which is too hot will smoke—and burn the batter—whereas that which is too cold will not give the desired crispness.

Keeping the oil clean is another secret of successful deep-frying. This is especially important when using the batter or bound-breading methods. Use a mesh skimmer, or a perforated metal spatula or spoon, to remove all particles of food and batter from the oil's surface. Most cooks skim after every two or three batches of ingredients have been cooked. Place the small particles of deep-fried batter skimmed from the oil into a large colander or bowl lined with absorbent paper, and allow to drain thoroughly. These may be used later

Deep-frying with wok

as tasty additions to soups, salads, sautéed vegetables, noodles-in-broth, or other grain dishes.

To ensure that deep-fried foods are served at their peak of texture and flavor, do your deep-frying just before you are ready to serve the meal, preferably after your guests have been seated at the table. If you have a large quantity of ingredients to deep-fry and wish to serve them simultaneously, keep freshly cooked pieces warm in a 250° oven.

After all foods have been deep-fried, allow the oil to cool in the wok or skillet, then pour it through a mesh skimmer or fine-weave strainer held over a funnel into your used-oil container. Seal the jar and discard any residue in the skimmer. Wipe all utensils with absorbent paper (washing is unnecessary) and store in a sealed plastic bag.

Crispy Lotus Root Stuffed with Miso & Onion

SERVES 4

1 teaspoon sesame oil
1 onion, minced
2 tablespoons red, barley, or Hatcho miso, creamed with 1 tablespoon water
1 lotus root, cut into ¾-inch-thick rounds (7 or 8)
Oil for deep-frying
3 tablespoons (whole-wheat) flour
1 egg, lightly beaten
Parsley sprigs

Heat a skillet and coat with the oil. Add onion and sauté for 4 minutes. Mix in creamed miso and sauté for 1 minute more. Remove from heat and allow to cool to body temperature. Use fingertips or a spatula to fill hollows in each round of lotus root with onion-miso mixture.

Heat the oil to 350° in a wok, skillet, or deep-fryer. Dust rounds in flour, dip in egg, and deep-fry for about 3 minutes, or until golden brown (p. 147). Drain well, then cut rounds horizontally into halves exposing the snowflake pattern of the miso-filled holes. Serve garnished with parsley.

For variety, roll in bread crumbs or bread crumb flakes after dipping in eggs.

Deep-fried Lotus Root Stuffed with Cheese & Miso

SERVES 4

A traditional favorite sold in Japanese delicatessens, this dish makes an excellent hors d'œuvre and is a joy to prepare.

1 cup grated cheese
2 tablespoons red, barley, or Hatcho miso
1 tablespoon minced onion or 1 clove of garlic, crushed (optional)
Dash of pepper
2 lotus roots, each 5 inches long
Oil for deep-frying
2 tablespoons (whole-wheat) flour
1 egg, lightly beaten
Shoyu (optional)

Combine the first four ingredients in a large cup, mixing well. Trim ends of lotus roots revealing hollow inner tubules. Cut each root crosswise into halves, parboil for 5 minutes, and drain briefly. Holding one lotus root section with a small cloth (to protect your hands from the heat), press the large end into the cheese-miso mixture, forcing the mixture up into the tubules until it fills them. Then press the end of the lotus root against the side of the cup while sliding it out to prevent the mixture from being withdrawn by suction. Repeat with the remaining sections.

Heat the oil to 350° in a wok, skillet, or deep-fryer. Dust each lotus root section liberally with flour, dip into the egg, and deep-fry until golden brown (p. 147). Drain well, then cut crosswise into ½-inch-thick discs. Serve hot or cold, seasoned, if desired, with a sprinkling of shoyu.

VARIATIONS

*Karashi Renkon: As an alternate filling use
    6 tablespoons sweet white or 4 tablespoons mellow white miso
    1 tablespoon red miso
    2 tablespoons minced leek or onion
    1 teaspoon hot mustard

*Sandwiched Hors D'oeuvres: Between two rounds of stuffed, deep-fried lotus root, sandwich any of the following: slices of cheese and/or fresh vegetables; deep-fried tofu (especially burgers or pouches); gluten meat.

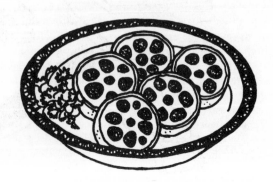

Creamy Corn Croquettes with Miso

SERVES 3 OR 4

Miso is the key to the flavor in these unique delicacies which have a crisp crust and soft melt-in-the-mouth center.

2½ tablespoons butter
½ cup whole-wheat flour
1¼ cups milk (soy or dairy)
2 tablespoons red, barley, Hatcho, or light-yellow miso
Dash of pepper
½ small onion, minced
½ cup fresh corn kernels
1 egg, lightly beaten
¾ cup bread crumbs or bread crumb flakes
Oil for deep frying

Use 1½ tablespoons butter, ¼ cup flour, the milk, 1½ tablespoons miso, and the pepper to make a Miso White Sauce (p. 114).

Melt remaining 1 tablespoon butter in a skillet. Add onion and corn, and sauté for 4 minutes. Mix in the miso, remove from heat, and stir into the white sauce. Allow to cool to room temperature, then cover and refrigerate for 30 minutes.

Using a large spoon or dipper, scoop out one-eighth of the vegetable-sauce mixture and drop in a ball into a bowl containing the remaining ¼ cup flour. Gently sprinkle flour over moist filling while using fingertips to form a sausage-shaped croquette about 4 inches long and 1½ inches in diameter. Carefully dip in eggs and sprinkle with bread crumbs. Repeat to make 8 croquettes, and allow to dry for 10 minutes.

Heat oil to hot (395°) in a wok, skillet, or deep-fryer. Slide in 2 croquettes at a time and deep-fry for about 1 minute or until golden brown and crisp. Drain and serve immediately, garnished, if desired, with lettuce, tomato slices, and parsley.

For an even richer texture, add ½ cup grated cheese to the white sauce.

Cheese & Miso Deep-fried Sandwich

SERVES 2

Known in Japan as *Hakata-agé*, this *nori*-wrapped preparation takes its name from the well-known *Hakata* kimono sash characterized by colorful horizontal stripes. Dried-frozen (or well-pressed regular) tofu is often used in place of bread.

4 bread slices, each 3½ inches square and 3/8 inch thick
2 teaspoons red, barley, or Hatcho miso
2 cheese slices, each 3½ inches square and ¼ inch thick
6 strips of *nori*, each 3½ inches wide and 8 to 10 inches long
2 eggs, lightly beaten
¼ cup whole-wheat flour
¼ cup bread crumbs, bread crumb flakes, or ground roasted sesame seeds (optional)
Oil for deep-frying
2 to 4 parsley sprigs

Spread one surface of each bread slice with ½ teaspoon miso, then sandwich 1 slice of cheese between 2 slices of bread to form 2 sandwiches (fig. 24). Cut each sandwich crosswise into thirds and wrap each third with a strip of *nori*, moistening one end of *nori* to seal. Combine eggs and flour, mixing lightly, to form a batter. Heat oil to 350° in a wok, skillet, or deep-fryer. Dip sandwiches into batter and, if desired, roll in bread crumbs or sesame. Drop into oil and deep-fry until golden brown (p. 147). Drain well. Cut each sandwich crosswise into thirds and serve with the cut surface facing upward, garnished with parsley.

VARIATIONS

*If *nori* is not available, pierce sandwiches in 2 places with foodpicks before deep-frying in batter.
*Tofu Hakata-agé: Cut a 12-ounce cake of well-pressed tofu (or a 5-ounce tofu cutlet) horizontally into fourths, then lengthwise and again crosswise into halves to make 16 rectangular pieces. Coat one surface of 8 pieces with a 1/8-inch-thick layer of Sweet Simmered Miso (p. 60), then top with the remaining tofu pieces. Dust each of the 8 sandwiches with flour, dip into beaten egg, and roll in bread crumbs. Deep-fry, cut, and serve as above, using lemon wedges and parsley as the garnish.

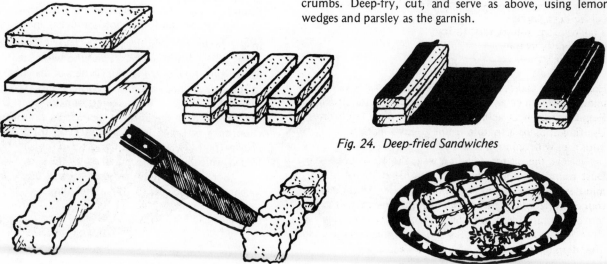

Fig. 24. Deep-fried Sandwiches

Deep-fried Potatoes in Miso & Onion Sauce

SERVES 2 OR 3

½ onion, minced
¼ cup water
Oil for deep-frying
4 small unpeeled potatoes (2-inch diameter), each cut into
    4 equal-sized chunks
1½ tablespoons red, barley, or Hatcho miso
2 tablespoons Parmesan cheese

Combine onion and water in a small saucepan, bring to a boil, and simmer for 5 minutes. Meanwhile heat oil to 350° in a wok, skillet, or deep-fryer. Drop in potato chunks and deep-fry until golden brown (p. 147); drain on absorbent paper.

Stir miso into simmering onions, then add potatoes and season with pepper; simmer for 1 minute. Serve topped with a sprinkling of the cheese.

Deep-fried Potato Chunks in Miso & Ginger Sauce

SERVES 3 OR 4

2 tablespoons red, barley, or Hatcho miso
2 to 2½ teaspoons honey
½ teaspoon powdered ginger or ¼ teaspoon grated ginger-
    root
¼ cup water or stock
2 small potatoes (2½-inch diameter), each cut into 4 chunks
    and patted very dry with a dishcloth
Oil for deep-frying

Combine the first four ingredients in a small saucepan, mixing well, and set aside on a back burner. Heat oil to 325° in a wok, skillet, or deep-fryer. Drop in potato chunks and deep-fry for about 6 minutes, or until golden brown and tender (p. 147). Meanwhile bring miso-ginger sauce to a boil and simmer over very low heat. Drain potatoes briefly, dip into sauce until covered, and transfer to individual plates. Serve hot or cold.

Eggs Deep-fried in Overcoats with Miso

SERVES 3

2 tablespoons butter
½ onion, minced
½ cup carrot, grated
2 cups cubed potatoes (1-inch cubes), boiled for 20 minutes,
    drained and mashed
1½ tablespoons red, barley, or Hatcho miso
½ teaspoon curry powder or dash of pepper
3 hard-boiled eggs, shelled and cooled to room temperature
3 tablespoons whole-wheat flour
1 egg, lightly beaten
1/3 cup bread crumbs
Oil for deep-frying
Ketchup-Worcestershire Sauce (p. 58)
Minced parsley

Melt the butter in a skillet. Add onion and carrot, and sauté for 3 minutes. Mix with mashed potato, miso, and curry powder and divide into 3 equal portions; allow to cool to at least body temperature. Completely enfold each egg with an even covering of the potato-miso mixture, then dust with flour, dip in beaten egg, and roll in bread crumbs. Heat oil to 375° in a wok, skillet, or deep-fryer. Deep-fry coated eggs until golden brown, lift out of oil with a slotted spoon or skimmer, and drain well. Allow to cool to at least body temperature, then cut each egg lengthwise into halves. Serve topped with the sauce and a sprinkling of parsley. If desired, arrange on a bed of lettuce or shredded cabbage garnished by tomato wedges.

For variety, omit the flour and beaten eggs in the coating, and use only bread crumbs; instead of deep-frying, bake at 350° for 20 minutes, or until nicely browned.

Sweet Miso Deep-fried in Yuba or Wonton Skins

MAKES 6

6 sheets of fresh yuba, each 4 inches square; or 6 wonton
    skins
9 tablespoons diced fresh yuba or wonton
3 tablespoons Yuzu Miso (p. 62) or Red Nerimiso (p. 60)
Oil for deep-frying
Shoyu

In the center of each yuba square layer 1 tablespoon diced yuba and 1½ teaspoons miso, and top with ½ teaspoon more of the yuba. Fold over the four corners of the yuba or wonton to form an envelope and fasten corners with a foodpick. Heat the oil to 350° in a wok, skillet, or deep-fryer. Drop in envelopes and deep-fry, turning them from time to time with chopsticks or tongs, for about 40 seconds, or until golden brown (p. 147). Drain well and serve (on sheets of neatly folded white paper) accompanied by the shoyu for dipping.

For variety, omit diced yuba and use 1 tablespoon Mushroom Miso Sauté (p. 65) as the filling.

Miso & Eggs

The use of miso in your favorite breakfast and luncheon egg preparations provides added aroma, flavor, and protein. For hors d'œuvres see Eggs with Miso and Sesame (p. 77).

Eggs Cooked Over Brown Rice with Miso

SERVES 3

1½ tablespoons oil
1 clove of garlic, minced
½ small onion, minced
4 mushrooms, minced
1 cup cooked Brown Rice (p. 57)
1 tablespoon red or barley miso, creamed with 1 tablespoon water
3 eggs
Dash of pepper

Heat a large skillet and coat with the oil. Add garlic and sauté for 30 seconds. Add onion and mushrooms, and sauté for 5 minutes more. Mix in brown rice, sauté for 2 more minutes, then stir in slightly more than half of the creamed miso. Spread rice in an even layer over bottom of skillet. Break eggs over rice and cook, covered, over low heat for 4 to 5 minutes, or until eggs are firm. Season with pepper and top each egg with a dab of creamed miso.

Fig. 25. Gashouse Eggs

Gashouse Eggs with Miso

SERVES 1

Also known as Cockeyed Egyptians, these innovative delicacies are a nice way of combining miso and wheat proteins in a breakfast egg dish.

1 teaspoon sweet or mellow white (or ½ teaspoon red) miso
5 teaspoons butter
1 slice of whole-wheat bread
1 egg

Spread first the miso and then 1 teaspoon butter evenly over one surface of the bread. Use the mouth of a small glass to cut a hole in the center of the bread (fig. 25) and remove the round. Melt the remaining 4 teaspoons butter in a skillet, put in the bread with the buttered side up, and break the egg into the hole. Place the round (buttered-side-up) next to the bread and fry both for 2 to 3 minutes, or until bottom is nicely browned and egg is half done. Turn and repeat until second side is slightly crisp and golden brown. Serve immediately.

Poached Eggs on Toast with White Miso

SERVES 2

2 eggs, poached
2 slices of buttered whole-grain toast
1 tablespoon sweet white or 2 teaspoons mellow white miso, creamed with 1 tablespoon boiling water

Place one egg atop the buttered side of each slice of toast, then pour on miso sauce. Serve immediately.

Scrambled Eggs or Omelets with Miso

SERVES 2 OR 3

4 eggs, lightly beaten
4 teaspoons red, barley, or Hatcho miso
2 to 3 tablespoons minced onion
3½ teaspoons oil
Dash of pepper
Sprigs of parsley

Combine the first three ingredients, mixing well. Heat one-half the oil in a large skillet. Pour in half the egg-miso mixture and scramble until firm, then press surface of eggs with the back of a spatula until bottom of eggs is lightly browned and fragrant. Turn and press the second side, then remove from skillet. Repeat with remaining egg-miso mixture. Serve seasoned with pepper and garnished with parsley.

To make omelets, reduce the amount of oil slightly and cook in two batches without scrambling. If desired, serve omelets filled with 1 tablespoon Sweet Simmered Miso (p. 60) and a pinch of alfalfa sprouts.

Scrambled Eggs
with Miso, Onions, and Tofu

SERVES 3

2 eggs, lightly beaten
1½ tablespoons red, barley, or Hatcho miso
7½ ounces (deep-fried) tofu, cut into ½-inch cubes
1 tablespoon oil
1 small onion, thinly sliced
Dash of pepper

Combine the eggs and miso in a small bowl, mixing well. Add tofu and set aside.

Heat a skillet and coat with the oil. Add onion and sauté for 4 to 5 minutes. Pour in tofu-egg mixture and scramble for 2 to 3 minutes, or until eggs are firm. Season with pepper. Serve hot or cold.

Egg Foo Yung with Miso

SERVES 2

1 tablespoon red, barley, or Hatcho miso
2¾ tablespoons stock or water
2 eggs, lightly beaten
1½ tablespoons oil, one-half of which may be sesame
¾ cup mung bean sprouts
3 mushrooms, thinly sliced
½ to ¾ cup chopped leeks or minced onions
Dash of pepper

Cream the miso with a little of the stock, then add eggs and remaining stock; mix well and set aside. Heat the oil in a large skillet. Add the next three ingredients and sauté over high heat for about 1 minute, or until leeks are lightly browned. Pour in miso-egg mixture to form a round pattie and fry on both sides until golden brown. Serve seasoned with pepper.

For variety, add diced (deep-fried) tofu and/or green peppers together with the sprouts. Top with Miso-Gingerroot Ankaké (p. 113) or Gingerroot Sauce (p. 118).

Layered Japanese Omelet
with Sweet Simmered Miso

SERVES 2 OR 3

Sweet Simmered Miso makes a good filling for many Western-style omelets. This subtly-sweet vegetable omelet is composed of alternating almost-crisp and creamy-soft layers.

4 eggs, lightly beaten
1 tablespoon brown sugar or honey
2 mushrooms, minced
1/3 cup finely-minced leeks, onions, or chives
Dash of salt
¼ cup dashi (p. 56), water, or stock
2 teaspoons oil
2½ teaspoons Red Nerimiso (p. 60)

Combine the first six ingredients, mixing well. Heat a large skillet and coat with 1 teaspoon oil. Fold a 4- by 6-inch piece of cheese cloth to form a small pad, grasp with tongs or chopsticks, and use to spread oil evenly over bottom and sides of skillet (fig. 26). Pour in one-fourth of the vegetable-egg mixture, swish it quickly around skillet to make a uniformly thin layer, and cook over high heat on one side only until omelet firms. Reduce heat to low and cook until bottom is almost crisp. Roll up omelet with a spatula, remove from skillet, and coat upper surface with ½ teaspoon Nerimiso. Re-oil skillet lightly and use cloth pad to free any particles of omelet clinging to skillet's walls. Prepare a second omelet. When it has finished cooking, place the first back into skillet atop the second. Fold one edge of bottom omelet over rolled omelet and, using spatula, roll up second omelet around first. Carefully remove roll from skillet and again coat upper surface with ½ teaspoon Nerimiso. Continue in this way to prepare a single roll composed of 4 omelets. Coat the top of the finished roll with 1 teaspoon Nerimiso and allow to cool to room temperature. Cut crosswise into 1-inch-wide sections before serving.

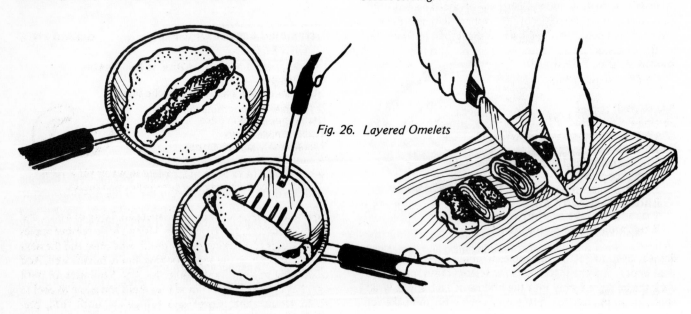

Fig. 26. Layered Omelets

Miso in Desserts

A little miso helps to evoke the natural sweetness of most fresh fruits—especially apples. The low salt content, subtle tartness, and mellow flavor of Hatcho often gives particularly good results in baked treats. Experiment also with Sesame Miso (p. 62), sweet or mellow white miso, or red miso in your favorite recipes for Apple Brown Betty, fruit fritters or turnovers, and pies.

Before the arrival of cane sugar in Japan, sweet and Finger Lickin' misos were served together with *mizuamé* and *amazaké* as the major natural sweetenings. They were—and still are—used in confections and tea treats, the most popular of which is *Kashiwa Mochi*, described below. Miso is also a key ingredient in the crisp Tokyo dessert crackers called *Kawara Senbei*, made by baking a mixture of wheat (or rice flour) dough, sweet red miso and sugar between two small roof tiles *(kawara)*, from which the crackers take their form. Sweet red miso is also mixed with sweet azuki-bean paste and used as a filling for the widely available steamed buns called *Miso Manju*.

Baked Apples Filled with Sesame-Raisin Miso
SERVES 5

5 large (red) apples
Sesame-Raisin Miso:
   1½ tablespoons sesame butter
   ¼ cup raisins
   1 tablespoon Hatcho, red, or barley miso
   1 tablespoon butter
   3 tablespoons brown sugar or 1½ tablespoons honey
   2 tablespoons water
   1 tablespoon sake or white wine (optional)
   ¼ teaspoon cinnamon (optional)

Preheat oven to 350°. Core apples to about seven-eighths of their depth. Mix the ingredients for sesame-raisin miso, then pack the mixture firmly into the hollow of each apple. Wrap apples in aluminum foil, place on a cookie tin and bake for about 20 minutes. Serve hot or chilled.

Apple Crisp with Miso
SERVES 4 TO 6

4 apples, thinly sliced
¼ cup raisins
1 tablespoon Hatcho, red, or barley miso
½ teaspoon grated lemon rind
1 tablespoon lemon juice
1 cup rolled oats or oatmeal (uncooked)
1/3 cup whole-wheat flour
2 tablespoons brown sugar (optional)
½ teaspoon cinnamon
¼ teaspoon nutmeg
Dash of salt
¼ cup oil (one-half of which may be butter)

Preheat oven to 350°. Combine the first five ingredients, mixing well, and spoon into a lightly oiled baking dish. Combine the remaining ingredients, mixing (or rubbing between palms) until oil is evenly distributed; sprinkle over surface of apples. Bake for about 30 minutes, or until apples are tender and surface is nicely browned. Delicious hot or chilled.

Jelled Apple-Miso Dessert
SERVES 5 TO 6

5 apples, peeled and cut lengthwise into fourths
1 cup water
1 tablespoon red, barley, or Hatcho miso
½ cup raisins
1 tablespoon lemon juice
2 tablespoons honey
2 tablespoons sesame butter
¼ teaspoon cinnamon
½ bar of agar (4 to 5 grams), soaked in water for 2 minutes, squeezed firmly and torn into small pieces

Combine apples and water in a saucepan, bring to a boil, and simmer, covered, for 10 minutes. Using a fork, remove apples and transfer to a baking pan or mold. Add miso and the next five ingredients to the apple cooking liquid, mixing well. Add agar, bring to a boil, and simmer for 4 to 5 minutes, or until agar has dissolved. Pour liquid into mold and allow to cool to room temperature. Cover and refrigerate until firm, preferably for 6 to 8 hours. Serve as is or topped with yogurt.

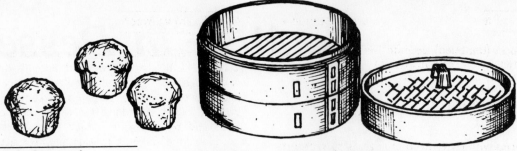

Japanese-style Steamed Miso-Cupcakes or Spongecake (*Miso-iri Mushipan*)

SERVES 2 OR 3

2 eggs separated into whites and lightly beaten yolks
1 tablespoon red or barley miso, creamed with 1½ teaspoons water
2/3 cup whole-wheat flour
½ teaspoon baking powder
6½ teaspoons honey
1 tablespoon finely chopped peanuts or roasted sesame seeds
Butter

Preheat a steamer (p. 55). In a large bowl, beat egg whites until stiff. Fold in yolks, creamed miso, flour, baking powder, and 2 tablespoons honey. Spoon batter into (paper-lined) cupcake molds or a small loaf pan lined with aluminum foil. Place in steamer and, unless using a bamboo steamer, stretch a moist cloth over steamer's mouth before covering. Steam for 20 to 25 minutes. Brush surface of cakes with ½ teaspoon honey, then sprinkle with peanuts or sesame seeds. Serve hot or cold with butter.

The Japanese and Chinese prefer steaming to baking since much less fuel is needed. Of course, the cupcakes may also be baked over a pan of water if desired.

Miso Mincemeat

MAKES ONE 9-INCH PIE

The mellow, slightly tart flavor of Hatcho miso provides the key to this unique and delicious dessert preparation.

4 (tart) apples, peeled, cored, and diced
½ cup apple juice
1½ cups raisins
Grated rind of 1 orange
Juice of 1 orange
2 cups nutmeats, preferably walnuts
¼ teaspoon cinnamon
¼ to ½ teaspoon cloves, allspice, or coriander
2 tablespoons Hatcho miso, or substitute 1½ tablespoons red or barley miso

Combine the first five ingredients in a heavy pot, bring to a boil, and simmer for 30 minutes. Add the next three ingredients and the miso creamed in a little of the cooking liquid; mix well, remove from heat, and allow to cool to room temperature. Use as a filling for a 9-inch mince pie or for turnovers. Also delicious as a spread for buttered toast or served like chutney with curried dishes.

Heavenly Sweet-potato Patties with White Miso

SERVES 6 OR 12

4 (Japanese) sweet potatoes, steamed for 20 minutes and mashed (2¼ cups)
¼ cup sweet white or 2 tablespoons mellow white miso
½ cup raisins
1 tablespoon honey
3 tablespoons butter

Combine the first four ingredients, mixing well, and shape into 12 patties. Melt 1 tablespoon butter in a heavy skillet, add 4 patties, and fry for 2 to 3 minutes on each side, or until lightly browned. Repeat until all ingredients are used. Serve hot or cold.

Banana, Peanut Butter & Sweet Miso Delight

SERVES 2 OR 3

2 tablespoons peanut or sesame butter
1 tablespoon sweet white miso
¼ cup raisins
1 teaspoon honey
2 tablespoons water
2 bananas, sliced into ½-inch-thick rounds

Combine the first five ingredients, mixing well, then spoon over banana slices. Mix lightly until slices are evenly coated. Serve immediately.

Miso Rice Pudding

SERVES 3 OR 4

The rich, creamy texture of rice porridge works like milk in most pudding recipes; raisins provide most of the sweetness.

½ cup brown rice, rinsed and drained
2½ cups water
1½ tablespoons Hatcho, red, or barley miso
½ cup raisins
1 tablespoon brown sugar or 1½ teaspoons honey
1 tablespoon butter
Dash of cinnamon

Combine rice and water in a pressure cooker and proceed as for rice porridge (p. 57). After opening cooker, stir in the last four ingredients. For best flavor, allow to stand for several hours before serving.

Miso Pumpkin Pie

24 ounces *kabocha* (unpeeled), cut into 1-inch cubes
2 tablespoons red, barley, or Hatcho miso
2 tablespoons honey or brown sugar
1½ tablespoons butter
Dash of nutmeg and/or allspice
Crust for an 8-inch pie

Combine *kabocha* with water to cover in a saucepan or pot, bring to a boil, and simmer for 20 minutes. Drain well, then combine with the next four ingredients and mash together. Line an 8-inch pie pan with the crust and bake in a 400° oven until lightly browned. Spoon in the *kabocha* mixture and re-bake for 20 to 30 minutes, or until nicely browned. For richest flavor, serve cold. This filling also works well in turnovers.

If pumpkin or squash is substituted for the *kabocha*, peel before boiling and drain very well; add 1 to 3 eggs to the mixture before baking.

Crêpes with Sweet Simmered Miso Filling

Red Sweet Simmered Miso Filling:
   3½ teaspoons red or barley miso
   2 teaspoons honey
   ½ teaspoon butter
   1 teaspoon sake or white wine
   ½ teaspoon grated lemon or orange rind
   2 teaspoons water
7/8 cup sifted whole-wheat flour
1 egg, lightly beaten
1 cup milk (soy or dairy)
1 tablespoon oil or butter

Using the filling ingredients, prepare Red Sweet Simmered Miso (p. 60) and set aside to cool. Combine the flour, egg, milk and 1 teaspoon oil, whisking lightly to form a smooth batter. Lightly oil a large skillet, then use batter to prepare 10 to 12 crêpes. Allow crêpes to cool, then spread one surface of each with about ½ teaspoon of the miso filling. Roll crêpes before serving.

Miso Kashiwa Mochi

Served once each year as a special treat on Children's Day—the fifth day of the fifth month—*Kashiwa Mochi* takes its name from the oak leaves generally used to wrap each portion. Widely prepared at commercial Japanese confectioneries, the filling is generally made of sweet white miso and puréed white kidney beans *(Ingen mamē)*, or occasionally of sweet red miso and sweet, azuki-bean paste *(an)*. Household recipes also call for a filling made with *kabocha* or chestnut purée.

7 ounces *kabocha*, pumpkin, or squash, peeled and cut into cubes
3¼ tablespoons sweet white miso
2½ teaspoons honey
1¼ cups glutinous rice flour
½ teaspoon salt
¾ cup boiling water

Steam *kabocha* for 15 to 20 minutes, then rub through a sieve. Add miso and honey, mixing well, to make a filling.

Combine flour and salt, mixing thoroughly. Gradually add boiling water while stirring vigorously for 3 minutes to develop a cohesive dough. Wrap dough in a moist cloth, place into a preheated steamer (p. 55) and steam for 20 minutes. Now transfer dough to a *suribachi* or mortar and pound for 5 to 10 minutes, or until dough develops a uniform, resilient texture. Divide dough into 8 parts and roll out each into 3½-inch rounds on a lightly floured board. Place equal portions of the filling at the center of each round, then fold over one side of the dough to form a half-moon shape. Seal edges by pinching dough with fingers. Wrap each portion in a large (6-to 8-inch-long) oak leaf, with the leaf's shiny surface touching the dough (or use a beech leaf or aluminum foil). Replace into preheated steamer and steam for 4 to 5 minutes. Allow to cool before serving.

Kashiwa Mochi

Miso Pickles

Selling miso pickles

Pickled vegetables are a basic condiment in the Japanese (and Chinese) diet, where they are the single most important source of salt, providing about 40 percent of the total intake. Served at almost every meal of the day, primarily as an accompaniment for rice or rice porridge, they are enjoyed for their slightly crisp texture and deep, rich flavor. There are six basic types of Japanese pickles and each takes its name from the pickling agent: miso, salt, salted moist rice-bran, vinegar, sake lees, and koji. Some scholars believe that the earliest Japanese pickles, called *konomono* or "fragrant things," were made with miso. And to this day, miso pickles (*miso-zuké*) are believed to aid the digestive process and promote long life and good health.

Commercially prepared miso pickles—made both at specialty shops and regular miso shops—are widely available at most food stores and miso retail outlets throughout Japan. More than 12 varieties of vegetables and seeds are used, the most popular of which are *daikon*, (wild) burdock root, cucumbers, eggplants, gingerroot, carrots, *uri* melons, beefsteak seeds, and *myoga*. Fish and meat pickles, usually prepared with sweet white miso, are generally sold at fish or meat markets. In farmhouses and temples, large batches of miso pickles are still prepared each year as part of the miso-making process, with vegetables buried in the keg at the start of fermentation and usually left there until the miso is fully mature (p. 192). In urban homes, small batches are made using storebought miso and special ingredients such as eggs and egg yolks, which are then often served as hors d'œuvres. Most farmers and homemakers prefer to make their miso pickles during the fall or winter; although the process takes longer due to the cold, the pickles' flavor is said to improve and it is easier to prevent the growth of unwanted mold on the miso surface.

Over a period of many centuries, Japanese craftsmen have raised the practice of miso-pickling to the level of a fine art. The country's most famous commercial makers enjoy a wide and lofty reputation, and they guard the secrets of their trade most carefully. Traditional masters call for a lengthy pickling believed to give vegetables a mellow saltiness and tender crunchiness, while extinguishing all bitter and strong flavors (such as those found in *daikon* or burdock root), accenting subtle indwelling flavors, and, above all, evoking a delightful aroma—which devotees refer to as "the life" of the product.

In this section, we will first discuss the rather simple method of preparing miso pickles at home, then go on to the complete 5-step process used by most commercial makers.

The Pickling Container

156

The type and size of the container used are determined by the scale of the household pickling process:

*Large Scale (2 to 10 pounds of fresh vegetable ingredients): Use a container of 2 to 10 gallons capacity, preferably an earthenware crock, a seasoned wooden keg (such as that used for shoyu or miso), a glass container (such as an aquarium), or an enamelware pot. If none of these are available, use a polyethylene tub or bucket. This scale is recommended for ingredients requiring 1 year or more of pickling.

*Medium Scale (½ pound to 2 pounds of ingredients): For kitchen use when pickling for less than one year, use a container of 2 to 4 quarts capacity such as an earthenware crock or casserole, a glass bowl, an enamel pot or shallow pan, or a tupperware container.

*Small Scale (less than 8 ounces of ingredients): Spread the miso in a ½-inch-thick layer over a piece of plastic wrap, arrange ingredients to be pickled on the miso, and roll up into a cylinder. This technique is especially good with small amounts of long, thin vegetables such as cucumbers and burdock root. Or you can use small glass jars or tupperware containers for small-sized ingredients such as egg yolks or garlic.

Fig. 27. Salt-pressing

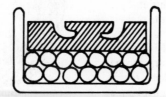
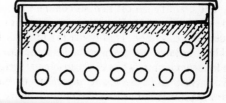

Preparatory Techniques

A vegetable's water content must be reduced to aid it in absorbing the miso's flavor, while preventing it from diluting the medium with excess water extracted by the miso's salt. The following procedures are used:

*Parboiling: Used to sterilize vegetables and soften their skins. Bring lightly salted water to a boil. Drop in well-washed vegetables, return to the boil, and simmer for 1 to 2 minutes. Drain thoroughly in a colander and allow to cool to room temperature.

*Salt Pressing: Use an amount of salt equal to about 10 percent of the weight of the fresh vegetables, about 2 tablespoons for every ½ pound. Place whole or cut ingredients in a large (earthenware, wooden, glass, or enamel) flat-bottomed container and sprinkle the entire surface of each vegetable with salt. Arrange ingredients compactly in parallel rows, top with a lid or another flat-bottomed container, and press with a stone or water-filled jar (fig. 27). For ingredients weighing less than 1 pound, use a 5- to 10-pound pressing weight; for 10 pounds of ingredients, use a 30-pound weight. Press for 2 days unless otherwise stated. After pressing, drain vegetables well, discard liquid, and wipe vegetables with a dry cloth.

*Wrapping in Cheesecloth: This technique helps soft ingredients to keep their form during pickling and makes it easier to remove them from the miso bed. Simply wrap in a single or double layer of cheesecloth before embedding.

Air-drying daikon

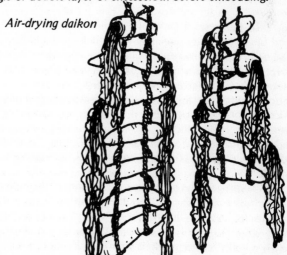

*Air-drying: Place vegetables in a shallow colander or tie in strands with string. Place or hang in a shady location during summer, in direct sunlight in very cold weather. Cover or bring indoors at night to protect from dew.

Air-drying turnips (kabu)

The Miso "Bed"

In Japanese, the pickling medium is called the "bed" and burying the vegetables in it is called "embedding." Use red or barley miso when pickling for several weeks or more; sweet white miso when the pickling time is less than one week. The latter gives a mild, subtly sweet flavor which is often given added zest by mixing in a small amount of sake, rice koji, or powdered mustard. The flavor of red miso can be enriched by the addition of (7-spice) red pepper, sake, or honey. Kinzanji and other varieties of Finger Lickin' Miso give delicious results with overnight pickles, especially egg yolks.

To prepare the bed, cover the bottom of the miso container with a ½- to 1-inch-thick layer of miso. On top of this lay a snug layer of the ingredients to be pickled, then cover with another layer of miso. Repeat until all ingredients are used. Cover the top miso layer with a double thickness of cotton cloth or a sheet of wax paper or plastic to keep out air and prevent mold formation. Store in a cool place or, if using sweet white, Finger Lickin', or small quantities of red miso, refrigerate. Large-scale containers should be further covered with a weighted pressing lid

Cleaning and Serving Pickles

Remove only as many vegetables from the miso as you need for 1 or 2 days. Using your fingers, scrape off excess miso and return it to the pickling container. Unless otherwise specified, rinse off any remaining miso under cold running water. Cut pickles crosswise or diagonally into thin slices, or mince.

Serve red-miso pickles as an accompaniment with plain or fried rice or noodles, or use as a granish for rice porridge, gruel, or tofu. Serve pickles made with sweet white or Finger Lickin' miso as an hors d'oeuvre. In Japan, thin rounds of either type are often arranged on tiny dishes (accompanied by chopsticks) and served together with green tea.

In most Zen temples (and some homes), each person reserves one fairly large slice of pickle until the end of the meal. This is held with a pair of chopsticks and used, together with a small amount of hot tea or water, to rinse out the eating bowls. The pickle is then enjoyed with the broth—and nothing has been wasted. Individuals then dry their own bowls, nestle them snugly one inside the other, and tie them into an attractive bundle, ready for the next meal. Thanks to the humble pickle, the kitchen crew is saved hours of dish washing.

When all homemade pickles have been removed from the container, the miso will be softer than usual due to the moisture extracted from the pickled vegetables. Use in cookery as you would regular miso or in the preliminary pickling of a similar second batch of vegetables (p. 161). After the removal of ingredients such as garlic or *daikon*, the miso will have been flavorfully enriched.

FOODS TO BE PICKLED

Asparagus

Peel 6 slender, young stalks and snap the tips. Cut lengthwise into halves, then into ½-inch lengths. Bring 2 cups water to a boil. Drop in asparagus and return to the boil. Drain, cool under cold running water, and pat dry with towels. Mix ½ cup sweet white miso and 1 tablespoon powdered mustard. Spread half the mixture in a shallow baking dish and cover with a double thickness of cheesecloth. Arrange asparagus in one layer on cloth, cover with a second double layer, and top with remaining miso mixture. Let stand for 3 hours at room temperature or refrigerate overnight. Serve as an hors d'oeuvre.

Beefsteak Leaves

Embed green leaves (fresh or salt-pressed) in a mixture of 4 parts red miso and 1 part *mirin* for 1 to 3 days. Silver and serve as a garnish.

Beefsteak Seeds

Salt-press about ½ cup red beefsteak seeds, then tie in a small cheesecloth bag. Embed in red miso for 1 month. Use as (1) a filling for rice balls or nori-wrapped sushi, (2) a garnish for soups, vegetable pancakes and grain dishes, or (3) an ingredient in tempura.

Burdock Root and Wild Mountain Burdock

Wild mountain burdock (*Yamagobo*) is one of Japan's most popular commercial varieties of miso pickle. Smaller and more richly flavored than regular burdock, it turns a handsome yellowish gold when pickled.

Use whole roots or fairly long lengths. If pickling for less than 1 month, cut roots lengthwise into halves. Parboil for 3 minutes and salt press for 1 to 3 days, then air-dry for several hours. Embed in red miso for at least 4 months, preferably 1 to 3 years.

Carrots

Prepare as for burdock root. For a firmer texture, salt-press or air-dry for about 1 week before pickling.

Celery

Cut stalks into 1-inch lengths. Embed in red miso for 24 to 36 hours. Serve as an hors d'œuvre.

Cucumbers

Use whole cucumbers. Salt-press for 1 to 2 days, then embed in red miso for 3 to 6 months, or in sweet white miso for 5 months.

Daikon or Turnips (*Kabu*)

Use whole *daikon.* Salt-press under heavy weights for 1 week or airdry for 5 to 10 days, or until soft and well contracted. Embed in red miso for at least 4 to 6 months; if desired, for 2 or 3 years.

For faster results, cut lengthwise into halves, then crosswise into 3- to 6-inch sections. Salt-press for 1 night or air-dry for 10 days. Embed in red miso (or a mixture of ½ teaspoon 7-spice red pepper for every 2 cups red miso) for 3 to 4 months, or in moromi miso for 5 months. *Takuan,* or *daikon* which has been pickled in moist salted rice bran, can be further pickled in miso for 3 to 4 weeks.

Eggplants

For best results use (Japanese-style) small and tender whole eggplants. Salt-press for 24 hours, then embed in red miso for 4 to 8 months, or as long as 1 to 2 years. Delicious also embedded in moromi miso or Finger Lickin' Miso for 70 days.

Eggs (*Hardboiled*)

*Sweet White Miso: Use 4 eggs, shelled. For the "bed" use ¾ cup sweet white miso (mixed, if desired, with 1 to 4 tablespoons *mirin,* sake or white wine). Cut two eggs lengthwise into halves and embed with the cut surface facing upward.

Embed remaining eggs whole. Cover container and refrigerate for 1 to 7 days. Remove excess miso but do not wash. Slice whole eggs into thin rounds. Serve as an hors d'œuvre as is, or on crackers or canapés.

*Red Miso: These eggs end up firmer and saltier. Use plain red miso (or mix with sake, etc., as above). Embed eggs whole. For use as an hors d'œuvre, pickle for 5 to 6 hours and serve as is, cut into halves. For use on crackers or canapés, pickle for 10 to 12 hours, then cut into thin rounds. For use as a rice garnish, pickle for 1 to 4 days, then dice or sliver.

*Sweetened Red Miso: Use as the pickling medium: ¾ cup red or barley miso, ¼ cup sugar and 3 tablespoons sake. Proceed as for red miso above.

*Finger Lickin' Miso: Cut eggs length wise into halves, remove yolks, and bury yolks and whites in (Kinzanji or moromi) miso for 24 hours. Remove and serve as for sweet white miso, above.

Egg Yolks (*Softboiled*)

Cover the bottom of a 6-inch square container with a 1-inch-deep layer of red miso. Press the large end of an egg into the miso in 4 places to make 4 depressions, then cover miso with a layer of cheesecloth and press cloth into depressions. Prepare four 3-minute eggs. Carefully remove yolks unbroken, and place one yolk in each of the 4 depressions. Cover with a layer of cheesecloth, gently top with miso, and wait for 1½ to 2 days. Serve yolks like cheese as an hors d'œuvre (garnished with slivered green beefsteak leaves if desired) or as a garnish atop hot rice.

Garlic or Shallots

*Red Nerimiso: Peel the thin outer skin from 10 to 12 cloves of garlic and parboil cloves for 3 minutes. Cut lengthwise into halves and dry on a (bamboo) colander in the shade for 6 to 12 hours. (For added fragrance, skewer and broil dried cloves until speckled.) Embed in about 1 cup hot, freshly-prepared Red Nerimiso (p. 60) for 3 to 6 months. Cut lengthwise into very thin slices before serving.

To reduce pickling time, cut (fresh or parboiled) garlic cloves into paper-thin slices; pickle for at least 2, preferably 3 weeks.

*Red Miso: Peel garlic cloves and cut lengthwise into halves. Embed in miso for at least 4, preferably 6 months. Serve diced or thinly sliced with rice or rice gruel. In rural Japan, these miso pickles are considered an excellent source of stamina and a cure for numerous diseases.

The miso which remains after pickling garlic is most delicious; use it like Garlic Miso (p. 64) or as a topping for tofu or hot rice.

Gingerroot

Use whole mature or young gingerroot. Salt-press for 1 to 3 days. Embed in red miso for at least 1, preferably 2 years. Or, for faster results, slice fresh gingerroot diagonally into paper-thin ovals. Embed for at least 2, preferably 3 weeks.

Green Peppers

Parboil 5 or 6 green peppers for 1 minute in lightly salted water. Remove seeds and stems, then cut lengthwise into 1-inch-wide strips. Combine 8 ounces sweet white miso, 2½ tablespoons *mirin*, and 1 tablespoon sake or white wine; mix well. Embed peppers, cover, and refrigerate for 1 week. Serve as a garnish for hot rice seasoned with a little sesame salt, or as an hors d'œuvre sprinkled with a few drops of shoyu. Cook leftover miso for 5 to 10 minutes in a skillet, stirring constantly, as for Sweet Simmered Miso.

Or cut fresh green peppers lengthwise into 1-inch-wide strips and salt-press for 24 hours; embed in red miso for 2 to 3 months.

Kabocha

Cut *kabocha* into ½-inch-thick slices; peel and trim off pulpy inner edge. Parboil for 1 to 2 minutes in lightly salted water. Drain and cool under cold running water. Air-dry for several hours. Embed in red miso for 2 to 4 months. For added tang, mix ½ teaspoon (7-spice) red pepper with each 2 cups of miso used.

Kombu

Use best grade *dashi kombu*. Wipe with a moist cloth, cut into 8-inch lengths, and steam or pressure cook in a little water for 20 to 30 minutes, or until tender. Spread upper surface of each *kombu* sheet with either a mixture of 1 cup sweet white miso and 1½ teaspoons sake, or with red miso. Roll up sheets from one end, embed in the miso with which they were spread, and wait for at least 6, preferably 12 months. (If using sweet white miso, cover and refrigerate during pickling.) Cut into very thin strips and serve as a garnish with rice.

Lotus Root

Cut 3 ounces of peeled lotus root into 2-inch lengths. Simmer until just tender in a mixture of 1 cup water and 1 tablespoon vinegar, then drain well. Embed in a mixture of ¾ cup sweet white miso, 1 teaspoon hot mustard, and 1 tablespoon *mirin*, pressing miso mixture into lotus root tubules to fill them. Wait for 24 hours. Scrape off miso, wash well, and cut into very thin rounds. Serve as a garnish or hors d'œuvre.

Myoga

Cut fresh *myoga* lengthwise into halves, then embed in red miso for 5 to 7 days. Serve as a garnish with rice.

Sansho Seeds

Salt-press *sansho* seeds for 2 to 3 days, then tie in a small gauze bag and embed in red miso for 1 to 2 weeks.

Tofu

Drain and press tofu (p. 55), then cut crosswise into ½-inch-thick slices. Parboil for 3 minutes, drain, and allow to cool to room temperature. Combine for the miso bed: ½ cup red miso, ½ teaspoon each grated gingerroot and sesame oil, 1 teaspoon sake or white wine, and a dash of (7-spice) red pepper or tabasco sauce. Embed tofu for 12 to 15 hours, then remove carefully and wipe miso from tofu surface with a damp cloth. Cut into ½-inch cubes and, for best flavor, broil on both sides until nicely speckled. This preparation has a soft cheeselike consistency, rich fragrance, and mellow saltiness. Served as is, it makes a tasty garnish for rice or a savory hors d'œuvre. Mashed with thinly-sliced vegetables, it goes well on crackers. To make a sandwich spread or dip, try mixing 3 parts pickled tofu with 2 parts sesame- or peanut butter, 1 part honey, and a little lemon juice.

Or, dry very well pressed tofu in a slow oven for about 1 hour. Cut each cake crosswise into thirds and embed in the miso for 1 year. Sold commercially in Japan, this product has a much firmer consistency than that described above; its appearance and aroma resemble those of a well-aged cheese. (Some varieties are wrapped in *kombu* and beefsteak leaves, and embedded in mellow barley miso.)

For a sweeter product, sprinkle parboiled tofu slices with ¼ teaspoon salt and embed for 2 days in a mixture of 1½ cups sweet white miso and 2 teaspoons sake (or white wine). Broil and serve as above.

Uri or White Melons

Cut each melon lengthwise into halves. Salt-press for 2 to 4 days. Embed in red miso for 3 months.

Wakame

Use 1 cup fresh or refreshed (uncut) *wakame*. Embed in 2 cups red miso for 1 week or in sweet white miso for 8 to 10 days. Serve thinly sliced as a garnish for rice or rice gruel.

Watermelon Rind

Remove green skin and pink flesh. Cut rind into 1-inch squares and parboil for 2 minutes in lightly salted water. Drain well, pat dry with a towel, and embed in sweet white miso; refrigerate for 2 to 3 weeks. Serve as an hors d'œuvre or garnish, or use in fruitcakes.

DAIKON MISO PICKLES
(Commercial Process)

The following process, used by most of Japan's large commercial makers of miso pickles, is said to create a long-lasting product with the best flavor, texture, and color. All vegetables are pickled in basically the same way; only the proportion of salt used and the pickling time varies. An increase or decrease in the weight of the *daikon* (or other vegetables) should be accompanied by an exactly proportional change in the weight of the other ingredients, and of the pressing weight.

In the commercial process, up to 1,200 pounds of *daikon* are pickled at one time in large polymer or concrete tanks; more traditional makers use wooden vats with a capacity of 175 pounds. The following recipe has been scaled down for use in households or communities.

10 pounds daikon, slender varieties used whole, fat varieties cut lengthwise into fourths
2 pounds salt
10 pounds red or barley miso, approximately

I. SALT PICKLING *(Shiozuké)*

1. *First Salt Pickling (Arazuké):* Wash *daikon* thoroughly and drain well. Place in a large (18 inch diameter, 18 inch deep) sturdy wooden, crockery, or plastic tub and sprinkle uniformly with 1.2 pounds salt (12 percent of the daikon's weight). Arrange *daikon* as snugly and compactly as possible in container, then top with a sturdy (wooden) pressing lid and a 20- to 30-pound weight. Cover container with a layer of plastic wrap or paper to keep out insects and dust, and allow to stand for 15 to 20 days.

2. *Second Salt Pickling (Chuzuké):* Pour off and discard any liquid that has accumulated in the pickling container. Drain *daikon* thoroughly, then sprinkle with 0.6 pounds salt (6 percent of *daikon's* original weight). Replace lid and re-press, this time using only a 20- to 25-pound weight; allow to stand for 60 to 90 days.

3. *Washing and Pressing (Shionuki):* Wash *daikon* well with water, then place in a tub of cold running water for 15 to 20 hours, or until the residual salt content of the *daikon* has dropped to about 10 percent. (Professional pickle makers determine this by measuring the relative density of a puréed sample of the *daikon* or of the liquid pressed from them.) Drain washed *daikon* well and place into an empty tub (preferably one with small drainage holes in the lower sides and bottom). Replace pressing lid and top with a 3- to 4-pound weight for 3 to 4 hours, or until liquid equal to about 15 percent of *daikon* weight is expelled. Remove *daikon* and discard liquid.

II. MISO PICKLING *(Misozuké)*

4. *Preliminary Miso Pickling (Shitazuké):* Measure out an amount of miso equal to 1.5 times the weight of the pressed *daikon*. (If possible, use miso which has already been used once in step 5 below). Arrange alternating layers of miso and *daikon* in the tub used in step 1, so that each daikon is completely surrounded by miso. Spread a double layer of cloth or sheet of plastic wrap directly over miso surface, top with lightly weighted (3-pound) pressing lid (to prevent mold growth), and allow to stand for 5 to 8 days.

5. *Basic Miso Pickling (Honzuké):* Remove *daikon* from miso, reserving miso (which now contains a fairly high proportion of liquid) for use in step 4 of your next batch of pickles, after which it is discarded. Measure out an amount of fresh miso equal in weight to that used in step 4 and mix into it 0.2 pounds of salt plus 1 to 2 ounces each of any or all of the following natural organic acids: racemic (grape), glutamic, citric, malic (apple), lactic. Embed *daikon*, cover, and allow to stand for at least 60, preferably 120 to 180 days, or until you are ready to use it. Remove only as much *daikon* from miso as you plan to serve in one week or less. Scrape miso from *daikon* by hand, returning miso to pickling container. Wash *daikon* and slice into thin rounds before use. When all *daikon* has been used, reserve miso remaining in keg for step 4 of a future batch.

OTHER MISO PICKLES *(Commercial Process)*

*Cucumbers and Uri Melons: In the first salt pickling, use an amount of salt equal to 16 percent by weight of the vegetables; in the second, 8 percent. Do basic miso pickling for at least 70 days.

*Daikon Moromi Pickles: Proceed as for *daikon* pickles but wash in step 3 until only 6 percent salt remains, then pickle in moromi miso for at least 70 days.

*Eggplants: In the first salt pickling use an amount of salt equal to 18 percent by weight of the vegetables; in the second, 6 percent. Do basic miso pickling for at least 120 days. (Note: burnt alum is sometimes used in place of salt in the first salt pickling.)

*Gingerroot: For best results, choose large, mellow-flavored roots. In the first salt-pickling use an amount of salt equal to 20 percent by weight of the vegetables; omit the second salt pickling. Pickle for at least 90 days in sweet white or mellow barley miso.

*Kombu: Use best quality, sweet kombu having a dark color tinged with black. Wash well in lukewarm water and steam for 15 to 20 minutes. Allow to cool to room temperature, then pickle (flat or rolled) in red miso for at least 120 days.

Miso pickles with tea

Koji Cookery

If you prepare your own koji at home (p.179) or purchase ready-made varieties, you may have a little left over after using it to make miso. The following recipes suggest ways of using koji in other preparations.

Amazaké
MAKES 3½ CUPS

Literally "sweet sake" (pronounced ah-mah-ZAH-kay), this creamy-thick hot rice drink has a rich, ambrosial flavor and virtually no alcohol content. A specialty at numerous teahouses and inns, it is often served with Dengaku (p. 144) and is most popular during the winter months—especially at New Year's. Rich in natural sugars (22.7% by weight vs. 34.8% in sweet white miso, 70.2% in honey, and 83.0% in *mizuamé*), it has long served as a sweetening agent in Japanese cookery. Amazaké is now being made by Grainaissance in Berkeley, CA; by Kendall Food Co. in Ashburnham, MA; by The Bridge in Middletown, CT; and by small companies in Los Angeles and Miami. All have received the eternal blessings of heaven and earth.

1 cup white, brown, or glutinous rice, washed and drained
2 cups water
2 cups firm granular rice koji

Combine rice and water in a pressure cooker and bring to full pressure (15 pounds). Reduce heat to low and simmer for 3 minutes if using white rice, or 20 minutes if using brown or glutinous rice. Remove from heat and allow pressure to come down naturally for 10 minutes. (Or cook in a regular pot as described on page 57.) Open crock, stir well, and allow to cool to 140°F. Mix in koji and pack mixture into a well-washed (or sterilized) wide-mouth jar or crock. Cover tightly and incubate at 140°F for 10 to 14 hours or at 90°F for 20 to 24 hours.

(To incubate, float the container in a large covered pot or tub partially filled with warm water, or wrap in towels and place over a hot water heater or in an insulated box next to hot water bottles.)

The fermentation is complete when the mixture has a rich, sweet fragrance and individual grains are very soft. Now stir well with a fork or several chopsticks to create a porridge-like consistency or, if using brown rice and a smooth texture is desired, purée in a blender or sieve. You now have amazaké base, which may be used in any of three ways:

*To Serve as Amazaké: Combine 1 part base with 1½ to 1¾ parts water in a saucepan and bring just to a boil. Season lightly with salt, pour into preheated cups, and top each portion with a dab of grated gingerroot.

*To Use as a Sweetener: Substitute 3½ tablespoons amazaké base for 1 tablespoon honey (or 2 tablespoons sugar) in any of your favorite preparations. Rich in enzymes, it is especially good in breads, cakes, pancakes, waffles, or muffins, where it assists in the leavening process and adds a rich moistness.

*To Make Doburoku (grog): Incubate for 7 to 10 more days at body temperature, or until the mixture develops a heady, slightly alcoholic aroma. Purée and serve as is, or dilute as above.

Bettara-zuké *(Daikon Pickled in Koji)*

In Japan, koji is used in the preparation of several types of pickles, including *daikon*, eggplant, and Chinese cabbage. As delectable as it is costly, *Bettara-zuké* has a unique mellow sweetness and juicy crunchiness combined with a heady aroma.

1 small *daikon*, peeled, cut lengthwise into quarters and then crosswise into fourths
2 tablespoons salt
1 cup white rice, cooked and cooled to body temperature
1 cup koji
¼ cup sake, white wine, or *shochu*
¼ teaspoon minced red peppers (optional)

Please begin by reading about Miso Pickles (p. 156). Air-dry *daikon* sections for 2 to 4 days until soft and well contracted, then salt-press using the 2 tablespoons salt. Pour off excess liquid and discard.

Meanwhile, combine warm rice, koji, and sake in a well-washed quart jar, cover tightly, and incubate at about 110°F for 2 days (or 80°F for 3 to 4 days), or until rice almost decomposes. Now combine salt-pickled *daikon* with rice-koji mixture and, if desired, sweetening and red pepper; allow to stand at room temperature for 6 to 10 days or until sweet and transparent. Remove *daikon* and scrape off koji mixture with your fingers; do not wash *daikon*. Slice into thin rounds and serve as an accompaniment for rice or as an hors d'œuvre.

Eggplants Pickled in Koji (*Nasu no Karashi-zuké*)

25 tiny Japanese eggplants (2 inches long, pick in autumn),
  caps removed, or substitute 18 ounces medium-sized
  eggplants
13 tablespoons salt
4¼ cups water
1½ cups koji
6 tablespoons mild mustard
4½ tablespoons *mirin*

Rub eggplants lightly with half the salt, then place (together
with this salt) in a pickling container (p. 156); top with a
pressing lid and 8-pound weight. Combine remaining half of
salt with the water, mix until dissolved, and pour into pickling container. Allow to stand for 20 to 30 days. Pour off
liquid and transfer eggplants to a bowl. Combine koji,
mustard and *mirin*, mixing well, then stir into eggplants.
Return to pickling container and press for 15 days more.
Serve as for Bettara-zuké.

VARIATIONS

*For a richer flavor use: 4¼ pounds salt-pressed eggplants, 2¼
cups (7 oz.) koji, 5 tablespoons honey, ¾ to 1 cup mild
mustard powder, 12 tablespoons sake or water, and 6 tablespoons shoyu. Mix all ingredients and press with a light
weight for 15 days.

Chinese Cabbage Pickled in Koji: In a pickling container,
place alternating layers of Chinese cabbage (total 2 pounds)
and salt (3 tablespoons). Salt-press for 2 to 3 days then discard liquid. Soak ½ cup koji in ¼ cup warm water for 15
minutes. Mix in 1 teaspoon honey, 2 tablespoons slivered
kombu, and 1 slivered red pepper. Squeeze cabbage well to
expel excess liquid then arrange alternating layers of cabbage
and koji mixture in the container. Press with a light weight for
4 to 5 days. Serve as for Bettara-zuké.

Amazaké at the Nakamura-ro restaurant

PART III

The Preparation of Miso

Making Miso at Home and in Communities

THE JAPANESE have long taken great pride in their homemade miso. During visits to the homes of friends, both in modern high-rise apartments and traditional farmhouses, we have been surprised again and again to discover how many people even to this day make their own. After mentioning our interest in the subject, we have found ourselves ushered to the kitchen, back porch, storeroom, or barn—where our hosts would proudly reveal their cache of 3 or 4 kegs or crocks—and treated to a taste of their favorite variety, followed by a detailed description of their personal miso-making process.

Indeed, the number of families and communities in Japan preparing their own miso is on the rise. For some, this is a response to rising food prices and the commercial trend toward standardization and deteriorating quality. But many are also rediscovering how enjoyable and easy it is to prepare miso with just the right flavor by choosing their own blend of ingredients and aging it for as long as they like. At least one large company is now doing a booming business selling *shikomi-miso*, a 44-pound mixture of high-quality koji, cooked soybeans, salt and water, packed into a keg and ready to be aged. Available in blends that produce either red or light-yellow miso, it is 10 to 20 percent less expensive than mature commercial brands and yields a product that is guaranteed to be both free of additives and, of course, unpasteurized. Yet whether they prepare it from scratch or use the new convenience mixture, most Japanese still maintain that the ancient proverb holds true: everyone prizes most the flavor of his or her family's homemade miso.

Starting in the late 1960s, a surprisingly large number of people in the United States started preparing homemade miso. Classes have been conducted by natural food companies and Japanese-American makers, and recipes for barley and red miso have been published and distributed. Names of organizations and individuals actively interested in such work are given on page 259.

The three most important factors affecting the quality of homemade miso are: 1) the quality of the koji; 2) the use of a proper fermentation container; and 3) the maintenance of a clean environment during preparation. Working with clean hands and utensils is of the utmost importance in keeping the influence of contaminating microorganisms to a minimum. Before making your own miso, please read Appendix C in order to get a sense of the chemical and microbiological changes you will be helping on their way.

Four Decisions

Before starting your miso, you will have to make four basic decisions:

1. **The Time of Year:** For best results, make miso during the cold months when the air is relatively free of contaminating microorganisms. Such molds and bacteria increase in number during the warmer part of the year and can impart an undesirable (sour or acidic) flavor to the finished product. Late November or early March are the best times for preparing homemade koji since the weather is cold but not *too* cold. Some Japanese prefer to make their miso in the fall when the new-crop soybeans and rice are at their peak of flavor; others prefer early spring, just before the warm months when most

of the transformation due to fermentation takes place in the kegs. Miso prepared during the cold months will be ready by October when the heat of summer is past and fall breezes begin to chill the air. In Japan, families generally make miso only once a year, preparing one vat of each of several varieties.

2. **To Make or Buy the Koji:** Homemade koji can be prepared for less than one-fourth the cost of storebought varieties, but the process takes about two days and it is not always possible to get a top-quality product on the first try. Nevertheless, if the instructions contained in the second half of this chapter are followed carefully, you should get good results. Most Japanese homemade miso is presently prepared with ready-made koji: the recipes are easy to follow, take very little preparation time, and are virtually foolproof. We have therefore placed them at the start of this chapter to encourage beginners to try them first.

3. **The Vat Size:** We will henceforth use the word "vat" to refer to all sizes and types of fermentation containers. The total amount of miso you wish to prepare determines the size of the vat you will need. It is generally agreed that *the larger the vat, the easier it is to produce delicious miso.* Why? Because the larger the vat, the smaller the total surface area (bottom, sides, and top) of the miso in proportion to the total volume. As shown in the figure below, the miso in the larger container has only one-third as much surface area per unit volume as the miso in the smaller.

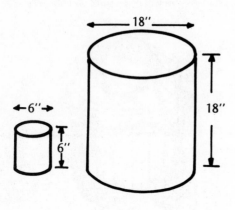

		SMALL	LARGE
Surface Area	(in²)	169	1526
Volume	(in³)	169	4578
Ratio	(S:V)	1.0	0.33

Thus large containers have a voluminous central core of miso totally sealed off from the surrounding environment; only a proportionally small surface area remains in contact with the walls, bottom, and top of the container where it is subject to gradual moisture losses through the container's pores and subtle outside (aerobic) influences. Miso in containers of only 1- to 2-quarts capacity may develop a slightly tart or alcoholic flavor, with moisture losses running as high as 5 to 7 percent of the original weight causing a concentration in salt content and an excessively "salty" flavor. For best results, your vat

should have a capacity of no less than 1 gallon, which is enough to hold 2 small-scale batches as described below. A Japanese family will typically make one 10-gallon or two 5-gallon vatfuls each year; individuals might consider pooling their efforts with friends to fill one such vat. Communities often use a wooden keg of 50 gallons capacity.

4. **Batch Size:** After you have determined the total amount of miso you wish to make, you are ready to decide how many individual batches will be required. The batch size is generally determined by the size of the cooking pots and mixing containers in your kitchen. Often two or three batches are needed to fill one vat. In the following section we give three batch sizes: small, medium, and large. A small batch makes about 2 quarts of miso, a medium batch 2 gallons, and a large batch 8 gallons. We have chosen a small-scale basic recipe so that the 2 cups of soybeans required can be cooked in a standard pressure cooker or 1-gallon pot found in most kitchens. However, if you have a large pressure cooker or pot, you will save time and fuel by doubling the basic recipe or using a larger batch size.

HOMEMADE MISO
(Using Ready-made Koji)

The following section contains recipes for six basic varieties of miso that are easily prepared at home. Each is actually only a variation on a basic theme, for in each recipe (for the same batch size) the amount of soybeans is the same (fig. 31, p. 172). The basic method calls for pressure cooking the soybeans, which takes much less time and fuel than boiling and prevents the beans from turning reddish-brown during cooking, thereby making it possible to produce light-colored misos as well as the standard darker varieties. Since a typical pressure cooker will hold just 2 cups of dry soybeans, larger batches should be prepared by multiple cooking. Overfilling may cause loose soybean hulls to clog the steam escape valve. If a pressure cooker is not available, use a pot (see Variation 1).

Using pressure-cooked soybeans, one batch of miso ingredients will be in the vat and ready to start fermentation within one hour after you begin work. The commercial miso retailed in the United States will cost you about 2½ times as much per pound as the miso in the following recipes, and 5½ times as much as miso prepared from homemade koji!

Utensils

To prepare miso on a small scale, you will need the following common kitchen utensils and a fermentation container (fig. 28):

A standard pressure cooker or pot of 1-gallon capacity

A mixing pot of 1½ to 2½ gallons capacity

A colander or bamboo *zaru*

A wooden pestle (a wooden rod about 2 inches in diameter, a tall thin bottle, or a potato masher also work well), or a grain mill or meat grinder

A measuring cup and measuring spoons

A large (wooden) spoon or spatula

A vat of at least 1-gallon capacity (see below)

A sealing sheet consisting of a 1½-foot square of butcher paper, brown kraft paper, or Japanese natural *washi* paper; or a double thickness of sturdy tightly-woven undyed cloth; or several sheets of wide *kombu;* or a piece of plastic wrap or cellophane

A pressing lid made of a piece of wood, plywood, firm plastic, or other sturdy material cut to fit inside the fermentation container atop the sealing sheet with a gap of 1/8 inch or less between the perimeter of the lid and the container's walls

A 3- to 4-pound pressing weight such as a well-washed stone or brick, or a water-filled jar

A piece of wrapping paper, newspaper, or polyethylene sheeting and a piece of string several feet long

A 3- by 5-inch index card

Fig. 28. Utensils for making miso

The key piece of equipment is the vat. The ideal small- or medium-scale vat (1- to 4-gallons capacity) is made of glazed or non-porous earthenware and is either cylindrical in shape or has a wide mouth. A traditional American crock (fig. 29), works perfectly; still used for pickling, and in natural food stores for storing and displaying grains, nuts, or dried fruits, it is available in various sizes at many natural food stores, Japanese hardware stores, or old-fashioned American hardware stores. Or order from the producer: Marshall Pottery Inc., 1400 Lake St., Marshall, TX 75670. Tel. 214-938-9201. A glass container, which has the advantage of permitting observation of the fermentation process, or an enamelware pot also work well. Small wooden kegs sometimes sold as containers for miso or shoyu are excellent for quantities of 4 gallons or more; be sure they are well seasoned and do not use them for smaller quantities since they may cause an excessive loss of moisture due to their slight porosity. Large wooden barrels (available in 30- and 55-gallon sizes for about $5.00 each from nail wholesalers or salted salmon importers) or used hogshead casks (available in 63- to 140-gallon sizes from some wineries) are ideal for community or large-scale production. Regardless of the vat's size, the diameter of its mouth should be no greater than its depth (preferably slightly less), and the miso should fill the vat to at least 80 percent of capacity.

Vats made of polyethylene or other plastics having 5- to 10-gallons capacity are now widely used in Japan, but experienced miso makers feel that natural materials yield a better flavor, and may be safer. Do not use a metal vat.

For larger batch sizes, increase the size of your utensils accordingly.

Fig. 29. Miso fermentation crocks

resembling the nap on a brand new tennis ball. This koji is used primarily to prepare homemade *Amazaké* (p. 162) but also works well in the preparation of both miso and salt-pickled vegetables.

Ingredients

Each of the basic ingredients for homemade miso is now available at reasonable prices in the United States. For a list of sources, see page 258.

Soybeans: Any variety of whole dry soybeans available at natural or health food stores, co-ops, and some supermarkets. Order in bulk for substantial savings. Soy grits (see Variation 4) may be either the coarse or fine varieties now available at better natural food stores. The larger sized and slightly more expensive "vegetable" type soybeans, bred from Japanese stock, are preferred by some to the smaller and more widely available U.S. "field" soybeans.

Corona hand-mill

Ready-made Dried Koji *(Urikoji):* This koji is prepared by drying fresh koji on large screens in an oven at 104°F. Both ready-made rice and barley koji are now available in the West at most natural food stores and at Japanese food markets (especially at New Years). The main U.S. producer is Miyako Oriental Foods in Los Angeles. In 1983 a 20-ounce tub of their white rice koji retailed for $3.46, or the equivalent of $2.77 a pound. Names of other makers, importers, and distributors are given on page 258. There are two basic types of ready-made dried koji:

Firm Granular Koji is composed of whole separate kernals of rice or barley with very little downy white mycelium visible on the surface of each grain. The beige or milky-white kernels look something like slightly puffed rice. One variety used primarily for making miso and one for salt-pickled vegetables *(tsukemono).* Miyako makes the miso type.

Soft Mat Koji is sold in sheets about 8 to 10 inches square and ¾ inch thick. It is composed of fluffy grains of steamed rice bound together by a felt-like white mycelium

Firm granular koji is the traditional form used to make miso and is still considered the best since it has more "strength" (ability to break down proteins and carbohydrates) than the soft mat variety. High-quality granular koji will have a very small percentage of "transparent" grains (those which the mycelium has not penetrated) among the milky-white majority. Individual grains, when broken in half, should show the white mycelium penetrating to the very center and not have a transparent core.

Since dried koji does not, in general, have quite as much "strength" as fresh koji, miso prepared with it takes slightly longer to come to maturity. This explains the difference in aging times between the following homemade varieties and their commercial counterparts as described in Chapter 4.

All koji should be kept well sealed in a cool dry place. For long-term storage, small quantities should be refrigerated (but not frozen). Koji with an olive-green or yellowish tint has probably stood too long in a warm place causing sporulation; it is best used whole or ground as koji starter (p. 178).

Ready-made Fresh Koji: Excellent quality fresh rice koji, produced by Miyako Oriental Foods in Los Angeles, is now widely available in the U.S. In Japan, fresh koji may be purchased directly from a koji or miso shop the day before the soybeans are cooked; it is immediately crumbled and mixed with all of the salt in the miso recipe, placed in a covered container, and stored in a cool, dry place. A given volume of fresh koji weighs about 14 percent more than dried granular koji. In the following recipes, when substituting fresh koji for dried, use only 60 percent of the required mixing liquid.

Salt: Any salt may be used, but to make miso with the best flavor and nutritional value, use sun-dried, unrefined natural sea salt, now available at some natural and health food stores and very rich in minerals (more than 63 varieties). You can prepare your own natural salt by simmering clean sea water in a large kettle until almost all of the moisture has evaporated, placing the moist salt in a cloth-lined colander or strainer, and allowing it to drain for several days; measure homemade salt by volume rather than weight when using it to make miso. (Save the liquid nigari that drips from the salt to use in preparing tofu.)

The salt in miso mellows as the fermentation proceeds; thus miso which tastes quite salty after six months may taste just right one year later. To compensate for this phenomenon, some recipes increase the proportion of salt together with the expected fermentation time. Whereas a 1-year red miso might, for example, require 2½ pounds of salt, the same product fermented for 2½ years would require 4 pounds.

People wishing to prepare low-salt misos should make either sweet red or sweet white varieties; do not simply try to reduce the salt in other types or they may spoil. As a general rule, the minimum amount of salt used with a given weight of grain or dried koji should *not fall below* the broken line in figure 30. The equation for this minimum amount is:

$$S = \frac{45 - G}{10}$$

where S is the weight in pounds of salt and G is the weight in pounds of grain or dried koji used with 10 pounds of dry soybeans. Thus a recipe calling for 10 pounds each soybeans and dried rice koji should not contain less than 3.5 pounds salt.

Fig. 30. Basic Proportions of Salt and Grain (or Dried Koji) used with 10 Pounds of Dry Soybeans for Different Miso Varieties

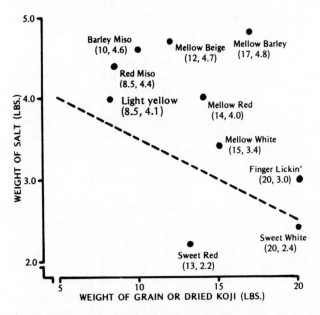

Water: Any water may be used for cooking the soybeans or as mixing liquid (below), but fresh pure water—from a deep well, spring, or distilled—has traditionally been considered to give the best flavor and most trouble-free fermentation. Water containing an abundance of chlorine or other chemicals may somewhat retard the activity of miso's microorganisms, while impure water may introduce contaminating microorganisms.

Seed Miso: Use any good-quality mature miso, either from a previous batch of your own making or commercial miso which has not been pasteurized and contains no preservatives. The use of a small amount of seed miso as an inoculum adds large numbers of yeasts and bacteria to the unfermented ingredients thereby enhancing the aroma and flavor of the finished product and reducing the fermentation time by up to 50 percent. It is best to use seed miso of the same variety as the miso you wish to prepare, but any miso will work.

Mixing Liquid: Either boiled water or the cooking liquid remaining after boiling the soybeans is mixed with the other ingredients to give the miso its proper moisture content. In Japan, this is called "seed water" (*tané mizu*). Fresh water, unless taken from a very pure deep well, is always boiled to assure that no contaminating microorganisms are present. From November until early April, soybean cooking liquid gives excellent results and helps make full use of the soybean nutrients. However, if the miso is prepared during the warm half of the year, water should be used since the soybean cooking liquid may encourage spoilage; in this case, cook the soybeans so that very little liquid remains at the end. If you want to try to use cooking liquid during the warmer part of the year, mix the liquid with 3 tablespoons salt as soon as it has drained from the beans, and reduce the salt added with the other ingredients accordingly.

The proper amount of liquid to be added to any given mixture of ingredients is difficult to specify exactly since it depends upon the moisture level of the koji and the moisture losses through the vat (which are determined by the vat's size and construction). If too much liquid is added, the miso can easily over-ferment and develop a strong alcoholic aroma. The miso's moisture content can be adjusted during fermentation by simply increasing or decreasing the pressing weight.

Alternate Carbohydrate Sources: For rice or barley koji, you may substitute up to 50 percent cornmeal or corn, sweet potatoes, Irish potatoes, or *kabocha;* these foods should be well steamed or boiled (see Variation 5). Wheat koji may be substituted in equal parts. See also page 44.

Alternate Protein Sources: For soybeans, you may substitute up to 100 percent broad, black, *azuki,* lima, or garbanzo beans, or others listed on page 44. Indian pulses (Bengal gram, Thur dhal, green gram, and Field beans) also work well. If 10 to 20 percent soybeans (and peanuts) are used together with these ingredients, the amino acid balance and total usable protein will be considerably enhanced (see p. 21).

Fig. 31. Proportions by Weight of Basic Ingredients for Various Homemade Misos

Type of Miso	Batch Size	Dry Soybeans	Dried Koji Soft Mat	Dried Koji Firm¹ Granular	Salt	Mixing Liquid	Seed Miso (Optional)
Red Miso	*BASIC RATIO* (WT)	10	8.5		4.4	11.1	0.4
	Small Batch	13 oz	11.1 oz 3.4c	2.4c	5.7 oz 8.9T	14.4 oz 1.7c	0.5oz 1T
	Medium	3 lb 4 oz	2 lb 12 oz 13.4c	9.7c	22.9 oz 2.2c	3 lb 9 oz 6.9c	2.1oz 4T
	Large	13 lb	11 lb 1 oz 53.5c	39.0c	5 lb 12 oz 9.0c	14 lb 7 oz 27.7c	8.3oz 1c
Barley Miso	*BASIC RATIO* (WT)	10	10		4.6	13.0	0.4
	Small Batch	13 oz	13 oz 3.9c	2.9c	6.0 oz 9.3T	16.9 oz 2.0c	0.5oz 1T
	Medium	3 lb 4 oz	3 lb 4 oz 15.7c	11.4c	23.9 oz 2.3c	4 lb 4 oz 8.1c	2.1oz 4T
	Large	13 lb	13 lb 62.7c	45.7c	6 lb 0 oz 9.4c	16 lb 14 oz 32.5c	8.3oz 1c
Light-yellow Miso	*BASIC RATIO* (WT)	10	8.5		4.1	11.1	0.4
	Small Batch	13 oz	11.1 oz 3.4c	2.4c	5.3 oz 8.3T	14.4 oz 1.7c	0.5oz 1T
	Medium	3 lb 4 oz	2 lb 12 oz 13.4c	9.7c	21.3 oz 2.1c	3 lb 9 oz 6.9c	2.1oz 4T
	Large	13 lb	11 lb 1 oz 53.5c	39.0c	5 lb 3 oz 8.4c	14 lb 7 oz 27.7c	8.3oz 1c
Sweet Red Miso	*BASIC RATIO* (WT)	10	13		2.2	12.3	0
	Small Batch	13 oz	16.9 oz 5.1c	3.7c	2.9 oz 4.5T	16.0 oz 1.9c	—
	Medium	3 lb 4 oz	4 lb 3 oz 20.4c	14.4c	11.4 oz 1.1c	4 lb 0 oz 7.7c	—
	Large	13 lb	16 lb 12 oz 81.5c	59.4c	2 lb 14 oz 4.5c	16 lb 0 oz 30.8c	—
Sweet White Miso	*BASIC RATIO* (WT)	10	20		2.4	19.2	0.4
	Small Batch	13 oz	1 lb 12 oz 8.4c	6.2c	3.1 oz 4.9T	25.0 oz 3.0c	0.5oz 1T
	Medium	3 lb 4 oz	7 lb 33.7c	24.6c	12.5 oz 1.2c	6 lb 4 oz 12.0c	2.1oz 4T
	Large	13 lb	28 lb 134.9c	98.5c	3 lb 2 oz 4.9c	24 lb 15 oz 48.0c	8.3oz 1C
Mellow Barley Miso	*BASIC RATIO* (WT)	10	17		4.8	16.3	0.4
	Small Batch	13 oz	1 lb 6 oz 6.6c	4.8c	6.2 oz 9.7T	21.2 oz 2.6c	0.5oz 1T
	Medium	3 lb 4 oz	5 lb 8 oz 26.5c	19.3c	25.0 oz 2.4c	5 lb 5 oz 10.2c	2.1oz 4T
	Large	13 lb	22 lb 2 oz 106.0c	77.3c	6 lb 4 oz 9.8c	21 lb 3 oz 40.9c	8.3oz 1c
Soybean Miso	*BASIC RATIO* (WT)	10	—		2.0	3.4	0.4
	Medium Batch	3 lb 4 oz 8c	—		10.4 oz 1.0c	16.6 oz 2c	2.1oz 4T
	Large	13 lb 32c	—		2 lb 10 oz 4.1c	4 lb 2 oz 8c	9.4oz 1c

Notes:
1) The ready-made firm granular dried koji produced in the U.S. by Miyako Oriental Foods weights 175 grams (6.17 ounces) per cup, or 36 percent more per cup than the figures given in this table. Since the basic proportions of the table are based on weight, use either the same weight as shown in the table or 66 percent the required volume. Example: to make a small batch of red miso using Miyako firm granular dried koji, use either 11.1 ounces or 1.58 cups of this koji.
2) If using fresh koji, use 1.14 times as much by weight as the dried koji.
3) If using fresh koji, use only 40 to 60 percent as much mixing liquid; for firm granular koji, only 80 to 90 percent as much.

Homemade Red Miso MAKES 6 CUPS OR 3.6 POUNDS
(Sendai Miso)

Basic proportions by weight: soybeans 10, dried rice koji 8.5, salt, 4.4, mixing liquid 11.1 (reduced to 6.7 if using fresh koji), seed miso 0.4.

- 2 cups (13 ounces) whole dry soybeans
- 3¼ cups water
- 9 tablespoons (5.7 ounces) natural salt
- 1 tablespoon seed miso (optional)
- 1¾ cups mixing liquid
- 11.1 ounces (315 grams) ready-made dried rice koji (about 3.4 cups well-crumbled soft mat koji or 2.4 cups homemade or firm granular koji)

PREPARE IN ADVANCE

Carefully remove any split soybeans (their loose hulls easily clog pressure cooker), then wash beans thoroughly in pressure cooker. Add 3¼ cups water, cover pot, and soak for 3 hours, or until beans have swelled to fill hulls tightly. Skim off any hulls floating in water.

To cook beans without pressure, see Variation 1.

If using a wooden vat, fill it with water and allow it to stand overnight to seal leaks.

1) Bring cooker to full pressure over medium-high heat. When steam first begins to jiggle vent cap, turn heat *immediately* to very low (to prevent foaming over); cook for 25 minutes at 15 pounds (30 minutes at 10 pounds, or 75 minutes at 5 pounds). Remove from heat and allow to stand for 10 to 15 minutes as pressure returns to normal. Open cooker and test for doneness; each bean should be soft enough to be easily crushed between your thumb and ring finger. Re-cover cooker.

2) See that all utensils are well washed, preferably doused with boiling water. Place colander over (or into) mixing pot, pour in cooked beans, and allow to drain for 3 to 5

minutes before returning beans to cooker. Using pestle or potato masher, mash beans until only about one-third remain whole. Or run two-thirds of the beans through a grain mill or meat grinder. (For smooth miso, mash or grind all beans.) Allow beans' temperature to cool to 110°F.

3) Remove cooking liquid from mixing pot and measure out 1¾ cups, reserving any excess for use in other cooking; if insufficient liquid remains, add the necessary amount of boiled water. Combine in the mixing pot all but 1½ teaspoons of the salt and, if used, the seed miso. Add ¼ cup liquid, mixing with a wooden spoon until smooth, then stir in the remaining 1½ cups liquid. Wash hands. Using fingertips,

crumble koji into mixing pot, then stir into liquid mixture. Now add soybeans and mix all ingredients thoroughly, using first the wooden spoon, then your hands to squeeze the ingredients together. After mixing, ingredients should have about the same consistency as mature miso.

4) Wash, rinse, and dry vat. Sprinkle ¼ teaspoon salt onto your moistened fingertips and rub salt over walls of vat. Sprinkle additional ¼ teaspoon salt over bottom of vat, then spoon in miso mixture, packing it down firmly to expel air pockets. Smooth miso surface, then sprinkle on and gently rub in the remaining 1 teaspoon salt. Cover surface with seal-

ing sheet, pressing it firmly against miso to expel surface air bubbles. Top with pressing lid and weight(s).

5) Within several days, make additional batches of mixed ingredients as described above; rub salt over vat's walls before packing in mixture but do not sprinkle additional salt over surface of previous batch. When vat is at least 80 percent full and contains a minimum of 12 cups unfermented miso, sprinkle surface with salt and top with sealing sheet, lid, and weight(s).

6) Cover container with a double layer of wrapping paper and tie in place with string. On index card, write type of miso prepared, exact ingredients used, the date, and date at which miso is expected to be ready. Make a note of this latter date on your yearly calendar and tape index card to paper-wrapped vat.

7) For natural fermentation, choose an unheated environment such as a garage, store-room, workshop, or barn; for faster (temperature-controlled) fermentation, see Variation 2. Choose a location that receives no direct sunlight and has adequate air circulation. Clean area well and set vat off floor on several blocks. Allow miso to ferment for at least 6 months including 1 full summer. The finest flavor will be attained after 12 months (or 18 to 24 months if seed miso is not used). Do not stir miso during fermentation.

8) As fermentation proceeds, you may wish to check the miso once every few months. However, do not open the vat more than is necessary since contact with the air encourages the growth of surface mold and contaminating organisms, and causes a slight darkening of the color and loss of aroma. If, after one month, no liquid tamari has risen to the miso's surface, increase the pressing weight. If tamari rises to a depth of more than ½ inch during the warm months, reduce the weight. To taste the miso, remove lid and sealing sheet and tilt vat so that tamari runs to one side. Using a clean spoon, open a small hole 3 to 4 inches deep at center of miso surface and retrieve a sample. Compare aroma, flavor, color, and texture with your favorite commercial miso and record your impressions on index card. If flavor is too salty or color too light, increase fermentation time. If texture is too soft, increase pressing weight and remove tamari for use in cookery (pp. 50 or 77). Overly alcoholic, acidic, or sour flavors cannot be remedied and may require that the miso be discarded. After each tasting, record date for next tasting on yearly calendar.

9) When miso is mature, remove all covering; carefully scrape off and discard any surface mold. (Although this mold is not harmful, it causes a slight decline in the miso aroma and flavor). Mix miso in container thoroughly from top to bottom to evenly distribute tamari and saltier surface layer. (Removal of tamari for use in cookery will cause a slight decline in the miso flavor.) Spoon a 1-month supply of miso into a small crock or jar and place in a refrigerator or other cool place for daily use. Smooth surface of miso remaining in container, re-cover, and weight as before. All non-sweet miso may be stored in its vat for 1 to 3 years; sweet miso should be stored in a very cool place and used within 1 to 2 months.

VARIATIONS

1) **Cooking Soybeans Without Pressure:** Wash beans thoroughly in cooking pot and drain well. Add 8 cups water, cover, and allow to stand for 12 to 14 hours at room temperature. (At temperatures below 50°F, increase soaking time to 18 hours.) Bring covered beans to a boil over high heat. Reduce heat to very low, set lid ajar, and simmer for about 2 hours, skimming off any foam and hulls that surface. Add 3 cups (hot) water and simmer for 2½ to 3 hours more, or until beans are soft (see Step 1). If necessary, add water from time to time so that about 2 cups cooking liquid remain when beans are done. Drain and proceed from Step 2.

2) **Temperature-controlled Fermentation:** Place the vat of mixed, unfermented ingredients in a warm dark place such as a water heater- or furnace room, above a stove, or in an insulated attic. During the first 2 months, choose a location

where the temperature is 70°F to 75°F. Then transfer for 2 months to a temperature of about 85°F. Finally, return to the original temperature for 2 months more. Allow the miso to stand in an unheated environment for 1 week before opening (fig. 49, p. 236). (For an even faster fermentation, place at 85°F for 1 week, 90°F for 2 to 3 months, 85°F for 1 week more, then ripen for 1 week in an unheated place.) Flavor will be improved if the miso is stirred thoroughly once or twice during this period. Fermentation time can also be decreased by packing mixed ingredients into vat while they are still hot (90°F to 100°F) and wrapping vat with several layers of thick towelling.

3) **Using Fresh Koji:** Substitute for the 11.1 ounces ready-made dried koji, 12.7 ounces fresh koji. Purchase or prepare this koji before starting to cook the soybeans, as explained on page 177. Use only 1 cup mixing liquid.

4) **Using Soy Grits:** The use of grits reduces the soaking, cooking, and fermentation times, and yields a lighter colored miso. Substitute as equal weight of grits for the soybeans in the basic recipe. a) To Pressure Cook: Soak as for whole soybeans, then pressure cook for 12 minutes. Continue as for the basic recipe. b) To Boil: Combine grits and 5 cups water in a large pot, cover, and soak for 2½ hours. Bring to a boil over low heat and simmer for 1 hour with lid slightly ajar.

5) **Using Alternate Protein and Carbohydrate Sources:** Lists of these are given to pages 44 and 171. All or part of the soybeans may be replaced by other beans. Soak, cook, and add these to the miso as for soybeans. If using alternate carbohydrate sources, add no more than 5½ ounces cooked weight and reduce the weight of koji by one half the weight of the carbohydrates added; mash well before mixing with koji. For example, to prepare a small batch of Sweet Potato Miso: Combine 5½ ounces each dried koji and mashed cooked sweet potatoes. Mix in the salt, cooked (mashed) soybeans, seed miso, and 1 cup mixing liquid (two-thirds the basic abount). Ferment as for red miso.

6) **Alternate Basic Ratios:** There are many different varieties of red miso, each determined by its ratio of basic ingredient weights. The ratio used by the Sendai Miso-shoyu Co., which makes most of the 1-year natural red miso sold in the West, is soybeans 10, koji 5.8, salt 4.5. Mr. Junsei Yamazaki (p. 241) uses 10:10:2.5 for 1-year red miso, increasing the salt to 3.5 for 2 year miso. Mr. Herman Aihara uses 10:10:3.0 for 8-month miso. Other ratios commonly employed in Japan are: a) soybeans 10, koji 6.4, salt 5.3; b) soybeans 10, koji 5.0, salt 4.1; c) soybeans 10, koji 7.2, salt 4.9. Notice that in the latter proportions, the salt is considerably higher than that used in America.

Homemade Barley Miso *(Mugi Miso)*

For basic ratios and amounts of raw materials, see page 172. Prepare as for Homemade Red Miso except: 1) Use barley koji instead of rice koji. 2) Increase the amount of water used in cooking the beans so that the necessary amount of mixing liquid remains when the beans have finished cooking. 3) Using natural fermentation, allow miso to ferment for at least 12 to 18 months; the finest flavor will be attained after 2 to 3

years. If using temperature controlled fermentation, reduce the above fermentation time by one half. 4) Virtually all barley miso calls for 10 parts each by weight of dry soybeans and dry koji. The ratio of salt used in America is as low as 3.5; in Japan it ranges for 4.6 to 6.0, with the latter proportion requiring 2 to 3 years fermentation.

Homemade Light-yellow Miso *(Shinshu Miso)*

For the basic ratio of raw materials, see page 172. Prepare as for Homemade Red Miso except: 1) After soaking, drain the beans, measure the amount of water drained, and add back an equal amount of fresh water. 2) For a lighter colored miso, rub the soaked beans between the palms of both hands to remove seedcoats before cooking. 3) Pressure cook beans to give a light color. 4) For an even lighter color (accompanied, however, by a loss of nutrients) discard all soybean cooking liquid and use boiled water as the mixing liquid. 5) Using natural fermentation, age for the same time as red miso. Using temperature controlled fermentation (to give a still lighter color) ferment for 1 week at 86°F, 3 weeks at 95°F, 1 more week at 86°F, and then allow to stand at room temperature for 1 week before serving. 6) For a slightly saltier miso, increase the ratio of salt from 4.1 to 4.5 and increase the aging time by 10 percent.

Homemade Sweet Red Miso *(Edo Miso)*

This is an excellent variety for those who don't want to wait more than one month to sample their homemade miso. Prepare as for Homemade Red Miso except: 1) Boil the soybeans for 8 to 10 hours, adding water as required. Or boil for 4 hours, allow to stand covered overnight, and return to the boil the next morning. Both procedures give the beans a deep reddish-brown color. 2) Drain beans for no more than 1 minute to prevent them from cooling. 3) Mash no more than 50 percent of the whole beans. 4) Mix beans with koji while beans are still quite hot (140°F to 158°F). Do not use seed miso lest the final miso sour slightly. 5) Pack the mixture into vat while mixture is still quite warm (122°F to 131°F). 6) Wrap vat with heavy towels to minimize heat loss, cover, and press as in the basic recipe. Place in a very warm environment (104°F to 113°F) for 3 weeks, then unwrap container and allow miso to ripen at room temperature for one week before serving. (Or wrap and ferment naturally for 4 to 5 weeks). Refrigerate the remaining miso to prevent spoilage.

Homemade Sweet White Miso *(Shiro Miso)*

Due to its high carbohydrate and low salt content, this miso takes less time to ferment than any other variety and is therefore excellent for homemade miso experimentation. Wash and cook soybeans as for Homemade Light-yellow Miso. Pack into vat while beans are quite warm and wrap as for Sweet Red Miso (above). Proceed as for light-yellow miso except: 1) Reduce fermentation time as follows: If using natural fermentation, age for 1 to 3 weeks in summer (taste frequently), 5 weeks in spring or fall, and 6 to 8 weeks in winter. If using temperature-controlled fermentation, age at 95°F for 1 to 3 weeks, or 113°F for 1 to 2 weeks. Commercial makers say this miso can be prepared in 24 hours if the basic ratio by weight is soybeans 10, dried koji 20, and salt 1.5, and if the temperature of the room is 140°F. Before serving, grind the miso in a grain mill or meat grinder to create a smooth texture.

Some makers suggest increasing the basic proportion of koji from 20 to 24 if dried rather than fresh koji is used, and increasing the proportion to 30 if the miso is prepared during the winter by natural fermentation. When using temperature-controlled fermentation, many makers mix the miso once midway through the fermentation.

Homemade Mellow Barley Miso
(Amakuchi Mugi Miso)

For the basic ratios of raw materials, see page 172. Prepare as for Homemade Red Miso except: 1) Use barley koji instead of rice koji. 2) Add enough water to the beans so that the necessary amount of mixing liquid remains when the beans have finished cooking. 3) Ferment the miso for the same lengths of time and at the same temperatures as for Homemade Sweet White Miso.

Homemade Hishio   MAKES 4½ CUPS

Also called *Namé-mono* or *o-namé*, hishio is a variety of country-style namémiso requiring a relatively short fermentation. It is generally prepared in farmhouses sometime between October and May. The koji is prepared both with and without soybeans depending on the locality. The method using soybeans is more difficult since, if the temperature rises, *natto* bacteria often propagate and the miso fails. In some localities, instead of stirring the miso daily, a pressing lid is used and the miso is left untouched. Hishio is thought to be the earliest ancestor of present-day shoyu.

    4 ounces eggplant, well washed
    5 ounces cucumber or *uri* melon, well washed
    8 tablespoons salt
    3 cups (13.4 ounces) ready-made dried wheat or barley
       koji
    2¼ cups boiled water
    2 ounces gingerroot, parboiled, and thinly sliced
       (optional)

Parboil eggplant and cucumber for about 1 minute to sterilize, then cool briefly and dice. Combine in a small bowl with 1 tablespoon salt, and gently rub salt into vegetables. Set a plate atop the layer of vegetables in bowl and place a 4- to 5-pound weight atop plate. Cover bowl with plastic wrap and press for 1 week.

On the same day vegetables begin to press, combine the koji, water, remaining 7 tablespoons salt and, if used, the gingerroot in the fermentation container. Cover container with a sheet of paper or plastic wrap held in place by a string, and place container in a clean location which receives no direct sunlight. Stir the mixture thoroughly once daily.

After 1 week, pour off all liquid from the pressed vegetables and discard. Wash hands, then squeeze vegetables firmly to expel any excess liquid. Mix vegetables into fermenting hishio. Allow hishio to ferment for 3 more weeks, stirring daily. The finished product should have a very moist texture (similar to applesauce) and pleasant, subtly sweet fragrance and flavor. Store covered in a cool place or refrigerator to prevent further fermentation.

To prepare the same miso using soybeans, use 3 1/3 cups rice koji, 1 cup soybeans and 1/3 cup salt, plus other ingredients as listed above. Cook beans, cool to body temperature and mash, then mix with the koji and cooking liquid. Add remaining ingredients and transfer to a crock. Allow to ferment, mixing daily, for about 1 to 2 weeks.

Indian Pulse & Soybean Miso

Developed in 1963 by Dr. T. N. Rao of the Central Food Technological Research Institute in Mysore, India, this flavorful product is a good example of how Japanese miso can be adapted to the tastes and ingredients of other countries. The use of a relatively small proportion of soybeans and peanuts together with local pulses greatly enhances the amino acid balance; the resultant product contains 11.2 percent protein when Bengal gram is used and 8.7 percent with Thur dhal. The percentages of salt are 5.0 and 5.4 respectively. To give a longer shelf life, powdered red peppers or chilies may be added to taste.

    2¾ pounds dehulled Bengal gram or Thur dhal, soaked
       for 15 hours in water to cover
    ½ pound whole dry soybeans, soaked for 12 hours
    ¾ pound chopped peanuts
    2½ pounds rice koji
    ¾ pound salt

Pressure-cook pulses like soybeans (25 minutes at 15 pounds), then drain and reserve. Combine soybeans and peanuts, and pressure cook as in the basic method above. Mix cooked ingredients with koji and salt (and spices if desired), add enough cooking liquid to give the desired consistency (45 to 47 percent moisture), and pack into vat. Ferment at 83°F for 5 to 10 days. Store in a very cool place, or refrigerate.

A square steamer

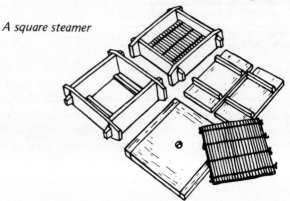

HOMEMADE KOJI AND KOJI STARTER

The preparation of good-quality koji is a fairly sensitive process requiring several pieces of special equipment (steamer and koji tray) that can be made or purchased without much difficulty. Don't be daunted: anyone can make good koji if he or she carefully follows the instructions given below, paying special attention to two basic points: 1) Keep your hands, all utensils, and the entire work area as clean as possible; 2) Keep the koji temperature within the recommended range throughout the 45-hour incubation period.

Most Japanese prepare koji at the same time of year they make miso, in the late fall or early spring, when the weather is cool and the number of contaminating microorganisms in the air is fairly low. The koji is generally prepared indoors in a room with a clean wooden floor. A typical batch calls for about 30 pounds of rice or barley so that the scale is considerably larger than in the following recipe. We have preferred to start with a smaller batch since the equipment is easier to obtain and you can easily increase all of the ingredients by as much as you like after your first small-scale success. The following recipe yields just enough koji for 1 medium-sized batch of Homemade Red Miso (p. 173). The amount of rice given just fills a typical steamer during one steaming.

To obtain a better perspective on the process of making koji, study the traditional miso shop method (Chapter 9), and to see how it fits into the integrated process of preparing Homemade Red Miso, study the flow chart in figure 33. The time schedule built into the following recipe ensures that all of the work can be done during ordinary waking hours. In all koji recipes, 1 pound of uncooked rice yields about 1.14 pounds of fresh koji. In the basic miso proportions on page 172, the weight of ready-made dried koji is the same as the weight of uncooked rice necessary to prepare fresh koji.

Utensils

A wooden koji tray about 16 by 10 by 2½ inches deep with a lid consisting of 1 or 2 thin boards. Japanese trays are made of cedar (*sugi*), but Douglas fir, cherry, or pine also work well. Join boards with dowels or pegs to prevent rusting. A desk or bureau drawer, a cloth-lined enamel or stainless steel tray, or a shallow fruit box may also be used.

A 1-gallon soaking container

A 1½- to 2-gallon kettle or wok. The kettle must have a flat rim and no handles rising above the rim to interfere with the steamer.

A 2- to 3-quart strainer or a cloth-lined colander

A square steamer (used with the kettle and easily made at home) or a round Chinese bamboo steamer with a woven bamboo lid (used with a wok and available at most Chinese hardware stores). Additional layers of steaming compartments may be added when using more than 6 to 8 cups of rice. The square steamer shown in figure 32 is made of ¾-inch-thick cedar boards; it is 9½ inches square and 4½ inches deep inside. Two ¾-inch-square boards near the bottom support a 9½-inch square bamboo mat which forms the steamer's floor. The base is a 13-inch-square board with a ¾-inch-diameter hole at the center. The steamer lid is composed of 2 boards reinforced on top to prevent buckling. An excellent Western-style steamer my also be improvised by placing a large colander atop several bricks or an inverted bowl inside an even larger kettle.

A steamer cloth made of coarsely-woven cotton or linen about 18 by 30 inches (or 24 inches square when used with the round steamer). Do not use ordinary dish-towel cloth; its relatively fine weave will not allow the passage of steam.

A wooden spatula or spoon

5 to 6 heavy-duty blankets (the oldest ones you have). A thick, flat cushion several feet square and a tarp may be substituted for 2 of them.

A clean linen sheet, or a piece of cotton cloth or *gyoza* mat of comparable size

A jar or bowl of several cups capacity

2 hot water bottles each wrapped in a small terrycloth towel or placed into a terrycloth sack with a drawstring mouth

2 thermometers (range 65°F to 130°F)

An incubation box, preferably one of sturdy carboard about 20 by 12 by 14 inches deep. It must be slightly larger than the koji tray. Poke a ¼-inch-diameter hole through lower left side of box, about 3 inches above the base.

Fig. 32. Utensils for making koji

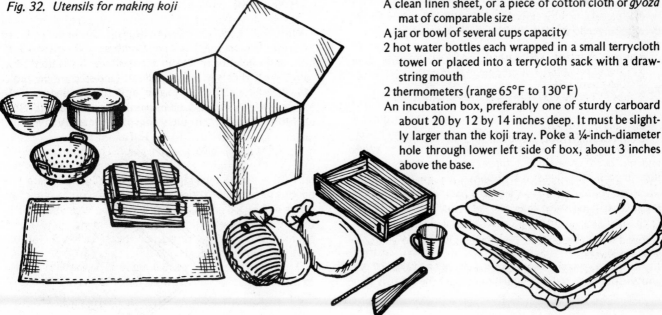

Fig. 33. Miso Flow Chart

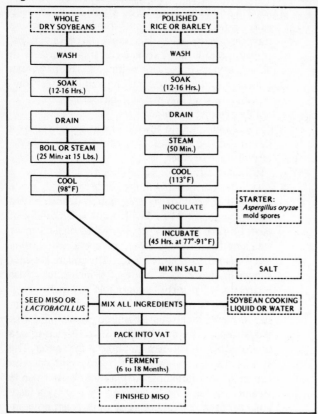

Fig. 34. Composition of Nutrients in 100 Grams of Basic Miso Ingredients

(Source: Standard Tables of Food Composition, Japan)

Ingredient	Food Energy	Protein	Fat	Carbo-hydrates (incl. fiber)	Ash
	Calories	*Percent*	*Percent*	*Percent*	*Percent*
Koji, Rice	334	6.0	0.7	73.4	0.4
Rice, white	351	6.2	0.8	76.9	0.6
Rice, brown	337	7.4	2.3	73.5	1.3
Barley, pearled	337	8.0	0.7	76.6	0.7
Barley, unpearled	335	10.0	1.9	71.7	2.4
Soybeans, whole	392	34.3	17.5	31.2	5.0
Soybean meal, defatted	322	49.0	0.4	36.6	6.0

softer and free of the residual "centerline" and hull characteristic of polished regular barley (*omugi*) so that it gives the miso what many consider to be a more agreeable texture.

Other Koji Grains: In some traditional miso shops and many farmhouses, whole wheat is used to make koji for *hishio* and Kinzanji miso. Cornmeal is also used as the koji substrate in order to create a less expensive miso. In the Shinshu area, where the latter technique originated, cornmeal is soaked in water for 1 hour, steamed for 40 minutes, cooled to body temperature, and then inoculated with starter as for rice koji. In some areas rye, oats, millet, corn kernels and even sweet potatoes are used as the substrate.

Koji Starter *(tané koji, koji kin):* Koji starter is now available from several natural food suppliers in the United States (p. 258) or in small quantities from the Northern Regional Research Center (p. 259). The best source, Westbrae, buys koji starter from Nihon Jozo Kogyo in Japan (p. 258), the producer of eight basic types: one each for red-barley, and mellow barley miso; two for soybean miso; and three for sweet white miso. Each type is available in at least one of three different forms (whole-grain, meal, or spore powder) and some types are fortified with yeasts and *Lactobacillus*. Most starters are a mixture of pure-culture mold strains, each having different capabilities in breaking down proteins, carbohydrates, and oils. Among the total of 17 different varieties and forms produced by Nihon Jozo, those most widely available in North America are the spore-powder starters for red, barley, soybean and light-colored misos, and for shoyu. Each comes sealed in a foil envelope weighing about 1½ ounces. Always keep starters well sealed in a refrigerator at 40°F to 59°F. Do not freeze.

All starter is olive green in color. The spore powder is 5 times as concentrated as the meal or whole grain forms and only 10 grams (1 tablespoon) are required to inoculate 110 pounds of (uncooked) rice. One tablespoon of the other two forms weighs 8.8 grams and will inoculate 19 pounds of rice. In cold weather or with small amounts of rice (less than 5 pounds), doubling the dosage of starter called for on the package yields good results.

If you already have a small amount of starter and wish to prepare more of your own see pages 182 and 249.

Ingredients

Rice: Most rice koji (for *amazaké* and *tsukemono* as well as for miso) is prepared from short-grain white (milled or polished) rice, most modern makers believing that the bran layers of brown rice inhibit the penetration and growth of the mycelium. For a discussion of the basic techniques and difficulties of preparing brown-rice koji, see page 36. Beginning koji makers may wish to experiment with a koji midway between the white and brown varieties by removing 50 to 75 percent of the bran layers and cracking the kernels into several pieces, thereby exposing the soft inner carbohydrate core to mycelium growth. Rice is always steamed, never boiled, to make koji; the latter process creates a wet texture which encourages the growth of undesirable bacteria. One cup raw rice (7.24 oz) yields 1.80 cups (8.25 ounces) fresh koji.

Barley *(O mugi, seimugi, hadakamugi):* For basically the same reasons that white rice is generally used to make rice koji, pearled barley (whole grains of unrolled natural barley with the bran layers removed) is used to prepare barley koji—and has been since ancient times. Barley contains slightly more protein, but slightly less carbohydrate and natural sugar than rice (fig. 34). Thus barley miso generally has a slightly higher nutritional value and is less sweet than rice miso. Other things being equal, the lack of sugars makes it necessary to ferment barley miso somewhat longer than rice miso.

Some miso makers prefer to use "naked" barley (*hadakamugi*) which is sometimes classified as a type of rye and yields miso with a unique aroma and flavor. It is also

Homemade Rice Koji
(Using Koji Starter)

MAKES 3.1 POUNDS (11 CUPS)

6.1 cups (2.7 pounds) white rice
5/8 teaspoon (1.9 grams) spore powder koji starter or 1½
   teaspoons (4.4 grams) meal or whole-grain starter
¼ cup (lightly roasted) white or whole-wheat flour

PREVIOUS AFTERNOON

Wash and scrub koji tray thoroughly, rinse with boiling water, and set upside-down to dry in a clean (sunny) place. Wash rice 3 or 4 times in soaking pot and soak for 12 to 16 hours in water to cover.

DAY 1:

1) 8:00 a.m.: Fill kettle (or wok) two-thirds full of water and bring to a boil. Meanwhile, transfer soaked rice to a large strainer or cloth-lined colander, rinse under cold running water, and drain well. Rinse off steamer, insert bamboo mat, and line bottom and sides with moistened steamer cloth. Place steamer and base atop kettle (or place round steamer into wok) and pour rice into steamer to a depth of about 2 inches. (For large batches of koji, if all rice will not fit into one steamer layer, either add a second layer or steam rice in several consecutive batches.) Using wooden paddle or spoon, press rice firmly into corners of steamer and smooth rice

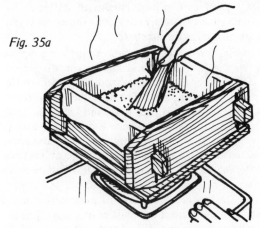

Fig. 35a

surface (fig. 35a). Fold over ends of cloth to cover. When steam rises through rice, cover with lid (fig. b), and turn heat to medium-high. Steam for 50 minutes.

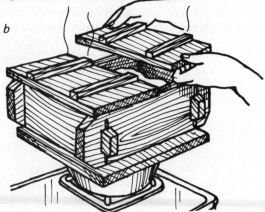

b

2) While rice is steaming, spread 2 blankets in a double layer atop a large table. Fold a clean sheet end to end and spread atop blankets.

Combine the flour and koji starter in a small cup. Mix well, cover, and place on table near blankets.

Fill a hot water bottle with boiling water; wrap in a small terrycloth towel or place in a towel sack.

3) Transfer hot steamed rice to center of sheet (fig. c). Using wooden paddle, mix rice thoroughly, breaking up all lumps, and spread to a depth of about 1 inch over a small area

c

at the center of sheet. Insert thermometer into rice and wait several minutes until temperature drops to 113°F (45°C). Sprinkle one-half of the starter-flour mixture over rice and stir vigorously with paddle until starter spores are evenly distributed throughout grain. Sprinkle on remainder of starter mixture and stir, breaking up any remaining small lumps (fig. d).

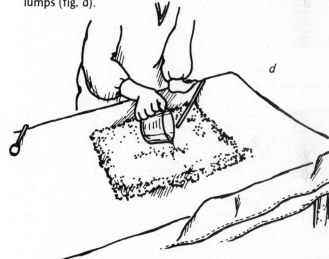

d

4) Mound and pack inoculated rice into a hemisphere at center of sheet. Insert thermometer into rice and fold edges of sheet snugly over hemisphere to form a compact bundle (fig. e). Use the 2 blankets on the table to wrap bundle firmly, to minimize heat loss. Place hot water bottle atop another thick blanket folded into fourths (or a large flat cushion). Place bundled rice directly on top of hot water bottle and cover with at least two more thick blankets. Place this entire insulated "package" in a clean, out-of-the-way place, preferably one that is fairly warm. (Avoid locations near circulating air heaters; the Japanese set their koji on boards over a warm bath.)

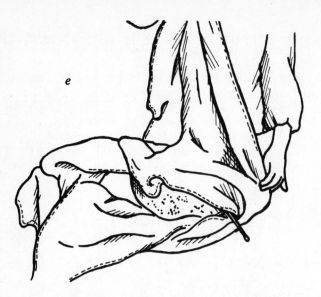

e

g

5) Check rice temperature every 2 to 4 hours, seeing that it stays between 77°F and 95°F (25°C and 35°C). To raise the temperature, add fresh or additional hot water bottles and/or more blankets; to lower, transfer hot water bottle to below the bottom blanket and/or remove topmost blankets. Just before retiring, check temperature and insert a fresh hot water bottle (fig. f).

up any small lumps. Shape koji into an oval mound (fig. h) 2 inches high at the highest points and slightly hollowed at the center. Insert one thermometer into koji and cover tray with

f

h

lid(s). Put tray into incubation box; beside tray place 2 fresh hot water bottles and an uncovered jar of hot water (to keep air humidity at 90 percent to 95 percent). Set box atop 6 to 8 thicknesses of folded blankets (or 1 or 2 thick cushions). Insert the second thermometer into the hole poked through the side of box and cover box with 2 or 3 thick blankets (fig. i). Check box air temperature from time to time; try to

DAY 2:

6) 8:00 a.m.: Check that koji temperature is within the range prescribed above. Adjust heat to bring temperature to about 95°F. Wash hands and open bundle. The young koji should now have a pleasant aroma, and individual grains should have a white, powder-like coating and be very loosely bound together by an almost invisible mycelium. If areas of bluish-green, black, or pink molds appear, carefully remove and discard. Now mix rice thoroughly and re-bundle.

7) 10:00 a.m.: Check koji temperature, wash hands, and open bundle. Re-check aroma and appearance, then transfer koji from sheet to koji tray (fig. g). Mix koji, breaking

i

keep it at 82°F, or at least within the range of 77°F to 91°F.

8) 2:30 p.m.: Wash hands and check that koji temperature is between 80°F and 98°F. In no case should it be allowed to fall below 77°F or rise above 104°F. Stir koji quickly but thoroughly in order to break up lumps (which can cause overheating), aid circulation, and ensure even mycelium growth. Remound koji into oval volcano shape, re-cover tray with lid set slightly ajar, and re-cover incubation box with blankets.

9) 6:00 p.m.: Check that temperature inside koji is within the range prescribed above. Stir koji thoroughly and spread it in an even layer (about 1 inch deep) over entire bottom of tray. Re-cover tray with lid set well ajar. Replenish hot water bottles and hot water in jar. (Begin to soak soybeans as described in the basic homemade miso recipe given on page 173.)

10) 10:00 p.m. (or just before retiring): Check that koji temperature is between 85°F and 96°F. If necessary, replenish hot water bottles.

DAY 3:

11) 11:00 a.m. (after 45 hours of incubation): Open box and examine koji for doneness. The individual rice grains should now be bound together with a delicate mycelium of fragrant white mold. Break open several grains (they should be soft enough to break easily) and check that the white mycelium roots have penetrated at least two-thirds of the way to the grain's center.

(If koji has a bluish-green color and a moldy or musty odor, sporulation has begun due to over-fermentation. If koji is black and slightly damp, contaminating molds have begun to grow due to overheating. In either case, place koji in a large colander, douse several times with hot water to wash off undesirable microorganisms, and re-incubate. Or discard koji and start again.)

12) Stir finished koji thoroughly, remove tray from incubation box and place in a cool, clean location for about ½ hour, or until koji temperature drops to room temperature. Measure into a large pot the amount of koji called for in the recipe you wish to prepare: a medium-sized batch of red miso, for example, requires 2 pounds 12 ounces times 1.14, or about 3 pounds 2 ounces. Mix this fresh koji with the amount of salt called for in your miso recipe, then proceed to mix with the cooked soybeans as described in variation 3 of the basic recipe for Homemade Red Miso (p. 175).

If any koji remains, transfer it to a separate container, seal well, and refrigerate; reserve for use in making *amazaké* or koji pickles (p. 162), or additional batches of miso.

STORING KOJI

If for some reason you cannot use the koji immediately, spread it in a thin layer on sheets of newspaper and allow to dry for 10 to 20 hours in a clean, warm place. Then seal and store in a cool, dry place. It will keep for 1 to 2 months in good condition, or for as long as 6 months, but with a slight decline in flavor and potency.

For even longer storage, spread the (plain or salted) koji on a clean sheet in direct sunlight (or on baking tins in a 113°F oven) until thoroughly dried. Sealed and stored in a cool, dry place, it will last for up to 1 year.

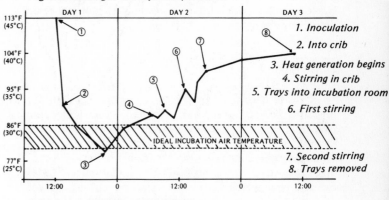

Fig. 36. Changes in Koji Temperature

1. Inoculation
2. Into crib
3. Heat generation begins
4. Stirring in crib
5. Trays into incubation room
6. First stirring
7. Second stirring
8. Trays removed

Homemade Brown Rice Koji

Soak and steam very lightly polished brown rice as described above for white rice. To prevent the growth of alien microorganisms, regulate the koji temperature very carefully, keeping it about 5°F below the average temperature when using white rice. Otherwise the process is the same.

Homemade Barley Koji MAKES 3.5 POUNDS (12.5 CUPS)
(Using Koji Starter)

To make enough fresh koji for one medium-sized batch of Homemade Barley Miso (p. 175) simply substitute polished (pearled) barley for white rice in the basic koji recipe. Prepare as for Homemade Fresh Koji except: 1) Soak the barley for only 2 to 3 hours. 2) Steam the barley for 90 minutes or until the grain becomes somewhat transparent and slightly rubbery. 3) For best results try to remove the incubating koji when the mycelium is pure white, after about 36 hours. A yellow mycelium is also satisfactory but will yield a sweeter miso. A black mycelium is unsatisfactory.

Homemade Rice or Barley Koji MAKES 12 CUPS
(Prepared Without Koji Starter)

Preparing this koji using wild mold spores is analogous to making sourdough bread without starter. The best results are obtained in areas where the air is clear and somewhat cold, or in places such as miso shops or rooms where miso is fermenting where there are large numbers of free *Aspergillus oryzae* mold spores in the atmosphere.

In Japan, it is said that the air is much more free of undesirable organisms (that could produce toxins in fermenting koji) than most air in the U.S. or other parts of the West. Thus, unless you live in an area where the air is very clean and preferably, cold, it is better to use koji starter.

Soak and steam the rice or barley as for Homemade Rice or Barley Koji. Spread the steamed grain on a sheet and allow to stand uncovered overnight so that it "catches" wild mold spores floating in the air. Transfer grain to the koji tray and spread it in an even layer over the bottom. Place tray in incubation box and proceed as for Homemade Rice Koji. Harvest the koji after about 3 to 4 days when it is covered with a white or light-yellow mycelium.

Homemade Koji Starter

Please begin by studying the commercial process for preparing koji starter (p. 233). The best starter is prepared from homemade koji incubated under carefully controlled conditions of temperature, humidity, and cleanliness. If contaminating microorganisms enter the koji, and the koji is then made into starter, their negative effect is multiplied. Starter can also be prepared from commercial koji, but the chances of obtaining a high degree of purity are somewhat less than with the homemade variety. Traditional Japanese homemade miso was generally started either by wild mold spores (described above) or by incubating a portion of each batch of homemade koji for 5 to 7 days, until the molds sporulated, then drying the product thoroughly and storing it for later use as starter. This latter process, known as the "cut-and-dry" method, was generally carried out without the use of brown rice or wood ash now used commercially—and good results were obtained.

To make your own starter, place about ½ cup finished homemade koji in a small wooden bowl, return it to the incubator, and keep at the same temperatures required for the commercial process until the mycelium turns from white to a soft olive green. Crumble, dry in a warm oven as described, and store sealed in a cool, dry place. Use as for whole-grain starter.

HOMEMADE MISO
(Using Homemade Koji)

In the following recipes, the preparation of the koji is an integral part of the miso-making process.

Homemade Hatcho or Soybean Miso

MAKES 6.4 POUNDS (10.6 CUPS)

We have had excellent results with this recipe. The key lies in keeping the temperature below 100°F, lest contaminating microorganisms begin to propagate and turn the soybeans into sticky *natto*. Some makers prefer to use a special soybean koji starter, however the regular starter used for rice or barley miso also works well. Please begin by studying the process for Homemade Rice Koji (p. 179), which the following recipe closely resembles, and the process for Commercial Hatcho Miso (p. 210).

- 8 cups (3¼ pounds) whole dry soybeans, soaked for 10 hours and drained
- ½ teaspoon (1.5 grams) spore-powder koji starter or 1½ teaspoons (4.4 grams) meal- or whole-grain starter
- 5 tablespoons (lightly roasted) white or whole-wheat flour
- 1 cup (10.4 ounces) salt (increase to 1¼ cups if aging miso for 2 years or more)
- 2 cups mixing liquid (boiled water)
- 4 tablespoons Hatcho or soybean miso

Place beans in a large steamer (p. 177) and steam for 6 hours, or until individual beans are soft enough to crush easily between the thumb and small finger. Combine starter and flour in a small bowl, mixing well. Cool beans to body temperature, then transfer onto a clean sheet and sprinkle with half the flour-starter mixture. Stir beans thoroughly with a wooden spoon, then sprinkle on the rest of the mixture and re-stir until each bean is covered with the inoculum.

Transfer inoculated beans into koji tray and place into incubation box with hot water bottles and water-filled jar as for Homemade Rice Koji. Keep air temperature inside box as close as possible to 86°F (and within the range of 79°F to 89°F), and stir following the same schedule as for Homemade Rice Koji. If the temperature rises above 100°F or if the beans become sticky, immediately remove hot water bottles and jar and open lid of box until temperature and humidity drop. Then return 1 water bottle but do not return jar for at least 4 hours, or until stickiness has disappeared. Continue incubating for 40 to 50 hours, or until beans are bound together by a dense mat of fragrant white mycelium. Mash or grind two-thirds of the soybean koji and combine in a large mixing pot with the salt, mixing liquid and mature miso; mix well. Transfer to vat, cover with sealing sheet and pressing lid, and top with weights: for Hatcho miso, use a weight equal to that of the fermenting mixture; for regular soybean miso, use one-third to one-fourth the weight. Allow to stand at the natural temperature of the environment for at least 12 months or, for best flavor, for 18 months or more, including two full summers.

*Tamari Miso: Please begin by reading the description of the commercial process on page 41. Prepare as for Homemade Hatcho except increase mixing liquid to 8 or 10 cups. Ferment in a regular vat (without central core or draining trough); mix thoroughly once a day for 1 year.

To extract *tamari*, pour mature *moromi* into a coarse-weave sack or a cloth-lined colander set over a large pot. Drain, then squeeze well to extract as much of the liquid as possible. Use tamari with hors d'œuvres or as an all-purpose seasoning like shoyu. Reserve pressing residue in sack for use as a topping.

Homemade Kinzanji Miso
(Prepared with both Whole-wheat and Rice Koji)

MAKES 20 CUPS

Traditionally, Kinzanji was prepared in farmhouses during the first week of October, when there is little rain and the air is cold and clear. The koji was made from equal weights of hulled soybeans and whole wheat, the proportions still believed to give the finest flavor. However, since this relatively large proportion of soybeans invites the entry of contaminating *natto* bacteria and since it takes a long time to hull the beans by hand, some non-commercial makers prefer to use 4 parts by weight of wheat to 1 part soybeans in order to ensure success and save time.

Commercial makers say repeatedly that it is extremely difficult to obtain the true Kinzanji flavor and aroma, and not simply a miso flavor. Some makers rely on a special ready-made Kinzanji koji (which is sold commercially in Shizuoka and Aichi prefectures and will hopefully soon be available in the West), while others use rice koji to give the miso additional sweetness. Careful control of the temperature during the koji incubation is essential.

45/8 cups whole wheat
4¼ cups whole dry soybeans
1¾ pounds eggplant, cut lengthwise into halves then crosswise into slices 3/8 inch thick
7¾ ounces gingerroot, cut into very thin rounds
2 or 3 white *uri* melons or large cucumbers cut into rounds 3/8 inch thick
½ cup thinly sliced rounds of burdock root (optional)
1¼ cups salt
4¼ cups well-crumbled rice koji
2 pieces of *kombu*, each 6 to 8 inches square, rinsed (optional)
6 to 8 green *shiso* leaves (optional)

Wash 4¼ cups wheat several times in a large pot, cover with plenty of water, and soak for 24 hours; drain well.

About 1 hour before wheat has finished soaking, place soybeans into a heavy skillet or pot and roast over medium heat, stirring constantly, until fragrant and light brown. Transfer warm beans to a wooden bowl and rub vigorously between the palms of both hands to remove hulls which are then discarded. (Or place roasted beans in a winnowing basket or on a mat and crush by rolling them under a small wooden box.) Soak beans in water for 30 minutes, then drain.

Place the wheat and beans in separate steamers. Steam the beans for about 5 hours until they are soft enough to be easily crushed between the thumb and ring finger. Steam the wheat for about 90 minutes or until the skins break open.

Roast the 3/8 cup uncooked wheat in a heavy skillet until light brown and fragrant, then purée in a blender or grind in a handmill to make flour. Spread the cooked beans and wheat in a large koji tray (p. 177), then sprinkle on and mix in the roasted flour. Place tray in incubation box and cover with blankets as when preparing Homemade Koji (p. 180); allow to ferment for about 4 days. Check temperature and mold growth from time to time. When the mycelium has a sweet aroma and is basically white interspersed with tiny dots of yellow, the koji is ready to harvest. (If it has begun to turn brown and develop a strong smell, it has fermented for too long and must be discarded.)

One day before you expect the koji to be ready, combine the four vegetables and salt in a large bowl; mix well. Cover vegetables with a large plate and press overnight with a 5- to 6-pound weight. Drain off liquid from vegetables and reserve.

Crumble the finished soybean-wheat koji, spread it on a clean surface in the sunlight, and dry for 6 hours. Allow koji to cool in the shade.

In a large vat combine soybean-wheat koji with crumbled rice koji; mix well. Add drained vegetables and reserved pickling liquid and mix again. Smooth surface of mixture and cover with one layer of *kombu*. If desired, top with a layer of green shiso leaves. Set a pressing lid on top of the miso and press with a weight of 2 to 3 pounds for at least 3 weeks and as long as 6 months. The miso may be served when the *uri* melons turn amber and become slightly transparent. (If using cucumbers in place of melons, add them 1 to 2 weeks before the miso is to be harvested.)

VARIATIONS

*Roast the whole beans, remove the skins and break the beans into halves. Mix the beans and whole wheat and steam them together until the beans are soft. Mix koji starter into the cooled mixture and ferment for 45 hours to make koji. Mix with a small amount of salt and water, pack into a fermentation container and allow to ferment for 2 months. Now add the salted, drained vegetables and ferment for 4 more months. Mix in a small amount of honey or *mizuamé* just before serving to give added sweetness and luster.
*In the above method use 4 parts by weight of wheat to 1 part soybeans. Prepare a 15% salt solution (100 parts water by weight to 15 parts salt) and add this to the finished koji to obtain the desired miso consistency. Omit use of rice koji.

Homemade Natural Shoyu
MAKES 3½ GALLONS

The process for making shoyu is very similar to that for making miso except: 1) The koji is made of a mixture of equal parts soybeans and roasted cracked wheat; 2) A different species of *Aspergillus* starter is used; 3) About three times as much mixing liquid and twice as much salt are used; and 4) the liquid is extracted by pressing after fermentation. Since extracting a large percentage of the liquid (shoyu) is the most difficult part of the process, in traditional Japan, men with special portable lever presses would make the rounds of farmhouses each year to do the job.

10 pounds (24.5 cups) whole dry soybeans
10 pounds (22 cups) whole wheat
1 tablespoon shoyu koji starter (*Aspergillus soyae*), or substitute *A. oryzae*
8 pounds (12½ cups) salt
28 pounds (3.4 gallons) mixing liquid (boiled or very pure water)

Wash soybeans, soak in water to cover for 12 hours, then drain well. Steam (do *not* boil) at 15 pounds for 75 minutes and allow pressure to come down naturally. (Or steam at atmospheric pressure for 5½ hours.)

Meanwhile, roast wheat in a heavy dry skillet until fragrant and golden brown, then grind coarsely (or crack) so that each kernel is split into an average of 4 pieces.

Allow soybeans and wheat to cool to body temperature, then combine with the starter, mixing well. Place about 3 quarts of the mixture into each of about 8 koji trays and incubate at 77°F to 86°F for 60 to 72 hours. Mix twice as for Homemade Koji and do not allow koji temperature to rise above 104°F.

Combine mixing liquid and salt in an 8- to 10-gallon vat; add koji and mix well. Leaving top open, allow to stand in a clean place at the natural temperature of the environment for exactly 12 months. Mix daily for the first three days, then once a week throughout most of the rest of the year (twice a week in summer); mixing incorporates oxygen, expels carbon dioxide, and prevents surface mold growth. (For a quicker fermentation, place vat in a heated room at 68°F to 77°F for 6 months; stir 2 to 3 times a week.) The finished *moromi* should have a deep reddish-brown color, applesauce-like consistency, and pleasant flavor and aroma.

The best way to extract shoyu from moromi on a small scale is to use a hydraulic press and press-ing sack, the type found at many tofu shops. Or, construct a pressing rack atop an empty wooden keg or sturdy pot using 4 to 6 sturdy broom handles or 2-by-4 boards laid parallel about 2 inches apart. Place a coarsely-woven sack atop the rack and pour *moromi* into sack; twist closed mouth of sack. Now have two people holding opposite ends of a sturdy wide plank place plank across top of sack and bear down with their full body weight to press liquid from sack. Repeat numerous times, squeezing neck of sack tighter from time to time, until as much liquid as possible has been extracted. Remove *moromi* residue from sack and reserve for use as a seasoning; refrigerate unused portions in a covered container. Pour shoyu into bottles and keep well sealed in a cool place. If soy oil accumulates or white mold forms on shoyu surface, remove and discard.

Homemade Namémiso
MAKES 2 GALLONS

This is the recipe for the delicious *namémiso* prepared at the Amanoya shop in Tokyo (p. 240). A typical batch of theirs is about nine times as large as the following recipe.

½ pound small eggplants
1½ ounces (21/3 tablespoons) salt
13.3 pounds (29 cups) wheat, roasted and split or cracked
1 pound (2½ cups) whole soybeans
1 tablespoon koji starter
1 gallon shoyu
¾ cup *mirin*
11/3 cups *mizuamé* or *bakugato* (millet or barley sugar syrup)
½ pound gingerroot, peeled and thinly sliced

Place uncut eggplants in a keg, sprinkle with the salt and press under 3- to 4-pound weight for 1 week. Drain, rinse, and cut lengthwise into halves, then into 3/8-inch cubes.

Mix wheat and soybeans and soak for 2 to 3 hours (longer in cold weather) or until soybeans just yield when pressed. Steam for 40 minutes, or until a piece of wheat broken open is no longer white inside. Cool to 80°F, then mix in koji starter. Prepare koji as for Homemade Rice Koji (p. 179). Combine finished koji with remaining ingredients and the salted eggplants. Ferment in kegs for 10 days in mid-summer, 20 days in fall or spring, and 30 days in winter.

Fig. 37. Equivalent Weights and Volumes of Miso Ingredients

Ingredient	Volume	Wt. (gm)	Wt. (oz)
Soybeans, whole dry	1 cup	185	6.52
Koji, dry soft mat (crumbled)	1 cup	94.1	3.32
Koji, dry firm granular	1 cup	129	4.55
Koji, fresh (crumbled)	1 cup	130	4.58
Salt	1 cup	290	10.2
Miso	1 cup	276	9.73
Water	1 cup	236	8.32
Rice or barley	1 cup	205	7.24
Miso	1 tablespoon	17.3	0.61

8
Japanese Farmhouse Miso

T HIS CHAPTER has two basic purposes: first, to describe the traditional art of preparing country-style miso and the role of that miso in Japanese culture and cookery; and second, to present this method and its tools as a model for the preparation of miso in communities in the West on a scale 2½ times the size of the largest recipe in the previous chapter.

Most of Japan's earliest miso was prepared by farmers and Buddhist priests. Indeed, throughout most of East Asia, the appearance of miso shops and professional craftsmen has been a rather recent development. Roughly 85 percent of all the miso found in present-day Korea, for example, is still made in private homes. And until the 1940s, most Japanese farmhouses and temples were totally self-sufficient in this regard.

Although there are more miso shops in Japan than in any other country in the Far East, the tradition of farmhouse miso remains alive, especially in remote rural areas and in the northeast provinces. This miso, an estimated 132,000 tons in 1974, accounts for about 17 percent of the nation's total output, with some 35,000 tons of soybeans used each year to produce it. Arriving at the right season in rural villages in any of Japan's famous farmhouse-miso provinces (Aomori, Nakano, Fukushima, Iwate, Yamanashi), one can still witness the art, craft, and ceremony involved in the ancient process. In most of these areas, one large batch of miso is made each year in March or April, during the peach-blossom season, when the farmers are awaiting the rice planting, the water is clear and cold, the air free of molds, and the temperature just warm enough to allow for the preparation of koji. In other areas, miso is made in the fall, during the lull following the harvest, for at this time, too, the weather is favorable, and the new-crop rice and soybeans are at their peak of flavor.

Every rural family that makes miso has its own distinctive variety in which it takes great pride. From this fact stems the famous proverb *temaemiso*, which literally means simply "homemade miso," but is a compact way of saying

that everyone likes his own miso best. In fact the Japanese term for self-glorification is *temaemiso;* when someone shows unusual satisfaction in something he has made or done himself, others may say in jest: "It's just like his pride in his homemade miso," or "There he goes, lining up his kegs of homemade miso."

In Japan, farmhouse miso is known as *inaka* or "rural" miso, and city dwellers speak nostalgically of the satisfying, down-to-earth goodness of the miso made in the village from which they trace their origin. During the major holiday seasons of New Year's and O-bon (all saints week), many return to the countryside to visit relatives, and most return with a large supply of farmhouse miso to help perpetuate the good memories of their visit. Although miso connoisseurs say that the finest country-style miso is made in areas where the air is clear and cold, or in the mountains where there is a sharp contrast between day- and nighttime temperatures, most Japanese simply refuse to believe that any miso can be more delicious than that prepared in their own native area.

Three different types of miso are prepared in Japanese farmhouses. The most common is either red or barley miso, prepared using a relatively large proportion of salt and the prevailing grain of the region, with a fermentation time of one to three years. In addition, many farmers also prepare one of the more than five varieties of Finger Lickin' Miso (p. 42). In a few parts of Japan, the main type is still soybean miso made with *miso-dama* or "miso balls" (p. 193). The first and third types are most widely used in miso soups and, on special occasions, in farmhouse-style Dengaku, Oden, or Nishimé. The second type is generally used as a topping for hot rice or, occasionally, as an hors d'œuvre with sake.

Part of each year's supply will usually be made with a relatively large proportion of salt and part will be made with less. The saltier varieties are used in soups throughout the summer months, since farmers feel they require an increased salt intake for their strenuous work under the hot sun. All are used abundantly, and even today miso consumption in rural Japan is about 20 percent higher than it is in the cities.

The work of preparing each year's supply is shared by the entire family, although in most villages it is primarily the responsibility of the womenfolk; the men help with the pounding and other heavy work but often know little of the technical details of the process. Always surrounded by an atmosphere of festivity, good cheer and excitement for the children, the work begins when the family's miso-making tools are brought out of storage from the barn, attic, or cellar. The huge wooden mortar and pestle used for mashing the cooked soybeans are charged with good memories of the New Year's season when they are used for pounding *mochi* (rice cakes). The main miso ingredients are gathered and made ready: home-grown soybeans often planted along the paths between the rice and barley fields, and grain freshly harvested and/or stored in the family barn. In some areas, miso making is a communal event, with an entire village or group of families coming together for 3 or 4 days and interspersing their work with song, dance, and great merriment.

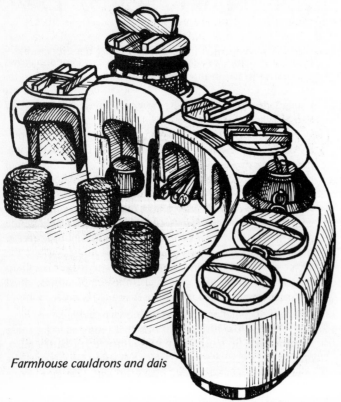

Farmhouse cauldrons and dais

Together with the sense of festivity is an even deeper sense of ritual, so often found in traditional societies where food is gratefully recieved as a life-sustaining gift from mother earth and its preparation is considered a sacred act. The work is timed to begin so that the third day, when fermentation in the vats begins, is highly propitious according to the ancient lunar calendar. Before lighting the fire under the massive kitchen cauldron (used only on special occasions), the entire family is assembled and two pinches of salt are placed at the corners of the cauldron's dais or on the cauldron's rim as an act of purification and offering to the many forces, great and minute, that will carry the miso fermentation to fruition. A year or more later, when the miso vats are ready to be opened, another propitious day is chosen and the family again gathers together. A small sample of the new miso is taken as a gift to neighbors, and the family tests the flavor in a special soup at the very next meal.

The koji prepared in many farmhouses is made without the use of a special starter; the ubiquitous natural mold spores, floating in the air and present in large numbers wherever other miso is fermenting, are found to be sufficient. In areas where grains or soybeans are scarce or expensive, or to produce unique flavors, rural miso makers sometimes add cooked starchy vegetables or corn to the basic mixture or even use the vegetables as the substrate for the koji.

In many farmhouses, various vegetables (which have been previously salt-pickled under pressure to reduce their moisture content) are buried in the miso just before it begins its fermentation. The art of pickling, in all of its many forms, is highly evolved in rural Japan as is its Western counterpart, the canning of fruits and jams. Homemade miso pickles are particularly prized by nursing mothers, since they are said to aid digestion and improve the flow and quality of breast milk.

When all is done, the family gathers to seal the 20-gallon wooden kegs or 10-gallon earthenware crocks. The relatively high salt content in most farmhouse miso, the often unheated (and generally very cold) environment, and the frequent lack of "strength" in koji prepared with wild mold spores, all combine to necessitate a relatively long aging, in most cases two to three years. In recent times, as farmers have moved to the cities, farms have been left abandoned throughout the remote countryside, and in the barns on a number of these we have found large kegs of (delicious) miso which were apparently too heavy to transport to the nearest road.

Despite its survival in some parts of Japan, the traditional farmhouse method is nevertheless gradually being forgotten and is in danger of dying out completely over the next few decades due largely to the spread of commercial miso to even the most remote regions of the nation. The estimated total rural production dropped 40 percent in the short period between 1966 and 1974, and many families that formerly prepared their own koji and cooked their soybeans now prefer to buy either ready-made koji or *shikomi-miso*, a mixture of the basic ingredients pre-packed in the vat and ready to ferment. Fortunately, however, there has been a recent revival of interest in preparing farmhouse miso among young Japanese. Living in rural communities devoted to a simple life of self-sufficiency and respect for tradition, they hope to stem the tide.

Fig. 38. Farmhouse Floorplan

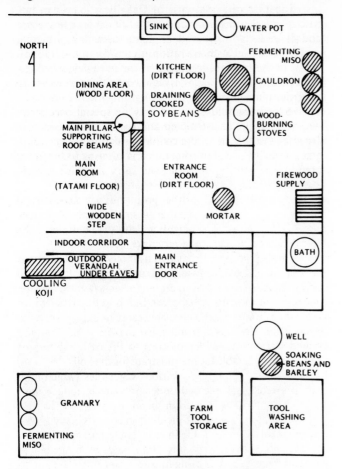

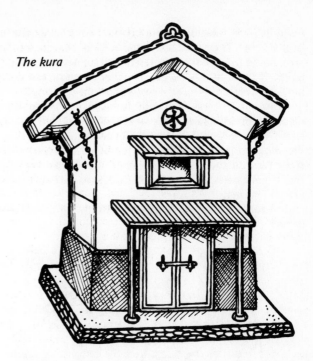

The kura

The Farmhouse as the Stage

Country-style miso is prepared and often fermented inside the farmhouse itself (fig. 38). The kitchen and entrance room usually have dirt floors well suited for the heavy work of pounding the beans and supporting the log fire that heats the caldron. The warm rice is usually allowed to cool on rice-straw mats spread under the eaves of an outdoor verandah or on the wide wooden step below which guests leave their shoes as they step up into the *tatami*-mat main room. The koji is often incubated at one end of this step next to the base of a huge, 2-foot-diameter wooden pillar that serves as the roofbeams' main support; there is access to this central area from both the entranceway and the main room. In some farmhouses, the miso is fermented indoors behind the wood-burning stoves, an area warmer than the rest of the house; this arrangement not only promotes faster fermentation but makes the mature miso easier to get at from the kitchen. In other farmhouses, the miso is fermented in a nearby barn, woodshed, granary, or *kura*, the family treasure storehouse. The fireproof *kura*, with its thick earthen walls, keeps the miso cool in summer and warm in winter and thereby works like a family wine cellar to promote even fermentation. Some families may have a special *kura* (called a *miso-gura*) used exclusively for aging miso. It generally has an earth floor and a slightly moist or humid interior enviornment compared with the dry environment in the family treasure storehouse.

Tools

Most of the tools used by farmhouse miso makers are made at home by hand. Wooden tools are generally made of fragrant and durable cedar (*sugi*), which has a high resistance to salt, water, and heat. The synthesis of utility and artistry in most traditional tools makes them models of folk-craftsmanship.

Caldron: A massive iron pot 24 to 30 inches in diameter at the mouth and 18 inches deep at the center of the rounded bottom. It is set atop a stone dais over a wood-burning stove and used only on special occasions (to prepare New Year's *mochi* and festival tofu, for example); each occasion is accompanied by the salt offering described previously. Most caldrons have a heavy wooden lid, its boards joined by dovetailing.

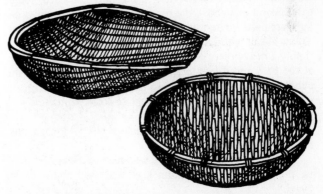

Colanders: Made of thin strips of woven bamboo, each *zaru* is about 42 inches in diameter and 14 inches deep. Bamboo winnowing baskets are also widely used.

Koji Trays or Thick Straw Mats: Two different sets of equipment are used for incubating the koji. Four or five wooden trays, each about 2½ feet square and 3 inches deep (used in some villages to store cakes of *mochi*) are used for large batches. They are stacked atop a 2½-foot-square insulating cushion (*zabuton*) and covered with gunney sacks and/or quilts. If more heat is needed, metal or porcelain hot water bottles are placed against the boxes under the covering.

In many areas, the koji is incubated inside thick *mushiro*, or insulating mats, made of tightly-woven rice straw. They are about 3½ by 6½ feet and ½ to ¾ inch thick. The *mushiro* mats are placed on top of a thick layer of rice straw for insulation. In cold weather, 4 to 5 mats are used, and in some cases a layer of clean cloth is placed between the koji and the mats.

Ladle: A 2-quart ladle with a sturdy 3-foot wooden handle.

Pounding Miso Ingredients

Mortar and Pestle: The massive wooden farmhouse mortar, 2½ feet in diameter and about 2 feet tall, is also used for pounding steamed glutinous rice to make *mochi*. Most mortars weigh several hundred pounds and the finest varieties are made of zelkovia (*keyaki*) using only the hard, tough trunk-wood just above the roots. Wooden pestles of two designs are used for pounding miso soybeans. One is shaped like a huge mallet with a heavy, slightly rounded head; the other is simply a heavy piece of wood about 3 to 4 inches in diameter at the base and 4 feet long. It is said that in some areas, the cooked soybeans are placed in a large wooden tub and crushed underfoot by workers wearing rice-straw sandals, as was the practice in traditional miso shops.

Rice Paddle: A wooden paddle about 9½ inches long, ordinarily used for serving rice.

Soaking Keg: A 19-gallon wooden container, identical to the wooden fermentation kegs described below under "vats."

Steamers and Cauldron Steaming Lid: A typical steamer consists of 4 to 6 wooden boxes, each about 5 inches deep and either 15 to 25 inches square or 22 inches in diameter. The bottom of each box is made of bamboo slats; the boxes are usually stacked one atop the other during steaming. A notch or hole in the extended sides of each box allows for the

insertion of a long pole so that it can be lifted off without having to touch the hot wood. A flat lid covers the top box, and all are set on a steaming lid placed over the mouth of the cauldron. A 1-inch-square hole in the center of this lid allows steam to rise from the cauldron. In some cases a steam disperser is placed over this hole to allow more uniform steaming of the grain in the bottom box.

Straw Cooling Mats: Either *mushiro* mats (see above) or *gyoza* mats of about the same size and made of *igusa* reeds are spread on the floor and covered with the freshly steamed grain. Usually two, but sometimes as many as four mats are used.

Vats: Either earthenware crocks or wooden kegs make excellent fermentation containers for the miso. A typical crock is 16 to 20 inches in diameter and 20 to 30 inches deep. The inside is glazed to prevent moisture loss and the mouth is wide enough to allow the insertion of a pressing lid. A typical wooden keg is either 9½ or 19 gallons in capacity. Ordinarily used as a sake container, it is bound with hoops of braided bamboo and must be well seasoned.

Each vat has a wooden pressing lid about 1 inch thick and ½ to 1 inch smaller in diameter than the mouth of the keg. Some kegs are sealed with a tight-fitting barrelhead that is used to keep out dust. Rope may be packed into the space between the head's outer rim and the vat's mouth to create a tighter fit. Or a regular wooden lid, grooved in a circle where it touches the mouth of the vat, may serve the same purpose.

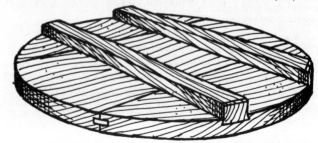

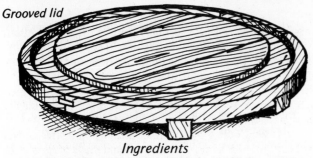

Grooved lid

Ingredients

Grain: All farmouse miso is made with the grain that is most available locally. Most families use grain they have grown themselves and which has been polished at the local rice shop. Traditionally, the word *inaka* (country-style) miso has generally connoted barley rather than rice or soybean miso. In some areas, wheat is used together with barley to give the miso a darker color.

Water: Water quality is believed to have a very important effect on the miso's flavor. Water drawn from the deep farmhouse well, whence it comes cold and pure, is preferred. It is generally boiled when used as the mixing liquid.

Koji Starter: At least four different methods are used to start koji. 1) *Natural Molds:* Perhaps the oldest, most difficult, and most time-consuming way of making koji, in which mold spores living in the air and on the koji trays or straw mats are used to inoculate the warm rice. It is said that in parts of Japan with clean air, molds that yield mycotoxins (such as aflatoxins) are rarer than in most countries. 2) *Cut-and-Dried Starter:* See page 182. 3) *Commercial Koji Starter:* Whole-grain starter purchased from the local koji maker or sake brewer. 4) *Regular Koji:* A small amount of commercial or homemade dried koji is mixed with the warm grain, which is then allowed to be inoculated further by natural mold spores; the addition of the dried koji simply hastens the process, however the results are generally not as good as when methods 2 or 3 are used.

Soybeans: Japanese soybeans are generally believed to yield the best miso. While many families grow their own, those that do not, purchase them from a local tofu or miso shop. New-crop beans have the best flavor.

Salt: Widely known as *nami-no-hana*, "the flowers of the waves," natural salt is preferred. Many farmers buy a large rice-straw sack filled with unrefined salt, allow it to drain (indoors) over a wooden tub for several weeks, and collect the liquid (*nigari*) that drips into the tub for use in making tofu. They then use the "naturally-refined" salt remaining in the sack to make their miso. Since the koji used in most farmhouse miso is not prepared under the controlled conditions prevailing in commercial shops, and since country-style miso is generally fermented for a long time, a relatively large amount of salt is used to prevent spoilage and the growth of contaminating microorganisms.

Alternate Carbohydrate and Protein Sources: Miso containing a large proportion of sweet potatoes or Irish potatoes is particularly popular (see p. 171).

Pickled Ingredients: In many farmhouses, salt-pressed vegetables are packed into the miso vat together with the basic ingredients and allowed to ferment until the miso is mature (see pp. 156 and 192).

Farmhouse Barley Miso   MAKES ABOUT 16 GALLONS

The following amounts are typical of an average batch, which makes a one-year supply. Our method uses koji starter which is easiest, fastest, and guarantees the best quality. Before starting, please study Homemade Koji (p. 179) and Homemade Miso (p. 172). Many of the illustrations accompanying the basic method are adapted with permission from *Miso Daigaku*.

4½ gallons (32½ pounds) pearled barley
2 tablespoons (17.6 grams) whole-grain koji starter
5 gallons (32½ pounds) whole soybeans
1½ gallons (14.9 pounds) natural salt
3 gallons (25 pounds) mixing liquid

DAY 1:

1) Start work early in the morning. Wash and rinse the barley several times in the soaking keg placed next to your water source, then soak for 2½ to 3 hours. Fill the cauldron half full of water and cover with the steaming lid. Light a wood fire beneath the cauldron and bring the water to a boil.

2) Line each of 3 steamers with a layer of cloth. Drain barley and divide among the 3 steamers, covering the bottom of each with an even layer about 1½ to 2 inches deep. Stack steamers congruently on top of each other over the center of

the steaming lid and cover barley in top steamer with lid or a layer of heavy cloth or burlap. Measuring from the time steam begins to rise through this cloth, steam barley for 60 to 90 minutes. Have two people use two poles to lift the top two steamer boxes while a third person removes the bottom one from the cauldron lid. Re-place the top two boxes, set the bottom one atop the other two, and cover the top box with the lid or cloth; continue steaming. Transfer the bottom box to the top in this way at 20- to 30-minute intervals until all barley has been steamed. (If desired, as each bottom box is removed, sprinkle barley lightly with water to hasten cooking, and stir vigorously with the rice paddle to break up lumps.)

3) Examine grain to see that it is somewhat transparent and resilient yet fairly soft. Arrange a double thickness of cooling mats (or blankets topped with a clean sheet) in the

shade outdoors and spread barley on mats in a layer 1 to 2 inches thick. Stir barley frequently with wooden paddle to hasten cooling and drying.

4) When grain temperature drops to about body temperature, and when its moisture level has decreased to the extent that only a few kernels stick to your palm if touched, sprinkle on the koji starter. Using the wooden paddle, lightly mix starter into barley, breaking up all lumps; then mix vigorously for 5 minutes. (If preparing koji without starter or if using koji boxes, see Variation 1.) Using your fingertips, crumble any remaining small lumps of grain, then gather inoculated barley into a mound at center of mat.

5) Fold ends and sides of mat over barley to form a compact bundle into which air cannot easily enter. Spread some dry straw as insulation to a depth of about 12 inches over an area the size of one of the mats (or use a mattress, thick cushions, or air mattress). Cover with the bottom cooling mat, then place bundle on top of mat. Cover with 2 or more straw mats, blankets, or quilts. If air temperature is low, place 2 to 4 hot water bottles beneath covering mats next to barley bundle; leave them in place for 10 to 12 hours, or until koji begins to develop its own heat. Check koji temperature every few hours and, if possible, once during the night, to see that it does not drop below 77°F or rise above 90°F. Add hot water bottles or covering mats to raise temperature; remove to lower.

DAY 2:

6) Early morning: Open bundle, check temperature, and mix barley thoroughly with paddle. Re-wrap, cover, and allow to stand for 2 hours more. Now unfold mat in which barley is wrapped and spread it flat on mat resting on straw. Spread barley in a layer 2 to 2½ inches deep over upper mat and cover with 2 to 4 more mats. At about 1:00 p.m. and again at 5:00 p.m., uncover barley, check that temperature is between 80°F and 95°F, and stir well. If temperature is too low, increase thickness of barley layer and/or add additional covering mats. Crumble any lumps with your fingertips; always re-cover.

In the evening, wash soybeans thoroughly, cover with water, and soak overnight in soaking keg placed near your water source.

DAY 3:

7) Early morning: Uncover and examine koji (p. 170). If barley is covered with a bloom of fragrant white mold, koji is at its best. With your fingertips, crumble thoroughly any small lumps. Leave koji uncovered for several hours as it cools to room temperature, then re-cover with a single mat to keep out contaminating microorganisms. (If koji mold is yellow and has a slightly sweet fragrance, it is satisfactory but not ideal; treat as for white mold. If mold is black, it must be removed; see p. 181). If koji is not yet done, re-cover with mats, bring temperature up to 94°F, and allow to stand until white mold appears.)

8) After beans have soaked for about 16 hours, drain and rinse well. Combine beans and about 15 gallons water in caldron, and light a wood fire beneath it. Cover caldron, bring water to a boil, and simmer for 5 to 6 hours, or until beans are soft. Add water occasionally if necessary. Near the end, adjust water so that about 3 gallons of liquid remain after cooked beans are drained.

9) Ladle beans into 1 or 2 colanders set over caldron and/or soaking keg and allow to drain thoroughly. Meanwhile, wash fermentation keg, mortar, and pestle(s).

10) When beans have cooled to about body temperature, shake colanders briefly, then transfer about 10 percent of the cooked beans to the mortar. With one to three people working together, pound beans thoroughly; chanting or singing helps keep the rhythm if several pestles are being used together.

11) Set aside 6 tablespoons salt. Measure out 3 gallons soybean cooking liquid. Add one-tenth each of the remaining salt, the koji and the cooking liquid to the mashed soybeans in mortar. Mix ingredients together with pestles, then pound briefly. Rub 2 tablespoons of salt over bottom and sides of vat, then pack in pounded mixture. (If preparing pickles in miso, see Variation 2).

1) Making Koji Without Starter in Koji Boxes: For this method to be successful, it is very important that the air be quite clear and preferably fairly cold, and that natural mold spores be present in the environment. Straw mats may be used in place of the boxes, as described in the method given above.

Spread steamed barley on cooling mats and allow to cool to no less than 113°F. Spread warm barley in a layer 1½ inches thick over bottom of each of 3 to 5 koji boxes. Place

12) Repeat mixing and packing procedure until all ingredients have been used and vat is at least 80 percent full. Now, using a long pestle or your fists, gently pound miso in keg to mix the various layers and expel air. Using a paddle, pack miso surface firmly, then smooth and level it precisely. Sprinkle remaining ¼ cup salt over miso surface, making sure to reach edges. Top miso with unweighted pressing lid, pushing lid about ¼ inch into miso. (In some areas, sheets of *kombu*, *ho* leaves [*Magnolia hypoleuca*], or cloth are placed between miso and pressing lid, and lid is weighted with an 8- to 10-pound stone.) Seal mouth of vat with a barrelhead or

one box on an insulating cushion, then stack on the remaining boxes so that each box completely covers the one below it and thereby prevents heat loss. Cover top and sides of stack with several layers of thick straw matting and/or quilts and

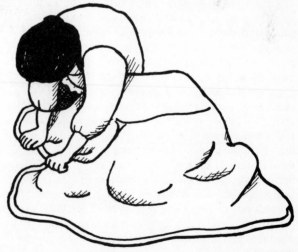

lid. Cover, if desired, with a large sheet of paper tied in place with string. Record exact miso ingredients, date, and expected date of maturity on an index card and attach it to vat. Place vat in appropriate fermentation area and allow to stand untouched for at least 18 months, preferably 2 to 3 years. Sample flavor from time to time.

To open: Stir miso thoroughly with paddle to mix in salty surface layers. Serve, reserving and storing unused portions as for Homemade Miso (p. 174).

blankets. In cold weather, heat with hot water bottles. After the first 24 hours of koji fermentation, mix the developing koji once daily with a paddle. When koji begins to develop its

own heat, stagger boxes slightly to allow the entry of oxygen and escape of carbon dioxide. The mycelium of white or yellow mold should appear after 4 to 7 days depending on the weather and the number of yeasts in the environment. Discard any koji covered with bluish-green mold. Proceed as for barley miso.

2) Making Miso Containing Miso Pickles: Miso pickles (*miso-zuké*) are prepared in most batches of farmhouse miso even though this practice is generally considered to cause a slight decline in the miso flavor.

A 19-gallon keg of miso may contain any or all of the following: 5 to 6 *daikon*, 10 small eggplants, 10 cucumbers, 15 gingerroots, 2 *kombu* rolls, 4 burdock roots and/or 5 carrots. Cut very large *daikon* lengthwise into quarters; cut regular-sized *daikon* lengthwise into halves. Use other vegetables whole. Wash and drain vegetables thoroughly, then place into separate tubs or large bowls and sprinkle with salt equal to about 7 percent of the vegetable weight. Place a pressing lid directly atop vegetables and press with a weight equal to four or five times the weight of the vegetables for about 1 week in summer and 2 weeks in winter. Rinse vegetables and discard briny pressing liquid. When one-fourth of miso has been packed into the fermentation keg, arrange one-third of each of the vegetables in a layer on top of the miso. Sprinkle vegetables with a few tablespoons of salt. When miso keg is one-half full and again when it is three-fourths full, insert layers of remaining vegetables. Cover third layer with remainder of miso. Do not stir miso after keg is full. Leave pickling vegetables untouched until miso has finished fermenting.

To use, remove vegetables from keg as they are needed. Rub excess miso from surface of each vegetable and return miso to keg. Rinse vegetables, slice into thin ovals or rounds, and serve (p. 156).

3) Making Sweet Potato Miso *(Imo Miso):* To the ingredients in the basic recipe, add 14 to 15 pounds steamed (sweet) potatoes or yams. (If desired, make potatoes into koji as for rice koji; p. 179.) Reduce the amount of salt to 4¾ quarts. Add potatoes to pounded soybeans together with koji; mash thoroughly. Pack into vats as above. Ferment for at least 5 to 6 months, starting in April or May.

In some areas, the sweet potatoes are cooked, pickled whole in salt, and mixed with commercial miso as an extender just prior to packaging. In some farmhouses, potato koji replaces the grain koji.

4) Making Date Miso *(Sotetsu Miso):* A farmhouse specialty on the island of Amami Oshima south of Kyushu. Use brown rice in place of barley to make the koji. Dry and grind to a powder 1 to 3 gallons of dried dates (the fruit of the sago palm, *Cycas revoluta*). Combine and mix with the other basic ingredients just before placing them to the vat.

NOTES AND ADDITIONAL INFORMATION

1) For a relatively sweet miso requiring only 6 to 9 months fermentation, use 65 percent of the salt in the basic recipe; for a saltier variety, increase the salt by 15 percent and age for 2 to 3 years.

2) For large-scale community production, the method used by a village we studied in Nagano prefecture might best serve as a model. Fifteen to twenty people work together. A building is equipped with a small (6 by 8 by 7-foot tall) koji incubating room containing 56 koji trays; it is similar to those in traditional miso shops. The room is kept at 77°F by a charcoal brazier throughout the koji fermentation. One part barley and 2 parts soybeans are mixed, soaked, steamed for 4 hours and made into koji. Sufficient portions of the finished soybean-barley koji is taken home by each family, mixed with salt, and fermented in kegs. Most people add only one-half the salt at the beginning and the rest 2 weeks later; some add the salt six times during the first 2 weeks. The miso is stirred daily for 6 months after which time it may be served, although most families ferment it for 1½ to 2 years to improve the flavor. Tamari is sometimes drawn from the miso in a long bamboo colander.

3) Rather than using hot water bottles, some farmers warm small batches of koji next to or under their living room *kotatsu*, a table covered with a large quilt and set over a sunken box at the bottom of which is a charcoal brazier heater. In many farmhouses, this is the only heat source for the entire family during the long, cold winter.

4) The soybeans are sometimes cooked for up to 24 hours. From morning until night, they are simmered in a covered pot over a low fire. Any logs remaining in the fire are removed and the beans are then cooked over low coals through the night.

5) In some villages, the miso is mixed once a month during the summer to prevent mold growth and hasten fermentation. The craftsman uses either his hands—well washed to the elbows—or a wooden paddle.

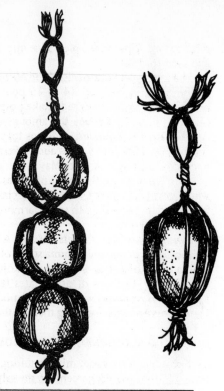

Farmhouse Soybean Miso made with Miso-dama
(Miso Balls)

Known as *Tama Miso* (miso made from balls), this is one of Japan's earliest farmhouse varieties. Unknown in China, the method for its preparation came to Japan from Korea where the balls (*miso-dama*) are still widely used to make both Korean miso (*jang*) and soy sauce.

In the basic process, cooked soybeans are mashed, shaped into balls, and tied with rice straw. Suspended from poles or placed on a special drying rack over the open-hearth fireplace (or the kitchen wood-burning stove), they are allowed to stand for about 30 days, or until the surface of each ball is covered with a bloom of fragrant mold. (In some areas, the balls are hung outdoors under the high farmhouse eaves for up to 60 days.) The inoculated balls are then crushed in a mortar, mixed with salt and water, and packed into vats, where the mixture is allowed to ferment for 1 year or more. Naturally, *miso-dama* are said to be quite difficult to prepare, except in areas blessed with clear, cold air in which the appropriate molds are found in abundance. Nowadays, miso made in this traditional, colorful way is gradually becoming a thing of the past.

Nevertheless, in a number of remote areas, it continues to thrive. In Nagano, Gifu, and Aichi prefectures, it is prepared in the late fall, while in Iwate and Miyagi prefectures it is made just after the spring equinox or the traditional lunar New Year, between late March and mid April. At both times in these places, the air is cold and clear enough to ensure that very few contaminating microorganisms are present, yet not so cold as to hinder fermentation.

Up until about 1600 A.D., most of the miso made in rural Japan was made from *miso-dama*. As the use of rice and barley koji grew in popularity (together with miso soup), the tradition of making pure soybean miso began to decline. Farmers began mixing rice- or barley koji with their *miso-dama* soybean koji just before the basic ingredients were packed into vats. And at a somewhat later stage, the *miso-dama* were largely abandoned in favor of rice or barley koji made in bundled straw mats or trays. At present, much of the farmhouse miso prepared with *miso-dama* contains rice- or barley koji purchased from a local koji or miso shop and mixed with the crushed balls. Adding grain koji decreases the fermentation time and increases the finished miso's sweetness and yield. Yet many farmers still prefer the flavor of the traditional product prepared with only soybeans, and we have been impressed by the flavor and aroma produced under even the simplest of brewing conditions.

We learned the following method from Mmes. Saiyo Miura and Kazuko Shinya in the remote mountain village of Kami Ugemura near Iwaizumi in Iwate prefecture. Since each family in the village makes all its own miso (as well as its own tofu), each farmhouse kitchen is equipped with a large cauldron (36 inches in diameter and 20 inches deep), a wooden tub (36 inches in diameter and 12 inches deep), and the other necessary pieces of equipment.

The following ingredients are for one batch. Four batches, usually prepared on four consecutive days, just fill a typical 48-gallon wooden fermentation keg.

9½ gallons whole soybeans, soaked overnight and drained
3½ (or as much as 4¾) gallons salt
Water

1) Combine beans in a caldron with about 20 gallons of water and simmer for 5 to 6 hours, or until soft. Place a 3-gallon bamboo basket on a draining rack set across one side of the caldron's mouth. Using a woven bamboo scoop (constructed like a concave badminton racket), ladle cooked beans

into the basket (fig. a), then transfer 2 basketsful of beans at a time into wooden mixing tub. Wearing (10-inch-high) woven-rice straw or rubber boots, tread beans for 15 to 30 minutes, or until thoroughly crushed (fig. b) (Or grind beans in a hand mill or pound in a mortar.) Combine remaining cooking liquid with the salt in a large crock or keg, cover, and store in a cool place.

2) Using both hands, shape crushed beans into slightly oval balls, each about 7 inches long.

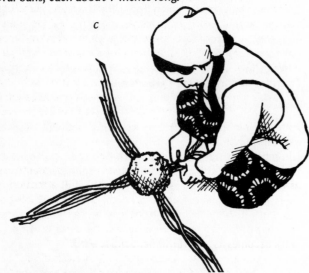

3) Tie together the ends of four 3-foot-long strands of dried rice straw. Arrange strands on a clean surface in the form of a cross, place one miso ball at intersection of strands (fig. c), and tie together at top of ball to form a supportive net. After preparing about 50, hang balls indoors from sturdy horizontal poles (fig. d) suspended from the ceiling 6 to 8 feet above a heat source (open hearth fireplace at center of main farmhouse room).

4) Allow balls to ferment for about 30 days until they are covered with a bloom of light bluish-green mold and are very hard.

5) Remove straw and immerse balls in water-filled mixing tub for several hours, or until the thin, slightly dusty surface layer dissolves in the water. Discard water and drain balls well. Transfer several balls at a time to a large wooden mortar, combine with a small amount of the salted soybean cooking liquid (and if necessary a little water), and pound with a pestle to give a consistency similar to that of regular miso. Repeat until all balls are pounded and mixed.

6) Line the bottom of a keg with a layer of garlic leaves (or sprinkle with salt) and place in the fermentation area (*kura* or barn). Transfer pounded soybean mixture into keg and pack firmly. Smooth miso surface and top with a ½-inch-thick layer of extra salt, then a layer of garlic leaves followed by a layer of (*sasa*) bamboo leaves. Top bamboo leaves with 6 flat rocks and cover keg with a wooden lid (fig. e). (A weighted pressing lid may be substituted for the garlic and bamboo leaves.)

7) Allow miso to ferment for at least 1 year, preferably 3 to 4 years for best flavor. When miso is ready, discard bamboo leaves. Scoop off upper layer of garlic leaves and salt, and mix in small amounts into fodder to feed to livestock. Mix miso well. Keep keg tightly covered when not in use.

9

The Traditional Miso Shop

AN EXAMPLE OF Japan's ancient heritage of fine craftsmanship, the traditional miso shop has a charm and rustic beauty similar to that found in fine old wineries: in the morning sunlight, golden soybeans soak in great wooden tubs; steam billows up from the massive black cauldron and wooden steamers through the arching rafters fashioned from the entire trunks of huge trees; basketfuls of steaming rice are spread with wooden pushing tools over a cedar floor; in a dark, warm-and-humid incubation room, row on row of shallow wooden boxes hold mounds of rice covered with a delicate bloom of pure white mold; the subtly sweet and pervasive fragrance of koji suffuses the atmosphere as it is crumbled between a craftsman's palms; men in straw sandals mash soft, warm soybeans underfoot in wooden tubs or pound them in sturdy mortars with large wooden pestles; tall cedar vats made of thick staves stand bound together by wide-girth hoops of exquisitely woven bamboo; men tread freshly mixed miso underfoot, packing it firmly into vats; others working with wooden spades shovel mature miso into wooden buckets; wife and children standing at the doorway of their home watch the men work in the adjoining shop: all while the master craftsman carefully, patiently helps it to happen.

The traditional craftsman takes deep pride in the quality of his miso, in his work and in the lineage of masters of which he is the living descendant. In many cases his apprenticeship was long and difficult and began at an early age. His master—who was often his father—customarily yielded each secret begrudgingly only after the young disciple had fully demonstrated his capacity for hard work, selfless service and devotion to the spirit of the craft. The work of a true master is a joy to watch. Years of patient and careful practice give rise to movements which flow effortlessly and gracefully. At one with his work, he cares, wasting nothing. He realizes that only by harmonizing his actions with the great rhythm of the four seasons and the microscopic chemical and biological forces at work within the huge fermentation vats can he enable fine miso to come to fruition. His work is a process of continually learning from nature, and his miso is an expression of the depth of his understanding. On the wall behind the great iron cauldron in many shops is a small but well-kept altar, an expression of gratitude.

For many master miso-craftsmen—as for fine sword makers or potters—daily work is seen as a spiritual practice or, as the Japanese say, a Way. Focusing his full attention on every detail moment after moment, the craftsman discovers a space in which the restrictions of time and self cease to operate. Since his main concern is neither fame nor fortune, his work becomes its own fulfillment and reward.

The method for preparing miso in the traditional shop has a number of basic distinguishing characteristics: the grains and beans are cooked over (or in) a large iron cauldron heated from below by a wood or charcoal fire; all of the work is done by hand without the use of motor-driven machines; the tools and containers are handmade and handsomely crafted from natural materials; the koji is prepared in small wooden trays in an incubation room heated, when necessary, by a small charcoal burner or stove; the miso is fermented naturally in huge cedar vats and contains only natural ingredients; it is packed into (5-gallon) wooden kegs for distribution and sale.

Japan's mild, relatively humid climate has proven itself ideal for supporting the growth of fermentation microorganisms. Thanks to this natural advantage and centuries of experience, Japanese craftsmen have developed a level of technical expertise second to none.

The first Japanese commercial miso shops were in operation as early as the year 700 A.D., but up until about 1600, the great majority of miso made in the country was prepared

195

non-commercially in private homes. As commercial miso shops developed, they used the basic farmhouse methods and tools but on an expanded scale. Some shops prepared miso only once each year, generally in the fall using new-crop soybeans and grains. Just as many farmers prepared shoyu as well as miso, so also did the earliest miso shops. Figure 39 shows the preparation of miso in a relatively large 17th century workplace. At the lower left, a fire is being stoked to heat the rice steamer above. The steamed rice is being carried in buckets to straw mats, where it is spread and cooled. After inoculation, the rice is rolled up in the mats and carried to the incubation room (upper center). The finished koji is carried out and mixed with salt in a large tub (lower right). Men bind staves with bamboo hoops to make wooden buckets in which they will sell the finished miso (upper right). The water carrier heads for the shop's well. In the storeroom, bales of rice in straw sacks and stacks of koji trays await use (upper center left).

Since earliest times, the word *kura* has been used to refer to miso shops. Ordinarily the term denotes the thick-walled storehouse or treasury in which a large and fairly well-to-do family keeps its valuables, and, in some cases, its homemade miso. Applied to miso shops, however, the term takes on a broader meaning, referring to the entire business and its tradition. It also refers to the buildings and incubation room, which are said to have their own *kura-gusé* or "unique individual characteristics." These are a product of the resident microorganisms, the buildings' structure and materials, the local climate, plus the intangible yet very real vibrations and living wisdom of all the shop's past masters. The soul and life-force of a shop, the *kura-gusé* is prized and nurtured above all, for it is believed to be the primary factor determining the quality of the miso prepared within its walls.

In most traditional shops throughout Japan, the basic tools and methodology remained virtually unchanged over a period of several centuries up until the end of World War II. At present, miso shops generally prepare miso throughout the year, either daily or at least 3 to 5 times each week. Some miso is seasonal, such as barley miso which, in many regions, is prepared only during the winter. Each master has his own preferred blend of ingredients and numerous secrets for giving a distinctive flavor, aroma, color and texture to his miso.

Today the traditional shop in its pure form is largely a thing of the past. The last examples, which were located in remote rural areas, are said to have disappeared during the mid 1950s. Although traditional tools are still widely used in modern shops, parts of the basic processes have been subject to mechanization in an effort to increase productivity and cut labor costs. The result has been what we shall call the "semi-traditional" shop. An excellent example of the use of middle-level technology, its basic characteristics are described on page 208.

In both traditional and semi-traditional shops the basic method for preparing miso is the same, and the key process is that of preparing fine koji. To master this process and make it work throughout the varying weather conditions of the four seasons requires many years of devoted study. Like the brewer of fine wines or the maker of delicious natural cheeses, the miso master is always learning. Koji is an essential part of many Japanese foods, including sake and shoyu, and a truly accomplished craftsman known for his expertise in preparing the koji for any of these is given the rare and honorific title of *toji* or "master brewer." Many *toji* are able to prepare at least seven varieties of koji, including, of course, the basic types made from white or brown rice, barley, and soybeans.

The latest statistics (1974) show that there are 2,400 commercial miso shops and factories in Japan, and they produce a total yearly output of 649,000 tons of miso retailing for 492 million dollars. Each year, they use 212,000 tons of soybeans, 101,000 tons of rice, 22,000 tons of barley, and 82,000 tons of salt. The great majority of these shops are relatively small scale, semi-traditional enterprises run by a single man and his family with the help of one or two relatives or hired craftsmen. Most shops produce several types of miso, and some also prepare special batches of koji which are sold fresh or dried as an independent item. During the cold months, a few use this koji to prepare commercial *amazaké* (p. 162).

Fig. 39. A 17th century workplace

The Miso Shop Building

Most traditional and semi-traditional shops are located adjoining the home of the miso maker. In the cities, the home and shop are often under the same roof, as in the *Tsujita* shop (fig. 40), whereas in the countryside, the home and various buildings used for miso making are usually located on the same piece of property.

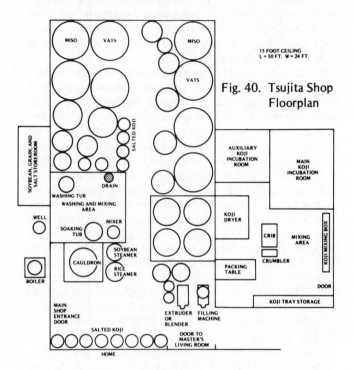

15 FOOT CEILING
L = 50 FT. W = 24 FT.

Fig. 40. Tsujita Shop Floorplan

The main building where most of the miso preparation takes place often looks like a large barn with a massive ridgepole 20 to 30 feet above ground level and an elaborate support system of beams and rafters joined without nails and fashioned from arching tree trunks. The high roof is generally covered with tile or thatch to keep out the summer heat and snowy winter cold. The walls are made of wood or mud plaster mixed with straw. Since there are generally few windows, the interior is often fairly dark. Parts of the floor are covered with large squares of hand-cut granite or concrete aggregate and, in some shops, parts are uncovered, packed dirt. In some set-ups, the caldron, koji incubation room and vats are all located in the main building; in others the koji room is in an adjacent building. A well is generally located within the main building fairly near the caldron or the washing-and-soaking area. A storeroom for soybeans, grain, and salt is situated either in the main building or nearby.

The koji incubation room, which is located near the center of many shops, is a well-insulated chamber usually constructed of 10-inch-thick stone or packed earth blocks, or of bricks. The floor is 12 by 9 feet and the low ceiling is never higher than 7 feet. The door is often very small (3 feet high) and thick to minimize heat loss when it is opened. One foot off the floor along both walls are benches on which the koji trays are stacked during fermentation. The room is heated by

a small charcoal brazier or gas stove, and a thermometer and hygrometer (to measure humidity) hang on the wall. At the center of many—but not all—incubation rooms there is a large wooden box called a "crib." In it the koji begins its incubation before being transferred to small wooden trays.

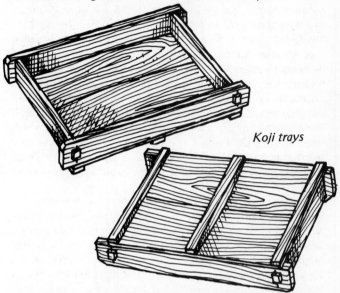

Koji trays

The koji mixing-floor generally runs across the entire front of the incubation room and is about 12 to 14 feet from front to back (p. 208). Made of tightly fitted, smooth cedar planks, it is elevated 6 to 8 inches above the shop's floor and used as the area for cooling the freshly steamed rice and inoculating it with starter. Some small shops use a large wooden mixing box measuring 6 by 9 by 1 foot deep in place of the floor; the box can be stood against a wall and the area used for other purposes as well.

Some traditional shops employ large insulated boxes, each big enough to house four medium-sized vats (fig. 41). After the vats are packed with the unfermented miso mixture and topped with individual pressing lids, an insulated wooden lid is placed over the entire affair. The heat generated by the miso fermentation raises the interior temperature, resulting in a sort of natural temperature-controlled fermentation and a considerable reduction in the required aging time.

Fig. 41. *Insulated fermentation box*

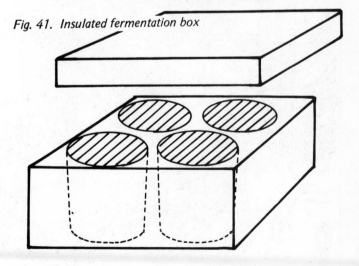

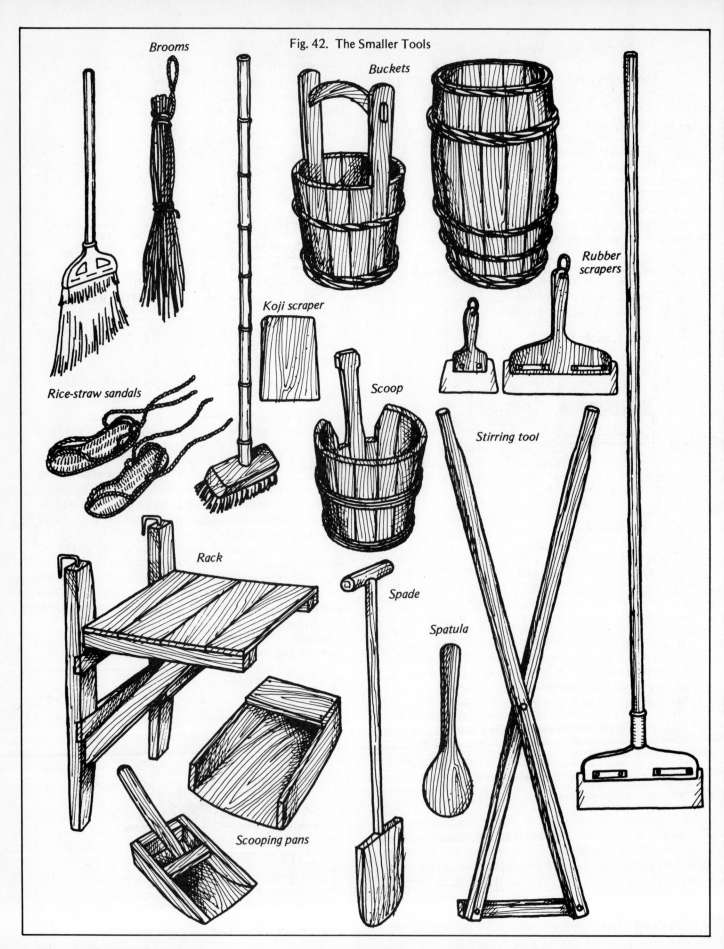

Fig. 42. The Smaller Tools

Brooms

Buckets

Koji scraper

Rubber scrapers

Rice-straw sandals

Scoop

Stirring tool

Rack

Spade

Spatula

Scooping pans

Traditional Tools and Equipment

The refining force of centuries of daily use has given the basic miso-making tools functionality and simple beauty. Most wooden implements are made of seasoned Japanese cedar (*sugi*) which is durable in the presence of water, heat, and salt, and has a pleasant fragrance. The principal smaller tools are shown in figure 42.

The most important large-scale pieces of equipment are the caldrons, the steamers, and the fermentation vats. Figure 43 shows a shop with a large caldron topped with the soybean steamer and small caldron topped with the grain steamer. Beneath each caldron is a firebox, access to which is gained by descending a small ladder into a pit 4-feet-wide and 5-feet-deep. Logs are stacked at one end of the pit and in the center is a cinder box in which burning logs are extinguished at the end of work for reuse later. Some shops have only one caldron (in which the soybeans are boiled) and one steamer used for the grain.

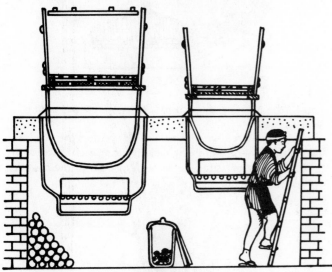

Fig. 43. *Steamer and caldron*

An exploded view of a steamer and cauldron is shown in figure 44. At the right are the steamer's bottom, a rack that sits on it, and a cloth that lines the rack and holds the rice. Note that the grain in the wood is radial, which enables the steamer to expand when heated. Bamboo (rather than metal) hoops are used to bind the staves so that in case the steamer catches fire, the hoops burn, the staves fall apart, and the steamer's moist contents extinguish the flames.

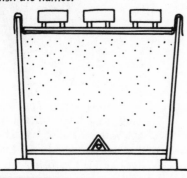

Fig. 44. *Steamer and cauldron*

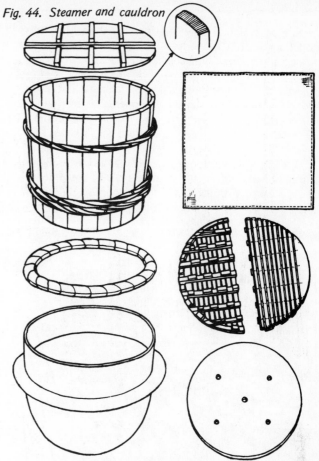

Two views of a fermentation vat are shown in figure 45. Capable of holding 4 to 6 tons of miso, a typical vat is 5½ feet deep and 7 feet in diameter at the mouth. Only the best quality, knot-free cedar is used, and if kept in constant use, the average vat will last 150 to 200 years; Western winery cooperage, which is equally long lasting, is usually made of white oak. Note that the wood grain of the slats is concentric with the vat to help prevent the leakage of tamari. Vats are always mounted on blocks to provide air circulation for the

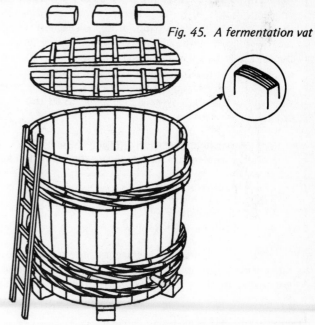

Fig. 45. *A fermentation vat*

base and ensure their long life. In some shops, the entire wood floor is built at the level of the vat's rim to provide easy access (fig. 46). Some contain a tamari trough (see also fig. 12, p. 41) and spout by means of which tamari that settles in the miso can be extracted when fermentation is complete. The fine art of Japanese cooperage is now almost totally extinct, and new vats are virtually impossible to find. Specially ordered they cost from $2,500 to $5,000 each.

Detailed descriptions of the sizes and construction of all traditional (and modern) miso making equipment is given in our *Miso Production: The Book of Miso, Volume II,* available exclusively from our Center (see p. 277).

Fig. 46. Shop floor at vat's rim

Preparing Traditional Rice Miso

The basic ingredients required to make a 1-ton batch of miso are given below; four batches fill one vat. The work is done by a miso master and two craftsmen who assist him. The following recipe is written for a shop that might wish to make only one batch of miso. To prevent overcrowding, small shops often prepare one batch of koji on each of four consecutive days, mixing each with salt and storing it. On each of the next four days, a batch of soybeans is cooked, mixed with one-fourth of the salted koji, and packed into the vats. Eight days are therefore required to fill one vat. The basic proportions of raw materials by weight are soybeans 10, rice 10, and salt 4.4.

528 pounds (white or lightly polished brown) rice
8 ounces whole-grain (or 1.6 ounces spore powder) koji starter
234 pounds natural salt
528 pounds whole dry soybeans
15 gallons seed miso
28 to 34 gallons mixing liquid

In the afternoon or evening the miso maker measures out the rice. If it has not been cleaned, he runs it through a winnowing machine to remove chaff, straw, or other debris.

He fills the washing keg about two-thirds full of grain and adds water to cover. Working the base of the stirring tool down to the bottom of the tub, he twists it vigorously back

and forth, agitating the rice for 30 to 60 seconds until it is well washed.

Using a large, wooden scoop, he transfers the rice into two baskets set on a draining rack. Dousing each basket with 2 or 3 scoops of water, he allows the grain to drain while washing more in the keg.

Now he rinses out a deep soaking tub, inserts a wooden plug in the tub's drainage hole, and covers the hole inside the tub with a small screen. The drained rice is then emptied into the tub and smoothed. Enough water to cover is added and the rice is left to soak overnight (12 to 16 hours).

THE FIRST DAY

At 6:30 a.m. the master fills his caldron two-thirds full of water, descends the ladder into the firebox pit, and lights a wood fire. After pulling the plug in the soaking tub to drain the rice, he places the steamer and its support on the

caldron's mouth then arranges the lower cloth to cover the steamer's wooden grating. He readies the koji mixing box, lining it with a large sheet of canvas (or, if using a mixing floor, sweeps then wipes it with a moist cloth).

When the water in the caldron comes to a boil, the master scoops his soaked rice into the steamer, smooths its surface, and covers it first with the upper cloth, then with two layers of gunny sacking. The edges of the sacks are tucked down firmly around all sides of the rice to help trap the steam which, after about 15 minutes, begins to rise through the sacks; measuring from this time, the rice is steamed for 40 minutes.

The master removes the sacks and upper cloth while an assistant hooks a rack over the steamer's side and places a basket on it. Using a wooden spade, the master turns over 10 to 12 spadefuls of rice, breaking up large clumps by whacking them with the spade's flat blade. Using the scoop, he then, fills the basket with steaming-hot rice.

While an assistant carries rice-filled baskets to the mixing box, the master continues to break up the firm rice still remaining in the steamer.

Emptied from the baskets into the large (6- by 9- by 1-foot-deep) mixing box, the rice is spread evenly in a 2½-inch-thick layer and allowed to cool.

Every five minutes, the master and one assistant mix and break up the rice with their spades, aiding the cooling process. The grain's temperature is measured (by touch or with a thermometer) after each mixing.

When the temperature has dropped to about 113°F, the master places a koji tray over the mixing box and measures in the koji starter together with approximately 3½ pounds of well-crumbled rice. Slowly and carefully, he mixes the two by hand.

After he has scattered half of this mixture over the rice, his assistants, using spades, mix the rice thoroughly until the mold spores are evenly distributed. After several minutes, the remaining inoculum is sprinkled on and mixed in. From time

to time, remaining clumps of rice are broken up with the spade's flat blade. It is now about noon.

As the rice continues to cool, the crib—a heavy wooden box about 4 by 4½ by 2 feet deep which may be located either in or outside the incubation room—is lined with clean canvas. When its temperature has dropped to 95°F, the rice is mounded at one end of the mixing box by pulling the box's cloth lining toward that end. Any remaining small clumps are broken up by hand as the rice is scooped into baskets, then poured into the crib. When all of the rice is in the crib, the surface is pressed firmly by hand to compact the interior and retard cooling. When the rice temperature reaches 91°F, the edges of the canvas are folded over and the crib's contents covered with 4 layers of thick rice-straw mats which serve as

insulation. The preparation of koji, the first fermentation process, is now well underway and will continue undisturbed throughout the night.

THE SECOND DAY

At 6:30 a.m., the master preheats the incubation room to between 80°F and 86°F using a small charcoal brazier or stove. (During the summer, preheating is often unnecessary.)

At 7:00 a.m., the two assistant craftsmen uncover the rice and check its temperature, which should be about 89°F but may be as high as 100°F. Using their spades and starting at one end of the crib, they turn over the warm rice, breaking up any lumps, and shovel it to the opposite end. After reaching the bottom at the first end, they work toward the opposite end, replacing the turned rice. In this way, oxygen is incorporated to nourish the growing koji molds, carbon dioxide is expelled, and the warm rice from the crib's center is mixed with the cooler portions from the sides and bottom. When all the rice has been turned, its surface is packed, smoothed, and re-covered.

By 9:00 a.m., about 160 clean koji trays have been neatly stacked (inverted to keep out alien mold spores) near the crib. The latter is uncovered and the rice thoroughly

turned and crumbled as before. As one assistant stacks nine koji trays across a corner of the crib, the other fills them one by one with (about 3¼ quarts or 3 pounds of) warm rice, poured in so as to form a mounded oval.

With one hand, the first assistant then quickly indents the center of each mound to form the "hollow oval" pattern, which will later prevent overheating at the koji's center.

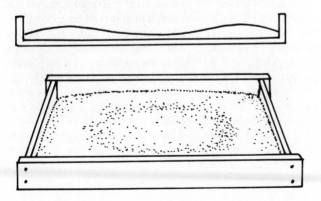

When 9 trays have been filled, hollowed, and stacked one atop the other, the master carries them to the incubation room where they are arranged in "vertical stacks" on a bench along one wall. When all of the trays are in the room (7 stacks of 22 trays each), an empty tray is inverted over the top of each stack, and the door of the room is tightly closed. The rice now continues its fermentation as it becomes koji.

After 1 hour, the master checks the room's temperature and humidity. In winter, the temperature should ideally be between 80°F and 86°F, and in no case must it be allowed to drop below 77°F. In summer, it may rise as high as 92°F but not above. The humidity should be 93 to 95 percent. To warm the room, the master stokes the brazier or stove (its fumes go out through a chimmney) and/or closes the ceiling vents; to cool it, he opens the vents or door. To raise the humidity, he sprinkles (hot) water over the floor.

At 1:00 p.m., the master and both assistant craftsmen wash their hands and test the koji's temperature (which should be about 95°F). They transfer the top tray in each stack to an empty section of the bench and stir the koji in it quickly with one hand to break up the young mycelium and thereby encourage its further growth; the mounded center is

indented to form a hollow as before. When all of the trays have been relocated and stirred, those which were formerly on the top of each stack are now on the bottom. This time the trays are arranged in "staggered stacks" to prevent the koji's overheating and provide more oxygen for growth.

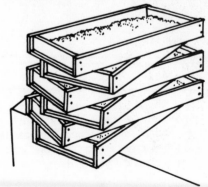

At 5:00 p.m., the master and his helpers once again wash their hands, test the koji (which should be about 100°F) and check the room's temperature and humidity which should be the same as described previously. They transfer the top tray from each stack onto an empty section of bench, and arrange them now in "bricklap stacks."

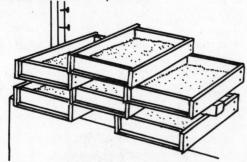

This time, the koji is stirred with both hands, which work quickly from the far to the near end of each tray making about eight openings and closings.

Finally, fingertips quickly shape the crumbled koji into the "three waves" pattern. When all of the koji has been stirred and re-stacked, it is incubated untouched overnight.

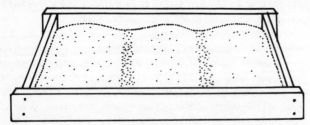

At 6:00 p.m. (or several hours earlier in winter), the soybeans are washed and drained using the same tools and procedures employed earlier for the rice. They are then soaked overnight in a tub reserved for this purpose, which is slightly larger than that used for the grain.

THE THIRD DAY

The morning hours are spent steaming a second batch of rice. At 10:00 a.m., the master and both assistant craftsmen check the koji's temperature (which may have risen as high as 104°F) and appearance. A fragrant white mycelium should now bind the soft rice kernels into a cohesive, ¾-inch-thick mat. The trays are carried from the incubation room and arranged in "staggered stacks" near the koji mixing-floor. Holding the trays one by one over a basket, one craftsman uses a wooden scraper to transfer the koji from tray to basket.

When the basket is full, the koji is crumbled into a large, flat strainer held over a second basket and any lumps are rubbed through.

All of the crumbled koji is now divided among a number of 34-gallon wooden kegs, which are placed around a special tub at the center of the mixing area. The master weighs the salt in a basket, then divides it into as many portions as there are kegs. In the mixing tub, he combines one keg of koji with one portion of salt.

Using a long-handled wooden "pusher," he mixes the two ingredients, then places the salted koji back into its keg. When all of the salt and koji have been mixed, the kegs are covered and set aside.

With the koji finished and the second batch of rice steamed, the work of cooking the soybeans takes center stage. The rice steamer is removed from atop the caldron and replaced by the slightly larger soybean steamer. (In some shops the beans are boiled in the caldron.) While the fire is being stoked, the master scoops the soybeans from the soaking tub into the steamer, then places a wooden lid directly atop the beans. After about 35 minutes, steam begins to rise through the lid. Measuring from this time, the beans are steamed for 5 to 5½ hours.

Meanwhile, the assistants prepare the vat in which the miso will be fermented. After constructing a walkway or ramp halfway up the vat's side, they scrub the interior with boiling water and stiff brushes, rinse the walls repeatedly, and

drain the water from a hole at the bottom of one side (or remove it with scooping pans if there is no hole.) The hole plugged, they wipe the vat clean and dry, then sprinkle approximately 1 pound of salt over its bottom. If the vat has a tamari trough it is set in place, its spigot closed.

When the soybeans are done, any logs in the firebox are removed and placed into a covered cinder pot. The soybeans are scooped into some 10 well-washed kegs and carried to the mixing area, together with a larger keg filled with about 40 gallons of boiled water drawn from the caldron. The beans and water are allowed to cool for 5 to 6 hours, or until they can be touched without discomfort (110°F-120°F).

Now all the basic ingredients in kegs around the mixing tub are ready to be combined. One keg each of soybeans and koji are poured into the tub, filling it to about one-half its capacity. While the master mixes the ingredients with a pusher or spade, an assistant rolls up his pantlegs, washes his feet *most* thoroughly and, sometimes, dons rice-straw sandals. Using a pusher to help maintain his balance, he treads the beans and koji underfoot for 2 to 4 minutes.

In an empty keg, meanwhile, the master combines a portion (about 6 quarts) of the seed miso with some of the mixing liquid (11 to 13½ quarts). He then adds the mixture a little at a time to the tub where it is mashed underfoot together with the koji and soybeans. When about half of the soybeans have been mashed and the mixture has approximately the same consistency as mature miso, it is scooped into empty kegs, carried up the ramp, and emptied into the

vat. The mixing and mashing process is repeated until all of the ingredients have been readied and transferred. The tools are carefully cleaned with scrapers, then washed. A layer of burlap sacking or cloth is placed over the unfermented miso during the night.

Preparing Subsequent Batches

For four consecutive days, the men steam soybeans, mash them with koji, and place the mixture into the vat. The latter is filled to within 6 inches of its rim with approximately 4 tons of tan, unfermented miso.

Using a spade, the master levels the miso surface while an assistant (having taken the same sanitary measures as before) treads the miso underfoot to pack it firmly and prevent the formation of air pockets. After extensive packing and a final leveling with the spade, the master lays a plank across the vat's mouth and, kneeling on the plank, proceeds to smooth and level the miso surface with a moistened spatula until it is perfectly flat. After sprinkling 3 cups of salt over the miso's surface (as a mold deterrent), he covers it with burlap sacking (sterilized with steam) which he tucks down firmly around the edges. Both halves of the pressing lid are set atop the sacks and 16 to 18 blocks (each weighing about 55 pounds) are arranged uniformly over the sturdy cross pieces joining the boards which comprise it.

Finally, the craftsmen cover the lid with several more layers of burlap (or, more recently, polyethylene sheeting).

On a large piece of heavy-duty paper the master records the quantities of ingredients he has used, the date, and the expected date of maturity. He attaches this paper to the vat or a nearby wall. The miso is allowed to ferment untouched at the natural temperature of the environment for a minimum of 6 months, including one full summer, and generally for 12 to 18 months.

Harvesting the Miso

When the miso is ready, the craftsmen remove the weights, lid, and sacking. Any tamari that has risen to the surface is ladled into a small keg and reserved. If the vat contains a tamari trough, its spigot is opened and the tamari that has settled to the bottom of the vat is collected, usually for use a mixing liquid in subsequent miso, but also as a household seasoning.

Now a ramp, stairway, or ladder is constructed to a few

feet below the vat's rim, to which a rack is hooked. On the rack are placed several kegs. After the master and his assistants have sampled—and given their approval to—the new miso, one man mounts the ramp. Using the pusher or spade, he mixes the saltier upper layers into the body of the miso, then begins filling the kegs.

After enough miso to meet outstanding orders has been carried to the packing room, the remainder in the vat is recovered with the sacking, but without the lid or weights.

Most of the miso is transferred to 5- or 20-gallon wooden shipping kegs, each sealed with a wooden lid. A small portion is kept for home consumption and gifting purposes.

Making Koji (Using Natural Mold Spores)

In some traditional miso shops, koji starter was not employed until the end of World War II. Rather, the multitudes of naturally-existing mold spores floating in the air inside the shop were used to start the koji fermentation and about 70 hours (as compared with 45 hours using starter) were required to finish it.

On the morning of the first day, freshly steamed barley was spread over a smooth wooden mixing-floor (located in front of the incubation room) which had been carefully wiped clean with a damp cloth. Wearing a special variety of *geta* footwear with stilt-like clogs to raise his feet above the

hot barley and prevent its being mashed, the master stirred the grain with a pusher until it had cooled to the point that it could be touched without discomfort. Having removed his clogs, rolled up his pantlegs, and washed his feet, he then used his toes to flip the barley into the air with each step, thereby hastening its cooling and exposing it to more of the airborne spores. After flipping all the barley, he allowed it to stand for about 3 hours. In the early afternoon, he used the pusher to transfer the barley onto half of the floor, making a layer 6 to 8 inches thick; this helped the barley develop internal heat during its fermentation. The grain was then left to stand uncovered overnight while mold spores settled on it.

On the morning of the second day, the koji incubating room was preheated to between 78°F and 86°F. About 3¼ pounds of barley were placed into each koji tray and the trays were arranged in "vertical stacks" of ten trays each on the floor of the room. If the room or koji were cold, an inverted koji tray was placed atop the stack, and the entire stack was covered with burlap sacking and, if necessary, doused with boiling water. The koji was allowed to stand overnight in the trays, untouched.

Early on the third day, the koji in each tray was mixed by hand as described above, and the trays were then arranged in "slanting stacks." Early on the fourth day, the mixing was repeated, and at the same time on the morning of the fifth, the koji was removed from the trays and mixed with salt. Later that morning the soybeans were cooked. The mixed ingredients were in the vat by nightfall.

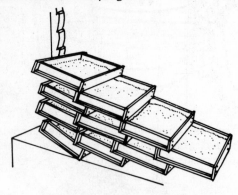

THE SEMITRADITIONAL SHOP

After World War II, many traditional shops began a process of modernization and mechanization in order to compete with large miso factories, increase output and lower labor costs. The resulting semitraditional shop is still much smaller than the modern miso factory, and most of its new equipment is simple and relatively inexpensive. While these electrically-powered machines make it possible to prepare miso with less work in a shorter time, though, they do give a different feeling to the work and result in a less rustic and quiet environment. But the miso-making process itself is almost identical to that used traditionally, and the use of the machines seems to have relatively little effect on the quality of the end-product. Many modernized makers have retained the spirit of traditional craftsmanship and take pride in their work. Some prepare both natural and quick miso, generally serving the former in their own homes and reserving the latter for sale to the many modern Japanese for whom flavor and quality have become less important than cost.

The transition from the traditional to the semitraditional shop was marked primarily by a change in basic equipment. The wood fires (or later fuel-oil burners) used to boil water in the caldron were replaced by a small boiler. Regulated by a time clock, it could be set to have steam ready as soon as the master began work, thereby saving him the time of lighting a fire and waiting for large amounts of water to come to a boil.

One of the boiler's pipes was run into the base of the steamer and used to cook the grain. In some shops, the steam was also used in this way to cook the soybeans, or it was run into the caldron and used to heat the water in which the beans were boiled. However, since cooking the soybeans traditionally took at least 5 hours, many semitraditional shops switched to a steam-heated pressure cooker which did the job in less than 1 hour with no decline in quality.

The time-consuming job of crumbling the finished koji by hand and rubbing it through a strainer was simplified by the use of a small crumbler.

Whereas the soybeans had formerly been mashed by treading them underfoot in a wooden tub, now they were simply run through an extruder or blender, together with a mixture of seed miso and mixing liquid. The same machine, heated by a jacket of circulating hot water, could be used later to pasteurize the miso, although many traditional masters preferred to omit this process.

The traditional wooden mixing tub was replaced by a motor-driven device. Built like a small cement mixer with a stainless steel body, it contained 4 rake-like "blades" that revolve slowly around a vertical axis to mix first the koji and salt, and later the blended soybeans and salted koji. The mixture is removed through a door at the base of the machine.

Finally, a small pneumatic filling machine was used to run the finished miso into polyethylene bags which replaced the traditional 5-gallon wooden kegs; each bag was thermally sealed with a small electric device.

Gradually, wells which were contaminated by industrial pollution came to be replaced with municipal water which almost always contained unwanted chemicals. Lightweight plastic buckets and kegs replaced their wooden forebears. Polyethylene film was used to cover the miso surface in the vats, and the koji incubation room was, in some cases, heated by a thermostat-controlled gas heater. Yet, with all these modifications, the basic process for preparing miso remained essentially unaltered in small shops. The truly fundamental changes were to begin with the rise of modern factories.

Making Hatcho Miso

The process for making Hatcho miso is a unique combination of the best of the traditional and modern techniques. Relatively large-scale, modern equipment is employed for cooking the soybeans and incubating the koji, but the fermentation of the miso takes place in huge cedar vats at the natural temperature of the environment over a period spanning at least two full summers. The finished product, although often packaged in sealed foil bags, is not pasteurized and contains no alcohol, preservatives, or other additives.

Traditionally, the cooked, mashed soybeans were shaped by hand into balls in a manner resembling the preparation of *miso-dama* (p. 193). The finished soybean koji was packed into the fermentation vats only during the cold months (from November to March), whereas now Hatcho miso is made throughout the year and four new vats are filled each week. Their lids piled high with stones, these centuries-old 6-foot-deep vats are housed in barn-like wooden buildings graced by massive arching rafters and high ceilings. The total atmosphere is a breathtaking remnant of an ancient tradition.

Until 1926, the soybean balls were placed on a bamboo gridwork in the attic and inoculated by allowing wild mold spores to settle on them. These were the famous *A. Hatcho* (or *A. oryzae* var. *hatcho*) spores. However, after 1926, regular *A. oryzae* fortified with *Lactobacillus* and purchased from specialty starter-shops in Kyoto and Toyohashi replaced the traditional product. Today, the unique Hatcho flavor comes not from the molds but from the unusual Okazaki climate (hot summers and mild winters); from the soybean koji and small proportion of water used; from the heavy pressing weight and long fermentation time employed; and from the Hatcho-makers' *kura-gusé* (p. 196). Hatcho is indeed difficult to reproduce outside its native birthplace.

Both of Japan's two Hatcho producers use basically the same methodology and equipment. The ingredients required to fill one vat are given below. The basic proportions of raw materials by weight are soybeans 10, salt 2, and mixing liquid 3.4.

> 5,500 pounds whole dry soybeans
> 3¼ cups. *A. oryzae* starter (spore powder)
> 27.5 pounds whole wheat, roasted then ground to a flour
> 1,100 pounds salt
> 1,850 pounds mixing liquid (water)

The dry soybeans are sorted and air-cleaned on a screen vibrator, washed in water, and soaked for 3 hours. After being drained, they weigh about 1.5 times their dry weight. The beans are transferred to a large rotary-type pressure cooker in which they are steamed for 3 to 4 hours; they then stand overnight under pressure.

The entire cooker is rotated on its horizontal axis to empty the cooked beans into a large grinder. Most (or all) of the beans are run through the machine's screw extruder into a metal die and cutter which grinds and shapes them into a three-dimensional "cross" about 2 inches thick and 2¼ inches in diameter; this shape creates a larger surface area for mold growth than if the beans were shaped into balls.

The Hatcho "cross"

Koji starter mold spores are mixed in a sifting machine with the roasted flour, and the soybean "balls" are passed under the sifter on a conveyer to inoculate them. They are then run by conveyor directly into one of several stainless steel incubating rooms, each about 30 by 50 by 7 feet high. Workers using shovels spread the balls to a depth of 1 foot over the stainless steel floors which are permeated with many tiny holes. Modern electronic temperature and humidity control equipment keeps the room's air temperature at 86°F and the temperature inside the koji at about 97°F during the 3 to 4 days of fermentation. At the interior of each ball, anaerobic *Lactobacillus* are actively producing substances which will later contribute to the miso's uniquely tart flavor. At the end of this first fermentation, the surface of each ball is covered with a pale yellowish-green bloom of fragrant mold, and the inside is mosit and brown. The koji balls (now weighing 6,600 pounds) are shoveled onto a conveyer and run between metal rollers in a crusher. In a 2½-foot-diameter, motor-driven mixer, batches of the crushed koji are mixed thoroughly with water and salt.

They are then transferred in wheelbarrows to huge cedar fermentation vats, each with a capacity of about 1,300 gallons. The miso mixture—which fills the vat to about 80 percent of capacity and weighs 9,500 pounds—is covered with a sturdy wooden pressing lid, atop which are piled large stones equal in weight to the total weight of the miso (frontispiece). In the large, unheated and uninsulated wooden buildings, the miso is allowed to ferment through at least 2 full summers. The lengthy fermentation is necessitated by the low percentage of carbohydrates and moisture in the substrate, and the heavy weight which creates a strictly anaerobic environment. The finished miso is removed from the vats on a first-in first-out basis as orders are received. If business is slow, some batches may ferment for 2½ or even 3 full years. The miso is packed into wooden or polyethylene kegs, or foil or polyethylene bags, for distribution.

Making Mellow White Miso

This process, developed in semi-traditional shops in Hawaii, is of particular interest for three reasons: 1) It allows for the preparation of a white and relatively sweet miso using only traditional, natural methods: 2) Low in salt, the miso requires only 1 month to prepare, yet is very delicious; 3) The process is easily adapted to community-scale production.

Steamed, inoculated rice is spread on 7- by 10-foot tables (made of stainless steel or wood and having a 3-inch-high rim around the perimeter), covered with canvas, and allowed to ferment at the natural room temperature—which in Hawaii is, of course, quite warm (77°F to 84°F) and humid; the mixture is stirred 2 or 3 times during the 45-hour koji incubation.

Soybeans (Kanrich variety work well) are soaked for 4 to 5 hours, then boiled for 1 hour at atmospheric pressure; they are then drained and the water discarded. The finished koji, cooked beans, and salt are mixed (without the addition of extra water), puréed in a grinder (which warms the mixture), and packed while still warm into 55-gallon wooden barrels (purchased for $5 each from a company that buys salted salmon in them). A double or triple thickness of heavy white cotton sacking (the type used to make rice sacks) is spread firmly over the miso's surface and tucked down around the edges to help minimize air contact. Atop the pressing lid is placed a 100-pound weight, and the mouth of the barrel is then covered with plastic sheeting to keep out dust. The miso is allowed to ferment at room temperature for 4 weeks. The liquid which accumulates at the surface (*miso-damari*) is removed and the miso packaged in plastic cottage cheese-type containers; no pasteurization, preservatives, or bleach need be used.

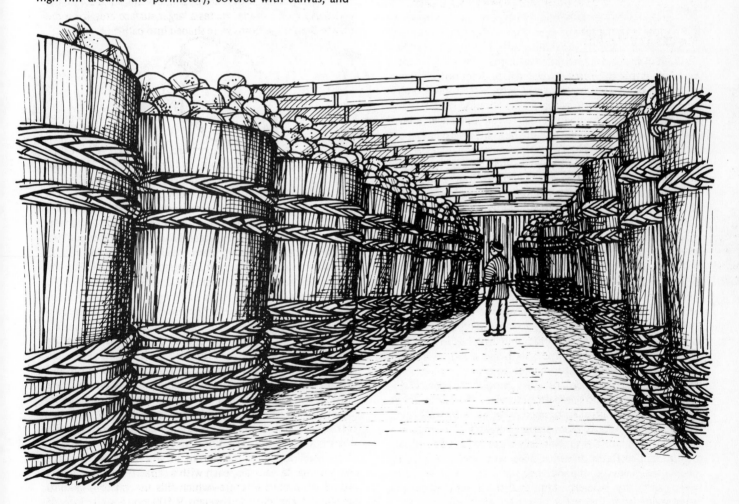

10
The Modern
Miso Factory

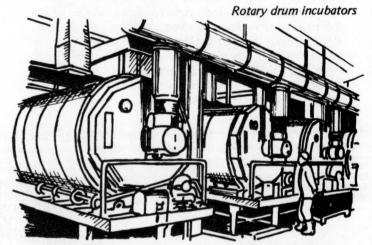

Rotary drum incubators

BEGINNING IN THE mid 1950s, a revolution began in the manufacture of miso. The application of modern technology to the entire miso-making process has resulted in the use of automated equipment, new ingredients, continuous process methodologies and packaging techniques, and new merchandising methods which have profoundly transformed the ancient craft as well as the miso itself.

By 1965, a number of the larger traditional manufacturers had amalgamated to form huge modern companies: twenty three factories had a yearly capacity of at least 4,100 tons each, and the ten largest produced 154,000 tons per year, or about 26 percent of the nation's total output. By 1974, the latter statistic had climbed to 30 percent and individual factories were turning out 264,000 pounds (twenty-two 6-ton vatsful) of miso daily! Today, the names of the "top ten" makers (p. 257) are household words in Japan, for they have been able for the first time in history to generate enough capital to do nationwide advertising via television, printed media, and billboards. Reaping the full benefits of a large-scale, low-margin enterprise, they distribute their standardized products to every part of Japan where they are sold in supermarkets and neighborhood grocery stores at heretofore unbelievably low prices. Recently, they have begun to export to North America and Europe, and one company is even starting a small branch factory in Los Angeles.

The first and perhaps most important technical innovation leading to the modern factory was the development of temperature-controlled fermentation, whereby total aging time could be reduced from one or two years to one month—and in the case of sweet misos, only three or four days! Heating the entire room in which miso was aged required, of course, extra energy expenditures, but the rapid turnover freed capital and space for additional production resulting in great savings.

Due to its quick aging, this miso was, by necessity, much lighter in color than most traditional miso. Aware of the modern Japanese tendency to associate whiteness in foods (bread, rice, sugar) with newness, prestige, and good flavor, the manufacturers added bleach to their product and pressure cooked it using special techniques to make it still whiter. Moreover, by using a large proportion of rice koji, they gave the product a sweet flavor, while further helping to reduce the fermentation time and lighten the color. By the mid 1960s, the sales of light-yellow and mellow beige miso had skyrocketed.

The second great technical innovation was the development of polyethylene bags for packaging. Formerly, all miso had been sold out of kegs at special retail outlets; the shop owner weighed and wrapped the miso for each customer, which of course raised its price. Suddenly, bagged miso was found on the shelves of virtually all food stores. At first, consumers did not realize that the new product contained preservatives (and/or had been pasteurized) to keep the bag from swelling and additional bleach to keep the color from darkening. In fact, it was not until 1975 that the government—in response to growing consumer concern—required makers to list all additives on their labels. Even before this time, however, sales had begun to fall as consumer interest in natural foods gained momentum.

The inside of a modern miso factory, in sharp contrast to its traditional forbear, reminds one of scenes from a science fiction film. Long conveyors carry freshly steamed rice up three floors in a reinforced concrete building. Huge pieces of stainless steel equipment carry out their functions with stopwatch precision in a highly sanitary environment. In research and testing laboratories, scientists in white coats examine mold cultures while engineers refine statistical methods of quality control and time-and-motion studies.

The development of new machinery has played a major role in reducing labor costs and increasing production speed. Electronic feedback systems link the entire process controlling the duration, temperature, and humidity of the various cooking and fermentation processes. The largest and most important pieces of new equipment include: *rotary-type soybean pressure cookers* capable of producing temperatures of 250°F, evenly cooking over 2,500 pounds of beans at a time by slowly rotating as the steam enters, preventing browning by having all their air quickly evaporated with a vacuum pump, and unloading their contents automatically onto a conveyor; *rotary drum incubators*, horizontally-mounted metal cylinders about 12 feet long and 6 feet in diameter, that slowly revolve to mix their load of koji under carefully controlled conditions of temperature and humidity; *continuous process rice and barley steamers*, in which the grain is loaded from chutes onto a stainless-steel mesh conveyor 3 feet wide and 20 feet long and passed slowly through four pressurized steaming chambers; and *automatic packaging machines* that seal miso in polyethylene bags at the rate of 30 per minute. The final mixture of ingredients is fermented in epoxy-lined steel tanks each having a capacity of 12 tons.

A number of new ingredients, too, have come into use since the 1950s, most important of which are pure culture inocula or fortifying agents including salt resistant yeasts and *Lactobacillus*. They serve much the same function as traditional seed miso in reducing the fermentation time and imparting a better flavor and aroma to the miso. As explained in Appendix I, a number of new chemical additives (preservatives, bleach, food coloring, chemical seasonings, artificial sweeteners, and vitamins) are also now employed. Although in the late 1950s up to 30 percent of all soybeans used in Japanese miso were in the form of defatted meal, the figure has fortunately dropped to less than 2½ percent.

The trend toward large-scale production and standardization seems to be slowing in Japan as affluence creates a growing demand for high quality. Yet it remains to be seen whether small, traditional makers can weather the storm.

For detailed descriptions of the equipment and methods used in producing miso in modern factories, see our *Miso Production, The Book of Miso, Volume II.*

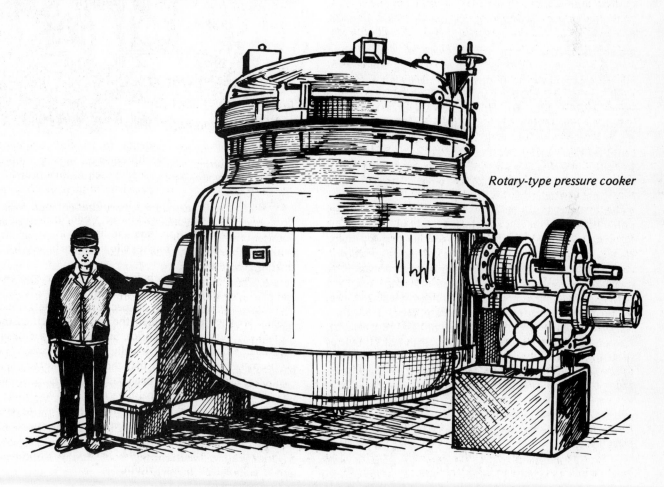

Rotary-type pressure cooker

Appendix A
A History of Miso and Soybean Chiang

THE HISTORY of both miso and soybean chiang is interwoven with the histories of soy nuggets (called *shih* or *tou-ch'ih* in China, *Hamanatto* in Japan, and generally "salted black beans" in the West) and soy sauce. The earliest evidence of soy nuggets is found in archaeological remains in China; they were excavated from the famous Western Han Tomb No. 1 at Ma-wang-tui, located at Ch'ang-sha, Hunan, and sealed in about 168 B.C. (Chang 1977). The earliest known literary reference to soy nuggets is found in the *Historical Records* (Chinese: *Shih chi;* Japanese: *Shiki*) by Ssu-ma Ch'ien, the great historian who died in about 85 B.C. (Watson 1961). Thus it seems likely that soy nuggets, an early ancestor of miso and soybean chiang, were known in China before the Han dynasty (206 B.C. to A.D. 220).

Soy sauce apparently originated in China at about this same time, for the earliest known appearance of the present characters of soy sauce, *chiang-yu*, is also in the *Historical Records (Shih chi)* of 85 B.C. It is not completely clear, however, if this liquid *chiang-yu* was made from a product containing soybeans; it could have been a meat or fish sauce. No clear indication of a soy sauce definitely made from soybeans appears until the time of the *Pen Ts'ao Kang-mu* in 1578 (Li 1965). This gap of 16 centuries raises many questions about the early origins of soy sauce in China. As we shall soon see, soybean chiang, a fermented soybean paste that is a close relative of miso, originated in China in the first century B.C. For most of its early history it was probably used in the form of a paste, rather than being pressed to extract a liquid soy sauce.

A single integrated history of soy nuggets, soy sauce, soybean chiang, and miso is given in the Ballantine edition of our *Book of Miso.* Our main sources of information on the early histories of chiang and miso in East Asia have been our own translations of the following works: Kawamura's *Miso no Hon* (1972; The Book of Miso), Ichiyama's *Kikkoman Shoyu Shi* (1968; History of Kikkoman Shoyu), Kawamura's *Miso Enkaku-shi* (1958; Historical Chronicles of Miso), Motoyama's *Inshoku Jiten* (1971; Encyclopedia of Food and Drink), and Morohashi's *Daikanwa Jiten (1955; Historical Chinese Character Dictionary).*

Etymology: While the general term *chiang*, referring to various pastes, appeared as early as the third century B.C., the first reference to chiang made from soybeans *(tou-chiang)* is found in the *Ch'i-min yao-shu* (Shih 1962) in A.D. 535. Since that time soybean chiang has always been known in standard Chinese (Mandarin) as *tou-chiang* ("bean chiang"); in Pinyin it is called *doujiang.* Other types

of chiang containing soybeans were also developed, as will be discussed later. As *tou-chiang* moved southward into southern China and Southeast Asia it became known as *tau cheung* in Cantonese, as *tau ch'iu* in Hokkien (from Fukien province), as *tauco* (pronounced taucho and formerly spelled tao-tjo; a corruption of the Hokkien for *tou chiang*) in Indonesian, as *tau-cheo* or *tau-chio* in Malaysian, as *tao-chio* or *tau-cheaw* in Thai, and as *tuong* (a term derived from *chiang*) in Vietnamese. To the east, in Korea, it became known as *jang.*

The Chinese word for soy sauce, *chiang-yu*, means "the liquid pressed from chiang." It clearly was derived from the earlier term *chiang.*

Pronounced *chiang* in China and *hishio* in Japan

Pronouned *chiang-yu* in China and *shoyu* in Japan

When the Chinese character *chiang* entered Japan (it first appeared in the *Man'yoshu* in A.D. 686) it was pronounced *hishio* (Pierson 1929). By 730 the character was being pronounced both *hishio* and *misho.* The present word for miso, written with the present characters, first appeared between 886 and 901. A more detailed discussion of the complex evolution of the new term will be given later.

Since miso has no close counterpart among Western foods, it has, since the time of earliest Western contact, usually been referred to in European languages by its Japanese name, *miso.* Only rarely has it been called "soybean paste." Chinese soybean chiang has never been widely known in the West, probably because it is a relatively unimportant food in China and because it is not nearly as appealing as miso to most Westerners. In 1976 Shurtleff and Aoyagi gave the first specific English names for each of the 6 basic types and 28 varieties of Japanese miso, as well as 9 varieties of Chinese chiang, 5 varieties of Korean Jang, and 4 varieties of Indonesian taucho. Miso is now known as *le miso* in French and *das miso* in German.

SOYBEAN CHIANG IN CHINA

Early Chinese Non-Soybean Chiang: Thought to have originated before the Chou dynasty (722-481 B.C.), chiang is undoubtedly the oldest condiment known to man, originally developed as a way of preserving protein-rich animal foods to be used either as seasonings or preserves. In effect, the peoples of East Asia discovered that when seafoods and meat (and, later, soybeans) were salted or immersed in a mixture of salt and rice wine (or water), their protein was broken down by enzymes into amino acids, which in turn stimulated human taste buds, augmenting the flavors of other foods. It was soon found that subsequent fermentation served to deepen and elaborate the primary flavor and aroma of the salt-pickled ingredients. The idea of combining these two distinct preservation techniques into a single process laid the foundation for the later development of miso, and enabled people long ago to break the vicious cycle of feast and famine, conserving foods from times of bounty to be enjoyed in times of scarcity.

The earliest varieties of Chinese chiang were probably made with fish, shellfish, and game. Their flesh—and in some cases bones, blood, and entrails—was ground or crushed, pickled in a mixture of salt and rice wine, and fermented in sealed earthenware vats for 100 days or more. This chiang closely resembled contemporary Asian fermented fish sauces and pastes such as the strong-smelling *nuoc mam* of Vietnam. But it was fundamentally different from modern miso (or shoyu) in that it contained no soybeans, grains, or koji. According to Shinoda (1974), Japan's most respected historian of Chinese foods, the earliest reference to koji appears in the *Shih Ching (Classic of Songs)*, the first of the Chinese Five Classics, consisting of 305 songs dating from the tenth to the seventh centuries B.C. Koji was added to pickled fish mixtures to speed the fermentation. Soybeans and grains were being used as ingredients in chiang by the first century B.C. The consistency of early chiang was probably neither as firm as that of miso nor as liquid as shoyu; rather it more than likely resembled applesauce, porridge, or the mash known as *moromi* from which today's shoyu is pressed. The various types of seafood miso (crab, shrimp, and red-snapper miso) still very popular in Japan are thought to be its direct descendants.

According to the *Daikanwa Jiten*, a remarkable dictionary showing the earliest uses of Chinese characters (Morohashi 1955), the written character for chiang made its first appearance in about the third century B.C. in two unrelated documents, the *Chou-li* (Japanese: *Shurai*) and the *Analects of Confucius (Lun yü)*. It is not clear which of these is the older. In the *Chou-li* (Rituals of the Chou Dynasty, a bureaucratic utopian vision of the administration that supposedly existed in the dynasty's royal court in the sixth to eighth centuries B.C.), chiang is mentioned several times. In the chapter "Contents of the Heavenly Palace Household" *(T'ien Kung Chia Tsai)* it is stated that "One hundred and twenty crocks of chiang were stocked for a party by the Chou government" (Biot 1851, Sun 1966). The work also states: "In preparing the eight basic

types of foods whose qualities harmonize with the four seasons, one should learn to use chiang from the hundred and twenty crocks ... Fasting from all foods is in the spring. Fasting from soups is in the summer. Fasting from chiang is in the autumn. Fasting from drinks is in the winter ... They selected the hundred delicacies, chiang products and rare things to make an offering." The *Chou-li* states that this chiang was made by mixing the meat of animals, birds, and fish with millet koji and salt, then pickling it in wine in a crock for a hundred days. It is quite remarkable that even at this early date the Chinese were consciously using the enzymes produced by the koji molds (whose spores fell on the substrate naturally, rather than by inoculation), to make fermented foods such as chiang and fermented grain-based alcoholic beverages (Sakaguchi 1979). It is also clear from the context that chiang was regarded as a highly prestigious food and a delicacy.

In the *Analects of Confucius (Lun yü*, Scroll 2, Chapter 10; Waley 1966; Lau 1979), chiang appears in a section where the sage is discussing proper etiquette and social behavior, the wise choice of foods, and fasting: "Foods not accompanied by the appropriate variety of chiang should not be served. Rather than using only one to season all foods, you should provide many to ensure harmony with each of the basic food types. Make grains central to your diet. Use wine in moderation to welcome guests, but by no means should you get drunk and act foolish." Confucius (c. 551-479 B.C.) did not write the *Analects* (or any other works); they were compiled by his disciples 100 to 200 years after his death.

In other texts of the same period, we learn that each of the 120 crocks mentioned above contained chiang made with a different combination of ingredients and having a distinctive flavor. One source mentions, for example, mustard chiang and says that it should be eaten only with *sashimi* (raw fish). A Chou dynasty legal document tells us that one government official was appointed director of chiang production, while another was made director of the closely affiliated bureau of medicine and foods.

The character for chiang next appears in several texts of the second or third century B.C. The *Chan Kuo*, in the section "The Intrigues of Eastern Chou," states that "Caldrons are not like pickle pots or chiang jars. If you pick up one and try to go to Ch'i, you will not get there as quick as a bird flying or a rabbit jumping or a horse galloping." This suggests that the containers in which chiang was pickled were relatively small. Five types of meat or fish chiang are mentioned in the *Li Chi* or *Record of Rituals* (Japanese: *Reiki*), the last of the Confucian Five Classics. This suggests the food's high status.

Chiang is next mentioned in the *Historical Records* (Chinese: *Shih chi;* Japanese: *Shiki*) by Ssu-ma Ch'ien, the great historian, who died in about 85 B.C. In "The Record of Prosperity" chapter it is stated that "Throughout Ta-i [possibly a district in today's Szechuan] in one year, one thousand fermented products and one thousand crocks of pickles and chiang are made. This is equivalent to a house of a thousand chariots (i.e. a dukedom)" (Watson 1961). Chiang is also mentioned in Chapter 135 (*Huo Ch'ih*

Lieh Chuan or "List of Various Products"); this is almost certainly a meat or fish chiang paste. The book also notes that in 140 B.C. a traveler in Canton ate a fermented food called *ku-chiang* prepared with a sweet wild fruit and probably resembling today's Kinzanji miso, but containing no soybeans. Since Canton was thousands of miles from the imperial capital at Chang-an and since we are told that this chiang was made in a remote town upstream from it, we may assume that the process for preparing various types of chiang was known throughout much of China before the Christian era. In this reference we also have the first known description of a chiang made without meat or fish.

The *Han Shu*, written by Pan Ku circa A.D. 90, stated in "The Collated Records of Yang Hsiung" section that the students of that age were such ignorant materialists that in the future, they might even use the sacred Taoist books "to cover chiang jars." The *Han shu* also mentioned the use of a starter *(chü)* in making two types of rice wines, *li* and *chiu*.

Early Chinese Soybean Chiang (*tou-chiang;* 100 B.C.-A.D. 599). The first reference to the use of soybeans as the basic protein source in chiang, as a substitute for the previously used meat and fish, appeared in the *Chi Chiu P'ien*, written by Shih Yu during the first century B.C. It stated, "Soy nuggets *(shih)* are made from black beans... chiang is made from (soy) beans and wheat flour... Wheat, rice, and (soy) bean gruel are what the country people and farmers eat." In the *Lun Heng*, written by Wang Chung in approximately A.D. 27-100, in the "Four Taboos" section, it is stated that "it is bad to hear thunder when making soybean chiang *(tou chiang)*." One wonders if it was believed that the thunder's static electricity affected the fermentation process.

The first detailed description of the process for making soybean chiang appeared in the *Ch'i-min yao-shu*, a remarkable ten fascicle agricultural encyclopedia, written in about A.D. 533 to 544 (Shih 1962). All of the fascicles 7 and 8 are about fermented foods and there is a long section on "Chiang." It states that the culture used for making chiang was called *huang-i* (yellow coating), *huang-cheng* (yellow mold) and *mai-yuan* (wheat must). These cultures of *Aspergillus* or *Rhizopus* molds were propagated on steamed wheat grains inoculated by spores that were airborne or attached to the leaves of certain plants (*Phragmites* or *Xanthium*). After describing the preparation of meat chiang and fish chiang, the *Ch'i-min yao-shu* stated that soybean chiang was prepared by fermenting a mixture of 30 parts presoaked steamed soybeans, 10 parts powdered wine starter, 10 parts yellow mold, and 5 parts white table salt. After incubation for three to five weeks (depending on the weather), the mixture ripened as a stock (now called chiang chiao). Thirty percent by volume of salt solution was then stirred into this and the mixture fermented for 100 days for best flavor, although it could be eaten after 20. It was thought that if a pregnant woman touched it during fermentation, it would go bad. In one place, the book advised making chiang during the twelfth and first months of the lunar calendar (January-February); in another it recommended fermentation under the hot summer sun. It also described the preparation of Chinese koji (called

ch'u or *k'u*) to produce fermented alcoholic beverages from millet or rice, and the preparation of "chiang-pickled vegetables" *(chiang tsai),* made by pickling half-dried vegetables in fermenting or well-fermented soybean chiang (Shih 1962).

During this period the Chinese learned to preserve a number of foods by pickling them in chiang: tofu was pickled to make *chiang toufu*, white uri melon to make *chiang kua*, and pork to make *chiang jou*. The use of soybeans in all of the above preparations marked a major step in the development of today's miso and shoyu. The early mention of soybean chiang in the *Chi Chiu P'ien* and *Lun Heng*, and the detailed description of this chiang's preparation in the *Ch'i-min yao-shu* indicate that the basic techniques for making soybean chiang had probably been established before the second century B.C.

These early varieties of Chinese chiang were used primarily as a seasoning. Their consistency was midway that of today's miso and soy sauce, resembling an applesauce or porridge. Considered both nutritious and tasty, they were popular daily foods, highly esteemed by all classes of people, and used as a dressing for cooked vegetables or grains (typically mixed with other ingredients such as vinegar or a sweetener), or for pickling.

The development of fermented soyfoods, a process that depends on a rather sophisticated (intuitive and conscious) understanding of microbiology and fermentation technology, was a remarkable achievement in the early history of China. It is also remarkable that the Chinese recognized and deliberately cultivated at least two types of molds, *Aspergillus* and *Rhizopus*, and used them to produce enzymes. The *Rhizopus* processes, used with soybeans or barley to make chiang or soy nuggets (both having koji with a crumbly consistency), were never transmitted to Japan. (The Japanese, however, developed a way for making saké with *Rhizopus* that was not found in China.)

600 to 1899: During the T'ang dynasty (618 A.D.-906 A.D.) chiang was referred to as the "ruler of foods" and in one well-known ceremony, a tray bearing its many varieties was placed on the palace altar, before which the Emperor showed his respect by formally bowing in public. A special official was appointed to guard the Imperial Household's supply as it fermented so that no one could steal the secrets of its production. In the *T'ang Shu* (The Old Book of T'ang, written by Liu Hsu, A.D. 887-946) at the "Records of the Hundred Officials" chapter it is stated that "In the department of the controller of pickles are 23 chiang craftsmen, 12 vinegar craftsmen, and 12 soy nugget *(shih)* craftsmen." The *Liu Shu Ku* written by Tai T'ung of the Sung dynasty (960-1126) noted cynically, "Nowadays people let soybeans and wheat go yellow, throw in some salt and water, and consider it chiang." Here we see mention of the use of both wheat and soybeans in chiang, the forerunner of today's shoyu. An early mention of the Chinese equivalent of miso soup appears in the *T'an Yuan*, written by Huang Chien in roughly 1027 A.D. "Someone asked if the people and officials of Hsiu-shui and Ch'ing-te were clear (i.e. honest). He replied, 'they are the color of *chiang shui* ("chiang water")—not clear and not thick (i.e.

corrupt)." This *chiang shui,* pronounced *shosui* in Japanese, later became the famous Zosui, a miso porridge. During the Southern Sung dynasty (1127-1279), chiang (probably soybean chiang) was considered one of the "Seven Necessities" in China. The other six were firewood, rice (or grain), oil, salt, vinegar, and tea.

The *Pen ts'ao kang mu,* a large and famous collection of botanical and medical writings by Li Shih-chen (1578, Ming Dynasty), mentioned various types of chiang, including soybean chiang, wheat chiang, and wheat & soy chiang. It mentioned five types of illnesses for which chiang was considered a potent remedy.

The *Kuang yang tsa chi,* written by Liu Hsien-t'ing during the late 17th century stated: "So if the sage did not get his chiang, he would not eat," attesting to the continued importance of chiang in the culture.

The Twentieth Century: Surprisingly little has been published about soybean chiang in China during the 20th century, although it still plays a very important role in the diet of the people.

The Englishman Shaw (1911) in Manchuria stated that "Chinese paste (chiang) is not the same article of diet as the Japanese paste miso. It is made by farmers, and eaten with fish, meat, and vegetables, while the more expensive soy (sauce) is only made by wealthy families and restaurant keepers and is not consumed by the very poor. There are two kinds of chiang: *ta* (great) and *hsiao* (small)." For great chiang, soybeans were boiled until soft, mashed in a mortar, shaped into flat cakes, and fermented on mats for 2 months. They were then ground to a powder, mixed with salt water, and fermented in a vat, with occasional stirring, for 15 days. The same method was used for small chiang, except that equal parts soybeans and maize (corn) were used in place of just soybeans.

In 1918 Shih in China wrote in detail about "Tou Chiang or Bean Sauce" but stated that it was generally made the "Water White Bean, *Phaseolus vulgaris.*" No mention of soybeans was made in the article, which described the fermentation process in detail.

The most detailed information seen on Chinese chiang is Nakayama's *Chugoku Meisaifu* (1973), published in four volumes in Japanese. It describes the numerous types of chiang and gives many recipes. Little else is known about the present status of the chiang industry or market in China. In the USA chiang is not nearly as widely known or used as Chinese soy sauce or Japanese miso, and only a few types (such as bean sauce and hoisin sauce) are mentioned in U.S. Chinese cookbooks, and then not frequently. Apparently it does not appeal to most American palates.

One interesting innovation is that in Taiwan the okara or soy pulp remaining from manufacture of soymilk or tofu is now sometimes used as an extender for soybeans in making miso.

The main varieties of soy-based Chinese chiang today are chunky soybean chiang *(tou-pan chiang),* hot chunky soybean chiang *(la tou-pan chiang),* Szechuan red-pepper soybean chiang *(ssu-ch'uan tou-pan chiang),* soy nugget chiang *(tou-ch'ih chiang),* and black soybean chiang *(hei chiang).*

SOYBEAN CHIANG IN KOREA AND SOUTHEAST ASIA

Dissemination of Chiang from China: By the early T'ang dynasty (618-906 A.D.), soybean chiang and soy sauce (the liquid seasoning extracted from chiang) had begun to move out of China into adjoining countries. There is considerable evidence that Buddhist priests played a key role in taking soybean chiang eastward into Korea and Japan, while Chinese traders from Canton and the surrounding Kwantung province, and from Fukien province were instrumental in disseminating it southward. As it entered new cultures, both its basic character and its name were altered slightly. Unfortunately, very little has been published about the history of soybean chiang as it entered the various countries surrounding China, except for Japan.

The various relatives of chiang in Southeast Asia are much more closely related to Chinese chiang in consistency (like applesauce) and flavor (strongly flavored) than to Japanese miso. As in China, most continue to be made non-commercially at home for home use, and they are most widely used as a base for sauces served with meat, seafood, poultry, or vegetable dishes, rather than as a soup base like Japanese miso. A detailed description of all the basic chiang-type foods with production information is given in Appendix B.

Korea: Korean records from A.D. 680 indicate that *jang* (soybean chiang) and *kan jang* (soy sauce) had entered the country in the customary exchange of gifts between ruling houses (Wang and Lee 1978). Today the main soy-based varieties of Korean jang are Korean soybean jang *(doen jang),* red-pepper soybean chiang *(kochu jang),* mild red-pepper soybean chiang *(mat jang),* and Japanese red jang *(wei jang* or *ilbon jang).* Traditional Korean miso is basically soybean miso, made by cooking and mashing soybeans, shaping them into 6-inch balls, tying these with strands of rice straw under the eves or rafters for 1 to 3 months until they are covered with a white bloom of mold. They are then crumbled to make *meju,* which serves as the base of jang or soy sauce.

Early Japanese mention a miso-like product or hishio from Korea. The *Wamyosho* (903-938), the earliest dictionary of the Japanese language referred to a Korean product called *koma-bishio,* a fermented soy and/or grain hishio. This product was further discussed in the *Honcho Shokkan* of 1695. While it is doubtful that miso came to Japan from Korea, it is very likely that Japanese miso and its name were influenced by its Korean forbears.

In 1976 in Korea, per capita daily consumption of soybean jang and red-pepper soybean jang were 15 grams and 10 grams respectively. Some 82% and 76% of each product respectively were produced in farmhouses and urban dwellings, and consumed directly by the families that made them (Wang and Lee 1978, Choe and Song 1960). Lee (1976) has given a detailed description of making Korean soybean jang and soy sauce.

Indonesia: The earliest reference to a relative of chiang in Southeast Asia was by the Dutch scientist Prinsen Geerligs in 1895 and 1896. He described Indonesian taucho, calling it *tao tsioe* in his Dutch article of 1895 and *tao tjiung* (after *tou-chiang*) in his German article of 1896. He indicated that the soybeans were inoculated with hibiscus leaves, called *waroe*. Ochse (1931) gave a detailed description of taucho, which he spelled *taotjo*. Burkill (1935) mentioned "*tao-cho*" saying that the cooked soybeans were mixed with roasted rice flour, then arenga palm sugar and a paste of glutinous rice.

The main soy-based varieties of Indonesian taucho, listed in order of popularity are soft sweet taucho (taucho Chianjur, which contains 25% by weight of palm sugar), salty liquid taucho (also called black bean sauce, a relative of *tausi*), firm dired taucho (*taucho kering*, sold in sun-dried cakes), and smoked dried taucho. Taucho is produced and consumed mainly in West Java, the center of production being the town of Chianjur, located midway between Bogor and Bandung. Figures on production and distribution have been given by Winarno (1976). Popular recipes include Sambal Goreng Taucho and Oseng-Oseng Taucho.

Vietnam: Vietnamese chiang is called tuong. The best and earliest description of tuong and its manufacture in North Vietnam (Tonkin) was given by BUI Quang Chieu (1905) and later summarized by Li (1912). Bui described two basic types of tuong, made with roasted soybeans and either glutinous rice or corn. For that made with glutinous rice: steam glutinous rice, cover on trays with banana leaves, and leave for 2 to 3 days until it molds to form koji *(moc)*. Roast the soybeans, grind to a powder, boil with water, and put in a jar for 7 days until sweet from autohydrolysis and fermentation. Then add salt plus 6 parts of the rice koji to 5 parts of the soy, ferment for 15 to 30 days, stirring before sunrise and covering at night; serve without filtering off the liquid. Tuong comes with either a chunky or a very smooth consistency; the chunky *(tuong ban)* is the most popular, while the smooth is made only in Cu-da, North Vietnam. A good tuong is mellow, thick, and brown; it is sweeter and smoother than *nuoc mam* fish sauces. Annamites (from central south Vietnam) say that only prosperous households succeed in making tuong. If tuong begins well but then sours, this is a bad omen. According to Mr. Hoang Van Chi (1981), owner of the first company to make smooth tuong in the West, since about 1950 there has been no soy tuong in North Vietnam because of a shortage of soybeans and rice caused by the protracted anticolonial war, and by the fact that the pre-Communist soy sauce makers were classified as landlords. Starting in the late 1970s efforts began to make soy sauce with peanut or cottonseed presscake.

Other Southeast Asia: Soybean chiang has long been used in Malaysia (where it is called *tau-cheo* or *tau-chio)* and in Thailand (where it is called *tao-chio* or *tau-cho cheaw)*, but little is known of the history or present status of these products.

HISTORY OF MISO IN JAPAN

The origins of miso are not clear, although most scholars agree that its earliest progenitor came from either China or Korea. Some set the date of arrival in Japan at shortly before the introduction of Buddhism (540-552 A.D.), whereas others feel that the lack of definite records demands the more conservative estimate of 663 A.D. The miso transmitted from Korea is thought to have been prepared using the *miso-dama* technique whereby cooked soybeans were mashed, shaped into balls, and inoculated with wild mold spores to form the koji. Crushed and mixed with salt and water, the balls were then fermented in crocks to make a variety of soybean miso. This special tradition, though largely unrecorded, is thought to have been the origin of much of Japan's earliest farmhouse miso. The product brought from China, on the other hand, is believed to have gained its first acceptance among the nobility and in monasteries.

Early Non-Soybean Hishios (Before A.D. 700): There is evidence that long before the arrival of miso-like foods from China and Korea, the Japanese had independently developed their own varieties of fermented sauces, resembling Chinese chiang and based on fish, shellfish, and meat. The earliest inhabitants of Japan were hunters and gatherers who are said to have arrived about 20,000 years ago. Long before the Chrisitan era, they learned to extract salt from sea water, and their earliest seasonings consisted of this natural salt, together with *sansho* pepper and ground shellfish. Starting in the late Jomon period and continuing through the succeeding Yayoi period (200 B.C.-25 A.D.), however, fish and meat sauces basically similar to chiang were independently developed, as attested to by pickling crocks recently excavated in the northeastern provinces and dating back 3,000 to 4,000 years. The Japanese word for these primordial seasonings was *hishio* (or *hishiho*), and when the first writing system was introduced from China, it was written with the character for chiang.

A number of these Japanese hishios (each made without the use of koji) can still be found: *shiokara* is squid, squid intestines, or bonito pickled in a mixture of mirin and salt; *shottsuru* (from Akita) is sardines and hard-finned *hatahata* pickled in salt; *shuto* is salted bonito intestines pickled in sake; and *gyoeki* is fermented fish liquid. Two lesser-known relatives are *ikanago shoyu* from Kagawa and *kurozukuri* from Hokuriku. (Ancient Rome had a similar fermented sauce called "garum," an ancestor of anchovy sauce.) All are aged for one week or more and served as toppings for rice or as hors d'oeuvres. Throughout the northerly regions characterized by long snowy winters and severe flooding, they have also long been used as emergency food staples (Kawamura 1972).

Today, the northeastern provinces are known as the "miso heartland" of Japan; the per-capita consumption there is the highest in the nation and the ancient homemade-miso tradition is still very much alive. These facts, combined with the archeological evidence indicating early mastery of salt-pickling and fermentation, move some scholars to go so far as to trace the origins of miso (and shoyu) to this part of Japan rather than to China or Korea.

The Nara Period (A.D. 710-784): The first written records of miso and hishio date from the Nara period; no documents or legends from before this time mention any varieties of fermented foods. And, strangely enough, no mention is made of them in either the *Kojiki* (712 A.D.)

or *Nihonshoki* (720 A.D.), which do mention soybeans and were written more than ten years after miso and a closely related variety of hishio are known to have been produced at the Imperial Palace.

One of the first references to this hishio appears in the *Man'yoshu,* an extraordinary collection of thousands of Japan's earliest songs and poems recorded from as early as the year 315 A.D. and compiled circa 760. In most of the poems, the Japanese words are elaborately spelled out with Chinese characters used phonetically. The character for hishio (chiang) appears in scroll 16 in a poem by Imiki Okimaru (686-707), a humorous bard who improvised at banquets for the court nobility. We and Pierson (1929) translate this as:

I want to eat red snapper *(tai)*
With a dressing of minced garlic and vinegar-hishio
So do not offer me a leek soup.

Another poem describes two comic crabs happily making themselves into crab hishio seasoned with pounded elm bark. Mention is also made of hishio containing wild game and deer meat. Unfortunately we are not told exactly what type of product this hishio was nor how it differed from miso and chiang, yet it is now generally believed that all of these products were well known at this period among the nobility and, to a lesser extent, the common people.

During the first several centuries of contact with the continent, miso and hishio were probably very similar to chiang, and many of the basic raw materials and complex fermentation techniques were undoubtedly acquired largely from the Chinese. However, Japanese and Chinese taste preferences have always been fundamentally different, the Chinese preferring to use relatively large amounts of spices, oil, and meat in their strongly flavored cookery and the Japanese preferring the simpler, more subtle flavors inherent in the foods themselves. Gradually, therefore, by altering the basic ingredients and preparatory techniques, the Japanese began to transform chiang into foods uniquely suited to their own tastes. Soybeans—used alone or together with rice or barley—came to be preferred to fish or meat as the basic ingredient, while wine and spices were generally reduced in quantity or omitted. Hishio probably retained much the same applesauce-like texture as chiang, but miso slowly evolved into a firmer product with a shorter aging time. Of the two foods, hishio was probably the more important and more varied. Both were initially served primarily as toppings for rice; the hishio still widely prepared in country farmhouses continues to be served mostly in this way.

Perhaps the most important event in the early development of miso and hishio was the establishment in 701 of the *Hishio Tsukasa* or Bureau for the Regulation of Production, Trade, and Taxation of Hishio and Miso, which was originally an annex of the emperor's kitchen *(kunaicho daishokuzen),* where hishio was made. Inaugurated by the Emperor Monmu in the *Taiho Ritsuryo* (Taiho Law Codes, one of Japan's earliest constitutions, which went into effect in 702), this bureau was located in the Imperial Palace. Using methods very similar to those developed in China, it transformed soybeans into high- and low-quality hishio, miso, and soy nuggets. These foods were consumed by the Imperial Household.

Another early reference to hishio, perhaps a soy-based product, appeared in the *Yoryo Ritsuryo,* written by Fujiwara Fuhito in 718. It mentioned various types of chiang and soy nuggets, plus *misho,* the second character of which was *chiang* (Ichiyama 1968).

The most detailed information to date on the early relatives of miso and the first clear reference to a soybean hishio appeared in the Todaiji Shosoin documents, written between 730 and 748, and still preserved in excellent condition in the Imperial Treasury of the Shosoin, connected with Nara's Todaiji temple. It records that in 730 taxes were being paid on hishio and on misho (a variety of hishio and an early relative of miso). A document from the next year mentions the same foods again. A document written prior to 748 clearly referred to soybean hishio (Ichiyama 1968). In a document of 740, first mention is made of *kasu hishio,* which may have been the lees remaining after the extraction of tamari. Records of about 750 show the following relative prices: highgrade hishio 15 *mon,* hishio 10.7 *mon,* ara-bishio 10 *mon,* and miso 7 to 8 *mon.* They also indicate that miso and hishio were sold in the markets of Nara; prices calculated on the basis of 1 *sho* (about 1.8 liters or 2 quarts) reveal that they were relatively inexpensive. These various fermented foods were most commonly written with the following characters; note that even the word "miso" contains the ideograph for hishio (chiang), indicating both origin and relationship:

Miso   Rice Hishio   Ara-bishio   Soy Nuggets

Much of Nara's miso was used at temples to provide free meals for the monks and laymen who donated their time to hand-copy Buddhist scriptures. Small quantities were used in side dishes and *aemono* (mixed salads) as well as with pickles, noodle dishes, *mochi,* and soups. Many of these preparations were served to the laborers who built Todaiji temple, then the largest wooden building in the world, and its immense cast statue of Buddha, the *Daibutsu,* which was completed the year 752.

One of the most colorful chapters in the history of miso concerns the great Chinese T'ang dynasty Buddhist master Chien-chen (Japanese: Ganjin). The founder of the Japanese Ritsu or "precepts" sect and of the well-known Toshodaiji temple in Nara, Ganjin spent over eleven years trying to reach Japan. After being blocked by pirates, shipwrecks, and storms, and having lost his eyesight during one of his six attempted crossings, he finally reached the

Buddhism-dominated Japanese court in 754 at the age of 66. The records of his ship's cargo show that in addition to 185 monks, sailors, and craftsmen, he brought with him 1,428 gallons of salt-free soy nuggets *(kan shih)*. Later records show that this same fermented soyfood was prepared at his temple in Nara, carried by foot to Kyoto, and peddled there in the streets.

It is not clear exactly what type of food Ganjin's salt-free soy nuggets were. They probably resembled soybean koji, but it is not clear what kept them from spoiling or how they were served or used in foods. Nevertheless, Ganjin is widely reputed to have brought the progenitor of Japanese miso to Japan from China. Yet records show that something called "miso" was already being sold in Nara's markets more than 20 years before Ganjin's arrival. Hence, some scholars have concluded that the popular "Ganjin theory" probably reflects more of a desire on the part of early miso makers and Buddhist priests to link their product to Ganjin's lofty reputation than to historical fact.

One of the key links in the transmission from China to Japan of the techniques for preparing the different varieties of chiang was the *Ch'i-min yao-shu*, the 6th-century encyclopedia mentioned above, which arrived in Japan during the late 700s. Its ten fascicles describe the preparation of koji, soy (and barley) nuggets, and numerous varieties of chiang. From it, the Japanese learned how to prepare red-snapper miso, crab miso, *yuzu* miso, savory soy nuggets (Hamanatto), and products closely related to Kinzanji miso. A veritable treasurehouse of accurate and detailed information, this tome had a profound effect on the development of Japanese farming methods and crafts as well as food preparation.

One of the historical puzzles concerning the early development of miso in Japan involves the origin of sweet white miso, which is still the favorite in the area of Japan's earliest capitals (Nara and Kyoto) and along the northern shores of the inland sea. The pattern of miso consumption in this area is very different from that of the rest of Japan: miso soup is relatively uncommon, only about one-third as much miso is consumed per capita as in Japan as a whole, and white miso's sweet flavor and light color are preferred to the regular miso's dark saltiness. These facts have given rise to the theory that at a very early period, sweet white miso was brought from China to the ancient Japanese capitals where it continued to preserve its aristocratic mien and distinctive usage in cookery.

Documents written near the end of the Nara period describe more than 22 varieties of hishio, miso, and soy nuggets. Of these, hishio was by far the most diversified, yet all its 15 or more varieties were generally grouped into three basic types:

1. *Fish, Shellfish, and Wild Game Hishio (Shishibishio):* Generally prepared by pickling crabs, sea urchins, or shrimp in a mixture of salt, water and sake. Deer meat, eggs and, occasionally, fowl were also used.
2. *Vegetable and Fruit Hishio (Kusa-bishio):* Foods such as *uri* melon, eggplant, *daikon*, green leafy vegetables, *kabu* turnips, *udo*, fresh green soybeans, *mizunegi* onions,

peaches and apricots pickled with salt and fermented. In some cases, vinegar and/or *mizuamé* sweetening was used with or in place of the salt. These preparations later evolved into *tsukemono* (salted pickles) and the various types of finger lickin' miso. During this period the first miso pickles were made using *uri* melons and eggplants.

3. *Soybean and/or Grain Hishio (Koku-bishio):* The last type of hishio to develop, these products contained soybeans, grain (rice, wheat, or barley), salt, and often sake or sake lees. The Chinese equivalent of this fermented soyfood was called *kara hishio* and that from Korea was called *komabishio* ("high-elegant hishio"). These three foods evolved into today's miso and shoyu.

The Heian Period (A.D. 794-1160): One of Japan's great Buddhist pioneers was Kukai (best known by his posthumos title Kobo Daishi). He went to T'ang China from 804 to 806, and in 816 founded a great Shingon monastery on Mt. Koya. In 811 he wrote a letter to Emperor Saga which concluded, "I made a mess writing on this white cloth you gave me, so please use it as a lid for your hishio." This indicates that hishio was widely popular at that time.

At the beginning of the Heian period, the word "miso" suddenly began to be written with a new combination of characters, which is used to this day. The character for "mi" meant "flavor" and the one for "so" meant throat. This second character was, itself, a Japanese invention and is presently used in no other words. It first appeared in an official Japanese document of 806 in connection with a food called *enso,* a salt seasoning. According to Kawamura (1972), the modern word "miso" made its first appearance in the *Sandai Jitsuroku,* a history book by Ogura Yoshiyuki that was published between 901 and 908 but had been widely circulated in manuscript form since 886. Ichiyama (1968), however, says that the modern word for miso first appeared in the *Fuso Ryakuki* of 938. The new word was written like this, just as it is to this day:

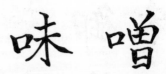

We may well inquire why the Japanese of this period deliberately invented a new character to replace the character chiang (hishio) that had been used during the previous two centuries, and why they introduced the character meaning "flavor" into the combination. It seems likely that by this time the Japanese had so thoroughly transformed chiang into a food suited to their own culture and tastes, that they felt it deserved a uniquely Japanese name. In fact, the *Sandai Jitsuroku* portrays miso as a truly Japanese food rather than as simply a Chinese import. But there were broader cultural changes too behind the change in characters. In 894, at the beginning of the Heian period, Japan essentially cut off contact with the outside world, and began an extended period of assimilating and transforming Chinese cultural imports. During this period, Japan also developed the *hiragana* and *katakana* writing styles, which were completed in the 10th century. It was as part of this larger cultural transformation that the change in miso and its characters took place.

Scholars generally agree that miso finally achieved its own identity during the 100 years prior to the emergence of its new name. Yet traditional writing habits were slow to change, and as late as the 18th century, the word miso was still written most frequently using the character for hishio or chiang, rather than the new Japanese *so*. The combination would have meant "hishio with a lot of flavor *(mi)*." The character for hishio could also have been pronounced *sho*, as it is in the word "shoyu." Thus if the combination were pronounced *misho*, it could have been the forerunner of the word "miso." The word "shoyu" would not appear for another 700 years.

Some scholars believe that the pronunciation "miso" originated with the *Wamyosho* (also called *Wamyo Ruijusho*), the earliest dictionary of the Japanese language, encyclopedic in scale and written between 903 and 938 by Minamoto no Shitagau. It was modeled after Chinese dictionaries and listed many types of hishio including ones pronounced *"miso," "misho,"* and *"kara hishio."* It also mentioned soy nuggets.

The earliest Japanese document to contain information about the production of miso and hishio was the *Engi Shiki,* an elaboration of old law codes, compiled in about 927 by Fujiwara Tokihira and others. In it we are told that miso was a fermented food with soybeans as its main ingredient, but also containing rice, rice koji, wheat, salt, and saké. The *Engi Shiki* gave detailed information about the Hishio Tsukasa government bureau, stated that hishio was given to the Emperor's civil and military officials as part of their annual wage, and listed at least ten different types of miso and hishio. Among these, the word "miso" was written using at least five different character combinations, all of which were pronounced "miso," or perhaps occasionally "misho."

It is not always clear whether each of these names refers to a different food, or whether the name of a single variety was simply being written with different character combinations. The book gives the amounts of basic raw materials used in preparing numerous different types of miso and hishio, but most of the quantities appear quite inaccurate

and cannot be used experimentally to make the products they describe.

Although notebooks dating from as early as the 8th century reveal that miso was bought and sold in the marketplaces of the former capital at Nara, the first shops specializing in its sale are said to have originated in about 925 in the new capital at Kyoto. The *Engi Shiki* records the presence of a miso retail shop in Kyoto's western market and a hishio outlet in the eastern market. Moreover, 50 other shops are reported to have carried hishio, and 32 miso, as one among numerous other foods. Thus by the middle of the 10th century, it seems that hishio and miso were becoming basic staples.

The *Engi Shiki* also mentions *kasu-hishio* and *hishio-kasu.* Perhaps the former was lightly pressed, yielding a smaller amount of the shoyu-like liquid, so that the moist residue could be used as a seasoning. And perhaps the latter was very firmly pressed, yielding more liquid and a dry presscake, which was discarded.

The *Utsuho Monogatari* (911-983) mentioned *kasu miso.* In the *Utsubo Monogatari* of 969, the word "miso" was first written in kana script, thus clearly indicating the pronunciation.

Records from the year 980 show that monks in Nara's Todaiji temple were provided with a large daily supply of miso which was used in mixed salads *(aemono),* foods simmered in seasoned broths *(nimono),* and soups. Meanwhile, Chinese-educated monks in other Nara temples had begun to prepare Kinzanji, abalone, and red-snapper miso.

In the epics of the Heian period, such as the *Tale of Genji* and *Konjaku Monogatari,* are found descriptions of all-night parties held by the court nobility in the Imperial palace. A typical dinner consisted of seven courses, each served consecutively on separate trays. Popular foods included abalone miso and red-snapper hishio, *uri* melons and eggplants pickled in miso, and red snapper, carp or other sea foods lightly marinated with miso sauces. Both hishio and miso were also apparently widely used as table seasonings. Among the palace women, miso was known as *ko,* meaning "fragrance or incense," or *higurashi* meaning "a clear-toned summer cicada" whose song is said to be able to penetrate even the hardest stone. Likewise the rich fragrance and fine flavor of miso were said to penetrate and season other foods. For this reason, in the Kyoto area miso is still occasionally called *mushi* or *bamushi* meaning "insect or honorable insect."

By the middle of the 10th century, miso-making had spread from the capital to the countryside. The *Wamyosho* (903-938) tells us that miso was being produced in the prefectures and usually bore the name of the area in which it was made: Shiga miso and Hida miso, still enjoyed to this day, were among the early favorites.

The Kamakura Period (1185-1333): In 1185, with the beginning of the Kamakura period, a great revolution occurred in Japan. A new and vital government, composed largely of samurai, took away control of the country from the degenerate and effete ruling aristocracy in Kyoto, and established its capital in remote Kamakura, just south of present-day Tokyo. Buddhism awoke as a new spiritual force, aimed at showing the common people how they could attain enlightenment by a simple life based on daily religious practice, faith, and meditation. Out of the basic, lean Buddhist lifestyle evolved a simple yet healthful way of eating which became the standard Japanese diet. A typical meal consisted of a large serving of cooked grain (rice, barley, or millet) accompanied by the newly discovered *takuan* (salt-pickled *daikon*) and miso soup containing tofu and vegetables.

Thus among miso historians the Kamakura period is famous as the the period in which miso soup developed. A preparation then unknown among the Japanese aristocracy and still unknown in China, it came to be a symbol of the "food of the people." Miso, tofu, and deep-fried tofu *(age)* became the basic, favorite foods both among the ruling Shoguns (Generalissimos) and in the Zen temples. Many Zen temples established shojin vegetarian restaurants within their own compounds as a way of making contact with the common people; here meatless meals, generally including a soup containing miso made at the temple, were served at reasonable prices in a quiet atmosphere of refined simplicity and beauty. Almost all temples made their own miso and gradually taught the process to people throughout the country, until in the hearts of many, the flavor of miso and the "flavor" of Zen became the same. In times of famine, the miso stored in large quantities in most farmhouses and city homes served as a lifesaving staple. Soon the saying *miso sae areba*, "Everything's all right as long as there is miso," came to be heard everywhere. Hence it was under the new Buddhist influence of the Kamakura period that the consumption of hishio containing fish or animal-derived products steadily declined, and that grain-and-soybean-based miso began to play its important role in the Japanese diet.

One new type of miso introduced to Japan during the Kamakura period was Kinzanji miso. In about 1255 A.D. the Japanese Buddhist monk Kakushin returned to Japan from China, where, according to the most widely held theory, he had learned to make this miso at Kinzanji, the Temple of the Golden Mountain, one of China's five great Sung dynasty Zen centers. This delectable, chunky, rather sweet miso contained a large percentage of barley koji plus minced eggplant, gingerroot, white *uri* melon, *kombu* (sea vegetable) and burdock root. Kakushin taught the method of Kinzanji preparation to the people of Yuasa in Wakayama prefecture, where the same ancient technique is used to this day. Yuasa has since become a famous center of shoyu production as well, and legend has it that shoyu's earliest progenitor, tamari, was discovered as the dark, fragrant liquid left over at the bottom or top of the Kinzanji barrel. A second theory holds that Kinzanji was transmitted to Japan by the *Ch'i-min yao-shu* in about 1650. A third theory suggests that it originated from the practice of soaking vegetables in hishio to make "vegetable hishio" *(kusa bishio)*.

The historical connection between miso, tamari, and shoyu that started in Japan in about 1200 in Yuasa bears further examination. The term *tamari* derives from the verb *tamaru*, meaning "to accumulate," as "water accu-

Making miso-damari

mulates in ponds." Originally the word *tamari* was written with the two characters shown below. The character on the left, *to*, means "soybean," and the one on the right, *yu*, means "a liquid extracted by filtering or pressing."

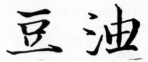

Later, however, a new character, the one used today, was adopted; it is the right-hand character in the word miso-damari, shown below. By 1260 tamari was being prepared for home consumption in the nearby towns of Yuasa and Hiromachi, and by 1290 the first Yuasa tamari, still a by-product of Kinzanji miso, is said to have been sold commercially, although no early documents exist. The tamari was always removed by either filtering or ladling, never pressing, as that would ruin the miso. Pressing the miso originated during the Muromachi (1336-1568), a period noted for its opulence. The term *miso-damari*, referring to the rich liquid tamari removed from miso, seems to have originated during the 1500s, when it came to be prepared and prized by the monks living in the five major temples of Kyoto.

Miso-damari

The word *shoyu* did not appear until a very late date, being first mentioned in a Japanese dictionary *(Ekirin Honsetsu Yoshu)*, published in 1597, but thought to have been written by a priest sometime between 1469 and 1503 and widely circulated in manuscript form.

醬 油

Shoyu

The Muromachi Period (1336-1568): During the Muromachi period, the seat of government returned to the Kyoto area and some of the formality, splendor, and aristocratic feeling of the Heian period was revived. But the period as a whole was characterized by social chaos and civil war. The famous samurai Takeda Shingen (1521-1573), lord of a large fief in the Shinshu area north of Tokyo, was the first to recognize miso's full potential as a soldier's food. Long-lasting, inexpensive, and highly nutritious, it took only minutes to make it into a warming soup. To ensure that his men had a large supply of it wherever they went, Takeda taught farmers throughout Shinshu to plant soybeans and process them into miso. The preparation of homemade miso soon flourished throughout the area and gradually spread to other nearby provinces. During the 16th century miso shops attached to private homes appeared in urban areas and gradually every region developed its own techniques and new varieties, which often came to be called by such lofty names as "morality" or "Bodhidharma" miso. Documents of this period show frequent references to miso in plays, stories and songs, indicating that it was not only a popular food but an integral and intimate part of the social fabric.

The Muromachi period saw the development of two new varieties of miso; Hatcho and sweet white. Oral tradition has it that Hatcho was first prepared as early as 1370, but scholars generally place the date somewhere between the late 1400s and early 1500s. A kabuki drama tells of how Hideyoshi Toyotomi (1536-1598), the child of poor farmers in central Japan's Aichi prefecture, rose to become one of Japan's most powerful feudal lords. When only ten years old, the child is said to have fallen asleep one night on a bridge near his home, wrapped only in a straw mat. A famous robber passing over the bridge scornfully kicked the urchin, who awoke and intrepidly grabbed the man's spear commanding him to stop such cruelty. The robber, impressed with the boy's courage, decided to raise him as his own son. In the play, the straw mat bears the trademark of one of the nearby Hatcho miso shops where it was used to prepare koji. Historians cite the incident to prove that Hatcho miso was being made as early as 1546. (The shop uses the same trademark to this day.) Later records show that by 1590, when Tokugawa Ieyasu left for the frontier town of Edo to found his new capital, both of Japan's present Hatcho miso makers were doing a thriving business.

Although some scholars support the previously mentioned theory that sweet white miso was transmitted from the Chinese to the Japanese capital during the Nara period, most believe that the present product was developed by Kyoto craftsmen during the 14th and 15th centuries to suit the tastes of the indolent court nobility. It is interesting to note that both Hatcho and sweet white miso still

The child Hideyoshi on a mat bearing the Hatcho miso mark (circa 1546).

retain a certain high-class image, a reflection, perhaps, of the era in which they originated.

In the late 1300s one of Japan's most famous miso recipes, Dengaku, is said to have originated, probably in rural villages. Miso spread on tofu was broiled over an open fire, as described in Chapter 6. Dengaku first became popular throughout Japan in the early 1600s and by 1775 was served in fashionable tea shops in Kyoto and Tokyo.

By the 15th century, the most widely available varieties of miso are said to have finally lost their luxury status and made their way into the homes of the common people. Yet at the same time, miso emerged as an essential and esteemed ingredient in the more famous schools of Japanese haute cuisine. Under the wise guidance of Senno-Rikyu, *shojin* cookery was carried to its peak of refinement and subtlety in Tea Ceremony Cuisine *(Kaiseki Ryori)*. It was in these newly emerging schools of fine cookery that sweet simmered, broiled, *yuzu*, and *kinomé* miso, together with many other of Japan's finest miso preparations, were first developed. From its earliest beginnings in simple peasant fare, miso now rose to attain the same level of honor among the people that it had enjoyed among the Japanese palace nobility eight centuries earlier, and that its predecessor *chiang* had enjoyed in China's Imperial Household twelve centuries before that.

Mention of miso was made in many cookbooks during this period. A work (the pronunciation of whose title is unknown) of 1467 discussed miso soup and its popularization. The *Hocho Kikigaki* (1487) discussed tarémiso. The *Shijoryu Hocho-gaki* (1489) talked of tarémiso, usutaré, and surimiso. The *Ogusaden Yori Soden no Kikigaki* (1504) described sumashi miso, tarémiso, and suri hishio.

The year 1593 is usually given as the year in which Sendai miso originated. Originally it was made for the soldiers of the great feudal lord and soldier Ida Masamune, and as a reserve food during times of famine. That same year they took Sendai miso to Korea (Ichiyama 1968).

The Edo or Tokugawa Period (1603-1867): In 1603 the capital of Japan was moved from Kamakura to Edo (later renamed Tokyo), where the Tokugawa Shoguns establsihed Japan's longest period of stability and peace. Miso made commercially in the towns of Shimousa and Saitama was sold in the huge markets of the new capital city. Because supply was insufficient to meet demand, however, the Shogun, Tokugawa Ieyasu, imported his favorite soybean and Hatcho miso by boat from his native town in central Japan. Although miso was consumed in increasingly large amounts, several factors prevented the many small miso makers of the period from growing into large-scale companies. First, miso, generally packed into large wooden kegs, was heavy and bulky, and the lack of good roads or river routes made long distance distribution difficult and expensive. Second, and perhaps more important, people enjoyed preparing their own miso at home at very little cost, making it difficult to price commercial miso competitively. Indeed, there was a saying popular at the time that a family that did not make its own miso would never have its own treasury-storehouse (kura), and many considered it a source of embarrassment if they had to use miso which they had not made themselves. Furthermore, most people preferred the flavor of the homemade or locally made product. Nevertheless, urbanization sped miso's commercialization and many of Japan's larger cities developed their own varieties. Here miso was first sold at saké stores; only later did outlets specialzing in miso and miso pickles come into existence.

It was during this period that many farmers and small miso-shop operators, who had formerly made only soybean miso, began to experiment with the use of barley or rice koji in order to obtain a wider variety of flavors. In the capital at Edo during the 1600s, the three most popular varieties were Sendai red miso, barley miso made in nearby Saitama prefecture, and the hometown specialty Edo sweet red miso. Salty rice miso was developed throughout the northeastern provinces and in the Shinshu area north of the capital. Both salty and sweet barley miso were produced in Kyushu and at the southern tip of Japan's main island, and new varieties of sweet white miso emerged in the Kyoto-Nara area. As grain koji became more widely used, the traditional practice of forming cooked soybeans into balls was abandoned in many areas and the grain koji was fermented in wooden trays.

By the early Tokugawa period, the first reports of Japanese miso had begun to reach Europe. The Italian Carletti mentioned it in 1597, the German Kaempfer gave a detailed account of its production in 1691-92, and Thunberg mentioned it in passing in 1795.

When the Chinese Zen master Ingen (founder of the famous Obaku sect) came to Japan in 1661, he was surprised to find miso totally different from the chiang he had known in his native country. Becoming extremely fond of it, he is said to have enjoyed miso soup each day and used it as an effective substitute for a Chinese herbal medicine that he had taken for many years.

In the early 1800s, Hokusai (1760-1849) did a nice woodblock print of a cedar vat, the type widely used until the 1970s for making miso and shoyu.

A Brief Overview of Origins: Before proceeding, it might be interesting, and indeed provocative, to reflect briefly on the origins and genealogies of miso and shoyu. The most widely held opinion among Japanese researchers and fermented-food historians is that both miso and shoyu trace their ancestry to Chinese chiang. However, Dr. Kinichiro Sakaguchi, Professor of Fermentation Science at Tokyo University, in his "Searching for the Roots of Shoyu" (1979) argues convincingly that today's miso traces its ancestry back through early Japanese misos and hishio to chiang, whereas shoyu traces its ancestry back through early shoyu, then through the four products of tamari shoyu, tamari miso, Hatcho miso, and savory soy nuggets (Hamanatto), and ultimately to Chinese soy nuggets (shih). In the shoyu lineage, the koji is always made from either soybeans alone or a mixture of soybeans and cracked wheat, whereas in the miso lineage the koji is always made from grain. Sakaguchi believes that the fundamental biochemical consequences of this difference are of much greater importance than the more superficial differences of form that have led researchers up until now to group solid or semisolid products in the miso lineage and liquid products in the shoyu lineage. Thus, in shoyu, the *Aspergillus oryzae* molds act directly on the soybeans during the koji fermentation, then their enzymes continue to act on the soybeans during the subsequent brine fermentation. This leads to the formation of more complicated metabolic compounds, a higher degree of protein hydrolysis and liquefaction, and the production of a sharper and stronger flavor in shoyu than in miso. Sakaguchi argues that miso has a 3,000-year history dating from the development of chiang during the Chou dynasty in China, whereas shoyu has a 2,000-year history dating from the development of soy nuggets (shih) during the Han dynasty. It is important to note here that most Chinese would probably disagree with Dr. Sakaguchi. They clearly trace the lineage of their soy sauce to *chiang*, not to *shih*, as evidenced by the Chinese word for soy sauce, *chiang-yu*, meaning "the liquid extracted from chiang." Moreover, most of their *chiang* and *shih* have always been made from a soy-based koji. We would say that both miso and shoyu trace their lineage back to both soy nuggets (*shih*, which existed prior to 206 B.C.) and to soybean chiang (which existed prior to A.D. 500).

Dr. Sakaguchi considers there to be three main reasons that shoyu and miso were not developed in the West: (1) Westerners did not know how to make koji using molds; (2) they had no soybeans until the 20th century; and (3) the basic flavoring components of shoyu and miso, especially natural L-glutamic acid and inosinic acid, were traditionally unknown in the West.

The Meiji and Pre-War Periods (1867-1939): From 1635 until 1854 Japan had lived in relative seclusion and isolation under the Tokugawa shoguns. The great advances made in Western science during this 220-year period passed largely unnoticed. There were few important developments in the production of miso or other fermented foods, and those which were made by local craftsmen were based on an empirical, trial-and-error process. In 1854 the American

Commodore Perry forced Japan to end its self-imposed isolation and begin trade with the West. In 1868 the Emperor replaced the declining Tokugawa shoguns as the political head of state, ushering in the Meiji Restoration. Openness, modernization, westernization, scientism, positism, and the ideal of progress all formed the dominant ethos of the Meiji Period, which lasted until 1912. In 1877 Tokyo Imperial University, the most famous of the new breed of government colleges and universities, was established, primarily for teaching western science and technology. By paying princely salaries and offering high positions, the Japanese were able to attract top European scientists to staff the new universities.

The imported European scientists and professors (mostly Germans and Englishmen) caused an almost immediate revolution in the field of Japanese food fermentations, for they brought with them the powerful tools of the Western scientific method and a host of new discoveries in the fields of fermentation and microbiology. Prior to 1870, makers of miso and other fermented foods were unaware of the basic nature of the fermentation process, of microorganisms, enzymes, and their respective interactions. Makers of koji had no idea what caused grains and/or soybeans to become covered with a fragrant white mycelium after several days incubation in a warm koji room, or what later transformed the koji almost magically into delicious, savory miso or shoyu. The microscope was essentially unknown in East Asia prior to the 1880s.

The pioneering first generation of European scientists in Japan studied the country's many fermented foods with great curiosity and enthusiasm. One of their first subjects for research was the koji mold, now known as *Aspergillus oryzae*, and the various foods in which it was used: saké, shoyu, and miso. In 1874 the German professor Dr. J.J. Hoffman wrote the earliest known description, detailed and scientific, of the process for making rice koji—although he did not use the word *koji*. In 1878 Korschelt, also a German, gave a long, detailed description of exactly how koji and koji starter were made. Although Hepburn had mentioned koji (and miso) in his Japanese-English Dictionary of 1867, Korschelt was the first western *scientist* to use the terms *koji* and *tané koji*. In a section of Korschelt's article and in a Japanese article written with Matsubara in 1878, Ahlburg, another German, who taught natural history at Tokyo University, gave the first detailed description of the koji mold, which he called *Eurotium Oryzae* Ahlburg. In 1884 the Polish botanist and mycological taxonomist F.J. Cohn first gave the koji mold its present name, *Aspergillus oryzae*. After 1884 the koji mold was referred to as *Aspergillus oryzae* (Ahlburg) Cohn, in recognition of Ahlburg's earliest accurate description. Other early pioneering research on koji and saké was done by the Englishman Atkinson (1878, 1881), the German Kellner (1889), and the Dutchman Wehmer (1895, 1901).

The first scientific study of miso in Japan was published, not by a Japanese, but by a German, Dr. Oscar Kellner, in conjunction with two Japanese scientists, M. Nagaoka and Y. Kurashima. In their "Researches on the Manufacture and Composition of Miso," published in Eng-

lish in 1889 in the *Bulletin of the College of Agriculture, Tokyo Imperial University*, they devoted 24 pages to miso's history, raw materials, manufacture, and chemical changes during fermentation, plus a description of eight types of miso and an analysis of three of these. The authors stated that miso was widely consumed by the lower classes and was especially favored in the northeastern provinces. In the countryside it was made by families in their homes, with special miso works being established only in large communitiies. Noting that no statistics on miso consumption were then available in Japan, Kellner made the rough estimate (which he was sure was on the low side) that since the smallest amount of miso consumed per day by one person was about 37.5 grams (10 monme or 2.16 tablespoons) and since an estimated 20 million of Japan's 39,000,000 inhabitants (51%) ate miso every day, the yearly miso consumption was nearly 30,000,000 kilograms. Actually Kellner's arithmetic was mistaken; even assuming that the remaining 49% ate no miso (an impossible but most conservative assumption), his figures show an average per capita consumption of 19.1 gm per day or 6.98 kg per year, for a total production of 274,000 metric tons per year, a more probable figure, but still probably much too low. He then concluded, whether by calculation or from original data is not known, that more than half of Japan's yearly production of soybeans (335,800 metric tons in 1883) were used to make miso.

In 1905 Oshima in Japan reported statistics showing that Japanese living in areas other than in the countryside consumed an average of 43 gm of miso a day, with a range of 13 to 100 gm; average rural consumption was estimated at 40 gm per person per day. Given that 80% of the population was rural, this would give an average daily consumption figure of 40.6 gm, or 14.8 kg per capita per year.

In 1911 Shaw, a British customs official in Manchuria, reported that, according to the latest statistics, the Japanese consumed 724,656 metric tons of soybeans and that the majority (393,768 metric tons or 54%) were used to make miso. Given that 1 kg of soybeans in those days yielded 2.5 pounds of miso, this would give an annual production of 1,984,419 metric tons of miso. The population of 49.85 million would then consume 19.7 kg per capita per year. These figures seem much too high.

In 1913 Takahashi and Abe estimated annual Japanese miso consumption at 45,000,000 kg or 45,000 metric tons, equivalent to 0.88 kg per capita per year. These figures are so far below the other estimates that they are highly suspect.

The figures of Kellner and Oshima show a rapid growth in total production and per capita consumption of miso from 1889 to 1911. Kawamura (1972), however, estimated Japanese per capita miso consumption to be roughly constant from the start of the Edo period (1600) to the beginning of World War II, at 35 gm per person per day or 12.78 kg per person per year. This assumption shows production increasing directly with population as indicated on page 226. The various production statistics (excepting Shaw's) from 1889 to 1940 show roughly similar trends. During this period, more than 50% of all Japanese miso was

THE MISO MARKET IN JAPAN (1930 - 1980)

Number of Manufacturers (1,000 plants)
Per Capita Consumption (Kg per person per year)
Production (100,000 metric tons)

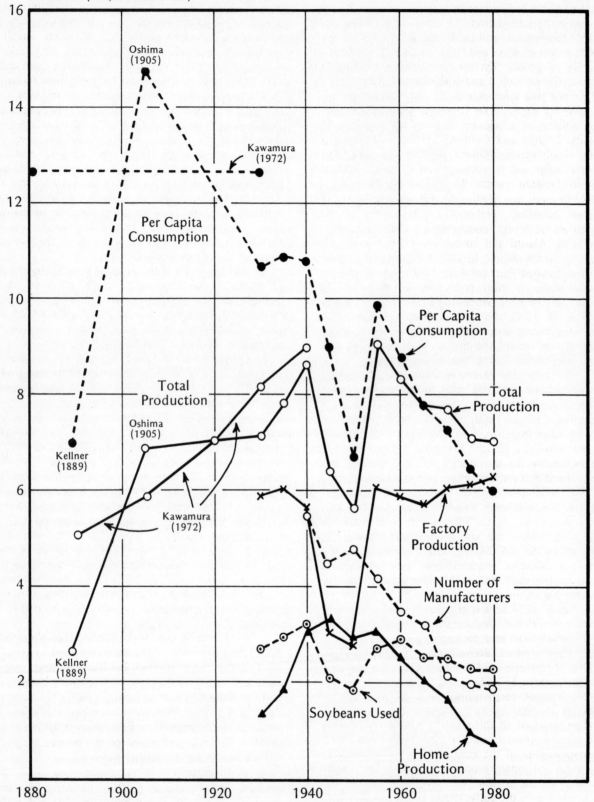

Sources: Pre 1930, journal articles, as noted. 1930 on, Japanese National Miso Association, personal communication, 1983.

made noncommercially in people's homes or farmhouses, where it was consumed by the family; in 1940 some 35 to 55% was made in homes and farmhouses.

Most of the early scientific research on miso and miso koji, during the period from the mid 1870s to 1905, was done by Europeans, as will be discussed later at "Europe." In 1889, however, Mori and Nagaoka assisted the German Kellner in an article "On the Manufacture, Composition and Properties of Koji," and Nagaoka and Kurashima assisted Kellner that same year in his classic article on miso. Starting in the early 1900s Japanese researchers began to write a number of articles on miso in European languages (primarily English and German) for both Japanese and European publications. Oshima (1905) discussed miso's nutritional value and its consumption in Japan. Takahashi (1908, in Japanese) wrote "A Preliminary Note on the Chemical Composition of Miso." Takahashi and Abe (1913, in English) published "Preliminary Notes on the Chemical Composition of Miso," containing an analysis of miso's amino acids. Akaghi and co-workers (1915) wrote "Researches on Hatcho-Miso." In 1921 Kinoshita wrote a 480-page tome entitled *Practical Miso Fermentation*, the most complete work on miso production to date. In 1924 Nishiwaki (in German) wrote about Hatcho miso koji and *tomé koji*. In 1935 and 1936 I. Iwamura wrote three articles in Japanese about miso in *Nippon Nogei Kagaku Kaishi*. He was one of the first to investigate the use of warming the miso during fermentation to shorten the fermentation time. The extent of other research articles on miso published in Japanese prior to World War II is not known.

During the late 1800s, paralleling the pioneering research on miso in Japan, was some extremely innovative research on koji by Jokichi Takamine. He was the person most responsible for introducing the koji process to the Western world and giving it important commercial applications there. As an early Japanese student of microbiology and fermentation science, Takamine had come to learn of the malting process in the West. He decided ambitiously to try to introduce the koji process in its place. After making considerable increases in the diastatic activity of the koji mold, he went to America in 1880, but met with opposition from the malt makers. He then undertook a new project to extract the enzymes from the koji mold for commercial use. In 1894 he was granted two U.S. Patents (No. 525,823 and 525,825) for a process for making diastatic enzyme, which was very successfully marketed as Takadiastase. This product, derived from the traditional miso and shoyu processes and containing a rich variety of enzymes, came to be widely used in the field of enzymology; it brought international fame to both Takamine and the koji mold.

The result of all this research was that the Japanese gained a better understanding of and control over the miso fermentation. One of the earliest major advances came in 1904, when the Japanese prepared their first pure-culture koji starters for use in miso.

Beginning in the early 1930s, the world of Japanese miso-production underwent a series of drastic changes which have continued to affect it up until the present.

With the rise of Japanese militarism, the conquest of new overseas territories in Korea, China, and Manchuria, and the development of Hokkaido and the islands to the north, many new markets for miso appeared and stimulated the growth of miso factories with international scope. By 1936, commercial miso production had soared to an all time estimated high of 600,000 tonnes (metric tons) or 600 million kg—a figure that would not be equalled again until the mid 1970s. But in 1936, most basic Japanese foodstuffs—including miso—were suddenly subjected to strict government price and quality controls. For purposes of standardization, government authorities grouped all miso varieties into three types (rice, barley, and soybean) and two grades (excellent and medium). Each type and grade had a fixed price. Although the designation of special varieties—such as Edo, Shinshu, or Hatcho miso—was allowed, the brand names of individual makers were outlawed. This system delivered a mortal blow to the production of many fine miso varieties and tended to encourage makers to lower their quality to the minimum, since they were assured that whatever they made would be sold.

World War II and the Postwar Period: Modern Times (1940-1983): To counter the growing threats to miso quality from oppressive controls, Japan's first nationwide miso trade association, the Japanese National Miso Association (*Zenkoku Miso Kogyo Kumiai Rengokai*) was founded in January 1940. In 1944 it came under government control, but in 1948 regained its original independence; in November 1960 it was rechartered under its original name and today it is very active with large offices and several publications in Tokyo.

With the founding of the Japanese National Miso Association in 1940, the provincial miso trade associations were unified under its leadership. Although its representatives worked with determination for the repeal of the oppressive controls, they were unsuccessful. During the war years, miso production decreased considerably, and although the control system was abolished after the war in 1946, the damage it did to the consciousness of both miso producers and consumers was never fully repaired. Many makers had lost pride in the quality of their product and had begun to adapt themselves to faster, lower-cost methods of production. And many consumers had begun to lose their sensitivity to and appreciation for fine natural miso as they grew accustomed to standardized, lower-quality products.

During the War, with the massive food shortages and dislocations throughout the Japanese food system, miso consumption and production inevitably dropped, and they continued to fall until about 1950 during the period of postwar austerity, but rebounded sharply with recovery, rising to a postwar peak in about 1955. Thereafter, however, miso consumption and production began a steady decline, that has continued to the present (page 226). There were various reasons for this trend.

After World War II, the entire value system of the Japanese people underwent a dramatic change. The process of Westernization that had begun in 1868 was suddenly accelerated in the areas of food, clothing, and housing. Western-style diets with higher contents of animal products, sugar, and refined foods, with white bread partially replacing white rice, gradually became the norm, partially replacing traditional Japanese eating patterns in which miso played a more important role. At the same time, mechanization in agriculture and other areas and the resulting more urban, sedentary lifestyle, greatly reduced physical labor, and with it both salt consumption and total food intake. This Westernization of the diet and mechnization with less physical labor were the main factors leading to reduced miso consumption. During the 1960s concern among Japanese over their excessive salt consumption (then twice that of most other nations) further accelerated the decline. Between 1955 and 1980, per capita miso consumption fell from 10 kg per person down to 6, a drop of 40%. The 1980 figure was still, however, 11.2 grams or about 1 tablespoon per day. During the 1970s, the per capita miso consumption of urban businessmen was only 58% of the national average.

With this decline in per capita miso consumption, total miso production also fell. Actually commercial or factory miso production after 1955 stayed quite constant, even rising slightly after 1965, in part because of slowly rising population. The main drop came in home miso production, as the country became more urbanized, commercial miso became more widely available at low prices, and people generally found less time or inclination to make their own. Thus from a peak of 336,000 tonnes in 1945 (homemade miso increased during the war), it fell to a mere 75,000 tonnes in 1980, a decline of 78%. The drop in total production combined with the larger proportion of rice used in miso led to a decline of total soybean usage in miso from about 288,000 tonnes in 1960 to 226,000 tonnes in 1980.

During the postwar period, dramatic changes in the structure of the miso industry also took place, in part because the entire economy was shifting from a rural-agricultural to an urban-industrial base, but more specifically because of government postwar taxes and incentives designed to stimulate modernization, mechanization, and amalgamation. Within the space of one generation, the primary center of miso production shifted from farmhouses and private homes to commercial shops; just before and during the war, 55% fo the country's total miso output was homemade, whereas in 1980 less than 11% was homemade. As shops grew into small factories and moved nearer to cities, the higher costs of land and labor demanded increased profitability from each unit of capital, space, and time; this led to extensive mechanization of the miso process including quick temperature-controlled fermentation, development of fast-maturing sweeter misos, and machine-paced packaging methods. As a result, the number of commercial manufacturers decreased from 5,500 during the 1930s (at which time they were mostly small and medium-sized shops) to 4,800 in 1950, then down to 1,900 in 1980, a 60% drop in 30 years. Meanwhile, the number of highly mechanized, large factories showed a steady increase. By 1958 a number of miso plants had a capacity of up to 10 tons per day. By 1965 a number of the larger traditional manufacturers had amalgamated to form huge modern companies; 23 factories had a yearly capacity of at least 4,100 tons each, and the ten largest made 154,000 tonnes per year, or about 26% of the nation's total miso output. By 1974 the latter statistic had climbed to 30% and individual factories were then turning out 15,000 to 20,000 tons a year. The names of the "top ten" miso companies (see App. E) had become household words in Japan. In 1980 Japan's 1,900 commercial miso manufacturers employed 10,600 workers and made miso with a net ex-factory value of $573 million.

During the postwar period Japanese research on microbiology and its application to food fermentations advanced rapidly; soon the Japanese became world leaders in this field. Important early publications on these subjects, all in Japanese, include the works of Tomoda and Sakaguchi (1956), Nakano, Ebine, and Ota (1967), Yoshii and Kaneko (1972), and Sakaguchi et al. (1974).

Research on miso and its fermentation increased substantially, along with the advances in applied microbiology. One of the first Japanese scientists to apply these new advances to miso production was Dr. Masahiro Nakano, Professor of Microbiology at Meiji University and the dean of modern miso researchers in Japan. Nakano (1967, 1976) published extensively in Japanese, and he taught many other fine miso researchers, including Dr. Hideo Ebine and Dr. Tsutomu Mochizuki. Dr. Ebine worked at the Japanese National Food Research Institute. Between 1966 and 1976 he and his co-workers published many miso studies; seven of the most important of these (a number of which are in English) are cited in our Bibliography. After April 1982 Dr. Ebine worked at the National Miso Association's Central Miso Research Institute. Dr. Mochizuki, director of the prestigious Shinshu Miso Research Center, also published extensively. In 1972, for example, Mochizuki and co-workers showed the importance of *Pediococcus halophilus* bacteria (which produced lactic acid) and *Saccharomyces rouxii yeasts* (which produced ethyl alcohol and higher alcohols) in the miso making process.

By the mid 1960s, various new "Advances in Miso Production" were being proudly hailed by Japanese food scientists. Halophilic (salt tolerant) lactic acid bacteria (*Pediococcus halophilus* and *Streptococcus faecalis*) and yeasts (*Saccharomyces rouxii* and *Torulopsis* species) were being used commercially as inocula by some miso makers. They remarkably reduced the fermentation time required to obtain a well-fermented miso with a pleasing flavor. Batch type rotary pressure cookers, which heated to 120°C, replaced traditional steel or iron caldrons; the rotary action gave even cooking. Mechanized rotary fermenters (huge horizontal-axis rotating drums), with regulated temperatures and humidities, and purified circulating air, were used in large plants to replace the traditional, labor-intensive koji rooms. Epoxy-lined steel and concrete tanks came to be used in place of the hugh, traditional cedar vats; coopers gradually were put out of business. Miso prepackaged in polyethylene bags rapidly replaced that sold out of wooden kegs. The combination of the sealed bags, nationwide distribution, supermarket retailing, and sweeter misos with less salt led to the use of pasteurization and preservatives (sorbic acid to keep the bags from bursting). Some research was done on the use of enzyme preparations to replace koji for hydrolysis of miso's protein and carbohydrates. They did not give satisfactory results except for soybean miso, for which they reduced the fermentation time by 33% and the yield by 8% (Watanabe 1969, 1971, 1974; Ebine 1971). By the late 1970s huge koji incubation rooms, with perforated stainless steel floors, had replaced the rotary fermenters in large factories; koji filled the room to a depth of 12 inches or more and was stirred and harvested mechanically. Ethyl alcohol preservatives began to replace sorbic acid.

Ingredients also changed after the mid 1960s. In 1971 Ebine wrote that Japanese soybeans were the best for making miso, followed by those from China and then the U.S.A. U.S. soybeans were generally considered "not suited for making miso of high quality." Extensive research by Shibasaki, Ebine, and others, however, located three U.S. varieties (Kanrich, Mandarin, and Comet) which were considered comparable to the best Japanese ones. Being less expensive, the U.S. soybeans soon became widely used. During the 1960s quite a bit of low-cost defatted soybean meal was also used in miso, but this resulted in an inferior product and the practice was largely abandoned; less than 0.5% was used after 1975. In addition, more rice and less barley and soybeans were used in miso to accelerate the fermentation process and give a lighter-colored, sweeter product. Water, previously drawn from deep wells was partially replaced by the chlorinated product supplied by municipal pipelines. Natural sea salt was abandoned for sodium chloride—the only product now produced by the Government Salt Monopoly Corporation. Japanese grown soybeans gave way to lower-cost, generally lower-quality American soybeans. And a wide variety of chemical additives, in addition to preservatives, came to be used quite uncritically in miso: coloring agents, MSG, rice anti-clumping agents, artificial sweeteners, bleach, and the like. Yet the basic ingredients remained the same. Ebine (1972) reported that in 1969 some 180,000 tons of soybeans, 9,200 tons of rice, 19,000 tons of barley, and 75,000 tons of salt were used to make 552,000 tons of various types of commercial miso. Note that, on average, 1 ton of soybeans yielded 3.06 tons of miso, and 4.8 times as much rice as barley was used.

One major and very unfortunate result of the modernization, mechanization, and concentration of control in Japan's miso industry was the gradual loss of the local and regional character of traditional misos. Nevertheless a considerable number of provincial (and some urban) miso masters continued to value the ancient way and the distinctiveness of their local, unique products. Like the many thousands of small European wine or cheese makers who have successfully resisted modern standardization by showing that real quality is found in tradition, individuality, and naturalness, these Japanese miso masters chose to view the modern rush toward uniform factory miso as a passing fad. Keeping in touch with the great natural cycles and with their own traditions and intuitions, they held on to their fine wooden tools and vats, searched for sources of natural ingredients, and never forgot the true meaning of "culture." Nourishing the secrets and wholeness of their craft, they worked hard—and waited. Some (such as Sendai Miso Shoyu and the major Hatcho miso companies) exported their misos to a growing market demanding such products in North American and Europe. In addition, there were efforts to revive traditional and unique misos. Mogi (1946) described the preparation of misos using unconventional carbohydrate sources, such as potatoes, chestnuts, buckwheat, millet, etc. Misumi Kan, a Kyushu-born novelist, worked to resuscitate homemade miso. Upon retirement he turned his spacious Tokyo home into a center for the study and preparation of miso and miso pickles. His two books about his work, *Miso University* and *Pickle University*, written in a highly literary and personal style, contain a wealth of information about the preparation of these two fermented foods in the traditional, natural way, plus many color and monochromatic photographs.

An important and colorful figure in the movement to revive traditional regional diversity of miso types and uses, explore miso history, and stamp out mass-produced uniform, modern misos was Wataru Kawamura, who became known throughout Japan as "Miso Sensei" (Miso Professor). In 1958 he wrote *Historical Chronicles of Miso*, an 815-page tome that was the first definitive work on the subject. In 1972 he and Ms. Hamako Tatsumi teamed up to write Japan's first *Book of Miso* (320 pages). In part I he discussed miso history in China and Japan (upon which we have drawn heavily), miso production and varieties, and the role in miso in the various Japanese provinces. In part II Ms. Tatsumi presented several hundred of Japan's best known miso recipes. In 1973 he wrote *Miso Soups Throughout the Provinces*, in 1974 *Encyclopedia of Miso Soups*, and in 1976 (with the Japanese National Miso Association), *Miso Digest*, a booklet of basic information about miso in Japan. Mr. Kawamura followed with delight the rising interest in natural miso in America and reported developments to the Japanese public.

Paralleling the revival of interest in traditional, natural misos was an interest in the ability of miso to promote long life and good health. One of the first publications in this area was the provocative *Physical Constitution and Food* (1965), written by Dr. Shinichiro Akizuki, a physician and hospital director in Nagasaki. He felt that miso had saved his life and that of his co-workers after the atomic blast at Nagasaki and that it could be used by anyone to help build a strong physical constitution. Other publications in this field included Kondo's *Japanese Long-Life Villages* (1972, showing a relationship between longevity and regular miso consumption), Morishita and co-workers' (1972*) investigations indicating that miso contained dipicolinic acid, which might protect the body from the effects of radioactivity, Iwadare's (1976) work on miso nutrition and healthful recipes, and *Asahi Simbun's* 1981 report of Dr. Hirayama's 13-year research project showing that people who drink miso soup regularly have the lowest rates of stomach cancer in Japan. For details on the above, see Chapter 2.

In 1960 aflatoxins (carcinogenic toxins produced by

two species of *Aspergillus* molds) came to the public attention when 100,000 turkeys and ducks died suddenly in England after consuming a poultry feed containing moldy Brazilian peanuts that had been contaminated with *Aspergillus flavus*. There was great concern that since miso and shoyu were fermented with another species of *Aspergillus*, *(A. oryzae)* they might also contain aflatoxins. Extensive investigations on samples of commercial koji, miso, and shoyu were conducted and from 1966 many reports were published on the subject. In Japan, for example, Manabe and Matsuura (1968) detected no aflatoxin on 238 samples of koji from koji makers, 28 koji samples from miso factories, 108 industrial miso samples, 30 homemade samples, and 20 shoyu samples collected nationwide. Other important early Japanese research showing that miso and shoyu were free of problems from aflatoxin contamination was done by Murakami et al. (1967-68), Matsuura (1970), Manabe et al. (1972), and many others.

Likewise, starting in about 1970, substances called nitrosamines, found in a number of Japanese protein foods (especially broiled, dried, or smoked fish and red frankfurters containing nitrites) were shown to be carcinogenic. Many foods (including fresh bread crumbs, spinach, green salads, miso, and shoyu) have low levels of nitrosamines, that are considered well within the limits of safety. Nagahori (1980) found that substances in miso and shoyu suppress formation of nitrosamines by 62 to 79%, keeping them at levels generally below 1 part per billion, which is of no concern.

During the 1960s, largely unnoticed in Japan, a major event in the history of Japanese miso was taking place; it was being transmitted to the West, largely by Japanese Macrobiotic teachers. By the mid to late 1960s, for the first time in history, large numbers of Caucasian Americans had begun to buy imported Japanese miso and use it in their cooking. A few Westerners began making miso, and more and more information about it began to appear, as described in the next section.

In Japan, by the early 1970s, a popular reaction had begun to set in against the processes of standardization and increased use of chemicals in traditional foods. People began to grow nostalgic for the taste of fine, natural miso and shoyu, and to speak out against the widespread use of preservatives, bleach, and other synthetic additives. In city apartments and communes, the tradition of preparing fine natural homemade miso began to be revived. Traditional miso and shoyu producers found that their products sold better if they advertised the fact that they were made from whole soybeans, fermented slowly at the natural temperature of the environment, and were free of chemical preservatives and other additives. In 1975 most larger producers stopped using chemical preservatives and switched instead to ethyl alcohol, a more natural preservative. Whereas in the 1960s traditional miso and shoyu were considered by many to be old fashioned, by the early 1980s they were increasingly viewed as the highest quality fruits of Japan's ancient tradition of fine craftsmanship.

Starting in the late 1960s a flood of cookbooks featuring miso began to hit the market. Among the better ones were the Women's College of Nutrition's 1969 seasonal miso cookbook, Lima Ohsawa's *Macrobiotic Cookery* (1971, with many miso recipes), Shufu-no-tomo's 1972 *Encyclopedia of Japanese Cookery*, Tsuda and co-workers' 1974 *Zen Temple Cookery*, and Egami's 1975 *Miso Soup and Miso Cookery*—to mention but a few.

Ichiyama's extremely interesting, 804-page *History of Kikkoman Shoyu* (1968), throws a great deal of light on the history of miso and fermented foods in general in Japan. Tamura's derivative 294-page *Book of Shoyu* (*Shoyu no Hon*, 1971) is more condensed, covering Ichiyama's key historical developments.

During the 1960s and 1970s dehydrated miso, both freeze-dried and spray dried, started to become quite popular in Japan, especially as the main ingredient in instant miso soups. First developed in 1959 by Ebine and Oguri, some 10,000 to 15,000 tons were made each year during the 1970s; this was roughly 2½ to 3½% of Japan's total miso production. Of the dehydrated product in 1979, an estimated 80% was freeze dried and the remainder was spray dried. By the mid 1970s instant miso soup, sold in small packets, was widely available.

Another new variety of miso was low salt (6.3% NaCl) or salt free miso. Early reports on this subject were published by Sano (1960*), Kobatake et al. (1964), Ito et al. (1965*), and Ebine (1966). Low salt miso was introduced commercially during the mid 1960s in response to the concern over high Japanese salt consumption (30 gm per capita per day in northern Japan and 18 gm in the rest of Japan, compared with 11 gm in the United States) and the corresponding high rates of stroke and high blood pressure (hypertension). A campaign throughout Japan to reduce salt intake was almost surely a key factor in lowering the death rate from strokes from 175 per 100,000 people in the period 1963-1970 down to 145 per 100,000 people in 1977, a 17% decrease. Low salt miso had become extremely popular by 1979, when most of the large manufacturers began to reduce the percentage of salt in their basic misos by 10 to 25%. In 1980 standards had been set for three low-salt products: mild-salt *(usujio)* miso had 10 to 25% less salt than normal; low-salt *(gen-en)* miso had less than half the normal amount of salt, and very-low salt *(tei-en)* had less than 1 gram of salt per 100 grams of miso. Thus standard Japanese misos came to contain only 9 to 12% salt. Ethyl alcohol was typically added as a preservative.

In 1977 Nagano Miso Company was the first to introduce a salt-free miso; in 1978 it started to be marketed as Jepron, and in 1982 the name was changed to GOLD 'N RICH. The first patent on such a product was issued to Nagano Miso Co. on 28 May 1981 (Japan Patent 1,048,853). By early 1983 Nagano Miso had applied for patents in nine countries; U.S. Patent No. 4,311,715 had been granted. Nagano Miso Co. also introduced a low-salt miso in 1979. For more details, see Chapter 4.

Starting in the early 1970s Japanese fermentation scientists began to investigate the possibility of using commercially available purified enzyme preparations in place of koji in the miso making process. This might allow greater control over the process, accelerate and simplify it, and eliminate the 10% loss of raw materials consumed by the mold during its growth. Kitaoka (1972) used protease enzymes to make a soybean miso, but the flavor of the resulting product was rather "flat and unbalanced." Saito et al. (1973) used a combination of protease enzymes with decreased amounts of koji to bring about a considerable reduction in miso aging time. Other research in this area during the 1970s has been reviewed by Aboise (1982). As of the early 1980s, purified enzyme preparations were not widely used in commercial miso manufacture, probably because their increased cost does not pay for itself in reduced fermentation time.

As of 1983, miso continued to be a basic part of the Japanese diet. An estimated 80 to 85% was used to make miso soup, with most of the rest used in sauces and simmered dishes, or as a topping for tofu. The three basic types of regular miso were rice miso, barley miso, and soybean miso. The six varieties of rice miso comprised about 81% of all regular miso made in Japan; the two varieties of barley miso comprised about 11%, and the two varieties of soybean miso comprised about 8%. There were also two types of special miso (Finger Lickin' and sweet simmered miso) and three varieties of modern miso (akadashi, dehydrated, and low-salt miso).

The various types of miso, though used largely as a seasoning, make a very substantial contribution to the protein intake of the Japanese. Rice misos contain an average of 115 gm of protein per kg of miso and Hatcho miso contains 217 gm per kg; shoyu contains 78 gm of protein per kg of shoyu. Thus in the late 1970s, miso contributed about 66,000 tonnes of vegetable protein to the Japanese diet, and shoyu contributed about 112,000 tonnes.

Starting in the mid 1970s, exports of miso from Japan began to increase steadily. In 1975 total miso exports were 828 metric tons (tonnes), with the largest importers being the U.S.A. (459 tonnes, 25% of which was for the natural food trade), EEC/Europe (156 tonnes), Brazil (58 tonnes), and Canada (36 tonnes). The net value in Japan was $680,000. Natural foods exporters shipped 117 tonnes, Mitoku shipping 67 tonnes and Muso 40. Of this roughly 22 tonnes were Sendai red miso, 50 tonnes were barley miso, and 35 tonnes were Hatcho or soybean miso. By 1981 miso exports had increased dramatically (by 84%) to 1524 tonnes. Of this 834 tonnes were exported to the U.S., 95 tonnes to Singapore, and 67 tonnes to the Netherlands, the three leading miso importing nations.

HISTORY OF MISO IN EUROPE

Miso has a surprisingly long history in Europe and the West. Miso was known to Europeans for almost 300 years before it was known in America. The earliest reference dates from the late 1500s, just before the beginning of the Edo period in Japan.

Early European References (1597 to 1899): The first known reference to miso (or to any soyfood) by a European or Westerner appeared in 1597, when the Florentine Francesco Carletti, a most literate and observant traveler who was very interested in Japanese cookery, visited Nagasaki during a two-year stay in Japan and wrote in his memoirs (first published in Italian in 1701): "They prepare various sorts of dishes from fish, which they flavor with a certain sauce of theirs which they call *misol*. It is made of a sort of bean that abounds in various localities, and which cooked and mashed and mixed with a little of that rice from which they made the wine already mentioned, and then left to stand as packed in a tub—turns sour and all but decays, taking on a very sharp, piquant flavor. Using this a little at a time, they give flavor to their foods . . ." (Carletti, 1701, 1964; first cited by Hymowitz and Newell, 1981).

The next reference to miso, which contained a much more detailed description of how it was made, was written in 1691-92 by Englebert Kaempfer, a brilliant self-educated German scientist and traveler who lived and traveled in Japan during these two years. His description, first published in Latin in his *Amoenitatum Exoticarum* in 1712 read:

> To produce miso, one takes one measure of *mamé* or *phaseolus daidsu* which is cooked with water for a long time then brayed or ground and mixed into a soft pap. Under continued braying, common salt is added, in summer four parts, in winter three. If less salt is added, one gets the product quicker, but shelf life is shorter. After reducing is repeated, one mixes the pap with *koos* or dehulled rice, and mixes the total by repeated braying. This rice in preparation has been boiled a little in the steam of unsalted water. One lets the mixture cool down and remain in a warm cellar one or two days and nights to ripen.
>
> This mixture, which has the texture of a pap or spread, is put into a bowl that has recently contained the popular *sacki*, a rice wine. Before using, one lets the bowl stand one or two months untouched.
>
> Koos lends to the product an agreeable taste, and its production requires like that of the Germans' "polenta," the experienced hand of the master. Those therefore who make it are held in high esteem, and they sell it ready made (Bening 1951).

Thereafter Kaempfer gave an equally detailed description of the shoyu making process. Prior to Kaempfer, numerous Western travelers had made mention of soyfoods (such as miso, tofu, and shoyu) but none of them had understood that these were made from soybeans. Through Kaempfer's description and illustration of the soybean and his descriptions of how miso and shoyu were made, the Western world first understood the relationship between soybeans and soyfoods.

In 1776 the Swedish doctor and botanist C.P. Thunberg mentioned miso in his famous *Travels*, which were published in English in 1795 and in French in 1796, based on his 14-month journey to Japan. In the chapter on "Japanese Foods" he wrote: "Three times a day, with each meal, the people eat miso soup prepared with fish and leeks. These miso closely resemble lentils. They are the small *dolic* beans of Japan. (He apparently thought soybeans were called "miso.") Miso or soy sauce constitute the principal food of the Japanese. People of all levels, great or small, rich or poor, eat them several times a day, year-round." He then described the method for making shoyu.

In 1783 the English botanist Charles Bryant discussed miso, apparently thinking that it was used as the basis for making soy sauce. Although some of his terminology was adapted from Kaempfer (1712), his observations were apparently original, although not very detailed or accurate: "The sauces prepared from miso are known under the name of 'Sooju or Soy.' The preparation of miso is rather complicated. A mass of soybeans are cooked in water until they become completely soft. These are then pounded several times with the addition of an approximately equal quantity of salt. This mass is mixed with a rice preparation called Roos *(koji)*. It is filled into a wooden vat and allowed to stand for several months. It is used in place of butter." He noted that the preparation of koji was a secret known to only a few people, who sold it in the streets to miso makers.

The earliest reference to Chinese chiang in Europe was in 1855 in a letter from Stanislaus Julien to the Society for Acclimatization in Paris. In discussing soyfoods, he mentioned in passing that "They also make *tsiang* (chiang), a sort of seasoning sauce."

When Japan began to introduce European scientific techniques during the Meiji period (1868-1912), one of the first areas of food research was the koji mold. The history of this early research and identification of the mold, *Aspergillus oryzae*, is described earlier at "Japan." Pioneering researchers included Hoffman (1874), Korschelt (1878), Ahlburg (1878), Atkinson (1878, 1881), Cohn (1884), Kellner (1889, 1895), and Wehmer (1895, 1901). The word *koji* was first mentioned by a Western scientist in 1878.

The most detailed early description of the process for preparing koji and koji starter was given in 1878 by the German Korschelt. He noted that all koji for sake was made only during the period from November to February. The steamed rice was inoculated with koji starter *(tané koji)* in the form of a fine yellow powder made by the koji maker, wrapped in straw mats, and incubated for three days in an underground chamber. On the evening of the third day it was put into wooden koji trays and incubated, with occasional mixing, until the morning of the fifth day. The koji starter was made at the end of the koji season using as a substrate a mixture of rice and wood ash. After a seven to ten day fermentation, in the same room with the koji, the trays were inverted and the spores tapped off on clean paper, then stored in a sealed crock until the next year.

In 1880 Paillieux of the Society for Acclimatization in France noted that the soybean "lends itself particularly well to the preparation of a puree, resembling puree of peas . . . According to my experience, one could also mix this paste, which the Japanese call miso, with other ingredients to keep them over the winter in barrels, for use in provisioning ships, etc." Paillieux had apparently tasted miso and conceived of miso pickles, long popular in East Asia.

In 1882 Prof. Edward Kinch of Cirencester, England, published the first chemical/nutritional analysis of miso; figures were given for both red miso and white miso. It is not known how he obtained this information.

The first European to publish a detailed scientific study of miso was the German Dr. Oscar Kellner (1851-1911). One of the great pioneers of German agricultural chemistry (along with Liebig and Hellriegel), Kellner accepted an invitation in 1880 to teach his specialty at Tokyo Imperial University. He stayed in Japan for 12 years, married a Japanese woman, and helped lay the foundations of agricultural chemistry and animal nutrition in Japan (Breirem 1952). In 1889 he and Japanese co-workers Mori and Nagaoka published "Researches on the Manufacture, Composition and Properties of Koji," which contained a chemical analysis of koji and noted that "The ferment of koji transforms gelatinized starch into maltose and dextrose, and also converts maltose to dextrose. It has strong diastatic properties." Also in 1889 Kellner, Nagaoka, and Kurashima wrote their classic "Researches on the Manufacture and Composition of 'Miso.'" Both these studies were in English. The latter 24-page work discussed miso's history, raw materials, manufacture, chemical changes during fermentation, and numerous miso varieties. It also contained chemical/nutritional analyses of four types of miso, whose fermentation time Kellner reported varied from as little as three to four days up to one to one and a half years. The various types of miso discussed by Kellner included Shiro Miso, Yedo Miso, Inaka Miso, Sendai Miso, Kinzanji Miso, Sakura Miso, Tekka Miso, and Kogo Miso. Kellner even discussed miso's early history: "The *Sandai Jitsuroku*, one of the oldest Japanese records, tells us that a Chinese priest named *Jingo* transmitted more than 1000 years ago a small quantity of miso to the then emperor of Japan . . . And the name *'Korei Shiwo'* sometimes, though not frequently used instead of the word 'miso,' points to its introduction from Korea." Kellner's remarkably detailed study is still one of the best ever published by a Westerner. It was long the main source of information for other Western articles on miso. Kellner continued his publications on miso with excellent articles in German, "Die Bereitung von Miso in Japan" (1895, in response to an inquiry that year), and "Ueber die Bereitung von Sake, Shoyu, und Miso" (1895).

Also in 1886 and 1889 the German Rein gave brief descriptions of miso and its production, with an analysis of its nutritional composition done by the College of Agriculture at Komaba, Tokyo. He said that miso "is said to be at its best when three years old."

Bretschneider (1893) cited numerous references to chiang in early Chinese literature.

The first descriptions of Indonesian miso-like foods *(taucho* or *tao tsioe* and *tao tjiung)* were given by Prinsen Geerligs, in Dutch in 1895 and in German in 1896. Both articles included nutritional analyses.

Prior to 1897 Europe's first commercial miso started to be manufactured in Switzerland. In 1897 the American Langworthy (using data from an unknown source) published a nutritional analysis of this miso; it must have been a dried product since it contained only 12.5% moisture (versus 48 to 50% for traditional Japanese misos), plus 26.4% protein and 13.9% fat. Langworthy also mentioned that numerous East Asian soyfoods had been made in

Switzerland but, again, unfortunately, he did not cite the source of his information. In 1907 Senft of Germany stated, "Recently the firm Jul. Maggi & Co. in Kempthal (Switzerland) has begun to make and market a type of miso." Maggi was also the first company in Europe to develop hydrolyzed vegetable protein (HVP), from which they are said to have made a type of unfermented soy sauce.

1900 to 1949: Senft (1907) in Germany called miso a "vegetable cheese" and described its preparation and composition, using information from Kellner. He also gave the first report on miso pickles *(misozuké)* then noted, as mentioned above, that Maggi in Switzerland had begun to make and market miso.

In 1910, Li Yu-ying, the Chinese soyfoods pioneer in Paris, discussed Chinese chiang in his book on *Soybeans*. In 1912, in French, Li discussed Chinese chiang and Vietnamese *toung*, based on the work of Bui (1905). In 1911 the Englishman Shaw in Manchuria described the manufacture of two types of Chinese chiang and reported that 54% of all soybeans consumed in Japan were used to make miso. In 1914 Winkler gave a description of miso making. Then in 1917 Fuerstenberg repeated information about miso from Kellner and Winkler. He, too, called miso a "vegetable cheese." Surprisingly, after Fuerstenberg, there was no reference to miso or chiang in scientific literature in Europe for over 40 years.

1950 to 1982. The late 1950s saw a rebirth of interest in miso in Europe. The person responsible for this was a remarkable Japanese gentleman named George Ohsawa, whose life and work are discussed later at "U.S.A." He began teaching a little about miso during his first stay in France from 1929 to 1935, then again more seriously and to a growing audience from 1956 (Kotzsch 1981). As a result of his teachings about Macrobiotics and Japanese natural foods, the first commercial miso company since Maggi in the early 1900s was started by the Gevaert family in Belgium in 1959. They continued to make traditional, natural barley miso from 1959 until 1966, then re-started in January 1981. In late 1981 they were making 1,200 kg a month of barley miso at plants in France and Belgium. The French miso plant was powered by hydropower. The macrobiotic community in Europe has continued to be the pioneering force in introducing, distributing, teaching about and using miso. By 1975 the European Economic Community (EEC) was importing 156 tonnes of miso from Japan; England, the largest importer, was importing 28 tonnes. By 1981 EEC miso imports from Japan had jumped to 230.7 tonnes; the leading importing nations were the Netherlands (67.8 tonnes), England (40.4 tonnes), West Germany (40.0 tonnes), and France (28.0 tonnes). Much of this miso was specially made in Japan using traditional, natural methods for the European natural-food and macrobiotic markets. Also in 1981 there were five miso plants in Europe: four in France and one in Belgium. In July 1980 *The Book of Miso* by Shurtleff and Aoyagi was published in Germany as *Das Miso Buch*; by December 1982 some 3,200 copies had been sold. For the first time in European history, largely because of macrobiotic influence but also because of emigration from and travel to East Asia, Europeans were beginning to use and enjoy miso.

Starting in the late 1970s the Department of Microbiology at the University of Strathclyde in Glasgow, Scotland began to do research on miso. Dr. Brian Wood, Sumbo Abiose (from Africa), and co-workers published numerous scientific papers on miso in prestigious journals. Abiose's 1979 PhD dissertation was entitled *Studies on Miso Fermentation*, and her 1982 journal article "Microbiology and Biochemistry of Miso Fermentation" is the best review to date of the world's research literature on this subject; it cites 137 references. Other important publications from the Glasgow group were by Wood and Yong (1975) and by Wood (1977, 1982).

HISTORY OF MISO IN THE UNITED STATES AND CANADA

Early Developments (1896-1929): The earliest known reference to miso in the U.S. was by Trimble in 1896. Writing about "Soybeans and Soybean Products" in the *American Journal of Pharmacy*, he gave a detailed and accurate account of miso, based on three earlier publications by Kellner. In 1897 in "Soy Beans as Food for Man," Langworthy mentioned miso briefly and published a collection of earlier nutritional analyses of red, white, and Swiss misos; he did not cite the source of his information. These nutritional analyses were also reprinted by Abel of the USDA in 1900.

During the period from 1900 until the early 1960s, virtually no important research and very few original publications related to miso appeared in the United States (or in Europe). The various reports from Japan written in English by Oshima (1905), Takahashi and Abe (1913), and Akaghi et al (1915) were presumably read by a few interested Americans. Piper Morse (1916) referred briefly to miso, calling it a "soybean cheese," apparently after Sawa (1902) or Senft (1907). Piper and Morse (1923) gave four pages of information on miso from earlier sources, plus three excellent photographs showing miso manufacture in Japan, the first such photographs published in the West. In 1927 Horvath summarized much of the earlier research on miso and mentioned chiang tofu, made in China by pickling tofu in chiang; it resembled a sharp cheese and could be used in the West in sandwiches.

Starting in the early 1920s pioneering research on the *Aspergillus* molds was done by Dr. Charles Thom and Dr. Margaret Church, both of the Microbiological Laboratory of the USDA Bureau of Chemistry. Thom, one of America's USDA culture collection, now housed at Peoria, Illinois. 1904 to 1942; in 1904 he started what later became the USDA culture collection, now housed at Peoria, Illinois. In 1921 Thom and Church wrote "Aspergillus Flavus, A. oryzae, and Associated Species," in which passing mention was made of miso, shoyu, and tamari shoyu. In 1923 Church wrote "Soy and Related Fermentations," which focused on Japanese shoyu but gave a short description of miso production and referred to the miso mold as *Aspergillus flavus oryzae*. Thom and Church's research culminated in 1926 with the publication of their classic 272-page monograph *The Aspergilli*. This was expanded by Thom's co-worker Kenneth Raper into *Manual of the Aspergilli* (1945), then by Raper and Fennell in 1965 into *The Genus Aspergillus*. The work of Thom and Church laid the foundation for much of the important work on miso done at the USDA Northern Regional Research Center in Peoria, Illinois, starting in 1959. Thom's culture collection, transferred to Peoria in about 1940, was the largest such collection in the world by 1983, containing some 55,000 cultures. . . . including those used for miso, shoyu, tempeh, and other fermented soyfoods.

In the early 1900s exports of miso from Japan (mostly to the West) began to increase, rising from 2.2 million pounds (1,000 tonnes) worth $34,647 in 1903 to 6.9 million pounds (3,130 tonnes) worth $135,800 in 1907 (Piper and Morse 1923). By 1930 some 308,104 pounds (140 tonnes) of Japanese miso were being imported to Honolulu. These foreign markets began to attract Japanese miso makers.

According to Wilcox (1909), miso was being made in Hawaii by 1908 and most of the soybeans were imported from Japan. The leading (and perhaps only) manufacturer was the Hawaiian Soy Company, with Mr. M. Yamakami as manager. They probably also made soy sauce (Kraus 1911). By 1911 the manufacture of both miso and soy sauce were being rapidly expanded in Hawaii, which was then a U.S. Territory; it was annexed in 1911 and became a state in 1959. The next miso company in Hawaii, the Kanda Miso Factory, was started in Honolulu in 1920 by Mr. Takejiro Kanda, and in 1921 the Takei Miso Factory was started on Maui by Mr. Shuji Takei. Other early Honolulu miso manufacturers were Ueno Miso Factory (1920s), Fukuda Miso Factory (1920s). Over the years a new and unique style of miso was developed in Hawaii. It originated in Okinawa, whence came many of Hawaii's early miso makers. The Hawaiian-style miso was sweeter and less salty than most Japanese misos, containing typically 70% rice and 30% soybeans. It was prized mostly for use with seafoods, rather than in miso soups or with vegetables. Many of the first miso makers in the continental USA were from Hawaii or had learned to make miso in Hawaii, and most of the miso made or used on the American mainland prior to World War II was this sweeter Hawaiian-style product.

The earliest known miso plant in the United States, the Fujimoto Miso Company, founded by Mr. Genpei Fujimoto, began operation in San Francisco in 1917. During World War II, about 1943 or 1944, because of the Japanese evacuation, the company was shut down and moved to 302 South Fourth West, Salt Lake City, Utah. It was re-established after the War by the son of the founder, Edward Kanta Fujimoto, and his wife Shizue. Edward died in 1958 and Mrs. Fujimoto continued to run the business until 1976, when she sold her equipment and the Kanemasa brand to Miyako Oriental Foods, which was established that year in Los Angeles.

The next commercial miso plant in the U.S. was the Norio Company, started in 1919 in San Francisco at 1531 Geary St. by Mr. Masaichi Norio; he made only *shiro miso* (probably sweet white, mellow white, or light yellow miso)

and exported most of it to Hawaii. In about 1932 the company was moved to 1532 Post St., where it was run by relatives, Mr. and Mrs. Minoru Arikawa and son. The U.S. government forced the family to close the business (then making about 82 tonnes of miso a year) when World War II started in 1941. They resumed after the War but retired in 1972 and the business was closed to make room for construction of a high-rise condominium (B.W. 1971; Arikawa 1982, personal communication).

According to George Tsuchiya, manager of T. Amano Co., there were several semi-commercial makers of miso and shoyu in Canada, in the Vancouver area, prior to World War I, and at least one commercial miso manufacturer was in the area prior to 1927. In that year, Mr. T. Amano, who stemmed from a family that made commercial miso and shoyu in Hiroshima, started a company called Amano Brothers on East Powell Street in Vancouver. He made his first miso in 1927 and his first shoyu in 1931. In 1982 the T. Amano company was making a red miso and a sweet white miso, as well as fermented shoyu.

Sometime between 1927 and 1932 the Tsuruda Miso Company was started in San Jose, California, by Mr. and Mrs. Tsuruda; it was shut down during World War II and never resumed.

1930 to 1959: When William Morse visited East Asia from 1929 to 1931 he wrote a lot about Japanese miso in his journals and included numerous photographs. He mentioned that Hatcho miso was then aged for 20 months and had been made in the same Hayakawa Kyuemon plant for about 300 years, that all miso was sold in wooden casks with braided bamboo hoops and, when retailed, was wrapped in the outer sheaves of bamboo shoots, that sweet white miso was most widely used for pickling fish, beef, etc., and that in making Sendai miso the steamed beans were still cooled by spreading them in wave patterns on the plant's wooden floors.

Miller (1933) discussed the use of miso in pickling vegetables such as eggplant, cucumbers, and the Oreintal pickling melon. A.K. Smith (1949) gave a good update on the manufacture and use of miso in Japan. This important article was partly responsible for the first real research on miso done in the West, at the USDA in Peoria, Illinois.

During this period a number of new miso manufacturers started production in Hawaii: Yamaju Miso Factory (1936, purchased by George Higa from Mr. Fukuda), American Hawaiian Soy Co. (1941; George Higa and co-workers), Fujii Miso Factory (c. 1941-54), Honolulu Miso Factory (c. 1942-50), and Hawaiian Miso & Soy Co. (1947; George and William Higa). In Los Angeles, the Yamaizumi Co. started making miso in about 1948 under the direction of Mr. Nagai, a craftsman from Fukuoka, Japan. During the 1960s their business declined, and in 1972, they started repacking Marufuku-brand miso, imported from the Hawaiin Soy Sauce Company in Honolulu, and selling it in America under the Yamaizumi brand. In 1975 Miyako Oriental Foods bought the rights to the Yamaizumi brand from Mrs. Nagai and the Yamaizumi company ceased operations.

In February 1942, shortly after the outbreak of

World War II, President Roosevelt signed Executive Order 9066, which permitted internment of 120,000 West-Coast Japanese-Americans in ten detention camps. All of the miso shops on the West Coast of the U.S. were forcibly shut down and their owners and workers sent to the camps. At that time Fujimoto was the largest miso company in the U.S. and Arimoto, making 82 tonnes a year, was probably second.

After the war there was little or no interest in miso among the non-Oriental Americans until the early 1960s.

Growth of Interest in Miso (1960-1982): The first real research on miso fermentation done in the Western world was carried out at the USDA Northern Regional Research Center in Peoria, Illinois, by Dr. Kazuo Shibasaki (a Japanese professor of agricultural chemistry, well trained in microbiology) and Dr. Clifford W. Hesseltine (Director of the NRRC fermentation laboratory and an eminent American microbiologist). Work began when Shibasaki arrived at the NRRC in 1957. Funded by various American groups promoting soybean exports, the team hoped to find new soybean varieties and processing methods to overcome some of the objections to American soybeans voiced by miso makers in Japan. But the research went much farther than anticipated; between 1960 and 1962 Shibasaki and Hesseltine published six pioneering scientific journal articles about miso and its fermentation and in 1961 a public service patent on "Preparation of Miso," was issued to Smith, Hesseltine, and Shibasaki. In 1959, in part because of this research, the first U.S. soybeans imported to Japan started to be used in making miso. And the NRRC miso research found other practical applications in Japan. It led to (1) the use of pure culture yeast inocula in the second stage of the miso fermentation, in place of the traditional mixed culture taken from a previous miso fermentation, (2) the development and use of solid substrate fermentations for the industrial production of enzymes and secondary metabolites, and (3) the development of the large-scale trommel (horizontal-axis tumbler) system of making koji, which produced more enzymes. Later, in April 1974, another Japanese researcher, Mr. Ichiro Ouchi, arrived at the NRRC then spent one year with Dr. Hesseltine developing new uses for miso in Western-style foods (such as barbecue sauce, spaghetti sauce, pizza, miso mayonnaise, and potato chips) to be introduced into the increasingly westernized diet of the younger generation in Japan. While the ultimate aim of this work, like Dr. Shibasaki's, was to increase soybean exports to Japan, some of the new recipes attracted interest in America as well. Hesseltine liked the barbecue sauce, thickened and seasoned with miso, and enjoyed introducing miso to visitors, served on a cucumber slice. From the early 1960s on, Hesseltine and co-workers at Peoria published information on miso in a wide variety of books and presented papers at many symposia. The early research at Peoria plus these publications on miso led to considerable interest in this savory fermented soyfood among western microbiologists and food scientists (an interest dormant since the 1880s), and helped to "legitimize" this ancient seasoning. As of early 1983 the NRRC was working with the University of Wisconsin to investigate the safety and storage life of low-salt misos, testing for possibilities of food poisoning from *Staphylococcus, Yersinia,* or botulism.

As noted previously at "History of Miso in Japan," the subject of aflatoxins came to the public attention in 1960 when contaminated peanuts killed 100,000 poultry in England. Despite the fact that by 1969 Japanese researchers had proved conclusively that aflatoxins were not a problem in miso or shoyu, in May of that year *TIME* magazine published a half-page article titled "Cancer: A Clue from Under the Eaves," about possible aflatoxins in homemade East Asian miso and soy sauce. Although the article's conclusions were highly speculative and the analytical techniques used strongly criticized, some Americans unfamiliar with the details and background of the issue became alarmed and wondered if it was perhaps unsafe to consume miso and soy sauce. In response to these concerns and much larger concerns with aflatoxins in U.S. livestock feeds, peanuts, and corn, researchers at the NRRC in Peoria began extensive investigations of aflatoxins. In 1979 Wang and Hesseltine, top American researchers on the subject, reviewed the literature, which showed repeatedly that soybeans are a poor substrate for aflatoxin production. The koji mold is completely different from molds of the same *Aspergillus* genus that produce aflatoxins, just as edible and poisonous mushrooms come from the same genus. Moreover, aflatoxins are most commonly found on peanuts, corn, cottonseeds, and copra. In short, then, fears concerning aflatoxins in miso are totally ungrounded, for none have ever been found in any commercial miso or soy sauce. The same is true of nitrosamines, as discussed previously at "History in Japan."

The single most important force in introducing miso to America and popularizing its use was the macrobiotic movement, founded by a remarkable Japanese couple, George and Lima Ohsawa. Their work began at about the same time as that at the USDA/NRRC in Peoria, although the two knew nothing of one another. In the early 1950s several of Ohsawa's macrobiotic students had arrived in New York City to prepare a beachhead and as early as March 1952 Herman Aihara was selling miso, imported from Ohsawa in Japan, in New York City. Ohsawa first arrived in America in December 1959. From January to March, 1960, he presented 30 lectures on macrobiotics and published a mimeographic edition of *Zen Macrobiotics*, which was sold for $0.50 at the lectures. The booket contained ten miso recipes (perhaps the first published in the U.S.) and introduced miso and shoyu as key components of a macrobiotic diet. Shoyu was spelled "syoyu;" Ohsawa did not call it *tamari*, as he later would. Soon Ohsawa's small but dedicated group of American students were using these new foods as part of their daily fare. During the late 1950s and early 1960s, two restaurants (Zen Teahouse and Musubi) and a macrobiotic food store (Ginza) were started by Ohsawa's Japanese students in New York City. They served and/or sold miso and natural shoyu, which Ohsawa had sent from Japan. In about November 1963 Michio Kushi opened the Genpei Restaurant in the Diamond Jim Building on 46th St. in

New York. In the basement, Junsei Yamazaki, just arrived from Japan via Chico, California, made his own barley koji then made about 100 pounds of miso in three 18-liter soy sauce vats. This was the first "macrobiotic" miso made in America; it was later moved to the basement of the Kushi home in Boston, where it finished its aging, then was enjoyed by the Kushis and their students.

For Ohsawa, as for all subsequent teachers and students of macrobiotics, miso was far more than just a savory high-protein seasoning and a source of natural digestion-aiding enzymes and bacteria. According to macrobiotic philosophy, it was, above all a very *yang* food (since it contained salt and was fermented under pressure for a long time) and, as such, it had intrinsic healing, almost medicinal effects that could be used to combat various diseases (the result of an excessively *yin* constitution) and aid in maintaining a balanced constitution or body/mind. For this reason most macrobiotic followers recommended the more *yang* barley and Hatcho misos for daily and healing use, rather than the various rice misos, which were considered more *yin*. It was primarily because of this belief in a deeper dimension to miso's value that Ohsawa and the macrobiotic movement took such a deep interest in miso. Indeed brown rice, cooked land and sea vegetables, and miso soup were considered the primary ingredients, to be used daily, in a healthful and healing macrobiotic diet.

From 1960 to 1966 Ohsawa lectured repeatedly about the virtues of miso and shoyu. In 1964 and 1966 editions of his popular macrobiotic cookbook, *Zen Cookery*, were published. It contined an entire chapter on "Miso Soy Bean Paste," including 13 recipes, which generated growing interest in this largely unknown soyfood. In 1965 a second edition of *Zen Macrobiotics* contained numerous miso recipes. At the time of Ohsawa's death in 1966 (he was 72), a rapidly growing number of young Caucasian Americans, interested in natural foods and macrobiotics, were using miso and shoyu regularly.

Ohsawa's students, both Japanese and American, actively continued his work. In late 1961 a group of students from New York had migrated to Chico, California, and in March 1962 they founded a new food company called Chico-San. They imported traditional miso from Japan and had it widely distributed under their label. Herman Aihara and Bob Kennedy lectured widely on miso and macrobiotics. In 1964 Junsei Yamazaki began experimental production of miso and shoyu at Chico-san and over the years he made 20 whiskey barrels full of 320 pounds miso each. When this miso matured, it was generally mixed with miso imported from Japan. In mid 1970 Yamazaki began to make large batches. Tragically in September 1972, when he had 4,500 to 5,000 pounds aging in wooden vats, the building burned down and all the miso was destroyed. After that Yamazaki taught miso making to small groups of students. In mid 1968 *Health Food Business Review* wrote an article about Chico-San's miso, calling it "Soy Bean Puree." This was the first popular article or health-food article about miso written in the U.S. In 1972 Aihara wrote and published *Miso and Tamari*, the first booklet about these foods in the West. It contained the first recipes for making miso and miso pickles at home; recipes for making barley, rice, and Hatcho miso were also given. In 1974 a revised and expanded edition of the book entitled *Soybean Diet* was published. Herman and Cornellia taught about miso extensively and published a number of other macrobiotic cookbooks containing miso recipes, such as the *Chico-San Cookbook* (1972). Chico-San continued to import, advertise, and distribute fine natural miso, expanding their efforts in the early 1980s. As of 1983 Chico-San had a three-stage plan to make miso in Chico. Working with a Japanese miso company they would first import bulk miso to Chico and practice aging it, then make miso at Chico using koji imported from Japan under refrigeration, and finally make the entire miso (including the koji) at Chico. They also hoped to make shoyu. In 1980 Yamazaki bought land in Orland in Northern California, where he hoped to start making high-quality miso using the finest natural ingredients, and to grow *ume* plums for *umeboshi* salt plums

Another center of activity for macrobiotics and miso was Boston, where Michio and Aveline Kushi taught, starting in September 1963. In April 1966 they opened Erewhon, a small macrobiotic food store that carried, among other things, natural miso and shoyu. The miso was purchased from Infinity Foods in New York, Chico-san in California, and a little from Lima Foods in Belgium. Hatcho miso was ordered from local Japanese trading companies, Japan Foods Corp. or Nishimoto. These misos were among the store's best-selling items. In 1968 Sanae, a macrobiotic restaurant, was started in Boston; it served miso and other soyfoods, as did all subsequent macrobiotic restaurants in Boston. Also in 1968 Erewhon started to import foods, including miso and shoyu, from Japan. A wholesale and distribution company was started that year and soon it was trucking a line of fine imported Japanese red, barley, and Hatcho misos to a growing number of natural food stores. The natural foods boom hit America in 1970, carrying Erewhon (and miso) along with it. Sesame miso and tekka miso were added to the Erewhon line. Other macrobiotic and natural food distributors sprang up across America and they too all carried and strongly promoted miso. In 1980 Erewhon sold roughly 150,000 pounds of its three basic misos. The *East West Journal*, founded in Boston in January 1971, soon became America's leading macrobiotic magazine. It played a major role in popularizing miso, with many excellent articles and recipes, as described later. Autumn Press, whose founder Nahum Stiskin studied macrobiotics in Boston, translated and published Lima Ohsawa's *The Art of Just Cooking* (1974), which contained many miso recipes, then in 1976 published the original edition of *The Book of Miso* by Shurtleff and Aoyagi. In 1978 Aveline Kushi wrote *How to Cook with Miso*, which was widely read. In 1980, after about a year of eating a strict macrobiotic diet and receiving consultations from Michio Kushi, Dr. Anthony Sattilaro, a physician and then chief administrator at Methodist Hospital in South Philadelphia, experienced an almost miraculous complete recovery from terminal cancer that had riddled his body. The dramatic story was published in the *East*

West Journal (March 1980 and March 1981), the Saturday Evening Post (August 1981), and LIFE magazine (August 1982) and eventually in a best-selling major book Recalled By Life (Sattilaro 1982). Through these publications miso, in the form of miso soup, which was a key part of his daily macrobiotic diet, was introduced to millions of Americans. In these and a host of other ways, the Boston macrobiotic community played a leading role in introducing miso to America.

During the 1960s New York remained active as a center of interest in macrobiotics and miso. Howard Rower's Infinity Foods, established in the mid-1960s, imported fine miso from a macrobiotic exporter in Japan and distributed it to natural food companies in the U.S. Michael Abehsera, a young Jewish French Moroccan who began studying and practicing macrobiotics in 1961, arrived with his wife in New York from Paris in 1964. Thereafter the couple ran a number of highly successful macrobiotic restaurants in New York City, all of which served miso, and he wrote two macrobiotic cookbooks, Zen Macrobiotic Cooking (1968) and Cooking for Life (1970), which sold very well and each contained four miso recipes. In 1969 the Abehseras toured the entire U.S., lecturing about macrobiotics, including miso.

Another key macrobiotic miso teacher was Noboru Muramoto, who immigrated to Amercia from Japan in 1971. In his popular book Healing Ourselves (1973) he suggested a number of medicinal uses for miso. From 1976, at his Asunaro Institute near Glen Ellen, California, he set up a regular shop for making miso and shoyu, developed (with his students) various American-style miso recipes, and taught many students these food crafts, including at least one (Elwell) who went on to open a commercial miso company (Lauchman and Elwell 1978). His newsletter Asunaro Notes published several articles on miso making. In late 1979 Muramoto relocated his Institute in Escondido, California, where he continued to give classes on miso and other Japanese foods.

The first four non-Oriental miso companies in America were all founded by students of macrobiotics: Thom Leonard of Ohio Miso Co., John Belleme of American Miso company in North Carolina, Christian and Gaella Elwell of South River Miso Co., in Massachusetts, and Dale Deraps of Imagine Foods/Moniteau Farm in Missouri. Strangely, many macrobiotic companies, teachers, and publications persisted in the use of Japanese names for miso (saying mugi for "barley," genmai for "brown rice," komé for "rice," etc.) which gave miso a slightly exotic image and probably slowed its introduction to America. They also were slow to accept the growing medical advice that less salt consumption is better. Despite these minor points, the macrobiotic community unquestionably played the leading role in introducing miso to the Western world.

Although students of macrobiotics were the first Caucasians seriously interested in miso and in using it daily, and although they opened the first Caucasian miso shops, they were not the very first Caucasians to make their own miso for food use. Students at Tassajara Zen Mountain Center in California have that distinction. In the fall of either 1968 or 1969 Kobun Chino-sensei, a Japanese Zen priest, worked with Ed Brown (head cook), William Shurtleff, and several other Americans in making miso. They obtained koji starter from Japantown in San Francisco, made rice koji which was incubated in handmade wooden trays above the Tassajara kitchen stove, cooked soybeans in large pots and ground them in a Corona hand mill, then mashed together the koji, soybeans and salt in a large brandy barrel (the charred interior had been scraped clean) using a wooden mochi pounder. After being aged in the basement for 12 months, the 35 to 50 gallons of excellent-quality miso was used in the community's meals – mostly in soups. It is interesting to note that the transmission of this ancient art was made by Buddhist priests, just as it had been in Japan 1200 years earlier.

After 1973 a growing number of Caucasian Americans, mostly students of macrobiotics, began to make their own miso. In about 1973 Aveline Kushi in Boston held some informal miso making classes using ready-made store-bought koji; one 18-liter keg of miso was made. In 1974 Blake Rankin, freshly returned from studying miso shops in Japan, worked with George Gearhart at Janus Foods in Seattle making small batches from store-bought koji. By 1975 they were making their own barley and wheat koji in redwood koji trays during 3-day workshops and teaching six students from the Seattle Zen Center. Eventually they made 500 pounds and published a description of the process. By 1976 Gearhart was teaching miso making classes in Washington and California, as was Bob Gerner at Westbrae Natural Foods in Berkeley. In the fall of 1974 Thom Leonard made his first batch of barley koji and barley miso in Lawrence, Kansas, using a recipe in Aihara's new book Soybean Diet. The 80-pound batch of miso was aged in a soy sauce keg from Hong Kong. He then made 80-pound batches of chunky wheat miso in early 1976. After moving to Fayetteville, Arkansas, he and Jim Heminger made larger scale miso equipment and on 15 April 1977 packed their first 35-gallon cedar vat with brown-rice miso. Soon over 1,000 pounds were aging in the vats (Leonard 1977). This miso was sold to and distributed by the Ozark Cooperative Warehouse. In the summer of 1980 Leonard taught miso classes at the macrobiotic Moniteau Farm in Missouri. Then from late 1980 on he taught about 15 classes on making miso and other soyfoods at the Kushi Institute and at his home in Boston. In 1983 he went to Ireland to start a miso plant in County Kilkenny; it never happened. Others who made miso on a home or community scale in the mid-1970s included Charlie Kendall, Robert Johnson, David Tucker, and The Farm in Tennessee.

In May 1974 William Shurtleff and Akiko Aoyagi, then living in Japan, started to write The Book of Miso. Shurtleff had been introduced to miso by poets Allen Ginsberg and Gary Snyder on a Circumambulation of Mt. Tamalpias in February 1967 (it was served with sesame tahini as a spread on crackers), had frequently used and twice made miso after June 1968 while working as a cook at Tassajara Zen Mountain Center near Big Sur in California, and in the spring of 1973 had made miso on Suwanose Island in southern Japan, then studied miso-like products in Taiwan and Korea. *The Book of Miso,* published in September 1976 by Autumn Press, was the first major book on miso in the West, and Shurtleff was the first westerner since Kellner in 1889 to do extensive research on miso in East Asia and the first ever to apprentice to a Japanese miso master. The book contained information on miso varieties, nutrition, history, production (on a home, community, traditional shop, or modern factory scale), and microbiology, plus 400 recipes and a lengthy bibliography. In 1981 an updated mass market edition was published by Ballantine Books; by late 1982 the two editions had sold 70,000 copies. In 1977 the Shurtleffs self-published *Miso Production,* describing how to start and run a commercial miso plant; the book was used in starting a number of such plants in the following years. These books helped to establish and standardize the English names of miso varieties and, in general, to introduce miso to the West.

With the growing demand for fine miso, a new wave of miso manufacturers started in America. The last company had been started in 1932. The first of the new companies was Miyako Oriental Foods, which opened in an 11,000-square-foot plant in Los Angeles (404 Towne Ave.) in June 1976, as a division of Yamajirushi Miso Company in Japan. The company was founded by Mr. Noritoshi Kanai, who had come to the U.S. in 1955 from Japan and noticed that no Japanese miso was being imported, so that only Hawaiian-style miso was available. He started to import Japanese miso to meet a growing demand from new Japanese immigrants. In 1975, to expand his line, Mr. Kanai bought the rights to the Yamaizumi brand of Hawaiian-style miso, then being imported to Los Angeles, and in 1976 his Miyako Oriental Foods began making this product in Los Angeles. Also in 1976 he bought the Kanemasa brand and some of the equipment from the former Fujimoto Miso Company and began to make a Japanese-style miso to supplement his imports. His main competitors were in Hawaii; in the early 1970s about 200 tons a year of Maruhi brand miso was being made and 100 tons a year of Murafuku brand (made by Hawaiian Soy Sauce Co.). During its first year of production in Los Angeles, Miyako made 150 to 200 tons of miso. Its bestseller was Yamajirushi brand (65%), followed by Kanemasa (25%) and Yamaizumi (10%). Most of the company's miso was sold in California. In 1978 Miyako introduced the Cold Mountain brand, marketed to the natural foods trade and started selling firm granular rice koji under that brand in tubs of 12 or 20 ounces, or 25 pounds for people wishing to make their own miso. By 1981 Miyako was producing four brands of miso plus rice koji, and also doing some private labeling. Ninety percent of their miso was sold to the Oriental trade; the remaining 10% was their Cold Mountain brand, with four varieties sold to the natural and health food trades. Eighty percent of their total sales were in California. Their production capacity was reported to be 454 tonnes (500 U.S. tons) a year in 1979, up 300% in five years and growing with the market at 15 to 25% a year. By late 1982 Miyako, now making 544 tonnes (600 U.S. tons) of miso a year, had outgrown its original plant.

In September the operation was moved into a sparkling new 20,000-square-foot plant with an annual capacity of 1,800 tonnes in Baldwin Park, California. The grand opening, costing $15,000, drew 500 miso enthusiasts. With sales now growing at 10 to 15% a year Miyako is considering production of powdered misos (Leviton 1983).

THE OHIO MISO COMPANY, INC.
ROUTE 2   MONROEVILLE, OHIO   44847
419/668-9512

The first Caucasian-run miso company in North America was Ohio Miso Co. in Monroeville, Ohio, founded by Thom Leonard and Richard Kluding; they began production on 13 March 1979. Thom had been making miso on a small, noncommercial scale since late 1974, as described earlier. By January 1980 Ohio Miso was making several varieties of miso: brown rice, barley (one or two year), mellow brown rice, mellow red, and black soybean; output was 2,400 pounds a week (Whole Foods 1979; Carr 1980; Leviton 1980).

Other early companies were Shin-Mei-Do Miso (opened April 1979 by Lulu Yoshihara; Denman Island, B.C., Canada); American Miso, Inc. (October 1981 by John Belleme; Rutherfordton, North Carolina); South River Miso Co. (having bought out Ohio Miso Co. in November 1980, Christian and Gaella Elwell started their own production in October 1982 in a beautiful traditional shop at Conway, Massachusetts). The founders of Shin-Mei-Do and American Miso, Inc. had both apprenticed with makers of traditional miso in Japan (Belleme 1981, 1981a). American Miso was the largest of the new Caucasian-run companies. Located on 100 acres of rural land, the company spent $325,000 for two buildings (3,500 square feet) and unique equipment, which combined both traditional and modern-mechanized components. The plant's capacity was 227 metric tons (500,000 pounds) of miso a year. Production grew steadily from 1,250 pounds a week in April 1982, to 3,000-4,800 pounds a week in late summer 1982, up to 6,000 pounds a week in early 1983, the latter being the equivalent of 131 tonnes a year. A detailed cover story by Leviton in the summer 1981 issue of *Soyfoods* magazine described the company's operations; it was making red (rice), mellow barley, and mellow white misos of excellent quality, with plans for miso dips and dressings, and from 1983, natural shoyu (see also Greenwood 1982). In 1982 Dale Deraps of Imagine Foods/Moniteau Farm in Jamestown, Missouri, and Mr. Chong of General Oriental Foods (225 tonnes a year capacity) in Holmdel, New Jersey, both began making miso. Most of these companies made naturally fermented, unpasteurized miso. As of 1983 a number of new companies and individuals were seriously considering starting miso plants in the U.S., which will certainly help create an expanding market.

The American media, and especially the macrobiotic and natural foods media, took a strong interest in miso. Major articles included "Soy Bean Puree: Miso. Ancient Oriental Health Food" (*Health Food Business Review*, July 1968), "Recipes from Aveline Kushi's Book of Miso" *(East West Journal* 1971), "Making Miso in America" (B.W. 1971, *EWJ*, a visit to the Norio Company in San Francisco), "How to Make Miso: An Excerpt from *The Book of Miso"* (*EWJ*, Nov. 1976), "Cooking: From the Book of Miso" *(EWJ*, June 1977), "Making Miso in America" *(EWJ*, Sept. 1978), "Cooking with Miso" (*Alternatives*, Nov. 1978), "Down-Home Miso" *(Whole Foods*, Oct. 1979), "Miso: Made in the U.S.A."*(EWJ*, Jan. 1980), "Make Way for Miso" *(Bestways*, July 1980), "The Miso Master's Apprentice" *(EWJ*, April 1981), "American Miso Makes a Big Move Down South" and "Miso-Cup" *(Soyfoods*, Summer 1982), and "Smokey Mountain Miso" *(EWJ*, Nov. 1982, about American Miso Co.). After the near nuclear reactor catastrophe at Three Mile Island in March 1979, a number of media articles recommended that Americans use miso since the dipicolonic acid it contains may partially protect the body from ingested radioactive materials.

Starting in the 1960s, there was a growing interest in Chinese and Japanese cooking in the U.S. Gloria Miller's *The Thousand Recipe Chinese Cookbook* (1966) was one of the first to have good information on and recipes for Chinese chiang. Good early Japanese cookbooks with many miso recipes included *Japanese Country Cookbook* (Rudzinsky 1969), The *Cookery of Japan* (Steinberg, 1969; a magnificent work), and *Zen Tastes in Japanese Cooking* (Tsuji 1971; the finest work available on Tea Ceremony Cuisine).

After the pioneering scientific research on miso and its fermentation by Shibasaki and Hesseltine in the early 1960s, there was surprisingly little such research subsequently. In 1974 C. Kao at Kansas State University published a PhD dissertation on miso (and other fermented foods) made from chickpeas, fava beans, and soybeans, then in 1977 Robinson and Kao wrote a jounral article summary of that research. In 1979 and 1981 Fukushima gave general information on miso and its status in Japan. Also, a number of Japanese patents for miso and koji began to be granted in the U.S. (Koyama 1976; Hayashi 1977).

American miso makers and marketers were innovative, developing a number of new products suited to American tastes. In the mid 1970s most of the miso in America was sold as such, in bulk or plastic bags, imported from Japan. The most popular varieties were red, barley, and Hatcho miso. A Finger Lickin' miso was also quite popular on the West Coast. America's first widely distributed product in which miso was used as an ingredient in a popular preparation was Instant Aka Miso Soup, introduced by Kikkoman in a foil packet in 1968 and sold in the Japanese food section at many West Coast supermarkets, as well

as Japanese food stores. By 1983 Kikkoman was offering an Instant Aka Miso Soup, Instant Shiro Miso Soup, and Instant Tofu Miso Soup, each in a large, colorful foil packet. In the fall of 1978 Edward & Sons Trading Co., under the direction of Joel Dee, introduced Miso-Cup, an instant natural dehydrated miso soup, packaged in foil pouches. By 1980 two flavors were available: golden light and rich savory with seaweed. Miso-Cup soon became the most widely advertised miso product in America (Leviton 1982). Year after year, full-page color or black-and-white ads in many U.S. natural and health food publications served to introduce millions of Americans to miso. Some people used Miso-Cup to help them kick the coffee/caffeine habit, finding its aroma and flavor as appetizing as those of coffee. In 1982 Edward & Sons introduced two powdered miso dip mixes, Miso-Plus Chive and Miso-Plus Jalapeno. Mixed with sour cream, yogurt, avocado, etc., they yielded quick and easy party dips or salad dressings. In the late 1970s San-J introduced a powdered soybean miso, containing 33% protein, which they sold to food processors as a natural substitute for MSG. White Wave in Colorado introduced a Yellow Miso Dressing, sold in an 8-ounce jar. In 1980 Marusan started importing two types of instant miso soups with red or white miso and ran full page color ads in trade magazines. In 1982 Fantastic Foods launched a widely advertised Quick Pilaf: Brown Rice with Miso, Health Valley introduced Vegetarian Baked Beans with Miso and Corn Chips with Miso and Wizard Baldour debuted a Hot Stuff with Miso. In early 1983 Westbrae Natural Foods presented their Instant Miso Soup in "white flavor and red flavor." Increasingly, then, miso was used as a key ingredient in other popular American foods.

American miso makers also experimented with using new basic ingredients to make new basic types of miso. Starting in about 1975 craftsmen began getting good results using peanuts, garbanzo beans (chick peas), black soybeans, and natto in place of regular soybeans, making their koji from corn, millet, wheat, or buckwheat, and using powdered kelp as a partial salt substitute. Yet except for the corn-soy miso and moromi wheat miso made by South River Miso Co. and Imagine Foods, relatively little of these new American-style misos were sold commercially.

During the 1970s and early 1980s the miso market in the U.S. grew steadily, with the growth coming from both increased imports and increased domestic production. Imports of miso from Japan to the U.S. grew from 219 tonnes in 1970 to 959 tonnes in 1982, for a 4.4-fold increase in just 12 years and a compound growth rate of more than 12% a year. Note that the growth rate increased markedly after 1968 (page 240). An estimated 20 to 25% of this imported miso was the traditional, natural style sold to the natural foods trade, with most of the rest going to Oriental food stores. Imported miso was subject to a 14% import duty. Interestingly miso and soy sauce were the only two soyfoods imported in large quantities to America; smaller quantities of soymilk and tofu in Tetra-Pak were also imported.

Despite the rapid increase in miso imports, it appears that production of miso in America grew at an even faster

U.S. MISO IMPORTS, PRODUCTION AND CONSUMPTION

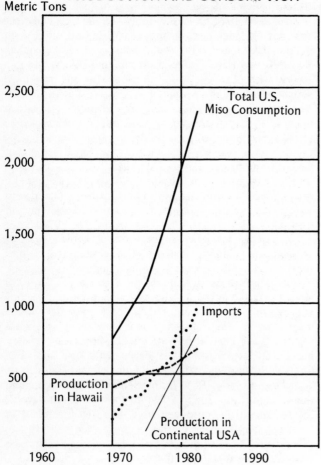

Metric Tons

- 2,500
- 2,000
- 1,500
- 1,000
- 500

Total U.S. Miso Consumption

Imports

Production in Hawaii

Production in Continental USA

1960   1970   1980   1990

Source: Japan Exports & Imports: Commodity by Country

$4.9 million. The total retail value of domestically made and imported miso was about $8.2 million.

This miso was consumed by both Asian and Caucasian Americans, both in growing numbers. During the 1970s the population of Asian and Pacific Americans grew by leaps and bounds, from 1,369,000 in 1970 to 3,500,000 in 1980, up 2.5-fold. The leading miso consumers in 1980 were probably Japanese-Americans, which numbered 700,747, up from 591,000 in 1970. The 806,000 Chinese-Americans and 774,000 Filipino-Americans were also important consumers. The main centers of Asian-American population, in order of importance, were Honolulu, New York, Los Angeles, San Francisco, Chicago, San Jose (California), Seattle, and Houston.

Caucasian miso consumers came from several groups. The great majority came from the closely related natural foods, macrobiotic, or vegetarian movements, but some came from the growing number of people interested in Japanese, Chinese, and other Asian cuisines. The prime consumer age group was 25 to 40. To each of these meatless or largely meatless diets, miso added its savory rich flavor plus some protein. Although the percentage of all miso in America consumed by Caucasians grew rapidly during the 1970s, as of 1983 it was probably still somewhat less than that consumed by Oriental Americans (primarily Japanese Americans).

From the mid 1970s to 1983 major changes took place in the miso market in America. Total miso consumption tripled and miso was increasingly sold as an *ingredient* in other popular foods rather than as miso itself. Misos with a lower salt content, lighter color, and sweeter flavor passed the darker, more traditional misos in popularity as Americans looked to reduce their salt intake. The market share of American-made misos steadily increased, even though they were generally more expensive than imports. The sale of domestically made misos in a cottage-cheese style round plastic tub with a pop-off lid made them easier to use than those in a sealed plastic bag and allowed them to be sold unpasteurized. Packaged miso (in tubs and bags) rapidly replaced the lower cost but messier bulk, self-serve misos. Important importers who distributed miso to the prime Caucasian markets (most also carried domestic misos) were, in approximate order of size, Westbrae Natural Foods in California, Tree of Life in Florida, Eden Foods in Michigan, Erewhon in Massachusetts, Chico-San in California, and Marusan in New Jersey. Major Japanese distributors, which serviced Oriental food stores and supermarkets, are listed in Appendix E. In 1982 a survey of 60,000 readers of *New Age* magazine showed that 36% purchased miso at least once a month. Yet more important, a steadily growing number of typical Americans were starting to use miso, usually as an ingredient in other popular foods. More and more natural foods restaurants (including soy delis, restaurants, and cafes) included miso dishes on their menu. The most popular use, at home and in restaurants, was in soups, followed by dips, dressings, sauces, and spreads. Most Americans greatly enjoy the flavor of a well-made miso soup.

In late 1982 JETRO, a Los Angeles based organization promoting Japanese exports, published a 32-page study

rate, although precise, prior to 1975, statistics are not available. Reliable estimates, however, indicate that between 1975 and 1982 miso production in the contiguous 48 states jumped from 120 to 750 tonnes, a remarkable 525%, while production in Hawaii grew steadily from 543 to 640 tonnes, some 18%. Thus total U.S. miso consumption (imports plus domestic production) grew from 756 tonnes in 1970 to 1,122 tonnes in 1975, up to 2,349 tonnes in 1982. By late 1982 Americans in the continental U.S. were consuming *three times* as much miso as they had in 1975 and the market was growing at about 10% a year!

As of 1983, the miso industry in the U.S. consisted of eight manufacturers (three in Hawaii), plus two more in Canada (see Appendix D). The largest producers were Miyako Oriental Foods (544 tonnes a year), Hawaiian Miso & Soy Co. (512 tonnes a year), American Miso, Inc. (125 tonnes a year), and American Hawaiian Soy Co. (125 tonnes a year). The U.S. miso industry used about 463 tonnes of soybeans and employed about 27 workers to make this miso, which retailed for about (in Japanese) on the American Miso Market. Surveys done in Los Angeles showed that 63% of miso buyers in stores were Asian Americans and 37% were Caucasians; the predominant buyers were in their thirties or fifties; there were seven major miso importers in Los Angeles; and in 20 of Los Angeles' 450 Japanese restaurants, the main dishes in which miso was served were miso soup (19), Ishikari Nabe (one pot cookery, 5), Tofu Miso Dengaku (5), Steak Grilled with Miso (4), and Salad with Vinegar Miso Dressing (2).

Miso was introduced to Caucasian Americans from the 1960s on as food that fostered good health. Starting in the late 1970s there was a rising concern by a growing number of Americans over their excessive consumption of salt (sodium). At least initially, this probably hurt miso's image as a healthful food, since it contains an average of 12% salt. The low-salt trend definitely led to a shift toward lower salt misos. Yet in the process more and more people came to realize that miso is actually and excellent food to help *reduce* salt intake (as explained in detail in Chapter 2). Research has shown that people who season their food with miso instead of straight salt typically end up using 50% less salt, since miso adds its own rich flavor. The extensive research done in Japan on the relationship between miso consumption and good health is described in Chapter 2. And finally, there is a growing consensus among nutritionists and physicians that diets containing less saturated animal fats and cholesterol (as are widely consumed in red meats) are healthier. As interest in meatless diets grows among those interested in good health, reduced food bills, world hunger, and animal rights, miso is increasingly being used to provide the savory flavors and protein once obtained from meats.

It is interesting to compare consumption of miso and soy sauce in both Japan and the United States. In 1980 in Japan the per capita yearly consumption of miso was 6.0 kg (13.2 lbs.) whereas that of shoyu was 11.86 kg or 10.1 liters (26.1 lbs. or 2.67 gallons). Thus Japanese consumed almost twice as much shoyu by weight as miso. In America the figures were, of course, much lower. Per capita yearly consumption of soy sauce in the U.S. was 254 gm or 0.254 kg or 0.216 liters or 14.7 tablespoons, roughly 2% of the per capita consumption in Japan. Per capita yearly consumption of miso in the U.S. was 7.37 gm or 0.007 kg or 1.3 teaspoons per year, roughly 0.1% of the per capita miso consumption in Japan. Thus the average Japanese consumes 50 times as much shoyu and 800 times as much miso as the average American, and the average American downs 35 times as much shoyu as miso.

One might be inclined to ask why, if both miso and shoyu are so widely used in Japan, miso is not nearly so well known nor widely used in the West. The reason for this unusual development lies, we feel, more in the difference in structure between the miso and shoyu industries, than in the basic appeal of the two foods. Most Japanese shoyu is produced by a few huge companies which have had the capacity and foresight to engage in international advertising and commerce. By comparison, the largest miso companies are quite small and have only a few decades of modern business experience. Therefore they have not yet been able to make their product known or available throughout the world. Nor, perhaps, have they become fully aware of the genuine interest in and potential market for fine miso in the United States and Europe. We are convinced that if a large (Japanese) miso company believed in the potential of miso as much as Kikkoman believes in that of shoyu (Japanese style soy sauce) and would promote miso as extensively and effectively as Kikkoman has promoted shoyu, miso's popularity would grow dramatically.

Miso's Future in the West: As of 1983 miso would seem to have a bright future in the West, as indicated by all major market trends except the concern with excess salt consumption, which can be turned to miso's advantage. In much the same way that the Japanese, over a period of 1,000 years, gradually transformed Chinese soybean chiang into unique and truly Japanese-style misos, so may we also expect that Westerners will continue the creative process, adapting miso to their own tastes, technology, and cuisine. There are many reasons to believe that miso will play an increasingly important role in America's evolving cuisine and become a standard household seasoning, just as soy sauce now is, as people discover the great variety of delicious flavors and aromas found in the many and varied types of fine miso.

MISO IN OTHER COUNTRIES

Miso has not yet attracted the attention it deserves in most Third World countries. We know of miso reasearch in only two countries not already mentioned:

Israel: Using United States P.L. 480 funds, Ilany-Feigenbaum and others (1967, 1969) and Diamant and Laxer (1967, 1968) developed misos from defatted soybean flakes and alternate carbohydrate sources such as corn, oats, potatoes, and sweet potatoes. Diamant and Laxer also developed a low-salt miso (4%), which had twice the P.E.R. of regular miso when fed to rats. Apparently the excess salt suppressed rat growth.

India: Rao et al. (1968, 1972) have done research on miso-like foods based in Indian oilseeds and pulses.

Latin America: The only Third World country we know of where miso is widely available is Brazil. However much of this miso is imported from Japan and most of it is consumed by the country's large Japanese population.

Friends of miso from Mexico have suggested that miso there might be marketed as "Super Miso," a play on words with *"Con su permiso,"* or "With your permission, I'd like some please."

Africa: The earliest known work on miso in Africa is very recent. In 1979 and 1982 Ms. Sumbo Abiose of Nigeria, working in Glasgow, Scotland, published excellent works on the miso fermentation process. Hopefully this will serve as an impetus to introduce miso to Africa, where soybean production is expanding rapidly and protein shortages are widespread.

Other East Asian Misos: Chinese Chiang, Korean Jang, and Indonesian Taucho

Dᴇᴠᴇʟᴏᴘᴇᴅ ɪɴ China long before the Christian era, chiang was the progenitor of the many varieties of miso and soy sauce that are now used throughout East Asia. As chiang was assimilated by various cultures, its name and basic character gradually changed to suit local conditions. In Korea it was transformed into *jang:* in Japan, it became miso and shoyu; in Indonesia and Thailand, *taucho;* and in Malaysia, *taucheo.*

Chiang in courtyard

CHINESE CHIANG

Although all varieties of Chinese-style miso are known collectivey as *chiang* (pronounced jiang), this term actually encompasses a remarkably wide range of foods, most of which are fermented with *Aspergillus oryzae* molds but many of which contain neither soybeans nor grain koji. Sharp in flavor, chaing often contains large amounts of fiery red peppers, plus small amounts of other spices such as garlic. Basic ingredients include nuts and seeds, broadbeans, flour or steamed bread, vegetables, and many sea foods. The most common varieties in China are Chunky Chiang *(tou-pan chiang)*, Sweet Wheat-flour Chiang *(t'ien mien chiang)*, and Red-pepper Chiang *(la-*

chiao chiang). In the West, the most widely available varieties— generally known by the Cantonese pronunciation of their names—are Bean Sauce *(yun-si* or *yuen-shi chiang)*, Hoishin Sauce *(hoisin chiang)*, Bean Paste or Chunky Chiang *(to-pan chiang)*, and Sweet Wheat-flour Chiang or Soy Jam *(t'inmin chiang)*; they are usually sold in 1-pound cans at Chinese food markets.

Whereas most Japanese miso is presently prepared commercially by professional craftsmen, the majority of Chinese chiang is prepared at home is much the same way that we in the West make our own jams, canned fruit, or pickles. Following centuries-old methodologies, both chiang and chiang-yu (the liquid pressed from chiang, i.e., soy sauce) are usually started in March or April; packed into 1- to 10-gallon earthenware crocks that are placed in courtyards or on rooftops or apartment balconies, they are allowed to ferment for 6 to 12 months. Most varieties are stirred daily, with rice wine added during the fermentation. The total production of chiang-yu is considerably larger than that of chiang. The Chinese have various terms for koji: *niang*, meaning "mother" is the general one, but it is often combined with the name for the type of fermentation for which it is used: *chiu niang* ("mother of alcohol") is koji used in making grain-based wines and *ts'u niang* ("mother of vinegar") for vinegar.

The flavor of homemade chiang varies greatly from household to household, and in many cases the strong aroma, high salt content, dark color, and extreme spiciness combine to create a product which appeals to only a small percentage of the population. In recent years, however, more uniform-tasting and universally appealing varieties have come to be prepared commercially on a large scale for distribution throughout the world. We find that sweet wheat-flour chiang—known to many Westerners as the basis for the delicious chocolate-brown sauce served with Peking Duck—is especially well suited to Western tastes.

In Taiwan and China, both homemade and commercial chiang scooped from open-top wooden kegs are sold at stores called "chiang gardens," which also deal in salt-pickled vegetables and soy sauce. Most shops sell only the three main varieties mentioned above, plus one or two local ones. Chiang is used in all of the major schools of Chinese cookery, usually as the base for sauces served with meat, seafood, or poultry

Fig. 47. Composition of Nutrients in 100 Grams of Chiang and Jang

Source: *Food Composition Tables for Use in East Asia (USDEW 1972) and Wang, (1979)*

Type of Chiang	Food Energy	Moisture	Protein	Fat	Carbo-hydrates (incl. fiber)	Fiber	Ash	Sodium	Calcium	Phosphorous	Iron	Potassium	Vit. B₁ (thiamine)	Vit. B₂ (riboflavin)	Vit. B₃ (niacin)
	Calories	Percent	Percent	Percent	Percent	Percent	Percent	Mg	Mg	Mg	Mg	Mg	Mg	Mg	Mg
Chunky Chiang (tou-pan chiang)	194	48.6	11.6	5.2	27.2	2.1	7.4	761	55	365	1.3	334	.07	1.19	1.2
Hot Chunky Chiang (la tou-pan chiang)	185	52.7	8.1	4.1	30.2	3.5	4.9	680	126	72	13.6	280	.35	.35	1.5
Sweet Wheat-flour Chiang (t'ien mien chiang)	192	47.0	5.4	1.2	40.1	2.7	6.3	570	32	104	5.7	183	.18	.80	0.9
Korean Soybean Jang (doen jang)	—	59.4	10.6	8.4	5.7	2.6	16.0	—	—	—	—	—	.002	.01	1.8
Korean Red-pepper Jang (kochu jang)	—	49.3	9.3	4.2	23.4	2.3	13.7	—	—	—	—	—	.08	.11	1.2
Korean Soybean Koji (meju)	—	23.2	43.0	17.8	11.9	5.7	4.1	—	—	—	—	—	—	—	—

dishes, and less commonly, with stir-fried tofu and vegetable preparations. (The Chinese have never adopted the Japanese practice of using chiang in soups.) At Chinese restaurants in the West, it can be sampled in a wide array of dishes listed as containing "bean sauce" or "bean paste."

The most common classification divides all chiang into four basic types: red or regular chiang, black chiang, assorted chiang, and chiang sauces. The varieties within each type are listed below in order of popularity. All Chinese names are written using the Wade-Giles system of romanization and standard Mandarin pronunciation, which has the following unique conventions: ch is pronounced like the j in jam, ch' like the ch in chard; k like the g in game, k' like the k in Korea; p like the b in bean, p' like the p in pea; t like the d in dough; t' like the t in tea.

Red or Regular Chiang

Chunky Chiang (*tou-pan chiang, topan chiang, or do-ban jiang*): Literally "bean petal chiang" or "board chiang" and also known as "Chinese soybean paste," this is a variety of wheat miso made with either soybeans or broadbeans and usually containing wheat flour. Soft in texture and very chunky due to the presence of unmashed beans, it ranges in color from warm chocolate to dark russet. Most varieties contain as much as 18 percent salt, and hence have a strong salty flavor, although modern commercial varieties are lower in salt and have a distinctive, yet milder taste. Prepared in basically the same way as the common Chinese soy sauce called *toyu* except that the percentage of liquid is much smaller, this chiang is fermented outdoors in large earthenware

crocks and stirred daily for 7 to 12 months. Some varieties contain whole roasted sesame seeds, oil, or fish. Typical proportions by weight of raw materials are: soybeans 10, barley 3.3, wheat flour 3.3, salt 5.

A well-known seasoning made by dissolving chunky chiang in water is called *huang-hsi chiang*.

Hot Chunky Chiang (*la tou-pan chiang* or *tou-pan la-chiang*): Also known as "hot bean paste," this hot-and-spicy variety is made by adding *togarashi* red peppers to chunky chiang. If dried red-pepper powder is also added, the product is known as *tou-pan yu la-chiao*.

Szechwan Red-pepper Chiang (*ssu-ch'uan tou-pan chiang*): Sharper in flavor than hot chunky chiang but not as hot as red-pepper chiang (see below), this spicy variety is specially prepared in Szechwan and renowned for its abundant use of red peppers. Often known in English as Szechwan Hot Soybean Paste, it plays a key seasoning role in Szechwan's fiery cuisine.

Hamanatto Chiang (*tou-ch'ih chiang*): Resembling a combination of chunky Japanese red miso and *hamanatto* (p. 42), this savory product is closely related to Chinese-style hamanatto (*tou-ch'ih* or *shang-ch'ih*), a seasoning made by fermenting lightly-salted soybeans. If hot red peppers are added, the product becomes Red-pepper Hamanatto Chiang (*tou-ch'ih la-chiao chiang*).

Cantonese Red Chiang (*mien-ch'ih chiang*): Made from beans particular to Canton, this variety also contains wheat flour.

Great Chiang (*ta chiang*): A variety using soybeans as the key ingredient.

Yellow-red Chiang (*huang chiang*): Literally "yellow chiang," this variety is made primarily with soybeans.

Black Chiang

Sweet Wheat-flour Chiang *(t'ien mien chiang, mien chiang, or t'ien chiang):* This chocolate-brown, sweet preparation, also called "sweet (soy)bean paste," "sweet flour paste," or "flour jam," is made from wheat flour, salt, and water. Its consistency is smooth and soft—like that of melted chocolate—and its flavor somewhat resembles that of Japanese akadashi miso (p. 44). When prepared commercially, the flour and water are combined to form a dough which is either shaped into 4½-inch-diameter dumplings *(man-t'ou* or *man-ju)* and steamed, or flattened into ¾-inch-thick sheets, dried until firm, then broken into pieces about 5 inches in diameter. The steamed buns or flat pieces are arranged on 4-foot diameter bamboo trays and allowed to ferment in an incubation room for about 4 days. (Or in some areas, the steamed buns are arranged on sorghum stalks in an outdoor shed and allowed to mold for 3 weeks during the month of May.) The molded buns or sheets are then transferred to large earthenware pots located in an outdoor courtyard or on a rooftop. Mixed with a small amount of water and about 5 percent salt, the steamed dough soon begins to soften and dissolve. The mixture is stirred daily and allowed to ferment for at least 3 to 4 months, and sometimes as long as 6 to 8 months. A small amount of additional water is sometimes added each day during the first week of fermentation. During the day and sometimes at night the lids of the pots are left open to give access to the supposedly beneficial effects of dew and moonlight.

When this variety of chiang is prepared at home, the steamed bun or moist dough (often inoculated with a yellow storebought koji starter mold) is placed on a platter in a warm, damp place for 7 to 15 days until mold forms. The molded product is then transferred to a small earthenware crock and covered with salty water; left uncovered under the sun and night sky for 5 days, the mixture is squeezed daily by hand. For the next 15 days the mixture is stirred with a bamboo pole, after which time the chiang is ready, although its fermentation may be continued for 2 months more to give a mellower flavor and darker color. In some areas, soy sauce pressing-residue is added to the mixture to make it saltier.

In Chinese restaurants, sweet wheat-flour chiang is often combined with small amounts of sugar, sesame oil, and rice wine to make the dipping sauce served with Peking Duck (p. 129) or Pancake Rolls (p. 128). In Japan, where chiang is not widely available, a similar sauce is prepared using Hatcho miso as the basic ingredient (p. 70). Sweet wheat-flour chiang is also served as a dip with thinly sliced meat hor d'œuvres or as a spread for steamed buns or baked bread topped with sliced leeks; as the basis of the sauce served with Mabo-doufu (tofu cooked with ground beef and red pepper); as a topping, mixed with ground beef, for the noodle dish Cha-chiang Mien; and as a seasoning with sautéed chicken or pork dishes. It is also widely used as a pickling medium.

Prepared commercially with the addition of plenty of minced red peppers, this variety becomes Red-pepper Wheat-flour Chiang *(la-mien chiang).*

Black Chiang *(hei chiang* or *he do-ban jiang):* Actually dark chocolate brown, black chiang (often sold as Black Bean Paste) is made from black soybeans, as is its close relative Bean Chiang *(tou chiang).* A well-known seasoning made by dissolving black chiang in water is called *hei-hsi chiang.*

Assorted Chiangs

The earliest varieties of chiang are said to have been sauces made by fermenting salted fish, shellfish, and meats. Similar to the well-known, strong-smelling *nuoc-mam* of Vietnam and *shiokara* or *shottsuru* of Japan, the modern descendents of these ancient foods are still widely used as both seasonings and sauces.

Red-Pepper Chiang *(la-chiao chiang* or *la-chiang):* An all purpose seasoning used like tabasco sauce, this hot-and-spicy preparation is made by fermenting salted red peppers. Containing no soybeans, it is vermilion red and has a soft, semi-liquid consistency similar to that of a thick chili sauce. At restaurants, it is often placed on the table in small bottles.

Canton Sweet Simmered Chiang *(hai-hsein chiang):* A close relative of Japanese Sweet Simmered Miso (p. 60). A variety made in the Fo-shan region near Canton containing fennel and spicy powder is called *chu-hou chiang.*

Dried Chiang *(kan chiang):* A general term for all chiang that has been dried after fermentation, this unique product has no counterpart among traditional Japanese misos.

Other Varieties, none of which contain soybeans or grain koji, include:

- *Sesame Chiang (chih-ma chiang):* The Chinese equivalent of Western-style sesame butter
- *Peanut Chiang (hua-chih chiang):* Chinese-style peanut butter
- *Umeboshi Chiang (shun-mui chiang):* With tart, salted *ume* plums
- *Shrimp Chiang (hsia chiang):* Often served with meat dishes
- *Cockle Chiang (hsien-chien chiang):* Featuring tiny salt-cured shellfish
- *Tangy Chiang (kuei-hua chiang):* Made from minced garlic, tangerine rind, and sesame seeds
- *Semi-fermented Chiang (chiang-p'i):* Made in large bun-shaped lumps

Chiang Sauces

Most of these sauces, which have a consistency similar to that of thick gravy, are presently available in cans at Chinese grocery stores in the West.

Bean Sauce *(yuan-shih chiang* or *yun-si-* or *yuen-shi chiang):* This chocolate-brown sauce, made from soybeans, flour, salt, and water has a thick consistency and rather salty flavor. The regular variety has a slightly chunky texture, whereas that labeled "ground bean sauce" *(mien-shih chiang* or *min see jeung,* i.e. flour and soy nugget sauce) is smooth. Also known as "soy jam or soybean condiment," this product is also called "yellow bean sauce" when yellow beans are used in place of the usual soybeans. In making soy sauce, the Chinese filter off the liquid from chiang. The lees or residue that remain are used as the basic ingredient in bean sauce. (Note that Japanese shoyu producers press the residue and then discard it.) Some varieties of bean sauce contain added sesame seeds, sugar, or caramel coloring, molasses, MSG, vinegar, and/or preservatives. Bean sauce is an essential seasoning with the famous Cha-chiang Mien (Soy Jam Noodles) and is also widely used in stir-fried preparations, as a pickling medium, and mixed with gingerroot and minced green onion as a seasoning atop steamed fish.

Hoisin Sauce *(hai-hsien chiang):* The Chinese name means "sea fresh chiang," i.e. "chiang to be eaten with fresh seafoods," which however, it usually isn't! Also known as "soy jam," this jet black paste is creamy smooth and very sweet; it looks and tastes quite like melted chocolate or like Sweet Wheat-Flour Chiang (above). After the light soy sauce is drawn off of chiang, the soybean lees are lightly pressed to extract some remaining soy sauce, ground to a smooth paste, then mixed with flour, sugar, vinegar, salt, chili powder, and water; some varieties also contain garlic, food coloring, and preservatives. Sold in the West in 1-pound cans or 14-ounce jars, it is a favorite sauce for Peking Duck or Mu Shu Pork, and Chinese style spareribs. It is prized for its spicy sweetish flavor when used as a barbecue sauce, especially with *yakitori* (Japanese-style grilled chicken).

Oyster Sauce *(hao-yu chiang or hao-wei chiang):* A widely-used seasoning made form the liquid that rises to the surface of salt-pickled, fermented oysters.

Barbecue Sauce *(sha cha chiang):* Known also as "shacha jam," this Cantonese or Taiwanese barbecue sauce is used mainly with *sukiyaki* and *yakitori* (grilled chicken), but is also served as a topping for rice, noodles, sea cucumber, pork, and fried beef.

Other Chiang Sauces, none of which contain soybeans or grain koji include:

Shrimp Sauce (hsia-yu or lu hsia-yu): Features tiny shrimps

Chinese Worcestershire Sauce (suan-la chiang, la-chiang yu, or chi-ch'ih): A close relative of its English counterpart

Chinese Ketchup (fan-ch'ieh chiang): Similar to Western tomato ketchup

Chunky Chiang *(tou-pan chiang):*	豆瓣醬，豆板醬，豆弁醬；
Huang-hsi Chiang:	黃稀醬
Hot Chunky Chiang *(la tou-pan chiang):*	瓣豆辣醬
Tou-pan Yu La-chiao:	豆瓣油辣椒
Szechwan Red-pepper Chiang	
(ssu-ch'uan tou-pan chiang):	四川豆板醬，豆瓣醬
Hamanatto Chiang *(tou-ch'ih chiang):*	豆豉醬
Red-pepper Hamanatto Chiang	
(tou-ch'ih la-chiao chiang):	豆豉辣椒醬
Cantonese Red Chiang *(mien-ch'ih chiang):*	麵豉醬
Great Chiang *(ta chiang):*	大醬
Yellow-red Chiang *(huang chiang):*	黃醬
Sweet Wheat-flour Chiang *(t'ien mien chiang):*	甜麵醬
Red-pepper Wheat-flour Chiang *(la-mien chiang):*	瓣麵醬
Black Chiang *(hei chiang):*	黑醬
Bean Chiang *(tou chiang):*	豆醬
Hei-hsi chiang:	黑稀醬
Red-pepper Chiang *(la-chiao chiang):*	辣椒醬
Canton Sweet Simmered Chiang	
(hai-hsien chiang):	海鮮醬，柱候醬
Dried Chiang *(kan chiang):*	干醬
Sesame Chiang *(chih-ma chiang):*	芝麻醬
Peanut Chiang *(hua-hsien chiang):*	花生醬
Umeboshi Chiang *(shun-mui chiang):*	酸梅醬
Shrimp Chiang *(hsia chiang):*	蝦醬
Cockle Chiang *(hsien-chien chiang):*	蜆介醬
Tangy Chiang *(kuei-hua chiang):*	柱花醬
Semi-fermented Chiang *(chiang-p'i):*	醬坯
Bean Sauce *(yuan-shin chiang):*	原豉醬
Hoisin Sauce *(hai-hsien chiang):*	海鮮醬
Oyster Sauce *(hao-yu chiang):*	蠔油醬，蠔味醬
Barbecue Sauce *(sha cha chiang):*	沙茶醬
Shrimp Sauce *(hsia-yu):*	蝦油，滷蝦油
Chinese Worcestershire Sauce	
(suan-la chiang):	酸辣醬　辣醬油　唸汁
Chinese Ketchup *(fan-ch'ieh chiang):*	番茄醬

KOREAN JANG

Korea's three main fermented soyfoods are soybean miso *(doen jang)*, soy sauce *(kan jang)*, and red-pepper miso *(kochu jang)*. These three products accounted respectively for 18.3 percent, 10.6 percent, and 6.6 percent of total Korean soybean utilization in 1976. In that year, the daily per capita consumption of the three products was about 15 grams, 20 grams (ml), and 10 grams respectively. As in China, most of the soybean miso (82 percent), soy sauce (64 percent) and red-chili miso (76 percent) are produced in farmhouses and urban dwellings, and consumed directly by the families that make them; each family is allotted 6 pounds of free salt per year for just this purpose. A typical downtown high-rise apartment in Seoul will have six to eight brown earthenware crocks containing homemade *jang* and *kan jang* on 80 to 90 percent of its balconies. For this reason, jang is sold on only a relatively small scale at the miso-and-pickle sections of outdoor markets and food stores. Jang is widely used in hot spicy soups *(chigé)* which are generally thicker than Japanese miso soups. *Kan jang,* sweeter and stronger than Japanese shoyu, is made with soybeans, salt, and water, without the use of koji grain.

Retailing Korean jang

The various types of Korean miso and soy sauce are made from a dried soybean koji called *meju*, which is prepared in much the same way as Japan's *miso-dama* (p. 193). To make *meju*, soybeans are soaked, cooked, pounded until well mashed in a mortar, shaped into balls and wrapped in rice straw (or put unshaped into rice straw sacks), then hung under the rafters or eaves for 1 to 3 months, until each ball is covered with a natural bloom of white mold. The material is then broken into chunks, dried in the sun, and generally ground to a fine powder, usually in a hand-turned stone mill. The resulting *meju* (dried and ground soybean koji) has a composition of nutrients as shown in figure 47; it contains almost no sodium chloride (0.2 percent). At present ready-made *meju* is sold in marketplaces and used as the basis for some homemade jang. And some families have recently begun to inoculate their cooked soybeans with koji starter *(Aspergillus oryzae* or *A. sojae)*, which is also sold in the markets. The starter is mixed with a little wheat flour and sprinkled over the cooked, air-dried soybeans. The beans are then incubated in a warm place (79-86°F) for 24 to 48 hours, or until they are covered with white mold. They are then dried, crushed, and mixed with salt and water as above.

Korean Soybean Jang *(doen jang):* The only traditional Korean jang, this variety is light grayish brown and slightly chunky from the small proportion of uncrushed soybeans it contains. Two varieties of this salty and very strong-flavored jang are found in traditional markets; neither contains grain koji and one is slightly more salty and lumpy than the other. Most of this jang is still made in private homes, even that which is sold commercially, since most Koreans prefer the homemade product.

To prepare Korean soybean jang, *meju* is mixed with an 18- to 22-percent salt brine (and sometimes with sesame seeds or sesame leaves) in an earthenware container of 1 to 10 gallons capacity. The container is covered (but has no pressing lid) and placed outdoors on a balcony or rooftop, or in a courtyard. Traditionally the fermentation lasted for six months, from March to September. If a commercial starter is used to make the *meju*, the fermentation may be reduced to 2 to 3 months, and even less if the *meju* is soaked in warm brine and the container kept exposed to sunlight. After the basic fermentation period, the liquid that has accumulated in the container is filtered off and pasteurized by simmering to make *kan jang* (Korean soy sauce). The remaining nonliquid portion left in the vat is allowed to age for at least a few months longer, until it is good quality *doen jang* (soybean miso).

In the United States, a commercial variety is now available in 1-pound cans at Korean and Japanese food markets. Labeled "Bean Mash" *(doen jang)*, it contains soybeans, wheat, salt, and water. Nutrient composition is shown in figure 47, page 243.

Red-Pepper Jang *(kochu jang):* This spicy hot Korean miso is bright brownish red, has a smooth texture, and is somewhat softer than Japanese miso; each of the three main varieties contain slightly different amounts of red pepper. To make red-pepper jang, dried, finely ground *meju* is mixed in crocks with cooked glutinous rice, ground red pepper, and either salt brine or Korean soy sauce. Typically the fermentation takes 2 to 3 months; however, it may be accelerated by placing the crocks in sunlight. A good red-pepper jang contains a combination of sweet, hot, sour, and salty flavors. In some areas, rice flour is mixed with water to form dumplings, which are dropped into boiling water and cooked, then mashed together with *meju* and ground red pepper. One-third of the salt is added daily for three days; the red-pepper jang may be served on the fourth day, but it is usually fermented for 6 months. It is said that some varieties are also prepared from rice koji and wheat flour, or from a mixture of cooked soybeans and mochi or glutinous rice. Red-pepper jang is the favorite base for a thick soup or stew containing thinly sliced or ground meat and a little sugar.

In the United States, a commercial variety is now available in 1-pound cans at Korean and Japanese food markets. Labeled "Hot Bean Mash" *(kocho jang)*, it contains rice, red peppers, soybeans, salt, and water.

Mild Red-Pepper Jang *(mat jang):* This variety is similar to red-pepper jang but it contains more *meju*, less ground red pepper, and less salt. Glutinous rice is generally used to add natural grain sugars and a sweet flavor. The jang is wrapped in blankets and fermented in a warm place for a relatively short time (about 2 weeks). Like Japanese Finger Lickin' Miso, it is often served with fresh vegetables or tofu as a dip, topping, or garnish.

Chinese Sweet Black Jang *(cha jang* or *chungkuk jang):* This soft, jet black miso is a close relative of Chinese Sweet Wheat-flour Chiang (p. 244). Most of the Korean varieties are made by Chinese in Korea or imported from China. It is most popularly served with noodles in a dish called Cha Jang Mien (p. 126). The words *cha* and *chung-kuk* both mean "Chinese."

Japanese Red Jang *(wei jang* or *ilbon jang):* This is a salty red rice miso similar to Japanese Sendai miso but with a flavor adapted to Korean tastes. It is saltier than the Japanese product. A smooth, reddish brown jang, it originated in Japan and was sold during the 36 years of Japanese occupation. It is now produced in large quantities in Korea. The words *wei* and *ilbon* both mean "Japanese."

Korean Jang

INDONESIAN TAUCHO

Formerly spelled tao-tjo (and now spelled tauco in Indonesia), this is a fermented soybean paste or chunky sauce, a variety of soybean miso with a long history that is produced and consumed mainly in West Java, the center of production being the town of Chianjur. There are four different flavors and consistencies of taucho, all of which are dark brown in color and usually known simply as *taucho:* 1) *Sweet soft taucho* (also called *taucho Chianjur*) is the most popular variety. It has a consistency of porridge or apple-sauce, interspersed with prominent soybean chunks. Its pronounced sweetness is due to the addition of 25 percent by weight of palm sugar. 2) *Salty liquid taucho* (also called black bean sauce, salted soybeans, or salted black beans) is a non-homogeneous mixture of firm reddish to black soybean halves immersed in a soy-sauce-like concentrate. It is extremely strong, pungent, and salty (much saltier than Japanese miso or shoyu). 3) *Firm dried taucho (taucho kering)* is a relatively new product made by sun-drying cakes of either of the previously mentioned taucho types. 4) *Smoked dried taucho* is a relatively uncommon product prepared mostly by Chinese.

The various types of taucho are used primarily as a seasoning in soups, vegetables, seafood, and noodle preparations, especially Lodeh, Taucho Ikan, Ikan Goreng Taucho, Sambal Taucho, Sambal Goreng Taucho, Oseng-Oseng Taucho, Mie Goreng Taucho, Tempeh Maska Taucho, and Tumis Udang.

Taucho differs from Japanese miso in that it is either sweeter or saltier and softer or firmer, is prepared by a much shorter natural fermentation, and contains a large proportion of glutinous rice flour. An estimated 84 cottage-industry shops produce taucho in Indonesia and 77 of these are located in West Java.

Taucho is traditionally made by a two-part fermentation process; a mold fermentation followed by a brine fermentation. One hundred kilograms of dry soybeans are washed and soaked in excess water for 15 to 20 hours, brought quickly to a boil, then dehulled underfoot or by hand. The beans are rinsed and the hulls usually floated off, boiled for up to 5 hours, drained, spread on 3-foot-diameter woven bamboo trays, where they are allowed to cool for 12 hours to air temperature (82°F). The beans are inoculated with a starter prepared by pounding to a powder 10 grams of sundried tempeh and mixing it with 190 grams of roasted glutinous rice flour. The active organisms in the starter are *Rhizopus oligosporus, Rhizopus oryzae,* and *Aspergillus oryzae.* This mixed culture inoculum has been shown to give taucho with the best flavor and aroma. Two hundred grams of this starter are mixed with 50 kilograms of roasted glutinous rice flour, mixed thoroughly with the soybeans, spread in a 1¼-inch-deep layer in the bamboo tray, sometimes covered with cheesecloth, and incubated in racks at 81°F for 3 to 4 days (traditionally as long as 7 to 14 days) until the beans are covered with a dense white mycelium. This koji-like substance is then broken into small pieces and put into 2½-gallon earthenware crocks with an 18 percent brine solution in the ratio of 100 kilograms koji to 200 liters brine. The resulting mash is allowed to stand outdoors in the sun for an average of 4 weeks and is mixed each morning. The crocks are covered each night. Beneficial bacteria and yeasts such as *Lactobacillus delbruekii* and *Hansenula spp.* become active and aid the brine fermentation. The finished product may be sold in small plastic bags as salty liquid taucho.

To make sweet soft taucho, 100 kilograms of the original taucho is combined with 25 kilograms each of palm sugar and water; the mixture is cooked until a homogenous, viscous consistency is obtained. Firm dried taucho is then prepared by sun-drying or smoking this product.

Taucho is the least important of Indonesia's four basic soyfoods, which include tempeh tofu, and kechap (soy sauce). It accounts for less than 1 percent of all Indonesian soybean utilization and the annual per capital consumption of all types of taucho is only 7.2 grams.

There are a number of publications on taucho. The best is F.G. Winarno's *Research on Taucho* (Phases I-III) published by FATEMETA, Bogor Agricultural University, Jalan Gunung Gede, Bogor, Indonesia, 1975. Additional information about this Indonesian miso is found in Winarno's *The Present Status of Soybeans in Indonesia* and *Indonesian Fermented Foods.* Publications by his colleagues include Nurhajati *et al.* (1975), Swastomo *et al.* (1975), and Zaenuddin *et al.* (1975).

For more details on taucho and a list of researchers, see the professional clothbound edition of our *Book of Tempeh* (Harper & Row).

A close relative of Indonesian taucho is Malaysian *taucheo.*

The Microbiology and Biochemistry of Miso Fermentation

THE PREPARATION of miso involves two consecutive fermentation processes. In the first, olive-green "koji starter" (*tané koji;* literally "koji seeds") consisting of dried mold spores is mixed with cooked rice, barley, or soybeans; the mixture is then incubated to produce the mold grain or soybeans called "koji." In the second, the koji is mixed with cooked soybeans, salt, water, and usually a little mature miso. Packed into vats, the ingredients are allowed to age while the dual processes of enzymatic digestion and fermentation transform them into the finished miso.

Let us enter this unfamiliar world, learn the names of its main dramateurs, and follow the interrelated processes of transformation. We will begin by discussing the nature of the basic molds used to prepare the koji starter, then go on to study the two fermentation processes mentioned above.

Koji Starter Molds

Select varieties of mold spores are the chief actors in the fermentation process, just as other varieties are used in the production of delicious natural cheeses, or yeasts are used in the making of wines or bread. What exactly are molds? Botanically, they are a family of lower plants which is part of a larger group known as fungi. The latter includes molds, mushrooms, yeasts, and mildews. All fungi lack chlorophyll, may be as small as a single cell, and can reproduce abundantly by the process of sporulation. Mycology—derived from the Greek stem *myco-* or *myc-* meaning fungus—is a special branch of botany dealing exclusively with the study of this vast world.

All molds and fungi grow on other organic substances called substrates. Bread, fruits, and vegetables allowed to stand too long in the cupboard often become the substrates for unwanted varieties. In the miso shop, cooked rice, barley, or soybeans are used intentionally as substrates. In addition to a suitable substrate, molds require a particular environment for hearty growth. For good miso, it must be fairly warm (about 80°F to 95°F), moist but not wet, and aerobic (i.e. containing plenty of free oxygen). Yeasts and anaerobic bacteria, however, can thrive in moist environments containing little or no free oxygen.

Molds are present in large numbers almost everywhere. Up until several decades ago, these wild spores were used as the "starter" for most of Japan's commercial miso, and they are still used in the preparation of some farmhouse varieties. Gradually, however, miso makers discovered that some mold varieties seemed to produce better quality miso than others; resorting largely to intuition and personal experience, they began to cultivate select strains in much the same way that prospectors nourished their sourdough cultures, Balkan peasants their yogurt starters, or cheesemakers their molds for mold-ripened cheeses such as Roquefort, Brie, Camembert, Blue or Bleu, Stilton, and Goronzolla. isolated pure cultures of miso molds, they discovered that virtually all varieties belonged to the single species *Aspergillus oryzae.*

The genus *Aspergillus* is part of the class Fungi Imperfecti, which also includes *Penicillium* molds. These fungi reproduce only asexually and are hence "imperfect." Their reproduction is by means of specialized spores called conidia (from the Greek meaning "fine dust"), which are born at the tips of special fungal filaments (modified hyphae) called conidiophores ("spore bearers"), shown in the figure on page 250.

The genus *Aspergillus* derives it's name from the term "aspergillum," which refers to a brush or small perforated container with a handle used, usually by priests or nuns, for sprinkling holy water in a liturgical service. The species name *oryzae* is probably derived from the Latin genus name for "rice" (*Oryza sativa*) since this mold was widely grown on rice by early East Asian cultures.

A close relative of *Apergillus oryzae* is *Aspergillus flavus,* (ass-per-JIL-us FLAY-vus), the main mold that produces aflatoxins on peanuts, corn, and a few other foods that are not stored properly. Aflatoxins, highly carcinogenic liver toxins, came to the public attention in 1960 when 100,000 turkeys and ducks suddenly died in England from consuming moldy Brazilian peanut presscake, contaminated by *A. flavus.* Since that time extensive tests around the world have been conducted to see if similar toxins might be produced in soyfoods such as miso, shoyu, tamari, or Hamanatto fermented by other species of *Aspergillus.* Dr. C.W. Hesseltine, one of the world's foremost authorities on aflatoxins (and on miso), has shown repeatedly that soybeans are a poor substrate for aflatoxin production, and there have been no reports of aflatoxins in miso or any other soyfoods fermented by *Aspergillus.*

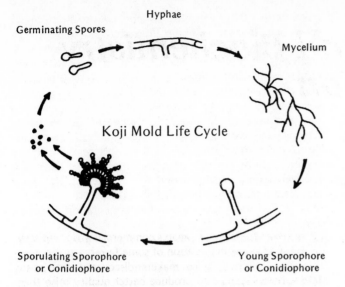

Germinating Spores

Hyphae

Mycelium

Koji Mold Life Cycle

Sporulating Sporophore or Conidiophore

Young Sporophore or Conidiophore

Within the single species *Aspergillus oryzae,* just as within the world of roses, there are a vast number of strains or subspecies—estimates range from 10,000 to 100,000—each with its own unique physical properties and name! Some mycologists, in fact, devote their entire lives to the study of *A. oryzae* and often specialize in the study of one or more of the important strains, those, that is, which yield koji with good fermentation "strength" and produce miso characterized by excellent flavor and aroma. Some strains are valued for their ability to produce large amounts of the enzyme amylase which digests or breaks down starches; these might be used in sweet white miso containing a large proportion of grains. Other strains are prized for their abundant production of the enzyme protease which breaks down proteins; these might be used to prepare the koji for soybean miso. Some molds have long "hairs" that create a firmly interlocking mycelium, excellent for commercial koji such as the soft mat variety available in grocery stores. Others have short "hairs" suited to modern factory koji production. Some molds have white "hairs" that give ready-made koji an attractive appearance. Others generate heat quickly and are used to make koji in short periods of time.

Most Japanese miso makers do not cultivate their own *A. oryzae* starter molds since the process requires extensive technical know-how and fairly complex equipment. Rather, this work is entrusted to a small number of specialty shops (fewer than ten), each of which tends a number of carefully bred strains, some of which may have been in their possession for centuries. These molds are bred and cross-bred over a period of many years as carefully as racehorses and chosen to give exactly the desired flavor and aroma to the miso. A shop's stock of molds is its most valued asset and the owner goes to great lengths—storing samples in vaults or caves—to guarantee their protection from fire or theft. Those portions of the stock in daily use are kept in their pure-culture state inside carefully sealed bottles in spotlessly clean laboratories to prevent even the slightest contamination by alien strains.

At the specialty shops, the molds are used to make "koji starter" (*tané koji*), later sold by special order to miso makers who use it in small amounts to make *koji*, the preparation of which precedes the making of miso itself.

Koji starter is prepared in basically the same way as koji itself except that the trays of inoculated steamed rice are allowed to stand for five (rather than just two) days in the warm incubation room until the mold turns from white to olive green indicating sporulation. The mycelium-bound grain is then dried in large rooms and sold in small sealed packages.

The substrate for koji starter is a mixture of cooked brown rice (or barley) and a small amount (about 2%) of the ash of a deciduous tree such as camellia or oak. Brown rather than white rice is used because the latter lacks the necessary nutrients for hearty mold growth. The alkaloid ash, in addition to preventing the excessively rapid generation of heat, provides the young mold with nutritious potassium and phosphorous salts, manganese, and other trace elements, and helps bring about the RNA/DNA balance required for proper sporulation. (It also prevents the rice from clumping.) After the warm rice-and-ash substrate is inoculated by mixing in pure-culture spores of a selected strain of *A. oryzae* mold, it is incubated for five days at 76°F in shallow wooden trays in a large humid room. Naturally, great care is taken to see that no contaminating microorganisms enter the culture during this time.

Soon after incubation begins, the mold spores send out hairlike shoots called hyphae. These growing filaments make the body of the mold, the white mycelium. Many hyphael cells make long erect shoots called "conidiophores" or "sporophores," which terminate in a bulbous head. After three to four days, these heads have formed bud clusters, which begin to sporulate luxuriously. It is at this stage that the color of the mold turns from creamy beige to soft olive green, the color of the spores themselves. Eventually each spore will have multiplied over 10 million times. The finished mats of mycelium-bound rice are transferred (in the trays) to drying rooms (113°F) for three to four days. Here the koji starter develops a tantalizing aroma similar to that of roasting chestnuts or almonds. Delicious as a snack, its flavor is richer and sweeter than that of regular koji.

Koji starter is made available commercially in three forms. The mycelium-bound grains are sometimes only lightly crumbled and sold as "whole-grain" starter. Or the spore-covered rice may be ground and sold as a "meal." About 50 percent of all koji starter sold today comes in the form of "spore powder" made by sifting whole-grain starter, discarding the mold-free rice grains, and collecting the olive-green spores; one gram of this pure powder contains from 6 to 10 billion spores. It is usually mixed with a powdered starch extender to make it easier to package and use.

Most modern starters contain not just one but several mold strains in a mixture carefully formulated to produce the right balance of enzymes needed to produce the particular type of koji desired. Some are also enriched with yeasts such as *Saccharomyces rouxii* or bacteria such

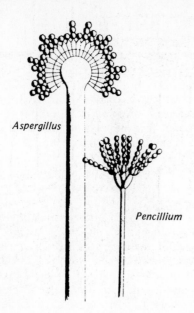

Aspergillus

Pencillium

Conidiophores of **Aspergillus** and **Penicillium**

as *Pedicoccus halophilus* and *Lactobacillus delbrueckii* which play important roles after the miso ingredients begin the second stage of their fermentation. A typical shop selling koji starter will offer eight or more basic types as explained on page 178.

Making Koji: The First Fermentation

Once in the miso-maker's hands, the starter is used to make koji in what is perhaps the most difficult but crucial part of the miso-making process. Koji (or "mold rice") is cooked grains or beans which have been inoculated with starter and allowed to ferment for about two days until covered with and bound together by a fragrant white mycelium. This mold produces the enzymes that eventually break down the complex molecules of protein, starch, and lipids (oils and fats) in the substrate, reducing them to simpler, more readily digestible products which are later fermented by yeasts and bacteria. Enzymes, complex substances produced by living cells, are actually only catalysts; they simply promote chemical reactions (such as hydrolysis or oxidation) without themselves undergoing marked change in the process. In the process of beer fermentation, malt is prepared by sprouting barley (without the use of molds) in order to develop enzymes. Thus, koji is to miso what malt is to beer.

The nature of koji is embodied in the very characters with which the word is written. In the more traditional form—used with most miso koji and especially with barley koji—the ideographs for "barley" and chrysanthemum" are placed side by side. In the more recent form—used especially with ready-made rice koji—the ideographs for "rice" and "flower" are conjoined. The first form is said to have originated in China, whereas the latter was developed in Japan about 1,000 years ago. In both, the notion of grain covered with a bloom of mold is vividly expressed.

To make koji, about one part by weight of starter is mixed with 1,000 parts substrate, cooked (usually steamed) grains or beans that have been allowed to cool to body temperature. The inoculated substrate is placed in a large, well-insulated, cloth-lined box called a crib, covered with thick insulating mats, and allowed to stand overnight. After a few hours, the temperature inside the crib begins to rise as heat is generated by the process of fermentation. Briefly uncovered the next morning, the ingedients are well mixed in order to replenish the oxygen supply, release carbonic acid gasses, and blend the warmer substrate at the crib's center with the cooler substrate near the sides, bottom, and top. The crib is re-covered, only to be opened several hours later. The young koji is then transferred into shallow wooden trays where it is mounded to help it retain the heat of fermentation. However, a small hollow—like the crater of a volcano—is dug at the top of each mound to prevent overheating. The koji trays are arranged in a special incubation room where the temperature is kept at 82°F to 86°F and the humidity at 90 to 95 percent. The koji's temperature rises slowly as shown in figure 36 on page 181.

To protect against the intrusion of contaminating microorganisms, the craftsman's hands and tools must be kept spotlessly clean and the koji kept within the required range of temperature and moistness. (Special care must be taken during the warm months when alien microorganisms are abundant and propagate more rapidly.) If the koji temperature is allowed to rise above 104°F, the production of enzymes decreases and undesirable bacteria (such as black and *natto* varieties) begin to flourish; as these bacteria multiply, additional overheating results and free water condenses on the substrate causing even more rapid bacterial growth. Koji containing black molds develops an unpleasant odor and may have to be discarded. If the koji temperature is allowed to rise above 113°F, the koji begins to die of its own heat; if it drops below about 77°F, fermentation gradually comes to a halt and non-toxic bluish-green molds (usually related to *Penicillium*) may flourish giving the koji and resultant miso a poor flavor.

If temperature and humidity are kept within the ideal range, only the *Aspergillus oryzae* molds propagate. To prevent overheating as the first fermentation progresses, and to remove carbon dioxide, provide oxygen, and help the mold penetrate the substrate more deeply, the mycelium is broken up at regular intervals and the koji is well stirred. After the second stirring, the mounded koji is spread in even layers over the trays.

The energy required to support the growth and metabolism of the molds and create the essential enzymes is supplied by the grain or soybean substrate. During the first fermentation, about 5 to 10 percent of the food energy in the substrate is consumed by the mold and is therefore ultimately lost as nutritional energy available to human beings from the finished miso. This is the small price we pay to obtain enhanced flavor, aroma, and digestibility.

After 40 to 50 hours, depending on the "speed" of the starter and the incubation temperature, the burgeoning molds will have thoroughly covered the substrate and bound it into a solid cake. The koji must be harvested while the conidiophores of the mold are still forming, before the olive-green color typical of sporulation has appeared. At this stage, there is maximum availability of desirable enzymes; further mold growth would result in an undesirable (moldy) flavor in the finished miso. Thus, the finest koji is characterized·by a felt-like white mycelium, a fragrant aroma, and—when tasted—a sweet delicious flavor.

Removed from the trays, the finished koji is now crumbled, cooled, and usually mixed with just the right amount of salt to prevent further mold growth. The first step of miso's two-step fermentation process is now finished.

Cooking the Soybeans

As the koji fermentation nears completion, soybeans are boiled or steamed until they are soft enough to be crushed easily between the thumb and ring finger. Thorough cooking makes their protein more receptive to enzyme activity and helps to inactivate the trypsin growth inhibitors present in uncooked beans. Cooking time and temperature influence the color and flavor of the finished product; the longer the cooking, the darker the miso. The soybeans for white and light-yellow miso are boiled under high pressure for a short time (30 to 60 minutes) and the cooking water then discarded. Sweet red miso is given its dark-red color by simmering the beans for six to eight hours, allowing them to stand overnight in the caldron and then returning the beans to a boil the next morning. After steaming or boiling, the beans for all types of miso are partially or completely crushed to facilitate the permeation of enzymes from the koji. Whereas koji is said to provide most of miso's aroma and sweetness, soybeans are thought to contribute most of its flavor.

Preparing the Miso: The Second Fermentation

The second fermentation is divided into four stages: the mixing of the basic ingredients; the digestion of protein, starch, and lipids in these ingredients by koji enzymes; the fermentation of the digested products by bacteria and yeasts; and the aging of the miso until it is fully mature.

The mashed soybeans are mixed with the salted koji, water or soybean cooking liquid, and "seed miso." The water—comprising about 10 percent of the total miso weight—is used to give the miso a moisture content of 48 to 52 percent. Regular water is almost always boiled before being added to eliminate contaminating microorganisms. A small amount of (unpasteurized) "seed miso" from a previous fermentation improves the miso aroma and flavor while decreasing the fermentation time by up to 50 percent by introducing hearty yeasts and bacteria. In modern miso factories the seed miso is often replaced by a pure-culture inoculum consisting of halophilic (salt resistant) yeasts such as *Saccharomyces rouxii* or *Torulopsis* and lactic acid bacteria such as *Pediococcus halophilus*, *Lactobacillus delbrueckii* or *Streptococcus faecalis;* the latter species are also used in cheese production. About 100,000

of these microorganisms are added for each *gram* of miso and, when used in temperature-controlled fermentation, they are kept at a maximum of 86°F, where they do their optimum work. Modern miso makers insist that the use of good inoculum is one of the secrets of preparing fine miso. The same type may be used for many different miso varieties.

Before packing the mixed ingredients into a huge wooden vat, the interior of the container is thoroughly scrubbed with boiling water and then sprinkled or rubbed with salt. In addition to removing contaminating microorganisms on the wood's surface, this serves to ferret out any mites or other tiny insects that can enter the chinks between the planks of vats which are allowed to stand empty. For broader protection, many producers now disinfect their entire buildings once or twice each year and sterilize (by steaming) all small kegs that enter the shop and the various cloths used in preparing the miso and koji. Although such insects cannot live in the miso and are not believed to represent a health danger, food inspectors and miso makers take every precaution to ensure that miso shops are free of them.

In the same way that grapes were traditionally treaded to make wine, the mixture in the vats is now mashed underfoot to remove air pockets in which alien molds might grow or liquid might accumulate. Its surface is carefully leveled and covered first with a cloth sealing-sheet and then a pressing-lid which fits snugly down inside the vat's mouth, thereby preventing the growth of surface molds. While not actually harmful, such molds cause a decline in the miso's aroma and flavor. The lid is then weighted with heavy stones to force a small amount of liquid (*miso-damari*) to the surface, creating a sealed, airtight (anaerobic) environment. This is ideal for the activity of the anaerobic bacteria and yeasts which will later gain predominance; it also prevents the entry of contaminating microorganisms. In many shops, a second sheet is tied over the the vat's mouth to keep out dust, insects, and the like.

During the first fermentation, the number of molds per gram of substrate had increased from about 13,000 to 295,000. Now, with the work of these molds finished the highly sensitive mycelium dies from the lack of oxygen and high salinity in the environment. But the work of enzymes left behind is about to begin.

Inside the vat, the enzymes begin breaking down—actually digesting—the nutritional components of soybeans and grains. Three basic enzymes are active: protease works on protein, amylase on carbohydrates, and lipase on lipids (oils and fats) (fig. 48). In this chemical process—technically known as hydrolysis—the reaction of water ions with the basic food nutrients produces a weak acid which transforms complex molecules into simpler ones that can be more easily assimilated by the body.

The enzyme protease converts soy protein molecules first into polypeptides and peptides, and then into more than 18 simple amino acids. The main soy protein is glycinin (80% to 90%) and the predominant resulting amino acid is glutamic acid, the active ingredient in the refined chemical seasoning known variously as MSG, monosodium glutamate, *aji-no-moto*, or Accent. These natural amino acids—and particularly glutamic—give the miso much of its flavor and some of its color, while also softening and mellowing the inherent sharpness of the miso's salt.

The enzyme amylase—with the help of a small amount of maltose—reduces starches in the koji to simple sugars and polysaccharides, primarily glucose, but also maltose, dextrose, and dextrin. These in turn serve as fermentable sugars for yeasts and bacteria which are soon to come upon the scene. About 80 to 90 percent of the proteins and starches in the soybeans and koji grains are broken down into simpler substances by the action of these microorganisms.

Since a large part of the starch is saccharified, miso that initially contained a large percentage of grain koji is sweet, whereas miso made from soybean koji (which is low in starch) is not.

The enzyme lipase transforms the 18 percent lipids contained in soybeans into simple free fatty acids, which assume a variety of different forms in the finished miso. The esters of some of these contribute to the miso's aroma.

At each stage of its development, miso is teeming with multitudes of living microorganisms. Continuous and multiple changes in the fermentation call forth different and specialized varieties one after another, each with its own part to play. These microorganisms are all *plants* (more specifically fungi and bacteria) that are halophilic (salt tolerant) and, in many cases, osmophilic (thriving in a medium of high osmotic pressure). Although anaerobic bacteria and yeasts are favored by the airtight environment, aerobic bacteria also manage to survive on the oxygen incorporated into the basic ingredients before they were packed into the vats.

As the process of enzymatic digestion nears completion, fermentation by yeasts and bacteria (many of which were supplied by the seed miso or pure-culture inoculum) assumes predominance. Working in a sealed environment with plenty of nutrients, the anaerobic bacteria suddenly increase in number from 10 million to 930 million per gram of substrate. One of the most important and abundant of these is *Lactobacillus*, the lactic acid bacteria used as yogurt, cheese, and butter starters. After the miso ingredients have been in the keg for two to three months under natural conditions, these bacteria assume dominance and begin to transform sugars into various acids (especially lactic and acetic); the acids in turn impart a subtle mellow

Fig. 48. The Interactions of Basic Miso Components (Adapted from *Miso Fermentation*, Shibasaki & Hesseltine, 1962)

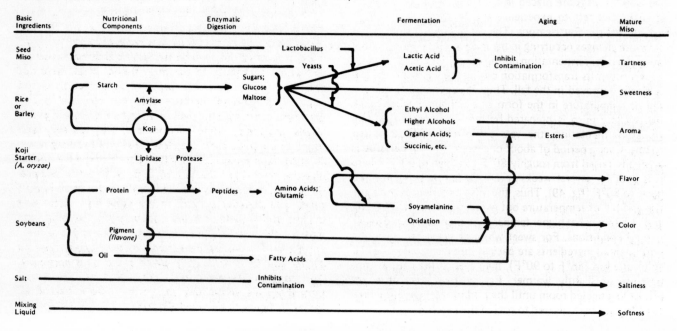

sourness to the finished miso and also assist in preventing spoilage.

Soon various yeasts begin their work of alcoholic fermentation. Consuming sugars, they produce alcohols (ethyl and higher varieties) and organic acids (especially succinic); the higher alcohols contribute to miso's pleasant bouquet and the organic acids to its flavor. Some varieties of yeasts make a film on the miso surface, while also contributing to the aroma.

As various substances are created by enzymatic digestion and bacterial or yeast fermentation, they begin to react chemically with one another. The full complexity of this interaction is illustrated in figure 48. Organic acids react with ethyl- and higher alcohols, with free fatty acids, or with acetic acid to produce esters (a primary aromatic element in fruits and flowers), which become the chief components of miso's bouquet. In quick miso, the distinctive fragrance of esters and alcohols often appears after only eight to ten days of fermentation. Amino acids react with sugars to produce red or brown pigments (soyamelanine), which combine with the soybean pigment flavone and deepen in color due to oxidation as the miso matures. Since amino acids play the dual role of enhancing flavor and deepening color, it is often said that miso with the richest color also has the richest flavor.

The cooking and fermentation processes deactivate trypsin inhibitors and other unfavorable substances such as hemagglutins and saponins, while simultaneously eliminating carbonyl compounds such as hexanol that sometimes carry a beany flavor. As these successive chemical changes continue quietly and leisurely inside the apparently dormant vats, the individual particles, first of the koji and then of the soybeans, slowly break down and merge to form the unique miso texture. Students of the biodynamic teaching of Rudolph Steiner feel that cosmic rays entering the miso during lengthy natural fermentation also have subtle but very beneficial effects.

When miso is fermented in the traditional natural way, the vats or kegs are placed in a covered area out of direct sunlight and left to experience the rhythmic temperature changes of the four seasons. These call forth, accelerate, or slow the changes occurring in the miso mixture. Most natural miso starts its fermentation during the colder months, undergoes most of its transformation during the warmer ones, and is finally removed in the fall. Thus, it experiences a rise and fall of temperature in the form of a bell curve. When quick light-yellow miso is prepared by modern temperature-controlled fermentation, the vats are placed in large heated rooms. Over a period of about one week, the temperature is gradually raised from roughly 80°F to a high of 90°F, where it is kept for several weeks or months before being lowered back to 80°F (fig. 49). Thus, the miso experiences the same rise and fall of temperature but over a shorter period of time and at a somewhat higher temperature than that found under natural conditions. For sweet white or sweet red miso, the unfermented ingredients are packed into insulated vats while still quite hot (86°F to 90°F), then aged at the natural temperature or slightly warmer. For mellow beige, they are placed in a heated room until their interior temperature rises to 90°F, and then allowed to cool of their own accord.

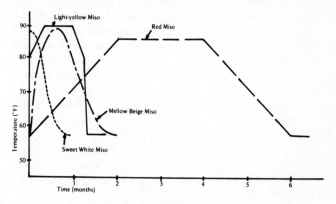

Fig. 49. Temperature Control Curves for Four Quick Misos

Whereas natural miso is usually allowed to stand untouched in the kegs or vats during the entire second fermentation, quick miso is generally mixed and transferred to a new vat or epoxy-lined steel tank once or twice during the process. Supplying the yeasts and aerobic bacteria with oxygen in this way hastens the fermentation process and raises the internal temperature. In some farmhouses, too, the miso is mixed at regular intervals or at least once during the summer for the same reason. After quick miso has been removed from its heated fermentation room, it is often allowed to stand for several weeks at room temperature; this final ripening (shown on the above graphs) further improves the flavor and aroma.

The Finished Miso

Unhurried aging in rhythm with the cycle of the seasons is one of the traditional secrets for evoking the finest miso flavor. Thus, natural miso is generally found to be of higher quality than its quick modern counterpart—and it therefore commands a premium price.

When natural miso is ready, each gram contains an immense number of active and beneficial microorganisms: 4,000 molds, 6,000 yeasts, 1.5 million aerobic bacteria, and 2 million anaerobic bacteria. Remarkably, the salt in miso exerts a selective action on the full range of microorganisms present, favoring those which are beneficial to human beings and which contribute to the miso flavor. If salt were not present, a toxic anaerobic bacterial fermentation would occur. Furthermore, because only the heartiest microorganisms can survive the rigors of months and years in miso's largely anaerobic, saline environment, they are very well suited to continue their ceaseless activity of breaking down complex food molecules after they have entered the human digestive tract. Thus the salt, in addition to acting as a preservative, also functions as a "sentient" agent for the human palate and digestive system. In the same way, lactic acid inhibits the growth of many contaminating bacteria, and most of the beneficial microorganisms present are actively antagonistic to the few dangerous varieties (*Staphylococcus aureus* and *Escherichia coli*) which cause food poisoning. Consequently, repeated tests conducted at laboratories throughout the world have shown that miso is free of all toxins, including those called aflatoxins.

The finest miso is sold in wooden kegs in the same form in which it emerges from the fermentation vats with all its microscopic flora alive and vital. Indeed, the principal reason miso is usually cooked only briefly—if at all—is precisely because the beneficial microorganisms (especially lactic acid bacteria) and enzymes they contain are easily destroyed by prolonged exposure to high temperatures. Unfortunately, much of the miso sold today in sealed polyethylene bags is pre-pasteurized by means of prolonged heating (140°F) in order to stop the microorganisms from producing carbon dioxide which causes the bags to swell. In some cases, preservatives are also added for the same purpose. Both of these newly-invented processes cause a definite decline in the miso fragrance and flavor—while also reducing its value as a food. Hence the best miso is that prepared by traditional natural fermentation methods and sold without additives or pasteurization. Many such varieites are now available throughout the West.

Edo period shoyu production

USA

CALIFORNIA
91706 Baldwin Park—Miyako Oriental Foods Inc., 4287 Puente Ave. Ph: 626-962-9633. Teruo Shimizu.

95963 Orland—Yamazaki Miso Co., 4192 County Road S. Ph: 530-865-5979. Kazuko Yamazaki.

HAWAII
96819 Honolulu, Oahu—American Hawaiian Soy Co., 274 Kalihi St. Ph: 808-841-8435. John Morita.

96819 Honolulu, Oahu—Hawaiian Miso & Soy Co., 1714 Mary St. Ph: 808-841-7354. William Higa.

MASSACHUSETTS
01341 Conway—South River Miso Co., South River Farm, Box 4. Ph: 413-369-4057. Christian Elwell.

NORTH CAROLINA
28139 Rutherfordton—American Miso Co. Inc., 4225 Maple Creek Rd. Ph: 828-287-2940. Greg Gonzales.

NEW YORK
10474 Bronx—MSB Food Enterprises, Inc., 710 Longfellow Ave. Ph: 718-617-4105. Michael Lee.

WISCONSIN
54631 Gays Mills—Earth Fire Products Co., P.O. Box 92, Corner of Grove & North Railroad Sts. Ph: 1-800-267-6918. Bob Ribbens.

CANADA

BRITISH COLUMBIA
V0R 1T0 Denman Island—Shin-Mei-Do Miso Co., 3906 Wren Road. Ph: 604-335-0253. Yasuo & Lulu Yoshihara.

V6V 1Z1 Richmond—Amano Foods Ltd., 5520 No. 6 Road. Ph: 604-303-9977. Graham Amano.

ONTARIO
L1Y 1A1 Claremont—Tradition Miso Inc., R.R. #4-2090. Ph: 905-649-2513. Jerry Lewycky.

EUROPE

Austria, A-2493 Lichtenwoerth—Sojvita Produktions GmbH, Hauptplatz 1. Ph: +43 02622-75494. Norbert Brunthaler.

France, F-47170 Andiran (near Mezin)—Danival-Gevaert, Moulin d'Andrian. Ph: +33 5-5397-0023. Daniel & Valerie Gevaert.

Germany, D-55232 Alzey-Mannheim—Noka Sojamanufaktur GmbH, Hauptstrasse 3. Ph: +49 0763 1-6892. Karl Selgmann.

Italy, 10078 Veneria Reale (TO)—Soy & Rice, Via A. Canale 8/c. Ph: +39 011-402-0380. Bosco Franca

Italy, 33040 Pradamano (UD)—Az. Agricola Biologica, Carlo Giacomelli, Via Roma, 41/1. Ph: +39 432 764683. Dario Benossi.

Portugal, 2775 Parede—Miso Producoes, Alt. Cult. E Almt., LDA, Rua do Douro, No. 92 r/c - Rebelva. Ph: +351 (1) 247 50 68. Miguel Azguime.

Yugoslavia, YU-11080 Zemun—Lion Health Food Co., Zagorska 12/9. Ph: +381 11-106073. Sladjan Randjelovic.

LATIN AMERICA

Brazil, Sao Paulo, S.P.—Maruviti, Rua Ibituruna 264, Jabaquara. Ph: +55 275-4533.

Brazil, Campinas, S.P.—Tozan, Barrio Carlos Gomes s/no. Ph: +55 011-278-2495.

Brazil, 13446 Sao Paulo, S.P.—Sakura-Nakaya Alimentos, C.P. 16131, Rua Ordenacoes 151. Ph: +55 295-4117.

Colombia, Santa Fe de Bogota 2—Alimentos de Oriente y Occidente., Apartado Aereo 57011. Ph: +57 674 1258. Nelson & Eunice Ortiz.

Martinique, 97226 Morne Vert—"Caplet." Ph: +596 55-56-57. Pascal Pinault.

Mexico, Veracruz, VER 91700—Organica-ecotienda, Xicotencatl 653-18, Col. Centro. Ph: +52 29-31-30-83. Pat Hayward

Peru, Lima—Fabrica de Siyau Kikko Sociedad de Responsibilidad Limitada., Av. Colombia 171, Pueblo Libre. Ph: +51 32-3754. Marco Kamego.

Peru, Lima 13—Nishii Super Shoyu, Renovacion 101-A, La Victoria. Ph: +51 14-31-81-05. Shinji Kawakami.

Appendix E
People and Institutions Connected with Miso

PEOPLE AND INSTITUTIONS IN JAPAN

In the following references, all Japanese personal names are written in the standard Japanese manner, last name first. All addresses are given in the Western style (street, ward [ku], city [shi], prefecture [ken], and zip code), rather than in the reverse Japanese style.

MISO RESEARCH SCHOLARS AND INSTITUTES

Akizuki Shinichiro: St. Francis Hospital, Hongen Machi 2-535, Nagasaki, Japan. A practicing physician and hospital director, Dr. Akizuki has experimented widely using miso and miso soup to prevent radiation sickness and maintain health (p. 26). His findings are presented in a pamphlet entitled *Physical Constitution and Food* (p. 248).

Ebine Hideo: Norinsho Shokuhin Sogo Kenkyujo, Shiohama 1-4-12, Koto-ku, Tokyo 135. Tel: 03-645-9911. Head of the fermentation division of the prestigious National Food Research Institute, Dr. Ebine is also the author of many English-language articles about miso.

Japanese National Miso Association: Zenkoku Miso Kogyo Kyodo Kumiai Rengokai, Shinkawa 1-26-19, Chuo-ku, Tokyo 104. Tel: 03-551-7161. Mr. Fujimori Denei, director; Mr. Miyachi Kazuo, executive vice president, and Mr. Matsushita Zenichi, fact finder. The coordinating body for all miso shops and factories in Japan. Also operates a large miso research lab.

Kawamura Wataru: Kugenuma 2373, Fujisawa-shi 251. Tel: 0466-22-1351. Author of several of Japan's most popular books about miso, widely known as Japan's "miso sensei" (teacher), and former director of publicity for the National Miso Association, Mr. Kawamura describes himself as a scholar (and lover) of miso soup.

Mochizuki Tsutomu: Director of the Shinshu Miso Research Institute in Nagano city (see below), Dr. Mochizuki is the leading expert on modern Shinshu miso.

Morishita Keiichi: Morishita Eiyo Kyoshitsu, Bunkyoku, Hongo 2-3-10, Tokyo. Tel:03-814-6786. An expert on the nutritional and health-given value of miso. Dr. Morishita is an M.D. who heads a hospital and nutritional research center in Tokyo. The author of more than 30 books, he has for many years advocated the value of traditional Japanese fermented soyfoods.

Murakami Hideya: Kokuritsu Jozo Shikenjo, Takinogawa, Kita-ku, Tokyo. Director of the National Fermented Foods Research Institute and a well-known scholar of *A. oryzae* molds.

Nakano Masahiro: Meiji Daigaku, Ikuta Kosha, Ikuta 5158, Kawasaki-shi, Kanagawa-ken 214. Tel: 044-911-8181. The dean of miso scholars and teacher of Drs. Ebine and Mochizuki, Dr. Nakano is professor of microbiology at Meiji University where he directs a laboratory engaged in the study of miso and other fermented foods.

Ouchi Ichiro, c/o Yamajirushi, Komome 3-15-1, Itabashi-ku, Tokyo. Tel: 03-972-3151. Formerly of the Shinshu Miso Research Institute, he spent one year in the U.S. at the Northern Regional Research Center developing new foods incorporating miso as a flavoring agent.

Sakaguchi Kinichiro: Takabon 3-17-4, Meguro-ku, Tokyo 152. Tel: 712-7033. A retired scholar of koji molds, Dr. Sakaguchi received the Emperor's medal of honor for his research work. He now publishes a magazine on foods with frequent articles on miso and shoyu.

Shibasaki Kazuo: Tohoku University, Nogaku-bu, Shokuhin Kagaku-ka, Kita 6 Banchi. Sendai-shi. Dr. Shibasaki spent 1958 and 1959 in the U.S. doing research on miso at the NRRL. He has co-authored many English-language articles on miso with Dr. Clifford Hesseltine and other researchers, and is now a consultant for the Sendai Miso-Shoyu Company.

Shinshu Miso Research Institute: Shinshu Miso Kenkyujo, 469-6 Nakagosho, Nagano-shi 380. Tel: 0262-28-1221. Under the directon of Dr. Mochizuki, this large and prestigious organization is doing basic scientific and technological research on miso production.

EXPORTERS OF NATURAL MISO AND KOJI TO THE WEST

Muso Co. Ltd., Export Dept. Otedori 2-5-1, Higashi-ku, Osaka 540 Japan. Tel: 06-945-0511. Yuko Okada.

Mitoku Co. Ltd., C.P.O. Box 780, Tokyo 100-91; Marunouchi Bldg., Marunouchi, Tokyo. Tel: 03-201-6706 thru 8. Mr. Akiyoshi Kazama, director.

TRADITIONAL OR SEMI-TRADITIONAL SHOPS MAKING NATURAL MISO

Amanoya: Makers of Finger Lickin'-and sweet red miso, as well as kohi and *amazaké* (see p. 258).

Arai Miso Ten: Suwa, Mitsukaido-shi, 2765, Ibaragi-ken. Tel: 0297-2-0274.

Fuchu Miso: Honmachi, Fuchu-shi, Hiroshima-ken. Tel: 0847-41-2080. Mr. Kanemitsu Yanosuke, director. The main supplier of natural barley miso to the West via Muso Shokuhin. Fuchu also produces natural Kinzanji miso and quick rice miso.

Hayakawa Kyuemon Shoten (also called Hatcho Miso Kakkyu Goshi-kaisha): Aza, Okan-dori 69, Hatcho-cho, Okazaki-shi, Aichi-ken 444. Tel: 0564-21-0151. Mr. Kaneko, director; Mr. Hayakawa Kyuemon, 18th proprietor. Located near Nagoya in Central Japan on the banks of the Yahagi river (once famous for its fine artesian wells and *Yahagi* soybeans), this company is the largest and best known of Japan's two very old makers of natural Hatcho miso—both of which are located on the same block. Said to have been established in 1362 (but thought by scholars to have originated in its present form about 350 to 400 years ago). Hayakawa is the proud supplier of the Imperial Household Agency. They presently transform about 50 percent of their Hatcho miso into akadashi miso.

Horikawa-ya: Gobo-shi, Toyota-shi, Aichi-ken. A traditional maker of natural Kinzanji miso.

Ikeda Kojiro Miso Shoten: Motogo 4-8-24, Kawaguchi-shi. Saitama-ken 332. Tel: 0482-22-6766. A traditional maker of natural barley miso located near Tokyo, Ikeda now exports to the U.S. and also produces quick rice miso.

Kantoya Shoten Matsumoto-cho 582, Ebisugawa Noboru, Gokochodori, Nakagyo-ku, Kyoto. Tel: 231-1728 or 211-4371. A maker of traditional red miso, this shop has a fine koji incubation room.

Kawasaki Shoten: Nishi Arie-cho, Minami Takagi-gun, Nagasaki-ken, Kyushu. A maker of traditional, natural Finger Lickin' (natto miso) and sweet barley miso.

Kawasho Miso Shoten: Kaizan-cho 3-145, Sakai-shi, Osaka 590. Tel: 0722-33-1061. A maker of delicious, traditional Kinzanji miso.

Meiji Seifun, Fuchu-machi 536, Fuchu-shi, Hiroshima-ken 726. Tel: 0874-41-2255. A maker of natural barley and red miso.

Nagata Tozaimon: Hatonaka 133, Aza, Taketoyo-cho, Kita-gun, Aichi-ken 470-23. Tel: 05697-2-0341. A maker of natural soybean miso and shoyu.

Ota Shoten: Okan-dori 52, Hatcho-cho, Okazaki-shi, Aichi-ken 444. Tel: 0564-22-0222. Mr. Kato Choichi, director. The second largest maker of Hatcho miso in Japan, Ota produces 1,000 tons annually and an additional 1,500 tons of one-year soybean miso (*waka Hatcho*). Their prices are relatively low.

Sendai Miso-Shoyu Inc.: Furujiro 1-5-1, Sendai-shi, 982. Tel: 0222-86-3151. Mr. Sasaki Kenichiro, director; Mr. Sasaki Shigeo, managing director; Mr. Haga Hiroshi, production director. The largest miso maker in the northeast provinces and the largest producer of Sendai-type red miso in Japan, this company produces much of the natural red miso (and shoyu) now imported into the United States. Their miso is aged 18 to 24 months, and their shoyu (made from whole soybeans) 18 months. They also make a natural brown-rice miso and a 6-month red miso using the most modern techniques of temperature-controlled fermentation. The company is now thinking about starting to produce miso in the United States. They have recently developed an excellent color film about the commercial production of miso and shoyu, available direct from Sendai or via Mitoku (above), and they hold an exclusive patent on the process of packaging (pasteurized) miso in sealed bags without the use of alcohol or other preservatives.

Shiromizu Shoten: Meihama-cho 3135, Nishi-ku, Fukuoka-shi, Fukuoka-ken 814. Tel: 092-881-0413. A maker of natural barley miso.

Suyamo Shoten: Ashida 2618, Tateshina-cho, Kitasaku-gun, Nagano-ken 384-23. Tel: 02675-6-1001. A maker of traditional Shinshu miso.

Tsuchiya Miso-shoyu: Higashi Yokomachi 383, Susaka-shi, Nagano-ken 383. Tel: 02624-5-0259. A producer of natural Shinshu miso.

Tsujita Miso Shoten: Kojiya Saburo Uemon, Nakamura 2-29-8, Nerima-ku, Tokyo 176. Tel: 03-999-2276. Mr. Tsujita Kiyoshi, master. A very old shop using traditional, natural methods, this firm makes 18- and 24-month brown-rice miso, 3-year chunky barley miso, ready-made dried koji, and brown-rice *amazaké*. Tsujita uses organic rice, natural sea salt, and the finest Hokkaido-grown *tsurunoko* soybeans. The producer of all brown-rice miso now sold in the West, this shop was the source of much of our information about making miso in traditional shops.

Yamatoya: Adzusa Kawamura, Adzusa, Nagano-ken. Tel: 026378-2280. Producer of natural miso using *miso-dama.*

JAPAN'S TEN LARGEST MISO FACTORIES

The following, listed in order of size (using 1974 production statistics), generally prepare light-yellow miso using quick temperature-controlled fermentation methods. Details are given in Chapter 9.

1. *Miyazaka Jozo* (Shinshu ichi), Nogata 2-4-5, Nakano-ku, Tokyo 165. Tel: 03-385-2121. Mr. Watanabe Yojuro, production director. This Tokyo factory produces about 15,000 tons per year; the Nagano and Yamanashi plants produce 9,300 and 3,300 tons respectively. All make Shinshu-type light-yellow miso. Tokyo makes freeze-dried miso.

2. *Hanamaruki:* Hirade 1560, Tatsuno-cho, Oaza, Kamiina-gun, Nagano-ken 399-04. Tel: 02664-2-1321. Also produce a mellow beige miso imported to the U.S.

3. *Takeya:* Kogan-dori 2-3-17, Suwa-shi, Nagano-ken 392. Tel: 02665-2-4000.

Busy Making Dengaku (from the "Tofu Hyaku Chin")

4. *Marukome:* Amori 833. Nagano-shi, Nagano-ken 380. Tel: 0262-26-0255. Yamamoto Yasuo, production mgr. The biggest single miso factory in Japan. Makes dehydrated miso.

5. *Kanesa:* Tamagawa 202, Hamada-aza, Aomori-shi 030. Tel: 0177-39-5211.

6. *Marudai:* Ohashi, Hamochi-machi, Sado-gun, Niigata-ken 952-05. Tel: Hamochi #3 or #4. Makers of Sado-style rice miso.

7. *Marusan:* Aza-arashita 1, Jingi-cho, Okazaki-shi 444-21. Operates 3 factories.

8. *Yamajirushi:* Komome 3-15-1, Itabashi-ku, Tokyo. Tel: 03-972-3151. Other factories in Maruko City (Nagano) and Moriya City (Ibaragi). Total output is 18,000 tons per year. The Moriya plant produces 6,000 tons of *shikomi-miso* (p. 167) yearly which is sold in 20-pound quantities to farm cooperatives, whence it is distributed to farm families.

9. *Ichibiki:* Shinto-machi 14, Atsuda-ku, Nagoya-shi. Also operates a factory in Toyohashi.

10. *Kaneko:* Aizumi-machi Okuno, Itano-gun, Tokushima-shi. Output is 11,000 tons per year.

OTHER MAKERS OF FINE MISO

Abumata Miso Co.: Honmachi 3-32-19, Nakano-ku, Tokyo. Tel: 372-5211. Mr. Takeyama, director of production. A large producer of sweet red miso.

Amadaya: Nakamura Fujio, Gobo 1, Gobo-shi, Wakayama-ken. Tel: 07382-2-0455. A maker of delicious Kinzanji and moromi misos, containing lots of koji and uri melons.

Ebiya: Azumbashi 1-15-55, Sumida-ku, Asakusa, Tokyo. Tel: 03-625-0003. A producer of high-quality Peanut and Tekka Miso.

Echigo Miso Jozo, Yoshida 5884, Yoshida Machi, Nishi Tanbaragun, Niigata-ken, Tel: 02569-2-4805. A maker of natural Kinzanji miso.

Ezaki Honten: Ebisu machi 902, Shimbara-shi, Nagasaki-ken 855. Tel: 2-3161. Mr. Shibata. A large and well-known producer of natural miso pickles.

Hagoromo Miso: Fuchu-machi 533-3. Fuchu-shi, Hiroshima-ken 726, Tel: 0847-41-2010. A main source of the natural barley miso sold in the U.S. Also makes a sweet white miso.

Hamamoto: Osaki 1-19-6, Shinagawa-ku, Tokyo. Tel: 03-493-0885. A maker of Kinzanji miso.

Hinode Miso Brewing Co., 3567 Shimo-Oyamada-Machi, Machida-shi, Tokyo 194-01. Mr. Tetsuo Fumoto. Tel: 0427-97-2311. Makers of Peanut Miso, Peanut & Raisin Miso, and Glutinous-rice Miso *(Mochigome miso),* each sealed in small plastic packets for easy export and sale.

Honda Miso Honten: Ichijo Agaru, Muromachi-dori, Kamikyo-ku, Kyoto 558. Tel. 075-441-1121. Mr. Honda Shigeru, fourth generation owner. One of Japan's best known makers of sweet white miso, Honda is a relatively traditional shop and is unique in preparing one natural variety without the use of preservatives (ethyl alcohol is used) or bleach. Honda's sweet white miso is sold under the registered brand name "Saikyo Miso" meaning "Western Kyoto Miso." Honda also produces akadashi and red miso.

Ichikyu Miso: Tokiwacho 2-15, Higashi-ku, Osaka. Tel: 941-09-4154. A maker of moromi miso.

Ishino Miso Co.: Ishiizutsu-cho, Shijo Kudaru, Aburakoji, Shimo-okyoku, Kyoto. Tel: 075-361-2336. One of Japan's two large producers of sweet white and akadashi miso. At present they do not export.

Ishiyama Miso Shoyu: Nigata-shi. Tel: 0252-28-2034. Mr. Kinji Ishiyama, exec. v.p. A maker of low-salt miso.

Iwanaga Shoyu Gomei-gaisha: Sashiki, Ashikita-machi, Ashikita-gun, Kumamoto-ken. A maker of natural chunky barley miso.

Kageju Shokuhin, Yawata 1-4-41, Shizuoka-shi, Shizuoka-ken. A maker of natural Kinzanji miso.

Kame-gen Jozo: Suwa 2-4-8, Suwa-shi, Nagano-ken. A maker of buckwheat miso containing buckwheat groats, soybeans, salt, and alcohol preservative.

Kirishima Food Co.: Okubo 65-1, Kirishima-cho, Kagoshima-ken. Japan's primary maker of Yubeshi Miso.

Marui Jozo: Azuma-cho 56, Iida-shi, Nagano-ken. Tel: 0265-22-6363. A maker of miso pickles. Uses wild mountain vegetables and Shinshu miso.

Nagano Miso Co.: Tenjin 3-9-29, Ueda-shi, Nagano-ken 386. Tel: 02682-4-7771. Mr. Hideki Oka, president. A maker of salt-free and traditional misos.

Nakamuraya Shoten: Yaji 3225, Tokuyama-shi, Yamaguchi-ken. Tel: 0834-62-3108 or 9. The maker of the delicious Hana-bishi brand sweet white miso now widely available in the U.S. both in 1-pound cartons or 35-pound kegs.

Sanjirushi Jozo: Meisei-dori 1-572-1, Kuwana-shi 511. Tel: 0594-22-3333. Tokyo office: 03-722-4433. Japan's largest maker of soybean miso. A larger maker of natural real tamari.

Sanman Kajimaya Shoten: Chuo 3-1-5, Okaya-shi, Nagano-ken. A maker of brown-rice miso.

Shinsho Miso Jozo: Sanjo-machi 3-12-23, Hiroshima-shi, Hiroshima-ken. A maker of Eiyaku brand brown-rice miso.

Shinshu Miso K.K.: Aramachi, Komoro-shi, Nagano-ken 384. Tel: 02672-2-0007. Mr. Koyama Masakuni, director. Head office: Shimo Ochiai 3-17-38, Shinjuku-ku, Tokyo 161. Tel: 03-951-1141. Mr. Koyama Kunitomo. A large producer of Shinshu miso, sold in the U.S. and Japan under the brand name "Yamabuki."

Shinshu Sennichi Miso K.K.: Kamimachi 82, Susaka-shi, Nagano-ken. Tel: 02624-5-0958. One of the first makers of natural miso to use natural (unrefined) salt.

Shoman K.K.: Nagisa 2-32, Matsumoto-shi, Nagano-ken. Makers of instant miso soup sold in a box with dehydrated tofu, leeks, *wakame,* dashi; and a tiny packet of fresh miso.

Yamanaga Miso: Hyakunin-cho 2-8-1, Shinjuku-ku, Tokyo. Tel: 03-371-9146. A maker of traditional-type miso.

Yorosho Honpo: Yuasa-machi Yokocho 519, Arita-gun, Wakayama-ken. Tel. 07376-2-2318. A maker of Kinzanji miso.

Yoshida Shohachi: Takashima-cho 382, Shimabara-shi, Nagasaki-ken 855. Tel: 09576-2-4107. The sole supplier of the natural natto (finger lickin') miso now sold in the U.S.

Yoshino-ya Jozo (Zenkoji Miso): Nishi-no-mon, Nagano-shi, Nagano-ken, Japan. Tel: 34-1171. A famous old maker of Shinshu light yellow miso.

MAKERS OF KOJI STARTER AND KOJI

Amanoya Kojiten: Soto Kanda 2-18-15, Chiyoda-ku, Tokyo. Tel: 03-251-7911. Mr. Amano Yaichi. A very old, traditional and beautiful shop preparing ready-made koji, some of which they use in the *amazaké* sold in their restaurant. The koji is fermented in long, earth-walled tunnels 20 feet beneath the streets of Tokyo. They also make delicious, natural Finger Lickin', and sweet red miso.

Hishiroku: A traditional Kyoto maker of koji starter. Tel: 075-541-4141.

Kojiya Sanzaemon Roho: Shimotachiuri-sagaru, Omiya-dori, Kamikyo-ku, Kyoto. A traditional koji maker.

Amanoya Kojiten: Soto Kanda 2-18-15, Chiyoda-ku, Tokyo. Tel: 03-251-7911. Mr. Amano Yaichi. A very old, traditional and beautiful shop preparing ready-made koji, some of which they use in the *amazaké* sold in their restaurant. The koji is fermented in long, earth-walled tunnels 20 feet beneath the streets of Tokyo. They also make delicious, natural Finger Lickin', and sweet red miso.

Hishiroku: A traditional Kyoto maker of koji starter. Tel: 075-541-4141.

Kojiya Takahashi: Agebocho, Toyota-shi, Aichi-ken 471. Tel: 0565-32-1323. A traditional maker of Kinzanji koji.

Nihon Jozo Kogyo: Sales office: Koishigawa 3-18-9, Bunkyo-ku, Tokyo 112. Tel: 03-816-2951. Factory: Higashiori-ue, Iishi-aza, Oaza, Juo-machi, Taga-gun, Ibaragi-ken. Tel: 0293-32-2307. Mr. Niimi Yasu, director; Mr. Chiba Akira, ass't. director. The Japan Brewing Co. is a large, reliable producer of koji starter used for both miso and shoyu and sold under the brand name of Marufuku Moyashi. This company was the source of much of our information on preparing koji starter.

Tokai Hakko Kagaku Kenkyujo: Ichigen 1712, Toyoda mura, Iwata-gun, Shizuoka-ken. A traditional maker of miso koji starter.

Cutting tofu for Dengaku
(from the "Tofu Hyaku Chin")

JAPANESE RESTAURANTS SPECIALIZING IN MISO CUISINE

Dengaku: Komachi 1-6-5, Kamakura-shi, Kanagawa-ken. Tel: 0467-23-2121. Dengaku cookery at its best in a charming atmosphere.

Nakamura-ro: Yasaka Jinja-nai, Higashiyama-ku, Kyoto. Tel: 075-561-4589. Delicious Dengaku and *amazaké.*

Shiru Hatchi: Ginza 8-chome, Tokyo. Tel: 571-0456. Popular and inexpensive miso soups.

PEOPLE AND INSTITUTIONS IN NORTH AMERICA

MISO RESEARCHERS AND INSTITUTES

Hesseltine, Clifford W.: Known for his outstanding research as a mycologist, Dr. Hesseltine has had a lifelong interest in miso and has written many articles on the subject. Past President of the Mycological Society of America, he is presently director of the fermentation laboratory of the NRRC (below).

Northern Regional Research Center (USDA/NRRC): 1815 North University St., Peoria, IL 61604. Tel: 309-685-4011. The main center for miso research in North America, the NRRC offers a good selection of scientific-journal articles on miso fermentation as well as pure-culture koji starters. Directed by Dr. Clifford W. Hesseltine, who is assisted by Dr. Hwa L. Wang, the fermentation laboratory has sponsored miso researchers from Japan, including Dr. Kazuo Shibasaki and Dr. Ichiro Ouchi.

Wang, Hwa L.: A woman working at the NRRC fermentation research lab, Dr. Wang has extensive experience in the field of miso and has written articles on the subject.

COMPANIES IMPORTING JAPANESE MISO, KOJI, OR KOJI STARTER

American Pacific Trading International Inc.: 2309 East 8th St., Los Angeles, CA 90021. Tel. 213-622-0422. Importers of Yamabuki brand miso from the Shinshu Miso Company in Komoro, Nagano prefecture.

Chico-San, Inc., P.O. Box 810, Chico, CA 95927. Tel: 916-891-6271. Importers of koji and various natural misos.

Eden Foods Inc., 701 Clinton-Tecumseh, Clinton, MI 49236. Tel: 517-456-7424. An importer of natural miso and shoyu.

Edward & Sons Trading Co., Route 1 Box 153, Saluda, NC 28773. Tel: 704-749-9666. Importers of instant freeze-dried miso soup sold as "Miso-Cup."

Erewhon Inc., 5 Waltham St., Wilmington, MA 01887. Tel: 617-657-8120. Importers of all basic miso types.

GEM Cultures, 30301 Sherwood Rd., Ft. Bragg, CA 95437. Tel: 707-964-2922. Gordon McBride. Presently America's best source of koji starters for many types of miso and shoyu. Their starter is imported from Japan's finest producers.

JFC International, Inc.: 445 Kaufman Ct., So. San Francisco, CA 94080. Tel: 415-873-8400. Or 1131 So. Mateo St., Los Angeles. Tel: 213-627-6534. Importers of more than 15 varieites of Japanese miso.

Kagemuri, T., 8578 Birnom St., Montreal, Quebec H3M 2V3, Canada. An importer of natural miso.

Kikkoman International, 50 California St., Suite 3600, San Francisco, CA 94111. Tel: 415-956-7750. Mr. Terumitsu Hattori. Importers of red miso which they dehydrate (and mix with dehydrated tofu plus land-and-sea vegetables) to make their instant miso soup, now sold in many supermarkets.

Lifestream, 12411 Vulcan Way, Richmond, B.C. Canada V6V 1J7. Tel: 604-278-7571. Or 91 Esna Park Dr., Markhah, Ont, Canada L3R 2S2. Tel: 416-475-6836. An importer of natural miso.

Manna Foods Inc., 112 Crockford Blvd., Scarborough, Ontario, M1R 3C3 Canada. Tel: 416-759-4108. An importer of natural miso.

Marusan Foods Corp., 8780 E. Valley Blvd., Rosemead, CA 91770. Tel: 213-571-8997. Importer of instant miso soups.

Mutual Trading Co., 431 Crocker St., Los Angeles, CA 90013. Tel: 213-626-9458. Mr. Noritoshi Kanai. Importers of light-yellow miso and distributors of miso and koji made by Miyako Oriental Foods, their subsidiary.

Nishimoto Trading Co.: 1884 E. 22nd St., Los Angeles, CA 90013. Tel: 213-747-4111. Importers of Hawaiian mellow white miso.

Soken Trading Co., Box 1705, Sausalito, CA 94965. Tel: 415-332-2313. Importers of various misos.

Tree of Life Inc., 315 Industrial Drive, St. Augustine, FL 32084. Tel: 904-829-3284. Importer of miso.

Westbrae Natural Foods, 4240 Hollis St., Emeryville, CA 94608. Tel: 415-658-7518. Importers of brown-rice, red, barley, Hatcho, and Finger Lickin' (natto) miso. Also distribute U.S.-made koji and miso.

INDIVIDUALS INTERESTED IN MISO

The following list of names, although quickly outdated, may prove helpful in bringing together people interested in miso.

Aihara, Cornellia and Herman: c/o GOMF, 902 14th St. Oroville, CA 95965. Tel: 916-533-7702 or 9900. Cornellia has given classes in miso making and miso cookery, and has prepared barley koji commercially. Herman has written and spoken extensively about miso; his books include *Miso and Tamari* and *Soybean Diet.*

Kendall, Charlie: Kendall Food Co., P.O. Box 69, Ashburnham, MA 01430. Tel: 617-827-6236. Research.

Kerrigan, Rick: 688 Capp St., San Francisco, CA 94110. Tel: 415-282-9909. Doing miso research.

Kushi, Aveline and Michio, 62 Buckminster Rd., Brookline, MA 02146. Tel: 617-232-6869. Aveline has taught miso making and cookery. Michio has taught thousands of people about the many virtues of miso, and numerous members of his macrobiotic community have experience making miso at home.

Muramoto, Noboru: 145 W. El Norte Parkway, Escondido, CA 92026. Tel: 714-743-6890. Teacher of many students now active in making miso. Note that his first name is spelled Noboru, not Naboru.

Shrift, Eric: P.O. Box 25, Andes Land Project, Andes, NY 13731. A student of N. Muramoto who plans to produce miso and teach miso-making classes.

Truslow, Will: 36 Hempstead Rd., Jamaica Plain, MA 02130. A student of N. Muramoto who makes miso at home and gives miso-making classes through the Kushi Institute in Boston.

Yamazaki, Junsei: See address at miso manufacturers, App. D. A highly skilled miso craftsman, he has taught miso-making classes throughout the U.S.

PEOPLE AND INSTITUTIONS IN EUROPE

Imported natural miso is now available throughout Europe. Macrobiotic teachers have played a major role in its popularization, and have already built one large miso production center in Belgium. Please send us other names if you know of them. For names of miso manufacturers, see Appendix D.

ENGLAND

Ceres, 269 Portabello Rd., London W.11, England. Attn. Craig Sams. An importer of natural miso and shoyu.

Harmony Foods, 1 Earl Cottages, Earl Rd., London S.E. 1, England. Tel: 01-237-8396. An importer of natural miso and shoyu.

Sunwheel Food Ltd., 12 Orpheus St., Camberwell, London S.E. 5-8RT, England. Tel: 01-701-7160. Attn. Peter Bradford or Robert Harropp. An importer of natural miso and shoyu.

FRANCE

Le Bol en Bois, 35 rue Pascal, 75013 Paris, France. Tel: 707.2724. Attn. Mr. Noboru Sakaguchi. A natural-food center and tofu shop that imports natural miso.

Mittler, Jacques: Route de la Montagne d'age, F-74330 Le Lechat, Poisy, France. Makes miso.

Roland, Jacquot: 10 Rue Bretagne, 91 390 Ris Orangis, France. Makes miso.

Yoshimi, Clim: Institute Yin/Yang-Tenryu of Paris, 8 rue Rochebrune, Paris 75011, France. Tel: 805-9135. Chief editor of the macrobiotic monthly magazine *Principe Unique.* Tenryu imports natural miso and shoyu.

GERMANY (WEST)

Nakamura, Jiro: Ubersetzung und Verlag, Münsterstrasse 255, 4 Düsseldorf, West Germany. Tel. 632-443. A translator, publisher, and teacher, he is one of the key figures introducing miso to Europe.

Rabenau, Detlef von: Am Seenfer 15, D-8194 Ambach, West Germany. Tel: 08177-8488. Interested in miso.

Weghaupt, Mascha and Thomas Lüttge: 800 Munchen 2, Theresienstr, 68, West Germany. Interested in miso.

ITALY

Bianchini, Gilberto: Centro Macrobiotico, Via Cuoco 9, 47037 Rimini, Italy. Tel: 0541-33670. Interested in miso and tofu production.

D'angella Giuseppe: V. Pasubio 16, 21047 Saronno (Varese), Italy. Making miso.

La Via Macrobiotica: C.P. 12032, 00135 Roma, Belsito, Italy. An importer of natural miso.

Romano, Silvio: Casale "Sosselva," 05010—Prado n. 123 (Terni), Italy. Interested in miso.

NETHERLANDS

Loo, Dr. Thio Goan: Dept. of Agricultural Research, Royal Tropical Institute, 63 Mauritskade, Amsterdam-Oost, Netherlands. Microbiologist interested in miso.

Manna Natural Foods, Meeuwenlaan 70, 1021 JK Amsterdam, Netherlands. An importer of natural miso and shoyu.

Nelissen, Adelbert: Stichting Oost West Centrum, Achtergracht 17-19, 1017 WL, Amsterdam, Netherlands. Tel: 020-240-203. A great place to learn about miso and natural foods.

Nelissen, Thomas: Overboslaan 13, Heemstede, Netherlands. Working with miso.

PORTUGAL

Edvardo Galamba de sa Pires: Apartado 5, Torres Novas, Portugal. An importer of natural miso.

UNIMAVE: Rua de Boa Vista. 55-2°, Lisbon-2, Portugal. Tel: 607283. An importer of natural miso.

PEOPLE AND INSTITUTIONS IN LATIN AMERICA

BRAZIL

Kikuchi, Tomio: Praca Carlos Comes 60, Sao Paolo, Brazil. A macrobiotic teacher who makes his own miso.

Zanatta, Flavio: Rua Almte Alexandrio, 3226/801, Rio G.B., Brazil. Interested in tofu and miso.

COSTA RICA

Prana: Av. Central Calles 21-23, San Jose, Costa Rica. A macrobiotic food store and importer of natural miso.

MEXICO

American Soybean Association: Rio Sena #26-201, Col. Cuauhtemoc, Mexico 5, D.F. Tel: 905-535-0659. Attn. Gil Harrison. The ASA is a source of information about buying and growing soybeans.

Takata, Maestro Ejo: Zen A.C., Avenida Revolucion #2036. San Angel, Mexico 20, D.F. A Japanese Zen priest teaching the local people about miso and other soyfoods.

Tovar, Dr. Raul: Faculty of Chemistry, Dept. of Food Science, University of Mexico, Mexico 20, D.F. An expert on miso.

Appendix F
Miso with Seafoods, Chicken and Meat

Although this is a meatless cookbook and we wholeheartedly support all the basic tenets of vegetarianism, the following information has been included for three reasons: 1) Fish and shellfish taken from un-polluted waters, barnyard fowl and hogs allowed to forage or fed scraps, and cattle or sheep grazed on land that cannot be used to grow crops can each serve as key sources of protein and other nutrients (especially in hungry countries) while also providing manure for the fields; 2) This book is, in part, a study of miso's role in Japanese cuisine and culture, and the omission of preparations using animal products would leave an incomplete picture; 3) Those moving toward a meatless diet (or away from meats and poultry toward seafoods) may like to use miso with small quantities of animal products (as most Japanese usually do) during the transition.

The various Japanese recipes fall into six basic categories, listed in the order they appear in the book. Within each category the preparations are listed in order of popularity.

Miso Toppings

Red-snapper Miso *(Taimiso):* Steam red snapper (or cod or salmon) until tender, then simmer briefly in a little sake. Add an equal weight of red or white Nerimiso and a little grated gingerroot; simmer until mixture is amber to reddish brown.

Clam Miso *(Shiguré Miso):* The word *shiguré* means "late autumn rains," reminiscent of the seashore weather at clam-digging time. Sauté clams in oil until just tender, then simmer for several minutes in a mixture of *mirin* and shoyu. Remove clams, add dashi, miso and sugar, and proceed as for Nerimiso. Add back clams and simmer briefly. Serve chilled, topped with *sansho* pepper, parsley, or grated gingerroot.

Oyster Miso *(Kaki Miso):* Combine sweet white miso, *mirin*, shoyu, and grated gingerroot in a saucepan. Add an equal volume of stock or dashi and bring to a boil. Add oysters and simmer for 5 minutes.

Pork- or Chicken Miso *(Buta- or Tori Miso):* Sauté ground or torn bits of pork or chicken in oil until tender. Add sweet white miso, sugar, *mirin* or sake, and shoyu; proceed as for Nerimiso. Serve as a topping for noodles, Cha-chiang Mien, Furofuki Daikon, Sang-chu, taro, or sweet potatoes.

Shrimp-, Abalone-, Bonita-, or Sweetfish Miso *(Ebi-, Awabi, Katsuo-, or Ayu Miso):* Prepare and serve as for Clam- or Oyster Miso.

Aemono

Nuta: Mix steamed or parboiled fish, shellfish, or squid with Vinegar Miso and one or two lightly cooked vegetables (especially leeks, wakame, or cucumbers).

Squid & Kinomé *(Ika no Kinomé-ae):* Combine fresh or lightly steamed squid with thinly-sliced, parboiled bamboo shoots. Mix with Kinomé Dressing.

Octopus & Gingerroot *(Tako no Shoga Miso-ae):* Broil octopus (or squid or abalone), slice, and mix with Gingerroot Miso Dressing.

Carp & Mustard-Vinegar *(Koi no Karashi Sumiso-ae):* Parboil whole (regular or Crucian) carp. Skin, bone, and tear into small bits. Mix with Mustard-Vinegar Miso Dressing.

Shrimp & Egg Yolk-Vinegar: Mix parboiled shrimps with Egg-Yolk Vinegar Miso.

Miso Soups and Stews

Carp Soup *(Koi Koku):* One of the few Japanese soups requiring the lengthy simmering of miso, this preparation is said to stimulate milk-flow in nursing mothers and is often used to invigorate the weak or sick. Sauté slivered burdock root in oil until tender. Add water to cover and bring to a boil. Add creamed miso and chopped carp and simmer for 2 hours (or pressure cook for 40 minutes). Stir in grated gingerroot and serve topped with slivered leeks and *sansho* pepper.

Chicken & Vegetable Miso Soup *(Satsuma-jiru):* Pre-cook chicken in water until tender. Strain stock and use to cook sliced carrot, burdock root, *daikon*, mushrooms, and leek. Add chicken and creamed miso; simmer until thick.

Pork & Vegetable Miso Stew *(Buta-jiru):* Simmer cubed pork in lightly salted water until tender. Add sliced spinach and leeks, and grated gingerroot. Stir in creamed miso and bring just to a boil.

Oyster or Fish Miso Soups *(Kaki or Sakana no Misoshiru):* Simmer seafoods in dashi until tender, then add vegetables and creamed miso. Bring just to a boil. Traditional Akadashi (p. 104) often featured oysters.

Simmered Dishes & Nabémono

Boston Mackerel Simmered with Miso *(Saba no Miso-ni):* Combine sweet white miso, sake, dashi, sugar, and grated gingerroot; bring to a boil. Add cutlets of unskinned mackerel and simmer for 15 minutes.

Oyster Nabé *(Kaki Nabé):* Combine miso, *mirin* and dashi, and bring to a boil. Add spring chrysanthemum leaves, chopped scallions, shelled oysters, and tofu; cook 3 to 4 minutes. Serve hot, dipping oysters in beaten raw eggs.

Doténabé with Oysters *(Kaki no Doténabé):* Substitute oysters for the tofu in Doténabé.

Salmon Nabé *(Ishikari Nabé):* Simmer chunks of salmon in a rich miso broth together with tofu, *konnyaku*, leeks, Chinese cabbage, carrots, *daikon*, green beans, and sliced leeks.

Chicken Nabé *(Tori Nabé):* Simmer chicken, green peppers, sliced onions, and mushrooms in dashi until tender. Add miso, *mirin*, sake, and sugar, and simmer several more minutes.

Grilled Preparations

Fish Dengaku *(Gyoden):* Sprinkle horse mackerel, sweetfish, or trout with salt, skewer, and broil over high heat till speckled. Spread both sides with Sweet Simmered Miso and rebroil briefly. Or sandwich the miso between broiled fish slices and steam in cherry or oak leaves.

Foods Pickled in Miso

Red Snapper, Mackerel, or Salmon *(Tai-, Saba-, or Sake no Misozuké):* Sprinkle fish lightly with salt, wrap in cheesecloth, and embed in a mixture of sweet white miso and a little sake or *mirin* for 2 to 3 days (or in red or barley miso for 1 to 2 days). Rub off excess miso and broil on both sides until cooked through. Serve as a topping for rice, an hors d'œuvre, a sandwich filling, or an ingredient in miso soups.

Pork *(Buta no Misozuké):* Arrange sliced pork on a plate and top with gingerroot slices. Sprinkle with sake and allow to stand for 1 hour, then steam for 40 minutes. Cool and embed with gingerroot in red or barley miso for 5 to 7 days. Rub off miso with fingertips, cut pork into thin strips, and serve as for red snapper above.

Chicken *(Tori no Misozuké):* Cut chicken into thin strips, sprinkle with sake, and allow to stand for 10 minutes. Wrap in cheesecloth and proceed as for red snapper.

Beef *(Gyuniku no Misozuké):* Pound meat lightly, cut into thin strips, and wrap in cheesecloth. Embed for 2 to 4 days in sweet white miso. Broil for 3 minutes on each side.

Traditional shoyu seller

Measures, Weights and Equivalents

TEMPERATURE

C = Celsius or Centigrade; F = Fahrenheit
C = 5/9 (F−32)
F = (1.8 x C) + 32
Freezing point of water = 32°F = 0°C
Boiling point of water = 212°F = 100°C
Body temperature = 98.6°F = 37.0°C

WEIGHT (MASS)

1 ounce (avoirdupois) = 28.3495 grams = 16 drams = 437.5 grains
1 pound (avoirdupois) = 16 ounces = 453.59 grams = 0.45359 kg
1 (short or U.S.) ton = 2,000 pounds = 0.907 tonnes or metric tons = 33.33 bushels of soybeans (used chiefly in the U.S. and Canada)
1 tonne or metric ton (MT) = 2,204.6 pounds = 1.1025 (short) tons = 36.75 bushels of soybeans
1 long ton = 2,240 pounds = 1.12 (short) tons = 1.016 tonnes or metric tons = 37.33 bushels of soybeans (used chiefly in England)
100 grams = 3.527 ounces
1 kilogram = 1,000 grams = 2.2046 pounds
1 quintal (qt) = 100 kg = 220.46 pounds
10 ppm = 0.01 gm/kg = .0045 gm/lb.

CAPACITY (U.S. LIQUID MEASURE)

1 teaspoon = 60 drops
1 tablespoon = 3 teaspoons = 14.75 ml or cc
1 fluid ounce = 2 tablespoons = 29.57 ml = 0.0296 liters = 1.8047 cu. in.
1 cup (U.S.) = 16 tablespoons = 8 fluid oz. = 236 ml
1 quart = 2 pints = 4 cups = 32 fluid oz. = 0.946 liters
1 gallon (U.S.) = 4 quarts = 231 cu. in. = 0.8333 imperial gallon = 3.785 liters
1 gallon (imperial) = 1.20 gallons (U.S.) = 4.456 liters
1 liter = 1,000 ml or cc = 1.0567 liquid quarts = 4.237 cups = 61.03 cu. in. = 33.814 fluid ounces = 0.264 gallons = 0.220 imperial gallons
1 kiloliter = 1,000 liters = 264.18 gallons (U.S.)= 33.315 cu. ft. = 2200.6 lb. water
10 ppm = 0.01 ml/liter = 0.38 ml/gallon

CAPACITY (U.S. DRY MEASURE)

1 quart = 2 pints = 67.20 cu. in. = 1.1012 liters
1 peck = 537.605 cu. in. = 9.309 quarts = 8.809 liters
1 bushel (bu) = 4 pecks (approximately 8 gallons) = 2,150.42 cu. in. = 35.2390 liters

CAPACTIY (JAPANESE)

1 *go* (Japanese) = 10 *shaku* = 180 cc = 0.763 cups (U.S.)
1 *sho* = 10 *go* = 1,903 quarts = 0.476 gallons = 1.800 liters
1 *koku* = 10 *to* = 100 *sho* = 47.6 gallons = 180 liters
1 tablespoon = 15 cc = 3 teaspoons
1 cup = 200 cc = 0.847 U.S. cups = 13.5 U.S. tablespoons

LENGTH (LINEAR MEASURE)

1 inch = 2.540 cm = 1,000 mils
1 foot = 12 inches = 30.48 cm
1 yard = 3 feet = 91.44 cm
1 mile = 5,280 feet = 320 rods = 1.609 km
1 mm = 0.03937 inches
1 cm = 0.3937 inches
1 meter = 39.37 inches = 3.2808 feet = 1.094 yards
1 km = 1,000 m = 0.621 miles = 3,280.8 feet

AREA (SQUARE MEASURE)

1 sq. in. = 6.452 sq. cm
1 sq. ft. = 144 sq. in. = 929.03 sq. cm = 0.0929 sq. m
1 sq. yd. = 1296 sq. in. = 0.836 sq. m
1 sq. mile = 640 acres = 2.593 sq. km
1 acre = 43,560 sq. ft. (208.7 ft. on a side) = 4840 sq. yds. = 4047 sq. m = 0.405 hectares
1 sq. cm = 0.1549 sq. in.
1 sq. meter = 1550 sq. in. = 10.764 sq. ft. = 1.196 sq. yd.
1 sq. km = 0.3856 sq. miles = 247.1 acres = 100 hectares
1 hectare (ha) = 10,000 sq, m (100 m on a side) = 2.471 acres

VOLUME (CUBIC MEASURE)

1 cu. in. = 16.387 cc
1 cu. ft. = 1728 cu. in. = 0.028 cu. m = 7.48 gallons
1 cu. yd. = 46,656 cu. in. = 0.765 cu. m
1 cc = 0.061 cu. in.
1 cu. m = 35.315 cu. ft. = 1.308 cu. yd. = 1 kiloliter

NATURAL AND SOY EQUIVALENTS

Atmospheric pressure = 14.7 lbs./sq. in. = 1.036 kg/sq. cm
1 gallon (U.S.) of water weighs 8.33 lbs. = 3.78 kg
1 cup of soybeans weighs 6.5 ounces = 182 grams
1 quart of soybeans weighs 1.62 lbs. = 0.736 kg
1 gallon of soybeans weighs 6.47 lbs. = 2.94 kg
1 bushel of soybeans weighs 60 lbs. = 27.24 kg; it yields 10.7 lbs. (17.8%) crude soy oil plus 47.5 lbs. (79.2%) defatted soybean meal plus 1.8 lbs. (3%) manufacturing loss
1 metric ton of soybeans contains 36.75 bushels; it yields 400 lbs. of oil and 1850 lbs. of meal
For equivalent weights of basic miso ingredients, see p. 184.

ENERGY, WORK & PRESSURE

A BTU (British Thermal Unit) is the quantity of heat required to raise the temperature of 1 pound of water one degree Fahrenheit (near 39.2°F)
A watt is a unit of power equal to the rate of work represented by a current of 1 amp under a pressure of 1 volt.
A horsepower (H.P.) = 746 watts = 0.746 kilowatts = 550 foot pounds per second
1 lb./sq. in. = 70.45 gm/sq. cm. = 0.070 kg/sq. cm.
1 kg/sq. cm. = 14.19 lb./sq. in.

Appendix H
So You Want to Study Miso in Japan?

A growing number of people have recently begun to consider the possibility of going to Japan to study miso making at its source. The traditional art and craft is best studied in depth under the guidance of a master. The problems to be expected in undertaking such an adventure are definitely not insurmountable.

1. *Time:* A basic apprenticeship will probably last at least 2 years, the first half of which will be devoted primarily to learning the language. A more thorough study might take three to four years. Or you could simply apply for a three-month tourist visa (which is readily obtainable and requires no letter of guarantee; see below), visit a number of shops to watch and get a feeling for the whole process, and make one good contact who would be willing to serve as your guarantor for a longer visit. You could then either go home, begin to practice what you have learned, and return later for a longer stay, or go to Korea with your letter of guarantee and return to Japan with a six-month visa.

2. *Money:* You will need money for your round trip transportation, daily food and housing, language study, and incidental expenses. As of this writing, a round-trip charter flight costs about $500. Living expenses range from $120 per month on up. Remember that Japan—and particularly any of its larger cities—is one of the most expensive places to live in the world. Monthly language school costs may average $100 per month or more. And incidentals including travel, entertainment, etc., usually go no lower than $25 per month. Before you start your trip, make sure you have enough money to last as long as you plan to stay—the Embassy will ask you to prove that you do. Do not expect to get an income from the miso master with whom you study. In fact, you should probably provide him with gifts from time to time as tokens of thanks.

3. *Visa:* Phone or write your nearest Japanese Consulate (offices in Anchorage, Atlanta, Chicago, Honolulu, Portland, New Orleans, New York, San Francisco, Seattle, and Vancouver) and ask them to send you the necessary application forms for a general-study visa No. 4-1-16-3 which is good for six months and can be renewed indefinitely. They will ask you to provide an explanation of the purpose of your trip, how long and where you intend to stay, and how you intend to support yourself. They will ask to see your passport, a letter of guarantee, your round-trip ticket, and perhaps your bank balance.

4. *Letter of Guarantee:* Obtaining this letter is the hardest part of getting a non-tourist visa. Your guarantor may be any Japanese or foreigner living in Japan who has lived there for one year or more. Send this person the form which explains exactly what information his letter of guarantee must contain together with a description of the purpose of your visit. If you are unable to locate a guarantor, explain this to the consulate and they will probably allow your parents or an American friend to serve as a substitute.

5. *Housing:* This problem is easiest to solve if you have a friend living in Japan who can lodge you when you arrive and then help you to find a place to stay. Travelers without a friend often start by staying in an inexpensive hotel or hostel. Many language schools have facilities for locating student housing. Living with a Japanese family will be a great aid to learning the language. Rent will range from about $30 per month on up.

6. *Language:* In order to study with a miso master, you will have to be able to speak some Japanese. The easiest and quickest way to learn is in an established language school. Some of the best include:

Tokyo Japanese Language School (Naganuma Tokyo Nihongo Gakko): Nanpeidai-machi 16-26, Shibuya-ku, Tokyo 150. Tel: 03-463-7261. They offer four semesters beginning in early January, April, July, and September.

Kyoto Japanese Language School (Kyoto Nihongo Gakko): Ichijo-dori, Muromachi Nishi, Kamikyo-ku, Kyoto 602. Tel: 075-414-0449. They offer three semesters beginning in early April, July, and September.

International Christian University (Kokusai Kirisutokyo Daigaku): Osawa 3-10-2, Mitaka-shi, Tokyo 181. Tel: 0422-31-3131. Yearly registration for the 3 successive semesters begins in early September.

At all three schools, classes are held three hours each morning five days a week at a cost of $300 to $365 per semester. At the first two schools, beginners may enter without previous application at the beginning of each semester. At the third school, admission applications (including numerous documents) must be at the school before May 1; not all applicants are accepted. After 6 months of intensive study, you should be able to carry on a conversation without difficulty; after one year, you should be fluent enough to continue language study on your own.

7. *Finding a Master:* If you were sponsored by an organization affiliated with miso, it should be able to assist you in finding the type of master you are looking for. If not, the list of names in Appendix D may well be of help. Or you may simply wish to begin visiting miso shops in your area and talking with the craftsmen until you find a situation that is mutually agreeable. Remember that you should generally call and make an appointment before visiting and take a small present with you when you go. Be careful not to be a nuisance and don't wear out your welcome. At first, you may wish to ask to visit the shop only once or twice each week while continuing your language studies. Later, you may be permitted to serve a full-time apprenticeship. At some time during your study, it would probably be helpful to visit a number of other shops throughout Japan to get a better perspective on your own work situation.

8. *Help from Your Friends:* Let us know if we can be of help to you in establishing contacts. We will probably be able to put you in touch with other people like yourself studying miso in Japan.

All traditional miso was prepared using only natural ingredients, and all of the varieties available today are prepared by at least some makers without the use of chemical additives. Following World War II, however, a number of additives began to be used in order to make miso more suited to mass distribution, to create whiter colors and sweeter flavors, and to counteract the negative effects of temperature-controlled quick fermentation. The use of additives increased steadily until about 1975 when consumer reaction developed momentum and a government law was passed requiring producers to list all ingredients and additives contained in packaged miso. Remember that most red, barley, and Hatcho miso is completely free of additives (except perhaps ethyl alcohol), whereas many varieties of sweet or white miso are not. The following, listed in order of frequency of occurrence, are presented here for the benefit of those who prefer natural foods and have developed the valuable habit of reading labels. Japanese equivalent terms are given to help natural-food importers double-check that no additives have been used.

Ethyl Alcohol Preservative *(shusei):* Also known simply as alcohol (C_2HO_5), this is the substance that occurs naturally in wine and liquor. Used to prevent sealed polyethylene bags from swelling, while halting fermentation and surface-mold growth, it is allowed at the legal limit of 2 percent by weight and is mixed with the miso just before packaging. Some companies use it only with miso packaged during the summer months. In Japan, it is legal to advertise miso as containing no additives even though it contains ethyl alcohol. For this reason it has recently replaced sorbic acid as the mostly widely employed preservative. It is most often used in misos which are relatively sweet, packaged in sealed bags or jars, and/or are prepared by quick temperature-controlled fermentation. Nevertheless, it is also frequently found in relatively salty, bulk-packed varieties prepared by natural fermentation. Traditional shops generally use it with unpasteurized miso, while modern makers may add it to reinforce the effects of pasteurization.

Food Coloring *(chakushokuzai):* Riboflavin (vitamin B_2) is occasionally used in light-yellow and semi-sweet beige misos. Added to the miso before fermentation, it improves the luster and gives a more natural yellow color which is lost during bleaching and quick fermentation.

Chemical Seasoning *(kagaku chomiryo):* Quick sweet white, light-yellow, and akadashi miso may contain monosodium glutamate (MSG, *aji-no-moto, gurutamin-san,* Accent) which appears to enrich the miso flavor by actually sensitizing the taste buds in the tongue. Unfortunately, many people find that MSG causes unpleasant physical and mental sensations if ingested in even moderate amounts. MSG is used because quick temperature-controlled fermentation and the discarding of the cooking water from light-colored varieties yield miso with a less than satisfactory flavor.

Non-clumping Agent: A chemical mixture with the brand name *Eimaruji* is sometimes cooked with the rice to prevent clumping.

Artificial Sweeteners *(kanmiryo):* Virtually all akadashi miso contains refined *mizuamé* (millet jelley) or malt sugar (*bakuga-to*). In a few cases, these are added to sweet white and sweet barley miso. Honey and sugar are virtually never used in miso of any type.

Vitamins: Vitamin B_1 is often added to the steamed rice together with the koji starter, and is meant to restore the nutrients in light-colored miso which are lost when the cooking water containing water soluble vitamins is discarded in order to give the miso a lighter color. In some misos methionine or its derivatives are added to miso at the end of fermentation to supplement the lack of sulfur-containing amino acids in soybeans. Other fortifiers occasionally added at the beginning of fermentation include vitamins A and B_2, plus calcium carbonate.

Sorbic Acid Preservative *(sorubin-san* or *sorubin-san kari):* This preservative or its potassium salt is allowed at the level of 1 gram per 1,000 grams of miso. Although still occasionally used in the same ways as ethyl alcohol, it is rapidly being replaced by the latter which is now generally considered safer and more natural.

Sodium Thiosulphate Bleach *(jiaryusan natorium* or *jiaryusan soda):* This bleach (also known as hyposulphite, SO_2) was used up until the late 1970s to bleach soybeans when making light-colored misos; at present its use has been discontinued.

Caramel: Used in most akadashi miso to add color and sweetness.

Shoyu: Often used in small amounts in akadashi miso to add color and flavor.

Bibliography

PUBLICATIONS ABOUT MISO

Additional publications relating to the manufacture of miso will be found in *Miso Production* by Shurtleff and Aoyagi.

Abbreviations: FSTA = Food Science and Technology Abstracts. *Chem. Abstr* = Chemical Abstracts.

Abehsera, Michel. 1968. *Zen Macrobiotic Cooking.* New York: University Books/Avon. 224 p.

Abehsera, Michel. 1970. *Cooking for Life.* New York: Swan House/Avon. 364 p.

Abel, Mary H. 1900. Beans, peas, and other legumes as food. *USDA Farmers Bulletin* No. 121. p. 9-11.

Abiose, Sumbo H. 1980. *Studies on Miso Fermentation.* Glasgow, Scotland: PhD thesis, University of Strathclyde.

Abiose, S.H., Allan, M.C. and Wood, B.J.B. 1982. Microbiology and biochemistry of miso (soy paste) fermentation. *Advances in Applied Microbiology* 28:239-65.

Ahlburg, H. 1878. (About Eurotium oryzae). In Korschelt 1878. p. 252-55.

Aihara, Cornellia. 1972. *The Chico-san Cookbook.* Chico, CA: Chico-san Inc. Reissued as Macrobiotic Kitchen by Japan Publications in 1982. 140 p.

Aihara, H. 1972. *Miso & Tamari.* San Francisco, CA: George Ohsawa Macrobiotic Foundation. 34 p.

Aihara, H. 1974. *Soybean Diet.* Oroville, CA: George Ohsawa Macrobiotic Foundation. 164 p.

Ajinomoto Inc. 1972. Dried miso preparation. Japanese Patent 26,719/72 (cited in FSTA 1973, No. 1J80).

Akaghi, T., Nakajima, I. and Tsugane, K. 1915. Researches on "Hatsucho-Miso." *Journal of the College of Agriculture,* Tokyo 5(3):263-69.

Akizuki, Shinichiro, 1965. *Taishitsu to Shokumotsu* (Physical Constitution and Food). Nagasaki: Self published. 40 p. An abridged edition, edited by Kawamura Wataru, is available from the Japanese National Miso Assoc. under the title *Taishitsu wa Shokumotsu de* (Your Physical Constitution Depends on What You Eat).

Akizuki, S. 1980. How we survived Nagasaki. *East West Journal.* Dec. p. 10, 12-13.

Aonuma, T. 1973. Soy and miso paste. U.S. Patent 3,764,708. By Kikkoman Shoyu Co.

Asahi Shimbun. 1981. Miso shiru igai na koyo. Tokyo. Sept. 27.

Atkinson, R.W. 1878. Brewing in Japan. *Nature* 18:521-23 (Sept. 12).

Atkinson, R.W. 1881. On the diastase of koji. *Proceedings of the Royal Society of London* 32:299-332.

Atkinson, R.W. 1881. The chemistry of sake brewing. *Memoirs of the Tokyo Imperial University Science Department* (Tokio Daigaku). No. 6. pp. 1-73.

Belleme, J. 1981a. The miso master with big heart. *Soyfoods.* Sum-April:50-54.

Belleme, J. 1981. The miso master with a big heart. *Soyfoods.* Summer. p. 64-66.

Biot, Edouard, trans. 1851. *Le Tcheou-Li ou Rites des Tcheou.* 3 Vols. Paris. Reprinted 1969, Taipei.

Breirem, K. 1952. Oscar Kellner. *J. of Nutrition* 47:3-10.

Bretschneider, Emilii Vasilevich. 1881-95. *Botanicon Sinicum.* Notes on Chinese Botany from Native and Western Sources. London: Trübner & Co. 3 Vols. Issued originally in the Journal of the Royal Asiatic Society, North China Branch. Series 2, Vols. 16, 25, 29.

Bryant, Carl. 1785. *Verzeichniss der zur Nahrung dienenden so wohl einheimischen als auslandischen Pflanzen.* Part 1. Leipzig: Weidemanns Erben und Reich. p. 378-80.

Bryant, Charles. 1783. *Flora diaetetica: or History of esculent plants, both domestic and foreign . . .* London: B. White. 379 p.

Bui, Quang Chieu. 1905. Les cultures vivrieres au Tonkin. *Bulletin Economique de l'Indo-Chine.* New Series 2. No. 48. p. 1152-53, 1157-68.

Burkill, I.H. 1935. *A Dictionary of the Economic Products of the Malay Peninsula.* London: Crown Agents. p. 1080-86. (The work is 2 volumes, 2400 p.)

Carletti, Francesco. [1701] 1964. *My Voyage Around the World.* Trans. by H. Weinstock. Pantheon Books, New York. p. 110. (Orig. Ragionamenti, 1594-1606).

Carr, B. 1980. Miso (Made in the U.S.A.). *East West Journal.* January. p. 68-69.

Chang, K.C. ed. 1977. *Food in Chinese Culture.* New Haven, CT: Yale University Press. 429 p.

Cheryan, M. 1980. Phytic acid interactions in food systems. *CRC Critical Reviews in Food Science & Nutrition* 13(4):297-335.

Choe, C. and Song, P. 1960. Fermented soybeans of Korea. *Bulletin of the Scientific Research Inst. of Korea* 5:29.

Church, M.B. 1923. Soy and related fermentations. *USDA Department Bulletin* No. 1152, May 12. 26 p.

Cohn, Ferdinand. 1884. Ueber Schimmelpilze aus Gaerungserreger. *Jahresberichte Schles. Ges. Vaterland Kultur.* 61:226. Breslau.

D.B. 1979. Down-home miso. *Whole Foods.* October. p. 62.

Diamant, Y., Ilany-Feigenbaum, J., Pinsky, E., Laxer, S., and Shor, F. 1963. "The preparation of Japanese miso for human consumption by fermentation of defatted soybean meal." *Israel J. of Chemistry* 1:184.

Diamant, E.J. and Laxer, S. 1968. Nutritional evaluation of miso. *Israel J. of Chemistry* 6:147.

Dyson, G.M. 1928. Mould food of the Far East. *The Pharmaceutical Journal and Pharmacist* 121:375-77. (Oct. 20, London).

Ebine, H. 1966. Manufacturing digestible proteinous foods from oilseeds and pulses by enzymatic treatment. *Japan Agricultural Research Quarterly,* Vol. 1, No. 1.

Ebine, H. 1967. Evaluation of dehulled soybean grits from United States varieties for making miso. *USDA Final Technical Report.* Public Law 480. Project UR-ALL-(40)-2.

Ebine, Hideo. 1968. *Fermented Soybean Foods in Japan.* Tokyo: Tropical Agricultural Research Center, Ministry of Agric. and Forestry. 20 p.

Ebine, H. and Yamamoto, K. 1968. Miso manufacturing from dehulled soybeans. 2. Evaluation of dehulled soybeans for miso making. *Shokuryo Kenkyusho Kenkyu Hokoku* No. 23:1.

Ebine, H. 1972. Miso in *Conversion and Manufacture of Foodstuffs by Microorganisms.* Proceedings of the sixth international fermentation symposium held in Kyoto, Japan, Dec. 5-9, 1971. p. 127-32.

Ebine, H. et al. 1972. Evaluation of U.S. soybeans as raw materials for making miso. *Report of the Central Miso Institute.* No. 7. July. 66 p. In Japanese with 4-page English summary.

Ebine, H. 1976. Fermented soybean foods. In Expanding the Use of Soybeans. *INTSOY Series* No. 10. pp. 126-29.

Egami, Tomi. 1975. *Miso Shiru to Miso Ryori.* (Miso Soup and Miso Cookery). Tokyo: My Life Series No. 46.

Fuerstenberg, Maurice. 1917. *Die Soja.* Berlin: Paul Parey. 43 p.

Fukushima, D. 1979. Fermented vegetable (soybean) protein and related foods of Japan and China. *J. of the American Oil Chemists' Society* 56(3):357-62, 379-80.

Fukushima, D. 1981. Soy proteins for foods centering around soy sauce and tofu. *J. of the American Oil Chemists' Society* 58(3):346-54.

Greenwood, R. 1982. Smokey Mountain miso. *East West Journal.* Nov. p. 50-53.

Hayashi, K. 1977. Process for producing koji for fermented food products. U.S. Patent 4,028,470.

Health Food Business Review. 1968. Soy bean puree: Miso. July. p. 44-45.

Hepburn, James C. 1867. *A Japanese and English Dictionary.* London: Treubner & Co. 558, 132 p. 2nd ed. 1872; 3rd ed. 1886; 4th ed. 1888. 5th ed. 1894; 7th ed. 1903.

Hesseltine, C.W. and Shibasaki, K. 1961. Miso: III. Pure culture fermentation with Saccharomyces rouxii. *Applied Microbiology* 9:515-18.

Hesseltine, C.W. 1962. Research at Northern Regional Research Laboratory on fermented foods. In *Proceedings of Conference on Soybean Products for Proteins in Human Foods.* USDA ARS-71-22. p. 74-82.

Hesseltine, C.W. 1965. A millennium of fungi, food, and fermentation. *Mycologia* 57:149-97.

Hesseltine, C.W. 1967. Fermented products—Miso, sufu, and tempeh. In *Proceedings of International Conference on Soybean Protein Foods.* USDA, ARS-71-35. p. 170-80.

Hesseltine, C.W. and Wang, H.L. 1972. Fermented soybean food products. In A.K. Smith and S.J. Circle. 1972. *Soybeans: Chemistry and Technology.* Westport, CT: AVI Publ. Co. p. 389-419.

Hesseltine, C.W., Swain, E.W. and Wang, H.L. 1976. Production of fungal spores as inocula for Oriental fermented foods. In *Development in Industrial Microbiology* 17:101-15.

Hesseltine, C.W. and Wang, H.L. 1977. Contributions of the Western World to Knowledge of Indigenous Fermented Foods of the Orient. Presented at *Fifth Intl. Conference on Global Impacts of Applied Microbiology*, Nov. 1977, Bangkok, Thailand. 32 p.

Hoang, Van Chi. 1981. *The Vietnamese and their favorite sauces.* Unpublished manuscript. 7 p.

Hoffmann, J.J. 1874. Ueber die bereitung von schoju, sake und myrin. *Mitteilungen der Deutsche Gesellschaft fur Natur- und Volkerkunde Ostasiens* 1(6):8-11.

Horvath, A.A. 1927. The soybean as human food. Peking: Chinese Government Bureau of Economic Information. *Bulletin Series* No. 3. 86 pp. Also published as a series in Chinese Economic Jnl. Sept. 1926 to April 1927.

Hymowitz, T. and Newell, C.A. 1981: Taxonomy of the genus Glycine, domestication and uses of soybeans. *Economic Botany* 35(3):272-88.

Ichiyama, M. 1968. *Kikkoman Shoyu-shi.* Noda, Japan: Kikkoman Shoyu K.K. 804 p.

Ilany-Feigenbaum, J. and Laxer, S. 1967. Color development in Israeli miso type products and its possible use for quality control. *Food Technology* 21:1527-28.

Ilany-Feigenbaum, J., Diamant, J., Laxer, S., and Pinsky, A. 1969. Japanese miso-type products prepared by using defatted soybean flakes and various carbohydrate-containing foods. *Food Technology* 23:554-56.

Ito, E., Ebine, H. and Nakano, M. 1965. About miso. *Report of the Food Research Inst.*, Tokyo. 20:127.

Iwadare, Shoji. 1976. *Miso, Tofu, Natto no Kenkoho* (Miso, Tofu, and Natto: The Way to Health). Tokyo: Yomiuri Shimbun.

Iwamura, I. 1935. Miso, a fermented soybean paste. *Nippon Nogei Kagaku Kaishi* (Bulletin of the Agricultural Chemical Socy. of Japan) 11(1):1-7.

Iwamura, I. 1936. Miso, a fermented soybean paste. *Nippon Nogei Kagaku Kaishi* 12:78-88.

Japanese National Miso Assoc. 1976. *Miso Digest.* Tokyo: Zenkoku Miso Kogyo Kyodo Kumiai Rengokai. 48 p.

JDAC: Japan Dietetic Assoc. Corp. 1964. *Standard Composition of Japanese Foods.* Tokyo: Daiichi Shuppan K.K. Bilingual: Japanese/English.

Julien, S. 1855. (Comments on tsiang/chiang in China). Cited in Paillieux 1880, p. 417.

Kaempfer, E. 1712. *Amoenitatum Exoticarum Politico—Physico—Medicarum.* Fasculi V. Lemgoviae, Germany: H.W. Meyerei. p. 837-40.

Kao, C. 1974. *Fermented Foods from Chickpea, Horsebean and Soybean.* Kansas State University. PhD thesis. 143 p.

Kawamura, W. 1958. *Miso Enkakushi* (Historical Chronicles of Miso). Tokyo: Zenkoku Miso Rengokai. 815 p.

Kawamura, W. and Tatsumi, H. 1972. *Miso no Hon* (The Book of Miso). Tokyo: Shibata Shoten. 320 p.

Kawamura, Wataru. 1973. *Miso Shiru Fudoki* (Miso Soups Throughout the Provinces). Tokyo: Mainichi Shimbun.

Kawamura, Wataru. 1974. *Miso Shiru Hyakka* (Encyclopedia of Miso Soups). Tokyo: Kosei Shuppansha.

Kellner, O., Mori, Y. and Nagaoka, M. 1889. Researches on the manufacture, composition, and properties of "koji." *Bulletin of the College of Agriculture, Tokyo Imp. Univ.* 1(5):9-33.

Kellner, O., Nagaoka, M. and Kurashima, Y. 1889. Researches on the manufacture and composition of "miso." *Bulletin of the College of Agriculture, Tokyo Imperial Univ.* 1(6):1-24.

Kellner, O.J. 1895. Die bereitung von miso in Japan. *Chemiker-Zeitung* 19(13):265.

Kinch, Edward. 1882. Die sojabohne. *Biedermann's Centrall-blat fur Agriculturchemie* 11:753-55.

Kinoshita, Asakichi. 1921. *Jitsuyo Miso Jozo* (Practical Miso Fermentation). Tokyo: Meibundo. 480 p.

Kitaoka, K. 1972. Soybean miso manufacturing with enzyme preparations. *Miso no Kagaku to Gijutsu* No. 218. p. 19-24. Cited in *Chem. Abstr.* 80 (1974), 81,090.

Kobatake, Y. et al. 1964. Nutritional value of protein in Japanese soybean products. *Eiyogaku Zasshi* 22(5):27-31.

Kondo, Akitani. 1972. *Nihon no Chojuson, Tanmeison* (Japanese Long-Life and Short-Life Villages). Tokyo: Sanrodo.

Korschelt, O. 1878. Ueber sake. *Mitteilungen der Deutsche Gesellschaft für Natur und Volkerkunde Ostasiens* 2(16):240-58.

Kotzsch, R.E. 1981. *Georges Ohsawa and the Japanese Religious Tradition.* PhD Thesis, History of Religions, Harvard University. 360 p.

Koyama, M. 1976. Process for producing processed low-salt soybean paste. U.S. Patent 3,937,844. Assigned to Shinshu Miso Co.

Krauss, F.G. 1911. Leguminous crops for Hawaii. *USDA Ag. Expt. Sta. Bull.* No. 23. p. 23-26.

Kushi, Aveline, 1971. Recipes from The Book of Miso. *East West Journal* 1(8):7.

Kushi, Aveline. 1978. *How to Cook with Miso.* New York: Japan Publications Trading Co. 127 p.

Lachman, G. and Elwell, C. 1978. Making miso in America. *East West Journal.* Sept., p. 54-58.

Langworthy, C.F. 1897. Soybeans as food for man. *USDA Farmers Bulletin* No. 58. p. 20-23.

Lau, D.C. 1979. *Confucius: The Analects.* New York: Penguin.

Lee, C-H. 1976. The effect of Korean soysauce and soypaste making on soybean protein quality. *Korean J. of Food Science and Technol* 8(1):12-32.

Leonard, T. 1977. Making brown rice miso in Arkansas. *Soycraft.* Autumn. p. 1.

Leviton, R. 1980. The Ohio Miso Company. *Soyfoods.* Summer. p. 26-31, 63-68.

Leviton, R. 1982. Miso-Cup. *Soyfoods.* Summer. p. 34-35.

Leviton. R. 1982. American Miso makes a big move down south. *Soyfoods.* Summer, p. 18-22.

Leviton, R. 1983. Cold Mountain Miso expands. *Soyfoods.* Winter. p. 7.

Li, Shih-chen. 1597. *Pen ts'ao kang mu.* 1965 ed. Hong Kong: Commercial Press (in Chinese). p. 360-71.

Li, Yu-ying. 1910. *Ta Tou: Le Soja.* Paris: Societe biologique de l'Extreme Orient. 65 p.

Li Yu-ying and Grandvoinnet, L. 1911-12. Le soja. *L'Agriculture Pratique des Pays Chauds* 11:177-96, 270-94, 360-75, 459-74. 12:28-38, 120-32, 213-23, 302-08.

Li Yu-ying and Grandvoinnet, L. 1912. *Le Soja. Sa Culture. Ses Usages Alimentaires, Therapeutiques, Agricoles et Industriels.* Paris, France: A. Challamel. 141 p.

Lockwood, L.B. and Smith, A.K. 1952. Fermented Soy Foods and Sauce. *Yearbook of Agric.*, 1950-51. p. 357-61.

MacDonald, W.C. and Deuck, J.W. 1976. Long term effect of shoyu (Japanese soy sauce) on the gastric mucosa of the rat. *J. of the National Cancer Inst.* 56(6):1143-47.

Manabe, M. et al. 1972. Fluorescent compounds in fermented foods: II. Tests on aflatoxin contamination of miso and miso-koji in Japan. *Nippon Shokuhin Kogyo Gakkai-shi* 19(2):76-80. Cited in *Chem. Abstr* 81 (1974), 167,973.

Matsuura, S. 1970. Aflatoxins and fermented foods in Japan. *Japan Agricultural Research Quarterly* 5:46-51. (Cited in FSTA 1971. 4066).

Miller, C.D. 1933. Japanese foods commonly used in Hawaii. *Hawaii Agric. Exp. Station. Bulletin* No. 68. p. 1-10, 28-43.

Miller, Gloria B. 1966. *The Thousand Recipe Chinese Cookbook.* New York: Antheneum.

Misumi, Kan. 1969. *Miso Daigaku* (Miso University). Tokyo: Bungeisha. He also wrote Tsukemono Daigaku (Pickle University).

Mochizuki, T. et al. 1972. Changes of several components during miso making. *Ferment. Technol. Today.* Proc. 4th Intl. Ferment. Symp. 663-68. (Cited in *Chem. Abstr.* 1976. 84, 29,405F).

Mogi, Masatoshi. 1946. *Taigai Miso* (Making Miso with Nongrain Koji). Tokyo: Seikatsu-sha.

Morohashi, Tetsuji. 1955-60. Daikanwa Jiten. Tokyo: Taishukan Shoten. 12 vols + Index.

Morse, W.J. 1929-31. *Log of the Dorsett-Morse Expedition to East Asia.* Typewritten manuscript in 17 volumes and handwritten notebooks. Only copy located at offices of American Soybean Assoc., St. Louis, Missouri. 6,000 p.

Motoyama, T. 1958. *Inshoku Jiten* (Encyclopedia of Food and Drink). Tokyo: Heibonsha. 604 p.

Murakami, H. et al. 1967-68. Non-productivity of aflatoxin by Japanese industrial strains of Aspergillus. *J. of General and Applied Microbiology* 13:323-34; 14:97-110, 251-62.

Muramoto, Noboru and Abehsera, Michel. 1973. *Healing Ourselves.* New York: Avon/Swan House. 150 p.

Nagahori, T. et al. 1980. On the substances in shoyu to suppress the nitrosation of dimethylamine. *Eiyo to Shokuryo* 33(3): 151-60.

Nakano, M., Ebine, H. and Ota, T. 1967. *Hakko Shokuhin* (Fermented Foods). Tokyo: Korin Shoin.

Nakano, M., Ebine, H. and Ito, H. 1976. On miso, a Japanese traditional fermented food. In *Proceedings of the Fifth International Fermentation Symposium* (held in Germany). p. 363.

Nakayama, Tokiko. 1973. *Chugoku Meisaifu* (Chinese Cuisine: Famous Recipes). Tokyo: Shibata Shoten. 4 Vols.

National Academy of Sciences. 1980. Recommended Dietary Allowances, 9th ed. Washington, D.C.: NAS.

Nishiwaki, Y. 1924. Biologische untersuchungen uber den koji-pilz des Okazaki-Hatchomiso-Koji und der kabocha-bana des tome-koji. *Centralblatt fur Bakteriologie* 63:25-28.

Norinsho. 1964. *Nihon Shokuhin Hyojun Seibunhyo.* (Standard Composition of Japanese Foods). Tokyo: Norinsho (Japanese Ministry of Agriculture and Forestry).

NRRC. 1976. Removal of phytic acid in soybeans to increase utilization of trace elements in soybeans and also the solubility of soybean protein. Peoria, IL: *Report of the USDA Northern Regional Research Center.* p. 11.

Ochse, J.J. 1931. *Vegetables of the Dutch East Indies.* Buitenzorg (Bogor), Java: Archipel Drukkerij. p. 366, 372, 389-93, 398, 407-08, 732, 943-71.

Ohsawa, G. 1960. *Zen Macrobiotics.* New York: Ohsawa Foundation. 103 p.

Ohsawa, Georges. 1965. *Zen Macrobiotics: The Philosophy of Oriental Medicine*, Vol. I. Los Angeles, CA: Ohsawa Foundation. 128 p.

Ohsawa, G. 1966. *Zen Cookery:* Practical Macrobiotics. Los Angeles, CA: Ohsawa Foundation. 84 p.

Ohsawa, Lima. 1971. *Makurobiotiku Ryori* (Macrobiotic Cookery). Tokyo: Nihon CI Kyokai. 199 p.

Ohsawa, Lima. 1974. *The Art of Just Cooking.* Brookline, MA: Autumn Press. 216 p.

Oshima, Kintaro. 1905. A digest of Japanese investigations on the nutrition of man. *USDA OES Bulletin* 159. p. 23-33, 145-53, 168-73.

Paillieux, A. 1880. Le soya, sa composition, chimique, ses varietes, sa culture et ses usages. *Bulletin de la Societe d'Acclimatization* 27 (or 3rd Series vol. 7): 414-71, 538-96.

Pierson, J.L. trans. 1929-63. *Man'yoshu.* Leiden (Leyden): E.J. Brill Ltd. 20 vols. 16:44. The only translation of the entire Man'yoshu.

Piper, C.V. and Morse, W.J. 1916. The soybean, with special reference to its utilization for oil, cake, and other products. *USDA Bull.* 439. 20 p.

Piper, C.V. and Morse, W.J. 1923. *The Soybean.* New York: Mc Graw-Hill. 329 p.

Prinsen-Geerligs, H.C. 1895. Eenige Chineesche voedingsmiddeln uit Sojaboonen bereid. *Pharmaceutisch Weekblad Voor Nederland* 32(33):1-2. Dec. 14.

Prinsen Geerligs, H.C. 1896. Einige chinesische Sojabohnenpräparate. *Chemiker-Zeitung* 20(9):67-69 (Jan. 29).

Rao, N.N., Dwarakanath, C.T. and Rao, T.N.R. 1968. Development of predigested protein-rich food based on Indian oil seed cakes and pulses. *J. of Food Science and Technology* (Mysore). Part I, 5:198-201. Part II (1972) 9:57-62.

Rao, N.N., Rao, T.N.R. and Shanthamma, M.S. 1972. Development of pre-digested protein-rich food based on Indian oilseed meals and pulses. II. *J. of Food Science and Technology* (Mysore) 9(2):57-62.

Raper, K.B. and Fennell, D.I. 1965. *The genus Aspergillus.* Baltimore, MD: Williams & Wilkins Co. 686 p.

Rein, J.J. 1899. *The Industries of Japan.* London: Hodder and Stoughton. p. 105-07. A translation of volume II of his *Japan nach reisen und studien.* publ. 1886.

Robinson, R.J. and Kao, C. 1977. Tempeh and miso from chickpea, horse bean, and soybean. *Cereal Chemistry* 54:1192-97.

Rudinsky, Russ. 1969. *Japanese Country Cookbook.* San Francisco: Nitty Gritty Productions. 192 p.

Saito, Y. et al. 1973. Miso manufacturing using enzymic preparations. *Miso no Kagaku to Gijutsu* 236:20-30. (Cited in *Chem. Abstr.* 1975. 82:169,030p).

Sakaguchi, K. 1972. Development of industrial microbiology in Japan. In *Proceedings of the International Symposium on Conversion and Manufacture of Foodstuffs by Microorganisms.* Kyoto, Japan. 5-9 Dec. 1971. p. 7-10.

Sakaguchi, Kinichiro, et al. 1974. Miso. *Shoku no Kagaku.* December.

Sakaguchi, Kinichiro. 1979. Shoyu no ruutsu o saguru. *Sekai.* Jan. p. 252-66.

Sawa, S. 1902. Note on Hamanatto, a kind of vegetable cheese. *Bulletin of the College of Agriculture, Tokyo Imp. Univ.* 4:419-20.

Senft, E. 1906-07. Ueber einige in Japan verwendete vegetabilische nahrungsmittel, mit besonderer berüchsichtigung der japanischen militärkonserven. *Pharmazeutische Praxis* 5(12):481-91, 6(3):81-89, 6(4):122-24.

Shaw, Norman. 1911. The Soya Bean of Manchuria. Shanghai: Statistical Dept. of the Inspectorate General of Customs. II. *Special Series No. 31.* 32 p.

Shibasaki, K. and Hesseltine, C.W. 1961. Miso I. Preparation of soybeans for fermentation. *J. of Biochemical and Microbiological Technology and Engineering* 3:161-74.

Shibasaki, K. and Hesseltine, C.W. 1961. Miso II. Fermentation. *Developments in Industrial Microbiology* 2:205-14.

Shibasaki, K. and Hesseltine, C.W. 1962. Miso Fermentation. *Economic Botany* 16:180-95.

Shih, Chi-yien. 1918. *Beans and Bean Products.* Shanghai: Soochow Univ. Biology Dept. 13 p.

Shih, Sheng-han. 1962. *A Preliminary Survey of the Book Ch'i Min Yao Shu: An Agricultural Encyclopedia of the 6th Century.* Peking: Science Press. 107 p.

Shinoda, Osamu. 1974. *Chugoku Shokumotsu-shi* ("History of Chinese Foods"). Tokyo: Shibata Shoten. 389 p.

Shufu-no-tomo. 1972. *Ryori Hakka* (Encyclopedia of Japanese Cookery). Tokyo: Shufu-no-tomo.

Shurtleff, W. and Aoyagi, A. 1976. *The Book of Miso.* Brookline, MA: Autumn Press. 256 p. Revised edition. 1981. New York: Ballantine Books, 620 p.

Shurtleff, W. 1977. Beikoku ni okeru miso. *Miso no Kagaku to Gijutsu.* No. 289, March, p. 11-15.

Shurtleff, W. and Aoyagi, A. 1977. *Miso Production.* Lafayette, CA: The Soyfoods Center. 62 p. Revised edition. 1979. 80 p.

Shurtleff, W. and Aoyagi, A. 1979. *The Book of Tempeh.* New York: Harper & Row. Paperback, 160 p. Professional hardcover, 248 p.

Shurtleff, W. and Aoyagi, A. 1980. *Das Miso Buch.* Soyen, W. Germany: Ahorn Verlag. 266 p.

Shurtleff, W. 1982. Miso soup-Safeguard against cancer. *East West Journal.* January. p. 42-43. Translation of *Asahi Shimbun* article.

Shurtleff, W. and Aoyagi, A. 1983. *Soyfoods Industry and Market: Directory and Databook.* Lafayette, CA: The Soyfoods Center. 116 p.

Smith, A.K. 1949. Oriental use of soybeans as food. *Soybean Digest.* Feb:15-17, March:26-34, April:23-31, May:24-30, June:15-22.

Smith, A.K. Hesseltine, C.W., and Shibasaki, K. 1961. Preparation of Miso. U.S. Patent No. 2,967,108.

Stahel, G. 1946. Foods from fermented soybeans as prepared in the Netherlands Indies. I. Taohoo, a cheese-like substance, and some other products. *J. of the New York Botanical Garden* 47:261-67.

Steinberg, Raphael. 1969. *The Cookery of Japan.* New York: Time-Life Books.

Sun Yi-jang, ed. 1966. *Chou-li Cheng-yi* (Ssu Pu Pei Yao edition). 6 Vols. Taipei.

Takahashi, J. 1955. Studies on sources of vitamin B-12. *Eiyo to Shokuryo* 8(2): 25-27.

Takahashi, T. 1908. A preliminary note on the chemical composition of miso. *J. of the Tokyo Chemical Socy.* 29(2).

Takahashi, T. and Abe, G. 1913. Preliminary notes on the chemical composition of miso. *J. of the College of Agriculture.* Tokyo 5(2):193-98.

Tamura, Heiji and Hirano, M. 1971. *Shoyu no Hon* (The Book of Shoyu). Tokyo: Shibata Shoten. 294 p.

Thom, Charles, and Church, M. 1921. Aspergillus flavus, A. oryzae, and associated species. *American J. of Botany* 8:103-26.

Thom, C. and Church, M. 1926. *The Aspergilli.* Baltimore, MD: Williams and Wilkens. 272 p.

Thom, Charles and Raper, Kenneth B. 1945. *Manual of the Aspergilli.* Baltimore, MD: The Williams and Wilkins Co. 373 p.

Thunberg, C.P. 1795. *Travels in Europe, Africa, and Asia, Made Between the Years 1770 and 1779.* London: F and C Rivington. 4 vols.

TIME magazine. 1969. Cancer, a clue from under the eaves. May 9. p. 81.

Tomoda Noritaka and Sakaguchi Kinichiro, ed. 1956. *Hakko Shokuhin: Biseibutsu Kogaku Koza* (Fermented Foods: Microbial Technology Course). Tokyo: Kyoritsu Shuppan.

Trimble, H. 1896. Recent literature on the soja bean. *American J. of Pharmacy* 68:309-13.

Tsuda, Tadao et al. 1974. *Shojin Ryori* (Zen Temple Cookery). Tokyo: Fujokai Shuppansha. 242 p.

Tsuji, Kaichi. 1971. *Zen Tastes in Japanese Cooking.* Tokyo: Kodansha. 207 p.

U.S. Dept. of Health, Education, and Welfare. 1972. Food Composition Table for Use in East Asia. Nutrition Program, Center for Disease Control, HEW, Atlanta, GA 30333. 334 p.

Waley, Arthur. 1938. *The Analects of Confucius.* London: George Allen & Unwin Ltd. U.S. ed. 1966 Random House, New York. 257 p.

Wang, H.L., Ellis, J.J. and Hesseltine, C.W. 1972. Antibacterial activity produced by molds commonly used in Oriental food preparations. *Mycologia* 64(1):218-21.

Wang, H.L. and Hesseltine, C.W. 1979. Mold-modified foods. In *Microbial Technology.* 2nd ed. Vol. II. H.J. Peppler ed. New York: Academic Press. p. 95-129.

Wang, Mrs. J.R. and Lee, Y.H. 1978. Traditional soybean foods in Korea. In *International Soya Protein Food Conference Proceedings.* Singapore, Jan. 25-27. p. 43-47.

Watanabe, T. 1969. Industrial Production of Soybean Foods in Japan. Presented at *Expert Group Meeting on Soya Bean Processing and Use,* Peoria, IL 17-21 Nov. 1969. United Nations Industrial Dev. Org. 38 p.

Watanabe Tokuji, Ebine Hideo, and Ota Teruo. 1971. *Daizu Shokuhin* (Soyfoods). Tokyo: Korin Shoin. 270 p.

Watanabe, T., Ebine, H. and Okada, M. 1974. New protein food technologies in Japan. In *New Protein Foods. Vol. 1A. Technology.* (A.M. Altschul, ed.). New York: Academic Press. p. 414-53. Ebine wrote the part of miso.

Wang, H.L., Swain, E.W. and Hesseltine, C.W. 1980. Phytase of molds used in Oriental food fermentation. *J. of Food Science* 45(5):1262-1266.

Watson, Burton, trans. 1961. *Records of the Grand Historian of China: From the Shih Chi of Ssu-ma Ch'ien.* 2 vols. New York: Columbia University Press.

Wehmer, C. 1895. Aspergillus oryzae, der Pilz der Japanischen Sake-Brauerei. *Centralblatt fur Bakteriologie und Parasitenkunde.* Series 2. 1(5):150-160 and 1(6):209-220.

Wehmer, C. 1901. *Die Pilzgattung Aspergillus.* Societe de Physique d'histoire Naturelle de Geneve, Memoirs. 23:1-157.

Wilcox, E.V. 1909. Soy Beans. *Hawaii Agric. Exp. Station Annual Report for 1908.* p. 83-84.

Winarno, F.G. et al. 1976. *The Present Status of Soybean in Indonesia.* Bogor, Indonesia; FATEMETA, Bogor Agricultural University. 128 p.

Winkler, G. 1914. *Die Sojabohne der Mandschurei.* Frankfurt am Main.

Women's College of Nutrition. 1969. *Tofu, Mame, Miso Ryori: Ju-ni Kagetsu* (Tofu, Soybean, and Miso Cookery Throughout the Twelve Months). Tokyo: Joshi Eiyo Daigaku.

Wood, B.J.B. and Yong, F.M. 1975. Oriental food fermentations. In *The Filamentous Fungi,* Vol. 1. J.E. Smith and D.R. Berry eds. London: Edward Arnold Ltd. p. 265-80.

Wood, B.J.B. 1977. Oriental food uses of *Aspergillus.* In *Genetics and Physiology of Aspergillus.* J.E. Smith and J.A. Pateman, eds. New York: Academic Press. p. 481-98.

Wood, B.J.B. 1982. Soy sauce and miso. In *Economic Microbiology,* Vol. 5, p. 39-86. (Academic Press).

Yoshi Hisao, Kaneko Yasuyuki, and Yamaguchi Kazuo. 1972. *Shokuhin Biseibutsu-gaku* (Food Microbiology). Tokyo: Gisho-do.

Yong, F.M. and Wood, B.J. 1974. Microbiology and biochemistry of soy sauce fermentation. *Advances in Applied Microbiology* 17:157-94.

Yoshihara, L. 1980. Shinmei-do Miso Company. *Soyfoods.* Summer. p. 10.

ABOUT WORLD HUNGER

The three most important works are starred.

Berg, Alan. 1973. *The Nutrition Factor*. The Brooklings Institute, 1775 Massachusetts Ave., N.W., Washington, D.C. 20036. A nutrition expert on the staff of the World Bank, Berg discusses the way hunger in the third world is linked to underdevelopment and malnutrition.

Borgstrom, Georg. 1974. *The Food/People Dilemma*. New York: Duxbury Press.

_____. 1973. *World Food Resources*. New York: Intext.

_____. 1972. *The Hungry Planet*. New York: Collier-Macmillan. A professor at Michigan State Univ., Borgstrom examines the food/population problem from an environmentalist's point of view, focusing on the effects of uneven food distribution between the rich and poor nations.

Brown, Lester R. 1974. *By Bread Alone*. New York: Praeger. One of the best books on the world food crisis. Head of the newly formed Worldwatch Institute in Washington, D.C., Brown is a highly articulate agricultural economist with a clear vision of the present problem and its solutions. His other recent writings include *In the Human Interest* (1973), *World Without Borders* (1972), and *Seeds of Change* (1970).

*Brown, Lester R. 1978. *The Twenty-Ninth Day: Accommodating Human Needs and Numbers to the Earth's Resources*. New York: W.W. Norton. 363 p. Outstanding!

Brown, Lester R. 1981. *Building a Sustainable Society*. New York: W.W. Norton & Co. 433 p. A great work.

George, Susan. 1977. *How the Other Half Dies: The Real Reasons for World Hunger*. Montclair, NJ: Allanheld, Osmun & Co. 308 p.

Lappé, Frances M. 1982. *Diet for a Small Planet* (Revised Edition), San Francisco: Ballantine/Friends of the Earth, 498 p. A two million-copy bestseller and one of the most influential books ever written concerning the world food crisis and basic nutrition. Emphasis on protein complementarity, meatless meals, and the wisdom of eating low on the food chain.

*Lappé, F.M., and Collins, J. 1978. *Food First: Beyond the Myth of Scarcity*. New York: Ballantine Paperback, Revised edition. 619 p. The finest and most up-to-date book on the world food crisis. A must! Available at reduced rates from the Institute for Food and Development Policy, 2588 Mission Street, San Francisco, CA 94110.

Lerza, Catherine, and Jacobson, Michael, ed. 1975. *Food for People Not for Profit*. New York: Ballantine. This official handbook for Food Day 1975 contains a wealth of up-to-date information concerning every aspect of the food crisis; each chapter written by an authority in the field.

Manocha, Sohan L. 1975. *Nutrition and Our Overpopulated Planet*, Springfield, Ill: Charles C. Thomas. An extensive and up-to-date treatment of the population/food crisis and means for its solution.

*Mesarovic, M., and Pestel, E. 1974. *Mankind at the Turning Point: The Second Report to the Club of Rome*. New York: Signet. The successor to *The Limits of Growth*, this highly readable and condensed book, based on sophisticated computer models, spells out clearly what we can and must do to avoid worldwide famine and catastrophe in the near future.

Miller, G. Tyler. 1975. *Living in the Environment*. Belmont, CA: Wadsworth. An excellent ecology textbook with extensive material concerning the population/food crisis and the means for its solution.

Glossary

Since the companion volume to this work, *The Book of Tofu*, has a lengthy and highly detailed glossary, this one will be kept short to avoid repetition. Basic ingredients are described in Chapter 5, and preparations (such as dashi) are listed in the Index. Most of the following foods are avilable in the West at Oriental grocery stores listed in the yellow pages under "Japanese (or Chinese) Food Products." Main outlets are listed on page 49.

Agar *(Kanten):* A sea-vegetable gelatin sold in light bars, strands, or flakes.

Amazaké: Literally "sweet sake"; see page 162.

Aona: Specifically a Chinese rape, generally all vegetable greens.

Asatsuki: A cross between a wild onion and a chive with a hint of garlic flavor.

Azuki beans: A small red bean, generally cooked with rice or used in desserts, and respected for both its nutritional and medicinal properties.

Bamboo shoots *(Takenoko):* Usually sold fresh in Japan, they appear in April and May and require lengthy cooking.

Bean sprouts *(Moyashi):* The sprouts of the mung bean, easily grown at home.

Beefsteak plant *(Shiso):* The fragrant green leaves *(aojiso),* aromatic red leaves *(shisonoha),* richly-flavored seeds *(shisonomi),* and tiny pink buds *(mejiso)* are each used fresh. The mint-like plant is now cultivated throughout the United States.

Bonito flakes *((Hanakatsuo):* The hard-as-wood dried, fermented bonito *(katsuobushi)* is shaved into paper-thin flakes and used as the basis for dashi or as a garnish.

Burdock root *(Gobo):* A long, dark-brown tapering root vegetable ½ to 1 inch in diameter and 18 to 24 inches long.

Butterbur *(Fuki):* The 4-foot-long, ½-inch-diameter stem of this spring vegetable has a flavor resembling that of celery. The young buds *(fuki-no-to)* are widely served with miso.

Carob: The chocolate-like brown powder made from the seed of a tree-borne pod; also called St. John's bread.

Chinese cabbage *(Hakusai):* A mild-flavored delicacy that may be used either like lettuce in salads or cabbage in simmered preparations. Very inexpensive.

Chrysanthemum leaves *(Shungiku):* Fragrant greens resembling spinach or trefoil.

Cloud-ear mushroom *(Kikuragé):* A delicate variety with a wavy cap, it grows on trees and has virtually no stem. Sold dried, it is also known as Dried Black Fungus or Wood Ear.

Daikon: The marvelously versatile Japanese giant white radish is often as thick as a man's arm and 18 to 24 inches long. Dried slivered *daikon (kiriboshi)* is sold in 4-ounce bags.

Eggplant *(Nasu):* The Japanese variety, sweeter and more tender than its American counterpart averages 4 inches in length, 1½ inches in diameter, and weighs 2 ounces.

Garbanzo beans: Also called chickpeas, this 3/8-inch-diameter tan variety is a favorite in Near Eastern cookery.

Gingerroot *(Shoga):* The 4-inch-long knobby tan root is peeled and freshly grated. Two parts powdered ginger may be substituted for 1 part fresh grated gingerroot.

Gingko nuts *(Ginnan):* These tender, ½-inch-long delicacies are sold fresh or canned.

Glutinous rice *(Mochigomé):* The natural unpolished form is also sold in the West as Sweet Brown Rice; the flour *(shiratamako)* is widely used for making the steamed balls called *dango.*

Glutinous yam *(Tororo imo):* When rubbed on a fine metal grater, these yams develop a highly cohesive, glutinous quality. Available fresh in many varieties.

Green nori flakes *(aonori):* A sea-vegetable seasoning made by crumbling the fragrant, bright-green fronds of dried *Enteromorpha prolifera;* delicious on noodles.

Hamanatto: A fermented, raisin-like soybean product with a mild flavor. Called "soy nuggets" in the West.

Hijiki: A stringy black sea vegetable *(Hizikja fusiforme)* sold in lengths about 1½ inches long. Often misspelled "hiziki" in the West.

Horsetails *(Tsukushi):* A wild spring plant the size of one's little finger.

Junsai: A "water shield" *(Brasenia purpurea),* this tiny wild pond plant, surrounded by a gelatinous slippery coating, is popular in soups.

Kabocha: Also called Hokkaido pumpkin, this delectable fall vegetable, with its dark-green edible skin, looks like a 6- to 8-inch-diameter acorn squash. Substitute winter squash or pumpkin.

Kampyo: Strips of shaved dried gourd used for tying foods into rolls or bundles.

Kinako: The delicious flour made by grinding roasted soybeans; widely used in confections.

Kinomé: The fragrant, bright-green sprigs of the *sansho (Xanthozylum piperitum)* tree, plucked in the spring.

Koji: Cooked rice, barley, or soybeans inoculated with *Aspergillus oryzae* mold and incubated in a warm, humid room for 45 hours until bound together with a fragrant white mycelium.

Kombu: A sea vegetable *(Laminaria species)* sold in leathery olive-brown sheets 3 to 6 inches wide and 2½ to 6 feet long. *Tororo kombu* is prepared by spraying the sheets briefly with a dilute vinegar solution, shaving them finely, and then shredding.

Konnyaku: Eight-ounce gray cakes made from the starch of *Amorphophallus konjac,* or devil's tongue plant, a member of the yam family. Konnyaku threads *(ito konnyaku)* and noodles *(shirataki)* are used in soups and *nabé* dishes.

Kudzu Powder *(Kuzu):* A high quality, rather expensive starch used somewhat like arrowroot or gelatin or as a highly effective medicine, and made from the root of the "kudzu" plant which grows throughout the United States. For details see *The Book of Kudzu* listed in the Bibliography.

Leek *(Negi):* The Japanese variety is milder and more slender than its Western counterpart.

Mandarin orange *(Mikan):* Japan's most popular and least expensive domestic fresh fruit, it is available from November until March. Delicious.

Matsutaké: The most expensive and most delicious of Japanese mushrooms, *Armilaria matsutake* grows a cap up to 8 inches in diameter.

Mirin: Also called sweet sake, mirin tastes like a mildly alcoholic mixture of sugar and water. Substitute for each tablespoon ½ teaspoon honey and 2 teaspoons sake or pale dry sherry. Or substitute 1½ teaspoons honey and 2½ teaspoons water.

Mizuamé: A natural grain sugar extracted from rice, millet, or barley, it looks like a solid pale-amber resin and may be softened by heating. Also sold as Amé, Rice Honey, or Millet Jelly. Close relatives are barley malt syrup and sorghum molasses.

Mochi: Cakes of steamed, pounded glutinous rice, each about 3 by 2 by ½ inches.

Myoga: The pinkish white buds of the *Zingiber mioga* that emerge from the plant's base each August.

Nameko: Tiny yellowish-brown mushrooms with a slippery coating; sold fresh or canned.

Nanohana: Rape blossoms; a springtime favorite in miso soups.

Natto: Sticky fermented whole soybeans.

Niboshi: Dried 2½-inch-long sardines used to make dashi.

Nira: A relative of the chive, *Allium odorum* has flat, dark-green leaves about 10 inches long and a rich fragrance, especially when sautéed.

Nori: A sea vegetable sold in paper-thin purplish-black sheets about 8 inches square and packaged in bundles of ten. The Japanese presently consume about 9 *billion* sheets each year. Other species of *Porphyra* are known in the West as laver. For details, see *The Book of Sea Vegetables*, listed in the Bibliography.

Osmund fern *(Zenmai):* The slender young fiddlenecks are a springtime delicacy.

Ramen: Crinkley yellowish-white Chinese noodles.

Red pepper *(Togarashi):* The Japanese variety are slender, 2½ inches long, and usually sold dried.

Rice flour *(Joshinko):* A fine-textured product usually made from white rice and widely used in the preparation of steamed desserts.

Sake: Rice wine contains about 15 percent alcohol and is widely used in cooking. The lees *(sake-no-kasu)* are used in dressings and soups.

Sansho pepper *(Kona-zansho):* A fragrant brownish-green pepper made from the seedpods of the *sansho* tree, the same tree which bears *kinomé* sprigs.

Sesame seeds *(Goma):* The delicious calcium-rich seeds come in white and black varieties and are usually lightly roasted then ground before use. Substitute one-half the amount of sesame butter or *tahini*.

Seven-spice red pepper *(Shichimi togarashi):* A zippy blend of red peppers and other spices including sesame, *sansho*, grated dried orange peel, green nori flakes, and white pepper.

Shiitaké: Japan's most popular mushroom, *Cornellius shiitake* is sold fresh or dried and widely used as the basis for stocks.

Shimeji: Small mushrooms with tan caps 1 to 1½ inches in diameter, *Tricholoma conglobatum* are usually sold fresh.

Shochu: A popular and very potent type of inexpensive spirits related to gin.

Shoyu: Japanese all-purpose soy sauce (see p. 49).

Snow peas *(Saya endo):* Also called edible-pod peas, these are the paper-thin type often associated with Chinese cookery.

Soba: Japanese buckwheat noodles.

Spinach *(Horenso):* Milder and slightly sweeter than its Western counterpart.

Sweet potato *(Satsuma imo):* One of Japan's most delicious and beloved foods, this variety has no exact counterpart in the West. About 1½ to 2½ inches in diameter and 4 to 8 inches long, they have a pale red skin and light-yellow richly-flavored meat.

Tahini: A smooth creamy paste made from unroasted (or very lightly roasted), hulled white sesame seeds. Due to the removal of the calcium-rich hulls, tahini is not as nutritious as sesame butter, and some commercial varieties use caustic soda in the cleaning and hulling process. Contains 19 percent protein.

Takuan: Dried whole daikon pickled for a long time in salted rice bran.

Tamari: A seasoning liquid resembling shoyu (p. 49).

Taro: A 2½-inch-diameter root vegetable also known in the West as dasheen or albi; the most popular of the many Japanese varieties are *Sato imo, yatsugashira*, and *akame imo*. Rich, creamy, and delicious.

Tempeh: Cultured soy cakes, see p. 50.

Tofu: For a description of the many types, see page 50.

Tororo imo: see Glutinous yam.

Trefoil *(Mitsuba):* Prized for its unique pungent aroma and handsome green leaves, *Crytotaenia japonica* is most widely used as a garnish.

Turnip *(Kabu):* The Japanese variety is a heart-shaped, white root about 3 inches in diameter having a mild, slightly sweet flavor.

Udo: Neither quite celery nor asparagus, *Aralia cordata* is a crisp and tender oddity with a unique hint of lemon flavor that is enjoyed fresh or cooked. The best varieties grow wild.

Udon: Fat white wheat-flour noodles similar to a No. 2 spaghetti.

Umeboshi salt plums: Salt-pickled plums from the *Prunus mumé* tree.

Uri melon: Also called "white melon" or "white gourd melon," this is a pale green fruit shaped like a cucumber, about 12 inches long and 3 inches in diameter.

Wakame: A dark-green sea vegetable *(Undaria pinnatifida)* with fronds about 3 inches wide and 12 to 18 inches long, it is sold both fresh and dried; widely used in soups and salads.

Wasabi: A hot green horseradish-like paste made from the grated root of the *wasabi* plant which is cultivated in terraced mountain stream beds.

Wheat gluten *(fu):* Both fresh and dried varieties sold in a multitude of different shapes are widely used in Japanese cookery.

Yuzu: A citrus fruit similar to a citron, lime, or lemon having a green and refreshingly fragrant rind which is slivered or grated; widely used in miso preparations, broths, and dipping sauces.

Index

273

ABOUT THE AUTHORS

William Shurtleff and Akiko Aoyagi spent their formative years on opposite sides of the Pacific. Born in California on 28 April 1941, Bill received degrees in engineering, honors humanities, and education from Stanford University. He taught physics for two years in Nigeria in the Peace Corps and has lived and traveled extensively in East Asia and Third World countries. He speaks seven languages, four fluently, including Japanese.

Akiko Aoyagi, born in Tokyo on 24 January 1950, received her education there from the Quaker-run Friends' School and the Women's College of Arts. She has worked as an illustrator and designer in Japan's modern fashion industry and America's emerging soyfoods industry.

Starting in October 1972, Bill and Akiko began working together, doing research and writing books about soyfoods. They worked together for six years in East Asia, mainly Japan, studying with top soyfoods researchers, manufacturers, nutritionists, historians, and cooks. Over 750,000 copies of their 53 books on soyfoods are now in print. The titles and publishers of some of these are listed on the copyright page at the beginning of this book.

In April 1976, Bill and Akiko founded the Soyfoods Center, and since that time they have worked to introduce soyfoods, especially traditional low-technology soyfoods, to the Western world. They feel that soyfoods can play a key role in helping to solve the world food crisis while providing high-quality, low-cost protein and healthier diets for people everywhere. Their work has led to the establishment of hundreds of soyfoods businesses making tofu, soymilk, miso, tempeh, and other soyfoods, and to the publication by others of more than 50 books about these foods. Their nationwide tours and many lectures, demonstrations, and media appearances have drawn widespread acclaim.

Soyfoods Center also produces SoyaScan, the world's largest bibliographic database on soybeans and soyfoods, containing more than 55,000 records (publications, original interviews, unpublished archival documents, and commercial soy products) from 1100 B.C. to the present. And the Soyfoods Center Library and Archives houses more than 50,000 documents—many unique.

Their global view and uniquely holistic, interdisciplinary approach are aimed at presenting the best of both traditional lore and modern scientific knowledge about soyfoods in a language accessible to both laymen and professionals.

By constantly addressing the problems of world hunger, the suffering of human beings and animals, and the perennial longing for good health and liberation, they hope to make their work relevant everywhere and a force for planetary renaissance.

As of 1998, William Shurtleff is director of Soyfoods Center. Akiko Aoyagi is a freelance illustrator and graphic designer. She runs her own art business in Walnut Creek, California.

If you would like to help in the larger work related to soyfoods and world hunger, if you have any questions or suggestions related to this book, or if you would like to receive a free copy of the Soyfoods Center Catalog, please contact or send a self-addressed, stamped envelope to Soyfoods Center.

SOYFOODS CENTER
P.O. Box 234
Lafayette, CA 94549 USA
(Phone: 925-283-2991)

Soyfoods Center

SOYFOODS CENTER, founded in 1976 by William Shurtleff and Akiko Aoyagi, has offices in California. Our basic goals and activities are related to soyfoods and world hunger.

Soyfoods: Our center is, above all, a source of information about soyfoods, especially tofu, soymilk, tempeh, and miso, about which we have done extensive research and written books and recipe pamphlets. Like a growing number of people, we feel that soybeans will be one of the key protein sources of the future on planet Earth, and that both traditional and modern soyfoods from East and West will serve as important sources of delicious, high-quality, low-cost protein in the diets of people everywhere, regardless of their income. We are interested in each of the following soyfoods, listed here in what we consider to be their approximate order of potential worldwide importance: tofu (soybean curd), soy flour, soymilk, tempeh, shoyu (natural soy sauce), textured soy protein (TVP), miso, whole dry soybeans, soy protein isolates and concentrates, roasted soybeans or soy nuts, fresh green soybeans, roasted full-fat soy flour (*kinako*), soy sprouts, yuba, and natto. We have developed hundreds of tasty and nutritious Western-style recipes for the use of these foods and compiled extensive, up-to-date information on their nutritional value, history, and production.

World Hunger: Presently more than 15,000,000 people die each year of starvation and malnutrition-caused diseases; three fourths of these are children. We constantly relate our work to this urgent problem of world hunger by studying and developing creative, low-cost, village-level methods for soyfood production using appropriate technology, by traveling and speaking in less developed countries, and by sending complementary copies of our publications to and communicating with key soyfoods researchers and producers in these countries.

Meatless Diets: Over half of all agricultural and in the United States is now used to grow crops (such as corn, soybeans, oats, and wheat) that are fed to animals. The affluent American diet is emerging as a major cause of world hunger as well as of degenerative diseases such as heart disease and cancer. Soyfoods, which are low in cost, high in protein, low in saturated fats, free of cholesterol, and relatively low in calories, can be used as delicious replacements for meats and dairy products as part of meatless or vegetarian diets. We encourage the adoption of such diets which help to make best use of the planet's precious food resources, are conducive to the development of a healthy body and clear mind, kind to animals, economical, and ecologically sound.

Commercial Soyfood Production: We encourage and aid people throughout the world in starting community or commercial production of soyfoods by providing technical manual, technical advice, materials, and equipment. We have helped to establish the *Soyfoods Association of North America* (SANA) and its international publication *Soyfoods*, to found *Bean Machines, Inc.* (a company selling tofu and soymilk equipment), and to develop catalogs of large and small scale equipment. We have compiled various technical manuals and presently serve as consultants for a wide variety of companies.

Lecture Demonstrations: We have done more than one hundred programs relating to soyfoods for natural food groups, research scientists, food technologists, nutritionists, commercial producers, university audiences, international symposia, home economists, and cooking schools. We have also done numerous television and radio programs and cooking classes throughout the world. We welcome invitations.

Soyfoods Center Network: Our main Center in California is devoted primarily to research and publication about soyfoods. We have the world's largest library (more than 3,500 documents) on soyfoods. Our growing International Soyfood Center Network, with branches around the world, is helping to introduce soyfoods around the world.

New Lifestyles: Our work is deeply involved in the development of lifestyles conducive to the welfare and survival of all beings on planet Earth. Thus we encourage voluntary simplicity, self-sufficiency (particularly food self-sufficiency on personal, regional, and national levels), right livelihood, a deeper understanding of selfless service, and of daily life and work as a spiritual practice, ecological awareness, holistic health, appropriate technology, the rapid development and adoption of solar energy, and the phasing out of nuclear energy.

Publications and Catalog: Our Center has published a number of full-sized specialty books on soyfoods including Tofu & Soymilk Production, Miso Production, Tempeh Production, Soyfoods Industry and Market: Directory and Databook, and History of Soybeans and Soyfoods. We also provide a free catalog listing of our other widely distributed books on tofu, miso, and tempeh, materials such as pamphlets, tofu kits, and slide shows related to soyfoods, and a list of soyfoods manufacturers in North America and Europe.

Your Financial Support and Help: Our work, now reaching people throughout the world, is not supported by government or corporate funds. We do, however, welcome contributions of any size from individuals and private foundations to aid us in furthering the soyfoods revolution and helping to put an end to world hunger. We have established Friends of the Center for supporters willing to contribute $35.00 or more; smaller contributions are also welcomed. If you would like to contribute your time and energy to our work, please contact us.